Intermarium

The Land between the Black and Baltic Seas

Marek Jan Chodakiewicz

Transaction Publishers
New Brunswick (U.S.A.) and London (U.K.)

First paperback printing 2016
Copyright © 2012 by Transaction Publishers, New Brunswick, New Jersey.

This book is printed on acid-free paper that meets the American National Standard for Permanence of Paper for Printed Library Materials.

Library of Congress Catalog Number: 2012009373
ISBN: 978-1-4128-4774-2 (cloth); 978-1-4128-6406-0 (paper)
eBook: 978-1-4128-4786-5
Printed in the United States of America

Library of Congress Cataloging-in-Publication Data

Chodakiewicz, Marek Jan, 1962-
    Intermarium : the Land between the Black and Baltic Seas / Marek Jan Chodakiewicz.
        p. cm.
    Includes bibliographical references and index.
    1. Europe, Central—History. 2. Europe, Eastern—History. 3. Europe, Central—Politics and government. 4. Europe, Eastern—Politics and government. 5. Europe, Central—Foreign relations. 6. Europe, Eastern—Foreign relations. I. Title.
    DAW1038.C48 2012
    943—dc23
                                                                    2012009373

To Helenka

Let us love one another!

—Adam Mickiewicz, *Pan Tadeusz, Book XII*

What is that sound high in the air
Murmur of maternal lamentation
Who are those hooded hordes swarming
Over endless plains, stumbling in cracked earth
Ringed by the flat horizon only

—T. S. Eliot, *The Waste Land*

Contents

Introduction

A good book is not one that persuades the whole world, for none would pass this test. It is the one that satisfies completely the class of readers to whom the work is particularly addressed and leaves no one to doubt either the author's good faith or his indefatigable labor to gain mastery of the subject. I naively flatter myself that every just reader will judge me acceptable on this score. Never has it been more necessary to surround a truth of the first order with all the light of evidence.[1]

—Joseph de Maistre

History and collective memories influence a nation, its culture, and institutions and, hence, its domestic politics and foreign policy. That is, of course, also the case in the Intermarium, the lands between the Black and Baltic Seas in Eastern Europe. The area is both the last unabashed rampart of Western Civilization in the East and a fascinating point of convergence of disparate cultures. Historically, the latter flourished because of the preponderance of the former in a fascinatingly synergetic relationship.

Defining precisely the physical setting of our inquiry is a daunting task. And it is an integral part of our project to explore various definitions. The very fact that no one seems to either know or agree what "Central and Eastern Europe" precisely is underscores the necessity for our study.

The most crucial task is to define "East" and "West." There are moral, ideological, cultural, geographical, and geopolitical definitions. For us "the West" consists of the sphere of freedom; "the East" denotes the opposite. At the moment, the eastern boundary runs along the western borders of Russia and Belarus. The nations to the west of that line are largely or fully free, if tenuously.

There is a certain relationship between freedom and cultural heritage in the area. Nations that adhere to Western Christianity tend to display characteristics more amicable to freedom than people who follow Eastern Orthodoxy or Islam. However, non-Western faiths do not preclude embracing freedom, as reflected in the democratic path followed by, say, Serbia and Bosnia-Herzegovina.

1

But where does Central Europe start? Where does it end? What of Eastern Europe? What about Central and Eastern Europe? Well, it depends. Geographically, the heart of Europe is located by the current border of northeastern Poland and western Lithuania.[2] The western rim of the continent rests on the Atlantic and the eastern part ends at the Ural Mountains. Geography is immutable. Geopolitically, however, the notion of the "East" and "West" shifts with the vicissitudes of the region. Thus, until 1989, the so-called German Democratic Republic was "the East," its position westerly of Sweden notwithstanding. Prague was also "the East," even though it is geographically located to the west of Vienna, which, however, ideologically belonged to "the West." This rule also applies to earlier periods in history. For example, historic south-eastern Hungary under the Ottoman rule in the sixteenth century was definitely "the East," but following its liberation in the seventeenth and eighteenth centuries, it must be squarely placed in "the West." Presently, as the European Union (EU) expands, so does the commodiousness of the "West." If a non-EU nation, Belarus, for instance, adhered to democratic standards, it would automatically be classified as belonging to the "West."

We have focused on the Intermarium, the land between the Black and Baltic Seas for several reasons. First, most importantly, it is culturally and ideologically most compatible with American national interests and political culture as the inheritor of the freedom and rights stemming from the legacy of the Polish-Lithuanian/Ruthenian Commonwealth. Second, it is the regional pivot and a gateway to both East and West. Third, since the Intermarium is the most stable part of the post-Soviet area (and most free and democratic), the United States should focus on solidifying its influence there to use it as a springboard to handling the rest of the successor states, including in the Caucasus, Central Asia, and the Russian Federation itself. Fourth, the ongoing political and economic success of the Intermarium states under American sponsorship undermines the enemies of freedom not only in the post-Soviet sphere but also all over the world. Fifth, the Intermarium is the most inclusive political concept that successfully operated in practice for several centuries within the framework of the Commonwealth and as such constitutes a direct challenge to any form of modern totalitarianism or xenophobic uniformity. Sixth, at its zenith, the Intermarium projected its might well beyond its borders, influencing events as far afield as Scandinavia and the Balkans, and it can do so again in congruence with America's objectives and its own interests. Last but not least, seventh, by reintroducing the concept of the Intermarium into the intellectual discourse, we would like to stress the autonomous and independent nature of the area (rather than either its nonexistence or submersion into conquering empires).

We acknowledge, of course, that there exist other ways to conceptualize the region. There were imperial efforts to deny the existence of the Intermarium or to imagine it as an extension of the conquering empires (e.g., nineteenth-century Russia's idea of "the Slavdom," invoking a block in need of a "Slavic monarch" to protect it, while ignoring both the majority that rejected such protection and the non-Slavic minority peoples; or Germany's contemporaneous concept of the *Mitteleuropa*, a German dominion and a passageway to the Middle East). In distinction to inimical imperial projects, most locally generated geopolitical ideas draw directly on the indigenous legacy of the Intermarium. For example, in the interwar period the "ABC" seas (Adriatyk–Bałtyk–Czarne/Adriatic–Baltic–Black) solution for the Intermarium was touted. This was a maximalist approach that included everything between the pre-1939 Soviet and German borders to be organized in a loose confederation. Later, the project was reduced to the Polish-Czechoslovak Federation, as unveiled in London during the war years. The Vyšehrad Triangle/Four (or Group) of Poland, Hungary, Slovakia, and the Czech Republic is the modern-day extension of this idea.[3] Therefore, sometimes, in particular while discussing the contemporary era, we shall venture a bit beyond the confines of the Black and Baltic Seas in our narrative.

The knowledge of the Intermarium entails the fluency with its component parts. Most focus on ethnic differences, indeed "ancient hatreds." While considering ethnic differences, we shall also underscore cultural affinities and other positive features (e.g., economy) which tend to unite, rather than divide the nations of the region. We shall dwell on particularities and peculiarities of each of the nation-states and suggest ways to address them to facilitate overcoming of their differences, or at least downplaying them for the sake of regional cooperation. We also shall differentiate between usually constructive cultural nationalism and potentially pernicious ethno(folk)-nationalism. The former is indispensable to reconstruct each nation's identity following the pestilence of Communism; the latter threatens to turn the reconstruction endeavor into a conflict of the local ethnicities, thus seriously jeopardizing the Intermarium project of cooperative nationalisms. It is within this context that our broad sweep of regional history ties to contemporary geo-politics as well as accounts for the major differences among the countries of the region that inevitably require a differentiated US policy approach to the individual states.

Thus, our focus on the Intermarium reflects not only the most efficient way to tackle the complexities of the region as a cohesive collection of a million indigenous component parts, but also reflects a tradition that the disparate people of the region will find most familiar and least threatening. Since the objective is to share the knowledge of the Intermarium with the English reading public, including American policymakers, it is crucial to explain the region in such terms that would help the United States influence the target populations. This is indispensable to break with the customary practice of talking only to their imperial overseers in Moscow or elsewhere.

Our journey into the Intermarium is a comprehensive narrative of a millennial panorama. However, the focus will be largely on the twentieth and early twenty-first centuries and their challenges, World War II and its aftermath, in particular. Crushing disasters, soaring triumphs, appalling horrors, and audacious rebirths will be reoccurring themes here. In this context, we shall also muse about remembering and forgetting. We shall delve into the Intermarium's history and people. We shall search for continuities and discontinuities of the past as manifested (or absent) in the present and projected into (or missing from) the future. Last but not least, in our journey, we shall offer some insights on the current issues, both domestic and foreign as they pertain to these lands. We shall dwell on post-Communism and post-colonialism, both sad legacies of the Soviet and, more broadly, foreign domination.[4] Our guiding leitmotif will be freedom, its manifestations, and travails in the area.

Freedom is indispensable for an unimpeded flow of individual recollections to coalesce gradually into collective memories and to process them critically into historical scholarship through an arduous process of verification against various other primary sources. No freedom interrupts the process of inheriting from the past and assessing it and leaves both persons and nations confused about their individual and collective identities. Further, the lack of freedom within hampers the free world without from understanding the enslaved. Therefore, at best, it results in flawed efforts to relate to their plight. At worst, it roots for their oppressors. This is the case with the post-Soviet successor states, in general, and the Intermarium, in particular.

For now freedom blooms in the region, waxing robustly in its north-western part but only shyly unveiling itself in the eastern and southern parts. Yet, despite the demise of the USSR in 1991, threats to the region's freedom persist. The Kremlin de facto refuses to accept Estonia, Latvia, Lithuania, Belarus, Ukraine, and Moldova as sovereign, referring to them as "the near abroad" (*blizhne zarubezhe/ближнее зарубежье*). It persistently meddles in their affairs. Moscow is equally irked with its former satellites, Warsaw, in particular. The relationship with the Poles is very complex, mixing freely the geopolitical and the metaphysical. The Kremlin's attitude stems from the historical competition between Muscovy and Poland–Lithuania over the Intermarium. The Russians also consider Poland as the main outpost of the West in the East, or as one leader uncharitably put it, "America's Trojan donkey in Europe." A sovereign Polish state encumbers Moscow's freedom of maneuver, including expansion, in regards to Europe. Consequently, to replace the dialectics of the class struggle and the world revolution, and to forge a new post-Soviet identity, Russia has embraced a historical narrative and symbols with Poland pitted as the main cultural challenger and the alleged pivot of much of the Kremlin's past misfortunes and potential threats.[5]

Resurgent Russia with imperial objectives has reemerged on the world stage. At the most alarming, its "neo-Eurasianist" ideology brazenly expresses itself in rabid anti-Americanism and unabashedly flirts with neo-Nazism. "If anything happens to the Unites States, we will occupy the Baltic states once again," proclaims menacingly its chief intellectual guru.[6] The most prevalent external manifestation of post-Soviet Russia is imperialism, and its weapon of choice has been mainly energy.[7] A shamelessly blooming Stalinist historical revisionism intellectually complements the Kremlin's political aggressiveness.[8] All this is part and parcel not only of Russia's imperial legacy but also of post-Communism, an attempt to salvage by transforming, covertly and overtly, as much as possible from the nefarious policies, institutions, arrangements, attitudes, legacies, myths, symbols, and personages of totalitarianism under the new conditions to retain power and undermine freedom.

The United States is failing to address this development sufficiently. This failure reflects a lack of imagination concerning potential consequences of this resurgence for American national interests. The result will most likely be the reabsorption of the former Soviet territories and satellite nations of Central and Eastern Europe, a development which cannot but undermine America's credibility and strategic interests. The sources of this potential failure stem from persistent ignorance of Russia's relationship with her neighbors. Thus, the chief remedy to avert the potential crisis should be learning the history of this relationship through a non-Moscow centric prism. Moscow-centrism is a condition where one not only concentrates almost exclusively on Moscow as the imperial command center, but also where one views and perceives Russia and its neighbors through the same prism that Moscow would like one to: as one realm, or, at least, very closely related. To avoid this necessitates studying the nature of the nations of the post-Soviet periphery, particularly those of the Intermarium, on their own terms and the strategic implications of the political and cultural affinities of these nations with the United States and the West.

The Intermarium, an area of coexistence, convergence, and clash of many cultures, has historically been a staunch defender of Western Civilization despite long spells of alien domination. The latest foreign occupations, during and after World War II (1939–1990), resulted in the near annihilation of the pluralistic essence of the Intermarium. The Jewish minority and its cultural legacy were exterminated wholesale between 1941 and 1944. As for the Christian majority, the extermination occurred both on the physical and spiritual planes. The former targeted chiefly the conscious national elites, which actively keep the flame of tradition burning. The spiritual extermination affected the common people, who were subjected to continuously perverse indoctrination to extirpate traditional reflexes from their subconscious and to create a new breed of humans by implanting a false consciousness in them.

In other words, the people were robbed of their traditional leaders and of their past. The occupiers quite literally killed the history of the occupied. They substituted it with totalitarian lies. Now the newly liberated nations have endeavored to reconstitute their collective memories. They have been trying to restitch their identities and rediscover themselves.[9] However, they are hampered in their efforts not only because of the totalitarian inheritance at home, but also because of the legacy of hostile propaganda of the empires ruling over them for the better part of the past two hundred and fifty years. In particular, Communist propaganda has proven durable beyond belief and continues to affect the way the West relates to the successor states of the Soviet Union.

The Intermarium is Central and Eastern Europe's easternmost part. We shall focus primarily on the Baltic States and interwar Poland's former eastern provinces. The latter are now the western parts of contemporary Belarus (Belorussia/White Ruthenia) and Ukraine. However, we shall also touch upon Moldova, western and central Poland (or ethnographic Poland), and eastern Ukraine and Belarus. In other words, historically speaking, we shall deal chiefly with the lands that once constituted an integral part of the Polish-Lithuanian Commonwealth (*Rzeczpospolita*) or depended on it. At its peak in the sixteenth century, the Commonwealth occupied about 80 percent of the Intermarium. It sprawled across an area larger than contemporary France, Belgium, and Holland combined. And, as Andrzej Nowak reminds us, its legacy continues to influence the region until the present day.[10]

Western scholars usually view the Intermarium as a peripheral area, a borderland. In fact, for them, the Intermarium is at best a space between civilizations. Most often, however, they habitually consider it through a Moscow-centric prism, treating the area as if it were synonymous with "Russia."[11] In other words, Western scholarship tends to mirror image the Muscovite diktat on the history of the Intermarium. We reject such a skewed approach. Instead, we consider it an eclectic and autonomous outpost of the West. Yet, neither completely of the West, nor of the East, the area retains the characteristics of both. At times, it serves as a Western rampart; at other times as a thoroughfare; and also as a launching pad for aggression both ways; but always as a meeting place for all and sundry. This is where the West and the East meet, interact, complement each other, and, occasionally, clash. This experience makes the Intermarium a sui generis phenomenon. However, it is sui generis only to the extent that it evolved a Western civilization on its own terms, creating its culturally unique off-shoot. Its chief organizing principle harkens from Poland, but there are also German, Italian, Scottish, French, Swedish, and other Western elements in the Intermarium. Historically it has aspired to be Western, but on its own peculiar terms. That has often produced tensions both within and without the Intermarium. At times these tremors have erupted in violence and war, almost invariably involving a vicious internecine element.[12]

For the past two hundred and fifty years, the experiences of the local people have been nothing short of calamitous if not outright apocalyptic, in the twentieth century, in particular.[13] The principal culprits were the foreign totalitarians, the Nazis and the Communists. However, the calamity had also a local dimension with all the indigenous ethno-cultural and religious groups involved in persecuting and even killing their own kind and, more often, each other. Those experiences were inimical, to say the least, to the profession of particular faiths as well as to the organic formation of nations and their salubrious cultural, social, economic, and political development in the former lands of the Polish-Lithuanian Commonwealth. It is in this context that we shall address the questions of individual recollections, collective memories, and false consciousness.

Collective memories are the sum of individual experiences woven together to form a national tapestry of remembering. Collective memories inform our cultural, political, and economic activities. Among other things, they influence the legislation and institutions of a free society. Therefore, a continuity of collective memories of Western Civilization is a sine qua non of freedom. Collective memories are necessary to empower the individual to achieve his best by creating a wholesome context for his action stemming from the past experiences. The degree of individual achievement is contingent both upon one's personal attributes and the degree of freedom one enjoys. And freedom is an inalienable part of Western Civilization, unattainable with false consciousness that is predicated on hostility to liberty.

By Western Civilization we mean the pluralistic heritage of Greek ethics, Roman law, and Christian religion stemming from Judaism.[14] The heritage blossomed in the idea of liberty flowing from the continuity of tradition as expressed by individual rights, including freedom to worship God and hold property. Its modern manifestation includes parliamentary democracy, rule of law, freedom of speech, unimpeded movement, and security for private property. In other words the West is freedom. (Thus, the trends which contradict the very essence of freedom, such as Nazism and Communism [both of them negating freedom through totalitarianism] as well as postmodernism and moral relativism [both denying freedom through their rejection of the absolute], are anti-Western, even if they originated in the West as indigenous heresies).

On the other hand, by alien domination we mean rule by various despotic systems inimical to human liberty. In the twentieth century their main forms were Nazism and Communism. To achieve freedom is to overcome the totalitarian legacy in the Intermarium. To resurrect the severed thread of history and to restore national continuity of memories require a sustained scholarly effort. Historians must find a way to reassemble links between the past and present to facilitate a smooth transition of the Intermarium into the future. Only when the national continuity in history is restored by each and all cultures involved, each will be able to verify the other's and one's own narrative and, eventually, undertake a general synthesis. The synthesis will fail if it is dominated by any one nationalistic strain or if it reverts to Moscow-centrism. Its organizing principle can be found in the old Commonwealth, which was a federation of "free with free, and equal with equal." By introducing the concept of the Intermarium to the general English-speaking reader, we attempt to suggest a scholarly framework for a future inquiry. It can be considered a preliminary synthesis, a general introduction to the Intermarium.

Notes

1.   Joseph de Maistre, "On the Pope" (1819), in *Critics of the Enlightenment: Readings in the French Counter-Revolutionary Tradition*, ed. and trans. Christopher Olaf Blum (Wilmington, DE: ISI Books, 2004), 168.

2.   See Paul Robert Magocsi, *Historical Atlas of Central Europe* (Seattle, WA: University of Washington Press, 2002); *The Historical Atlas of Poland* (Warszawa and Wrocław: Państwowe Przedsiębiorstwo Wydawnictw Kartograficznych, 1986); Filip Sulimierski, Bronisław Chlebowski, and Władysław Walewski, *Słownik geograficzny Królestwa Polskiego i innych krajów słowiańskich* (*Geographic Dictionary of the Polish Kingdom and Other Slavic Countries*), 15 vols (Warszawa: Wydawnictwa Artystyczne i Filmowe, 1975–1977), and its early edition (Warszawa: Nakładem Władysława Walewskiego, 1884), which has been digitalized, is available on the internet at http://www.mimuw.edu.pl/polszczyzna/SGKPi/ (accessed April 25, 2012). See also James Stuart Olson, Lee Brigance Pappas, and Nicholas C. J. Pappas, *Ethnohistorical Dictionary of the Russian and Soviet Empires* (Westport, CT: Greenwood Press, 1994); Ronald Wixman, *The Peoples of the USSR: An Ethnographic Handbook* (Armonk, NY: M.E. Sharpe, 1984); Michael Bruchis, *The USSR: Language and Realities: Nations, Leaders, and Scholars* (New York: Columbia University Press, 1988); James H. Bater, *The Soviet Scene: A Geographical Perspective* (New York: Edward Arnold, 1989); Mikhail Bernstam, "The Demography of Soviet Ethnic Groups in World Perspective," in *The Last Empire: Nationality and the Soviet Future*, ed. Robert Conquest (Stanford, CA: Hoover Institution Press, 1986), 314–68; Viktor Kozlov, *The Peoples of the Soviet Union* (The Second World Series), trans. Pauline M. Tiffen (Bloomington, IN: Indiana University Press, 1988); *The First Book of Demographics for the Republics of the Former Soviet Union, 1951–1990* (Shady Side, MD: New World Demographics, 1992); Richard Frucht, *Eastern Europe: An Introduction to the People, Lands, and Culture* (Santa Barbara, CA: ABC-CLIO, 2005). For mandatory postmodernist musings about Central and Eastern Europe as "invented" see, e.g., Tomasz Kamusella, "Central Europe in the Distorting Mirror of Maps, Languages and Ideas," *The Polish Review* 57, no. 1 (2012): 33–94.

3.   We shall elaborate on this in Part III in the chapter on "Geopolitics and Foreign Policy in the Intermarium."

4.   For a brief overview of post-Communism see Marek Jan Chodakiewicz, "The nature and future of Communism," remarks delivered at the Heritage Foundation's conference "Captive Nations: Past, Present, and Future?" http://www.iwp.

edu/news_publications/detail/the-nature-and-future-of-communism (accessed July 22, 2009). On post-colonialism see Ewa M. Thompson, *Imperial Knowledge: Russian Literature and Colonialism* (Westport, CT and London: Greenwood Press, 2000); and Henry F. Carey and Rafal Raciborski, "Postcolonialism: A Valid Paradigm for the Former Sovietized States and Yugoslavia?" *East European Politics and Societies* 18, no. 2 (Spring 2004): 191–235.

5.   See Marek Jan Chodakiewicz, "Poland and the Future of NATO," *The Sarmatian Review* 19, no. 3 (September 1999): 655–59; Marek Jan Chodakiewicz, "America's Eastern Tier: Poland between NATO and United Europe," *Periphery* 8/9 (2002–2003): 4–12, also published in Polish as "Wschodnia flanka Ameryki," *Templum* no. 2/3 (2002): 39–53; Joanna A. Gorska, *Dealing with a Juggernaut: Analyzing Poland's Policy towards Russia, 1989–2009* (Lanham, MD: Rowman & Littlefield Pub Inc., 2010).

6.   Aleksandr Dugin interviewed by Konstantin Ameliushkin, "Александр Дугин: если с США что-то случится, мы еще раз оккупируем страны Балтии," ("If anything Happens to the United States, We Will Occupy the Baltic States Once Again"), http://ru.delfi.lt/archive/print.php?id=38456403 (accessed November 15, 2010).

7.   On Russia and its current mission from a bevy of leading post-Soviet intellectuals see a collection of interviews by Filip Memches, *Słudzy i wrogowie Imperium: Rosyjskie rozmowy o końcu historii* (*Servants and Enemies of the Empire: Russian Conversations about the End of History*) (Kraków: Dziennik-Arcana, 2009). See also Bruce Clarke, *An Empire's New Clothes: The End of Russia's Liberal Dream* (London: Vintage, 1996); Janusz Bugajski, *Cold Peace: Russia's New Imperialism* (Westport, CT: Greenwood Publishing Group, 2004); Andrei P. Tsygankov and Pavel A. Tsygankov, eds., *New Directions in Russian International Studies* (Stuttgart and Hannover: Ibidem-Verlag, 2005); Marlene Laruelle, ed. *Russian Nationalism and the National Reassertion of Russia* (London: Routledge, 2009); Marlene Laruelle, *In the Name of the Nation: Nationalism and Politics in Contemporary Russia* (New York: Palgrave Macmillian, 2009); Marlène Laruelle, *Russian Eurasianism: An Ideology of Empire* (Washington, DC: Woodrow Wilson Center Press, 2008); Marshall I. Goldman, *Petrostate: Putin, Power and the New Russia* (New York: Oxford University Press, 2010); Andreas Umland, ed., *The Nature of Russian "Neo-Eurasianism": Approaches to Aleksandr Dugin's Post-Soviet Movement of Radical Anti-Americanism* (Armonk: M.E. Sharpe, 2009), which is vol. 47, no. 1 (January–February 2009) of *Russian Politics and Law*. On the Russian public's concurrent attitudes toward the West see Richard Rose and Neil Munro, "Do Russians See Their Future in Europe or the CIS?" *Europe-Asia Studies* 60, no. 1 (January 2008): 49–66. Only one-third of the respondents desires integration with "Europe." However, two-thirds envision Russia's integration with the Commonwealth of Independent States (CIS), or, to put it simply, the post-Soviet sphere. The Western rim of the post-Soviet sphere is Europe's Intermarium. This suggests the Russian public wish, or at least passive permission, for imperial reintegration, even if Rose and Munro deny that.

8.   Tomasz Sommer and Marek Jan Chodakiewicz, "Average Joe: The Return of Stalinist Apologists," *World Affairs: A Journal of Ideas and Debate* (January/February 2011): 75–82.

9.   On this topic, the most indispensable is a multifarious debate in Zdzisław Krasnodębski, Stefan Garsztecki, and Rüdiger Ritter eds., *Last der Geschichte? Kollektive Identität und Geschichte in Ostmitteleuropa: Belarus, Polen, Litauen,*

Ukraine (Hamburg: Verlag Dr. Kovač, 2008). A nostalgic look at the legacy of the Intermarium, in particular, of its Commonwealth period, has produced musings on "neo-Sarmatism," an ideology and identity uniting all local ethnicities into one, common "Polish" ethos grounded in freedom and practiced in a republican form. See Jan Filip Staniłko, "Neosarmacki republikanizm: Źródła i teraźniejszość polskiej tradycji politycznej," ("Neosarmatian Republicanism: The Sources and the Presence of a Polish Political Tradition") *Arcana* no. 2–3 (86–87) (2009): 6–24; Jakub Brodacki, "Debata neosarmacka," (A Neosarmatian Debate) *Glaukopis: Pismo społeczno-historyczne* no. 19–20 (2010): 36–43.

10.   Andrzej Nowak, "From Empire Builder to Empire Breaker, or There and Back Again: History and Memory of Poland's Role in Eastern European Politics," in *Od Imperium do Imperium: Spojrzenie na historię Europy Wschodniej*, ed. Andrzej Nowak, (*From Empire to Empire: A Look at the History of Eastern Europe*) (Kraków and Warszawa: Arcana and Instytut Historii PAN, 2004), 356–93.

11.   Moscow-centrism and Russophilia afflicting Western academia deserve a monograph of their own. During the Cold War, an astute observer remarked that Slavic departments at American universities were the best embassies of the USSR. That applies to the rest of the Western world as well in reference to contemporary Russia, although, mercifully, its current government is not universally hailed as an agent of progress like the Soviet one was. For a rather typical example of Moscow-centrisim see Isabel de Madariaga, *Ivan the Terrible: First Tsar of Russia* (New Haven, CT and London: Yale University Press, 2005), who, inexplicably, calls the Duchy of Moscow—Russia; and she supports every Muscovite claim, based on dynastic and religious rationale, to the Intermarium. Madariaga is quite conversant in Russian sources as well as in Western ones, as well as their scholarly interpretation; however, she is practically oblivious to anything emanating from the Intermarium, in particular, the Polish-Lithuanian Commonwealth. She hardly bothered to study any sources and has practically failed to consult any Polish scholarship with, perhaps, one or two exceptions, which made no impact on her. She also appears to understand the systemic differences between Muscovy and the Commonwealth on the most superficial level only, sneeringly dismissing the Polish King's claim to defend freedom and comparing it disparagingly with propaganda akin to the one deployed during the US intervention in Iraq (320, 441, n. 14).

12.   For a general overview see Piotr S. Wandycz, *The Price of Freedom: A History of East Central Europe from the Middle Ages to the Present*, 2nd ed. (London and New York: Routledge, 2001). For a Moscow-centric view of Ruthenian history see George Vernadsky, *A History of Russia* (New Haven, CT: Yale University Press, 1969); George Vernadsky, *Political and Diplomatic History of Russia* (Boston, MA: Little, Brown, and Company, 1936); Jesse D. Clarkson, *A History of Russia* (New York: Random House, 1969); Edward Acton, *Russia: The Present and the Past* (London and New York: Longman, 1990); Helene Carrere D'Encausse, *The Russian Syndrome: One Thousand Years of Political Murder* (New York and London: Holmes & Meier, 1992); Martin Sixsmith, *Russia: A 1000-Year Chronicle of the Wild East* (New York: The Overlook Press, 2011). For a non-Moscow centric view of the Intermarium, or its component parts, see Mikhaylo Hrushevsky, *History of Ukraine-Rus'*, vol. 1: *From Prehistory to the Eleventh Century* (Edmonton, AB: Canadian Institute of Ukrainian Studies, 1997), (a publishing project-in-progress which encompasses ten volumes; in addition to vol. 1, there have been three more volumes published [1999–2002] dealing with *History of the Ukrainian Cossacks*: vol. 7: *The Cossack Age, 1600–1625*; vol. 8:

The Cossack Age, 1626–1650; and vol. 9: *The Cossack Age, 1650–1653*; Ihor Sev-
cenko, *Ukraine between East and West: Essays on Cultural History to the Early
Eighteenth Century* (Edmonton, AB: Canadian Institute of Ukrainian Studies,
1996); Paul Robert Magocsi, *A History of Ukraine* (Seattle, WA: University of
Washington Press, 1996); Orest Subtelny, *Ukraine: A History* (Toronto, Buf-
falo, and London: The University of Toronto Press and Canadian Institute of
Ukrainian Studies, 1994); Jan Zaprudnik, *Belarus: At a Crossroads in History*
(Boulder, CO, San Francisco, CA, and Oxford: Westview Press, 1993); Henryk
Paszkiewicz, *The Making of the Russian Nation* (Westport, CT: Greenwood
Press, 1977); Jan Kucharzewski, *The Origins of Modern Russia* (New York: Polish
Institute of Arts and Sciences in America, 1948); Oscar Halecki, *Borderlands of
Western Civilization: A History of East Central Europe* (New York: The Ronald
Press Company, 1952). For a very competent discussion of competing historical
narratives of the Grand Duchy of Lithuania see Katarzyna Błachowska, *Wiele
historii jednego państwa: Obraz dziejów Wielkiego Księstwa Litewskiego do
1569 roku w ujęciu historyków polskich, rosyjskich, ukraińskich, litewskich i
białoruskich w XIX wieku* (*Many Histories of One State: The Picture of the Past
of the Grand Duchy of Lithuania until 1569 According to Polish, Russian, Ukrainian, Lithuanian, and Belorussian Historians in the 19th Century*) (Warszawa:
Wydawnictwo Neriton, 2009). For a case study of competing contemporary
Polish and Russian remembering and historiography about the Ukraine in the
seventeenth century see Martin Aust, *Polen und Russland im Streit um die
Ukraine: Konkurrierende Erinnerungen an die Kriege des 17. Jahrhunderts in den
Jahren 1934 bis 2006* (Wiesbaden: Harrassowitz Verlag, 2009). For intellectual,
cultural, and artistic aspects of Polish-Russian rivalry over the centuries see
David L. Rensel and Bozena Shallcross, eds., *Polish Encounters, Russian Identity*
(Bloomington, IN: Indiana University Press, 2005).

13. For some demographic data see Andrzej Maryański, *Przemiany ludnościowe
w ZSRR* (*Demographic Transformations in the USSR*) (Warszawa and Kraków:
Centrum Badań Wschodnich Uniwersytetu Warszawskiego i Wyższa Szkoła
Pedagogiczna w Krakowie, 1995); Piotr Eberhardt, *Przemiany ludnościowe
na Ukrainie XX wieku* (*Demographic Transformation in Ukraine in the 20th
Century*) (Warszawa: Biblioteka "Obozu," 1994); Piotr Eberhardt, *Przemiany narodowościowe na Białorusi* (*Demographic Transformation in Belarus*) (Warszawa: Editions Spotkania, 1994); Piotr Eberhardt, *Przemiany
narodowościowe na Litwie* (*Demographic Transformation in Lithuania*)
(Warszawa: Przegląd Wschodni, 1997); Piotr Eberhardt, "Kresy wschodnie—granice, terytorium, ludność polska," ("The Eastern Borderlands: Borders,
Territory, and the Polish Population") in *Europa nieprowincjonalna: Przemiany
na ziemiach wschodnich dawnej Rzeczpospolitej (Białoruś, Litwa, Ukraina,
wschodnie pogranicze III Rzeczpospolitej Polskiej) w latach 1772–1999* (*Non-
Provincial Europe: Transformations in the Eastern Lands of the Old Com-
monwealth [Belarus, Lithuania, Ukraine, and the Eastern Borderlands of the
III Polish Commonwealth], 1772–1999*) ed. Krzysztof Jasiewicz (Warszawa
and London: Instytut Studiów Politycznych Polskiej Akademii Nauk, Oficyna
Wydawnicza Rytm, Polonia Aid Foundation Trust, 1999), 29–39 (afterward
Europa nieprowincjonalna); Piotr Eberhardt, *Ethnic Groups and Population
Changes in Twentieth-Century Central-Eastern Europe: History, Data, Analy-
sis* (Armonk, NY and London: M.E. Sharpe, 2003); Piotr Eberhardt, "Political
Migrations in Poland, 1939–1948," TMs, Warsaw 2006, http://www.igipz.pan.
pl/zpz/Political_migrations.pdf; Raul Hilberg, *The Destruction of the European*

Jews, 2nd revised edition (New York and London: Holmes & Meier, 1985), 338–39; Lucy S. Dawidowicz, *The War against the Jews, 1933–1945* (Toronto, New York, London, Sydney, and Auckland: Bantam Books, 1986), 403.

14. See an elegant explication in Christopher Dawson, *Religion and the Rise of Western Culture* (New York: Doubleday, 1991). For a militant one see Feliks Koneczny, *On the Plurality of Civilisations* (London: Polonica Publications, 1962). See also T. S. Eliot, *Notes towards the Definition of Culture* (New York: Harcourt, Brace, and Company, 1949).

Background

American attempts to study the peoples of the post-Soviet sphere, and, more precisely, the Intermarium, in particular, have been hampered by several obstacles.[1] The most important is the cultural gap. Namely, there is historical discontinuity as far as this part of the world is concerned. The fact that the United States did not exist during much of Europe's history and the fact that North America was colonized principally by peoples from Western Europe created a void of tradition of first-hand knowledge about the Old Continent's central and eastern parts. First, the United States had yet to be conceived when the Intermarium had arguably reached its peak of salubrious development under the auspices of the Polish-Lithuanian Commonwealth in the sixteenth century. Second, during most of the United States' existence as an independent nation, the lands between the Black and Baltic Seas remained subjugated by outside powers—first the Russian, German, Austrian, and Turkish empires and then the USSR. Thus, the Intermarium largely lacked its own voice in the exchange between the Old World and the New.

There were several other external and internal reasons the United States remained unfamiliar with the Intermarium. The first one was propaganda. The Great Powers successfully sold their version of history of the conquered lands to the outside world, including the United States.[2] Thus, as Americans came to understand it, a multitude of captive peoples functioned simply as Russians, Germans, Austrians, or, to a lesser extent, Turks. On the one hand, the historical discourse of the imperial apologists depicted their captive nations as either congenitally anarchical, and thus in need of order, or inherently infantile, and thus in need of supervision. On the other hand, the empires, for the most part, stressed unity and uniformity under their sovereigns.

America could easily relate to both imperial narratives. After all, native Americans, black slaves, and non-WASP immigrants were viewed as both anarchical and infantile. The language of unity fared particularly well in the United States which fought a bloody fratricidal war to preserve its own national cohesion in the mid-nineteenth century. The United States consequently tended to consider most domestic rebellions within the empires as civil wars. This was particularly the case with Poland's anti-Russian January Rising of 1863.[3]

Our lack of direct expertise in the matters of the Intermarium can also be traced back to American isolationism and exceptionalism. For large stretches of our history, Americans neither cared about the outside world nor imagined that we had much to learn from it. We considered ourselves uniquely blessed, simply the best of them all. Thus, we failed to identify possible sources of affinity and compatibility between the American system and those of other nations, excluding perhaps Great Britain. This was especially true of the Polish-Lithuanian Commonwealth and its tradition of freedom, in particular (which the empires in unison derided as anarchy)—a mixed republican-executive tradition arguably as close to that of America as the tradition of any other country in the world, and a history with lessons of special value to the United States. This was a pity, nay, a disservice to America's national interest. Affinity usually translates into intellectual curiosity. The latter spurs a drive for knowledge of a particular phenomenon or a region and creates a degree of expertise to serve America's national interest, which, however, can, but does not have to, contradict the affinity and empathy stemming from it. (The congenial relationship between the United States and China before 1949 perhaps serves as a good example of this mechanism.) Thus, we missed the opportunity to produce a homegrown talent to understand the Intermarium on both its and America's own terms, and not through the skewed prism of the empires with systems inimical to that of the United States.

Moscow was particularly successful in purveying its colonial discourse to the point where the world has largely failed to recognize Tsarist Russia (and later the Soviet Union) for what it really was: the greatest colonial empire on Earth. Russia conquered through an old-fashioned land expansion drive, grabbing one region after another with the imperial logic of protecting its previous conquests. In the Anglo-Saxon world, especially, this was almost completely overlooked because Russia was not a sea-born empire. Further, by false association one could perhaps mistake Muscovy's invariably bloody expansion across a continent for America's enthusiastic fulfillment of its "Manifest Destiny," which, occasionally, turned brutal against the indigenous people. Thus, explorations into Imperial Russia's actions were studiously avoided in the United States lest they invite unwanted comparisons with our own conduct.

Consequently, the Americans remained rather unfamiliar with the astonishing variety of cultural, religious, ethnic, and national forms in the Intermarium. This was despite the fact that by the end of the nineteenth century these very lands became an important source of emigration to the United States. As the immigrants came mostly from the uneducated peasantry or the urban lower classes, their unsophisticated knowledge of the Intermarium reflected their humble social station. They spoke languages distant from English; and they were overwhelmingly non-Protestants: Catholic, Uniate, Orthodox, and Jewish. Theirs was largely a preliterary folk tradition. Hence, there was little they could impart that would be intellectually appealing to their fellow Americans, the traditional Anglo-Saxon Protestant elite, in particular. To be fair, the newcomers from the Intermarium were thrilled to be in the United States and, for the most part, enthusiastically embraced "the American way," while practicing some of the old customs in their own ethno-cultural neighborhoods. It was only upon their assimilation that a few of their admirably Americanized children found the ways to share their stories with other Americans. A few of those entered the mainstream only much later.

In any event, the conceptual failure to comprehend the Intermarium continued during and after the rise of the Soviet Union, its successful struggle against Nazi Germany, and the Kremlin's subsequent mastery over much of the central and eastern European lands and peoples in the twentieth century. Although the United States became intimately involved in world affairs during World War II and its aftermath, providing leadership to the forces of freedom and democracy, America's understanding of the Intermarium became mired in, and colored by, the ideological struggles of Communism, anti-Communism, and anti-anti-Communism.

Already following World War I, in the wake of the Bolshevik Revolution of 1917, America's discourse on the Intermarium reflected heavily the sensitivities of the Left. Disparate leftists and Communist agents of influence in the media, government, and academia tended to treat the Soviet-occupied part of the region with sympathy for the new rulers and indifference to the captive population. Similarly, the Left imbibed the Kremlin's hostility toward the successor states created after 1918. Its discourse reduced the newly independent nations to "reactionary" and "fascist" dictatorships whose "oppressed" people allegedly yearned to the "liberated" by the Communists to join the USSR. Meanwhile, on the American Right, so far as its existence even penetrated a formidably isolationist mind-set, the free part of the Intermarium was reduced merely to that of a *cordon sanitaire* against Bolshevism. The largest and strongest of the local nations, Poland, served as its pivot. But who would take Poland seriously in America? Generally, the successor states were too weak and too small to matter in the grand scheme of geopolitical and ideological struggles, even had the United States not been isolationist. They simply were of little consequence.

Yet, in the 1920s and 1930s, the Soviets showed an inordinate concern for the Intermarium in general and Poland in particular. The Politburo obsessively referred to Poland as "the main enemy." This seemingly strange perception of a rather weak nation contrasts glaringly with the Soviet attitude toward powers that by American standards were a much greater threat to the USSR, including Germany, Japan, and Great Britain. Why would Poland bring such a Communist ire on itself? True, it halted the Bolshevik advance to the West in the war of 1920. But the real reason was much more profound. The threat to the USSR was not ethnic Poles or the state they recreated and dominated in the interwar period (1918–1939). The threat was in the idea of the old Polish-Lithuanian-Ruthenian Commonwealth whose ethos, culture, and "ideology" of freedom held sway in the Intermarium between the fifteenth and nineteenth centuries. It was the ancient political ethos that Stalin and his comrades feared. In the era of ethnic nationalism, the ethos failed to be translated into the language of modernity, but for the Soviets it loomed large as a threat because of its potential universalism. The Kremlin feared neither ethnic nationalism nor modern ideology to the same degree. It feared a freedom-loving principle that potentially could have organized the Intermarium and the rest of the region as an effective dam against Communism and other totalitarian threats, including Nazism. Muscovy also feared that the "Polish disease" of freedom would afflict other captives as well as its own Russian people: hence, Moscow's congenital hatred of "the Polish lords," a Comintern propaganda boogey man concocted to express the Communist detestation of liberty. All this remained a secret for the United States. As far as Washington was concerned, the interwar successor states were irrelevant and dispensable.

The willingness to sacrifice them for the sake of political expediency became all too evident when America emerged as the leading power on the world scene during World War II. So far as it existed at all as a function of US foreign policy, the question of the Intermarium was mostly viewed through the lens of Poland's situation or, more precisely, through the prism of Soviet–Polish relations. At the conferences in Tehran (November 28–December 1, 1943) and Yalta (February 4–11, 1945), the United States and Great Britain assigned Central and Eastern Europe to the Soviet sphere of influence. For all purposes, the Intermarium ceased to exist as a factor in US foreign policy until the 1980s (the exception was the perennially symbolic, if practically meaningless, American nonrecognition of the Soviet incorporation of the Baltics).

Aside from the diplomatic acquiescence in the Soviet takeover, American policy adopted the strategy of containment but this was predicated on an eminently defensive premise. Namely, the United States aimed to "contain" the Soviets in "their" own sphere, which de facto and de jure was considered as legitimate and, thus, reduced the early Cold War rhetoric of "liberation" of the captive nations and the "rollback" of Communism to mere propaganda of electoral politics.

Thus, American policy served to legitimize the Soviet domination. First, for the American people the war was over in 1945; we were ready to return to the business of peace. Second, our government and academic establishment, even at the height of Cold War hostilities, never let us forget that the Soviets had been America's allies against the Nazis. World War II-era propaganda persevered long after the conflict and both erstwhile partners in the East and West continued its dissemination, each for his own purpose. The Soviets promoted the image of the "Great Fatherland War" and their "victory over Fascism" because it served as an indispensable auxiliary instrument to legitimize their power, thereby serving both the purposes of domestic control and foreign propaganda (which catered mostly to the West's "progressive Left").[4]

Meanwhile, Americans maintained that there was such a thing as a war-time alliance with Moscow in fusing the term "alliance" with its most positive connotations of common values, and not just common interests. We perpetuated the myth of such a war-time alliance because it stressed the nation's commitment "never again" to permit Nazi-style genocide. This both justified American wartime losses and countered the arguments of the domestic Left which, consistently, but especially during the counter-cultural revolution of the 1960s and afterwards, claimed that the United States was really "AmeriKKKa," a "fascist" and "racist" entity akin to Nazi Germany. The celebration of the war-time alliance further endowed the postwar status quo of the division of the world into two antagonistic blocs with a hopeful promise that the two superpowers leading them could cooperate as they once had.

In the study of the past, as Norman Davies argues, the myth necessitated maintaining the supremacy of "the Allied scheme of history."[5] According to this scheme, World War II was a "good" war fought by the forces of "democracy" and "freedom" against Hitler. Once the Nazis were defeated, "democracy" and "freedom" triumphed. No thought was given to the fact that Berlin conspired with Moscow to launch the conflict in September 1939 and that until June 1941 the USSR was the most faithful ally of the Third Reich. Further, it was studiously avoided that Stalin had killed more people than Hitler and that both totalitarians threatened humanity with particularly genocidal brands of socialism, international and national. Last but not least, the fact that we pragmatically used one totalitarian against the other, failed to assert itself openly in American academia and, thus, in our historical consciousness. Hence, even from beyond his grave, the persistent significance of the myth of "Uncle Joe" Stalin in American thinking utterly outweighed the freedom of the Intermarium (and even Russia itself).

In America's mass culture, the myth has endured to this very day. It has naturally fluctuated, changing shape and form in congruence with succeeding intellectual fashions and political challenges. For half a century, we essentially projected our hopes, worries, and fears onto our relationship with the Soviet Union. First, the original rendition of the myth was thoroughly naive, stressing that the Soviets were just like us. Next, the myth adopted the wishful thinking of the early Cold War era: Why did the Soviets suddenly stop being like us? Then, the pendulum swung and some asked why we were not more like the Soviets with their equality and social justice in place of inhuman capitalism and "so-called" bourgeois democracy. Or, perhaps, the New Left chimed in, why would not we become even better than the bureaucratically ossified Soviets who, admittedly, were superior to us but not as good as revolutionary China or Cuba? In the 1970s, with moral relativism asserting itself, some resigned themselves that we were just as bad as the Soviets. It was in this context that we saw the "convergence" theory. In the 1980s, the larger part of the foreign policy establishment, Ronald Reagan notwithstanding, held that if we only treated the Soviets like good citizens of the world, while simultaneously permitting them to achieve strategic parity with us, they would become good citizens, and thus our friends once more. If popular sentiments were any gauge, we never wanted to destroy the Soviets. We simply wanted to get along just as we did, briefly, during World War II. None of America's attitudes, on the cultural level, left any room for the Intermarium.

This strategic reason was also largely absent in academia. In international relations and political science, the realists accepted the USSR as an unpleasant, yet permanent reality and devised the policy of containment to deal with it. The regnant "realism" of the Kissingerian variety assented to a spheres of influence division of the world as the optimal model of strategic stability, and this concept, which bred the "Sonnenfeldt Doctrine" of accepting Soviet subjugation of East-Central Europe, viewed movements for national independence within the Soviet sphere as irritants that threatened to disrupt the hard-won modus vivendi—the apogee of realist strategic ambitions: the "balance of power."[6] The intensity of the realists' commitment to spheres of influence was such that under the influence of NSC Soviet Affairs Advisor, Condoleezza Rice, Secretary of State, James Baker, and National Security Advisor, Brent Scowcroft, President George H. W. Bush worked to preserve the territorial integrity of the collapsing USSR and, in his "Chicken Kiev" speech, denounced Ukrainian aspirations for independence as grounded in a "suicidal nationalism."[7] The realists effectively maintained that stance for half a century. The idealists were torn between, initially, their admiration of the allegedly progressive "fatherland of the world proletariat" and, increasingly, concerns about human rights, Jewish emigration, and, later, also labor rights because of the rise of "Solidarity" in Poland. The old Wilsonian concept of nationality rights yielded to minority rights. Thus, both the realists and the idealists, for different reasons, were rather wary of nationalism, particularly of the anti-Kremlin type. That meant that the Intermarium was ignored at best, or viewed as a threat at worst.

Elsewhere in social sciences, the Left emerged dominant in the rapacious Gramscian wake of the 1960s. The Communists, their liberal-left apologists, conscious and subconscious Soviet agents of influence, anti-anti-Communists, and other leftist scholars whose behavior was indistinguishable from those later revealed to be agents of influence, exercised disproportionate influence over America's discourse on the USSR.[8] Moscow was their main point of reference. It was the center. The progressives stuck to this concept despite widely deriding the totalitarian paradigm of the study of the USSR, which, after all, was predicated on the supremacy of the center. That contradiction, of course, did not stop them. The peripheries, including the Intermarium, hardly mattered for them. Or, if they did, these regions were to be reduced to a folkloristic phenomena or postmodernistically deconstructed to be shown as, allegedly, "imagined communities" with "invented traditions." Thus, American academia was largely at war with small nationalisms.

The anti-Communists, mostly conservative but occasionally liberal as well, were the exception. Even though they held fast to the totalitarian model, which was by definition Moscow-centric, they paid attention to the peripheries. The anti-Communists kept the memory of the captive nations alive. And that was enough to provoke the ire of the anti-anti-Communists who liked to dismiss the people of the Intermarium, including the émigrés in the United States, as inveterate "reactionaries," "fascists," and, since the 1960s, increasingly, "anti-Semites." The last label, in particular, has enjoyed a wide currency for a while now. It has tarred not only the Poles but also the Balts, Ukrainians, Belarusians, and others collectively with the merciless brush of being Nazi collaborators, virtual co-executors of the Holocaust of the Jews. In this rendering, the denizens of the Intermarium were the radical opposite of our war-time Soviet allies and, thus, unworthy of our help.

The Soviets, for their part, chimed in with eerily identical propaganda. Anyone who opposed the Communists was a "fascist" and a "reactionary," thwarting progress. Any alternative to Communism could only be more oppressive, theocracy, for example. In fact, had "Solidarity" not been crushed by martial law in 1981 and 1982, Poland would have surely become a "second Iran," according to the Kremlin canard. Further, the Communist secret police staged numerous provocations to smear nationalism with a brush of "Nazism." It infiltrated nationalist underground and dissident circles. It set up false nationalist organizations, which spewed hatred, racism, and anti-Semitism.[9] It even went so far as to discredit Russian nationalism as a chauvinistic and anti-Semitic movement or cultural impulse so as to bolster the failing legitimacy of the regime and to win Western support for it.

Russia's own *Pamyat* (Remembrance) is a case in point. Initially, a decentralized grass roots effort to preserve the nation's historical monuments and sites, it was promptly taken over by the Soviet secret police, the Committee of State Security Komitet Gosudarstvennoy Bezopastnosti (KGB) in the early 1980s. *Pamyat* then became the chief purveyor of gross intolerance and shrill chauvinism.[10] All this was a Soviet operation to disinform the West. Yes, the sirens of the KGB crooned, the Communist dictatorship may have its disagreeable features but at least it keeps the genocidal nationalist maniacs trampled underfoot. If Communism falls, Nazism will rise, or at least something similarly repulsive.

The disinformation played well in the West. In combination with anti-anti-Communism and all flavors of academic Leftism, it seriously conditioned and limited America's response to the pleas for freedom emanating from the western peripheries of the USSR. As a result, the people of the Intermarium were largely left to their own devices when they made their bid for liberty, starting in the late 1980s. Once successful, because of the implosion of the Moscow center, their emergence has slowly begun to register in the United States and infiltrate our reality. This is mostly because America enjoys an inordinate degree of popularity in the Baltics, in particular, but also in Ukraine and Belarus. Even American academia has taken note and a number of works, of various quality, have resulted. Nonetheless, the prejudice stemming from home-grown ideologies and Soviet disinformation has persisted.[11] Western scholars tend to focus their ire almost exclusively on nationalism and give post-Communism a free ride.[12] The result is that academics are yet to devise a fair lense to study the area in its own right and politicians are yet to elucidate a coherent US policy toward the Intermarium. We shall endeavor to remedy the problem.

Notes

1. There have been very few works on the Intermarium by Western-born scholars, in the United States, in particular. See Jonathan Levy, *The* Intermarium *: Wilson, Madison, & East Central European Federalism* (Boca Raton, FL: Dissertation. com, 2006); Oliver Schmidtke and Serhy Yekelchyk, *Europe's Last Frontier? Belarus, Moldova, and Ukraine between Russia and the European Union* (New York: Palgrave Macmillan, 2008). See also "The Western States," *Russia and the Independent States*, ed. by Daniel C. Diller (Washington, DC: Congressional Quarterly, 1993), 275–94; and the following two essays in Daniel Hamilton and Gerhard Mangott, eds., *The New Eastern Europe: Ukraine, Belarus, Moldova* (Washington, DC: Center for Transatlantic Relations, 2007): Angela Stent, "The Lands in between: The New Eastern Europe in the Twenty-First Century," (1–24) and Gerhard Mangott, "Deconstructing a Region," (261–86), http://transatlantic. sais-jhu.edu/bin/o/y/new_eastern_europe_text.pdf (accessed April 23, 2012). The twentieth century, in particular, World War II and its aftermath, has generated most interest so far, but here émigrés and native scholars predominate with a few exceptions, most notably a liberal Timothy Snyder, *Bloodlands: Europe between Hitler and Stalin* (New York: Basic Books, 2010). See also a post-Soviet Jewish voice of Alexander V. Prusin, *The Lands between: Conflict in the East European Borderlands, 1870–1992* (New York and Oxford: Oxford University Press, 2010); and various contributors to Peter Gatrell and Nick Baron, eds., *Warlands: Population Resettlement and State Reconstruction in the Soviet-East European Borderlands, 1945–50* (Houndmills: Palgrave Macmillan, 2009).
2. The United States was influenced, in particular, by the German version of history, as American universities were positively captivated by German scholarship, philosophy, and propaganda. See, e.g., Vejas Gabriel Liulevicius, *The German Myth of the East, 1800 to the Present* (Oxford and New York: Oxford University Press, 2009). This was a simple function of Germany commandeering, in the nineteenth century, the intellectual explication of Western philosophy and history. Freedom itself was supposed to have been born amongst the pre-Christian Germanic tribes. See John Burrow, *A History of Histories: Epics, Chronicles, Romances, and Inquiries from Herodotus and Thucydides to the Twentieth Century* (New York: Alfred A. Knopf, 2008), 380–96, 425–37.
3. See Pawel Styrna, *Poland and the New York Times* (forthcoming from Leopolis Press and the Kościuszko Chair of Polish Studies at the Institute of World Politics).

4.   See Chris Bellamy, *Absolute War: Soviet Russia in the Second World War* (New York: Vintage Books, 2008).

5.   Norman Davies, *No Simple Victory: World War II in Europe, 1939–1945* (New York: Viking, 2006).

6.   Henry Kissinger, *Diplomacy* (New York: Simon & Schuster, 1994).

7.   Zbigniew Brzezinski, *Second Chance: Three Presidents and the Crisis of American Superpower* (New York: Basic Books, 2007), 46–47, 53, 58, 61, 78. Dissident voices in the US government included very few intrepid souls, perhaps most notably Paul Goble, who specialized in the USSR's non-Russian nationalities at the State Department. Even earlier, under Ronald Reagan, it was quite hard to overcome the ingrained prejudice of Moscow-centric bureaucracies, even in the intelligence community including, for instance, the CIA's Office of Soviet Affairs within the Directorate of Intelligence. Such clairvoyants as James Bruce or Ken deGraffenreid were strictly exceptional. See, e.g., James Bruce, "Dimensions of Civil Unrest in the USSR," *Top Secret Memorandum* (National Intelligence Council, 1983), 1–29 (forthcoming in *Glaukopis*); and "Prof. deGraffenreid discusses Reagan's intelligence and security policies," April 26, 2012, posted at http://www.iwp.edu/news_publications/detail/prof-degraffenreid-discusses-reagans-intelligence-and-security-policies.

8.   See John Earl Haynes and Harvey Klehr, *In Denial: Historians, Communism & Espionage* (San Francisco, CA: Encounter Books, 2003); Paul Kengor, *Dupes: How America's Adversaries Have Manipulated Progressives for a Century* (Wilmington, DE: ISI Books, 2010).

9.   Established in the late 1980s, the extremist nationalist Social-National Party in Soviet Ukraine was "outright led by the KGB," for example. See Grzegorz Górny, "Ukraiński kłopot z Banderą," ("The Ukrainian Problem with Bandera") *Rzeczpospolita, Plus-Minus*, October 17–18, 2009. See also Sławomir Cenckiewicz, "'Endekoesbecja': Dezintegracja Polskiego Związku Katolicko-Społecznego w latach 1982–1986," ("'The Endek-Commie Secret Police': The Disintegration of the Polish Catholic-Social Union, 1982–1986") in Sławomir Cenckiewicz, *Śladami bezpieki i partii: Studia-źródła-publicystyka* (*Tracking the Secret Police and the Party: Studies, Sources, Journalism*) (Łomianki: LTW, 2009), 421–561.

10. According to Vadim Belotserkovsky, Pamyat—"Russia's first fascist organization"—was launched on the explicit orders of the top Communist leadership for the domestic consumption to counter Poland's "Solidarity" in 1981. The Soviet authorities, including KGB head Yurii Andropov himself, denounced the free Polish trade union as an example of "self-administration which draws toward anarcho-syndicalism" and, of course, "a conspiracy of the CIA and the Zionists." However, the Kremlin praised Poland's Grunwald Patriotic Association which was national-bolshevik, anti-Jewish, chauvinistic, and enjoyed the sponsorship of the secret police. Pamyat was conceived as a similar extremist force against "anarcho-syndicalism" in the USSR. After the suppression of "Solidarity," Moscow kept Pamyat largely under wraps only to reactivate it in the late 1980s. See Вадим Белоцерковский, "Происхождение организованного фашизма в России," *Civitas: Вестник гражданского общества*, http://www.vestnikcivitas.ru/pbls/1354 (accessed March 29, 2011); Paul Goble, "Moscow Prosecutors Refuse to Ban 'Protocols of the Elders of Zion' as Extremist," *Window on Eurasia*, http://windowoneurasia.blogspot.com/2011/03/window-on-eurasia-moscow-prosecutors.html (accessed March 30, 2011). See also John Garrard, "A Pamyat Manifesto:

Introductory Note and Translation." *Nationalities Papers* 19, no. 2 (Fall 1991): 135–45. The practice has continued with the Kremlin stage managing nationalist extremists, soccer hooligans, and skinheads against the opposition and the minorities. See Charles Clover, "'Managed Nationalism' Turns Nasty for Putin," *Financial Times*, http://www.ft.com/cms/s/0/046a3e30-0ec9-11e0-9ec3-00144feabdc0.html#axzz1BdrkNvR1 (accessed December 23, 2010).

11. For a nefarious convergence of Communist propaganda and postmodernism see Marek Jan Chodakiewicz, "Poland in America's Crooked Mirror: An Installment in Culture Wars," *The International Affairs Review* no. 1–2 (157–58) (2008): 42–56, with a version posted at http://www.iwp.edu/docLib/20080222_MirrorImagingAmerica.pdf; and a short version in Polish as "Polska w krzywym zwierciadle Ameryki," *Najwyższy Czas!*, March 8, 2008.

12. One prominent scholar was even seriously concerned about the possibility of a monarchical restoration in Russia, while the post-Communists were stealing the country blind and the post-KGB men were preparing to assume power openly. See Walter Laqueur, *Black Hundred: The Rise of the Extreme Right in Russia* (New York: Harper Perennial, 1993). Compare it with: Jarosław Bratkiewicz, *Rosyjscy nacjonaliści w latach 1992–1996: Od detradycjonalizacji do retradycjonalizacji* (*Russian Nationalists in 1992–1996: From De-Traditionalism to Re-Traditionalism*) (Warszawa: Instytut Studiów Politycznych Polskiej Akademii Nauk, 1998) and Andreas Umland, ed., *Theorizing Post-Soviet Russia's Extreme Right: Comparative Political, Historical and Sociological Approaches* (Armonk, NY: M.E. Sharpe 2008), which is vol. 46, no. 4 (July–August 2008) of *Russian Politics and Law*. And see, in a broader context, Michael Minkenberg, *Historical Legacies and the Radical Right in Post-Cold War Central and Eastern Europe* (Stuttgart and Hannover: Ibidem-Verlag, 2010).

Sources and Method

Ours is a synthesis of the Intermarium's past. Although we rely heavily on various archival collections and published primary sources, we also extensively refer to scholarly monographs and other secondary sources. But we further delve into contemporary matters. That entails consulting electronic and print media as well as investigating through travels and interviews. The Internet expedited both parts of our research and writing endeavor.[1]

Researching history should be rather straight-forward, if there is unimpeded access to the archives. That is the case in much of the Intermarium, except for Belarus and, to a lesser extent, Russia and Ukraine. We have thus worked in a score of archives in North America, Central and Eastern Europe, and Russia. However, this monograph is intended mainly for the English-speaking reader and the beginner student. Therefore, for the most part, we have elected to list chiefly secondary sources in English, occasionally annotating them. The most prominent exception is the section of World War II and its aftermath, where the reader can find some references to primary sources and many secondary sources written in the languages of the Intermarium. We have also occasionally included notable works in their original languages in other sections of this work. Most original research can be found fully annotated in our other historical works on related topics.[2]

Researching and writing about the events in real time is quite challenging. Contemporary developments tend to seem always red-hot; they often defy the scholar's attempts at prudence and balance. This is not only because of one's emotional investment in here and now, but also because of the lack of reliable sources. Here, one must rely on newspapers, radiobroadcasts, Internet podcasts, news, blogs, and postings, TV programs, and video documentaries as well as direct interviews with the participants and observers. Consequently, the historian has a hard time discerning the relative importance of the emerging trends, and even the significance of these trends can escape him or her altogether. Phenomena and personages appearing important at the moment can be utterly meaningless in the long run. Even truly cardinal developments can escape the scholar's scrutiny undetected. In the present the teleological forward thrust of history remains largely obscure, except in theological terms of Christianity or Judaism.

A scholar's inquiry would be incomplete without a traveler's journey to the heart of his interest. Therefore, we organized a three-part expedition to the post-Soviet sphere during the summer of 2010.[3] This was to follow up on our ventures into those lands undertaken periodically over twenty years since 1989. This time, we sojourned throughout the area, as opposed to only a few selected destinations as before. We went to the Baltics, Ukraine, Russia, and Belarus. We visited nearly everywhere between Tallinn and Odessa: all major cities, most medium-size ones, and much of the countryside around Marijampolė, Kaunas, Šiauliai, Jelgava, Riga, Salacgrīva, Pärnu, Tallinn, Narva, Jõgeva, Tartu, Põlva, Kanepi, Ape, Smiltene, Ruana, Rēzekne, Krāslava, Daugavpils, Zarasai, Utena, Molėtai, Švenčionys, Vilnius, Šalčininkai, Druskininkai, Lazdijai; Lviv, Ivano Frankyvsk, Chernovtsi, Kamianets Podil-skyi, Khmelnytskyi, Vinnytsia, Zhytomyr, Kyiv, Korosten, Novohrad Volynskyi, Rivne, Sarny, Lutsk, Kovel; Brest, Baranovichi, Minsk, Orsha, Vitebsk, Stoubtsy, Navahrudak, Lida, Hrodna; and Smolensk. In other words, this time we covered all areas of the Intermarium which were once within the borders of the Polish-Lithuanian Commonwealth, and even beyond, because we extended our trip as far as Odessa.

The chief objective of the field expedition was to collect primary and secondary sources as well as mine raw data from the encounters with the locals and their environment. The method was an immersion into, and the penetration of, the local communities along with sampling their cultural and social fare and offerings as a means of learning their concerns and soliciting their opinion on the current situation. Further, we paid attention to material culture, including scholarship, archival material, bookstore contents, exhibits, monuments, and architecture. Last but not least, we inquired about politics and economics on the microscale.

A word on methodology of the interviews is warranted. A journalistic approach was the rule. The selection of the witnesses was random and hap-hazard. Our sampling method should not be confused with scientific polling Western-style. Instead, we encouraged unguarded sharing of whatever information the interlocutors felt important. The conversations were rather unstructured. The tone ranged from casual to venting. Since the interlocutors felt uncomfortable about being recorded in any way, we made mental notes and, later, we sometimes jotted down a few of the salient points. We also discussed with our research assistants the exchanges we had had with the local people. This was necessary because the natives of the post-Soviet sphere are acutely suspicious of any official polling. They tend to either give the pollster the answers they think one expects, or to lie spitefully to distort the poll, or to express the opinion most prevalent in the media and at the official level, which does not necessarily reflect the opinion of the persons polled. Thus, our sampling method allows for discovering some of the concerns of the local people but is not quantifiable in any scientific way. This was one of the serious challenges encountered on the journey. Another one was geography.

The geography of the place is often daunting to the outsider.[4] In particular, the place names can appear confusing. Therefore, we have decided, while initially identifying a place, to list all of its historical names. Later, as we move through history, the names will alternate to reflect the demographic make up of the majority population or to denote the oft-changing state jurisdiction it fell under. Therefore, we shall initially refer to Lithuania's capital as Vilnius/Wilno/Vilna; but in, say, 1919, we shall call it Wilno, its Polish designation. Medieval Ruthenia's Kiev becomes contemporary Ukraine's Kyiv. Same applies to Soviet Belarussia populated with Belarussians, and the successor state Belarus inhabited by Belarusians as well as Moldavia/Moldova and Moldavians/Moldovans. We shall also use English names, if possible: hence, Volhynia rather than Wołyń.

The question of national identity in the Intermarium is truly tricky. Roughly until the mid-nineteenth century most people there had a "local" identity. They were simply peasants (usually of unconscious Ruthenian ethnicity) and their most important frame of reference was their religion (usually Eastern Orthodoxy), their village, and their lord. Only the nobility, the political (historic) nation, which uniquely constituted about 10 percent of the population, developed something akin to national consciousness already in the premodern times. They identified themselves generically as "Poles." However, because the population was eminently multi-ethno-cultural, it was not unusual to encounter a person self-dubbed as *natione Polonus, gente Ruthenus, civitas Magnum Ducatus Lithuanorum, origine Judaeus*—of the Polish nation, of the Ruthenian people, of the citizenship of the Grand Duchy of Lithuania, and of Jewish origin. That simply meant that, in the sixteenth-century context, the person was a Polish Catholic noble of Jewish origin assimilated among the Ruthenians in the Grand Duchy of Lithuania, which was a federated part of the Polish-Lithuanian Commonwealth. It is quite appropriate to consider a historical Pole of the Intermarium through a similar prism as we would a contemporary American, who can at the same time be Irish, German, Polynesian, Mexican, Cherokee, and African, for example. Therefore, we have eschewed an ethno-nationalist definition of one's nationality: "blood." Biological ethnicity as derived from DNA research interests us least, if at all. Instead, we have stressed self-identification, culture, and language. Thus, "Polish" will denote willful adherence to a culture, rather than an ethnic label, unless otherwise noted. On the other hand, nonhistoric ("peasant" or "folkish") nations usually recognize themselves, and are considered by others, as ethno-nationalist groups, e.g., Ukrainians. Thus, Ukrainian in this context refers to local, regional, and national levels; Polish has an additional universal dimension between the Black and Baltic Seas.[5]

For cultural, historical, and political reasons, Poland and the Poles will constitute an important point of reference throughout our journey in the Intermarium. "Polishness" will signify a historically alternative—Western and universalist—organizing principle in the region, in distinction to Communism, Nazism, ethno-nationalism, and other competing "isms."

Last but not least, in the process of our journey we shall try to explicate a variety of phenomena in the Intermarium that the locals have found obvious and the outsiders baffling. For example, some Westerners have been surprised at the growing importance of religion in the post-Soviet zone. But the same persons are prone to frown at the religious institutions and spirituality of the Deep South in the United States. They are also discreetly embarrassed by the strong religiosity of the African-American community, even when it serves leftist and liberal goals. In each case, one should shed one's prejudices and approach the phenomenon of faith with an open mind.

Among the most enduring institutions, none is arguably harder to grasp for a Western reader than the secret police. This is partly because the Westerner is hard pressed to find anything analogous in contemporary times in his own society. Further, this is because the secret police operates, well, in secret. Thus, it tries to leave as few traces of its activities as it is possible. The lack of access to its archives, in turn, fertilizes the imagination and results in a plethora of conspiracy theories which, of course, are out of fashion in any polite society. Yet, the secret police has been one of the most nefarious phenomena in the Intermarium.

Inaugurated under the Romanovs, the Habsburgs, and the Hohenzollerns in the eighteenth century, those domestic spy organizations were designed to monitor the elites and the people to ferret out the enemies of the rulers and, thus, to maintain the stability of the state. During the nineteenth century the secret services became professionalized and evolved some basic procedures of enduring quality. They combined repression with domestic and foreign intelligence gathering. Provocation emerged as their favorite tool. They achieved their most grotesque and horrific shape under the totalitarian regimes of the Soviet Union and the Third Reich. The secret police simply became converted into terror apparatus. They also improved on old modes of operation and applied them in the totalitarian context. The Soviet secret services, in particular, perfected the art of subterfuge, deception, infiltration, disintegration, and provocation to control their own citizens, counter foreign espionage activities, and manage Western perceptions of Communism and its aims. In comparison, their Nazi counterparts were rather less accomplished in deception. Their methods were cruder and intelligence-gathering missions less successful. However, the secret policemen of both systems plied intelligence and terror interchangeably. It was quite common for an officer of the *Sicherheitsdient* (SD), the Nazi security office, to alternate between cracking Polish underground networks and attending to the mass murder of the Holocaust. Likewise, in a similarly flawless exchange, an operative in the *Narodnii Komissariat Vnutrennikh Del* (NKVD), the Kremlin's security police, having prepared the Katyn Forest massacre of the Polish POWs, would be dispatched to spy on America's nuclear secrets. There was no contradiction perceived between the two roles; they were viewed as complementary by the perpetrators themselves.[6]

Whereas the Nazi secret police structures were utterly destroyed with the collapse of the Third Reich, the Communist ones endured, albeit in a transformed manner. The first important watershed was Stalin's death in 1953 when mass terror was suspended. It continued to be a possibility until the implosion of the USSR in 1992 because, simply, the secret police maintained the capacity to rain mass death if the Politbureau so desired. Under post-Communism, the secret services of the successor states retained the structure, personnel, and the net of agents of the USSR, initially at least in the Baltics, partly in Ukraine and Moldova, and permanently in Belarus. As the chief purveyor of terror, misery, pathology, and mischief, the Intermarium's secret services would like to be perceived as ubiquitous and omnipotent. They are no longer either; but they continue to exercise undue influence everywhere to a varied degree and, hence, should be kept in mind accordingly as a tool of power.

Our work is divided into four parts. First, a brief outline of the history of the Intermarium over the past millennium or so will culminate with the sanguinary experience of World War I, and the Bolshevik Revolution and the bloodshed it wrought. Second, the pivot of our story, the region's near destruction at the hands of the Nazis and Communists during World War II, as well as its sordid aftermath, will cheerfully conclude with the liberation of the 1990s. Third, a discussion will follow of the challenges of the current times, including domestic and foreign policy of the component parts of the Intermarium. Last but not least, we shall delve into the issue of collective memory, individual recollections, and false consciousness within the post-totalitarian context of the newly liberated states.

A brief history is necessary to provide a proper framework to understand the Intermarium. Without it, the experiences of its people would not make much sense and we would simply continue to clone the Muscovite imperialist spin still pervading much of Western historiography. Our brief telling of the Intermarium's past should be satisfactory to the untainted beginner, stimulating to the general scholar, and challenging to the specialist hitherto captive of the standard Moscow-centric tale or an ethno-centric myth of any of the nationalities inhabiting the space. The focus on World War II and its aftermath serves to demonstrate, on the one hand, how the Muscovite spin came to dominate our understanding of the area through the simple device of "winners writing history." On the other hand, it shows the destruction of the peoples and their institutions that could have provided an alternative narrative (or, more precisely, narratives) of the Intermarium. Last but not least, we shall discuss the results of the implantation of false consciousness by the totalitarians on the inhabitants of the Intermarium. To understand the violence perpetrated on the collective memory of its people is to appreciate the necessity of resurrecting individual recollections to make the civic societies of the area whole again. The process should commence with the individual fusing with other experiences in his or her locality and immediate region; their sum should then converge into a national framework to result in an all-Intermarium synthesis of many narratives, ultimately reconcilable under the rubric of freedom.

Intermarium has been with me since my childhood. First, I imbibed it from family stories, of Wilno and Lwów, in particular, and then from literature and poetry: Adam Mickiewicz, Henryk Sienkiewicz, Eliza Orzeszkowa, Zygmunt Krasiński, Henryk Rzewuski, and many others. As an undergraduate and graduate student I benefited from lectures, seminars, and informal instructions of such inspiring teachers as Robert Conquest, Martin Malia, Anthony D'Agostino, Dwight van Horn, Richard Wortman, Mark von Hagen, Mihai Maxim, and, last but not least, Istvan Deak, who all taught me to navigate the area between the Black and Baltic Seas, as well as between Berlin and Moscow (sometimes with a detour via Vienna).

The present monograph germinated in me for decades. It finally grew out of a mammoth paper delivered at the panel on "The National Resistance Movements and Collaboration in World War II on the Territory of the Old *Rzeczpospolita*: History and Memory," during the conference on "Politics with History and Collective Memory in Public Discourses in East Central Europe," held at Bremen University, in Germany, on October 14–16, 2005. I am grateful to Professor Zdzisław Krasnodębski (Bremen University) for conceiving the idea of the conference and for suggesting the general thrust of the paper.[7]

Between 2005 and 2010, I spoke at various public functions, ranging from conferences to brown bag lectures, on selected topics of the Intermarium. These included, most notably, "East Goes West: The EU and Poland," at the Heritage Foundation, Hudson Institute, Discovery Institute, and Global Britain Conference "Is the European Union in the Interest of the United States of America?" Washington, DC, in June 2005 (I would like to thank Dr. Lee Edwards for his invitation); "The United States, Poland, and Estonia: Public Diplomacy and Individual Efforts," Respublica Student Fraternity, University of Warsaw, Warsaw, Poland, in June 2006 (I would like to thank Dr. Piotr Gontarczyk for facilitating this event); "Polish-Jewish Relations in the 20th and 21st Centuries from the American Perspective," The Institute of National Remembrance, Warsaw, Poland, in June 2006 (I would like to thank late Professor Janusz Kurtyka for organizing this lecture); "Poland and Post-Soviet Russia," a public lecture at "Poland in the Rockies," Canmore, Alberta, Canada, in July 2006 (I would like to thank Tony Muszyński for inviting me); "The Soviet Invasion against the Eastern Borderlands," a public lecture series,

The Polish-Canadian Association, The Polish House (Dom Polski), Calgary, Canada, in May 2007 (I would like to thank Szymon and Krysia Apanowicz for organizing this event); "Transformation: Continuity and Discontinuity in Post-Soviet Europe between 1988 and 1993," at the Department of International Relations, Florida International University, Miami, FL, in February 2008 (I would like to thank Professor Ralph Clem for inviting me to speak); and "The Nature and Future of Communism," Conference on "Captive Nations: Past, Present-and Future?" the Heritage Foundation, in July 2009 (I would like to acknowledge Helle Dale for encouraging my participation).

At my academic home at the Institute of World Politics, Washington, DC, I lectured periodically on various topics related to my research interest for the purpose of this monograph. These included "The Collapse of Communism and Its Aftermath: The Case of the Secret Police in East Central Europe," a brown bag lecture, in July 2006; "Poland, the US, and the Transformation, 1985–2008," at The Kościuszko Chair unveiling ceremony, in November 2008; "Hubal: Guerrilla Warfare in Poland," IWP Movie Night Lecture Series, in June 2009; and "The Katyn Forest Massacre," IWP Movie Night Lecture Series, in June 2010. Most importantly, during the academic year 2011–2012, I presented a fifteen-part lecture series based upon draft chapters of the present monograph. The assistance of Katie Bridges, Tricia Lloyd, Colin Parks, Jason Johnsrud, Charles van Someren, Brooks Sommer, and Dominic Bonaduce was indispensable in this undertaking. The questions from the students and colleagues were very helpful in honing in my arguments.

While working on the monograph, I also published articles on the Intermarium in various scholarly periodicals and popular press. Both are mentioned in the footnotes. Among many others, I would like to thank Mrs. Carole Foryst for putting in a good word for me at the *Journal of Intelligence and Counterintelligence.* Edwin Dyga and Derek Turner took great care of me at the *Quarterly Review.* Jerzy Kłosiński of *Tygodnik Solidarność* and Dr. Tomasz Sommer of *Najwyższy Czas!* deserve credit for consistently opening up their pages for my feullietons and analyses of selected topics of the Intermarium.

I would like to acknowledge my colleagues and friends who read and commented on various drafts of my book as well as answered some of my questions, including Ambassador (Dr.) Aldona Wos, Professor Ewa M. Thompson (Rice University), Professor Dariusz Tołczyk (University of Virginia), Professor John Radziłowski (University of Alaska South-East), Professor Peter Stachura (University of Sterling), Professor Stephen Baskerville (Patrick Henry College), Professor Carolyn C. Guile (Colgate University), Professor Juliana Pilon (The Institute of World Politics), Professor John Tierney (IWP), Professor Herbert Romerstein (IWP), Professor Paul Goble (IWP), Professor John Lenczowski (IWP), General Walter Jajko (IWP), late Professor Brian Kelley (IWP), Professor Tania Mastrapa (IWP), Professor Alexander Osipian (Department of History and Cultural Studies, Kramatorsk Institute of Economics and Humanities, Kramatorsk, Ukraine), Dr. Jack Dziak, Dr. Nadia Schadlow, Dr. Tomasz Sommer, Dr. Wojciech Jerzy Muszyński, Dr. Jerzy Targalski (a.k.a. "Józef Darski"), Vladimir Bukovsky, and Richard Tyndorf. Aside from reading and commenting extensively on my manuscript, Dr. Targalski and Mark Paul, an independent scholar from Canada, also shared generously with me their extensive research on the Intermarium.

At the Institute of World Politics, I would further like to recognize the invaluable assistance of our chief librarian Jim Stambaugh, library manager Dmitry Kulik, his sidekick Christopher Fulford, and, especially, our superb assistant for academic affairs, Mallorie (Lewis) Marino, without whom we would often be lost. After her departure, Daniel Acheson piloted the project at the very end. Paweł Styrna deserves applause for working on the technical side of this project and picking my brain with his provocations. Further, his contributions to research were second to none. Our interns Victoria Vlad, Jordan Harms, and Ian Myre's dedication to this undertaking was exemplary. Mackenzi Jo Siebert of Patrick Henry College deserves our gratitude, too, for helping with research. I would also like to thank my students in our IWP seminar on "Russian Politics and Foreign Policy," which I co-teach with Dr. John Lenczowski (and whose influence and incisiveness have been paramount), for helping me better elucidate some of the concepts presented here (2005–2011), in particular, Daniel Acheson, Lucie Adamski, Anna Akopyan, Emily Betson, Erin Carrington, Tim Coakley, Scott Copeland, Kevin Cyron, Julien Duval-Leroy, William Elliot, Darren Fazzino, Alexandra Filipowicz, Chris Fulford, Kate Harrison, Emily Hawkes, Katherine Humphries, Richard Koyomji, James P. Kromhout, Daniel Lips, Colin McIntosh, Donald McCann, Christopher Miller, Lance Mogard, Mark Moody, Travis Molliere, David Ray Pate, Apostolas Pittas, John Rose, David Shaw, Cordelia Sinclair, Brian Scicluna, Herpreet Singh, Oksana Skidan, Chris Smith, Storm Swendsboe, Santee Vasquez, Nicole Villescas, Megan Watson, and Kereth Wein.

I owe a great deal of thanks to numerous individuals who facilitated my research, travel, and contacts, among them most notably Lady Blanka Rosenstiel, Ava and Adam Bąk, John Niemczyk, Ron Trzciński, and Dr. Maria Michejda; and, in the Intermarium itself, Jolanta Mysiakowska, Tadeusz Kadenacy, Sebastian Bojemski, Kaziu Ujazdowski, Adam Wojtasiewicz, and Radek Pyffel. All others wish to remain anonymous, in particular, in Belarus, but also in the intelligence community.

This project would have been impossible without a network of friends. Accordingly, I would like to thank, in addition to individuals mentioned above, Dr. Janusz Subczynski; Magdalena and Iwo Pogonowski; Wanda and Zenon Wos; Lydia and Władysław Poncet; and Vincent Knapczyk, Anton Chrościelewski, Marian Dorr-Dorynek, Jerzy Włodarczyk, Anthony Domino,

Dr. Teofil Lachowicz, Christopher Olechowski, Sylvia Pełka, and their comrades-in-arms at the Polish American Veterans Association (PAVA-SWAP). Last but not least, gratitude is due to my foster father Zdzisław Zakrzewski and to my sister Anna Wellisz for their suggestions, and my toddler Helenka for providing much needed comic relief at home.

Special thanks are due to the team at Transaction: Mary E. Curtis, Hannah K. Jones, Mindy Waizer, Jennifer A. Nippins, Jeffrey Stetz, and, last but not least, the late Dr. Irving Horowitz. They were all fantastic and contributed, each in her or his way, to the birthing of our monograph.

The completion of this opus was possible thanks to the generous assistance of the Earhardt Foundation and the Smith Richardson Foundation. I shall gladly take the blame for all the mistakes in this work, both real and postmodernistically imagined.

Notes

1. Many resources are available on line. Habitually, we set our favorites to the Library of Congress (http://catalog.loc.gov/), Columbia University libraries (http://library.columbia.edu/), and Biblioteka Narodowa in Warsaw (http://alpha.bn.org.pl/screens/opacmenu_pol.html). There are very many other helpful websites for the study of the Intermarium. For example, see "Modern History of Ukraine, 1848–Present: A List of English-Language Secondary Sources (Monographs, Book chapters, Collections, Articles)," comp. by Orest T. Martynowych, Centre for Ukrainian Canadian Studies, University of Manitoba (Spring 2011), http://umanitoba.ca/faculties/arts/departments/ukrainian_canadian_studies/media/Modern_Ukrainian_History_biblio.pdf. And see below.

2. So far, we have authored, coauthored, edited, and coedited fifteen monographs and documentary collections on the history of the region, including biography, microhistory, general history, and history of ideas. Most of our works are cited below.

3. A full report of the trip in Marek Jan Chodakiewicz, "Notatki z post-Sowiecji (część I)," ("Notes from the Post-Soviet Lands, Part I") *Najwyższy Czas!*, October 9, 2010, XXXV; "Notatki z post-Sowiecji (część II)," ("Notes from the Post-Soviet Lands, Part II") *Najwyższy Czas!*, October 16, 2010, XXXV; "Notatki z post-Sowiecji (część III)," ("Notes from the Post-Soviet Lands, Part III") *Najwyższy Czas!*, October 23, 2010, XXXV; "Notatki z post-Sowiecji (część IV)," ("Notes from the Post-Soviet Lands, Part IV") *Najwyższy Czas!*, October 30–November 6, 2010, XLIII.

4. For a brief and neat presentation of the geography and history of the western rim of the Intermarium and its immediate neighbors, see Wojciech Roszkowski, "The Lands between: The Making of East-Central Europe," in *New Europe: The Impact of the First Decade*, vol. 1: *Trends and Prospects*, ed. Teresa Rakowska-Harmstone, Piotr Dutkiewicz, and Agnieszka Orzelska (Warsaw: Institute of Political Studies Polish Academy of Sciences and Collegium Civitas Press, 2006), 13–55. And for a very useful discussion of the Intermarium and its Polish connection see Agnieszka Biedrzycka, Fr. Roman Dzwonkowski, Janusz Kurtyka, and Janusz Smaza interviewed by Barbara Polak, "Kresy pamiętamy," ("We Remember the Borderlands") *Biuletyn Instytutu Pamięci Narodowej* no. 1–2 (96–97) (January–February 2009): 2–26; and Adam Hlebowicz, Tomasz Łabuszewski, and Piotr Niwiński interviewed by Barbara Polak, "Kresy utracone"

("The Lost Borderlands") In *Stół bez kantów i inne rozmowy Biuletynu IPN z lat 2003–2005* (*A Non-Crooked Table and Other Conversations of the Biuletyn IPN, 2003–2005*) (Warszawa: Instytut Pamięci Narodowej, 2008), 255–75, which was first published in the *Biuletyn Instytutu Pamięci Narodowej* no. 12 (47) (December 2004).

5. For an interesting discussion see Fredrika Björklund, "The East European 'ethnic nation' – Myth or reality?" *European Journal of Political Research* 45, no. 1 (January 2006): 93–121.

6. Vasily Zarubin ("Zubilin") was the chief interrogator in Stalin's camps for Polish POWs who were subsequently shot. Zarubin was then posted in New York to oversee Moscow's American *agentura*. See Anna M. Cienciala, Natalia S. Lebedeva, and Wojciech Materski, eds., *Katyn: A Crime without Punishment* (New Haven, CT and London: Yale University Press, 2008).

7. Marek Jan Chodakiewicz, "The Chain of Memory, Interrupted: The Eastern Borderlands of the West, 1939–1947 and After," TMs, June 2005, 1–127. For a heavily edited version see Marek Jan Chodakiewicz, "Chain of Memory, Interrupted: The Eastern Borderlands of the West, 1939–1947 and After," in *Politics, History and Collective Memory in East Central Europe*, ed. by Zdzisław Krasnodębski, Stefan Garsztecki, and Rüdiger Ritter (Hamburg: Krämer, 2012).

Part I

Intermarium: A Brief History

The Muscovite was an enemy to all liberty under heavens.[1]

—Zygmunt II August (Sigismund Augustus), King of Poland, Grand Duke of Lithuania, the Lord and Master of Ruthenia, to Elisabeth I, Queen of England, 1560

Polonized Germans, Tatars, Armenians, Gypsies, [and] Jews can belong to the Polish nation if they live for the common ideal of Poland . . . A Negro or a Redskin can become a real Pole, if he adopts the spiritual heritage of the Polish nation, which is contained in its literature, art, politics, customs, and if he has an unwavering will to contribute to the development of the national life of the Poles.[2]

—Wincenty Lutosławski, 1939

A rat crept softly through the vegetation
Dragging its slimy belly on the bank
While I was fishing in the dull canal
On a winter evening round behind the gashouse
Musing upon the king my brother's wreck
And on the king my father's death before him.
White bodies naked on the low damp ground
And bones cast in a little low dry garret,
Rattled by the rat's foot only, year to year.[3]

—T. S. Eliot, *The Waste Land*

1

The Origins

Intermarium refers to the space between the Black and Baltic Seas, which circumscribe it in the north and south, respectively. Its geographic boundaries are perhaps best explained by rivers. The latter, however, approximate the area's sprawl, rather than strictly delineate it. In the north the boundaries follow the Baltic coast from the estuary of the Vistula and, then, the Neman until the Gulf of Finland, where they slope south through Lake Peipus into Velikaya River. They proceed toward the general area where the Western Dvina bends, the Svir originates, and the Berezina, Sozh, and Desna, in turn, meet the Dnieper as it flows into the Black Sea. The boundaries hug its coast until the delta of the Danube to move sharply north from there following the Prut toward the Dniester and the Bug as it veers west to meet the Vistula and complete the cycle in its estuary at the Baltic.

As far as its topography, the Intermarium consists mostly of flatlands. Steppes dominate its southern part, the Ukraine, in particular. Post-glacial lakes dot the sylvan countryside in the north, specifically in what is now Estonia, Latvia, and Lithuania, as well as contemporary Poland's Mazuria (East Prussia, Borussia). In between the southern steppes and northern lakes, there are the Pripet marshlands, primarily in contemporary Belarus, but also creeping into Ukraine. The area is also heavily forested there. The Carpathian mountains are the only formidable topographical obstacle, delineating the south-western boundary of the Intermarium.

The region's climate produces hot, humid summers and cold, frigid winters with extreme temperature shifts. Because of the proximity to the North Pole, the north-eastern parts of the Intermarium experience long days in summertime. In winter and fall, daylight appears for a brief spell only. Early spring and late fall are customarily rainy and dreary. A cyclical thaw and ubiquitous mud cause arguably greater obstacles to humans than blinding snow and freezing temperatures.

Human transactions in the region date back several millennia. Most archeological activities have focused on the rim of the Intermarium. In particular, the Black Sea coastal area has yielded some interesting finds from the Scythian culture. In the west, the Roman influences infiltrated through Dacia, or present-day Romania. Eclectic artifacts from a variety of cultures have also been discovered in burial sites in the southern steppes. The north has been less bountiful for archeologists.

H. J. Mackinder famously referred to the Intermarium as the "geographic pivot of history."[4] He who mastered the pivot, controlled the world. Hence, constant struggles for the Intermarium ensued. Geographic determinism aside, the Intermarium has indeed witnessed its share of invasions. Most of them, however, were incursions from the east. Much of the time, before the early modern times, in particular, it was the case of the nomads simply passing through. During the *Völkerwanderung* before the fifth century and after, successive waves of visitors from Asia spilled across the southern areas of the Intermarium. The Goths, Vandals, Huns, Langobards, and others sojourned there, sometimes remaining for a century only to proceed further west. The Slavs who arrived in their wake settled the area permanently.[5]

The name Slav comes from the Slavic designation for "word" (Polish: *słowo*; Russian: *slovo*). The Slavs called everyone who spoke a related Slavic language "*Słowianie*" (Russian: *slaviane*), or "people of the word." Anyone who did not was considered a foreigner. The Germans had the dubious distinction of being known as "the mute ones" (*Niemcy*—stemming from *niemi*). Apparently, the ancient Slavs assumed that the German language sounded like the guttural noises made by the speech-impaired. On the other hand, the Germans and others, including Romans and Byzantines, tended to use the word "Slav," or *sclavus* (σκλάβος), to denote "a slave." Slavic lands were customary poaching grounds for the human animal and the destination of choice for slavers from as far afield as Muslim-dominated Iberia. They also craved amber which originated chiefly on the Baltic coast.

We should keep in mind that at that time much of central and eastern Europe consisted of impassable primeval forest. Interaction with others was rare and limited to trade and war. By the same token, the boundaries were not drawn firmly and borders were left mostly open. On the periphery of the Slavic world, but also sometimes in its midst, there were settlements of other ethnic groups, including the Norsemen, Goths, and others.

In time, the Slavs soon split into three distinct groups: western, southern, and eastern. Western Slavs chose central European lands between the Bug and Elbe rivers. In the future they would become Poles, Czechs, Slovaks, and Lusatian Sorbs. To the west, across the Elbe, they bordered the Germanic tribes, including the Saxons. Southern Slavs claimed the Balkans. There the ancestors of the Serbs, Croats, Slovenes, Bulgarians, and Macedonians cohabitated with the Greeks (Byzantines), the Illyrians (future Albanians), the Vlahs, the Dacians (future Romanians), the Avars, the Magyars (Hungarians), and others.

Eastern Slavs settled in the middle of the Intermarium. Theirs was arguably the most inaccessible realm. Naturally, these ancestors of the modern-day Russians, Ukrainians, and Belarusians at first lacked any coherent national consciousness. Instead, they identified themselves with their tribes: Polochians, Radimichians, Tivertsians, Dulebians, and others. The names of the tribes stemmed often from their place of settlement. For example, the Polianians were the people of the fields, while the Derevlians were the folk of the forest. Their institutional arrangements were similar to other Slavic peoples. Tribes were divided into clans that consisted of families following the patriarchical principle. The eldest male issue presided over an extended family dwelling under one roof or a small encampment. On important occasions families would hold a clan assembly (*veche*). All could speak but the elders presumably had the final vote. Periodically, women were left in charge for extended spells as able-bodied males embarked upon hunting and war expeditions. By the eighth century, these eastern Slavic people were firmly established in what collectively would soon be known as Ruthenia (*Rus'*) and its inhabitants as the Ruthenians.[6]

The word "Ruthenians" derives most probably from a Scandinavian name for rowers. It was the Viking raiders who, through trade and war, first settled in the far north-east of the Intermarium in the late eighth century. They dominated the local Finno-Ungaric and Slavic people. Eventually, these Norsemen took over Kiev, the principal city of the eastern Slavs. According to an ancient chronicle, the Kievians themselves invited Viking chieftain Rurik and his men to establish order or settle a dispute. They remained permanently. They developed rudimentary state institutions to control the surrounding Slavic population which they exploited and looted. Their prince owned all the land of *Rus'*. His was a patrimonial realm. He could grant land, and take it away just as easily. It was from Rurik that each Ruthenian prince (*knyaz*) traced his descent, hence the Rurikovich dynasty. The Scandinavians, or Varangians, as they were known locally, supplied much of the ruling caste of the eastern Slavs.

Soon, however, the Varangians became assimilated in language and customs. They underwent Slavicization and shared the lot of their people. They also inserted more dynamism in the activities of the supposedly relaxed east Slavs. Trade, dynastic disputes, and war-making boomed. The rulers of the Ruthenian lands involved themselves in a multitude of projects both within and without. At home, they built mostly wooden fortresses and towns. They burned and uprooted forests for cultivation. They fostered trade and settlement. But most of all each Ruthenian-Varengian prince endeavored to advance up the hierarchical ladder to capture the ultimate prize: the overlordship of Kiev. Hardly any of the princelings bid for the prize on his own; most schemed in a variety of convoluted alliances within the extended family. Some called for foreign assistance, including quite commonly from Poland and Hungary. The winners rewarded their followers with loot taken from neighboring countries and the realms of the losing Ruthenian princes. Those who failed in their bid for Kiev died or fled into exile. The exiles often concluded alliances with their foreign hosts and the deals often would be sealed with marriages. A few, invariably female, married exotic Western Europeans and, thus geographically removed, were out of the power game. However, some Ruthenian blue bloods took Polish and Hungarian spouses; others aimed for the Byzantine "born in purple" imperials (and, less glamorously, the nomadic Polovtsian chieftains). And thus the process of seeking the ultimate prize in Kiev would inevitably repeat itself.[7]

To appreciate the medieval dynamic of love and war-making, we should briefly introduce the neighbors of *Rus'*. To the west the Ruthenians connected with the Poles, Slovaks, Hungarians, and the descendants of the Dacians (Wallachians and Moldavians). To the north the Ruthenian living space abutted territories settled by the Balts. These included the ancestors of present-day Estonians, who were part of the Finno-Ungaric migration from beyond the Altai, just like the Hungarians. However, Samogitians, Lithuanians, Latvians, and other linguistically related Baltic groups were the last Indo-Europeans settlers in the Intermarium. In the east, between the eighth and eleventh centuries, the Ruthenians came into contact with the Khazars, Pechenegs (Patzinaks), Polovtsy (Cumans), and other Turkic people of the steppe. It was from there that the Muslim traders penetrated the lands of Ruthenia and reached as far north as the Baltic Sea. In the south, the Ruthenians occasionally extended their presence to the Black Sea and even the Byzantine Empire.[8]

Notes

1. Quoted in Isabel de Madariaga, *Ivan the Terrible: First Tsar of Russia* (New Haven, CT and London: Yale University Press, 2005), 418, n. 14.
2. Wincenty Lutosławski, *Posłannictwo polskiego narodu* (*The Task of the Polish Nation*) (Warszawa, 1939), 23–24, quoted in Marek Jan Chodakiewicz and Wojciech Jerzy Muszyński, eds., *Złote serca czy złote żniwa? Studia nad wojennymi losami Polaków i Żydów* (Warszawa: The Facto, 2011), 331, also in English as *Golden Harvest or Hearts of Gold: Essays on Wartime Poles and Jews* (Washington, DC: Leopolis Press, 2012), 305, which was further edited by Paweł Styrna. Professor Lutosławski was a renowned philosopher at the public level associated closely with the National Democratic movement (Poland's Christian nationalists) and, at the personal level, a very good friend of Roman Dmowski, the movement's undisputed leader.
3. T. S. Eliot, *The Waste Land*, 1922, http://www.bartleby.com/201/1.html (accessed April 23, 2012).
4. More precisely, the reference was to the southern chunk of Intermarium, and the rest of what the geopolitician considered to be the steppe of "Russia." See H. J. Mackinder, "The Geographical Pivot of History," *The Geographical Journal* 23, no. 4 (April 1904): 421–37.
5. See Paul M. Barford, *The Early Slavs: Culture and Society in Early Medieval Eastern Europe* (Ithaca, NY: Cornell University Press, 2001); Florin Curta, *The Making of the Slavs: History and Archaeology of the Lower Danube Region, ca. 500–700* (Cambridge and New York: Cambridge University Press, 2001); Francis Dvornik, *The Slavs in European History and Civilization* (New Brunswick, NJ:

Rutgers University Press, 1962); David W. Anthony, *The Horse, the Wheel, and the Language: How Bronze-Age Riders from the Steppes Shaped the Modern World* (Princeton, NJ and Oxford: Princeton University Press, 2007).

6. For the latest interpretation see Serhii Plokhy, *The Origins of the Slavic Nations: Premodern Identities in Russia, Ukraine, and Belarus* (Cambridge and New York: Cambridge University Press, 2006); and for a very brief explanation see Matthew Bielawa, "An Understanding of the Terms 'Ruthenia' and 'Ruthenians,'" *Genealogy of Halychyna/Eastern Galicia* (2002), http://www.halgal.com/ruthenian.html (accessed April 23, 2012). See also an exchange by Michel Bouchard, "The Medieval Nation of Rus': The Religious Underpinnings of the Russian Nation," *Ab Imperio* no. 3 (2001): 97–121; and Ildar Garipzanov, "Searching for 'National' Identity in the Middle Ages (the Response of a Europeanist)," *Ab Imperio* no. 3 (2001): 143–46.

7. See Wladyslaw Duczko, *Viking Rus: Studies on the Presence of Scandinavians in Eastern Europe* (Leiden and Boston, MA: Brill, 2004). And see the following essays in Ildar H. Garipzanov, Patrick J. Geary, and Przemysław Urbańczyk, eds., *Franks, Northmen, and Slavs: Identities and State Formation in Early Medieval Europe* (Turnhout: Brepols Publishers, 2008): Oleksi P. Tolochko, "The Primary Chronicle's 'Ethnography' Revisited: Slavs and Varangians in the Middle Dnieper Region and the Origin of the Rus' State," (169–88); and Przemysław Urbańczyk, "Slavic and Christian Identities During the Transition to Polish Statehood," (205–22). Urbańczyk suggests a Viking component in the founding of the modern Polish state. See Przemysław Urbańczyk, *Trudne początki Polski (Difficult Beginnings of Poland)* (Wrocław: Wydawnictwo Uniwersytetu Wrocławskiego, 2008).

8. Florin Curta and Roman Kovalev, eds., *The Other Europe in the Middle Ages: Avars, Bulgars, Khazars, and Cumans* (Leiden and Boston, MA: Brill, 2008); Harry Norris, *Islam in the Baltics: Europe's Early Muslim Community* (London and New York: Tauris Academic Studies, an imprint of I.B. Tauris Publishers, 2009), 4–17.

2

Medieval Ruthenia and the Mongols

Byzantium played an important role in the history of Ruthenia. At first, the lands of the Eastern Roman State were a lusty target for looting expeditions. But trade also flourished there. In time, the ruling Ruthenian princes intermarried with the Byzantine dynasts. It was directly from Constantinople that the Ruthenian rulers adopted Orthodox Christianity. A lengthy process of the conversion commenced in 867 with the establishment of an Eastern Orthodox bishopric of *Rus'*. It concluded, in 988, with the ceremonial baptism of the dukes and people of Kiev, by then the principal city and fortress of the Ruthenians. The latter also accepted high culture from Constantinople, including Old Church Slavonic with its Cyrillic alphabet for liturgy and administration.

Along with Eastern Orthodoxy the masters of Kiev and its off-shoots adopted its peculiar doctrine of caesaro-papism, the idea of the supremacy of the lay ruler over the spiritual guardian of the Faith. The State dominated the Church. Thus, with great detriment to the development of freedom, the Ruthenians rejected the Augustinian division of the body politics into the sacred and the profane spheres. Naturally, the degree of adherence to this caesaro-papist paradigm varied. It depended on the relative strength of the local prince. In the best case, Novgorod "the Great" enjoyed a mixed oligarchic–popular–clerical constitution which kept its princes in check. Hence, the city was the freest of all medieval and early modern Ruthenian towns, a virtual mercantile republic. The Novgorodians gladly traded with all and sundry. Novgorod was the shining exception, though. Moscow was its polar opposite, as we shall see. But until its ascendancy in the fourteenth century, the Ruthenian principalities generally coexisted with their neighbors.[1]

Until roughly the thirteenth century, the Intermarium was divided into the pagan north and the Orthodox Christian south. In many places these beliefs coexisted and overlapped for a time. After the conversion of Kiev, however, Eastern Orthodoxy spread rather quickly among the Ruthenians. Yet, pagan influences persisted in the region, particularly in the north-eastern areas of Suzdal and Rostov through the eleventh century. They also continued to reach the Ruthenian lands from the Baltics and Scandinavia with periodic military reinforcements of the Varengians. The last Viking war outfit joined their kith and kin in Kiev in the early twelfth century. By that time Scandinavia had been converted to Western Christianity. The Swedish warriors interacted with the Ruthenians, sharing their Norse ways and their new faith, before being themselves absorbed into the culture of *Rus'* and its Byzantine confession, or returning home faithful to Rome.

Latin Christendom coexisted with Eastern Orthodoxy on a much more permanent basis along the Intermarium's westernmost reaches. Intermarriage was relatively frequent between the ruling Ruthenian princes and their Polish and Hungarian counterparts. Soon, the Ruthenians began looking farther out to western and northern Europe for their nuptials. In the most prominent case, Yaroslav the Wise (978–1054) and his children were wed to the representatives of the royal houses of Hungary, Sweden, Norway, Spain, and France. Despite confessional differences, a vigorous interaction continued with Ruthenia's western neighbors even after the Great Schism between Rome and Constantinopole in 1054.[2]

Intermarriage, commerce, and war with their western neighbors facilitated steady contact with Latin culture and its political system. But the adaptation of Western ways was rather selective and tentative. In Kievian *Rus'* there was at least superficial familiarity with Western chivalry, if little emulation of it. Ruthenia knew no Western-style property-rights and freedoms. Feudalism failed to take root as Ruthenian principalities remained firmly wed to the patrimonial principle. The prince apportioned the land to be used in common by the people within the commune (*mir*) system. All principalities adhered to the ancient system of "counseling" within the noble advisory board (*rada*) and the popular assembly (*veche*). A council of sorts, the *veche*'s purpose was to limit the power of the prince. The system depended on the ruler's personal attributes and political, social, and economic circumstances. A ruthless sovereign of independent means needed no counsel. A weak prince heeded the council of his nobles (*boyars*), and sometimes even the people. Natural autocratic tendencies of the rulers were reinforced through Byzantine and steppe influences. Caesaro-papism and nomadic ways coexisted in a curious mix with traditional Slavic and Viking arrangements. But with the decline of Kiev those largely failed to translate into a centralized system for all of *Rus'*. Because of the nature of the succession laws, where each princely offspring stood to inherit a part of the realm, the Ruthenian lands experienced their own version of "feudal" partitioning of the patrimonial domain. By the thirteenth century, there were almost three hundred *Rus'* principalities in the Intermarium and its immediate vicinity. Most were locked in sanguinary internecine combat for the mantle of the ruler of Kiev. Eventually, several alternative centers of power emerged at various times but none were able to dominate the whole of Ruthenia.

The lack of unity and the failure to understand nomadic military tactics translated into a fearsome calamity: the Mongol invasion and the khans' domination of the Ruthenian lands. The Mongols (also called Tartars or Tatars) dealt with the haplessly disunited Ruthenian princes usually one by one in a series of gory battles in 1223 and 1238–1242. The resistance was uneven: eastern Ruthenian areas submitted practically without a fight. They were spared. The southern and western parts of Ruthenia fought desperately and suffered disproportionately. Kiev, Chernihov, Suzdal, and other countless cities were razed to the ground. Half the Ruthenian population perished. Subsequent resistance to the Tatars and their local collaborators was essentially a defense of local—and by extension "Western"—ways by the Ruthenians. The resisting areas shook off the Mongol domination within 150 years mostly as a result of the Lithuanian offensive in the fourteenth century. In the eastern Ruthenian lands, the so-called "Mongol yoke" lasted until 1480, despite a symbolic Muscovite victory over the Tatars in 1380.

Ironically, it was the Mongols who facilitated and sponsored the ascendancy of Muscovy. Hitherto a minor trading outpost in the far east, rather grandiosely referred to as a principality, and well outside the periphery of the Intermarium, Moscow came to exercise a nefarious influence on the region. Following the initial conquest of the Ruthenian lands, the Mongols eschewed colonization and direct control. Instead, their khans acted as remote sovereigns bestowing and accepting princely titles, in effect adjudicating Ruthenian succession struggles. Most importantly, the Mongols turned to local collaborators for tax collection, including human beings for slavery. After a few princes demurred or rebelled, most notably in Tver, the ruler of Muscovy joined the Mongols against that principality and helped crush it in 1327. He then begged for and accepted the *yarlik*, the plenipotentiary privilege from the khan. He also received the title of the "Grand Duke" from the Tatars. Henceforth, in official correspondence, the khan referred to him as his "slave" (*khlop*). This symbolic moniker reflected Muscovy's unsavory role in the Tatar occupation system. The Kremlin collected the taxes for the Mongols and curbed rebellious Ruthenians for their distant overlords. It also participated in some punitive Tatar expeditions against the recalcitrant *Rus'* cities, which were conducted periodically with great fierceness. Within this occupation system, Moscow had the license to tyrannize others, thus enhancing the power of its duke. Further, the Muscovites adopted a variety of Asiatic ways, including the sequestration and veiling of women and ghettoization of foreigners. Moreover, intermarriage occurred at the top of the social ladder between the Ruthenians and the Tatars. Last but not least, the Kremlin wholeheartedly embraced the Mongol way of government, which some scholars used to call "oriental despotism."[3]

In Muscovy, there was no law but that of the ruler and his whim. Dispensing with the ancient Slavic institution of *veche*, the Muscovite dukes used the power of the state in an arbitrary and despotic manner. Their power was mightily enhanced on the theological and political levels when they also claimed the mantle of the Byzantine Emperors after the fall of Constantinople to the Ottoman Turks in 1453. The dukes of Muscovy took to calling themselves "autocrats" and "emperors" (*tsars*). Moscow became "the Third Rome" in the Muscovite eyes. This was also an ex post facto justification of their imperial expansion and the drive to subjugate all the lands of the *Rus'*. Having completed the conquest of the Rostov-Suzdal principalities, which were its closest neighbors, the Kremlin crushed the Novgorod Republic in 1478, which was the first serious acquisition outside of the inner core. By then, with their power waxing, the rulers of Muscovy had turned increasingly against their erstwhile Tatar overlords in the east and against the dukes of Lithuania in the west. Eventually, the Muscovites would begin to refer to themselves as "the Russians," for external propaganda purposes, and "Great Ruthenians" (*velikiye Russy*), for internal use; and they dubbed their realm as "Russia" and "Great Ruthenia" (*velikaia Rus'*) to the same ends. Eventually, they would rename their state as the Russian Empire, and continue their expansions in all directions. The avowed aim of "Holy Russia" and its rulers was to "gather all the lands of Rus'," which they dubbed "Russian lands." That put the Muscovites on a collision course with many of their fellow Ruthenians and other inhabitants of the lands they coveted as well as with several neighboring powers.[4]

Notes

1.   In the fifteenth century, Novgorod sought the assistance of Poland-Lithuania against Muscovy. As punishment, Moscow's Ivan III exterminated much of the population of Novgorod. On Novgorod's system, see Michael C. Paul, "Was the Prince of Novgorod a 'Third-rate bureaucrat' after 1136?" *Jahrbücher für Geschichte Osteuropas* 56, no. 1 (Spring 2008): 72–113; Michael C. Paul, "Secular Power and the Archbishops of Novgorod before the Muscovite Conquest." *Kritika: Explorations in Russian and Eurasian History* 8, no. 2 (Spring 2007): 231–70; Michael C. Paul, "Episcopal Election in Novgorod, Russia 1156–1478," *Church History: Studies in Christianity and Culture* 72, no. 2 (June 2003): 251–75; Michael C. Paul, "The Iaroslavichi and the Novgorodian Veche 1230–1270: A Case Study on Princely Relations with the Veche," *Russian History/ Histoire Russe* 31, no. 1–2 (Spring–Summer 2004); Janet Martin, *Treasure of the Land of Darkness: the Fur Trade and Its Significance for Medieval Russia* (Cambridge: Cambridge University Press, 1985); Gail Lenhoff and Janet Martin. "Marfa Boretskaia, Posadnitsa of Novgorod: A Reconsideration of Her Legend and Her Life," *Slavic Review* 59, no. 2 (2000): 343–68.

2.   See Nora Berend, ed., *Christianization and the Rise of Christian Monarchy: Scandinavia, Central Europe, and Rus' c. 900–1200* (Cambridge: Cambridge University Press, 2007); Florin Curta, ed., *East Central and Eastern Europe in the Early Middle Ages* (Ann Arbor, MI: University of Michigan Press, 2005); Jean W. Sedlar, *East Central Europe in the Middle Ages, 1000–1500* (Seattle, WA and London: University of Washington Press, 1994); George Ostrogorsky, *History of the Byzantine State* (New Brunswick, NJ: Rutgers University Press, 1969); Peter F. Sugar, Peter Hanak, and Tibor Frank, eds., *A History of Hungary*

(Bloomington and Indianapolis: Indiana University Press, 1990); Hugh Agnew, *The Czechs and the Lands of the Bohemian Crown* (Stanford, CA: Hoover Institution Press, Stanford University, 2004); Przemysław Urbańczyk, ed., *The Neighbours of Poland in the 11th Century* (Warsaw: Wydawnictwo DiG, 2002); Pawel Jasiennica, *Piast Poland* (Miami, FL and New York: The American Institute of Polish Culture and Hippocrene Books, 1985); Paul W. Knoll, *The Rise of the Polish Monarchy: Piast Poland in East Central Europe, 1320–1370* (Chicago, IL and London: The University of Chicago Press, 1972); Jerzy Braun, ed., *Poland in Christian Civilization* (London: Veritas Foundation Publication Centre, 1985). See also Stanisław Bylina, ed., *Ruś Kijowska i Polska w średniowieczu (X–XIII w.) (Kievan Rus' and Poland in Medieval Times (10–13th Centuries))* (Warsaw: IH PAN, 2003); Jacek Banaszkiewicz, ed., *Imagines Potestatis: Rytuały, symbole i konteksty fabularne władzy zwierzchniej. Polska X–XV w. (z przykładem czeskim i ruskim) (The Images of Power: Rituals, Symbols, and Contexts of the Supreme Power: Poland, 10th–15th Centuries (with the Czech and Ruthenian examples))* (Warsaw: IH PAN, 1994).

3.   On the initial Mongol conquest of the Ruthenian lands see Leo de Hartog, *Genghis Khan: Conqueror of the World* (New York: St. Martin's Press, 1989), 118–23, 164–69. See also George Vernadsky, *A History of Russia*, vol. 3: *The Mongols and Russia* (New Haven, CT and London: Yale University Press, 1953); Boris Rybakov, *Киевская Русь и русские княжества XII–XIII вв. (Kievan Rus' and Russian Principalities in XII–XIII Centuries)* (Moscow: Nauka, 1993); Donald G. Ostrowski, *Muscovy and the Mongols: Cross-Cultural Influences on the Steppe Frontier, 1304–1589* (Cambridge, MA and New York: Cambridge University Press, 1998).

4.   On "Holy Russia" see Michael Cherniavsky, *Tsar and People: Studies in Russian Myths* (New York: Random House, 1969); and Andrzej Walicki, *A History of Russian Thought: From the Enlightenment to Marxism* (Stanford, CA: Stanford University Press, 1979). On Moscow's imperial expansion see W. Bruce Lincoln, *The Conquest of a Continent: Siberia and Russians* (New York: Random House, 1994); Dominic Lieven, *Empire: The Russian Empire and Its Rivals* (New Haven, CT and London: Yale University Press, 2001); Robert D. Crews, *For Prophet and Tsar: Islam and Empire in Russia and Central Asia* (Cambridge and London: Harvard University Press, 2006); and Ewa M. Thompson, *Imperial Knowledge: Russian Literature and Colonialism* (Westport, CT and London: Greenwood Press, 2000).

3

The Balts, the Germans, and the Poles

The Balts were the least numerous and the weakest people of the Intermarium. Their coastal location along the Baltic also made them easily accessible and, thus, a tempting prey for the Scandinavians and the Germans. Inland, the Ruthenians and the Balts had both clashed and cooperated from the earliest times.[1] In the twelfth and thirteenth centuries, the north-eastern Ruthenian princes invaded Estonia numerous times. Commerce was arguably more prevalent than fighting, though. The Ruthenians and the Balts occasionally united to fend off a common enemy: the Germans and the Tatars, in particular. In the fourteenth century, mostly because of the Mongol threat, some western and southern Ruthenian princes established a particularly close relationship with the dukes of Lithuania. They even briefly succeeded in converting the Lithuanian rulers to Orthodox Christianity. Ruthenian became the dominant language of the court in Vilnius and Lithuania's official documents were written in Cyrillic (Old Church Slavonic). Nonetheless, the Lithuanians continued to worship their pagan gods until roughly the end of the fourteenth century when they peacefully converted *en bloc* to Latin Christianity as the basis of their dynastic alliance with the Poles.

Earlier, peaceful attempts at the Christianization of the Balts from Scandinavia and Germany came to naught. The Prussians, Livonians, Latgalians, and Ests defended their pagan ways zealously. They were thus to be converted by fire and sword. The Christianization of some of them occurred during the so-called Northern Crusades, which commenced at the end of the twelfth century. For the next 150 years the Danes, Swedes, and Germans sailed and marched against the Balts. Ultimately, the Swedes took Karelia, to the north of the Intermarium proper. The Danes captured a large chunk of contemporary Estonia. Last but not least, the Germans conquered the lands of the Prussians, Latgalians, Ests, and Livonians along the Baltic coast.

The chief architects of the German victory were the so-called Knights of Christ, or Brethren of the Sword, who eventually affiliated with the Teutonic Knights (*Deutsche Orden*), or the Knights of the Hospital of St. Mary. Those were military monks who originated as a crusading order in the Holy Land.

After their defeat by the Muslims and, next, their expulsion following a lackluster performance against the pagan nomads in eastern Hungary, they were invited by a minor Polish prince to defend his northern frontier of Mazovia against the raiding Baltic Prussians in 1226. The Teutonic Knights promptly falsified land deeds from the Poles and conquered to the north-east, exterminating the pagans in their path. Whenever weak they shrewdly sought the assistance of the Pope and western European courts; waxing strong, they lashed out mercilessly at their neighbors. Between the thirteenth and fourteenth centuries, in a late medieval manifestation of the *Drang nach Osten*, the ironclad monks established a crusading state stretching from Pomerania to Estonia along the shores of the Baltic. Dilligent administrators, the Teutonic Knights fostered settlement and commerce. They cooperated closely with the Hanseatic League, a formidable trading alliance of prominent German and Scandinavian towns. The Teutonic Knights also continued their expansion into the Intermarium and adjacent lands.

Eventually, in the north-east, the Ruthenians checked the momentum of the Western crusaders, beating first the Swedes and then the Teutonic Knights in 1240 and 1242, respectively. That merely caused the invaders to eschew expanding into the Ruthenian interior. They hugged the coast, but consistently attacked Samogitia and other Lithuanian areas throughout the thirteenth and fourteenth centuries. Suddenly, while at their peak, the mighty Teutonic Knights were crushed by an alliance of the Poles, Lithuanians, Ruthenians, and Tatars at the battle of Grunwald in 1410. From then on, their power slowly waned. Yet, the threat posed by the German crusaders persisted for sometime after. Ultimately, after a series of wars, the Teutonic State became a fief of the King of Poland-Lithuania as a secularized Protestant principality in 1525. Its chunk was incorporated directly into Poland as Royal Prussia.[2] By that time the Polish-Lithuanian Commonwealth stretched beyond Livonia on the Baltic in the north, past Smolensk in the east, approached the Black Sea in the south, and stopped at Silesia and Pomerania in the west, which the Polish kings had lost to the Germanic rulers in the preceding centuries.

The Commonwealth of Poland-Lithuania was, first, a personal (1385) and, then, a federal (1569) union between the Kingdom of Poland and the Grand Duchy of Lithuania. The former absorbed Halich (Galicia)—the south-westernmost part of Ruthenia in the middle of the fourteenth century. The Grand Duchy of Lithuania expanded greatly east and south by taking advantage of the waning of the Mongol power and the affinities of the remnants of the Ruthenian principalities of the Intermarium in the fourteenth and fifteenth centuries. Western and southern Ruthenians were averse both to the Mongols and their Muscovite collaborators, the wielders of the yoke. They viewed the dukes of Moscow as usurpers, upstarts, and traitors. They looked with irritation and hostility at the avowed aim of the Muscovites to "gather the lands of Rus." To their chagrin the rulers of Moscow claimed to be the heirs to the

Grand Dukes of Kiev. However, that honor had meanwhile been acquired also by the Grand Dukes of Lithuania through intermarriage, acculturation, and reconquest of the Kievian lands from the Mongols. The territories of western and southern Ruthenia had been largely depopulated and devastated because of the Mongol depredations. Now, under the Grand Duchy of Lithuania they began to recover. This process was greatly accelerated after the union with the Kingdom of Poland, concluded at Lublin in 1569.[3]

Notes

1. See Alan V. Murray, ed., *The Clash of Cultures in the Medieval Baltic Frontier* (Surrey, UK: Ashgate Publishing Limited, 2009); Alan Palmer, *The Baltic: A New History of the Region and Its People* (Woodstock and New York: The Overlook Press, 2006); Andrejs Plakans, *A Concise History of the Baltic States* (Cambridge and New York: Cambridge University Press, 2011); Andrejs Plakans, *The Latvians: A Short History* (Stanford, CA: Hoover Institution Press, Stanford University, 1995); Toivu U. Raun, *Estonia and the Estonians* (Stanford, CA: The Hoover Institution Press, 2001); Saulius Suziedelis, *The Sword and the Cross: A History of the Church in Lithuania* (Huntington, IN: Our Sunday Visitor Publishing, 1988); V. Stanley Vardys and Judith B. Sedaitis, *Lithuania: The Rebel Nation* (Boulder, CO and Oxford: Westview Press, 1997); Norman Davies, *Vanished Kingdoms: The Rise and Fall of States and Nations* (New York: Viking, 2011), chap. 5: "Litva," at 229–308. For a brief history of some of the Ruthenian lands that accrued to the Grand Duchy of Lithuania and, later, the Polish-Lithuanian Commonwealth, see Andrew Wilson, *Belarus: The Last European Dictatorship* (New Haven, CT, and London: Yale University Press, 2011), 3–59.

2. See Norman Davies, *Vanished Kingdoms: The Rise and Fall of States and Nations* (New York: Viking, 2011), chap. 7: "Borussia," at 325–93; Marian Biskup and Gerard Labuda, *Dzieje Zakonu Krzyżackiego w Prusach: Gospodarka – Społeczeństwo – Państwo – Ideologia* (*A History of the Teutonic Order in Prussia: Economy, Society, State, Ideology*) (Gdańsk: Wydawnictwo Morskie, 1988); Karin Friedrich, *The Other Prussia: Royal Prussia, Poland, and Liberty, 1569–1772* (Cambridge and New York: Cambridge University Press, 2006); Jerzy Dygdała, ed., *Lustracje dóbr królewskich XVI–XVIII wiek: Prusy Królewskie 1765*, vol. 1: *Województwo pomorskie*, part 2 [*A Review of the Royal Estates, 16th-18th Century: Royal Prussia, 1765, Province of Pommerania*] (Toruń: Towarzystwo Naukowe w Toruniu, Uniwersytet Mikołaja Kopernika, IH PAN, 2003 [2004]).

3. Pawel Jasienica, *Jagiellonian Poland* (Miami, FL: The American Institute of Polish Culture, 1978); Harry E. Dembkowski, *The Union of Lublin: Polish Federalism in the Golden Age* (New York and Boulder, CO: East European Monographs and Columbia University Press, 1982); Harry Norris, *Islam in the Baltics: Europe's Early Muslim Community* (London and New York: Tauris Academic Studies, an imprint of I.B. Tauris Publishers, 2009), 18–29.

4

The Commonwealth

The resulting Commonwealth of Poland-Lithuania (*Rzeczpospolita, Respublica*) embraced most of the Intermarium. It was the largest and the freest nation in Europe.[1] It ably defended itself from external enemies and maintained domestic concord for over two centuries. It was also economically prosperous thanks to its rich farmland. The bounty of its agriculture was complemented by the commercial success of its towns. Trading routes crisscrossed it from the west to the east and from the south to the north. The Vistula carried most cargo. Danzig (Gdańsk) on the Baltic served as its most important maritime trade port. The Commonwealth was known as the "granary of Europe." Its trade flowered; its population boomed both through natural increase and through immigration as the Commonwealth was a safe haven for all ethnicities and religious dissidents. Its opulence reflected itself in outstanding art and architecture, unmistakably Western (classical), and predictably with a local flavor.

The success of the Polish-Lithuanian-Ruthenian state was unprecedented because it came to fruition through peaceful means and blossomed as a "noble democracy," or a "county democracy," according to Andrzej Sulima-Kamiński who poignantly reflects on the robust nature of its local self-rule. The Commonwealth combined three branches of government: the royal, the aristocratic, and the noble. It was a mixed system—a noble monarchical republic. At its origin lay the very same ancient Slavic institution that used to function in the Intermarium prior to the Mongols. However, the Poles interpreted them differently than the Ruthenians. They adapted the institutions of Latin Christendom to peculiarly Polish arrangements. Thus, gradually, the local assemblies (*wiece*) became local dietines (*sejmiki*), which eventually spawned the national Parliament (*Sejm*). The medieval ducal council (*rada*) evolved into the royal council and the Senate.

By the sixteenth century, the nobility (*szlachta*), which constituted about 10 percent of the population (and most of them, petty gentry, owned no serfs, but farmed on their own), wielded political power by electing their representatives to local dietines and the national Parliament. They also elected the Commonwealth's King for life. His executive power was limited, principally by the so-called Henrician articles of 1573 and other laws. The Senate, where the aristocratic senators occupied appointable posts, served as a device to check both the royal prerogative and the noble, lower-house power. In addition, the nobility had the right of legal uprising, the so-called confederacy (*konfederacja*), to prevent royal tyranny. On the other hand, an illegal rebellion (*rokosz*) was completely unconstitutional. For the nobles the political system of the Commonwealth was the vaunted "golden freedom" (*złota wolność*). We should stress that, despite the fact that the franchise was limited to the nobility only, the sheer size of the noble estate guaranteed such extensive participation in the government that it would not be achieved anywhere in Europe until the English parliamentary reforms of the early nineteenth century. Perhaps as many as one million "Poles" enjoyed their civic rights. Further, the ranks of the nobility grew exponentially not only because of ennobling commoners and foreigners alike but also because the Commonwealth had no primogeniture for much of its ascent. All children stood to inherit, including women, a custom that, once again, was not matched in most of Europe until the nineteenth century. The Polish nobles considered themselves superior not only to their subjects but also to the rest of Europe's nobility. The former compared their Commonwealth to Republican Rome as the source of virtue. They also evolved a fascinating myth of their own origin. Accordingly, they were not Slavs at all but Sarmatians, an ancient warrior people of the steppe near the northern tip of the Black Sea.[2]

The political rights of the nobility grew out of a series of privileges granted to them by Polish rulers in late medieval times. The most important of those were the Act of Cienia in 1228, which mirrored England's *Magna Carta* in limiting the royal prerogative and establishing a lordly council to advise the sovereign, the precedent of calling of the national assembly (*wiec*) at Chęciny in 1331, which initiated the transfer of local councils (*wiece/sejmiki*) onto the national parliamentary level; and the Act of Košice of 1374, which effectively eliminated most royal taxes on the nobility and seriously limited the royal power to wage war without the consent of the nobles. Thus, unlike the *Magna Carta*, which remained an unfulfilled promise for several centuries, Poland's progress of freedom was consistent. In the Grand Duchy perhaps the single-most important privilege was bestowed upon the nobility in 1386, when those who accepted Western Christianity were automatically granted hereditary rights to all their possessions, including land. That was a dramatic break with the patrimonial tradition of the Kievian *Rus'* and, simultaneously, a logical step to congruity with the system of the Kingdom of Poland. It thus de facto privileged Latin Christians, mostly ethnic Lithuanians, over the Orthodox Christians, mostly ethnic Ruthenians, and encouraged conversion to Catholicism and the adoption of Western ways.

Under the Commonwealth, some customary rights of the Grand Duchy of Lithuania were added into the mix of the Polish medieval privileges. The intention was to make both federative parts legally and culturally compatible. Thus, the Union of Horodło of 1413 admitted Lithuanian and Ruthenian *boyars* to the Polish heraldic clans (*rody*). That made all Latin-faith nobles equal by symbolically bestowing on them the Polish coats of arms. The Orthodox *boyars* were included in several subsequent charters of rights. In 1436, the monarch granted his nobles the crucial right of *Neminem captivabimus nisi jure victum*. This brilliant law guaranteed that no one would be arrested without a valid court sentence, predating England's *Habeas corpus* by 143 years. The king's town and county administrators (*starosta*) were also ordered to desist interfering with local courts. Judges became electable. The royal act of 1493 established a bicameral Parliament (*Sejm*) with elective lower chamber and appointable upper house, the Senate. The supremacy of parliament was enshrined in the *Nihil Novi* constitution of 1505 which guaranteed "nothing new without our consent," a sentiment that would be expressed over three centuries later across the Atlantic as "no taxation without representation." Further, the Sejm guaranteed religious liberty in the Act of the Confederation of Warsaw of 1573.

Last but not least, the right of the free veto (*liberum veto*) safeguarded the freedom of the individual by mandating that acts of parliament be approved unanimously. This curious, but ultimately politically lethal device, stemmed from the early medieval Polish custom of seeking consensus. It was intended to protect the minorities, including a minority of one. If a law was disagreeable even to a single deputy, he could interrupt the parliamentary proceedings with his *liberum veto*. That would force the sponsors of the legal bill to adjourn and hammer out a compromise with the dissenters. The *liberum veto* served its purpose rather well until the middle of the seventeenth century, when it spiraled out of control with gross acts of abuse fueled through corruption by Polish magnates and foreign powers. But that was the law of unintended consequences, which hardly anyone safeguarding freedom of the minorities had anticipated.

It was clearly the nobility which enjoyed most of the Commonwealth's privileges. However, the burghers maintained and extended various rights stemming from many Polish cities adherence to the Magdeburg Law. These privileges were sometimes extended to the cities in the Intermarium, even though many of them were founded as private towns by the local magnates. Thus, the burghers flowered under the Commonwealth despite noble attempts to curb them. The peasants, mostly feudal serfs, enjoyed only limited local customary privileges usually observed at the discretion of their lords. The status of the peasantry was the most humane on the royal estates. On middle and small estates it depended on the individual master. It was usually horrible on large aristocratic estates, particularly in the Ukraine where absentee landlordism prevailed. Nonetheless, Protestant and Catholic lords did not usually seek to convert their peasant subjects to their brand of Christianity. Also the Muslims and Jews were left alone to practice their faith. Protestant denominations multiplied, including extremist sects like the Antitrinitarian Aryan Brothers. And various political and religious refugees were gladly given asylum in Poland-Lithuania. These included thousands of Muscovy's Old Believers, random aristocrats, and droves of peasants who fled to the Commonwealth in search of freedom.

The exception to the rule of religious coexistence germinated within Eastern Orthodoxy. More than a few of the Ruthenians, including many of the nobility and some of the upper Orthodox clergy, in particular, felt that a salutary development of the body politics of the Commonwealth necessitated a rapprochement with Rome. The reformers hoped both to foster unity at home and to preempt the angry usurpations of Moscow's "Third Rome" on the Commonwealth's Orthodox Ruthenians. Latin Christians among the Poles and Lithuanians encouraged them vigorously. Accordingly, some of the Orthodox bishops signed an Act of Union with the Catholic Church at the synod at Brześć (Brest) in 1569. This is the origin of the Uniate (Greek Catholic) confession. The Uniates (Greek Catholics) remained Orthodox in rite but they recognized the Pope. They were immediately condemned by the majority of the Commonwealth's Eastern Orthodox bishops who wanted no communion with Rome. The Moscow Patriarchate promptly anathematized the Uniates. The situation was further exacerbated because many of the leading Ruthenian magnates gradually converted to either Catholicism or Protestantism (mostly Calvinism), thus causing the Orthodox to lose their champions in the Senate and other prominent institutions of the Commonwealth. The strife within and without the Orthodox Church would eventually boil over into a sustained violent internecine conflict in the middle of the seventeenth century.[3]

Meanwhile, at its peak in the sixteenth century, the Commonwealth amply earned its appellation as "a state without stakes."[4] For the most part, there was no religious persecution and there were considerably fewer witch hunts than in the West. Even for Jews, the Commonwealth was a "paradise" (*paradisus Judeorum*).[5] The Statute of Kalisz of 1264, a local Jewish privilege by a Polish prince, was extended over the next century to include all the Jews of the medieval Kingdom of Poland. Under the Commonwealth, more privileges accrued to the Jewish community. The Jews enjoyed complete autonomy with their own self-government, the Council of Four Lands (*Va'ad Arba' Aratzot*), which deliberated usually in Lublin, between 1580 and 1764, and which is correctly considered as the forerunner of the Knesset, the Israeli parliament. The bulk of the adherents of the Mosaic faith preferred a separate existence based on diaspora Judaism and Yiddish culture. The Jewish community boasted its own legal courts and privileges. In towns they operated under royal and aristocratic protection. Even the instances of conflict with the Christians were adjudicated by the royal officers and courts, rather than the local Christian judiciaries. Jewish transactions with the gentile population were almost always strictly economic. However, the gates to assimilation were wide open to those willing to convert. In fact, in the Grand Duchy of Lithuania if a Jew was baptized into the Catholic faith, he was automatically ennobled.[6]

The Commonwealth was a multiethnic state assembled on a voluntary basis. It encompassed Poles, Ruthenians, Lithuanians, Armenians, Jews, Tartars, Germans, Dutch, Scots, Swedes, Italians, French, and others joined together by common culture and institutions. Since Poland and the Poles were the conduits of the Western culture, including indigenous Polish political freedom that surpassed anything available in the West at that time, a gradual Polonization of the Intermarium meant its Westernization (Europeanization). Hence, any Ruthenian or Lithuanian identifying himself also as "a Pole" testified to the fact that not only was he a Polish nobleman with all the liberties his status entailed but also that culturally he was a Westerner, a European. Simply put, in the Eastern Borderlands of the West, Polishness became thus synonymous with "Europe." However, paradoxically, the Commonwealth was also antithetical to much of what "Western Europe" stood for between the fifteenth and nineteenth centuries: royal absolutism, religious intolerance, civil strife, and constant wars. Further, Poland-Lithuania was a jarring contradiction to the patrimonial tyranny of both the Russian-Muscovite and the Ottoman empires.[7]

At its peak in the fifteenth and sixteenth centuries, the Commonwealth was able to hold these rapacious powers off with relative ease. In fact, it was known as the *Antemurale Christianitatis*, the Rampart of Christianity. The dynastic ambitions of its powerful Jagiellonian rulers and, later, the strategic vision of its dynamic King István Báthory (Stefan Batory), extended far beyond the traditional understanding of the Intermarium. From their dual capitals at Cracow and Wilno, the Jagiellonians expanded into north-eastern, central, and south-eastern Europe. They ascended the thrones in Prague and Budapest. They challenged the Habsburgs, defied the Ottomans, and routed the Rurikids of Moscow. The Polish-Lithuanian-Ruthenian armies operated as far afield as the Balkans, Crimea, and Livonia. Cracow vied for influence with Istanbul in the Danubian Principalities. The Croats wrote poems about Polish victories, hoping for the liberation from the Muslim yoke. It was under the Jagiellonians and their early successors that a broader interpretation of the Intermarium began to take shape, including all lands of Central and Eastern Europe, between the Baltic, Adriatic, and Black seas.

Notwithstanding their prolonged martial success, the Poles projected their unique domestic philosophy onto the international arena, in law and foreign policy. As early as 1414, at the Congress of Constance, Polish diplomats argued before an astonished "civilized" audience of western European potentates that one should not convert pagans with fire and sword, but with love. The Poles simply posited the possibility of coexistence of Christian and non-Christian powers. A century before Hugo Grotius and Jean Bodin, the Polish Renaissance thinkers preached and practiced religious tolerance; wrote about just war; explicated the idea of national self-determination, championed state sovereignty; pondered humanitarian aspects of war; and condemned wars of aggression; stressed the importance of diplomatic immunity and validity of treaties; and proposed a modern system of diplomatic relations.[8]

By the middle of the seventeenth century, however, the Commonwealth entered a period of decline and calamity. Its deterioration and fall stemmed from several factors. The most important was the abuse of freedom which led to the breakdown of parliamentarism. Next, there came the pauperization of the nobility because of the demographic pressure, a consolidation drive for the aristocratic latifundia, and the lack of land. Middle nobility declined and a yawning gap appeared between the petty gentry and magnates. Then there was the mounting conflict between Western Christianity and Eastern Orthodoxy. It was especially acute in the southern Ruthenian lands, the Ukraine. To exacerbate the situation, the Orthodox also quarreled with the Uniates. Increasingly, Eastern Orthodoxy was tied to the social question of the lower classes, the peasants and the Cossacks. The Ruthenian elites either embraced the Uniate rite or converted to Catholicism. Last but not least, the predatory neighbors pounced upon Poland-Lithuania.

Gradually, liberty turned to license. The domestic malady rendered the Commonwealth susceptible to foreign afflictions which in turn exacerbated internal weaknesses. It was a vicious circle perpetuating the disfunction and the gradual decay of the internal institutions and body politics of the state. Poland-Lithuania's political system, the *liberum veto* in particular, began to be abused by domestic and foreign forces seeking to foster anarchy. Power-hungry aristocrats and agents of alien powers bribed corrupt parliamentary deputies either to swing the vote their way or to implode the Sejm through the use of the *liberum veto*. A veto unresolved by compromise simply nullified all legislation of the parliament's contemporary session. It was a constitutional kiss of death for the device contrived to protect the minorities could not be abolished except through unanimity. The latter was unobtainable because vested interests opposed the renewal of the Commonwealth. Russian and Prussian envoys intervened surreptitiously with gold numerous times to prevent any reform, in particular the raising of the taxes for military defense. Poland-Lithuania was perhaps the only nation to permit foreign lobbies on its soil, eventually to its peril. Under such foreign meddling and native prejudices, once vaunted religious tolerance gradually deteriorated. Civic mindedness yielded to purely selfish pursuits also on the social level. Noble jealousy of burgher prosperity and the attempts by the latter to enter the ranks of the nobility through land ownership caused a legislative backlash against towns, which soon undercut their prosperity. By the seventeenth century the burghers were banned from owning landed estates. Onerous taxes were levied on commerce and industry, while landed nobility enjoyed tax exemptions. To steer business away from the burghers, and avoid relying on them, the magnates increasingly turned to Jews to provide financial, trade, and other services. Jews often held leases on aristocratic monopolies on alcohol production, tax farming, toll roads, and estate management in the Intermarium's south-east, in particular. The Ruthenian peasants harshly resented them as much as they hated the nobility and Jesuit priests. The burghers throughout the Commonwealth complained bitterly about undue Jewish influences. Social unrest festered on many levels and it finally blew up in the middle of the seventeenth century. The situation became further exacerbated by prolonged civil and foreign wars. In effect, between 1648 and 1667 the Commonwealth lost 30 percent of its population: over 3 million out of 10 million people, an enormous figure by early modern European standards.

The Ukrainian (Zaporozhian) Cossacks were arguably the most restless element of the Commonwealth. These freebooters were predominantly of Eastern Orthodox faith. Many of the rank-and-file were runaway serfs. Denizens of southern Ukraine, they congregated in their war camp, the *Sich*, beyond the breaks of the Dnieper. Polish nobles, customarily of Ruthenian background, commanded the Zaporozhian Host (*wojska zaporoskie*). A minority of the Cossacks was registered with the Polish-Lithuanian armies and drew regular salaries. Most were unregistered, however. The military registries grew only in the time of war. The Cossack host loyally and bravely fought against the Muscovites, Swedes, Turks, and other enemies of Poland-Lithuania. In times of peace, the Cossacks periodically launched unauthorized looting expeditions against the Ottoman Empire. But they also vigorously defended the Commonwealth against seasonal slave raids by the Crimean Tatars, an off-shoot of the Mongol hordes of yore. (It is estimated that over some 200 years these fierce Crimean warriors carried off about 3 million people into Ottoman slavery.) Proud of their military service, the Cossacks clamored to be ennobled. Foolishly myopic, the Polish-Ruthenian magnates and much of the Polish nobility opposed granting political rights to them. Many of the great lords of the Ukraine hoped to enserf the Cossack rank and file. The latter responded with mutinies.

The most violent of the Cossack rebellions occurred in 1648. It enjoyed wide support among the Orthodox peasantry. It targeted Jews and Catholics, Polish nobility of all ethnic backgrounds, in particular. It would have been put down with a customary cruelty by the Polonized Catholic magnates of Ruthenian origin and their private armies with some support of the Commonwealth troops, had it not been for the involvement of the Muscovite State and the Ottoman Empire. Both foreign powers rendered assistance to the Cossacks. The Sublime Porte allowed their Crimean Tartar vassals to support the rebels militarily. In consequence, the Commonwealth had to fight a civil war and two foreign invasions simultaneously. To boot, the Swedes invaded to pursue dynastic claims of their own in 1655.[9] They overran nearly the entire country before the Poles put them to flight. Having expelled the

Swedes, Poland-Lithuania faced an invasion from Transylvania and, more menacingly, from Muscovy. In 1667, the Commonwealth lost the eastern part of the Ukraine along the Dnieper, including Kiev, to the Tsar. There was no respite from war, though. Soon the regular Ottoman armies and their Tatar auxiliaries invaded Poland. They were repulsed in 1673 but only after the loss of the province of Podolia in the south-west of the Ukraine. The Ottoman menace was finally checked by the Polish-Lithuanian forces and their allies under King John III Sobieski at the battle of Vienna in 1683.

Afterward, however, the Commonwealth grew too exhausted to continue as an independent player on the international scene. It became unable to defend its own territory, including the Intermarium. It watched passively as the Muscovites defeated the Swedes in 1709, crushed the Ukrainian Cossacks in 1775, and conquered the Crimean Tartars in 1783. Much of the fighting took place on the Polish territory. Its cities destroyed, villages depopulated, economy devastated, and parliamentary system moribund, Poland-Lithuania suffered horribly. It became a convenient battlefield for great European power politics. For instance, during the War of the Polish Succession (1733–1735), the Russians, Prussians, French, Saxons, and Austrians vied with one another for the prize of imposing a king of their liking on the hapless country.

Throughout the eighteenth century, the Commonwealth slowly slipped into an informal state of vassalage to the Russian Empire and its Prussian and Austrian allies. All three took to stationing their troops in the Commonwealth. They also perpetrated untold violations of national sovereignty. For instance, the Austrians forcibly collected supplies in the countryside. The Prussians routinely shanghaied Polish subjects to press them into their army and deluged the country with falsified Polish coin. The Russians did all that and they further periodically marched their soldiers into the House of Parliament to interrupt any proceedings aimed at reform. They also arrested reformist deputies and dispatched them to Siberia. In fact, the practice of carrying off Polish serfs and prisoners of war and settling them in Muscovy and its lands, which commenced in the fifteenth century, now spilled from the rim of the Intermarium into central and western Crownlands of Poland itself. The Russians kidnapped and deported nobles, peasants, burghers, and Jews with impunity as the nation sunk into anarchy and impotence.[10]

Meanwhile, internal factions in the Commonwealth, led by various aristocratic clans, vied for dominance in alliance with various foreign governments, usually of the Muscovite Tsar. Some of those aristocrats championed reforms; others stuck with tradition. The traditionalists enjoyed the support of most of the nobility. The reformers, however, were more dynamic. Nonetheless, the traditionalist Poles were the first to stage an armed rebellion, the conservative Bar Confederacy (1768–1772), against both foreign domination and revolutionary transformation. Others soon rebelled in favor of radical reform and against external oppression.

These reformist "enlightened" rebels voted for the Constitution of May 3, 1791, Europe's first ever written instrument of government modeled after the American paradigm, but also inspired by the Revolution in France. The Constitution eliminated many of the crippling facets of Poland's traditional parliamentarism, including the *liberum veto*. It enfranchised the burghers, making them practically equal in rights with the nobility (many of whom among the petty gentry, however, became legally disadvantaged for failing to meet property qualifications). The constitution further extended the protection of the government to the peasantry. Last but not least, the cardinal legal document of the land established a constitutional monarchy in Poland. However, after a bit over a year, the Russians invaded to stop the reforms. They met with armed resistance in the Constitution's defense in 1792 and in the Insurrection of 1794. With Prussian assistance, the Muscovites defeated both armed efforts to preserve the Commonwealth's independence. The subsequent Polish alliance with revolutionary France, and its emperor Napoleon in particular, suffered a crushing defeat as well by 1815.[11]

Notes

1.　See Norman Davies, *God's Playground: A History of Poland*, vol. 1: *The Origins to 1795* (New York: Oxford University Press, 1982); Adam Zamoyski, *The Polish Way: A Thousand-Year History of the Poles and Their Culture* (New York and Toronto: Franklin Watts, 1988); Daniel Stone, *The Polish-Lithuanian State, 1389–1795* (Seattle, WA and London: University of Washington Press, 2001); Richard Butterwick, ed., *The Polish-Lithuanian Monarchy in European Context, c. 1500–1795* (Houndmills, Hampshire, and New York: Palgrave, 2001); Harold B. Segel, ed., *Political Thought in Renaissance Poland: An Anthology in English* (New York: PIASA Books, 2003); Samuel Fiszman, ed., *The Polish Renaissance in Its European Context* (Bloomington and Indianapolis: Indiana University Press, 1988); *Polska na tle Europy XVI–XVII wieku: Konferencja Muzeum Historii Polski, Warszawa, 23–24 października 2006* (*Poland and Europe, 16th–17th Centuries*) (Warszawa: Muzeum Historii Polski and InPlus, 2008); Krzysztof Koehler, "The Heritage of Polish Republicanism," *The Sarmatian Review* XXXII, no. 2 (April 2012): 1658–66; and Dalibor Roháč, "'It is by Unrule That Poland Stands': Institutions and Political Thought in the Polish-Lithuanian Commonwealth," *The Independent Review* 13, no. 2 (Fall 2008): 209–24. On art and architecture see, in particular, Carolyn C. Guile, *Borderland: Art and History in the Early Modern Polish-Lithuanian Commonwealth* (forthcoming from Pennsylvania State University Press); and Carolyn C. Guile, "'According to the Polish Sky and Customs': Art and Architecture in Early Modern Poland," a presentation delivered at The Fourth Annual Kościuszko Chair Lecture, The Institute of World Politics, Washington, DC, November 12, 2011.

2.　See Maria Bogucka, *The Lost World of the Sarmatians: Custom as the Regulator of Polish Social Life in Early Modern Times* (Warsaw: IH PAN, 1996); and, especially, Jan Chryzostom Pasek, *Memoirs of the Polish Baroque: The Writings of Jan Chryzostom Pasek, a Squire of Poland and Lithuania*, ed. by Catherine S. Leach (Berkeley, CA: University of California Press, 1980).

3.　Andrzej Sulima Kaminski, *Republic vs. Autocracy: Poland-Lithuania and Russia, 1686–1697* (Cambridge, MA: Distributed by Harvard University Press for the

Harvard Ukrainian Research Institute, 1993); Frank E. Sysyn, *Between Poland and the Ukraine: The Dilemma of Adam Kysil, 1600–1653* (Cambridge, MA: Harvard University Press and the Harvard Ukrainian Research Institute, 1985); Pawel Jasiennica, *The Commonwealth of Both Nations*, vol. 1: *The Silver Age*, vol. 2: *Calamity of the Realm*, vol. 3: *A Tale of Agony* (Miami, FL: The American Institute of Polish Culture, 1987–1992); Andreas Kappeler, Zenon E. Kohut, Frank E. Sysyn, and Mark von Hagen, eds., *Culture, Nation, and Identity: The Ukrainian-Russian Encounter, 1600–1945* (Edmonton and Toronto: Canadian Institute of Ukrainian Studies Press, 2003); Barbara Skinner, *The Western Front of the Eastern Church: Uniate and Orthodox Conflict in Eighteenth-Century Poland, Ukraine, Belarus, and Russia* (DeKalb, IL: Northern Illinois University Press, 2009).

4.   Janusz Tazbir, *A State without Stakes: Polish Religious Toleration in the Sixteenth Century* (New York and Warsaw: The Kościuszko Foundation, Twayne Publishers, and Państwowy Instytut Wydawniczy, 1973).

5.   See Salo Wittmayer Baron, *Social and Religious History of the Jews*, vol. 16: *Late Middle Ages and Era of European Expansion, 1200–1650; Poland-Lithuania, 1500–1650* (New York: Columbia University Press, 1976); Antony Polonsky, *The Jews in Poland and Russia*, vol. 1: *1350 to 1881* (Oxford and Portland, OR: The Littman Library of Jewish Civilization, 2010), 7–221; Chimen Abramsky, Maciej Jachimczyk, and Antony Polonsky, eds., *The Jews in Poland* (New York and Oxford: Basil Blackwell, 1986); Jacob Litman, *The Economic Role of Jews in Medieval Poland: The Contribution of Yitzhak Schipper* (Lanham, MD, New York, and London: University Press of America, 1984); M. J. Rosman, *The Lords' Jews: Magnate-Jewish Relations in the Polish-Lithuanian Commonwealth during the 18th Century* (Cambridge, MA: Distributed by Harvard University Press for the Center for Jewish Studies, Harvard University and the Harvard Ukrainian Research Center, 1990); Hillel Levine, *Economic Origins of Antisemitism: Poland and Its Jews in Early Modern Period* (New Haven, CT and London: Yale University Press, 1991); Gershon David Hundret, *Jews in Poland-Lithuania in the Eighteenth Century: A Genealogy of Modernity* (Berkeley and Los Angeles: University of California Press, 2004); Magda Teter, *Jews and Heretics in Catholic Poland: A Beleaguered Church in the Post-Reform Era* (New York: Cambridge University Press, 2006). More broadly, about the interaction of the Jewish people with the Intermarium majority population, see Wolf Moskovich, Shmuel Shvarzband, and Anatoly Alekseev, eds., *Jews and Slavs* (Jerusalem and St. Petersburg: Israel Academy of Sciences and Humanities, Hebrew University of Jerusalem, Department of Russian and Slavic Studies, Center for the Study of Slavic Languages and Literature, Slavonic Bible Foundation, Russian Academy of Sciences, 1993–2005), in particular vol. 4: *Judeo-Slavic Interaction in the Modern Period*; vol. 5: *Jews and Ukrainians*; vol. 7: *Jews and Eastern Slavs*; vol. 11: *Jewish-Polish and Jewish-Russian Contacts*; vol. 13: *Anti-Semitism and Philo-Semitism in the Slavic World and Western Europe*; vol. 16: *Khazars*; vol. 19: *Jews, Ukrainians, and Russians*; vol. 21: *Jews, Poles, and Russians: Jewish-Polish and Jewish Russian Contacts*.

6.   The legal basis of granting nobility to Jews (and Muslims) was "according to the law of the statue of the G[rand] D[uchy] of Lit[huania], article 6, chapter 12, paragraph VI quinto; [and] the 1764 Constitution of the Titles for Neophytes." See "Herbarz Oszmiański" [The Oszmiany Book of Heraldry] published as Dm. Iv. Dovgiallo [Dimitrii Ivanovich Dovgiallo], *Istoriko-iuridicheskee materialy, izvlechennee iz aktovykh knig gubernii vitebskoi i mogilevskoi, khraniachis v'*

tsentral'nom arkhiv' v Vitebske i izdannye pod' predaktsiei Dm. Iv. Dovgiallo, vypusk dvadtsat' os'moi (Vitebsk: Gubernskaia Tipo-Litografiia, 1900), 28, 31. There were also very rare examples of the ennoblement of Jews who remained faithful to Judaism, for example, the royal banker Meir (Leliwa) Ezofowicz in 1525. See Robert Szuchta, "Pierwszy Żyd szlachcicem – Meir Ezofowicz, podskarbi litewski," ("First Jew as a Nobleman: Mir Ezofowicz, the Sub-Treasurer of Lithuania") *Rzeczpospolita*, April 28, 2008.

7. See, in particular, the output of the superb Ottomanist Halil Inalcik, *Essays in Ottoman History* (Istanbul: Eren, 1998); Halil Inalcik and Donald Quataert, eds., *An Economic and Social History of the Ottoman Empire, 1300–1914*, 2 vols. (Cambridge: Cambridge University Press, 1994). See also Donald Quataert, *The Ottoman Empire, 1700–1922* (Cambridge: Cambridge University Press, 2000); Stanford J. Shaw and Ezel Kural Shaw, *History of the Ottoman Empire and Modern Turkey*, 2 vols. (Cambridge: Cambridge University Press, 1976); Lord Kinross, *The Ottoman Centuries: The Rise and Fall of the Turkish Empire* (New York: Perennial, 2002); Peter Sugar, *Southeastern Europe under Ottoman Rule, 1354–1804* (Seattle, WA and London: University of Washington Press, 1977). See also Harry Norris, *Islam in the Baltics: Europe's Early Muslim Community* (London and New York: Tauris Academic Studies, an imprint of I.B. Tauris Publishers, 2009), 31–73; Dariusz Skorupa, *Stosunki polsko-tatarskie 1595–1623 (Polish-Tatar Relations, 1595–1623)* (Warsaw: IH PAN and Neriton, 2004); Piotr Borawski and Aleksander Dubiński, *Tatarzy Polscy: Dzieje, obrzędy, legendy, tradycje (Polish Tatars: History, Rituals, Legends, and Tradition)* (Warszawa: Wydawnictwo Iskry, 1986).

8. Polish thinkers based themselves on Roman law, the Bible, Church Fathers, and various medieval and Renaissance philosophical traditions. Chronologically, the following thinkers were crucial for the formation and maintenance of the so-called Polish school of international law: Stanisław ze Skarbmierza/Stanislaus de Scarbimiria (ca. 1365–1431), *Sermones super Gloria in excelsis* (Warszawa: ATK, 1978, written ca. 1390), and *Sermones sapientiales* (Warszawa: ATK, 1979, written between 1414–1430), e.g., the sermon on *De bello iusto*; Paweł Włodkowic/ Paulus Vladimiri (ca. 1370–1436), in particular, *Tractatus de potestate papae et imperatoris respectu infidelium* (1415); Jan Ostroróg (1436–1501), *Monumentum pro rei-publicae ordinatione* (ca. 1477); Jakub Przyłuski (ca. 1512–1554), *Leges seu statuta ac privilegia Regni Poloniae*, 6 vols. (1548); Jan Tarnowski (1488–1561), *Consilium Rationis Bellicae* (1558); and Krzysztof Warszewicki/ Christophori Varsevicii (1543–1601), *Ad Stephanum regem Poloniae oratio, qua cum Ioanne Magno Moscorum Duce XV. Ianuarii ad Zapotsiam confectam pacem gratulatur* (1582) and *De consilio et consiliariis principis liber* (1595). They were complemented by a bevy of other Polish thinkers, who concentrated on domestic reforms, including Andrzej Frycz Modrzewski/Andreias Fricius Modrevius (ca. 1503–1572), *Commentariorum de Republica emendanda*, 5 vols. (1554) and *Silvae quator* (1594, posthumously), which advocated abolishing serfdom and equal rights to all citizens from all classes; and Wawrzyniec Grzymała Goslicki/Laurentii Grimali Goslici (ca. 1533–1607), *De optimo senatore* (1568), which affirmed the subordination of the ruler to law, denied his right to rule without the consent of his subjects, preached the right to rebellion against a tyrant, and introduced a tri-division of power (executive, legislative, and judiciary), getting published in English as *The Accomplished Senator* (1607). See also Harold B. Segel, ed., *Political Thought in Renaissance Poland: An Anthology in English* (New York: PIASA Books, 2003); Samuel Fiszman, ed., *The Polish*

Renaissance in Its European Context (Bloomington and Indianapolis: Indiana University Press, 1988); and C. H. Alexandrowicz, "Paulus Vladimiri and the Development of the Doctrine of Coexistence of Christian and Non-Christian Countries," *British Yearbook of International Law* 39 (1963): 441ff.

9.   See Robert I. Frost, *After the Deluge: Poland-Lithuania and the Second Northern War, 1655–1660* (Cambridge: Cambridge University Press, 2004); and, more broadly, Robert I. Frost, *The Northern Wars: War, State and Society in Northeastern Europe, 1558–1721* (Harrow: Longman, 2000). See also Andrzej Rachuba, ed., *Metryka Litewska: Rejestry podymnego Wielkiego Księstwa Litewskiego: Województwo brzeskie litewskie 1667–1690 r.* (Warsaw: Neriton, IH PAN, 2000); Henryk Lulewicz, ed., *Metryka Litewska. Rejestry podymnego Wielkiego Księstwa Litewskiego: Województwo trockie 1690 r.* (Warsaw: Neriton, IH PAN, 2000); Henryk Lulewicz and Andrzej Rachuba, eds., *Metryka litewska: Rejestry podymnego Wielkiego Księstwa Litewskiego: Województwo nowogródzkie 1690 r.* (Warsaw: IH PAN, Neriton, 2002); Andrzej Karpiński, *W walce z niewidzialnym wrogiem: Epidemie chorób zakaźnych w Rzeczypospolitej w XVI–XVIII w. i ich następstwa demograficzne, społeczne i polityczne* (*Fighting the Invisible Enemy: Infectious Disease Epidemics in the Commonwealth, 16th–18th centuries*) (Warsaw: Neriton, IH PAN, 2000).

10. See Marek Jan Chodakiewicz, "Siberian Exile in Polish History," in *Oh Land of Siberia! Land Eternally Mournful: Polish Poetry from the Soviet Gulags*, ed. by Halina Abłamowicz (Lewiston, NY, Queenston, ON, and Lampeter, Wales: The Edwin Mellen Press, 2008), 9–82.

11. For internal developments see Jerzy Lukowski, *Liberty's Folly: The Polish-Lithuanian Commonwealth in the Eighteenth Century, 1697–1795* (London: Routledge, 1991). For a study of imperial politics leading to the destruction of Poland-Lithuania see H. M. Scott, *The Emergence of the Eastern Powers, 1756–1775* (Cambridge: Cambridge University Press, 2001). See also Richard Butterwick, *Poland's Last King and English Culture: Stanisław August Poniatowski, 1732–1798* (Oxford: Oxford University Press, 1998); Adam Zamoyski, *The Last King of Poland* (London: Jonathan Cape, 1992).

5

The Partitions

Ultimately, the Romanovs, the Hohenzollerns,[1] and the Habsburgs[2] partitioned Poland in 1772, 1793, and 1795 (with Vienna abstaining from the second partition), respectively. The Commonwealth thus disappeared as a state.[3] And the Intermarium for the first time found itself mostly under the control of the Muscovites and their Russian Empire. Only the south-western areas of Galicia, Transcarpathia, and Bukovina fell under the House of Austria.[4] The Habsburg partition fared much better, particularly starting in the middle of the nineteenth century, from a cultural, political, and, to a lesser extent, economic standpoint. Even Vienna's official policy of Germanization was rather tepid by the standard of Berlin's *Kulturkampf*, not to mention the crude ruthlessness of Moscow's aggressive Russification. Naturally, the latter entailed an onslaught on Western Christianity, Roman Catholicism in particular, but also the Uniate rite.[5]

From the point of view of the heirs to the legacy of freedom of the Commonwealth, the next 120 years of the history of the Intermarium is a tale of resistance and accommodation. On the one hand, former citizens of the Commonwealth rebelled periodically. On the other hand, in between, they also sought a modus vivendi with the partitioning powers. The Poles repeatedly resorted to arms to restore the Commonwealth. Many enthusiastically sided with Napoleon, in particular, during his invasion of Russia in 1812, which was dubbed "the war for Polish liberation." Later, the insurrections of 1830–1831 and 1863–1864 in the ethnic Polish lands inevitably spilled over with decreasing intensity into the Kremlin's Intermarium. There were also separate risings in Austrian Galicia in 1846 and 1848 (as well as Prussia's western Polish provinces during the Spring of Nations), but they failed to affect the Russian partition, except with a few anemic incursions and conspiracies. The Rising of 1863 was particularly important because it was the last time that the representatives of all ethno-religious groups of the old Commonwealth acted in concert and solidarity against the common, Muscovite enemy.[6]

For the most part, the insurrections were noble Polish affairs. And the nobles paid for them disproportionately. The nobility constituted the bulk of an estimated 100,000 insurgents and members of various conspiracies, including their families, deported to Siberia from 1772 until 1914. About

300,000 members of the petty gentry lost their noble status in the process of disenfranchisement and repression following the destruction of the Commonwealth. Nonetheless, the nobility continued to play a paramount role in the leadership of Polish politics in all orientations, including ultraloyalism, conservatism, socialism, populism, and nationalism. Even though the lordly houses supplied their fair share of rebels, the aristocratic elite oscillated between accommodation and collaboration for the most part. At the end of the nineteenth century many of them even advocated "triloyalism," dutiful cooperation with Vienna, Berlin, and Moscow. The middle and petty nobility often provided leadership to revolutionary and radical movements. The majority of the nobility, however, simply tried to live their lives as best they could under alien regimes. Their aim was that in the countryside, social, cultural, and economic ways would continue largely as they had under the Polish-Lithuanian state. As a result, it can be argued that the Commonwealth survived intact on the noble estates of the Intermarium; in the personal relations within noble families and between them; and in the transactions between the nobility, the peasantry, and the Jews. In Latgalia, for instance, the Polish nobility lived nearly autonomously despite the onerous and even hostile attitude of the imported Russian Imperial occupation bureaucracy.[7]

The nobility was under siege politically, culturally, and economically. In addition to routine political oppression, the partitioning powers disenfranchised anyone who failed to meet their property requirements. That stripped most of the petty gentry of their noble status. More importantly, each rising resulted in massive confiscations, deportations, and cashiering of the Polish nobility, in particular, in the Russian Empire. The dispossessed nobility moved to towns, where they formed much of the intelligentsia in the former lands of the Commonwealth. The nobles also tended to intermarry with the entrepreneurial and professional classes who were often of foreign origin, Germans, Italians, Scots, Jews, Armenians, and others, and who generally prospered under the partitions so long as they did not rebel openly. Nonetheless, it was the nobility and the intelligentsia that resisted the official policy of Russification most successfully. The policy made some inroads among the humble classes, except Catholic peasants.[8]

Accommodation was the norm among the peasantry. In fact, the Orthodox peasants became perhaps the most loyal subjects of the Tsar in the Russian partition. However, a few of the Catholic and Uniate farmers of the Intermarium resisted. As late as 1863, Catholic Lithuanians, Catholic Latvians, and some Unite Ruthenians flocked to the insurgent side in Samogitia, Latgalia, and the north-eastern lands as far as Volhynia. In the south-east, in the Ukraine, the attempts to rally the Orthodox population to the cause of freedom under the banner of the legacy of the Commonwealth failed for the most part. Likewise in the Habsburg lands, the peasantry usually remained loyal to the sovereign in Vienna. However, by the end of the nineteenth century some of the

Orthodox in the Austrian partition looked with hope toward the Tsar. Many, however, under the leadership of the Uniate clergy and their offspring, began converting their Ruthenian brethren into Ukrainian nationalists. Meanwhile, the Baltic peasants found a cause of their own: Estonian, Latvian, and Lithuanian nationalism. A thin layer of the intelligentsia (including priests in Lithuania) and entrepreneurs emerging from the sea of peasantry provided the leadership stratum. For instance, in Estonia the nationalist movement originated and persevered within a few university student fraternities established by Estonian burgher and peasant boys. But the nationalizing and modernizing of the rural masses could really only occur in earnest after the freeing of the serfs, which took place in the Russian Empire only following 1861. Overall, the peasants mattered at the dawn of the era of mass politics in the Intermarium, if only because they constituted the majority of the population. Some moved to the cities to swell the ranks of the urban proletariat. A number emigrated overseas. Most stayed put.[9]

Throughout the nineteenth century the Romanov and the Habsburg partitions remained severely underdeveloped from the economic standpoint. The Intermarium plodded on as an agricultural area. Scarcely any industrialization took place. There were food and wood processing enterprises thinly scattered around White Ruthenia and the Ukraine. The Baltic Sea coastal areas in the north and the Black Sea rim with the robust port of Odessa were the industrialized exceptions and commercial hubs. Galicia had a small oil industry center and a few industrial enterprises mostly in Lwów/Lviv/Leopolis/Lvov/Lemberg.[10] This economic neglect of the peripheries of the Russian Empire and the Dual Monarchy of Austro-Hungary seriously retarded the emergence of an indigenous working class which was often artisan and Jewish in origin. Hence, the radical social movements of the Intermarium were frequently heavily Jewish (but by no means all[11]). For example, the Bund, or the Jewish Workers Union, founded in Wilno/Vilnius/Vilna, was Imperial Russia's largest Marxist party until the revolution of 1905.[12] Jewish social radicalism reflected not only the downtrodden station of the Jewish proletariat but also the official discrimination of the Jewish community at large by the Imperial government. Until the end of the eighteenth century Jews were usually barred from settling anywhere in the Russian Empire. After the partitions of the Commonwealth, Jews were not permitted to reside outside of the so-called Pale of Settlement (which basically was identical with the Intermarium and the central lands of ethnic Poland). The bulk of the Jewish population lived in small towns. They were also largely confined to traditional Jewish economic pursuits such as trade, crafts, petty loans, and inn-keeping. Like the rest of the population, the Jews were subjected to Russification and, hence, usually spoke Russian, rather than Polish, in addition to Yiddish.

Facing challenges from without, the Jewish community experienced dynamic transformation within at the end of the nineteenth century. The masses of the traditionalist ultra-Orthodox Jewry were somewhat depleted through modernization and emigration. A thin layer of assimilated intelligentsia and professionals arose in the wake of the *Haskalah* (enlightenment) movement. Some of them embraced Polish culture and a few even the Christian faith. Most of the assimilationists, however, underwent Russification, to advance under the Romanov reign, or Germanization, to succeed in the Habsburg realm. Much of the unassimilated Jewish population, however, sought modernity through socialism or nationalism (Zionism) or a combination of both. Simply put, the processes within the Jewish minority reflected the developments within the Christian majority. That included also a demographic explosion by the end of the nineteenth century.[13]

Dynamic social and cultural changes far outpaced the outdated political and economic arrangements of the Intermarium, the part under Russian Imperial control, in particular. The traditionalist framework cracked seriously during the Revolution of 1905. The Intermarium erupted with violence. It was limited to the Russian partition. The countryside burned as the peasants attacked the manors and estates of Baltic German, Russian, and Polish nobles. In fact, in the Baltics the revolution acquired a distinctly nationalist flavor. The industrial peripheries saw massive worker strikes and military mutinies, in Odessa most notably. The Russians put the upheaval down with their customary ruthlessness. But some reforms followed.[14] The nobility and intelligentsia were permitted to develop a variety of local organizations of a charitable, educational, and cultural nature. A few even participated in limited elections to the imperial parliament, the *Duma*. Some land distribution took place as well, which benefited the peasantry. In the agricultural heartland, however, change was very slow to come. For the most part, some basic social and economic arrangements dating back to the Commonwealth remained firmly entrenched until 1914.

Notes

1. On Prussia and Germany see Hajo Holborn, *A History of Modern Germany: 1648–1945*, 3 vols. (Princeton, NJ: Princeton University Press, 1982).
2. On the Habsburgs see Robert A. Kann, *A History of the Habsburg Empire, 1526–1918* (Berkeley, Los Angeles, and London: University of California Press, 1980); Alan Sked, *The Decline and Fall of the Habsburg Empire, 1815–1918* (New York: Dorset Press, 1989); A. J. P. Taylor, *The Habsburg Monarchy, 1809–1918: The History of the Austrian Empire and Austria-Hungary* (Harmonsworth: Penguin Books, 1964).
3. For the mechanisms of the dismemberment of the Commonwealth see G. Shaw-Lefevre Baron Eversley, *The Partitions of Poland* (New York: H. Fertig, 1973); and Jerzy Lukowski, *The Partitions of Poland 1772, 1793, 1795* (London and New York: Longman Publishing Group, 1999). For a standard work on the subsequent fate of the Intermarium see Piotr S. Wandycz, *The Lands of Partitioned Poland, 1795–1918* (Seattle, WA and London: University of Washington Press, 1984). For a very detailed treatment of the Intermarium from the Partitions to the modern times by a variety of scholars see Krzysztof Jasiewicz, ed., *Europa*

nieprowincjonalna: Przemiany na ziemiach wschodnich dawnej Rzeczpospolitej (Białoruś, Litwa, Ukraina, wschodnie pogranicze III Rzeczpospolitej Polskiej) w latach 1772–1999 (Non-Provincial Europe: Transformations in the Eastern Lands of the Old Commonwealth [Belarus, Lithuania, Ukraine, and the Eastern Borderlands of the III Polish Commonwealth], 1772–1999) (Warszawa and London: Instytut Studiów Politycznych Polskiej Akademii Nauk, Oficyna Wydawnicza Rytm, Polonia Aid Foundation Trust, 1999) (afterward *Europa nieprowincjonalna*). See also Timothy Snyder, *The Reconstruction of Nations: Poland, Ukraine, Lithuania, Belarus, 1569–1999* (New Haven, CT and London: Yale University Press, 2003); and Waclaw Lednicki, *Russia, Poland and The West: Essays in Literary and Cultural History* (New York: Roy Publishers, 1953).

4. See Norman Davies, *Vanished Kingdoms: The Rise and Fall of States and Nations* (New York: Viking, 2011), chap. 9: "Galicia," at 439–89; and Larry Wolff, *The Idea of Galicia: History and Fantasy in Habsburg Political Culture* (Stanford, CA: Stanford University Press, 2010). On the Ruthenes of Bukovina see Robert A. Kann and Zdeněk V. David, *The Peoples of the Eastern Habsburg Lands, 1526–1918* (Seattle, WA and London: University of Washington Press, 1984), 178–81, 272–79, 415–23. And on their montagnard brethren, the Hutsuls, in the adjacent Huculszczyzna and Pokucie, who also were assigned to the Habsburg realm see a folkloristic, anthropological, and literary *tour de force* by Stanisław Vincenz, *Na wysokiej połoninie: Prawda starowieku: Obrazy i gawędy z wierchowiny huculskiej (Up on the Highest Mountain Side: The Ancient Truth: Vignettes and Tales from the Hutsul Peaks)* (Sejny: Pogranicze, 2002), which was originally published in 1938.

5. See Hugh Seton-Watson, *The Russian Empire, 1801–1917* (Oxford: The Clarendon Press, 1990); Nicholas Riasanovsky, *Nicholas I and Official Nationality in Russia, 1825–1855* (Berkeley, Los Angeles, and London: University of California Press, 1959); Theodor R. Weeks, *Nation and State in Late Imperial Russia: Nationalism and Russification on the Western Frontier, 1863–1914* (De Kalb, IL: Northern Illinois University Press, 1996); Darius Staliūnas, *Making Russians: Meaning and Practice of Russification in Lithuania and Belarus After 1863* (Amsterdam and New York: Rodopi, 2007); Sergei I. Zhuk, *Russia's Lost Reformation: Peasants, Millennialism, and Radical Sects in Southern Russia and Ukraine, 1830–1917* (Washington, DC, Baltimore, MD, and London: Woodrow Wilson Center Press and The John Hopkins University Press, 2004); Dennis J. Dunn, *The Catholic Church and Russia: Popes, Patriarchs, Tsars and Commissars* (Hants and Burlington: Ashgate, 2004); John-Paul Himka, *Religion and Nationality in Western Ukraine: The Greek Catholic Church and the Ruthenian National Movement in Galicia, 1867–1900* (Montreal, Kingston, Ontario, London, and Ithaca, NY: McGill-Queen's University Press, 1999); Henryk Głębocki, *Kresy Imperium: Szkice i materiały do polityki Rosji wobec jej peryferii (XVIII–XXI wiek) (The Borderlands of the Empire: Essays and Materials on Russia's Policy toward Its Peripheries between the 18th and 21st Centuries)* (Kraków: Arcana, 2006).

6. See Adam Zamoyski, *1812: Napoleon's Fatal March on Moscow* (London: HarperCollins, 2004); W. H. Zawadzki, *A Man of Honour: Adam Czartoryski as a Statesman of Russia and Poland, 1795–1831* (Oxford: The Clarendon Press, 1993); Angela T. Pienkos, *The Imperfect Autocrat: Grand Duke Constantine Pavlovich and the Polish Congress Kingdom* (Boulder, CO and New York: East European Monographs and Columbia University Press, 1987); Adam Zamoyski, *Holy Madness: Romantics, Patriots, and Revolutionaries, 1776–1871* (New

York: Viking, 2000); R. F. Leslie, *Reform and Insurrection in Russian Poland, 1856–1865* (London and New York: University of London and The Athlone Press, 1963); R. F. Leslie, *Polish Politics and the Revolution of November 1830* (Westport, CT: Greenwood Press Publishers, 1969). Leslie is a Stalinist but his works are virtually the only available in English on the nineteenth-century Polish insurrections. For a recent history of the 1863 insurrection in the Intermarium see Dawid Fajnhauz, *1863: Litwa i Białoruś* (1863: Lithuania and Belarus) (Warszawa: Wyd. Neriton, IH PAN, 1999).

7.   See Mikhail Dolbilov, "The Stereotype of the Pole in Imperial Policy: The 'Depolonication' of the Northwestern Region in the 1860s," *Russian Studies in History* 44, no. 2 (Fall 2005): 44–88; Darius Staliūnas, "Russländische 'Kollaborationsangebote' an nationale Gruppen nach dem Januaraufstand von 1863 im so genannten Nordwestgebiet," in *"Kollaboration" in Nordosteuropa: Erscheinungsformen und Deutungen im 20. Jahrhundert*, ed. by Joachim Tauber (Wiesbaden: Harrassowitz Verlag, 2006), 88–100 (afterward *"Kollaboration" in Nordosteuropa*); Janina z Puttkamerów Żółtowska, *Inne czasy, inni ludzie (Different Times, Different People)* (London: Polska Fundacja Kulturalna, 1998); Dorota Samborska, "Ludzie i miejsca Inflant polskich początku XIX wieku we wspomnieniach Kazimierza Bujnickiego z Dagdy," ("People and Places of the Polish Inflanty at the Beginning of the 19th Century According to the Memoirs of Kazimierz Bujnicki of Dagda") *Verbum Nobile: Pismo środowiska szlacheckiego*, no. 16 (2007): 64–71; Jerzy Żenkiewicz, *Dwór polski i jego otoczenie: Kresy Północno-Wschodnie (The Polish Manor and Its Surroundings: The North-Eastern Borderlands)* (Toruń: Adam Marszałek, 2008); Krzysztof Zajas, *Nieobecna kultura: Przypadek Inflant polskich (Absent Culture: The Case of the Polish Inflanty)* (Kraków: Universitas, 2008); and, in particular, Gustaw Manteuffel, *Inflanty polskie oraz listy znad Bałtyku (The Polish Inflanty and the Letters from the Baltic Coast)* (Kraków: Universitas, 2009), which is a nineteenth-century account by a noted scholar and nobleman. See also Priscilla Roosevelt, *Life on the Russian Country Estate: A Social and Cultural History* (New Haven, CT and London: Yale University Press, 1995); Geroid Tanquary Robinson, *Rural Russia Under the Old Regime: A History of the Landlord Peasant World and a Prologue to the Peasant Revolution of 1917* (Berkeley and Los Angeles: University of California Press, 1960); Daniel Beauvois, *The Noble, the Serf, and the Revizor: The Polish Nobility between Tsarist Imperialism and the Ukrainian Masses (1831–1863)* (Chur, Switzerland and New York: Harwood Academic Publishers, 1991). Beauvois is a Moscow-centric post-Marxist. See Jakub Brodacki, "'Idąc rakiem,' czyli ab ovo," *Glaukopis: Pismo społeczno-historyczne* [Warsaw] no. 5–6 (2006): 438–49.

8.   See Jolanta Sikorska-Kulesza, *Deklasacja drobnej szlachty na Litwie i Białorusi w XIX wieku (The Process of Becoming Déclassé among the Petty Gentry of Lithuania and Belarus in the 19th Century)* (Warszawa: Oficyna Wydawnicza "Ajaks," 1995); Czesław Malewski, *Rody Szlacheckie w powiecie lidzkim na Litwie w XIX wieku (Noble Families in the County of Lida in Lithuania in the 19th Century)* (Wilno: Wydawnictwo Czas, 2002); Stanisław Dumin and Sławomir Górzyński, *Spis szlachty wylegitymowanej w guberniach grodzieńskiej, mińskiej, mohylewskiej, smoleńskiej i witebskiej (The Register of Verified Nobility in the Grodno, Minsk, Mohilev, Smolensk, and Vitebsk gubernias)* (Warszawa: DiG, 1992); Natalia Czyżewska and Przemysław Czyżewski, "Nad Niemnem: Drobna szlachta grodzieńska w XVI–XX wieku," ("By the Niemen River: Petty Gentry of the Grodno Area in 16th–20th Centuries") *Verbum Nobile: Pismo*

środowiska szlacheckiego, no. 16 (2007): 6–10; Wiktoria Śliwowska, *Zesłańcy polscy w Imperium Rosyjskim w pierwszej połowie XIX wieku: Słownik biograficzny* (*Polish Exiles in the Russian Empire in the First Half of the 19th Century: A Bibliographical Dictionary*) (Warsaw: Wydawnictwo DIG, 1998); Tadeusz Epsztein, *Edukacja dzieci i młodzieży w polskich rodzinach ziemiańskich na Wołyniu, Podolu i Ukrainie w II połowie XIX wieku* (*Education of Children and Youth in Polish Noble Families in Volhynia, Podolia, and Ukraine in the Second Half of the 19th Century*) (Warszawa: IH PAN, Wyd. DiG, 1998); Mirosław Ustrzycki, *Ziemianie polscy na Kresach w latach 1864–1914: Świat wartości i postaw* (*Polish Landed Nobility in the Borderlands, 1864–1914: Their World of Values and Attitudes*) (Kraków: Arcana, 2006); Tadeusz Epsztein, *Piórem i paletą. Zainteresowania intelektualne i artystyczne ziemiaństwa polskiego na Ukrainie w drugiej połowie XIX wieku* (*With a Pen and a Palette: Intellectual and Artistic Pursuits of the Polish Landed Nobility in the Ukraine in the Second Half of the 19th Century*) (Warsaw: IH PAN, Neriton, 2005); Ryszard Kołodziejczyk, ed., *Image przedsiębiorcy gospodarczego w Polsce w XIX i XX wieku* (*The Image of the Entrepreneur in Poland in the 19th and the 20th Centuries*) (Warszawa: IH PAN, Wyd. DiG, 1993).

9.   See Andrei S. Markovits and Frank E. Sysyn, eds., *Nationbuilding and the Politics of Nationalism: Essays on Austrian Galicia* (Cambridge, MA: Harvard University Press, 1982); Paul Robert Magocsi, *The Roots of Ukrainian Nationalism: Galicia as Ukraine's Piedmont* (Toronto: University of Toronto Press, 2002); Christopher Hann and Paul Robert Magocsi, eds., *Galicia: A Multicultured Land* (Toronto, Buffalo, and London: University of Toronto Press, 2005); Alexander V. Prusin, *The Lands between: Conflict in the East European Borderlands, 1870–1992* (New York and Oxford: Oxford University Press, 2010), 11–71; Jan Molenda, *Chłopi, naród, niepodległość: Kształtowanie się postaw narodowych i obywatelskich chłopów w Galicji i Królestwie Polskim w przededniu odrodzenia Polski* (*Peasants, Nation, Independence: The Shaping of Nationalist and Civic Attitudes of the Peasants of Galicia and the Kingdom of Poland on the Eve of Poland's Rebirth*) (Warsaw: Wyd. Neriton, IH PAN, 1999). See also the following essays in Jasiewicz, *Europa nieprowincjonalna*: Albis Kaseperavičius, "Kształtowanie się narodu litewskiego" ("The Shaping of the Lithuanian Nation"), 217–23; Sokrat Janowicz, "Kształtowanie się narodu białoruskiego" ("The Shaping of the Belarusian Nation"), 242–48; Regina Grejtiane, "Wokół kształtowania się narodu łotewskiego: Narodowe odrodzenie w Latgalii w XIX i XX wieku" ("Concerning the Shaping of the Latvian Nations: The National Rebirth in Latgalia in the 19th and 20th Centuries"), 261–69; Ēriks Jēkabsons, "Polska mniejszość narodowa na Łotwie: Krótka charakterystyka i zarys działalności" ("Polish National Minority in Latvia: A Short Description of Its Activities"), 297–98; Valters Ščerbinskis, "Przedstawiciele narodów muzułmańskich oraz Karaimi na Łotwie od końca XIX wieku do czasów obecnych" ("The Representatives of Muslim and Karaites in Latvia from the End of the 19th Century until the Modern Times"), 299–308; Włodzimierz Tugaj, "Mniejszość łotewska na ziemiach białoruskich w XIX i XX wieku" ("Latvian Minority in the Area of Belarusia in the 19th and 20th Centuries"), 320–36; Iwan Hreczko, "Uwagi do dziejów Cerkwi greckokatolickiej na ziemiach wschodnich dawnej Rzeczypospolitej (XVIII–XX w.)" ("Some Remarks toward the History of the Greek Catholic Church in the Eastern Lands of the Former Commonwealth [18th–20th Centuries]), 355–62. See also Andrew Wilson, *Belarus: The Last European Dictatorship* (New Haven, CT and London: Yale University Press, 2011), 60–89; Oleg Łatyszonek, *Od Rusinów Białych do*

Białorusinów: U źródeł białoruskiej idei narodowej (*From White Ruthenians to Belarusians: The Sources of Belarusian National Idea*) (Białystok: Wydawnictwo Uniwersyteckie, 2006); Jerzy Turonek, *Odrodzenie Białorusi: Rzecz o Wacławie Iwanowskim* (*The Rebirth of Belarus: On Wacław Iwanowski*) (Warszawa: WOW "Gryf" and IH PAN, 1992); Bazyli Białokozowicz, "U źródeł kształtowania się nowożytnej białoruskiej świadomości narodowej," (*The Origins of the Shaping of Modern Belarusian National Consciousness*) *Białoruskie Zeszyty Historyczne* no. 4 (1996); Алесь Смалянчук, "Беларускі нацыянальны рух і краёвая ідэя," ("The Belarusian National Movement and the Homeland Idea") *Białoruskie Zeszyty Historyczne* no. 14 (2000), http://kamunikat.fontel.net/www/czasopisy/bzh/14/14art_smalanczuk.htm (accessed September 20, 2010); Ігар Кузняцоў, "Носьбіты ідэі беларускай дзяржаўнасці—ахвяры таталітарнага рэжыму," ("The Idea of the Belarusian Statehood as a Victim of the Totalitarian Regime") *Białoruskie Zeszyty Historyczne* no. 16 (2001) http://kamunikat.fontel.net/www/czasopisy/bzh/16/16art_kuzniacou.htm (accessed September 20, 2010); and a rather pedestrian effort, lacking a sufficient comparative perspective, by Pers Anders Rudling, "The Battle Over Belarus: The Rise and Fall of the Belarusian National Movement, 1906–1931," PhD Dissertation, University of Alberta, 2010, http://uni-greifswald.academia.edu/PerAndersRudling/Books/353834/_The_Battle_Over_Belarus_The_Rise_and_Fall_of_the_Belarusian_National_Movement_1906-1931_ (accessed April 23, 2012). See further Edward Allworth, ed., *Tatars of the Crimea: Their Struggle for Survival: Original Studies from North America, Unofficial and Official Documents from Czarist and Soviet Sources* (Durnham and London: Duke University Press, 1988); Alan Fisher, *The Crimean Tatars* (Stanford, CA: Hoover Institution Press, 1987); Azade-Ayşe Rorlich, *The Volga Tatars: A Profile in National Resilience* (Stanford, CA: Hoover Institution Press, 1986); and Louis Guy Michael, *More Corn for Bessarabia: The Russian Experience, 1910–1917* (East Lansing, MI: Michigan State University Press, 1983).

10. Daniel Chirot, ed., *The Origins of Backwardness in Eastern Europe: Economics and Politics from the Middle Ages until the Early Twentieth Century* (Berkeley, Los Angeles and London: University of California Press, 1989); Marc Ben-Joseph, *Adversities of Autonomy: Bank Krajowy Królestwa Galicyi i Lodomeryi and the Politics of Credit in Galicia 1870–1913* (Kraków: Wydawnictwo Uniwersytetu Jagiellońskiego Kraków, 1999); John Czaplicka, ed., *Lviv: A City in the Crosscurrents of Culture* (Cambridge, MA: Harvard University Press, 2005). For a critical review of *Lviv* see Marek Jan Chodakiewicz, "Ni ma jak Lviv?" ("There Ain't Nothing Like Lviv?") *Glaukopis* no. 5–6 (2006): 490–97.

11. John-Paul Himka, *Socialism in Galicia: The Emergence of Polish Social Democracy and Ukrainian Radicalism (1860–1890)* (Cambridge, MA: Distributed by Harvard University Press for the Harvard Ukrainian Research Institute, 1983).

12. Henry J. Tobias, *The Jewish Bund in Russia: From Its Origins to 1905* (Stanford, CA: Stanford University Press, 1972); Hans Rogger, *Jewish Policies and Right-Wing Politics in Imperial Russia* (Berkeley and Los Angeles: University of California Press, 1986).

13. See Antony Polonsky, *The Jews in Poland and Russia*, vol. 1: *1350 to 1881* (Oxford and Portland, OR: The Littman Library of Jewish Civilization, 2010), 223–438; Antony Polonsky, *The Jews in Poland and Russia*, vol. 2: *1881 to 1914* (Oxford and Portland, OR: The Littman Library of Jewish Civilization, 2010);

Nancy Sinkoff, *Out of the Shtetl: Making Jews Modern in the Polish Borderlands* (Providence, RI: Brown Judaic Studies, 2004).

14. Robert E. Blobaum, *Rewolucja: Russian Poland, 1904–1907* (Ithaca, NY and London: Cornell University Press, 1995); Alvin Marcus Fountain II, *Roman Dmowski: Party, Tactics, Ideology, 1895–1907* (Boulder, CO and New York: East European Monographs and Columbia University Press, 1980); Robert Blobaum, *Feliks Dzierzynski and the SDKPiL: A Study of the Origins of Polish Communism* (Boulder, CO and New York: East European Monographs and Columbia University Press, 1984); Andrzej Walicki, *Philosophy and Romantic Nationalism: The Case of Poland* (Oxford: The Clarendon Press, 1982); Brian Porter, *When Nationalism Began to Hate: Imagining Modern Politics in Nineteenth-Century Poland* (Oxford and New York: Oxford University Press, 2002). For reviews of Porter's deeply flawed work see John Radzilowski, *Kosmas: Czechoslovak and Central European Journal* 15, no. 1 (Fall 2001): 97–99, and Marek Jan Chodakiewicz, "Nacjonalizm wyobrażony" (Nationalism Imagined), *Arcana* no. 6 (60) (2004): 167–86.

6

World War I and the Revolution

World War I broke out with the Russian invasion of the Intermarium's peripheral East Prussian area in August 1914. Repulsed in the north, the Russians meanwhile registered some successes in Austrian Galicia. They captured Lwów and pushed south-west toward the Carpathians. However, by the fall of 1915, the Germans and Austro-Hungarians expelled the Russians completely from the periphery and pursued them into their own empire. By the mid-1916, the Germanic powers occupied much of the territories of the old Commonwealth.

In March 1917, a revolution convulsed Russia. The Tsar abdicated. His former realm was crippled by the phenomenon of dual power: an ineffectual liberal regime and a radical central council (Soviet). Replicated a thousandfold regionally, the Soviets mushroomed throughout the Romanov lands to disable effective government everywhere. The police disappeared along with civilian administrators; industrial unrest paralyzed the Empire's economic life; the infrastructure collapsed; most state functions ceased; the Russian armies dissolved and the deserters headed home in droves. The peasants attacked noble estates on a massive scale setting the countryside ablaze. General anarchy ruled.

In November 1917, the revolution entered its Communist phase. The Bolsheviks under Vladimir Lenin seized power. Practically, all political orientations of the Russian Empire opposed them but failed to unite militarily against the Reds. Meanwhile, many of the captive minorities rebelled and proclaimed their independence. The Communists suavely played the nationalities card, cynically supporting the independence of all and sundry, only with a slight hint that the "freedom" implied a future duty to submit one's nation to Bolshevism. Further, the Reds encouraged universal anarchy by advancing the slogan: "rob that which was robbed" (*grab' nagrablennoe*). This was both a strategic and a tactical approach. The greater the number of people implicated in revolutionary crimes, the greater the fear of the return of the forces of law and order. The greater the destruction, the easier it would be to build socialism on the ruins of the old system. Despite fostering the disintegration of the Russian state within and without, the Communists nonetheless themselves teetered on the verge of collapse. Therefore, to stave off the most serious threat to its existence, the "Republic of the Soviets" decided to compromise with Germany.[1]

In March 1918, prostrated, Red Moscow consented to ceding practically the whole of the Intermarium to triumphant, imperial Berlin (with Vienna playing an increasingly subsidiary role).[2] From their arrival in the eastern zone of occupation in 1915, the Germanic powers played competing nationalities against one another. However, the occupiers also permitted the establishment of the local authorities along a national basis. They supported chiefly the nationalisms of the non-Poles. In particular, Germany sponsored Ukrainian nationalism and set up a puppet buffer Ukrainian state, under the *Hetmanate*, in the east in 1917. But Berlin also assisted the Latvians, Estonians, Lithuanians, and Belarusians. The rationale was that their nationalisms were less developed and less threatening as largely devoid of the educated and wealthy elite. According to this line of reasoning, only the Poles were capable of offering any meaningful resistance to Berlin. Ultimately, however, Germany's plans came to naught because of her collapse in the west in November 1918.

As the German and Austro-Hungarian troops retreated home, a free-for-all ensued in the vacated space of the Intermarium. The further east, the more anarchy and violence prevailed. Wherever the Bolsheviks appeared, they lustfully unleashed Red Terror and War Communism. The latter was a policy of merciless economic exploitation of the peasantry and others, including wholesale food confiscations which triggered a massive famine. The reaction of the victims of Bolshevism was predictably violent. It also fueled the political struggles. Warlords of different shade and hue appeared in small localities and major regions. Whites, Reds, Blacks, and Greens fought it out against each other fiercely. The Russian political scene witnessed a convoluted combination of tactical alliances usually dictated by the relative threat of the day. The Blacks were anarchists, the Greens equaled agrarian populists, and the Whites meant monarchists. To confuse things further, many of the putative "Whites" were really non-Bolshevik, or even anti-Bolshevik, Reds, like the Social Revolutionaries (SRs), for example. This was because the Bolsheviks branded anyone who disagreed with them as "Whites."

In addition to the Russian revolutionaries and counterrevolutionaries, various ethno-cultural groups set up their own outfits, for instance, the Cossacks or Chechens. To confuse things, they also split along political lines of Reds and Whites. Nonetheless, a disciplined ethnic military unit amidst the sea of Russian anarchy could turn the tide, as was the case with the Latvian Rifles who declared for the Bolsheviks. A multitude of "volunteer armies" appeared on the scene. These included the German *Freikorps* and Polish detachments as well as monarchist, or, more broadly, non-Bolshevik, Russians, and various erstwhile foreign POWs struggling to return home, win fame and fortune, and overthrow the Reds or whoever else was in power in the area. Everyone killed without mercy one's ideological opponents or persons perceived as such. Class struggle overlapped ethnic struggle. The nobility and the Jews had the dubious distinction of being on almost everyone's enemy list. The obvious exception was the monarchist Whites and the Poles who—because of their interest in law and order as well as preservation of the old elite—protected the nobles (as well as the middle classes and the non-Red intelligentsia) and, to an extent, the Jews. The latter could also sometimes count on the support of the Reds. Nonetheless, massive pogroms that took the lives of between 50,000 and 100,000 Jews marked nearly all revolutionary, counterrevolutionary, and military activities.[3]

But pogroms were completely perennial to the political objectives of the combating forces. The Bolsheviks stood for a revolutionary tyranny; the Whites fought for an imperial restoration; and the captive nations struggled for freedom. In the western part of the Intermarium, the Poles clearly had the upper hand. In November 1918, Poland proclaimed its independence. Between 1918 and 1922, it fought nine wars at the center and on all its frontiers: against the Germans, Ukrainians, Lithuanians, Czechs, and the Bolsheviks. Occasionally, the Poles combated also the Whites, the Blacks, and the Greens, as disparate Polish forces slashed their way home from the depth of the flaming Russian Empire. By the force of inertia, the wars raged in the Eastern Borderlands. Warsaw sent assistance after the local Poles had claimed Wilno/Vilnius and Lwów/Lviv and clamored for a union with central Poland. Both cities were populated by a Polish majority, with the Jews constituting the most sizable minority. The Lithuanian ethnic group in Wilno was miniscule, as confirmed by the German census of 1916, and it was rather small outside the city, where the Poles also predominated. Whereas the Ukrainian inhabitants of Lwów were relatively few, they constituted a clear majority in the surrounding countryside. However, the Ukrainians, Lithuanians, and others failed to translate their numerical superiority into a nationalist victory in most places of mixed ethnic composition. The Poles were rather successful in establishing their government in the western belt of the Intermarium between Wilno and Lwów and in garrison cities strategically perched on railroad junctions. In the countryside, revolution and partisan warfare raged unabated.

Throughout the Intermarium, the local peasant communities formed their "Green" self-defense forces to protect themselves, including the land and other loot captured at the expense of the nobility. The Greens were particularly successful in eastern White Ruthenia (Belarus). There they also often allied themselves with the forces of Belarusian populist nationalism which proclaimed its state's short-lived independence from the capital of Minsk in March 1918. The Belarusian republic was crushed by the Bolsheviks in 1919. Some "Green Oak" units continued to struggle against the Reds until 1921, and the remnant found asylum in Poland afterward.

Active principally in eastern and southern Ukraine, the Blacks established their anarchist outposts that were more akin to the Cossack *Sich* than to the utopian communes of their Bakuninian ideology. They raged against all forces of order. After temporarily allying themselves with the Reds against the Whites, the anarchists were completely routed by the Bolsheviks in 1920. And so were the eastern Ukrainian populist nationalists who briefly ruled from Kiev. They proclaimed their independence in 1918 and fought against the Reds, Whites, and Blacks in central and eastern Ukraine. In the west, in Galicia, a separate nationalist Ukrainian government operated principally against the Poles, but also against the Romanians, Hungarians, and even Czechoslovaks, until its forces were defeated in 1919 by Poland. A year later, the eastern Ukrainian populist nationalists under Semyon Petlura joined the Poles in the war against the Bolsheviks.[4] After the Communist rout, Warsaw agreed to a compromise peace with Moscow and jettisoned its erstwhile Ukrainian confederates, who had failed to gain the support of the Ukrainian masses. Poland also pragmatically maintained its neutrality toward Russia's monarchists. That predictably allowed the Reds to crush the Whites in the south and north of the Intermarium.

In the north, in a variety of kaleidoscopic alliances, the Balts fiercely defended their freshly won freedom. Both Estonia and Lithuania proclaimed their independence in February 1918, followed by Latvia in November 1918. The Lithuanians of Kaunas unsuccessfully collaborated with the Bolsheviks against the Poles in the regional conflict over Wilno/Vilnius, Lithuania's historic capital. Their anti-Polish offensive in the Suwałki/Suvalkai area failed as well. On the other hand, the Lithuanians succeeded in wrestling the Klaipėda/Memelland region from the Germans in 1923. Meanwhile, Latvia and Estonia vigorously fought against the Bolsheviks, the Germans, and the Whites. The Latvians initially suffered a defeat, first, at the hands of the Bolsheviks and, then, the Germans in early 1919. The former established a "Soviet Latvia," which controlled much of the country; the latter proclaimed "The Baltic Duchy," which stretched over northern and western Latvia and part of Estonia. For that reason, and others, the Estonians assisted the Latvians to defeat the Germans. The Latvians meanwhile additionally allied themselves with the Poles against the Reds. The ultimate defeat of the Bolsheviks by the Latvian-Polish forces came with some German assistance in 1920. At the same time, the Estonians prevailed over the Communists with some White Russian, British, Finnish, and Swedish aid. Nonetheless, Baltic independence was very tenuous and fragile. It persevered only because of the triumph of the Polish forces over the Red Army in 1920.[5]

The western and northern parts of the Intermarium emerged free from the carnage of World War I, revolution, and civil strife. In the process, each nation state concentrated on its own narrowly defined interests. Most quarreled violently with their neighbors. All fought against the Bolsheviks but, their anti-Communism notwithstanding, each was eager separately to find a modus vivendi with Red Russia usually to the detriment of other nationalities in the Intermarium. Thus, nationalist selfishness undermined the region's unity. Poland's pragmatic abandonment of free Ukraine is a case in point. Further, an important factor behind the failure to unite against Communism had to do with leftist affinities of some of the major players. For example, Poland's Commander-in-Chief, Marshal Józef Piłsudski, was a nationalistic socialist. He viewed the Whites, and their avowed aim of the restoration of autocracy, as a greater threat than the Reds, and their utopian promise of a socialist paradise on earth. At the crucial juncture of 1919, Piłsudski elected to remain neutral in Russia's Civil War, which was a gift to Lenin. Other factors behind the failure to crush the Communists had to do with a poorly conceived *Realpolitik*. For example, already in 1919, the Estonians falsely convinced themselves that, following the expulsion of the Bolsheviks from their country, the Reds would leave them alone. The Lithuanians misguidedly thought that the Communist help against the Poles would both benefit their nationalist cause and allow them to retain their independence. By the same token, Ukrainian nationalists crossed over to the Reds to oppose the Poles and the Whites. The Russian monarchists and other counterrevolutionaries meanwhile failed to endorse the independence of the former imperial lands resolutely, exacerbating well-founded fears of future White Russia among the newly free nation states. Some even suicidally supported the Reds during the Polish eastward offensive in 1920. Thus, nationalist selfishness, leftist affinities, and imperialist predilections resulted in a failure to create an alliance that would help secure the Intermarium's freedom and anchor it on a permanent basis by destroying the Bolshevik power in Russia forever.[6]

Admittedly, to be fair, only the Entente powers had the resources to roll back the Red tide permanently. Alas, the assistance of the Western allies to the anti-Communist forces was half-hearted at best. The only exception was the generous aid of the United States, which equipped and trained about 20,000 Polish-American Catholic volunteers who, along with a handful of Protestant American daredevil pilots, arrived to fight for Poland's freedom. Also significantly, American relief volunteers, led by the formidable Herbert Hoover, fed, clothed, and nursed Polish citizens back to health as famine and diseases were rampant.[7] But America soon withdrew from world affairs. Its idealistic President Woodrow Wilson's diplomatic assistance for the Poles, so crucial during World War I, ceased. The remaining Western powers largely failed to aid Poland. Instead, London and Paris inexplicably tried to engineer Warsaw's diplomatic surrender to Moscow at the most threatening moment of Lenin's westward offensive in 1920. As for the Russian Whites, France and Great Britain simply abandoned them. Thus, totalitarianism triumphed in much of the former Russian Empire, casting a menacingly Spenglerian shadow upon the bloodied and shell-shocked Europe, "The Wasteland" of T. S. Eliot's paralyzingly horrific imagination, and, indeed, the world.

Notes

1. W. Bruce Lincoln, *Passage through Armageddon: The Russians in War and Revolution, 1914–1918* (New York: Simon and Schuster, 1986); George Katkov, *Russia 1917: The February Revolution* (New York: Harper and Row Publishers, 1967); Richard Pipes, *The Russian Revolution* (New York: Vintage Books, 1990); Robert V. Daniels, *Red October: The Bolshevik Revolution of 1917* (New York: Charles Scribner's Sons, 1967); William Henry Chamberlain, *The Russian Revolution*, 2 vols. (Princeton, NJ: Princeton University Press, 1987).

2. John W. Wheeler-Bennett, *Brest Litovsk: The Forgotten Peace, March 1918* (New York: W.W. Norton and Company, 1971); John-Paul Himka and Hans-Joachim Torke, eds., *German-Ukrainian Relations in Historical Perspective* (Edmonton and Toronto: Canadian Institute of Ukrainian Studies Press, 1994); Vejas G. Liulevicius, *War Land on the Eastern Front: Culture, National Identity, and German Occupation in World War I* (Cambridge and New York: Cambridge University Press, 2000). The latter monograph projects too much of World War II experience onto the preceding global conflict. The Prussian-commanded Germans of 1914 were not the Nazi-led Germans of 1939.

3. See W. Bruce Lincoln, *Red Victory: A History of the Russian Civil War* (New York and London: Simon and Schuster, 1989); Evan Mawdsley, *The Russian Civil War* (Edinburgh: Birlinn Ltd., 2000); Geoffrey Swain, *The Origins of the Russian Civil War* (London and New York: Longman, 1996); Oliver H. Radkey, *The Agrarian Foes of Bolshevism: Promise and Default of the Russian Socialist Revolutionaries, February to October 1917* (New York and London: Columbia University Press, 1962); Richard Luckett, *The White Generals: An Account of the White Movement and the Russian Civil War* (New York: The Viking Press, 1971); Vladimir N. Brovkin, *Behind the Front Lines of the Civil War: Political Parties and Social Movements in Russia, 1918–1922* (Princeton, NJ: Princeton University Press, 1994). According to a recent Russian study, Ukrainian, Russian, and Belarusian factions, both nationalist and Communist (including the Red Army), murdered at least 100,000 Jews. The claim that Poles were responsible for 2.6 percent of the victims has no foundation in fact, as the American mission under Henry Morgenthau sent to Poland in 1919 to investigate allegations of anti-Semitic excesses established that the number of Jews killed amounted to about 280. See Lidia B. Miliakova, ed., *Kniga pogromov: Pogromy na Ukraine, v Belorussii i evropeiskoi chaste Rossii v period Grazhdanskoi voiny 1918–1922 gg. Sbornik dokumentov* (*The Book of Pogroms: Pogroms in Ukraine, Belarus, and European part of Russia during the Civil War, 1918–1922: A Collection of Documents*) (Moscow: ROSSP-EN, 2007), xii–xiv; Oleg Vital'evich Budnitskii, *Rossiiskie evrei mezhdu krasnymi i belymi, 1917–1920* (Moscow: ROSSP-EN, 2005), which was translated by Timothy J. Portice as *Russian Jews between Reds and Whites, 1917–1920* (Philadelphia, PA: University of Pennsylvania Press, 2012); Henry Abramson, *A Prayer for the Government: Ukrainians and Jews in Revolutionary Times, 1917–1920* (Cambridge, MA: Harvard University Press, 1999); Benjamin Lieberman, *Terrible Fate: Ethnic Cleansing in the Making of Modern Europe* (Chicago, IL: Ivan R. Dee, 2006), 140–46 ; "Mission of The United States to Poland, Henry Morgenthau, Sr. Report," *Wikipedia*, http://en.wikisource.org/wiki/Mission_of_The_United_States_to_Poland,_Henry_Morgenthau,_Sr._Report; Hugh Gibson, "Polska 1919 oczami amerykańskiego dyplomaty" ("Poland

in 1919 through the Eyes of an American Diplomat"), *Glaukopis*, no. 17–18 (2010): 10–52. More broadly on the Jewish predicament during World War I and its aftermath in the Intermarium, see Antony Polonsky, *The Jews in Poland and Russia*, vol. 3: *1914 to 2008* (Oxford and Portland, OR: The Littman Library of Jewish Civilization, 2012), 3: 5–54; and in its southern part Alexander Victor Prusin, *Nationalizing a Borderland: War, Ethnicity, and Anti-Jewish Violence in East Galicia, 1914–1920* (Tuscaloosa, AL: University of Alabama Press, 2005). On Polish military endeavors, see Dariusz Radziwiłłowicz, *Polskie formacje zbrojne we wschodniej Rosji oraz na Syberii i Dalekim Wschodzie w latach 1918–1920 (Polish Armed Formations in Eastern Russia and Siberia as well as the Far East between 1918 and 1920)* (Olsztyn: Wydawnictwo Uniwersytetu Warmińsko-Mazurskiego w Olsztynie, 2009); Kazimierz Krajewski, "Nie tylko Dowborczycy," ("Not Only the Troops of Dowbor"), *Biuletyn Instytutu Pamięci Narodowej* no. 1–2 (96–97) (January–February 2009): 27–36; and further the following two essays in *"Kollaboration" in Nordosteuropa: Erscheinungsformen und Deutungen im 20. Jahrhundert*, ed. by Joachim Tauber (Wiesbaden: Harrassowitz Verlag, 2006): Alfred Eislef, "Deutsche in der Region Odessa 1917–1920: Loyalität, Autonomie, Emigration," (364–78); Nikolas Katyer, "Heut Weiße, Morgen Rote: 'Kollaboration' als Grenzerfahrung im Russichen Bürgerkrieg," (379–405).

4. L. I. Petrusheva, E. F. Teplova, and G. A. Trukan, eds., *Rossiia antibol'shevistskaia: Iz belogvardeiskikh i emigrantskikh arkhivov (Anti-Bolshevik Russia: From White Guard and Emigré Archives)* (Moscow: Institut Rossiiskoi istorii RAN, 1995); P. A. Aptekar', L. B. Chizhov, and N. E. Eliseeva, eds., *Krest'ianskoe vosstanie na Tambovshchine (1921–22 gg.): Komplekt dokumentov iz fondov TsGASA (Peasant Rising in the Tambov Area: A Collection of Documents)* (Moscow: TsGASA, 1991); P. A. Aptekar', L. B. Chizhov, and N. E. Eliseeva, eds., *Povstancheskie dvizheniia na Ukraine 1921 g.: Komplekt dokumentov iz fondov TsGASA (Insurgent Activities in the Ukraine: A Collection of Documents)* (Moscow: TsGASA, 1991); V. F. Verstiuk et al., eds., *Ukrainska Tsentralna Rada: Dokumenty i materialy (Ukrainian Central Council: Documents and Materials)*, 2 vols. (Kiev: Naukova dumka, 1996–1997).

5. See Wiktor Sukiennicki, *East Central Europe During World War I: From Foreign Domination to National Independence*, 2 vols. (Boulder, CO: East European Monographs, 1984); Norman Davies, *White Eagle, Red Star: The Polish-Soviet War, 1919–20* (London: Orbis Books Ltd., 1983); Adam Zamoyski, *Warsaw 1920: Lenin's Failed Conquest of Europe* (London: Harper Press, 2008); Jerzy Borzęcki, *The Soviet-Polish Peace of 1921 and the Creation of Interwar Europe* (New Haven, CT and London: Yale University Press, 2008); Alexander V. Prusin, *The Lands between: Conflict in the East European Borderlands, 1870–1992* (New York and Oxford: Oxford University Press, 2010), 72–97; I. I. Kostiushko, ed., *Pol'sko-sovetskaia voina, 1919–1920: Ranee ne opublikovannye dokumenty i materialy (Polish-Soviet War, 1919–1920: Formerly Unpublished Documents and Material)*, 2 vols (Moscow: Institut slavianovedeniia i balkanistiki RAN, 1994); Vasyl' Kuchabsky, *Western Ukraine in Conflict with Poland and Bolshevism, 1918–1923* (Edmonton and Toronto: Canadian Institute of Ukrainian Studies Press, 2009); Michał Klimecki, *Polsko-ukraińska wojna o Lwów i Wschodnią Galicję 1918–1919 r.: Aspekty polityczne i wojskowe (Polish-Ukrainian War for Lwów and Eastern Galicia)* (Warszawa: Wojskowy Instytut Historyczny, 1997); Andrew Ezergailis, *The 1917 Revolution in Latvia* (New York and Boulder, CO: Columbia University Press and East European Monographs, 1974);

Véjas Gabriel Liulevičius, "Das Land Ober Ost im Ersten Weltkrieg: Eine Fallstudie zu den deutsch/litauischen Beziehungen und Zukunftsvorstellungen," in *"Kollaboration" in Nordosteuropa: Erscheinungsformen und Deutungen im 20. Jahrhundert*, ed. by Joachim Tauber (Wiesbaden: Harrassowitz Verlag, 2006), 118–27 (afterward *"Kollaboration" in Nordosteuropa*). See also Joanna Gierowska-Kałłaur, *Zarząd Cywilny Ziem Wschodnich (19 lutego–9 września 1920)* (*The Civilian Government of the Eastern Lands, 19 February–9 September 1920*) (Warsaw: IH PAN and Neriton, 2003). For a predictably post-modernist interpretation, obsessed with minorities and ethnicity, disregarding the fact that the contemporaries saw their struggles as a fight for territory, see Piotr Wróbel, "The Seeds of Violence: The Brutalization of an East European Region," *Journal of Modern European History* 1, no. 1 (2003): 44–59; Julia Eichenberg, "The Dark Side of Independence: Paramilitary Violence in Ireland and Poland after the First World War," *Contemporary European History* 19, no. 3 (2010): 231–48; Joshua Sanborn, "The Genesis of Warlordism: Violence and Governance during the First World War and the Civil War," *Contemporary European History* 19, no. 3 (2010): 195–213. For the aftermath of the Polish-Ukrainian alliance see Timothy Snyder, *Sketches from a Secret War: A Polish Artist's Mission to Liberate Soviet Ukraine* (New Haven, CT: Yale University Press, 2005); Alexander J. Motyl, "Ukrainian Nationalist Political Violence in Inter-War Poland, 1921–1939," *East European Quarterly* 19, no. 1 (March 1985): 45–55; Anton Shekhovtsov, "By Cross and Sword: 'Clerical Fascism' in Interwar Western Ukraine," *Totalitarian Movements and Political Religions* 8, no. 2 (June 2007): 271–85; Christopher Gilley, "A Simple Question of 'Pragmatism'? Sovietophilism in the West Ukrainian Emigration in the 1920s," Koszalin Institute of Comparative European Studies, KICES Working Papers, no. 4 (March 2006); Jan Jacek Bruski, *Petlurowcy: Centrum Ukraińskiej Republiki Ludowej na wychodźstwie (1919–1924)* (*The Petlurites: The Center of the Ukrainian People's Republic in Exile, 1919–1924*) (Kraków: Wydawnictwo Arcana, 2004); Włodzimierz Mędrzecki, *Inteligencja polska na Wołyniu w okresie międzywojennym* (*The Polish Intelligentsia in Volhynia during the Interwar Period*) (Warsaw: IH PAN and Neriton, 2005); Robert Potocki, *Polityka państwa polskiego wobec zagadnienia ukraińskiego w latach 1930–1939* (*The Policy of the Polish State Toward the Ukrainian Question between 1930 and 1939*) (Lublin: Instytut Europy Środkowo-Wschodniej, 2003); Roman Wysocki, *Organizacja Ukraińskich Nacjonalistów w Polsce w latach 1929–1939: Geneza, struktura, program, ideologia* (*OUN in Poland between 1929 and 1939: Origins, Structure, Program, Ideology*) (Lublin: Wydawnictwo Uniwersytetu Marie Curie-Skłodowskiej, 2003); Lucyna Kulińska, *Działalność terrorystyczna i sabotażowa nacjonalistycznych organizacji ukraińskich w Polsce w latach 1922–1939* (*Terrorist and Sabotage Activities of the Ukrainian Nationalist Organizations in Poland, 1922–1939*) (Kraków: Fundacja Centrum Dokumentacji Czynu Niepodległościowego and Księgarnia Akademicka, 2009). For the Belarusian predicament in the first half of the twentieth century, see Andrew Wilson, *Belarus: The Last European Dictatorship* (New Haven, CT and London: Yale University Press, 2011), 90-117; for the situation of the Belarusian minority see Krystyna Gomółka, "Polityka rządów polskich wobec mniejszości białoruskiej w latach 1918–1939," ("Polish Government Policy toward the Belarusian Minority between 1918–1939") *Białoruskie Zeszyty Historyczne* no. 4 (1996); Сяргей Токць, "Культурнае жыццё беларускай вёскі ў міжваеннай Польшчы (па матэрыялах Гарадзеншчыны)," ("Cultural Life of Belorussian Countryside in Interwar Poland [Based upon Documents from the Grodno region]) *Białoruskie Zeszyty Historyczne* no. 18 (2002) http://kamunikat.fontel. net/www/czasopisy/bzh/18/18art_tokc.htm (accessed September 20, 2010). And on interwar Polish-Lithuanian relations see Piotr Łossowski, *Po tej i tamtej stronie Niemna: Stosunki polsko-litewskie 1883–1939 (On this and that Side of the Niemen: Polish-Lithuanian relations, 1883–1939)* (Warszawa: Czytelnik, 1985); and Piotr Łossowski, *Stosunki polsko-litewskie 1921–1939* (Warsaw and Łowicz: IH PAN and Mazowiecka Wyższa Szkoła Humanistyczno-Pedagogiczna, 1997).

6. Józef Mackiewicz, *The Triumph of Provocation* (New Haven, CT and London: Yale University Press, 2009), 48–59.

7. Robert F. Karolevitz and Ross S. Fenn, *Flight of Eagles: The Story of the American Kosciuszko Squadron in the Polish-Russian War, 1919–1920* (Sioux Falls, SD: Brevet Press, Inc., 1974); Teofil Lachowicz, *Polish Freedom Fighters on American Soil: Polish Veterans in America from the Revolutionary War to 1939* (Minneapolis, MN: Two Harbors Press, 2011), 73–111; Jerzy Jan Lerski, *Herbert Hoover and Poland: A Documentary History of Friendship* (Stanford, CA: Hoover Institution Press, 1997).

7

Interwar

Ultimately, four successor states emerged in northern and western Intermarium: Estonia, Latvia, Lithuania, and Poland. In addition to its ethnic core, the Second Polish Republic (*Rzeczpospolita Polska*) encompassed also predominantly Ukrainian and Belarusian lands which had been part of the old Commonwealth. Further, Romania recouped Bessarabia/Moldavia. A Russian possession since its capture from the Ottomans in the early nineteenth century, this rimland area of the Intermarium contained Romanians, Ukrainians, Belarusians, Jews, Poles, and others.

The Baltics and Poland successfully undertook the Herculean task of constructing viable states. That required legislative, institutional, infrastructural, political, and cultural efforts carried out mostly by their own autonomous efforts. At first, the newly free states constituted themselves as liberal democracies. However, by the 1930s, dictatorships arose everywhere. Poland was the first to succumb in 1926. Lithuania followed suit that same year. Latvia lived under a rather mild dictatorship from 1934 to 1940. Estonia's was the most benign case, with the parliament suspended only from 1934 to 1938. The critics of the successor states have simplistically branded their systems as "fascism." In fact, they were military dictatorships that retained a broad range of liberal freedoms, including, to a various extent, an unfettered press and parliament. Those center-left technocratic regimes combined elements of nationalism, progressivism, socialism, etatism, corporatism, and authoritarianism. The veterans of the wars for independence played key roles in the regimes. Their rule waxed and waned with spurts of liberalism and authoritarianism. Their attitude toward the minorities oscillated between leniency and protection to prejudice and discrimination. Whatever the government policy, the minorities, for the most part (with some exceptions like the Poles in Lithuania and the Belarusians in Poland), enjoyed a broad cultural autonomy and a myriad of their own institutions in the realm of education, economy, and welfare. Their situation, in Poland in particular, compared quite favorably with the harsh conditions for minorities in Germany, France, Italy, Spain, Sweden, and Great Britain.[1] All in all, those authoritarian regimes in the Intermarium were usually friendlier toward the minorities than were the majority populations they ruled over. However, only in Poland was the military dictatorial government judiciously moderated by the conservative and monarchist elements of the traditional landed nobility and industrialist-banking class. Thus, the Second Republic really never strayed from the nationalist-authoritarian mould with a progressive slant of modernizing etatism. Lacking an indigenous conservative elite, the Baltic countries tended to be more radical along nationalist lines. That was both a response to the trends emanating from the West and the threats looming in the East.[2]

The Soviet Communists never ceased to subvert the newly independent states. Moscow's revolutionaries took advantage of the economic collapse across Europe following World War I and, later, the Great Depression of the 1930s. The Bolsheviks also capitalized on the class and minority discontent. They supported the irredentist nationalisms of restive minorities. The minorities were considered a burden everywhere. Relatively few in Estonia and more numerous in Latvia, they were quite prominent in Lithuania. In Poland's Eastern Borderlands the Ukrainians, Belarusians, Jews, and others together constituted the majority of the population. They all chafed at the nationalism of the ethnicity controlling the state, countering it with their own brands. Although the minorities uneasily accommodated with the Estonian, Latvian, and Lithuanian states, in Poland some of the non-Poles contested the state's borders, and even resorted to subversive activities, aided by foreign governments such as German, Lithuanian, and Soviet. The Ukrainians were the most separatist and hostile followed by the Belarusians. Feeling excluded, the Jews were indifferent at best. The response of the dominant nationality was to crack down on the perceived minority dissenters. Anti-Semitism was ubiquitous among the opposition majority nationalist parties and dissatisfied ethnic minority groups. From the mid-1930s, it increasingly enjoyed official support. Anti-Jewishness was also coupled with other antiminority measures. The Polish authorities chiefly targeted the minority extremists, but they also alienated the mainstream, for instance, through an intermittent anti-Orthodox Church campaign (which was perceived as anti-Ukrainian and anti-Belarusian) and through the majority affirmative action in higher education and the economy (which was considered antiminority, anti-Jewish, in particular). That caused further radicalization of the most active parts of the minorities along nationalist or Communist lines. Thus, competing nationalisms contributed to the destabilization of the region, which also experienced serious economic problems in the Great Depression, in Poland, in particular.[3] Nonetheless, during the interwar period, even the minority experience was relatively speaking rather mild in the northern and western parts of the Intermarium. Each minority group could cultivate its own political, economic, educational, social, and cultural institutions. Law and order were maintained, and property rights respected for the most part. There was no mass terror and wholesale persecution of any group—unlike in the Soviet Union.

Poland's victory of 1920 spared the northern and western parts of the Intermarium the terrible fate of its east and south, where the Bolsheviks reconquered much of the territories of the old Russian Empire. They claimed swaths of the Ukraine, including Kiev, the Crimean Peninsula, and about half of White Ruthenia (Belarus) with Minsk for themselves. Eastern and southern Intermarium became the separate administrative entities of Soviet Ukraine and Soviet Belorussia in the putatively happy proletarian family of peoples of the Union of Soviet Socialist Republics (USSR).

Communism was an alien transplant in Soviet Russia and its "republics." But it soon found some pleasingly agreeable features in the host organism. The Communists inherited not only much of the Empire of the Tsars but also the legacy of autocracy, oriental despotism, patrimonial state, Third Romism, and Great Russian chauvinism. Bolshevism swiftly absorbed and gradually deployed them against the captive population. The Reds ruled through deception. They established a dual system. While certain institutions ably parodied a "democratic" government in a well-orchestrated performance, the Bolshevik dictatorship really dictated the script for the *danse macabre* in the land of the Soviets. Accordingly, the USSR was commanded from Moscow by a secretive body called the Politbureau with its chairman, who was at the same time the first secretary of the Communist party. The Central Committee of the party ran the daily affairs. The top party people, including the secret police and military leaders, became the new elite: the *nomenklatura*. The Bolsheviks, however, maintained a fiction of a "parliament" (Soviet) and "elections," where everyone was forced to "vote" for candidates handpicked by the Communist bosses.

The leaders ruled through a series of convoluted, yet apparently pragmatic, policy shifts justified in terms of "Marxist-Leninist dialectics." They rejected "bourgeoisie morality," that is the moral legacy of Western Civilization and the spiritual heritage of (Eastern Orthodox) Christianity. Instead, the Bolshevik leadership relativistically embraced "values" that "objectively" expedited the cause of the "world revolution," "socialist construction," and "Communist triumph" at a given moment. Those relative "values" were cyclically discarded at will to be replaced by yet another set of "values" as dictated by the immediate Soviet policy needs. At home, whenever the utopian pursuits of the rulers threatened the death of the host organism, the Bolsheviks would introduce brief spells of "liberalization" to allow the people to recuperate before another political campaign or Five Year Plan to "achieve Communism." Abroad, whenever the Soviets felt weakened from their exertions of "achieving Communism," they would pursue openly a policy of appeasement or détente with their "imperialist enemies," while, of course, never abandoning clandestine activities which included espionage, assassination, sabotage, deception, propaganda, and support for local Communist parties and so-called "national liberation movements" throughout the world. Moscow's agents waged ruthless political warfare against the "imperialists" and "capitalists," while the Kremlin's diplomats sweetly talked peace and trade with them. Thus, the utter lack of morality allowed the bosses of the *nomenklatura* consistently to pursue seemingly contradictory policies. The resulting policy shifts allowed the Communist party to cling to power for the next seventy years.[4]

The dialectics of power became obvious only in time. Initially, however, there was hope that Bolshevism would moderate itself, perhaps peter out. The signs were promising. In 1921, the Reds abandoned War Communism in favor of the New Economic Policy (NEP). The new line combined a carefully supervised system of state control with some market mechanisms in the economy of the USSR. The idea was to encourage the peasants voluntarily to supply food to the starving population for fair prices. Red Terror abated to a large extent, relatively speaking by Soviet standards at least. "Only" an estimated one million people perished in this most economically, politically, and culturally liberal decade in the USSR. The concomitant liberalization also entailed a certain license for the pro-Communist and Communist local ethnic elites to foster Ukrainian, Belarusian, Polish, Jewish, and Tartar *ersatz*-cultures, naturally in a highly Sovietized form.[5]

In 1929, however, Moscow changed its line. Under the newly ascendant Bolshevik party hegemon, Joseph Stalin, the Kremlin embarked upon a policy of forced industrialization and collectivization of agriculture,[6] which led to millions of deaths. Others were killed when the Muscovite center turned on the western periphery's non-Russian, Bolshevik-nationalist elites, despite their Soviet form. As far as the sheer volume of victims is concerned, the Ukrainians fared the worst of all the majority peoples of the Intermarium. This was, in particular, true during the Terror-Famine of 1932–1933 and the Great Purge of 1937–1938. Overall, between eight and fifteen million Soviet citizens died in mass starvation, deportations, and shootings when the Communists collectivized agriculture. The victims included between three and six million Ukrainians who perished in the *Holodomor* (artificial famine). Many more Soviets perished in the mass repressions that followed. The majority ethnic Russians figured prominently among the victims (as well as the perpetrators).[7]

The minorities seem to have been proportionally represented among the repressed except for the Jews who were significantly underrepresented.[8] In distinction, the Soviet Poles were grossly overrepresented among the targets of the Great Purge. Between 1937 and 1938, at least 144,000 (out of an official population of 636,000) fell victim to the so-called "Polish operation" of Stalin's secret police. They constituted about 9 percent of the 1.6 million Soviet citizens seized during the Great Purge. Of these, 111,000 Poles were executed (or almost 80 percent). In addition, several hundred thousand Poles were deported to the interior from the western parts of Soviet Ukraine and Belarus. If the deaths by starvation and diseases as well as other causes among the deported families are taken under the consideration, the total body count can be estimated at up to 250,000 people of Polish origin or identified as such.

The USSR considered Poland to be "the enemy number one" and the Soviet Poles, quite falsely, to be a hotbed of anti-Communist Polish agents. Thus, the Poles were targeted with appropriate ferocity. Many Soviet Poles were repressed in St. Petersburg/Leningrad. Further, two Polish "autonomous" regions in the Ukrainian Soviet Socialist Republic and Belorussian Soviet Socialist Republic were disbanded and their inhabitants either shot or deported to the Gulag. Aleksandr Gurianov and Andrzej Paczkowski estimate that Poles accounted for almost 10 percent of the total number of victims of the Great Purge and for around 40 percent of the victims of purges directed against national minorities. Amir Weiner points out that by 1939, 16,860 Poles in Gulag camps accounted for 1.28 percent of the inmate population, while their share in the entire Soviet population was only 0.37 percent. With the exception of the Russians, the 0.91-percent gap was the largest among the ethnic groups in the Gulag system.[9] Terry Martin states that the Poles were "subjected to the greatest degree of popular and local communist hostility during collectivization. . . . Poles were bluntly told, 'you are being dekulakized not because you are a kulak, but because you are a Pole.' This reflected a widespread sentiment of popular ethnic cleansing." Based on his calculation of the percentage of each nationality in the population of Leningrad city and oblast, Martin continues: "Poles were 30.94 times more likely to be executed than non-Poles. For other diaspora nationalities, the targeting was not yet so extreme."[10]

Since Poland and the Poles were "the enemy number one," Moscow laid its war plans accordingly. The Kremlin ignored the Polish-Soviet Non-Aggression Treaty of 1932 and cozied up to the Nazis, welcoming their wooing. The mutual plans culminated in a clandestine alliance between the USSR and the Third Reich of August 23, 1939 (and its follow up on September 28). The secret pact provided for the division of central and eastern Europe into Nazi and Soviet spheres, including the partition of Poland, the annexation of the Baltics, and the truncation of Finland and Romania. The pact de facto launched World War II.[11]

Notes

1.   On Sweden's treatment of its minorities see "The Sami: An Indigenous People in Sweden," http://www.sweden.gov.se/content/1/c6/03/97/05/4ef76212.pdf (accessed February 15, 2008); "Norway," December 2000, Institute for Jewish Policy Research and American Jewish Committee, http://www.axt.org. uk/antisem/countries/norway/norway.htm (accessed April 24, 2012); Paul Gallagher, "The Man Who Told the Secret," *Columbia Journalism Review* January/February 1998, http://backissues.cjrarchives.org/year/98/1/sweden.asp. For France's Alsatians see Mark Mazower, *Hitler's Empire: How the Nazis Ruled*

Europe (New York: Penguin, 2008), 39; Regional Dossier for German (Alsace), http://mercator-education.org (accessed February 15, 2008). For Italy and Spain and their minorities see Klaus Bochmann, "Racism and/or Nationalism: Minorities and Language Policy under Fascist Regimes," *Racial Discrimination and Ethnicity in European History* CLIOH Notebook, http://www.stm.unipi.it/Clioh/tabs/libri/book7.htm (accessed April 24, 2012); Regional Dossiers for German(South Tyrol), http://mercator-education.org and for a direct link: http://www.mercator-research.eu/fileadmin/mercator/dossiers_pdf/german_in_france2nd.pdf; Rolf Steininger, *South Tyrol: A Minority Conflict of the Twentieth Century* (New Brunswick, NJ: Transaction Publishers, 2004); R. J. B. Bosworth, *Mussolini's Italy: Life under the Dictatorship, 1915–1945* (New York: The Penguin Press, 2006), 155–58, 179; Giles MacDonogh, *After the Reich: From the Liberation of Vienna to the Berlin Airlift* (London: John Murray, 2007), 503–6. For Lithuania's attitude to its minorities see, e.g., Krzysztof Buchowski, *Polacy w niepodległym państwie litewskim 1918–1940* (*Poles in Independent Lithuanian State*) (Białystok: Instytut Historii Uniwersytetu w Białymstoku, 1999). On the United Kingdom's treatment of the Welsh see Philip Jenkins, *A History of Modern Wales, 1536–1990* (London and New York: Longman, 1992). For Germany's minorities see Edmund Pjech, "Niemiecka polityka oświatowa a mniejszości narodowe w latach 1918–1990: Sytuacja Serbołużyczan na tle innych miejscowości," ("German Educational Policy and the National Minorities, 1918–1990: The Situation of the Lusytian Serbs in Comparison to Other Minorities") *Dzieje Najnowsze* no. 2 (2009): 15–33.

2. See Joseph Rothschild, *East Central Europe between the Two World Wars* (Seattle, WA and London: University of Washington Press, 1990); Edward D. Wynot, *Cauldron of Conflict: Eastern Europe, 1918–1945* (Wheeling, IL: Harlan Davidson, 1999); Alexander V. Prusin, *The Lands between: Conflict in the East European Borderlands, 1870–1992* (New York and Oxford: Oxford University Press, 2010), 98–124; Antony Polonsky, *The Jews in Poland and Russia*, vol. 3: *1914 to 2008* (Oxford and Portland, OR: The Littman Library of Jewish Civilization, 2012), 3: 56–357; Ezra Mendelsohn, *The Jews of East Central Europe between the World Wars* (Bloomington, IN: Indiana University Press, 1987); Wojciech Roszkowski, *Land Reforms in East Central Europe after World War One* (Warsaw: Institute of Political Studies, Polish Academy of Sciences, 1995); Ivan T. Berend, *Decades of Crisis: Central and Eastern Europe Before World War II* (Berkeley, Los Angeles, and London: University of California Press, 2001); Hugh Seton-Watson, *Eastern Europe between the Wars 1918–1941* (New York, Evanston, and London: Harper and Row, Publishers, 1967); Wojciech Roszkowski, *Landowners in Poland, 1918–1939* (Boulder, CO and New York: East European Monographs and Columbia University Press, 1991); Antony Polonsky, *Politics in Independent Poland, 1921–1939: The Crisis of Constitutional Government* (Oxford: The Clarendon Press, 1972); Edward D. Wynot, Jr., *Polish Politics in Transition: The Camp of National Unity and the Struggle for Power, 1935–1939* (Athens, GA: University of Georgia Press, 1974); Richard M. Watt, *Bitter Glory: Poland and Its Fate, 1918 to 1939* (New York: Simon and Schuster, 1979); Peter Stachura, *Poland, 1918–1945: An Interpretive and Documentary History of the Second Republic* (London and New York: Routledge, 2004); Walter C. Clemens, Jr., *Baltic Independence and Russian Empire* (New York: St. Martin's Press, 1991); Georg Von Rauch, *The Baltic States: The Years of Independence: Estonia, Latvia, Lithuania, 1917–1940* (New York: St. Martin's Press, 1995); Andrejs Plakans, *A Concise History of the Baltic States*

(Cambridge and New York: Cambridge University Press, 2011); Andrejs Plakans, *The Latvians: A Short History* (Stanford, CA: Hoover Institution Press, Stanford University, 1995); Toivu U. Raun, *Estonia and the Estonians* (Stanford, CA: The Hoover Institution Press, 2001); Andres Kasekamp, *The Radical Right in Interwar Estonia* (New York: St. Martin's Press, 2000); Algimantas Kasparavičius, "The Historical Experience of the Twentieth Century: Authoritarianism and Totalitarianism in Lithuania," in *Totalitarian and Authoritarian Regimes in Europe: Legacies and Lessons from the Twentieth Century*, ed. Jerzy W. Borejsza and Klaus Ziemer (New York and Oxford: Berghahn Books, 2006), 297–312; David Smith, "Retracing Estonia's Russians: Mikhail Kurchinskii and Interwar Cultural Autonomy," *Nationalities Papers* 27, no. 3 (September 1999): 455–74. On the national minorities in interwar Poland see, e.g., Jerzy Ogonowski, *Uprawnienia językowe mniejszości narodowych w Rzeczypospolitej Polskiej 1918–1939* (*Language Rights of National Minorities in the Republic of Poland, 1918–1939*) (Warszawa: Wydawnictwo Sejmowe, 2000). On the minorities at a regional level see Joanna Januszewska-Jurkiewicz, *Stosunki narodowościowe na Wileńszczyźnie w latach 1920–1939* (*Nationality Relations in the Wilno Region, 1920–1939*) (Katowice: Wydawnictwo Uniwersytetu Śląskiego, 2010). For peerless contemporary investigative journalism on the non-Soviet part of the Intermarium, mostly the northern section (Wilno land in particular), in the interwar period, see Józef Mackiewicz's three volumes of dispatches: *Bulbin z jednosielca* (*Bulbin of the Single Farm Settlement*) (London: Kontra, 2001); *Bunt rojstów* (*The Rebellion of Marshes*) (London: Kontra, 2002); and *Okna zatkane szmatami* (*Windows Patched Up with Rugs*) (London: Kontra, 2002).

3.	The Great Depression hit Poland harder than any other European country. Real output in Poland fell by more than 20 percent, thus exceeding Austria and Germany's drop. The rate of decrease in most other countries was substantially smaller. See Niall Ferguson, *The War of the World: Twentieth-Century Conflict and the Descent of the West* (New York: The Penguin Press, 2006), 234. According to another source, between 1928 and 1932 the wage index fell by 61 percent and industrial output declined by 40 percent. See Prusin, *The Lands between*, 114.

4.	See John Lenczowski, *The Sources of Soviet Perestroika* (Ashland, OH: Ashbrook Center, Ashland University, 1990); Martin Malia, *The Soviet Tragedy: A History of Socialism in Russia, 1917–1991* (New York: The Free Press, 1994); Brian Crozier, *The Rise and Fall of the Soviet Empire* (Roseville, CA: Forum and Prima Publishing, 2000); Alain Besancon, *The Soviet Syndrome* (New York and London: Harcourt, Brace, Jovanovich, 1978); Anthony D'Agostino, *Soviet Succession Struggles: Kremlinology and the Russian Question from Lenin to Gorbachov* (Boston, MA: Allen and Unwin, 1988). Compare with the Moscow-centric and philo-Soviet works of Jerry Hough and Merle Fainsod, *How the Soviet Union is Governed* (Cambridge, MA and London: Harvard University Press, 1979) (which is an outrageous revision of late Merle Fainsod's fine *How Russia is Ruled* (Cambridge, MA: Harvard University Press, 1953); John N. Hazard, *The Soviet System of Government* (Chicago, IL and London: The University of Chicago Press, 1980); Stephen Cohen, *Rethinking the Soviet Experience: Politics and History since 1917* (New York and Oxford: Oxford University Press, 1986).

5.	See Leonard Schapiro, *The Origin of the Communist Autocracy: Political Opposition in the Soviet State, First Phase, 1917–1922* (Cambridge, MA: Harvard University Press, 1977); Stephen F. Cohen, *Bukharin and the Bolshevik Revolution: A Political Biography, 1888–1938* (Oxford and New York: Oxford

University Press, 1980); Gregory Carleton, *Sexual Revolution in Bolshevik Russia* (Pittsburgh, PA: University of Pittsburgh Press, 2005); Terry Martin, *The Affirmative Action Empire: Nations and Nationalism in the Soviet Union, 1923–1939* (Ithaca, NY and London: Cornell University Press, 2001).

6. John A. Armstrong, *The Politics of Totalitarianism: The Communist Party of the Soviet Union from 1933 to the Present* (New York: Random House, 1961); Alec Nove, *An Economic History of the USSR* (New York and Harmondsworth: Penguin Books, 1984); Sheila Fitzpatrick, *The Russian Revolution, 1917–1932* (Oxford and New York: Oxford University Press, 1985); Theodore Hermann von Laue, *Why Lenin? Why Stalin? A Reappraisal of the Russian Revolution, 1900–1930* (New York and Hagerstown: JB Lippincott Company, 1971). Nove is a Stalinist; Fitzpatrick a Stalinist apologist; and von Laue believes that the need to modernize Russia required Communist tyranny, a thesis infamously proposed on a global scale first by Barrington Moore, *The Social Origins of Dictatorship and Democracy: Lord and Peasant in the Making of the Modern World* (Boston, MA: Beacon Press, 1966).

7. On the ambivalent nature of the attitude of the Russian majority toward the Soviet power see Geoffrey Hosking, *Rulers and Victims: The Russians in the Soviet Union* (Cambridge, MA and London: The Belknap Press of Harvard University Press, 2006). See further H. M. Mykhailychenko, I. P. Shatalina, and S. V. Kul'chyt'skyi, eds., *Kolektyvizatsiia i holod na Ukraini, 1929–1933. Zbirnyk dokumentiv i materialiv (Collectivization and Hunger in the Ukraine: A Collection of Documents and Materials)* (Kiev: Naukova dumka, 1993); R. Ia. Pyrih et al., ed., *Holod 1932–1933 rokiv na Ukraini. Ochyma istorykiv, movuiu dokumentiv (Hunger of 1932–1933 in the Ukraine: According to Historians and Documents)* (Kiev: Vydavnytstvo politichnoi literatury Ukrainy, 1990); Andrea Romano, N. S. Tarkhova, and Fabio Bettanin, eds., *Krasnaia Armiia i kollektivizatsiia derevni v SSSR, 1928–1933 gg. Sbornik dokumentov iz fondov Rossiiskogo gosudarstvennogo voennogo arkhiva (Red Army and Collectivization of Agriculture in the USSR, 1928–1933: A Collection of Documents from the Russian State War Archive)* (Napoli: Istituto universitario orientale, 1996); Valerii Vasil'ev and Lynne Viola, eds. *Kollektivizatsiia i krest'ianskoe soprotivlenie na Ukraine (noiabr' 1929-mart 1930 gg.) (Collectivization and Peasant Resistance in the Ukraine [November 1929–March 1930])* (Vinnitsia: Logos, 1997); *Holodomor v Ukraini 1932–1933; Wielki głód na Ukrainie 1932–1933,* collective work (Warszawa and Kyiv: Instytut Pamięci Narodowej, 2008); *Holodomor: The Great Famine in Ukraine, 1932–1933* (Warsaw-Kiev: The Institute of National Remembrance-Commission of the Prosecution of Crimes against the Polish Nation, Ministry of Interior and Administration, Republic of Poland, The Security Services of Ukraine Branch State Archives, Institute of Political and Ethno-National Studies at the National Academy of Sciences of Ukraine, 2009); Jacques Vallin, France Meslé, Serguei Adamets, and Serhii Pyrozhkov, "A New Estimate of Ukrainian Population Losses during the Crises of the 1930s and 1940s," *Population Studies* 56, no. 3 (November 2002): 249–64. Compare with M. [Moshe] Lewin, *Russian Peasants and Soviet Power: A Study of Collectivization* (New York and London: W. W. Norton and Company, 1975); the author is a Leninist and much of his writing is Communist propaganda. See also Yuri Shapoval, ed., *The Famine-Genocide of 1932–1933 in Ukraine* (Kingston, ON: The Kashtan Press for the Ukrainian Canadian Civil Liberties Association, 2005); Robert Conquest, *The Harvest of Sorrow: Soviet Collectivization and the Terror-Famine* (New York and Oxford: Oxford University Press, 1986); Robert

Conquest, *The Great Terror: A Reassessment* (New York and Oxford: Oxford University Press, 1990); Robert Conquest, *Kolyma: The Arctic Death Camps* (Oxford and New York: Oxford University Press, 1979); Anne Applebaum, *Gulag: A History* (New York and London: Doubleday, 2003); Paul R. Gregory and Valery Lazarev, eds., *The Economics of Forced Labor: The Soviet Gulag* (Stanford, CA: Hoover Institution Press, Stanford University, 2003); Dariusz Tolczyk, *See No Evil: Literary Cover-Ups and Discoveries of the Soviet Camp Experience* (New Haven, CT and London: Yale University Press, 1999); Barry McLoughlin and Kevin McDermott, eds., *Stalin's Terror: High Politics and Mass Repression in the Soviet Union* (London: Palgrave Macmillan, 2003); Pavel Polian, *Against Their Will: The History and Geography of Forced Migrations in the USSR* (Budapest: Central European University Press, 2004).

8.   Jews were least likely to suffer repression during the 1930s. According to Yuri Slezkine, in 1937–1938, only about 1 percent of all Soviet Jews were arrested for political crimes, as compared to 16 percent for Poles. By early 1939, the proportion of Jews in the Gulag was 15.7 percent lower than their share of the total Soviet population. As Slezkine makes clear, "The reason for this was the fact that the Jews were not targeted as an ethnic group. . . . Indeed, Jews were the only large Soviet nationality without its own 'native' territory that was not targeted for a purge during the Great Terror." The impact on the groups most affected was horrific: about 80 percent of all those arrested in the operations targeting Greeks, Finns, and Poles were executed. See Yuri Slezkine, *The Jewish Century* (Princeton, NJ and Oxford: Princeton University Press, 2004), 273–74. For a case study of an anti-Jewish purge in the Crimea and southern Ukraine, which netted about thirty "counterrevolutionaries" and "spies," most of them shot, see Mikhail Mitsel, "The Final Chapter: Agro-Joint Workers—Victims of the Great Terror in the USSR, 1937–1940," *East European Jewish Affairs* 39, no. 1 (2009): 79–99.

9.   For the persecution and slaughter of the Poles in the USSR see Maciej Korkuć, Jarosław Szarek, Piotr Szubarczyk, and Joanna Wieliczka-Szarkowa, *W cieniu czerwonej gwiazdy: Zbrodnie sowieckie na Polakach (1917–1956)* (*In the Shadow of Red Star: Soviet Crimes against the Poles [1917–1956]*) (Kraków: Wydawnictwo Kluszczyński, 2010), in particular, the chapter by Jarosław Szarek and Joanna Wieliczka-Szarkowa, "Zbrodnie bolszewickie, 1917–1939," (Bolshevik Crimes, 1917–1939) at 21–110; Aleksander Gurjanow, "Sowieckie represje wobec Polaków i obywateli polskich w latach 1936–1956 w świetle danych sowieckich" ("Soviet Repressions against Poles and Polish Citizens in the Years 1936–1956"), in *Europa nieprowincjonalna: Przemiany na ziemiach wschodnich dawnej Rzeczypospolitej (Białoruś, Litwa, Łotwa, Ukraina, wschodnie pogranicze III Rzeczypospolitej Polskiej) w latach 1772–1999*, ed. Krzysztof Jasiewicz (Non-Provincial Europe: Transformations in the Eastern Lands of the Former Commonwealth [Belarus, Lithuania, Latvia, Ukraine, Eastern Borderlands of the Third Polish Republic, 1772–1999]) (Warsaw and London: Instytut Studiów Politycznych PAN, Rytm, and Polonia Aid Foundation Trust, 1999), 972–79 (afterward "Sowieckie represje," in *Europa nieprowincjonalna*); Andrzej Paczkowski, "Poland, the 'Enemy Nation,'" in *The Black Book of Communism: Crimes, Terror, Repression*, ed. Stéphane Courtois et al. (Cambridge, MA and London: Harvard University Press, 1999), 363–93; Amir Weiner, *Making Sense of War: The Second World War and the Fate of the Bolshevik Revolution* (Princeton, NJ and Oxford: Princeton University Press, 2001), 142–46; Terry Martin, *The Affirmative Action Empire: Nations and Nationalism in the*

Soviet Union, 1923–1939 (Ithaca, NY and London: Cornell University Press, 2001), 311–43. See also Ewa M. Thompson, *Imperial Knowledge: Russian Literature and Colonialism* (Westport, CT and London: Greenwood Press, 2000); G. N. Mozgunova, A. V. Korsak, and M. N. Levitin, eds., *Sud'by natsional'nykh men'shinstv na Smolenshchine, 1918–1938 gg. Dokumenty i materialy Arkhivnogo upravleniia Administratsii Smolenskoi oblasti (The Fate of National Minorities in the Smolensk Region, 1918–1938: Documents and Materials from the Archival Authority of the Administration of the Smolensk Region)* (Smolensk: Gosudarstvennyi arkhiv Smolenskoi oblasti, 1994); Leon Piskorski and Eugeniusz Wolski, eds., *"Przechodniu powiedz Polsce . . .": Księga Pamięci Polaków-ofiar komunizmu-pochwanych na Lewaszowskim Pustkowiu pod Sankt Petersburgiem ("Passer-By, Tell Poland": The Book of Remembrance of Poles—Victims of Communism—Buried at the Levashovske Pustkove Near St. Petersburg)* vol. 1 (Sankt Petersburg: Rada Ochrony Pamięci Walk i Męczeństwa, 1995); Stanisław Morozow, "Deportacje polskiej ludności cywilnej z radzieckich terenów zachodnich w głąb ZSRR w latach 1935–1936" ("The Deportations of the Polish Civilian Population from the Western Soviet Territories to the Interior of the USSR in the Years 1935–1936"), *Pamięć i Sprawiedliwość: Biuletyn Głównej Komisji Badania Zbrodni przeciwko Narodowi Polskiemu—Instytutu Pamięci Narodowej* no. 40 (1997–1998): 267–81; Mikołaj Iwanow, *Pierwszy naród ukarany: Polacy w Związku Radzieckim, 1921–1939 (The First Nation To Be Punished: Poles in the Soviet Union)* (Warszawa and Wrocław: Polskie Wydawnictwo Naukowe, 1991); Mikołaj Iwanow, "Matka premiera: O Polakach w Dowbyszu," ("The Mother of the Prime Minister: About the Poles in Dovbish") *Biuletyn Instytutu Pamięci Narodowej* no. 1–2 (96–97) (January–February 2009): 37–43; Wojciech Lizak, *Rozstrzelana Polonia: Polacy w ZSRR, 1917–1939 (The Executed Polonia: Poles in the USSR)* (Szczecin: Prywatny Instytut Analiz Społecznych, 1990); Janusz M. Kupczak, *Polacy na Ukrainie w latach 1921–1939 (Poles in the Ukraine)* (Wrocław: Wydawnictwo Uniwersytetu Wrocławskiego, 1994); Hieronim Kubiak et al., eds., *Mniejszości polskie i Polonia w ZSRR (Polish Minorities and the Polonia in the USSR)* (Wrocław, Warszawa, and Kraków: Zakład Narodowy imienia Ossolińskich, Wydawnictwo Polskiej Akademii Nauk, 1992); Wojciech Materski, *Pobocza Dyplomacji: Wymiana więźniów politycznych pomiędzy II Rzecząpospolitą a Sowietami w okresie międzywojennym (The Undercurrents of Diplomacy: Prisoner Exchanges between the 2nd Republic and the Soviets in the Interwar Period)* (Warszawa: ISP PAN, 2002); Wojciech Grzelak, *Rosja bez złudzeń: Uroki demokracji suwerennej (Russia without Delusions: The Joys of Sovereign Democracy)* (Warszawa: 3SMedia, 2008), 125–30; Ewa Ziółkowska, "Kuropaty: Cmentarzysko polskich ofiar sowieckiego terroru," (Kuropaty: The Graveyard of Polish Victims of the Soviet Terror) *Biuletyn Instytutu Pamięci Narodowej* no. 1–2 (96–97) (January–February 2009): 44–53; Paweł Zyzak, "Zapomniane ludobójstwo: Los Polaków w Związku Sowieckim w latach 30. XX w.," *Glaukopis* no. 21–22 (2011): 131–55; Zdzisław J. Winnicki, *Szkice kojdanowskie: Kojdanowsko-Polski Region Narodowościowy w BSRR: Uwagi o genezie oraz o przesłankach funkcjonowania: Stan badań problematyki (The Koydani Sketches: Kozdani-Polish Nationality Region in the BSSR: Some Remarks on the Origin and Reasons for Functioning: Researching the Problem)* (Wrocław: Wydawnictwo GAJT, 2005); Father Roman Dzwonkowski, ed., *Bez sądów, świadków i prawa . . . Listy z więzień, łagrów i zesłania do Delegatury PCK w Moskwie 1924–1937 (No Courts, Witnesses, and Law: Letters from Jail, Camps, and Exile to the Office of the Polish Red Cross in*

Moscow, 1924–1937) (Lublin: Towarzystwo Naukowe KUL, 2002); Father Roman Dzwonkowski, ed., *Głód i represje wobec ludności polskiej na Ukrainie, 1932–1947: Relacje* (*Famine and Repressions against the Polish Community in Ukraine, 1932–1947: Recollections*) (Lublin: Towarzystwo Naukowe KUL, 2005); Józef Świderski, *Śmierć na czarnoziemie* (*Death on Black Soil*) (Łódź: By the author, 2000) (which is a memoir of the Terror-Famine from Podolia); Wasyl Haniewicz, *Tragedia syberyjskiego Białegostoku* (*The Tragedy of Siberian Białystok*) (Pelplin: Bernardinum, 2008) (which is a monograph of a single village where almost all men were shot at the end of the 1930s); Mieczysław Łoziński, *Polonia nieznana* (*The Unknown Polonia*) (Kłodawa and Konin: Drukarnia Braci Wielińskich, 2005) (which is a memoir of a Pole from Zhitomir/Żytomierz in Soviet Ukraine between 1918 and 1939); Maria Kuberska, *To było życie . . . Wspomnienia z Kazachstanu 1936–1996* (*This Was Life: A Memoir from Kazakhstan, 1936–1996*) (Warszawa: Pax, 2006) (which is a memoir of seventy years of a Polish family in the USSR's Ukraine and Kazakhstan); Walenty Woronowicz, *Przypadki XX wieku: 20 lat na Wyspach Sołowieckich i Kołymie, 1935–1955* (*Events of the 20th Century: 20 Years on the Solovki Islands and in Kolyma*) (Warszawa: Instytut Historii PAN and Gryf, 1994) (which is a memoir of a Soviet Pole in the Gulag); Andrzej Nowak interviewed by Kamila Baranowska, "Polacy w ZSRR ginęli, bo byli Polakami," *Rzeczpospolita* (May 6, 2008); Bartosz Marzec, "Sprawa POW," *Rzeczpospolita* (April 4, 2008); and Jan Maria Jackowski, "'Operacja polska,' czyli nieznane ludobójstwo," ("'The Polish Operation' or an Unknown Genocide"), *Nasz Dziennik* (February 12, 2009); Mikołaj Iwanow interviewed by Waldemar Moszkowski, "Zapomniany holocaust Polaków," ("A Forgotten Holocaust of the Poles") *Nasz Dziennik* (March 5, 2003). See also Father Roman Dzwonkowski, *Kościół katolicki w ZSRR 1917–1939: Zarys historii* (*Catholic Church in the USSR, 1917–1939: A History*) (Lublin: Towarzystwo Naukowe KUL, 1997); Father Roman Dzwonkowski, *Losy duchowieństwa katolickiego w ZSRR 1917–1939: Martyrologium* (*The Fate of Catholic Clergy in the USSR, 1917–1939: Martyrology*) (Lublin: Towarzystwo Naukowe KUL, 1998); Tadeusz Madała, *Polscy księża katoliccy w więzieniach i łagrach sowieckich od 1918 r.* (*Polish Catholic Priests in Soviet Jails and the Camps since 1918*) (Lublin: Retro, 1996); Dennis J. Dunn, *The Catholic Church and Russia: Popes, Patriarchs, Tsars and Commissars* (Hants and Burlington: Ashgate, 2004).

10. Terry Martin, *The Affirmative Action Empire: Nations and Nationalism in the Soviet Union, 1923–1939* (Ithaca, NY and London: Cornell University Press, 2001), 311–43.

11. See Bogdan Musial, *Kampfplatz Deutschland: Stalins Kriegspläne gegen den Westen* (Berlin: Propyläen, 2008); I. I. Kostiushko, ed., *Materialy 'Osoboi papki' Politbiuro TsK RKP(b)-VKP(b) po voprosu sovetsko-pol'skikh otnoshenii 1923–1944 gg. Sbornik dokumentov* (*Documents from the personal file of the Politburo on the Soviet-Polish relations, 1923–1944*) (Moscow: Institut slavianovedenie i balkanistiki RAN, 1997); Hugh Seton-Watson, *From Lenin to Malenkov: The History of World Communism* (New York: Frederic A. Praeger, 1953).

8

World War II and the Liberation*

In March 1939, before the war broke out, Adolf Hitler's Third Reich had reclaimed Memelland from Lithuania by a threat of force. More significantly, for years both Berlin and Moscow had separately courted Warsaw to participate in the partitioning of the Intermarium. Stalin offered a joint condominium in the Baltics. Hitler promised eastern Ukraine with the access to the Black Sea. Poland flatly refused both overtures. In particular, Warsaw firmly turned down the Nazi dictator's invitation for a joint anti-Bolshevik crusade. The rejection sealed Poland's fate. It also led to signing of the Ribbentrop–Molotov Pact whereby Germany and the Soviet Union partitioned her, the Intermarium, and Central and Eastern Europe among themselves. Poland succumbed to a combined Nazi-Soviet attack in September 1939. Her Eastern Borderlands were incorporated into the Soviet Union. The Baltic countries were annexed the following year, in June 1940. At the time Stalin also claimed Bessarabia and Bukovina, the Moldavian part of Romania. Sovietization, Red terror, and mass deportation of the Poles, Jews, Ukrainians, Belarusians, Romanians, Balts, and others ensued. Only the German invasion of June 1941 interrupted the Soviet depredations. The wheels of terror failed to stop, though. The Nazi ferocity focused on the Jewish minority in a largely successful attempt at its total extermination. The Germans also decimated the traditional elites of the Intermarium, mostly ethnic Polish intelligentsia and nobility. Slavic peasants suffered as well from the brutal economic exploitation and ruthless police and military reprisals. However, the Balts were the least affected by the Nazi occupation.

After the return of the Soviets in 1944, the mass deportations to the Gulag recommenced one more time. Further, Stalin expelled most of the Poles of the western Intermarium to the Communist Polish state. In turn, smaller numbers of Ukrainians and Belarusians were deported from "people's" Poland eastward. Also, various Soviet military, police, and party personnel, often ethnic Russians, were brought in from the interior of the USSR. Many settled with their families, particularly in the Baltics. The newly conquered lands were subject to a thorough re-Sovietization, including the collectivization of agriculture and wholesale property confiscation. Industrialization took place throughout the area and the rural population shifted to the cities in large numbers. Naturally, the Soviets also reintroduced their system of *nomenklatura* and rule through secret directives of the Politbureau.

Following the initial period of resistance, the captive peoples increasingly adjusted to the Soviet occupation. The process of accommodation became the norm after 1956. Many of the natives in the Baltics, Belarus, and Ukraine joined the Communist party and operated as agents of the Soviet power. Dissent was perennial and ineffectual. Its residue was mostly of both a nationalist and religious type, in western Ukraine and Lithuania in particular. Only when the Kremlin commenced reforms in the mid-1980s, did long-suppressed nationalist aspirations bubble to the surface. "People power" movements appeared everywhere in the Intermarium. Grass-roots nationalist organizers and erstwhile Soviet collaborators joined hands to restore freedom to their nations. Some of the local Communists simply wanted to cling to power and opportunistically donned the nationalist garb. Others defected earnestly. A few undoubtedly feigned support for freedom, fully expecting the Kremlin to reassert itself in no time. As it were, the Moscow center disappointed its followers. Preoccupied with its own myriad problems, the Kremlin grudgingly allowed the peripheries to tend to their own affairs. This was a gradual process, amidst increasingly feeble protestation from the center. Soon, Moscow was unable to control the centrifugal forces which were gaining momentum all over the USSR, and particularly in the Intermarium.[1]

From 1988 the republics of the western Soviet rim proclaimed sovereignty. At first their aim was not freedom, but autonomy. The intention was to negotiate a new "union" pact with Moscow. However, soon, separatism won the day. Lithuania was the first Soviet Republic to proclaim its independence in March 1990, followed by Latvia in May 1990. Ukraine and Belarus issued statements of sovereignty in July 1990, but became officially independent, along with Estonia and Moldova, after August 1991. The Baltic states are full-fledged liberal democracies; Ukraine a struggling one; and Moldova even more so. Belarus remains Europe's last dictatorship. It also largely eschews Western ties. All newly free states of the Intermarium became full-fledged members of the United Nations without Russia's supervision. The Baltics joined NATO and the European Union (EU). Ukraine and Moldova would like to, but not Belarus. All but Belarus enjoy rather cordial relations with their immediate western neighbors, Poland in particular. On the eastern periphery, however, uneasy peace persists for now. Moscow indulges in petty harassment of the Baltics over their close relationship with the West and their alleged mistreatment of the Russian minority. Further, the Kremlin has applied the energy weapon against the successor states, Ukraine in particular. It has waged cyberwarfare against them, Estonia for example. Last but not least, the Russian Federation ominously refers to the Intermarium as "near abroad" (ближнее зарубежье), thus implying that the newly free nations are but *Saisonstaaten*. In other words, it seems that new, post-Soviet Russia has rejected the hopeful legacy of Novgorod and reembraced the ruthless heritage of Muscovy.[2]

Arguably, the greatest challenge for the post-Soviet western periphery is to reverse the outcome of World War II and its aftermath. In other words, the objective of the newly free countries is to restore the cultural, political, and economic pluralism inherent in the Intermarium at least since the days of the old Polish-Lithuanian Commonwealth. Thus, our next step is to show what was destroyed, how, and why.

Notes

* For detailed notes see Part II.

1. See Constantine Christopher Menges, *Transitions from Communism in Russia and Eastern Europe: Analysis and Perspectives* (Washington, DC: George Washington University Press, 1993); Illan Berman and J. Michael Waller, eds., *Dismantling Tyranny: Transitioning beyond Totalitarian Regimes* (Lanham, MD, Boulder, CO, Toronto, and London: Rowman & Littlefield, 2006); Lee Edwards, ed., *The Collapse of Communism* (Stanford, CA: Stanford University, 2000); Steven L. Solnick, *Stealing the State: Control and Collapse in Communist Institutions* (Cambridge, MA: Harvard University Press, 1999); Stephen K. Carter, *Russian Nationalism: Yesterday, Today, Tomorrow* (New York: St. Martin's Press, 1990); Gerhard Simon, *Nationalism and Policy toward the Nationalities in the Soviet Union: From Totalitarian Dictatorship to Post-Stalinist Society* (Boulder, CO: Westview Press, 1991); Alexander J. Motyl, ed., *The Post-Soviet Nations: Perspectives in the Demise of the USSR* (New York: Columbia University Press, 1992); Ronald Grigor Suny, *The Revenge of the Past: Nationalism, Revolution, and the Collapse of the Soviet Union* (Stanford, CA: Stanford University Press, 1993); Hélène Carrère d'Encausse, *The End of the Soviet Empire: The Triumph of the Nations* (New York: Basic Books, 1993); Mark R. Beissinger, *Nationalist Mobilization and the Collapse of the Soviet State* (Cambridge and New York: Cambridge University Press, 2002); Ian Bremmer, *New States, New Politics: Building the Post-Soviet Nations* (Cambridge and New York: Cambridge University Press, 1997); Georgiy I. Mirsky, *On Ruins of Empire: Ethnicity and Nationalism in the Former Soviet Union* (Westport, CT: Greenwood Press, 1997); Walter C. Clemens, Jr., *Baltic Independence and Russian Empire* (New York: St. Martin's Press, 1991); Clare Thomson, *The Singing Revolution: A Political Journey through the Baltic States* (London: Michael Joseph, 1992); Priit Vesilind with James and Maureen Tusty, *The Singing Revolution* (Tallinn: Kirjastus Varrak Publishers Ltd., 2008); Roman Szporluk, *Russia, Ukraine, and the Breakup of the Soviet Union* (Stanford, CA: Hoover Institution Press, Stanford University, 2000); Timothy Snyder, *The Reconstruction of Nations: Poland, Ukraine, Lithuania, Belarus, 1569–1999* (New Haven, CT and London: Yale University Press, 2003); Herman Pirchner, Jr., *Reviving Greater Russia? The Future of Russia's Borders with Belarus, Georgia, Kazakhstan, Moldova and Ukraine* (Washington, DC: The University Press of America and American Foreign Policy Council, 2005); Keith Smith, *Russian Energy, Politics in the Baltics, Poland, and Ukraine: A New Stealth Imperialism* (Washington, DC: The CSIS Press, 2005); Romuald Misiunas and Rein

Taagepera, *The Baltic States: Years of Dependence, 1940–1990* (Berkeley, CA: University of California Press, 1993); Anatol Lieven, *The Baltic Revolution: Estonia, Latvia, Lithuania, and the Path to Independence* (New Haven, CT: Yale University Press, 1993); Rein Taagepera, *Estonia: Return to Independence* (Boulder, CO: Westview Press, 1993); Toivu U. Raun, *Estonia and The Estonians* (Stanford, CA: The Hoover Institution Press, 2001); David J. Smith, *Estonia: Independence and European Integration* (London and New York: Routledge, 2001); Ernest Gellner, "Ethnicity and Faith in Eastern Europe," in *Eastern Europe . . . „Central Europe . . ., Europe*, ed. Stephen R. Graubard (Boulder, CO, San Francisco, CA, Oxford: Westview Press, 1991), 275–78 (on Estonia); Grigory Ioffe, *Understanding Belarus and How Western Foreign Policy Misses the Mark* (Lanham, MD: Rowman & Littlefield Publishers, Inc., 2008); Vitali Silitski and Jan Zaprudnik, *Historical Dictionary of Belarus* (Lanham, MD, Toronto, and Plymouth: Scarecrow Press, 2007); Charles King, *The Moldovans: Romania, Russia, and the Politics of Culture* (Stanford, CA: The Hoover Institution Press, 2000); Stefan Ihrig, *Wer sind die Moldawier? Rumänismus versus Moldowanismus in Historiographie und Schulbüchern der Republik Moldova, 1991–2006* (Stuttgart and Hanover: Ibidem-Verlag, 2008); Matthew H. Ciscel, *The Language of the Moldovans: Romania, Russia, and Identity in an Ex-Soviet Republic* (Lanham, MD: Lexington Books, 2007); Andrei Brezianu and Vlad Spânu, *Historical Dictionary of Moldova* (Lanham, MD, Toronto, and Plymouth: Scarecrow Press, 2007); Michael Bruchis, *The Republic of Moldova: From the Collapse of the Soviet Empire to the Restoration of the Russian Empire* (New York and Boulder, CO: Columbia University Press and East European Monographs, 1997); Nicholas Dima, *Moldova and the Transdnestr Republic* (New York and Boulder, CO: Columbia University Press and East European Monographs, 2001); Wim P. Van Meurs, *The Bessarabian Question in Communist Historiography* (New York and Boulder, CO: Columbia University Press and East European Monographs, 1994); Anne Applebaum, *Between East and West: Across the Borderlands of Europe* (New York: Pantheon Books, 1994); Andrew Wilson, *Ukrainian Nationalism in the 1990s: A Minority Faith* (Cambridge and New York: Cambridge University Press, 1997); Andrew Wilson, *The Ukrainians: Unexpected Nation* (New Haven, CT and London: Yale University Press, 2002); Anna Reid, *Borderland: A Journey through the History of Ukraine* (Boulder, CO: Westview Press, 2000 and 2nd edn. Orion Publishing Company, 2003); Hiroaki Kuromiya, *Freedom and Terror in the Donbas: A Ukrainian-Russian Borderland, 1870s–1990s* (Cambridge: Cambridge University Press, 1998); Tatiana Zhurzhenko, *Borderlands into Bordered Lands: Geopolitics of Identity in Post-Soviet Ukraine* (Stuttgart and Hanover: Ibidem-Verlag, 2010); Mikhail Molchanov, *Political Culture and National Identity in Russian-Ukrainian Relations* (College Station, TX: Texas A&M University Press, 2002); Kataryna Wolczuk, "Catching Up with 'Europe'? Constitutional Debates on the Territorial-Administrative Model in Independent Ukraine," in *Region, State and Identity in Central and Eastern Europe*, ed. Judy Batt and Kataryna Wolczuk (London: Frank Cass, 2002), 65–88; Kataryna Wolczuk, *The Moulding of Ukraine: The Constitutional Politics of State Formation* (Budapest: Central European University Press, 2001); Katja Yafimava, *Post-Soviet Russian-Belarussian Relationships: The Role of Gas Transit Pipelines* (Stuttgart and Hanover: Ibidem-Verlag, 2006); Coit Blacker and Condoleezza Rice, "Belarus and the Flight from Sovereignty," in *Problematic Sovereignty: Contested Rules and Political Possibilities*, ed. Stephen D. Krasner (New York: Columbia University Press, 2001), 224–50. See also the following essays, whose authors, regrettably, focus almost exclusively on Poland and Ukraine, in Andrzej Dumała and Ziemowit Jacek Pietraś, eds., *The Future of East-Central Europe* (Lublin: Maria Curie-Skłodowska University Press, 1996): Orysia Lutsevych, "The Case for Ukraine to Maintain Its Nukes," (260–65); Beata Surmacz, "The International Role of Ukraine," (300–11); Stepan Trohimchuk, "Polish-Ukrainian Integration as a Foundation of Peace and Security in East-Central Europe," (311–13); Paul Kubicek, "Delegative Democracy in Post-Soviet States," (424–43); Ostap Semkiv, "Ukraine: From Totalitarianism to Democracy," (453–59); Natalya Lutsyshyn, "Transitions to Democracy in Ukraine: Reality and Prospects," (459–60); Anatoliy Romanyuk, "Integration and Disintegration Processes in the Party System of Ukraine," (504–9); Oleg Protsyk, "The Influence of Ukrainian Parliamentary Elections of 1994 on the Process of Political Transformation in Ukraine," (509–14); Michał Łesiów, "An Important New Role of National Languages in the Former Soviet Republics which became Independent States in 1991," (605–9). See further the following essays, whose authors include most of the post-Soviet Intermarium in their inquiry, considering them now to belong to East Central Europe, in *New Europe: The Impact of the First Decade*, vol. 2: *Variations on the Pattern*, ed. Teresa Rakowska-Harmstone, Piotr Dutkiewicz, and Agnieszka Orzelska (Warsaw: Institute of Political Studies Polish Academy of Sciences and Collegium Civitas Press, 2006): Lars Johannsen, "The Baltic States: A Miracle?" (49–100); David Riach, "Post-Soviet Belarus," (101–53); Wim van Meurs, "Moldova," (329–70); Tadeusz Andrzej Olszański, "Ukraine," (487–523). See also *New Europe: The Impact of the First Decade*, vol. 1: *Trends and Prospects*, ed. Teresa Rakowska-Harmstone, Piotr Dutkiewicz, and Agnieszka Orzelska (Warsaw: Institute of Political Studies Polish Academy of Sciences and Collegium Civitas Press, 2006): Teresa Rakowska-Harmstone, "Dynamics of Transition," (91–137); and "Economic Transformation," (139–76).

2. On the struggle between the "Novgorodian" and the "Muscovite" factors in contemporary Russia see Nicolai N. Petro, *The Rebirth of Russian Democracy: An Interpretation of Political Culture* (Cambridge, MA and London: Harvard University Press, 1995); and Leszek Wołosiuk, "Nowogród Wielki: Atlantyda Rosji – o prawdziwych narodzinach Rusi," ("Novgorod the Great: The Atlantis of Russia – The True Birth of Ruthenia") *Arcana* no. 2–3 (2009): 249–74. See further Richard F. Starr, *The New Military in Russia: Ten Myths that Shape the Image* (Annapolis, MD: Naval Institute Press, 1996); J. Michael Waller, *Secret Empire: The KGB in Russia Today* (Boulder, CO: Westview and Harper Collins, 1994); Stephen Kotkin, *Armageddon Averted: The Soviet Collapse, 1970–2000* (Oxford and New York: Oxford University Press, 2001); Yegor Gaidar, *Collapse of an Empire: Lessons for Modern Russia* (Washington, DC: Brookings Institution Press, 2007); Stephen White, Rita di Leo, and Ottorino Cappelli, eds., *Soviet Transition: From Gorbachev to Yeltsin* (London and Portland, OR: Frank Cass, 1993); David Remnick, *Resurrection: The Struggle for a New Russia* (New York: Vintage, 1998); Michael McFaul, Nikolai Petrov, and Andrei Riabov, *Between Dictatorship and Democracy: Russian Post-Communist Political Reform* (Washington, DC: Carnegie Endowment for International Peace, 2004); Lilia Shevtsova, *Russia: Lost in Translation: The Yeltsin and Putin Legacies* (Washington, DC: Carnegie Endowment for International Peace, 2007); Susan Glasser, *Kremlin Rising: Vladimir Putin's Russia and the End of Revolution* (New York: Scribner, 2005); Andrew Jack, *Inside Putin's Russia* (New York: Oxford University, 2004); Roy Medvedev, *Post-Soviet Russia: A Journey through the*

Yeltsin Era ed. and trans. by George Shriver (New York: Columbia University, 2000); Mark Kramer, *Travels with a Hungry Bear: A Journey to the Russian Heartland* (New York: Houghton Mifflin, 1996); Heyward Isham, *Remaking Russia: Voices from Within* (New York: M.E. Sharpe, 1995); Richard Sakwa, *Russian Politics and Society* (New York: Routledge, 1993, 2nd ed., 2002); Bruce Clarke, *An Empire's New Clothes: The End of Russia's Liberal Dream* (London: Vintage, 1996); David D. Laitin, *Identity in Formation: The Russian-Speaking Populations in the Near Abroad* (Ithaca, NY: Cornell University Press, 1998); Anna Politkovskaya, *Putin's Russia: Life in a Failing Democracy* (New York: Henry Holt and Company, 2007); Susanne Michele Birgerson, *After the Breakup of a Multi-Ethnic Empire: Russia, Successor States, and Eurasian Security* (Westport, CT: Praeger/Greenwood, 2002). For an eyewitness of Polish diplomat perspective on the implosion of the USSR and its aftermath see Włodzimierz Marciniak, *Rozgrabione imperium: Upadek Związku Sowieckiego i powstanie Federacji Rosyjskiej* (*A Looted Empire: The Collapse of the Soviet Union and the Foundation of the Russian Federation*) (Cracow: Arcana, 2001).

Part II

The Armageddon and Its Aftermath (1939–1992)

Verily, since they were overrun by the Hitler-Stalin armies, we can talk about the lands of the Grand Duchy of Lithuania as if about Atlantis: No voice is heard from Lithuania; we can barely guess the sound of the bells from a sunken city . . . Painting, sculpture, architecture – all this are expressions of the soul, which cannot express itself where there is no law and, thus, no freedom. And there is a void in the lands of the Grand Duchy of Lithuania . . . Atlantis.[1]

—X. Walerian Meysztowicz

Hatred grew into the hearts and poisoned the blood of brothers.[2]

—Henryk Sienkiewicz

9

An Overview

Because of decades of Communist censorship and propaganda, scholars have only now begun to unearth the hidden past of the Intermarium during the last century. We can presently outline with some confidence the salient points of history of the people of the Baltic states, Ukraine, Belarus, and Moldova during World War II and its aftermath. First, we shall depict the mechanisms at play. Next, we shall recount the most important developments under the Soviet and Nazi occupations.[3]

The experience of the Intermarium between 1939 and 1947 was a Hobbesian conflict of all against all. It was an Armageddon on an unprecedented scale with millions of victims. The driving forces of the unspeakable carnage were the Nazis and the Communists. Within the context they dictated, this apocalyptic scenario applied to governments, political organizations, and many individual citizens. Mass terror, extermination, and deportations were the trademark of both the Germans and the Soviets. Both thus bear the bulk of the blame for what they unleashed. The Ukrainian nationalists were the only other group to embark on ethnic cleansing as part of their political agenda. Consequently, civilian losses at the hands of other organized participants in the Armageddon were not substantial. That does not apply to numerous local collaborators in the Holocaust, who usually volunteered individually to assist the Nazis and should be considered as an auxiliary category of its own, rather than a state player since their own governments had ceased to exist overtly (except Romania, Hungary and Slovakia which operated in the south-east).

The conflict in the Intermarium did not preclude acts of kindness on the part of individuals, communities, and even some organized groups (e.g., religious orders), or day-to-day coexistence between members of various ethnic groups. In fact, there was no predetermined pattern of conduct as far as any given individual was concerned. Under extreme circumstances, he or she could act with courage and dignity or malice and cowardice or anything in between. Sometimes those occurred interchangeably. For most, consistency of attitude was an anomaly, not the rule. One could and often did vary in one's responses to the daily exigencies. And the challenges posed by two totalitarianisms were daunting.

For the majority of individuals, human behavior spanned the spectrum between collaboration, accommodation, and resistance. Accommodation was the most common attitude. It was dictated primarily by the instinct of self-preservation, and, despite all, the basic decency of the average person who was neither a hero nor a villain.[4] Indigenous political organizations in the Intermarium applied collaboration, accommodation, and resistance with different intensity and nuance as viable responses to both local competitors and foreign invaders. The degree of involvement in collaboration, accommodation, and resistance varied with individuals, communities, organizations, and ethnic groups. It was conditioned first and foremost by the occupation policies of the totalitarian powers but also by other factors, including chance, timing, circumstances, ideological preferences, and personal inclinations of the occupied. Within such context, victims could and did become victimizers; collaborators turned into victims or resisters; and resisters into collaborators. And even though accommodation was the most prevalent attitude, to complicate things, the endeavor to accommodate sometimes required an occasional dabbling in collaboration and a vigorous venture into resistance. Tellingly, nationalism virtually everywhere drove resistance, but it also could, and did, justify collaboration.[5]

As for the organized resistance, most clandestine groups were set up along ethnic lines, with the notable exception of the Soviet underground. The non-Soviets customarily limited their area of operation to their own ethnic territories.[6] Uniquely for a "nationalist" outfit, the Polish underground operated in all regions, from Estonia in the north to Moldavia in the south and, eventually, far in the east. It also admitted anyone who pledged loyalty to traditional "Polishness" (*polskość*), his or her ethnic background notwithstanding. In the north-east, the Poles accepted Polish sympathizers from all groups, particularly Catholic and Orthodox Belarusians, and, exceptionally, a few unassimilated Jews. Assimilated Jews were usually converts to Catholicism, and, thus, as a rule they were treated as Poles. In the south-east, Volhynia, in particular, the Poles admitted unacculturated Jews more gladly as well as the Czechs and others.[7] The Communists, once they were forced underground following the Nazi invasion in 1941, accepted anyone, in theory at least, his or her ethnic background notwithstanding. In practice, the Communists tended to reject, abuse, and even murder unarmed Jewish refugees, women, children, and the elderly, in particular. Stalin's clandestine groups operated virtually everywhere in the Eastern Borderlands. Forcible conscription was a practice of the Soviet guerrillas, as it was with the Ukrainian nationalist underground.

The centerpiece of the conflict was the struggle of the totalitarian giants, Nazi Germany and the Soviet Union, against one another.[8] The clash occurred over the subjugated bodies of a multitude of small nations. Their governments and citizens vainly endeavored to sit the calamity out. Ultimately, however, they sided with one giant against the other. Only exceptionally did they fight against both the Third Reich and the USSR. The small nations were quickly overrun and their governments overthrown. The totalitarian invaders deployed a whole array of social engineering schemes against the captive populations, including most often mass terror. The denizens of the captive nations suffered ordinary terror, which included expropriations, forced labor, imprisonment, deportations, and random killing.[9] Exceptionally, some of the captive people faced mass extermination, or extraordinary terror, in particular, the Jews during the Holocaust.[10] Also the local traditional elite, which was mostly Polish Catholic, faced extermination, albeit on a much smaller scale.[11]

The conflict not only pitted the German Nazis against the Soviet Communists, but also the citizens of each overrun state against one of the occupiers or, less frequently, both. Further, each ethnic group focused on its own predicament and often turned against other groups, both internal minorities and external neighbors.[12] Also members of a particular national group feuded with their peers within the same ethnicity for ideological, criminal, or personal reasons. At times, all these aspects of violence overlapped.

In other words, the conflict was not only a total war involving foreign invaders but also a series of local conflicts between the majority population and the minorities in each region; national minority groups pitted against each other; political organizations, both covert and overt, against one another, including within the same ethnic group; and communities against other communities as well as individuals against one another. The conflict was permanent but it was also cyclical, escalating and deescalating in congruence with local exigencies and general developments spurred by the warring giants. The conflict also forced the participants to collaborate with one or the other occupier, and sometimes both, against other local peoples.[13] The results of the conflict were catastrophic. Not only was an entire ethnic group nearly exterminated, namely the Jews, and others were decimated and displaced, but there ensued a nearly complete destruction of the fabric of the old Polish-Lithuanian Common-wealth. Almost all age-sanctified customs and arrangements that had been formed organically during the preceding half a millenium nearly vanished.[14] In the Intermarium, to put it bluntly, modernity expressed in its extremist, totalitarian form virtually obliterated tradition and history.

Then, in the wake of the Armageddon, there came modernization Soviet-style. The gaping wounds of the war were slimed with a paralyzing puss of Marxist-Leninist ideology and a crippling crust of Communist institutions. Free life barely pulsated underneath, squelched. The ensuing demographic, social, and economic changes wrought upon the hapless captive people by the Soviets were intended to eliminate the burden of history forever and to usher in a red paradise on Earth, the Intermarium in this instance. Chialism of this kind had inflicted itself upon its eastern part already in the wake of World War I; now the western part settled in to the dubious pleasures of utopianism.

Yet, after 1953, the Red terror subsided. To be sure, brutality persisted for decades, including more than a few killings, but mass murder stopped. Its specter loomed menacingly almost until the end. "The peace of the prison" reigned in the USSR and its colonies, as Angelo Codevilla and Paul Seabury put it.[15] The totalitarian police state remained in place, and the luckless captives, traumatized by terror and its memories, largely froze or, at best, settled into inertia. Only in the second half of the 1980s, when the Communist leadership openly showed no more stomach for mass repression, did the Soviet slaves rebel. Theirs was largely a nonviolent insurrection. Modeling itself after the Polish way to resist as pioneered by "Solidarity," the Intermarium was the first to show the will for freedom in the USSR.

Nonviolence entailed gradualism. The legacy of totalitarianism meant social atomization. That, in turn, spelled poor organization and headless grass-roots activism on the part of the captives. The lack of traditional elites equaled reliance on the Soviet-made leaders. The persistence of Communist mentality and Soviet institutions, including the secret police, revealed itself in disintegration and confusion of the righteous drive for liberty. All this translated into a gradual transformation, rather than a singular eruption of freedom in the Intermarium, as well as, afterward, lingering pathologies inherited from the Communist era. Freedom, nonetheless, did dawn there after half a century, if tenuously.

Notes

1. X. Walerian Meysztowicz, *Poszło z dymem: Gawędy o czasach i ludziach* (*Up in Smoke: The Tales of Times and People*) (London: Polska Fundacja Kulturalna, 1973), 257, 316. Born in a prominent noble Polish-Lithuanian family, Father Meysztowicz was a veteran of the Polish-Bolshevik War, a Roman Catholic priest, a lecturer at the University of Wilno, and an important émigré intellectual resident in Rome.

2. Henryk Sienkiewicz, *With Fire and Sword*, tran. by Jeremiah Curtin (Boston, MA: Little, Brown, and Company, 1897), 776.

3. The English-language bibliography on the Nazi and Soviet occupations is growing, but not yet adequate (except for the study of the Holocaust). For the Intermarium as a whole see Timothy Snyder, *Bloodlands: Europe between Hitler and Stalin* (New York: Basic Books, 2010). For the Baltic States see Geoffrey Swain, *Between Stalin and Hitler: Class War and Race War on the Dvina, 1940–1946* (London and New York: RoutledgeCurzon, 2004); Valdis O. Lumans, *Latvia in World War II* (New York: Fordham University Press, 2006); Andrejs Plakans, *Experiencing Totalitarianism: The Invasion and Occupation of Latvia by the USSR and Nazi Germany 1939–1991, A Documentary History* (Bloomington, IN: Author House, 2007); Andrew Ezergailis, *Stockholm Documents: The German occupation of Latvia, 1941–1945: What Did America Know?* (Riga: Publishers of the Historical Institute of Latvia, 2002); Modris Eksteins, *Walking Since Daybreak: A Story of Eastern Europe, World War II, and The Heart of Our Century* (Boston, MA and New York: Houghton Mifflin Company, 1999); Valters Nollendorfs and Erwin Oberländer, eds., *The Hidden and Forbidden History of Latvia under Soviet and Nazi Occupations, 1940–1991: Selected Research of the Commission of the Historians of Latvia* (Riga: Institute of the History of Latvia, 2005); Vello Salo et al., eds., *The White Book: Losses*

Inflicted on the Estonian Nation by Occupation Regimes, 1940–1991 (Tallinn: Estonian Encyclopaedia Publishers, 2005); Toomas Hiio, Meelis Maripuu, and Indrek Paavle, eds., *Estonia 1940–1945: Reports of the Estonian International Commission for the Investigation of Crimes against Humanity* (Tallinn: Estonian Foundation for the Investigation of Crimes Against Humanity, 2006); Toomas Hiio, Meelis Maripuu, and Indrek Paavle, eds., *Estonia since 1944: Reports of the Estonian International Commission for the Investigation of Crimes against Humanity* (Tallinn: Estonian Foundation for the Investigation of Crimes Against Humanity, 2009); Saulius Suziedelis, *The Sword and the Cross: A History of the Church in Lithuania* (Huntington, IN: Our Sunday Visitor Publishing Division, 1988), 182–200; Judith B. Sedaitis and V. Stanley Vardys, *Lithuania: The Rebel Nation* (Boulder, CO: Westview Press, 1997), 46–60; Gertrude Schneider, "The Two Ghettos in Riga, Latvia, 1941–1943," in *The Holocaust in the Soviet Union: Studies and Sources on the Destruction of the Jews in the Nazi Occupied Territories of the USSR, 1941–1945*, ed. Lucjan Dobroszycki and Jeffrey S. Gurock (Armonk, NY and London: M.E. Sharpe, 1990), 181–93; Georg von Rauch, *The Baltic States: The Years of Independence: Estonia, Latvia, Lithuania, 1917–1940* (New York: St. Martin's Press, 1974), 217–34; Roswitha Czollek, *Faschismus und Okkupation: Wirtschaftspolitische Zielsetzung und Praxis des faschistischen deutschen Besatzungsregimes in den baltischen Sowjetrepubliken während des Zweiten Weltkrieges* (Berlin: Akademie-Verlag, 1974). For Lithuania alone, see the reports of the International Commission of the Evaluation of the Crimes of the Nazi and Soviet Occupation Regimes in Lithuania at http://www.komisija.lt/en/body.php?&m=1194863084. For Ukraine see Taras Hunczak and Dmytro Shtohryn, eds., *Ukraine: The Challenges of World War II* (Lanham, MD: University Press of America, 2003) (afterward *Ukraine*); Orest Subtelny, *Ukraine: A History*, 2nd ed. (Toronto, Buffalo, and London: University of Toronto Press in association with the Canadian Institute of Ukrainian Studies, 1994), 453–95; Paul Robert Magocsi, *A History of Ukraine* (Seattle, WA: University of Washington Press, 1996), 611–51; Andrew Wilson, *The Ukrainians: Unexpected Nation* (New Haven, CT and London: Yale University Press, 2002), 127–51. For Belarus see Jan Zaprudnik, *Belarus: At a Crossroads in History* (Boulder, CO, San Francisco, CA, and Oxford: Westview Press, 1993), 75–119; and see below. On the Poles see, inter alia, Bogusia J. Wojciechowska, ed., *Waiting to be Heard: The Polish Christian Experience under Nazi and Stalinist Oppression, 1939–1955* (Bloomington, IN: Author Houe, 2009); and see below. For a neo-Stalinist explication of Polish–Soviet relations during World War II and its aftermath see Elena V. Iakovleva, *Polsha protiv SSSR, 1939–1950* (*Poland against the USSR*) (Moscow: Veche, 2007). For Poland's losses at the hands of the Germans only see Krystyna Daszkiewicz, *Niemieckie ludobójstwo na narodzie polskim (1939–1945)* (*German Genocide against the Polish Nation*) 2 vols. (Toruń: Wydawnictwo Adam Marszałek, 20009). The only solid study to consider all human losses, one's ethnic background notwithstanding, concerns Poland. Wojciech Materski and Tomasz Szarota, eds., *Polska 1939–1945: Straty osobowe i ofiary represji pod dwiema okupacjami* (*Poland 1939–1945: Individual Losses and Victims of Repression under Both Occupations*) (Warszawa: Instytut Pamięci Narodowej, 2009); and a short summary of the book by Waldemar Grabowski, "Raport: Straty ludzkie poniesione przez Polskę w latach 1939–1945," (A Raport: Human Losses of Poland between 1939 and 1945) *Nasz Dziennik* (September 1, 2009). However, see also Mark Harrison, "Counting Soviet Deaths in the Great Patriotic War: Comment," *Europe-Asia Studies* 55, no. 6 (September 2003): 939–44; and Boris Sokolov, "How to Calculate Human Losses during the Second World War," *The Journal of Slavic Military Studies* 22, no. 3 (July 2009): 437–58.

4. All these matters and more are considered in a microstudy of a single county (Janów Lubelski-Kraśnik in Lublin Province) in central Poland. See Marek Jan Chodakiewicz, *Between Nazis and Soviets: Occupation Politics in Poland, 1939–1947* (Lanham, MD: Lexington Books, 2004). For a short explication see Marek Jan Chodakiewicz, "Accommodation, Collaboration, and Resistance in Poland, 1939–1947: A Theory of Choices and the Methodology of a Case Study," *The Dekaban Lecture Series in Polish and Polish-American Studies* (Detroit, MI: The Piast Foundation) no. 1 (2002): 6–20. For comparison in southeastern (contemporary) Poland's Rzeszów area see Bart Nabrdalik, "South-Eastern Poland between 1939 and the Final Soviet Frontier Demarcation in 1951—The Destruction of an Ethnic Mosaic," *The Journal of Slavic Military Studies* 21, no. 1 (January 2008): 17–37; and a case study of a locality in the Intermarium during both occupations by Alexander Brakel, *Unter Rotem Stern und Hakenkreuz: Branovicze 1939–1944: Das westliche Weißrussland unter sowjetischer und deutscher Besatzung* (Paderborn: Schöningh, 2009). For some general points on collaboration and resistance on the national level in Lithuania see Sigitas Jegelevičius, "Okupacija ir kolaboravimas Lietuvoje Antrojo pasaulinio karo metais," *Genocidas ir reistencija* no. 1 (13) (2003): http://www.genocid.lt/Leidyba/13/sigitas.htm (accessed April 24, 2012). On a more general level, Umbreit stresses that it was not only the nationalists and fascists who collaborated with the Nazis. Certain collaborators were simply opportunists who wanted to further their careers. However, collaboration should not be equated with treason. It was an attempt "to preserve the political, social and economic order" and to prevent the Nazis from becoming more directly involved in the affairs of the occupied countries. See Horst Umbreit, "Auf dem Weg zur Kontinentalherrschaft," in *Das Deutsche Reich und Der Zweite Weltkrieg, Band 5: Organisation und Mobilisierung des Deutschen Machtbereichs. Kriegsverwaltung, Wirtschaft und Personelle Ressourcen, 1939–1941,* ed. Bernhard R. Kroener et al. (Stuttgart: Deutsche Verlags-Anstalt, 1988), 28–46, 265–97. Rings believes collaboration and resistance were two main pivots of life under Nazi occupation. See Werner Rings, *The Life with the Enemy: Collaboration and Resistance in Hitler's Europe* (London: Weidenfeld and Nicolson, 1982). Focusing on similar problems, Gross proposes to look at "collusion or complicity" (rather than the inflexible "collaboration") in the context of the phenomenon of "war as revolution" in Eastern Europe—with any discussion of resistance conspicuously lacking (except for a brief mention of Poland). In this scheme the Nazi revolution cleared the way for the Communist system of "complicity *cum* social atomization," where, with the blessing of the Western Powers, the Soviets divided the conquered societies into "democratic" forces and "fascist" elements. The latter were purged mercilessly, even though overwhelmingly they had nothing to do with fascism. See Jan Gross, "War as Revolution," in *The Establishment of Communist Regimes in Eastern Europe, 1944–1949,* ed. Norman Naimark and Leonid Gibianskii (Boulder, CO: Westview Press, 1997), 25, 34 (afterward *The Establishment*). Deák uses the terms "collaboration" and "accommodation" interchangeably and stresses that "active collaborators and active resisters were but a small minority among the many who just wanted to get by." Passivity characterized the bulk of the population, which (along with resisters and collaborators) simply "reacted to

the behavior of the German, Soviet, and other occupying powers." See István Deák, "Introduction," In *The Politics of Retribution in Europe: World War II and Its Aftermath*, ed. István Deák, Jan T. Gross, and Tony Judt (Princeton, NJ: Princeton University Press, 2000), 3–14. For a detailed discussion of collaboration in Germany, Poland, the Baltics, and "Russia" see the following essays in *"Kollaboration" in Nordosteuropa: Erscheinungsformen und Deutungen im 20. Jahrhundert*, ed. by Joachim Tauber (Wiesbaden: Harrassowitz Verlag, 2006): Joachim Tauber, "'Kollaboration' in Nordosteuropa: Erscheinungsformen und Deutungen im 20. Jahrhundert," (11–18); Werner Röhr, "Kollaboration: Sachverhalf und Bergriff: Methodische Überlegungen auf der Grundlage vergleichender Forschungen zur Okkupationspolitik der Achsenmächte im Yweiten Weltkrieg," (21–39); Christian Koller, "Fremdherrschaft und nationale Loyalität: Das Fremdherrschaftskonzept in der politischen Sprache Deutschlands der ersten Hälfte des 20. Jahrhunderts," (56–74); Tomasz Szarota, "Kollaboration mit deutschen und sowjetischen Besatzern aus polnischer Sicht – damals, gestern und heute," (324–41). See further *Pamięć i Sprawiedliwość* no. 1 (12) (2008); Ryszard Kaczmarek, "Kolaboracja na ziemiach wcielonych do Rzeszy Niemieckiej," ("Collaboration in the Lands Incorporated into the German Reich") (159–82); and Grzegorz Motyka, "Kolaboracja na Kresach Wschodnich II Rzeczpospolitej, 1941–1944," ("Collaboration in the Eastern Borderlands of the 2nd Republic, 1941–1944") (183–98). For arguably the most poignant insights both on general and regional levels on the topic of collaboration, accommodation, and resistance (and much more) by a contemporary libertarian conservative observer see Józef Mackiewicz's two volumes of commentary *Nudis Verbis* (London: Kontra, 2003); and *Fakty, przyroda, ludzie* (*The Facts, Nature, and People*) (London: Kontra, 1984). His fiction is equally stimulating. See, e.g., *Nie trzeba głośno mówić* (*One Should Not Say That Out Loud*) (London: Kontra, 1980).

5.   The degree of involvement varied with ethnic groups because both occupiers applied different nationalities policies to individual groups at various times. See some preliminary remarks on the Polish, Russian, German, and Jewish minorities in Vinnytsia/Winnica (Ukraine) under the Soviets and Nazis (1935–44) in Amir Weiner, *Making Sense of the War: The Second World War and the Fate of the Bolshevik Revolution* (Princeton, NJ and Oxford: Princeton University Press, 2001). Weiner is a leftist with pronounced pro-Soviet sympathies but he at least retains a soft spot for the Jewish minority. For other case studies see, Longin Tomaszewski, *Wileńszczyzna lat wojny i okupacji 1939–1945* (*Wilno-Land during the Years of War and Occupation*) (Warszawa: Oficyna Wydawnicza "Rytm," 2001); Stanisława Lewandowska, *Życie codzienne Wilna w latach II wojny światowej* (*Everyday Life in Wilno during the Second World War*), 2nd ed. (Warszawa: Bellona, 2001); Stanisława Lewandowska, *Losy wilnian: Zapis rzeczywistości okupacyjnej. Ludzie, fakty, wydarzenia 1939–1945* (*The Fate of the Residents of Wilno: A Record of the Reality of the Occupation*), 3rd ed. (Warszawa: Neriton, 2004). The participation of the captive people in police and military formations of the occupying powers is a particularly contentious point. On October 10, 2002, a conference on "Citizens of the Occupied Countries in World War II," was held in Vilnius/Wilno. It was sponsored by the Genocide and Resistance Research Centre of Lithuania and Lithuanian War History Association. The participants of the conference recognized that collaboration can only occur if there is the will to collaborate on both sides. Further, the stronger party in the collaborationist project almost invariably

dictates the conditions for collaboration. However, the weaker party can twist certain aspects of the collaborationist project to its advantage. Several papers were devoted to the topic including: Petras Stankeras, "The Nazi German Policy of Involving People of the Occupied Baltic Countries in the Military-Police Units During World War II," Eriks Jekabsons, "The Fate of the 24th Territorial Latvian Riflemen Corps in June–July 1941," Stasys Knezys, "Transition Period: From the 29th Corps to the Self-Preservation Battalions," Arūnas Bubnys, "Activity and Evaluation of the Lithuanian Police Battalions," Uldis Neiburgs, "Latvian Soldiers in German and Red Armies During World War II: Problems of Research," and Arvydas Anušauskas, "Forced Mobilisation During World War II," http://www.genocid.lt/GRTD/Konferencijos/eng/war.htm (accessed January 20, 2005). See also Peter J. Potichnyj, "Ukrainians in WW II Military Formations: An Overview," in Hunczak and Shtohryn, *Ukraine*, 201–8; and the following essays in *"Kollaboration" in Nordosteuropa: Erscheinungsformen und Deutungen im 20. Jahrhundert*, ed. Joachim Tauber (Wiesbaden: Harrassowitz Verlag, 2006): Kathrin Reichelt, "Kollaboration: Zwei Beispiele aus der Judenverfolgung in Lettland, 1941–1944," (77–87); Christoph Dieckmann, "Kollaboration? Litauische Nationsbildung und deutsche Besatzungsherrschaft im Zweiten Weltkrieg," (128–39); Saulius Sužiedėlis, "Lithuanian Collaboration During the Second World War: Past Realities, Present Perception," (140–63); Michael McQueen, "Collaboration as an Element in the Polish-Lithuanian Struggle Over Vilnius," (164–73); Egidius Aleksandravičius, "Lithuanian collaboration with the Nazis and Soviets," (174–91).

6. See David G. Williamson, *Poland Betrayed: The Nazi-Soviet Invasions 1939* (Barnsley, South Yorkshire, UK: Pen & Sword, 2009); Bogdan Chrzanowski and Piotr Niwiński, "Okupacja sowiecka i niemiecka: Próba analizy porównawczej (Wybrane problemy)," ("Soviet and German Occupations: An Attempt of a Comparative Analysis") *Pamięć i Sprawiedliwość* no. 1 (12) (2008): 13–40; Piotr Niwiński, ed., *Opór wobec systemów totalitarnych na Wileńszczyźnie w okresie II wojny światowej (Anti-Totalitarian Resistance in Wilno Land during the Second World War)* (Gdańsk: Instytut Pamięci Narodowej, Komisja Ścigania Zbrodni przeciwko Narodowi Polskiemu, 2003); N. I. Vladimirtsev and A. I. Kokurin, eds., *Sbornik dokumentov: NKVD-MVD SSR v bor'be s banditizmom i vooruzhennym natsionalisticheskim podpol'em na Zapadnoi Ukraine, v Zapadnoi Belorussii i Pribaltike (1939–1956) (A Collection of Documents: NKVD-MVD of the USSR against Banditry and Armed Nationalist Underground in Western Ukraine, Western Belarus, and the Baltics)* (Moskva: Ob'iedinennaia redaktsia MVD Rossii, 2008); Arvydas Anušauskas, ed., *The Anti-Soviet Resistance in the Baltic States* (Vilnius: Akreta, 2002) (afterward *The Anti-Soviet Resistance in the Baltic States*), a publishing project of the Genocide and Resistance Research Centre of Lithuania. For a critical review of this work see Rafał Wnuk in *Pamięć i Sprawiedliwość* no. 2 (4) (2003): 366–75.

7. See Waldemar Grabowski, *Polska tajna administracja cywilna, 1940–1945 (Polish Secret Civilian Administration)* (Warszawa: Instytut Pamięci Narodowej, KŚZpNP, 2003), 108–10, 412–81; Rafał Wnuk, "Za pierwszego Swieta": Polska konspiracja na Kresach Wschodnich II Rzeczypospolitej (wrzesień 1939–czerwiec 1941) ("Under the First Soviet": Polish Conspiracy in the Eastern Borderlands of the 2nd Republic (September 1939–June 1941))* (Warszawa: Instytut Pamięci Narodowej, K ŚZpNP and PAN ISP, 2007); Rafał Wnuk, "Polska konspiracja antysowiecka na Kresach Wschodnich II RP w latach 1939–1941 i 1944–1952," in *Tygiel Narodów: Stosunki społeczne i etniczne na dawnych ziemiach wschod-*

nich Rzeczpospolitej, 1939–1953, (A Melting Pot of Nations: Social and Ethnic Relations in the Former Eastern Borderlands of the Second Polish Republic) ed. Krzysztof Jasiewicz (Warszawa: ISP PAN, Rytm, and Polonia Foundation Trust, 2002), 157–250 (afterward "Polska konspiracja," in *Tygiel Narodów*); *Dzieje polskiego podziemia na Białostocczyźnie w latach 1939–1956: Materiały z sesji naukowej – 24 kwietnia 1992 r. – w Instytucie Studiów Politycznych PAN (A History of the Polish Underground in the Bialystok Region between 1939 and 1956)* (Toruń: Wydawnictwo Adam Marszałek, 1992); Jerzy Węgierski, *Lwowska konspiracja narodowa i katolicka, 1939–1946 (The Lvovian Nationalist and Catholic Conspiracy, 1939–1946)* (Kraków: Wydawnictwo Platan, 1994); Grzegorz Mazur and Jerzy Węgierski, *Konspiracja lwowska, 1939–1944: Słownik biograficzny (Lvovian Underground, 1939–1944: A Biographical Dictionary)* (Katowice: Wydawnictwo Unia, 1997); Father Stanisław Bizuń, *Historia krzyżem pisana: Wspomnienia z życia Kościoła katolickiego na Ziemi Lwowskiej 1939–1945 (History Written with the Cross: Recollections from the Life of the Catholic Church in the Lwów Land)* (Lublin: Wydawnictwo Oddział Lubelski Stowarzyszenia Wspólnota Polska, 1994); Grzegorz Hryciuk, *Polacy we Lwowie 1939–1944: Życie codzienne (Poles in Lwów: Everyday Life)* (Warszawa: KiW, 2000); Grzegorz Mazur, *Pokucie w latach drugiej wojny światowej: Położenie ludności, polityka okupantów, działalność podziemia (Pokucie during the Second World War: The Situation of the Civilian Population, the Policy of the Occupiers, and the Activity of the Underground)* (Kraków: Nakładem Uniwersytetu Jagiellońskiego, 1994). For a microscale focus on the Polish mainstream underground during World War II and its aftermath see Edward Jaworski, *Lwów—Kleparów: Rejon SZP-ZWZ-AK w latach 1939–1945 (Lwów-Kleparów: The ZSP-ZWZ-AK Command between 1939 and 1945)* (Warszawa: Kanon, 1990); for the underground press, including in the Eastern Borderlands, of the Polish Nationalists see Marek Jan Chodakiewicz and Wojciech Jerzy Muszyński, *Żeby Polska była polska: Antologia publicystyki konspiracyjnej podziemia narodowego, 1939–1950 (Let Poland be Polish: An Anthology of the Underground Nationalist Press)* (Warszawa: Instytut Pamięci Narodowej, 2010).

8. The literature on the Nazi Germany's invasion of the Soviet Union is vast and growing. An important recent study is Chris Bellamy, *Absolute War: Soviet Russia in the Second World War: A Modern History* (London: Macmillan, 2007). Its main flaw is that the author either does not know or ignores sources perennial to his main focus, in particular, documents and monographs regarding the nations of the Intermarium. See for instance his inadequate treatment of the Katyn Forest massacre at 87–88. Further, instead of regarding the conflict as a clash of similarly repulsive totalitarians, he favors the Soviets. Why wax lyrical about, say, the Red Army snipers, and not the sharpshooters of the *Wehrmacht*? Would not it be right to treat both with similar detachment?

9. For the ebbs and flows of ordinary terror in a single locality see Marek Jan Chodakiewicz, "Ordinary Terror: Communist and Nazi Occupation Politics in Jedwabne, 1939–1949," *Glaukopis* 1 (2003): 266–76. For an account of a single terror institution see Sergei Chertoprud, *НКВД - НКГБ в годы Великой Отечественной войны: Неизвестные страницы (NKVD-NKGB during the Great Fatherland War: The Unknown Chapters)* (Moscow: Iaza/Eskimo, 2005). Confiscations and expropriations were the trademark of foreign occupations between 1772 and 1992 with the greatest intensity felt between 1917 and 1945. See Jan Pruszyński, "Grabież i niszczenie dziedzictwa kulturalnego Kresów Wschodnich Rzeczypospolitej," ("Pillage and Destruction of the Cultural

Heritage of Eastern Borderlands of the Commonwealth") in Jasiewicz, *Europa nieprowincjonalna*, 198–213. The bibliography on Soviet and Nazi deportations is very extensive. See below and see e.g., *Deportatsii z zakhodni zemli Ukrainy kintsia 30-kh – pochatku 50-kh r.r.: Dokumenty, materiali, spokhadi, (Deportations from Western Ukraine from the End of the 1930s until the Beginning of the 1950s: Documents, Materials, Essays)* 3 vols. (Lviv: Natsional'na Akademia Nauk Ukrainy im. I. Krypiakevycha, 2003).

10. See Krzysztof Jasiewicz, ed., *Świat Niepożegnany: Żydzi na dawnych ziemiach wschodnich Rzeczpospolitej w XVIII-XX wieku (An Unmourned World: Jews in the Old Territories of the Commonwealth between the 18th and 20th Centuries)* (Warszawa and London: ISP PAN, Oficyna Wydawniczya Rytm, and Polonia Aid Foundation, 2004) (afterward *Świat Niepożegnany*); R. A. Chernoglazova, ed., *Tragediia evreev belorussii v gody nemetskoi okkupatsii (1941–1945): Sbornik materialov i dokumentov (The Tragedy of the Jews of Belarussia during the German Occupation)* (Minsk: Ia. B. Dremach, 1995); and Sara Bender, *The Jews of Białystok During World War Two and the Holocaust* (Waltham, MA: Brandeis University Press, and Hanover and London: New England University Press, 2008). And see below.

11. See Szczepan Kurzymski, *Losy Polaków na terenach wschodnich w latach 1939–1945 (The Lot of the Poles in the Eastern Territories between 1939 and 1945)* (Gdańsk: Roxan, 2003); *Represje Związku Sowieckiego wobec obywateli państwa polskiego w latach 1939–1956: Materiały z V Ogólnopolskiej Konferencji Naukowej poświęconej Polakom, którzy w latach 1939–1956 przebywali w więzieniach śledczych (Repression of the Soviet Union against the Citizens of the Polish State between 1939 and 1956: Material from the 5th all Polish Scholarly Conference Devoted to the Poles, Who Were in Investigative Prisons between 1939 and 1956)* (Koszalin: Stowarzyszenie Humanistów i Artystów, 2005); Sławomir Kalbarczyk, Tomasz Łabuszewski, and Kazimierz Krajewski interviewed by Barbara Polak, "O sowieckich represjach wobec Polaków," ("Soviet Repression against the Poles") in *Stół bez kantów i inne rozmowy Biuletynu IPN z lat 2003–2005 (A Non-Crooked Table and Other Conversations of the Biuletyn IPN, 2003–2005)* (Warszawa: Instytut Pamięci Narodowej, 2008), 101–23, which is *Biuletyn Instytutu Pamięci Narodowej* no. 11 (34) (November 2003); and see the following essays in Jasiewicz, *Europa nieprowincjonalna*: Tomasz Plejakowski, "Represje sowieckie wobec obywateli polskich w latach 1939–1991 w świetle polskiej historiografii emigracyjnej i źródeł archiwalnych" ("Soviet Repressions against Polish Citizens between 1939 and 1991 According to Polish Emigre Historiography and Archival Sources") (951–71); Aleksander Gurjanow, "Sowieckie represje wobec Polaków i obywateli polskich w latach 1936–1956 w świetle danych sowieckich" ("Soviet Repressions against Poles and Polish Citizens between 1939 and 1956 According to Soviet data") (972–82); and Roman Dzwonkowski, "Represje władz sowieckich wobec duchowieństwa polskiego na ziemiach wschodnich dawnej Rzeczypospolitej w latach 1939–1941 i 1944–1966" ("Repression by the Soviet Authorities against Polish Clergy in the Eastern Lands of the Former Commonwealth between 1939 and 1941 as well as 1944 and 1966") (1145–54).

12. The Polish–Ukrainian conflict was arguably the most acute. See Ryszard Torzecki, *Polacy i Ukraińcy: Sprawa ukraińska w czasie II wojny światowej na terenie II Rzeczypospolitej (Poles and Ukrainians: The Ukrainian Cause during the Second World War in the Second Commonwealth)* (Warszawa: Wydawnictwo Naukowe PWN, 1993); Timothy Snyder, *Sketches from a Secret War: A Polish*

Artist's Mission to Liberate Soviet Ukraine (New Haven, CT: Yale University Press, 2005); Timothy Snyder, *The Reconstruction of Nations: Poland, Ukraine, Lithuania, Belarus, 1569–1999* (New Haven, CT: Yale University Press, 2003), especially part II, "The Causes of Ukrainian-Polish Ethnic Cleansing, 1943;" Alexander V. Prusin, "Revolution and Ethnic Cleansing in Western Ukraine: The OUN-UPA Assault against Polish Settlements in Volhynia and Eastern Galicia, 1943–1944," in *Ethnic Cleansing in Twentieth Century Europe*, ed. Steven Béla Várdy, T. Hunt Tooley, and Agnes Huszár Várdy (New York and Boulder, CO: Social Science Monographs and Columbia University Press, 2003), 517–35; Adria Pelensky, "The Unknown Genocide in Volhynia and Galicia," *Undergraduate Journal of Slavic Studies* 1, no. 1 (Spring 2005): 49–62; Grzegorz Motyka, "Postawy wobec konfliktu polsko-ukraińskiego w latach 1939–1953 w zależnożci od przynależności etnicznej, państwowej i religijnej," ("Attitudes toward the Polish–Ukrainian Conflict between 1939–1953 According to Ethnicity, Citizenship, and Religion") in Jasiewicz, *Tygiel Narodów*, 279–408; Iaroslav Isaievych, ed., *Volyn i Kholmshchyna 1938–1947 rr.: Polsko-ukrainske protystoiannia ta ioho vidlunnia. Doslidzhennia, dokumenty, spohady* (*Volhynia and the Chełm Area, 1938–1945: Polish–Ukrainian Relations*) (Lviv: Natsionalna akademiia nauk Ukrainy, Instytut ukrainoznavstva im. I. Krypiakevycha, 2003); the bilingual collection of documents *Polacy i Ukraińcy między dwoma systemami totalitarnymi, 1942–1945* (*Poles and Ukrainians between Two Totalitarian Systems, 1942–1945*) (Warszawa and Kiev: Wydawnictwo Rytm, Instytut Pamięci Narodowej KŚZpNP, Archiwum MSWiA RP, Państwowe Archiwum Służby Bezpieczeństwa Ukrainy, 2005); Grzegorz Hryciuk, *Przemiany narodowościowe i ludnościowe w Galicji Wschodniej i na Wołyniu w latach 1931–1948* (*National and Demographic Transformations in Eastern Galicia and Volhynia between 1931 and 1948*) (Toruń: Adam Marszałek, 2005); Maria Dębowska, *Kościół katolicki na Wołyniu w warunkach oku pacji, 1939–1945* (*Catholic Church in Volhynia under the Occupations, 1939–1945*) (Rzeszów: Instytut Pamięci Narodowej, 2008). See also the deeply flawed and one-sided early article by Timothy Snyder, "'To Resolve the Ukrainian Problem Once and for All': The Ethnic Cleansing of Ukrainians in Poland, 1943–1947," *Journal of Cold War Studies* 1, no. 2 (1999): 86–120; and a more developed argument in Timothy Snyder, "The Causes of Ukrainian-Polish Ethnic Cleansing 1943," *Past & Present* 179, no. 1 (May 2003): 197–234. And see the following essays in Hunczak and Shtohryn, *Ukraine*: Edward Wynot, Jr., "Background to Tragedy: Polish-Ukrainian Relations on the Eve of World War II" (127–40) and Taras Hunczak, "Ukrainian-Polish Relations during World War II" (141–52). For relations between Belarusians, Poles, Jews, and others in the Province of Białystok see Wojciech Śleszyński, "Polityka narodowościowa władz sowieckich na obszarze przedwojennego województwa białostockiego w latach 1939–1941," ("The Nationalities Policy of the Soviet Authorities in the Pre-War Bialystok Province between 1939–1941") *Dzieje Najnowsze* no. 4 (2001): 57–64. For the predicament of Poland's Belarusians see Wiesław Balcerak, ed., *Polska-Białoruś, 1918–1945* (*Poland-Belarus, 1918–1945*) (Warszawa: Instytut Historii PAN, Stowarzyszenie Współpracy Polska-Wschód, Stowarzyszenie Polska-Białoruś, 1994); Marek Wierzbicki, "Białorusini polscy w okresie przełomu (1939–1945)," ("Polish Belarusians during the Period of the Rupture [1939–1945]") *Pamięć i Sprawiedliwość* no. 2 (6) (2004): 83–113. For the fate of all ethnic groups of the north-east see Sokrat Janowicz, "Zderzenie wielu światów, czyli Kresy białoruskie w latach 1939–1953," ("The Clash of Many Worlds, or the Belarusian

Borderlands between 1939–1953") in Jasiewicz, *Tygiel Narodów*, 145–56. For two interesting microstudies focusing on Jews, Poles, and Ukrainians in Galicia see Rosa Lehmann, *Symbiosis and Ambivalence: Poles and Jews in a Small Galician Town* (New York and Oxford: Berghahn Books, 2001); Shimon Redlich, *Together and Apart in Brzezany: Poles, Jews, and Ukrainians, 1919–1945* (Bloomington, IN: Indiana University Press, 2002). Naturally, conflict in the borderlands predated the war. Without the war, however, it would have lacked the revolutionary ferocity which became its benchmark. For Jewish–Ukrainian relations on the eve and during the war see Maksym Hon, "Konflikt ukraińsko-żydowski na ziemiach zachodnioukraińskich w latach 1935–1939," ("The Ukrainian–Jewish Conflict in Western Ukraine between 1935 and 1939") in Jasiewicz, *Świat Niepożegnany*, 244–58; Taras Hunczak, "Ukrainian and Jewish Relations during the Soviet and Nazi Occupations," in Hunczak and Shtohryn, *Ukraine*, 107–26. Compare that with prewar Jewish relations with Polish Catholic military settlers in Janina Stobniak Smogorzewska, "Osadnicy wojskowi a ludność żydowska na Kresach Wschodnich 1920–1940," ("Military Settlers and the Jewish Population in the Eastern Borderlands, 1920–1940") in Jasiewicz, *Świat Niepożegnany*, 559–69. For Jewish–Polish coexistence in Wilno before the war see Jarosław Wołkonowski, "Model wileński współistnienia polsko-żydowskiego w latach międzywojennych," ("The Vilenian Paradigm of Polish–Jewish Coexistence in the Interwar Period") in Jasiewicz, *Świat Niepożegnany*, 391–99; Jarosław Wołkonowski, *Stosunki polsko-żydowskie w Wilnie i na Wileńszczyźnie 1919–1939 (Polish–Jewish Relations in Wilno and Its Environs, 1919–1939)* (Białystok: Wydawnictwo Uniwersytetu w Białymstoku, 2004). For Jewish–Polish affairs in interwar Lwów see Grzegorz Mazur, "Szkic do dziejów stosunków polsko-żydowskich we Lwowie w okresie międzywojennym," ("An Outline of the History of Polish–Jewish Relation in Lwów in the Interwar Period") in Jasiewicz, *Świat Niepożegnany*, 400–417. For a comparison of the situation of Jews under Polish rule and under the Soviet and Nazi occupations in Volhynia see Szmuel Spektor, "Żydzi wołyńscy w Polsce międzywojennej i w okresie II wojny światowej," ("Volhynian Jews in the Interwar Period and during the Second World War") in Jasiewicz, *Europa nieprowincjonalna*, 566–78; Timothy Snyder, "Żydzi wołyńscy pod rządami polskimi oraz w okresie okupacji sowieckiej i nazistowskiej," ("Volhynian Jews under Polish Rule and during the Soviet and Nazi Occupations") in Jasiewicz, *Świat Niepożegnany*, 266–91. For the Nazi view of the Jewish community in Latvia before the war and during the first Soviet occupation see Karlis Kangeris, "Stosunki żydowsko-łotewskie z perspektywy Trzeciej Rzeszy (1933–VI 1941)," ("Jewish–Latvian relations from the point of view of the Third Reich [1939–June 1941]") in Jasiewicz, *Świat Niepożegnany*, 298–312. For Jewish–Lithuanian relations before and during the war see Algis Kasperavičius, "Stosunki litewsko-żydowskie w latach 1935–1944," (Lithuanian–Jewish Relations, 1935–1944) in Jasiewicz, *Świat Niepożegnany*, 313–29; and Dov Levin, "Dlaczego Żydzi byli mordowani przez swoich litewskich sąsiadów," ("Why Were Jews Murdered by Their Lithuanian Neighbors") in Jasiewicz, *Świat Niepożegnany*, 718–32. For Jews and Gentiles in Belarus during the Nazi occupation see Laryssa Michajlik, "'Sąsiedzi' obok 'sąsiadów'? Ratowanie Żydów na terytorium Białorusi w latach 1941–1944," ("'Neighbors' Next to 'Neighbors'? Rescuing Jews in Belorussia, 1941–1944") in Jasiewicz, *Świat Niepożegnany*, 773–41.

13.   Tadeusz Piotrowski's work is perhaps the only study that looks comprehensively at the question of collaboration with the Nazis and Communists in Eastern

Europe before, during, and after World War II. Aside from the occupiers, certain members of minority ethnic groups, especially the Ukrainians, were enemies of Polish independentists. While a few Poles collaborated with both invaders, small, but very dynamic factions within the ethnic minorities failed to be loyal to the Second Polish Republic or even to their own conationals. In particular, Piotrowski argues, it seems that Jews were more likely to collaborate with the Soviet authorities whereas the opposite was true for the Ukrainians, Lithuanians, and Belarusians. He proposes to apply "the term 'Holocaust'...to include the victims of both of these genocidal régimes [i.e., the Nazi and Soviet regimes] and their collaborators." Moreover, Piotrowski insists that "the inhuman policies of both Hitler and Stalin were clearly aimed at the total extermination of the Polish citizens, both Jews and Christians. Both régimes endorsed a systematic program of genocide." Piotrowski claims that the Nazi theory and practice threatened a general genocide of the Poles, therefore limiting the utility of collaboration. According to him, a "collaborator" or "accomplice" was "any Polish citizen who voluntarily offered services to Nazi Germany at any time throughout the war, to the detriment of Poland or its citizens... The services include military, paramilitary, police, political, economic, literary, and other types of assistance, as well as any assistance given... in the conduct of genocide." Piotrowski distinguishes, however, between "collaboration" and "conscription." Conscripts were those Polish citizens who were forced to accept the Volksliste, and serve in the German military, or become slave laborers and concentration camp inmates (including, to a certain extent, the informers among them). There were also other collaborators, including the Polish police en bloc and all Polish editors of the Polish-language Nazi press as well as "some" employees of the officially approved welfare organization. Finally, against their standing orders from Warsaw, some local commanders of the independentist underground in the Eastern Borderlands maintained contact with the Germans as a self-defensive measure against the Soviet partisans. See Tadeusz Piotrowski, *Poland's Holocaust: Ethnic Strife, Collaboration with Occupying Forces and Genocide in the Second Republic, 1918–1947* (Jefferson, NC: McFarland & Company, 1998), 1, 32, 83–84.

14.   For a general picture see Alexander V. Prusin, *The Lands between: Conflict in the East European Borderlands, 1870–1992* (New York and Oxford: Oxford University Press, 2010), 125–223. For changes in the countryside see Marek Wierzbicki, "Zmiany społeczne i gospodarcze wsi kresowej w latach 1939–1953" ("Social and Economic Changes in the Countryside of the Borderlands between 1939–1953") in Jasiewicz, *Tygiel Narodów*, 95–144; and Bart Nabrdalik, "South-Eastern Poland between 1939 and the Final Soviet Frontier Demarcation in 1951—The Destruction of an Ethnic Mosaic," *The Journal of Slavic Military Studies* 21, no. 1 (January 2008): 17–37, which concerns southeastern (contemporary) Poland's Rzeszów area. For a day-by-day microaccount from a single city see Grzegorz Mazur, Jerzy Skwara, and Jerzy Węgierski, eds., *Kronika 2350 dni wojny i okupacji Lwowa, 1 IX 1939 – 5 II 1946* (*A Chronicle of 2350 Days of War and Occupation in Lwów*) (Katowice: Wydawnictwo Unia, 2007).

15.   Angelo Codevilla and Paul Seabury, *War: Ends and Means*, 2nd ed. (Washington, DC: Potomac Books, 2006), 266–68, 270–72.

10

The First Soviet Occupation (1939–1941)

World War II started with the joint invasion of Poland by the Third Reich and the USSR in September 1939.[1] The political planks for the invasion were laid out in the Ribbentrop–Molotov Pact of August 23, 1939. Its Secret Protocol provided for the partition of Poland and the Baltic States between Hitler and Stalin. Subsequently readjusted, the agreement resulted in the incorporation of western Poland into Germany, and creation of a Nazi-run colony, the so-called Government General, in central Poland. Meanwhile, Poland's eastern provinces were absorbed into the USSR.[2] Initially, the Baltic States were merely assigned to the Soviet sphere of influence. However, in June 1940, Stalin invaded Estonia, Latvia, and Lithuania and incorporated them directly into the Soviet Union. The Red Army simultaneously marched into Romania's Bessarabia and Bukovina, absorbing them likewise. By fusing them with much of the territories of the erstwhile Moldavian Autonomous Soviet Socialist Republic, which included Transnistria, the Kremlin thus created the Moldavian Soviet Socialist Republic (MSSR) in August 1940.

The MSSR was the most heterogeneous of the new Soviet republics. Its population consisted of Romanians ("Moldavians"), Ukrainians, Russians, Bulgarians, Germans, Poles, Jews, the Gagauz, and others. The minorities constituted about 30 percent of the people. Estonia was the most homogenous of the three Baltic states, with a small sprinkling of Russians, Jews, Germans, Swedes, and others. Latvia had significant Russian, Jewish, German, and Polish minorities. They accounted for about 25 percent of the country's population. Lithuania's Jewish, Polish, Russian, and German minorities were almost as numerous percentagewise. Their numbers increased significantly, once the Soviets facilitated the incorporation of Poland's Wilno/Vilnius area into Lithuania in October 1939.

Divided between three Soviet republics, Stalin's newly conquered eastern provinces of Poland were the most diverse ethnically. In the north-east, the Belarusians dominated, while the Ukrainians were the most numerous in the south-east. Although they constituted a majority in the Second Republic at large, the Poles found themselves in a minority in the eastern provinces.

Like the Jews, who lived throughout the Eastern Borderlands, the Poles often clustered in towns. However, there were also large and numerous Polish pockets scattered in the countryside. This particularly concerned the areas around Lwów and Tarnopol, and they formed the majority population in the countryside in the Wilno region. The Poles included large noble landowners, numerous petty nobility, military settlers, officials, and ordinary villagers, either surrounded by or mingling with Ukrainian and Belarusian peasants. Throughout, in the center-east Prypiats'/Prypeć Marsh area, in particular, there were numerous settlements of people calling themselves "locals" (*tutejsi*), Eastern Orthodox by faith and speaking a dialect between Belarusian and Ukrainian. In addition to a relatively limited number of Lithuanians, there were smaller numbers of Germans, Czechs, and some White Russian émigrés. A few Polish Tatar Muslims[3] and Talmudless Jewish Karaites (Karaim)[4] added an exotic twist into the mix.

Thus, the Soviets acquired quite a heterodox population in western Intermarium. Most of the captive people defined themselves by their religion and nationality. For many of them the integral nationalist (folkish) definition of ethnicity applied. That was, in particular, the case with the so-called nonhistoric nations, who had a largely stateless past (Estonians, Latvians, Ukrainians, and Belarusians) or had been assimilated to a large extent into another culture (Lithuanians). As for the Romanian-speakers of the MSSR, they displayed a mix of national and local consciousness, with pan-Romanian nationalism at its strongest in Bessarabia and Bukovina. Although of ancient pedigree, the Jews were a stateless people, yet acutely aware of their own ethnic and religious distinctiveness. Like the Poles, they were present in every state between Estonia and Moldavia.[5]

The Poles were the only *bona fide* historic nation. As elsewhere, nationalism was in vogue in interwar Poland and "Polish and Catholic" fused as the most common denominator for the majority population. However, in reality, being Polish, in the eastern provinces particularly, remained to a large extent a matter of culture, rather than ethnicity. Hence, almost all willing to assimilate were welcomed in practice, including acculturated Poles of Jewish origin who converted to Christianity and, to a much lesser extent, the so-called Poles of Mosaic faith.

That sort of heterodox plurality was repulsive to the Communists, though. It defied and contradicted the uniformism of Sovietization. Therefore, to control his new subjects, Stalin cordoned off the newly conquered areas both from the Nazi-dominated lands and the Soviet Union proper. Nominally, however, Poland's northeastern provinces were incorporated into the Belorussian Soviet Socialist Republic and the southeastern provinces into the Ukrainian Soviet Socialist Republic. The area around Wilno/Vilnius/Vilna was temporarily handed over to Lithuania (October 1939–June 1940). There the largely Christian Polish population was targeted for aggressive Lithuanization, persistent discrimination, and sporadic violence.[6] Following the conversion of the area into the Lithuanian Soviet Socialist Republic, everyone experienced Sovietization.

Stalin subjected his captive peoples to a crash course in social engineering that had taken twenty years to implement in the USSR. The Soviet occupation administration not only appropriated all state property of Poland, Estonia, Latvia, and Lithuania but also community and private possessions of all ethnic groups in the conquered territories. Private property, except that of small farmers, was confiscated on the spot. Some owners of small and middle-sized urban enterprises were permitted to remain at their posts in a technical or managerial capacity. However, large landed estate owners (in general, Christian Poles but also a few Jews) were uniformly repressed.[7] The countryside was increasingly collectivized. The authorities demanded food quota from the villages. Many of the industrial plants, cargo warehouses, and department stores were looted and their contents shipped to the Soviet Union. Shortages of commercial products and foodstuff occurred frequently.

Churches and synagogues were taxed heavily and sometimes even confiscated. Some were converted to warehouses, Communist "culture" clubs, or military garrisons. Religious figures were persecuted, some arrested, and a few shot, Christians, in particular. All prewar state, political, social, private, and community organizations were dissolved and their leaders repressed. Schools were Sovietized. Some teachers, mostly Poles, were purged, arrested, deported, or even executed. The Polish and Hebrew languages as well as Christian and Jewish religious instruction were removed from schools. All children were forced to learn Russian. Local languages, Ukrainian, Belarusian, and Yiddish, were also taught but used only as conduits for Communist propaganda. Polish culture was banned except when it could be expressed in a Soviet and Communist form. The occupiers fostered a Stalinist version of Ukrainian, Belarusian, and Jewish folk culture *sans* religion as a means to Sovietize the captive peoples.[8]

The Communists held sham elections and established Soviet republics. Everywhere they ruled by terror.[9] In theory, Soviet repression in the Baltics and Poland's eastern provinces was class based. It targeted the ruling elite, state officials, and the well-to-do. However, its members, more often than not, came from the majority ethnic group dominating an occupied state.[10] Hence, the terror had both a class and an ethnic character. This was the case, in particular, with the repression of the "Polish lords." Nearly anyone associated with the Polish state and institutions qualified as such, including, for instance, a Ukrainian Orthodox Christian former hamlet head in Volhynia. Further, because the definition of a "class enemy" was infinitely flexible, the Soviet repressions took on a universal dimension.

There are still no ironclad statistics of death, and perhaps they will never be produced. Russian scholar Alexandr Gurianov concentrated exclusively on

Poland's Eastern Borderlands. According to his very conservative estimate, which is a revision down of his previous calculations, between September 1939 and August 1941, 58,000 Polish citizens lost their lives under the Soviet rule. This includes 33,000 who were executed and 25,000 who died in jail, camps, and various places of exile. The smallest category of victims, 2,000 people, consists of deported refugees, mostly Jewish, who had fled into the Soviet zone before the advancing Nazis. However, Gurianov's periodization fails to provide for the fact that the deportees suffered their greatest losses within a year or so after having been amnestied by Stalin in the bowels of the Gulag in August 1941. They died by their tens of thousands because of maltreatment, diseases, exposure, and malnutrition not only in the USSR but also after their evacuation to Iran. For instance, regional studies from the Białystok region show that the death rate among deportees from individual localities examined was closer to 20 percent, according to Jan Jerzy Milewski. That quadruples most other estimates. Moreover, Gurianov fails to account for the victims of revolutionary fury of the Communists and their collaborators either during the Soviet invasion in September and October 1939 or the Soviet escape in June and July 1941.[11]

To confuse the picture further, there are serious problems with the statistics of mass deportations in the Intermarium, its western part, in particular. There is a tendency to revise the old émigré estimates downwards. It may be warranted to a point, however. Let us consider the evidence.[12]

As early as May 1939, the Soviet government founded the Resettlement Authority with the Council of People's Commissars of the USSR.[13] The purpose of this body was ostensibly to remedy the problem of underpopulation in the northeastern regions of the Soviet Union. In reality, the Resettlement Authority busied itself with organizing another wave of deportations of the so-called undesirable element. After the Soviet invasion of Poland and the occupation of her Eastern Borderlands, the jurisdiction and workload of the Resettlement Authority increased.

On October 27, 1942, a senior Soviet official responsible for the "evacuees," reported that

> in 1939 a total of about 10,000 households [*khoziaistva*] was resettled. The plan for 1940 initially envisioned resettling 29,500 farmsteads. However, the quota was increased to 105,000 households to be deported to Siberia and north-eastern areas of the Kazakh SSR according to resolution no. 572 of the SNK SSSR [Soviet of People's Commissars of the Union of Soviet Socialist Republics] and the TsK VKP(b) [the Central Committee of the Communist Party (Bolsheviks)] of January 21, 1940, on the 'Deportation to the Eastern Areas of the USSR.' Additional resettlement operations, which occurred between the regions, affected 142,880 households and, in total, 162,127, including actions that took place within the republics and special operations.

In fact, in 1940, 135,061 households were resettled, which included over 600,000 people.

According to the plan for 1941, the Resettlement Authority was already obliged to resettle over 200,000 households, mostly to the eastern areas of the Soviet Union—to Siberia and the Far East.[14]

It is unknown to what extent the plan for 1941 was fulfilled. Until the deportation project was terminated in late June 1941, up to 100,000 households may have been affected. Thus, on the basis of the aforementioned document, it can be estimated that, between May 1939 and July 1941, the Soviets deported to the Gulag a minimum of one million and a maximum of two million people.[15] Because the Resettlement Authority was established before the outbreak of World War II, its plan for deportations in 1939 was to be fulfilled primarily, if not only, within the pre-September 1939 territories of the USSR. However, even if the Resettlement Authority did not anticipate the Nazi–Soviet Pact of August 23, 1939 (and thus failed to plan its mass deportations of Polish and other foreign citizens a priori), it can be safely assumed that after the conquest of Poland's Eastern Borderland, the Kremlin, first, automatically extended the jurisdiction of the Resettlement Authority onto the newly acquired territories and, second, increased the overall quota of households to be deported. It can be thus estimated that at least a portion of 10,000 households deported in 1939 came from eastern Poland. Further, it is obvious that after the 1940 plan was increased from 29,500 to 135,061 households, the bulk of the deportees originated from the newly conquered territories of eastern Poland, the Baltics, Finland, and Romania. The same applies to the 200,000 households slated for deportation in 1941. The inhabitants of the Eastern Borderlands bore the brunt of the operation from October 1939 to June 1940; later they were joined by other unfortunates from newly acquired lands.

To summarize, just under the aegis of the Resettlement Authority, the Soviets deported to the Gulag from one to two million people between May 1939 and July 1941. Most of the deportees came from the newly conquered territories, chiefly eastern Poland. The Resettlement Authority worked hand in glove with the Soviet secret police, or People's Commissariat of Internal Affairs (Narodnyi Komissariat Vnutrennykh Del, NKVD), but not all persons in its custody fell under the jurisdiction of the former institution. Individuals and groups arrested, interrogated, imprisoned, and shipped east by the NKVD for any other purpose than "resettlement" are most likely not included in the count above. That means that the estimate of between one and two million persons deported excludes prisoners of jails as well as labor, concentration, and POW camps under the direct supervision of the NKVD.

Granted, our preliminary inquiry outlined above is based upon an interpretation of a single Soviet report. However, this very important document needs yet to be explained by the revisionist scholars who, it seems, have managed to locate only a portion of the records regarding deportations but tend to treat them as the final word.[16]

Pending further research, let us scrutinize the entire process of the deportations, diligently examining each of its stages. Let us retrace the mechanism of the deportations. First, the Politburo gave orders to deport and approved the quota. Second, the details of the plan were worked out by the NKVD high command and disseminated down to the raion level.[17] Third, at the raion and village level the lists of the individual "enemies of the people" and their families, which had been generated through the operations of the *agentura* at the grassroots, were harmonized with the general categories of the undesirables to be deported, which had been sent in from the center. Fourth, armed with the deportation lists thus compiled, the NKVD troikas descended on particular settlements and individual households. At this stage, the lists were not closed for it was left at the discretion of the NKVD and its local collaborators to include additional victims. This way they could claim "revolutionary vigilance" which allowed them to overfulfill the plan of repression locally.

Fifth, having rounded up entire families and having expropriated their entire property but hand luggage, the NKVD and its auxiliary militia escorted the victims to a place of concentration, usually a railway depot. At this point, the deportees were handed over to the railroad troops of the NKVD, who counted them and compared their tally against the lists supplied by the local secret police authorities. Similarly, sixth, at the end of the trip to the eastern and northern parts of the USSR, the railroad NKVD surrendered the victims to the local NKVD officers, who—after counting the human cargo and checking the lists—would then escort the unfortunates to their place of resettlement. Most of the times the deportees were assigned to a kolkhoz, a labor camp really; but occasionally they were just dumped in the middle of nowhere and left to fend for themselves.

We need to look carefully at the prisoner transfer mechanism because it is mostly based on the documents of the railroad NKVD that the revisionist historians stake their claim to the lower victim count. As Tadeusz Piotrowski points out, Polish émigré victim estimates are based upon approximations regarding the capacity of trains used in the deportation process. Another way to estimate the number of deportees is to calculate the average victim load per cattle car. On October 11, 1939, NKVD General Ivan Serov ordered that "an estimate of 25 persons to a car should be observed" but that "it is not permitted to break up a family." Yet, the thousands of Jewish and Christian survivors attested in unison that at a minimum there were twenty-seven persons per car, but more often "about 50" and even the maximum of up to seventy. Thus, it seems, that the NKVD railroad troops violated the order, or perhaps overinterpreted it so as not "to break up a family."[18]

Why would the railroad NKVD ignore their orders? Well, there could be an insufficient number of railway cars available, so people had to be crammed into fewer cars than anticipated. Also, if the railway police troops were issued with food for twenty-five people per car, that was not only insufficient to feed the actual number of about fifty people per car but also it left little for the guards to steal for themselves. This would explain why the deportees suffered hunger on the way to their places of exile. Strange as it may seem, on paper, there were strict regulations against starving deportees and prisoners. And the plan—a Soviet deity—which stipulated that "an estimate of 25 persons per car" were to be fed was an ironclad guarantee that prevented the guards from drawing additional rations for any additional prisoners. Hence, on paper, to tally with the omniscient plan, a transport of a hundred boxcars with 5,000 people would have to be reported as an echelon of 2,500 deportees who were fed that many food rations per day. As often was the case in the Soviet Union, fiction masqueraded as reality. According to Anne Applebaum, who studied the Gulag extensively, Soviet statistics are notoriously unreliable. Why would it be any different with the NKVD railroad records?

On the face of it, the NKVD railway troops should have accepted the deportees at the point of origin, transported them, and passed them on to the appropriate authorities at the destination. However, it appears that invariably the railroad NKVD was forced to accept a number of people which exceeded "an estimate of 25 persons per car," thus violating Serov's order. If the cattle cars were thus stuffed with more deportees than permitted, as they were, it was in the interests of the NKVD train guards to lower the count. Mortality among the deportees, estimated by some at 10 percent, certainly helped. But it was not sufficient enough to eliminate the overpopulation on cattle trucks to the desired level of "an estimate of 25 persons." Instead, since both the deportees had to be delivered and at least lip-service had to be paid to the standing orders, the NKVD railway troops may have doctored the deportation lists, revising them downward. Those lists would be submitted to the superiors at the NKVD railway command. Next, while passing the deportees on to the local NKVD at destination, it was enough to produce the original lists generated by the local NKVD at the point of origin. Those would contain accurate counts with individual names of the deportees listed. And these individual lists remained forever at the local level. Most likely only some general summary reports from each locality were sent up to the raion and then oblast authorities of the NKVD (but not railway NKVD). There, they were further diluted and combined with other similar reports to be dispatched to the republican and, lastly, central commands of the NKVD. And at that point, they were never checked against the separate, and doctored, lists of the railway NKVD. The lists then disappeared into the inscrutable and inaccessible bowels of Soviet secret police archives. This way both the regular NKVD could brag about overfulfilling the plan of repression at the local level, and the railway NKVD could claim that it obeyed the orders and followed the plan. The historians are thus left with "an estimate 25 people per car," as ordered by General Serov.

It seems that the key is to refocus on the deportation process at the point of origin and at destination. And even more appropriately, scholars should begin by scrutinizing the Soviet occupation on a microscale, compiling databases with names of victims of Communism. Juxtaposing them against official Soviet lists would allow us to reign in the chaos of the official statistics. Alas, hitherto there have been almost no case studies of small localities under the Soviet occupation.

Another problem is that historians may be looking at partial evidence for they have focused on narrowly ethnic and regional concerns, such as the deportations from eastern Poland, instead of Soviet imperial considerations. After all, small deportations from a periphery could be easily subsumed under large deportations at the center, and thus overlooked.

Then, there is the question of Communist nomenclature. It is possible that in the Soviet bureaucracy there was a separate category to denote the deportations of "enemies of the people" referred to in ethnic terms as Poles, Jews, and other "former Polish citizens," and yet another, perhaps partly overlapping category, that described "enemies of the people" strictly in class terms. Hence, it is possible that scholars have overlooked, say, some "kulak" deportations, with their point of origin unspecified, which at a closer scrutiny may prove to have occurred in eastern Poland.

We should thus start looking at the Soviet terror from the point of view of the imperial victimizers, and not solely individual victims. This approach forces us to recognize that "the Polish problem" was subsumed under all other imperial considerations and was just one factor, among many, behind Stalin's terror.

Last but not least, scholars are looking at fragmentary evidence because the post-Soviet archives are still not fully accessible. To overcome this handicap at least partly, microstudies of accessible localities should urgently be undertaken to understand better the period between 1939 and 1941.

Keeping the above in mind, for the western part of the Intermarium, occupied by the Soviets, we can estimate that about 100,000 people were executed, including about 22,000 in the so-called Katyn[19] affair and about 40,000 shot during the evacuation of prisons following the Nazi invasion in June 1941. A minimum of 500,000 (according to secret Soviet records) and a maximum of 1.2 million people were deported to the Gulag, where many of them perished. Estonia alone lost 32,000 people to deportations (10,000 in 1941 and 22,000 in 1949), which constituted about 3 percent of the country's population. In addition, the NKVD and People's Comissariat of State Security (Narodnyi Komissariat Gosudarstvennoi Bezopastnosti, NKGB) imprisoned some 7,000 Estonian citizens in 1940–1941. Some were executed locally, but the overwhelming majority of them were convicted and sent to prison camps in the Soviet interior where most of them died. Latvia's losses were equally staggering: almost 15,500 were deported in 1941 including political prisoners, and more than 42,000 in 1949. The corresponding figures for Lithuania were 17,500 in 1941, including political prisoners, of whom around 75 percent were ethnic Lithuanians; and 118,000 were deported in 1944–1953, with a further 70,000 arrested and imprisoned. In addition, at least 5,000 Balts were killed during the brief first Soviet occupation. As for the MSSR, including the occupied Romanian territories, at least 32,000 (and a maximum of 90,000) were deported in 1940 and 1941 (including around 29,000 in the largest operation of June 12–13, 1941) and a minimum of 45,000 experienced similar fate between 1944 and 1953 (including circa 36,000 in the massive action of July 6–7, 1949). Over 30,000 Moldovans suffered arrest, and perhaps 8,000 were executed.

In absolute numbers, a plurality of the victims of Soviet repression in the Intermarium were ethnic Polish Catholics[20]—a minimum of 400,000 out of some five million of their fellow ethnic coreligionists living in the Eastern Borderlands. (Poles constituted some 70 percent of the civilian deportees, while Jews accounted for about 20 percent and Ukrainians and Belarusians around 10 percent.) Within two years, the terror against the Poles leveled off however. The opposite was true for the Ukrainians, as well as the Baltic peoples, because the incidence of repression against them increased as the occupation progressed. The Belarusians meanwhile were treated rather leniently in relative terms throughout. Jewish refugees from central and western Poland were overrepresented among the deportees from eastern Poland, but local Jews were hardly affected. In the Baltics, the victims were overwhelmingly ethnic Estonians, Latvians, and Lithuanians (except in the Wilno area).[21] However, members of every ethnic group, several million in total, were proportionally and forcibly drafted into the Red Army, a clear violation of international law as applied to occupied territories. Many of them were used as cannon fodder by Stalin.

The Soviet occupation policy fluctuated and varied somewhat from one conquered state to the next. As far as Stalin's nationalities policy was concerned, there were a few local peculiarities. These even included occasional concessions to the captive peoples, if temporary and disingenuous.[22] In general, the Soviet dictator aimed at exacerbating tensions between ethnic groups, which already harbored suspicion and even ill-will toward one another.[23] As one local Soviet secret police commander claimed on September 20, 1940, "the Jews have supported us and only they have been visible at all times. It's been fashionable for every [Communist] supervisor of a [state] institution or an enterprise to brag that not a single Pole is employed with him. Many of us were simply afraid of the Poles."[24] This statement certainly applied to some of the Jewish youth, the lumpenproletariat, and more than a few intellectual sympathizers of Communism but not to the Jewish community at large. Local

Jews suffered less terribly than others but, as mentioned, Jewish refugees from central and western Poland were overrepresented among the victims of Soviet repression. In reality, only local ethnic Germans avoided repression for the most part, because, under an agreement with Nazi Germany, they were transferred *en masse* from eastern Poland and the Baltic states to the Polish territories occupied by the Third Reich.[25] Thus, they escaped the tender mercies of Stalin. Other nationalities faced Communist terror and social engineering.

Chronologically, beginning already in September 1939, the Soviets concentrated their ire on the Poles. The latter were at the time also the most frequent victims of attacks by Ukrainian, Belarusian, and Jewish Communists, nationalists, and criminals. At least several thousand Poles—state officials, soldiers, large landowners, and settlers—are believed to have been killed in a wave of murders that mirrored those committed by the German invaders and Fifth Columnists in western Poland in 1939. (These murders augured, albeit on a much smaller scale, the massacres that were to occur when the Nazis turned on the Soviets in June and July 1941). Likewise, some members of the Jewish middle and upper classes were targeted by the same radical and criminal perpetrators in the eastern provinces in the fall of 1939. The Soviets aided and abetted at least some of those actions.[26]

Meanwhile, pro-Soviet revolutionary committees and militias, consisting for the most part of members of the minorities, installed themselves in power. Under the tutelage of the Soviet secret police, NKVD, and Red Army, the militias took part in arresting Polish officials and oversaw the imposition of the Communist rule upon the area. Later, by the end of 1940, the initial revolutionary authorities drawn from the local people were gradually replaced with Soviet citizens, usually ethnic Russians, brought in from the USSR proper.[27]

During the early stage of the Soviet occupation (October 1939–June 1940), it was once again mainly the Christian Poles who felt the brunt of Stalin's wrath. Members of the broadly understood elite, state officials, in particular, down to the village head, political and social activists, and large landowners in toto, were slated for arrest, deportation, or execution.[28] Four massive waves of roundups and deportations took place in February 1940, April 1940, June 1940, and May–June 1941. However, by the fall of 1940, Stalin checked the all-out anti-Polish animus of the NKVD and sought to accommodate his Polish subjects. For example, he even allowed the Polish language to be taught in some schools where the pupils were ethnically Polish.

Nonetheless, the hunt for individual Polish "enemies of the people" and underground groups continued unabated until June 1941. The NKVD rather aptly destroyed the provincial command centers of the Polish underground.[29] Still, local cells survived, albeit they usually lacked contact with the regional and central leadership as well as with one another. A few large Polish partisan units in the field were annihilated by the Soviets by the summer of 1940. However, small survival groups of guerrillas persevered until the summer of 1941.[30]

Of the remaining clandestine movements, the Ukrainian nationalists were the strongest and the most dynamic. They not only maintained links with their counterparts in Nazi-occupied Poland, where they enjoyed German protection, but also with the Nazis themselves. Further, the Ukrainian nationalists managed, initially at least, to infiltrate their operatives into the local administration and, in particular, the revolutionary militia. After the preliminary period, when the NKVD was busy dealing mainly with the Poles, the Soviet secret police turned also against the non-Communist Ukrainian elite, the nationalist underground, in particular. Although it largely limited itself to self-help and seeking out escape routes, the Jewish underground became likewise the focus of Soviet scrutiny.[31] However, the lot of the Belarusian underground under Stalin remains unknown. It is not even obvious that there was any anti-Communist conspiracy except for a few dispersed cells and individuals. However, the Soviet secret police did arrest a few Belarusian nationalists who were considered "counterrevolutionaries" and their much more numerous coethnics who were regarded (and regarded themselves) as acculturated Poles and, thus, members of the educated elite. Some Belarusian victims also fell into the category of Polish state officials, including hamlet heads, foresters, or railroad workers. The same applied to some Ukrainians.

Poland's eastern provinces served as a model for other hapless states conquered by Stalin. After June 1940, the Polish scenario was replayed in the Baltics. The difference was that, before invading, the Soviets forced the Balts to establish Red Army bases in Estonia, Latvia, and Lithuania. Consequently, the Balts put up hardly any armed resistance to the Soviet invasion of June 1940. Also, the initial revolutionary chaos seems to have been much less acute than in Poland in September 1939. Moreover, there was a pronounced participation of ethnic Estonians, Latvians, and, perhaps to a lesser extent, Lithuanians in the revolutionary committees and militias that seized power in the wake of the Red Army and NKVD takeover of their countries.

Otherwise, the Soviet occupation of the Baltic states followed its traditional pattern. Terror ensued. It included arrests, mass deportations, and executions. It was coupled with property confiscation, suppression of organized religion, smashing of the independent political, social, and community life, and the wholesale Sovietization of culture and education. Food shortages became common. Commercial wares disappeared. Discontent quickly set in.[32]

Meanwhile, the nationalist underground movements in Estonia, Latvia, and Lithuania built up their cells in cities and the countryside. They concentrated largely on intelligence gathering and training for the anticipated rising. They also established links with the émigrés who enjoyed the support of the Germans because of the long-range anti-Moscow plans of Berlin. Despite cruel repression by the NKVD, the underground survived until the summer of 1941.

By spring 1941, dissatisfaction with the Soviet occupation was widespread from Estonia to Moldavia. At least some of the erstwhile Soviet supporters cooled in their pro-Communist ardor. Even the lower classes, the putative beneficiaries of the revolution, were rather disappointed with the Communist regime. So were the minorities, excluding the poorest among them and those who benefited from the system. The remnants of the former elite positively seethed with hatred. Except for the Poles[33] and Jews, all nationalist underground movements that maintained contact with the Germans were preparing themselves for an insurrection.[34]

Notes

1. On the Soviet military activities against Poland in September 1939 see Czesław Grzelak, ed., *Agresja sowiecka na Polskę w świetle dokumentów, 17 września 1939*, (*The Soviet Aggression against Poland According to Documents, 17 September 1939*) 3 vols. (Warszawa: Bellona, 1994–1996); Czesław Grzelak, *Kresy w czerwieni: Agresja Związku Sowieckiego na Polskę w 1939 roku* (*The Borderlands in Red: The Aggression of the Soviet Union against Poland in 1939*) (Warszawa: Wydawnictwo Neriton, 1998); Ryszard Szawłowski (Karol Liszewski), *Wojna polsko-sowiecka 1939: Tło polityczne, prawnomiędzynarodowe i psychologiczne; Agresja sowiecka i polska obrona; Sowieckie zbrodnie wojenne i przeciw ludzkości oraz zbrodnie ukraińskie i białoruskie,* (*The Polish–Soviet War, 1939: Political, International-Legal, and Psychological Background; Soviet Crimes against Humanity and Ukrainian and Belarusian Crimes*) 2 vols. (Warszawa: Antyk–Marcin Dybowski, 1997); Jerzy Prochwicz, "Walki oddziałów KOP na obszarach północno-wschodniej Polski," ("Combat of the Units of the Borderlands Defense Corps in North-Eastern Poland") *Białoruskie Zeszyty Historyczne* no. 13 (2000): http://kamunikat.fontel.net/www/czasopisy/bzh/13/13art_prochwicz.htm.

2. See Jan Tomasz Gross, *Revolution from Abroad: The Soviet Conquest of Poland's Western Ukraine and Western Belorussia* (Princeton, NJ: Princeton University Press, 1988); Keith Sword, ed., *The Soviet Takeover of the Polish Eastern Provinces, 1939–41* (New York: St. Martin's Press, 1991); Piotr Chmielowiec, ed., *Okupacja sowiecka ziem polskich (1939–1941)* (*The Soviet Occupation of Polish Lands*) (Rzeszów and Warsaw: Instytut Pamięci Narodowej—Komisja Ścigania Zbrodni przeciwko Narodowi Polskiemu, 2005); Albin Głowacki, "Ogólne założenia sowieckiej polityki okupacyjnej w Polsce," ("General Outlines of the Soviet Occupation Policy in Poland") *Pamięć i Sprawiedliwość* no. 1 (12) (2008): 61–78; Jerzy Węgierski, *Lwów pod okupacją sowiecką, 1939–1941* (*Lwów under the Soviet Occupation*) (Warszawa: Editions Spotkania, 1991); Iurii Shapoval, "Western Ukraine at the Beginning of WW II: Unknown Documents and Facts," in Hunchak and Shtohryn, *Ukraine*, 1–12.

3. See Juljan Talko-Hryncewicz, *Muślimowie czyli tak zwani Tatarzy litewscy* (*Moslems or the So-Called Lithuanian Tatars*) (Kraków: Nakładem Księgarni Geograficznej "Orbis", 1924), also at http://ciekawepodlasie.pl/artykuly/2010/10/muslimowie-czyli-tak-zwani-tatarzy-litewscy/; Jan Tyszkiewicz, *Z historii Tatarów polskich, 1794–1944* (*From the History of Polish Tartars, 1794–1944*) (Pułtusk: Wyższa Szkoła Humanistyczna im. Aleksandra Gieysztora w Pułtusku, 2002); Ali Miśkiewicz, *Tatarzy Polscy, 1918–1939: Życie*

społeczno-kulturalne i religijne (*Polish Tatars, 1918–1939: Socio-Cultural and Economic Life*) (Warszawa: Państwowe Wydawnictwo Naukowe, 1990); Aleksander Srebrakowski, "Tatarzy i Karaimi wileńscy wobec powojennej ewakuacji ludności polskiej i żydowskiej z Litewskiej SRR," ("The Wilno Tatars and Karaites vis-a-vis the Post-War Evacuation of the Polish and Jewish Population from the Lithuanian SSR") *Wrocławskie Studia Wschodnie* no. 3 (1999): 145–54. And see the following essays in Jasiewicz, *Europa nieprowincjonalna*: Stanisław Witold Dumin, "Szlachta tatarska na ziemiach wschodnich dawnej Rzeczypospolitej (1795–1999)," ("Tatar Nobility in the Eastern Lands of the Old Commonwealth") (536–49); and Selim Chazbijewicz, "Represje wobec ludności tatarskiej na byłych ziemiach wschodnich Rzeczypospolitej w I połowie XX. wieku," (The Repressions against the Tatar Population in the Former Eastern Lands of the Commonwealth in the First Half of the 20th Century) (1132–39). For an overview on Muslims in the northern and northwestern part of the Intermarium see the following essays in Göran Larsson, ed., *Islam in the Nordic and Baltic Countries* (London and New York: Routledge, 2009): Aysha Özkan, "Estonia," (90–101); Emin Poljarevic and Ingvar Svangerg, "Latvia," (116–30); and Egdūnas Račius, "Lithuania" (116–30).

4.   One theory is that the Karaites were the descendants of the Khazars, whose leadership converted to Talmudless Judaism. See Grzegorz Pełczyński, *Karaimi polscy* (Polish Karaites) (Poznań: Poznańskie Towarzystwo Przyjaciół Nauk, 2004); Nathan Schur, *History of the Karaites* (Frankfurt a.M. and New York: Peter Lang, 1992).

5.   On the Jewish predicament during the Soviet occupation see Ben-Cion Pinchuk, *Shtetl Jews under Soviet Rule: Eastern Poland on the Eve of the Holocaust* (London: Basil Blackwell, 1990); Don Levin, *The Lesser of Two Evils: East European Jewry under Soviet Rule 1939–1941* (Philadelphia, PA and Jerusalem: The Jewish Publication Society, 1995); Maciej Siekierski and Feliks Tych, eds., *Widziałem Anioła Śmierci: Losy deportowanych Żydów polskich w ZSRR w latach II wojny światowej: Świadectwa zebrane przez Ministerstwo Informacji i Dokumentacji Rządu Polskiego na Uchodźstwie w latach 1942–1943* (*I Saw an Angel of Death: The Fate of the Deported Polish Jews in the USSR during World War Two: Testimonies Collected by the Ministry of Information and Documentation of the Polish Government-in-Exile, 1942–1943*) (Warszawa: Rosener i Wspólnicy, 2006); Evgenii Rozenblat, "Евреи в системе межнациональных отношений в западных областях Беларуси. 1939–1941 гг.," ("Jews in the System of International Relations of the Western Provinces of Belarusia, 1939–1941") *Białoruskie Zeszyty Historyczne* [Białystok] no. 13 (2000): 89–103, http://kamunikat.fontel. net/www/czasopisy/bzh/13/13art_rozenblat.htm; Andrzej Szuchcitz, "Żydzi wobec upadku Rzeczpospolitej w relacjach polskich z Kresów Wschodnich 1939–1941," ("Jews and the Collapse of the Commonwealth According to Polish Testimonies from the Eastern Borderlands, 1939–1941") in Jasiewicz, *Świat Niepożegnany*, 259–65; Grzegorz Motyka and Rafał Wnuk, "Żydzi w Galicji wschodniej i na Wołyniu w latach 1939–1941," ("Jews in Eastern Galicia and Volhynia, 1939–1941") in Jasiewicz, *Europa nieprowincjonalna*, 579–90.

6.   Prewar Lithuania had no foreign policy; it had the so-called "Vilnius question," which dictated nearly all its reactions vis-à-vis Poland up until and after the outbreak of World War II. Like in 1920, in 1939 the Soviets played the Lithuanian cards against the Poles and the Lithuanians were only too happy to oblige. For the background to the Lithuanian occupation of Wilno and its course, including the collusion with the Third Reich and the Soviet Union, see

Šarūnas Liekis, *1939: The Year that Changed Everything in Lithuania's History* (Amsterdam and New York: Rodopi, 2010). For some data on the Lithuanian and Soviet occupations of Wilno between 1939 and 1941 see Poczta do Rządu, Archiwum Akt Nowych, Delegatura Rządu (afterward DR), file 202/I-45, vol. 4, 873–85; Sytuacja Polaków na Litwie i Wileńszczyźnie, Archiwum Zakładu Historii Ruchu Ludowego in Warsaw, the collection of Professor Stanisław Kot, file 92 (afterward, AZHRL, the Kot Collection); the testimonies in Województwo Wileńskie, the Hoover Institution Archives, Polish Government Collection and the General Anders Collection, Ministerstwo Informacji i Dokumentacji (afterward HIA, PGC, GAC, MID); Jarosław Wołkonowski, "Penetracja polskiego podziemia na Wileńszczyźnie przez litewską policję bezpieczeństwa w latach 1939–1941," ("Penetration of the Polish Underground by the Lithuanian Security Police during 1939–1941") in *Społeczeństwo białoruskie, litewskie i polskie na ziemiach północno-wschodnich II Rzeczypospolitej (Białoruś Zachodnia i Litwa Wschodnia) w latach 1939–1941*, ed. by Małgorzata Giżejewska and Tomasz Strzembosz (*Belarusian, Lithuanian, and Polish Communities in the NorthWestern Lands of the 2nd Commonwealth [Western Belorussia and Eastern Lithuania] between 1939–1941*) (Warszawa: ISP PAN, 1995), 340–55; Piotr Łossowski, ed., *Likwidacja Uniwersytetu Stefana Batorego przez władze litewskie w grudniu 1939 roku* (*The Liquidation of the Stefan Batory University by the Lithuanian Authorities in December 1939*) (Warszawa: Wydawnictwo Interlibro, 1991); Andrzej Bogusławski, *W znak Pogoni: Internowanie Polaków na Litwie, wrzesień 1939-lipiec 1940* (*In the Name of the Chase: The Internment of the Poles in Lithuania, September 1939–July 1940*) (Toruń: Europejskie Centrum Edukacyjne, 1994); Tomas Balkelis, "War, Ethnic Conflict and the Refugee Crisis in Lithuania, 1939–1940," *Contemporary European History* 16 (2007): 461–77.

7. A notable exception was the brother of Felix Dzerzhinsky (Feliks Dzierżyński), the founder of the Soviet secret police, who was permitted to remain at his estate in the Nowogródek area. Władysław Dzierżyński was a decent man and a Polish patriot, who participated in the underground and was subsequently shot by the Nazis in 1942. The future Communist dictator of Poland, Wojciech Jaruzelski, and his family were deported to the Gulag on June 14, 1941, from Henryk Hawrykiewicz's estate of Vinkšnupiai in the community of Bartininkai, the County of Vilkaviškis, near Kaunas/Kowno, where they had fled from the Nazis and Soviets. Jaruzelski's father died in exile. See Jerzy Surwiło, *Rachunki nie zamknięte: Wileńskie ślady na drogach cierpień* (*The Unsettled Accounts: The Vilenian Traces on the Road of Suffering*) (Wilno: Biblioteka Magazynu Wileńskiego, 1992), 102–4. For the fate of Poland's landed nobility under the Soviets see Krzysztof Jasiewicz, *Zagłada polskich kresów: Ziemiaństwo polskie na Kresach Północno-Wschodnich Rzeczpospolitej pod okupacją sowiecką, 1939–1941: Studium z dziejów zagłady dawnego narodu politycznego* (*The Destruction of the Polish Borderlands: Polish Landed Nobility in the Northeastern Borderlands of the Commonwealth under the Soviet Occupation, 1939–1941: A Study of the History of the Extermination of the Former Political Nation*) (Warszawa: Oficyna Wydawnicza Volumen and Instytut Studiów Politycznych PAN, 1997). For their lot under both occupiers see Krzysztof Jasiewicz, *Lista strat ziemiaństwa polskiego* (*The List of the Losses of the Polish Landed Nobility*) (Warszawa: Pomost-Alfa, 1995).

8. See Ewa M. Thompson, "Nationalist Propaganda in the Soviet Russian Press, 1939–1941," *Slavic Review* 50, no. 2 (Summer 1991): 385–99; Ewa M. Thompson,

Imperial Knowledge: Russian Literature and Colonialism (Westport, CT: Greenwood Press, 2000); Władimir A. Niewieżyn (Vladimir A. Nevezhin), *Tajne plany Stalina: Propaganda sowiecka w przededniu wojny z Trzecią Rzeszą 1939–1941 (The Secret Plans of Stalin: Soviet Propaganda on the Eve of the War with the Third Reich, 1939–1941)* (Kraków: Arcana, 2000), 79–94; Wojciech Śleszyński, *Okupacja sowiecka na Białostocczyźnie w latach 1939–1941: Propaganda i indoktrynacja (The Soviet Occupation of the Bialystok Region, 1939–1941: Propaganda and Indoctrination)* (Białystok: Agencja Wydawnicza Benkowski and Białostockie Towarzystwo Naukowe, 2001); Янка Трацяк, "Рэлігійная і нацыянальная палітыка КП(б)Б у Заходняй Беларусі ў 1939–1941 гг.," ("Religious and Nationalities Policy of the Communist Party of Belorussia in Western Belarus between 1939 and 1941") *Białoruskie Zeszyty Historyczne* no. 13 (2000): http://kamunikat.fontel.net/www/czasopisy/bzh/13/13art_traciak.htm; Сяргей Токць, "Арганізацыя савецкай уладай агітацыйна-прапагандысцкай работы ў Беластоцкай вобласці ў 1939–1941 гг.," ("The Organization by the Soviet Authorities of Agitation and Propaganda Work in the Bialystok Region between 1939 and 1941") *Białoruskie Zeszyty Historyczne* no. 13 (2000): http://kamunikat.fontel.net/www/czasopisy/bzh/13/13art_tokc.htm; Сяргей Яцкевіч, "Палітыка савецкіх улад адносна нацыянальнага школьніцтва ў Заходняй Беларусі ў 1939–1941 гг.," ("The Policy of the Soviet Authorities toward National Education in Western Belarus") *Białoruskie Zeszyty Historyczne* no. 14 (2000): http://kamunikat.fontel.net/www/czasopisy/bzh/14/14art_jackievicz.htm; В. А. Астрога, "Палітычныя і нацыянальна-культурныя праблемы Заходняй Беларусі 1939–1941 гг. у гістарыяграфіі БССР (1939–1941 гг.)," ("Political and National–Cultural Problems of Western Belarus between 1939 and 1941 in the Historiography of the BSSR") *Białoruskie Zeszyty Historyczne*, no. 13 (2000): http://kamunikat.fontel.net/www/czasopisy/bzh/13/13art_astroha.htm.

9. On the Soviet terror apparatus see Juozas Starkauskas, "The NKVD-MVD-MGB Army," in *The Anti-Soviet Resistance in the Baltic States*, 46–63; Ігар Кузняцоў, "Палітычныя рэпрэсіі ў Беларусі ў 1939–1941 гадах," ("Political Repression in Belarus between 1939 and 1941") *Białoruskie Zeszyty Historyczne* no. 13 (2000): http://kamunikat.fontel.net/www/czasopisy/bzh/13/13art_kuzniacou.htm; Сяргей Сноп, "Асаблівасці дзейнасці судовых органаў СССР на тэрыторыі далучаных абласцей Заходняй Беларусі ў перыяд 1939–1941 гадоў," ("The Peculiarities of the Activities of the Judiciary Organs of the USSR on the Territories of the Incorporated Provinces of Western Belarus between 1939 and 1941") *Białoruskie Zeszyty Historyczne* no. 13 (2000): http://kamunikat.fontel.net/www/czasopisy/bzh/13/13art_snop.htm; Tomasz Bereza, Piotr Chmielowiec, and Janusz Grechuta, *W cieniu "linii Mołotowa": Ochrona granicy ZSRR z III Rzeszą między Wisznią a Sołokiją w latach 1939–1941 (In the Shadow of the Molotov Line: The Protection of the Border between the Third Reich and the USSR between Wisznia and Solkija between 1939 and 1941)* (Rzeszów: Instytut Pamięci Narodowej, KŚZpNP, 2002).

10. See e.g., Nijolė Maslauskienė, "Valdininkijos šalinimas iš okupuotos Lietuvos administracijos ir jos keitimas okupantų talkininkais 1940 m. birželio–gruodžio mėn," ("The Purge of Civil Servants in Soviet Occupied Lithuania between June–December 1940") *Genocidas ir reistencija* no. 2 (8) (2000): http://www.genocid.lt/Leidyba/8/arunas8.htm.

11. See the following two essays in Marcin Zwolski, ed., *Exodus: Deportacje i migracje (wątek wschodni). Stan i perspektywy badań (Exodus: Deportations and*

Migrations [the Eastern Factor]. Research and Its Perspectives) (Warszawa and Białystok: Instytut Pamięci Narodowej – Komisja Ścigania Zbrodni przeciwko Narodowi Polskiemu, 2008): Aleksander Gurjanow, "Sowieckie represje polityczne na ziemiach wschodnich II Rzeczypospolitej w latach 1939–1941," ("Soviet Political Repression in the Eastern Lands of the 2nd Republic, 1939–1941), 21–30, in particular the table on 23; and Jan Jerzy Milewski, "Deportacje z Białostockiego w latach okupacji sowieckiej (1939–1941)," ("Deportations from the Białostok Area during the Soviet Occupation, 1939–1941"), 39.

12. The following section is based upon Marek Jan Chodakiewicz, "Losy Sybiraków: Rozważania o metodologii badań nad czystkami etnicznymi na okupowanych przez Związek Sowiecki ziemiach polskich, 1939–1947," *Glaukopis* no. 4 (2006): 74–96, also in English as "The Fate of the Siberian Exiles," at http://www.iwp. edu/news/newsID.448/news_detail.asp; and Marek Jan Chodakiewicz, "Żydzi na Syberię! Sowiecka polityka wobec żydowskich 'wrogów ludu' na okupowanych Kresach Wschodnich II RP w latach 1939–1943," ("Jews to Siberia! Soviet Policy against Jewish 'Enemies of the People' in the Occupied Eastern Borderlands of the 2nd Republic"), *Glaukopis* no. 11–12 (2008): 425–72.

13. The Resettlement Authority had analogous subordinate bodies on the republican, oblast, and krai levels. Among other things, the Resettlement Authority assumed the functions of two Jewish agencies recruiting and settling "toiling Jews" in various "Jewish settlements" in the USSR. The Jewish agencies were "liquidated by the NKVD." See Spravka, I. Karpov, 27 October 1942, Gosudarstvennyi Arkhiv Rossiyskoi Federatsii (afterward GARF), fond A-327, opis 1, dela 1, lista 45–47.

14. See Spravka, I. Karpov, 27 October 1942, GARF, fond A-327, opis 1, dela 1, lista 45–47.

15. Of course, Soviet official statements made public subsequently denied such estimates. For example, a Soviet official misquoted and lowered the 1940 figure of deportees, depicting it as cumulative for the whole first occupation period: "during the period of 1939–1941 around 135,000 families of up to 500,000 people were resettled to the areas of the Far East, Siberia, and other regions." Nonetheless, during the same meeting, the Soviet officials admitted that in the eastern parts of the Russian Federative Soviet Socialist Republic alone there were over 5 million "evacuees." Were all of them truly "evacuees?" See Zapiska t. A.V. Gritsenko, K.p. povestki Zasedaniia Biuro Sovnarkoma RSFSR, September 1945 (no daily date entered), GARF, fond A-327, op. 1, d. 1, l. 12.

16. The most prominent purveyors of this figure are Stanisław Ciesielski, Grzegorz Hryciuk, and Aleksander Srebrakowski, *Masowe deportacje ludności w Związku Radzieckim* (Toruń: Wydawnictwo Adam Marszałek, 2003), 260–61. At page 246, these authors claim that between 1940 and 1941, the Soviets deported 4.5 percent of the prewar population of Poland's Eastern Borderlands or "over 300,000" people, including about 200,000 ethnic Poles, ca. 70,000 Jews, ca. 25,000 Ukrainians, ca. 15,000 Belorussians, and several thousand Germans, Czechs, Lithuanians, Russians, and others. It seems that the authors overlook those Polish citizens who found themselves in the USSR as prisoners, draftees, refugees, and by other involuntary means. These latter categories are noted, however, in Daniel Boćkowski, *Czas nadziei: Obywatele Rzeczypospolitej Polskiej w ZSRR i opieka nad nimi placówek polskich w latach 1940–1943* (*The Time of Hope: Citizens of the Polish Republic in the USSR and Their Welfare Provided by Polish Outfits, 1940–1943*) (Warszawa: Neriton and Instytut Historii PAN, 1999).

17. See strictly secret Order of the People's Commissar Serov for the Interior of Lithuanian SSR in 1940, Order No. 0054, Kaunas, 28 November 1940; and Appendix, Instructions regarding the manner of conducting the deportations of the anti-Soviet element from Lithuania, Latvia, and Estonia, Strictly Secret, 11 October 1939, *Lituanus: Lithuanian Quarterly Journal of Arts and Sciences* 34, no. 4 (Winter 1988): http://www.lituanus.org/.

18. See strictly secret Order of the People's Commissar Serov for the Interior of Lithuanian SSR in 1940, Order No. 0054, Kaunas, 28 November 1940; and Appendix, Instructions regarding the manner of conducting the deportations of the anti-Soviet element from Lithuania, Latvia, and Estonia, Strictly Secret, 11 October 1939, *Lituanus: Lithuanian Quarterly Journal of Arts and Sciences* 34, no. 4 (Winter 1988): http://www.lituanus.org/, also reproduced as Documents A and B in Tadeusz Piotrowski (ed.), *The Polish Deportees of World War II: Recollection of Removal to the Soviet Union and Dispersal Throughout the World* (Jefferson, NC and London: McFarland & Company, Inc., Publishers, 2004), 203–9. Piotrowski publishes about a score of testimonies of Christians. For a sample of further Christian recollections see Siberian Society of U.S.A., *The Mass Deportation of Poles to Siberia: A Historical Narrative based on the Written Testimony of the Polish Siberian Survivors* (Chicago, IL: Classic Printing, 2009). For Jewish testimonies, which are similar, as far as dynamics and deportation statistics per rail car, see Maciej Siekierski and Feliks Tych, eds., *Widziałem Anioła Śmierci: Losy deportowanych Żydów polskich w ZSRR w latach II wojny światowej: Świadectwa zebrane przez Ministerstwo Informacji i Dokumentacji Rządu Polskiego na Uchodźstwie w latach 1942–1943 (I Saw an Angel of Death: The Fate of the Deported Polish Jews in the USSR during World War Two: Testimonies Collected by the Ministry of Information and Documentation of the Polish Government-in-Exile, 1942–1943)* (Warszawa: Rosener i Wspólnicy, 2006).

19. See Anna M. Cienciala, Natalia S. Lebedeva, and Wojciech Materski, eds., *Katyn: A Crime without Punishment* (New Haven, CT and London: Yale University Press, 2008); Wojciech Materski, ed., *Katyn: Documents of Genocide: Documents and Materials from the Soviet Archives Turned Over to Poland on October 14, 1992* (Warsaw: Institute of Political Studies, Polish Academy of Sciences, 1993); J.K. Zawodny, *Death in the Forest: The Story of the Katyn Forest Massacre* (Notre Dame, IN: University of Notre Dame Press, 1962); Allen Paul, *Katyn: Stalin's Massacre and the Seeds of Polish Resurrection* (Annapolis, MD: Naval Institute Press, 1996); George Sanford, *Katyn and the Soviet Massacre of 1940: Truth, Justice and Memory* (London and New York: Routledge, 2005); Eugenia Maresch, *Katyn 1940: The Documentary Evidence of the West's Betrayal* (Stroud: The History Press, 2010); Jędrzej Tucholski, *Mord w Katyniu: Kozielsk, Ostaszków, Starobielsk – Lista ofiar (The Murder in Katyn: Kozielsk, Ostaszkow, Starobielsk)* (Warszawa: Instytut Wydawniczy PAX, 1991); Sławomir Kalbarczyk, ed., *Zbrodnia katyńska w kręgu prawdy i kłamstw (The Katyn Crime in Light of the Truth and Lies)* (Warszawa: Instytut Pamięci Narodowej, 2010); Natalia Lebiediewa, "Proces podejmowania decyzji katyńskiej," ("The Process of Making the Katyn Decision") in Jasiewicz, *Europa nieprowincjonalna*, 1155–74. For the latest on post-Soviet revisionism and genocide denial as far as Katyn is concerned see Inessa Jażborowska (Inessa Yazhborovskaya), "Russian Historical Writing About the Crime of Katyn," *The Polish Review* LIII, no. 2 (2008): 139–57.

20. NKVD sources indicate the overall number and the destination of the deportations. However, we still lack detailed case studies of the scale of the arrests,

deportations, and executions in each locality in the Borderlands affected by the Soviet terror. For the overall picture on deportations and other aspects of the Soviet terror see Poczta do Rządu, AAN, DR, file 202/I-45, vol. 4, 1039–44; *"Zachodnia Białoruś," 17 IX 1939-22 VI 1941*, vol. 2: *Deportacje Polaków z północno-wschodnich ziem II Rzeczpospolitej, 1940–1941* (*"Western Belarus," 17 September 1939-22 June 1940: Deportations of the Poles from the Northeastern Lands of the 2nd Commonwealth, 1940–1941*) (Warszawa: Oficyna Wydawnicza Rytm, 2001); a bilingual (Polish and Russian) documentary collection *Deportacje obywateli polskich z Zachodniej Ukrainy i Zachodniej Białorusi w 1940 r.* (*Deportations of Polish Citizens from Western Ukraine and Western Belarus in 1940*) (Warszawa and Moscow: Wydawnictwo Rytm, IPN KŚZpNP, MSWiA RP, FSB Federacji Rosyjskiej, 2003); Tomasz Strzembosz, ed., *Okupacja sowiecka (1939–1941) w świetle tajnych dokumentów: Obywatele polscy na Kresach północno-wschodnich II Rzeczypospolitej pod okupacją sowiecką w latach 1939–1941* (*The Soviet Occupation [1939–1941] According to Secret Documents: Polish Citizens in the Northeastern Borderlands of the 2nd Commonwealth under the Soviet Occupation between 1939 and 1941*) (Warszawa: ISP PAN, 1996); Irena Grudzińska-Gross and Jan Tomasz Gross, eds. and comp., *War through Children's Eyes: The Soviet Occupation of Poland and the Deportations, 1939–1941* (Stanford, CA: Hoover Institution Press, 1981); Jan T. Gross and Irena G. Gross, eds., *W czterdziestym nas matko na Sybir zesłali. . .: Rosja a Polska 1939–42* (*They Shipped us, Mother, to Siberia in 1940: Russia and Poland, 1939–42*) (London: Aneks, 1983); Stanisław Ciesielski, Grzegorz Hryciuk, and Aleksander Srebrakowski, *Masowe deportacje radzieckie w okresie II wojny światowej* (*Massive Soviet Deportations during the Second World War*) (Wrocław: Instytut Historyczny Uniwersytetu Wrocławskiego and Wrocławskie Towarzystwo Miłośników Historii, 1994), 26–82; Wojciech Materski, ed., *Z Archiwów sowieckich*, vol. 1: *Polscy jeńcy wojenni w ZSSR* (*From the Soviet Archives: Polish POWs in the USSR*) (Warsaw: ISP PAN, 1992), 9, 21; Daniel Boćkowski, *Czas nadziei: Obywatele Rzeczypospolitej Polskiej w ZSRR i opieka nad nimi placówek polskich w latach 1940–1943* (*The Time of Hope: The Citizens of the Polish Commonwealth in the USSR and Caring for Them by Polish Outposts between 1940 and 1943*) (Warszawa: Neriton and Instytut Historii PAN, 1999); Stanisław Kalbarczyk, "Zbrodnie sowieckie na obywatelach polskich w okresie wrzesień 1939–sierpień 1941: Próba oceny skali zjawiska oraz szacunku strat ludzkich," ("Soviet Crimes against Polish Citizens between September 1939 and August 1941: An Attempt to Estimate the Phenomenon and the Human Losses") *Pamięć i Sprawiedliwość: Biuletyn Głównej Komisji Badania Zbrodni przeciwko Narodowi Polskiemu-Instytut Pamięci Narodowej* 39 (1996): 16–21; Marek Jan Chodakiewicz, "Losy Sybiraków: Rozważania o metodologii badań nad czystkami etnicznymi na okupowanych przez Związek Sowiecki ziemiach polskich, 1939–1947," *Glaukopis* no. 4 (2006): 74–96, also in English as "The Fate of the Siberian Exiles," at http://www.iwp.edu/news/newsID.448/news_detail. asp; Eugeniusz Mironowicz, "Zmiany struktury narodowościowej w zachodnich obwodach Białorusi w latach 1939–1941," ("Changes of National Structure in the Western Provinces of Belarus between 1939 and 1941") *Białoruskie Zeszyty Historyczne* no. 20 (2003): http://kamunikat.fontel.net/www/czasopisy/bzh/20/09.htm; Анатоль Трафімчык, "Зводная табліца дэмаграфічных ацэнак Віленшчыны першай паловы XX стагоддзя: нацыянальны аспект (лакалізацыя вакол тэрыторый, якія адышлі Літве ў 1939 і 1940 гг.)," ("A Table to Assess Demographic Changes in the Wilno Region during the First Half of the 20th Century: The National Aspect [Focusing on the Area Handed Over to Lithuania in 1939 and 1940]") *Białoruskie Zeszyty Historyczne* no. 22 (2004): 173–82: http://kamunikat.fontel.net/pdf/bzh/22/09.pdf; Daniel Boćkowski, "Losy żydowskich uchodźców z centralnej i zachodniej Polski przebywających na Kresach północno-wschodnich w latach 1939–1941," ("The Fate of the Jewish Refugees from Central and Western Poland Who Sojourned in the Northeastern Borderlands between 1939 and 1941") in Jasiewicz, *Świat Niepożegnany*, 91–121; Эмануіл Іофе, "Яўрэйскія бежанцы на тэрыторыі Беларусі (1939–1940 гг)," ("Jewish Refugees in Belarus [1939–1940]") *Białoruskie Zeszyty Historyczne* no. 13 (2000): http://kamunikat.fontel.net/www/czasopisy/bzh/13/13art_iofe.htm; N. S. Lebedeva, "The Deportation of the Polish Population to the USSR, 1939–41," *The Journal of Communist Studies and Transition Politics* 16, no. 1/2 (March/June 2000): 28–45; Natalija Lebedeva, "Lenkijos ir Baltijos šalių gyventojų trėmimas į SSRS 1939–1941 m.: panašumai ir skirtumai," ("The Deportation of the Polish and Baltic Population to the USSR in 1939–1941: Its Regional Specifics"), *Genocidas ir reistencija* no. 2 (10) (2001): http://www.genocid.lt/Leidyba/10/natalija.htm#Polish; Elmārs Pelkaus ed., *Aizvestie: 1941. gada 14. jūnijā* (Rīga: Latvijas Valsts arhīvs and Nordik, 2001) (which is a trilingual work: English, Russian, and Latvian). And see the following essays in Jasiewicz, *Europa nieprowincjonalna*: Daniel Boćkowski, "Masowe deportacje ludności polskiej z tak zwanej Zachodniej Białorusi jesienią 1939 roku" ("Mass Deportations of the Polish Population from the So-Called Western Belarus in the fall of 1939"), 983–92; Albin Głowacki, "Przesiedlenie części ludności z obwodu Lwowskiego do Mołdawi na przełomie lat 1940/1941" ("The Resettlement of a Portion of the Population from the Lwow Region to Moldavia at the End of 1940 and the Beginning of 1941"), 993–1007; Arūnas Bubnys, "Represje sowieckich organów bezpieczeństwa wobec Polaków mieszkających na Litwie i polskiego podziemia w latach 1940–1941" ("The Repressions of the Soviet Security Organs against the Poles Residing in Lithuania and against the Polish Underground, 1940–1941"), 1025–34; and Wojciech Materski, "Z martyrologii narodu estońskiego w latach II wojny światowej: Pierwsza masowa deportacja (czerwiec 1941 roku)" ("From the Martyrology of the Estonian Nation during the Second World War: The First Mass Deportation"), 1175–83.

21. Albert Kalme, *Total Terror: An Expose of Genocide in the Baltics* (New York: Appleton-Century-Crofts, Inc., 1951); Arvydas Anušauskas, *Pirmoji sovietinė okupacija: Teroras ir nusikaltimai žmoniškumui—The First Soviet Occupation: Terror and Crimes against Humanity* (Vilnius: Margi raštai, 2006); Anton Weiss-Wendt, "The Soviet Occupation of Estonia in 1940–41 and the Jews," *Holocaust and Genocide Studies* 12, no. 2 (1998): 308–25.

22. For example, in October 1940, Stalin allowed the Jews of Lwów to have a day off to celebrate the Day of Atonement. See Dimitri Volkogonov, *Lenin: A New Biography* (New York: The Free Press, 1994), 385. In another case, in December 1940, the NKVD proclaimed a local amnesty in the Jedwabne *rayon* to entice the Polish underground fighters to give themselves up. No evidence of a similar offer has surfaced in any other regions under Soviet occupation, notwithstanding that most Poles foolish enough to turn themselves in were subsequently arrested or forced to become secret police snitches. See Marek Jan Chodakiewicz, *The Massacre in Jedwabne, July 10, 1941: Before, During, After* (New York and Boulder, CO: Columbia University Press and East European Monographs, 2005). For the initial period of the Soviet occupation in Poland's southeastern territories, particularly as it impacted the Ukrainian population, see Mikola Litvin, Ostap

Lutskyi, and Kim Naumenko, *1939: Zakhidni zemli Ukrayini* (*1939: Western Ukraine*) (Lviv: Institut ukrainoznastva im. I. Krypayakevicha NAN Ukrainyi, 1999).

23. On ethnic conflict in Poland's eastern provinces under the Soviet occupation see Andrzej Żbikowski, "Konflikty narodowościowe na polskich Kresach Wschodnich (1939–1941)," ("National Conflicts in the Polish Eastern Borderlands [1939–1941]") (in:) Jasiewicz, *Tygiel narodów*, 409–27; Elazar Barkan, Elizabeth A. Cole, and Kai Struve, eds., *Shared History – Divided Memory: Jews and Others in Soviet-Occupied Poland, 1939–1941* (Leipzig: Leipziger Universitätsverlag, 2007). On Polish–Jewish relations during the first Soviet occupation see Marek Wierzbicki, *Polacy i Żydzi w zaborze sowieckim: Stosunki polsko-żydowskie na ziemiach północno-wschodnich II RP pod okupacją sowiecką (1939–1941)* (*Poles and Jews under the Soviet Partition: Polish–Jewish Relations in the North-Western Lands of the Second Republic under the Soviet Occupation [1939–1941]*) (Warszawa: Fronda, 2001); Marek Wierzbcki, "Polish-Jewish Relations in the City of Vilna and the Region of Western Vilna under Soviet Occupation, 1939–1941," in *Polin: Studies in Polish Jewry*, vol. 19: *Polish-Jewish Relations in North America* (Oxford and Portland, OR: The Littman Library of Jewish Civilization, 2007), 487–516; Marek Wierzbicki, "Western Belarus in September 1939: Revisiting Polish-Jewish Relations" in Barkan et al., *Shared History – Divided Memory*; Bogdan Musiał, "Stosunki polsko-żydowskie na kresach wschodnich R.P. pod okupacją sowiecką 1939–1941," ("Polish-Jewish Relations in the Eastern Borderlands of Poland under the Soviet Occupation, 1939–1941") *Biuletyn Kwartalny Radomskiego Towarzystwa Naukowego* 34, no. 1 (1999): 103–25; Jerzy Robert Nowak, *Przemilczane zbrodnie: Żydzi i Polacy na Kresach w latach 1939–1941* (*The Crimes Kept Silent About: Jews and Poles in the Borderlands, 1939–1941*) (Warszawa: Wydawnictwo von borowiecky, 1999); Andrzej Żbikowski, *U genezy Jedwabnego: Żydzi na Kresach Północno-Wschodnich II Rzeczypospolitej. Wrzesień 1939–lipiec 1941* (*Genesis of Jedwabne: Jews in the North-Eastern Borderlands of the Commonwealth, September 1939–July 1941*) (Warszawa: Żydowski Instytut Historyczny, 2006); Mark Paul, *Neighbours on the Eve of the Holocaust: Polish-Jewish Relations in Soviet-Occupied Eastern Poland, 1939–1941*, http://www.kpk-toronto.org/archives/sovocc.pdf. On Polish–Belarusian relations see Marek Wierzbicki, *Polacy i Białorusini w zaborze sowieckim: Stosunki polsko-białoruskie na ziemiach północno-wschodnich II Rzeczypospolitej pod okupacją sowiecką, 1939–1941* (*Poles and Belarusians under the Soviet Partition: Polish–Belarusian Relations in the Northeastern Lands of the Second Republic under the Soviet Occupation, 1939–1941*) (Warszawa: Oficyna Wydawnicza Volumen, 2000); Marek Wierzbicki, "Stosunki polsko-białoruskie pod okupacją sowiecką (1939–1941)," ("Polish-Belarusian Relations under the Soviet Occupation, 1939–1941") *Białoruskie Zeszyty Historyczne* 20 (2003): 172–202. And see a critical review of Wierzbicki's monograph by Eugeniusz Mironowicz in *Białoruskie Zeszyty Historyczne* 18 (2002): 251–62.

24. Quoted in Michał Gnatowski, *W radzieckich okowach: Studium o agresji 17 września 1939 r. i radzieckiej polityce w regionie łomżyńskim w latach 1939–1941* (*In Soviet Chains: A Study of the Aggression of September 17, 1939, and the Soviet Policy in the Łomża Region, 1939–1941*) (Łomża: Łomżyńskie Towarzystwo Naukowe im. Wagów, 1997), 159.

25. See Vladis O. Lumans, *Himmler's Auxiliaries: The Volksdeutsche Mittelstelle and the German National Minorities of Europe, 1933–1945* (Chapel Hill, NC:

University of North Carolina Press, 1993); John Basarab, "The 1939–1940 German-Soviet Population Exchange in Western Ukraine," in Hunczak and Shtohryn, *Ukraine*, 311–34.

26. Some Ukrainian nationalists were carrying out these attacks as a part of an anti-Polish offensive designed jointly with the Germans, in the Province of Stanisławów, for example. The Communists were naturally working for Stalin, and the criminal elements took advantage of the breakdown of law and order. Sometimes all three phenomena overlapped. See Ryszard Szawłowski (Karol Liszewski), *Wojna polsko-sowiecka 1939: Tło polityczne, prawnomiędzynarodowe i psychologiczne; Agresja sowiecka i polska obrona; Sowieckie zbrodnie wojenne i przeciw ludzkości oraz zbrodnie ukraińskie i białoruskie* (*The Polish-Soviet War, 1939: Political, International-Legal, and Psychological Background; Soviet Crimes against Humanity and Ukrainian and Belarusian Crimes*) 2 vols. (Warszawa: Antyk–Marcin Dybowski, 1997); Ryszard Szawłowski, "Antypolskie wystąpienia na Kresach Wschodnich (1939–1941)," ("Anti-Polish Actions in the Eastern Borderlands, 1939–1941") in *Encyklopedia "Białych Plam"* (Radom: Polskie Wydawnictwo Encyklopedyczne, 2000) vol. 1, 165–69; "*Zachodnia Białoruś, 17 IX 1939-22 VI 1941*, vol. 1: *Wydarzenia i losy ludzkie, 1939* ("*Western Belarusia," 17 September 1939–22 June 1941: Events and the Fate of the People, 1939*) (Warszawa: Oficyna Wydawnicza Rytm, 1998); Marek Wierzbicki, *Polacy i Białorusini w zaborze sowieckim: Stosunki polsko-białoruskie na ziemiach północno-wschodnich II Rzeczypospolitej pod okupacją sowiecką, 1939–1941* (*Poles and Belarusians under the Soviet Partition: Polish–Belarusian Relations in the North-Eastern Lands of the Second Polish Republic under the Soviet Occupation, 1939–1941*) (Warszawa: Oficyna Wydawnicza Volumen, 2000); Andrzej Szefer, "Dywersyjno-sabotażowa działalność wrocławskiej Abwhery na ziemiach polskich w przededniu agresji hitlerowskiej w 1939 r.," ("Diversion and Sabotage by the Breslau Abwehr in Poland on the Eve of the Nazi Aggression in 1939") *Biuletyn Głównej Komisji Badania Zbrodni Hitlerowskich w Polsce* 32 (1987): 274. The Wrocław-based periodical *Na Rubieży* also provides many examples of these occurrences. To compare with conditions in western Poland see Alexander B. Rossino, *Hitler Strikes Poland: Blitzkrieg, Ideology, and Atrocity* (Lawrence, KS: University Press of Kansas, 2003), 14–16; Czesław Pilichowski, ed., *Zbrodnie i sprawy: Ludobójstwo hitlerowskie przed sądem ludzkości i historii* (Warsaw: Państwowe Wydawnictwo Naukowe, 1980), 504–18; Karol Marian Pospieszalski, "Straty osobowe mniejszości niemieckiej w Polsce we wrześniu 1939 roku: Przeglądowe studium źródłowe nad tzw. sprawą 58 000 Volksdeutschów," ("The Losses of the German Minority in Poland in September 1939: A Review of Sources Concerning the So-Called Case of 58,000 Ethnic Germans") *Studia źródłoznawcze: Commentationes* 35 (1997): 101–8; Janusz Kutta, ed., *Pierwsze dni września 1939 roku w Bydgoszczy: Materiały z sympozjum* (*First Days of September 1939 in Bydgoszcz: Conference Material*) (Bydgoszcz: Miejski Komitet Ochrony Pamięci Walk i Męczeństwa, 2001); Tomasz Chinciński, "Niemiecka dywersja w Polsce w 1939 r. w świetle dokumentów policyjnych i wojskowych II Rzeczypospolitej oraz służb specjalnych III Rzeszy, część 1 (marzec–sierpień 1939 r.)," *Pamięć i Sprawiedliwość* no. 2 (2005): 159–95; Tomasz Chinciński, "Niemiecka dywersja w Polsce w 1939 r. w świetle dokumentów policyjnych i wojskowych II Rzeczypospolitej oraz służb specjalnych III Rzeszy, część 2 (sierpień–wrzesień 1939 r.)," *Pamięć i Sprawiedliwość* no. 1 (2006): 165–97; Tomasz Chinciński and Paweł Machcewicz, eds., *Bydgoszcz 3–4 września 1939: Studia i dokumenty*

(Warsaw: Instytut Pamięci Narodowej–Komisja Badania Zbrodni przeciwko Narodowi Polskiemu, 2008), passim, especially 170–204, 338–52; Christian Jansen and Arno Weckbecker, *Der "Volksdeutsche Selbstschutz" in Polen 1939/40* (München: Oldenbourg, 1992).

27. See Wojciech Śleszyński, "Sowieckie kadry na Białostocczyźnie (1939–1941)," ("Soviet Cadres in the Bialystok Region, 1939–1941") *Arcana* no. 4–5/46–47 (July–October 2002): 239–50; Krzysztof Jasiewicz, ed., *Pierwsi po diable: Elity sowieckie w okupowanej Polsce 1939–1941 (Białostocczyzna, Nowogródczyzna, Polesie, Wileńszczyzna) (The First After the Devil: Soviet Elites in Occupied Poland, 1939–1941 [The Regions of Białystok, Nowogródek, Polesie, and Wilno])* (Warsaw, London, and Paris: PASFT, ISP PAN, Oficyna Wydawnicza "Rytm," 2002); Krzyszytof Jasiewicz, "Aparat sowiecki na ziemiach wschodnich II Rzeczpospolitej jako model patologicznego funkcjonowania klasy politycznej (1939–1953)," in Jasiewicz, *Tygiel narodów*, 39–94; Міхаіл Васілючак, "Кадравая палітыка саветаў у Крынкаўскім раёне Беластоцкай вобласці (верасень 1939–чэрвень 1941 гг.)," ("The Cadre Policy of the Soviets in the Krynki Area of the Bialystok Region") *Białoruskie Zeszyty Historyczne* no. 20 (2003): http://kamunikat.fontel.net/www/czasopisy/bzh/20/11.htm; Nijolė Maslauskienė, "Lietuvos komunistų tautinė ir socialinė sudėtis 1939 m. pabaigoje–1940 m. rugsėjo mėn.," ("The Social and National Composition of the Communists of Lithuania from the End of 1939 to September 1940"), *Genocidas ir reistencija* no. 1 (5) (1999): http://www.genocid.lt/Leidyba/5/nijole5.htm; Nijolė Maslauskienė, "Lietuvos komunistų sudėtis 1940 m. spalio–1941 m. birželio mėn," ("Composition of the Communist Party of Lithuania between October 1940 and June 1941"), *Genocidas ir reistencija* no. 2 (6) (1999): http://www.genocid.lt/Leidyba/6/nijole6.htm#Composition%20of%20the%20Communist%20Party%20of%20Lithuania%20between%20October%201940%20and%20June; Nijolė Maslauskienė, "Lietuvos tautinių mažumų įtraukimas į LSSR administraciją ir sovietinės biurokratijos tautiniai santykiai 1940–1941 m.," ("The Involvement of Ethnic Minorities in the Administration of the LSSR and Ethnic Relations in the Soviet Bureaucracy between 1940 and 1941"), *Genocidas ir reistencija* no. 1 (9) (2001): http://www.genocid.lt/Leidyba/9/nijole.htm#Nijolė. For a regional study see Michał Gnatowski, *"Sąsiedzi" w sowieckim raju: Rejon jedwabieński pod radziecką władzą 1939–1941 ("Neighbors" in Soviet Paradise: The Jedwabne Region under the Soviet Rule, 1939–1941)* (Łomża: Łomżyńskie Towarzystwo Naukowe im. Wagów, 2002).

28. On a microscale see, for example, the lot of the foresters, their families, and their property in Michał Gnatowski, "Deportacja osadników i służby leśnej oraz ich rodzin z regionu łomżyńskiego na wschodnie obszary ZSRR w lutym 1940 roku," ("Deportations of the Settlers and Foresters as well as Their Families from the Łomża Region to the Eastern Parts of the USSR in February 1940") *Studia Łomżyńskie* 7 (1996): 49–66.

29. There was a plethora of local and regional Polish secret outfits. However, the Union of Armed Struggle (Związek Walki Zbrojnej, ZWZ) was the largest resistance group active in both zones of occupation of Poland. Later, in 1942, after absorbing other clandestine organizations, it became known as the Home Army (AK). See the bilingual (Polish and Russian) documentary collection *Polskie podziemie na terenach Zachodniej Ukrainy i Zachodniej Białorusi w latach 1939–1941, (Polish Underground in Western Ukraine and Western Belarus between 1939 and 1941)* 2 vols. (Warszawa and Moscow: Wydawnictwo Rytm, Ministerstwo Spraw Wewnętrznych i Administracji Rzeczpospolitej

Polskiej and Służba Bezpieczeństwa Federacji Rosyjskiej, 2001); the bilingual (Polish and Ukrainian) documentary collections: *Polskie podziemie 1939–1941: Lwów, Kołomyja, Stryj, Złoczów (Polish Underground, 1939–1941: Lwów, Kołomyja, Stryj, Złoczów)* (Warszawa and Kiev: Wydawnictwo Rytm, IPN KŚZpNP, Archiwum MSWiA RP, Państwowe Archiwum Służby Bezpieczeństwa Ukrainy, 1998); *Polskie podziemie 1939–1941: Od Wołynia do Pokucia, (Polish Underground, 1939–1941: From Volhynia to Pokucie)* parts 1–2 (Warszawa and Kiev: Wydawnictwo Rytm, IPN KŚZpNP, Archiwum MSWiA RP, Państwowe Archiwum Służby Bezpieczeństwa Ukrainy, 2004), which are, respectively, volumes 1 and 3 of *Polska i Ukraina w latach trzydziestych i czterdziestych XX wieku. Nieznane dokumenty z archiwów służb specjalnych (Poland and Ukraine in the 1930s and 1940s of the 20th Century: Unknown Documents from the Archives of Secret Services)*. See also Piotr Kołakowski, "Sowiecki aparat bezpieczeństwa wobec podziemia polskiego na Kresach Wschodnich 1939–1941: Zarys problematyki," ("The Soviet Security Apparatus against the Polish Underground in the Eastern Borderlands, 1939–1941: An Outline") in *Polska i jej wschodni sąsiedzi w XX wieku: Studia i materiały ofiarowane prof. dr. hab. Michałowi Gnatowskiemu w 70-lecie urodzin, (Poland and Her Eastern Neighbors in the 20th Century: A Festschrift for Prof. Gnatowski)* ed. by Hanna Konopka and Daniel Boćkowski (Białystok: Wydawnictwo Uniwersytetu w Białymstoku, 2004), 295–309; Michał Gnatowski, *Niepokorna Białostocczyzna: Opór społeczny i polskie podziemie niepodległościowe w regionie białostockim w latach 1939–1941 w radzieckich źródłach (The Unbending Bialystok Region: Civil Resistance and the Polish Independentist Underground in the Bialystok Area, 1939–1941, According to Soviet Documents)* (Białystok: Instytut Historii Uniwersytetu w Bialymstoku, 2001); Elżbieta Kotarska, *Proces czternastu (Trail of the Fourteen)* (Warszawa: Oficyna Wydawnicza Volumen, 1998).

30. For a case study of a single local Polish guerrilla outfit and its underground backers see Tomasz Strzembosz, *Antysowiecka partyzantka i konspiracja nad Biebrzą: X 1939– VI 1941 (The Anti-Soviet Partisan Movement and Conspiracy around Biebrza, October 1939–June 1941)* (Warszawa: Neriton, 2004); and Tomasz Strzembosz and Rafał Wnuk, *Czerwone Bagno: Konspiracja i partyzantka antysowiecka w augustowskiem, wrzesień 1939-czerwiec 1941 (Red Swamp: Anti-Soviet Underground and Partisan Movement in the Augustów Area, September 1939–June 1941)* (Gdańsk and Warszawa: Wydawnictwo Naukowe Scholar and Muzeum II Wojny Światowej, 2009). On the Polish underground under the first Soviet occupation see the following essays in Jasiewicz, *Europa nieprowincjonalna*: Andrzej Krzysztof Kunert, "Powołanie Komendy Obszaru Nr. 3 ZWZ we Lwowie i Komendy Okupacji Sowieckiej ZWZ w świetle dokumentacji Komendy Głównej ZWZ w Paryżu" ("The Founding of the Region 3 Command of the ZWZ in Lwów According to the Documents of the ZWZ High Command in Paris") (662–68); Grzegorz Mazur, "Walka NKWD ze Związkiem Walki Zbrojnej na Kresach Południowo-Wschodnich w świetle dokumentów z polskich archiwów w Londynie" ("The Struggle of the NKVD against the ZWZ in the Southeastern Borderlands According to the Documents in the Polish Archives in London") (669–78); Jędrzej Tucholski, "Polskie podziemie antysowieckie w województwie wołyńskim w latach 1939–1941 w świetle materiałów NKWD" ("The Polish Anti-Soviet Underground in the Volhynia Province between 1939 and 1941 According to the NKVD Sources") (679–95); and Bernadetta Gronek, "Początek konspiracji antysowieckiej na terenie 'Zachodniej Białorusi' (wrzesień 1939-lipiec 1940) w świetle dokumentów NKWD" ("The Origins of the

Anti-Soviet Conspiracy in 'Western Belarus' According to NKVD Documents") (696–719).

31. Clandestine Jewish organizations were simply avatars of prewar parties, including the far-right Zionists Revisionists (who were the most anti-Soviet). No Jewish underground group preached or practiced armed resistance. They chiefly limited themselves to political agitation and self-assistance for its members. In most cases, except briefly in Lithuanian-occupied Wilno/Vilnius, the Jews refused to cooperate with the Polish underground as they claimed that they were not interested in the restoration of the Polish state but in establishing the state of Israel. See Piotr Gontarczyk, ed., "Komunistyczny antysemityzm kontra żydowski antykomunizm, 1939–1941," (Communist Anti-Semitism vs. Jewish Anti-Communism, 1939–1941) *Glaukopis* 2/3 (2004–2005): 330–42; Bogdan Musiał, "Jewish Resistance in Poland's Eastern Borderlands during the Second World War, 1939–1941," *Patterns of Prejudice* 38, no. 4 (December 2004): 371–82. In his study on Jews in Soviet-occupied Eastern Poland, Dov Levin concludes that the activity of Jewish underground organizations was not of a military nature nor was it opposed to Soviet rule in principle: "These movements did not regard themselves as enemies of the regime, instead hoping that over time the regime would change its policies regarding Judaism and Zionism. . . . even though the Zionist youth movements were hounded by the security services throughout this period, none of them (not even Betar) professed hostile trends or thoughts, and all were careful to avoid any manifestation of anti-Sovietism." Consequently, he questions whether it was an underground at all and poses the question: "did these activities and undertakings conform to the conventional model of a 'classic' underground, or were they no more than a string of illegal activities?" See Levin, *The Lesser of Two Evils*, 235–56, especially 255–56. As a result, the reaction of the authorities to Jewish underground activities was muted: "While the authorities cracked down on non-Jewish underground activity, they usually countered such operations by Jewish groups (almost all of which were Zionist youth movements) with propaganda only. Arrests, trials, and deportations were ordinarily invoked only when centers of activity were exposed by chance or by informers." Ibid., 296. The Soviets did not put obstacles in the way of some Bundists and other Jewish political activists who applied for permission to leave the Soviet Union after the Red Army entered Lithuania in June 1940. According to Daniel Blatman: "the Soviets refrained from harassing Jewish political activists and even allowed many of them to leave." Several thousand Jews managed to leave the Soviet Union legally, depleting the Jewish community of its leadership cadres. See Daniel Blatman, *For Our Freedom and Yours: The Jewish Labour Bund in Poland, 1939–1949* (London and Portland, OR: Vallentine Mitchell, 2003), 26–30.

32. For various evolving attitudes of the civilian population toward the Soviet occupation see Wojciech Wrzesiński, "Postawy i nastroje Polaków po klęsce wrześniowej na terenie okupacji sowieckiej," ("Attitudes of the Poles Following the September Defeat Under the Soviet Occupation") in *Komunizm: Ideologia, system, ludzie, (Communism: Ideology, System, People)* ed. Tomasz Szarota (Warszawa: Wydawnictwo Neriton and Instytut Historii PAN, 2001), 27–39. For a case study of property confiscation see Vidas Grigoraitis, "Lengvųjų automobilių nacionalizavimas Lietuvoje," (Nationalization of Motorcars in Lithuania during the Soviet Occupation) *Genocidas ir rezistencija* no. 1 (5) (1999): http://www.genocid.lt/Leidyba/5/vidas.htm#Nationalisation%20of%2 0motorcars%20in%20Lithuania%20After%20Soviet%20Occupation.

133

33.   Although the Polish underground did not collaborate with the Nazis, at least
       one junior rank underground leader of the *Kresowe Bataliony Śmierci* went
       rogue and cooperated with the Germans in the Białystok border area. On the
       other hand, at least one Polish NCO worked with the NKVD against the Nazis
       on the southeastern border near Przemyśl. Naturally, Poland's Communists
       collaborated with the Soviets en bloc. For example, Mykola Demko (a.k.a
       Mieczysław Moczar), an ethnic Ukrainian, was a Soviet military intelligence
       (GRU) agent. His assignment was border penetration missions.

34.   See the following essays in *The Anti-Soviet Resistance in the Baltic States*:
       Valentinas Brandiškas, "Anti-Soviet Resistance in 1940 and 1941 and the Revolt
       of June 1941" (8–22), Juris Ciganovs, "The Resistance Movement against the
       Soviet Regime in Latvia between 1940 and 1941" (122–30), and Tiit Noormets,
       "The Summer War: The 1941 Armed Resistance in Estonia" (186–208). See also
       Wolodymyr Stojko, "Ukrainian National Aspirations and German Designs on
       Ukraine," in Hunczak and Shtohryn, *Ukraine*, 13–22.

11

The Nazi Occupation (1941–1944)

In June 1941, Hitler attacked his erstwhile ally, Stalin. As Nazi-led coalition troops pounced east, an insurrection broke out from Estonia to Moldavia. In many areas, the captive peoples rose against the hated Soviets. Some insurgent leaders coordinated their rising with the Germans. Others rebelled spontaneously. Occasionally, they attacked the retreating Red Army troops and, more often, meted out rough justice to local Communists and their collaborators. Simultaneously, during the retreat, the Soviet leadership issued an order to "shoot counterrevolutionary elements." No prisoner was to fall into the hands of the Germans. As mentioned, an estimated 40,000 inmates were massacred in jails and during the evacuation on the roads east.[1]

At the same time, acting upon a preconceived scenario, the Nazis began mass murdering Jews. This was a new development. For the first two years of the war, as mentioned already, the majority of victims tended to be Christian, Catholics in particular. Now, the Intermarium witnessed the onset of the Holocaust.[2] The initial phase lasted from June 1941 until January 1942, by which time most of the Jews in the Baltic states were killed. First, special police execution squads, the *SS-Einsatzgruppen*, took to the field, directing and carrying out executions. Second, Nazi police leaders incited and led the riffraff, anti-Communist insurgents, and others among the local population to assault Jews. Third, during the summer of 1941, some locals, usually from the majority group, killed a number of Jews spontaneously without any encouragement. Most perpetrators justified their actions by anti-Communism, alleging that they thus dealt harshly with Soviet collaborators. The argument is spurious because in most instances the local Jewish communities were subjected to collective reprisals, although many individual Soviet collaborators were also targeted.[3]

During the initial period of anarchy, Ukrainian, Lithuanian, Latvian, and Estonian underground activists and émigré politicians attempted to reestablish their own governments and independent states, if allied with Germany. Although only the Balts had enjoyed a twenty-two-year spell of peace, independence, and freedom (1918–1940), the period of Ukrainian self-determination was brief (1918–1921). Nonetheless, there had been a Ukrainian government and a Ukrainian state, albeit without any fixed borders, in 1918–1921. The effort to set up a Ukrainian regime in the summer of 1941 should be viewed as a continuation of an earlier bid for independence which was terminated by the Soviets and the Poles.

Like the Romanians, Hungarians, Bulgarians, and others, except the Poles and Jews, the Balts and Ukrainians banked on Hitler. The Nazi dictator would have none of that. Instead, the Germans imposed direct rule on the initially friendly peoples. Undoubtedly, after the nightmare of the Soviet occupation, at least some of the Jewish community awaited the Germans with considerable relief and sometimes even hope. Most Poles rejoiced to see the Red Army routed and some even greeted the conquering German soldiers for freeing them from Soviet oppression. The Balts overwhelmingly and actively welcomed the troops of the Third Reich as did Ukrainians and many Belarusians, hoping to receive support for their own statehood. The new masters cared about the local displays of enthusiasm only to the extent that the Nazis channeled the pro-German animus of many of the denizens of the Intermarium against the Jews and Communists. Everywhere from Estonia to Moldavia, the SS and the *Wehrmacht* used the locals, usually drafted from the majority populations, as their civilian and police auxiliaries at the middle and lowest rungs of the administrative system. A new occupation commenced. The only exception was Moldavia, which, to the joy of most of its inhabitants, and the relief of some, was reincorporated into Romania. Henceforth, pro-Nazi collaboration on anti-Jewish and anti-Communist level took place within the framework of Bucharest's internal and external policy. Most notably, a mass slaughter of Bessarabian and Bukovinian Jews commenced after their deportation to Transnistria.

As the front rolled off to the east, the Nazis civilian bureaucrats appeared in the Intermarium. They divided the newly captured territories into artificial administrative units.[4] Whereas the immediate front area was controlled by the military, the civilian and police authorities vied for influence in the so-called *Reichskommissariat Ostland* and *Reichskommisariat Ukraine*. The former comprised the Baltic states, Poland's northeastern provinces, and a chunk of formerly Soviet Belorussia. The latter consisted of Poland's Volhynia (Province of Wołyń) and erstwhile Soviet Ukraine.[5] Smaller areas in the north-west (around Białystok, renamed *Bezirk Białystok*) and south-west (Eastern Galicia, dubbed *Distrikt Galizien*) were incorporated, respectively, into Germany proper and the General Government (*Generalgouvernement*).

In the newly occupied territories, the Third Reich automatically appropriated all Soviet state property (which had been originally seized from the Baltic states and Poland as well as their community groups and individual citizens). The Nazis also refused to return confiscated private property to the rightful owners. Nonetheless, the new occupiers allowed the locals to manage small and medium-size enterprises with some German oversight. In the countryside, this benefited, in particular, the remnants of the Polish landed nobility, who emerged from hiding. Significantly, the new occupiers did not decollectivize the countryside. The Nazi authorities also completely expropriated the Jews.

As far as religion is concerned, Christianity was tolerated, Protestantism in particular. There was a virtual Eastern Orthodox renaissance, especially in the areas of erstwhile Soviet Belorussia and Ukraine remaining under direct German military rule. Churches were returned to their pastors. The clergy was left largely unmolested except when the Nazis considered its individual representatives as sources of resistance. Catholicism was cyclically repressed because the Nazis deemed it to be the chief expression of Polish nationalism. Hundreds of Polish priests and nuns were imprisoned, and many even shot, usually in collective reprisals but also for assisting the underground and Jews. On the other hand, the Lithuanian Catholic clergy and Uniate (Ukrainian) Catholic Church remained virtually untouched.[6]

Judaism was outlawed altogether, at least officially (along with any form of Jewish education, whether in Hebrew or Yiddish, though Jewish schools did flourish in the Wilno ghetto from 1942 to mid-1943 and for periods in other ghettos). The Nazis inherited from the Soviets the synagogues, ritual baths, schools, and cemeteries and, additionally, they immediately confiscated those precious few Jewish assets not previously expropriated by the Communists. The religious and community properties were sometimes converted to other use; more often than not, they were destroyed. Having already been deracinated, atomized, and persecuted and having had their community institutions pulverized by the Soviets, the rabbis and their flocks constituted an easy target for extermination.

Meanwhile, the Estonians, Latvians, and Lithuanians were allowed to reestablish their own educational systems up to, and occasionally including, the university level. The Ukrainians and Belarusians were permitted to continue school instructions in their own languages, naturally in a nationalistic vain and deferent to the Nazis. They were also encouraged to cultivate their folk culture. Meanwhile, the Poles were only admitted to elementary and, less frequently, basic-level vocational education. Polish culture continued to be banned. Likewise, almost all Polish community, social, and political institutions remained outlawed. Exceptionally, distinctly Polish charity organizations were permitted in the southeastern region of Lwów/Lviv/Lemberg/Leopolis/Lvov.[7]

The Nazis ruled by terror. Terror was a tool of race struggle and policy objectives as dictated by racial, economic, political, and military considerations. Soon, terror, along with the policies of total economic and labor exploitation, led to the breakdown of law and order and fostered anarchy in the countryside. Nazi policies also facilitated and encouraged, sometimes inadvertently, a war of all against all within and without the captive nations.

There were two facets of terror: extraordinary and ordinary. Extraordinary terror was reserved for the Jews: total extermination, plain and simple. Ordinary terror was meted out to the Christian Poles, especially, and, in descending order, to other Slavic ethnicities and the Balts.[8] Ordinary terror meant cyclical extermination of the elite and an ever-escalating repression of the people. However, ordinary terror could be, and sometimes was, mitigated by policy consideration. On the other hand, extraordinary terror against the Jews was not. Namely, they were slated for wholesale extermination, a policy that usually overrode even the exigencies of the Nazi battle for victory. In other words, Jews were ultimately slaughtered even if it was detrimental to the German war effort.

In the initial stage of the Holocaust, between June 1941 and January 1942, about one million Jews were killed. After a brief respite, in spring 1942, the Germans and their Lithuanian, Latvian, Belarusian, and Ukrainian auxiliaries recommenced the Jewish mass murder. The Romanians joined in autonomously and vigorously, while the Hungarians only half-heartedly and rarely. A series of mass-shootings took place usually just outside of towns and villages inhabited by Jews. The most famous execution sites include Ponary outside of Wilno/Vilnius and Babi Yar near Kiev. Jews from Eastern Galicia were often deported to the death camps, especially Bełżec. As a result, during the second stage of genocide, in 1942 and 1943, an estimated one million more Jews died in the lands between Estonia and Moldavia, including about 500,000 Soviet Jews. Altogether about two million Jews perished in the east.[9]

As for the non-Jewish victims of ordinary terror, there were multiple perpetrators, chiefly the Germans. For the Intermarium as a whole, in absolute numbers, the Ukrainians qualify as the most victimized, followed by the Belarusians and Poles. The latter, however, suffered the largest number of casualties proportionally to their population in the region. In the Intermarium's western part (in the Wilno, Nowogródek, and Polesie areas which belonged to the prewar Polish state), between 150,000 and 200,000 Poles and Belarusians perished, according to Grzegorz Hryciuk. Most of the victims were Belarusian. In Volhynia and eastern Galicia, the estimates of the statistics of death stand at between 275,000 and 375,000 Ukrainians and Poles, the former outnumbering the latter. Nonetheless, cumulatively, the Poles led the way in victim count in the Eastern Borderlands (excluding pre-1939 Soviet territories). During the Nazi occupation, it can be estimated that cumulatively between 250,000 and 300,000 Christian Poles died. A minimum of 150,000 Poles were killed by the Germans in Poland's old eastern provinces and adjacent lands. About 5,000 Poles were shot by Soviet partisans and their Communist allies. Larger numbers died at the hands of Lithuanian police and military formations in the service of the Germans, including an estimated 2,000 in Ponary alone. Lithuanian and Belarusian nationalists killed several thousand Poles. Between 80,000 and 120,000 Poles died in a wave of ethnic cleansing operations by the Ukrainian nationalist underground (spearheaded by the Organization of Ukrainian Nationalists and the Ukrainian Insurgent Army) which commenced in Volhynia in early 1943 and spread southward and westward later.[10]

Meanwhile, the Germans killed a minimum of 100,000 Ukrainians who were Polish citizens and a further 400,000 in Soviet Ukraine. Tens of thousands of Ukrainians also perished at the hands of Communist partisans and rival nationalist factions for such crimes as speaking out against their opponents, refusing to serve in or deserting from the partisan ranks, and assisting endangered Poles or Jews. Thousands of Ukrainians died while serving in various German police and military formations. And hundreds of thousands of Ukrainians perished in the ranks of the Red Army.[11]

About 150,000 of Poland's Belarusians died at the hands of the Germans, who also killed up to 500,000 non-Jewish Soviet Belorussians.[12] Belarusian/Belorussian military casualties ran into the hundreds of thousands, mostly Soviet but also some in German police and military formations. The Poles killed about 10,000 Ukrainians in combat and reprisal during the anti-Polish ethnic cleansing campaign and for supporting the Nazis or Soviets; as well as circa 1,500 Belarusians and several hundred Lithuanians for their real and alleged anti-Polish collaboration with the USSR and the Third Reich. Last but not least, the Germans shot an estimated 15,000 Balts, including many actual or suspected Communists.[13] In 1944 and 1945, around 20,000 Estonians, Latvians, and Lithuanians died during the Red Army offensive and in the mass escape to the West, as the eastern front was collapsing, including under Allied bombs. All in all, several million human beings perished in the Intermarium. The largest category of victims was Jewish trailed by the Soviet POWs, Ukrainians, Belarusians, Poles, and others.

The carnage took place within the context of the Nazi occupation policy. It fluctuated as dictated by the demands of the war effort and as pushed by the persistent power tug between the most important institutions of the Third Reich: the military, the police, and the civilian administration. The Nazi nationalities policy, as mentioned, was driven by racism. The occupation authorities accordingly differentiated between the captive peoples. The *Reichsdeutsche* led the rooster, followed by the *Volksdeutsche*.[14] The Balts were considered superior to the Slavs. Of the latter, the Christian Poles were considered as the most odious, and, at the outset, their elite was slated for gradual liquidation.[15] Although naturally inferior to the German *Herrenvolk* (Master Race), the Ukrainians[16] and Belarusians[17] were courted, initially at least. The Jews were slated for a wholesale extermination in ever-increasing installments.

Within such a rigid and genocidal framework, there coexisted, on the one hand, consistent features congruent with the Nazi ideology and, on the other, frequent departures from racist fantasies dictated by German pragmatism. The latter was informed by the requirements of war economy and by the specter of shifting war fortunes. The Nazi racism fostered resistance, the German pragmatism accommodation.

Like the Soviets, the Nazis encouraged the participation of local collaborators in the occupation system.[18] Auxiliary policemen were recruited among the Estonians, Latvians, Lithuanians, Ukrainians, and Belarusians. There were about 100,000 Ukrainians serving in the local police forces, according to Dieter Pohl. Many of them joined the Ukrainian nationalist militias which emerged spontaneously to fight the Soviets in the summer of 1941; many of them participated in the anti-Jewish pogroms orchestrated by the Germans. Soon after, these Ukrainian militias were purged and reassembled as police auxiliaries. They played a key role in the slaughter of the Jews.

On the other hand, the Poles of the Intermarium did not participate in the Holocaust in the Nazi collaborationist units. Nonetheless, quite a few Poles joined the Belarusian auxiliary police, especially in the early stages. In some places the Poles set up local home guard forces that were later vetted, purged, replaced with Belarusians, and reassembled as the local police for the Germans. Afterward, a few Poles remained as policemen passing as non-Poles but, in reality, serving as infiltrators at the behest of the Polish underground, at least in some instances. Meanwhile, hundreds of thousands of Balts (including 50,000–60,000 Estonians and 115,000 Latvians), Ukrainians, and Belarusians joined various German military formations, including the Waffen-SS, for the most part as conscripts but many as volunteers. (Tens of thousands of them perished in combat, and many were taken prisoner by the Soviets and sent to penal camps in the Soviet interior, where some died.)

Further, the middle and lower rungs of the Nazi civilian administration were staffed by the locals. The rule was to employ the natives at all posts dealing directly with the conquered populations. The local officials were usually tasked with the most unsavory and onerous undertakings, including collecting the food quota and procuring "volunteers" for forced labor projects. Even the Jews had their own hierarchical structure within the ghetto. The so-called *Judenräte* (Jewish councils) served as conveyer belts between the Jewish community and the occupation authorities. The Jewish police often became a tool for anti-Jewish measures in the ghettos. Ultimately, many of the Jewish policemen participated in the destruction of their own communities.[19]

As a rule, the Nazis wanted the power structure to reflect their racist fantasies. Therefore, while the Germans from the Reich served in top positions, they aimed to recruit, first, the ethnic Germans and, then, the Balts to occupy important middle rung positions. Because there were very few ethnic Germans left and the Balts tended to stick to their own ethnic areas (except for their mobile police and military auxiliaries), the Nazis were forced to deal with the Slavs. The Ukrainians and Belarusians were considered inferior but friendly, initially at least. The Poles were deemed hostile and undesirable from the very beginning (except at the outset in the western Belarusian areas). However, the Poles were generally better educated than other Slavs. Therefore, the German-speaking and educated remnant of the Polish elite was able to infiltrate the lower and medium rungs of the local administration. Most individual Poles did so on their own, to secure a livelihood; some entered the system on orders from the resistance; other Polish officials joined the resistance only later. However, to remain employed (and alive), they were expected to carry out the tasks assigned to them by the Germans.[20]

It seems that many native low- and middle-level officials of the Nazi occupation system wanted not only to improve their own lot but also to assist the captive populations. Most frequently, however, the native officials tended to help their own coethnics. For example, some Poles who infiltrated the system in the summer of 1941 initiated their careers by denouncing to the Nazis certain Belarusians and Ukrainians as Communists. Many of these persons indeed had served in the Soviet administration but some were not Communists at all but, rather, opportunists and even closet nationalists. Nonetheless, those Poles thus used the Nazis to avenge themselves for the bloody purges and deportations carried out by the Soviet secret police in collaboration with the non-Polish local people. By mid-1942, the Nazis had caught on to the Polish scheme. They partly purged the Poles, from nontechnical official posts, in particular, and replaced them with more reliable Belarusians and Ukrainians.

Meanwhile, to the north of Poland's former eastern provinces, the events developed in a very similar manner. During the initial stage of the Nazi occupation of the Baltics, Estonian, Latvian, and Lithuanian nationalists squared accounts with their fellow ethnics, local Russians, and Jews who were considered Communist collaborators. A number of those Baltic nationalist activists returned to their low- and medium-level official posts and continued their anti-Communist and antiminority operations. However, soon, the Germans purged some of the native officials as too overtly nationalistic and, thus, potentially unreliable for the occupation authorities. The Nazis further employed ethnic auxiliary policemen and paramilitaries not only on their home turf but also in other regions. And, therefore, Lithuanian Special Units under Nazi command executed masses of Jews in Poland's western Belarus; Latvian SS-*Wachtmänner* guarded the Warsaw ghetto; Estonian volunteers served as antiaircraft gun crews inside the Third Reich; and Ukrainian and Belarusian SS-personnel defended the beaches of Normandy and other places in Western Europe. In the initial period of the Holocaust, in particular, some of these auxiliary units played an extremely lethal role in western, northern, and central Intermarium. Afterward, the local uniformed and armed collaborators continued to provide valuable services in the killing fields of the Shoah and elsewhere.[21]

Elsewhere in the Intermarium, to the far east and south of its periphery, military and police collaboration with the Third Reich was also widespread. In the most successful case, the *Wehrmacht* encouraged the local Russians in the Orel, Bryansk, Kursk, and Polotsk areas to set up the Lokot Autonomy (*Lokotskoe Samoupravlyene*). Its anti-Communist self-defense force, dubbed the Russian National Liberation Army (*Russkaiia Osvoboditelnaia Narodnaia Armiia*—RONA), was eventually incorporated into the Waffen-SS. The much larger Russian Liberation Army (*Russkaia Osvoboditel'naia Armiia*—ROA) was likewise recruited among ethnic Russians to operate under the command of the German army. And so did numerous Cossack units and others, including the Crimean Tartars. Some served in the *Wehrmarcht's* Eastern Legions (*Ostlegionen*) along with the erstwhile Soviet citizens of the Caucasus and Central Asia. Others enrolled in the SS. Some were enthusiastic volunteers, whereas many elected to enlist to avoid death in German POW camps. In perhaps the most bizarre case of collaboration, SS-*Reichsführer* Heinrich Himmler himself authorized Judaic prayers to accommodate the soldiers of two battalions of the SS consisting of Karaites (Karaim), Talmudless Jews of the Crimea. The Karaites of the Wilno-Troki region excluded themselves from this enterprise. Some estimates of armed collaboration in the east are as high as two million.[22] Let us keep in mind, however, that many more inhabitants of the Intermarium were drafted, some of them illegally in territories occupied by the Soviet Union, into the Red Army and fought against the Third Reich throughout the war.

Meanwhile, the lot of the civilians in the Intermarium was much more dramatic than that of the soldiers and policemen in either the German or Soviet forces. The Nazis subjected the captive nations to total labor and economic exploitation. Christians were expected to perform labor duty (*Arbeitspflicht*) and Jews were ordered to carry out forced labor (*Zwangsarbeit*). Forced labor for the Jews was more supervised, exploitative, and burdensome than what befell the Christian population outside of concentration camps. Labor duty meant that one had to perform occasional tasks (constructing roads, removing snow, transporting lumber) on demand for the occupation authorities, in addition to maintaining steady employment (in agriculture, industry, or the service sector). Those who were unemployed were slated to be deported for slave labor in the Reich. Nonetheless, Christians working on their own farmsteads, in small enterprises, and offices were usually not closely supervised. That gave them more leeway in dealing with the authorities. While virtually lethal for the Jews, obligatory labor was much more onerous for the Slavs than the Balts. All captive peoples were forced to contribute economically to the Nazi war effort. That included high taxes, confiscation of liquid assets, periodic forced contributions of cash, jewelry, and other valuables, including art and clothing. Jewish property was confiscated wholesale, as mentioned.[23] An enormous food quota was imposed on the peasants. Its execution was invariably ruthless. Food shortages became acute. Hunger set in. Again, it seems that the terror and want were considerably more severe in Poland's eastern provinces than in the Baltic states. By mid-1942, dissatisfaction with the

Nazi rule was widespread. It translated into both organized and spontaneous grassroots resistance, especially outside the Baltics.

Both forms of resistance were divided along ethnic lines, although there were examples of spontaneous individual and organized group resistance that transcended national exclusivity. The Communists, of course, operated among all ethnicities. Nonlocal Slavs and Jews were overrepresented in the Soviet underground. In many cases the participation of the Jews (mostly fugitives from the ghettos) reflected an effort to save themselves rather than a desire to grace humanity with Communist totalitarianism. Eventually, according to their memoirs, at least some fugitives identified with Soviet goals over Jewish ones. Christian Poles were notably underrepresented among the Communist partisan movement (except possibly in Volhynia),[24] followed by the Balts. In theory, the Polish underground claimed to accept all loyal citizens of Poland. In practice, this was limited only to the individuals who considered themselves culturally "Polish," one's ethnic background notwithstanding, as well as some Belarusians and a few Jews, the former particularly in the Wilno and Nowogródek areas and the latter mostly in Volhynia. Individual Russians and Polonized Tatars did fight in the Polish ranks. However, the participation of the Ukrainians and Lithuanians in Polish clandestine activities was strictly exceptional.[25]

Organized resistance against the Nazis was largely a continuation of the underground activities aimed at the Soviets. There were some differences among the participants. The Communists were an obvious exception here. They naturally strove for the return of Stalin's rule and directed all their efforts to that end. On the other hand, the Jews concentrated on surviving by whatever means necessary, including some who dreamed of fighting for the future State of Israel. Jewish Communists were a mixed bag: from Stalinist fanatics to opportunists, as evidenced by the experience of the Minsk ghetto and some guerrilla units and survival groups operating outside.[26] Other, national underground movements shared common enemies and a common strategy. They struggled for full independence from all invaders. Yet, they failed to unite their efforts.

The Estonian, Latvian, Lithuanian, Ukrainian, Belarusian, and Polish clandestine organizations varied in tactics. The Poles resorted now to armed clandestine struggle, but not the Balts. The latter limited themselves almost exclusively to nonviolent political and cultural resistance against the Germans.[27] So did the Belarusians. The Ukrainian nationalists kept their military operations against the Nazis to a bare minimum.[28] Instead, from early 1943, they concentrated on the ethnic cleansing of the Poles, the struggle against the Soviets, and the bloody purges of Ukrainian Communist sympathizers and other dissidents.[29]

The Polish underground Home Army (*Armia Krajowa*, AK) operated as far afield as the outskirts of Moscow. As far as its military viability, it was arguably the most powerful and best organized clandestine organization in the west of the Intermarium. In the east, the Communists in Nazi-occupied Soviet Belorussia and Ukraine, armed and supplied by the Kremlin, were the strongest. The Ukrainian nationalist formations in Volhynia and Eastern Galicia dominated regionally. Aside from the AK, there were also other Polish clandestine organizations active in Poland's eastern provinces but, by 1943, almost all of them became subordinated to the Home Army. Unlike the Soviet partisans, most soldiers of the Polish resistance remained underground, living a double life as civilians and reserve fighters. Some of them were part-time fighters, occasionally participating in military activities. Only a few took to the field full time as intelligence operatives, long-range commandos, or local guerrillas. Their anti-Nazi activities were characterized by precision strikes on crucial military, industrial, transportation, and communications targets as well as individual assassinations of police and military personnel. Later, by mid-1943, the AK partisan units engaged German outfits and garrisons and their auxiliaries. Unlike the Communist and Ukrainian nationalist partisans, the Home Army did not as a rule conscript its fighters by force.[30]

Although officially at war with the Third Reich only, the AK fought against everyone regarded as enemy of Poland. In revenge for collective reprisals against Polish civilians by Ukrainian, Lithuanian, and Belarusian policemen and soldiers, who were usually directed by the Germans, the Polish underground targeted the perpetrators. However, it also carried out its own retaliatory actions against enemy civilians. That, in particular, concerned Ukrainian villagers, who were also singled out by the Poles for assisting the Ukrainian nationalist underground. Further, some Belarusian civilians were shot by the AK in revenge both for supporting the Nazis and the Soviets. However, revenge killings of Lithuanian civilians were rather exceptional.[31]

The relationship between the Home Army and the Soviets was complex. It was uneasy at best and hostile at worst. Officially, the Soviets were "allies of our allies." Unofficially, they were enemies. The conflict was driven, first, by the Communist hostility as expressed by Stalin against the Polish government-in-exile in London and its plenipotentiary administration in Warsaw; and, second, by local altercations pitting everyone in the underground against each other, in particular, the Poles, the Soviets, the Ukrainian nationalists, and the Jewish fugitives. A series of local wars within war erupted.

In the north-east the AK clashed with Soviet partisans as early as 1942. That was because the latter assassinated members of the Polish elite and robbed, and often mistreated, Polish and other villagers to secure supplies.[32] Jewish fugitives also perpetrated robberies. Simply, they robbed to survive. This was one of the by-products of the Holocaust. As mentioned, after a brief respite, the Nazi mass murder of Jews commenced anew with the action to liquidate the ghettos in spring 1942. By then the Jewish extermination became a very orderly affair. Most executioners were local collaborators enrolled as volunteer auxiliary policemen under German command. Afterward, a few survivors remained as slave laborers under Nazi tutelage, a few individuals hid with sympathetic Christians, and groups of fugitives either roamed in the forests alone or clustered in survival camps. Eventually, most of them subordinated themselves to the Soviet partisans. Initially, the bulk of Soviet guerrillas consisted of fugitive Red Army men. Some escaped from POW camps and formed loose groups in the forests. Others avoided capture after the defeat of 1941 and survived hiding with the local people. By mid-1942, after a failed Nazi operation to capture them, some of these fugitives began organizing forest survival groups. They eventually established links with the Communist underground and NKVD commandos dropped behind the front lines to commence guerrilla war. The Soviet partisans did accept some Jews, armed young men in particular. But the relationship between Jews and Soviets was problematic, the Jewish side often falling victim to anti-Semitism. Like the Soviets, the Jews lacked support among the local population and, therefore, attacked the locals to obtain the supplies necessary to survive. Often these raids would become violent, especially if the farmers showed any resistance.[33]

The Germans meanwhile proved unwilling and unable to defend the civilian population. At best, they allowed and even encouraged the locals to establish self-defense groups, primarily to fend off raids by Soviet partisans.[34] Usually, however, the Nazis imposed collective punishment on villages suspected of aiding and abetting any and all partisan units and bandit groups. Hence, the Nazis left the population largely to its own devices. To protect the locals, the Home Army clashed with Soviet, Jewish, and common bandit groups. The conflict with the AK was exacerbated significantly after many fugitive Jews subordinated themselves to the Soviets, who, from mid-1943, unilaterally launched a war against the Polish underground in the Wilno and Nowogródek areas by killing Polish partisans surreptitiously after luring them to "friendly" meetings at Soviet bases. This assassination campaign escalated from individuals to small squads and, finally, entire Polish guerrilla units.[35] In response, lacking material support from either the West or central Poland, a few local AK commanders concluded a temporary, informal truce with the Germans, who even supplied the Poles with some weapons. Yet, the Home Army refused to participate in joint operations with the Germans against the Soviet partisans and continued to engage in skirmishes with the German military and Belorussian police.[36]

Between December 1943 and May 1944, the Polish underground units in the north-east nonetheless fought more frequently against the Communists than against the Nazis. On the other hand, in the southeastern provinces the AK cooperated more often with the Soviet partisans than struggled against them. Particularly in Volhynia the Poles allied themselves tactically with the Soviets against the Ukrainian nationalists and, much less often, against the Nazis.[37] The Polish underground also sided with and assisted the Jewish fugitives in Volhynia against the common Ukrainian nationalist enemy. Further, Polish self-defense formations, which were often connected to the Home Army, occasionally solicited and obtained local German assistance against the Ukrainian nationalists. The Germans supplied the Poles with a few arms and even intervened a few times to protect them from Ukrainian onslaughts. Granted, the Nazis did much more for the Ukrainians, albeit unwittingly. After all, the bulk of the Ukrainian auxiliary police in Volhynia, which had been trained, armed, and directed to put their exterminationist skills into practice during the Holocaust, deserted *en bloc* in the spring of 1943 and joined the Ukrainian nationalist guerrillas.[38] The general Nazi policy of virtual noninterference in the Ukrainian–Polish conflict in Volhynia caused the Polish population, the underground included, to seek a tactical rapprochement with the Soviets.

The apogee of the tactical cooperation with the Stalin's forces occurred gradually everywhere in Poland between January and October 1944, including most intensively until August 1944 in the eastern provinces in the Intermarium. In January 1944, the Red Army crossed the old Polish–Soviet frontier. Accordingly, the Home Army High Command in Warsaw launched a rolling insurrection codenamed Operation "Tempest." An apparent paradox, the "Tempest" was both anti-Nazi and anti-Soviet. Its military edge was directed at Germany but its political animus was aimed at the USSR. The operation endeavored to expel the Nazis before the arrival of the Soviets to establish a free Polish administration in every locality of prewar Poland against Stalin's express wishes.

Nonetheless, the Home Army units in the field were given orders to cooperate tactically with the Red Army. As a result, they harried the retreating *Wehrmacht* and captured some localities on their own. The AK troops fought jointly with the Soviet troops to liberate major cities, including Wilno/Vilnius and Lwów/Lviv. The "Tempest" was much more successful, at least temporarily, in the areas where the Poles dominated or constituted a plurality or a sizable minority. It nonetheless ended the same everywhere. The Soviets surrounded and disarmed most of the Polish fighters. Some officers were shot. Others were arrested and dispatched to the Gulag. The rank and file was given a choice: to join the Communist forces or share the fate of their commanders. Many elected the latter, some the former. Many of them deserted the Communist-led military soon after. Probably most of the AK fled the Soviet round-ups and returned underground.

The "Tempest" culminated in an ill-fated and tragic rising in Warsaw which lasted from August until October 1944. The decision to launch the insurrection in Poland's capital was influenced in no small degree by the events in the Eastern Borderlands. By defeating the Nazis on their own and establishing a free government in Warsaw, the Polish underground leadership vainly hoped to forestall the Soviet takeover of Poland.[39]

But the Rising collapsed; the "Tempest" proved an utter failure. The Western Allies did virtually nothing to assist the Poles. The Polish government-in-exile in London was unable to help in any way either. It was a "guest" in Great Britain, really a hostage to the policy of the Allies toward the Kremlin. It protested in vain; it faithfully stood by the United Kingdom and the United States. Its army in exile, the fourth largest in the field, shed blood on all battlefields of Europe, Africa, and the Middle East. Yet, all the sacrifice and effort of the Poles in exile failed to influence the Allies and deliver freedom for Poland. At home, the strategy of the Polish underground proved likewise untenable and ineffective. Despite having incurred enormous human and material losses against the Nazis, the Poles were unable to find any modus vivendi with the Soviets to safeguard their nation's independence.

The Polish underground's experience with Stalin in 1944–1945 mirrors to a certain extent the history of the Baltic and Ukrainian nationalist movements with Hitler. The captive nations and their national leaderships each vainly attempted to salvage their freedom while operating on the stomping ground of the giants, the totalitarian dictators. Each clandestine national movement and the peoples each represented were disappointed in their endeavors. However, the defeat was much more bitter for the Poles than the others. Poland had stood by the western Allies against Hitler from September 1939. It was to Warsaw's peril that it stood alone against Stalin, however. The Western democracies were rather selective about tangling with their totalitarian enemies. Having defeated Hitler, the United States and the United Kingdom gave Stalin free reign over half of Europe.

Notes

1. Bogdan Musiał estimates that 30,000 were shot in the Polish eastern provinces occupied by the Soviets alone. See Bogdan Musiał, *"Konterrevolutionäre Elemente sind zu erschiessen": Die Brutalisierung des deutsch-sowjetischen Krieges im Sommer 1941* (Berlin and Munich: Propyläen, 2000), 193; an expanded edition was published as Bogdan Musiał, *Rozstrzelać elementy kontrrewolucyjne! Brutalizacja wojny niemiecko-sowieckiej latem 1941 roku* (Warszawa: Fronda, 2001). See also *Zbrodnicza ewakuacja więzień i aresztów NKWD na Kresach Wschodnich II Rzeczypospolitej w czerwcu-lipcu 1941 roku: Materiały z sesji naukowej w 55. rocznicę ewakuacji więźniów NKWD w głąb ZSRR (Łódź, 10 czerwca 1996 roku) (The Criminal Evacuation of Jails and Prisons of the NKVD in the Eastern Borderlands of the 2nd Commonwealth in June and July 1941)* (Warszawa and Łódź: Główna Komisja Badania Zbrodni przeciwko Narodowi Polskiemu—Instytut Pamięci Narodowej i Okręgowa Komisja Badania Zbrodni przeciwko Narodowi Polskiemu w Łodzi, 1997); Krzysztof Popiński, Aleksander Kokurin and Aleksander Gurianow, *Drogi śmierci: Ewakuacja więzień sowieckich z Kresów Wschodnich II Rzeczpospolitej w czerwcu i lipcu 1941 roku (The Roads of Death: The Evacuation of Soviet Jails from the Eastern Borderlands of the 2nd Republic in June and July 1941)* (Warszawa: Karta, 1995). And see Juozas Jankauskas, *1941 m. Birželio sukilimas Lietuvoje (The Insurrection of June 1941 in Lithuania)* (Vilnius: Lietuvos gyventojų genocido ir rezistencijos tyrimo centras, 2010).

2.   See Rolf-Dieter Müller and Gerd R. Ueberschär, *Hitler's War in the East, 1941–1945: A Critical Assessment*, 2nd revised edition (New York and Oxford: Berghahn Books, 2002), 222–25; Richard Rhodes, *Masters of Death: The SS-Einsatzgruppen and The Invention of the Holocaust* (New York: Alfred A. Knopf, 2002); Hans-Heinrich Wilhelm, ed., *Rassenpolitik und Kriegführung: Sicherheitspolizei und Wehrmacht in Polen und in der Sowjetunion 1939–1942* (Passau: Wissenschaftsverlag Richard Rothe, 1991); Helmut Krausnick and Hans-Heinrich Wilhelm. *Die Truppen des Weltanschauungskrieges: Die Einsatzgruppen der Sicherheitspolizei und des SD* (Stuttgart: Deutsche Verlags-Anstalt, 1981); Hans Joachim Neufeldt and Georg Tessin, *Zur Geschichte der Ordnungs Polizei 1936–1945, Teil 1: Entstehung und Organisation des Hauptamtes Ordnungpolizei im 2. Weltkrieg, Teil 2: Die Stäbe und Truppeneinheiten der Ordnungspolizei* (Koblenz: no publisher, 1957); Jan Jerzy Milewski and Anna Pyżewska, eds., *Początek wojny niemiecko-sowieckiej i losy ludności cywilnej (The Origin of the German-Soviet War and the Lot of the Civilian Population)* (Warszawa: Instytut Pamięci Narodowej, 2003); Witold Mędykowski, ed., "Part VII: Pogromy 1941 roku na terytorium byłej okupacji sowieckiej (Bukowina wschodnia, województwa RP, państwa bałtyckie) w relacjach żydowskich," ("The Pogroms of 1941 in the Formerly Soviet-Occupied Area [Eastern Bukowina, Provinces of the Commonwealth, and the Baltic States] According to Jewish Recollections") in Jasiewicz, *Świat Niepożegnany*, 761–809; and Grzegorz Hryciuk, "Represje niemieckie na Kresach Wschodnich II Rzeczpospolitej, 1941–1944," ("German Repression in Eastern Borderlands of the 2nd Republic") *Pamięć i Sprawiedliwość* no. 1 (12) (2008): 79–112.

3.   The initial phase is most evident from the Nazi police orders and reports. See Marek Jan Chodakiewicz and Wojciech Jerzy Muszyński, "W cieniu 'Barbarossy': Wybór niemieckich dokumentów policyjnych (maj 1941–kwiecień 1942)," ("In the Shadow of 'Barbarossa': A Selection of German Police Documents [May 1941–April 1942]") *Glaukopis* 1 (2003): 239–65; Yitzhak Arad, Shmuel Krakowski, and Shmuel Spector, eds. *The Einsatzgruppen Reports* (New York: The Holocaust Library, 1989); Peter Klein ed., *Die Einsatzgruppen in der besetzten Sowjetunion 1941/42: Die Tätigkeits- und Lageberichte des Chefs der Sicherheitspolizei und des SD* (Berlin: Edition Hentrich, 1997); Andrzej Żbikowski, "Lokalne pogromy Żydów w czerwcu i lipcu 1941 roku na wschodnich rubieżach II Rzeczypospolitej," *Biuletyn Żydowskiego Instytutu Historycznego w Polsce* no. 162–63 (1992): 3–18, and the abridged English version, "Local Anti-Jewish Pogroms in the Occupied Territories of Eastern Poland, June–July 1941," in *The Holocaust in the Soviet Union: Studies and Sources on the Destruction of the Jews in the Nazi Occupied Territories of the USSR, 1941–1945*, ed. Lucjan Dobroszycki and Jeffrey S. Gurock (Armonk, NY and London: M.E. Sharpe, 1990), 173–79; Delhine Bechtel, "De Jedwabne à Zolotchiv pogromes locaux en Galicie, juin–juillet 1941," *Cultures d'Europe Centrale*, vol. 5: *La destruction des confines*, compiled and ed. by Delphine Bechtel and Xavier Galmiche (Paris: CIRCE, 2005), 69–92. See also Alexander B. Rossino, "Polish 'Neighbors' and German Invaders: Contextualizing Anti-Jewish Violence in the Białystok District during the Opening Weeks of Operation Barbarossa," *Polin: Studies in Polish Jewry* 16 (2003): 431–52; Marco Carynnyk, "Furious Angels: Ukrainians, Jews, and Poles in the Summer of 1941," http://www.timeandspace.lviv.ua/index.php?module=academic&section=sessi on&id=47 (accessed September 14, 2009); Marco Carynnyk, "'Jews, Poles, and Other Scum': Ruda Różaniecka, Monday, 30 June 1941," Fourth Annual Danyliw

Research Seminar in Contemporary Ukrainian Studies, Chair of Ukrainian Studies, University of Ottawa (Canada), October 23–25, 2008, http://www. ukrainianstudies.uottawa.ca/pdf/P_Danyliw08_Carynnyk.pdf (accessed September 14, 2009); Andrzej Żbikowski, "Pogromy i mordy ludności żydowskiej w Łomżyńskiem i na Białostocczyźnie latem 1941 roku w świetle relacji ocalałych Żydów i dokumentów sądowych," ("Pogroms and Murder of the Jewish Population in the Łomża and Bialystok Regions in the Summer of 1941 According to the Testimonies of Jewish Survivors and Court Documents") and Edmund Dmitrów, "Oddziały operacyjne niemieckiej Policji Bezpieczeństwa i Służby Bezpieczeństwa a początek zagłady Żydów w Łomżyńskim i na Białostocczyźnie latem 1941 roku," ("The Operational Units of the German Security Police and Security Service and the Onset of the Extermination of the Jews in the Łomża and Białystok Regions") in Wokół Jedwabnego, ed. Paweł Machcewicz and Krzysztof Persak, 2 vols. (Warszawa: Instytut Pamięci Narodowej, 2002), 1: 159–352; Tomasz Szarota, "'Selbstreinigungsaktionen' SIPO i SD na Litwie i w Polsce a udział miejscowej ludności w Holokauście (na przykładzie pogromów w Kownie i Jedwabnem)," ("'Self-Cleansing Actions' of the SIPO and SD in Lithuania and Poland and the Participation of the Local Population in the Holocaust") in Jasiewicz, Świat Niepożegnany, 686–701. For a case study of a locality in the Province of Białystok where a mass killing of Jews took place see Marek Jan Chodakiewicz, The Massacre in Jedwabne, July 10, 1941: Before, During, After (New York and Boulder, CO: Columbia University Press and East European Monographs, 2005). For a seriously flawed and woefully underresearched account of the same see Jan Tomasz Gross, Neighbors: The Destruction of the Jewish Community in Jedwabne, Poland (Princeton, NJ: Princeton University Press, 2001). See also some Polish punditry on the topic in Antony Polonsky and Joanna B. Michlic, eds., The Neighbors Respond: The Controversy over the Jedwabne Massacre in Poland (Princeton, NJ and Oxford: Princeton University Press, 2004); Robert Jankowski, ed., Jedwabne: Spór historyków wokół książki Jana T. Grossa "Sąsiedzi" (Jedwabne: The Quarrel of Historians about the Book of Jan Tomasz Gross, "Neighbors") (Warsaw: Fronda, 2002).

4. See The Historical Atlas of Poland (Warszawa and Wrocław: Państwowe Przedsiębiorstwo Wydawnictw Kartograficznych, 1986), 50.

5. On the Nazi occupation policy in Belarus and Ukraine see Jerzy Turonek, Białoruś pod okupacją niemiecką (Belarus under the German Occupation) (Warszawa: Książka i Wiedza, 1993); Christian Gerlach, Kalkulierte Morde: Die deutsche Wirtschafts-und Vernichtungspolitik in Weissrussland 1941 bis 1944 (Hamburg: Hamburger Edition, 1999); Babette Quinkert, Propaganda und Terror in Weißrußland 1941–1944: Die deutsche "geistige" Kriegführung gegen Zivilbevölkerung und Partisanen (Paderborn: Ferdinand Schöningh Verlag, 2009); Karel C. Berkhoff, Harvest of Despair: Life and Death in Ukraine under Nazi Rule (Cambridge, MA and London: The Belknap Press of Harvard University Press, 2004); Alexander Dallin, German Rule in Russia, 1941–1945: A Study of Occupation Policies (London: Macmillan, 1957); and the following essays in Hunczak and Shtohryn, Ukraine: Rudolf A. Mark, "The Ukrainians as Seen by Hitler, Rosenberg, and Koch" (23–36), Bohdan Krawchenko, "Soviet Ukraine Under Nazi Occupation, 1941–1944" (37–62); and Arkady Joukovsky, "Ukrainian Territories under Romanian Occupation During World War II, 1941–1942" (153–70).

6. See the following essays in Hunczak and Shtohryn, Ukraine: Andrew Turchyn, "The Ukrainian Catholic Church during World War II" (261–76) and "The

Ukrainian Orthodox Church during World War II" (277–300). See also Włodzimierz Osadczy, "Kościoły wobec konfliktu polsko-ukraińskiego w czasie II wojny światowej," ("Churches Facing the Polish-Ukrainian Conflict during the Second World War") *Biuletyn Instytutu Pamięci Narodowej* no. 1–2 (96–97) (January–February 2009): 68–76; Leonid Rein, "The Orthodox Church in Byelorussia Under Nazi Occupation (1941–1944)," *East European Quarterly* 36, no. 1 (March 2005): 13–46.

7. For some preliminary observations on Germany's nationalities policies in the Wilno land see Arūnas Bubnys, "Etniniai santykiai nacių okupuotoje Lietuvoje 1941–1944 m.," ("Ethnic Relations in Nazi-Occupied Lithuania") *Genocidas ir rezistencija* no. 1 (29) (2011): http://www.genocid.lt/centras/lt/1408/a/#eng.

8. For the supervisors of terror in Nazi-occupied Lithuania see Petras Stankeras, "Aukščiausioji vokiečių SS ir policijos vadovybė Lietuvos generalinėje srityje 1941–1944 m. ("The Highest German SS and Police Authorities in the Lithuanian General Region in 1941–1944")," *Genocidas ir reistencija* no. 2 (10) (2001): http://www.genocid.lt/Leidyba/10/petras.htm.

9. The total of Jews killed in the Borderland States and the Soviet Union needs to be recalculated. Scholars often count as "Soviet Jews" all Jews killed in the territories occupied by the USSR in 1939 and 1940. At the same time, they double count the same victims as Polish, Latvian, and other Jews. Jews from the Wilno/Vilnius region may even be counted three times as Polish, Lithuanian, and Soviet citizens. Compare Dawidowicz, *The War against the Jews*, 403; and Raul Hilberg, *The Destruction of the European Jews* (New Haven, CT and London: Yale University Press, 1985), vol. 3: 1308–21. See also Antony Polonsky, *The Jews in Poland and Russia*, vol. 3: *1914 to 2008* (Oxford and Portland, OR: The Littman Library of Jewish Civilization, 2012), 3: 359–589; Yitzhak Arad, *The Holocaust in the Soviet Union* (Lincoln, NE: University of Nebraska Press, 2009); CAHS symposium presentations, 2004, "Lithuania and the Jews: The Holocaust Chapter," http://www.ushmm.org/research/center/publications/occasional/2005-07-03/paper.pdf. For the Holocaust in the Ukraine, in general, see Ray Brandon and Wendy Lower, eds., *The Shoah in Ukraine: History, Testimony, Memorialization* (Bloomington and Indianapolis: Indiana University Press, 2008); for Poland's southeastern provinces see Dieter Pohl, *Nationalsozialistische Judenverfolgung in Ostgalizien, 1941–1944: Organisation und Durchführung eines staatlichen Massenverbrechens* (Munich: R. Oldenbourg Verlag, 1996); Thomas Sandkühler, *"Endlösung" in Galizien: Der Judenmord in Ostpolen und die Rettungsinitiativen von Berthold Beitz, 1941–1944* (Bonn: Verlag J. H. W. Dietz Nachfolger, 1996); and for the Holocaust in the region of Zhytomir in Soviet Ukraine see Wendy Lower, *Nazi Empire-Building and the Holocaust in Ukraine* (Chapel Hill, NC: University of North Carolina Press, 2005). For the extermination of the Jews in some of the northeastern provinces and in Soviet Belarus see Christian Gerlach, *Kalkulierte Morde: Die deutsche Wirtschafts- und Vernichtungspolitik in Weißrußland 1941 bis 1944* (Hamburg: Hamburger Edition, 1999); and Monika Tomkiewicz, *Zbrodnia w Ponarach 1941–1944 (The Crime in Ponary)* (Warszawa: IPN-KŚZpNP, 2008); Philip W. Blood, "Securing Hitler's *Lebensraum*: The Luftwaffe and Białowieża Forest, 1942–1944," *Holocaust and Genocide Studies* 24, no. 2 (2010): 247–72. On the Baltic States see Andrew Ezergailis, *The Holocaust in Latvia, 1941–1944: The Missing Center* (Riga: Historical Institute of Latvia, 1996); Bernhard Press, *The Murder of the Jews in Latvia, 1941–1945* (Evanston, IL: Northwestern University Press, 2000); Andris Caune et al., eds., *Holokausts Latvijā: Starptautiskās*

konferences materiāli, 2004. gada 3.–4. jūnijs, Rīga, un 2004.–2005. gada pētījumi par holokaustu Latvijā—Holocaust in Latvia: Materials of an International Conference 3–4 June 2004, Riga and the Holocaust Studies in Latvia in 2004–2005 (Riga: Latvijas vēstures institūta apgāds, 2006); *Holokausta pētniecības problēmas Latvijā: 2006.–2007. gada pētījumi par holokaustu Latvijā un starptautiskās konferences materiāli, 2007. gada 6.–7. novembris, Rīga (Problems of Holocaust Research in Latvia: Holocaust Studies in Latvia 2006–2007 and Proceedings of an International Conference, 6–7 November 2007, Riga)* (Riga: Latvijas vēstures institūta apgāds, 2008); Andrew Ezergailis, "'Sąsiedzi,' nie zabili Żydów," (Neighbors Did Not Kill Jews) in Jasiewicz, *Świat Niepożegnany*, 658–84; Christoph Dieckmann and Saulius Sužiedėlis, *Lietuvos žydų persekiojimas ir masinės žudynės 1941 m. vasarą ir rudenį: Šaltiniai ir analize⁻ –The Persecution and Mass Murder of Lithuanian Jews during Summer and Fall of 1941: Sources and Analysis* (Vilnius: Margi raštai, 2006); Anton Weiss-Wendt, *Murder without Hatred: Estonians and the Holocaust* (Syracuse: Syracuse University Press, 2009); Eugenia Gurin-Loov, *Eesti juutide katastroof 1941–Holocaust of Estonian Jew 1941* (Tallinn: Eesti Juudi Kogukond, 1994); Ruth Bettina Birn, "Collaboration with Nazi Germany in Eastern Europe: The Case of the Estonian Security Police," *Contemporary European History* 10 (2001): 181–98; Ruth Bettina Birn, *Die Sicherheitspolizei in Estland 1941–1944: Eine Studie zur Kollaboration im Osten* (Paderborn: Schöningh, 2006); David Vseviov, "Estońscy Żydzi – prosperity i tragedia," (Estonian Jews: Prosperity and Tragedy) in Jasiewicz, *Świat Niepożegnany*, 204–14.

10. For detailed contemporary Polish underground reports about the conflict in Poland's eastern territories, in particular, as it pertained Poles and Ukrainians, see Jan Brzeski and Adam Roliński, eds., *Archiwum Adama Bienia: Akta narodowościowe (1942–1944) (The Archive of Adam Bień: The Nationalities Papers, 1942–1944)* (Kraków: Nakładem Biblioteki Jagiellońskiej i Księgarni Akademickiej, 2001); Lucyna Kulińska and Adam Roliński, eds., *Antypolska akcja nacjonalistów ukraińskich w Małopolsce wschodniej w świetle dokumentów Rady Głównej Opiekuńczej, 1943–1944 (Anti-Polish Action of the Ukrainian Nationalists in Eastern Małopolska According to the Documents of the Main Welfare Council, 1943–1944)* (Kraków: Fundacja Centrum Dokumentacji Czynu Niepodległościowego, 2003); Lucyna Kulińska, ed., *Dzieje Komitetu Ziem Wschodnich na tle losów ludości polskich Kresów, (A History of the Committee of Eastern Lands against the Backdrop of the Fate of the Population of Polish Borderlands)* 2 vols. (Kraków: Oficyna Wydawnicza Abrys, 2001–2002). See also Tadeusz Piotrowski, *Genocide and Rescue in Wołyń: Recollections of the Ukrainian Nationalist Ethnic Cleansing Campaign Against the Poles During World War II* (Jefferson, NC: McFarland and Company, 2000); Władysław Siemaszko and Ewa Siemaszko, *Ludobójstwo dokonane przez nacjonalistów ukraińskich na ludności polskiej Wołynia 1939–1945, (Genocide Perpetrated by the Ukrainian Nationalists against the Polish Population of Volhynia, 1939–1945)* 2 vols. (Warszawa: von borowiecky, 2000); Władysław Filar, *Wołyń 1939–1944: Eksterminacja czy walki polsko-ukraińskie. Studium historyczno-wojskowe zmagań na Wołyniu w obronie polskości, wiary i godności ludzkiej (Volhynia, 1939–1944: Exterminaion or Polish-Ukrainian Struggles: A Historical-Military Study of the Struggles in Volhynia to Defend Polishness, Faith, and Human Dignity)* (Toruń: Adam Marszałek, 2003) (afterward *Wołyń 1939–1944*); Henryk Komański and Szczepan Siekierka, *Ludobójstwo dokonane przez ncjonalistów*

ukraińskich na Polakach w województwie tarnopolskim 1939–1946 (Genocide Perpetrated by the Ukrainian Nationalists against the Poles in the Province of Tarnopol, 1939–1946) (Wrocław: Nortom, 2004); Szczepan Siekierka, Henryk Komański and Krzysztof Bulzacki, *Ludobójstwo dokonane przez nacjonalistów ukraińskich na Polakach w województwie lwowskim 1939–1947 (Genocide Perpetrated by the Ukrainian Nationalists against the Poles in the Province of Lwów, 1939–1947)* (Wrocław: Stowarzyszenie Upamiętnienia Ofiar Zbrodni Ukraińskich Nacjonalistów we Wrocławiu, 2006); Szczepan Siekierka, Henryk Komański, and Eugeniusz Różański, *Ludobójstwo dokonane przez nacjonalistów ukraińskich na Polakach w województwie stanisławowskim 1939–1946 (Genocide Perpetrated by the Ukrainian Nationalists against the Poles in the Province of Stanisławów, 1939–1946)* (Wrocław: Stowarzyszenie Upamiętnienia Ofiar Zbrodni Ukraińskich Nacjonalistów we Wrocławiu, [2008]); Iaroslav Isaievych et al., eds., *Volyn i Kholmshchyna, 1938–1947 rr: Polsko-ukrainske protystoiannia ta ioho vidlunnia. Doslidzhennia, dokumenti, spohadi* [Volhynia and the Chelm region, 1938–1947] (Lviv: Natsionalna akademiia nauk Ukrainy, Instytut ukrainoznavstva im. I. Krypiakevycha, 2003); Zdzisław Konieczny, ed., *Zbrodnie nacjonalistów ukraińskich na ludności cywilnej w południowo-wschodniej Polsce (1942–1947) (The Crimes of Ukrainian Nationalists against the Civilian Population in South-Eastern Poland, 1942–1947)* (Przemyśl: Polski Związek Wschodni w Przemyślu, 2001); "Ukraińska walka o ziemię i ludzi: Lubelszczyzna 1940–1943," ("The Ukrainian Struggle for Land and People: The Lublin Area, 1940–1943") in Czesław Partacz and Krzysztof Łada, *Polska wobec ukraińskich dążeń niepodległościowych w czasie II wojny światowej (Poland and the Ukrainian Independentist Aspirations during the Second World War)* (Toruń: Centrum Edukacji Europejskiej, 2003), 97–132; Romuald Niedzielko, "Sprawiedliwi Ukraińcy: Na ratunek polskim sąsiadom skazanym na zagładę przez OUN-UPA," ("Righteous Ukrainians: Rescuing Polish Neighbors Sentenced to Extermination by the OUN-UPA") *Biuletyn Instytutu Pamięci Narodowej* no. 1–2 (96–97) (January–February 2009): 77–85; Berkhoff, *Harvest of Despair*, 285–300.

11. Berkhoff estimates that about one million people, including POWs, lost their lives under the Nazi regime in the territory of *Reichskommissariat Ukraine* or after deportation to the Reich. Jews likely accounted for half the victims. Hryciuk argues that up to 150,000 Ukrainians were killed by the Germans in Poland's Eastern Galicia and Volhynia; most of the victims were in Volhynia, which was part of the *Reichskommissariat Ukraine* at that time. See Berkhoff, *Harvest of Despair*, 307; Grzegorz Hryciuk, "Zmiany ludnościowe i narodowościowe w Galicji Wschodniej i na Wołyniu w latach 1939–1948," ("Demographic and National Transformations in Eastern Galicia and Volhynia between 1939 and 1948") in *Przemiany narodowościowe na Kresach Wschodnich II Rzeczypospolitej, 1931–1948 (National Transformations in the Eastern Borderlands of the Second Republic)*, ed. Stanisław Ciesielski (Toruń: Adam Marszałek, 2003), 195–96, 215–18; Grzegorz Hryciuk, *Przemiany narodowościowe i ludnościowe w Galicji Wschodniej i na Wołyniu w latach 1931–1948 (National and Demographic Transformations in Eastern Galicia and Volhynia between 1931 and 1948)* (Toruń: Adam Marszałek, 2005), 238–42, 266–71. See also Snyder, *The Reconstruction of Nations*, 164; Wiktor Poliszczuk, *Gwałt na prawdzie o zbrodniach OUN Bandery (Raping the Truth about the Crimes of the Bandera OUN)* (Toronto: n.p., 2003); Taras Hunczak, "The

Ukrainian Losses During World War II," in Hunczak and Shtohryn, *Ukraine*, 335–50.

12. According to German estimates, some 345,000 civilians are reckoned to have died in Belarus as a result of punitive operations, together with perhaps 30,000 partisans. See Gerlach, *Kalkulierte Morde*, 884 seq.

13. All statistics of death should be considered approximations. My estimates on the Baltic victims of the Germans are similar to those of Paul Goble, the leading specialist on the non-Russian post-Soviet nationalities. See Paul Goble to Marek Jan Chodakiewicz, May 30, 2005. See also, inter alia, Eugeniusz Mironowicz, "Zmiany struktury etnicznej na Białorusi w okresie okupacji niemieckiej," ("Changes of the Ethnic Structure of Belarus during the German Occupation") *Białoruskie Zeszyty Historyczne* no. 21 (2004): 104–16, http://kamunikat.fontel. net/pdf/bzh/21/06.pdf; Stanisław Ciesielski, ed., *Przemiany narodowościowe na Kresach Wschodnich II Rzeczypospolitej, 1931–1948* (*Population Changes in Eastern Borderlands of the 2nd Republic, 1931–1948*) (Toruń: Wydawnictwo Adam Marszałek, 2003); Christoph Dieckmann, Vytautas Toleikis, and Rimantas Zizas, *Karo belaisvių ir civilių gyventojų žudynes Lietuvoje 1941–1944—Murders of Prisoners of War and of Civilian Population in Lithuania, 1941–1944* (Vilnius: Margi rastai, 2005).

14. On the ethnic Germans in the Intermarium see Valdis O. Lumans, "A Reassessment of Volksdeutsche and Jews in Volhynia-Galicia-Narew Resettlement," in *The Impact of Nazism: New Perspectives on the Third Reich and Its Legacy*, ed. Alan E. Steinweis and Daniel E. Rogers (Lincoln and London: University of Nebraska Press, 2003), 81–100; Дзмітрый Крывашэй, "Насельніцтва нямецкага паходжання ў Беларусі ў 1941–1944 гадах," ("People of German Origin in Belarus, 1941–1944") *Białoruskie Zeszyty Historyczne* no. 22 (2004): 155–72, http://kamunikat.fontel.net/pdf/bzh/22/08.pdf.

15. See Arūnas Bubnys, "Etniniai santykiai nacių okupuotoje Lietuvoje 1941–1944 m.," ("Ethnic Relations in Nazi-Occupied Lithuania") *Genocidas ir rezistencija* no. 1 (29) (2011): http://www.genocid.lt/centras/lt/1408/a/#eng; Maria Wardzyńska, *Sytuacja ludności polskiej w Generalnym Komisariacie Litwy, czerwiec 1941–lipiec 1944 (The Situation of the Polish Population in the General Commissariat of Lithuanian, June 1941–July 1944)* (Warszawa: Instytut Pamięci Narodowej, GKBZpNP, 1993).

16. According to John Armstrong and Wiktor Poliszczuk, because some Ukrainian nationalists collaborated with the Nazis, Ukrainian cultural life flourished under the Germans in central Poland's Government General (but not in the *Reichskommissariat* Ukraine in the East). Nonetheless, there was a great deal of opposition to the Ukrainian nationalists within the Ukrainian community, as well as divisions within the Ukrainian political leadership, not only among the nationalists themselves, who were split into pro- and anti-Nazi factions and often fought bitterly, but also between the nationalists and the Communists. Furthermore, the Ukrainian people suffered fully the horrors of the war. Therefore, although they had initially welcomed the Germans, they began resisting them in 1942, for a time at least. Then, after 1944, some of them resisted the Soviet and Polish Communists. Others collaborated, but majority remained neutral. See John A. Armstrong, *Ukrainian Nationalism*, 3rd ed. (Engelwood, CO: Ukrainian Academic Press, 1990); Wiktor Poliszczuk, *Bitter Truth: The Criminality of the Ukrainian Nationalists (OUN) and the Ukrainian Insurgent Army (UPA)* (Toronto: n.p., 1999); Wiktor Poliszczuk, *Integralny nacjonalizm ukraiński jako odmiana faszyzmu: Zasady ideologiczne nacjonalizmu ukraińskiego; Ukraiński*

ruch nacjonalistyczny: struktura organizacyjna i założenia programowe; Dowody zbrodni OUN i UPA; Nacjonalizm ukraiński w dokumentach, (Ukrainian Integral Nationalism as a Form of Fascism: Ideological Principles of Ukrainian Nationalism; Ukrainian Nationalist Movement: Its Organization and Program; Proof of the Crimes of the OUN and UPA; Documents on Ukrainian Nationalism) 5 vols. (Toronto: n.p., 1998–2003); Grzegorz Motyka, *Ukraińska partyzantka 1942–1960: Działalność Organizacji Ukraińskich Nacjonalistów i Ukraińskiej Powstańczej Armii* (Warszawa: Instytut Studiów Politycznych PAN, and Rytm, 2006).

17. See Уладзімер Сакалоўскі and Уладзімер Ляхоўскі, "Нямеччына й беларускі нацыянальны рух напярэдадні й у першыя гады Другое Сусьетнае Вайны," ("Germany and the Belarusian Nationalist Movement before and during the First Years of the Second World War") *Białoruskie Zeszyty Historyczne* no. 13 (2000): http://kamunikat.fontel.net/www/czasopisy/bzh/13/13art_sakalouski.htm; Алег Гардзіенка, "Беларуская Народная Самапомач: яшчэ адна спроба атрымання незалежнасці (1941–1943)," (Belarusian National Self-Help: One More Way to Achieve Independence) *Białoruskie Zeszyty Historyczne* no. 16 (2001): http://kamunikat.fontel.net/www/czasopisy/bzh/16/16kom_hardzijenka.htm.

18. Bernhard Chiari, *Alltag hinter der Front: Besatzung, Kollaboration und Widerstand in Weißrußland 1941–1944* (Düsseldorf: Droste Verlag, Schriften des Bundesarchivs 53, 1998).

19. Truman Anderson, "Germans, Ukrainians and Jews: Ethnic Politics in *Heeresgebiet Süd*, June–December 1941," *War in History* 7, no. 3 (2000): 325–51; Jewgienij Rosenbłat, "Strategia przetrwania: Żydzi Zachodniej Białorusi w okresie Holocaustu," ("The Strategy of Survival: Jews of Western Belarus during the Holocaust") in Jasiewicz, *Świat Niepożegnany*, 122–42; Isaiah Trunk, *Judenrat: The Jewish Councils in Eastern Europe under Nazi Occupation* (Lincoln: University of Nebraska Press, 1972); Arūnas Bubnys, "Kauno ir Vilniaus getų žydų policija (1941–1944 m.)" ("The Jewish Police in the Kaunas and Vilnius Ghettos [1941-1944]"), *Genocidas i reistencja* no. 1 (17) (2005): http://www.genocid.lt/Leidyba/17/bubnys.htm.

20. For a scathingly unfair depiction of a high-ranking Polish underground officer who occupied a prominent position in the civilian structure of the German administration in the area of Wilno see the Lithuanian author Juzoas Lebionka, "Moje Glinciszki," ("My Glinciszki") in Jasiewicz, *Europa nieprowincjonalna*, 854–58. For a scholarly treatment of the situation of the Polish population under Nazi-ruled northeastern Poland and Lithuania see Maria Wardzyńska, *Sytuacja ludności polskiej w Generalnym Komisariacie Litwy, czerwiec 1941–lipiec 1944 (The Situation of the Polish Population in the General Commissariat of Lithuanian, June 1941–July 1944)* (Warszawa: Instytut Pamięci Narodowej, GKBZpNP, 1993). Compare with Arūnas Bubnys, "Etniniai santykiai nacių okupuotoje Lietuvoje 1941–1944 m.," ("Ethnic Relations in Nazi-Occupied Lithuania") *Genocidas ir rezistencija* no. 1 (29) (2011): http://www.genocid.lt/centras/lt/1408/a/#eng.

21. For the activities of Einsatzgruppe A reinforced by Baltic ethnic auxiliaries see the infamous SS-*Standartenführer* Jäger Report of December 1, 1941 (Einsatzkommando 3, Gesamtaufstellung der im Bereich des EK.3 bis zum 1.Dez. 1941 durchgeführten Exekutionen, Kauen, am 1. Dezember 1941), at the Osobyi Archiv in Moscow (501-1-25, fol. 109–117). A microfilmed copy of this report is available at the United States Holocaust Memorial Museum in Washington,

DC (USHMM RG-11.001M, reel 183). Documents concerning the operations of Einsatzgruppe A and its helpers in the Wilno region have been published in part by Raul Hilberg (ed.), *Documents of Destruction: Germany and Jewry, 1933–1945* (Chicago, IL: Quadragle Books, 1971), 47–55. See also Michael MacQueen, "The Context of Mass Destruction: Agents and Prerequisites of the Holocaust in Lithuania," *Holocaust and Genocide Studies* 12, no. 1 (Spring 1998): 27–48; Konrad Kwiet, "Rehearsing for Murder: The Beginning of the Final Solution in Lithuania in June 1941," *Holocaust and Genocide Studies* 12, no. 1 (Spring 1998): 3–26; Leonid Rein, "Local Collaboration in the Execution of the 'Final Solution' in Nazi-Occupied Belorussia," *Holocaust and Genocide Studies* 20, no. 3 (Winter 2006): 381–409; Gabriel N. Finder and Alexander V. Prusin, "Collaboration in Eastern Galicia: The Ukrainian Police and the Holocaust," *East European Jewish Affairs* 34, no. 2 (Winter 2004): 95–118; Martin Dean, *Collaboration in the Holocaust: Crimes of the Local Police in Belorussia and Ukraine, 1941–45* (Houndmills, Basingstoke, Hampshire, and London: Macmillan, 2000; New York: St. Martin's Press, 1999), 21, 46, 52, 74; Frank Buscher, "Investigating Nazi Crimes in Byelorussia: Challenges and Lessons," http://muweb.millersville.edu/~holo-con/buscher.html; Arūnas Bubnys, "Vokiečių ir lietuvių saugumo policja (1941–1944)," (German and Lithuanian Security Police, 1941–1944) *Genocidas ir rezistencija* no. 1 (1997): http://www.genocid.lt/Leidyba/1/arunas1.htm#GERMAN%20AND%20LITHUANIAN%20SECURITY%20POLICE%20IN%201941-1944; Arūnas Bubnys, "Lietuvių viešoji policija ir policijos batalionai (1941–1944)," ("Lithuanian Public Police and Police Battalions in 1941–1944") *Genocidas ir reistencija* no. 2 (4) (1998): http://www.genocid.lt/Leidyba/3/arunas2.htm#Lithuanian%20Public%20Police%20and%20Police%20Battalions%20in%201941–1944; Arūnas Bubnys, "253-iasis lietuvių policijos batalionas (1943–1944)," ("The Operation of the 253rd Lithuanian Police Battalion in 1943–1944") *Genocidas ir reistencija,* no. 2 (4) (1998): http://www.genocid.lt/Leidyba/4/arunas3.htm; Arūnas Bubnys, "Lietuvių policijos 2-asis (Vilniaus) ir 252-asis batalionai (1941–1944)," ("The Activities of the 2nd and the 252nd Police Battalions between 1941–1944") *Genocidas ir reistencija* no. 2 (8) (2000): http://www.genocid.lt/Leidyba/8/arunas8.htm; Arūnas Bubnys, "Penktasis lietuvių policijos batalionas (1941–1944)," ('The 5th Battalion of the Lithuanian Police [1941–1944]") *Genocidas ir reistencija* no. 1 (9) (2001): http://www.genocid.lt/Leidyba/9/arunas.htm; Arūnas Bubnys, "Lietuvių policijos batalionai Pskovo srityje ir Kurše: 13-asis ir 10(256)-asis batalionai (1942–1945)," ("Lithuanian Police Battalions in Pskov Region and Kursk: The 13th and 10(256)th Battalions [1942–1945]") *Genocidas ir reistencija* no. 2 (10) (2001): http://www.genocid.lt/Leidyba/10/arunas.htm#Pskov; Arūnas Bubnys, "Lietuvių saugumo policija ir holokaustas (1941–1944)," ("Lithuanian Security Police and the Holocaust (1941–1944]") *Genocidas ir reistencija* no. 1 (13) (2003): http://www.genocid.lt/Leidyba/13/bubnys.htm; Knut Stang, *Kollaboration und Massenmord: Die litauische Hilfspolizei, das Rollkommando Hamann und die Ermordung der litauischen Juden* (Frankfurt am Main: Peter Lang, 1996), 156–71; Christoph Dieckmann, "The Role of the Lithuanians in the Holocaust," in *Facing the Nazi Genocide: Non-Jews and Jews in Europe,* ed. Beate Kosmala and Feliks Tych (Berlin: Metropol, 2004), 149–68; Ēriks Jēkabsons and Uldis Neiburgs, "Łotewskie bataliony policyjne w ochronie getta warszawskiego (VIII-X 1942)," ("Latvian Police Battalions Guarding the Warsaw Ghetto [August–October 1942]") in Jasiewicz, *Świat Niepożegnany,* 531–58. See also Karen Sutton, *The Massacre of the Jews of Lithuania: Lithuanian*

Collaboration in the Final Solution, 1941–1944 (Jerusalem and New York: Gefen Publishers, 2008); Alvydas Nikžentaitis, Stefan Schreiner, and Darius Staliūnas, eds., *The Vanished World of Lithuanian Jews* (Amsterdam and New York: Rodopi, 2004), in particular Yitzhak Arad, "The Murder of the Jews in German-Occupied Lithuania (1941–1944)," (175–203), Arūnas Bubnys, "The Holocauast in Lithuania: An Outline of the Major Stages and their Results," (205–21), and Martin C. Dean, "Lithuanian Participation in the Mass Murder of Jews in Belarus and Ukraine, 1941–1944," (283–96). Further see David Gaunt, Paul A. Levine, and Laura Palosuo, eds., *Collaboration and Resistance During the Holocaust: Belarus, Estonia, Latvia, Lithuania* (Bern: Peter Lang, 2004), and, in particular, Martin Dean, "Microcosm: Collaboration and Resistance during the Holocaust in the Mir Rayon of Belarus, 1941–1944," (223–59) and Evgenij Rosenblat, "Belarus: Specific Features of the Region's Jewish Collaboration and Resistance," (261–82). Lastly, see Martin Dean, "The 'Local Police' in Nazi-Occupied Belarus and Ukraine as the 'Ideal Type' of Collaboration: In Practice, in the Recollections of Its Members and in the Verdicts of the Courts," in *"Kollaboration" in Nordosteuropa: Erscheinungsformen und Deutungen im 20. Jahrhundert*, ed. Joachim Tauber (Wiesbaden: Harrassowitz Verlag, 2006), 414–33.

22.   See Catherine Andreyeva, *Vlasov and the Russian Liberation Movement: Soviet Reality and Émigré Theories* (Cambridge and New York: Cambridge University Press, 1989); Samuel J. Newland, *Cossacks in the German Army, 1941–1945* (London and Portland, OR: Frank Cass, 1991); Leonid Rein, "Untermenschen in SS Uniforms: 30th Waffen-Grenadier Division of Waffen SS," *The Journal of Slavic Military Studies* 20, no. 2 (April 2007): 329–45; Warren Paul Green, "The Nazi Racial Policy toward the Karaites," *Soviet Jewish Affairs* 7 (1978): 36–44; Emanuela Trevisan-Semi, "The Image of the Karaites in Nazi and Vichy France documents," *Jewish Social Studies* 32 (December 1990): 81–93. See also the following essays in *"Kollaboration" in Nordosteuropa: Erscheinungsformen und Deutungen im 20. Jahrhundert*, ed. Joachim Tauber (Wiesbaden: Harrassowitz Verlag, 2006): Iskander Gilyazov, "Die Kollaboration der türk-muslimischen Völker der Sowjetunion während des Zweiten Weltkrieges als Erscheinungsform des Nationalismus," (406–13); Matthias Schröder, "'Denkmal Vlasov' – Zur politischen Instrumentalisierung des russischen Kollaborateurs General Vlasov im Zweiten Weltkrieg und zur Rezeptionsgeschichte nach 1945," (434–42). See further Jarosław Gdański, "*Ostlegionen* – 'Legiony Wschodnie' Niemieckich Wojsk Lądowych," ("Eastern Legions of the German Land Forces") *Glaukopis* no. 15–16 (2009): 127–64.

23.   For property confiscations in Poland by the Nazis see Bernhard Rosenkötter, *Treuhandpolitik: Die "Haupttreuhandstelle Ost" und der Raub polnischer Vermögen, 1939–1945* (Essen: Klartext Verlag, 2003). For Jewish property seized in the European context see Martin Dean, *Robbing the Jews: The Confiscation of Jewish Property in the Holocaust, 1933–1945* (New York: Cambridge University Press, 2010). For the question of Jewish property in Lithuania see Valentinas Brandišauskas, "Lietuvos žydų turto likimas Antrojo pasaulinio karo metai," ("The Fate of Lithuanian Jews' Assets during the Second World War") *Genocidas ir reistencija* no. 1 (15) (2004): http://www.genocid.lt/Leidyba/15/valentin. htm; Valentinas Brandišauskas, "Žydų nuosavybės bei turto konfiskavimas ir naikinimas Lietuvoje," ("Expropriation of the Jewish Property, and Destruction in Lithuania during the Second World War") *Genocidas ir reistencija* no. 2 (12) (2002): http://www.genocid.lt/Leidyba/12/valentin.htm.

24. Polish ethnic Communists constituted the smallest contingent of Soviet patriots. The Communist underground was nonexistent in western Poland (i.e., territories incorporated directly into the Reich). In the General Government, the Communists fielded around 6,000 people at the peak of the party's expansion in July 1944. It must be remembered that, in addition to a sizable contingent of Jews, many Communist partisans were either common criminals or fugitives who were generally unaware of the Soviet agenda, reacting instead to the gospel of "national liberation" preached by the party at the time. In Poland's eastern provinces, there were hardly any indigenous Communists left following the first Soviet occupation. Nonetheless, there were Poles who were forcibly inducted into Soviet partisan units. Some of these draftees promptly escaped; others were shot as unreliable. Only a few remained, including in a single guerrilla outfit (the "Kościuszko unit"), operating within a Soviet detachment in the Nowogródek area. The only region where there was anything approaching a large-scale participation of Poles in the Soviet underground was Volhynia. To save themselves from the ethnic cleansing operation of the Ukrainian nationalist underground, whenever they were unable to join Polish resistance units (which were late in forming), about 5,000 Poles entered Soviet guerrilla detachments or accepted Soviet (including NKVD) leadership of and equipment for their self-defense forces. The Soviets, on their part, for propaganda purposes, had orders to create partisan units "Polish in form, Bolshevik in substance," most notably the "Poland Has Not Perished Yet" outfit under Robert Satanowski. Last but not least, individual Poles, who were NKVD officers or agents, did infiltrate the pro-Western, independentist underground, everywhere. For a brief case study of Volhynia see Oksana Petruszewicz, "Polacy i Sowieci na Wołyniu," ("The Poles and the Soviets in Volhynia") *Myśl Polska*, June 22–29, 2008; and Andrzej Szutowicz, *Gen. Robert Satanowski – życiorys żołnierski* (*Gen. Robert Satanowski – A Soldier's Biography*) (Drawno: Kawaliera, 2005). For a comparison with Stalin's underground in central Poland see Marek Jan Chodakiewicz, Piotr Gontarczyk, and Leszek Żebrowski, eds., *Tajne Oblicze: Dokumenty GL-AL i PPR, 1942–1945*, 3 vols. (*Secret Face: Documents of the Communist Underground*) (Warszawa: Burchard Edition, 1997–1999). And see a rather sympathetic rendering of their ideology in Stanisław Ciesielski, *Myśl polityczna polskich komunistów w latach 1939–1944* (*Political Thought of Polish Communists between 1939 and 1944*) (Wrocław: Wydawnictwo Uniwersytetu Wrocławskiego, 1990).

25. See Jarosław Wołkonowski, "ZWZ-AK a problem mniejszości etnicznych na Wileńszczyźnie," *Opór wobec systemów totalitarnych na Wileńszczyźnie w okresie II wojny światowej* (*Resistance Against Totalitarian Systems in the Wilno Region during the Second World War*), ed. Piotr Niwiński (Gdańsk: Instytut Pamięci Narodowej, Komisja Ścigania Zbrodni przeciwko Narodowi Polskiemu, 2003), 38–59; Jarosław Wołkonowski, "Wileński Okręg ZWZ-AK a problem mniejszości żydowskiej w okresie okupacji niemieckiej," ("The Wilno Region of the ZWZ-AK and the Problem of the Jewish Minority during the German Occupation") in Jasiewicz, *Świat Niepożegnany*, 526–30; Bernhard Chiari, "Polski ruch oporu a Żydzi: Uwagi do rozważań o II wojnie światowej," ("Polish Resistance Movement and the Jews: Some Remarks about the Second World War") in Jasiewicz, *Świat Niepożegnany*, 516–26; Marc Bartuschka, *Der Partisanenkrieg in Weißrußland 1941–1944: Jeder gegen Jeden? Ursprünge, Strukturen und Parteien des Konflikts* (Saarbrücken: VDM Verlag Dr. Müller, 2008).

26. Reuben Ainsztein, *Jewish Resistance in Nazi-Occupied Eastern Europe with a Historical Survey of the Jew as Fighter and Soldier in the Diaspora* (London: Paul Elek, 1974); Jerzy Węgierski, "Konspiracja i walka Żydów na Kresach południowo-wschodnich: Zarys i próba hipotezy motywów," ("Conspiracy and the Struggle of the Jews in the South-Eastern Borderlands: An Outline and a Hypothesis of Their Motives") Jasiewicz, *Świat Niepożegnany*, 495–505; Grzegorz Berendt, "Rewolta więźniów getta w Łachwie (3 września 1942 r.)," ("The Revolt of Prisoners of the Łachwa Ghetto, 3 September 1942") *Glaukopis*, no. 23–24 (2011–2012): 46–61; Barbara Epstein, *The Minsk Ghetto, 1941–1943: Jewish Resistance and Soviet Internationalism* (Berkeley, CA: University of California Press, 2008).

27. See Vineta Rolmane, "The Resistance in Latvia during the Nazi Occupation (July 1941–May 1945)," in *The Anti-Soviet Resistance in the Baltic States*, 131–48; Arūnas Bubnys, *Nazi Resistance Movement in Lithuania, 1941–1944* (Vilnius: VAGA Publishers, 2003) (the title of Bubnys's work is clearly a mistranslation: "anti-Nazi Resistance" was meant); Linas Venclauskas "Lietuvos įvaizdžiai antinacinėje lietuvių spaudoje," ("The Vision of Lithuania in the Lithuanian Anti-Nazi Press") *Genocidas ir reistencija* no. 1 (15) (2004): http://www.genocid.lt/Leidyba/15/linas.htm.

28. The Ukrainian underground was divided, roughly, into two factions: the Melnyk and the Bandera groups of the Organization of Ukrainian Nationalists (OUN-M and OUN-B, respectively). The former opted for complete collaboration with the Nazis and eschewed armed struggle against them altogether, while maintaining some conspiratorial political activities. The OUN-B fielded the Ukrainian Insurgent Army (UPA), which engaged in occasional low-level melees with German forces and more frequent weapon seizures from German outposts. There were also autonomous secret Ukrainian nationalist organizations, for instance, in Volhynia, which were eliminated by the OUN-B. In practice, the rank-and-file membership of all nationalist groups often overlapped. For example, there were UPA men of OUN-B serving with the OUN-M-sponsored 14th Waffen-SS Division. Ukrainian nationalists of all orientations served in the *SS-Schutzmanschaften* and other Nazi auxiliary police formations. See Roman Drozd, ed., *Ukraińska Powstańcza Armia: Dokumenty-struktury* (Warszawa: Burchard Edition, 1998) (afterward *UPA dokumenty*); Marek Jan Chodakiewicz, "'Dwie drogi, jeden cel,': Ukraińcy w brygadach międzynarodowych Hitlera" ("'Two Roads, One Aim': Ukrainians in Hitler's International Brigades"), *Templum* no. 2/3 (2002): 102–109; Michael O. Logusz, *Galicia Division: The Waffen-SS 14th Grenadier Division, 1943–1945* (Atglen, PA: Schiffer Military History, 1997); Basil Dmytryshyn, "The SS-Division Galicia, 1943–1945,"in Hunczak and Shtohryn, *Ukraine* 209–230; Edward Prus, *UPA: Armia Powstańcza czy kurenie rizunów* (*UPA: An Insurgent Army or Bands of Killers*) (Wrocław: Nortom, 1994); Henryk Pająk, *Za samostijną Ukrainę* (For Independent Ukraine) (Lublin: Wydawnictwo Retro, 1992); *Ukrains'ka Powstan'ska Armia: U borbot'i proty totalitarnikh rezhimiv* (*UPA: Fighting against Totalitarian Regimes*) (Lviv: Natsional'na Akademia Nauk Ukrainy im. I. Krypiakevycha, 2004), the last named being vol. 2 of *Ukraina: Kul'turna spadshchina, natsionalna svidomist', derzhavnist* (Ukraine: Cultural Heritage, National Consciousness, Statehood).

29. For an excellent historiography of the Ukrainian–Polish conflict see Krzysztof Łada, "Creative Forgetting: Polish and Ukrainian Historiographies on the Campaigne [sic] Against the Poles in Volhynia During World War II," *Glaukopis* 2/3

(2004–2005): 343–78. The conflict eventually spilled into the eastern fringes of central Poland (General Government). For a case study see Robert Ziętek, "Konflikt polsko-ukraiński na Chełmszczyźnie i południowym Podlasiu w okresie okupacji niemieckiej" (Polish–Ukrainian Conflict in the Chełm Area and in Southern Podlasie during the German Occupation), *Rocznik Chełmski* 7 (2001): 251–89. While ignoring earlier massacres of Poles, Ukrainian historians claim that the Polish underground started killing Ukrainians in the Podlasie and Chełm areas in the summer of 1942, pointing specifically to villages in the vicinity of the Parczew Forest and Dratów. However, the former villages, according to Jewish sources, were attacked by Jewish partisans in revenge for the villagers' anti-Jewish activities, and it was the Germans who carried out the executions in Dratów. See Harold Werner, *Fighting Back: A Memoir of Jewish Resistance in World War II* (New York: Columbia University Press, 1992), xvii, xix–xx, 99 (Zamołodycze), 110 (Hola), 161 (Pachole), 169 (Krzywowierzba), 176 (Zahajki), 178 (Krzywy Bór, Chmielów, Krasówka, Zienki), 179 (Zamołodycze, Kapłonosy), 185 (Kapłonosy), 187 (Ostrów Lubelski), 196 (Marianka); Ryszard Tyndorf, "Przyczynek do historii stosunków polsko-ukraińskich na Chełmszczyźnie," [A Detail of History of Polish-Ukrainian Relations in the Chełm Area] *Glaukopis* 5/6 (2006): 485–89. On the attitude of the Ukrainian nationalist underground toward the Jews see Grzegorz Motyka, "Ukraińska Powstańcza Armia a Żydzi," (UPA and the Jews) in Jasiewicz, *Świat Niepożegnany*, 483–94.

30. See the following essays in Jasiewicz, *Europa nieprowincjonalna*: Marek Ney-Krewicz, "Ziemie wschodnie Rzeczypospolitej Polskiej w koncepcjach walki Armii Krajowej: Zarys problemu" (Eastern Lands of the Polish Commonwealth in the Conceptual Plans of Struggle of the Home Army: An Outline) (638–45); and Andrzej Chmielarz, "Organizacja i działalność wywiadu wschodniego ZWZ-AK" ("The Organization and Activities of the Eastern Intelligence Gathering Operation of the ZWZ-AK") (656–61). And see Cezary Chlebowski, *Wachlarz: Monografia wydzielonej organizacji dywersyjnej Armii Krajowej, wrzesień 1941–marzec 1943 (The Fan: A Monograph of the Autonomous Diversionary Organization of the Home Army, September 1941–March 1943)* (Warszawa: Instytut Wydawniczy Pax, 1990); Aleksander Szemiel, *23 Brasławska Brygada partyzancka Armii Krajowej we wspomnieniach dowódców i żołnierzy (The 23rd Braslavian Partisan Brigade of the Home Army According to the Recollections of Its Commanders and Soldiers)* (Warszawa: Oficyna Wydawnicza Adiutor, 2002); Kazimierz Litwiejko, *Narodowa Organizacja Wojskowa Okręg Białystok, 1941–1945 (National Military Organization of the Bialystok District, 1941–1945)* (Białystok: Wydawnictwo Benkowski, n.d. [2002]); Kazimierz Krajewski, *Uderzeniowe Bataliony Kadrowe, 1942–1944 (Storm Cadre Battalions, 1942–1944)* (Warszawa: Instytut Wydawniczy Pax, 1993).

31. The most notorious case occurred on June 20, 1944, in Glinciszki, where a Home Army unit ambushed a Lithuanian auxiliary police detachment of the Nazis, killing four policemen. As punishment, the Lithuanian police executed thirty-nine Polish hostages, including women and children as well as the AK quartermaster for the Wilno/Vilnius area. In revenge, the Home Army shot twenty-seven persons, mostly Lithuanian peasants, but also including a few Lithuanian policemen, in Dubinki/Dubingiai. See Jarosław Wołkonowski, "Starcie polsko-litewskie," ("The Polish–Lithuanian Clash") *Karta* no. 32 (2001): 64–89.

32. See Biuro Prezydialne, Poczta dla Rządu, Sowiecka partyzantka na Kresach (Wileńszczyzna), AAN, DR, file 202/I-36, 70–71; Raport o Kresach za 14-27

marca 1943, AAN, DR, file 202/I-42, 21; Informacje o komunistycznej partyzantce na Mińszczyźnie, AAN, Narodowe Sły Zbrojne (afterward NSZ), file 207/17, 24; Eugeniusz Iwaniec, "Napad sowieckiej partyzantki na Kosów Poleski, 3 sierpnia 1942 r. (sukces czy klęska?)," ("The Assault of the Soviet Partisan Movement on Kosov Poleski, August 3, 1942 [a success or a failure?]") Białoruskie Zeszyty Historyczne, nr. 25 (2006): 259–96; Bogdan Musiał, ed., Sowjetische Partisanen in Weißrußland: Innenansichten aus dem Gebiet Baranoviči, 1941–1944: Eine Dokumentation (Munich: R. Oldenbourg Verlag, 2004); Bogdan Musiał, Sowjetische Partisanen 1941–1941: Mythos und Wirklichkeit (Paderborn: Schöningh, 2009); Michał Gnatowski, "Kontrowersje i konflikty między ZWZ-AK i radzieckim podziemiem na północno-wschodnich ziemiach Polski w latach 1941–1944," ("Controversies and Conflicts between the ZWZ-AK and the Soviet Underground in the North-Eastern Lands of Poland between 1941 and 1944") in Granice i pogranicza: Historia codzienności i doświadczeń, vol. 2, ed. Marzena Liedke, Joanna Sadowska, and Jan Tyrkowski (Białystok: Instytut Historii Uniwersytetu w Białymstoku, 1999), 177–92; Alexander Brakel, "'Das allergefährlichste ist die Wut der Bauern': Die Versorgung der Partisanen und ihr Verhältnis zur Zivilbervölkerung. Eine Fallstudie zum Gebiet Baranowicze 1941–1944," Vierteljahrshefte für Zeitgeschichte 55, no. 3 (2007): 393–424; Leonid D. Grenkevich, The Soviet Partisan Movement, 1941–1944: A Critical Historiographical Analysis (London and Portland, OR: Frank Cass Publishers, 1999); Kenneth Slepyan, Stalin's Guerrillas: Soviet Partisans in World War II (Lawrence, KS: University Press of Kansas, 2006).

33. See Sarunas Liekis, "Jewish Partisans and Soviet Resistance in Lithuania," in Gaunt, Levine, and Palosuo, Collaboration and Resistance, 459–78; Leonid Smilovitsky, "Antisemitism in the Soviet Partisan Movement, 1941–1944: The Case of Belorussia," Holocaust and Genocide Studies 20 (2) (2006): 207–34; Adam Puławski, "Postrzeganie żydowskich oddziałów partyzanckich przez Armię Krajową i Delegaturę Rządu," ("Perception of the Jewish Partisan Units by the Home Army and the Office of the Delegate") Pamięć i Sprawiedliwość no. 2 (4) (2003): 271–300; Mikołaj Iwanow, "Partyzantka żydowska na Kresach północno-wschodnich i jej stosunek do Armii Krajowej, 1942–1945," ("The Jewish Partisan Units in the North-Eastern Borderlands and Their Attitude toward the Home Army") in Jasiewicz, Świat Niepożegnany, 506–15.

34. See Rimantas Zizas, "Vietinė savisauga (savigyna) Lietuvoje nacių Vokietijos okupacijos metais (1941–1944)," ("Local Defence [Self-Defence] in Lithuania during the Nazi German Occupation [1941–1944]") (part 1) Genocidas ir reistencija no. 2 (10) (2001): http://www.genocid.lt/Leidyba/10/rimantas.htm; and Rimantas Zizas, "Vietinė savisauga (savigyna) Lietuvoje nacių Vokietijos okupacijos metais (1941–1944)," ("Local Defence [Self-Defence] in Lithuania during the Nazi German Occupation [1941–1944]") (part 2) Genocidas ir reistencija no. 1 (11) (2002): http://www.genocid.lt/Leidyba/11/zizas.htm#Defence.

35. See Zygmunt Boradyn, Niemen – rzeka niezgody: Polsko-sowiecka wojna partyzancka na Nowogródczyźnie, 1943–1944 (Niemen – the river of discord: Polish–Soviet partisan war in the Nowogródek region, 1943–1944) (Warszawa: Oficyna Wydawnicza Rytm, 1999) (afterward Niemen – Rzeka niezgody); Marek Jan Chodakiewicz, Narodowe Siły Zbrojne: "Ząb" przeciw dwu wrogom (National Armed Forces: "Ząb" against Two Enemies) (Warszawa: Fronda, 1999), 77–88 (afterward Narodowe Siły Zbrojne); Maria Wardzyńska, "Mord popełniony latem 1943 r. przez partyzantów radzieckich na żołnierzach AK z oddziału 'Kmicica,'" ("The Murder Perpetrated by the Soviet Partisans on the

Home Army Soldiers of the "Kmicic" Unit in the Summer of 1943") *Pamięć i sprawiedliwość: Biuletyn Głównej Komisji Badania Zbrodni przeciwko Narodowi Polskiemu Instytutu Pamięci Narodowej* no. 39 (1996): 134–50; Rimantas Zizas, "Raudonųjų partizanų ir Pietryčių Lietuvos kaimų savisaugos ginkluoti konfliktai 1943 m.," ("Soviet Partisans of Lithuania and the Conflict of 1943") *Genocidas ir reistencija* no. 1 (15) (2004): http://www.genocid.lt/Leidyba/15/zizas.htm.

36. See DSW, Agencja A., Tygodnik nr. 14, AAN, DR, 202/II-24, 5; DIP, Tygodniowy Przegląd Najważniejszych Wydarzeń w Kraju, M.I. II/44 (February 1944), AAN, DR, file 202/III-20, 35; Przegląd Najważniejszych Wydarzeń w Kraju, nr. 11/44, March 16, 1944, AAN, DR, file 202/I-42, 139; Chodakiewicz, *Narodowe Siły Zbrojne*, 322–23; Michael Foedrowitz, "W poszukiwaniu 'modus vivendi': Kontakty i rozmowy pomiędzy okupantami a okupowanymi dotyczące porozumienia polsko-niemieckiego w czasie II wojny światowej," ("Searching for the 'Modus Vivendi': Contacts and Conversations between the Occupiers and the Occupied Concerning a Polish–German Agreement during the Second World War") *Mars* 2 (1994): 165–80; Jarosław Wołkonowski, "Wileńskie rozmowy polsko-niemieckie w lutym 1944 roku," ("The Wilno Polish–German Talks in February 1944") *Mars* 2 (1994): 181–202; Krzysztof Tarka, *Komendant Wilk: Z dziejów wileńskiej Armii Krajowej* (*Commander Wolf: A History of the Wilno Home Army*) (Warszawa: Oficyna Wydawnicza Volumen, 1990), 66–70; Zygmunt Szczęsny Brzozowski, *Litwa-Wilno, 1910–1945* (Lithuania-Wilno, 1910–1945) (Paris: Editions Spotkania, 1987), 150–55; Jarosław Wołkonowski, *Okręg Wileński Związku Walki Zbrojnej Armii Krajowej w latach 1939–1945* (*The Wilno District of the Union of Armed Struggle-Home Army, 1939–1945*) (Warszawa: Adiutor, 1996), 171–84 (afterward *Okręg Wileński Związku Walki Zbrojnej Armii Krajowej*). See also Bernhard Chiari, *Alltag hinter der Front: Besatzung, Kollaboration und Widerstand in Weißrußland 1941–1944* (Düsseldorf: Droste Verlag, Schriften des Bundesarchivs 53, 1998), 285–86; Bernhard Chiari, "Reichsführer-SS—Kein Pakt mit Slaven: Deutsch-polnische Kontakte in Wilna-Gebiet 1944," *Osteuropa-Archiv* 50, no. 4 (April 2000): A133–53.

37. Jerzy Węgierski, *W lwowskiej Armii Krajowej* (*In the Lvovian Home Army*) (Warszawa: Pax, 1989); Michał Fijałka, *Wołyńska 27 Dywizja Piechoty Armii Krajowej* (Warszawa: Pax, 1986).

38. See Józef Turowski and Władysław Siemaszko, *Zbrodnie nacjonalistów ukraińskich dokonane na ludności polskiej na Wołyniu 1939–1945* (*The Crimes of the Ukrainian Nationalists against the Polish Population in Volhynia, 1939–1945*) (Warszawa: Główna Komisja Badania Zbrodni Hitlerowskich w Polsce–Instytut Pamięci Narodowej and Środowisko Żołnierzy 27 Wołyńskiej Dywizji Armii Krajowej, 1990), 11–13; Ryszard Kotarba, "Zbrodnie nacjonalistów ukraińskich na ludności polskiej w województwie tarnopolskim w latach 1939–1945: Próba bilansu," ("The Crimes of the Ukrainian Nationalists against the Polish Population in the Province of Tarnopol between 1939 and 1945: An Attempt to Summarize") in *Polska–Ukraina: Trudne pytania*, vol. 6: *Materiały VI międzynarodowego seminarium historycznego "Stosunki polsko-ukraińskie w latach II wojny światowej," Warszawa, 3–5 listopada 1999* ("Poland-Ukraine: Difficult Questions: The Materials from the 6th International Historical Seminar on the 'Polish-Ukrainian Relations during the Second World War'") (Warsaw: Światowy Związek Żołnierzy Armii Krajowej, Związek Ukraińców w Polsce, and Karta, 2000), 262. Certainly not all Ukrainians deserted from the police, and a sizable contingent remained outside of Volhynia.

39.   The bibliography of the Rising is rather extensive in Polish and quite inadequate in Western languages. The most important English-language positions are J. K. Zawodny, *Nothing but Honour: The Story of the Warsaw Uprising, 1944* (Stanford, CA: Hoover Institution Press, 1978); Jan M. Ciechanowski, *Warsaw Rising 1944* (London and New York: Cambridge University Press, 1974); and Norman Davies, *Rising'44: The Battle for Warsaw* (New York: Viking, 2004). For the latest research on the insurrection see the bilingual (Polish and Russian) collection *Powstanie Warszawskie 1944 w dokumentach z archiwów służb specjalnych* (Warszawa and Moscow: Instytut Pamięci Narodowej, Komisja Ścigania Zbrodni przeciwko Narodowi Polskiemu, Ministerstwo Spraw Wewnętrznych i Administracji Rzeczpospolitej Polskiej and Służba Bezpieczeństwa Federacji Rosyjskiej, 2007). See also Marek Jan Chodakiewicz, "The Varsovian Rising, 1944: Perception and Reality," *Glaukopis* no. 2/3 (2004–2005): 61–75, http://www.warsawuprising.com/doc/chodakiewicz1.pdf; Marek Jan Chodakiewicz, "The Uprising Retold," *Neue Politische Literatur* 47, no. 2 (2002): 344–46, and an expanded version as "Der Warschauer Aufstand," *The Sarmatian Review* [Houston] 22, no. 2 (April 2002): 875–80.

12

The Second Soviet Occupation (1944–1992)

After the torchlight red on sweaty faces
After the frosty silence in the gardens
After the agony in stony places
The shouting and the crying
Prison and place and reverberation
Of thunder of spring over distant mountains
He who was living is now dead
We who were living are now dying
With a little patience[1]

       —T. S. Eliot, The Waste Land, 1922

Poland had to wait for one thousand years for the appearance of the
slogan that the Commonwealth should be inhabited solely by the Poles.
It was only the Soviet agentura that advanced and implemented this
slogan here; we will not encounter it proposed by any Polish thinker.[2]

       —Adam Doboszyński, 1946

What dominates the current political situation in the world, what the
cardinal feature of the domination is — which we tend to forget about
because we would indubitably like to forget about it — it is not any
division but ... a joint venture. A joint Soviet-British-American one.
The company, founded for the duration of the war and its aftermath,
continues, formally and officially, to function and to fulfill its role. The
latter consists of the division between the participants of other people's
property, both political and material, left over by the states which lost
the war. The objects of this transaction, or, to put it in moral terms,
the victims of the joint venture are, first of all, the following states:
Poland, Lithuania, Latvia, Estonia, Finland, Germany, Italy, Romania,
Hungary, Czechoslovakia, Bulgaria, Yugoslavia, Albania, Greece, Persia,
Manchuria, Korea, and Japan. In addition, in congruence with the

waxing of the power of the joint venture, indirectly or directly, it came to bear its influence over numerous other states and nations in Europe, Asia, and Africa.

This is the way things truly are. Stemming from this general picture, a secondary issue reveals itself in a variety of misunderstandings between the partners, which — given the volume of the loot to be divided — are quite natural. The partners quarrel, sometimes even jump one another, and shake their fists at each other. Sometimes it comes near to breaking up the partnership. This does not mean, however, that the break has occurred . . . The partnership endures . . . [because] Great Britain and the United States want to maintain peace, and the states, which fell victim to that peace, can only be saved by a war. It is difficult to find more contradictory intentions among the parties involved.

The error of Great Britain and the United States rests in their lack of appreciation for this specific [Communist] threat, which is unprecedented in history . . . [Therefore] our effort should be to undermine and torpedo the joint venture of the Soviet Union-Great Britain-the United States.[3]

—Józef Mackiewicz, 1947

As the Red Army stormed west in 1944–1945, Stalin approached the newly enslaved peoples in a dual manner. First, the once Soviet-occupied territories reconquered from the Nazis were immediately reincorporated into the Soviet Union.[4] Second, the newly seized countries were subjected to occupation by proxy with the assistance of the local Communists whose presence camouflaged the Soviet military and police colonial rule over those nations. Hence, Estonia, Latvia, Lithuania, Belarus, and Ukraine reverted to the status of Soviet republics. A truncated Poland and other East Central European nations became "people's democracies." Stalin ruled the former directly and the latter less directly, through his proxies.

As during the previous occupation, the Soviet system based itself on terror.[5] Like before, terror was carried out with the assistance of native collaborators. Since the local Communists were few and far between, most collaborators were opportunists. Many, technical experts (e.g., engineers), in particular, simply accommodated the occupiers to survive. In addition, Stalin and his proxies made a skillful use of the minorities. For example, the Poles and Jews in Volhynia and Eastern Galicia were invited, and often even conscripted, to the so-called *istrebitelnye batal'ony* ("destruction battalions") of the NKVD to avenge themselves on the Ukrainian nationalists. The latter were now fighting chiefly the Soviets but they also continued their campaign of ethnic cleansing against the Poles. To avoid the Gulag or service in the Red Army, some Poles and Jews did enroll as NKVD auxiliaries. The surviving Jews in the Minsk and Wilno/Vilnius regions, many of whom had been Soviet partisans, were likewise recruited in the auxiliary militia to mete out punishment to real and alleged Nazi collaborators among the local Lithuanians, Belarusians, and Poles, and to assist in the effort to wipe out the remnants of the Home Army.[6] Naturally, there was always a sufficient contingent of home-grown traitors of the majority ethnicity willing to assist the Soviets. The NKVD and its local proxies employed many Ukrainians on a significant scale, against the Ukrainian underground, for instance.[7] These developments mirrored similar processes which took soon after in the "people's democracies."

Terror was one tool of totalitarian rule. Deception was the other. Stalin bragged about "liberating" East Central Europe and introducing "democracy" there. In reality, until the attempt at a full Sovietization between 1948 and 1956, the "people's democracies" experienced *ersatz* political pluralism, sham coalition governments (invariably dominated by the Communists), falsified elections, censorship, ban on travel abroad (except for the migration of Jews from Poland), and police terror. Mass terror included assassinations, routine torture of prisoners,[8] overloaded jails, concentration camps, and internal[9] and external deportation, the latter to the Gulag. At least 100,000 people were shipped off to Siberia from the territory of "people's" Poland alone.[10] Probably altogether twice as many individuals were seized and dispatched to forced labor from other "people's democracies," Hungary and Romania, in particular, between 1944 and 1946.[11] Last but not least, there were massive purges, pacification actions in the countryside, and a Soviet-led, full-scale counterinsurgency war against the independentist underground movements, which persisted into the 1950s. On the other hand, until 1948, the denizens of the "people's democracies" enjoyed some religious and cultural freedoms, a modicum of safeguards on small property holdings, the possibility of changing employment easily, and a chance to travel within their countries rather unimpeded.

None of that was granted to the captive peoples from Estonia to Moldavia whose territories were reincorporated into the USSR.[12] In essence, these nations were reliving the nightmare of 1939–1941. Private property was reconfiscated again. There was only very limited property restitution for the Jewish survivors.[13] The important exception was that recollectivization was temporarily postponed until 1948, a lethal famine of the previous two years quite possibly a factor as well as the raging anti-Communist insurgency. Nonetheless, Christian churches were suppressed, though with less ferocity than before.[14]

All in all, it was business as usual for the Communists. Mass deportations commenced immediately upon the return of the Red Army to the Intermarium. A minimum of 180,000 Balts were sent to the Gulag and probably 200,000 Ukrainians, half as many Belarusians, and at least 45,000 denizens of the Moldavian Soviet Socialist Republic, most of them real and alleged "Nazi collaborators" and "enemies of the people."

The Poles of the eastern provinces were relatively luckier than the rest of the locals. An estimated 50,000 of them were dispatched to Siberia. Between 1944 and 1946 in the Provinces of Wilno and Nowogródek alone, the NKVD arrested 13,000 Home Army soldiers, killed up to 3,000, and sent more than 20,000 people (including Polish civilians) to the Gulag. Between July 1944 and March 1945 in the area of Lwów/Lviv, the Soviet secret police killed or captured 60,000 persons, probably half and half Poles and Ukrainians. In the Grodno region, during the NKVD sweeps of the fall of 1945 alone, about 2,000 Polish underground soldiers were seized. Slightly to the north-west, on the very edge of the Intermarium, abutting East Prussia, in the area of Augustów, a single massive Soviet operation in July 1945 netted about 7,000 Poles. Up to 1,420 of the victims disappeared forever without a trace, almost certainly shot.[15]

The bulk of Poles, over two million, fled or suffered expulsion from their households. They were expropriated and shipped off, destitute and down-trodden, to "people's" Poland. However, the expulsion mostly concerned the southeastern provinces.[16] After a short period, in the north-east, Stalin halted the process of "repatriating" Poles, who had "opted" for resettlement. Hence, a sizable Polish minority remained behind in the Lithuanian and Belorussian Soviet Socialist Republics.[17] Most of the tiny band of the Jewish survivors of the Holocaust, along with a much more sizable group of the Jewish survivors of the Gulag, elected not to linger in the Soviet-occupied Eastern Borderlands and moved uninhibited to central Poland, later escaping to the West.[18]

As for human losses after 1944, we can conservatively estimate that about 145,000 people perished on the Soviet side of the border in the Intermarium, including 85,000 Ukrainians, 30,000 Belarusians, 15,000 Balts, 10,000 Poles, and 5,000 Romanians (Moldovans). Thus, the human toll in situ is compa-rable to the first Soviet occupation of 1939–1941. This excludes, however, the many victims of the horrible famine of 1946–1947, which afflicted the entire territory of the USSR, and the tens of thousands of prisoners from the Intermarium who perished in the Gulag after 1944.

Naturally, the re-Sovietization and the concomitant repression fueled resis-tance. The resistance was simply a continuation of the effort initiated during the first Soviet occupation and the Nazi rule. Various national underground movements operated separately for the most part. However, now even the Balts resorted to armed guerrilla struggle,[19] and so did the Moldovans (Romanians). The Ukrainians shifted the bulk of their effort against the Soviets. Yet, determined to drive out the remaining Poles, the anti-Polish atrocities continued, albeit on a smaller scale, mainly in Eastern Galicia. The Poles responded in kind, if to a much more limited extent. On the other hand, there were some instances of tactical cooperation of the Ukrainian anti-Communist partisans with the Polish clandestine formations[20] as well as between the Polish guerrillas and the Lithuanian secret groups. The former took place mostly in "people's" Poland; the latter in Soviet Lithuania.[21]

As for the Belarusians, their nationalist underground hardly existed at all. A few guerillas remained behind, mostly from local self-defense forces active already during the Nazi occupation. Some of them consciously carried on the legacy of the anti-Bolshevik Green Oak movement. There were also a few espionage and sabotage outfits, like the "Black Cat," cooperating with western intelligence agencies.[22] Most of the Belarusian people, however, accommodated pliantly like others did. In a few cases, real and alleged Soviet collaborators among them were targeted by the Poles.[23] Some Belarusians who considered themselves Polish patriots continued their anti-Soviet struggle within the framework of the Polish underground. The latter was now greatly weakened and, hence, limited the territory of its operations largely to the pockets of Polish settlements in Lithuanian and Belorussian Soviet Socialist Republics. The Polish clandestine activities were the weakest in the south-east because the expulsion of Poles was most complete there and the threat of the Ukrainian nationalist underground most acute. The Polish underground largely withdrew into major cities, Lwów/Lviv, in particular. It focused chiefly on nonmilitary resistance, including publishing and disseminating of the underground press. Nonetheless, throughout the Intermarium, the armed struggle of the Balts, Ukrainians, Poles, Belarusians, and others lasted into the 1950s.[24] The last Estonian insurgent died in a KGB dragnet only in 1978.[25]

In the USSR's Central and Eastern European satellites, concomitantly to eradicating the underground, the Communists also dealt with the parliamentary opposition. The Soviet proxies applied the so-called salami tactics against them. Most of the parties initially licensed by Stalin as the opposition were left-ist or liberal. However, a few above-ground center-right groups were legalized by the regime and also permitted to operate temporarily. By 1948, however, the opposition parties in all the "people's democracies" were either destroyed or absorbed into their collaborationist equivalents which marched to the Kremlin chimes. Some, the Socialists, in particular, after the mandatory purges, were incorporated into the ranks of the Communists. In Poland, uniquely, a couple of collaborationist parties were permitted to exist as nominally separate entities, but totally emasculated by the Soviet proxies, in the rubber stamp parliament until 1989. In essence, these sham "coalition partners" of the satellite Communists were retained as mock remnants of the prewar parliamentary system within a totalitarian framework. This was a direct legacy of the deception operation necessitated by Yalta.

In the newly reabsorbed Intermarium, no such frivolities were allowed. The indigenous political, social, and cultural institutions were immediately crushed by the totalitarian juggernaut. The Kremlin permitted no departures from the central paradigm pioneered in the Soviet Russia. On the surface, practically nothing remained of the sphere of freedom, save for a few religious institutions, which experienced periods of fierce persecution punctuated by the occasional bouts of liberalization by the authorities. Religion remained a refuge, openly practiced mostly by the elderly and females. Religion sustained the memories of freedom. Even more exceptionally, during nearly half a century of Soviet occupation, it was the individual recollections about the interwar liberty and wartime and postwar underground resistance that animated the spirit of free thought and independence among the horribly battered elites of the captive nations between Estonia and Moldavia. Eventually, the spirit prevailed after nearly half a century.

However, when the liberation came, it occurred in an entirely different context than the one prevailing before 1939. The old framework was either annihilated completely, or lingered on openly in a warped form, or, at best, survived frozen underground. The old institutions could only persevere in the public sphere for a heavy price of collaboration, for example, churches serving as museums of atheism. The clergy was thoroughly penetrated by the secret police, the hierarchs, in particular. The old forms persisted in deep hiding and their flame keepers tended to harbor unreconstructed and reflexive, mostly optimistic stereotypes of the prewar times. The sphere of freedom was practically nonexistent in the Soviet Union even within the family for the elders were scared to share anything with their children for fear of punishment. Thus, freedom existed only in the imagination of a few bold souls who either kept the flame going from before 1939; or received the torch from the freedom fighters to pass it on to the future generations; or completely invented liberty for themselves *ex nihilio*.

Before freedom bloomed from those feeble seeds, however, the Intermarium experienced seven crucial, often overlapping and mutually enforcing, phenomena under the Soviet rule. First, after waiting about a decade in vain for a nuclear war between the East and West, the captive people psychologically resigned themselves to the defeat of liberty and permanence of Communism. They accommodated the occupier. Passive resistance faded, and collaboration became increasingly prevalent. Second, there occurred a cultural Russification, which affected Belarus and Ukraine the most, and Estonia and Latvia the least, with Lithuania and Moldova in the middle. Third, the urbanization and industrialization took place, in the Baltics to the relatively greatest extent and in some regions of Ukraine with Moldova and Belarus lagging behind. Fourth, there was migration from the village to the city both in and out of a particular "union republic." Fifth, internal migration was accompanied by the influx of other "Soviet peoples," the Russians, in particular, into the Intermarium, especially the Baltics.

Sixth, the phenomenon of the nationalization of Communism took place. Simply, as time went by, the conquered locals increasingly participated in the Soviet institutions of the totalitarian state. They frequently enrolled in the Communist party, administration, and secret services. One can truly talk about the Lithuanization of the local Communist party apparatus, for example. Consequently, strong "national Bolshevik" tendencies emerged within some republican parties which until perhaps 1956 had been perceived almost exclusively as vehicles of foreign (Russian) domination and their local participants as traitors. The reasons many natives joined the Communist party spanned the spectrum from accommodationist survivalism through sheer opportunism and ugly careerism to love of power and seduction by utopianism. Nearly all forms of the participation in the Communist party required consciousness alteration, i.e., choosing Russification and Sovietism as either an overriding or complementary factor to one's original ethno-cultural identity. For many cognitive dissonance became the norm employed to continue to function in a system that crushed the variegated heritage of the Intermarium.[26]

Last but not least, seventh, the active resistance to the Soviet rule practically disappeared. The local, postinsurgent dissident circles were but miniscule affairs of a few idealists in the realm of human rights, environmentalism, and history.[27] They were thoroughly infiltrated by the secret police and quite impotent in political terms. Yet, their emphatic protest, the mere fact of their existence, sounded a moral note that should not be ever underestimated. For one, it denoted continuity, whether consciously or not, with prewar freedom of what became the western periphery of the Soviet Union after 1944.

All of the above phenomena impacted enormously the Intermarium's liberation in the late 1980s and the early 1990s.[28] But the principal stimulus that created the conditions paving the way to freedom paradoxically came from the Kremlin. And its principal laboratory was not the Intermarium but neighboring Poland. What occurred then in the western periphery of the Soviet Union was a transformation based upon a model first implemented by the Poles. Its main attribute was nonviolence. It was emulated by nearly all the Soviet slaves in the western rim of the Empire. The transformation itself was initially a carefully engineered and guided process that eventually spun out of control and acquired a momentum of its own, erupting, at long last, in liberty. The process occurred alongside and fed off of a groundswell of counterrevolutionary, anti-Communist popular upheavals, which were, first, appropriated and, later, defused by the (post)Soviet elites eager to maintain power.

Notes

1. T. S. Eliot, *The Waste Land*, 1922, http://www.bartleby.com/201/1.html.
2. Adam Doboszyński, *W pół drogi (Halfway Along)* (Warsaw: "Prolog," 1993). Doboszyński was a leading Endek thinker and activist. This work was written right after World War II but had to wait for half a century to be published.
3. Józef Mackiewicz, "Wielka spółka trwa," ("The Joint Venture Endures") *Wiadomości* no. 41 (1947) reprinted in *Nudis Verbis* (London: Kontra, 2003), 395–97.
4. Exceptionally, Stalin permitted the overwhelmingly Polish Province of Białystok, which had been incorporated into "Soviet Belarus" after the invasion of September 1939, to revert to "people's" Poland.
5. See *Pogranichnye voiska v gody velikoi otechestvennoi voiny, 1941–1945: Sbornik dokumentov (Borderland Troops during the Great Fatherland War, 1941–1945:*

A Collection of Documents) (Moskva: Izdatelstvo "Nauka," 1968); *Pogranichnye voiska SSSR, mai 1945–1950: Sbornik dokumentov i materialov (Borderland Troops of the USSR, May 1945–1950: A Collection of Documents and Materials)* (Moskva: Izdatel'stvo "Nauka," 1975); A. F. Noskova et al., eds., *NKVD i polskoe podpole, 1944–1945 (Po "Osobym papkam" I. V. Stalina) (NKVD and the Polish Underground, 1944–1945 (Stalin's Personal File))* (Moskva: Institut slavianovedeniia i balkanistiki RAN, 1994); Giennadij A. Bordiugow et al., eds., *Polska–ZSRR: Struktury podległości: Dokumenty WKP(b), 1944–1949 (Poland–USSR: The Structures of Dependence: Documents of the VKP(b), 1944–1949)* (Warszawa: ISP PAN and Stowarzyszenie Współpracy Polska-Wschód, 1995); *Z Archiwów Sowieckich, (From the Soviet Archives)* 5 vols. (Warszawa: ISP PAN, 1992–1995); Franciszek Gryciuk and Piotr Matusak, eds., *Represje NKWD wobec żołnierzy podziemnego Państwa Polskiego w latach 1944–1945: Wybór źródeł, (Repressions of the NKWD against the Soldiers of the Underground Polish State between 1944 and 1945: A Selection of Sources)* 2 vols. (Siedlce: WSRP, 1995); Tomasz Strzembosz, ed., *NKWD o polskim podziemiu 1944–1948: Konspiracja polska na Nowogródczyźnie i Grodzieńszczyźnie (The NKVD about the Polish Underground, 1944–1948: The Polish Conspiracy in the Nowogródek and Grodno Regions)* (Warszawa: ISP PAN, 1997); Piotr Kołakowski, "NKWD-NKGB a podziemie polskie: Kresy Wschodnie," ("The NKVD-NKGB and the Polish Underground: The Eastern Borderlands") *Zeszyty Historyczne* no. 136 (2001): 59–86; Waldemar Strzałkowski, ed., *Proces Szesnastu: Dokumenty NKWD (Trail of the Sixteen: NKVD Documents)* (Warszawa: Rytm, 1995); Наталля Рыбак, "Метады і сродкі ліквідацыі акаўскіх і постакаўскіх фарміраванняў у заходніх абласцях Беларусі ў 1944–1954 гг.," (*Methods and Means of Liquidating the AK and Post-AK Units in the Western Provinces of Belarus, 1944–1954*) *Białoruskie Zeszyty Historyczne* no. 14 (2000): http://kamunikat.fontel.net/www/czasopisy/bzh/14/14art_rybak.htm; Peter J. Potichnyj, "Pacification of Ukraine: Soviet Counterinsurgency, 1944–1956," in Hunczak and Shtohryn, *Ukraine*, 171–200; Aigi Rahi-Tamm, Ritvars Jansons, and Peeter Kaasik, "Estonia i Łotwa," (Estonia and Latvia) in *Czekiści: Organy bezpieczeństwa w europejskich krajach bloku sowieckiego, 1944–1989 (The Chekists: Security Organs in the European Countries of the Soviet Bloc, 1944–1989)*, ed. Krzysztof Persak and Łukasz Kamiński (Warszawa: Instytut Pamięci Narodowej, 2010), 151–88; Juozas Starkauskas, "Fronto užnugario apsaugos NKVD kariuomenės veikla Lietuvoje (1944–1945)," ("The Activities of NKVD Forces of Rear Defence Fronts in Lithuania [1944–1945]"), *Genocidas ir reistencija* no. 1 (1997): http://www.genocid.lt/Leidyba/1/Juozas_%20Starkauskas.htm; Inga Petravičiūtė, "Sovietinio saugumo struktūra ir funkcijos Lietuvoje (1941–1954)," (The Structure and Functions of Soviet Security in Lithuania (1941–1954)), *Genocidas ir reistencija* no. 1 (1997): http://www.genocid.lt/Leidyba/1/Inga1.htm; Mindaugas Pocius, "MVD-MGB specialiosios grupės Lietuvoje (1945–1959)," ("Special MVD-MGB Troops in Lithuania [1945–1959]"), *Genocidas ir reistencija* no. 1 (1997): http://www.genocid.lt/Leidyba/1/mindaugas_pocius_mvd.htm; Nijolė Žemaitienė, "MGB–KGB agentūra okupuotoje Lietuvoje," ("MGB–KGB Agent Net in Occupied Lithuania"), *Genocidas ir reistencija* no. 2 (1997): http://www.genocid.lt/Leidyba/2/nijole2.htm#MGB–KGB%20Agencies%20in%20Occupied%20Lithuani; Juozas Starkauskas, "Sovietinė vidaus kariuomenė. Jos taktika ir veiklos metodai (1944–1953)," ('Soviet Homeland Defense Force, Its Strategy and Tactics in 1944–1953"), *Genocidas ir reistencija* no. 2 (1997): http://www.genocid.lt/Leidyba/2/Starkausk1.htm#Soviet%20Home%20Army,%20Its%2

0Strategy%20and%20Tactics%20in%201944–1953; Aleksandras Kokurinas, "SSRS NKGB–MGB struktūra," ("USSR NKGB–MGB Structure"), *Genocidas ir reistencija* no. 2 (1997): http://www.genocid.lt/Leidyba/2/aleksand.htm; Kęstutis Kasparas, "Okupantų veiksmai siekiant demoralizuoti ir dezorganizuoti pasipriešinimą 1945 m. vasarą," ("Soviet Occupation Operations to Demoralize and Destroy the Lithuanian Resistance in Summer 1945"), *Genocidas ir reistencija* no. 1 (3) (1998): http://www.genocid.lt/Leidyba/3/Kestutis_Kasparas. htm; Juozas Starkauskas, "Čekistai pasieniečiai Lietuvoje pokario metais," ("KGB Frontier Guards in Lithuania After the War"), *Genocidas ir reistencija* no. 1 (3) (1998): http://www.genocid.lt/Leidyba/3/Juozas_Starkauskas. htm#KGB%20Frontier-Guards%20in%20Lithuania%20After%20the%20War; Juozas Starkauskas, "MVD vidaus kariuomenės 4-osios divizijos antrasis veiklos periodas. 1946 m.," (The MVD 4th Division Operations in Lithuania in 1946), *Genocidas ir reistencija* no. 2 (4) (1998): http://www.genocid.lt/Leidyba/4/juozas.htm; Juozas Starkauskas, "Komunistų partijos įtaka čekistams 1944–1953 m.," ("The Communist Party Influence on the Chekists, 1944–1953"), *Genocidas ir reistencija* no. 1 (15) (2004): http://www.genocid.lt/Leidyba/15/juozas.htm; Juozas Starkauskas, "Apie dar vieną stalinio laikotarpio teroro organą – troikas ir petiorkas," ("About One More Organ of the Stalinist Period – Troikas and Petiorkas"), *Genocidas ir reistencija* no. 1 (11) (2002): http://www.genocid. lt/Leidyba/11/starkaus.htm#Troikas. For comparison see Liesbeth van de Grift, *Securing the Communist State: The Reconstruction of Coercive Institutions in the Soviet Zone of Germany and Romania, 1944-1948* (Lanham, MD: Lexington Books, 2012). On the totalitarian assault on the arts see Raili Nugin, *The Implementation of Stalinist Art Model in Estonia in 1945–1950: A Story of Defeat of Artists' Free Will* (Köln: LAP Lambert Academic Publishing, 2009). On the assault on religion see Otto Luchterhandt, "Die Kollaborationsproblematik im Verhältnis von Religionsgemeinschaften und kommunistischen Einparteistaat (ausgehend vom Fall 'Sowjetunion')," in *"Kollaboration" in Nordosteuropa: Erscheinungsformen und Deutungen im 20. Jahrhundert*, ed. by Joachim Tauber (Wiesbaden: Harrassowitz Verlag, 2006), 443–52. For a dated assessment of the Soviet occupation see Clarence A. Manning, *Ukraine under the Soviets* (New York: Bookman Associates, 1953).

6.   For a brief period after the Soviet "liberation," the Poles constituted a plurality, if not majority, of the *istrebitelnye batal'iony* in the southeastern Borderlands, having joined what were essentially self-defense units (later incorporated into the *istrebitelnye batal'ony* of the NKVD) to protect the remaining Polish settlements from continued attacks by the Ukrainian Insurgent Army. See Tomasz Balbus, "Polskie *istriebitelne bataliony* NKWD w latach 1944–1945," ("Polish Destruction Battalions of the NKVD between 1944 and 1945") *Biuletyn Instytutu Pamięci Narodowej* no. 6 (June 2002): 71–75. For a preliminary study of Jewish factor in the Soviet terror apparatus after the return of the Red Army to Belarus see Leonid Smilovitskii, "The Participation and the Role of the Jews in the Belarusian Militia, 1944–1953," *Shvut: Studies in Russian and East European Jewish History and Culture* 12, no. 28 (2004–2005): 47–66. There are no comprehensive studies concerning the Soviet police auxiliaries in the Wilno region. However, some participants talk about "revenge" as the reason for joining. See, for example, Joseph Riwash, *Resistance and Revenge, 1939–1949* (Montreal: No publisher, 1981), 66; Marek Jan Chodakiewicz, *After the Holocaust: Polish–Jewish Conflict in the Wake of World War II* (New York and Boulder, CO: Columbia University Press and East European Monographs,

2003), 67–102. For the fate of the Jewish community in Lithuania after the war see Irena Mikłaszewicz, "Żydzi w Litewskiej SSR, 1944–1990," ("Jews in the Lithuanian SSR, 1944–1990") in Jasiewicz, *Świat Niepożegnany*, 183–92.

7. Jeffrey Burds, "AGENTURA: Soviet Informants' Networks & the Ukrainian Rebel Underground in Galicia, 1944–1948," *East European Politics and Societies* 11, no. 1 (Winter 1997): 89–130.

8. See Marek Jan Chodakiewicz, "The Dialectics of Pain: The Interrogation Methods of the Communist Secret Police in Poland, 1944–1955," *Glaukopis* no. 2/3 (2004–2005): 99–144, http://www.glaukopis.pl/index.php?menu_id=3&id=10 and http://www.projectinposterum.org/docs/chodakiewicz1.htm.

9. For example, the remnant of the Ukrainian population was deported from southeastern territories of the new Polish satellite state of the USSR and resettled in the north. See Jan Pisuliński, *Przesiedlenie ludności ukraińskiej z Polski do USRR w latach 1944–1947 (The Resettlement of the Ukrainian Population from Poland to the Ukrainian Soviet Socialist Republic between 1944 and 1947)* (Rzeszów: Wydawnictwo Uniwersytetu Rzeszowskiego, 2009); Eugeniusz Misiło, ed., *Akcja "Wisła": Dokumenty (Operation "Vistula": Documents)* (Warszawa: Archiwum Ukraińskie, 1993); Jan Pisuliński, ed., *Akcja "Wisła" (Operation "Vistula")* (Warszawa: Instytut Pamięci Narodowej, KŚZpNP, 2003); Andrzej Tłomacki, *Akcja "Wisła" w powiecie bialskim na tle walki politycznej i zbrojnej w latach 1944–1947 (Operation "Vistula" in the County of Bielsk against the Backdrop of Political and Military Struggle between 1944 and 1947)*: (Warszawa and Biała Podlaska: Drukarnia Calamus, 2003); and the trilingual (Polish, Russian, and Ukrainian) documentary collection in *Akcja "Wisła," 1947* (Warszawa and Kiev: Instytut Pamięci Narodowej KŚZpNP, Archiwum MSWiA RP, Państwowe Archiwum Służby Bezpieczeństwa Ukrainy, 2006), which is volume 6 of *Polska i Ukraina w latach trzydziestych i czterdziestych XX wieku*.

10. The victims of deportations included not only Polish underground fighters but also ethnic Germans and autochthons from Silesia and Pomerania whom the Soviets classified as Germans. The figure of 100,000 excludes of course the German POWs who were sent east by the millions. On the mass deportations after 1944 and prisoner releases from the Gulag see Stanisław Ciesielski, ed., *Przesiedlenie ludności polskiej z Kresów Wschodnich do Polski, 1944–1947 (Resettling the Polish Population from the Eastern Borderlands to Poland, 1944–1947)* (Warszawa: Wydawnictwo Neriton and Instytut Historii PAN, 1999); Hubert Orłowski and Andrzej Sakson, eds., *Utracona Ojczyzna: Przymusowe deportacje i przesiedlenia jako wspólne doświadczenia (The Lost Fatherland: Forced Deportations and Resettlements as a Common Experience)* (Poznań: Instytut Zachodni, 1997); Andrzej Paczkowski and Wojciech Materski, eds., *Z archiwów sowieckich, (From the Soviet Archives)* vol. 5: *Powrót żołnierzy AK z sowieckich łagrów (The Return of the AK Soldiers from the Gulag)* (Warszawa: ISP PAN, 1995) (afterward *Powrót żołnierzy AK*); Eugeniusz Misiło, *Akcja Wisła: Dokumenty (Operation Vistula: Documents)* (Warszawa: Wydawnictwo Łódzkie DWN, 1993); Jan Snopko, "Sprawozdanie z międzynarodowej konferencji naukowej 'Repatriacje i migracje ludności pogranicza polsko-litewsko-białoruskiego,' Białystok, 23–24 października 2003," ("A Report from the International Scholarly Conference 'Repatriation and Migrations of the Population of the Polish–Lithuanian–Belarusian Borderlands") *Dzieje Najnowsze* XXXVI, no. 1 (2004): 243–46; Siarhiej Tokć, "Zmiany struktury narodowościowej na pograniczu białorusko-polskim w BSRR (1945–1959)," ("Changes in the National Structure of the Belarusian–Polish Borderland in

BSSR, 1945–1959") *Białoruskie Zeszyty Historyczne* no. 21 (2004): 117–32: http://kamunikat.fontel.net/pdf/bzh/21/07.pdf.

11. See Mečislav Borák, *České stopy w Gulagu: Z výzkumu perzekuce Čechů a občanů ČSR v Sovetském svazu* (*Czech Footprints in the Gulag*) (Opava: Slezské zemské museum, 2003); Raphael Rupert, *A Hidden World* (London: Collins, 1963); István Fehérváry, *The Long Road to Revolution: The Hungarian Gulag, 1945–1956* (Santa Fe, NM: Pro Libertate Publishing, 1984); Lászlo Karsai, "The People's Courts and Revolutionary Justice in Hungary, 1945–1946," in Deák, Gross, and Judt, *The Politics of Retribution in Europe*, 233–51.

12. So far, the most thoroughly researched are the experiences of Latvia and Estonia under the Soviet yoke, in particular, until 1956. See Valters Nollendorfs and Erwin Oberländer, eds., *The Hidden and Forbidden History of Latvia under Soviet and Nazi Occupations, 1940–1991: Selected Research of the Commission of the Historians of Latvia* (Riga: Institute of the History of Latvia, 2005); Vello Salo et al., eds., *The White Book: Losses Inflicted on the Estonian Nation by Occupation Regimes, 1940–1991* (Tallinn: Estonian Encyclopaedia Publishers, 2005); Toomas Hiio, Meelis Maripuu, and Indrek Paavle, eds., *Estonia 1940–1945: Reports of the Estonian International Commission for the Investigation of Crimes against Humanity* (Tallinn: Estonian Foundation for the Investigation of Crimes Against Humanity, 2006); Toomas Hiio, Meelis Maripuu, and Indrek Paavle, eds., *Estonia since 1944: Reports of the Estonian International Commission for the Investigation of Crimes Against Humanity* (Tallinn: Estonian Foundation for the Investigation of Crimes Against Humanity, 2009); Aigi Rahi-Tamm, Ritvars Jansons, and Peeter Kaasik, "Estonia i Łotwa," (Estonia and Latvia) in *Czekiści: Organy bezpieczeństwa w europejskich krajach bloku sowieckiego, 1944–1989* (*The Chekists: Security Organs in the European Countries of the Soviet Bloc, 1944–1989*), ed. Krzysztof Persak and Łukasz Kamiński (Warszawa: Instytut Pamięci Narodowej, 2010), 151–88.

13. See Leonid Smilovitsky, "The Struggle of Belorussian Jews for the Restitution of Possessions and Housing in the First Postwar Decade," *East European Jewish Affairs* 30, no. 2 (2000): 53–70. For the general European context see Martin Dean, Constantin Goschler, and Philipp Ther, eds., *Robbery and Restitution: The Conflict over Jewish Property in Europe* (New York and Oxford: Berghahn Books, Published in Association with the United States Holocaust Memorial Museum, 2007), and, in particular Dariusz Stola, "The Polish Debate on the Holocaust and the Restitution of Property," 240–55. For the property restitution problem in central and western Poland see Marek Jan Chodakiewicz, "*Restytucja*: The Problems of Property Restitution in Poland, 1939–2001," in *Poland's Transformation: A Work in Progress*, ed. Marek Jan Chodakiewicz, John Radzilowski, and Dariusz Tolczyk (Charlottesville, VA: Leopolis Press, 2003), 159–93. See also Adam Hlebowicz, "Straty materialne kultury polskiej na Wschodzie," ("Material Losses of Polish Culture in the East") *Biuletyn Instytutu Pamięci Narodowej* no. 3 (March 2007): 23–28.

14. See Mihai Gribincea, *Agricultural Collectivization in Moldavia: Bessarabia during Stalinism, 1944–1950* (New York and Boulder, CO: Columbia University Press and East European Monographs, 1996); and for comparison, Gail Kligman and Katherine Verdery, *Peasants under Seige: The Collectivization of Agriculture in Romania, 1949–1962* (Princeton, NJ: Princeton University Press, 2011). See further Otto Luchterhandt, "Die Kollaborationsproblematik im Verhältnis von Religionsgemeinschaften und kommunistischen Einparteistaat (ausgehend vom Fall 'Sowjetunion')," in *"Kollaboration" in Nordosteuropa: Erscheinungsfor-*

men und Deutungen im 20. Jahrhundert, ed. by Joachim Tauber (Wiesbaden: Harrassowitz Verlag, 2006), 443–52; Irena Mikłaszewicz, "Kościół katolicki na Wileńszczyźnie w latach 1944–1990," ("The Catholic Church in the Wilno Region, 1944–1990") in Jasiewicz, *Europa nieprowincjonalna*, 368–74; Arūnas Streikus, "Bažnyčios ir sovietų valdžios santykiai Lietuvoje, Latvijoje ir Estijoje 1940–1990 m.: Panašumai ir skirtumai," ("The Relationship between the Church and Soviet Regime in Lithuania, Latvia and Estonia in 1940–1990: Similarities and Differences"), *Genocidas ir rezistencija* no. 2 (12) (2002): http://www.genocid.lt/Leidyba/12/arunas.htm; Arūnas Streikus, "Lietuvos Katalikų Bažnyčia ir ginkluotasis pasipriešinimo sąjūdis Lietuvoje," ("The Church and the Armed Resistance Movement"), *Genocidas ir rezistencija* no. 2 (1997): http://www.genocid.lt/Leidyba/2/streikus2.htm.

15. See Henryk Piskunowicz, "Zwalczanie polskiego podziemia przez NKWD i NKGB na kresach północno-wschodnich II Rzeczypospolitej," ("Fighting against the Polish underground by the NKVD and NKGB in the North-Eastern Borderlands of the 2nd Commonwealth") in *Wojna domowa czy nowa okupacja? Polska po roku 1944 (A Civil War or a New Occupation? Poland after 1944)*, ed. Andrzej Ajnenkiel (Wrocław, Warszawa and Kraków: Wydawnictwo Zakładu Narodowego im. Ossolińskich, 1998), 70 (afterward "Zwalczanie polskiego podziemia," in *Wojna domowa*); Tomasz Łabuszewski, "Grodzieński WiN: Paradoksy i sprzeczności," ("The Grodno WiN: Paradoxes and Contradictions") *Biuletyn Insytutu Pamięci Narodowej* no. 1–2 (January–February 2008): 64–70; Kazimierz Krajewski and Tomasz Łabuszewski, "Ostatni obrońcy Kresów północno-wschodnich: Armia Krajowa na Wileńszczyźnie, Nowogródczyźnie, Grodzieńszczyźnie i Polesiu w latach 1944–1945," ("The Last Defenders of the North-Western Borderlands: The Home Army in the Areas of Wilno, Nowogródek, and Grodno as well as Polesie, 1944–1945") *Biuletyn Instytutu Pamięci Narodowej* no. 1–2 (96–97) (January–February 2009): 95–106; Kazimierz Krajewski and Tomasz Łabuszewski, "Jan Borysewicz 'Krysia': Legenda Nowogródzkiej Armii Krajowej," (The Legend of the Nowogródek Home Army) *Biuletyn Instytutu Pamięci Narodowej* no. 1–2 (96–97) (January–February 2009): 111–16; Elżbieta Kotarska, "Lwowski epizod epistolarny 1944–1945," ("The Lvovian Epistolarian Period, 1944–1945") in Jasiewicz, *Europa nieprowincjonalna*, 1276. See also Dariusz Rogut, *Polacy z Wileńszczyzny w obozach sowieckich 'saratowskiego szlaku' (1945–1949) (Poles from the Wilno Region in the Gulag of the 'Saratov Road')* (Toruń: Wydawnictwo Adam Marszałek, 2003). On the Augustów dragnet see two secret memoranda by Abakumov to L.I. Beria, July 21 and 24, 1945, Tsentralnii arkhiv FSB RF (Central Archive of the Federal Security Service of the Russian Republic), Moscow, reproduced in Adam Leszczyński, "Obława augustowska 1945: IPN zdobył w Moskwie rozkazy rozstrzelania Polaków" ("The Augustów Dragnet: In Moscow, the Institute of National Remembrance Acquired the Orders to Shoot the Poles"), *Gazeta Wyborcza*, 17 April 2012; Krzysztof Jasiewicz interviewed by Piotr Zychowicz, "Zabili ich w pałacyku Göringa?" ("Were They Killed in Göring's Hunting Lodge?") *Rzeczpospolita, Plus-Minus*, 25–26 June 2011; Piotr Falkowski, "Memoriał pyta prokuraturę o obławę," ("Memorial Inquires with the Prosecutors Office about the Dragnet") *Nasz Dziennik*, 9 June 2011.

16. According to a secret Soviet report as of August 15, 1946, there were 247,460 "former Polish citizens" in exile in the USSR. Almost certainly this concerned ethnic Poles and Jews only, and not other ethnicities. See Sekretno, Zametiteliu predsedatelia Soveta Ministrov Soiuza SSR tovarishchu Kosiginu A.N., Dokla-

dnaia zapiska o realizatsii sovetsko-polskogo soglashenia ot 6–20 1945 goda, 4 September 1946, GARF, fond A-327, op. 1, d. 14, l. 26–36. In April 1946 Stalin complained that "more than a million have been sent to Poland, while they sent us only 400,000 Ukrainians and Byelorussians." It is unclear if Stalin included in this number about 217,000 Polish Christians and Jews, including refugees, deportees, and inmates of the Gulag, who were allowed to return to Poland by 1947. See Bela Zhelitski, "Postwar Hungary, 1944–1946," in Naimark and Gibianskii, *The Establishment*, 81; Ciesielski, Hryciuk, and Srebrakowski, *Masowe*, 79; Peter Gatrell and Nick Baron, eds., *Warlands: Population Resettlement and State Reconstruction in the Soviet-East European Borderlands, 1945–1950* (Basingstoke and New York: Palgrave Macmillan, 2009), and, in particular, Kateryna Stadnik, "Ukrainian-Polish Population Transfers, 1944–46: Moving in Opposite Directions" (165–87); Konrad Zielinski, "To Pacify, Populate and Polonise: Territorial Transformations and the Displacement of Ethnic Minorities in Communist Poland, 1944–49," (188–209); and Peter Gatrell and Nick Baron, "Violent Peacetime: Reconceptualising Displacement and Resettlement in the Soviet-East European Borderlands after the Second World War" (255–67). See further Irena Matus, "Repatriacja Białorusinów z terenów województwa białostockiego do Białoruskiej Socjalistycznej Republiki Radzieckiej we wspomnieniach mieszkańców," ("The Repatriation of the Belarusians from the Province of Białystok to the BSSR According to the Testimonies of the Inhabitants") *Białoruskie Zeszyty Historyczne* no. 3 (1995): http://kamunikat. fontel.net/www/czasopisy/bzh/03/03art_matus.htm; Анатоль Вялікі, "На раздарожжы Беларусы Беласточчыны ў час перасялення ў БССР (1944–1946)," ("Belarusians of the Bialystok Region at the Crossroads at the Time of the Resettlement to the BSSR, 1944–1946") *Białoruskie Zeszyty Historyczne* no. 18 (2002): http://kamunikat.fontel.net/www/czasopisy/bzh/18/18art_vialiki.htm; Eugeniusz Mironowicz, "Przesiedlenia ludności z Białorusi do Polski i z Polski do Białorusi w latach 1944–1946," ("The Resettlement of the Population from Belarus to Poland and Poland to Belarus") *Białoruskie Zeszyty Historyczne* no. 19 (2002): http://kamunikat.fontel.net/www/czasopisy/bzh/19/19art_miranovicz. htm; a bilingual (Polish and Ukrainian) collection of documents *Przesiedlenie Polaków i Ukraińców, 1944–1946 (The Resettlement of the Poles and Ukrainians)* (Warszawa and Kiev: Wydawnictwo Rytm, Instytut Pamięci Narodowej KśZpNP, Archiwum MSWiA RP, Państwowe Archiwum Służby Bezpieczeństwa Ukrainy, 2000), which is volume 2 of *Polska i Ukraina w latach trzydziestych i czterdziestych XX wieku. Nieznane dokumenty z archiwów służb specjalnych (Poland and Ukraine in the 1930s and 1940s: Unknown Documents from the Secret Police Archives)*; and on everyday predicament of the Polish inhabitants of Lwów see Ryszard Gansiniec, *Notatki lwowskie (1944–1946)* (Wrocław: Oficyna Wydawnicza "Sudety", 1995).

17. See Agnieszka Grędzik, "Polacy na Białorusi w polityce władz sowieckich po II wojnie światowej," ("Poles in Belarus in the Policy of the Soviet Authorities after the Second World War") *Nasz Czas* [Vilnius] 5 (630) (2004): http://www.nasz-czas.lt; Alicja Paczoska, *Dzieci Jałty: Exodus ludności polskiej z Wileńszczyzny w latach 1944–1947 (The Children of Yalta: The Exodus of the Polish Population from Wilno between 1944 and 1947)* (Toruń: Wydawnictwo Adam Marszałek, 2002); A. F. [Anatol Fiodaravich] Vialiki, *Na razdarozhzhy: Belarusy i paliaki ŭ chas peresialennia, 1944–1946 hh.* (Minsk: BDPU, 2005); Anatol F. Vialiki, *Belarus'—Pol'shcha u XX stahoddzi:Neviadomaia repatryiatsyia,1955–1959 hh.: Manahrafyia* (Minsk: BDPU, 2007); Jan Czerniakiewicz, *Przemieszczenia*

Żydów i Polaków na kresach wschodnich II Rzeczypospolitej i w ZSRR 1939–1959 (Warszawa: Centrum Badań Radzieckich UW, 1991); Jan Czerniakiewicz, *Repatriacja ludności z ZSRR 1944–1948* (Warszawa: Państwowe Wydawnictwo Naukowe, 1987).

18. For overall statistics see Irena Hurwic-Nowakowska, *Żydzi polscy (1947–1950): Analiza więzi społecznej ludności żydowskiej (Polish Jews [1947–1950]: An Analysis of the Social Links of the Jewish Population)* (Warszawa: Wydawnictwo Instytutu Filozofii i Socjologii Polskiej Akademii Nauk, 1996), 24–32; Alina Cała, "Mniejszość żydowska," ("The Jewish Minority") in *Mniejszości narodowe w Polsce: Państwo i społeczeństwo polskie a mniejszości narodowe w okresach przełomów politycznych (1944–1989), (National Minorities in Poland: The Polish State and Society and the National Minorities during the Time of Political Crises [1944–1989])* ed. Piotr Madajczyk (Warszawa: Instytut Studiów Politycznych Polskiej Akademii Nauk, 1998), 245–46 (afterward "Mniejszość żydowska," in *Mniejszości narodowe w Polsce*); Albert Stankowski, "Nowe spojrzenie na statystyki dotyczące emigracji Żydów z Polski po 1944 roku," in Grzegorz Berendt, August Grabski, and Albert Stankowski, *Studia z historii Żydów w Polsce po 1945 r.* (Warsaw: Żydowski Instytut Historyczny, 2000), 103–51; Lucjan Dobroszycki, *Survivors of the Holocaust in Poland: A Portrait Based Jewish Community Records, 1944–1947* (Armonk, NY and London: M.E. Sharpe, 1994), 12–14, 16, 21, 22–26, 67–85; Helga Hirsch, *Gehen oder bleiben? Juden in Schlesien und Pommern, 1945-1957* (Göttingen: Wallstein Verlag, 2011); Albert Kaganovitch, "Stalin's Great Power Politics, the Return of Jewish Refugees to Poland, and Continued Migration to Palestine, 1944-1946," *Holocaust and Genocide Studies* 26, no. 1 (Spring 2012): 59–94; Zorach Warhaftig, *Refugee and Survivor: Rescue Efforts during the Holocaust* (Jerusalem: Yad Vashem and Torah Education, 1988), 296–97; Timothy Snyder, *Bloodlands: Europe between Hitler and Stalin* (New York: Basic Books, 2010), 339–77.

19. See the following essays in *The Anti-Soviet Resistance in the Baltic States*: Nijolė Gaškaite-Žemajtienė, "The Partisan War in Lithuania from 1944 to 1953" (23–45), Arvydas Anušauskas, "A Comparison of the Armed Struggles for Independence in the Baltic States and Western Ukraine" (63–70), Heinrihs Strods, "The Latvian Partisan War between 1944 and 1956" (149–60), Heinrihs Strods, "The Nonviolent Resistance Movement in Latvia (1944–1958)" (161–74), and Mart Laar, "The Armed Resistance Movement in Estonia from 1944 to 1956" (209–41). See also the bilingual (Lithuanian and English) *Kovojanti Lietuva, 1944–1953: Fighting Lithuania, 1944–1953*, ed. Eugenijus Jakimavičius (Vilnius: Petro Ofsetas, 1996); Arvzdas Anušauskas, "Litewska antysowiecka partyzantka i konspiracja w latach 1944–1965," ("The Lithuanian Anti-Soviet Guerrillas and Conspirators between 1944 and 1965") in Jasiewicz, *Europa nieprowincjonalna*, 845–53; Ričardas Čekutis, "Partizanų spauda 1944–1953 m.," *Genocidas ir rezistencija* no. 2 (16) (2004): http://www.genocid.lt/Leidyba/16/cekutis.htm; Arvydas Anušauskas, "Kai kurie lietuvių rezistencijos fenomeno bruožai," ("Some Features of the Lithuanian Resistance Phenomenon"), *Genocidas ir reistencija* no. 1 (13) (2003): http://www.genocid.lt/Leidyba/13/arvydas.htm#Some; Nijolė Žemaitienė, "Generolo Jono Žemaičio vaidmuo partizaniniame kare," ("General Jonas Žemaitis's Contribution to the Partisan War in Lithuania"), *Genocidas ir reistencija* no. 2 (4) (1998): http://www.genocid.lt/Leidyba/4/nijole3.htm#General%20Jonas%20Žemaitis's%20Contribution%20to%20the%20Partisan%20War%20in%20Lithuania; Oleksandr Vovk, "Paskutinis karinis ir politinis sąjūdis dėl Ukrainos nepriklausomybės," ("The

Latest Armed and Political Movement for the Independence of Ukraine"), *Genocidas ir reistencija* no. 2 (1997): http://www.genocid.lt/Leidyba/2/Vovk. htm#The%20Latest%20Armed%20and%20Political%20Movement%20for%20 the%20Independence%20of%20Ukraine.

20. In "people's" Poland, the mainstream Polish underground endeavored to cooperate with the Ukrainian Nationalists against the Communists. However, the UPA burned 160 Polish villages in the Province of Rzeszów alone, massacring the inhabitants in at least some of them. The Polish partisans torched far fewer Ukrainian villages in retaliation. Further, the Polish Nationalists killed Ukrainian peasants in at least three localities, and the mainstream underground in at least one. Ukrainian Nationalists also murdered Ukrainians suspected of siding with the Poles or Communists. On Polish–Ukrainian battles and cooperation in central Poland see Dionizy Garbacz, *Wołyniak: Legenda prawdziwa* (*The Volhynian: A True Legend*) (Stalowa Wola: Wydawnictwo "Sztafeta", 1996), 69–86; Grzegorz Motyka, *Tak było w Bieszczadach: Walki polsko-ukraińskie, 1943–1948* (*That's How It Was in Bieszczady: Polish–Ukrainian Struggles, 1943–1948*) (Warszawa: Oficyna Wydawnicza "Volumen," 1999); Wiktor Poliszczuk, *Dowody zbrodni OUN i UPA: Działalność ukraińskich struktur nacjonalistycznych w latach 1920–1999* (*Evidence of the Crimes of the OUN and UPA: The Activities of the Ukrainian Nationalist Structures between 1920 and 1999*) (Toronto: n.p., 2000), 421–92, 538–47, 556–63, 615–50; Grzegorz Motyka and Rafał Wnuk, *Pany i rezuny: Współpraca AK-WiN i UPA, 1945–1947* (*Lords and Slaughterers: Cooperation between AK-WiN and the UPA, 1945–1947*) (Warszawa: Oficyna Wydawnicza Volumen, 1997) (afterward *Pany i rezuny*); Ihor Iljuszyn (Ihor Ilushin), *UPA i AK: Konflikt w Zachodniej Ukrainie (1939–1945)* (*The UPA and the AK: A Conflict in Western Ukraine*) (Warszawa: Związek Ukraińców w Polsce, 2009); Robert Ziętek, "Służba Bezpieczeństwa OUN w Nadrejonie 'Łewada' w latach 1945–1947," ("The Security Service of the OUN in the 'Lewada' Region between 1945 and 1947") *Rocznik Bialskopodlaski* 8–9 (2000–2001): 105–48.

21. Jarosław Wołkonowski, "ZWZ-AK a problem mniejszości etnicznych na Wileńszczyźnie," ("The ZWZ-AK and the Problem of Ethnic Minorities in the Wilno Region") in *Opór wobec systemów totalitarnych na Wileńszczyźnie w okresie II wojny światowej*, (*Resistance against Totalitarian Systems in the Wilno Region during the Second World War*) ed. Piotr Niwiński (Gdańsk: Instytut Pamięci Narodowej, Komisja Ścigania Zbrodni przeciwko Narodowi Polskiemu, 2003), 56–59.

22. See Jerzy Targalski, "Intermarium: Uwagi," ("Intermarium: Remarks") TMs, Warsaw, December 8, 2011, 1–12 (a copy in my collection); Nina Strużyńska, "Antysowiecka konspiracja i partyzantka Zielonego Dębu na terenie Białorusi w latach 1919–1945," ("Anti-Soviet Conspiracy and Partisans of the Green Oak in Belorussia between 1919–1945") in Jasiewicz, *Europa nieprowincjonalna*, 859–66.

23. The Polish–Belarusian conflict was limited mostly to the Province of Białystok but it has not been yet studied comprehensively. Even the Communist sources remarked that "the attitude of the Belarusian population is very bad toward the Polish people and authorities." See Sprawozdanie sytuacyjne z terenu Województwa Białostockiego za listopad 1945, December 17, 1945, Archiwum Państwowe w Białymstoku, Urząd Wojewódzki w Białymstoku (afterward APB, UWB), file 231, 28. The Polish independentists targeted some Belarusian villages for confiscation and burned a few, killing a number of Belarusian peasants for alleged

collaboration with the NKVD and UB. The most notorious cases occurred in the County of Bielsk Podlaski in January and February 1946, when a Polish guerrilla unit killed seventy-nine Belarusians. Most of the killings were unjustified for they targeted innocent civilians. However, some of those actions stemmed from substantiated suspicion about the Belarusian–Communist connection. According to the Belarusian scholar Eugeniusz Mironowicz, the Belarusians of the Province of Białystok were overrepresented in the local agencies of the Communist proxy regime, the terror apparatus in particular. Documents bear his opinion out. For example, "at the beginning of 1945 Belarusians constituted 10% of the militiamen in the province and 50% of the secret police functionaries." In May 1945, in the County of Białystok, which was no more than 25 percent Belarusian, representatives of that minority accounted for over 75 percent of the membership of the Polish Workers Party (175 out of 228 Communists). In the County of Bielsk Podlaski, which was 45 percent Belarusian, Belarusian Communists dominated the local party structure (84.3 percent or 437 persons). See Protokół w związku z napadami bandy i spalenia wsi Zaleszany, January 31, 1946, Protokół strat wsi Szpaki, February 3, 1946, Protokół strat wsi Zanie, February 5, 1946, Archiwum Państwowe w Białymstoku, Urząd Wojewódzki w Białymstoku (afterward APB, UWB), file 496, 42–62; Rejonowy Przedstawiciel Rządu Jedności Narodowej do Spraw Ewakuacji na rejon Siemiatycze, Bielsk Podlaski, do Głównego Przedstawicielstwa Rządu Jedności Narodowej do Spraw Ewakuacji w Białymstoku, February 1, 1946, Powiatowa Rada Narodowa w Bielsku Podlaskim, Telefonogram do Urzędu Wojewódzkiego w Białymstoku, February 6, 1946, APB, UWB, file 55, 2–3; Informacja o ustaleniach końcowych śledztwa S 28/02/Zi w sprawie pozbawienia życia 79 osób - mieszkańców powiatu Bielsk Podlaski w tym 30 osób tzw. furmanów w lesie koło Puchał Starych, dokonanych w okresie od dnia 29 stycznia 1946r. do dnia 2 lutego 1946r. przez członków oddziału NZW dowodzonego przez R. Rajsa ps "Bury", www.ipn. pl.gov; "Zbrodnie oddziału PAS NZW dowodzonego przez Romulda Rajsa ps. "Bury" popełnione na Białorusinach w styczniu- lutym 1946 r. w dokumentach polskich władz komunistycznych," ("The Crimes of the PAS NZW Unit Under the Command of Romuald Rajs 'Bury' Perpetrated against Belarusians in January and February 1946 According to the Documents of the Polish Communist Authorities") Białoruskie Zeszyty Historyczne no. 8 (1997): http://kamunikat. fontel.net/www/czasopisy/bzh/08/08kryn_bury.htm; Eugeniusz Mironowicz, "Białorusini," ("Belarusians") in Madajczyk, Mniejszości narodowe w Polsce, 15; Jerzy Kułak, "Pacyfikacja wsi białoruskich w styczniu 1946 roku," ("The Pacification of the Belarusian Villages in January 1946") Biuletyn Instytutu Pamięci Narodowej no. 8 (September 2001): 49–54; Sławomir Iwaniuk, "Białoruska samoobrona na Białostocczyźnie w latach 1945–1947 (przyczyny tworzenia i działalność)," ("Belarusian Self-Defense in the Bialystok Region between 1945 and 1947 [the reasons for its forming and activities]" "Białoruskie Zeszyty Historyczne no. 3 (1995); Wiesław Choruży, "Spalenie wsi Zanie przez oddział PAS NZW kpt. Romualda Rajsa Burego," ("The Burning of the Village of Zanie by the PAS NZW Unit of Romuald Rajs Bury") Białoruskie Zeszyty Historyczne 18 (2002): 167–77; and Jerzy Kułak, Rozstrzelany oddział: Monografia 3 Wileńskiej Brygady NZW – Białostocczyzna, 1945–1946 (The Executed Unit: A Monograph of the 3rd Wilno Brigade of the NZW in the Białystok Region) (Białystok: Godruk, 2007).

24. See Grzegorz Wąsowski and Leszek Żebrowski, eds., Żołnierze wyklęci: Antykomunistyczne podziemie zbrojne po 1944 roku (The Anti-Communist Armed

Underground after 1944) (Warszawa: Oficyna Wydawnicza Volumen and Liga Republikańska, 1999), and the second, expanded edition of this work by Kazimierz Krajewski et al., (Warszawa: Oficyna Wydawnicza Volumen and Liga Republikańska, 2002); and Rafał Wnuk et al., eds., *Atlas polskiego podziemia niepodległościowego: The Atlas of the Independence Underground in Poland, 1944–1956* (Warszawa and Lublin: Instytut Pamięci Narodowej, 2007). And see the trilingual (Polish, Russian, and Ukrainian) selection of documents on the crushing of the Polish underground in Lwów and other southeastern areas after the war in *Operacja "Sejm" 1944–1947* (Warszawa and Kiev: Instytut Pamięci Narodowej KŚZpNP, Archiwum MSWiA RP, Państwowe Archiwum Służby Bezpieczeństwa Ukrainy, 2007), which is volume 6 of *Polska i Ukraina w latach trzydziestych i czterdziestych XX wieku*. See also Piotr Niwiński, *Okręg Wileński AK w latach 1944–1948* (*The Wilno District of the AK between 1944 and 1948*) (Warszawa: Oficyna Wydawnicza Volumen, 1999); Kazimierz Krajewski and Tomasz Łabuszewski, *Białostocki Okręg AK–AKO, VII 1944–VIII 1945* (*The Bialystok District of the AK-AKO, July 1944–August 1945*) (Warszawa: Oficyna Wydawnicza Volumen and Dom Wydawniczy Bellona, 1997); Piskunowicz, "Zwalczanie polskiego podziemia," in Ajnenkiel, *Wojna domowa*, 49–72. Further, see the following essays in Jasiewicz, *Europa nieprowincjonalna*: Piotr Niwiński, "Ewakuacja struktur Okręgu Wileńskiego AK z terytorium Wileńszczyzny w 1945 r." ("The Evacuation of the Structures of the AK Wilno District from the Wilno Region") (743–54); Jerzy Węgierski, "Internowanie dowódców i żołnierzy lwowskiej Armii Krajowej i organizacji NIE w latach 1944–1949" ("The Internment of the Soldiers of the Lvovian AK and the NIE Organization between 1944 and 1949") (780–89); Tomasz Łabuszewski, "Poakowskie oddziały partyzanckie w byłym Inspektoracie Grodzieńskim AK-AKO-WiN, 1945–1950" ("Post-AK Partisan Units in the Former Grodno Inspectorate of the AK-AKO-WiN, 1945–1950") (806–19); Kotarska, "Lwowski epizod" (1262–76).

25. Laar, *War in the Woods*, 203–6.
26. On the early stages of the Kremlin's postwar policies see Jan Szumski, *Sowietyzacja zachodniej Białorusi, 1944–1953: Propaganda i edukacja w służbie ideologii* (*Sovietization of Western Belarus: Propaganda and Education in the Service of Ideology*) (Kraków: Arcana, 2010). For a case study of Sovietization of a single town, see William Jay Risch, *The Ukrainian West: Culture and the Fate of Empire in Soviet Lviv* (Cambridge, MA: Harvard University Press, 2011). On the vicissitudes of the national Bolsheviks in Latvia, where they suffered purges in 1959, see Monika Michaliszyn, "Działalność i upadek łotewskich narodowych komunistów," ("The Rise and Fall of the Latvian National Communists") TMs, Warsaw, no date (2010), 1–35 (a copy in my collection). See further Otto Luchterhandt, "Die Kollaborationsproblematik im Verhältnis von Religionsgemeinschaften und kommunistischen Einparteistaat (ausgehend vom Fall 'Sowjetunion')," in *"Kollaboration" in Nordosteuropa: Erscheinungsformen und Deutungen im 20. Jahrhundert*, ed. by Joachim Tauber (Wiesbaden: Harrassowitz Verlag, 2006), 443–52; Timothy Snyder, *The Reconstruction of Nations: Poland, Ukraine, Lithuania, Belarus, 1569–1999* (New Haven, CT and London: Yale University Press, 2003), 90–102, 202–14; Alexander V. Prusin, *The Lands between: Conflict in the East European Borderlands, 1870–1992* (New York and Oxford: Oxford University Press, 2010), 201–23; Romuald Misiunas and Rein Taagepera, *The Baltic States: Years of Dependence, 1940–1990* (Berkeley, CA: University of California Press, 1993); Dietrich Al., V. Stanley Vardys, and Laurence P. Kitching, eds., *Regional Identity under Soviet Rule: The Case of*

the Baltic States (Hackettstown, NJ: AABS, Published for the Institute for the Study of Law, Politics, and Society of Socialist States, University of Kiel, 1990); Tönu Parming and Elmar Jarvesoo, eds. *A Case Study of a Soviet Republic: The Estonian SSR* (Boulder, CO: Westview Press, 1978); Ralph S. Clem, ed., *The Soviet West: Interplay between Nationality and Social Organization* (New York: Praeger Publishers, 1975); Michael Bruchis, *Nations – Nationalities – People: A Study of the Nationalities Policy of the Communist Party in Soviet Moldavia* (New York and Boulder, CO: East European Monographs and Columbia University Press, 1984); William E. Crowther, "Ethnicity and Participation in the Communist Party of Moldavia: Research Note," *Journal of Soviet Nationalities* 1, no. 1 (Spring 1990): 119–20; Stephen Fischer-Galati, "Moldavia and the Moldavians," in *Handbook of Major Soviet Nationalities*, ed. Zev Katz (New York: Free Press, 1975), 415–33; Sherman David Spector, "The Moldavian S.S.R., 1964–1974," in *Nationalism in the USSR and Eastern Europe*, ed. George W. Simmonds (Detroit, MI: University of Detroit Press, 1977), 260–69; Michael Ryan and Richard Prentice, *Social Trends in the Soviet Union from 1950* (New York: St. Martin's Press, 1987); and Antony Polonsky, *The Jews in Poland and Russia*, vol. 3: *1914 to 2008* (Oxford and Portland, OR: The Littman Library of Jewish Civilization, 2012), 3: 591–760. See also James Stuart Olson, Lee Brigance Pappas, and Nicholas C. J. Pappas, *Ethnohistorical Dictionary of the Russian and Soviet Empires* (Westport, CT: Greenwood Press, 1994).

27. For an informative essay on Lithuania's dissent see Jerzy Targalski, "Litwa: Opozycja," (Lithuania: The Opposition) TMs, Warsaw, no date [2008], 1–153, especially pages 1–7, which focus on the 1970s and early 1980s (a copy in my collection); on Ukraine see Jerzy Targalski, "Ukraina: Opozycja," (Ukraina: The Opposition) TMs, Warsaw, no date (2008), 1–78, especially pages 1–12, which focus on the period between the 1960s and early 1980s (a copy in my collection).

28. For a useful chronology see Melanie Newton and Vera Tolz, eds., *The USSR in 1989: A Record of Events* (Boulder, CO: Westview Press, 1990); Melanie Newton and Vera Tolz, eds., *The USSR in 1990: A Record of Events* (Boulder, CO: Westview Press, 1992); Melanie Newton and Vera Tolz, eds. *The USSR in 1991: A Record of Events* (Boulder, CO: Westview Press, 1993); Raymond E. Zickel, ed., *Soviet Union: A Country Study* (Washington, DC: GPO, 1991). See also World Bank, *Statistical Handbook: States of the Former USSR* (Studies of Economies in Transformation, No. 3) (Washington, DC: The World Bank, 1992).

13

Transformation*

I now think I should have used that occasion to form a new party and should have insisted on resigning from the Communist party. It had become a brake on reforms even though it had launched them. But they all thought the reforms only needed to be cosmetic. They thought that painting the facade was enough, when actually there was still the same old mess inside the building.[1]

—Mikhail Gorbachev,
recalling a Politburo meeting in April 1991

No other country played a greater role in the ending of the Soviet empire in Central and Eastern Europe than Poland.[2]

—Paul Goble

Transformation can be a tactical tool to reshape a phenomenon so that its innate qualities alter as little as possible or even not at all. That is exactly what happened in the USSR and its satellites. Let us consider the tool in light of the changes in the Soviet empire in its twilight.

In terms of logic, there is a plethora of ways to explicate the transformation of a phenomenon (an entity or a concept) into another. The most popular, perhaps, is a teleologically deterministic explanation. In short, its cause, projection, and shape lead to a predetermined goal. This interpretation assumes that if a transformation occurred, its end result is precisely as it was intended to be. Of course, this can be one of our logical assumptions. Another purely speculative one is the proposition that if we transform anything we cannot be certain about the outcome. The actual outcome can unexpectedly materialize quite far from the intended goals. In fact, one can apply any number of permutations to the possible outcome.

From the stand point of logic, the same should also apply to the interpretations of the so-called "systemic transformation from Communism to democracy" which took place in the USSR and its satellites, including Poland.

However, for a variety of reasons, the most prevalent narrative of the Polish events that transpired in the late eighties and early nineties there posits the existence only of the most teleologically deterministic explanation. It is said that the transformation of Communism led to democracy. Some even insist that the goal of the transformation of Communism was democracy. This ultimate outcome is ascribed to virtually everyone participating in the process, the Communists included. The latter were the driving force of the process. They had the power. They initiated the transformation. And that is the official story.

Tellingly, following 1989, most intellectuals in Poland and elsewhere in the post-Soviet zone avoided the words "independence" or "freedom." Instead, to describe the sociopolitical process under way, they referred to "transformation." Partly, this can be explained by the fact that the process was not sudden and violent; there was no interruption, but rather intellectual, personal, and institutional continuity with the past. Thus, from the technical point of view, transformation fits the bill rather well. Further, one recoiled from such concepts as "independence" or "freedom" because some, the adherents to moral relativism, in particular, were repulsed by their absolutist connotations. Many on the Communist-cum-liberal Parnassus were outright scared that these idealistic formulas might be translated into the language of Polish nationalism. According to them, an eruption of Polish or any other nationalism could have interrupted the transformation.

And now for a little laboratory demonstration. Please lift up a flat piece of paper. This is Communism. Please crunch it into a ball. The crunching is transformation. The ball is post-Communism, and not democracy. Transformation means that we change the shape and form of an object or material but its qualities remain the same.

In the context of the "Round Table" negotiations between the Communists and the so-called "constructive opposition" in the spring of 1989 in Poland, was the transformation of Communism predetermined to result in democracy? Not necessarily. All options were on the table. There could have been a variety of outcomes, including the return of hard totalitarianism *à la* North Korea or the ascent of soft totalitarianism like in China after the Tiananmen Square massacre of June 1989. In Poland, as we shall see, elsewhere in the Intermarium, the phenomenon of transformed Communism has manifested itself in a different form. While retaining all its ill-gotten gains and advantages accruing from having had ruled dictatorially for decades, as well as its pathological character and dialectical modus operandi, Communism has merely accepted for tactical reasons the rules of the democratic game. Thus, post-Communism is Communism transformed *sans* its ideology. Instead, post-Communism prefers nihilism and moral relativism as handy weapons to eliminate the odium of its old ideological legacy and to undermine the absolute which characterizes anti-Communism. Further, post-Communism retains the old immoral Marxist-Leninist dialectical modus operandi as a handy tool to maintain power. It also cultivates Communism's institutions and personnel, albeit adjusted to the new post-Communist reality. Last but not least, post-Communism is deception that allows the transformation to be seen as a wholesome operation of restoring and maintaining freedom and democracy. It thus attracts non-Communists and even former anti-Communists who adopt, unwittingly or not, the post-Communist narrative and objectives as their own. This allegedly allows for safeguarding democracy, but really permits one to prosper in post-Communism. The resulting system is not democracy. Instead, post-Communism is a fiction of democracy where the disenfranchisers continue to dominate the disenfranchised via economic means, media monopoly, and active measures, rather than sheer terror. That is what obtained in Poland after 1989.

However, many would angrily disagree. According to the post-Communist/liberal historical *Diktat* of the past two decades, something altogether different occurred at the end of the eighties and the beginning of the nineties. The Communists, jointly with the "constructive opposition," brought about a democratic system in Poland (and elsewhere in the former Soviet Bloc).[3] As a rather primitive propaganda version of mainstream opinion has it, "Polish patriot" General Wojciech Jaruzelski and the "man of honor" General Czesław Kiszczak, the Communist dictator and his chief of the secret police, respectively, benevolently invited the tolerant and open-minded leftist dissident and their hand-picked allies to deliberate at the so-called "Round Table," which gave birth to democracy and civil society. Then everyone lived happily ever after. Everything else is footnotes.

Is it really? What happened in reality? The documents are in Moscow. And the Kremlin refuses to share them. However, based upon leaks and shreds of information, we can extrapolate and deduce rather differently about the sources and mechanisms of the complex changes in Poland. But we must start with the masters, not the servants, with Moscow, and not Warsaw.

The Soviet Union

In the seventies of the last century, the USSR reached the apex of its power.[4] Communism spread brutally across the world. It appeared unstoppable. The Kremlin was triumphant. This situation was related chiefly to the moral malaise gripping the United States as a result of the countercultural revolution of the sixties and the related American defeat in Vietnam. Moscow's power was also bankrolled by outrageously high energy prices. It seemed that nothing would threaten the Soviets.

Yet, at the zenith of the Communist success, the first serious turning point materialized inexplicably. In 1978, the Pole Karol Wojtyła was elected Pope. John Paul II's triumphant return to his native Poland a year later resounded with a hope-inspiring message: "Fear not!" This, in turn, emboldened the

Polish and other peoples of the Communist empire to nonviolent resistance. "Solidarity" erupted from this combustive spirit in 1980. In the guise of a trade union, this was a national liberation movement, a champion of freedom, and a defender of human rights. Also at the same time, inspired by Islam and tradition, the Afghans defended themselves with arms against the Soviets. They were followed by the Nicaraguan anti-Communist insurgents. "Solidarity" men and women, the mujahideen, and the Contras received moral, spiritual, political, and material support not only from the Vatican but also Washington, where conservative anti-Communists enjoyed power under Ronald Reagan's leadership since 1980. Britain's conservative prime minister Margaret Thatcher supported this policy loyally and vigorously. The contribution of the West's strategic sanctions and economic warfare; funds for the anti-Communists (either for violent and nonviolent resistance); public diplomacy and political warfare, in particular, via Radio Liberty and Radio Free Europe were stupendous factors in shaking the foundations of the USSR and its satellites. The American-led offensive paved the way for momentous changes in the "Evil Empire," as Reagan famously dubbed it.

Patriotic anti-Communists on the peripheries of the Red hegemon irritated the Kremlin, through violent or nonviolent resistance, but on their own they were unable to destroy the Soviet Union, of course. Yet, other factors intervened in their favor. Significantly, the dramatic decline of the price of gas and oil as well as economic warfare and sanctions initiated by the West as punishment for the imposition of martial law in Poland in December 1981 seriously undermined the USSR's economic standing. Further, multiple colonial ventures of Moscow in Africa and South America cost the Politburo gargantuan financial outlays. Moreover, the progressive collapse of the Soviet economy was exacerbated by the subsidies for the "fraternal parties" around the world and to the Central and Eastern European satellites, including the People's Republic of Poland, which was mired in a structural crisis of its own. Socialism failed to deliver. Feature looked bleak.

In 1985, Mikhail Gorbachev assumed power as the General Secretary in the Kremlin. His inheritance was in shambles. His aim was to reform and save socialism and the Soviet Union, and not their destruction. Gorbachev touted his reforms as "restructuring" (*perestroika*). This was, in essence, a modernized version of Lenin's New Economic Policy (NEP) of the 1920s. A radical turn away from the horrors of War Communism, this pseudoliberal solution limited to a certain extent government intervention in the economy. The NEP was implemented to stave off the collapse of Soviet Russia. In essence, it de-criminalized some aspects of free economic activity.

Thus, it legalized much of the so-called "black market," along with genuine businessmen and criminals as well as their detractors and enablers in the secret police. The policy allowed farmers to sell food at market prices. Small entrepreneurs and artisians were permitted to produce partly unimpeded. However, from its inception, the well-heeled people with access to power fared best and benefited handsomely from the NEP. That included the nascent Communist nomenklatura which grew rich by controlling credit, wholesale, and distribution as well as by enjoying preferential access to the choicest items.

The economic plank of Lenin's reform was accompanied by a political and cultural liberalization. Intraparty dissidents and Bolshevik literati and artists benefited from it most. To goad the reluctant to follow the NEP, the propagandists, journalists, and writers denounced them as did other party activists at factory floor mass meetings. In fact, both the "infantile leftist" opponents of the NEP and its abusers, so-called "speculators" in particular, bore the brunt of the regime's propaganda campaign in favor of dialectical ("market") economic reforms. However, as soon as the Communist party and state administration regained their strength, the "liberal" economic policies was discontinued and dissent repressed. Thus, the NEP fully proved its tactical utility already under Lenin and Stalin in the 1920s, and Nikita Khrushchev employed some of its elements successfully in the mid-1950s as well.

Thirty years later, Gorbachev anchored his reforms on this twice-tested Leninist legacy. Inspired by his illustrious predecessors, the General Secretary unveiled a carrot and stick policy: "restructuring" (*perestroika*) would be complemented by "openness" (*glasnost'*). The latter was devised to expedite the former because the policy of economic reforms met with staunch opposition from the *nomenklatura*. Gorbachev's economic course was being sabotaged by the high and middle *apparat*. The Communists realized that the reforms threatened the system mortally and any liberalization could cause an explosion of popular anger at the heart of the empire.

Yet, perestroika held a powerful incentive for the nomenklatura. It expanded their privileges by authorizing an ever-increasing range of economic activities, which, gradually, would turn into massive privatization and state property appropriation by the apparat. What was de facto under the nomenklatura control would become de jure under theirs by the mid-1990s. This was obviously not Gorbachev's aim at all, at least not without the Communist party and state's continued domination over the process, as is the case in China today. Eventually, the economic incentives and opportunities offered by perestroika would weaken the resistance of the apparat against reforms because the Communist upper and middle rung leaders realized that they would be their chief beneficiaries. Extremely tenuous at first, the process would evolve from its initial stage of low level, and even primitive, economic transactions in service, food, trade, and credit sectors. The well-connected launched start-up cooperatives which were authorized to operate outside the rigid confines of the planned economy. Small entrepreneurs were also permitted to hawk their wares. Some of the black marketers emerged in the open, in cooperation with their secret police contacts. Within several years the low level cooperative and individual economic activity morphed into the stealthy, dynamic, and kleptocratic privatization of state assets by the nomenklatura. However, this was by no means apparent in the mid-1980s. At the time, the apparat sabotaged perestroika, and the country remained moribund. Gorbachev realized that the USSR needed a further radical jolt to shake things up.

The Communist leader believed that without the reforms the USSR would collapse. Therefore, to force the *apparat* to carry his policies out obediently, the General Secretary invoked the old Leninist-Stalinist method: denunciation in the form of criticism and self-criticism. He called his own version of it "openness." It was supposed to complement and propel *perestroika*.

Glasnost' was intended to signify a political thaw, liberalization. It was based upon a simple mechanism of denunciation. Initially, the so-called "party grassroots" were encouraged to criticize the management at state enterprises. The factory KGB men were instructed to encourage young Communist activists to denounce the plant supervisor and party secretary for sabotaging the resolutions of the Central Committee and even the General Secretary himself. The public theater at first tied in neatly with the ongoing KBG campaign against corruption.[5] *Perestroika* and *glasnost'* were good; "speculators" and "saboteurs" were bad. After a time, such criticism at industrial enterprises became increasingly spontaneous. The emboldened grassroots used the cover of *perestroika* and *glasnost'* to complain not only about unfulfilled party decrees, but also about real problems of ordinary people, like the lack of hygienic products. The management soon began to apologize for a variety of failures. This caused general confusion, in particular, since the critics gradually grasped their apparent impunity. The onlookers took note and the ranks of the persons willing to register their dissatisfaction openly mushroomed. They felt that they enjoyed protection at the highest place. After all, the campaign of openness was based upon the authority of Gorbachev himself.

The people began to test the limits of the official tolerance. The initially demure dissatisfaction snowballed into loud dissent on a massive scale. The criticism increased, sharpened, and spilled out of the enterprises into the society at large. It penetrated into housing projects and sports clubs. It even reached the media. Here a similar mechanism was at play. Young journalists were encouraged to write the truth. They focused on history, Stalin's mass terror, in particular. These who refused to condemn the crimes were roundly criticized. The critics initially invoked the "proud ideals of Leninism," "socialist legality," and "Communist morality." All of them were supposed to have been violated by Stalin. *Nota bene*, the stalwart apologists of Stalinist crimes (or, rather, more precisely, the opponents of the reforms) also claimed to be guarding the Leninist orthodoxy and socialist legality. But they failed to check their detractors who were becoming emboldened by their own apparent impunity.

Soon, a portion of the editorial boards of the press, radio, and television openly backed *perestroika*. Some even began to over interpret Gorbachev's policies. They pushed hard for freedom. Their enemies in the media leadership were increasingly shouted down. Aesopian and cryptic editorial allusions about various transgressions turned into bold and outrageous barbs of investigative journalism. The subterfuge of the "letters to the editor" to convey one's position yielded to open punditry. Regular duels took place both between and within editorial boards, where journalists denounced each other as insufficiently in tune with the party line. And the party line was *glasnost'*. They clamored for more openness. The participants in the latest round of *kto kovo* also outbid each other in pledging loyalty to Leninism. Ultimately, the boldest supporters of reforms arrived at a spot where it was no longer possible to remain within the straight-jacket of the Marxist-Leninist discourse and express one's hopes and dissatis-faction and, indeed, a desire for freedom. Thus, they emancipated themselves from the Communist discourse. Some invoked liberalism, others nationalism. The latter concerned the Russian center to an extent but, perhaps in particular, also the peripheries of the Soviet empire. History accelerated again.[6]

Open ferment in the industry, media, and housing projects obscured a much more fierce, if clandestine, power struggle at the top, in the Kremlin itself. On the outside, the Communist leadership presented a veneer of unity. Inside, meanwhile, Gorbachev clashed with his foes over the best tactics to save socialism and strengthen the Soviet Union. Foreign policy served as an important field of ideological and political struggle.

When there was no unity among the leaders, the Soviet grassroots had to be pacified through reforms so they would stay quiet as their masters bickered. Similarly, the top Communists wanted the West to relax its anti-Soviet politi-cal, military, and propaganda readiness so that the Politburo could deal with its differences unencumbered by any immediate outside threats. Thus, in the second half of the 1980s, Moscow, in congruence with its old dialectical rule, began supporting détente with the West. This was also a tactical ruse to solicit credit and aid from the United States and its allies to shore up *perestroika*. It was also to demonstrate to Western public that the Soviet Union was no longer a threat which would in turn increase grass roots pressure for nuclear disarmament and, perhaps, American withdrawal from Europe.

Tactically, the success of the détente enhanced the prestige of Gorbachev. To strengthen his position further, the General Secretary also shook his fist at the Soviet satellites in Central and Eastern Europe. They were ordered to "reform" in congruence with the Moscow paradigm of *glasnost'* and *perestroika*. Their obedience was indispensable for the fostering of the continued uniformity of the Soviet Bloc. The "fraternal" parties emulated Stalin and his terror in the 1940s and 1950s, then Khrushchev with his "thaw" and "de-Stalinization," and later Brezhnev and his "stagnation." Therefore, Gorbachev expected that the Communists of Central and Eastern Europe would mimic his "socialist renewal."[7] Their compliance was indispensable to legitimize the *bona fides* of the Kremlin's new master. Obedience of the satellites to the General Secretary was also necessary to placate his Politbureau comrades always apprehensive about centrifugal tendencies in the USSR's Central and European colonies. Last but not least, an apparent "liberalization" in the Soviet Bloc could lead to Western credits, not to mention the idea of Finlandization of Europe, or "a common European home from the Atlantic to the Pacific," as Gorbachev dubbed it. For all those reasons the General Secretary's ideas were tried in the satellites.

The Soviet Bloc

Most of the Central and European Communist leaders balked at Moscow's new orders. Erich Honecker in East Germany, Todor Zhivkov in Bulgaria, Nicolae Ceaușescu in Romania, and Gustáv Husák in Czechoslovakia resisted *glasnost'* and *perestroika* openly. Of course, they paid some lip service to the "reforms," but they angrily rejected their spirit. They vainly turned to their anti-Gorbachevian allies in the USSR itself for succor. To enforce obedience to the Kremlin line, Moscow deployed its influence in the satellites, including in the secret police. Thus, the Soviets shaped the developments in Central and Eastern Europe from above and below, by their *agentura* among the ranks of the local comrades. The old guard defended itself with various success. Thus, Miloš Jakeš substituted Husák already in 1987, although the former continued the country's glacial pace for a couple of years more. The local Gorbachevian "reformers" succeeded in pushing out Honecker and Zhivkov only in the fall of 1989. Ceaușescu was overthrown in a bloody palace coup before the year was over.

Where either the old guard or its successors were not sufficiently obedient, the Kremlin grew impatient with its clients, sometimes resorting to employing "active measures" from below. This, in turn, triggered an outcome that could best be described as resulting from the law of unintended consequences. Namely, the Gorbachevian reforms and the ways of their implementation ushered in freedom. That was not the Kremlin's intension. Moscow and its followers in the satellites deluded themselves that the process of reform was reversible as long as the Red Army stayed in place and the secret police kept things under control. Accordingly, to force the Soviet Bloc leadership to obey Gorbachev, the Kremlin appears to have authorized some reckless operations by the KGB and its *agentura* (or, perhaps, Moscow must have issued a general order, and the local secret services under their Soviet supervisors were improvising). Most importantly, in East Germany the secret police and the entire repression apparatus uncharacteristically refrained from shooting at the crowd milling around the Berlin Wall on and off at least since September 1989. The demonstrations were not crushed and served as an excuse for the leadership change in October. East Germany's Gorbachevian "reformers" were not firmly entrenched yet, though. Then, in November, someone mysteriously rescinded the order to fire at the border violators. Rumors spread rapidly about the possibility to cross to the West with impunity. The Communist-controlled media encouraged the crossing, as did a top official. The bravest of the people breached the structure unimpeded. Many others joined joyously. The floodgates were opened. The Wall thus fell in November 1989. The German Democratic Republic outlived the Wall by nearly a year. It succumbed only in October 1990, when the Gorbachevian line failed utterly and the USSR found itself imploding. Germany reunified, certainly not an outcome envisioned by the Kremlin in early 1989.

In Czechoslovakia, the secret police and its net of agents inspired and infiltrated the student demonstrations also in November 1989. This provided the unwitting protesters with a protective umbrella and encouraged many others to join in spontaneously. The paradox is only apparent. The objective was to force a leadership change and an acceleration of the pro-Gorbachevian course by the Czechoslovak party, just like earlier its East German counterpart. And that was accomplished. This time the limits of *perestroika* and *glasnost'* were stretched beyond their party "reformist" boundaries. The Velvet Counter-revolution of the Czechs and Slovaks resulted in a parliamentary democracy in December 1989. The secret police however remained in charge as did the nomenklatura, firmly convinced at the time at the apparent imminence and feasibility of the reversal of the reformist Kremlin line.

Also in December 1989, in Romania, a part of the Soviet *agentura* in Ceaușescu's secret services staged a provocation against the old party leadership. The Communist dictator was talked into addressing an outdoors mass rally. He expected to receive standard support for his anti-Gorbachevian line. This was supposed to be a routine, serpentine public speech and a choreographed outburst of approval. The *Conducător*, however, was unexpectedly shouted down. Visibly shocked, he lost his resolve and retreated. Violence erupted among the rally participants. In particular, fighting broke out among the ranks of the secret police; the military jumped into the fray; and then the people joined spontaneously. Ceaușescu was apprehended and shot. His erstwhile Communist comrades seized power and talked about ushering in freedom and democracy.

In Romania, Czechoslovakia, and East Germany, the "reform" Communists took the reins initially as envisioned by the Kremlin. Of course, the Soviet KGB maintained its "reformist" *agentura* in influential posts, including some of the executors of the latest operations now in top positions. In late 1989 and early 1990, everything in the satellites seemed to progress more or less in congruence with the intentions of Gorbachev. Every Communist state had its own version of *perestroika* and *glasnost'*, which appeared genuine and which tallied with the post-1956 fashion to allow "separate national roads to socialism."

This concerned also Poland and Hungary. Between 1986 and 1989, both Warsaw and Budapest obediently fulfilled Moscow's directives, pleasing the Soviet General Secretary. Therefore, he granted the native dictators a relatively large measure of autonomy to follow his lead on *glasnost'* and *perestroika*. Let us concentrate on Poland, because it triggered some of the irreversible changes and pioneered some of the trademark processes that ultimately led to the transformation of Communism into post-Communism throughout the Soviet Bloc.[8]

"People's" Poland

In Poland, the situation developed according to a very sophisticated scenario laid out by the Kremlin and implemented by the local Communists between 1986 and 1989. The objective was to maintain power through a suave deception operation. The task appeared rather difficult. Nowhere else was there a more rebellious nation in the Soviet Bloc than in Poland.[9] In the 1980s, the Polish desire for freedom manifested itself in the form of the quintessential national liberation movement masking as the free-trade union "Solidarity." Forced underground after martial law in 1981, it created an independent civic society, complete with education and publishing. It was a virtual state within state run by dissidents of various shade and hue, from integral nationalists and anachronistic Pilsudskites through liberals and social democrats to post-Stalinists and neo-Trotskites. The leftists received most of the Western media coverage and, thus, enjoyed a great deal of public recognition as "freedom fighters."[10]

The strength of Poland's dissident movement undermined the relative position of Warsaw's Communist party. It made the native reds feel less secure in their bailiwick. Therefore, nowhere else in the Soviet Bloc was there a Communist regime more compliant with the Kremlin. The historical track record of obedience to Moscow by the Polish Communists was perhaps second only to that of the Bulgarian apparatchiks, if for different reasons. Except for an eccentric episode in 1956,[11] the leadership of the Polish United Workers Party (*Polska Zjednoczona Partia Robotnicza*—PZPR) obeyed Moscow with exemplary servility for decades. Poland's party first secretary General Wojciech Jaruzelski and his faithful Chekist General Czesław Kiszczak faithfully followed Gorbachev's lead. The Soviet General Secretary trusted them most, because they needed the Kremlin's protection most.

Let us stress that the same rules that applied to Gorbachev's "reforms" also pertained to Jaruzelski and Kiszczak's transformative endeavors. Their aim was to preserve socialism, the Polish People's Republic, and their own power which was guaranteed by their subservience to the Kremlin. Their aim tallied with the concomitant orders from Moscow and with their own interests as Polish Communists. Hence, what took place in the Polish People's Republic after 1985 was a gargantuan deception and disinformation operation.[12] The Communist objective was to retain control, while simultaneously to feign reforming and "sharing" power. The key steps of the operation consisted of the so-called Mieczysław Wilczek economic reform and the Round Table maneuver. The latter was the means to divide and neutralize "Solidarity" and other pro-independence dissident groups. The Wilczek economic "reform" was a set of legal measures freeing some areas of Poland's economy from state control, essentially a modernized version of the NEP. However, it went well beyond anything attempted in the USSR at the time.

The Wilczek "reform" was Poland's *perestroika*. It was also a device to bribe the top and middle Communist *apparat*. This way the *nomenklatura* was reassured about its future. The apparatchiks were encouraged to continue the process of enriching themselves individually. They had had the party's unofficial blessings before but now they could operate, technically and legally, outside of its confines. State assets were theirs for a fraction of their value. Thus, the party leaders of various rungs who ran state enterprises for the government would take them over as independent "capitalists." They initially created privately held shell companies which leased the enterprises. They privatized them next with loans from their party chums from state-owned banks. Thus, the Communists solidified their grip on power in a mixed sociopolitical environment of socialist power and crony "capitalist" economy.

However, this was essentially a *faux* free market because it was based not on competition but on grants of government monopolies and tax exemptions and access to state credit. And there was virtually no business risk because the loans came with state guarantees. And the Polish Communists remained in firm control of the system. If, as was expected, the party dialectically soon changed its line and retreated from the neo-NEP, the enterprises would be reintegrated into the state-party command economy with ease and under the same management. They would thus revert from the "capitalist" charade to the traditional *apparatchik* role. Simply, the *nomenklatura* would switch from "private entrepreneurs" back to party hacks again, relinquishing their temporarily "private" stewardship of banking and industry. The party leadership anticipated a smooth reversal. In the end, nothing would have changed, essentially from the original, pre-Round Table paradigm. Any benefits accruing meanwhile from the Wilczek "reform" to small and medium size nonparty businessmen would be likewise reversed, as they were a purely tactical concession by the Communists, a useful by-product of the deception operation. That, at least, was the general plan grounded in the usual Marxist dialectics. The objective of the Communist party was, once again, to maintain power.[13]

As far as the Round Table maneuver, it was supposed to be Poland's *glasnost'* writ large. This was arguably the most brazen and outrageous provocation (*provokatsia*) ever, except for the Trust caper of the 1920s. Whereas the Wilczek "reform" was the economic plank of the effort to maintain power, the Round Table charade was the political aspect of the deception operation. It necessitated for the Communist rulers of the Polish People's Republic to replicate the same active measures paradigm that had served them so well between 1944 and 1948.[14]

When the Red Army entered once again the Polish territories and the NKVD maintained the order of the grave over the Poles, Stalin commanded his Polish Communists to wield power in such a deceitful way that it would appear that they were sharing government control. Thus, the Kremlin dictator denied he was violating the spirit of Yalta, which guaranteed freedom and democracy. Instead, the Soviet leader claimed he was, first, "liberating" the Poles from the "German fascists" and, then, protecting the "Polish democrats" from the "Polish fascists." The Kremlin initially covered up the Communist takeover by obscuring and camouflaging its power over Poland by trucking out a bevy of witting and unwitting collaborators, only some of whom were either open or secret reds. Stalin's puppets were ordered to appear moderate even to the point of denying their Communist ideology. These local plenipotentiaries of Moscow were further tasked with conducting a disinformation and deception operation to fool the West externally and to neutralize the Polish independentists (anti-Nazis and anti-Communists) internally.

The offensive followed the blueprint outlined by Stalin. It commenced accordingly on several fronts. First, Communist propaganda entered the fray. The Soviet system of the occupation by proxy was dubbed "democracy." The Communists and their followers were described as "democrats," while their opponents were tarred as "fascists." This concerned virtually the entire Polish independentist camp, which was a successor to the war-time Polish Underground State and its Home Army (AK). After 1944, under the Soviet occupation, the camp consisted of a largely leftist and civilian part, which functioned openly, and its chiefly rightist and military component, which operated clandestinely.

Next, Soviet agents masquerading as the independentists entered into open collaboration with the Communists. This concerned primarily the activists who usurped control over the Polish Socialist Party and the People's Party. Real leaders were either in the West, in the Gulag, or underground. Further, Moscow's orders were to woo liberal "useful idiots," in particular, among the artists and literati, but also various technocratic pragmatics, specifically in the administration, infrastructure, and industry. They were all co-opted and showcased as a façade of the Soviet system of occupation by proxy. None were either coerced or required to join the Communist party.

Moreover, deploying salami tactics, to demobilize the underground, the Communists concluded an apparent compromise with the left wing of the independentist camp: the Polish Peasant Party (PSL). The ferocious stick of military assault on the Polish guerrillas was coupled with the hopeful carrot of forgiveness. Accordingly, an "amnesty" was proclaimed in 1945 and another in 1947. In each instance, the insurgents who turned themselves in were repressed or used to penetrate the ranks of the stalwart clandestine remnant. By the mid-1945, most anti-Communist political forces accommodated the Kremlin's system of the occupation by proxy. The PSL joined the *faux* coalition with the Communists. The latter also permitted fake "free" press, some of it tied to the aboveground opposition. In reality, the mass media was tightly controlled and censored only to be stifled totally by 1948. The Communists further blocked property restitution for the victims of the Nazis and Soviets. Then, the proxy regime falsified a "popular referendum" in 1946 and a "parliamentary election" in 1947. The reds trumpeted their fake "democratic" mandate and their triumph echoed in Western leftist fanfares about the "smashing of fascism" and the alleged "victory of progress" in Poland. Meanwhile, the Soviets and their local auxiliaries completely crushed the anti-Communist insurgency and destroyed the aboveground opposition, absorbing its collaborationist part. In 1948, Stalin was in total control. No need to pretend either at home or abroad, the deception and disinformation operation was concluded. Poland became subject to open Sovietization and full-blown totalitarianism.

This gradual and sophisticated deception operation was to serve as the paradigm for Jaruzelski and Kiszczak who undertook a similar maneuver between 1986 and 1992. And the analogies of that time period with the immediate post-war situation are simply uncanny. In the mid-1980s the Kremlin's orders were to implement a local version of *perestroika* and *glasnost'*. It was supposed to be another dialectical turn for the Polish Communist party. It was all about retaining power. The proxy regime in Warsaw drew on its successful experience in the 1940s.

The key, once again, was to divide the opposition and to neutralize it via propaganda and agents. Accordingly, official propaganda condemned the "Solidarity extremists" and lionized the "constructive opposition." The former tended to be conservative and Christian nationalist. They clamored for free elections and independent Poland. The "constructive opposition" consisted of ex-Stalinists and post-Trotskites, most of them former Communist party members-turned-dissident. They wanted to reform socialism and to strip it of its national Bolshevik face which had been put in place in 1956 to legitimize the Communist rule in Poland. The erstwhile dissident Marxists were joined by liberal Catholics, who, through quiet pragmatism, had endeavored to achieve and maintain, in an evolutionary and legalistic manner, a sphere of semiautonomy around the Catholic Church and its institutions. They also did not mind socialism, seeing it as the fulfillment of "social justice." The remaining confederates in the "constructive opposition" consisted of various collaborators and accommodationists, who had been comfortable in the Polish People's Republic, because they were its products from the lower classes and because they owed their professional career to Communism, either as servile winners in a contest of negative selection or as cynical opportunists, who, having had brownnosed their privileges from the proxy regime, flirted with the dissidents only to sell themselves back to their original masters.

At the latest in 1988, the "constructive opposition" broke with the "Solidarity" underground to meet the conditions dictated by the Communists. The latter then selected the leading collaborators, outright agents, and compliant accommodationists to negotiate a *faux* agreement at the so-called "Round Table" (February–April 1989). Accordingly, the deal provided for an openly rigged parliamentary "election," where only 35 percent of all seats were open to democratic contest in June 1989. Further, in a staunchly conservative, Catholic, and anti-Communist country, the regime and the "constructive opposition" colluded to exclude almost all conservative Catholic anti-Communist candidates from the opposition electoral list (which was, inexplicably, described as "the 'Solidarity' ticket"). And, of course, 65 percent of the seats went to the Communists and affiliated "parties" uncontested. The deception and falsification was touted as "free elections," a fiction also purveyed by the Western media. This demobilized the underground and other alternative resistance forms against the Communists, channeling practically the entire energy of "Solidarity" supporters toward the open "legal" venue.

Meanwhile, the proxy regime allowed a "free" press to operate without, of course, abolishing censorship. Further, this concession benefited only the participants in the "constructive opposition." The media under their command naturally supported the Communist party's "reformist" line. After nearly half a century of Marxist-Leninist monopoly of information, the people lapped up the propaganda of the Communist collaborators from the "constructive opposition" as the truth revealed. Simultaneously, the Communists and their allies opposed property restitution to prevent the rebirth of traditional elites. Next, the partners created a *faux* coalition government, where the key positions in the police and the military remained in the hands of the Communists. Their "transformed" and "democratized" secret police conducted active measures against the "Solidarity extremists" at least well into 1991 and almost certainly after. The Communist clandestine services continued to observe closely the collaborators and accommodationists. They also maintained their old *agentura*. There was no lustration of the newly ascendant elite, no vetting of agents.[15]

In other words, the Communists remained structurally prepared for the change of the party line and the return to the hard version of totalitarianism. Lo and behold, something altogether different, and miraculous, occurred in 1991: the implosion of the Soviet Union. The local Communists under Jaruzelski and Kiszczak never saw it coming. They failed to predict it. After the implosion they simply continued the role they had played within the framework of *perestroika* and *glasnost'*. But there was no going back. The fast spinning wheels of history outpaced the party leadership in Warsaw. The Polish Communists engineered a neo-NEP and expected its reversal. But the Kremlin never gave them the sign. Moscow never did anything substantial itself to initiate the return of its own affairs to the Soviet norm. Instead, the empire simply disappeared. The scenario for saving socialism and the Communist power in Poland failed to unfold according to the carefully laid plans. Thus, Jaruzelski, Kiszczak, and others had to transform themselves quickly into democrats.

Since one could not tame the roaring wave of liberty, one had to join it. Accordingly, lesser-known comrades were tapped to spearhead the transition to post-Communism. Already in early 1990, they had rebranded their party as a "social-democratic" one. This was done in response to the events elsewhere in the satellites, and before the loss of their Moscow center. Next, the post-Communists simply sat back and waited as their leftist and liberal collaborators among the "constructive opposition" compromised themselves in government. The post-Communists next rode the wave of popular discontent to win Poland's democratic elections. In 1993, the erstwhile proxies of the Kremlin were back in power in Warsaw. The Polish post-Communists capitalized on the electorate embittered by the hard-biting economic reforms introduced in the wake of the Round Table by the "constructive opposition." The people generically blamed "Solidarity" for general hardship and misery. And because "Solidarity" was erroneously perceived as "the right," the electorate turned to a leftist alternative. The post-Communists disguised as "social democrats" were the most obvious contradiction of "Solidarity," and, hence, economic collapse. Thus, the "social democrats" won.

From the long-range perspective, the post-Communist victory was possible because there was neither de-Communization nor deagenturalization in Poland. From the short-range point of view of electoral politics, all it took was some demagoguery about "Solidarity" government mismanagement and a slick campaign financed with ill-gotten gains of the transformation and propelled by the American expertise. From a medium-range perspective, there were several factors accounting for the post-Communist triumph: first, the macabre state of Poland's economy; second, a disastrous cultural nadir inherited from the Polish People's Republic; third, the absence of traditional, conservative elite to avoid the perils of post-Communism. The nation was plagued by a rampant lack of competence among mainstream "Solidarity" activists (now union liberals); the lackluster professionalism and lack of imagination among liberal Catholics; the obsessive pro-post-Communism and anti-anti-Communism among the erstwhile Trotskites and Stalinists (now secular liberals); and rapacious avarice among the rest of the former "constructive opposition" (now avowedly economic classical liberals of sorts). Most importantly perhaps, to perpetuate the post-Communist-cum-liberal coalition of the spirit, the former party elites and their leftist collaborators deployed the most potent weapon paralyzing their "extremist" opponents: cultural nihilism and moral relativism, which purveyed in unison by the media seeped into society and destroyed the collective spirit of "Solidarity." This moral malaise, inaugurated with the Round Table agreement and the

195

rigged elections of 1989, served handsomely to demobilize and deradicalize the Polish people and their anti-Communism.

Under the circumstances, only a few individual romantics soldiered on for justice and freedom, mocked and vilified by Poland's triumphant leftists. The "extremists" were feverish, disorganized, and capable only of reacting to the unfolding reality being forged by the post-Communists and liberals, rather than offering and delivering a viable vision of a free country. The "extremists" further failed to learn how to transform themselves. They failed to abandon the defensive ramparts of their minds where they had been imprisoned first by the Nazi carnage, next, the Communist terror of the 1940s and 1950s, and then by the ensuing trauma of the sanguinary repression. Finally, the "unconstructive opposition" was incapable of physically destroying Communism and tackling its poisonous legacy.

Therefore, until this very day an informal post-Communist-liberal coalition ascribes to itself shamelessly the role of the founding fathers of democracy and freedom who gave Poland her independence. Of course, this was not their objective. They shrewdly transformed themselves so nothing would change. They deceptively took on a democratic form to preserve as much of the old system as possible. They opportunistically constructed the system in response to the implosion of the USSR and the surge of freedom and anti-Communism, improvising dialectically to remain relevant and congruent with the changing winds. They failed to predict that the spirit of freedom would break its chains all over the Soviet sphere. They watched in utter terror as the Moscow center collapsed. The implosion of the external and internal empire caught them by complete surprise.

The Communist collapse occurred chiefly because Gorbachev refrained from mass repression. His attempts at violence were embarrassing by the Communist standards (Georgia and Lithuania suffered but a few score of dead nonviolent resisters). The lack of ruthless resolve on the part of the General Secretary only encouraged the slaves of Communism to further rebellion. In 1992, the Soviet Union was no more. Communism fell as the state system of the empire. It would have been enough to kill a few million people and things would have returned to their Marxist-Leninist totalitarian norm. The Communists would have preserved their power in an unadulterated manner, reversing the neo-NEP and its concomitant "democratic" charade of the late 1980s and early 1990. This failed to pass because of indecisiveness and ineptness of Gorbachev.

Post-Communism in Poland

After the implosion, the post-Communist comrades, initially scared, but still more sophisticated, dynamic, operative, and flexible than anyone else in the empire, continued to shore up their position. They increased their wealth through privatization, legitimized their power through elections, and, thus, transformed themselves into "capitalists" and "democrats." They suavely perfected the tools of the democratic game (both for the sake of the West and their own people), but they also retained the means to play that game better than anyone else: banks, enterprises, media, and secret services. Moreover, after 1989, the post-Communists immediately co-opted practically anyone who wanted to transform with them, in particular, as far as the privatization of the economy was concerned. The post-Communists practiced flexibility and pragmatism with a gusto. It did not go unnoticed. For example, some of the so-called economic liberals instantaneously joined the former party kleptocrats.

The pathological processes observed first in Poland would be replicated throughout the former Soviet empire. Thus, the transformation from Communism to post-Communism ushered in a very specific system. It was neither Communism nor democracy as we know it in the Anglo-sphere or Western Europe. In Poland, the Third Republic failed to emerge. Instead, the Poles found themselves in a curious half-way house. This was a post-Polish People's Republic with the post-Communists and some post-dissidents holding power. As a popular song writer put it, "so much has changed but nothing has changed" (*tyle się zmieniło/a nic się nie zmieniło*). And Polish wags quipped that "Communism fell and the Communists fell down on golden parachutes" (*komuna padła na cztery łapy*).

Yet, in all fairness, could it have happened differently? In the context of the Round Table of spring 1989, let us remember that at the time the Soviet Empire was still holding out; the Berlin Wall remained in place; and the Communists were the only ones with the tanks and guns. Therefore, perhaps, any tactical method was good to neutralize their advantage and power. At that time, one could legitimately promise the Communists anything and everything until they were actually overthrown. For example, the "promises" of allowing the children of the *nomenklatura* to inherit their family's ill-gotten wealth were justified. That would have never lasted had democracy and its concomitant rule of law obtained immediately. Whereas empty promises can be understood as tactical tools of neutralizing the totalitarians, it is much tougher to swallow the betrayal of democracy by agreeing to the rigged elections of June 1989. For some such tactical moves could still be palatable under one condition, however. Namely, while applying such dialectical contortions one should never lose sight of the ultimate objective: freedom. Therefore, one should always keep in mind that the Round Table agreements were neither about executing transformation; nor reforming socialism; nor extending the autonomy of the Church; nor accommodating another phase of the Soviet occupation by proxy; nor shining as Communist collaborators of the Kremlin. The Round Table agreements should have been about Poland's freedom and independence, plain and simple. They were not, alas. Instead of serving as a tactical stepping stone, they became a strategic outcome freezing Poland in time when history accelerated. There was a pronounced lack of leadership except on the Communist side.

Unfortunately, *ex definitio*, the "constructive opposition" was never qualified to serve as leaders of a movement which advocated national solidarity, freedom, and democracy. Neither their history nor their program nor their temperament reflected those goals. They were post-Stalinists, neo-Trotskites, and Communist collaborationists of various ilk. Why expect freedom to be their priority? But they hardly had any competition. After so many years of terror, trauma, discrimination, pauperization, and environmental degradation, the alternative force—rightist, conservative, libertarian, nationalist, and independentist—simply was not prepared to handle the enormous challenge that materialized at the end of the 1980s and the beginning of the 1990s in the Soviet Bloc. The alternative force simply did not exist outside of a small constellation of Christian nationalist groups, which were bitterly divided. The Polish nation did exist. And, although anti-Communist to the core, it was also atomized and confused. Soon, the people became demobilized and deradicalized which was one of the key objectives of the transformation to facilitate the endurance of post-Communism and its supporters.[16]

The Polish scenario would be successfully replicated with various local twists throughout the Intermarium.

Notes

*   A version of this and next sections was published as Marek Jan Chodakiewicz, "Active Measures Gone Awry: Transformation in Central and Eastern Europe, 1989–1992," *International Journal of Intelligence and Counterintelligence* 24, no. 3 (Fall 2011): 467–93.

1.   Mikhail Gorbachev quoted in Jonathan Steele, "Mikhail Gorbachev: I should have abandoned the Communist party earlier," *Guardian* (August 16, 2011): http://www.guardian.co.uk/world/2011/aug/16/gorbachev-guardian-interview. This was Gorbachev's commentary on the fact that some of his comrades in the Politburo wanted to impose martial law and reintroduce censorship in the USSR in April 1991. According to a news agency dispatch, "He insisted Wednesday that the U.S.S.R. could have been preserved through gradual democratic changes and acknowledged making mistakes that led to the August 1991 coup, which dealt a deadly blow to the Soviet Union. Gorbachev admitted that he had placed excessive trust in some of his aides and allies and was too slow in reforming the Communist Party, where the old guard was fiercely resisting reforms. He also recognized that ill-conceived economic reforms resulted in empty shelves, fueling public discontent. Gorbachev insisted that his main focus at the time was to avoid bloodshed. 'There could have been a civil war,' he said. 'A civil war in a country rigged with nuclear weapons.'" See Vladimir Isachenkov, "Gorbachev says Russia needs change," Associated Press, August 17, 2011: http://hosted. ap.org/dynamic/stories/E/EU_RUSSIA_GORBACHEV?SITE=AP&SECTION =HOME&TEMPLATE=DEFAULT&CTIME=2011-08-17-08-44-28.

2.   Paul Goble quoted in Judith Latham, "Revolutions of 1989 - Poland Sets the Stage," *Voice of America News* (September 24, 2009): http://www.voanews. com/english/NewsAnalysis/2009-09-24-voa38.cfm, http://sofiaecho.

com/2009/09/25/789453_revolutions-of-1989-poland-sets-the-stage, http://
www.turkishweekly.net/news/89597/-revolutions-of-1989-%E2%80%93-
poland-sets-the-stage.html, and http://www.thelinguist.com/en/en/library/
item/61493/.

3.   For the most thoughtful short piece on the collapse of Communism and its
aftermath see John O'Sullivan, "The Road from 1989: Reflections on the Greatest Peaceful Transformation in History," *National Review* (November 23, 2009):
44–47. For another incisive, yet brief analysis see George Friedman, "Twenty
Years after the Fall," (November 9, 2009): http://www.stratfor.com/week-
ly/20091109_russian_dilemma?utm_source=GWeekly&utm_
medium=email&utm_campaign=091109&utm_content=readmore. For an
appreciation of the spiritual factors and actors, in particular John Paul II and
Ronald Reagan, in overthrowing Communism see Newt Gingrich, Callista
Gingrich, Vince Haley, "The Victory of the Cross," *The Daily Standard* (November 9, 2009): http://www.aei.org/article/101286. For a useful chronology
of the events see Steven F. Hayward, "The Berlin Wall, 20 Years Later," *The
American* (November 2009): http://www.american.com/archive/2009/novem-
ber/the-berlin-wall-20-years-later. As mentioned, there is a plethora of theories
about the causes of the collapse of Communism. Some of them correctly consider a multitude of factors. However, most pundits are fiercely partisan. Unlike
the conservatives and neoconservatives, the liberal and leftists pundits tend to
deny or at least minimize the role of Ronald Reagan, Margaret Thatcher, and
even Pope John Paul II in the victory over totalitarianism. For example, *The
Economist* ("The Beginning of the End," November 12, 2009: http://www.
economist.com/world/europe/displayStory.cfm?story_id=14843274), was
virtually alone among the mainstream media to praise Reagan's contribution.
Most credit Gorbachev alone (e.g., Rodric Braithwaite). A couple give the
Soviet General Secretary the palm of primacy but also appreciate the role of
other actors (e.g., while Paul C. Demakis credits both Gorbachev and Reagan,
Joshua Muravchik acknowledges John Paul II, Ronald Reagan, "Solidarity," and
others). Very few focus on the nefarious role of the Communist secret police
in the transformation. Some overemphasize the importance of the dissident
intellectuals (e.g., Timothy Garton Ash) or "reform Communists" and the
nomenklatura, who allegedly shifted to democracy out of their own economic
self-interest (e.g., Stephen Kotkin). Others overstress the significance of the
popular factor in the rebellion against Communism, in particular, as it pertains
to "the Velvet Revolution" in Czechoslovakia, (e.g., Michael Meyer). There are
also competing opinions about the actual trigger of the collapse. One notable
theory advanced by, among others, Patricia H. Kushlis, is the role of "the Sinatra doctrine" which the Soviets proposed, out of economic necessity, to shed
the external empire, including Poland, but not the internal one. Another one
concerns the crucial role of Poland's "Solidarity," in particular the Round Table
agreement and "free" elections of June 1989 (e.g., Judith Latham and Doug
Saunders). Andrew Nagorski credits both Poland and Hungary for the collapse.
Others focus exclusively on Hungary's opening of its Western border which
precipitated mass emigration from East Germany, initiating changes there (e.g.,
Mitchell Koss and Michael Meyer again). In fact, Neal Acherson, Quentin Peel,
Ross Douthat claim that the fall of the Berlin Wall is not only a symbol of
Communism's collapse (as Newt Gingrich would have it), but also the actual
crowning of Germany's role in the process through patient diplomacy (*Ostpo-
litik*) and other actions, thus giving that nation a pivotal role in defeating

totalitarianism. Nonetheless, a few, virtually unknown, observers, including Tanya Koncheva and Anca Paduraru, offer tantalizing glimpses of what increasingly seems to have been a palace coup in Bulgaria and Rumania, respectively. Even fewer commentators (e.g., Jeffrey T. Kuhner and Roger Scruton) have been brave enough to admit that the so-called "collapse of Communism" in 1989 and later was a sham. The Communists simply transformed into post-Communists, Social Democrats, and liberals. Last but not least, Gerard DeGroot, basing himself on the confused account of Constantine Pleshakov, champions a curious synthesis where everyone, including good Communists, unite to end Communism. This is the infamous theory of convergence brought to its logical conclusion. See Timothy Garton Ash, "1989!" *The New York Review of Books* 56, no. 17 (November 5, 2009); Timothy Garton Ash, "1989 Was a Very Good Year," *The Los Angeles Times* (November 5, 2009): http://www.latimes.com/news/opinion/la-oe-gartonash5-2009nov05,0,5820196.story; Joshua Muravchik, "After the Fall: 1989, Twenty Years On," *World Affairs: A Journal of Ideas and Debate* (Summer 2009): http://www.iwp.edu/news/newsID.572/news_detail.asp; Paul C. Demakis, "Who Ended the Cold War?" *The Boston Globe* (November 5, 2009): http://www.boston.com/bostonglobe/editorial_opinion/oped/articles/2009/11/05/who_ended_the_cold_war/; Rodric Braithwaite, "Gorbachev was key in freeing eastern Europe," *The Financial Times* (November 5, 2009): http://www.ft.com/cms/s/0/c62f605e-ca41-11de-a3a3-00144feabdc0,dwp_uuid=5725f986-bc9d-11de-a7ec-00144feab49a.html; Gerard DeGroot, "Who Killed Communism? Look Past the Usual Suspects," *The Washington Post* (November 1, 2009); Neal Ascherson, "They're Just Not Ready," *The London Review of Books* 32, no. 1 (January 7, 2010): 18–20; Newt Gingrich, "Berlin Wall Is Well Worth Remembering," *The Washington Examiner* (November 6, 2009): http://www.aei.org/article/101276; Quentin Peel, "Failure of Imagination," *The Financial Times* (November 5, 2009): http://www.ft.com/cms/s/0/27f6ee9c-ca42-11de-a3a3-00144feabdc0.html?nclick_check=1; Ross Douthat, "Life after the End of History," *The New York Times* (November 9, 2009): http://www.nytimes.com/2009/11/09/opinion/09douthat.html?ref=opinion; Michael Meyer, "The Triumph of the Powerless," (November 24, 2009): http://www.themoscowtimes.com/opinion/article/the-triumph-of-the-powerless/390204.html; Michael Meyer, "In One of History's Hidden Turning Points, a Gambit by Hungarian Officials Opened the Door to the Collapse of the Eastern Bloc," *The Los Angeles Times* (September 13, 2009); Mitchell Koss, "Hungary Was the First Rip in Iron Curtain: Months before the Berlin Wall fell, Hungarians Had Marched to Demand Democracy," *The Los Angeles Times* (November 9, 2009): http://www.latimes.com/news/opinion/commentary/la-oe-koss9-2009nov09,0,2886067.story; Judith Latham, "Revolutions of 1989 - Poland Sets the Stage," (September 24, 2009): http://www.voanews.com/english/NewsAnalysis/2009-09-24-voa38.cfm; Doug Saunders, "Beyond the Berlin Wall: Poland's Round Table Laid Out Course for Freedom: Innovative and Risky Discussions in Warsaw Became a Template for Europe's Non-violent Transition Back to Democracy," *The Globe and Mail* (Toronto) (October 26, 2009): http://v1.theglobeandmail.com/servlet/story/GAM.20091026.WAL-L26ART2258/TPStory/TPComment#; Andrew Nagorski, "The Berlin Wall Fell Later: By Nov. 9, 1989, When Germans Breached the Berlin Wall, a Long Line of Regimes Were Already Toppling," *Newsweek* (November 3, 2009): http://www.newsweek.com/id/220832; Tanya Kancheva, "Remembering Bulgaria's 'Palace Revolution,'" *RFE/RL* (November 9, 2009): http://www.rferl.org/content/

Remembering_Bulgarias_Palace_Revolution/1873558.html; Anca Paduraru, "Why Rumanians Died for Democracy," (December 15, 2009): http://www.isn. ethz.ch/isn/Current-Affairs/Security-Watch/Detail/?lng=en&id=110548; Patricia H. Kushlis, "The Soviets, The Sinatra Doctrine and the Beginning of the Cold War's End," *Whirled View* (November 9, 2009): http://whirledview. typepad.com/whirledview/2009/11/the-soviets-the-sinatra-doctrine-and-the-beginning-of-the-cold-wars-end.html; Jeffrey T. Kuhner, "Rebirth of an Old Scourge," *The Washington Times* (November 8, 2009): http://www.washington-times.com/news/2009/nov/08/rebirth-of-an-old-scourge/; Roger Scruton, "The Flame That Was Snuffed Out by Freedom," *The Times [London]* (November 7, 2009). And see Frederic Bozo, ed., *Europe and the End of the Cold War: A Reappraisal* (London and New York: Routledge, 2008); Leon Aron, "Everything You Think You Know About the Collapse of the Soviet Union Is Wrong," *Foreign Policy* (July/August 2011): http://www.foreignpolicy.com/articles/2011/06/20/everything_you_think_you_know_about_the_collapse_of_the_soviet_union_is_wrong?page=full. This is a "trailer" of Aron's forthcoming *Roads to the Temple: Truth, Memory, Ideas, and Ideals in the making of the Russian Revolution, 1987–1991* (where he argues that it was idealism and a quest for the moral imperative that drove the reformers and, later, revolutionaries who overthrew Communism in Russia).

4.   For the implosion of Communism at the Moscow center and its aftermath see Nicolai N. Petro, *The Rebirth of Russian Democracy: An Interpretation of Political Culture* (Cambridge, MA and London: Harvard University Press, 1995); Stephen Kotkin, *Armageddon Averted: The Soviet Collapse, 1970–2000* (Oxford and New York: Oxford University Press, 2001); Yegor Gaidar, *Collapse of an Empire: Lessons for Modern Russia* (Washington, DC: Brookings Institution Press, 2007); Richard B. Dobson and Steven A. Grant, "Public Opinion and the Transformation of the Soviet Union," *International Journal of Public Opinion Research* 4, no. 4 (Winter 1992): 302–20; David Remnick, *Resurrection: The Struggle for a New Russia* (New York: Vintage, 1998); Michael McFaul, Nikolai Petrov, and Andrei Riabov, *Between Dictatorship and Democracy: Russian Post-Communist Political Reform* (Washington, DC: Carnegie Endowment for International Peace, 2004); Richard F. Starr, *The New Military in Russia: Ten Myths that Shape the Image* (Annapolis, MD: Naval Institute Press, 1996); J. Michael Waller, *Secret Empire: The KGB in Russia Today* (Boulder, CO: Westview and Harper Collins, 1994); Lilia Shevtsova, *Russia — Lost in Translation: The Yeltsin and Putin Legacies* (Washington, DC: Carnegie Endowment for International Peace, 2007); Susan Glasser, *Kremlin Rising: Vladimir Putin's Russia and the End of Revolution* (New York: Scribner, 2005); Andrew Jack, *Inside Putin's Russia* (New York: Oxford University, 2004); Roy Medvedev, *Post-Soviet Russia: A Journey through the Yeltsin Era*, ed. and trans. George Shriver (New York: Columbia University, 2000); Mark Kramer, *Travels With a Hungry Bear: A Journey to the Russian Heartland* (New York: Houghton Mifflin, 1996); Heyward Isham, *Remaking Russia: Voices from Within* (New York: M.E. Sharpe, 1995); Richard Sakwa, *Russian Politics and Society* (New York: Routledge, 1993, 2nd edn., 2002); Bruce Clarke, *An Empire's New Clothes: The End of Russia's Liberal Dream* (London: Vintage, 1996); Anna Politkovskaya, *Putin's Russia: Life in a Failing Democracy* (New York: Henry Holt and Company, 2007). For a very interesting analysis of the role of the KGB in the transformation of the USSR compare Jerzy Targalski, "Rola służb specjalnych i ich agentury w pierestrojce i demontażu komunizmu w Europie Sowieckiej," ("The Role of Special

Services and Their Agentura in Perestroika and in Dismantling of Communism in Soviet Europe"), TMs, Warszawa, 2010, pp. 1–549 (a copy in my collection); and Anatoliy Golitsyn, *The Perestroika Deception: Memoranda to the Central Intelligence Agency*, ed. Christopher Story (New York and London: Edward Harle Limited, 1998). See further Marek Jan Chodakiewicz, "Jak Gorbaczow zatopił Sowiety," ("How Gorbachev sank the USSR") *Uważam Rze*, March 19–25, 2012; and see below.

5.　Luc Duhamel, *The KGB Campaign against Corruption in Moscow* (Pittsburgh, PA: University of Pittsburgh Press, 2010).

6.　See John Lenczowski, *The Sources of Soviet Perestroika* (Ashland, OH: John M. Ashbrook Center for Public Affairs, 1990); Anthony D'Agostino, *Soviet Succession Struggles: Kremlinology and the Russian Question from Lenin to Gorbachev* (Boston, MA: Allen and Unwin, 1988) (where the author got Gorbachev the Leninist dialectician right in the short run only, but failed to anticipate his evolution and lack of resolve); Constantine Christopher Menges, *Transitions from Communism in Russia and Eastern Europe: Analysis and Perspectives* (Washington, DC: George Washington University Press, 1993); Illan Berman and J. Michael Waller, eds., *Dismantling Tyranny: Transitioning Beyond Totalitarian Regimes* (Lanham, MD, Boulder, CO, Toronto, and London: Rowman & Littlefield, 2006); Lee Edwards, ed., *The Collapse of Communism* (Stanford, CA: Stanford University, 2000); Jonathan Luxmoore and Jolanta Babiuch, *The Vatican and the Red Flag: The Struggle for the Soul of Eastern Europe* (London and New York: Geoffrey Chapman, 2000); Steven L. Solnick, *Stealing the State: Control and Collapse in Communist Institutions* (Cambridge, MA: Harvard University Press, 1999); Stephen K. Carter, *Russian Nationalism: Yesterday, Today, Tomorrow* (New York: St. Martin's Press, 1990); Gerhard Simon, *Nationalism and Policy Toward the Nationalities in the Soviet Union: From Totalitarian Dictatorship to Post-Stalinist Society* (Boulder, CO: Westview Press, 1991); Alexander J. Motyl, ed., *The Post-Soviet Nations: Perspectives in the Demise of the USSR* (New York: Columbia University Press, 1992); Ronald Grigor Suny, *The Revenge of the Past: Nationalism, Revolution, and the Collapse of the Soviet Union* (Stanford, CA: Stanford University Press, 1993); Hélène Carrère d'Encausse, *The End of the Soviet Empire: The Triumph of the Nations* (New York: Basic Books, 1993); Mark R. Beissinger, *Nationalist Mobilization and the Collapse of the Soviet State* (Cambridge and New York: Cambridge University Press, 2002); Anatoliy Golitsyn, *The Perestroika Deception: Memoranda to the Central Intelligence Agency*, ed. Christopher Story (New York and London: Edward Harle Limited, 1998); and Jerzy Targalski, "Rola służb specjalnych i ich agentury w pierestrojce i demontażu komunizmu w Europie Sowieckiej," ("The Role of Special Services and Their Agentura in Perestroika and in Dismantling of Communism in Soviet Europe"), TMs, Warszawa, 2010, pp. 1–549 (a copy in my collection).

7.　For the Kremlin's relationship with its Central and Eastern European colonies see Joseph Rothschild and Nancy M. Wingfield, *Return to Diversity: A Political History of East Central Europe since World War II* (New York and Oxford: Oxford University Press, 2000); Hugh Seton-Watson, *The East European Revolution* (Frederick A. Praeger, Publisher 1962); Zbigniew K. Brzezinski, *The Soviet Bloc: Unity and Conflict* (Cambridge, MA and London: Harvard University Press, 1977); Hans-Hermann Hohmann, et al., *The New Economic Systems of Eastern Europe* (Berkeley and Los Angeles: University of California Press, 1975); Stanislaw Wellisz, *The Economies of the Soviet Bloc: A Study of Decision Making and Resource Allocation* (New York and Toronto: McGraw-Hill Book Company, 1966); Sarah Meiklejohn Terry, ed., *Soviet Policy in Eastern Europe* (New Haven, CT and London: Yale University Press, 1984); Charles Gati, *The Bloc that Failed: Soviet-East European Relations in Transition* (Bloomington and Indianapolis: Indiana University Press, 1990); Charles Gati, *Hungary and the Soviet Bloc* (Durham: Duke University Press, 1986); Charles Gati, *Failed Illusions: Moscow, Washington, Budapest, and the 1956 Hungarian Revolt* (Washington, DC and Stanford, CA: Woodrow Wilson Center Press and Stanford University Press, 2006); Jiri Valenta, *Soviet Intervention in Czechoslovakia 1968: Anatomy of a Decision* (Baltimore, MD and London: The Johns Hopkins University Press, 1991); Milovan Djilas, *The New Class: An Analysis of the Communist System* (New York: Frederick A. Praeger, Publisher, 1957); Paul Neuburg, *The Hero's Children: The Post-War Generation in Eastern Europe* (New York: William Morrow and Company, Inc., 1973); Frantisek Silnitsky, et al., eds., *Communism and Eastern Europe: A Collection of Essays* (New York: Karz Publishers, 1979); Teresa Rakowska-Harmstone and Andrew Gyorgy, eds., *Communism in Eastern Europe* (Bloomington, IN: Indiana University Press, 1981).

8. See Mark Kramer, "The Collapse of East European Communism and the Repercussions within the Soviet Union," published in three parts in the *Journal of Cold War History* 5, no. 4 (Fall 2003); 6, no. 4 (Fall 2004); 7, no. 1 (Winter 2007). See also the following essays in Sir Adam Roberts and Timothy Garton Ash, eds., *Civil Resistance and Power Politics: The Experience of Non-violent Action from Gandhi to the Present* (Oxford: Oxford University Press, 2009): Mark Kramer, "The Dialectics of Empire: Soviet Leaders and the Challenge of Civil Resistance in East-Central Europe, 1968–1991," (91–109); Kieran Williams, "Civil Resistance in Czechoslovakia: From Soviet Invasion to 'Velvet Revolution," 1968–1989 (110–26); Alexander Smolar, "Towards 'Self-Limiting Revolution,' Poland: 1970–1989," (127–43); and Charles S. Maier, "Civil Resistance and Civil Society: Lessons from the Collapse of East Germany," (260–76). On the role of the secret police see Alexandra Grúňová, ed., *NKVD/KGB Activities and Its Co-operation with Other Secret Services in Central and Eastern Europe, 1945–1989: Anthology of the International Conference, Bratislava 14.-16.11.2007* (Bratislava: Nation's Memory Institute, 2008); Krzysztof Persak and Lukasz Kaminski, *A Handbook of Communist Security Apparatus in East Central Europe 1944–1989* (Warsaw: Institute of National Remembrance, 2005); Mike Dennis, *The Stasi: Myth and Reality* (London and Harlow: Pearson Longman, 2003); Andreas Glaeser, *Political Epistemics: The Secret Police, the Opposition, and the End of East German Socialism* (Chicago and London: The University of Chicago Press, 2011); Benjamin B. Fischer, ed., *At Cold War's End: US Intelligence on the Soviet Union and Eastern Europe, 1989–1991* (Langley, VA: Center for the Study of Intelligence/Central Intelligence Agency, 1999); Roman David, *Lustration and Transitional Justice: Personnel Systems in the Czech Republic, Hungary, and Poland* (Philadelphia, PA: University of Pennsylvania Press, 2011). See further Charles Gati, *The Bloc That Failed: Soviet-East European Relations in Transition* (Bloomington and Indianapolis: Indiana University Press, 1990); Matthew A. Kraljic, ed., *The Breakup of Communism: The Soviet Union and Eastern Europe* (New York: H. W. Wilson, 1993); Timothy Garton Ash, *The Uses of Adversity: Essays on the Fate of Central Europe* (New York: Vintage Books, 1990); Timothy Garton Ash, *The Magic Lantern: The Revolution of '89 Witnessed in Warsaw, Budapest, Berlin and Prague* (New York: Random House, 1990); Bernard Gwertzman and Michael T. Kaufman, *The Collapse of*

Communism: Revised and Updated (New York and Toronto: The New York Times Company, 1991); Mark Frankland, *The Patriots' Revolution: How East Europe Won Its Freedom* (London: Sinclair-Stevenson Limited, 1990); Gale Stokes, *The Walls Came Tumbling Down: The Collapse of Communism in Eastern Europe* (New York and Oxford: Oxford University Press, 1993); Stephen R. Graubard, ed., *Exit from Communism* (New Brunswick, NJ and London: Transaction Publishers, 1993); Stephen R. Graubard, *Eastern Europe... Central Europe... Europe* (Boulder, San Francisco and Oxford: Westview Press, 1991); John S. Micgiel, ed., *The Transformations of 1989–1999: Triumph or Tragedy?* (New York: The East Central European Center, 2000); Peter Schweizer, *Victory: The Reagan Administration's Secret Strategy that Hastened the Collapse* (New York: The Atlantic Monthly Press, 1994); Romesh Ratnesar, *Tear Down this Wall: A City, a President, and the Speech that Ended the Cold War* (New York: Simon and Schuster, 2009); Carole Foryst, "US Intelligence and the Oval Office as the USSR Collapses: Bush Plays Gorbachev as an Asset in Place," TMs, Honors Thesis, The Institute of World Politics, Washington, DC, May 8, 2010; Dick Combs, *Inside the Soviet Alternate Universe: The Cold War's End and the Soviet Union's Fall Reappraised* (University Park, PA: Pennsylvania State University Press, 2008);Vladimir Tismăneanu, ed., *The Revolutions of 1989: Rewriting Histories* (London and New York: Routledge, 1999); Sorin Antohi and Vladimir Tismăneanu, eds., *Between Past and Future: The Revolutions of 1989 and Their Aftermath* (Budapest and New York: Central European University Press, 2000); Mary Elise Sarotte, *1989: The Struggle to Create Post–Cold War Europe* (Princeton, NJ: Princeton University Press, 2009); Stephen Kotkin and Jan T. Gross, *Uncivil Society: 1989 and the Implosion of the Communist Establishment* (New York: Modern Library, Random House, 2009); György Dalos, *Der Vorhang Geht Auf: Das Ende der Diktaturen in Osteuropa* (Munich: C.H. Beck, 2009); Michael Meyer, *The Year that Changed the World: The Untold Story Behind the Fall of the Berlin Wall* (New York: Scribner, 2009); Victor Sebestyen, *Revolution 1989: The Fall of the Soviet Empire* (New York: Pantheon Books, Random House, 2009); Jeffrey A. Engel, ed., *The Fall of the Berlin Wall: The Revolutionary Legacy of 1989* (New York: Oxford University Press, 2009); Constantine Pleshakov, *There Is No Freedom Without Bread! 1989 and the Civil War that Brought Down Communism* (New York: Farrar, Straus and Giroux, 2009); Susan Rose-Ackerman, *From Elections to Democracy: Building Accountable Government in Hungary and Poland* (Cambridge and New York: Cambridge University Press, 2005); Ignac Romsics, *From Dictatorship to Democracy: The Birth of the Third Hungarian Republic, 1988–2001* (New York, Highland Lakes, NJ, and Boulder, CO: Social Science Monographs, Atlantic Research and Publications, Inc., Columbia University Press, 2007); Peter Sinai-Davies, *The Romanian Revolution of December 1989* (Ithaca, NY: Cornell University Press, 2005); Juliana Geran Pilon, *The Bloody Flag: Post-Communist Nationalism in Eastern Europe: Spotlight on Rumania* (New Brunswick, NJ and London: Transaction Publishers, 1992); Tom Gallagher, *Modern Rumania: The End of Communism, The Failure of Democratic Reform, and the Theft of a Nation* (New York: NYU Press, 2008); Annabelle Townson, *We Wait for You: Unheard Voices from Post-Communist Romania* (Lanham, MD: Hamilton Books, 2005); Ilko-Sascha Kowalczuk, *Endspiel: Die Revolution von 1989 in der DDR* (Munich: C.H. Beck Verlag, 2009); Timothy Garton Ash, *In Europe's Name: Germany and the Divided Continent* (New York: Random House, 1993). See also Jerzy Targalski, "Republiki zachodniosowieckie – legitymizacja komunistów narodowych i rządy koalicyjne," ("Western Soviet Republics: Legitimizing the National Communists and Coalition Governments") TMs, Warsaw, no date (2010), pp. 1–279, including on Hungary (150–52), Slovakia (152–54), Czech Republic (154–81), Bulgaria (181–85), and Romania (185–254), (a copy in my collection). Lastly, see the symposium on 1989 in *Pamięć i Sprawiedliwość* (*Memory and Justice*) (Warsaw), no. 2 (18) (2011), and in particular, Jiři Suk, "Rozłam pomiędzy 'totalitaryzmem' a 'demokracją': Czechosłowacki rok 1989 – możliwości," ("A Split between 'Totalitarianism' and 'Democracy': 1989 in Czechoslovakia: Possibilities"), 13–52; Dragoş Petrescu, "Revolucje 1989 roku. Schemat wyjaśniający," ("Revolutions of 1989: An Explanatory Scheme"), 53–79; "Rok 1989 w państwach Europy Środkowej: Dyskusja z udziałem Adama Burakowskiego, Antoniego Dudka i Pawła Ukielskiego. Dyskusję poprowadziła Małgorzata Choma-Jusińska," ("1989 in Central Europe: A Debate between Adam Burakowski, Antoni Dudek and Paweł Ukielski Moderated by Małgorzata Choma-Jusińska"), 81–101; and Ilko-Sascha Kowalczuk, "Rewolucja 1989 roku w NRD," ("The Revolution of 1989 in East Germany"), 197–216.

9. For dissent and resistance elsewhere in the Soviet Bloc see Gary Bruce, *Resistance with the People: Repression and Resistance in Eastern Germany, 1945–1955* (Lanham, MD: Rowman & Littlefield Publishers, Inc., 2003); John P.C. Matthews, *Tinderbox: East-Central Europe in the Spring, Summer, and Early Fall of 1956* (Tucson, AZ: Fenestra Books, 2003); Paul E. Zinner, ed., *National Communism and Popular Revolt in Eastern Europe: A Selection of Documents on Events in Poland and Hungary, February–November 1956* (New York: Columbia University Press, 1957); Sandor Kopacsi, *In the Name of the Working Class: The Inside Story of the Hungarian Revolution* (New York, NY: Grove Press, 1986); Vojtech Mastny, ed., *East European Dissent*, vol. 1, 1953–1964, and vol. 2, 1965–1970 (New York: Facts on File, Inc., 1972); Rudolf L. Tokes, ed., *Opposition in Eastern Europe* (Baltimore, MD and London: The Johns Hopkins University Press, 1979).

10. Poland's nonviolent resistance to Communism achieved its postwar peak under "Solidarity" but there had always been a rather substantial measure of dissent. See Peter Raina, *Political Opposition in Poland, 1954–1977* (London: Poets and Painters Press, 1978); Peter Raina, *Independent Social Movements in Poland* (London: London School of Economics and Political Science and Orbis Books Ltd., 1981); A. Ostoja-Ostaszewski, ed., *Dissent in Poland: Reports and Documents in Translation, December 1975–July 1977* (London: Association of Polish Students and Graduates in Exile, 1977); Jane Leftwich Curry, ed. and trans., *The Black Book of Polish Censorship* (New York: Vintage Books, 1984); Michael H. Bernhard, *The Origins of Democratization in Poland: Workers, Intellectuals, and Oppositional Politics, 1976–1980* (New York: Columbia University Press, 1993); Keith John Lepak, *Prelude to Solidarity: Poland and the Politics of the Gierek Regime* (New York: Columbia University Press, 1988); David Ost, *Solidarity and the Politics of Anti-Politics: Opposition and Reform in Poland since 1968* (Philadelphia, PA: Temple University Press, 1990); Lawrence Weschler, *The Passion of Poland: From Solidarity through the State of War* (New York: Pantheon Books, 1984); Michael T. Kaufman, *Mad Dreams, Saving Graces: Poland: A Nation in Conspiracy* (New York: Random House, 1989); Roman Laba, *The Roots of Solidarity: A Political Sociology of Poland's Working-Class Democratization* (Princeton, NJ: Princeton University Press, 1991); Lawrence Goodwyn, *Breaking the Barrier: The Rise of Solidarity in Poland* (New York and Oxford: Oxford University Press, 1991); Andrzej Paczkowski and Malcolm Byrne, eds., *From*

Solidarity to Martial Law: The Polish Crisis of 1980–1981: A Documentary History (Budapest and New York: Central European University Press, 2007); Abraham Brumberg, ed., *Poland: Genesis of a Revolution* (New York: Random House, 1983); Adam Michnik, *Letters from Prison: And Other Essays*, trans. Maya Latynski (Berkeley, Los Angeles and London: University of California Press, 1987); Andrzej Swidlicki, *Political Trials in Poland, 1981–1986* (London, New York and Sydney: Croom Helm, 1988); Charles Wankel, *Anti-Communist Student Organizations and the Polish Renewal* (New York: St. Martin's Press, 1992); Shana Penn, *Solidarity's Secret: The Women Who Defeated Communism in Poland* (Ann Arbor, MI: The University of Michigan Press, 2005); Maryjane Osa, *Solidarity and Contention: Networks of Polish Opposition: Social Movements, Protest, and Contention, Volume 18* (Minneapolis and London: University of Minnesota Press, 2003); Marta Toch, ed., *Reinventing Civil Society: Poland's Quiet Revolution, 1981–1986, December 1986* (New York and Washington: The U.S. Helsinki Watch Committee, 1986); Steve W. Reiquam, ed., *Solidarity and Poland: Impacts East and West* (Washington, DC: The Wilson Center Press, 1988); Marciej Lopinski, Marcin Moskit, and Mariusz Wilk, *Konspria: Solidarity Underground*, trans. Jane Cave (Berkeley, Los Angeles, and Oxford: University of California Press, 1990); Timothy Garton Ash, *The Polish Revolution: Solidarity* (New Haven, CT and London: Yale University Press, 2002); Jean-Yves Potel, *The Summer Before the Frost: Solidarity in Poland*, trans. Phil Markham (London: Pluto Press, 1982); Benjamin Weiser, *A Secret Life: The Polish Officer, His Covert Mission, and the Price He Paid to Save His Country* (New York: Public Affairs, 2004); Douglas J. MacEachin, *U.S. Intelligence and the Confrontation in Poland, 1980–1981* (University Park, PA: The Pennsylvania State University Press, 2002); Leopold Labedz and the Staff of *Survey* Magazine, eds., *Poland under Jaruzelski: A Comprehensive Sourcebook on Poland during and after Martial Law* (New York: Charles Scribner's Sons, 1984); Solidarity Support Committee in Southern Sweden, *Poland, December 13th 1981 - . . . The War against the Nation* (Lund: Nowa, Krag, CDN and Rahms, 1982).

11. Marek Jan Chodakiewicz, "A Bid for Autonomy: Destalinisation in Poland and the Victory of the Right-nationalist Deviation," *Glaukopis* no. 5/6 (2006): 275–327.

12. See Sławomir Cenckiewicz, "Służba Bezpieczeństwa Okrągłego Stołu: Transformacja ustrojowa w Polsce w latach 1988–1990 była wspierana przez bezpiekę," ("Security Service of the Round Table: Systemic Transformation in Poland Was Assisted by the Secret Police, 1988–1990") in Sławomir Cenckiewicz, *Śladami bezpieki i partii: Studia-źródła-publicystyka* (*Tracking the Secret Police and the Party: Studies, Sources, Journalism*) (Łomianki: LTW, 2009). And see below.

13. For a good introduction to the history of "people's Poland" see Antoni Dudek, *PRL bez makijażu* (*The Polish People's Republic with No Make Up*) (Cracow: Znak, 2008). See also Andrzej Paczkowski, *The Spring Will Be Ours: Poland and the Poles from Occupation to Freedom* (University Park, PA: The Pennsylvania State University Press, 2003); A. [Anthony] Kemp-Welch, *Poland under Communism: A Cold War History* (Cambridge and New York: Cambridge University Press, 2008); Marjorie Castle, *Triggering Communism's Collapse: Perceptions and Power in Poland's Transition* (Lanham, MD: Rowman & Littlefield, 2005); Leszek Balcerowicz, *Socialism, Capitalism, Transformation* (Budapest, London, and New York: Central European University Press, 1995); Janine R. Wedel, ed., *The Unplanned Society: Poland during and after Communism* (New York: Columbia University Press, 1992); Bartlomiej Kaminski, *The Collapse of State*

Socialism: The Case of Poland (Princeton, NJ: Princeton University Press, 1991); Zbigniew Gluza, ed., *The End of Yalta: Breakthrough in Eastern Europe, 1989/90* (Warsaw: The Karta Center, 1999); Jon Elster, ed., *The Roundtable Talks and the Breakdown of Communism* (Chicago, IL and London: The University of Chicago Press, 1996), in particular Wiktor Osiatynski, "The Roundtable Talks in Poland," 21–68; David R. Pichaske, *Poland in Transition, 1989–1991* (Granite Falls, MN: The Ellis Press, 1994); David Ost, *The Defeat of Solidarity: Anger and Politics in Postcommunist Europe* (Ithaca, NY and London: Cornell University Press, 2005); Elizabeth C. Dunn, *Privatizing Poland: Baby Food, Big Business, and the Remaking of Labor* (Ithaca, NY and London: Cornell University Press, 2004); Marjorie Castle and Ray Taras, *Democracy in Poland* (Cambridge and Boulder: Westview Press, 2002). See also the following essays in *New Europe: The Impact of the First Decade,* vol. 1: *Trends and Prospects,* ed. Teresa Rakowska-Harmstone, Piotr Dutkiewicz, and Agnieszka Orzelska (Warsaw: Institute of Political Studies Polish Academy of Sciences and Collegium Civitas Press, 2006): Teresa Rakowska-Harmstone, "Dynamics of Transition," (91–137); and "Economic Transformation," (139–176). And see below.

14.   See Tadeusz Piotrowski, *Poland's Holocaust: Ethnic Strife, Collaboration with Occupying Forces and Genocide in the Second Republic, 1918–1947* (Jefferson and London: McFarland & Company, Inc., Publishers, 1998); M. K. Dziewanowski, *The Communist Party of Poland: An Outline of History* (Cambridge, MA: Harvard University Press, 1959); Jan B. de Weydenthal, *The Communists of Poland: An Historical Outline,* Revised Edition (Stanford, CA: Stanford University Press, 1986); Krystyna Kersten, *The Establishment of Communist Rule in Poland, 1943–1948* (Berkeley, CA: University of California Press, 1991); *Padraic Kenney, Rebuilding Poland: Workers and Communists, 1945–1950* (Ithaca, NY and London: Cornell University Press, 1997); Anita J. Prazmowska, *Civil War in Poland, 1942–1948* (Hampshire and New York: Palgrave Macmillan, 2004), which is a confused and flawed account of the Soviet takeover of Poland, where the leftist author fails to notice that one cannot talk about civil war when the center of command of one of the combatants is located in a foreign capital (Moscow) and is controlled by a foreign government (Stalin), and the bulk of the forces involved are foreign (the Red Army and the NKVD) with some native auxiliaries, a few volunteer renegades and others forced conscripts; Arthur Bliss Lane, *I Saw Poland Betrayed: An American Ambassador Reports to the American People* (New York and Indianapolis: The Bobbs-Merrill Company Publishers, 1948); Antony Polonsky and Boleslaw Drukier, *The Beginnings of Communist Rule in Poland* (London, Boston, and Henley: Routledge & Kegan Paul, 1980); Richard F. Staar, *Poland, 1944–1962: The Sovietization of a Captive People* (New Orleans, LA: Louisiana State University Press, 1962); Hansjakob Stehle, *The Independent Satellite: Society and Politics in Poland since 1945* (New York, Washington and London: Frederick A. Praeger, Publishers, 1965). See also Konrad Rokicki and Robert Spałek, eds., *Władza w PRL: Ludzie i mechanizmy* (*Power in the Polish People's Republic: People and Mechanisms*) (Warszawa: IPN-KŚZpNP, 2011).

15.   See Roman David, *Lustration and Transitional Justice: Personnel Systems in the Czech Republic, Hungary, and Poland* (Philadelphia, PA: University of Pennsylvania Press, 2011); Piotr Grzelak, *Wojna o lustrację* (*War for Lustration*) (Warsaw: Trio, 2005); Sławomir Cenckiewicz, *Długie ramię Moskwy: Wywiad wojskowy Polski Ludowej, 1943–1991* (*Moscow's Long Arm: Military Intelligence of People's Poland*) (Poznań: Zysk i Ska, 2011), 327–426; Sebastian Pilarski, ed.,

Służba Bezpieczeństwa wobec przemian politycznych w latach 1988–1990: Region Łódzki (*Security Service and the Political Transformation, 1988–1990: The Łódź Region*) (Warszawa and Łódź: Instytut Pamięci Narodowej, 2009); Janusz Borowiec, ed., *Kryptonim "Ośmiornica": Służba Bezpieczeństwa wobec rzeszowskiego oddziału Solidarności Walczącej, 1982–1990* (*Codename "Octopus": The Security Service against the Rzeszów Outfit of Fighting Solidarity*) (Warszawa and Rzeszów: Instytut Pamięci Narodowej, KŚZpNP, 2009). And see below.

16. See Marek Jan Chodakiewicz, "Transformacja: Przekształcenie ku ocaleniu," ("Transformation: Changing to Preserve") in *Racja stanu: Janowi Olszewskiemu w 80. rocznice urodzin* (*Raison d'etat: A Festschrift to Jan Olszewski for His 80th Birthday*) (Poznań: Zysk i ska, 2011), 69–82, which is a record of the proceedings of a conference: *Dwie koncepcje państwa: Księga dedykowana premierowi Janowi Olszewskiemu i sędziemu Bogusławowi Nizieńskiemu jako dodatek do pokłosia konferencji "Pomiędzy PRL a III RP – 20 lat transformacji," która odbyła się 4 czerwca 2009 r. w Sejmie RP* (*Two Concepts of a State: A Festschrift for Prime Minister Jan Olszewski and Judge Bogusław Nizieński as an Addition to the Conference Material on "Between the PRL and the 3rd RP – 20 Years of Transformation"*), with some essays appearing at http://www.vetsc.org; Marek Jan Chodakiewicz "Opcja Okrągły Stół," ("The Round Table Option") *Najwyższy Czas!*, February 21, 2009; Marek Jan Chodakiewicz, "Transformacja ustrojowa," (Systemic Transformation) *Tygodnik Solidarność*, June 5, 2009; and Marek Jan Chodakiewicz, *Ciemnogród? O Prawicy i Lewicy* (*Hicksville? On the Right and the Left*) (Warsaw: Ronin Publishers, 1996 [1995]), 257–61. See also Antoni Dudek, *Reglamentowana rewolucja: Rozkład dyktatury komunistycznej w Polsce, 1988–1990* (*A Rationed Revolution: The Disintegration of the Communist Dictatorship in Poland, 1988–1990*) (Cracow: Arcana, 2004); Antoni Dudek, Grzegorz Sołtysiak and Krystyna Trembicka interviewed by Barbara Polak and Jan M. Ruman, "Stół bez kantów," (A Non-Crooked Table) in *Stół bez kantów i inne rozmowy Biuletynu IPN z lat 2003–2005* (*A Non-Crooked Table and Other Conversations of the Biuletyn IPN, 2003–2005*) (Warszawa: Instytut Pamięci Narodowej, 2008), 167–90; Sławomir Cenckiewicz, "Służba Bezpieczeństwa Okrągłego Stołu: Transformacja ustrojowa w Polsce w latach 1988–1990 była wspierana przez bezpiekę," ("Security Service of the Round Table: Systemic Transformation in Poland Was Assisted by the Secret Police, 1988–1990") in Sławomir Cenckiewicz, *Śladami bezpieki i partii: Studia-źródła-publicystyka* (*Tracking the Secret Police and the Party: Studies, Sources, Journalism*) (Łomianki: LTW, 2009); Tadeusz Kisielewski, *Partii portret własny: Polityka i świadomość w PZPR: Studium upadku* (*A Self-Portrait of the Party: Policy and Consciousness in the Polish United Workers Party: A study in Collapse*) (Warszawa: Wydawnictwo Neriton and Instytut Historii PAN, 2011); Paweł Kowal, *Koniec systemu władzy: Polityka ekipy gen. Wojciecha Jaruzelskiego w latach 1986–1989* (*The End of a System of Power: The Policy of the Jaruzelski Regime, 1986–1989*) (Warszawa: Instytut Studiów Politycznych PAN, Instytut Pamięci Narodowej, and Wydawnictwo Trio, 2012); Paulina Codogni, *Okrągły Stół czyli polski Rubikon* (*Round Table or the Polish Rubicon*) (Warszawa: Collegium Civitas and Prószyński i S-ka, 2009); Sławomir Cenckiewicz, *Długie ramię Moskwy: Wywiad wojskowy Polski Ludowej, 1943–1991* (*Moscow's Long Arm: Military Intelligence of People's Poland*) (Poznań: Zysk i Ska, 2011), 327–426; Janusz Borowiec, ed., *Wybory '89 w Polsce południowo-wschodniej w dokumentach SB* (*The Elections of 1989 in South-East Poland According to the*

Secret Police Documents) (Warszawa and Rzeszów: Instytut Pamięci Narodowej, KŚZpNP, 2009); Sebastian Pilarski, ed., *Służba Bezpieczeństwa wobec przemian politycznych w latach 1988–1990: Region Łódzki (Security Service and the Political Transformation, 1988–1988: The Łódź Region)* (Warszawa and Łódź: Instytut Pamięci Narodowej, 2009); Antoni Dudek, ed., *Zmierzch dyktatury: Polska lat 1986–1989 w świetle dokumentów*, vol 1: *(lipiec 1986–maj 1989) (The Twilight of the Dictatorship: Poland during 1986–1989 According to Documents [July 1986–May 1989])* (Warszawa: Instytut Pamięci Narodowej, KŚZpNP, 2009); Artur Kubaj, ed., *Koniec pewnej epoki: Wybory parlamentarne 1989 roku w województwie szczecińskim w dokumentach (The End of a Certain Epoch: Parliamentary Elections of 1989 in the Szczecin Province According to Documents)* (Warszawa and Szczecin: Instytut Pamięci Narodowej, 2010); Janusz Borowiec, ed., *Kryptonim "Ośmiornica": Służba Bezpieczeństwa wobec rzeszowskiego oddziału Solidarności Walczącej, 1982–1990* (Codename "Octopus": The Security Service against the Rzeszów Outfit of Fighting Solidarity) (Warszawa and Rzeszów: Instytut Pamięci Narodowej, KŚZpNP, 2009); Henryk Głębocki, "'Jak znaleść numer telefonu na Kreml?' Rosja w strategii politycznej 'konstruktywnej opozycji' w PRL (1985–1989)," ("'How to Find the Phone Number for the Kremlin?' Russia in the Political Strategy of the 'Constructive Opposition' in the Polish People's Republic [1986–1989]") *Arcana* no. 2–3 (2009): 39–97; Tomasz Mianowicz, "1989: Transformacja – konwergencja," (1989: Transformation – Convergence) *Arcana* no. 2–3 (2009): 98–114; Paweł Wierzbicki, "Strategie polityczne opozycji demokratycznej wobec władz PRL w latach 1986–1989," ("The Political Strategies of the Democratic Opposition vis-à-vis the Authorities of the Polish People's Republic, 1986–1989") *Arcana* no. 2–3 (2009): 115–41; David Morgan, "Radomska 'wojna na dole': 'Solidarność' jej reaktywacja i wewnętrzne konflikty w latach 1988–1989," *Wybierzmy wolność 1989* (Radom: "Resursa Obywatelska," 2009), 25–45, also published in English as "The War from Below: The 1989 June Election in Radom," *Glaukopis* no. 17–18 (2010): 191–206. For an opinion that as a result of the transformation Poland became a "neo-colony" of the West see an interview with Witold Kieżun, "Polska neo-kolonią," ("Poland as a Neo-Colony") March 12, 2011: http://tysol. salon24.pl/286593,polska-neo-kolonia. For an eyewitness view from the US Embassy in Warsaw by a participant sympathetic to the liberals and leftists, in particular the Communists, for pragmatic reasons of power, see, John Davis, "Postwar Relations: The Long Climb From Yalta and Potsdam to Gdańsk and the Round Table," *The Polish Review* LIV, no. 2 (2009): 195–228. And for an insider's view by a post-Trotskite dissident in Poland see Adam Michnik, "Will Year of Miracles Be Squandered? Cynicism Threatens to Destroy Gains of 1989," *Spiegel* online, (October 23 2009): http://www.spiegel.de/international/world/0,1518,656961,00.html; Matthew Kaminski, "From Solidarity to Democracy: A Polish Dissident Reflects on the Liberation of Eastern Europe 20 Years Later," *The Wall Street Journal* (November 6, 2009): http://online.wsj.com/article_email/SB10001424052748704795604574519463075074956-lMyQjAx-MDA5MDAwNjEwNDYyWj.html; Adam Michnik, "Solidarity Under Strain: We in Poland Began the Berlin Wall's Collapse. But for All the Gains, People Remain Deeply Dissatisfied," *The Guardian* (November 9, 2009): http://www.guardian. co.uk/commentisfree/2009/nov/09/solidarity-poland-berlin-wall-1989. See also, in similar vein, Konstanty Gebert interviewed by Irena Maryniak, "Table Talk," *Index on Censorship* no. 3 (2009), republished in Eurozine.com, September 30, 2009: http://www.eurozine.com/articles/2009-09-30-gebert-en.html.

For the aftermath, in particular as far as the lustration, the vetting of agents, and the "transformed" Communist secret police, see Roman David, *Lustration and Transitional Justice: Personnel Systems in the Czech Republic, Hungary, and Poland* (Philadelphia, PA: University of Pennsylvania Press, 2011); and Piotr Grzelak, *Wojna o lustrację* (*War for lustration*) (Warsaw: Trio, 2005). On the environmental degradation and efforts to overcome it see Marek Jan Chodakiewicz, "An Environmental Battleground: Eco-Politics in Poland," in *Managing the Environment: An East European Perspective*, ed. O.P. Dwivedi and Joseph G. Jabrra (Willowdale, ON: de Sitter, 1995), also published in *International Journal of Comparative Sociology and Anthropology* 1 (1995): 64–90.

14

The Liberation

A foreign policy based on our bedrock principles allows us to offer a practical solution to the suffering peoples of the world, a means of achieving the prosperity and political stability that all Americans take for granted as their birthright. So while our hopes today are for a new era, let us remember that if that new era is indeed upon us, there was nothing inevitable about it. It was the result of hard work—and of resolve and sacrifice on the part of those who love freedom and dare to strive for it. Let us remember, too, that at this critical juncture our responsibilities grow more, not less, serious. We must remain strong and free of illusion—for only by doing so can we reach out and embrace this new era and transform this hope of peace and freedom for all the world into reality . . . What we wanted was a chance to try our ideas out on the world stage. We have. And, my friends, I hope you are as proud as I, because, despite the naysayers and the conventional wisdom, the words of the pundits, and the false prophecies of false Cassandras who proclaimed we could not succeed, we knew we were right. And I believe that, yes, we have been vindicated. And nowhere is that more true than in the realm of foreign policy. We came to Washington together in 1981, both as anti-Communists and as unapologetic defenders and promoters of a strong and vibrant America. I am proud to say I am still an anti-Communist. And I continue to be dedicated to the idea that we must trumpet our beliefs and advance our American ideals to all the peoples of the world until the towers of the tyrants crumble to dust.[1]

—Ronald Reagan, 1988

The 'new world order' was implied in my discussions with the Pope and his senior staff. There was generally convergence. In the case of Lithuania I, under instructions, informed the Holy Father that the pressure of Lithuanian leaders on the Moscow leadership for immediate independence was jeopardizing the role of Gorbachev. In this case I spoke to the senior Vatican authority on the subject and I believe that the Holy See was

211

instrumental in getting Lithuanian leaders to postpone their pressure for immediate independence from Moscow.

—Thomas Patrick Melady,
US Ambassador to the Vatican (1989–1993)[2]

The liberation of the Intermarium at the end of the twentieth century was a gradual process. It started with the offensive unleashed by John Paul II, Ronald Reagan, and Margaret Thatcher. The offensive seized the high moral ground by supporting freedom and democracy. The United States took the lead in practical aspects of the undertaking. It armed anti-Communist resistance around the globe and supported nonviolent opposition to the Kremlin within its empire. It deployed public diplomacy and political warfare against the totalitarians. Western broadcasting, in particular, was crucial in breaking the Communist monopoly on interpreting the Intermarium's reality.[3] The offensive both emboldened the USSR's captive peoples and challenged Moscow's leadership. The latter elected to reform first before clamping down again. The pivot of the process of the liberation was at the Kremlin. Moscow's reform policies of restructuring (*perestroika*) and openness (*glasnost'*) inadvertently unleashed centrifugal forces on the peripheries. The policies caused a series of chain reactions of fluctuating intensity and nature throughout the Soviet republics. The irregular jolts of energy emanating from the center circulated around the empire, reviving the comatose body politic all over the Soviet Bloc.

Impacted by the reforms and power struggles in Moscow, each of the "union republics" displayed nonetheless a dynamic of its own, predicated upon its local peculiarities. Conflict developed within the republican branches of the Communist party, administration, and security services. Tiny dissident circles quarreled about strategy and tactics. The republican minorities were restive, often looking to Moscow for assistance. All this played itself out concomitantly with widespread grassroots upheavals by the majority populations. We should note the paramount role of momentous historical events, old and current, like the Ribbentrop–Molotov Pact or the Chernobyl nuclear disaster (along with national symbols, for instance, Kuropaty for the Belarusians) to account for the radicalization and unification of the grassroots behind the anti-Soviet upheaval.[4] Further, any novel developments in a particular Soviet republic or its region could and did influence the other regions and republics. Each would try in turn to copy and outbid the others in its demands within the republic's own confines and without, targeting the Moscow center. This emulating and bidding ball game occurred with increasing intensity at all levels. It started with the highest republican echelons of party, state, and security apparatus and descended down to the grassroots in the cities and villages. And then the ball would often boomerang up to the top leadership again with an increasing intensity. The Kremlin's responses usually reinvigorated social and national mobilization from the Soviet elite all the way to the grassroots.

Last but not least, there was the Polish factor. Various social, political, and cultural processes, which eventually resulted in independence for the republics, were also informed by the dramatic events outside of the USSR proper, in particular, in Central and Eastern Europe between 1988 and 1991. Thus, first, the KGB copied the Hungarian and Bulgarian models to facilitate the creation of the opposition where there had been none. But those dissident groups could not be easily controlled. They attracted popular support and turned into mass movements. Next, the Intermarium's national liberation organizations modeled themselves, to an extent, upon Poland's "Solidarity." They were inspired by the latest installment in the Polish anti-Communist struggle which, by 1990, after ten years, was widely perceived to have succeeded. This wishful perception was further reinforced because a small cadre of intrepid anti-Communist Poles was training the anti-Soviet freedom fighters and carrying the nonviolent struggle into the USSR itself. After 1989, official Warsaw provided the liberationist movements in the empire with diplomatic support. This concerned, in particular, the Baltics, Belarus, and Ukraine.[5]

Initially, in the west of the USSR, the local elites, mostly Communist, took advantage of the policy of liberalization ordered by Moscow. However, at first, the independence of their "union republics" was simply not on their agenda. Instead, they claimed to support nebulous "reforms." The elites reacted both to the developments at the Kremlin and on the streets. They nonetheless pushed the boundaries of freedom, frequently surprised at their unexpected flexibility. Yet, none among the mainstream Soviet republican elites allowed himself to dream of sovereignty for the nations of the Intermarium. That was considered utterly and hopelessly romantic. Worse, it was deemed totally unrealistic. Soviet experience dictated the following: Any attempt to bring freedom about would end in bloodshed, and, consequently, in severe punishment for the local elites. Only the grassroots anti-Communist nationalists refused to compromise on the dream. They wanted full independence for their nations: Estonia, Latvia, Lithuania, Ukraine, Belarus, and Moldova. They set the agenda and jammed it through, step by step, and leap by leap, despite the outraged fury of the Kremlin and its local supporters. The romantic nationalists also had to face serious opposition on the part of the realists, minimalists, and provocateurs. Gradually, the nationalist dream was realized. The nationalists, however, were excluded from its fruits. Ultimately, it was the post-Communists who stole the thunder of the nationalists and emerged victorious in most of the newly independent states of the Intermarium.

It is *au courant* to consider nationalism as the root of all evil. It allegedly leads to violence and destruction. Yet, nationalism depends largely on the sources of its ideology (for example, a Christian religious component tends to moderate it). It also depends on the elites who undertake a nationalist mobilization and their goals (e.g., the elites who mobilized the Japanese for postwar reconstruction had peace and prosperity on mind, unlike their predecessors who wanted war and regional domination). Further, nationalism of the small and medium size people reacts primarily to the challenges that greater powers have in store for their countries. The end game in the west of the Soviet Union shows that nationalism can be rather peaceful and constructive. There was virtually no bloodshed and no nationalist agitation for violence.[6]

Nationalism was one of the most important forces which propelled the erstwhile Soviet colonies toward freedom. It was distilled from long-submerged individual recollections and long-suppressed collective dreams. Grassroots and, eventually, elite postulates in the Baltics, Belarus, Ukraine, and Moldova were expressed in nationalist terms. At the outset, they took on the form of ecological and human rights concerns, as well as oral history projects, the latter admirable endeavors to reclaim eradicated memories. Powerful, spontaneous national movements were formed subsequently to support them. Initially, however, most republican politicians were far behind the popular dreams of freedom.

Local hard-line Communists of the western Soviet periphery opposed most of Mikhail Gorbachev's reforms, including *glasnost'* and *perestroika*. Other Communists (so-called party "liberals" or "reformers") tactically supported the General Secretary. The most dynamic ones among the latter came from the ranks of the Communist Youth (*Komsomol*). Some of the "reform" Communists also flirted with "national Bolshevism/Communism," which was an effort to win more autonomy from Moscow within the framework of the Soviet republic. To outmaneuver their old guard detractors, the "reform" Communists needed popular support. The appeal to nationalism was the surest way to gain the people's backing. This could be initially accomplished just by virtue of invoking one's party work on behalf of a particular Soviet republic. Later, the local "reform" reds pondered autonomy within the USSR. By then, the grassroots expected more straightforward declarations of nationalism.

Starting around 1988 the "reformers" also tried to steal the thunder of the anti-Communist nationalists by monopolizing dissent. As "national Bolsheviks/Communists," they initially controlled various "popular front" (or "national front" or "people's power") movements that arose in virtually each of the Soviet republics. Some viewed the "reformer" participation as efforts to neutralize the drive for freedom from within. From without, aside from employing the KGB and other instruments of power, to counter its "national front" detractors, the anti-Gorbachevian old guard everywhere set up "Interfronts" (or "Internationalist Fronts"). Those were, in essence, officially sanctioned assemblies of pan-Soviet patriots, both Communists and nonparty. As the USSR began to unravel, the Kremlin increasingly relied upon them to counter the "popular fronts" in the republics.

In the long run such attempts to stem freedom failed, however. The events forced the temporizers and procrastinators, who acted out of prudence and Soviet inspiration, either into irrelevance or into a more radical stance. The grassroots nationalists came to the fore, symbolically and rhetorically at least. They dominated the discourse. Everywhere they demanded independence for their nations to a stormy applause of the local populations, the Russian minority, most notably, excluded.[7] The nationalists initially worked within the Communist system, utilizing institutions created by the occupiers, including the local pseudoparliaments, or republican Supreme Soviets. Applying popular pressure from the streets and outvoting the Soviet patriots, various "popular fronts" pushed for freedom. They also established and reestablished parallel government and social structures outside of the framework of the Soviet institutions. Thus, "popular fronts" held their own congresses and assemblies. Eventually, even the local "reform" Communists split from the Soviet party to create its zygotic national Bolshevik outfits, later often renamed "social democratic" parties.

Demonstrations, strikes, and rallies spilled across the thawing Intermarium. There was very little violence but massive acts of civil disobedience did take place. The most spectacular of them was the creation of a human chain of 600 km in length with about 2 million people holding hands between Tallinn, Riga, and Vilnius to mark the fiftieth anniversary of the Ribbentrop–Molotov Pact on August 23, 1989. However, the "Singing Counterrevolution" in the Baltics was indubitably the most sustained expression of the will to freedom for it continued in a series of concerts and musical events for almost five years (1987–1992).

Paradoxically, in most places it was the Communists (and soon-to-be post-Communists) who presided over the proclamation of their nations' independence. In fact, perhaps the most poignant moment came when the erstwhile Communist leaders of Russia, Ukraine, and Belarus met at the Belavezha Forest (Białowieża/Belavezhskaya Pushcha) and proclaimed the USSR dissolved on December 8, 1991. The trio, and perhaps also others, resolved to associate voluntarily in a loose confederation, the Commonwealth of Independent States (CIS). This was an attempt to fold the USSR into the CIS, to find a new façade for the old edifice, and to encourage republican national Bolshevik supporters of autonomy to form a horizontal confederation by circumventing the Politbureau and other central Soviet authorities. It ended up driving the final nail into the unholy creation of Lenin and Stalin.[8] Afterward, the Soviet Union was practically no more.

Following independence, the nationalist movements everywhere inevitably split into a plethora of political parties of the right, center, and left. However, almost invariably, across the Intermarium, the nationalists lost free elections to the post-Communists. The latter suavely rode the wave of post-independence disillusion propelled by economic hardships. Also, there had been neither a de-Communization nor vetting of the secret police agents. Continuity of the Soviet institutions in their national forms was the norm. There was virtually no restoration of the pre-Soviet state institutions and legal forms. Instead, the Communist nomenklatura's initial staunch resistance to the reforms turned to a giddy enthusiasm as the avowed goal of the newly independent states was to create "capitalism." There is no capitalism without capitalists, so the post-Communists converted themselves into "capitalists" by privatizing state assets and precluding any competition by virtually monopolizing the key sectors of the economy, including banking and industry. No state economic plan was needed to maintain control anymore. An informal net of relationships based on the old nomenklatura structure sufficed to maintain a chokehold on the system. Thus, the post-Communists were well positioned to maintain their customary supremacy under new conditions. This amounted to a golden parachute to much of the old Soviet elite. The nationalists of various strain and the post-Communists have been rotating in office since. The latter remain firmly in control economically. The successor states of the western rim of the erstwhile USSR thus faithfully copied the Polish model of the transformation with local idiosyncrasies, of course.[9]

Between 1987 and 1992, history accelerated in the Intermarium. There were, of course, some general similarities between its national component parts and some peculiarities within each region. The Baltic states were the first ones to assert themselves and make their bid for freedom.[10]

Estonia

Estonia is the optimal example of success because by reestablishing spiritual, legal, and material continuity with its prewar independent predecessor state it alone denied power to the post-Communists upon reclaiming freedom.[11] First, however, in the mid-1980s, the Estonian nationalists expressed themselves publicly in songs. The anti-Communist "Singing Counterrevolution" attracted hundreds of thousands in the spring of 1987 and later. For the next five years the Estonians assembled in small groups and huge crowds to sing about freedom for their nation.[12] Meanwhile, grassroots nationalists organized themselves as the Estonian Heritage Society (*Eesti Muinsuskaitse Selts*). They collected oral history accounts of the anti-Soviet struggle. Initially, such unabashed patriots were overshadowed by the Popular Front of Estonia (PFE—*Eestimaa Rahvarinne*). However, because of its all too often "reform" Communist leaders and their minimalist aspirations for autonomy, rather than independence, the PFE soon began to lose its appeal in favor of the triumphantly patriotic Estonian National Independence Party (*Eesti Rahvusliku Sõltumatuse Partei*—ERSP).[13]

In February 1990, the ERSP won the first free elections to the Estonian Congress, a new body created in distinction to the Soviet institutions. Soon after, however, the competing *Rahvarinne* carried the elections to the

Supreme Soviet of the Estonian Soviet Socialist Republic. The Popular Front won mainly because it lacked electoral competition on the nationalist side. The ERSP and others boycotted it as Communist, Soviet, and, thus, un-Estonian. A period of dual power ensued. The ERSP and its allies fought for the affirmation of the continuity of Estonian statehood, anchored upon the prewar republic, which de jure existed and enjoyed recognition by major foreign powers. The *Rahvarinne* wanted a completely new state declared. That would have entailed maintaining some Soviet arrangements. Eventually, however, in the face of a hostile Soviet reaction to Tallinn's bid for freedom, the sides temporarily reconciled. In September 1991, Estonia officially reasserted its independence based upon the continuity of statehood. Gradually, the ERSP and other nationalist groups led the nation to liberty. *Rahvarinne* melted away. In 1992, the prewar constitution was resurrected in an updated form. Because of the nationalist insistence on the continuity of statehood, with all its legal and cultural implications, the post-Communists and their "social democratic" successors were practically neutralized at the outset. They have not been able to achieve power since, except sometimes in coalition governments. Consequently, the internal influence of the Kremlin has been reduced mostly to the Russian minority and the former KGB *agentura*.[14]

Latvia

In Latvia's march to freedom, the formula of the "Singing Counterrevolution" caught on as well.[15] At first, the nascent Latvian human rights circles and environmentalist dissidents quickly sided with the newly created Popular Front of Latvia (*Latvijas Tautas Fronte*—LTF). The latter, under the leadership of "reform" Communists, supported the nation's autonomy within the USSR. This was too timid, however, for the majority of Latvians. Many backed the Latvian National Independence Movement (*Latvijas Nacionālās Neatkarības Kustība*—LNNK) instead. However, parallel, non-Communist institutions, like the Civic Congress, were marginalized. The LNNK proved unsuccessful in challenging the LTF.[16] The latter won the elections to the Supreme Soviet of the Latvian Soviet Socialist Republic and formed a government. The "reform" Communist–nationalist coalition, backed by the Russian minority, proclaimed Latvian independence in May 1990. The following year the nation introduced its new constitution which incorporated a significant portion of the prewar fundamental law, virtually restoring the original document.[17] In the first free elections in June 1993, however, the LTF imploded. A center-right coalition government was established. Subsequently, following successive polls, several other coalition governments emerged, including the post-Communists usually as "social democrats." They are Moscow's main allies as well as of the Russian minority, which maintains strong presence in the parliament.

Lithuania

Lithuania's bid for freedom predated those of its Baltic neighbors. Both the Estonians and Latvians closely watched the ginger maneuvers and bumbling missteps of the Lithuanians. Tallinn learned from them more successfully than Riga as far as nationalism and anti-Communism are concerned. Vilnius had to improvise on its own. It was a trailblazer in the Intermarium.[18] Lithuania was the first to undertake a nationalist mobilization from below on Gorbachev's watch. It entailed all the disadvantages of the Soviet straightjacket and no blueprint of resistance, except the nonviolent Polish one, which had to be adjusted to square with quite different conditions. The Lithuanians avoided openly identifying with the Poles for emotional, nationalist reasons and for practical, Soviet ones. The applicability of "Solidarity" to Lithuania had to be first tested. The nonviolence plank worked well. So did relying on religion, tradition, and history. However, any reference to the universalism of the old Commonwealth was eschewed as inimical to Lithuanian ethno-nationalist aspirations. The Lithuanians correctly rejected the façade of trade unionism and suavely opted for the form of an ethno-cultural organization which they later proclaimed to be a national liberation movement. Thus, although partly copied from Poland's experience, the Lithuanian way masqueraded as a sui generis thrust for independence. And it built on Warsaw's path to transformation: Nonviolent resistance and negotiations were the rule. Yet, Vilnius had to improvise its march to freedom to the extent that it was a pioneer of the endeavor within the Soviet frontiers. It was arguably the first union republic to cry freedom.

Further, there was coordination with the other two Baltic nations. For example, Lithuania copied Estonia's approach of mobilizing through music. In addition to nationalist and folk songs, the locals also sang Catholic hymns giving their "Singing Counterrevolution" a distinct flavor. The significance of including the fight for religious freedom in its nationalist message was a factor that further distinguished Lithuania from its other Baltic neighbors. Likewise, the leadership of its "popular front" organization, Reform Movement of Lithuania (*Lietuvos Persitvarkymo Sąjūdis*), later simply Sąjūdis, was dominated by the non-Communists from the start. It coupled the support for Gorbachev with cultural and linguistic demands that very quickly evolved beyond the postulate for autonomy to the demand for independence.

In October 1988 Sąjūdis won the elections to the Congress of People's Deputies. This was intended as a new Soviet rubber-stamp "parliament." Instead, it became an official perch for Sąjūdis. In February the Congress officially expressed its wish for independence. In May 1989 it proclaimed Lithuania's incorporation into the USSR null and void, thus invoking the principle of sovereignty of the nation. In February 1990 Sąjūdis swept the elections to the Supreme Soviet of the Lithuanian Soviet Socialist Republic. In March 1990 it officially announced the nation's independence, despite opposition from the Kremlin as well as the national minorities, the Russians and Poles. The latter, fearing Lithuanian nationalism, demanded autonomy. Sąjūdis ruled Lithuania briefly but buckled under the strain of economic and political crisis, receding into obscurity and impotence. In February 1992, the post-Communists, renamed the Democratic Labor Party, won the parliamentary elections and returned to power. They also oversaw the adoption of the new constitution which is a hybrid of Western legal ideas, Soviet institutional arrangements, and a few prewar Lithuanian symbols.[19] Since then the nationalists of various strain have fluctuated in power with the post-Communists. The Kremlin's influence with the latter remains rather solid as it does with the minorities, the Russians and, to a lesser extent, the Poles.

Ukraine

In Ukraine (and Belarus) the feeble dissident circles were galvanized by the Chernobyl nuclear disaster of April 26, 1986. Its horror also mobilized the grassroots. The environmentalists quickly began elucidating nationalist postulates. Further, at the top, the political fall-out of the catastrophe enfeebled the opponents of reforms, emanating from the Moscow center, in the republican Communist party machines. "Reform" Communists emerged dominant and spearheaded the drive to assert their autonomy from the Kremlin. As the central authority crumbled, the Ukrainian "reform" Communists (and national Bolsheviks, in particular) and their allies declared their intention to see their state sovereign on July 16, 1990, and actually voted for independence on August 24, 1990.[20]

This occurred also because of the pressure from below, most notably from the National (or People's) Movement of Ukraine (*Narodnyi Rukh Ukrainy*; *Народний Рух України*). Headed largely by grassroots nationalists, environmentalists, and human rights activists (sometimes these categories being interchangeable), the *Rukh* derived its strength chiefly from western Ukraine. Much of its appeal stemmed from its staunch defense of the Ukrainian language, culture, and history, including Ukraine's brief statehood in the early twentieth century and its defenders. Although it failed to rout the "reform" and "national Bolshevik" Communists in the elections to the republican Supreme Soviet in the spring of 1990, the Ukrainian nationalist movement was instrumental in rallying support for the independence referendum in December 1991. At the time also the eastern Ukrainians and the minority eastern and southern Russians and others supported Ukraine's sovereignty for the most part. Their industrial strikes were important factors on the road to freedom. But all was not well. The nation's early progress was marred by the Tatar–Russian–Ukrainian altercations in the Crimea.[21] Further, rather suspicious of the western nationalists, including the Rukh, the easterners and southerners tended to organize along free trade union basis, in Donbas, in particular. They supported the "reform" Communists and, later, the post-Communists.

Donning a variety of guises, the post-Communists kept the reins of power, preventing the nationalists from forming a government. The former subsequently presided over the writing and enacting a predictably post-nomenklatura friendly constitution for Ukraine. The final product only managed to sow confusion and preserve much of the legal arrangements from the Soviet times, albeit somewhat amended. The post-Communists lost their total grip on power only after the victory of the nationalist-led Orange Revolution of 2004.[22]

Belarus

Ukraine is now better off than Belarus. In the 1980s, however, Minsk stirred earlier than Kyiv. Belarusian human rights activists were even tinier a band than their almost as insignificant Ukrainian counterparts. Yet, Minsk's dissident intellectuals first responded to the tactical chink in the totalitarian armor afforded by Moscow's reforms via appealing for cultural freedom already at the end of 1986. Namely, they wanted rights for their native tongue, Belarusian. The intellectuals objected to the Russian remaining overwhelmingly the language of politics and education. In addition to emphasizing Belarusian literary and political tradition, in particular the nation's brief independence in 1918, but also the national Bolshevik-led cultural revival of the 1920s, they further advanced an environmentalist agenda in the wake of the nuclear accident at Chernobyl.[23]

The greatest jolt for mass mobilization occurred, however, following the discovery of the mass graves of the victims of Communist (and most likely also Nazi) terror at Kuropaty outside of Minsk in spring 1988. This was a true catharsis. Intellectuals who spearheaded the excavations immediately formed the Martyrology Society of Belarus (*Martyraloh Belarusi; Мартыралёг Беларусі*), modeled after Russia's Memorial Society (*Memorial; Мемориал*). The objective was to commemorate all the murdered, including Belarusians, Jews, Poles, Ukrainians, Russians, and others.[24] The *Martyraloh* activists also began popularizing other important symbols and facts from the history of Belarus. These events inspired the grassroots which were arguably the most feeble among all the popular movements in the western rim of the USSR. They also led to the formation of and the Belarusian National Front "Rebirth" (*Belaruski Narodny Front "Adradzhenne"*, BNF; *Беларускі Народны Фронт "Адраджэньне,"* БНФ), in 1988. While the grassroots took to the streets, the increasingly anti-Communist leadership of the BNF demanded democracy, independence, and an alliance with the West. It further advocated a Belarusian–Baltic–Ukrainian union, a virtual restoration of the Grand Duchy of Lithuania in the Intermarium.

The BNF failed to take power. It secured only 10 percent of the votes in the elections to the Supreme Soviet of the Soviet Socialist Belorussian Republic in March 1990. However, it continued to play a vocal role as the opposition both in the streets and the parliament. Meanwhile, the real struggle was taking place within the Communist party leadership. It pitted, on the one hand, almost uniformly Russian-speaking party hacks who wanted to remain within the Soviet Union, and, on the other hand, both Belarusian and Russian-speaking *apparatchiks*, who moved from the support for autonomy to the embrace of independence. The latter group prevailed. Accordingly, under the aegis of the national Bolsheviks and "reform" Communists, the Supreme Soviet first declared the nation sovereign on July 27, 1990, and then independent on August 25, 1991. Having transformed themselves, the post-Communists remained in power first in a post-Communist, flawed democracy of sorts and, then, from 1994, in a dictatorship. They are also the authors of the nation's constitution, a hybrid retaining old Soviet and contemporary Russian elements, while paying lip service to some Western sentiments. Belarus remains unfree.[25]

Moldova

The endgame in Moldova was almost as unsatisfactory as in Belarus with the post-Communists assuming power, albeit in a "democratic" parliamentary form. Initially, however, Moldova's path to independence resembled the Baltic way. It oscillated between the Estonian and Lithuanian examples. One of the most important early symbols was the fight for the restoration of the Latin alphabet.[26] Moldova uniquely produced an irredentist orientation which endeavored to rejoin Romania. It further spawned a Ukrainian, Russian, and Gagauz separatist movements. The Gagauz initially proclaimed independence, but then they settled for autonomy.[27] However, some of the others, namely mostly Russian-speakers, established a de facto independent state, Transnistria, under the Kremlin's informal protection in September 1990. (Incidentally, this was a scenario that Moscow failed to implement regarding Lithuania's Polish and Russian minority autonomists, as will be shown below.) Ultimately, between March and July 1992, with Russian backing, the so-called Pridnestrovan Moldovan Republic defeated Moldova's military efforts to reassert the latter's control over the area.[28] Thus, Transnistria should be considered primarily through the lense of Chişinău's foreign policy. It nonetheless has functioned as a factor in its domestic affairs as well.

The dynamics of Moldova's emancipation from the USSR followed a familiar pattern. At first, "reform" Communists and pan-Romanian nationalists of the Moldavian Soviet Socialist Republic (MSSR) focused on advancing the goals of *glasnost'* and *perestroika*. In 1988 they jointly established the Democratic Movement of Moldova (*Mişcarea Democratică din Moldova*, MDM). A mostly intellectual endeavor, the MDM quickly gained popular support and began voicing nationalist postulates. Initially, the movement focused on culture. It even emulated "The Singing Counterrevolution" and adopted it to the local conditions. In 1989 the MDM converted itself into the National (or Popular) Front of Moldova (*Frontul Popular din Moldova*, FPM).

The FPM advocated restoring the primacy of the Romanian ("Moldovan" in Soviet parlance) language written in the Latin script. It also began organizing mass rallies and demonstrations. The greatest of them all materialized as "The Grand National Assembly" in Chişinău in late summer of 1989. To the great chagrin of its heavily "reformed" Communist and national Bolshevik leaders, it featured a massive grassroots anti-Communist and nationalist mobilization.

Under the pressure from the streets, the Supreme Soviet of the MSSR adopted the FPM's language postulate into law in August 1989. Russian was relegated to the second official language. This upset the ethnic nationalists among the minorities. To placate them, provisions were made to establish semiautonomous administrative entities for the Gagauz and Russians in their newly recognized ethnic enclave of Gagauzia, with Gagauzian and Russian as the official languages. More concessions were made to the Russian and Ukrainophone secessionists in Transnistria. However, as mentioned, Tiraspol proclaimed itself a separate Soviet republic in September 1990. This eventually translated into a de facto independence. Chişinău's half-hearted efforts to suppress the rebellion faltered when the post-Soviet military assisted the Transnistrians.

Meanwhile, in February and March 1990, an election took place in Moldova where all political organizations, save the Communist party, were barred. Yet, running as nonparty individual candidates, the FPM candidates did very well against the pro-Moscow Communists. The nationalists now were the single largest group in the Supreme Soviet. Consequently, the FPM ruled in alliance with the "reform" Communists both within and without its ranks, as well as Moldovan "national Bolsheviks," who wanted to assert more autonomy from the Kremlin. In May 1990, the nationalist-led government triumphantly opened the border with Romania. On June 23, 1990, the FPM and its allies declared their country sovereign and renamed it Soviet Socialist Republic of Moldova (SSRM). This stop-gap measure of the autonomists would not do. Ultimately, on August 27, 1991, the post-Communists dropped both "Soviet" and Socialist" from the official name and proclaimed their Republic of Moldova (RM) independent officially.

A vigorous debate about reunifying with the mother country reached its fever pitch. Romania, however, failed to provide appropriate assistance because, bereft of Nicolae Ceauşescu, its own "reform" Communists and post-Communists were frankly reluctant to antagonize Moscow and to assist the pan-Romanian nationalists who were at the same time their enemies at home. At this point, in late 1990 and early 1991, Moldova's "reform" Communists gradually abandoned the pan-Romanian nationalists of the FPM. The former allied themselves with the minorities, also led by the erstwhile Communists, for example, the Russians of the Unity group (*Yedinstvo*). Together, they would win all subsequent elections. The Moldovan post-Communists thus executed successfully a maneuver that failed in the German Democratic Republic (East Germany). They preserved the MSSR-SSRM under a different name, the Republic of Moldova, and managed to maintain themselves in power. The FPM lost the pan-Romanian momentum and imploded. Its remnant reconstituted itself as the Christian Democratic Popular Front (*Frontul Popular Creştin Democrat*), but it remained impotently in the opposition. The post-Communists have continued to dominate Moldova since under various guises.[29]

The lessons of the bid for freedom in the Intermarium clearly indicate that the romantic notions of "people's power" winning independence for the successor states should be dismissed. The popular factor undoubtedly played an important and conspicuous role. Oftentimes, however, the popular enthusiasm became a vehicle for frantic, if often unsavory, old Communist elite maneuvers to maintain themselves in power. The actions of the Soviet leaders in the Intermarium were initially intended to prevent a nationalist and anti-Communist radicalization of the masses and to salvage as much as possible from the old system and its institutions. Hence, instead of freedom one should talk about transformation. Once the dissolution of the USSR occurred, the former Communist masters continued to exercise power over their former captive peoples. This time they could boast democratic legitimacy, sometimes even plausibly. And the exercise of power was connected to economics, rather than police terror, for the most part at least. Nonetheless, the transformation, with all its unsavory features, the Soviet continuities, and the post-Communists survivals, did extend the sphere of liberty by ushering in various measures of democracy and freedom in the Intermarium.

Now the newly liberated successor states had to learn how to deal with the challenges of post-Communism, post-Soviet Russia, and postmodern West.

Notes

1. See Ronald W. Reagan, "Building Up to Tearing Down the Wall," AEI Online, no. 15 (November 2009): http://www.aei.org/issue/100014. This is a consistent theme in the fortieth President's messages. See Marek Jan Chodakiewicz and Paweł Toboła-Pertkiewicz, eds., *Ronald Reagan: Moja wizja Ameryki* (*Ronald Reagan: My Vision of America*) (Warszawa: Wydawnictwo ARWIL, 2004).
2. Thomas Patrick Melady, "My Experiences with John Paul II, TMs," March 23, 2011, (a copy of a draft in my collection). Ambassador Melady was appointed by President George H. W. Bush and served between 1989 and 1993.
3. A. Ross Johnson and R. Eugene Parta, eds., *Cold War Broadcasting: Impact on the Soviet Union and Eastern Europe* (New York: Central European University Press, 2010).
4. See Keiji Sato, "The Molotov-Ribbentrop Commission and Claims of Post-Soviet Secessionist Territories to Sovereignty," *Demokratizatsiya: The Journal of Post-Soviet Democratization* 18, no. 2 (Spring 2010): 148–59.
5. A few Polish anti-Communists became involved inside the Soviet Union itself. There was always a trickle of visitors from Poland to study, sightsee, and visit family. In the 1970s, some began smuggling Bibles and religious literature and

aiding the Catholic Church in a variety of illegal ways. Home Army veterans were often involved in those clandestine activities. See, e.g., Longin Łokuciewski, "Druga podróż do Wilna," ("My Second Trip to Wilno") *Glaukopis* no. 15–16 (2009): 22–33. Very few individuals looked for political connections. For example, Zbigniew Romaszewski, a foreign student in physics in Moscow in the 1970s, approached successfully the famous dissident Andrei Sakharov for cooperation. However, first serious anti-Communist political initiatives took place only after 1982 and entailed smuggling Russian and Ukrainian language underground press into the USSR. The radical liberationist group behind the effort was "Fighting Solidarity" (*Solidarność Walcząca*), an extremely effective and dynamic clandestine anti-Communist group. Unlike mainstream "Solidarity," from which it stemmed, this arguably the most apt Polish conspiratorial outfit did not forswear violence as it believed in the right to self-defense from Communist terror. It also was rather successful in preventing secret police infiltration. From 1986, its activists, grouped in the Eastern Department of "Fighting Solidarity" (*Wydział Wschodni "Solidarności Walczącej"*), in particular Piotr Hlebowicz, Jadwiga Chmielowska, and others, began infiltrating into the Soviet Union to establish contact with anti-Communists there. The idea was to assist them in the anti-Soviet struggle by providing the organizational know how and the printing equipment. Initially, the Poles focused on the Grodno (Hradna) area and the Polish community there. Next, they secured introduction to the Gulag survivors in Wilno/Vilnius, which became the "Fighting Solidarity's" Soviet hub. The Poles reached out to the Lithuanian freedom fighters. Those grizzled Lithuanian veterans provided introduction to their former fellow camp inmates in Estonia and Latvia. Accordingly, the Poles branched out into the Baltics, where—through the *largerniki*—they met young anti-Communist Balts. Meanwhile, in Vilnius "Fighting Solidarity" activists became acquainted with young Ukrainians who brought them to Kyiv, where the Poles, once again, capitalized on their Gulag references to legitimize themselves with some anti-Communist Ukrainian veterans. The Crimean Tatars were next. Here "Fighting Solidarity" used its Polish connections in Turkey to introduce the Crimeans to the Tatar Polish diaspora in Istanbul. Meanwhile, they further reached out to Poland's Georgians who provided introductions to the hermetic Georgian émigré circles in France and Germany as well as to Georgian nationalists in Soviet-occupied Georgia. The Poles were also in touch with Russian anti-Communists in Moscow itself. Soon, Hlebowicz and others of "Fighting Solidarity" were reaching as far afield as Chechnya, Kazakhstan, Kyrgyzstan, and the Soviet Far East. In 1989 at the latest, the Poles began coordinating their activities with former Soviet dissident Vladimir Bukovsky in the United Kingdom and former Polish dissident Irena Lasota in the United States. Both made funds available to them, in particular through the National Endowment for Democracy. "Fighting Solidarity" set up Coordinating Center "Warsaw '90" to facilitate training and communications for anti-Communist freedom fighters in nearly all Soviet republics. See Piotr Hlebowicz, "Organizacja podziemna 'Solidarność Walcząca': Wydział Wschodni 'Solidarność Walcząca," ("Clandestine Organization 'Fighting Solidarity': The Eastern Department of 'Fighting Solidarity'") *Glaukopis* no. 23–24 (2011–2012): 227–48.

6.   For the factor of violence via comparison of the Basque country and Catalonia, on the one hand, with Ukraine and Georgia at the cusp of their independence from the USSR on the other, see David D. Laitin, "National Revivals and Violence," *European Journal of Sociology* 36, no. 1 (1995): 3–43.

7.   For a general discussion of the Russian minority in the post-Soviet sphere at the outset of freedom see Leon Gudkov, "The Disintegration of the USSR and Russians in the Republics," in *Soviet Transition: From Gorbachev to Yeltsin*, ed. Stephen White, Rita di Leo, and Ottorino Cappelli (London and Portland, OR: Frank Cass, 1993), 75–88. See also Geoffrey Hosking, *Rulers and Victims: The Russians in the Soviet Union* (Cambridge, MA and London: The Belknap Press of Harvard University Press, 2006).

8.   The creation of the Commonwealth of Independent States was a tactical move to preempt a similar initiative on the part of Gorbachev. It was also an attempt to counter the model of the USSR's Stalinist leadership under Gorbachev with a post-Stalinist paradigm of collective leadership. This solution was attempted before, in the wake of Stalin's death in 1953, but only at the Politburo level. In 1991, Russian republican leader Boris Yeltsin contrived a variation of the plan by plotting with his counterparts at the (horizontal) republican level. The idea was to create a republican collective leadership, circumventing the Politburo. Yeltsin invited his Ukrainian and Belarusian comrades to outmaneuver the General Secretary of the CPSU by establishing a collective leadership of the Soviet Union, now renamed the CIS. It was a plot against Gorbachev and the Politburo, but not against the USSR per se. With the benefit of hindsight it is perhaps natural to credit Yeltsin and other comrades with introducing state sovereignty of Russia and other republics under the guise of the CIS. However, initially at least, they intended neither to destroy the USSR nor to champion secessionism of the republics. Instead, they wanted a new union treaty that would allow for far-reaching autonomy of the republics. The republican leaders followed the Soviet succession struggle model that they were very familiar with. Eventually, they ran out of their Leninist moves; the utility of the paradigm ended. Instead of being the final solution to chaos in the USSR, the CIS proved to be an unworkable stop gap measure, a half way house. Thus, the republican leaders, undoubtedly surprised, took the logical step of emancipating themselves from the framework of the USSR. It took some time to conceptualize life outside of the Leninist box. When it did happen, the participants, observers, and scholars reflexively and deterministically adjusted the outcome to fit their preconceived notion of Yeltsin's alleged intentions. It is usually ignored that the final implosion of the USSR was a case of the law of unintended consequences resulting from the Leninist tactics at the center. This phenomenon is generally misunderstood by scholars and contemporaries. Gorbachev's take on this is very revealing. He casts himself as the proper Leninist centrist: between the "reactionaries" of Gennady Yanayev and the secessionists of Boris Yeltsin. In fact, all parties involved wanted to save the USSR with the Russian Soviet Socialist Republic as its pivot, but they advocated competing visions. Gorbachev wanted a Union Treaty which provided for a confederative structure: The Union of Sovereign Nations. Yeltsin wanted the same but without Gorbachev and other top people in the Politburo. Instead, he championed parallel/horizontal structures between the republican leaderships to circumvent and replace the old center. Yanayev and his comrades wanted to save the USSR in its unadulterated Stalinist glory. Thus, they carried out a failed palace coup against Gorbachev. None of the leaders had a strategic vision of anything beyond the familiar framework of the USSR. Ultimately, however, Yeltsin fell victim to his own Leninist tactics of outmaneuvering his opponents and pushed his concept too far to continue accommodating the old Soviet paradigm. Thus, the center failed to hold. As Gorbachev himself put it: "Participants in the [Yanayev] conspiracy

said, and some still say, that they wanted to save our union [the USSR]. But, as I said from the start, they ended up destroying the country. Although the coup collapsed three days later, it damaged the principle of a common state, speeding the republics' 'run on the Union'—a process that Russia's leaders had initiated long before the putsch. One after another, the republics began declaring independence. The situation we faced was indeed grave. But we were able to convene the congress of People's Deputies, which approved preparation of another draft of the Union Treaty, based on the concept of a confederative state. We ran into all kinds of problems, but we soon had a new draft and began presenting it to the republics. Once again, the prospect existed that we could work together to end the crisis. Had it not been for the collusion of the leaders of Russia, Ukraine and Belarus, meeting at Belovezhskaya Puschcha, the new treaty could have been signed before the end of 1991. The union, which would have been known as the Union of Sovereign States, would have been saved—in a different form, and with much greater rights to the republics. Had that happened, I am convinced that economic reforms would then have been less painful, the collapse of industrial production would have been avoided and the dangerous decline in Russians' living standards would not have occurred." See Mikhail Gorbachev, "Looking back, moving forward," *The Washington Post* (August 21, 2011).

9.   See Jerzy Targalski, "Republiki zachodniosowieckie – legitymizacja komunistów narodowych i rządy koalicyjne," (Western Soviet Republics: Legitimizing the National Communists and Coalition Governments) TMs, Warsaw, no date (2010), pp. 1–279 (a copy in my collection). See further Mark Kramer, "The Collapse of East European Communism and the Repercussions within the Soviet Union," published in three parts in the *Journal of Cold War History* 5, no. 4 (Fall 2003); 6, no. 4 (Fall 2004); 7, no. 1 (Winter 2007); Ronald J. Hill, "Managing Ethnic Conflict," in *Soviet Transition: From Gorbachev to Yeltsin,* ed. Stephen White, Rita di Leo, and Ottorino Cappelli, (London and Portland, OR: Frank Cass, 1993), 57–74; Georgiy I. Mirsky, *On Ruins of Empire: Ethnicity and Nationalism in the Former Soviet Union* (Westport, CT: Greenwood Press, 1997); Alexander V. Prusin, *The Lands between: Conflict in the East European Borderlands, 1870–1992* (New York and Oxford: Oxford University Press, 2010), 224–52; Anne Applebaum, *Between East and West: Across the Borderlands of Europe* (New York: Pantheon Books, 1994); Nadia Diuk and Adrian Karatnycky, *New Nations Rising: The Fall of the Soviets and the Challenge of Independence* (New York: Wiley, 1993); Timothy Snyder, *The Reconstruction of Nations: Poland, Ukraine, Lithuania, Belarus, 1569–1999* (New Haven, CT and London: Yale University Press, 2003), 232–55; Susanne Michele Birgerson, *After the Breakup of a Multi-Ethnic Empire: Russia, Successor States, and Eurasian Security* (Westport, CT: Praeger/Greenwood, 2002); Petr Kopecký and Cas Mudde, eds., *Uncivil Society? Contentious Politics in Post-communist Europe* (New York and London: Routledge, 2003); David D. Laitin, *Identity in Formation: The Russian-Speaking Populations in the Near Abroad* (Ithaca, NY: Cornell University Press, 1998); Adam Roberts and Timothy Garton Ash, eds., *Civil Resistance and Power Politics: The Experience of Non-violent Action from Gandhi to the Present* (Oxford: Oxford University Press, 2009), 231–46, 317–53; Rich Fawn, ed., *Ideology and National Identity in Post-communist Foreign Policies* (London: Frank Cass, 2004), 60–82, 156–76; United States Congress, Joint Economic Committee, Richard F. Kaufman and John Pearce Hardt, eds., *The Former Soviet Union in Transition* (Armonk, NY and London: M.E. Sharpe, 1993), 961–70, 990–92,

1003–18; Teresa Rakowska-Harmstone, Piotr Dutkiewicz, and Agnieszka Orzelska, eds., *New Europe: The Impact of the First Decade*, vol. 2: *Variations on the Pattern* (Warsaw: Institute of Political Studies Polish Academy of Sciences and Collegium Civitas Press, 2006), 49–153, 329–70; 487–523; Maruska Svasek, *Postsocialism: Politics and Emotions in Central and Eastern Europe* (New York: Berghahn Books, 2006); Sharon L. Wolchik and Jane L. Curry, *Central and East European Politics: From Communism to Democracy* (Lanham, MD: Rowman & Littlefield Publishers, 2008); Jarosław Dudek, Daria Janiszewska, and Urszula Świderska-Włodarczyk, eds., *Europa Środkowo-Wschodnia: Ideologia, historia a społeczeństwo* (*East-Central Europe: Ideology, History, and Society*) (Zielona Góra: Uniwersytet Zielonogórski [Zielona Góra University], 2005); Richard B. Dobson and Steven A. Grant, "Public Opinion and the Transformation of the Soviet Union," *International Journal of Public Opinion Research* 4, no. 4 (Winter 1992): 302–20; William M. Reisinger, Arthur H. Miller, Vicki L. Hesli, and Kristen H. Maher, "Political Values in Russia, Ukraine and Lithuania: Sources and Implications for Democracy," *British Journal of Political Science* 24, no. 2 (1994): 183–223. And see below.

10. See "Starting Anew Amidst the Rot of the Old: Interviews with Lenart Meri, Valery Kalabugin, Tunne Kelam, Ilmars Bisers, Romualdas Razukas, Aigars Jirgens, Zigmas Vaisvila," *Uncaptive Minds* 4, no. 4 (18) (Winter 1991–1992); Walter C. Clemens, Jr., *Baltic Independence and Russian Empire* (New York: St. Martin's Press, 1991); Clare Thomson, *The Singing Revolution: A Political Journey through the Baltic States* (London: Michael Joseph, 1992); Romuald Misiunas and Rein Taagepera, *The Baltic States: Years of Dependence, 1940–1990* (Berkeley, CA: University of California Press, 1993); Anatol Lieven, *The Baltic Revolution: Estonia, Latvia, Lithuania, and the Path to Independence* (New Haven, CT: Yale University Press, 1993); Mark R. Beissinger, "The Intersection of Ethnic Nationalism and People Power Tactics in the Baltic States, 1987–1991," in *Civil Resistance and Power Politics: The Experience of Non-violent Action from Gandhi to the Present*, ed. Adam Roberts and Timothy Garton Ash (Oxford: Oxford University Press, 2009), 231–46); Lars Johannsen, "The Baltic States: A Miracle?" in *New Europe: The Impact of the First Decade*, vol. 2: *Variations on the Pattern*, ed. by Teresa Rakowska-Harmstone, Piotr Dutkiewicz, and Agnieszka Orzelska (Warsaw: Institute of Political Studies Polish Academy of Sciences and Collegium Civitas Press, 2006), 2: 49–100.

11. Jerzy Targalski, "Republiki zachodniosowieckie – legitymizacja komunistów narodowych i rządy koalicyjne," ("Western Soviet Republics: Legitimizing the National Communists and Coalition Governments") TMs, Warsaw, no date (2010), pp. 1–279, in particular pp. 1–19 on the period between 1989 and 1990 (a copy in my collection).

12. See Priit Vesilind with James and Maureen Tusty, *The Singing Revolution* (Tallinn: Kirjastus Varrak Publishers Ltd., 2008). For the role of singing as an expression of anti-Communist dissent in Poland in the 1970s and 1980s, see Marek Payerhin, "Singing Out of Pain: Protest Songs and Social Mobilization," *The Polish Review* 57, no. 1 (2012): 5–31. For a thoughtful review of a documentary on the Singing Counter-revolution see Jay Nordlinger, "Songs and Tanks," *National Review* (August 15, 2011): 45–46. Conservative Nordlinger, of course, misnames it as "Singing Revolution." As a matter of fact, most sources refer to the Singing Counter-revolution as the "Singing Revolution" because of leftist prejudices in Western scholarly discourse. Further, the American culture's positive connotations of "the American revolution," another misnomer, are at

fault. The War for Independence, which broke out in the English colonies in North America in 1776, was a traditionalist rebellion by elite men of property against a revolutionary monarch who encroached upon the rights of his colonial subjects as Englishmen. The response was to restore freedom within a republican framework in an independent state, thus, a secession and hardly a radical revolution totally overturning the social order. Simply, traditional representative English institutions were Americanized and endowed with a republican form.

13. "Not Waiting for Gorbachev: An Interview with Tiit Madisson," *Uncaptive Minds* 1, no. 2 (June–July–August 1988); Józef Darski [Jerzy Targalski], "Between Anti-Stalinism and Anti-Communism," *Uncaptive Minds* 1, no. 3 (September–October 1988); "Opposition as Self-Defense: An Interview with Heiki Ahoen," *Uncaptive Minds* 1, no. 3 (September–October 1988); "Breaking Away: The Estonian Political Scene in 1989: An Interview with Tunne Kelam," *Uncaptive Minds* 3, no. 1(10) (January–February 1990); Jerzy Kropiwicki, "Estonia is short of cash," *Uncaptive Minds* 3, no. 4 (13) (August–September–October 1990); "Democracy without Parties: An Interview with Riho Laanemaae and Mart Nutt,"*Uncaptive Minds* 4, no. 2 (16) (Summer 1991).

14. For a short introduction to Estonia's case see "The Restoration of Estonian Independence," http://www.einst.ee/factsheets/factsheets_uus_kuju/the_restoration_of_estonian_independence.htm. See further Rein Taagepera, *Estonia: Return to Independence* (Boulder, CO: Westview Press, 1993); Toivu U. Raun, *Estonia and The Estonians* (Stanford, CA: The Hoover Institution Press, 2001); David J. Smith, *Estonia: Independence and European Integration* (London and New York: Routledge, 2001); Ernest Gellner, "Ethnicity and Faith in Eastern Europe," in *Eastern Europe . . . , Central Europe . . . , Europe*, ed. Stephen R. Graubard (Boulder, CO, San Francisco, Oxford: Westview Press, 1991), 275–78; John T. Ishiyama, "Founding Elections and the Development of Transitional Parties: The Cases of Estonia and Latvia, 1990–1992," *Communist and Post-Communist Studies* 26, no. 3 (1993): 277–99; David J. Smith, "'The Devil and the Deep Blue Sea': European Integration, National Identity, and Foreign Policy in Post-Communist Estonia," in *Ideology and National Identity in Post-communist Foreign Policies*, ed. Rich Fawn (London: Frank Cass, 2004): 156–76; and, for constitutional issues, see Rett Ludwikowski, *Constitution Making in the Region of Former Soviet Dominance* (Durham, NC: Duke University Press, 1996), 81–89.

15. On Latvia's progress between 1989 and 1990 see Jerzy Targalski, "Republiki zachodniosowieckie – legitymizacja komunistów narodowych i rządy koalicyjne," ("Western Soviet Republics: Legitimizing the National Communists and Coalition Governments") TMs, Warsaw, no date (2010), pp. 1–279, in particular pp. 19–39 (a copy in my collection).

16. See "Our Goal Is to Restore Latvian Independence: An Interview with Ivars Godmanis," *Uncaptive Minds* 3, no. 1(10) (January–February 1990); Olgerts Dzenitis, "Latvia: An Independent State?" *Uncaptive Minds* 5, no. 3 (21) (Fall 1992); Alexei Grigorievs, "The Russian Army in Latvia," *Uncaptive Minds* 5, no. 3 (21) (Fall 1992); Monika Michaliszyn, "Działalność i upadek łotewskich narodowych komunistów," (The Rise and Fall of the Latvian National Communists) TMs, Warsaw, no date (2010), pp. 1–35 (a copy in my collection).

17. John T. Ishiyama, "Founding Elections and the Development of Transitional Parties: The Cases of Estonia and Latvia, 1990–1992," *Communist and Post-Communist Studies* 26, no. 3 (1993): 277–99; Diana Stukuls, "Imagining the

Nation: Campaign Posters of the First Postcommunist Elections in Latvia," *East European Politics and Societies* 11, no. 1 (1997): 131–54.

18. For an insightful analysis of Lithuania's opposition and the actions of the local Communist authorities, including active measures by the KGB, see Jerzy Targalski, "Litwa: Opozycja," (Lithuania: The Opposition) TMs, Warsaw, no date (2008), pp. 1–153, in particular pages 7–103 (from 1985 to 1991); Jerzy Targalski, "Republiki zachodniosowieckie – legitymizacja komunistów narodowych i rządy koalicyjne," ("Western Soviet Republics: Legitimizing the National Communists and Coalition Governments") TMs, Warsaw, no date (2010), pp. 1–279, in particular pp. 39–80 on the period between 1989 and 1991 (a copy in my collection); and Józef Darski [Jerzy Targalski], "Litwa," [Lithuania] n.d., http://www.abcnet.com.pl/files/TRANSFORMACJA%20NA%20LITWIE%2 0(WERSJA%20ROBOCZA).doc. For contemporary eyewitness accounts see "The Man from Sajudis: An Interview with Arunas Degutis," *Uncaptive Minds* 2, no. 3 (7) (May–June–July 1989); "We Are Helping Ourselves: An Interview with Kazimieras Uoka," *Uncaptive Minds* 3, no. 1(10) (January–February 1990); "No More Games: An Interview with Egidijus Meilunas," *Uncaptive Minds* 3, no. 3 (12) (May–June 1990); "Soviets Go Home! Photographs from Vilnius," *Uncaptive Minds* 3, no. 3 (12) (May–June 1990); "Moscow's Game Plan Has Failed (Lithuania): An Interview with Francois Thom," *Uncaptive Minds* 4, no. 1 (15) (Spring 1991); "No Other Choice (Lithuania): An Interview with Vytautas Landsbergis," *Uncaptive Minds* 4, no. 2 (16) (Summer 1991); Egidijus Meilunas, "A Short History of Liberty (Lithuania)," *Uncaptive Minds* 4, no. 3 (17) (Fall 1991); "Why the Communist Won: An Interview with President Vytautas Landsbergis," *Uncaptive Minds* 5, no. 3 (21) (Fall 1992); "Perspectives on Lithuanian Elections," *Uncaptive Minds* 5, no. 3 (21) (Fall 1992).

19. See Rett Ludwikowski, *Constitution Making in the Region of Former Soviet Dominance* (Durham, NC: Duke University Press, 1996), 73–81, and Lithuania's constitution reproduced at pp. 484–509.

20. For the influence of the KGB on the Soviet Ukraine's opposition between 1985 and 1992 see Jerzy Targalski, "Ukraina: Opozycja," (Ukraina: The Opposition) TMs, Warsaw, no date (2008), pp. 1–78, especially pages 12–64 (a copy in my collection); Jerzy Targalski, "Republiki zachodniosowieckie – legitymizacja komunistów narodowych i rządy koalicyjne," ("Western Soviet Republics: Legitimizing the National Communists and Coalition Governments") TMs, Warsaw, no date (2010), pp. 1–279, in particular pp. 95–136 on the period between 1989 and 1992 (a copy in my collection). See Roman Solchanyk, *Ukraine: The Road to Independence* (New York: St. Martin's Press, 1993); Bohdan Nahaylo, *The Ukrainian Resurgence: Ukraine's Road to Independence* (Toronto: University of Toronto Press, 1998); Alexander J. Motyl, *Dilemmas of Independence: Ukraine after Totalitarianism* (New York: Council on Foreign Relations, 1993); Taras Kuzio, "Ukraine under Gorbachev," *Uncaptive Minds* 1, no. 3 (September–October 1988); "To Save a Culture: An Interview with Mykola Rudenko," *Uncaptive Minds* 1, no. 3 (September–October 1988); "A Complex Road to Independence: An Interview with Mykhaylo Osadchy," *Uncaptive Minds* 3 no. 2(11) (March–April 1990); Ilona Kiss, "The Coal Miners: Spearhead of the Soviet Working Class," *Uncaptive Minds* 3, no. 4 (13) (August–September–October 1990); Antoni Pospieszalski, "Catholics, Orthodox, Uniates, and Others (Ukraine)," *Uncaptive Minds* 3, no. 5(14) (November–December 1990); "The Ukrainian Piedmont: An Interview with Vyacheslav Chornovil," *Uncaptive Minds* 4, no. 1 (15) (Spring 1991); "History Is Working to Our Advantage,

but Very Slowly: An Interview with Yevhen Proniuk," *Uncaptive Minds* 4, no. 1 (15) (Spring 1991); Taras Kuzio, "Political parties in Ukraine," *Uncaptive Minds* 4, no. 2 (16) (Summer 1991); "The Story of Democracy in a Ukrainian Town: An Interview with Bohdan Voloshynsky," *Uncaptive Minds* 4, no. 3 (17) (Fall 1991); David Abraham, "From the Spirit of Helsinki to Independence: Interview with Levko Lukyanenko," *Uncaptive Minds* 4, no. 3 (17) (Fall 1991): 53–54; Jan Rozdzynski, "What Kind of Independence," *Uncaptive Minds* 4, no. 4 (18) (Winter 1991–1992): 97–104; Józef Darski [Jerzy Targalski], "Quo vadis Ukraine?" *Uncaptive Minds* 5, no. 1 (19) (Spring 1992): 59–74; Taras Kuzio, *Ukraine: The Unfinished Revolution* (London: Alliance, 1992); Peter J. Potichnyj, "The Referendum and Presidential Elections in Ukraine," *Canadian Slavonic Papers* 33, no. 2 (June 1991): 123–38; Vitaly Korotich, "The [sic] Ukraine Rising," *Foreign Policy* 85 (Winter 1991–1992): 73–82; Adrian Karatnycky, "The Ukrainian Factor," *Foreign Affairs* 71, no. 3 (Summer 1992): 90–107; Jan Feldman, "Longing for the 'Good Tsar': In Russia and Ukraine," *New Leader* (April 6, 1992): 9–10; Charles Furtado, "A Tree Grows in Ukraine," *Nationalities Papers* 20, no. 2 (Fall 1992): 79–83; Nadia Diuk and Adrian Karatnycky, "Ukraine: Europe's New Nation," *The World and I* 7, no. 3 (March 1992): 96–101; Solomea Pavlychko, "Between Feminism and Nationalism: New Women's Groups in the Ukraine," in *Perestroika and Soviet Women*, ed. Mary Buckley (Cambridge: Cambridge University Press, 1992), 82–96; Anatoli Rusnachenko, "The Workers' and National-Democratic Movements in Contemporary Ukraine," *Journal of Ukrainian Studies* 18, no. 1–2 (Summer–Winter 1993): 123–49; Serhiy Holovaty, "Politics after Communism: Ukraine: A View from Within," *Journal of Democracy* 4, no. 3 (July 1993): 110–13; Bohdan Krawchenko, "Ukraine: The Politics of Independence," in *Nations and Politics in the Soviet Successor States*, ed. Ian Bremmer and Ray Taras (Cambridge: Cambridge University Press, 1993), 75–98.

21.　　　During a period of hectic secessionist clamor after 1991, the Tartar minority wanted a separate state and the Russians, under hard-core Communists, proclaimed independence, promulgated a constitution, swore in a president, and endeavored to integrate with Russia. The separatist push was eventually defeated by Kyiv. The Crimea was ultimately denied political autonomy but was granted a legislature of sorts without an executive as well as a range of local economic and cultural rights to appeal to its largely non-Ukrainian populations. See "The Tatars against the Empire: An Interview with Rafael Farkiievich Mukhametdinov," *Uncaptive Minds* 3, no. 5 (14) (November–December 1990); Urszula Doroszewska, "Crimea: Whose Country?" *Uncaptive Minds* 5, no. 3 (21) (Fall 1992); "Reclaiming a Homeland: An Interview with Mustafa Dzhemilev," *Uncaptive Minds* 5, no. 3 (21) (Fall 1992); "Why Crimea is Peaceful? An Interview with Mustafa Dzhemilev," *Uncaptive Minds* 7, no. 2 (26) (Summer 1994); Volodymyr Prytula, "Where to Go from Here? (Crimea)," *Uncaptive Minds* 7, no. 2 (26) (Summer 1994); Volodymyr Prytula, "The Crimean Deadlock," *Uncaptive Minds* 8, no. 9 (29) (Summer 1995); Urszula Doroszewska, "Sevastopol - City of Russian Glory," *Uncaptive Minds* 8, no. 9 (29) (Summer 1995); "We Prefer Ukraine. An Interview with Nadir Bekirov," *Uncaptive Minds* 8, no. 9 (29) (Summer 1995); Refat Chubarov, Natalie Belitser and Urszula Doroszewska, "Different Nationalisms: The Case of Crimea," *Uncaptive Minds* 9, no. 3–4 (Summer–Fall 1997): 43–52; Andrew Wilson, "Parties and Presidents in Ukraine and Crimea, 1994," *The Journal of Communist Studies and Transition Politics* 11, no. 4 (December 1995): 362–71; Denis J. B. Shaw, "Crimea: Background and Aftermath of Its 1994 Presidential Election," *Post-Soviet Geography* 35, no. 4 (1994):

221–34; Edward Allworth, ed., *Tatars of the Crimea: Their Struggle for Survival: Original Studies from North America, Unofficial and Official Documents from Czarist and Soviet Sources* (Durham, NC and London: Duke University Press, 1988); Alan Fisher, *The Crimean Tatars* (Stanford, CA: Hoover Institution Press, 1987).

22. See Lewis H. Siegelbaum and Daniel J. Walkowitz, *Workers of the Donbass Speak: Survival and Identity in the New Ukraine, 1989–1992* (Albany, NY: State University of New York Press, 1995); David J. Meyer, "Why Have Donbas Russians Not Ethnically Mobilized Like Crimean Russians Have? An Institutional/Demographic Approach," in *State and Nation Building in East Central Europe: Contemporary Perspectives,* ed. John S. Micgiel (New York: Institute on East Central Europe, Columbia University, 1996), 317–30; Grigorii Nemirya, "A Qualitative Analysis of the Situation in the Donbass," in *Post-Soviet Puzzles: Mapping the Political Economy of the Former Soviet Union* (4 vols.), ed. Klaus Segbers and Stephan De Spiegeleire, vol. 2: *Emerging Geopolitical and Territorial Units: Theories, Methods and Case Studies* (Baden-Baden: Nomos, 1995), 2: 451–66; Theodore Friedgut, "Perestroika in the Provinces: The Politics of Transition in Donets'k," in *Local Power and Post-Soviet Policies,* ed. Theodore H. Friedgut and Jeffrey W. Hahn (Armonk, NY: M.E. Sharpe, 1994), 162–83; Vitaly Timofeev and Rex A. Wade, "Kharkiv in the Post-Perestroika Days: Some Political Tendencies," *Soviet and Post-Soviet Review* 21, no. 1 (1994): 85–98; Stanley Bach, "From Soviet to Parliament in Ukraine: The Verkhovna Rada during 1992–94," in *The New Parliaments of Central and Eastern Europe,* ed. David M. Ollson and Philip Norton (London: Frank Cass, 1996), 213–30; Sarah Birch, "Electoral Behavior in Western Ukraine in National Elections and Referendums, 1989–91," *Europe-Asia Studies* 47, no. 6 (1995): 1145–75; Roman Szporluk, *Russia, Ukraine, and the Breakup of the Soviet Union* (Stanford, CA: Hoover Institution Press, Stanford University, 2000); Taras Kuzio and Andrew Wilson, *Ukraine: Perestroika to Independence* (Edmonton: Canadian Institute of Ukrainian Studies Press, 1994); Verena Fritz, *State-Building: A Comparative Study of Ukraine, Lithuania, Belarus, and Russia* (Budapest: Central European University Press, 2007), Chapter 6, "Ukraine: From Soviet breakdown to disordered independence," 109–36; Rett Ludwikowski, *Constitution Making in the Region of Former Soviet Dominance* (Durham, NC: Duke University Press, 1996), 89–95; Andrew Wilson, *Ukrainian Nationalism in the 1990s: A Minority Faith* (Cambridge and New York: Cambridge University Press, 1997); Andrew Wilson, *The Ukrainians: Unexpected Nation* (New Haven, CT and London: Yale University Press, 2002); Anna Reid, *Borderland: A Journey through the History of Ukraine* (Boulder, CO: Westview Press, 2000, and 2nd edn. Orion Publishing Company, 2003); Hiroaki Kuromiya, *Freedom and Terror in the Donbas: A Ukrainian-Russian Borderland, 1870s–1990s* (Cambridge: Cambridge University Press, 1998); Tatiana Zhurzhenko, *Borderlands into Bordered Lands: Geopolitics of Identity in Post-Soviet Ukraine* (Stuttgart and Hannover: Ibidem-Verlag, 2010); Anders Åslund and Michael McFaul, eds., *Revolution in Orange: The Origins of Ukraine's Democratic Breakthrough* (Washington, DC: Carnegie Endowment for International Peace, 2006); Paul D'Anieri, *Understanding Ukrainian Politics: Power, Politics, and Institutional Design* (Armonk, NY: M.E. Sharpe, 2007); Mikhail Molchanov, *Political Culture and National Identity in Russian-Ukrainian Relations* (College Station, TX: Texas A&M University Press, 2002); Kataryna Wolczuk, "Catching up with 'Europe'? Constitutional Debates on the Territorial-Administrative Model in Independent

Ukraine," in *Region, State and Identity in Central and Eastern Europe*, ed. Judy Batt and Kataryna Wolczuk (London: Frank Cass, 2002), 65–88; Kataryna Wolczuk, *The Moulding of Ukraine: The Constitutional Politics of State Formation* (Budapest: Central European University Press, 2001); Steven J. Woehrel, "Political-Economic Assessment: Ukraine," in United States Congress, Joint Economic Committee, in *The Former Soviet Union in Transition*, ed. Richard F. Kaufman and John Pearce Hardt (Armonk, NY and London: M.E. Sharpe, 1993): 961–70; Andrew Wilson, "Ukraine's 'Orange Revolution' of 2004: The Paradoxes of Negotiation," in *Civil Resistance and Power Politics: The Experience of Non-violent Action from Gandhi to the Present*, ed. Adam Roberts and Timothy Garton Ash (Oxford: Oxford University Press, 2009), 335–53; Tadeusz Andrzej Olszański, "Ukraine," in *New Europe: The Impact of the First Decade*, vol. 2: *Variations on the Pattern*, ed. Teresa Rakowska-Harmstone, Piotr Dutkiewicz, and Agnieszka Orzelska (Warsaw: Institute of Political Studies Polish Academy of Sciences and Collegium Civitas Press, 2006), 2: 487–523. See also the following essays in Andrzej Dumała and Ziemowit Jacek Pietraś, eds., *The Future of East-Central Europe* (Lublin: Maria Curie-Skłodowska University Press, 1996): Orysia Lutsevych, "The Case for Ukraine to Maintain Its Nukes," (260–65); Beata Surmacz, "The International Role of Ukraine," (300–311); Stepan Trohimchuk, "Polish-Ukrainian Integration as a Foundation of Peace and Security in East-Central Europe," (311–13); Paul Kubicek, "Delegative Democracy in Post-Soviet States," (424–43); Ostap Semkiv, "Ukraine: from Totalitarianism to Democracy," (453–59); Natalya Lutsyshyn, "Transitions to Democracy in Ukraine: Reality and Prospects," (459–60); Anatoliy Romanyuk, "Integration and Disintegration Processes in the Party System of Ukraine," (504–9); Oleg Protsyk, "The Influence of Ukrainian Parliamentary Elections of 1994 on the Process of Political Transformation in Ukraine," (509–14); Michał Łesiów, "An Important New Role of National Languages in the Former Soviet Republics which became Independent States in 1991," (605–9).

23. For contemporary commentary by participants see "A Difficult Start: An Interview with a Byelorussian Activist," *Uncaptive Minds* 2, no. 3 (7) (May–June–July 1989); "That's Something You Don't Forget: An Interview with Zenon Pazniak," *Uncaptive Minds* 2, no. 4 (8) (August–September–October 1989); Dorota Macieja, "Where Communism Is Dying of Radiation Sickness (Byelorussia)," *Uncaptive Minds* 3, no. 4 (13) (August–September–October 1990); Jan Rozdzynski, "There Will Not Be Civil War," *Uncaptive Minds* 5, no. 2 (20) (Summer 1992); Jakub Lapatka, "In Defense or Offense?" *Uncaptive Minds* 5, no. 2 (20) (Summer 1992); Wojciech Gorecki, "Alosha Capone," *Uncaptive Minds* 5, no. 2 (20) (Summer 1992). See also for comparison Taras Kuzio, "Radical Nationalist Parties and Movements in Contemporary Ukraine Before and After Independence: The Right and Its Politics, 1989–1994," *Nationalities Papers* 25, no. 2 (June 1997): 211–42. For an insightful analysis of the early period (1988–1992), including the influence of the KGB, see Jerzy Targalski, "Białoruś," ("Belarus") TMs, Warsaw, no date (2011), pp. 1–23 (a copy in my collection); and Jerzy Targalski, "Republiki zachodniosowieckie – legitymizacja komunistów narodowych i rządy koalicyjne," ("Western Soviet Republics: Legitimizing the National Communists and Coalition Governments") TMs, Warsaw, no date (2010), pp. 1–279, in particular pp. 30–95 on the period between 1989 and 1991 (a copy in my collection).

24. David R. Marples, "Kuropaty: The Investigation of a Stalinist Historical Controversy," *Slavic Review* 53, no. 2 (Summer 1994): 513–23.

25. See Andrew Wilson, *Belarus: The Last European Dictatorship* (New Haven, CT and London: Yale University Press, 2011), 140–67; Grigory Ioffe, *Understanding Belarus and How Western Foreign Policy Misses the Mark* (Lanham, MD: Rowman & Littlefield Publishers, Inc., 2008); Vitali Silitski and Jan Zaprudnik, *Historical Dictionary of Belarus* (Lanham, MD, Toronto, and Plymouth: Scarecrow Press, 2007); David Riach, "Post-Soviet Belarus," in *New Europe: The Impact of the First Decade*, vol. 2: *Variations on the Pattern*, ed. Teresa Rakowska-Harmstone, Piotr Dutkiewicz, and Agnieszka Orzelska (Warsaw: Institute of Political Studies Polish Academy of Sciences and Collegium Civitas Press, 2006), 2: 101–53; Katja Yafimava, *Post-Soviet Russian-Belarussian Relationships: The Role of Gas Transit Pipelines* (Stuttgart and Hannover: Ibidem-Verlag, 2006); Coit Blacker and Condoleezza Rice, "Belarus and the Flight from Sovereignty," in *Problematic Sovereignty: Contested Rules and Political Possibilities*, ed. Stephen D. Krasner (New York: Columbia University Press, 2001), 224–50; Kathleen Mihalisko, "Political-Economic Assessment: Belarus," in United States Congress, Joint Economic Committee, *The Former Soviet Union in Transition*, ed. Richard F. Kaufman and John Pearce Hardt (Armonk, NY and London: M.E. Sharpe, 1993): 1003–18; and Rett Ludwikowski, *Constitution Making in the Region of Former Soviet Dominance* (Durham, NC: Duke University Press, 1996), 95–102 and Belarus's constitution reproduced at 332–50.

26. A. Morar, N. Movilyanu, and I. Shishkanu, "Vvedeniye latinitsi: kak eto bylo" ("The Introduction of the Latin Alphabet: How It Was"), *Sovetskaya Moldavia* [Chisinau] (June 17, 1989): 3; A. Morar, N. Movilyanu, and I. Siskanu, "Cum a fost arestata Grafia Latina" ("How the Latin Alphabet Was Arrested"), *Moldova Socialista* [Chisinau] (June 17, 1989): 3.

27. See Jonathan Eyal, "Moldovans," in *The Nationalities Question in the Soviet Union*, ed. Graham Smith (New York: Longman, 1990), 123–41; William E. Crowther, "The Politics of Ethno-national Mobilization: Nationalism and Reform in Soviet Moldavia," *Russian Review* 50, no. 2 (April 1991): 183–203; Nicholas Dima, "The Soviet Political Upheaval of the 1980s: The Case of Moldova," *Journal of Social, Political, and Economic Studies* 16, no .1 (Spring 1991): 39–58; Nicholas Dima, "Recent Changes in Soviet Moldavia," *East European Quarterly* 24, no. 2 (Summer 1991): 167–78; Jeff Chinn and Steven D. Roper, "Territorial Autonomy in Gagauzia," *Nationalities Papers* 26, no. 1 (March 1998): 87–101; "Gagauz Proclaim Republic; Situation 'Explosive,'" *Moscow Domestic Service* [Moscow] (August 21, 1990), Foreign Broadcast Information Service, Daily Report: Soviet Union. (FBIS-SOV-90-162.), August 21, 1990, 92.

28. In September 1990, Transnistria's Russian and Ukrainian speakers proclaimed the Pridnestrovian Moldovan Soviet Socialist Republic; later, it changed its name to the Pridnestrovian Moldovan Republic. Tiraspol serves as its capital and its system is a presidential dictatorship with a rubber stamp parliament. Armed clashes commenced in November 1990 between the Moldovans and the Transnistrians, the latter assisted by out-of-area Cossacks and other Russian-speaking volunteers. The conflict escalated into a regular war in March 1992. Moldova lost because of a Russian military intervention by parts of the Red Army (14th Guards Army) left behind in the area. A cease fire was called in July 1992. Transnistria remains separate from Moldova as a virtual protectorate of the Russian Federation. Initially, however, in 1990 the Kremlin spurned the PMSSR, rejecting its separation from the MSSR, because Moscow feared that its endorsement of a secessionist movement would encourage similar centrifugal phenomena elsewhere in the USSR). See E. Kondratov,

"Moldavia Hit by Three-way Ethnic Strife," *Current Digest of the Soviet Press* 42–43 (November 28, 1990): 1–7; "The Dniestr Republic: The Stalinist State Format Kept in Readiness," *Soviet Analyst: An Intelligence Commentary* 22, no. 5 (1993): 1–12; Ioan Chiper, "Bessarabia and Northern Bukovina," in *Contested Territory: Border Disputes at the Edge of the Former Soviet Empire*, ed. Tuomas Forsberg (Aldershot: Edward Elgar, 1995), 107–27; Steven D. Roper, "From Frozen Conflict to Frozen Agreement: The Unrecognized State of Transnistria," in *The Quest for Sovereignty: Unrecognised States in the International System*, ed. Tozun Bahcheli, Barry Bartmann, and Henry Srebrnik (London: Frank Cass and Taylor and Francis, 2004), 102–17; No author, "The Republic of Moldova Armed Forces and Military Doctrine Introduction and Background: Military-political Developments," Defence Academy of the United Kingdom, Conflict Studies Research Centre, Central & Eastern European Series, (no date [1997?, April 2007]): 1–18, http://www.da.mod.uk/colleges/arag/document-listings/cee; Graeme P. Herd, "Moldova & The Dniestr Region: Contested Past, Frozen Present, Speculative Futures?" Defence Academy of the United Kingdom, Conflict Studies Research Centre, Central & Eastern European Series, 05/07 (February 2005): 1–17, http://www.da.mod.uk/colleges/arag/document-list-ings/cee/05%2807%29-GPH.pdf; Igor Munteanu, "Social Multipolarity in Moldova," Defense Academy of the United Kingdom, Conflict Studies Research Centre, Central and East European Series Publication, G80 (November 1999): 1–38, http://www.da.mod.uk/colleges/arag/document-listings/cee/G80-im.pdf; Roman Solchanyk, "The Politics of State Building: Centre-Periphery Relations in Post-Soviet Ukraine," *Europe-Asia Studies* 46, no. 1 (1994): 47–68; Pål Kolstø, Andrei Edemsky, and Natalya Kalashnikova, "The Dniester Conflict: Between Irredentism and Separatism," *Europe-Asia Studies* 45, no. 6 (1993): 973–1000. For contemporary reports see Aleksandr Takiy, "Complex Situation Persists in Moldavia," TASS [Moscow], August 2, 1990, Foreign Broadcast Information Service, Daily Report: Soviet Union (FBIS-SOV-90-190), August 3, 1990, 61; "Russia and Moldova Reach Accord on Dniester Region," *New York Times* (July 22, 1992): A9; Lee Hockstader, "In Moldova's East Bank, Separatists Still Cling to the Bad Old Days," *Washington Post* (March 25, 1994): A31; "Russia, Moldova Agree on Pullout," *Washington Post* (August 11, 1994): A24; Carlotta Gall, "Moldova, Transdnestr Agree to Pursue Peace," *Moscow Times* [Moscow] (International Weekly Edition) 2, no. 34 (January 8, 1995): 20; "Moldovan Women Force Out General," *New York Times* (June 18, 1995): 10.

29.   For an insightful description of the events see Jerzy Targalski, "Republiki zach-odniosowieckie – legitymizacja komunistów narodowych i rządy koalicyjne," ("Western Soviet Republics: Legitimizing the National Communists and Coalition Governments") TMs, Warsaw, no date (2010), pp. 1–279, in particular pp. 136–43 on the period between 1989 and 1992 (a copy in my collection). See further Darya Fane, "Moldova: Breaking Loose from Moscow," in *Nations and Politics in the Soviet Successor States*, ed. Ian Bremmer and Ray Taras (New York: Cambridge University Press, 1993), 191–253; Charles King, *The Moldovans: Romania, Russia, and the Politics of Culture* (Stanford, CA: The Hoover Institution Press, 2000); Stefan Ihrig, *Wer sind die Moldawier? Rumänismus versus Moldowanismus in Historiographie und Schulbüchern der Republik Moldova, 1991–2006* (Stuttgart and Hannover: Ibidem-Verlag, 2008); Matthew H. Ciscel, *The Language of the Moldovans: Romania, Russia, and Identity in an Ex-Soviet Republic* (Lanham, MD: Lexington Books, 2007); Andrei Brezianu and Vlad Spânu, *Historical Dictionary of Moldova* (Lanham, MD, Toronto and

Plymouth: Scarecrow Press, 2007); Michael Bruchis, *The Republic of Moldova: From the Collapse of the Soviet Empire to the Restoration of the Russian Empire* (New York and Boulder, CO: Columbia University Press and East European Monographs, 1997); Nicholas Dima, *Moldova and the Transdnestr Republic* (New York and Boulder, CO: Columbia University Press and East European Monographs, 2001); Wim P. Van Meurs, *The Bessarabian Question in Communist Historiography* (New York and Boulder, CO: Columbia University Press and East European Monographs, 1994); Sergiu Verona, "Political-Economic Assessment: Moldova," in United States Congress, Joint Economic Committee, *The Former Soviet Union in Transition*, ed. Richard F. Kaufman and John Pearce Hardt (Armonk, NY and London: M.E. Sharpe, 1993): 990–92; Wim van Meurs, "Moldova," in *New Europe: The Impact of the First Decade*, vol. 2: *Variations on the Pattern*, ed. Teresa Rakowska-Harmstone, Piotr Dutkiewicz, and Agnieszka Orzelska (Warsaw: Institute of Political Studies Polish Academy of Sciences and Collegium Civitas Press, 2006), 2: 329–70; Charles King, "Marking Time in the Middle Ground: Contested Identities and Moldovan Foreign Policy," in *Ideology and National Identity in Post-communist Foreign Policies*, ed. Rich Fawn (London: Frank Cass, 2004), 60–82; Igor Munteanu, "Social Multipolarity in Moldova," Defense Academy of the United Kingdom, Conflict Studies Research Centre, Central and East European Series Publication, G80 (November 1999): 1–38, http://www.da.mod.uk/colleges/arag/document-listings/cee/G80-im.pdf; V. G. Baleanu, "In the Shadow of Russia: Romania's Relations with Moldova and Ukraine," Defense Academy of the United Kingdom, Conflict Studies Research Centre, Central and East European Series Publication, G85 (August 2000): 1–28, http://www.da.mod.uk/colleges/arag/document-listings/cee/G85; William E. Crowther, "Moldova after Independence," *Current History* 93, no. 585 (October 1994): 342–47; Piotr Pacholski, "The Country without a Nation (Moldova)," *Uncaptive Minds* 5, no. 3 (21) (Fall 1992).

Part III

Post-Soviet Continuities and Discontinuities: Domestic and Foreign Challenges

*Having been excluded for decades from the rewards of worldly advance-
ment, our friends [in the post-Soviet Bloc] had failed to cultivate those
arts—hypocrisy, treachery and realpolitik—without which it is impossible to stay in government. They sat in their offices for a while, pityingly
observed by their staff of former secret policemen, while affable and much
travelled rivals, of the kind with whom German Social Democrats and
French Gaullists could both 'do business', carefully groomed themselves
for the next elections. Not since 1945 had so many records of party membership disappeared, or so many dissident biographies been invented.
Within two years the real dissidents had returned to their studies, while
the world outside was racing on, led by a new political class that had
learnt to add a record of outspoken dissidence to all its other dissimula-
tions. We were witnessing what [Czechoslovak Communist Alexander]
Dubcek had promised, socialism with a human face. The most urgent
preoccupation of this new political class was to climb on to the European
Union gravy train, which promised rewards of a kind that had been
enjoyed, in previous years only by the inner circle of the secret police.*[1]

—Roger Scruton

*This is truly an event of great interstate and geopolitical significance
... For the first time since the collapse of the Soviet Union, the first real
step has been made towards restoring natural economic and trade ties
in the post-Soviet space.*[2]

—Vladimir Putin
on a Russian-led economic union, August 2011

15

An Overview

Powerful forces exert enormous pressure on the Intermarium's political, social, cultural, and economic life. Since the liberation, those forces have been post-Communism, nationalism, and globalism.

Post-Communism is Communism transformed. Post-Communism shrewdly eschews any ideological labels, preferring moral relativism and nihilism instead. However, it retains the Marxist-Leninist dialectical modus operandi with its immorality to allow for utmost political flexibility. And it conserves the old institutions and personnel under a different guise. All this allows post-Communism to maintain its grip on power.

Nationalism denotes social organization according to the idea of the unity of the language, geography, culture, religion, and history. Nationalism reflects the belief that common tradition, institutions, and faith translate into a community of shared interests. This community will guarantee a harmonious internal development within the nation, and it does not have to be a source of conflict with the neighboring nations.

Globalism is confusing hybrid of the traditional and the new issuing from the West. It is not a simple function of Westernization. Instead, it is a mixed offering of traditional Western values and countercultural fads created in opposition to these very values. The Western values include the rule of law, individual liberty, free market, parliamentary democracy, responsible patriotism, and traditional families. The countercultural fads pertain to the platitudes of postmodernism, deconstruction, and moral relativism served both in academic and pop-cultural forms. The countercultural entails a rebellion against everything that historically made the West unique, in particular its absolutist values regarding the obtainability of truth. This currently relativist antithesis of the West is yet another Western-born and bred heresy. In a way, then, globalism offers both Western and anti-Western elements all wrapped in one and arriving from the same Western destination, confusingly and enticingly, a daunting project to disentangle for a shell-shocked survivor of Soviet totalitarianism.

Yet the task before the survivor should be straightforward: both to re-Westernize and to de-Communize himself or herself to move forward into modernity. In other words, the objective is to achieve freedom.

Freedom and its promise, hope, anger, and desperation, all at once, project themselves onto the political scene of each of the nation state of the Intermarium, domestically and internationally. Various traditions, or their lack, impact internal and external political developments in a variety of ways: by fostering affinities, by encouraging coalitions, and by shouting dissent. The political scene thus may appear chaotic to the casual observer. Yet, it is eminently logical and generally predictable, to a certain extent at least.

Within this context we shall discuss the phenomena of post-Communism and anti-Communism. We shall introduce the patriots and the post-Communists; the liberals and social democrats; the "pinks" and "reds"; the nationalists and the conservatives; and, finally, extremists of all stripes and shapes: from unreconstructed Communists to radical nationalists and others. These categories are not dichotomous, denoting right and left. Instead, they tend to be overlapping to a certain extent. And they are impacted by various undercurrents, including the business world, the criminal underworld, and the spiritual universe, institutionalized and otherwise.

Overtly and covertly, the Intermarium grapples with the legacy of post-Communism. It also tackles current problems, such as the global recession and cultural changes. Most importantly, on the one hand, it faces the specter of a resurgent Russia. On the other hand, it engages the West, including NATO, the European Union, and the United States. The post-Soviet sphere faces a crucial dilemma: reintegration into the empire or integration with the West?

We shall now look at the internal and external political considerations of the Intermarium's elites, weave social and economic impressions of the region, and consider its majorities and minorities.[3]

Notes

1. Roger Scruton, "The Flame that Was Snuffed Out by Freedom," *The Times* [London] (November 7, 2009).
2. Putin quoted in Neil Buckley, "Putin sets sights on Eurasian economic union," *Financial Times* (August 16, 2011): http://www.ft.com/intl/cms/s/0/a7db2310-b769-11e0-b95d-00144feabdc0.html#axzz1VL1UnMTl. The customs union was launched in 2010.
3. In addition to the sources listed above and below, Part III is based upon daily reading of mainstream papers in Russian, Polish, and a variety of other languages and watching Russian, German, Polish, and English-language TV satellite news services. Further, for the past seven years we have also edited an Internet weekly newssheet concerning the region, "Eurasia, etc.," which contains both mainstream and eccentric sources for the study of current issues of the world, in general, and the Intermarium, in particular. However, the most indispensable English-language sources on the post-Soviet world remain the daily commentaries by Paul Goble, "Window on Eurasia," distributed via the Internet (about 5,500 entries between its launch in 2006 and termination in 2011) and www.windowoneurasia.blogspot.com (after a brief hiatus it was relaunched in 2012 as www.windowoneurasia2.blogspot.com); the daily analysis of Vladimir Socor and others in the *Eurasia Daily Monitor* (2004–present) published by the

Jamestown Foundation and http://www.jamestown.org/programs/edm/; and the dispatches of Radio Free Europe/Radio Liberty, http://www.rferl.org/. Of the mainstream papers, we regularly consult: the *Wall Street Journal, New York Times, Washington Post, Financial Times, Guardian,* and *Economist* as well as *Der Spiegel* and *Frankfurter Allgemeine Zeitung.* Agency dispatches are often much more useful because they tend to be devoid of excessive editorializing: Agence France Press (http://www.afp.com/afpcom/en/), Reuters (http://www.reuters.com), Associated Press (http://www.ap.org), and Bloomberg (http://www.Bloomberg.com) are recommended. National and regional news sites can also be helpful, for example, "All Moldova," http://www.allmoldova.com/en/moldova-news/index.html. Some graduate student research undertakings may be more insightful than others. See, for instance, the University of Aarhus, Department of Political Science, Demstar Project: Democracy, the State, and Administrative Reforms, http://www.demstar.dk/. For a variety of resources on contemporary issues (including videos of conferences) see Intermarium: On-Line Journal of the East Central European Center, Columbia University, http://ece.columbia.edu/research/intermarium/index.html. Other Internet resources are listed below.

16

Contemporary Politics

The key to the transformation, or the recycling of the nomenklatura:

1. *Ideological nomenklatura (party ideology apparat): Social demo-crats or liberals (so-called intellectuals)*

2. *Economic nomenklatura and secret police colonels and up: Liberals*

3. *Remaining nomenklatura (industrial, etc.)*

   a) upper level apparat: Liberals

   b) middle level apparat: Social democrats

4. *lower ranks of the secret police: Nationalist parties, anti-Semitic groups, radical outfits*

—Jerzy Targalski aka Józef Darski[1]

What follows is not a comprehensive coverage of the contemporary politics in the Intermarium.[2] Even though we deal with the period between roughly 1992 and 2012, this is not a straightforward chronological narrative of facts, people, places, and events.[3] Instead, first, we shall concentrate on some general issues applicable everywhere in the region. Then, we shall scrutinize certain important local phenomena in each of the post-Soviet successor states. In each case, our focus will vary slightly as we bow to the local conditions and flesh out the most salient characteristics and concerns of the newly liberated nations. Some countries' personalities therefore will receive more scrutiny than others. Their careers best reflect and symbolize the ambiguous nature of the transformation. This notably concerns Moldova, where post-Communist pathologies are arguably at their most brazen, and, hence, it serves us as a convenient laboratory to study them. We shall further look at the institutions of the Intermarium: both old and new. We shall point out continuities and discontinuities among and between them. Although often purposefully obscured, personal continuities outnumber institutional ones.

Regional idiosyncrasies abound. There will be, however, two overarching and contradictory themes: post-Communism and Westernization (or, more precisely, re-Westernization). The latter is the restoration of liberty; the former its denial. Post-Communism is present everywhere in the Intermarium. And everywhere it displays both its common features and divergent peculiarities. So does Westernization. The latter is most advanced in the Baltics. It has made some inroads in Ukraine, but fewer in Moldova. Belarus lags far behind. However, post-Communism is strongest there in its most unadulterated form. It is quite recognizable in Ukraine and Moldova, but in the Baltics it has transformed itself to a great extent as a legitimate and mainstream democratic avatar. In Estonia, Latvia, and Lithuania a putatively democratic face of post-Communism has resulted from both a high level of Westernization and a particular flavor of political culture there. The latter is fueled by the strong national identity of the Estonians, Latvians, and Lithuanians who perceive Communism as an alien implant and post-Communism as its bastard child left behind after the implosion of the USSR. Thus, under such hostile conditions, post-Communism in the Baltics had to transform itself more radically than anywhere else in the post-Soviet zone.[4]

The objective of contemporary politics in the Intermarium should be to restore its Western tradition and to eliminate post-Communism. The "return to the West," as some put it grandiloquently, is indispensable to reanchor the local communities and nations within the salubrious framework of liberty to execute closure on totalitarianism, to reestablish a moral high ground, and to achieve modernization, and, hence, prosperity. The latter objective is achieved by emulating a system, parliamentary democracy and free market capitalism, which have produced the desired results elsewhere, most notably in the West, in particular the United States, where tradition fuels modernization. Parliamentary democracy, rule of law, respect for private property, widespread religious faith, freedom, individualism, and patriotism have blessed America with exceptional power and prosperity that have been the inspiration, and envy, of the entire world. This includes the Intermarium where the American way has had its impressive share of enthusiastic admirers. The vaunted "American way" means strategic continuity of the immutable original intent of the Founding Fathers, tactically updated and readjusted to meet the challenges of the ever-fluctuating times. This resulted in a stunning success of the United States as far as its development and power are concerned. Therefore even now democracy, capitalism, and the rule of law remain at least an avowed aim of most mainstream political players in the Intermarium. And they still find a fair amount of support among the people, although it has lately declined from effusively exuberant to cautiously conditional.

Generally, the people have been disappointed by the lack of instantaneous success. More specifically, one expected the Western thesis of freedom to overcome its Soviet antithesis of post-Communism, which is Communism transformed. Instead, a synthesis of both occurred to produce a hybrid of both nefarious pathology and hopeful promise. Within it, post-Communism endures and reaps the benefits of freedom and democracy. Hence, because there has been no de-Communization, no lustration of the *agentura*, and no reckoning for Communist crimes, Communism has triumphed in its post-Communist form. Freedom and prosperity have failed to bloom as expected. Instead, their progress has been retarded by various pathologies stemming from post-Communism. Consequently, confusion and cynicism have set in among the people. They have reflected themselves in indifference, weathervane emulation of the powerful, and a deep distrust of the elite.[5] That is because in most places in the Intermarium the majority of political leaders recoil from the full implications of the oft-declared desire toward re-Westernization and modernization. Without removing the legacy of Communism, there can be no triumph of freedom. By commission or omission, the elites of the Intermarium invariably facilitate the survival of post-Communism. Why? They themselves are of it.

Post-Communism finds succor not only in the post-Soviet institutional, ideological, and personal survivals,[6] but also in the philosophical, political, social, and cultural bowels of the countercultural trends of postmodernistic deconstruction, moral relativism, and nihilism, which, like, say, Communism and National Socialism, originated in the West as the contradictions of its rich heritage of freedom. The postmodernist heresies currently in vogue in the West are based upon the conviction that, first, everything is a social construct and, thus, imagined, propagated, and enforced by whoever holds power; and, second, that therefore the truth does not exist and no difference obtains between right and wrong. This heretical denial of the absolute in essence equates Communism with democracy, as simply yet another emanation of power of the currently ruling elite. It also absolves the Communists of all crimes as relative. It further shifts the blame from the individual perpetrators to some nebulous "social construct" that simply served as a framework for dialectically ruthless and impersonal forces of history. In this convoluted discursive framework everyone is guilty, even the victims, but everyone is equally innocent, including the perpetrators.[7]

Wait! Someone did suffer: "The Other," which is defined collectively as "the minorities." With a dialectical twist, the postmodernist intellectual heresy replaces the individual, his or her origin notwithstanding, as the victim of the totalitarians by anointing the eccentric "Other" as the sole depository of all pain and persecution. This new paradigm of real and alleged victimhood was foisted upon the post-Soviet zone by the globalist commissars of political correctness from the West. Reinforced by the preachers of the Western media, they rather swiftly impregnated their ideological mates among the post-Communists and liberals with the cult of the "Otherness." The native clones of globalism quickly seized the opportunity to be postmodern. The trend was pioneered in Poland and Hungary and then spread to the Baltics. Ukraine and Moldova pay it a lip service domestically, but bow to it internationally. Belarus largely ignores it. In the EU member states minority suffering is publicly commemorated *de rigueur*; similar commemorations by the majorities in the Intermarium are perceived as threats and stigmatized as manifestations of, allegedly, nationalism, fascism, sexism, xenophobia, racism, anti-Semitism, and homophobia. Consequently there is a widespread impression among the majority populations in the post-Soviet zone that, first, the historic wrongs were not righted; second, one is not allowed to grieve about them in public; or one is expected to yield the space at the apex of suffering to the new false gods of "Otherness." It is singularly unhelpful that the postmodernists dominating the historical discourse in the European Union refuse to equate Nazism and Communism, or even acknowledge the crimes of Moscow, for example, the Katyn Forest massacre.[8]

Last but not least, the purveyors of postmodernism have conveniently introduced the following deceitful trick into the elite cultural discourse. They "critically" deconstructed the "corrupt" Western power structure and its systemic symbols, most gladly the Cross. Then, they enshrined "nothing" in its stead. By disallowing any other set of beliefs, the traditional ones in particular, branded as "oppressive" (racist, sexist, and so on), the "tolerant" ones claimed to have ushered in a just and egalitarian system with no particular power structure. Instead, they claim, there should be "nothing." However, "nothing" in and of itself by excluding all others becomes a dominant system with a self-anointed radical elite guarding its orthodoxy. Thus, in reality, the new power elite has championed nihilism as its tool of total control.

This postideology of the postmodernists of the West fits the post-Communists of the Intermarium just fine. They could now conveniently claim not only to have abandoned Communism but they also could set out to discredit anti-Communism. Their disingenuous argument ran as follows: Any ideology is bad. Anti-Communism is hateful and the anti-Communists resort to "Bolshevik" methods to impose their views on everyone. Let us forget the past. Let us choose the future. We shall march there together under the stewardship of the only orientation which not only fosters harmony, compromise, and tolerance through social democratic empathy but which also possesses professional cadres to accomplish the national goal of modernization: the post-Communists and left-liberals. (Incidentally, this insidious propaganda line, or "discourse," if you will, although unmistakably of Western countercultural theoretical origin, was pioneered in practice in Poland during 1989. Afterward it spread to the Intermarium like a wild fire.)[9]

Thus, Communism may be "dead" but the nefarious leftist ideas which birthed it are well and alive. They not only serve a theoretical purpose to provide ideological continuity to the post-Soviet power elite, but they are also applied in practice to glorify and deploy the state as the alleged vehicle of all progress. And post-Communism thrives because of the unholy relationship between the state and economy. The former showers privileges on those who control its institutions, and, thus, they are able to prosper in the competition-proof environment of crony capitalism.

Accordingly, the post-Communists rebranded their party as social democratic. This was originally intended as a temporary maneuver. In fact, as mentioned before, it was a deception operation in a dual manner. Had the Soviet power been restored, the "social democrats" could have reverted to their previous shape once that was ordered dialectically by the Kremlin. If, however, the Communists were to operate successfully in a "transformed" environment, where the very word "Communism" carried a serious stigma initially, they needed to alter their image by changing the façade: hence a new name for the old party. Naturally, some Communist stalwarts retained their old name and old ways. They were soon marginalized, however, throughout the Intermarium, even in Belarus, leaving Moldova as the sole exception in the twenty-first century. Everywhere else, the transformed Communists proved the wave of the future.

Their most significant psychological break at the level of perception and propaganda came when Western politicians, journalists, and academics conceptualized them as "post-Communists." Only their most hard core domestic and foreign opponents continued to refer to them as "Communists," or, most often, "Commies." In a knee jerk reaction of anti-anti-Communism, liberal media and the glitterati at home and abroad immediately branded that widespread moniker as primitive, intolerant, and potentially threatening to democracy. That was both to stigmatize anti-Communism in the mainstream and to assist the former Communists in entering it.

The post-Communists, meanwhile, swore that they had never believed in Communism in the first place. They demurely objected in their offended innocence that they were really "social democrats." As such, undoubtedly to their own initial surprise, the erstwhile Communists discovered that they were then rather effusively greeted by liberal Western intellectuals and other leftist activists. Ideological affinities of the Western progressives allowed the post-Communists to make a smooth transition from the henchmen of totalitarianism to the champions of socialist humanism. In addition, the erstwhile Bolsheviks began waxing eloquent about the wisdom of the theory of convergence, initially castigated by the East, and mothballed by the West since the 1970s, but now conveniently resurrected. Convergence meant that both the West and the East took correct, albeit distinct, paths to the same goal: European socialist unity. So now the post-Communists were not only "social democrats" but also the eastern apostles of the European Union. Some Western conservatives, meanwhile, pragmatically rejoiced at this apparent taming of the totalitarians, preferring "social democrats" over chaos and anarchy.

To guarantee institutional and political continuity from the Soviet times as well as to manipulate parliamentary democracy, the post-Communists everywhere endeavored to introduce a "superpresidential," or at least semi-presidential, system. The greater degree of success in this operation, the greater and more durable the power of the post-Communists. Hence, they remain dominant in Belarus and, to a lesser extent, Ukraine and Moldova.[10] On the electoral scene, they invariably capitalized on a wave of popular resentment against the corruption inherent in crony privatization and the unemployment stemming from de-etatization, including some free-market reforms. Among the elderly, the post-Communists milked the mushy nostalgia for the alleged "security" of the Soviet times. They promised to tame "wild capitalism" of the "liberals." Simultaneously, they wooed the young with their self-proclaimed professionalism and vigorous championing of globalism.[11]

After a while, delighted at their impunity at home and abroad (hardly anyone was persecuted for Communist crimes and de-Communization failed to materialize), the comrades began switching parties.[12] Social democracy was no longer good enough. Other options beaconed. Some of that occurred already at the threshold of independence; as mentioned, the "people power" national liberation movements were full of Communists. A few of them turned in their party cards altogether. Some others also left the Communist party soon to join or establish various political groups. Undoubtedly, it is safe to assume that at least a few of them were Soviet agents on assignment practicing the art of infiltration and disintegration. That is just standard operating procedure of any totalitarian secret police.[13] But others were looking to redeem themselves; after all, people do change, at least some of them do. Still other former Communists were looking for more fertile hunting grounds, especially on the right which sorely lacked in the professional talent. They also continued to be very active in the business world, relying routinely on their political connections to ensure financial success. In free Intermarium it hence became possible to have a prosperous career under virtually any umbrella. Politicians with post-Communist background could be thus found practically everywhere.

By design from the above, by the force of inertia, and by spontaneous reflexes from below, the processes that expedited the ascent of the post-Communists to new democratic heights have come to a full bloom in the Baltics, in particular. They are robustly budding in Ukraine and, to a lesser extent, in Moldova. In Belarus they are sprouting very gradually and under careful control of the dictatorial overseer. The post-Communist success could not have happened without a hospitable political and philosophical reception from the Western cheerleaders. And the cheering was reciprocal.

Since postmodernistic deconstruction, moral relativism, and nihilism invaded the Intermarium from the West, the post-Communists and other local leftists conveniently have hailed them as new and true essence of contemporary Europe and America. The native conservatives and other right wingers, however, have reacted to them pretty much like their Western counterparts: they deny the haughty claim of the postmodernists to override the ancient logocentric heritage of the West. Generally, the conservatives strive to re-Westernize and de-Communize. Their leftist detractors at best offer the impossible mirage of the Westernization through a convergence of European and American postmodernist heresies with eastern post-Communist pathologies. At worst, the unspoken specter of the reintegration of the Intermarium with Russia beacons invitingly in the subconscious of some of the post-Communists. The Right staunchly opposes both.

Logically, to achieve re-Westernization and, hence, freedom, one should endeavor to debunk oneself from the principal impediment: the pathologies stemming from the legacy of Soviet totalitarianism. In other words, to allow freedom to bloom fully, one needs to de-Communize fully. That entails phasing out from politics, economy, culture, and society the nefarious influences of the Soviet occupation and its aftermath, including present pathological connections to the Kremlin, the oligarch, the mafia, and Russia's secret services. In practical terms it requires maintaining the rule of law, including punishment for Communist crimes, property restitution, and guarantees for private property ownership. Openness, transparency, honesty, and integrity of public life can be obtained best by implementing the policies of lustration. That means openly vetting all public individuals to ascertain whether or not they collaborated with the KGB and other Communist secret agencies and whether the surreptitious parasitical relationship has continued into the present. The Left vehemently opposes this.

Yet, it is obvious that the deeper a break with the inheritance of Communism, the closer one gets to recreating the Western conditions locally, the stronger the flowering of freedom, and the greater the chances of a successful modernization. The story of the Intermarium in the last two decades is the tale of the endeavors to complete the project to re-Westernize.

There are naturally geographic variations of the process. The greater the degree of the identification with the West present, the higher the level of achievement in terms of democracy and economy. Generally, by that standard, the Baltics tend to be the most pro-Western and the closest to the democratic ideal. Estonia leads the pack, followed by Latvia and Lithuania. Ukraine and Moldova trail behind. Belarus fails to measure up to most Western political litmus tests. The nature of internal political forces of each state reflects these geographic trends.

However, domestic politics of the Intermarium are by no means a straightforward contest between righteous "patriots" backed by the people who support the West and dastardly "post-Communists" alienated from the mainstream who kowtow to Russia. Neither do the former necessarily support parliamentary democracy, nor do the latter readily advocate a dictatorship. The political character and ideological profile of the "patriots" and the "post-Communists" vary geographically and are determined by a number of factors, including history and the degree of involvement of the West, the United States in particular, but also the European Union, in a Soviet successor state. They are also conditioned by the intensity of a particular brand of populism or ethno-nationalism, the depth of popular disenchantment and malaise, and the level of political and social corruption.

The terms "patriots" and "post-Communists" can be infinitely flexible and need a very careful explanation. The latter term is simpler. A post-Communist is a Communist transformed who maintains himself in power with as little substantial reform as possible. While adjusting to, and accommodating, change, or the "transformation," with impressive agility, he or she supports the most extensive possible continuity of the old Communist ways at the present and into the future. The post-Communist champions a predicament where the people maintain their Soviet-style mentality and endure the misery inflicted by the on-going legacy of Marxism-Leninism, while the elite perpetuates the conditions conducive to the continuity of such malady and enjoys Western-style privileges. Usually, but not always, it is of secondary matter whether the status quo can be maintained within a dictatorship or a parliamentary democracy. The post-Communist is apt at operating in both environments with dialectical suaveness.

He or she is usually a former member, or a fellow traveler, of the Communist party, or one of its successor organizations. To maintain himself in power politically and economically, the post-Communist clings to the network of comrades, contacts, and institutions, usually transformed, stemming from the time of the Soviet occupation. He or she sometimes continues to adhere, either genuinely or cynically, to a diluted version of the Marxist-Leninist ideology, usually in a social–democratic form. Even if barren of any ideological belief, the post-Communist nearly always falls back to the trusty modus operandi of Marxism-Leninism as far as the dialectical exercise of power is concerned. Deception remains the key here. The post-Communist will frequently deny his past or feign ignorance about any connection, however tenuous, to anything Soviet. At the same time he or she is apt at dirty tricks. He or she is a master of *kto kavo* (who does whom in). Thus, Marxism-Leninism remains the tool of power for him or her, if in deep disguise. The post-Communist wields the tool usually by the means of a post-Communist successor party, most often renamed "social democratic," or any other party, including a number of freshly minted ones on any side of the political spectrum.

However, there are also genuine, unreconstructed Communists of various stripes who resent the post-Communists as traitors. The unreformed Communists are ruthlessly brazen about their preferences for the bad old days, but are insufficiently dialectical to succeed in their schemes at the present, except for a time in Moldova.[14] Last but not least, being a post-Communist is not a permanent condition. One can always exercise free will and become a patriot. Or one can retreat into privacy. There is no obligation to remain a post-Communist.

It is a matter of convenience, however. It is the opposite on the other side of the barricade among the patriots.

In the Intermarium, a patriot usually denotes an anti-Communist. Or at least it used to be the case until recently. And, in a perfect world, an anti-Communist is a person who has always opposed all manifestations of Communism, before, during, and after World War II, including, now, post-Communism. Clearly, very few have survived with a sustained record of uninterrupted anti-Communist activism or even passive anti-Communist attitudes. Over almost half a century, very few in the Intermarium can claim no flirtation with Soviet Communism whatsoever, either for idealistic or pragmatic reasons. Very few can boast of no nefarious dealings with the Soviet secret police. In addition to a handful of grizzled veterans with impeccable credentials, almost invariably the Gulag survivors, there are also middle-aged people, who became adults before and during the heyday of the counterrevolution of the late 1980s and early 1990s, and even very young individuals who are entering politics now and embracing the anti-Communist legacy as theirs. These are the ideal patriots, at least in theory.

Although anti-Communism suffices to describe the ideology of perhaps most of them, particularly in the early 1990s, in reality the patriots adhere to a variety of theoretical propositions and practical stances. Sometimes they are complementary, and at other times dissonant. A patriot is obviously interested in the welfare of his nation and that is why he primarily opposes Communism. A patriot can be a nationalist, but not necessarily. In fact, a patriot can be anything between a radical nationalist and an absolutist monarchist, including social democrat, liberal, Christian democrat, libertarian, conservative, or any other.

Most of the patriots tend to be pro-Western, in the Baltics, Moldova, and Belarus, in particular, but fewer in Ukraine. Some of them exude a healthy dose of Euroskepticism.[15] Most distrust the national minorities or can even be hostile toward them to an extent, which impacts the pace of internal civic integration and fosters conflict. Everywhere in the Intermarium an anti-Western radical ultranationalist fringe rejects the West as a hot spot of decadence, ruled by "Jews," "freemasons," and "homosexuals." The radical nationalists and populists condemn free-market capitalism and parliamentary democracy. The canard of a Jewish conspiracy rears its ugly head from time to time.[16] These attitudes are most prevalent among the extremists everywhere, but are a case for concern particularly in Ukraine where the ultranationalists constitute a serious force in the western parts of the nation among the majority population. Ironically, some of the ideological preferences of radical nationalists, a penchant for autarchy in particular, show affinity with both the unreconstructed Communists of various stripes and the post-Communist reigning dictatorship in Belarus.[17]

To confuse things further, over time, some of the patriots have suspended or even foresworn their erstwhile anti-Communism to cooperate with some of the post-Communists, for either pragmatic or ideological reasons. Usually the liberal or social-democratic patriots who support the European Union tend to collaborate with the post-Communists of similar preferences. Generally, a pro-Western stance by a post-Communist tends to elicit the support of many former anti-Communists, some of whom have increasingly espoused however the anti-anti-Communist position.

Meanwhile, a number of the post-Communists (and most unreformed Communists) maintains links with Moscow, in Belarus, Ukraine, and Moldova primarily, but also in the Baltics, where they are best friends of the Russian minority. Paradoxically, however, as mentioned, some of the post-Communists tend to be also pro-Western. There is no clear division of roles here necessarily; sometimes prominent post-Communists of the Intermarium seem supportive of both the West and the East simultaneously. That may be ideological pragmatism at its best, shrewd political tactics, or, simply, a deception operation, the standard modus operandi dictated by the Marxist-Leninist dialectics.

Although the proportions vary from country to country, the greatest number of the post-Communist "fans" of the West resides in the Baltics; some in Ukraine and Moldova; and practically none in Belarus. The pro-Western types can also be explicitly pro-US, as reflected in their support of Washington during the conflict in Iraq and, more broadly, War on Terror, in Ukraine for example. To a large extent this was to demonstrate to the electorate that the post-Communists were no longer pro-Russian traitors, but, instead, pro-American patriots, and, hence, pro-Western. The post-Communists have further been casting about in search of foreign sponsors in a changed world. Having grown used to Moscow's *Diktat*, they do not mind instructions from Washington or Brussels. In this way, through demonstrating obedience, they have also maintained their indispensability on the political scene. The West has been rather pleased reciprocating with aid, although also forgetting that those bought do not stay bought for long.

To retain power, or at least to remain in the democratic game, increasing numbers of the post-Communists support the European Union. They have quickly realized that Brussels does not really threaten their lofty positions in the successor states, if they can be perceived as playing by the democratic rules and regurgitating progressive slogans. And perception tends to trump reality. Also, that helps the former nomenklatura and its allies consolidate their grip on state institutions in a new, transformed way. The truth is that, according to Lars Johannsen and Ole Nørgaard, even the Soviet successor states who have acceded to the EU, have so far failed to reform state administration and bureaucracy and to provide for a clean break with post-Communism. In a long run the accession will eventually smooth the way to another gradual soft landing of the erstwhile totalitarians.[18] What is there not to like in Brussels for a former red apparatchik? The post-Communists further back the EU because of their leftist ideological affinities for social democracy and liberalism, which presently hold the Old Continent in their grip. Precisely because of such ideological affinities, the post-Communists moreover can rest confident that the EU will guarantee them impunity from prosecution for the past crimes. Hence, they have heartily welcomed the support of the anti-anti-Communist liberal and social democratic wing of the erstwhile patriots in the Intermarium.

This inevitably logical alliance of the "pinks" and "reds" reflects the convergence of ideologies and the reassessment of priorities. On a broader scale, it also signifies what one scholar has aptly described as mentality and personality change: "Post-Socialist Transformations as Identity Transformations."[19] Accordingly, in the 1990s, as part and parcel of the transformation process, the liberals and social democrats have abandoned their earlier nationalism and have begun to orient themselves internationally, toward the European Union in particular. Some were seduced by the gospel of globalization; others pragmatically joined the apparent juggernaut because, after all, was it not blessed by America's President Bill Clinton? Further, former anti-Communists have lately adopted the causes that used to range from perennial through irrelevant to nonexistent in their struggle for independence against the Soviet Union but are now quite *au courant* in the Western liberal universe.

The best examples here are the trajectories of the growth and development of environmentalism, feminism, and gay liberation. Only a portion of those ideologies is indigenous to the Intermarium. Much of it is transplanted, or, more precisely, imposed by *fiat* by visiting Western leftists or brought back home by the native beneficiaries of Western scholarships which are most gladly dispensed to the politically correct, in the social sciences and the humanities in particular. Thus, a new *Weltanschauung* endeavors to supplant an intellectual universe annihilated by the Soviets. It is to be accomplished by transforming the Communist ideological legacy by marrying it with Western post-modernist theories.

As mentioned, the integral part of postmodernist deconstruction and moral relativism is the worship of "The Other." In the Intermarium, as elsewhere, it translates into the championship of multiculturalism and minority rights, including the adherents of the "alternative life styles." Countercultural radicals from the European Union and the United States, via their government pressure and NGO work, wield impressive lobbying powers backed up by substantial funds. They are most robust in the Baltics, visible in Ukraine, present in Moldova, but largely absent in Belarus.[20] What are the results of this kind of social engineering? How does it relate to the indigenous environmentalist, feminist, and gay dynamics?

In the 1980s and early 1990s a conservationist counterrevolution broke out against the Soviet environmental pollution. Conservation and stewardship of nature were its buzzwords. Nationalism and anti-Communism propelled it. Now, however, it is transformed into a full-fledged green movement with all its doctrinaire aberrations, deifying nature and de-anthropophying our environmental concerns. As a political proposition, extremist nature worship is, however, somewhat moderated within the parliamentary context because of the requirements of maintaining mainstream respectability and coalitions with disparate partners. Moreover, the nexus between nationalism and environmentalism remains, albeit in a more diluted form.[21]

During the struggle for freedom in the late 1980s and early 1990s, feminism was consigned to a complete fringe; now it aspires to bloom with "gender" quotas, sensitivity trainings, and indoctrination on sexual harassment and alleged patriarchal violence in the family. Virtually a nonexistent factor in the fight for independence, gay liberation is still far from rampant, but homosexual frolic takes place quite openly at the art and entertainment levels, if at political and academic ones still to a much lesser degree. Again, the Baltics lead the way in gender and lifestyle matters. To challenge the EU's radicalism on cultural issues, socially conservative Latvia, for example, has constitutionally defined marriage as a compact between a man and a woman. And its citizens fail to embrace so-called "gay pride" parades. Other nations only now begin to address such postmodernist contrivances usually with bans, pickets, and counter-marches.[22] In Ukraine environmentalism is a waxing minority concern, feminism is a performance art,[23] and gay liberation is a butt of public jokes. Moldova lags behind Ukraine in Western-imported sensitivities. And Belarus has largely relegated underground its environmentalism, feminism, and gay liberation.

And never mind that the environmentalists, feminists, and, to a lesser extent, gays (who remain mostly closeted) attack occasionally the post-Communist establishment and its allies. That is simply an expression of angry frustration of the lifestyle radicals at the slow pace of the mainstream "red–pink" alliance in leading the countercultural charge to transform the Intermarium's societies along the postmodernist lines as in the West. The lifestyle radicals are much more adamantly opposed to the conservative and nationalist orientations, anti-Communists, in general. The latter have not succumbed to nihilism and moral relativism because their frame of reference is usually Christian. Hence, their normative world view threatens "alternative life styles" and green quasi cults.

Another, perhaps most important, reason for the convergence of the "pink" and "red" orientations is that the liberals and social democrats of patriot background see no utility for anti-Communism anymore. They find it only of historical relevance, if at all. In contemporary times, they consider anti-Communism divisive. It may even be an excuse for authoritarianism, xenophobia, illiberalism, and opposition to parliamentary democracy. And, as we have mentioned above, the fringe of the anti-Communist nationalists has indeed championed such nefarious views, including anti-Semitism. However, most have not. Like in the United States, the liberal *reductio ad Hitlerum* is a handy device to delegitimize the conservative and patriotic orientation. Scaremongering about the alleged imminence of "fascism" is also a convenient tool to mobilize and close the ranks on the left-liberal side.

Last but not least, the "pinks" have recognized the importance of the business world to the economic welfare of their countries and to their own financial well-being. Remaining involved in politics is costly. Serious funds are necessary to win elections. And who has the money? Not the anti-Communists. The convergence of the "pinks" with the "reds" is greatly facilitated by that realization, some would say at least at times undoubtedly self-serving. Most of the business milieu of the Intermarium harkens from the former Communist *nomenklatura*. It has even be alleged that the greatest Russian oligarchs, whose power used to radiate everywhere in the post-Soviet space, but has now waned somewhat, were connected to the old secret police, the dreaded KGB. And, it was rumored widely, they had strong mafia ties. Sometimes all categories overlapped.

We should recognize, in passing at least, these three important groups of political players in the Intermarium: the successful businessmen, the secret agents, and the ruthless mafiosi. The historian is reluctant to delve into a topic that lacks crucial documentation, indeed really any sources save for journalistic dispatches and fantastic gossip. However, preliminary research has allowed us to establish the following basic facts about the elusive trio.

The Intermarium's most successful businessmen (*biznesmeny*), the oligarchs in particular, usually have Communist roots. At least some of them maintained ties to the secret police in the past. They are also often perceived as utterly corrupt, dabbling with the criminal underworld.[24] Initially, the businessmen supported the post-Communists almost exclusively. Now they are split. The disunity reflects, firstly, their personal preferences, which surfaced with an ever-increasing boldness after gaining the self-empowerment that vast wealth affords and following their self-emancipation from the slavish forms of the totalitarian system. Secondly, the high profile lack of agreement among them stems from tactical differences and pragmatism: the oligarchs compete against one another in both economics and politics and like to be on the winning side in every business deal and every new election. Nonetheless, most of the oligarchs agree on the fundamentals. Since much of the business class harkens from the *nomenklatura* and many enjoy their ill-gotten wealth because of the orgy of embezzlement condoned and facilitated by the post-Communists in the 1990s, the post-Soviet entrepreneurs tend not to support the conservative forces of law and order in the Western meaning of the concept, except so far as such forces promise to maintain the status quo, guarantee them impunity for past, present, and future misdeeds, and continue to reward the *nouveau riche* with government contracts and access to power. There are virtually no true conservatives in the Intermarium willing to facilitate this, but plenty of others are happy to oblige across the political spectrum. Thus, the businessmen are connected to prominent politicians, some even flaunt such links indeed, in Ukraine in particular, and more than a few have entered politics themselves. Thus, the perception is that the oligarchs frequently fight among themselves and often make shady, backdoor deals to patch things up. [25]

Foreign businesses and their principals are another story. Initially, these expatriate Westerners hired mostly post-Communists on the account of their connections and management skills, however pathological for acquired under totalitarianism. Thus, the local "managers" provided foreigners with, in criminal parlance, "the roof" (*krisha*), or protection. It was nearly impossible to do business otherwise. And, in their turn, the foreigners provided their "business partners" with access to Western credit and contacts. That was the case virtually everywhere. It impacted practically everyone, even the proverbially straight-as-an-arrow Scandinavian entrepreneurs. As far as enabling the system, businessmen from the Russian Federation lead the wolf pack in the Intermarium. Although Russian businesses officially qualify as foreign, their owners feel quite at home everywhere in the former Soviet Union. For a variety of reasons described above, they unofficially can even claim an indigenous status. In fact, it appears that the Russian businessmen have virtually overshadowed the local entrepreneurs in the Baltics, Estonia in particular. And Moldova is virtually at their mercy. All businessmen operate in an unforgiving environment that requires connections to facilitate deals. Often the contacts are not, strictly speaking, legal. They come from the spy world and the criminal underground.[26]

As for secret agents,[27] Soviet successor states, including primarily Russia, but also other nations, maintain their nets of the *agentura* in the Intermarium. There are several categories of secret operators. First, there are field officers of the KGB's heir, the Service of Foreign Intelligence (SVR) of the Federal Security Service (FSB), and the Military Intelligence (GRU), and their local successor organizations. They are hardly reconstructed at all in Belarus, transformed somewhat in Ukraine and Moldova, and largely reinvented in the Baltics but based upon an ill-conceived compromise attempting to reconcile the old and the new. Thus, in Estonia, Latvia, and Lithuania some fresh blood flows in the veins of their secret services in an allergic disharmony with the diseased blood clots left behind by the KGB. Next, in each nation of the Intermarium there are the sources (agents) handled by the FSB and other agencies. They may be agents of influence, active in the media, politics, and academia; and there are outright spies, a few of whom get caught occasionally, as was the case in Estonia recently.[28]

Some agents are new recruits. Others used to be snitches for the KGB during the Soviet times. Some of them continue under a new umbrella. Usually it is either the FSB or GRU. However, it can also be their local successor or a Western (or other foreign) spy entity, sometimes operating under a false flag.

Here, the continuity of informing is likely predicated on blackmail. Although the Communists destroyed much of the local secret police archives in the Intermarium, the Moscow center retained all the important files. Further, some of the material was delivered or sold to Western intelligence agencies by defectors as the Soviet empire was crumbling. Finally, some documents were saved from destruction by the locals and are slowly revealed to the world. That means that Moscow, in particular, wields undue influence among the entrepreneurial, political, cultural, and media elite of the Intermarium, a situation that can only be remedied through a lustration, the vetting of agents.[29]

Only a partial lustration has been undertaken so far against great opposition of the vested interests. The vetting has proceeded in spurts and spasms, spurred by high-profile cases. There have been more than a few revelations about the identities of the informers, most of them either defunct or sleepers. Most of the information is mainly of historical value. It is admittedly shocking to discover some heroes of the struggle for independence to have been in the employ of the KGB.[30] It is also painful personally for many to learn that their close relatives and friends spied on them for the Soviet secret police. Yet it is all very necessary to make a clean sweep, put the past behind, and to ensure the national security of the newly liberated post-Soviet successor states.

At any rate, the clandestine operations involve the whole of the Intermarium's political spectrum, not just the post-Communists.[31] But the size of the spy net, the extent of the penetration, and the real value of its influence will remain unknown until the unlikely event that the powers involved, Russia in particular, resolve to open their archives to independent research. So why mention the *agentura* at all? Because it is a factor on the political scene; to pretend otherwise would be disingenuous; it would further rob us of a valuable perspective, that of remaining attentive to the possible influence of a secret tool of power; and, ultimately, glossing the spy issue over in silence would stoke the fires of paranoia of the conspiracy theorists.

This also applies, albeit to a lesser extent, to the mafia. In most places it is referred to as "the Russian mafia." It is a misnomer. If anything, "the post-Soviet mafia" is much more accurate, as the gangsters are of various ethnicities and are bound by their common, Soviet origin and post-Communist legacy. However, some gangs are of a single ethnicity, clan, or even family (e.g., "the Chechen mafia"). There are also local "mafias," sometimes autonomous, and at other times loosely affiliated with the ubiquitous "Russian mafia." The smartest of the set, well-connected to the KGB, moved up the ladder, proclaimed themselves "businessmen," legalized their loot, and bought into respectability, of sorts, including on the political scene. Whether or not they have retained their connections to the criminal underworld is anyone's guess. Probably, yes, some of them did. And the same applies to their links to the secret services.[32] The ones who remained stuck in the criminal underground appear to be on the wane as the Intermarium slouches toward re-Westernization. As with the spies, their influence on the political scene is quite hard to gauge. The educated guess would be that they are more influential locally than nationally. From the point of view of geography, the mafiosi are most rampant in Ukraine and Moldova. They are much more under control in the Baltics. The gangsters are quite invisible in Belarus. A dictatorship bears no competition in thuggery.[33]

The mafiosi, the spies, and the oligarchs amply reinforce the popular conviction that post-Communism oozes corruption, practices deception, and celebrates nihilism. Paradoxically, however, having embraced the West's postmodernist heresies with delight, the post-Communist elites have incongruously also championed the resurrection of traditional Christian religion throughout the Intermarium.[34] This dialectical strategy serves several purposes. First, it gives post-Communism an instrument of control over the masses, institutional and spiritual. Second, it further legitimizes the post-Communists in the public eye as alleged traditionalists or, at least, restorers of tradition. Third, after the demise of the cult of Marxism-Leninism, the new strategy channels the human need for spirituality into yet another officially sanctioned venue. Fourth, it harnesses in support of post-Communism the old religious institutions and their personnel, some of them secret police agents, as useful props of the successor regime for the domestic and foreign perception as alleged signs of "religious freedom" and "liberalism" of the system.

All this suggests that far from being a hopeful discontinuity with the Communist past, the official utilization of the traditional faiths in the Intermarium bears all the marks of an obvious continuity with the Communist practice, albeit in a transformed form. Hence, most post-Soviet states actively support organized religion. The official state holidays and functions often feature religious elements. The state sponsors church building and restoration. Public TV consistently airs prayer and masses, daily in Ukraine and much less frequently in Estonia. Whether the post-Communist system can continue to control the religious impulse is another story. The law of the unintended consequences suggests the opposite.

That is not to say that the rejuvenating power of faith reveals itself uniformly across the Intermarium. On the contrary, there is a great deal of diversity, not only in the official approach to religion and the variety of religious offerings but also in the intensity of belief among the denizens. Generally, four Christian denominations are present in the area: the Orthodox, Uniate Catholic, Roman Catholic, and Protestant. There are also pockets of Judaism and Islam as well as a sprinkling of such exotic groups as the Mormons and the Bahai, among others. The Muslims continue in their traditional domiciles: the Crimea, eastern Moldova, and the environs of Vilnius as well as in major towns, where the Jews congregate as well. The mainstream Lutherans are mostly limited to Estonia and Latvia, but various Christian evangelical groups operate virtually in each of the successor states. The Orthodox Christians are present everywhere, overwhelmingly in the east and decreasingly in the west of the Intermarium. The Uniates cluster mostly in western Ukraine. The Roman Catholics are strong in the west, and their numbers recede towards the east. Most of them are settled in rural pockets within the old boundaries of the Polish Lithuanian Commonwealth, but there is also a bit of the Latin Church's presence beyond, in larger cities in particular, including, for example, Odessa. In the official and popular perception Roman Catholicism remains "the Polish faith," a stereotype greatly reinforced not only by historical memories but also the recent pontificate of late Pope John Paul II (1920–2005). This perception has not been affected by the Vatican's latest attempt, which commenced in the early twenty-first century, to limit, if not outright eliminate, the mass in Polish in some Catholic churches in Ukraine and Belarus and replace it with the majority languages.[35]

The importance of religion in the public square and individual life fluctuates from country to country. Estonia is the most irreligious of the lot with its formerly traditional, Protestant (Lutheran) Christianity barely registering any influence among the people. Even the Russian minority, generally a religiously tepid lot, is more devout in its Orthodox worship. Yet, even in Estonia the state sometimes draws on religious symbols and ceremonies and at least some politicians find it efficacious to make a pro-religious gesture, like endowing or restoring a church. Latvia's Lutheranism is more firmly ensconced in its population's national consciousness, as is Orthodoxy among the Russian minority. Nonetheless, the role of religion in public squares is largely ceremonial. Lithuania is nominally Roman Catholic and the state puts great store in maintaining cordial relations with the Church and involving it in official business. That predictably includes the attempt to Lithuanize the Polish minority, which has historically deployed its Catholic faith in the service of its own identity protection and nationalism. Meanwhile, Lithuania's Russians and Belarusians remain Orthodox of a various level of commitment. Their Orthodox faith, however, meshes weirdly with their devotion to the Soviet mythology and past.

The Ukrainian state officially supports all religions, but it openly champions the Orthodox and the Uniate churches. Yet, Ukraine faces an uneasy coexistence of the Christian denominations, which sometimes even degenerates into outright violence. In particular, the Orthodox fight among themselves over their allegiance to Moscow and Kyiv. The Uniates have maintained a near monopoly on Ukraine's ethno-nationalism, but the Uniate Church manifests its strength almost exclusively in the western part of the country. The Uniates assert themselves often against the Roman Catholics, who are mostly of the Polish minority and largely subdued, congregating primarily in the west of Ukraine.[36]

In Belarus, like in Russia, there is a symbiotic relationship between the state and the Orthodox Church. However, any unauthorized actions by the clergy, in particular support for the opposition, are not tolerated. Since the hierarchy is traditionally obedient, the official ire targets the lower clergy, however infrequently. The same applies to Roman Catholicism, a domain of both some Belarusians and minority Poles. The Church is tolerated and even encouraged so long as the Vatican continues to agree gradually to replace its Polish parish priests with the Slovaks or, better yet, Germans. Minsk is concerned about Roman Catholicism as a conduit for Polish nationalism.

Moldova's relationship with the Orthodox Church resembles both Belarus and eastern Ukraine, as the population is overwhelmingly Orthodox. The state dominates the Orthodox Church and it enjoys the support of the religious hierarchs. There is a mild degree of harassment of the lower clergy, in particular those connected to pan-Romanian nationalism. Nonetheless, orthodoxy underpins some of the state ceremonies but mostly for decorative purposes. The official concern has been about the undue influence of Romania in Moldova's religious life. Therefore, at least until recently, the authorities seemed to have favored the Orthodox Church of Moldova with its seat in Chişinău, which is an autonomous entity within the Russian Orthodox Church and its Moscow Patriarchate. Its main competitor is the Orthodox Metropolis of Bessarabia, which is also an autonomous structure but under the autocephalous Romanian Orthodox Church and its Bucharest Patriarchate. Of other faiths, Roman Catholicism is the strongest, but it mostly is limited to the tiny Polish minority. The Catholics are largely left alone. Aside from the Romanian-affiliated Orthodox, it seems that the Muslims have born the brunt of official harassment, but that has to do with global fears of Islamism more than with Moldavian internal politics.[37]

Religion has proven to be extremely resilient in the face of almost impossible odds of the twentieth century. It will remain a factor in the public and individual life of the Intermarium. However, after the initial burst, there has been no massive return to the faith in most instances but religion has recovered some of its ground and has been making progress to attract new souls and stray sheep. The clergy does particularly well when spiritual care is combined with material assistance for the sick, elderly, orphans, and unemployed. Church-led sobriety initiatives and morality drives tend to resonate positively among some of the people. Faith-based charities and schools are enormously popular and fulfill a very important function in post-Soviet societies, the Catholics and evangelicals excelling on this field in particular. Further, throughout the Intermarium various confessions have also served to maintain separate identities by the national minorities, for instance Jews and Poles. Internationally, the Kremlin has used faith as a tool to exercise control over the Russian minority and to interfere in the affairs of the sovereign states there (including, most recently, with the so-called "Compatriot Program"). However, generally, religion will not be of major importance in domestic politics except regionally, where it reinforces local nationalism in western Ukraine in particular.

Post-Communism, globalism, nationalism, crime, and religion influence and impact, covertly and overtly, the visible political scene of the Intermarium. To an untrained eye, the public landscape looks eminently ordinary. After the hectic early 1990s, and the implosion of "popular fronts," the region settled to politics as usual. New constitutions are now enacted.[38] Political parties compete and parliamentary democracy functions everywhere, except in Belarus. On the negative side, cheating at the ballot box occurs, starting at the local level, even in the Baltics, however infrequently. It has registered as a serious problem in Ukraine and Moldova. In Belarus electoral fraud is of course institutionalized through the dictatorship.[39] Incumbent parties take over state bureaucracies and treat them as spoils of the system and tools of coercion to perpetuate themselves in power, a practice known as "the use of administrative resources" (adminresurs).[40]

The number of parties tends to dwindle if there is political stability. Sometimes this denotes a victory for freedom, but most often a shift to authoritarianism. Some parties practice brazen deception, mislabeling themselves and switching ideologies and programs. That is done sometimes out of opportunism (e.g., to weather tough times for leftism) and sometimes to cover up their past and real intentions. Parties often morph and conclude strange electoral alliances.[41] They alternate in power. The dynamics of the alternance is based upon seemingly familiar Western patterns of the electorate's initial support for hard-biting economic reforms, introduced usually by the Right, and the people's exhausted rejection of the belt-tightening measures, in favor of the Left. And there is also the popular anger against official corruption, which leads to periodic government changes and manifests itself in political discontinuity at the parliamentary level.[42]

That has been, at least, the case in the Baltics, to a various extent.[43] Ukraine only reached that particular mode of democracy in 2004, and Moldova in 2007 and 2009. Prior, the post-Communists had virtually monopolized power there. But both have relapsed since. The harder the grip of post-Communism, the more intense the popular protest ultimately erupts in favor of reform, as evident in the Ukrainian and Moldovan cases of their "color" revolutions.[44] Evidently, two decades later the citizenry and the opposition elites still find it indispensable to finish the fight for freedom that began in the late 1980s. That also pertains to Belarus, which, protest or no, has remained frozen in the dictatorial mode.

The Intermarium strives to emulate the West but the local peculiarities create different dynamics of the political systems. Further, unlike in the West, there is constant churning under the surface as disparate forces have now resorted to a democratic joust to settle their disputes, except in Belarus. The political scene thus appears normal only, of course, if we discount the history of the Intermarium, in particular Nazism and Communism, as well as post-Communism, anti-Communism, the "pink"–"red" nexus, extremists of various home-bred ilk, radicals of Western counterculture, and the conjoined triplets of the entrepreneurial, agent, and criminal worlds as well as the religious dimension, both institutionalized and not.

Notes

1. See Jerzy Targalski, "Intermarium: Uwagi," ("Intermarium: Remarks") TMs, Warsaw, December 8, 2011, pp. 1–12, the "Recycling of the nomenklatura," at page 7 (a copy in my collection).

2. A version of the following section was published as Marek Jan Chodakiewicz, "Post-Soviet Domestic and Foreign Challenges," *The International Chronicles: Journal of Contemporary Political Culture* (September 2011): http://www. theinternationalchronicles.com/en/index.html?info=561&menuks=154.

3. For the initial period, until the mid-1990s, see Timothy J. Colton and Robert Legvold, eds., *After the Soviet Union: from Empire to Nations* (New York: W.W. Norton & Company, 1992); Ian Bremmer and Ray Taras, eds., *Nations and Politics in the Soviet Successor States* (New York: Cambridge University Press, 1993); Carol R. Saivetz and Anthony Jones, eds., *In Search of Pluralism: Soviet and Post-Soviet Politics* (Boulder, CO: Westview Press, 1994); Bogdan Skajkowski, ed., *Political Parties of Eastern Europe, Russia and the Successor States* (London: Longman, 1994); Jane Shapiro Zacek and Ilpyong J. Kim, eds., *The Legacy of the Soviet Bloc* (Gainesville, FL: University Press of Florida, 1997); John W. Blaney, ed., *The Successor States to the USSR* (Washington, DC: Congressional Quarterly Books, 1995); Reimund Seidelmann, ed., *Crises Policies in Eastern Europe: Imperatives, Problems and Perspectives* (Baden-Baden: Nomos, 1996); *Shaping Actors, Shaping Factors in Russia's Future* (New York: St. Martin's Press, 1998); Robert J. Kaiser, *The Geography of Nationalism in Russia and the USSR* (Princeton, NJ: Princeton University Press, 1994); "The Western States," *Russia and the Independent States*, ed. by Daniel C. Diller (Washington, DC: Congressional Quarterly, 1993), 275–94; Signe Landgren, "Post-Soviet Threat to Security," in *SIPRI Yearbook, 1992: World Armaments and Disarmament* (New York: Oxford University Press, 1992), 546–47; Zvi Y. Gitelman, "Ethnopolitics and the Future of the Former Soviet Union," in *The Politics of Nationality and the Erosion of the USSR*, ed. Zvi Y. Gitelman (New York: St. Martin's Press, 1992), 1–25; Kelvin Gosnell, *Belarus, Ukraine and Moldova* (Brookfield, CT: Millbrook Press, 1992). See further Maruska Svasek, *Postsocialism: Politics and Emotions in Central and Eastern Europe* (New York: Berghahn Books, 2006); Sharon L. Wolchik and Jane L. Curry, *Central and East European Politics: From Communism to Democracy* (Lanham, MD: Rowman & Littlefield Publishers, 2008); Jarosław Dudek, Daria Janiszewska, and Urszula Świderska-Włodarczyk, eds., *Europa Środkowo-Wschodnia: Ideologia, historia a społeczeństwo* (*East-Central Europe: Ideology, History, and Society*) (Zielona Góra: Uniwersytet Zielonogórski [Zielona Góra University], 2005); and Oliver Schmidtke and Serhy Yekelchyk, *Europe's Last Frontier? Belarus, Moldova, and Ukraine between Russia and the European Union* (New York: Palgrave Macmillan, 2008).

4. There are actually three political cultures in the Baltics, and, to a certain extent, elsewhere in the Intermarium: nationalism, post-Sovietism, and globalism. We should keep in mind, however, that sometimes they overlap. And they are often

modified by individualism, which is more prevalent, say, among the Estonians (and even the Russians from Estonia), than among the Russians from Muscovy. The latter show highly collectivistic trends. On the other hand, Estonians, both émigré and domestic, display rather high levels of ethnic pride and belonging. Perhaps then nationalism is the prime beneficiary of the collectivistic reflexes among the Estonians. See Sten Berglund, Bernd Henningsen, and Mai-Brith Schartau, eds., *Political Culture: Values and Identities in the Baltic Sea Region* (Berlin: Berliner Wissenschafts-Verlag, 2006); Cynthia S. Kaplan, "Political Culture in Estonia: The Impact of Two Traditions on Political Development," in *Political Culture and Civil Society in Russia and the New States of Eurasia*, ed. Vladmir Tismăneanu (Armonk, NY: M.E. Sharpe, 1995), 227–68; Aune Valk and Kristel Karu, "Ethnic Attitudes in Relation to Ethnic Pride and Ethnic Differentiation," *The Journal of Social Psychology* 141, no. 5 (October 2001): 583–601; Li Bennichi-Bjorkman, "The Cultural Roots of Estonia's Successful Transition: How Historical Legacies Shaped the 1990s," *East European Politics and Societies* 21, no. 2 (Spring 2007): 316–48; Mart Nutt, "Different National-isms: The Case of Estonia," *Uncaptive Minds* 9, no. 3–4 (Summer–Fall 1997): 33–42; Juri Adams and Janusz Bugajski, "Different Nationalisms: The Lessons of Estonia," *Uncaptive Minds* 9, no. 3–4 (Summer–Fall 1997): 149–60; Tovio U. Raun, "Estonia after 1991: Identity and Integration," *East European Politics and Societies* 23, no. 4 (Fall 2009): 526–35; and two essays in by Pål Kolstø, ed., *National Integration and Violent Conflict in Post-Soviet Societies: The Cases of Estonia and Moldova* (Lanham, MD: Rowman & Littlefield, 2002): Raivo Vetik, "The Cultural and Social Makeup of Estonia" (71–104), and Aleksej Semjonov, "Estonia: Nation–building and Integration – Political and Legal Aspects" (105–58). For comparison see Taras Kuzio, "Political Culture and Democracy: Ukraine as an Immobile State," *East European Politics and Societies* 25, no. 1 (Winter 2011): 88–114; Pål Kolstø and Hans Olav Melberg, "Integration, Alien-ation, and Conflict in Estonia and Moldova at the Societal Level: A Comparison," in *National Integration and Violent Conflict in Post-Soviet Societies: The Cases of Estonia and Moldova*, ed. Pål Kolstø (Lanham, MD: Rowman & Littlefield, 2002), 31–70; Orest Subtelny, "Russocentrism, Regionalism, and the Political Culture of Ukraine" in *Political Culture and Civil Society in Russia and the New States of Eurasia*, ed. Vladmir Tismăneanu (Armonk, NY: M.E. Sharpe, 1995), 189–207; Anu Realo and Jüri Allik, "A Cross-Cultural Study of Collectivism: A Comparison of American, Estonian, and Russian Students," *The Journal of Social Psychology* 139, no. 2 (April 1999): 133–42.

5. On the rule of law see Martin Krygier, Adam Czarnota and Wojciech Sadur-ski, eds., *Rethinking the Rule of Law in Post-communist Europe: Past Legacies, Institutional Innovations, and Constitutional Discourses* (Budapest: CEU Press, 2005). On the economic aspect of the "transformation" see Kazimierz Z. Poznanski, "Building capitalism with communist tools: Eastern Europe's defective transformation," *East European Politics and Societies* 15, no. 2 (Spring 2001): 320–37; Ross E. Burkhart, "Economic Freedom and Democracy: Post-Cold War Tests," *European Journal of Political Research* 37, no. 2 (March 2000): 237–53; Thilo Bodenstein and Gerald Schneider, "Capitalist Junctures: Explaining Economic Openness in the Transition Countries," *European Journal of Political Research* 45, no. 3 (May 2006): 467–97; Karl C. Kaltenthaler, Ste-phen J. Ceccoli, and Andrew Michta, "Explaining Individual-Level Support for Privatization in European Post-Soviet Economies," *European Journal of Politi-cal Research* 45, no. 1 (January 2006): 1–29; Marcus A. G. Harper, "Economic

Voting in Postcommunist Eastern Europe," *Comparative Political Studies* 33, no. 9 (2000): 1191–227; Byong-Kuen Jhee, "Economic Origins of Electoral Support for Authoritarian Successors: A Cross-National Analysis of Economic Voting in New Democracies," *Comparative Political Studies* 41, no. 3 (March 2008): 362–88. For the initial support for democracy (1990–1992), stronger in Lithuania among both urban and rural dwellers, than in Ukraine and Russia, where city inhabitants were more pro-democratic than the villagers, according to opinion polls, see William M. Reisinger, Arthur H. Miller, Vicki L. Hesli, and Kristen H. Maher, "Political Values in Russia, Ukraine and Lithuania: Sources and Implications for Democracy," *British Journal of Political Science* 24, no. 2 (1994): 183–223. But see also Lars Johannsen, "The Foundations of the State: Emerging Urban-Rural Cleavages in Transition Countries," *Communist and Post-Communist Studies* 36, no. 3, (2003): 291–309. More on public attitudes see Richard B. Dobson and Steven A. Grant, "Public Opinion and the Transformation of the Soviet Union," *International Journal of Public Opinion Research* 4, no. 4 (Winter 1992): 302–20; Arthur H. Miller, Vicki L. Hesli, and William M. Reisinger, "Conceptions of Democracy among Mass and Elite Post-Soviet Societies," *British Journal of Political Science* 27, no. 2 (April 1997): 157–90; Arthur H. Miller, Vicki L. Hesli, and William M. Reisinger, "Public Behavior and Political Change in Post-Soviet States," *The Journal of Politics* 57, no. 4 (November 1995): 941–70; Arthur H. Miller, Vicki L. Hesli, and William M. Reisinger, "Comparing Citizen and Elite Belief Systems in Post-Soviet Russia and Ukraine," *Public Opinion Quarterly* 59, no. 1 (Spring 1995): 1–40; Richard Smoke, ed., *Perceptions of Security: Public Opinion and Expert Assessments in Europe's New Democracies* (New York: Manchester University Press, 1996); Martin Aberg and Mikael Sandberg, *Social Capital and Democratisation: Roots of Trust in Post-Communist Poland and Ukraine* (Burlington, VT: Ashgate, 2003).

6.   See Georges Mink and Jean-Charles Szurek, "Adaptation Strategies of the Former Communist Elites," in *The Political Analysis of Postcommunism: Understanding Postcommunist Ukraine*, ed. Volodymyr Polokhalo (College Station, TX: Texas A&M University Press, 1997), 197–204; Kazimierz Z. Poznanski, "Building Capitalism with Communist Tools: Eastern Europe's Defective Transformation," *East European Politics and Societies* 15, no. 2 (Spring 2001): 320–37; Anton Steen and Juri Ruus, "Change of Regime – Continuity of Elites? The Case of Estonia," *East European Politics and Societies* 16, no. 1 (Spring 2001): 223–27; Andrew Konitzer-Smirnov, "Serving Different Masters: Regional Executives and Accountability in Ukraine and Russia," *Europe-Asia Studies* 57, no. 1 (January 2005): 3–33; Renske Doorenspleet, "The Structural Context of Recent Transitions to Democracy," *European Journal of Political Research* 43, no. 3 (May 2004): 309–35; Klaus Armingeon and Romana Careja, "Institutional Change and Stability in Postcommunist Countries, 1990–2002," *European Journal of Political Research* 47, no. 4 (June 2008): 436–66; Jan Pakulski, "Poland and Ukraine: Elite Transformation and Prospects for Democracy," *Journal of Ukrainian Studies* 20, no. 1–2 (Summer–Winter 1995): 195–208. And compare with Andrew Barnes, "Comparative Theft: Context and Choice in the Hungarian, Czech, and Russian Transformations, 1989–2000," *East European Politics and Societies* 17, no. 3 (Summer 2003): 533–65; Catalin Augustin Soica, "From Good Communists to Even Better Capitalists? Entrepreneurial Pathways in Post-Socialist Romania," *East European Politics and Societies* 18, no. 2 (Spring 2004): 236–78; Roger Schoenman, "Captains or Pirates? State-Business

Relations in Post-Socialist Poland," *East European Politics and Societies* 19, no. 1 (Winter 2005): 40–76.

7. For the intellectual sources of nihilism and moral relativism see William F. Buckley, Jr., *God and Man at Yale: The Superstitions of "Academic Freedom"* (Chicago: Henry Regnery Company, 1951); Roger Kimball, *Tenured Radicals: How Politics Has Corrupted Our Higher Education* (Chicago, IL: Elephant Paperbacks, 1998); Alan Bloom, *The Closing of the American Mind: How Higher Education Has Failed Democracy and Impoverished The Souls of Today's Students* (New York: Simon and Schuster, 1987); Dinesh D'Souza, *The Illiberal Education: The Politics of Race and Sex on Campus* (New York and Toronto: The Free Press, 1991); R. V. Young, *At War With the Word: Literary Theory and Liberal Education* (Wilmington, DE: ISI Books, 1999); Hilton Kramer and Roger Kimball, eds., *The Future of the European Past* (Chicago: Ivan R. Dee, 1997); Keith Windschuttle, *The Killing of History: How Literary Critics and Social Theorists are Murdering Our Past* (San Francisco: Encounter Books, 2000); Gertrude Himmelfarb, *The De-Moralization of Society: From Victorian Virtues to Modern Values* (New York: Alfred A. Knopf, 1995); Thomas Sowell, *The Vision of the Anointed: Self-Congratulation as a Basis for Social Policy* (New York: Basic Books, 1995); Robert H. Bork, *Slouching Towards Gomorrah: Modern Liberalism and American Decline* (New York: Regan Books, 1996); Digby Anderson, ed., *The Loss of Virtue: Moral Confusion and Social Disorder in Britain and America* (New York: The Social Affairs Unit and a National Review Book, 1992); Paul Edward Gottfried, *The Strange Death of Marxism: The European Left in the New Millennium* (Columbia and London: University of Missouri Press, 2005). For the worrisome implications of Western intellectual heresies in the post-Soviet sphere, including Russia itself, see, e.g., Tomasz Sommer and Marek Jan Chodakiewicz, "Average Joe: The Return of Stalinist Apologists," *World Affairs: A Journal of Ideas and Debate* (January/February 2011): 75–82.

8. See Marek Cichocki, "New Countries, Old Myths: A Central European Appeal for an Expansion of European Understanding," *Intermarium* 12, no. 2 (2008–2009): http://www.columbia.edu/cu/ece/research/intermarium/vol12/NewCountries.pdf; Kenneth Christie, *Historical Injustice and Democratic Transition in Eastern Asia and Northern Europe: Ghosts at the Table of Democracy* (London: RoutledgeCurzon, 2002); Will Kymlicka and Magda Opalski, eds., *Can Liberal Pluralism Be Exported? Western Political Theory and Ethnic Relations in Eastern Europe* (Oxford: Oxford University Press, 2001); Rachel A. Epstein, *In Pursuit of Liberalism: International Institutions in Postcommunist Europe* (Baltimore, MD: Johns Hopkins University Press, 2008); Alex Pravda and Jan Zielonka, eds., *International Influences on Democratic Transition in Central and Eastern Europe* (Oxford: Oxford University Press, 2001).

9. See Rafał Ziemkiewicz, *Michnikowszczyzna: Zapis choroby* (*Michnikitis: A Record of Illness*) (Warszawa: Red Horse, 2006). The title is a clever pun on a Communist slogan reflecting the penchant to brand a deviation from the party line after a leading comrade accused of such a transgression, in this instance the leading post-Trotskyite Adam Michnik.

10. See Kimitaka Matsuzato, "Differing Dynamics of Semipresidentialism across Euro/Eurasian Borders: Ukraine, Lithuania, Poland, Moldova, and Armenia," *Demokratizatsiya: The Journal of Post-Soviet Democratization* 14, no. 3 (Summer 2006): 317–46; John T. Ishiyama and Ryan Kennedy, "Superpresidentialism and Political Party Development in Russia, Ukraine, Armenia and Kyrgyzstan," *Europe-Asia Studies* 53, no. 8 (December 2001): 1177–91.

11. See John P. Robinson, Ted Robert Gurr, Erjan Kurbanov, Stephen McHale, and Ivan Slepenkov, "Ethnonationalist and Political Attitudes among Post-Soviet Youth: The Case of Russia and Ukraine," *Political Science and Politics* 26, no. 3 (September 1993): 516–21; Ellen Carnaghan and Richard Rose, "Generational Effects on Attitudes to Communist Regimes: A Comparative Analysis," *Post-Soviet Affairs* 11, no. 1 (January–March 1995): 28–56; Viktoriya Topalova, "In Search of Heroes: Cultural Politics and Political Mobilization of Youths in Contemporary Russia and Ukraine," *Demokratizatsiya: The Journal of Post-Soviet Democratization* 14, no. 1 (Winter 2006): 23–41.

12. See Andrey A. Meleshevich, *Party Systems in Post-Soviet Countries: A Comparative Study of Political Institutionalization in the Baltic States, Russia, and Ukraine* (New York: Palgrave Macmillan, 2007), in particular Chapter 7: "The Role of the Old Communist Elites during the Formative Stage of the Party System," 115–37. See also Anatoly Kulik and Susanna Pshizova, eds., *Political Parties in Post-Soviet Space: Russia, Belarus, Ukraine, Moldova, and the Baltics* (Westport, CT and London: Praeger Publishers, 2005).

13. Józef Darski [Jerzy Targalski], "Police Agents in the Transition Period," *Uncaptive Minds* 4, no. 4 (18) (Winter 1991/1992): 27–28; Jerzy Targalski aka [Józef Darski] interviewed by Łukasz Wiater, "W systemie sowieckim agenturalność jest dziedziczna, a w post-komuniźmie zapewnia karierę," ("In the Soviet System Being an Agent Is Inherited, and in Post-Communism It Facilitates a Career") March 12, 2011, http://www.portal.arcana.pl/W-systemie-sowieckim-agenturalnosc-jest-dziedziczna-a-w-postkomunizmie-zapewnia-kariere,910.html and http://portal.arcana.salon24.pl/286650,targalski-w-postkomunizmie-agenturalnosc-zapewnia-kariere.

14. See John T. Ishiyama, ed., *Communist Successor Parties in Post-Communist Politics* (Hauppauge, NY: Nova Science Publishers, 1999), and its next edition: András Bozóki and John T. Ishiyama, eds., *The Communist Successor Parties of Central and Eastern Europe* (Armonk, NY: M.E. Sharpe, 2002); John T. Ishiyama, "The Communist Successor Parties and Party Organizational Development in Post-Communist Politics," *Political Research Quarterly* 52, no. 1 (March 1999): 87–112; and Eitan Tzelgov, "Communist Successor Parties and Government Survival in Central Eastern Europe," *European Journal of Political Research* 50, no. 4 (June 2011): 530–58.

15. Paul Taggart and Aleks Szczerbiak, "Contemporary Euroskepticism in the Party Systems of the European Union Candidate States of Central and Eastern Europe," *European Journal of Political Research* 43, no. 1 (January 2004): 1–27. But see Ainius Lasas, "Guilt, Sympathy, and Cooperation: EU-Baltic Relations in Early 1990s," *East European Politics and Societies* 22, no. 2 (Spring 2008): 347–72.

16. For a rather typical rant on how "the Jews" took over Ukraine, in particular its banks and media (having earlier, "of course," subjected it to Communist terror, including the collectivization), see Vladimir Borisov, "Who Controls the [sic] Ukraine," [November 2005?], http://iamthewitness.com/Ukraine.html.

17. For a single case see Aleksej Semjonov, "Estonia: Nation-building and Integration – Political and Legal Aspects," in *National Integration and Violent Conflict in Post-Soviet Societies: The Cases of Estonia and Moldova*, ed. Pål Kolstø (Lanham, MD: Rowman & Littlefield, 2002), 105–58. See further Taras Kuzio, *Soviet and Post-Soviet Politics and Society: Theoretical and Comparative Perspectives on Nationalism* (Stuttgart and Hannover: Ibidem-Verlag, 2007); Andrew Wilson, *Ukrainian Nationalism in the 1990s: A Minority Faith* (Cambridge: Cambridge

University Press, 1997); Peter F. Sugar, ed., *Eastern European Nationalism in the Twentieth Century* (Washington, DC: The American University Press, 1995); Luciano Cheles, Ronnie Ferguson, and Michalina Vaughan, eds., *The Far Right in Western and Eastern Europe* (London and New York: Longman 1995); Paul Hockenos, *Free to Hate: The Rise of the Right in Post-Communist Eastern Europe* (New York and London: Routledge, 1994); Tore Bjorgo and Rob Witte, *Racist Violence in Europe* (London and New York: St. Martin's Press, 1994); Geoffrey Harris, *The Dark Side of Europe: The Extreme Right Today* (Edinburgh: Edinburgh University Press, 1994).

18.   See Lars Johannsen and Ole Nørgaard, "Governance in Central and Eastern Europe: A Cross-Sectional Perspective: How the EU Accession Broke Institutional Path Dependencies in Post-Communist Regimes," Paper prepared for the 12th NISPAcee Annual Conference: "Central and Eastern European Countries Inside and Outside the European Union: Avoiding a New Divide," Vilnius, Lithuania, May 13–15, 2004, pp. 1–18, http://www.demstar.dk/papers/Vilnius2004JohannsenNorgaard.pdf. The authors have based themselves upon a study of the elite of fifteen post-Communist successor states. To appreciate how the accession to the EU coddles the post-Communists as far as the law, by completely overlooking their persistence in political and economic power as a legal issue, see Andreas Bågenholm, "Understanding Governmental Legislative Capacity: Harmonization of EU legislation in Lithuania and Romania," Department of Political Science, University of Gothenburg (2008): 1–192, http://gupea.ub.gu.se/bitstream/2077/18372/1/gupea_2077_18372_1.pdf.

19.   Mikko Lagerspetz, "Post-Socialist Transformations as Identity Transformations," in *Political Culture: Values and Identities in the Baltic Sea Region*, ed. Sten Berglund, Bernd Henningsen, and Mai-Brith Schartau (Berlin: Berliner Wissenschafts-Verlag, 2006), 13–22. See also Mark Cichock, "Transitionalism vs. Transnationalism: Conflicting Trends in Independent Latvia," *East European Politics and Societies* 16, no. 2 (Spring 2001): 446–65.

20.   See Will Kymlicka and Magda Opalski, eds., *Can Liberal Pluralism Be Exported? Western Political Theory and Ethnic Relations in Eastern Europe* (Oxford: Oxford University Press, 2001); Rachel A. Epstein, *In Pursuit of Liberalism: International Institutions in Postcommunist Europe* (Baltimore, MD: Johns Hopkins University Press, 2008); Alex Pravda and Jan Zielonka, eds., *International Influences on Democratic Transition in Central and Eastern Europe* (Oxford: Oxford University Press, 2001); Bernd Rechel, ed., *Minority Rights in Central and Eastern Europe* (London: Routledge, 2009).

21.   See Wolfgang Rüdig, "Is Government Good for Greens? Comparing the Electoral Effects of Government Participation in Western and East-Central Europe," *European Journal of Political Research* 45, Supplement S1 (October 2006): S127–54. On the nexus between environmentalism and nationalism see Katrina Z. S. Schwartz, "'The Occupation of Beauty': Imagining Nature and Nation in Latvia," *East European Politics and Societies* 21, no. 2 (Spring 2007): 259–93. For comparison with Poland see Marek Jan Chodakiewicz, "An Environmental Battleground: Eco-Politics in Poland," in *Managing the Environment: An East European Perspective*, ed. O.P. Dwivedi and Joseph G. Jabrra (Willowdale, ON: de Sitter, 1995), 64–90.

22.   See Gordon Waitt, "Sexual Citizenship in Latvia: Geographies of the Latvian Closet," *Social & Cultural Geography* 6 no. 2 (April 2005): 161–81; Laura Sheeter, "Latvia Defies the EU over Gay Rights," *BBC News* (June 16, 2006): http://news.bbc.co.uk/2/hi/europe/5084832.stm; Aleks Tapinsh, "Homophobic Attitudes

Remain Entrenched," *East of Center: Daily Arts, Culture, Politics, Media, Law & Order, Society, Economics & Business, from Transitions' Editors, Transitions Online: Regional Intelligence,* (June 4, 2007): http://www.tol.org/client/article/18756-homophobic-attitudes-remain-entrenched.html. Elsewhere in the Intermarium, the gay community does not even contemplate marriage. It is not permitted to march openly. In 2008 in Moldova, gay pride bus riders were met with threats of violence. In 2011 in Chişinău and Bălţi Orthodox clergy led the faithful in numerous anti-gay actions. The Orthodox Church consistently opposes gay rights. In Bălţi the Communist-dominated city council even voted to ban "homosexual propaganda," which meant that in practice gays were barred from the municipality. Gay pride parades remain forbidden. See Piotr Kościński, "Bielce – miasto bez gejów," ("Bălţi: A Town with no Gays"), *Rzeczpospolita,* 25 February 2012, posted at http://www.rp.pl/artykul/828648.html; Matthew Jenkin, "Moldova city bans 'gay propaganda,'" *Gay Star News,* February 24, 2012, posted at http://www.gaystarnews.com/article/moldova-city-bans-gay-propaganda; Christopher Brocklebank, "Anti-discrimination bill in Moldova being challenged by Orthodox Church," *Pink News: Europe's Largest Gay Newsservice,* April 9, 2012, posted at http://www.pinknews.co.uk/2012/04/09/anti-discrimination-bill-in-moldova-being-challenged-by-orthodox-church; Tony Grew, "Police look on as fascists attack gays at Moldova's banned Pride," *Pink News: Europe's Largest Gay Newsservice,* May 8, 2012, posted at http://www.pinknews.co.uk/2008/05/12/police-look-on-as-fascists-attack-gays-at-moldovas-banned-pride/.

23. Ukrainian feminists have developed a tactic of naked attacks. In November 2010, the Ukrainian activists of Femen stormed, half-naked, into an Iranian cultural center to object an impending execution of a Persian woman for adultery. In October 2010 they marched bare-chested to protest Putin's visit to their country. In July 2010, they stripped publicly to oppose sex tourism. In February 2010, they burst half-naked into a polling station to express their outrage at business as usual in politics. See "Half naked women of feminist group Femen protest Ukrainian election," (February 8, 2010), http://www.whatsonxiamen.com/news10195.html; André Eichhofer, "Students Fight Prostitution in Ukraine," *Der Spiegel* (July 30, 2010): http://www.spiegel.de/international/europe/0,1518,639246,00.html; "Naked Feminists to Putin: 'We Are Not Thrahnesh,'" *Zhizn na Ukraine* (October 28, 2010): http://www.promes.org/en/s59/5996.html; "Topless Ukrainian Feminists Storm Iranian 'Cultural Event' to Protest Planned Stoning," *The Blaze* (November 15, 2010): http://www.theblaze.com/stories/topless-ukrainian-feminists-storm-iranian-cultural-event-to-protest-planned-stoning/. On the problems of women in the Intermarium in a more scholarly vein see Scott D. Orr, "Identity and Civil Society in Latvia, Poland, and Ukraine: Women's NGOs," *East European Politics and Societies* 22, no. 4 (Fall 2008): 856–79; Alexandra Hrycak, "Foundation Feminism and the Articulation of Hybrid Feminism in Post-Socialist Ukraine," *East European Politics and Societies* 20, no. 1 (Winter 2006): 68–101; Alexandra Hrycak, "Coping with Chaos: Gender and Politics in a Fragmented State," *Problems of Post-Communism* 52, no. 5 (September–October 2005): 69–81; Vicki L. Hesli and Arthur H. Miller, "The Gender Base of Institutional Support in Lithuania, Ukraine and Russia," *Europe-Asia Studies* 45, no. 3 (1993): 505–32; Solomea Pavlychko, "Between Feminism and Nationalism: New Women's Groups in the Ukraine," in *Perestroika and Soviet Women,* ed. Mary Buckley (Cambridge: Cambridge University Press, 1992), 82–96; Solomea Pavlychko, "Feminism and Post-Communist Ukrainian Society," in *Women in*

Russia and Ukraine, ed. and trans. Rosalind Marsh (Cambridge: Cambridge University Press, 1996), 305–14; and the following two essays in Mary Buckley, ed., *Post-Soviet Women: From the Baltic to Central Asia,* ed. Mary Buckley (Cambridge: Cambridge University Press, 1997): Nijole White, "Women in Changing Societies: Latvia and Lithuania," (203–18), and Solomea Pavlychko, "Progress on Hold: The Conservative Faces of Women in Ukraine," (219–34).

24.　See Georges Mink and Jean-Charles Szurek, "Adaptation Strategies of the Former Communist Elites," in *The Political Analysis of Postcommunism: Understanding Postcommunist Ukraine,* ed. Volodymyr Polokhalo (College Station, TX: Texas A&M University Press, 1997), 197–204. On graft, in general, see Ase B. Grodeland, Tatyana Y. Koshechkina, and William L. Miller, "'Foolish to Give and Yet More Foolish Not to Take': In-depth Interviews with Post-Communist Citizens on Their Everyday Use of Bribes and Contacts," *Europe-Asia Studies* 50, no. 4 (June 1998): 651–77; Alexandru Grigorescu, "The Corruption Eruption in East-Central Europe: The Increased Salience of Corruption and the Role of Intergovernmental Organizations," *East European Politics and Societies* 20, no. 3 (Summer 2006): 516–40. On the Baltics see Karin Hilmer Pedersen and Lars Johannsen, "The Talk of the Town: Comparing Corruption in the Baltic States and Poland," in *Political Culture: Values And Identities In The Baltic Sea Region,* ed. Sten Berglund, Bernd Henningsen, and Mai-Brith Schartau (Berlin: Berliner Wissenschafts-Verlag, 2006), 117–34; David J. Galbreath, "Still 'Treading Air'? Looking at the Post-Enlargement Challenges to Democracy in the Baltic States," *Demokratizatsiya: The Journal of Post-Soviet Democratization* 16, no. 1 (Winter 2008): 87–96; Mel Huang, "Wannabe Oligarchs: Tycoons & Influence in the Baltic States," Defense Academy of the United Kingdom, Conflict Studies Research Centre, Central and East European Series Publication, G111 (May 2002): 1–11, http://www.da.mod.uk/colleges/arag/document-listings/cee/G85. On oligarchic corruption in Ukraine see Ararat L. Osipian, "Political Graft and Education Corruption in Ukraine: Compliance, Collusion, and Control," *Demokratizatsiya: The Journal of Post-Soviet Democratization* 16, no. 4 (Fall 2008): 323–44; Taras Kuzio, "Ukrainian Economic Policy after the Orange Revolution: A Commentary on Åslund's Analysis," *Eurasian Geography and Economics* 46, no. 5 (2005): 354–63; Andrew Konitzer-Smirnov, "Serving Different Masters: Regional Executives and Accountability in Ukraine and Russia," *Europe-Asia Studies* 57, no. 1 (January 2005): 3–33; Valentyn Yakushyk, James Mace, and Kostiyantyn Maleyev, "Corruption as a Political Phenomenon under Communism," in *The Political Analysis of Postcommunism: Understanding Postcommunist Ukraine,* ed. Volodymyr Polokhalo (College Station, TX: Texas A&M University Press, 1997), 163–76. On some legal and logistical problems prosecuting the mafia in the post-Soviet sphere see George Ginsburgs, *The Soviet Union and International Cooperation in Legal Matters* (Norwell, MA, and Dordrecht, the Netherlands: Martinus Nijhoff Publishers and Kluwer Academic Publishers, 1994), 281–323, which is Chapter VI: "Russia and the Successor States." See also David Satter, *Age of Delirium: The Decline and Fall of the Soviet Union* (New Haven, CT and London: Yale University Press, 2001); David Satter, *Darkness at Dawn: The Rise of the Russian Criminal State* (New Haven, CT and London: Yale University Press, 2003); Arkady Vaksberg, *The Soviet Mafia* (New York: St. Martin's Press, 1991); Federico Varese, *The Russian Mafia: Private Protection in a New Market Economy* (New York: Oxford University, 2001, 2nd ed. 2005); Stephen Handelman, *Comrade Criminal: Russia's New Mafiya* (New Haven, CT: Yale University Press, 1995); Paul Klebnikov,

Godfather of the Kremlin: Boris Berezovsky and the Looting of Russia (New York: Harcourt, Inc., 2000); Marek Jan Chodakiewicz, "Czekiści, mafia i państwo" ("The Chekists, Mafia, and the State") *Tygodnik Solidarność* (August 6, 2010).

25.   Ukraine's wealthiest oligarch, Rinat Akhmetov (worth over $30 billion in 2008), supports the Russofile post-Communists of eastern Ukraine headed by current president Viktor Yanukovich of the Party of Regions. However, the billionaire Sergey Taruta opposes him. Another tycoon, Viktor Pinchuk ($8.8 billion), who is the son-in-law of former President Leonid Kuchma, got himself elected as a parliamentary deputy, straddled the fence between the "easterners" and "westerners," and, finally, retreated into privacy after the Orange Revolution. Yulia Tymoshenko, one of the leading political contenders, herself emerged from the kleptocratic milieu. In one of her more controversial moves as prime minister, Tymoshenko stripped Pinchuk of a business and helped resell it, which reaped a profit of several billion dollars to benefit other oligarchs, including investment banker Igor Kolomoyski ($6.6 billion), who, in 2005, thus switched sides, dropping post-Communist Yanukovich and shifting his support to Tymoshenko. This and other shady deals served as handy excuses to land her in jail in 2011. President Yanukovych decided to square his account with her under the pretext of having personally benefited from (or abused power during) a disastrous energy agreement with Russia in 2009; a tender for medical vehicles; and carbon credits. Tymoshenko is no stranger to political vendetta. She did a brief stint in jail under President Kuchma in 2001. See James Marson, "Trials and Tribulations in Ukraine," *Business New Europe* (June 27, 2011): http://www.bne. eu/story2754/Trials_and_tribulations_in_Ukraine; Stefan Wagstyl and Roman Oleachyk, "Ukraine Election Divides Oligarchs," *Financial Times* (January 15, 2010): http://www.ft.com/cms/s/0/ab42016a-0174-11df-8c54-00144feabdc0. ht#axzz1B2FScxPm; Taras Kuzio, "Oligarchs Wield Power in Ukrainian Politics," *Eurasia Daily Monitor* 5, no. 125 (July 1, 2008): http://www.jamestown. org/single/?no_cache=1&tx_ttnews%5Btt_news%5D=33765; Judy Dempsey, "Ukraine's Dance of the Oligarchs," *The New York Times* (December 23, 2005): http://www.nytimes.com/2005/12/23/business/worldbusiness/23iht-wbolig. html; Helen Fawkes, "Ukraine Fears the Rise of New Oligarchs," *BBC News* (June 23, 2005): http://news.bbc.co.uk/2/hi/business/4114342.stm. By comparison, the "oligarchs" of the Baltics appear puny. Take, for example, Andris Šķēle, who served twice as prime minister (1995–1997, 1999–2000). His worth is estimated barely at 60 million Euros. Initially "non-party", Šķēle founded his own Popular (or People's) Party in 1998. He resigned his office in 2000 and, subsequently, party membership in 2003 because of the allegations of corruption. However, in 2009, Šķēle returned to active politics. See "Šķēle Back as a Leader of People's Party," *The Baltic Times* (October 15, 2009): http://www.baltictimes.com/news/ articles/23705/. See also Mel Huang, "Wannabe Oligarchs: Tycoons & Influence in the Baltic States," Defense Academy of the United Kingdom, Conflict Studies Research Centre, Central and East European Series Publication, G111 (May 2002): 1–11, http://www.da.mod.uk/colleges/arag/document-listings/ cee/G85.

26.   For a solid discussion of the issue of corruption and overlap between business, mafia, and secret services, by The Organized Crime and Corruption Reporting Project (OCCRP), see "The Proxy Platform," http://www.reportingproject. net/proxy/ and http://www.reportingproject.net/proxy/the-proxy-platform. Most of the illicit business cases discussed stem from Russia, but the focus is on Moldova. The culprits have established presence (mostly for money laundering)

as far afield as New Zealand, Vietnam, Latin America, the United States, and the EU, the Baltics in particular but also the UK. Some stories also touch upon the murder of Sergei Magnitskii, a Russian whistle blower who died while in police custody after discovering the involvement of Russia's secret servicemen in a tax fraud and corporate scam crime. On Russia see "Russian Laundering Machine," http://www.reportingproject.net/proxy/russian-laundering-machine; "The Invisible Empire of the Diplomat," http://www.reportingproject.net/proxy/the-invisible-empire-of-the-diplomat; "Tormex Users: A Proxy World," http://www.reportingproject.net/proxy/tormex-users-a-proxy-world; "Death of a Lawyer," http://www.reportingproject.net/proxy/death-of-a-lawyer. On Latvia see "Latvian Bank Woes," http://www.reportingproject.net/proxy/latvian-bank-woes; "Laundering at a Family Bank," http://www.reportingproject.net/proxy/laundering-at-a-family-bank. On Moldova see "Opening the Door: Proxy Platform Revealed," http://www.reportingproject.net/proxy/opening-the-door-proxy-platform-revealed; "The Phantom Accounts," http://www.reportingproject.net/proxy/the-phantom-accounts; "The Money Carousel," http://www.reportingproject.net/proxy/the-money-carousel; "Slum Millionaire: The Moldovan Proxy," http://www.reportingproject.net/proxy/slum-millionaire-the-moldovan-proxy; and "Money from Moldova," http://www.reportingproject.net/proxy/money-from-moldova. For a legal take at the international level see "Laws Still Needed to Combat Laundering," http://www.reportingproject.net/proxy/laws-still-needed-to-combat-laundering. For the mafia-political class nexus at the highest level see Taras Kuzio, "Yanukovych Provides a Krysha for Organized Crime," *Eurasia Daily Monitor* 9, no. 34 (17 February 2012), posted at http://www.jamestown.org/single/?no_cache=1&tx_ttnews%5Btt_news%5D=39024&tx_ttnews%5BbackPid%5D=7&cHash=692b e4a3bb7db2b91eae3373c738437e. For a brief historical essay on the nexus of the state and the criminal underworld in Russia see Marek Jan Chodakiewicz, "Wolność i patologia a Rosja (część 1)," ("Freedom and pathology and Russia [part 1]") *Najwyższy Czas!*, 16 June 2012, XXXIV–XXXV; Marek Jan Chodakiewicz, "Wolność i patologia a Rosja (część 2)," ("Freedom and pathology and Russia [part 2]") *Najwyższy Czas!*, 23 June 2012, XXXIV–XXXV.

27.   The problem of the Communist and post-Communist secret services has been seriously understudied. We know practically next to nothing about Belarus and Ukraine. One leading expert on the Baltics claims that as late as 1991, the Lithuanian KGB force of about 1,200 officers ran approximately 6,000 secret agents. Latvia's KGB employed 564 Chekists who controlled about 4,300 informers. Lithuania's population was about 3 million, while Latvia's stood at 2.7 million (including approximately 1.4 ethnic Latvians). Thus, the proportion of the agents to the citizens was similar in both countries. See Jerzy Targalski aka [Józef Darski] interviewed by Łukasz Wiater, "W systemie sowieckim agenturalność jest dziedziczna, a w post-komunizmie zapewnia karierę," ("In the Soviet System Being an Agent Is Inherited, and in Post-Communism it Facilitates a Career") (March 12 2011): http://www.portal.arcana.pl/W-systemie-sowieckim-agenturalnosc-jest-dziedziczna-a-w-postkomunizmie-zapewnia-kariere,910.html and http://portal.arcana.salon24.pl/286650,targalski-w-postkomunizmie-agenturalnosc-zapewnia-kariere. Aside from the sources listed below, the following is culled from interviews with intelligence professionals and other experts on the area who would like to remain anonymous.

28.   In 2012, a former Soviet militiamen, Alexei Dressen, who served at the top of free Estonia's secret services, was caught, along with his wife Viktoria, passing

classified information to Russia. See Marek Jan Chodakiewicz, "Estońskie szpiegowanie," ("Estonian spying") *Tygodnik Solidarność*, March 9, 2012; Jari Tanner, "Estonians held on allegations of spying for Russia," Associated Press, February 22, 2012; David Mardiste, "Estonia shaken by a new Russian spy scandal," February 22, 2012. A high-ranking Estonian defense official, Herman Simm, who was the head counterintelligence officer for the Defense Ministry, was sentenced for spying for Russia in 2009. He commenced carrying out tasks for the SVR in 1995, apparently re-recruited through a combination of bribes and blackmail. However, his ties to the KGB date back to 1966. He was a Communist party member and a secret policeman, a graduate of the elite Interior Ministry Academy of the USSR. He reached the rank of a colonel. During the fight for independence, Simm apparently switched sides, although some perceived him as still aiding the Soviets. He served as the nation's top policeman. Eventually, he was drummed out of the service for corruption. Simm then contacted, or was contacted by, his old handlers. Yet, his background somehow failed to raise a red flag for over a decade. What happened to Putin's favorite adage: "Once a Chekist, Always a Chekist"? See Fidelius Schmid and Andreas Ulrich, "New Documents Reveal Truth on Nato's 'Most Damaging' spy," *Der Spiegel* (April 30, 2010): http://www.spiegel.de/international/europe/0,1518,691817,00.html; "Estonian Spy Sold Nato Secrets," *BBC News* (February 25, 2009): http://news. bbc.co.uk/2/hi/7910814.stm; Roger Boyes, "Russian Spy in Nato Could Have Passed Missile Defence and Cyber-War Secrets," *Times on Line* (November 16, 2008): http://www.timesonline.co.uk/tol/news/world/europe/article5166227. ece; "How Many More? A Senior Russian Spy in NATO Is Convicted," *Economist* (February 28 2009): http://www.economist.com/node/13184989?story_id=13184989.

29. Exceptionally, the Vilnius KGB archives escaped destruction to a large extent. See "Maciej Siekierski and Richard Sousa, "Agents of History," *Hoover Digest* no. 1 (Winter 2010): 155–59. Riga and Tallinn's KGB documentary legacy is partly accessible to selected scholars. The Minsk KGB archives are inaccessible at all as are the ones in Chișinău, while the Kyiv KGB documentary depositories have just been re-sealed by the newly elected post-Communist government. For the best-known case of KGB and GRU files landing in the West's lap see Christopher Andrew and Vasili Mitrokhin, *The Mitrokhin Archive: The KGB in Europe and the West* (London and New York: Allen Lane and The Penguin Press, 1999); Christopher Andrew and Vasili Mitrokhin, *The World Was Going Our Way: KGB and the Battle for the Third World* (New York: Basic Books, 2005). It is much less known that the CIA acquired the Stasi archive.

30. Lithuania's Virgilius Cepaitis ("Juozas") of Sąjūdis was one of the first prominent activists to be exposed. See N. Lashkevich, "The passions over KGB agent known as 'Juozas," *The Current Digest of Post-Soviet Press* 43, no. 48 (1 January 1992): 16–17.

31. In 1994, Lithuania's prime minister and Latvia's foreign minister were forced to resign after their ties to the KGB became known. Kazimiera Pruskine ("Shatri"), reported on her foreign contacts. Georgs Andrejevs ("Ziedonis"), was one of the very few to confess; he was recruited in 1963 to inform on his friends and co-workers. See Matt Bivens, "Wanted Alive: Ex-KGB Agents and Informers Baltic States Hunt Down Former Soviet Operatives with a Vengeance: Already, a Prime Minister and a Foreign Minister Have Been Toppled," *The Los Angeles Times* (August 2, 1994): http://articles.latimes.com/1994-08-02/news/wr-22515_1_prime-minister. The Latvians are arguably most serious of all Balts

about the lustration. They have vetted at least some of their politicians and revealed the names of some 4,500 informers. See "Latvia to Disclose the Names of Former KGB Agents March 1, 2007," *RIA Novosti* (October 26, 2006): http://www.globalsecurity.org/intell/library/news/2006/intell-061026-rianovosti01. htm. At the time, the Estonians, who lag far behind, published only thirty-two names of former KGB informers. However, in congruence with the amnesty law, 1,153 had people turned themselves in as former KGB agents by April 1, 1996. Their names remain confidential. See Aadu Oll, "Estonia: Toward Post-Communist Reconstruction," in *Dismantling Tyranny: Transitioning beyond Totalitarian Regimes*, ed. Illan Berman and J. Michael Waller (Lanham, MD, Boulder, CO, Toronto, and London: Rowman & Littlefield, 2006), 84. For hysterical Islamist allegations about the KGB-FSB operations in Estonia (and one of the reasons why very few serious scholars venture into this particular field of research) see "KGB Agents in Helsinki Tried to Stage Protest against Kavkaz Center," (November 28, 2010), Kavkazcenter.com, http://kavkazcenter. com/eng/content/2010/11/28/12987.shtml.

32. In 1995, former KGB agents-cum-gun runners wiretapped Estonia's prominent politicians, at the behest of Edgar Savisaar, a former Communist *apparatchik*, a participant in the independence drive, a post-Communist, and free Estonia's first prime minister. At the time of the scandal, Savisaar was the Minister of the Interior, in charge of the police. The operation was conducted by the employees of the Security Intelligence Agency (SIA), which was, ostensibly, a private firm owned by two ex-KGB officers. Savisaar ordered his aide, who worked for the SIA at one point, to record sensitive conversations. She did. This was most likely a part of the effort to facilitate secret arms sales. It is unclear whether the undertaking was private business, an SRV (or GRU) operation, or a joint venture between the mafia and post-Soviet secret services. At any event, after Savisaar, at the time a cabinet minister, stonewalled, he was fired by Prime Minister Tiit Vahi, whose government promptly fell as a result of the scandal. See Stephen Kinzer, "Political Wiretapping Scandal Reminds Estonians of Soviet Era," *The New York Times* (October 18, 1995): http://www.nytimes.com/1995/10/18/world/political-wiretapping-scandal-reminds-estonia-of-soviet-era.html. Currently the head of the Center Party (drawing its support heavily from the Russian minority) and the Mayor of Tallinn, Savisaar continues to live dangerously. At the end of 2010, he was accused of accepting money from Vladimir Yakunin, the President of Russian Railways. Savisaar counterclaimed that the money was donated to build an Orthodox church. It is unclear, however, whether the full amount was applied to that worthy goal or whether at least some of the funds were used for political campaigning. At any rate, his detractors charged Savisaar with being "an agent of Russian influence." See "'Truth Commission' Clears Tallinn Mayor of Wrongdoing," ERR News, Estonian Public Broadcasting, (January 6, 2011): http://news.err. ee/politics/60751922-4047-4eb1-be07-b06f0710487d; "Calm after Storms: Austerity Can Sometimes Be Popular. Just Ask the Estonians," *The Economist*, (March 10, 2011): http://www.economist.com/node/18333141. Kaunas's former small time black marketer turned multi-millionaire Vladimir Romanov is another interesting player. He associated with the mafia, including notorious gangster Henrikas Daktaras, and had dealings with ex-KGB men. His business focused on privatization and banking (e.g., Romanov co-founded Ukio bank) at home and other ventures in the post-Soviet sphere and the Balkans (where he owns the Birac aluminum plant in Bosnia-Herzegovina's Republika Srpska).

However, according to his supporters, Romanov turned on his past associates to earn legitimacy and respectability. His detractors accuse him of nefarious and corrupt practices, for example asset stripping at Dirbtinis Pluostas, a Lithuanian textile company Romanov controlled, which went bust after falling in debt to the tune of nearly $100 million USD. In Ukraine he bought privatization vouchers and shares from workers at a pittance. Romanov also clashed with another Russian oligarch with Lithuanian citizenship, Viktor Uspaskich, over Krekenavoi Agrofirma, a meat processing plant both coveted. Most of his business dealings are now abroad; Romanov even purchased a Scottish soccer team. And reportedly he is a religious fellow. For an uncritical profile see Ian Johnston, "How Big Player Took on the Russian Mafia and a KGB Agent: Romanov Unravelled," *The Scotsman* (March 7, 2005): http://sport.scotsman.com/vladimirromanov/How-big-player-took-on.2608473.jp.

33. A few observations on the criminal underworld in Marek Jan Chodakiewicz, "Czekiści, mafia i państwo" (The Chekists, Mafia, and the State) *Tygodnik Solidarność* (August 6, 2010); Marek Jan Chodakiewicz, "Notatki z post-Sowiecji (część I)," (Notes from the Post-Soviet Lands, Part I) *Najwyższy Czas!* (October 9, 2010): XXXV; and Marek Jan Chodakiewicz, "Notatki z post-Sowiecji (część II)," (Notes from the Post-Soviet Lands, Part II) *Najwyższy Czas!* (October 16, 2010): XXXV. And see David Satter, *Darkness at Dawn: The Rise of the Russian Criminal State* (New Haven, CT and London: Yale University Press, 2003); Arkady Vaksberg, *The Soviet Mafia* (New York: St. Martin's Press, 1991); Federico Varese, *The Russian Mafia: Private Protection in a New Market Economy* (New York: Oxford University, 2001, 2nd edn. 2005); Stephen Handelman, *Comrade Criminal: Russia's New Mafiya* (New Haven, CT: Yale University Press, 1995); Paul Klebnikov, *Godfather of the Kremlin: Boris Berezovsky and the Looting of Russia* (New York: Harcourt, Inc., 2000); Misha Glenny, *McMafia: A Journey through the Global Criminal Underworld* (New York: Alfred A. Knopf, 2008).

34. For some insights on the role of religion (and nationalism) see Marek Jan Chodakiewicz, "Notatki z post-Sowiecji (część I)," ("Notes from the Post-Soviet Lands, Part I") *Najwyższy Czas!* (October 9, 2010): XXXV; Marek Jan Chodakiewicz, "Notatki z Post-Sowiecji (część II)," ("Notes from the Post-Soviet Lands, Part II") *Najwyższy Czas!* (October 16, 2010): XXXV; Marek Jan Chodakiewicz, "Notatki z Post-Sowiecji (część III)," ("Notes from the Post-Soviet lands, Part III") *Najwyższy Czas!* (October 23, 2010): XXXV; Marek Jan Chodakiewicz, "Notatki z Post-Sowiecji (część IV)," ("Notes from the Post-Soviet Lands, Part IV") *Najwyższy Czas!* (October 30–November 6, 2010): XLIII; Marek Jan Chodakiewicz, "Rumuno Post-Sowieci," ("Rumanian Post-Soviets") *Tygodnik Solidarność* (May 15, 2009); Marek Jan Chodakiewicz, "Mołdawskość" ("Moldavian Identity") *Tygodnik Solidarność* (July 30, 2010); Marek Jan Chodakiewicz, "Co z Ukrainą," (What about Ukraine?) *Tygodnik Solidarność* (October 22, 2010); Marek Jan Chodakiewicz, "Ni ma jak Lviv?" ("There Ain't Nothing Like Lviv?") *Glaukopis* no. 5–6 (2006): 490–97. See also Otto Luchterhandt, "Die Kollaborationsproblematik im Verhältnis von Religionsgemeinschaften und kommunistischen Einparteistaat (ausgehend vom Fall 'Sowjetunion')," in *"Kollaboration" in Nordosteuropa: Erscheinungsformen und Deutungen im 20. Jahrhundert*, ed. by Joachim Tauber (Wiesbaden: Harrassowitz Verlag, 2006), 443–52.

35. See Father Roman Dzwonkowski, *Polacy na dawnych Kresach Wschodnich: Z problematyki narodowościowej i religijnej* ("Poles in the Former Eastern Borderlands: Nationality and Religion Problems") (Lublin: Oddział Lubelski Wspólnoty

Polskiej, 1994); and Teresa Siedlar-Kołyszko, *Byli, są. Czy będą...?* ("They Were, They Are. Will They Be...?") (Kraków: Oficyna Wydawnicza "Impuls," 2006).

36. See Sophia Senyk, "The Ukrainian Catholic Church Today: Universal Values versus Nationalist Doctrines," *Religion, State & Society* 30, no. 4 (2002): 320–32; Grzegorz Górny, "Dwie Ukrainy," (Two Ukraines) *Rzeczpospolita* (December 3, 2004); Eugeniusz Tuzow-Lubański and Anna Wiejak, "Zagrabione kościoły nie wrócą do właściciela," ("Expropriated Churches Will Not Return to the Owner") *Nasz Dziennik* (August 7, 2008); Mariusz Kamieniecki, "Ukraińcy wolą filharmonię: Sąd administracyjny we Lwowie odrzucił prośbę o zwrot Polakom kościoła rzymskokatolickiej parafii pw. św. Marii Magdaleny," ("The Ukrainians Prefer a Philharmonics: Administrative Court in Lwów Rejected the Request to Return to the Poles the Roman Catholic Church of Marie Magdalen") *Nasz Dziennik* (March 28, 2011).

37. Islamic Human Rights Commission, "Briefing: Moldova's Unoffical [sic unofficial] Muslims," (July 2, 2003): http://www.ihrc.org.uk/show.php?id=677.

38. On constitution writing and implementation see Rett Ludwikowski, *Constitution Making in the Region of Former Soviet Dominance* (Durham, NC: Duke University Press, 1996), 73–81 (Lithuania), 81–89 (Estonia), 89–95 (Ukraine), and 95–102 (Belarus) as well as Belarus's constitution reproduced at 332–50 and Lithuania's at 484–509.

39. See, at the general level, Daniel Calingaert, "Election Rigging and How to Fight It," *Journal of Democracy* 17, no. 3 (2006): 138–51. For Ukraine see Kerstin Zimmer, "The Comparative Failure of Machine Politics, Administrative Resources and Fraud," *Canadian Slavonic Papers* 47, no. 3/4 (September–December 2005): 361–84; Misha Myagkov, Peter C. Ordeshook, and Dimitry Shakin, "The Disappearance of Fraud: The Forensics of Ukraine's 2006 Parliamentary Elections," *Post-Soviet Affairs* 23, no. 3 (2007): 218–39.

40. See Jessica Allina-Pisanno, "Social Contracts and Authoritarian Projects in Post-Soviet Space: The Use of Administrative Resource," *Communist and Post-Communist Studies* 43, no. 4 (December 2010): 373–82. The author's evidence comes mostly from Ukraine and its neighbors.

41. See Ferdinand Müller-Rommel, Katja Fettelschoss, and Philipp Harfst, "Party Government in Central Eastern European Democracies: A Data Collection (1990–2003)," *European Journal of Political Research* 43, no. 6 (October 2004): 869–94; Paul G. Lewis, *Political Parties in Post-Communist Eastern Europe* (New York and London: Routledge, 2000); Paul G. Lewis, ed., *Party Development and Democratic Change in Post-Communist Europe: The First Decade* (London and Portland, OR: Frank Cass Publishers, 2001); Janusz Bugajski, *Political Parties in Eastern Europe: A Guide to Politics in the Post-Communist Era* (Armonk, NY: M.E. Sharpe, 2002); Sten Berglund, Joakim Ekman, and Frank H. Aarebrot, eds., *The Handbook of Political Change in Eastern Europe* (Cheltenham, Glos, and Northampton, MA: Edward Elgar Publishing, Inc., 2004); Anatoly Kulik and Susanna Pshizova, eds., *Political Parties in Post-Soviet Space: Russia, Belarus, Ukraine, Moldova, and the Baltics* (Westport, CT and London: Praeger Publishers, 2005); Suzanne Jungerstam-Mulders, ed., *Post-Communist EU Member States: Parties and Party Systems* (Aldershot, Hampshire, and Burlington, VT: Ashgate Publishing, 2006); Paul Webb and Stephen White, eds., *Party Politics in New Democracies* (New York and Oxford: Oxford University Press, 2007); Andrey A. Meleshevich, *Party Systems in Post-Soviet Countries: A Comparative Study of Political Institutionalization in the Baltic States, Russia, and Ukraine* (New York: Palgrave Macmillan, 2007).

42. See Hubert Tworzecki, *Learning to Choose: Electoral Politics in East-Central Europe* (Stanford, CA: Stanford University Press, 2003); Richard Rose and Neil Munro, *Elections and Parties in New European Democracies* (Washington, DC: CQ Press, 2003), and the 2nd edn: *An Interactive Process* published in 2010 by European Consortium for Political Research Press. See also Margit Tavits, "On the Linkage between Electoral Volatility and Party System Instability in Central and Eastern Europe," *European Journal of Political Research* 47, no. 5 (August 2008): 537–55; Tatiana Kostadinova, "Voter Turnout Dynamics in Post-Communist Europe," *European Journal of Political Research* 42, no. 6 (October 2003): 741–59; Byong-Kuen Jhee, "Economic Origins of Electoral Support for Authoritarian Successors: A Cross-National Analysis of Economic Voting in New Democracies," *Comparative Political Studies* 41, no. 3 (March 2008): 362–88.

43. For free election results in the Baltics up to, and including, 2004 see Centre for the Study of Public Policy, University of Aberdeen, "Baltic Voices: Elections," http://www.balticvoices.org/estonia/estonian_elections.php, http://www.balticvoices.org/latvia/latvian_elections.php, and http://www.balticvoices.org/lithuania/lithuanian_elections.php. See also Richard Rose and Neil Munro, *Elections and Parties in New European Democracies* (Washington, DC: CQ Press, 2003), 166–78 (Estonia), 194–209 (Latvia), 210–25 (Lithuania).

44. For an analysis of the upheavals in Serbia, Georgia, Ukraine, Moldova, and Kyrgyzstan see Menno Fenger, "The Diffusion of Revolutions: Comparing Recent Regime Turnovers in Five Post-Communist Countries," *Demokratizatsiya: The Journal of Post-Soviet Democratization* 15, no. 1 (Winter 2007): 5–28; Taras Kuzio, "Democratic Breakthroughs and Revolutions in Five Postcommunist Countries: Comparative Perspectives on the Fourth Wave," *Demokratizatsiya: The Journal of Post-Soviet Democratization* 16, no. 1 (Winter 2008): 97–109. In addition to the five nations mentioned above, Kuzio also considers Slovakia, Central and Eastern Europe's arguably most post-Communist nation. He argues that it was rescued from its pathological hibernation by the EU, which failed to extend the same assistance to Ukraine and Georgia, however.

17

The Baltics

How does this post-Soviet mish mash translate into party politics and democracy? It does rather well in the Baltics.[1] Even if its progress is marred by an unsettled relationship with Russia, Estonia, in particular, appears to be a paradigm of freedom and parliamentarism. Its Baltic sisters have been similarly successful. We shall now discuss their political systems, their main personalities, and their major parties.

Estonia

Estonia has a mixed, presidential and prime ministerial system.[2] Between 1992 and 2011, Tallinn had ten governments with eight prime ministers as well as three presidents. A largely symbolic president is chosen by the parliament. If a candidate fails to garner a two-thirds majority the electoral college casts the vote. Lennart Meri, twice elected president (1992–2001), was the nation's anchor in its first stages of statehood but his tenure was marred by the allegations of collaboration with the KGB. The next president, Arnold Rüütel (2001–2006), had been a reform Communist at the cusp of Estonia's independence and afterwards championed the post-Communists, in particular the Popular Union of Estonia. The allegations of corruption and, to put it charitably, Rüütel's status as a "consultant" for the KGB, as well as his poor health, caused him to lose the next election. Afterwards, former emigrant in the United States, the Swedish-born Toomas Hendrik Ilves took the presidency (2006–present). He was initially an agrarian conservative but now identifies himself as a social democrat.

The unicameral parliament (*Riigikogu*) is the highest legislative institution of the land. The deputies are chosen by direct vote. Usually the leader of the largest scoring party or, more often, coalition becomes prime minister, when appointed by the president. Since independence, Estonia has had fifteen governments led by eight prime ministers, two of them holding the office thrice and one twice. Andrus Ansip has been the nation's longest serving prime minister (2005–present).[3] Edgar Savisaar was its most scandal-ridden, including ties to the KGB and oligarchic corruption (1991–1992).[4] However, arguably the most successful of the Estonian heads of government is conservative Christian Democrat Mart Laar (1992–1994, 1999–2002), former staunch anti-Communist dissident, and a robust conservative-libertarian.[5]

276

In 1992, Laar was the architect of the National Coalition Party (NCP) "Pro Patria" which resulted from a merger of four organizations: two separate Christian Democratic parties, Populist Conservatives, and the Republican Coalition. Three years later, the Estonian National Independence Party joined the NCP and the Pro Patria Union (PPU) resulted. In 2006, the Res Publica party, although avowedly libertarian and conservative, in fact pragmatic and technocratic, combined with the PPU to form the Union of Pro Patria and Res Publica (*Isamaa ja Res Publica Liit*), currently the largest right-wing political entity in Estonia.[6] It champions free markets, tradition, nationalism, and lustration, the vetting of public figures to weed out foreign agents, an issue which has not been satisfactorily resolved yet. Some of its staunchest competition comes from the libertarian and libertine Reform Party,[7] an off and on coalition partner of both Pro Patria and Res Publica, as well as, rather incongruously, the Social Democratic Party (SDP).

The history of the SDP is rather instructive in terms of political confusion and, perhaps, electoral deception. It came about through a series of mergers. First, in 1990 the socialists and social democrats, both domestic and émigré, post-Communist and anti-Communist, joined together to form the Estonian Social Democratic Party. Second, it entered an electoral coalition with the center-right peasant Estonian Rural Center Party, and, in 1996, both agreed to merge as the Moderates. In 1999, the Moderates further attracted to their ranks the center-right Popular Party of Republicans and Conservatives, which earlier had absorbed the right-wing Peasant Party. At this point the amalgam began campaigning as the Moderate Popular Party (MPP). In 2004, the MPP ultimately renamed itself the Social Democratic Party and openly moved to the left.[8] On the other hand, the SDP's coming out of the closet may have been an attempt to neutralize the social democrats and communists of the Russian minority.

Other important parliamentary contenders are the socialist and liberal Estonian Center Party, which relies heavily on the ethnic Russians for support; populist agrarian and social democratic Popular Union of Estonia;[9] and leftist and environmentalist Greens of Estonia. The environmentalists fluctuate in and out of the parliament. Of many other extraparliamentary entities, two are notable: the Estonian United Left Party, which represents unabashed socialism and aggrieved Russian minority (along with the Constitution Party and the Russian Party in Estonia); and the Estonian Party of Independence (EPI), a nationalist outfit opposed to the European Union. More precisely, the EPI oscillates between Eurosceptic and Europhobic. Virtually all other Estonian parties are Euroenthusiastic and even Euroeuphoric. We shall elaborate on this phenomenon later.

Incredibly, despite so many impediments Estonia is a flowering democracy. Its coalition governments are miracles of compromise, to an extent resembling the beleaguered, quarrelsome, contradictory, and fragile, yet enduring,

Israeli governmental alliances, *sans* the religious pivot. But unlike Jerusalem, Tallinn is not beholden to the moribund socialist, welfarist, and etatist ways. By implementing libertarian and conservative policies, the successive Estonian governments oversaw, until the recent global recession, a consistently sustained and dynamically stupendous economic growth based upon new technologies, tourism, and trade, mainly with Scandinavian and other European countries, but also Russia and the United States. Estonia's *Tiigrihüpe* (Tiger Leap) into communication technologies is particularly impressive and promising.[10]

Latvia

Latvia's economy boomed much as Estonia's. And it likewise crashed terribly because of the global recession and socialist excesses of its politicians.[11] There are other similarities between the two Baltic neighbors. The number of parties was overwhelming in the 1990s, although it was whittled down somewhat in the 2000s. And coalition building remains an admirable art, encompassing all and sundry. In other words, Riga's political system is very akin to Tallinn's.[12]

Latvia has a unicameral parliament (*Saeima*) which is elected in direct elections, and which, then, chooses the president who, in turn, appoints the prime minister. Since independence, Latvia has experienced sixteen governments, twelve prime ministers,[13] and four presidents. The presidents have displayed various levels of commitment to tradition and continuity, as well as various faces of modernity.

Guntis Ulmanis aka Guntis Rumpītis (1993–1999) was elected initially on the strength of his family ties to free Estonia's last prewar president Kārlis Ulmanis: he was his grand nephew. A Gulag survivor, upon return home, the younger Ulmanis concealed his background and as Rumpītis joined the Communist party to advance his career as an economist. He was nonetheless fired in 1970 when his family's heritage was revealed. Laying low, the future president waited until 1989 to quit the Communist party, to revert to his true family name, and to oppose the system openly. A leader of the agrarian Latvia Farmer's Union party, a resurrected namesake of its prewar parliamentary predecessor, Ulmanis provided much needed stability to his nation and a symbolic sense of continuity with the prewar republic. The allegations of his ties to the KGB were never proven.[14]

His successor, Vaira Vīķe-Freiberga (1999–2007), although born in Latvia in 1937, spent almost her entire life in Canada as an émigré and a scholar, a clinical psychologist. She returned to the old country only in 1998. Unburdened personally by any legacy of the past association with the Soviets, Vīķe-Freiberga injected a welcome dose of civility, pragmatism, and sophistication into the nation's political discourse. And she projected a fabulous image abroad, in the European Union and North America, in particular. She is, after all, a liberal Western academic. On the other hand, her detractors accused her of political correctness and mushy multiculturalism. In particular, her apparently excessive attentiveness to the demands of the Russian minority raised some eyebrows. Further, the detractors charged, the lack of personal exposure to the Soviet occupation rendered the president much less sensitive to the matters of de-Communization and lustration. Running and serving as a nonparty, independent politician, Vīķe-Freiberga expected to fail to please everyone. She was a one-term president.[15]

Also an independent, Valdis Zatlers (2007–2011) assumed the presidency next. For an average Latvian his was a candidacy even more obscure than his predecessor's. And he had even less political experience than she did. A medical doctor, Zatlers was involved with the anti-Soviet "people's power" movement from 1988. Following Latvia's achievement of freedom, Zatlers returned to medical practice. A decade later he rendered his tacit support to the ostensibly "conservative" Folk (Popular or People's) Party, an outfit founded by a controversial oligarch. Accordingly, Zatlers's tenure as president was marred by the allegations of impropriety, corruption, and tax evasion. Naturally, none of the charges have stuck so far.[16] And the president actually attempted to crack down on corruption, which proved to be his undoing.

In 2011, after approving a police raid on an alleged kleptocrat, Zatlers was unexpectedly outmaneuvered by Andris Bērziņš (2011–present). Originally an engineer by training, this oligarchic banker-cum-parliamentarian successfully challenged the incumbent for Latvia's presidency. Before Bērziņš became the nation's fourth president, he had been Soviet Latvia's member of the *nomenklatura*: from an electronic enterprise executive to a deputy government minister. At the end of the 1980s he became a Gorbachevian "reform" Communist and, later, sided with the independence movement as a delegate of the Latvian Soviet. After 1992, Bērziņš plunged vigorously into economic transformation, privatizing the Bank of Latvia and emerging as a chairman of a major private bank as well as board member of several large corporations. Although in 2010 Bērziņš was elected to the parliament for the center-left Union of Greens and Farmers, he is widely held to be a front man for the post-Communist kleptocrats and other allied monied interests.[17]

Of the twelve Latvian prime ministers, some of them rather lackluster, the most outstanding and intrepid so far is the current government head, Valdis Dombrovskis. He has held the office twice. It would be premature to issue a definite verdict, but his performance has been quite impressive. Polish by origin, the youthful politician (born in 1971) is a physicist. Educated and trained in Latvia, Germany, and the United States, Dombrovskis earlier served as his nation's finance minister (2002–2004) and the EU's parliamentary deputy. In February 2009, he was tapped for prime ministership at the height of the financial crisis which caused a wholesale meltdown of the Latvian economy and spiraled into serious street riots. Dombrovskis succeeded in forming a minority government. Then he instituted severe austerity measures which halted the economic collapse and elicited solid support of the electorate. He handily won the parliamentary elections of October 2010. At the head of a majority coalition government in Riga, he promised more budget cuts.[18]

The coalition dubbed itself the "Unity" bloc (*Vienotība*).[19] Most of the participants are veteran political fighters. Most are backed either by the local oligarchs or Moscow. Most have emerged from various convoluted groups and alliances. Latvia's strange bedfellows include the Greens, who were established in 1991 and became an important feature in the legislature. They only failed to enter the parliament once: between 1998 and 2002. Afterwards they united with the center-right Latvian Peasant Union (LPV),[20] which was originally founded in 1917 and relaunched itself in 1990. LPV sat outside of the parliament following every other election since 1993 until blocking itself with the environmentalists in 2002 to form the Union of Greens and Peasants (a vehicle of an oligarch). It proved to be a winning formula, bringing serious electoral gains in 2004, 2006, and 2010.[21] Next, there was, at least initially, the conservative nationalist "For Fatherland and Freedom" party. Put together in 1993, the conservative nationalists uniquely and successfully crossed the 5 percent electoral threshold in each of the parliamentary elections between 1993 and 2006. In 2010, they did so again together with the nationalist "Everything for Latvia!" party under the umbrella of the right-wing National Alliance. But they proved troublesome partners for Dombrovskis.[22]

Because of the truculence of the "old" parties, the prime minister has bet on fresh entities. The leading engines of the "Unity" bloc are new parties and coalitions founded in the twenty-first century: the center-right New Era Party (NEP), the conservative-nationalist Civic Union (CU), and the socialist-liberal Society for Different (or Other) Politics (SDP). The rightist CU came into the existence in 2008 as an off-shoot of "For Fatherland and Freedom" and a splinter of the NEP. The leftist SDP was founded likewise in 2008 by, among others, refugees from the oligarchic Popular (People's) Party. In truth, most of the participants in the "Unity" bloc are tainted by oligarchic ties. But so is almost everyone else.[23]

Dombrovskis's main support comes from the center-right NEP (*Jaunais Laiks*), a clean government political entity founded in 2001. It is conservative and, sometimes, libertarian with a healthy dose of moderate nationalism and populism. The NEP is Latvia's prime anticorruption advocate and force. It sharply differentiates itself from all other political parties because of their alleged oligarchic connections. Its economic approach is pragmatic. Ebulliently pro-free market before the implosion of the economy, the NEP turned to hands-on etatism to tackle the crisis, successfully so far.

There are, however, problems with the opposition. Alienating seriously his erstwhile right-nationalist allies, Dombrovskis even attempted to include the communists and social democrats of the Russian minority Harmony Center party to make his coalition cabinet as broad as possible. The result was that the nationalists reacted angrily and were expelled, while the Russians rejected the offer. The Harmony Center was hoping to win the election and form a government itself. In 2010 it came in second after the "Unity" bloc.[24] A year later, the Russian-dominated party scored highest in a snap election (followed by the Reform Party of Zatlers and the "Unity" bloc of Dombrovskis). This time the Russians wanted in. However, Dombrovskis was able to put together a fragile governing coalition without the Harmony Center.[25] Snubbed, the Russians reacted angrily. Outside the parliament the Harmony Center can count not only on the Kremlin, which will be addressed below, but also on another socialist, Russian minority outfit: For Human Rights in United Latvia. But in the parliament the Russians and other leftists are opposed by the right conservative National Alliance and the ostensibly conservative libertarian For a Good Latvia party, the latter also controlled by oligarchs.[26] This allows Dombrovskis a freedom of maneuver.

There are several interesting features of Latvia's political scene. As mentioned, the current political contenders are rather new entities. Most of them accepted refugees from older political organizations which spectacularly imploded or became completely marginalized. For example, the Democratic Party "Saimnieks" materialized suddenly as an ad hoc coalition of left-liberals to win the parliamentary election in 1995. It fared so horribly in power and, later, at the polls that it never reached the parliament again and self-disbanned in 2005. Meanwhile, its members joined a variety of parties without any strongly pronounced ideological preferences. Except for the Greens, the peasants, the nationalists, and the communists of the Russian minority, most of the successful mainstream Latvian parties have tended not to be overtly and overly ideological. Founded in 1993, the "liberal democratic" Latvian Way Party is the case in point. It produced five prime ministers (including one, Ivars Godmanis, who officially joined it only after resigning from office). In 2007, having exhausted all possibilities for further shape-shifting, the ultimate survivor clique folded into the avowedly conservative, Christian Democratic Latvia's First Party.

Most of such parties are perceived as utterly corrupt, hence the utility of frequent label changes. By the same token, the mainstream parties tend to be extremely flexible and pragmatic. Hence, they are successful in coalition building. But so are, apparently, some of the overtly ideological parties. For example, the Greens and the Peasants have constituted an electoral bloc since 2002 based upon their preference for small, single-family "sustainable" farms: both tally with the objectives of agrarianism and the fantasies of environmentalism. But the glue that binds most of them together was fashioned by the oligarchic interests and largesse.[27] All in all, Latvia's political system shares many of its features with those of Estonia and, to a lesser extent, Lithuania.

Lithuania

Lithuania displays a few sui generis political, institutional, and economic particularities that set her apart from her Baltic kin and kith.[28] Among other things, she appears less stable with more frequent government changes than among her neighbors. This is because Vilnius was at a distinct disadvantage of having been the very first in the USSR to launch its struggle for freedom. It had to innovate and compromise more than others. Initially, as mentioned already, Lithuania was forced to implement the Polish "Solidarity" way under much more adversarial circumstances. Next, therefore, she had to improvise her tactics more imaginatively than its soon-to-be Baltic and other emulators. Further, shocked with the apparent success and fast pace of change, but pessimistic about its durability and extent, she had to allow for an earlier and deeper compromise which provided for a much more extensive survival of the Soviet institutions and ways well into Lithuania's independence. The implosion of the USSR proved, retroactively, such compromise to have been too far reaching and even, sometimes, unnecessary. It retarded Lithuania's progress as it ensnared her deeper in post-Communism than the other two Baltic states.

The circumstances for Lithuania then may be a bit different than for Estonia and Latvia. And so are some of the institutional and legal arrangements. Like Riga and Tallinn, Vilnius has a unicameral parliament (*Seimas*) and a robust prime minister. But unlike them, it elects its presidents in direct, general elections. Hence, they are not exactly toothless. Since 1992, Lithuania has experienced fifteen governments; eleven chiefs of cabinet, including two who served twice and three interim; and seven heads of state, one of them acting president.

Some of the most notable facts about Lithuania's presidents (and other leaders) highlight the concerns about the nefarious influence of the Soviet legacy.[29] They also reflect what can be termed as the neutral cruelties of democracy in the post-Communist context, where neither de-Communization nor lustration occurred. Simply, like everywhere else, the electorate usually votes for the most flexible and palatable candidate, and not necessarily for the most righteous or qualified one. And, as always, perception trumps reality. Missing a common point of reference, confused with the siren song of moral relativism, and atomized after nearly half a century of totalitarianism, the Lithuanians lack a reflexive unity even on the most basic issues, ethical ones in particular.[30] However, sometimes the good guys win, even in post-Communism, and that is indeed a triumph for freedom and democracy. We shall elaborate on that by following briefly the careers of four chief executives: Algirdas Brazauskas, Valdas Adamkus, Rolandas Paskas, and Dalia Grybauskaitė.

Ironically, the introduction of democracy in Lithuania resulted at first in a post-Communist victory. Algirdas Brazauskas was initially acting president

(November 1992–February 1993) and then the first freely elected president (February 1993–February 1998), and, finally, a prime minister.[31] For many his electoral success, in particular, in the run for the presidency, was shatteringly shocking for two reasons. First, it was highly distasteful because Brazauskas had been the First Secretary of Central Committee of the Communist Party of Lithuania (CPL), an integral component of the Communist Party of the Soviet Union (Bolsheviks) (1988–1989). Within a few years, he morphed from a life-long dour *apparatchik* into a Gorbachevian "reform" Communist. Then, he donned the garb of a national Bolshevik, a "rebellious" party head who publicly broke with Moscow by taking the CPL out of the CPSU.

Second, Brazauskas's victory was very disturbing because the patriots anticipated the triumph of Stasys Lozoraitis, Jr. A Lithuanian émigré, he represented the Lithuanian government-in-exile as its ambassador to the United States and the Vatican. Like his father and namesake before him, Lozoraitis was a symbol of Lithuania's uninterrupted, free statehood. In fact, technically, Lozoraitis became the head of the government-in-exile after his father's death. After 1989, the son returned home and accepted deputy premiership from the Sąjūdis government. However, a slew of monumental problems of the post-Communist transformation, including the mishandling of the shattered economy by the etatist amateurs of the "people's power" movement and the hysteria regarding KGB agents amidst the leadership of the organization and its opponents, caused voter anger and the former Communist *apparatchik* trumped the symbol of Lithuanian freedom. In free, unfettered, and democratic elections, the erstwhile Communist party gensek defeated the president-in-exile. Nothing could be more earth shattering for the patriots, except perhaps Lozoraitis's alleged dealings with the KGB, which were revealed later.[32] At any rate, after his presidential ride, Brazauskas briefly retired and then served as Lithuania's longest lasting prime minister (2001–2006), resigning because of corruption charges among his cabinet.

In fairness, all Lithuanian presidents have had rumors swirling around them about their alleged corruption, mafia links, or KGB–FSB connections, past and present. Arguably, only the nation's second and fifth chief executive, President Valdas Adamkus (1998–2003 and 2004–2009), a US citizen, an American military veteran, and a former anti-Communist "forest brother," seems the closest to an ideal beyond reproach. But that is because he left Lithuania in 1944 and returned only in 1997. And Adamkus is no Western liberal, but, instead, indeed, a staunch conservative. A Republican in the United States, Adamkus ran and ruled as an independent in his home country. By all accounts he impressed his fellow citizens with personal honesty and integrity. During his first term, in 2000, after some misgivings, he supported the implementation of the law to vet former Communist secret police agents among politicians and other public figures.[33] Accordingly, Adamkus prevailed upon the conservative-dominated *Seimas* to oust a conservative prime minister, Gediminas Vagnorius, who opposed the vetting and who, incidentally, turned out to have been an alleged KGB informer. During his second term, President Adamkus oversaw his nation's access to the European Union and NATO in 2004.

Corruption charges took its toll on Lithuania's third president, Rolandas Paksas (2003–2004), who has the dubious distinction as Europe's only contemporary head of state to be impeached and removed from office.[34] During Soviet times Paksas studied in Leningrad (St. Petersburg), where he indulged in his passion for aviation and established many a useful contact. He became a Communist party member. After 1989, Paksas automatically transitioned to its direct successor, the post-Communist Democratic Labor Party, and prospered as a successful businessman. However, in 1995, he reinvented himself as a populist nationalist and joined the right-wing Homeland Union (Lithuanian Conservatives). That move propelled him to the office of prime minister in 1999. A year later he discovered somewhat of a liberal in himself. Accordingly, Paksas established the ostensibly center-right and Europhoric[35] Liberal Democratic Party, which he chaired. That earned him the mayoralty of the capital city of Vilnius. In 2003, running on a loud populist and liberal platform,[36] Paksas unexpectedly defeated the understated conservative incumbent for presidency. However, the charade unraveled almost immediately as the winner's chumminess with the mafia and, possibly, the FSB surfaced. Within a bit over a year, Paksas was forced out.[37] Although ostracized and banned from the public sphere at home he sued his country abroad and continued standing for elections, renaming his political vehicle as Order and Justice party, and self-identifying as center-left and Europhoric. Currently, Paksas enjoys his post as a deputy of the European Parliament. He also sports a fresh halo of victimhood since in early 2011 the European Court of Human Rights ruled that the presidential impeachment had violated his human rights.[38]

Paksas is not the only Lithuanian politician with a sordid past and suspicious acquaintances. There were at least two alleged KGB agents among the nation's prime ministers.[39] Research to identify the agents of the Soviet period has barely begun. As for the present, it is truly unknown how many, if any, top Lithuanian leaders willfully have continued to maintain links to foreign intelligence services, including Russia's FSB-SVR or GRU.

The same applies to second-tier politicians and civil servants. The dust barely had settled after the Paksas scandal when it was revealed that Foreign Minister Antanas Valionis was not just an informer of the Communist secret police, but a KGB reserve officer. The top officer of Lithuania's counterintelligence (State Security Department Director General), Arvydas Pocius, also admitted to serving in the KGB reserve.[40] These high-profile cases and others finally forced the political elite of Lithuania to tackle lustration. In arguably one of the most notable acts of her tenure so far, President Dalia Grybauskaitė

(2009–present) at last ordered all Soviet-era secret police files to be made available to the public in February 2010.[41] The laudable decision was long overdue. In the short run, there will be much bitterness. In the long run, it should clear the atmosphere and allow the Lithuanians to move on. It is a significant victory of openness and transparency over post-Communism. It will strengthen enormously the national security. Last but not least, it is significant that the freedom to consult the archives and, thus, to vet public figures and others came from Grybauskaitė. A former Communist party member, a graduate of elite Soviet schools, and, thus, a beneficiary of the Soviet occupation, the current president is a prime example of a post-Communist who has, however, been Westernized by her subsequent education and work in the United States and the European Union and who, therefore, earned the endorsement of the patriots of the conservative Homeland Union in her victorious electoral bid for the presidency.

The stories of Brazauskas, Adamkus, Paksas, and Grybauskaitė amply illustrate the best and the worst in Lithuania, the constant tug of war between re-Westernization and post-Communism. The process repeats itself manifold down the political ladder. It overlaps with other phenomena among parties, coalitions, and individual politicians. At times it appears to threaten to paralyze the country but, instead, it brings about salubriously cathartic qualities. The business of government continues as it should in a democracy.

Lithuania has had eleven prime ministers, including two who held the job twice, and three who served as acting heads of the cabinet. Since 1992, five of them have been overt post-Communists. Six premiers have been ostensibly either conservative nationalists or were endorsed by them. However, as the Paksas case demonstrates, one should not assume that they were necessarily what they proclaimed themselves to be. The same applies to political parties and their activists. Virtually everyone old enough to have been an adult in the USSR is a great unknown. We shall briefly look at two groups: the conservatives and the post-Communists.

Initially, in the 1990s, there was an explosion of parties which led to a serious fragmentation of Lithuania's political scene. However, two orientations really mattered: the conservatives on the right, and the post-Communists on the left. In the early 2000s, the latter lost some of their influence as they faced competition from new orientations, some of them liberal or leftist modeling themselves on the Western paradigm, at times of a countercultural kind. Yet parties have become fewer as disparate groups began uniting or at least forming rather durable electoral coalitions.

On the patriot side, the conservatives have displayed a remarkable staying power on the nation's parliamentary scene. Even under the most calamitous of circumstances, the patriotic center-right has consistently managed to get the necessary votes to cross the 5 percent threshold to qualify for the *Seimas* in the past two decades.[42] Given their scarce resources, dearth of professional cadres, and other limitations, this is no mean achievement. After the complete marginalization of the Sąjūdis by 1992, its right wing, led by Vytautas Landsbergis, formed a new party, the conservative, libertarian, and Christian democratic Homeland Union (Lithuanian Conservatives, HU). Landsbergis was a celebrated hero of the struggle for independence. He was one of the guiding lights of the Sąjūdis and also the first Chairman of the Supreme Council (Soviet/Taryba) of Lithuania, the nation's proto-parliament. In the 1990s, Landsbergis was at the height of his popularity, at least until the allegations of his involvement with the KGB surfaced.[43] His party scored a spectacular success in the parliamentary elections of 1996 but it barely survived the voting contest of 2000.[44] During that decade, however, all other right-wing groups fared even worse. A centripetal trend developed among them. Consequently, the HU absorbed a Christian democratic party and an association of the victims of Soviet persecution (the Union of Political Prisoners and the Exiled). In 2008, the HU further united with the right-wing Lithuanian National Union and the center-right Lithuanian Christian Democrats and adopted the name of the HU—Lithuanian Christian Democrats (HU-LCD).[45] It has poised itself to face and, perhaps, weather the challenges not only of post-Communism but also of the counterculture from the West.

Whereas the conservatives have been slowly consolidating their forces, the post-Communists have been gradually dissipating them.[46] At first, the future of overt post-Communism looked bright. Although the Communist party was delegalized in 1991, its successor was inexplicably permitted. This allowed the post-Communists, during the 1990s, to alternate in power with various conservative and liberal coalitions. But now the overt post-Communists are no longer the power brokers of the Lithuanian scene. There are several reasons behind their waning. In December 1990, the Communist Party of Lithuania converted itself into the Democratic Labor Party of Lithuania (DLPL) and rebranded itself as social democratic for reasons of tactics and deception. First, at that point any association with Communism carried a stigma. Second, the return of the Soviet power was considered imminent by many and the cadres needed a political shell corporation to hide behind until then. Since the USSR failed to reimpose itself upon Lithuania, however, Moscow's erstwhile Janissaries briskly marched on as Vilnius's transformed social democrats. The domestic electorate believed their empty promises. They were also readily accepted by their Western European comrades practically on equal terms.

In the mid-1990s, freedom's permanence in Lithuania began to look assured. It manifested itself, among other things, in the periodic electoral punishment of the post-Communists at the hands of the deceived voters. Cut off from the state through, the DLPL began hemorrhaging cadres and resources. Some of that occurred already at the threshold of independence; there were at least twelve Communist party members elected as deputies of Sąjūdis, for example. Most gave up their party membership. Afterwards the CPL and DLPL defectors joined other parties, some of them rival leftist, tepidly centrist, and even unequivocally rightist. Significantly, whenever the post-Communists founded or cofounded entirely new parties, they tend to be either business friendly ("liberal") or populist ("center-left"). Of the former, the New Union (Social Liberals) remains perhaps the most influential.[47] Of the latter, the ephemeral Liberal Union of Lithuania eventually merged with the SDP. The SDP remains influential. Practically no post-Communist commandeering of radical nationalism, Russian or Yugoslav-style, occurred in Lithuania. However, like everywhere else, some post-Communist pragmatics and careerists have been able to find even more rewarding pursuits outside of the DLPL in the business world. The departure from under the party's protective umbrella was also connected to the obvious fact that no Communists were truly persecuted for their crimes, and de-Communization (and lustration) remained largely just an impotent right-wing slogan.[48]

Economically, the post-Communists came out on top. Politically, by 2000, their flagship, the DLPL, began to falter. It failed to find succor by entering into various electoral alliances and coalitions. It continued to shed electoral support and cadres. By now the post-Communists who remained loyal to the party have established their social democratic credentials to the point where other, non-Communist, or even formerly anti-Communist, social democrats take them seriously. That led to the merger of the DLPL and the Lithuanian Social Democratic Party (LSDP) in 2001. The latter used to be a rather respectable entity, drawing on the historical legacy of Lithuanian socialism and populism dating from before the Revolution of 1905.[49] The LSDP's institutional form was preserved in exile in the West. The new leftist party is thus an official hybrid of the totalitarian legacy of the USSR and the émigré heritage of free Lithuania. It renamed itself Social Democratic Party of Lithuania (SDPL).[50] It is now firmly ensconced in the mainstream, and enjoys a degree of respectability outside of the anti-Communist circles. SDPL's pro-EU rhetoric is pronounced. However, its pro-Muscovite stance is still palpable, perhaps second only to Russian-born oligarch Viktor Uspaskich's Labor Party (LP), which, nonetheless, also flirts with Brussels to gain legitimacy. Parenthetically, the LP caters to the Russian minority and sometimes cooperates with the Polish minority, which will be discussed separately.[51]

Notes

1.   Two Scandinavian scholars first prematurely proclaimed the Baltics as failures, but then they corrected themselves somewhat, still having problems keeping up with the fast pace of change. See Ole Nørgaard and Lars Johannsen, *The Baltic States after Independence*, 2nd edn. (Cheltenham and Northampton, MA: Edward Elgar Publishing, 1999). See further Józef Darski [Jerzy Targowski], "Baltic Politics," *Uncaptive Minds* 6, no. 3 (24) (Fall 1993); Vello Pettai and Marcus Kreuzer, "Party Politics in the Baltic States: Social Bases and Institutional

Context," *East European Politics and Societies* 13, no. 1 (Winter 1999): 148–89; Luise Pape Møller, "Moving Away from the Ideal: The Rational Use of Referendums in the Baltic States," *Scandinavian Political Studies* 25, no. 3 (2002): 281–93; Centre for the Study of Public Policy, University of Aberdeen, "Baltic Voices," http://www.balticvoices.org/index.php.

2.   For a brief overview of Estonia see Linda Drengsgaard and Ole Hersted Hansen, "State of the State in Estonia," Demstar Research Report no. 12, Department of Political Science, University of Aarhus (March 2003): 1–56, http://www.demstar.dk/papers/EstoniaSOTS.pdf; Vello Petai, "Understanding Politics in Estonia: The Limits of Tutelary Transition," ed. Ole Nørgaard and Lars Johannsen, Demstar Research Report no. 25, Department of Political Science, University of Aarhus (April 2005): 1–42, http://www.demstar.dk/papers/UnderstandingEstonia.pdf; Centre for the Study of Public Policy, University of Aberdeen, "Baltic Voices: Estonian Government," (before 2004), http://www.balticvoices.org/estonia/estonian_government.php; US State Department's Bureau of European and Eurasian Affairs, "Background Note: Estonia," (November 12, 2010), http://www.state.gov/r/pa/ei/bgn/5377.htm; Central Intelligence Agency, "Estonia," *The World Factbook*, https://www.cia.gov/library/publications/the-world-factbook/geos/en.html; and consistent coverage in the 2000s by Vello Pettai, "Estonia," in *European Journal of Political Research* 41, no. 7–8 (December 2002): 947–51; 42, no. 7–8 (December 2003): 935–39; 43, no. 7–8 (December 2004): 993–99; 44, no. 7–8 (December 2005): 1002–7; 45, no. 7–8 (December 2006): 1094–100; 46, no. 7–8 (December 2007): 943–48; 47, no. 7–8 (December 2008): 962–68; 48, no. 7–8 (December 2009): 951–55; 49, no. 7–8 (December 2010): 955–63. And see Jean-Jacques Subrenat, ed., *Estonia: Identity and Independence* (Amsterdam and New York: Editions Rodopi B.V., 2004); John T. Ishiyama, "Electoral Systems Experimentation in the New Eastern Europe: The Single Transferable Vote and the Additional Member System in Estonia and Hungary," *East European Quarterly* 29, no. 4 (1995): 487–507; Jüris Ruus, "Estonian Riigikogu and the Institutionalization of Its Committees," in *Committees in the New Democratic Parliaments of Central Europe*, ed. David M. Olson and William E. Crowther (Columbus, OH: The Ohio State University Press, 2003), 117–33. See also "Problems on Problems (Estonia): An Interview with Lagle Park," *Uncaptive Minds* 6, no. 3 (24) (Fall 1993); Siergiei Matiunin, "Independence after Occupation (Estonia)," *Uncaptive Minds* 7, no. 2 (26) (Summer 1994); "Who Needs a Conflict? A Conversation between Two Estonians," *Uncaptive Minds* 7, no. 2 (26) (Summer 1994); Jueri Luik, "The Use and Abuse of Peacekeeping (Estonia)," *Uncaptive Minds* 7, no. 3 (27) (Fall–Winter 1994); Cynthia S. Kaplan, "Political Culture in Estonia: The Impact of Two Traditions on Political Development," in *Political Culture and Civil Society in Russia and the New States of Eurasia*, ed. Vladmir Tismăneanu (Armonk, NY: M.E. Sharpe, 1995), 227–68; R. A. Panagiotou, "Estonia's Success: Prescription or Legacy?" *Communist and Post-Communist Studies* 34, no. 2 (June 2001): 261–77; Li Bennich-Bjorkman, "The Cultural Roots of Estonia's Successful Transition: How Historical Legacies Shaped the 1990s," *East European Politics and Societies* 21, no. 2 (Spring 2007): 316–48; Tovio U. Raun, "Estonia after 1991: Identity and Integration," *East European Politics and Societies* 23, no. 4 (Fall 2009): 526–35; Aleksej Semjonov, "Estonia: Nation-Building and Integration – Political and Legal Aspects," in *National Integration and Violent Conflict in Post-Soviet Societies: The Cases of Estonia and Moldova*, ed. Pål Kolstø (Lanham, MD: Rowman & Littlefield, 2002), 105–58; Aadu Oll, "Estonia: Toward Post-Communist

Reconstruction," in *Dismantling Tyranny: Transitioning Beyond Totalitarian Regimes*, ed. Illan Berman and J. Michael Waller (Lanham, MD, Boulder, CO, Toronto, and London: Rowman & Littlefield, 2006), 75–88; Ferdinand Müller-Rommel and Georg Sootla, "Estonia," in *Cabinets in Eastern Europe*, ed. Jean Blondel and Ferdinand Müller-Rommel (Basingstoke: Palgrave, 2001), 17–28. On Estonia's economy and its efforts to join the EU, see John Gillingham, *European Integration, 1950-2003: Superstate or New Market Economy?* (New York: Cambridge University Press, 2003), 422–26.

3. "Calm after Storms: Austerity Can Sometimes Be Popular. Just Ask the Estonians," *The Economist* (March 10, 2011): http://www.economist.com/node/18333141.

4. Savisaar was Estonia's first (acting) prime minister. On scandals surrounding him and his Soviet secret police links see Stephen Kinzer, "Political Wiretapping Scandal Reminds Estonians of Soviet Era," *The New York Times* (October 18, 1995): http://www.nytimes.com/1995/10/18/world/political-wiretapping-scandal-reminds-estonia-of-soviet-era.html; "'Truth Commission' Clears Tallinn Mayor of Wrongdoing," ERR News, Estonian Public Broadcasting, (January 6, 2011): http://news.err.ee/politics/60751922-4047-4eb1-be07-b06f0710487d; "Calm after Storms: Austerity Can Sometimes Be Popular. Just Ask the Estonians," *The Economist* (March 10, 2011): http://www.economist.com/node/18333141. And see above.

5. "Reasons for Our Success: An Interview with Mart Laar," *Uncaptive Minds* 7, no. 3 (27) (Fall–Winter 1994).

6. For the party's website see http://www.irl.ee/.

7. See http://www.reform.ee/

8. See http://www.sotsdem.ee/.

9. See http://www.erl.ee/.

10. By some accounts, Skype was developed by Estonian software engineers in cooperation with a Swede and a Dane who put up the capital and patented the invention. See Leo Siemann, "Top 10: Estonian Inventions and their Inventors," *Estonian Inventor/Eesti Leiutaja*, 2009–2011, http://www.estinventor.com/?page_id=34. On Estonia's new technologies see, e.g., Kaisa Saarenmaa and Osma Suominen, "'The Tiger Leap': Information Society in Estonian Frames," TMs, University of Tartu, Centre for Baltic Studies (Autumn 2002): 1–19, http://sange.fi/~ozone/Tigerleap.pdf. For the developments in telecommunications in the post-Soviet zone in general see Ole Nørgaard and Luise Pape Møller, "Telecom Development and State Capacity in Transition Countries: A Framework for Analyses," Demstar Research Report no. 5, University of Aarhus, Department of Political Science (January 2002): 1–73, http://www.demstar.dk/papers/Telecom1.pdf.

11. See Alexei Grigorievs, "High Dive into the Market (Latvia)," *Uncaptive Minds* 6, no. 1 (22) (Winter–Spring 1993); Mark Broad, "Latvia's Economic Boom Turns Sour," *BBC News* (December 3, 2008): http://news.bbc.co.uk/2/hi/business/7760440.stm; "Latvia's Economy Shrinks Rapidly," *BBC News* (February 9, 2009): http://news.bbc.co.uk/2/hi/business/7879529.stm.

12. For basic facts see Latvijas Institūts, "Welcome to online Latvia!" http://www.li.lv/; Ole Nørgaard, Ole Hersted Hansen, Ilze Ostrovska, and Louise Pape Møller, "State of the State in Latvia," Demstar, Research Report no. 1, University of Aarhus, Department of Political Science (May 2000): 1–51, http://www.demstar.dk/papers/LatviaStateOf.pdf; Central Intelligence Agency, "Latvia," *The World Factbook*, https://www.cia.gov/library/publications/the-world-factbook/

geos/lg.html; US State Department's Bureau of European and Eurasian Affairs, "Background Note: Latvia," (May 28, 2010): http://www.state.gov/r/pa/ei/ bgn/5378.htm; and Centre for the Study of Public Policy, University of Aberdeen, "Baltic Voices: Latvian Government," http://www.balticvoices.org/latvia/latvian_government.php?PHPSESSID=924e591e55b5bb67afdd246ab2d75b43, but updated only until 2004. For electoral results between 1993 and 2010 see Wolfram Nordsieck, "Parties and elections in Europe: Latvia," 2010, http://www. parties-and-elections.de/latvia2.html and http://www.parties-and-elections.de/ latvia.html; and consecutive installments by Jānis Ikstens, "Latvia," in *European Journal of Political Research* 41, no. 7–8 (December 2002): 1010–14; 42, no. 7–8 (December 2003): 1003–09; 43, no. 7–8 (December 2004): 1054–58; 44, no. 7–8 (December 2005): 1077–85; 45, no. 7–8 (December 2006): 1162–65; 46, no. 7–8 (December 2007): 1012–18; 47, no. 7–8 (December 2008): 1039–47; 48, no. 7–8 (December 2009): 1015–21; 49, no. 7–8 (December 2010): 1049–57. See also Juris Dreifelds, *Latvia in Transition* (Cambridge, New York, and Melbourne: Cambridge University Press, 1996); Andrejs Plakans, "Latvia: Normality and Disappointment," *East European Politics and Societies* 23, no. 4 (Fall 2009): 518–26.

13.   Ole Nørgaard and Ferdinand Müller-Rommel, "Latvia," in *Cabinets in Eastern Europe*, ed. Jean Blondel and Ferdinand Müller-Rommel (Basingstoke: Palgrave, 2001), 29–39; The Cabinet Ministers of the Republic of Latvia, "History of the Cabinet of Ministers," (January 14, 2001): http://www.mk.gov.lv/en/mk/ vesture/.

14.   Ulmanis was alleged to have informed for the KGB under the code-name "Hugo." However, given the timing and the source (a "Russian Palestinian newspaper" *Al Quds*) of the revelations, it appears entirely possible that Latvia's President was targeted by Moscow's active measures, a disinformation campaign. See Matt Bivens, "Wanted Alive: Ex-KGB Agents and Informers Baltic States Hunt Down Former Soviet Operatives with a Vengeance: Already, a Prime Minister and a Foreign Minister Have Been Toppled," *The Los Angeles Times* (August 2, 1994): http://articles.latimes.com/1994-08-02/news/wr-22515_1_prime-minister.

15.   See "Latvian President: No Top Politicians in KGB Agent Files," *The Baltic Times* (November 20, 2006): http://www.baltictimes.com/news/articles/16852/; "Latvia to Disclose the Names of Former KGB Agents March 1, 2007," *RIA Novosti* (October 26, 2006): http://www.globalsecurity.org/intell/library/news/2006/ intell-061026-rianovosti01.htm; Nadine Vitols-Dixon, *A Life's Journey: Vaira Vīķe-Freiberga, President of Latvia* (Riga: Pētergailis, 2006); and for the former President's personal website see "Vaira Vīķe-Freiberga," http://www.vvf. lv/vvf/.

16.   Zatlers is tied to the oligarch, and twice prime minister, Andris Šķēle. The doctor's election to presidency had all the markings of a typical backdoor deal. For Šķēle see above. And see Talis Saule Archdeacon, "Unknown Surgeon Elected President," *The Baltic Times* (June 6, 2007): http://www.baltictimes.com/ news/articles/18004/; "PROFILE: Valdis Zatlers - surgeon, political newcomer, president," (May 31, 2007): http://web.archive.org/web/20070930190628/http:// eux.tv/article.aspx?articleId=8967. For the Popular (People's) Party website see http://www.tautaspartija.lv/.

17.   See "Curriculum Vitae: Latvijas Valsts prezidents Andris Bērziņš," http://www. president.lv/pk/content/?cat_id=8806; "Bērziņu ievēlē par Valsts prezidentu," http://www.tvnet.lv/zinas/latvija/379748-berzinu_ievele_par_valsts_prezidentu; "Andris Berzins elected new president in Latvia," *BBC News* (June 2,

2011): http://www.bbc.co.uk/news/world-europe-13628945; Martin Quinn, "Challenger Andris Berzins Wins Latvia's Presidential Election," *Associated Press* (June 2, 2011): http://ca.news.yahoo.com/challenger-andris-berzins-wins-latvias-presidential-election-153850333.html.

18.   See Anders Åslund and Valdis Dombrovskis, *How Latvia Came through the Financial Crisis* (Washington, DC: Peterson Institute for International Economics, 2011), which is a well-deserved, but a self-congratulatory piece, perhaps a bit premature. See also the interview with Valdis Dombrovskis by Katarzyna Zuchowicz, "Najgorsze już za Łotyszami," ("The Worst Is Already Behind the Latvians") *Rzeczpospolita* (July 12, 2010): http://www.rp.pl/artykul/2,507768. html; "Dombrowskis Chosen as Latvian PM," *BBC News* (February 26, 2009): http://news.bbc.co.uk/2/hi/europe/7911983.stm; "Valda Dombrovska Blog," http://valdisdombrovskis.lv/; "Latvia PM Valdis Dombrovskis Wins Election, to Hold Coalition Talks," *The Times of India* (October 3, 2010): http://timesofindia. indiatimes.com/world/europe/Latvia-PM-Valdis-Dombrovskis-wins-election-to-hold-coalition-talks/articleshow/6675375.cms; "Guts and Glory: Latvians Defy Conventional Wisdom by Re-electing an Austerity Government," *The Economist* (October 7, 2010): http://www.economist.com/node/17204851; "Same Old Saeima?" *The Economist* (July 26, 2011): http://www.economist. com/blogs/easternapproaches/2011/07/latvia.

19.   See the "Unity" bloc's website at http://www.vienotiba.lv/.

20.   For the Latvian Peasant Union see http://www.lzs.lv/.

21.   For the Green-Peasant coalition see http://www.zzs.lv/. Its chief sponsor is oligarch Aivars Lembergs.

22.   Descending originally from the Latvian National Independence Movement (LNNK) of 1988–90, the right-nationalists of the National Alliance stem from two main groups: National Conservative Party and "For Fatherland and Freedom." Both joined forces in 1995, when the latter absorbed the former. Later, they were joined by a more hard-core nationalist outfit "Everything for Latvia!" The nationalists served in Dombrovskis's first government but failed to join the second cabinet. The break came because of the nationalist demands to repatriate Russian speakers to Russia. For the National Alliance's website see http://www.visulatvijaidodu.lv/. See also Aaron Eglitis, "Latvia's Dombrovskis to Form a Two-Party Government as the Nationalists Left out," *Bloomberg* (October 25, 2010), http://www.bloomberg.com/news/2010-10-25/latvia-s-dombrovskis-to-form-two-party-government-as-nationalists-left-out.html; "Latvia PM Party Has Fresh Doubts Over 3-Party Govt," *Reuters* (October 25, 2010): http://www.reuters.com/article/idUSLDE69O0IF20101025. For the electoral durability of the nationalists see Wolfram Nordsieck, "Parties and Elections in Europe: Latvia," 2010, http://www.parties-and-elections.de/latvia2. html; and Centre for the Study of Public Policy, University of Aberdeen, "Baltic Voices: Latvian Government," http://www.balticvoices.org/latvia/latvian_ elections.php.

23.   "Same Old Saeima?" *The Economist* (July 26, 2011): http://www.economist. com/blogs/easternapproaches/2011/07/latvia.

24.   For Latvia's election results of October 2010 see http://www.parties-and-elections.de/latvia.html.

25.   The Harmony Center received 28.71 percent of the vote (thirty-one seats); the Reform Party – 20.31 percent (twenty-two seats); and "Unity" bloc – 19.16 percent (twenty seats). The parliament sits one hundred deputies. See "Prorosyjskie Centrum Zgody Wygrywa na Łotwie," *Rzeczpospolita* (September 17, 2011):

http://www.rp.pl/artykul/26,718902-Wybory--prorosyjskie-Centrum-Zgody-na-czele---exit-polls.html; "Latvia's Election: Reboot in Riga: A Low-Key Election Marks a Big Shake-Up. But More Is to Come," *The Economist* (September 24, 2011): http://www.economist.com/node/21530161; Vladimir Socor, "After Elections, Latvia Can Have a Latvian Government Again (Part One)," *Eurasia Daily Monitor* 8, no. 175 (September 23, 2011): http://www.jamestown.org/programs/edm/single/?tx_ttnews%5Btt_news%5D=38443&tx_ttnews%5Bbac kPid%5D=27&cHash=bd167a24531d05d28250ac0435903c53; Vladimir Socor, "After Elections, Latvia Can Have a Latvian Government Again (Part Two)," *Eurasia Daily Monitor* 8, no. 176 (September 26, 2011): http://www.jamestown.org/programs/edm/single/?tx_ttnews%5Btt_news%5D=38447&tx_ttnews%5Bb ackPid%5D=27&cHash=47bd818d3021923f25ad1cbcb2695f15; Vladimir Socor, "A Latvian Government for Latvia," *Eurasia Daily Monitor* 8, no. 197 (October 26, 2011): http://www.jamestown.org/single/?no_cache=1&tx_ttnews%5Btt_news%5D=38573.

26. E.L. and K.S., "Latvia: Phew," *The Economist* (October 3, 2010): http://www.economist.com/blogs/easternapproaches/2010/10/latvia.

27. See Mike Collier, "Latvia Prepares for a Three-Way Split," *Business New Europe* (August 19, 2011): http://www.bne.eu/story2848.

28. For an introduction to Lithuania see Linda Drengsgaard, Ole Hersted Hansen, and Line Brøgger, "State of the State in Lithuania," Demstar Research Report no. 19, University of Aarhus, Department of Political Science (July 2004): 1–41, http://www.demstar.dk/papers/SotSLithuania[1].pdf; Algimantas Jankauskas and Darius Žeruolis, "Understanding Politics in Lithuania," ed. Ole Nørgaard and Lars Johannsen, Demstar Research Report no. 18, University of Aarhus, Department of Political Science (February 2004): 1–32, http://www.demstar.dk/papers/UnderstandingLithuania.pdf; Lars Johannsen and Tom Y. K. Nielsen, "The Political Economy of Agrarian Reform: Lithuania in Comparative Perspective," Demstar Research Report no. 8, University of Aarhus, Department of Political Science (September 2002): 1–38, http://www.demstar.dk/papers/Agrarian-Reform.pdf; Central Intelligence Agency, "Lithuania," *The World Factbook*, https://www.cia.gov/library/publications/the-world-factbook/geos/lh.html; US State Department's Bureau of European and Eurasian Affairs, "Background Note: Lithuania," (July 2, 2010): http://www.state.gov/r/pa/ei/bgn/5379.htm; Centre for the Study of Public Policy, University of Aberdeen, "Baltic Voices: Lithuanian Government," http://www.balticvoices.org/lithuania/lithuanian_government.php?S776173303132=32238329d605a6f7c35ac88272097d11, but updated only until 2004. For electoral results between 1990 and 2008 see Wolfram Nordsieck, "Parties and Elections in Europe: Lithuania," http://www.parties-and-elections.de/lithuania2.html and http://www.parties-and-elections.de/lithuania.html. For consistent electoral and political coverage of the nation in the twenty-first century see Algis Krupavicius, "Lithuania," *European Journal of Political Research* 41, no. 7–8 (December 2002): 873–79; 42, no. 7–8 (December 2003): 1010–20; 43, no. 7–8 (December 2004): 1059–69; 44, no. 7–8 (December 2005): 1086–101; 45, no. 7–8 (December 2006): 1166–81; 48, no. 7–8 (December 2009): 1022–36; 49, no. 7–8 (December 2010): 1058–75. See also A. E. Senn, *Lithuania Awakening* (Berkeley, CA: University of California Press, 2002); Rawi Abdelal, *National Purpose in the World Economy: Post-Soviet States in Comparative Perspective* (Ithaca, NY: Cornell University Press, 2001), Chapter 4, "Lithuania: Toward Europe and the West," 84–102; Verena Fritz, *State-Building: A Comparative Study of Ukraine, Lithuania, Belarus,*

and Russia (Budapest: Central European University Press, 2007), Chapter 10, "Lithuania: Moving towards Western Models," 243–84; Alvidas Rukošaitis and Darius Žeruolis, "Dynamics of Institutionalization of Standing Committees in the Lithuanian Parliament, 1990–92: First Democratic Term," in *Committees in the New Democratic Parliaments of Central Europe*, ed. David M. Olson and William E. Crowther (Columbus, OH: The Ohio State University Press, 2003), 134–53. For the best depiction of the manipulation of Lithuania's politics by the KGB and its FSB successor see Jerzy Targalski, "Litwa: Opozycja," (Lithuania: The Opposition) TMs, Warsaw, no date (2008), 1–153, in particular pages 104–53 (1991–2008).

29. Alfred Erich Senn, "Post-Soviet Political Leadership in Lithuania," in *Patterns in Post-Soviet Leadership*, ed. Timothy J. Colton and Robert C. Tucker (Boulder, CO: Westview Press, 1995), 123–40; Ole Hersted Hansen and Ferdinand Müller-Rommel, "Lithuania," in *Cabinets in Eastern Europe*, ed. Jean Blondel and Ferdinand Müller-Rommel (Basingstoke: Palgrave, 2001), 40–49.

30. Mindaugas Jurkinas and Ainė Ramonaité, "Divergent Perceptions of Political Conflict in Lithuania," in *Political Culture: Values And Identities in the Baltic Sea Region*, ed. Sten Berglund, Bernd Henningsen, and Mai-Brith Schartau (Berlin: Berliner Wissenschafts-Verlag, 2006), 183–203.

31. On Brazauska's ride in free Lithuania see Ausra Park, "The End of the Lithuanian Political 'Patriarch's' Era: From Rise to Decline and Legacies Left Behind," *Demokratizatsiya: The Journal of Post-Soviet Democratization* 18, no. 2 (Spring 2010): 160–81.

32. Thomas Lane, *Lithuania: Stepping Westward* (London and New York: Routledge, 2001), 141–42; Alexandra Ashbourne, *Lithuania: The Rebirth of a Nation, 1991–1994* (Oxford and Lanham, MD: Lexington Books, 1999), 41; Anatol Lieven, *The Baltic Revolution: Estonia, Latvia, Lithuania and the Path to Independence* (New Haven, CT: Yale University Press, 1993), 235–36, 271; "Lithuania," in *Freedom in the World, 1997–1998: The Annual Survey of Political Rights and Civil Liberties, 1997–1998*, ed. Adrian Karatnycky (New York: Freedom House, 1998), 338.

33. See "Lithuanian Court Deems Lustration Law Constitutional," *RFE/RL NEWSLINE*, 3, no. 45, Part II, (March 5, 1999): http://warrencountychronicle.com/friends/news/omri/1999/03/990305II.html(opt,mozilla,mac,russian,koi8,new); Neil J. Kritz, ed., *Transnational Justice: How Emerging Democracies Reckon with Former Regimes*, vol. 2: *Country Studies* (Washington, DC: United States Institute of Peace, 1995), Chapter 21: "Lithuania," 763–70. For the record, even Adamkus has been accused of working for the KGB. A leading Polish expert has alleged that the Lithuanian president was a Soviet agent operating under the code-name "Fermeris." See Jerzy Targalski aka [Józef Darski] interviewed by Łukasz Wiater, "W systemie sowieckim agenturalność jest dziedziczna, a w post-komuniźmie zapewnia karierę," ("In the Soviet System Being an Agent Is Inherited, and in Post-Communism It Facilitates a Career") (March 12, 2011) http://www.portal.arcana.pl/W-systemie-sowieckim-agenturalnosc-jest-dziedziczna-a-w-postkomunizmie-zapewnia-kariere,910.html and http://portal.arcana.salon24.pl/286650,targalski-w-postkomunizmie-agenturalnosc-zapewnia-kariere.

34. See Ginta T. Palubinskas, "Democratic State Building in Post-Communist Lithuania," *Lituanus: Lithuanian Quarterly Journal of Arts and Sciences* 51, no. 4 (Winter 2005): http://www.lituanus.org/2005/05_4_2Palubinskas.htm; Zenonas Norkus, "Carl Schmitt as a Resource for Democratic Consolidation

Studies: The Case of the President's Impeachment in Lithuania (Rolandas Paksas)," *East European Politics and Societies* 22, no. 4 (Fall 2008): 784–802.

35. This is coined as a contraction of Euroeuphoric.

36. The ever naïve American newspaper of record inexplicably reported: "Rightist Wins Presidency in Lithuania," *The New York Times* (January 6, 2003): http://www.nytimes.com/2003/01/06/world/rightist-wins-presidency-in-lithuania.html?ref=rolandaspaksas.

37. An avid flier, Paksas was chummy with a murky Russian aviation businessman, Yuri Borisov, who donated at least $400,000.00 to the politician's election campaign. In return, the president-elect restored Borisov's Lithuanian citizenship by decree. He further shared with his pal secrets of the police investigation against the businessman as well as assisted him in commercial dealings regarding privatization of state property. To expedite the process, the businessman threatened the politician, as wiretaps by Lithuania's security services demonstrated. Borisov's main contact with Paksas was the President's national security advisor, Remigijus Acus. Borisov was connected to Almax, a Russian consulting firm with alleged links to the FSB. The Russian businessman was also involved with supplying weapon systems (helicopter parts) to Sudan in violation of EU laws. Aside from being impeached and barred from holding public office, Paksas was not punished for his crimes. The scandal should be seen in the context of Western intelligence warnings about the penetration of the nation by the Russian capital (money laundering being one of the concerns) before Lithuania's imminent entry into the NATO and the EU, which eventually happened in May 2004. See Vaidotas A. Vaičaitis, "Transitional Democracy and Judicial Review: Lithuanian Case," no page number, note 8, a paper delivered at the VII World Congress of the International Association of Constitutional Law, Zappeion Megaron, Athens, Greece, June 11–15, 2007, http://www.enelsyn.gr/papers/w5/Paper%20by%20Prof%20Vaidotas%20A.%20Vaicaitis.pdf; Stephen Lee Myers, "A New Role on Lithuania's Horizon; a New Scandal, Too," *The New York Times* (December 28, 2003): http://www.nytimes.com/2003/12/28/world/a-new-role-on-lithuania-s-horizon-a-new-scandal-too.html?ref=rolandaspaksas; "Borisov Not Packing His Bags Yet," *The Baltic Times* (January 8, 2004): http://www.baltictimes.com/news/articles/9226/; Steven Paulikas, "Borisov's Lawyers Battle Deportation Orders," *The Baltic Times* (January 15, 2004): http://www.baltictimes.com/news/articles/9260/; Stephen Lee Myers, "Lithuanian Parliament Removes Country's President after Casting Votes on Three Charges," *The New York Times* (April 7, 2004): http://www.nytimes.com/2004/04/07/world/lithuanian-parliament-removes-country-s-president-after-casting-votes-three.html?pagewanted=1; Milda Seputyte, "Government Prepared to Deport Borysov," *The Baltic Times* (July 8, 2004): http://www.baltictimes.com/news/articles/10375/; Jerzy Targalski aka [Józef Darski] interviewed by Łukasz Wiater, "W systemie sowieckim agenturalność jest dziedziczna, a w post-komuniźmie zapewnia karierę," ("In the Soviet System Being an Agent Is Inherited, and in Post-Communism It Facilitates a Career") (March 12, 2011): http://www.portal.arcana.pl/W-systemie-sowieckim-agenturalnosc-jest-dziedziczna-a-w-postkomunizmie-zapewnia-kariere,910.html and http://portal.arcana.salon24.pl/286650,targalski-w-postkomunizmie-agenturalnosc-zapewnia-kariere. Paksas sued Lithuania in the European Court of Human Rights and won his case. According to EU judges, the impeachment violated Paksas's human rights as did the barring of the politicians from future elections. Lithuania promised to "accept" the ruling. See "Grybauskaite Bows to EU Court Ruling," *The Baltic*

Times (January 12, 2011): http://www.baltictimes.com/news/articles/27706/; "Lithuania Loses Euro Court Case Over Ex-Leader Paksas," *BBC News* (January 6, 2011): http://www.bbc.co.uk/news/world-europe-12126217. For the verdict see GRAND CHAMBER, CASE OF PAKSAS v. LITHUANIA (Application no. 34932/04), JUDGMENT, STRASBOURG, (January 6, 2011): http://cmiskp.echr.coe.int/tkp197/view.asp?action=html&documentId=879540&portal=hbkm&source=externalbydocnumber&table=F69A27FD8FB86142BF01C1166DEA398649.

38.   For his party's website see http://www.ldp.lt/.

39.   Premier Gediminas Vagnorius of the Homeland Union (Lithuanian Conservatives) was allegedly a KGB informer. Although her own father was killed by the NKVD in 1944, the heroine of the Sąjūdis and two-times prime minister Kazimiera Prunskiene reported, under the code name "Shatri," about her academic contacts abroad. Unabashed, Prunskiene became an agrarian populist and keeps running for president with decent results. See Tomas Skucas, "Lithuania: A Problem of Disclosure," in *Dismantling Tyranny: Transitioning Beyond Totalitarian Regimes*, ed. Illan Berman and J. Michael Waller (Lanham, MD, Boulder, CO, Toronto, and London: Rowman & Littlefield, 2006), 89–106, especially 102–3; Matt Bivens, "Wanted Alive: Ex-KGB Agents and Informers Baltic states hunt down former Soviet operatives with a vengeance: Already, a prime minister and a foreign minister have been toppled," *The Los Angeles Times* (August 2, 1994): http://articles.latimes.com/1994-08-02/news/wr-22515_1_prime-minister; Olga S. Opfell, *Women Prime Ministers and Presidents* (Jefferson, NC: McFarland and Co., 1993), 161–68.

40.   See Milda Seputyte, "Leaked KGB Documents Stir Fresh Round of Political Intrigue," *The Baltic Times* (January 12, 2005): http://www.baltictimes.com/news/articles/11744/; "Lithuania Still Up in Arms Over KGB Collaborators," *The Baltic Times* (January 12, 2005): http://www.baltictimes.com/news/articles/11765/; "'Ketvirtoji valdžia': Antanas Valionis – apie KGB šmėklas, šių dienų realijas ir ateities vizijas," Balsas.lt, 17 January 2005, http://www.balsas.lt/naujiena/269012/ketvirtoji-valdzia-antanas-valionis-apie-kgb-smeklas-siu-dienu-realijas-ir-ateities-vizijas.

41.   See Adam Mullett, "KGB Secrets To Be Published," *Baltic Reports: Daily News from the Baltic States* (February 24, 2010): http://balticreports.com/?p=11541.

42.   This refers, in particular, to the Homeland Union and the Christian Democrats. See Centre for the Study of Public Policy, University of Aberdeen, "Baltic Voices: Lithuanian Government," http://www.balticvoices.org/lithuania/lithuanian_government.php?S776173303132=32238329d605a6f7c35ac88272097d11, but updated only until 2004. For electoral results between 1990 and 2008 see Wolfram Nordsieck, "Parties and Elections in Europe: Lithuania," http://www.parties-and-elections.de/lithuania2.html and http://www.parties-and-elections.de/lithuania.html.

43.   Tomas Skucas, "Lithuania: A Problem of Disclosure," in *Dismantling Tyranny: Transitioning beyond Totalitarian Regimes*, ed. Illan Berman and J. Michael Waller (Lanham, MD, Boulder, CO, Toronto, and London: Rowman & Littlefield, 2006), 102–3; "Lithuania," in *Freedom in the World, 1997–1998: The Annual Survey of Political Rights and Civil Liberties, 1997–1998*, ed. Adrian Karatnycky (New York: Freedom House, 1998), 338; "Lithuanian Premier Slams Charges against Landsbergis," *RFE/RL NEWSLINE* 1, no. 131, Part II, (October 3, 1997): http://www.friends-partners.org/friends/news/omri/1997/10/971003II.

html(opt,mozilla,unix,english,,new). And see Vytautas Landsbergis, "The Road to Citizen," *Uncaptive Minds* 7, no. 2 (Summer 1994).

44. See Terry D. Clark, "The 1996 Elections to the Lithuanian Seimas and Their Aftermath," *Journal of Baltic Studies* 29, no. 2 (1998): 135–48; and Terry D. Clark and Nerijus Prekevičius, "Explaining the 2000 Lithuanian Parliamentary Elections: An Application of Contextual and New Institutional Approaches," *Slavic Review* 62, no. 3 (2003): 548–69.

45. See the party's website at http://www.tsajunga.lt/.

46. See David Burgess, "Farewell to Postcommunism (Lithuania)," *Uncaptive Minds* 9, no. 1–2 (31–32) (Winter–Spring 1997); Diana Janusauskiené, "The Metamorphosis of the Communist Party of Lithuania," in *The Communist Successor Parties of Central and Eastern Europe*, ed. András Bozóki and John T. Ishiyama (Armonk, NY: M.E. Sharpe, 2002), 224–39.

47. It is led by former deputy chief prosecutor of the Soviet Lithuanian Socialist Republic, Arturas Paulaskas, who later served as the chief prosecutor of free Lithuania. Paulaskas's father was a KGB snitch. See "Lithuania," in *Freedom in the World, 1997–1998: The Annual Survey of Political Rights and Civil Liberties, 1997–1998*, ed. Adrian Karatnycky (New York: Freedom House, 1998), 338. For the party website see http://www.nsajunga.lt/Default.aspx?Lang=EN.

48. Józef Darski [Jerzy Targalski], "De-Communization: The Case of Lithuania," *Uncaptive Minds* 6, no. 1 (Winter–Spring 1993): 78–81; Claire Bigg, "Interview: Former Lithuanian President Says 'Communism Was Never Defeated,'" *Radio Free Europe/Radio Liberty*, (March 2, 2010): http://www.rferl.org/content/Interview_Former_Lithuanian_President_Says_Communism_Was_Never_Defeated/1972668.html.

49. The LSDP was an urban-based Marxist party which attempted to attract the Lithuanian peasant masses. It failed because the peasants ultimately chose Lithuanian nationalism instead, and the LSDP was left with its Polish and Jewish urban followers. See Dalius Vasys, "The Lithuanian Social Democratic Party and the Revolution of 1905," *Lituanus: Lithuanian Quarterly Journal of Arts and Sciences* 23, no. 3 (Fall 1977): http://www.lituanus.org/1977/77_3_02.htm.

50. For the party's website see http://www.lsdp.lt/.

51. Uspaskich founded and bankrolled the Labor Party, which did very well in the elections of 2004. His hard-core electorate consists mostly of the Russian minority. Subsequently, he became the minister of economy in the cabinet of prime minister Brazauskas. He promptly quarreled with his boss over the privatizing of the strategic oil refinery at Mažeikiai. He opposed its sale to a Polish-owned company, and advocated Russian ownership instead. In May 2006, following the allegations of corruption, Uspaskich suspended his party leadership and fled to Moscow, where he asked for political asylum. After holding him briefly in September 2006, the Kremlin ultimately refused to extradite the oligarch to Vilnius. In September 2007 Uspaskich nonetheless returned to Lithuania where he continues to run the Labor Party. Despite his legal problems, including fresh allegations of embezzlement, his party performs decently in national elections and the oligarch even got himself voted into the European Parliament in 2009. See Vladimir Vodo and Gennady Sysoev, "Uspaskich at the Gate: A Russian-born Businessman Could Become Prime Minister of Lithuania," *Kommersant* (October 12, 2004): http://www.kommersant.com/p514113/r_1/Uspaskich_at_the_Gate/; "Founder of Lithuanian Labor Party Viktor Uspaskich Released from Custody," *Regnum* (September 28, 2007): http://www.regnum.ru/english/891492.html; Adam Mullet, "Labor Party

Invited into Ruling Coalition," *Baltic Reports: Daily News from the Baltic States* (October 23, 2009): http://balticreports.com/?p=3252; Jerzy Targalski aka [Józef Darski] interviewed by Łukasz Wiater, "W systemie sowieckim agenturalność jest dziedziczna, a w post-komuniźmie zapewnia karierę," (In the Soviet System Being an Agent Is Inherited, and in Post-Communism It Facilitates a Career) (March 12, 2011) http://www.portal.arcana.pl/W-systemie-sowieckim-agenturalnosc-jest-dziedziczna-a-w-postkomunizmie-zapewnia-kariere,910.html and http://portal.arcana.salon24.pl/286650,targalski-w-postkomunizmie-agenturalnosc-zapewnia-kariere.

18

Southern and Central Intermarium

Lithuania seems to be the least Westernized of the Baltic states. However, with all its quirks and problems, its overall positive condition is a far cry from the divisive predicament that Ukraine, Belarus, and Moldova find themselves in. The largest and most populous of all the Intermarium's newly independent nations, Ukraine is mired in a plethora of challenges. We shall discuss its geographic, historical, cultural, and confessional divisions. But first, we shall focus on the political differences stemming from them.

Ukraine

Ukraine has struggled to maintain a parliamentary democracy.[1] After a lackluster start, Kyiv approximated it closely, in particular, between 2004 and 2010, even though it has lately suffered an apparent reversal. The significance and extent of the relapse cannot be gauged at the moment. However, if anything, it has pushed the nation closer to Moscow's model of "sovereign democracy," rather than Minsk's brazen dictatorship.

In some ways, Kyiv's political system resembles that of Tallinn, Riga, and Vilnius. It combines Western and post-Soviet ingredients, favoring the latter. In other ways, it is sui generis, or at least imparts a strong local flavor into the Western-cum-post-Soviet mix.

Ukraine's chief cultural feature is a de facto bilingualism: Ukrainian being prevalent in the west, and Russian in the east. This carries serious political and social implications to be discussed later.[2] It is not a bilingualism of aliens as in Estonia and Latvia. It would be similar to the intractable bilingualism of Belgium if the pacific Netherlands was the menacing Russian Federation. In Ukraine the Russian-speakers are largely native to the region, in the east, in particular, and not postwar colonial leftovers. Moreover, Ukraine is confused, or at least divided, about its national identity and the role of the state in fostering it. Yet, nationalism legitimizes the new nation state. All political contenders make use of it to mobilize the population and claim power for themselves, including, conveniently, the post-Communists.[3]

Ukraine's political economy and institutional structures seem akin to Russia's. So does its high level and character of oligarchy and corruption. Thus, rather than strengthening democracy and free markets, necessary reforms like privatization primarily fuel post-Communists pathologies, in a short run at least. This adversely impacts public opinion and voter preferences, which are also influenced by party machine politics and voter fraud.[4] Further, the Ukrainian judiciary is beholden to the politicians to a much greater extent than in the Baltics.[5] The Ukrainian political landscape is pockmarked moreover by extreme forms of post-Soviet and post-Communist personal and institutional survivals.[6] Next, its main administrational oddity is the Autonomous Republic of Crimea. Other features, however, conform to the general standard prevalent in the Intermarium.

Like the Baltics, Ukraine has a unicameral parliament, the Supreme Soviet/Council (*Verkhovna Rada*), which is subject to popular elections.[7] The nation's executive branch is dual: a powerful president and a strong prime minister. The former is elected by direct vote; the latter is appointed by the president but must be confirmed by the parliament. Further, the president retains the right to name foreign and defense ministers as well as provincial administrators, the latter put forth by the prime minister. The lack of concord between both chief executives may lead to a paralysis of the state and, in the worst case scenario, a constitutional crisis.

The power of Ukrainian presidency has waxed and waned over the past twenty years. This fluctuation has reflected institutional continuity with the Soviet system, the personalities of the successive presidents, the need for stability, and the drive for authority.[8] Or to put it more crudely, strong presidency has served the post-Communists rather well. Having virtually monopolized power in Ukraine into the twenty-first century, they have justified it in terms of maintaining stability. The Orange Revolution of 2004 halted and reversed this trend, although it is unclear how durable this particular victory for democracy will remain. Let us consider the presidents before and after this watershed.

Ukraine's first postliberation president Leonid Kravchuk (1991–1996) was perhaps the weakest of all chief executives.[9] An ethnic Ukrainian, Kravchuk was born in the countryside of Poland's western Ukraine in 1934. His father served as a cavalryman in the Polish army, perishing during World War II. In its wake, Kravchuk became a Communist party member, earning his wings in the propaganda apparatus. Later, as a Gorbachevian reform Communist, he was co-opted to the Soviet Ukraine's Politburo in 1989. He failed to reform and "nationalize" the Communist party and quit it in August 1991 to join the independence movement. Thus, he went the national Bolshevik way. Meanwhile, banking on his popularity as the Speaker of the Supreme Soviet (*Rada*), Kravchuk defeated the celebrated dissident and nationalist leader Viacheslav Chornovil for national presidency. Later, however, the chief executive flirted with western Ukraine's nationalists for expediency's sake.

Although he surrendered Ukraine's nuclear weapons, the president eschewed close cooperation with Russia within the Commonwealth of Independent States (CIS). In particular, he opposed a common army and currency with Russia. His term in office saw an economic collapse and massive fraud during the privatization of state assets.[10] The chief executive was implicated in a number of financial scandals which came to surface despite the silence of almost uniformly sycophantic media. Upon losing the presidency, in the wake of a prolonged clash with prime minister Leonid Kuchma (1992–1993), Kravchuk openly joined the oligarchs of Kyiv, the so-called "Dynamo Group," a staunchly Russophile and anti-Western outfit, which on the political arena branded itself as the Social Democratic Party of Ukraine-United.[11]

His successor, Leonid Kuchma (1994–2004), carried himself like a true strongman.[12] Born in a village in the east of Soviet Ukraine, he also lost his father in the war and joined the Communist party upon adulthood. A rocket engineer by training, Kuchma's career advanced on a dual track as a scientific apparatchik and an industrial executive in several places including the space ship launching center at Baikonur in Soviet Kazakhstan and the mammoth "Yuzhny" machine plant at Dnipropetrovsk (Dnepropetrovsk) in eastern Ukraine. He used the resources of the latter to maintain himself in politics during and after the implosion of the USSR. Elected to the *Rada*, Kuchma allied himself with other eastern Ukrainian oligarchs and their industrial complex. After serving as prime minister (1992–1993), he quit to challenge the sitting president. Subsequently, Kuchma was elected to the highest office twice. First, in 1994, he mildly trounced the incumbent Kravchuk, who lost the support of the Russian-speaking east and south. Next, he won handily against the unreconstructed Communist Petro Symonenko. Kuchma's perhaps more viable challenger, the romantic nationalist Chornovil, died in a mysterious car crash shortly before the election in 1999.[13]

Ukraine's second president executed a policy of *rapprochement* with Russia, on the one hand. On the other, he eschewed preventing the policy of nation-building (mostly by the force of inertia)[14] and pleased the international community with his economic reforms, including expedited privatization. Yet, the economy failed to recuperate until well into his second term, and then briefly. Kuchma and his family[15] meanwhile became mired in massive corruption scandals, including illicit acquisition of state assets and illegal weapon system sales in the Middle East. There were allegations of links to the local mafia, its Russian overbosses, and even Columbian drug cartels. The president clamped down on the media, which ultimately led to a high-profile grizzly murder of an opposition investigative journalist.[16] Kuchma also fought bitterly with his successive prime ministers. Arguably the most contentious and protracted power struggle involved premier Viktor Yushchenko (1999–2001). The president helped the unreformed Communists and oligarchs oust his prime minister amidst much mutual recrimination. Kuchma's star began to wane however and many of his eastern oligarchic/industrial associates abandoned him. That is perhaps why, in 2004, the president refused to support their favorite and, at the same time, his own last prime minister, Viktor Yanukovych (2002–2004), against Yushchenko during the so-called Orange Revolution.

The Orange (Counter)Revolution has been so far the most important watershed in free Ukraine's contemporary affairs.[17] In essence, it was a counterrevolution against post-Communism. It was an endeavor to put the nation on par with the Baltics in terms of democratic development. It dealt a serious, if not yet lethal, blow to post-Communism. It unleashed an unprecedented wave of grassroots activism. The popular enthusiasm rivaled that of the heyday of the proindependence surge between 1988 and 1992, but it was much more polarizing for the nation. On one level, the Orange Revolution was, of course, a battle of various oligarchic and post-Communist coteries. But on the most visible and dynamic level, it pitted the easterners against the westerners, and the post-Communism of the former against the nationalism of the latter. In addition, the followers of the Orthodox Moscow Patriarchate squared off with the Uniates, while the Autocephalic Ukrainian Orthodox remained divided in their loyalties, mostly according to their geographic location in the nation. Further, the Ukrainian young faced off with the old. Yet, not all of the seniors objected to the Orange Revolution. There were plenty of the elderly in the Orange ranks, and enough of the youth opposing them. Region, not age, determined one's political stance. Last but not least, at the lowest level, the frustrated individual petitioners took on the stony-faced government bureaucrats via the Orange way.

The Orange Revolution broke out in November 2004 in reaction to strong-arm violence, candidate intimidation, voter coercion, and massive electoral fraud. The Orange camp supporters feared that business as usual would enthrone another dour former Communist *nomenklaturshchik*, Yanukovych, as Ukraine's president. The grassroots were already agitated because of the assassination attempt by poisoning of the leading presidential candidate, Yushchenko, in September 2004. A nationalist mobilization of students and others took place throughout the nation, most enthusiastically and massively in western Ukraine. However, the most crucial part of the Orange Revolution played itself out in Kyiv. In the capital city the throngs assembled to protest in a nonviolent way against the post-Communist pathologies in the nation's life. When electoral returns were reported favoring Yanukovych, demands went out for a recount and, then, a rematch. In addition, the demonstrators advanced a variety of postulates, including economic, social, and cultural. Transparency of public life was one of the most popular demands as was the fight against corruption. Other proposals were of economic and standard of living character. Anti-Communism and anti-post-Communism undergirded nearly all of them. Freedom once again was the *cri du coeur et du jour* in the streets of Kyiv and elsewhere. The presidential contest was duly replayed and Yushchenko won the highest office in January 2005. The Orange camp proclaimed a victory for Ukraine.

Victory perhaps it was, but an imperfect and impermanent one, of course. The Orange orientation concentrated on the immediate: a fair election. However, it lacked a strategic vision for Ukraine's feature. It was short of cadres, resources, and the know-how of political warfare. Except emotionally and briefly, the grassroots largely failed to connect to the leadership and vice versa. The political victors at the top almost immediately fell at each other's throats. Yet, the Orange Revolution has left in its wake an enduring legacy of grassroots mobilization and regional solidarity, even if of the opposing orientations. Its most durable result was the presidency of Viktor Yushchenko (2004–2010).

Born in an eastern Ukrainian village after the war, Yushchenko is a child of teachers. His father was not only a Red Army POW of the Nazis and an Auschwitz survivor, but also a defiantly nonparty person. An Orthodox Christian, Yushchenko adheres to the Ukrainian Autocephalic Church. An economist by training, during the Soviet occupation he worked as a midlevel official in an economic institution. Yushchenko was a rank-and-file Communist party member. He first surfaced as a Gorbachevian technocratic "reformer" in 1989. Following Ukraine's independence, Yushchenko parlayed his Soviet-time employment in the financial sector into an impressive banking career. Appointed by the parliament, he headed the National Bank of Ukraine from 1993 to 1999. Occupying a crucial banking post during the orgy of embezzlement of the early to mid-1990s, Yushchenko certainly associated on the professional field with the oligarchs and kleptocrats but personally steered clear of major scandals, as much as it was possible, of course, for a person in his capacity.[18] During his travails as prime minister he garnered an impressive mass following. The banker-turned-politician capitalized on it handsomely when he entered the presidential joust in 2004.

His campaign experienced a dramatic turning point when, as mentioned, Yushchenko was allegedly poisoned by the deputy head of Ukraine's secret police, Volodymyr Statsyuk, who promptly fled to Russia. The presidential candidate survived, if badly disfigured. Rumors of a government conspiracy swirled, and Moscow's hand was seen behind the Kyiv cabal that was implicated in the assassination attempt. And the cabal and its allies defended themselves with self-contradictory counterclaims that the poisoning was a hoax and, besides, it was America's CIA that orchestrated the whole sordid affair, undoubtedly in cahoots with Yushchenko's American wife, Katherine.[19]

Yushchenko's presidential record is rather ambivalent, at least in a short run. On the one hand, he followed into the footsteps of his predecessors by quarreling violently with his prime ministers. Most notably, in September 2005 the head of state fired the flamboyant oligarch-turned-populist politician, Yulia Tymoshenko, a powerful force in the Orange Revolution. The president also promptly dismissed a number of his other erstwhile Orange allies. Thus, he undermined the ad hoc parliamentary coalition and destabilized the country. To add insult to injury, but also to return a measure of stability, Yushchenko appointed his erstwhile rival Yanukovych as prime minister (2006–2007). The vituperation among the Orange elite thus paved the way to the restoration of the post-Communist leadership of eastern Ukraine and its allies. Most importantly, it demobilized the civic grassroots behind the Orange Revolution. The waning of popular support was blamed on Yushchenko's bumbling ways and inability to compromise.[20] Ukraine's economic performance on the president's watch also left much to be desired, but that had much to do mostly with inimical global trends and Russia's periodic flexing of its energy muscle, which we shall address later. Last but not least, the head of state's vigorous efforts to join NATO and the European Union came to naught.

On the other hand, Yushchenko conducted a vigorous anticorruption drive, for example, dismissing nearly all uniformed commissioned police officers at one point. This applied to traffic inspectors, in particular, the hive of graft. Most importantly, he clung fast to democracy and never violated its rules. In fact, the third president's greatest achievement was to ensure, for the first time in Ukraine's history, fair elections between 2006 and 2010.

His historical policy was more controversial, but, at least partly, rather laudable.[21] Yushchenko introduced the commemorations of the victims of the Terror-Famine (*Holodomor*) on the countrywide scale as a major binding element of Ukrainian nationalism. Both the eastern and western parts of the country have related well to the restoration of common history, the former because it was the epicenter of Stalin's extermination through hunger and latter because of its high levels of national solidarity and anti-Communism. However, casting the Terror-Famine as mainly, or even solely, a Ukrainian tragedy, and narrating it publicly so that it is incorrectly perceived as such, has alienated needlessly Ukraine's minorities, as well as other victims of Stalin's forced collectivization throughout the Soviet sphere, from Belarus through Russia to Kazakhstan.

Also the endeavor to endow Ukraine with the Ukrainian Cossack mythology, focusing on the *Zaporizhian* Sich as the mythical heart of Ukrainian statehood and Hetman Bohdan Khmelnytsky (Bohdan Chmielnicki, ca. 1595–1657) as its founding father, failed to carry the day. Khmelnytsky was a rebellious Polish noble with a Catholic father and an Orthodox mother in the old Commonwealth, which is not exactly a trump card among either Ukrainian ethno-nationalists or Moscow-centric Russophiles. Besides, the latter prefer their own Cossack myth: the Russian imperial Cossacks of the Don and elsewhere. Further, geographically, it is hard to showcase the Hetmanate as an all-Ukrainian state. It never controlled more than a portion of the central and north-eastern Ukrainian lands and that for a rather short period. For nationalistic reasons its appeal is obvious in the Ukrainophone central and western parts of the nation. However, it largely failed to impress in the Russian-speaking regions in the east and south. Even the recently recreated historic site of the Sich on an islet on the lower Dnieper is symbolically dwarfed by a nearby gigantic Soviet-era dam and a power plant of the Kakhovka Reservoir that the eastern Ukrainian population nostalgically relates to much more eagerly.

Last but not least, Yushchenko's consistent endorsement of the ultraradical Ukrainian Nationalist Organization (OUN) of the interwar and war years, including the last-minute presidential lionizing of one of its top leaders, the late extremist Stepan Bandera, proved very divisive. In addition to Jewish groups at home and abroad, as well as Russia and the European Union officially, and some Poles unofficially, it angered many in eastern Ukraine, where the locals, including the Ukrainians, reject Bandera and his followers as "fascists" and, instead, celebrate the "victorious Red Army."[22]

By the end of his presidency Yushchenko was at the nadir of his popularity. He ran nonetheless but failed abysmally to qualify for the second round which pitted the populist oligarch Tymoshenko against the post-Communist easterner Yanukovych. The latter won a tight race and became Ukraine's fourth president.

Viktor Yanukovych (2010–present) was born in a village in eastern Ukraine to a Ukrainian mother, who worked as a nurse, and a father, who was an engine driver but harkened from a Polish Catholic petty gentry hamlet of Yanuki (Januki), which is now in Belarus.[23] Yanukovich was orphaned early. As a teenager he inclined to, in Soviet parlance, hooliganism. Robbery and assault earned him jail time and he continued having brushes with the law, including an alleged gang rape, until early adulthood in the 1970s. Then, the exconvict enrolled at a vocational school for electricians and, miraculously, traveled to western Europe, which was a privilege virtually unheard among Soviet citizens without strong party and secret police backing. Afterward, Yanukovych climbed steadily the apparatchik's ladder, complete with a "correspondence" course for a university degree in engineering, a Communist party membership, and a succession of managerial posts in the transportation industry.

In 1996 the industrial manager was appointed for the first time to an administrative political post at a local level. The next promotion was to a regional governorship in eastern Ukraine's Donetsk area. At that time, although evidence of his either attending school or studying remotely is very scant, Yanukovych also collected a graduate degree in international law, a doctorate in sciences, and a "professorship" in economics. Thus credentialed, the Donetsk politician was tapped by Kuchma to become his prime minister (2002–2004). Yanukovych favored massive subsidies to the coal industry in his native east. He also preferred close ties to Russia, while paying lip service to the EU. The politician further opposed Ukraine's membership in NATO, but supported with troops America's "War on Terror" in Iraq. Yanukovych has continued in a similar vein as president, to an extent at least. However, occupying the highest office in the land has also allowed him to indulge some of the more menacing post-Communist impulses. The new head of state has reverted to the pre-Orange Revolution modus operandi as far as democratic practices are concerned. Ominously, in January 2011 Yanukovych amended the constitution to extend the term of the current sitting parliament, which is dominated by his Party of the Regions, from four to five years. This essentially amounts to postponing the general elections for another year. Meanwhile, his officials intimidate the media and the opposition. Former prime minister Yulia Tymoshenko has been indicted, tried, sentenced, and imprisoned for corruption in 2011. The guilty verdict came as no surprise: The president himself averred that she would have to prove her innocence, a clear reversal of standard legal procedures in a democracy. Yanukovych has reserved his harshest vituperations, however, against his predecessor's historical policy, the Terror-Famine, in particular. Ukraine's new leader has flatly denied that the Holodomor was genocide. He adamantly opposed the remembrance of the victims of forced collectivization and famine. Whether Yanukovych can turn back the clock is debatable, but possible. The Belarus option beacons invitingly as arguably the most convenient systemic solution for the post-Communists, if they are outside of the EU.[24]

As mentioned, the evolution of the power of the presidency in Ukraine reflects the authoritarian leanings of the post-Communist leadership which, by the mid-1990s, almost completely dominated the Ukrainian political scene. Some have argued, however, that a strong president is necessary to offset the inherent instability resulting from a proliferation of parties that translated into a lack of unity in the legislative body. Also, a firm head of state is indispensable to reconcile the nationalist-leaning and Russophobe western regions and the Communist-supporting and Russophile east.[25] Whatever the merits of such arguments, it is indubitable that Ukraine's party scene is, well, wild.

Ukraine's legislature, the *Rada*, is elected directly by the people. Until the Orange Revolution, the elections were afflicted by vote rigging. Naturally, there are serious issues at stake in each election and, despite fraud, the vote has reflected the electorate's wishes at least to an extent. The rank-and-file citizens rather like their democratic institutions and arrangements, their imperfections notwithstanding.[26]

With the electoral threshold at 3 percent, a proliferation of parties enlivens the parliament and positively swamps the extraparliamentary scene. To cross the electoral threshold and to matter in the *Rada*, larger parties tend to form electoral blocks and parliamentary coalitions. At the moment, following the elections of 2007, there are seventeen separate parties in the parliament. Three of them stand alone. The rest assembles in electoral blocks. Because of the penchant of the coalitions and parties to split, their number can easily change in and out of parliament. The origins of some parties are often obscure; their ideology contradictory; their tactics convoluted; their funding unclear; and their connections dubious. Ukrainian parties can represent ideologies, personalities, localities, tasks, or businesses. Sometimes all those categories may overlap. And their champions are quite brazen about it. The most effective parties usually enjoy oligarchic backing. A short explication follows.[27]

Of the ideological set, Ukraine's political parties cover the spectrum from the most extreme to the mildest. The latter seem to be in short supply, though. Most of the parties are outspokenly leftist, very often populist.[28] There is a veritable flood of socialist groups. Most are beholden to the Leninist-Stalinist past.[29] The unreconstructed Communist Party of Ukraine (CPU) under Petro Symonenko would basically like the bad old days back, *sans* the Soviet Union for now at least.[30] The CPU enjoys enough popular support to remain outside of any block, although it has naturally allied itself at various times with a variety of partners, including the Orange camp, if briefly. Likewise, the Socialist Party of Ukraine (SPU) chaired by Oleksandr Moroz is powerful enough to operate on its own but seeks tactical ties to other parties when necessary. There are also the Social Democratic Party-United (SDPU-o) of Yuriy Zahorodniy; the Social Democratic Party (SDP) of Yevhen Kornichuk; and the Progressive Socialist Party under Natalya Vitrenko.

We ought to keep in mind that the alleged socialist (or any other) ideological façade can merely be hiding a broadly conceived lobbying group. For example, Social Democratic Party of Ukraine-United is a cover for the oligarchic interests of Kyiv. Yanukovych's Party of the Regions, one of the three stand-alone entities, represents the eastern industrial oligarchs. Soviet youth movement apparatchik turned billionaire banker Serhiy Tihipko's Strong Ukraine is his own electoral vehicle in the nation's east.

Even tiny and ostensibly moderate parties can serve as springboards for their ambitious leaders and as conveyer belts for oligarchic interests. Let's take the *Viche* (Assembly), for example. Until 2005 it operated in an extraparliamentary manner as the Constitutional Democratic Party (CDP). Even when, in 1998, it entered a coalition endearingly known as "The Elephant—The Social Liberal Union," it failed to cross the electoral threshold. After the Orange Revolution it renamed itself *Viche* and cooperated closely with the Party of the Regions. But it never merged with it, thus maintaining a façade of respectability. *Viche's* purpose is to channel mild leftists and liberals into an entity which garners their votes for the eastern oligarchic machine.

Of mainstream nationalist orientations of various ilk,[31] People's Movement of Ukraine (*Rukh*) under Borys Tarasyuk still lingers on as the reminder of the heyday of the struggle for independence. The Defenders of Fatherland Party and its leader Yuriy Karmazin combine nationalism and socialism to woo the voters. And so do, to various degrees, the People's Self-Defense of

Yuriy Lutsenko and The Time Has Come! (*Pora!*) of Vladyslav Kaskiv. Both were of the Orange orientation. The latter is an institutionalized avatar of the grassroots Orange youth activists.[32] The Civic Movement "People's Self-Defense" was originally an ad hoc gathering of some leftist defectors of post-Communist origin who ostensibly favored EU-style social democracy. The movement, eventually, upon absorbing "Forward Ukraine," another nebulous entity, became a political party, People's Self-Defense, in 2010.

Of the fringe groups, extremist nationalist outfits like Freedom (*Svoboda*) remain mercifully outside of the parliament for now but tend to be somewhat important in local elections, in the west, in particular. Freedom is unapologetically national socialist. However, the Organization of Ukrainian Nationalists, which unabashedly stresses its prewar pedigree, is less rabid and more effective in the western regions than Freedom and other neo-Nazi outfits.[33] At the same time, Western-style conservative and libertarian parties are hard to find in Ukraine, although United Center (UC) comes close. Known as the Party of Private Property until 2008, the UC has openly espoused classical liberal solutions and principled anti-Communism.

As far as leaders, aside from Tihipko's Strong Ukraine, there are three other coalitions based on personality "cults" of sorts. The Lytvyn Bloc comprises of the Labor Party of Ukraine and the People's Party. It is led by Volodymyr Lytvyn, an erstwhile Kuchma retainer and inveterate post-Communist.[34] Meanwhile, the iron-willed diva of Ukrainian politics heads the Yulia Tymoshenko-Baktivshchizna (Fatherland) Bloc, symbolically uniting herself and her homeland. Former president Viktor Yushchenko is more modest and dispensed with naming a party after himself. Nonetheless, the currently eclipsed *Nasha Ukraina* (Our Ukraine) basically represents him. These personality-oriented parties tend to bank on the symbolic power of their leaders. They also tend to be rather pragmatic, if etatistic. For public consumption they proclaim a combination of populist, socialist, and nationalist sentiments, while sometimes quietly promising economic reforms grounded in free-market principles. All in all, they tend to be the vehicles of the oligarchic power of various degree.

In Ukraine, parties are still learning democracy. Or, more precisely, they operate in a context resembling democracy. They sometimes employ democratic means to maintain themselves afloat and even in power, but often to nondemocratic, murky ends. And, conversely, they employ undemocratic means to remain in the democratic game. Until the Orange breakthrough of 2004, all elections had been marred by electoral fraud, manipulation, and clientelism. Sarah Birch has referred to it perceptively as "nomenklatura democratization."[35] And little wonder: There has been no de-Communization and no lustration in Ukraine. Re-Westernization (in the west) and Westernization (in the east) are far off, although some unmistakable signs of globalism, both traditional and countercultural, have been spotted comfortably embedded with post-Communism. Civil service is often corrupt and unprofessional. The judiciary is a fiefdom of the parties in power. State bureaucracy is virtually rotten, beholden to party machine politics of patronage.[36] Even local politics have but a few redeeming features, although there may be a ray of hope there at least.[37] All this breeds cynicism among citizens and embitters the voters. Trust is notoriously in short supply toward public figures like elsewhere in the post-Soviet sphere.[38] As a result, Ukraine remains a halfway house between the Baltics and Belarus.

Belarus

Post-1991 Belarus is an oddity even in the Intermarium.[39] In some ways, as far as the contemporary frame of reference, "Europe's last dictatorship" resembles the post-Soviet central Asian republics, albeit with less violence and repression. There is also an extremely high degree of continuity among the Belarusian elite from the Soviet times to the present. The ambition of the government in Minsk is to emulate and improve Moscow's "sovereign democracy," including its symbiotic relationship with the Orthodox Church. However, the Belarus regime refuses to practice the Kremlin's schizoid attempt to reconcile the White and Red elements of Russia's past. Instead, it preaches an oxymoronic "Belarusian Soviet nationalism."[40] Accordingly, the transformation of Belarus has consisted of preserving much of the Communist institutional and personal inheritance as well as the Soviet historical myths. Its dictatorial government goes out of its way to stress continuities with the totalitarian past. Its systemic discontinuities with the legacy of the Soviet occupation concern the shape and form only, rather than the content.[41]

Like Ukraine, Belarus has two official languages: Belarusian and Russian. However, the authorities in Minsk promote and use the latter, rather than the former. Consequently, in conjunction with centuries-long Russification, most intensive under the Soviets, in particular, hardly anyone speaks literary Belarusian. Linguistic Belarusian nationalism is limited to a tiny band of the opposition intelligentsia; and the Belarusian vernacular is spoken as "the simple tongue" (*prosty*) only to an extent by the locals, primarily in the western parts of the nation's countryside. This has greatly retarded the development of Belarusian national consciousness and nationalism, vis-à-vis Russia, in particular. That, in turn, has allowed the post-Communist dictatorship in Minsk to endure largely unchallenged.[42]

The tale of Belarus after its declaration of independence in 1991 is one of inertia and missed opportunities. The transformed Soviet system retained the chairman of the Supreme Soviet as the head of state. Although he was not elected democratically by the people, the chairman was no longer a rubber stamp candidate imposed by Moscow. Instead, he was elected indirectly by the deputies of the Supreme Soviet. The chairman then handpicked his prime minister as was the case in Soviet times. However, without enforced "democratic centralist" unanimity of Marxism-Leninism, the leader of the government could defy the chairman. During a brief spell of post-Soviet chaotic "democracy," the head of state and his handpicked prime minister tended to neutralize each other. This rendered the business of government impotent. To disentangle the mess, calls went up to introduce a system with a single chief executive. This paved the way to a rigid presidential dictatorship which was introduced in 1994.

Neither the post-Communist "democrats" first nor the dictator later bothered much about changing the symbols, institutions, and substance of the system inherited from the USSR. To neutralize the nationalists, in 1991, the "democrats" did introduce a new flag and a new coat of arms based upon historic symbols. But that really exhausted their enthusiasm for "change." Only in 1996 did Belarus get around to renaming its Supreme Soviet as the National Assembly of the Republic of Belarus. It is a rubber stamp bicameral parliament. The Soviet (Council) of the Republic stands in for the upper house, while the lower one calls itself the House of Representatives.[43] Belarusian bicameralism is a unique feature in the Intermarium, and, perhaps, a strange nod toward the constitution of the old Polish-Lithuanian Commonwealth. In addition, Belarus established at the time the All-Belarusian People's Assembly. It is a corporatist consultative body encompassing the representatives of the government, industry, and "the people." It replicates the functions of the congresses of the Communist party. It gathers every five years (1996, 2001, 2006, and 2010).

Thus, Belarus retains institutionally a dual government–party system, albeit renamed and devoid of overt Communist ideology. The most important office of the land, however, is that of the head of state. It replicates the functions of both the erstwhile general secretary of the Communist party and of the chairman of the Supreme Soviet. The president still appoints his prime ministers but dominates them completely. We shall look at the personalities involved, their policies, and a variety of other actors, including political parties.

In the early 1990s, the Communist "reformers" and, later, the national Bolsheviks under Stanislau Shushkevich (Stanisław Szuszkiewicz) completely stole the thunder from the puny Christian nationalist movement under Zenon Pozniak.[44] The post-Communists outmaneuvered their domestic enemies in two ways. First, the former flatly refused to deal with the nationalists directly but appropriated their symbols and language. Second, meanwhile, they froze and saved as much of the Soviet institutional forms and personnel as was possible. Shushkevich engineered much of this strategy. That he could pass for a Belarusian nationalist is strange enough. He openly declares himself a Catholic of Polish origin. However, he donned the halo of a martyr of the Bolsheviks as the son of a prominent Belarusian literary figure victimized during Stalin's rule. A mathematician and physicist of some renown, Stanislau

Shushkevich served as the head of state in the crucial era of the transformation (September 1991–January 1994). He was the chairman of the Belarusian Supreme Soviet which under his tutelage was falsely perceived to be evolving into a democratic parliament.

On December 8, 1991, along with Russia's Boris Yeltsin and Ukraine's Leonid Kravchuk, Shushkevich oversaw the attempted transformation of the Soviet Union into the Commonwealth of Independent States at the Belaviezha (Białowieża/Belavezhskaya Pushcha) Forest. Thus, he participated in the final act of the dissolution of the USSR. Further, under his watch, Soviet nuclear weapons stationed on Belarusian soil were claimed by the Russian Federation and withdrawn. The chairman failed to parley the nuclear disarmament of Minsk into any concessions or aid from either the Kremlin or the West. Instead, Shushkevich spoke nebulously in favor of world peace, free market, and parliamentary democracy. However, hardly any meaningful reform took place in Belarus. Neither de-Communization nor lustration were ever contemplated. Parliamentarism became tantamount with shady backdoor deals and dirty party politics. Capitalism was deemed synonymous with corruption and embezzlement of state property. The nation was seriously destabilized under the chairman's watch.

In addition, Shushkevich quarreled violently with his prime minister, Communist technocratic apparatchik Vyacheslav Kebich (1990–1994). This feud practically paralyzed the political process.[45] Kebich first opposed the dissolution of the USSR and then pushed for a Russo-Belarusian fusion in politics and economics. Shushkevich defended the existence of Belarus as a separate entity, which earned him some credibility among the nationalist grassroots. However, the chairman became a champion of Belarusian nationalism by default. His anti-Kebich tactical maneuvers tallied with his earlier posturing to neutralize Pozniak and his followers. Shushkevich lacked a strategic vision for a free Belarus. Instead, he copied Gorbachev with a series of tactically shrewd dialectical policy shifts that ultimately led to disaster for freedom. The chairman's attitude evolved in congruence with the unfolding of events and the concomitant propaganda requirements. At first, Belarus was to be autonomous within the USSR and run by the Communist "reformers"; next, a sovereign state constituted as a liberalized version of the Soviet Union and commanded by the local national Bolsheviks; then, a separate people's democracy of sorts ruled by the national Bolsheviks and other post-Communists; finally, a social democracy Western European style governed by the post-Communists with most Soviet institutions and personnel left intact.

Throughout all this, free and fair elections simply failed quite to materialize.[46] Instead, various political coteries struggled for power within the narrow confines of Soviet institutions, singularly maladaptive to liberal parliamentarism. In essence, former Communists fought each other for power and spoils. Some openly continued to call themselves Marxists-Leninists. Many pretended to be nonparty whatsoever. Competing cliques clashed in and out of the Supreme Soviet of Belarus. The end game pitted the Communists against the post-Communists, some of them national Bolsheviks, while others morphed into social democrats or liberals, whether out of opportunism or pragmatism. The outnumbered and outmatched Belarusian Christian nationalists clumsily sulked around on the margins. No viable challenger emerged to combine anti-Communism, freedom, and parliamentarism.

Political, social, and economic chaos resulted. A miasma of embezzlement and corruption engulfed the country in a scenario eerily similar everywhere in the post-Soviet sphere. Political players quarreled over this and other issues including the limits of democracy and media freedom. Meanwhile, the economy spiraled out of control. The electorate grew embittered. The people universally and genuinely mistook the post-Communist pathologies for freedom, democracy, and capitalism. They recoiled from them in disgust. Serious popular discontent set in. A clamor went up for a strong man to step in and clean the house.[47]

Emerging from complete obscurity, one Oleksandr Lukashenka swiftly volunteered.[48] A former KGB border guard, a Red Army man, a collective farm manager, a provincial Communist apparatchik, and a deputy in the Supreme Soviet from 1990, his only distinction to date had been to have cast the lone vote opposing the dissolution of the USSR. Otherwise he showboated as the leader of a parliamentary group oxymoronically dubbed "Communists for Democracy." In 1993, Lukashenka shrewdly used his perch of the head of the anticorruption committee of the Supreme Soviet as a bully pulpit to launch his presidential campaign. He promised honesty and transparency. He and his comrades accused Shushkevich and his cronies of corruption. In January 1994, Lukashenka and his allies forced a vote of nonconfidence against Shushkevich, ousting him from the chairmanship of the Supreme Soviet. The chairman's two replacements, in brief succession, the faceless Vyacheslau Kuznyatsou and the Sovietostalgic Myechyslau Hryb, proved to be toothless nonentities as heads of state, serving but fleetingly and perfunctorily. The political scene was ready for a major change.

In July 1994 in an apparently free, if not exactly fair, election Lukashenka trounced both Shushkevich and Kebich to lead Belarus. He assumed a new office created especially for the winner: the Presidency.[49] Under his rule, Belarus became a full-fledged dictatorship. He remains in power still. The dictator appoints and dismisses his prime ministers at will. He controls two rubber stamp bodies, established in 1996, that pretend to be a legislature and a consultative entity; respectively, a bicameral National Assembly and the All-Belarusian People's Assembly. The constitution, enacted in 1999, was also tailor-made for the president. This was preceded by a series of steps intended to guarantee a durability of his tenure based upon the most rigid version of post-Communism in the Intermarium.

The dictator has considered Belarusian nationalism as potentially the greatest threat to his power. Therefore, while shrewdly transforming and restoring Soviet idiosyncrasies, Lukashenka (1994–present) almost immediately eliminated traditional and nationalist symbols of the free Belarusian state, including its flag and coat of arms. They were replaced with hideous and ominous contraptions modeled after the Soviet paradigm. This particular choice was a part and parcel of a vigorous, if ultimately failed, campaign to resurrect the USSR with Lukashenka at its head in Moscow. It was also tied to the new president's ambitious "foreign" policy, which we shall deal with later. The same concerns his other similar Sovietostalgic moves.

Most importantly, the new leader made the Russian language official on a par with the Belarusian. In practice, because of the highly successful Russification of the population, the official lingual parity simply means the enshrining of the primacy of the Russian language in the public square. Further, Lukashenka's historical policy has celebrated the Soviet Union, equating it with his nation's statehood. In fact, the dictator has openly posited a continuity of his regime with the Soviet one as expressing the unity of the Belarusian past. For example, most notably, the Soviet partisans of World War II became the main paragons of Belarusian patriotism. The president has also unabashedly celebrated all Soviet heroes, including democidal monsters like Felix Dzherzhinsky (Feliks Dzierżyński), the founder of the Communist secret police.

Moreover, in his avowed bid to reintegrate with the Russian Federation (in the form of the Belarus–Russia Union), as a halfstep to the resurrection of the USSR, Lukashenka resorted to a clever historical manipulation. He claimed the mantle of the Grand Duchy of Lithuania, a position earlier championed by both the nationalists of Pozniak and the reform Communists of Shushkevich. A deceptive rouse intended for domestic consumption, this was also done to intimidate Vilnius. Minsk dropped that act, however, when it began zig-zagging in its relations with Moscow, and balking at integration, as we shall see later.[50]

As for the economy, after putting a stop to the kleptocratic freewheeling of the 1990s, Lukashenka has moved very gingerly from a liberalized Khrushchevian Soviet stage through an interim phase that an expert has dubbed "goulash Communism" to what now appears to be a very fastidious and tentative imitation of China's neo-NEP of the late 1980s. There are unmistakable, if subdued signs of globalization, including the ubiquity of cell phones and computers as well as Western garb among the population, the young, in particular. Freeways have appeared and other infrastructural changes, including in the service industry. In 2009, to spur investments and entrepreneurship, the government introduced "a flat rate personal income tax (12 percent)," as the initiator of the reform has gushed proudly.[51] Private businesses tend to be small operations. Industry and banking remain state-owned. Some foreign investments have materialized, often as joint ventures with state enterprises. But lately Belarus has been hit by the global financial crisis, which augurs trouble.[52]

The dictator values stability above all and free markets invite volatility. Hence, he prefers state control. This tactic serves his power well also because it apparently pleases the average Belarusian, who is interested in stability and confuses freedom with chaos. The fact that corruption registers at fairly low levels further reinforces a positive grassroots perception of the dictatorship. Moreover, no oligarchs have emerged to flaunt their wealth before the people or to threaten the president, whose popular nickname is *"Bat'ko"*—daddy. Thus, Lukashenka's tame and taming economic policy allows him to deal with, among other things, the opposition as he pleases.[53]

From the outset, the new president intimidated his political detractors. The dictator resorted to ham-fisted tactics, quite literally violence, against his most vocal opponents. The most prominent ones, like Pozniak and Shushkevich, fled to the West. They have been followed by an uninterrupted stream of minor objectors. A score or more disappeared, most famous among them Viktor Gonchar and Yuri Zakharenko, former deputy chairman of the Supreme Soviet and former minister of the interior, respectively. The victims of an alleged death squad also included the president's erstwhile personal photographer, Dmitri Zavadski.[54] Others were beaten or intimidated. Lukashenka's secret police, the KGB, which creepily retained its Soviet-time personnel, moniker, and modus operandi, routinely lashes out at the opposition leaders and their grassroots supporters.

Nonetheless, there are periodic demonstrations against the regime. The most violent ones occurred during the aborted Denim Revolution in March 2006 and its feeble continuation (albeit without the blue jeans as the rallying color) in December 2010.[55] Both burned themselves out in the context of unfree and unfair presidential elections and fierce police repression. The opposition thus changed its tactics. Pickets appeared on street corners with signs complaining about the price of gas and such other mundane issues. They were promptly dispersed by the police. The opposition also tried silent flash-mob tactics, but the regime promptly banned any large crowd from gathering. Some of the leaders were promptly packed off to jail. Same applies to independent journalists.

By the fall of 2011 the momentum had petered out among the antidictatorship activists. They never seriously threatened Lukashenka. Their protest has been mainly limited to Minsk. Further, it has attracted chiefly the young and other usual suspects. The rest of the citizenry is either placid or even appears rather satisfied with Lukashenka.[56] Why? Fear is a factor, of course. There persists the insidiously lingering memory of the Soviet legacy of ruthlessly silencing, and even exterminating, dissent, all and sundry. The failure of the political opposition to unite and elucidate its message in a form attractive to most citizens is another factor. The anti-Communist nationalists have no idea how to preach their gospel. Moreover, the president is genuinely popular in some circles. Lukashenka is almost invariably perceived as an agent of stability and order and a protector against the encroachment by the West. To synthesize the official propaganda, having halted the anarchy, corruption, and chaos of the transformation of the early 1990s, in congruence with the fraternal post-Soviet Russian people, although not always their Kremlin leadership, the intrepid Lukashenka has made sure the pensioners get their meager dole promptly and the trains run punctually despite US, NATO, and EU interference, including their Belarusian "agents" who camouflage themselves as the opposition, often, if not always, so obviously in the pay of Poland.[57]

None of the above in itself is a guarantee of the dictator's permanence. Major economic problems can trigger popular unrest and so can power struggles at the top or a foreign intervention. Further, the lord of Minsk should not expect victory in a fair and unfettered electoral contest. But by controlling the polling environment, Lukashenka can continue to win. The president has ascertained that the opposition enjoys no or little access to the media; that its activists are intimidated; and that the KGB proceeds apace with its disintegrative clandestine operations (*dezintegratsyia*) which artificially reinforce the already uneasy and quarrelsome relationships within, and between, the opposition groups as well as among their leaders. Meanwhile, the power of Lukashenka has waxed continuously. In the unmistakably totalitarian fashion of yore, although a trait of any satrapy really, the president decides even which pop musicians should succeed.[58]

Lukashenka has little use for political parties. The dictator has even eschewed setting up his own presidential party per se. On the one hand, this is partly to cater to the popular revulsion of the apparent political anarchy of the early 1990s, when the multiple parties jousting for power were perceived as nothing but corrupt coteries devoid of any decency and idealism. On the other hand, the Belarusian president takes no chances lest a viable competitor emerge from within the ruling party to challenge him. Consequently, most deputies in the so-called "parliament," the National Assembly of Belarus, are nonparty. They call themselves "independents." And that is the presidential party. They are handpicked corporatist-style from social, economic, and cultural associations. They have consistently formed the largest political bloc since the elections in 1995, when ninety-five of them were "elected" (out of 260 deputies). In 2000, following a radical trimming of the size of the "legislature," eighty-one "independents" took their seats (out of 110 "parliamentarians"); in 2004—ninety-five; and in 2008—one hundred and three. The "independents" are reliable rubber-stampers for Lukashenka. While in parliament, almost half of them (fifty-one persons) affiliated as the Belarus (*Belaya Rus'*) party, a clear copy of the Kremlin's United Russia. In essence, therefore, partylessness (or nonpartyness) denotes membership in Lukashenka's own kabal.

Of the remaining political entities, three, all of them reliably pro-dictator of course, have been permitted consistently to elect a few members to the parliament: the Agrarian Party, which was founded in 1992; the Liberal Democratic Party (LDP), which appeared in 1994[59]; and the Party of Belarusian Communists (PBK), which was created in 1991 but morphed into the Communist Party of Belarus (KPB) in 2006.[60] Modeled after its Russian namesake under the infamous Vladimir Zhirinovski, the LDP has consistently fielded a single representative in the All-Belarusian People's Assembly between 1995 and now. The Agrarian Party, which champions rural populism and bolshevism, boasted thirty-three deputies in 1995, one in 2000, three in 2004, and one once again in 2008. The communists fluctuated from the high of forty-two deputies in 1995 to six in 2000, eight in 2004, and, once again, six in 2008. Simply, most of them joined the "nonparty" presidential contingent, rather than the KPB. The liberal democrats and the communists share but one dream: the unification with Russia. Along with the agrarians, they also advance a nebulous platform of socialism, populism, and official state nationalism. Last but not least, all three party entities slavishly obey Lukashenka.[61]

Naturally, kowtowing to the dictator does not guarantee one a spot in the parliament, as the Belarusian Socialist Sporting Party and the Republican Party of Labor and Justice found out, for instance. But opposing the government is a virtual kiss of death, whether one calls himself a communist or an ultranationalist. This is plainly evident in and out of the electoral game.

International monitors have agreed that the vote in Belarus is rigged at all levels.[62] Thus, the elections matter in so far as they reflect the nature and will of the dictatorship. They can signify the latest maneuver by Lukashenka and allow one to ascertain which individual cronies the president has anointed or reannointed lately. His treatment of the opposition has also served as a political weather vane. Killing is very infrequent; beating more prevalent; and arresting rather common. The intensity of the repression fluctuates according to the will of the dictator.[63]

So far mostly extraparliamentary parties and their activists have been targeted. By Soviet standards, the repression in Belarus has been mild. By civilized standards, it is unacceptable of course. It has affected a number of political groups, most of them failing to agree on anything but their loathing for President Lukashenka. The opposition's largest umbrella group, the United Democratic Forces (UFD), combines the post-Communists, social democrats, agrarians, populists, liberals, and some nationalists. Their competitors include the Belarusian National Front Party (BNF Party), launched in 1988, which fuses nationalism and Christian democratic conservatism[64]; and the United Civic Party (UCP), established in 1995, which advocates libertarian conservatism.[65] The self-proclaimed heirs to Belarus's traditional rural social democracy, which traces back its origins to 1902, refounded their party in 2005 as the Belarusian Social Democratic Party "Hramada." The Communists

315

who refused to worship Lukashenka reinvented themselves in 2006 as the Belarusian Party of the Leftists "Just World." These parties interchangeably quarrel and cooperate, even concluding ephemeral coalitions which embrace such unlikely bedfellows like the BNF and the Leftists. There are others, even less significant groups, including the now-banned feminists of the Belarusian Women's Party "Hope"; the greens (*Zialonya partia*)[66]; and the radical nationalists. Their persistence, however, should be more a subject of an irksome folkloristic curiosity rather than a topic of serious scholarly inquiry.[67]

Because of the ruthless effectiveness of the Belarusian secret police, the opposition parties have been rather impotent and their leaders ineffectual. However, the mere fact of their continued existence, form, and operation testifies to the fact that Belarus is not the USSR, which tolerated no dissent and dealt with its dissidents mercilessly. Yet, Minsk's attitude toward its opposition oscillates between tacit tolerance and mild repression. This *faux* pluralism reminds one eerily of Central and Eastern Europe in the 1970s. There are striking similarities to the people's democracies, the pre-"Solidarity" People's Republic of Poland, in particular. There are some features straight out of China in the late 1980s and early 1990s. Taras Kuzio correctly points out eery Belarusian analogies with Moldova and its Transnistrian breakaway region. Yet, despite cyclical predictions of its impending doom, the Belarusian regime has proven quite durable so far.[68]

Moldova

This judgment also applies to a certain extent to Moldova, in particular, before 2009. The nation is extremely interesting for a student of the Intermarium because it functions as a hybrid, combining and showcasing with great clarity virtually all features of post-Communism, globalism, and nationalism at once, which are present, to a varied degree, in other countries of the post-Soviet zone. Thus, we shall dwell on it at length.

Even though it lacks a bona fide dictator, Moldova remains the most Sovietized and Communistic of all the nations in the Intermarium. It is also the poorest one there.[69] Its system retains a great deal from the Soviet times, and has acquired rather little from the West, except for a bit via post-Communist Romania. Moldova is also the only post-Soviet successor state in the Intermarium with a recent past of challenging the international boundaries of the old USSR. This stems from its ethno-cultural and historical connection to a country outside of Soviet frontiers, namely, Romania. Ultimately, however, Chişinău's relationship with Bucharest is perhaps a bit like that between Minsk and Moscow, where unification has long been touted—sometimes as a promise, and sometimes a threat for both internal and external consumption. But it actually is not intended to happen anytime soon.[70]

Moldova's most distinct peculiarities are its three nationalist movements: an autonomist, an integrationist, and a secessionist. The autonomists are essentially the Gagauz, a tiny minority of perhaps 150,000. The integrationists are Romanian speakers, a majority of about 3.4 million. The secessionists tend to be Ukraino- and Russophone Slavs (some 700,000), although they briefly made common cause with the Turkic Gagauz. The latter fielded a nascent nationalist movement that flirted in turn with democratic anti-Communism, in the late 1980s, and with retrograde philo-Sovietism, in the early 1990s. To counter pan-Romanian nationalism, the Gagauz first proclaimed their independence in August 1990 and then supported the integrity of the USSR. Ultimately, however, after some stormy altercations with the majority, they achieved a de jure autonomy in 1994. The Gagauz tacitly rely on the Kremlin in case of perceived problems with Chişinău. They are particularly concerned about the integrationists.[71]

As far as their ideology, the integrationists are Christian nationalist pan-Romanians. They would like Moldova to join Romania, which is insufficiently irredentist for their liking however. Their claims are based upon the fact that a significant part of Moldova had been Romanian before World War II and that the vast majority of the population is Romanian-speaking.[72] Meanwhile, the secessionists, who control the de facto independent eastern region of Transnistria, either would like to remain alone, or unify with Ukraine, or, better yet, subordinate themselves to some future neo-Soviet Union. For now, strung along the western bank of the Dniester River, Transnistria remains an oppressive presidential dictatorship with all pathologies of post-Communism in full bloom. Among other things, its government persecutes the Romanian speakers. Its president-almost-for-life Igor Smirnov (1990–2011), a former industrial apparatchik from a nomenklatura family, was practically untouchable because of his brutal suppression of any dissent, steady support from the Kremlin, and a torrent of Russian economic investments in the region. His recent post-Communist youth replacement, Yevgeny Shevchuk (2011–present), has so far continued in a similar vein. He runs Transnistria's affairs completely independently from the government of the rest of Moldova.[73]

In essence, then, Chişinău has failed to control a chunk of its territory in the east. Further, a significant portion of its political class, with waning and waxing popular support, yearns consciously or subconsciously to be absorbed by Romania. This has led to a chronic crisis of power and identity. Because the secessionists enjoy the backing of Moscow, Moldova has no power to bring them to heel. Chişinău could only take serious measures against the pan-Romanian integrationists. Their official opponents, who may be called anti-integrationists (but, in reality, they are opportunistic post-Communists), have combined police repressions with a robust propaganda campaign promoting "Moldovanism" as an alternative to pan-Romanianism. "Moldovanism" was conceived and implemented between 1991 and 1994 as a project to champion a separate national identity grounded both in very real historical experiences of the region and in Soviet mythology. In the nationalist discourse it was *de rigueur* to invoke "the villages" as the heart of the nation.[74] It was also the key image of pan-Romanian nationalism appropriated by the post-Communists. Using the image, the latter stole the thunder of the integrationists, fostering "Moldovan nationalism," or "Moldovanism." According to the anti-integrationist dichotomy, the "Moldovan-speaking Moldovians" have been pitted against Romanian-speaking integrationist traitors to the Moldovan fatherland. Nonetheless, the "Moldovanist" orientation has also rather contradictorily fostered a "re-Russification," according to Trevor Waters.[75] Thus, it seems that "Moldovan nationalism" is a tactical ploy to allow the post-Communist opponents of the pan-Romanian orientation to retain power which is possible most likely so long as Moldova remains separate from Romania.[76]

As for its system, Moldova is a gyrating post-Communist hybrid among the post-Soviet successor states. In fact, its main institutional pillar of stability seems to be the army. Everything else tends to oscillate between semistability and flux at various times. This reflects a chronic crisis of the state.[77] Moldova falls in between Ukraine and Belarus culturally, economically, politically, and ideologically. But it has also drawn inspiration from other nations, including Romania. Like Kyiv and Minsk, Chişinău has avoided de-Communization and lustration to a large extent. Further, its kleptocracy rivals that of Ukraine's, in methods, rapaciousness, and aspirations, if not in the size of the loot. Its economy has fluctuated between dirigisme and a free for all, or at least to all who are well-connected former Communists, their cronies, and anyone morally flexible enough to operate in such a dubious environment.[78]

In Moldova democracy was manipulated, at times even perverted, to accommodate the soft landing of the post-Communists. The latter have maintained virtual reigning dynasties where nepotism and cronyism rules supreme.[79] They control all the principal institutions of the state, which are periodically transformed to perpetuate their rule. Although some Moldovan schemes are *sui generis*, the post-Communists and their allies have also borrowed various institutional arrangements from their Intermarium neighbors. Moldova's unicameral parliament resembles that of the Baltics and Ukraine. Initially, the nation's president was elected by popular vote like in Lithuania and Ukraine. However, in 2000 Chişinău switched to the indirect method of selecting the chief of state, which reflects the experience of Tallinn and Riga. In theory, Moldova has a dual system of power with a president and a prime minister. In practice, a strong president tends to dominate his prime minister, which is similar to Ukraine and Belarus. Like in Ukraine and the Baltics, the chief of state formally selects his premier and the parliament then approves him. If the president dominates the parliament, the selection and approval process of the head of government proceeds rather smoothly. Otherwise, a protracted crisis may ensue. Thus, much hinges on the composition of the parliament and its congruity with the chief of state. In a way, at the executive level, Moldova has displayed similar features as Belarus. However, instead of degenerating from the chaotic tug of war between an indirectly elected chief of state and his handpicked head of government to a rigid presidential dictatorship, Chișinău has fluctuated between these two models, never settling on one permanently. It often seems that the dictatorship is a step away, but other contenders for power pull any would be strong man away from the throne at the last minute. In this manner Moldova resembles Ukraine more than Belarus.[80]

It is in Moldova that the two main forms of post-Communism are perhaps most evident: the dictatorial presidential and the chaotic parliamentarian.[81] Even in times of parliamentary chaos the presidential role is important, paramount sometimes, however. This is because the chief executive has usually served as both the trigger and the focus of the deliberative democratic fracas.

Moldova's first chief of state was a lifelong Communist apparatchik, Mircea Ion Snegur (1990–1996).[82] Born in a peasant family in 1940, he graduated with a degree in agriculture. Later, Snegur advanced up the nomenklatura ladder to assume, in 1985, the secretaryship of the Central Committee of the Communist Party of the Moldavian Soviet Socialist Republic (MSSR). He evolved from a Brezhnievite apparatchik to a Gorbachevian "reform" Communist and a national Bolshevik. In July 1989, other "reform" comrades appointed him to the chairmanship of the Presidium of the Supreme Soviet of the MSSR. After the electoral victory of the pro-independence National Front of Moldova (*Frontul Popular din Moldova*, FPM) in spring 1990, however, the new chairman began to flirt with the newly ascendant patriotic orientation. He courted its Christian nationalist pan-Romanian leaders and supporters. Therefore, in April 1990, Snegur was able to retain his leading post on the Supreme Soviet; and in September he became Moldova's first president. In essence, the former perch was simply converted into the latter, thus giving Snegur incredible symbolic legitimacy and continuity. Both times he was elevated as a result of internal arrangements and indirect vote in the Supreme Soviet, rather than by popular elections.

Snegur's task was to maintain himself and his party comrades in power against a seemingly unstoppable wave of liberation, anti-Communism, and reunification. He faced three formidable challenges: an economic collapse, an anti-Soviet and pan-Romanian radicalization at home, and a rapidly changing international situation which culminated in the dissolution of the USSR. The president rode the wave just fine. Basically, he blamed the horrible state of the economy on the pan-Romanians.

At the beginning of his tenure, Snegur patiently used his Communist party base in the Supreme Soviet to undermine the majority orientation, the anti-Communist nationalists. The latter entered the hitherto rubber stamp legislature to change it on a popular mandate for the National Front of Moldova following the free, if heavily unfair elections of March and February 1990. The FPM majority consisted of a variety of individuals, some of them committed nationalists and anti-Communists, many others "reform" Communists and national Bolsheviks in the process of becoming post-Communists. Still others were quite accidental opportunists and starry-eyed idealists, and at least a few Soviet secret police agents. Because of the lack of experience among its cadres, the continued suppression of the nationalist rank-and-file in the countryside, the ban on registration as a political party, and the disintegration measures applied by the KGB, the FPM lacked a cohesive structure and party discipline in and out of the parliament. It soon proved quite ineffectual in government and suffered defeat.

For a while, however, the FPM was riding high. Its popularity fueled by nationalist rhetoric reached a high pitch in the spring and summer of 1990. But as elsewhere in the Intermarium, there were no calls for counter-revolutionary direct action and firmness to remove the Communists, as if the latter would just politely disappear. Yet, physically attacking the Soviet state and its functionaries would have been suicidal and premature so long as a direct military intervention by the Kremlin loomed large. Instead, therefore, the nationalists limited themselves largely to sloganeering. The reintegration with Romania and the re-Romanization of education and culture, including the reintroduction of the Latin alphabet, became the FPM government's leading priorities.[83] Sadly, the FPM failed to apply itself to the less lofty tasks of solving mundane problems and lost its momentum and support. The precipitous crumbling of the economy, a disgusting display of graft, a deterioration of public security, the secessionist agitation of the Russians, Ukrainians, and the Turkic Gagauz, the menacing ethno-nationalist agitation, and the sheer ineptness of the pan-Romanian and anti-Communist prime minister Mircea Druc (May 1990–May 1991) caused popular anger and a backlash against the FPM. This naturally facilitated a successful post-Communist counteroffensive.

As a result, the shrewd President Snegur outsmarted and outmaneuvered the clueless premier Druc, who was duly dismissed by the Supreme Soviet. His lackluster successor was a bland "reform" Communist technocrat, Valeriu Muravschi (May 1991–July 1992), an erstwhile member of the *nomenklatura*, who insinuated himself into the FPM leadership as an economic expert. The new premier picked virtually no fights with President Snegur. In December 1991 the latter was confirmed in power directly by a popular election that, in effect, was a plebiscite against the FPM, which continued its precipitous decline. From then until the election of February 1994, in which the nationalists were virtually annihilated, the chief of state laid the ground work for post-Communism in Moldova.[84] Snegur's leading assistant in this masterful power play was his post-Communist prime minister Andrei Sangheli (July 1992–January 1997), who operated under the banner of "agrarianism."

Most importantly, with the backing of Moscow, the president and his comrades checked and reversed the integrationist sentiment of the pan-Romanianism. Ironically, one of the key arguments used by the post-Communists was nationalistic: First, Chişinău must subdue the secessionists of Tiraspol, and only then it should undertake a union (or reunion) with Romania. Next, the argument shrewdly evolved: If Moldova joined Romania, it would have to forget about Transnistria. Further, the post-Communists argued, there were allegedly insurmountable social and economic incompatibilities between Moldova and Romania. They would have to be overcome in the short run before contemplating a union in a long run. Ultimately, neither reunification with Bucharest nor reabsorption of Tiraspol occurred. Under Snegur's stewardship, the post-Communists ensconced themselves firmly in power as "patriotic," "pro-Western" "agrarians" and "socialists". They remained the masters of a separate post-Soviet successor state. Thus, Moldova was barred from the logical path accorded to East Germany, which led the latter ultimately to the *Wiedervereinigung*.[85]

Snegur's years in power were thus devoted to shoring up post-Communism and conserving as much of Moldova's Soviet symbols, structures, and servants as it was possible. Briefly reestablished during the patriotic fever of 1990 and 1991, the national anthem (identical to Romania's) was dropped. Moldova became de facto bilingual, Russian vying for influence with Romanian. Under the president's watch, the nationalist opposition experienced serious persecution and the unconstructed Communists some fleeting harassment. The original Communist Party of the MSSR was even formally banned in August 1991 in response to the *Putsch* in Moscow. But that was just a brief inconvenience.

On the economic field, free-market reforms were largely limited to privatizing state enterprises and pegging the local currency to the dollar, in January 1992, which caused hyper-inflation. Decollectivization of the farmland fragmented rural holdings making them less efficient and destroyed collective and state farms. Along with ending state subsidies for farming, crumbling of state distribution networks, and disappearing of mandatory, plan-driven purchases, the decollectivization virtually crippled the agricultural nomenclature dynasty based upon the Soviet paradigm. With the private seed capital for the expansion and modernization of farms lacking and cheap foreign food and related products flooding the market, Moldova's agricultural production shrunk to almost autarkical levels. Deindustrialization proceeded apace as state-driven demand disappeared and inferior and defective wares, product of socialist planning, failed to attract consumers. Public-owned companies collapsed one after another. On the bright side, eventually the service industry came to dominate the national economy. And agriculture recuperated some, wine production, in particular.[86]

But the recovery took a very long time. Meanwhile, the ensuing structural crisis virtually crippled the economy and persisted until the end of the decade. Among other things, it triggered massive illegal labor migration of the young from Moldova to western Europe and Russia. Moldova relied heavily on the hard currency remittances the labor migrants sent home. And the volume of the monies dispatched home fluctuated with the vicissitudes of the global economy. The situation has persisted into the present time.[87] Meanwhile, the embezzlement of state properties proceeded apace by the post-Communists and their cronies. Ruined rural and urban enterprises were picked up for a pittance.

Things looked bleak in at the political and civic levels as well. In 1993, the unabashed Bolsheviks were officially permitted to reassemble as the Party of Communists of the Republic of Moldova (PCRM). Within a fortnight, they became once again a serious force in the country's "democratic" politics. However, democratic institutions, including the parliament, were painfully slow to develop. Feeble and underfunded, the nongovernmental sector could hardly compete with the omnipotent state. Moldova's civil society took a long while to grow and achieve any noticeable level of success. Intellectual and artistic circles did better than grassroots organizations of the ordinary people. In a marked departure from Soviet practice, the president and his cronies generally eschewed crushing such spontaneous low-level efforts so long as they were not overtly nationalist and political.[88]

Further, under Snegur's stewardship, the Supreme Soviet was renamed as the Parliament of Moldova with its deputies and the country's president elected directly by the people. The first post-Soviet constitution was finally enacted in 1994. It confirmed Moldova as a separate and neutral republic with Romanian as the official language written in Latin but the minorities were granted extensive linguistic rights as well.[89] As for the fading, pan-Romanian challenge, the post-Communists continued to handle nationalism by appropriating it as "Moldovanism." Ultimately, however, Snegur's "Moldovaness" campaign petered out and cost him the re-election. Right before the vote the incumbent belatedly backpedaled on the minority issues. Quite cynically, he objected to the Russifying educational "reforms" and supported nationalist student demonstrators in 1995. Meanwhile, his main rival, Petru Lucinschi, went a logical step farther from mere "Moldovaness," campaigning on the platform of reconciliation of the "ethnic Moldovans" with the Slavic minorities under the post-Communist leadership. In other words, taking a clue from Belarus, the challenger successfully promoted a neo-Soviet model of coexistence within an independent Moldovan state.[90]

Petru Chiril Lucinschi (1997–2001) was the "agrarian" speaker of the Supreme Soviet/parliament who denied Snegur a second term in a bitter contest of 1996.[91] A peasant child born in 1940, the new president boasted of a doctorate in Marxist-Leninist philosophy. In 1973, he was promoted to the Politburo of the Communist Party of the MSSR, as the only native Romanian (Moldovan), and entrusted with the first secretaryship of the party's prestigious Chişinău organization. However, his bosses dispatched Lucinschi to Moscow in 1978, where he embarked upon an impressive "all-union" career. The philosopher became an imperial Communist apparatchik of the highest echelon in the USSR. After a promising sojourn at the top in the Soviet capital, the Kremlin sent Lucinschi to assume the second secretaryship of the Communist party in Tajikistan in 1986.

In 1989 Gorbachev dispatched Lucinschi back home to Chişinău to take over as the first secretary of the Communist Party of the MSSR.[92] Having had failed to arrest the march of freedom locally, the "reform" Communist was recalled to Moscow in 1991, where the Kremlin nonetheless elevated him to the prestigious post of secretary of the Central Committee of the Communist Party of the USSR. But two years later the imperial apparatchik re-emerged in Chişinău once again. He became one of the leading lights of the "agrarian" orientation and secured the speakership of the Supreme Soviet as its post-Communist representative in 1993.[93]

Lucinschi's bewildering return to newly liberated Moldova was a seemingly stunning demotion comparable only to the career eclipse of former Soviet foreign minister Eduard Shevardnadze, who, after the implosion of the Moscow center, settled for the mere presidency of Georgia. It is hard to establish whether Lucinschi's second return to his native land was a job search; a professional relocation after corporate downsizing; a post-Soviet consolation prize; or a part of a wider plan by the Kremlin to check and reverse the centrifugal tendencies in the crumbling empire. Perhaps it was all that and more, topped with the unintended consequences of freedom.

As president, Lucinschi attempted to rule by distancing himself from the "agrarians" and opposing the unreformed Communists. Instead, he fostered Moldova's first genuine coalition government, The Alliance for Democracy and Reforms. It consisted of all post-Communist orientations and the Christian democrats descendent from the FPM. The coalition was inherently unstable, and, during his tenure, the chief of state was forced to appoint four prime ministers in quick succession.[94] Further, Lucinschi's presidency was marked by a chronic economic crisis and other post-Communist pathologies which had likewise characterized the reign of his predecessor. In fact, the new head of state exacerbated the situation by elevating the parasitical relationship between the government and the new post-Communist ownership class to ridiculous heights. His choices for prime ministers, in particular the post-Communist "nonparty" Dumitru Braghiş (1999–2001), who had been previously involved in privatization and foreign economic contacts in top posts at the Ministry of Finance and the Ministry of Economy and Reforms, only solidified the widespread popular perception of pervasive corruption in the government.[95]

Organized crime ran rampant in Moldova. Much of it was indigenous, some foreign, Russian, in particular.[96] Halfhearted reforms, such as they were, failed to improve the lot of the people. Their anger at the post-Communists manifested itself in their deep disappointment with the political system itself. Much of the electorate became mired in apathy and cynicism. In 2000, some of them also widely, if falsely, perceived that the amendment to the Constitution instituting indirect presidential elections would benefit Lucinschi and his cronies. On the contrary, the idea was to demote the president in favor of the legislature. In fact, as the insiders planned, the amendment was custom-made for any dominant party in the parliament. In 2001, the unreformed Bolsheviks of the PCRM were able to mobilize enough of their supporters to win the parliamentary election overwhelmingly. Thus, the erstwhile imperial apparatchik Lucinschi overplayed his hand and lost his presidency to the unabashed Communist leader Vladimir Voronin.

Thoroughly Russified and Sovietized, the winner is partly of ethnic Romanian/Moldovan background.[97] Born in 1941 in a rustic family of Romanian-speaking Orthodox Christian anti-Communists on his mother's side, Voronin completely discarded the dangerous baggage of his personal past. He studied food processing and began to climb the nomenklatura ladder in the agricultural sector, in particular bread baking industry. Soon, the provincial bakery director was shifted to the apparat. Voronin worked on local executive committees. Following his graduation from the top-tier Academy of Social Sciences of the Central Committee of the CPSU in 1983, other nomenklatura appointments followed in party and administration, including with the Council of Ministers of the MSSR in Chişinău and with the city party committee of Bender.

In the late 1980s and early 1990s Voronin was a good Gorbachevian Communist and a national Bolshevik, trying to neutralize nonviolently the swelling wave of anti-Sovietism. In 1988, he was promoted to serve as the Minister of Internal Affairs in Chişinău, where he supervised MSSR's secret and uniformed police. In 1990, the country's top security man was transferred to Moscow, where, a year later, he finished the infamous Academy of the Ministry of Internal Affairs of the USSR. Meanwhile, he was twice tipped for the Supreme Soviet of MSSR and, later, Moldova. Following his return from Moscow, Voronin focused on restoring the Bolshevik party, which had been banned from 1991 to 1993. It re-emerged as the PCRM with the erstwhile Chekist at its head in 1994.

In 1996 Voronin ran for president unsuccessfully. His bid for parliament both in 1998 and 2001 succeeded, though.[98] After the Constitution was amended to allow for indirect presidential elections, the PCRM, taking advantage of its dominant position in the parliament, appointed its leader as Moldova's chief of state. The original idea behind indirect elections, naturally, was to diminish the power of the presidency. In practice, however, because the Communist party controlled the legislature unchallenged, its candidate individually wielded the most power ever in the postindependence history of Moldova. Vladimir Voronin (2001–2009) was no rubber stamp president. "Although Moldova is a parliamentary republic where the president's powers are clearly circumscribed, Voronin tends to act in practice as the state's chief executive," according to a perspicacious student of the region.[99]

The new chief of state was the first unreformed and unabashed Communist ever to be democratically (albeit indirectly) elected to presidency in the post-Soviet sphere after the implosion of the USSR.[100] There was no post-Communist deception on his part. Voronin brazenly promised to restore the alleged wholesomeness of Marxism-Leninism with all it entailed. Naturally, his message was crafted in a positive way, featuring such alluring slogans as providing "full employment," curtailing "evil capitalism," and promising good times for all. The new president planned to recollectivize and otherwise reverse the puny advances of free market in Moldova. All that, of course, necessitated intensifying the nation's re-Russification and re-Sovietization. Post-Communism would no longer do, ran Voronin's message. It was a venal betrayal of the Red Revolution. They were to return to the glorious Soviet past. His fiery rhetoric earned him the scary sobriquet: "the Moldavian Mao."

Consequently, rather than the feeble and inconsequential pan-Romanians, it was the post-Communists under different guises, who constituted the president's most formidable foes during his first tenure in power (2001–2005). They formed the bulk of the opposition. A fractious parliament resulted as the kleptocratic post-Communists battled it out with the retrograde Communists about the future of the nation. The latter under Voronin held sway and won the next parliamentary elections comfortably enough to reappoint their leader to yet another presidential term (2006–2009). Throughout, the president worked hand-in-glove with his Communist prime minister, Vasile Tarlev (2001–2008), the longest continuously serving head of the government in the post-Soviet sphere.[101]

The Communist electoral victories were expedited by a modest revival of Moldova's economy which commenced, ironically, in 2001 and continued for much of the decade. Voronin, of course, took credit for the upturn and tied it to his re-Sovietizing economic policies. The truth is that under his watchful eye Moldova continued very gingerly on the path of economic reform, even joining such "imperialist" and "capitalist" outfits like The World Trade Organization in 2001. And zero rate corporate tax introduced in 2008 to encourage foreign investments hardly squared with "Maoism." The government also began preaching about the benefits of joining the EU. The regime even cooled down somewhat its Russophilism, in particular, because the Transnistrian problem festered on with the Kremlin's blessings. Gradually, the Communist president and his cronies began to resemble increasingly their post-Communist rivals also as far as corruption and embezzlement. Sweetheart deals involving selling of state property at preferential prices continued. A thief is preferable to a doctrinaire implementing democidal ideology of Marxism-Leninism. According to an Intermarium joke, it is corruption that gives socialism its human face. Clearly it was neither 1940 nor 1945, nor even 1984 in Chișinău.

The national Bolshevik government failed to live up to its utopian Communist promises. Nonetheless, it continued with its incendiary revolutionary rhetorics at least until 2005. It is like simultaneously preaching anti-Semitism, on the one hand, and favoring the Jewish minority, on the other. Consequently, in the eyes of the disillusioned electorate Voronin and his Communist comrades appeared only marginally better than everyone else since independence.

The rural folk remained demobilized and apathetic but the urban dwellers, in the capital city of Chișinău, in particular, simmered with discontent. There were serious opposition rallies and demonstrations between January and April 2002 against the Russification campaign of the government.[102] Voronin was able to neutralize them by waiting the irritated nationalists out. No force was used. Next, some in the opposition promised to emulate Ukraine's Orange Revolution with their own Grape Revolution but failed to spark unrest in the wake of the parliamentary elections in 2005.[103] Afterward, the anger of the nationalists and others increased over their president's zig zags in Russian–Moldovan relations, including Transnistria. Having first distanced himself from Russia, Voronin then dealt directly with Putin, staking his credibility on bilateralism and sidelining the EU and the United States in the Transnistrian negotiations. The Moldovan president got nowhere with his Russian counterpart and had to reverse himself once again. He breathed fire about the secessionist region, which slightly assuaged some of his critics.[104] However, when the Communists were charged with electoral fraud in April 2009, the streets of Moldova's major towns became restive and, finally, erupted. Dubbed as the Twitter Revolution, it was put down by the authorities after much rioting and violence. The demonstrators raised social, economic, and pan-Romanian demands. Freedom was their leitmotif. They attacked government buildings, and chanted anti-Communist slogans. National solidarity was riding high again.[105]

Voronin won in the short run by crushing the demonstrators. However, in a long run, because enough of the active voters switched their preferences to deny the PCRM an absolute majority in the parliament, the national Bolsheviks lost. Thus, the legislature came to a grinding halt. The president was forced to resign in June 2009 (but continued on as acting president until September 2009).[106] The deadlock seemed permanent.

Despite repeated elections, no clear majority has emerged and Moldova remains in the state of a chronic constitutional crisis. No amount of behind the scenes deals in the parliament can change that. Three successive *pro tempore* presidents, all of them anointed by the avowedly libertarian and conservative opposition, but of the pro-EU moderate brand with strong ties to the post-Communists, have failed to resolve the political paralysis. Acting chiefs of state Mihai Ghimpu[107] (September 11, 2009–December 28, 2010), Vladimir Filat[108] (28–30 December 2010), and Marian Lupu[109] (December 30, 2010–March 16, 2012) concentrated on the symbolic, rather than the concrete. For example, Ghimpu instituted The Soviet Occupation Day (28 June) as a national holiday.

He also breathed new life into the rhetorics of pan-Romanianism at the highest levels of public life. Further, he celebrated the anti-Communist resistance, including not only the hard-core guerrillas of the 1940s and 1950s but also the folks of the Twitter Revolution. Last but not least, the president *pro tempore* stepped up his pro-EU propaganda. Moldova's intended de jure integration with the EU conveniently equals a de facto reunification with Romania.

The blink-of-an-eye acting president Vlad Filat was merely a convenient bridge between Ghimpu and Lupu. Yet, the liberal Filat has provided much-needed stability and continuity as Moldova's prime minister (2009–present). His successor as president, Lupu, avoided the embarrassing topic of anti-Communism. He also toned down the pan-Romanian rhetoric but amplified the pro-EU propaganda. The chief of state *pro tempore* further worked to smooth relations with Russia. Lupu was definitely an asset in terms of foreign perceptions. But even he could neither fix the economy that has registered a precipitous decline, because of the global downturn, since 2009, nor solve the quandary of Moldova's party politics. In general, the acting presidents tended to the day-to-day business of the government, but were not able to resolve most of the burning issues, including the constitutional stalemate. Nor is there much hope with the newest president, Nikolae Timofti (2012–present). Elected indirectly by a razor thin majority, Timofti promises more of the same. Despite the mirage of recent successful presidential elections, in reality the *pro tempore* regime has evolved into a permanent system of limbo. The electorate is too polarized to give victory to a clear-cut winner. Obviously, most of the people in Moldova failed to get the appropriate tweet after their "revolution."[110]

That, by the way, has been, more or less, the case throughout much of Moldova's post-1990 history. The flaw is systemic. Post-Communism virtually guarantees that elections tend to be free but unfair.[111] This is partly because Moscow continues to meddle in internal politics of the nation. The Kremlin's approach has evolved from ham-fisted to more subtle. Its focus is the Russian minority. But electoral fraud is also a function of post-Communism. Most importantly, there has been no real de-Communization, except for the temporary and symbolic banning of the party in the early 1990s.[112] The Communists, in all their avatars, were the only ones with the means, the know-how, and an apparatus in place, formal and informal, capable of organizing consistently and exerting nefariously official and unofficial pressure to mobilize, demo-bilize, encourage, and intimidate the voter, in the countryside, in particular. In short, only when the spirit of liberation and nationalism briefly held sway in the early 1990s was there a chance to discard the legacy of the Soviet past. But the elections took place within the Soviet context and the nationalists failed to push the issue of liberation all the way to its logical, democratic, and pan-Romanian conclusion. A paradigm shift proved impossible without getting rid of the nomenklatura elites who opposed de-Communization and reunification.

Soon, it was too late. By 1994, anti-Soviet nationalism was no longer a viable electoral force. Various mutations of post-Communism vied for influence, some of them in reform Communist garb, others in agrarian, social democratic, and liberal attires. Some of these post-Communists either joined with or absorbed moderate nationalists. The system seemed to have solidified under the leadership of the transformed cadres of the Soviet regime with a sprinkling of moderate, liberal, and pragmatic nationalists to legitimize them. The transformed post-Communists and their allies carried the day at the exit polls in 1994 and 1998. But, increasingly, they faced the angry challenge of the brazen unreformed Communists. The latter have emerged from the last five elections victorious: in 2001, 2005, 2009 (twice), and 2010.[113] The opposition was helpless except in the last case when it managed to clobber together an eclectic parliamentary confederation to run a minority government. An apparently shaky coalition holds united to various degrees by its opposition to the Communists. But in practice the system pro tempore has kept Moldova in a limbo.

An unsettled situation in the parliament has had at least one positive result, though: it forced the contumacious Moldovans to compromise. Perhaps its most shocking manifestation was a legislative collusion between the Christian democrats and unreformed Communists in 1999 and 2005.[114] For a Western observer that would be politics as usual. For a Moldovan citizen, however, that shocking switch confirmed the popular prejudice, common across the post-Soviet sphere, that all politicians are the same, Marxist-Leninist or not. As a popular wag would have it, "the pigs change; the trough remains the same." To appreciate this perception, we shall have a look at Moldova's main political parties.[115]

Most of the "pigs" on the national forum are either post-Communist or unreconstructed Communist. Therefore, we should first disentangle the confusing organizational and institutional legacy of Marxism-Leninism. Aside from making the obscure origins and roots of the major individual players transparent (see above), we must decipher the twists and turns of their chameleonic electoral vehicles. We need to keep in mind that the political parties in Moldova primarily serve the individual would be strong men and their entourages, rather than their avowed constituencies. There is quite a bit of deception involved, in terms of cyclical party rebranding, coalition building, and ideology changing. This is similar to Ukraine, and, to a much lesser extent, the Baltics.

The unreformed Communists are the easiest to describe because there is hardly any deception involved in their activity. However, even they have evolved from staunch Soviet patriots of the USSR into post-Soviet national Bolsheviks of Moldova. That means that the PCRM resembles somewhat the pre-1989 Communist parties of the Soviet satellite people's democracies of Central and Eastern Europe, except that their autonomy from Moscow is currently only constrained by the extent of their own voluntary devotion to the Kremlin. Russia largely lacks the will, if not the means, of direct coercion to discipline and to extract obedience from Moldova's Communists. As far as their nationalities policy, the national Bolsheviks endeavor to accommodate the Romanian-speaking majority as well as the Slavic and Turkic minorities. Simultaneously, the non-Romanian/Moldovan-speaking unreformed Communists akin to the PCRM maintain a grip on their own ethnic communities via minority national Bolshevism. It applies in particular to Transnistria and to a much lesser extent to Gagauzia. But it also concerns the Russian-speaking minority within the direct jurisdiction of the government in Chișinău. In other words, virtually every ethnic group has Russophilic national Bolsheviks who control their various minority organizations and parties. They also transformed themselves and embraced post-Communism.

Initially, in 1991, the Communists and nonparty Soviet patriots of the Moldavian Interfront (Internationalist front) became doubly homeless with the dissolution of the CPSU and the implosion of the USSR.[116] The rank-and-file dispersed, while the Russophile leaders either remained in Chișinău or departed for Tiraspol and Moscow. Their objective was to relaunch a new Bolshevik organization. However, some of them, ethnic Russians and Ukrainians, in particular, either joined or reactivated their membership in the socialist Yedinstvo-Unitatea (Unity) Intermovement, founded already in 1989, that purported to represent Moldova's minorities best. In fact, some had maintained dual membership in both the Moldavian Interfront and the Unity Intermovement. Yedinstvo attracted mostly Russian-speaking minority national Bolsheviks and Soviet patriots, basing itself permanently in Transnistria. Likewise, the Gagauz Halkî (Gagauz People) united Turkic minority national Bolsheviks and local nationalists. Both have maintained representatives in Chișinău, including at the parliament.

Meanwhile, other unreformed Communists concentrated on the Romanian-speakers, while courting the minorities. As mentioned, the CPSU was briefly banned. Because of their effort, the Marxist-Leninists re-emerged quite reinvigorated in 1993 as the PCRM under the erstwhile secret police supervisor Vladimir Voronin. His group quickly became a formidable political force. Between 1994 and 2000 it was the largest opposition party in the parliament. From 2001 to 2009 the PCRM controlled the legislature and presidency. It remains the strongest and most popular single orientation in Moldova.[117]

Initially, however, when the outlook for the unreformed Communists appeared bleak, many of their reform comrades endeavored to reinvent themselves in a variety of different ways. Consequently, they are to be found throughout the political spectrum of Moldova. After the banning of the Communist party, a few of its members almost immediately established the Socialist Party of Moldova (SPM) in 1992. It played a secondary role in various coalitions in the parliament, including with the national Bolshevik minorities, during the first decade of independence, only to recede into irrelevance after 2005.[118]

Other former reform Communists became much more powerful and relevant. Arguably, in the first decade, those who transformed themselves into the "agrarians" were the most successful of all. After the CPSU was delegalized, many of the cadres, in particular an influential contingent of provincial deputies at the Supreme Soviet, magically rediscovered their rustic roots and tapped into the illustrious legacy of the indigenous peasantist, populist activism with origins in the nineteenth century and a staunch anti-Communist pedigree in the first half of the twentieth century. Hence, in 1991, the post-Communists conveniently established the Democratic Agrarian Party of Moldova (DAPM).[119] It was an alliance of former party technocrats, rural apparatchiks, collective farm managers, and nascent oligarchs. The objective was to maintain power and to privatize agriculture and food processing industry to benefit themselves. While courting Russia and the national minorities, the DAPM was also the party of "Moldovanism." This initially ad hoc agrarian special interests group remained the most powerful force in the country until 1998. Afterward it receded into obscurity along with its main off-shoot, the ephemeral Socialist Workers' Party (SWP) under post-Communist prime minister Valeriu Muravschi (1991–1992, FPM, DAPM), representing a portion of the former urban CPSU apparat.

Other comrades, the reform Communists, in particular, first, in the late 1980s and early 1990s, found themselves in the pan-Romanian National Front of Moldova (FPM), while maintaining their CPSU membership. Before and after the ban on the Bolshevik party, they established and joined various informal factions within the FPM, many of them national Bolshevik. Thus, they continued to enjoy control and power as allies of the Christian nationalists within the National Front which dominated the Supreme Soviet at the time. Soon, some of them abandoned national Bolshevism and began flirting with social democracy, others with liberalism. Most of the FPM affiliated post-Communists invoked nationalism, opportunistically vacillating between pan-Romanianism and Moldovanism. As the FPM was burning itself out impotently, its post-Communists detached themselves gradually from its cause.

Already in 1990, some of them split from the FPM, to object to its waxing nationalism, and formed the Social Democratic Party of Moldova (SDP).[120] Its leaders were mostly nomenklatura intellectuals. The SDP's influence was largely limited to the capital but it also wooed the national minorities. It has never entered the parliament, and functions largely as an unfulfilled symbol for its Western supporters. Even the ascent of former prime minister Dumitru Braghiş at its helm in 2006 failed to reverse the party's abysmal electoral results.

Other post-Communist FPM defectors included the intellectuals who set up the social-liberal Congress of the Intelligentsia (CI) in 1993. The following year it entered the parliament jointly with the Congress of the Peasants (CP), an electoral springboard dominated by the former rural nomenklatura masking as rustic traditional populists. In 1998, the CI fused with the avowedly center-right Party of Reform (PR). The latter appeared already in 1993, invoking Christian democratic and nationalistic values. In 1997 it was taken over by the now irrelevant FPM's former post-Communist leader Mihai Ghimpu. The PR was an umbrella organization which absorbed, at one time or another, various homeless politicians and their organizations. At one point, the LP's leadership used to be heavily "agrarian," including former president Mircea Snegur (DAPM) and former prime minister Valeriu Muravschi (FMP, DAPM, and SWP). Subsequently, in 2005, the PR dumped its Christian democratic pretenses and reinvented itself as the modern (as opposed to classical) Liberal Party (LP).[121] Meanwhile, in 2003, it had been submerged, on an autonomous basis, into the social-liberal Our Moldova Alliance (OMA). Thus, in a variety of avatars, the LP has become merely an ad hoc electoral vehicle of the post-Communists [122]

That has also been the case with Moldova's other "liberal" outfits. In 1993, a number of former CPSU's social democratic and liberal-minded members of the intelligentsia, some after an unsatisfying stint with the FPM, established the Democratic Party for the Rebirth and Prosperity of Moldova (DPRPM). Other erstwhile comrades of the intelligentsia origin enrolled also in the Democratic Party (DP) and the Democratic Labor Party (DLP). All three failed to win seats in the legislature and, essentially, faded away. Then, in 1997, the post-Communist President Lucheschi became desperate for an electoral vehicle. Accordingly, his henchmen of the so-called "Pro Lucinschi" parliamentary bloc picked up and reassembled some of the pieces of several failed liberal and social–democratic outfits to forge the ostensibly centrist Movement for a Democratic and Prosperous Moldova (MDPM). In 2000, it restyled itself as the center-left Democratic Party of Moldova (DPM).[123] Thus, Moldova's social democracy and social liberalism largely remain dominated by the post-Communists.

A few post-Communists who earnestly propitiated for their Marxist-Leninist past stuck with the much-diminished FPM, which first renamed itself the Christian Democratic National Front (CDNF) in 1992, and then the Christian Democratic National Party (CDNP) in 1999.[124] The CDNP continues to be staunchly pan-Romanian. However, it has strayed from its initial anti-Communism. In 2005, the party entered the parliament because it made a deal with Voronin's PCRM. But that was its undoing. Many of its followers defected to the freshly established Liberal Democratic Party of Moldova (LDPM).[125] In 2009, the CDNP failed to cross the electoral threshold, joining many other extraparliamentary entities. Most of them are fly by night outfits that vanish as fast as they appear. There are a few exceptions, in particular, on the nationalist side.[126] Moldova's hard-core pan-Romanians and anti-Communists include the historic National Liberal Party (NPL)[127] and the new ultraintegrationist National Romanian Party (NRP).[128] They continue to clamor for reunification with Romania but no one really pays much attention anymore, at least not to their terms.

Among the extraparliamentarians, in addition to the nationalists, it behooves us to name a couple of fresh Western imports: the feminists and the environmentalists. The Women's Association of Moldova, which ran for election in 1994, and the Christian Democratic League of Women, which fought to enter the parliament in 1998, failed to stand on their own. The former became an NGO. The latter fused with other leftist outfits to form the Social Liberal Party in 2001, which, in turn, was gobbled up by the post-Communists of the center-left DPM seven years afterward. Meanwhile, the environmentalists never entered the legislature even after they changed their rather manageable "Green" label to the rather serpentine Green Alliance Ecological Party of Moldova.[129]

Feminism and environmentalism are obviously not priorities to the national electorate. Gay issues hardly register at all. Instead, for nearly twenty years, the Moldovan voter has been served with a choice between unreformed Communists and post-Communists of various ilk and shape, and a sprinkling of largely ineffectual Christian democrats whose once mighty pan-Romanianism has turned itself into a symbolic protest song delivered consistently out of tune. Yet, at least the extraparliamentary Christian democrats and pan-Romanians seem honest. The *faux* ideological façade across the board, from radical left to conservative right, of the parties in the legislature belies their nearly uniform organizational pedigree stemming from Marxism-Leninism.

The main parliamentary players now are the eternal Party of the Communists of the Republic of Moldova (PCRM),[130] the DPM, Liberal Party (LP), and the LDPM, which virtually absorbed, in 2011, the OMA. Despite their incongruous overt ideologies, confusing alliances, changing monikers, and fractious leadership, the DPM, LP, and LDPM have formed a minority governing coalition, the Alliance for European Integration (AEI). In a way, this is a re-hash of the post-Communist-cum-Christian democrat coalition—a new version of The Alliance for Democracy and Reforms—against the unreformed Communists of 1998–2001. Yet, it appears more stable. Despite their differences, contradictions, and the nine-hundred-day long constitutional crisis with an acting president, the AEI continues to hold together for now. Vladimir Socor perhaps prematurely dubbed the situation as "post-post-Communism."[131]

The political geography of Moldova seems quite confusing. The legacy of the Soviet occupation persists to an astonishing degree. It is hard to gauge whether even hard-core anti-Communist parties are indeed free of the post-Communists, or secret police agents. Over the past twenty years, scores of political parties imploded, morphed, joined others, and/or changed names and orientations. Leaders and rank-and-file members switched sides, beliefs, and affiliations, sometimes multiple times, or they simply disengaged themselves temporarily or permanently. To look for ideological purity and a wholesome pedigree is mostly futile. The current participants in the public square are usually tainted by their past associations and they are much better than an average Western politician in obscuring their personal history.

Former members of the Communist party are virtually everywhere and they have monopolized the political discourse of Moldova in practically all its shades. It was perhaps inevitable. After all Moldova was one of the most Sovietized parts of the USSR. Its totalitarian system allowed for political participation only within the nefarious confines of the Bolshevik machine. Hence, we witness the continuous persistence of the post-Communists in post-Communism. Without legally and physically banning them from participation in the public square they are here to stay, mostly for worse.[132]

Waiting for the younger generation to replace the aging former party apparatchiks and to reform Moldova may be false hope. After all, it is the former nomenklatura who has trained most of the young, including instilling in them the admiration for the ideology of Marxism-Leninism and its utility as a dialectical tool of exercising power. It is the post-Communists who set the example for the young how to rule kleptocratically and cynically. It is the exparty apparatchiks who created the "democratic" and "free market" system of Moldova that the young grew up in.[133] Of course, while others tacitly acknowledge it, the unreformed Communists are the most brazen about this: "Moldovan Communist Party leaders argued that the hard-left connection truly reflected their party's identity, which they were not about to change. Significantly, this is the view of the Party's young leadership echelon, people in their twenties and thirties who are being groomed to take over soon from the Soviet-bred generation of party leaders."[134]

The post-Communists as well as their supporters and enablers remain on top in Moldova. The sad remnant of the traditional elite continues to be inept and ineffectual. The people are confused and alienated, feeling left behind.[135] To change all this would require not just a transformation, but a bold, peaceful conservative and libertarian counterrevolution. This applies as well to a various degree to other nations in the Intermarium. However, given the current cultural climate and geopolitical considerations, it is hardly in the cards.

Notes

1. For a brief introduction see "Government Portal: Web Portal of the Ukrainian Government," http://www.kmu.gov.ua/control/; Central Intelligence Agency, "Ukraine," *The World Factbook*, https://www.cia.gov/library/publications/the-world-factbook/geos/up.html; US State Department's Bureau of European and Eurasian Affairs, "Background Note: Ukraine," (May 24, 2010): http://www.state.gov/r/pa/ei/bgn/3211.htm; "Ukraine," European Forum For Democracy and Solidarity, Socialist International, http://www.europeanforum.net/country/ukraine. For pre-2004 free Ukraine see Taras Kuzio, *State and Nation Building*

in *Ukraine* (London: Routledge, 1998); Robert S. Kravchuk, *Ukrainian Politics, Economics and Governance, 1991–1996* (Basingstoke: Macmillan, 1999); Mykola Ryabchuk, "Between Civil Society and the New Etatism: Democracy in the Making and State Building in Ukraine," in *Envisioning Eastern Europe: Postcommunist Cultural Studies*, ed. Michael D. Kennedy (Ann Arbor, MI: University of Michigan Press, 1994), 125–48; Denis J. B. Shaw and Michael J. Bradshaw, "Problems of Ukrainian Independence," *Post-Soviet Geography* 33, no. 1 (January 1992): 10–20; Ilya Prizel, "Ukraine's Hollow Decade," *East European Politics and Societies* 16, no. 2 (Spring 2002): 363–85; and the bilingual work of Halyna Koscharsky, ed., *Ukraine Today: Perspectives for the Future* (Commack, NY: Nova Science, 1995), which includes interesting data on historiography, education, religion, culture, emigration, and foreign relations (even with Australia!). On the KGB and post-KGB factor in contemporary Ukrainian politics see Jerzy Targalski, "Ukraina: Opozycja," (Ukraina: The Opposition) TMs, Warsaw, no date (2008), 1–78, especially pages 64–78 (a copy in my collection).

2.   See Orest Subtelny, "Russocentrism, Regionalism, and the Political Culture of Ukraine," in *Political Culture and Civil Society in Russia and the New States of Eurasia*, ed. Vladmir Tismăneanu (Armonk, NY: M.E. Sharpe, 1995), 189–207; Dominique Arel, "Voting Behavior in the Ukrainian Parliament: The Language Factor," in *Parliaments in Transition: The New Legislative Politics in the Former USSR and Eastern Europe*, ed. Thomas F. Remington (Boulder, CO: Westview, 1994), 125–58; Dominique Arel, "Language Politics in Independent Ukraine: Towards One or Two State Languages?" *Nationalities Papers* 23, no. 3 (September 1995): 597–622; Sven Holdar, "Torn between East and West: The Regional Factor in Ukrainian Politics," *Post-Soviet Geography* 36, no. 2 (February 1995): 112–32; Nikolai Shulga, "Regionalisation, Federalisation and Separatism in Ukraine: Historical Roots, New Realities and Prospects," in *Post-Soviet Puzzles: Mapping the Political Economy of the Former Soviet Union* (4 vols), ed. Klaus Segbers and Stephan De Spiegeleire, vol. 2: *Emerging Geopolitical and Territorial Units: Theories, Methods and Case Studies* (Baden-Baden: Nomos, 1995), 2: 467–88; Vicki L. Hesli, "Public Support for the Devolution of Power in Ukraine: Regional Patterns," *Europe-Asia Studies* 47, no. 1 (January 1995): 91–121; Serhiy Makeyev and Svitlana Oksamytna, "Problems of Internal Political Geography: The Ukrainian Example," in *The Political Analysis of Postcommunism: Understanding Postcommunist Ukraine*, ed. Volodymyr Polokhalo (College Station, TX: Texas A&M University Press, 1997), 205–12; Paul Kubicek, "Regional Polarisation in Ukraine: Public Opinion, Voting and Legislative Behaviour," *Europe-Asia Studies* 52, no. 2 (March 2000): 273–94; Lyudmyla Pavlyuk, "Extreme Rhetoric in the 2004 Presidential Campaign: Images of Geopolitical and Regional Division," *Canadian Slavonic Papers* 47, no. 3/4 (September–December 2005): 293–316; Iryna Maryniak, "Belarus and Ukraine: Nation Building in Babel," *Index on Censorship* 22, no. 2 (March 1993): 20–33; Dominique Arel and Valentyn Khmelko, "The Russian Factor and Territorial Polarization in Ukraine," *The Harriman Review* 9, no. 1–2 (March 1996): 81–91; George Liber, "Imagining Ukraine: Regional Differences and the Emergence of an Integrated State Identity," *Nations and Nationalism* 4, no. 2 (April 1998): 187–206; Sarah Birch, "Interpreting the Regional Effect in Ukrainian Politics," *Europe-Asia Studies* 52, no. 6 (September 2000): 1017–41; Gwendolyn Sasse, "The 'New' Ukraine: A State of Regions," in *Ethnicity and Territory in the Former Soviet Union: Regions in Conflict*, ed. James Hughes and Gwendolyn Sasse (London and Portland, OR: Frank Cass, 2002), 69–100;

Paul S. Pirie, "National Identity and Politics in Southern and Eastern Ukraine," *Europe-Asia Studies* 48, no. 7 (November 1996): 1079–104.

3.   See Taras Kuzio and Paul D'Anieri, *Dilemmas of State-Led Nation Building in Ukraine* (Westport, CT: Praeger, 2002); Catherine Wanner, *Burden of Dreams: History and Identity in Post-Soviet Ukraine* (University Park, PA: Pennsylvania State University Press, 1998); Peter J. S. Duncan, "Ukraine and Ukrainians," in *The Nationalities Question in the Post-Soviet States*, ed. Graham Smith, (London: Longman 1996), 188–209; Paul D'Anieri, Robert Kravchuk, and Taras Kuzio, *Politics and Society in Ukraine* (Boulder, CO: Westview, 1999); Sharon L. Wolchik and Volodymyr Zviglyanich, eds., *Ukraine: The Search for a National Identity* (Lanham, MD: Rowman and Littlefield, 2000); Bohdan Harasymiw, "Ukrainian Nationalism and the Future," in *Nationalism and the Breakup of an Empire: Russia and Its Periphery*, ed. Miron Rezun (New York: Praeger, 1992), 57–70; John A. Armstrong, "Whither Ukrainian Nationalism?" *Canadian Review of Studies in Nationalism*, 23, no. 1–2 (1996): 111–24; Tadeusz O. Olszanski, "Ukrainian People or Ukrainian Nation?" *Canadian Review of Studies in Nationalism* 27, no. 1–2 (2000): 45–48; Yaroslav Bilinsky, "Are the Ukrainians a State Nation?" *Problems of Communism* 41, no. 1–2 (January–April 1992): 134–35; Yaroslav Bilinsky, "Primary Language of Communication as a Secondary Indicator of National Identity: The Ukrainian Parliamentary and Presidential Elections of 1994 and the 'Manifesto of the Ukrainian Intelligentsia' of 1995," *Nationalities Papers* 24, no. 4 (December 1996): 661–78; Julian Birch, "Ukraine – A Nation-State or a State of Nations?" *Journal of Ukrainian Studies* 21, no. 1–2 (Summer–Winter 1996): 109–24; David Saunders, "What Makes a Nation a Nation? Ukrainians since 1600," *Ethnic Groups* 10 (1993): 196–207; Stephen C. Shulman, "Sources of Civic and Ethnic Nationalism in Ukraine," *Journal of Communist Studies and Transition Politics* 18, no. 4 (December 2002): 1–30; Stephen C. Shulman, "The Contours of Civic and Ethnic National Identification in Ukraine," *Europe-Asia Studies* 56, no. 1 (January 2004): 35–56; Oxana Shevel, "Nationality in Ukraine: Some Rules of Engagement," *East European Politics and Societies* 16, no. 2 (Spring 2002): 386–414; Yevhen Bystrytsky, "Nationalism and Legitimation of Postcommunist Regimes," in *The Political Analysis of Postcommunism: Understanding Postcommunist Ukraine*, ed. Volodymyr Polokhalo (College Station, TX: Texas A&M University Press, 1997), 51–66; Mikhail A. Molchanov, "Post-Communist Nationalism as a Power Resource: A Russia-Ukraine Comparison," *Nationalities Papers* 28, no. 2 (June 2000): 263–88; William Zimmerman, "Is Ukraine a Political Community?" *Communist and Post-Communist Studies* 31, no. 1 (1998): 43–55; Stephen Rapawy, *Ethnic Reidentification in Ukraine*, IPC Staff Paper No. 90 (Washington, DC: US Bureau of the Census, 1997); Taras Kuzio, "National Identity in Independent Ukraine: An Identity in Transition," *Nationalism and Ethnic Politics* 2, no. 4 (Winter 1996): 582–608; Taras Kuzio, "Identity and Nation Building in Ukraine: Defining the 'Other,'" *Ethnicities* 1, no. 3 (December 2001): 343–66. On the peripheries of Ukrainian nationalism see Hugo Lane, "Rusyns and Ukrainians Yesterday, Today, and Tomorrow: The Limitations of National History," *Nationalities Papers* 29, no. 4 (December 2001): 689–96; Raymond A. Smith, "Indigenous and Diaspora Elites and the Return of Carpatho-Ruthenian Nationalism, 1989–1992," *Harvard Ukrainian Studies* 21, no. 1–2 (June 1997): 141–60; Susyn Yvonne Mihalasky, "Ethno-National Orientation among Lemkos in Poland," in *National Identities and Ethnic Minorities in Eastern Europe*, ed. Ray Taras (New York: St. Martin's, 1995), 208–24. For beyond nationalism

see Ray Taras, Olga Filippova, and Nelly Pobeda, "Ukraine's Transnationals, Far-Away Locals and Xenophobes: The Prospects for Europeanness," *Europe-Asia Studies* 56, no. 6 (September 2004): 835–56.

4. For the insights by one of the most clear sighted observers of the oligarchs see Józef Darski [Jerzy Targalski] "Oligarchiczny system polityczny na Ukrainie," ("The Oligarchical Political System in Ukraine") TMs, Warsaw, no date (2005?), 1–19 (a copy in my collection). See also Robert S. Kravchuk, *Ukrainian Political Economy: The First Ten Years* (New York: Palgrave Macmillan, 2002); Rawi Abdelal, *National Purpose in the World Economy: Post-Soviet States in Comparative Perspective* (Ithaca, NY: Cornell University Press, 2001), Chapter 5, "Ukraine: Between East and West," 103–26; Hans van Zon, Andre Batako, and Anna Kreslavska, *Social and Economic Change in Eastern Ukraine: The Example of Zaporizhia* (Aldershot: Ashgate, 1998); Andrij A. Halushka, "Presidential Elections and Structure of Industry in Ukraine," (Vienna: Institut für Höhere Studien, East European Series, no. 14, December 1994), http://www.ihs.ac.at/publications/eco/east/ro-14.pdf; James L. Gibson, "Political and Economic Markets: Changes in the Connections between Attitudes toward Political Democracy and a Market Economy within the Mass Culture of Russia and Ukraine," *The Journal of Politics* 58, no. 4 (November 1996): 954–85; Taras Kuzio, "Prospects for the Political and Economic Development of Ukraine," in *The New Eastern Europe: Ukraine, Belarus, Moldova*, ed. Daniel Hamilton and Gerhard Mangott (Washington, DC: Center for Transatlantic Relations, 2007), 25–44, http://transatlantic.sais-jhu.edu/bin/o/y/new_eastern_europe_text.pdf; Alexander J. Motyl, "Structural Constraints and Starting Points: The Logic of Systemic Change in Ukraine and Russia," *Comparative Politics* 29, no. 4 (July 1997): 433–47.

5. Alexei Trochev, "Meddling with Justice: Competitive Politics, Impunity, and Distrusted Courts in Post-Orange Ukraine," *Demokratizatsiya: The Journal of Post-Soviet Democratization* 18, no. 2 (Spring 2010): 122–47.

6. See John A. Armstrong, "Persistent Patterns of the Ukrainian Apparatus," *Soviet and Post-Soviet Review* 20, no. 2–3 (1993): 213–31; Bohdan Harasymiw, "Ukraine's Political Elite and the Transition to Post-Communism," *Journal of Ukrainian Studies* 21, no. 1–2 (Summer–Winter 1996): 125–46; Jan Pakulski, "Poland and Ukraine: Elite Transformation and Prospects for Democracy," *Journal of Ukrainian Studies* 20, no. 1–2 (Summer–Winter 1995): 195–208; Andrew Konitzer-Smirnov, "Serving Different Masters: Regional Executives and Accountability in Ukraine and Russia," *Europe-Asia Studies* 57, no. 1 (January 2005): 3–33; Vladimir Pigenko, Charles R. Wise, and Trevor L. Brown, "Elite Attitudes and Democratic Stability: Analysing Legislators' Attitudes towards the Separation of Powers in Ukraine," *Europe-Asia Studies* 54, no. 1 (January 2002): 87–107; Evgenii Golovakha, "Elites in Ukraine: Evaluation of the Project's Elite Survey," in *Emerging Societal Actors – Economic, Social and Political Interests, Theories, Methods and Case Studies*, ed. Klaus Segbers and Stephan De Spiegeleire (Baden-Baden: Nomos, 1995), 3: 167–242 (this is vol. 3 of a four volume work on *Post-Soviet Puzzles: Mapping the Political Economy of the Former Soviet Union*). See also Kerstin Zimmer, "The Comparative Failure of Machine Politics, Administrative Resources and Fraud," *Canadian Slavonic Papers* 47, no. 3/4 (September–December 2005): 361–84; Jessica Allina-Pisanno, "Social Contracts and Authoritarian Projects in Post-Soviet Space: The Use of Administrative Resource," *Communist and Post-Communist Studies* 43, no. 4 (December 2010): 373–82; Paul Kubicek, "Delegative Democracy in Russia

and Ukraine," *Communist and Post-Communist Studies* 27, no. 4 (December 1994): 423–41; Paul D'Anieri, "Structural Constraints in Ukrainian Politics," *East European Politics and Societies* 25, no. 1 (Winter 2011): 28–49; Volodymyr Polokhalo, ed., *The Political Analysis of Postcommunism: Understanding Postcommunist Ukraine* (College Station, TX: Texas A&M University Press, 1997), in particular the following essays: Valentyn Yakushyk, James Mace, and Kostiyantyn Maleyev, "Corruption as a Political Phenomenon under Communism," (163–76), Georges Mink and Jean-Charles Szurek, "Adaptation Strategies of the Former Communist Elites," (187–204), and Yevhen Holovakha, "The Social Pathology of the Postcommunist Society" (227–40).

7.   The post-Soviets in Ukraine did not bother to change the name of their principal democratic institution. Perhaps this should be viewed as yet another example of compromise. The *Verkhovna Rada* is both the Ukrainian translation of the Russian word for "Soviet" and a nod toward Ukrainian history: a *rada* was a medieval boyar assembly, an early modern Cossack council, and also the embryonic legislature (*Tsentralna Rada*) of the ephemeral Ukrainian People's Republic established by the end of the First World War. The Bolsheviks, initially, extinguished all non-Communist forms and symbols of Ukrainian state institutions replacing them with revolutionary ones, which replicated all things "Soviet" on the republican level. In 1938, however, in the wake of the Terror-Famine and the Great Purge, Stalin changed the name of All Ukrainian Congress of Soviets's Central Executive Committee of the Ukrainian Soviet Socialist Republic to the Supreme Soviet of the Ukrainian SSR, also referred to interchangeably in Ukrainian as the *Verkhovna Rada*. This is significant to stress because from its inception the newly independent Ukraine has endeavored to reconcile both Soviet and Ukrainian elements of its history, rather than eliminate the totalitarian legacy wholesale, in particular as far as such a symbolic institution. It could have been called Rada Ukrainy, Sobor Ukrainy, or even Seym Ukrainy, in congruence with its tradition. See Stanley Bach, "From Soviet to Parliament in Ukraine: The Verkhovna Rada during 1992–94," in *The New Parliaments of Central and Eastern Europe*, ed. David M. Ollson and Philip Norton (London: Frank Cass, 1996), 213–30; Sarah Whitmore, *State-Building in Ukraine: The Ukrainian Parliament, 1990–2003* (London: Routledge Curzon, 2004).

8.   See Kimitaka Matsuzato, "Semipresidentialism in Ukraine: Institutionalist Centrism in Rampant Clan Politics," *Demokratizatsiya: The Journal of Post-Soviet Democratization* 13, no. 1 (Winter 2005): 45–60; Oleh Protsyk, "Ruling with Decrees: Presidential Decree Making in Russia and Ukraine," *Europe-Asia Studies* 56, no. 5 (July 2004): 637–60; Oleh Protsyk, "Troubled Semi-Presidentialism: Stability of the Constitutional System and Cabinet in Ukraine," *Europe-Asia Studies* 55, no. 7 (November 2003): 1077–95; Andrew Wilson, "Ukraine," in *Semi-Presidentialism in Europe*, ed. Robert Elgie (Oxford: Oxford University Press, 1999), 260–315; Charles R. Wise and Trevor R. Brown, "The Separation of Powers in Ukraine," *Communist and Post-Communist Studies* 32, no. 1 (March 1999): 23–44; Paul D'Anieri, *Understanding Ukrainian Politics: Power, Politics, and Institutional Design* (Armonk, NY: M.E. Sharpe, 2007).

9.   See Alexander J. Motyl, "The Conceptual President: Leonid Kravchuk and the Politics of Surrealism," in *Patterns in Post-Soviet Leadership*, ed. Timothy J. Colton and Robert C. Tucker (Boulder, CO: Westview Press, 1995), 103–21.

10.   Serhiy Naboka, "A Lack of Everything," *Uncaptive Minds* 6, no. 3 (24) (Fall 1993); Taras Kouzmov, "Ukraine: A Long Way to Go," *Uncaptive Minds* 7, no. 2 (26) (Summer 1994): 59–64; Józef Darski [Jerzy Targalski], "Which Way

Independence?," *Uncaptive Minds* 7, no. 3 (27) (Fall–Winter 1994): 117–28; Dominique Arel, "Ukraine: The Muddle Way," *Current History* 97 (1998): 342–46; Sarah Birch, "The Ukrainian Parliamentary and Presidential Elections of 1994," *Electoral Studies* 14 no. 1 (1995): 93–99; Oxana Prisiajniuok, "The State of Civil Society in Independent Ukraine," *Journal of Ukrainian Studies* 20, no. 1–2 (Summer–Winter 1995): 161–76.

11. Kravchuk and his family were involved in a number of shady deals, including the selling off the nation's merchant marine. As late as 2010, the former president continued to enjoy his ill-gotten gains, including in state-owned real estate and land. And so do Leonid Kuchma and Viktor Yanukovych, the latter settling down in a forest preserve. In 2009, Kravchuk ditched the SDPU(u), switching over to Yulia Tymoshenko. See Svitlana Tuchynska, "Ukrayinska Pravda Exposes President's Mezhygirya Deal," *Kyiv Post* (May 6, 2010): http://www.kyivpost. com/news/nation/detail/66006/; "Kravchuk Leaves Social Democratic Party of Ukraine (United)," Interfax.com.ua, (September 25, 2009): http://www.interfax. com.ua/eng/main/20944/.

12. See Andrew Wilson, "Ukraine: Two Presidents and Their Powers," in *Postcommunist Presidents*, ed. Ray Taras (New York: Cambridge University Press, 1997); Marko Bojcun, "Leonid Kuchma's Presidency in Its First Year," *Journal of Ukrainian Studies* 20 no. 1–2 (Summer–Winter 1995): 177–93; Marko Bojcun, "Ukraine under Kuchma," *Labour Focus on Eastern Europe* 52 (Autumn 1995): 70–83; Kataryna Wolczuk, "Presidency in Ukraine: A Mid-Term Review of the Second Presidency," *Democratization* 4 no. 3 (Autumn 1997): 152–71; Oleh Protsyk, "Constitutional Politics and Presidential Power in Kuchma's Ukraine." *Problems of Post-Communism* 52, no. 5 (September–October 2005): 23–31; Hans van Zon, "Political Culture and Neo-Patrimonialism under Leonid Kuchma," *Problems of Post-Communism* 52, no. 5 (October/September 2005): 12–22; Paul D'Anieri, "Leonid Kuchma and the Personalization of the Ukrainian Presidency," *Problems of Post-Communism* 50, no. 5 (September–October 2003): 58–65; Sarah Whitmore, "State and Institution Building under Kuchma," *Problems of Post-Communism* 52, no. 5 (September–October 2005): 3–11. And see Taras Kuzio, *Ukraine under Kuchma: Political Reform, Economic Transformation and Security Policy in Independent Ukraine* (New York: St. Martin's Press, 1997); Elizabeth Pond, "An End, Maybe, to Sleepwalking in Ukraine," *Washington Quarterly* no. 18 (Winter 1995): 73–81; Leonid Kistersky and Serhii Pirozhkov, "Ukraine: Policy Analysis and Options," in *Perceptions of Security: Public Opinion and Expert Assessments in Europe's New Democracies*, ed. Richard Smoke (New York: Manchester University Press, 1996), 209–27; Adrian Karatnycky, "Ukraine at the Crossroads," *Journal of Democracy* 6, no. 1 (January 1995): 117–30; Nadia Diuk, "Ukraine: A Land in between," *Journal of Democracy* 9, no. 3 (July 1998): 97–111; Ilya Prizel, "Ukraine between Proto-Democracy and 'Soft' Authoritarianism," in *Democratic Changes and Authoritarian Reactions in Russia, Ukraine, Belarus, and Moldova*, ed. Karen Dawisha and Bruce Parrott (Cambridge: Cambridge University Press, 1997), 330–69.

13. See Taras Kuzio, "Kravchuk to Kuchma: The 1994 Presidential Elections in Ukraine," *The Journal of Communist Studies and Transition Politics* 12, no. 2 (June 1996): 117–44; Sarah Birch, "The Presidential Election in Ukraine, October 1999," *Electoral Studies* 21, no. 2 (June 2002): 339–45; Thomas F. Klobucar, Arthur H. Miller, and Gwyn Erb, "The 1999 Ukrainian Presidential Election: Personalities, Ideology, Partisanship, and the Economy," *Slavic Review* 61, no. 2

(Summer 2002): 315–44; Olena Nikolayenko, "Press Freedom during the 1994 and 1999 Presidential Elections in Ukraine: A Reverse Wave?" *Europe-Asia Studies* 56, no. 5 (July 2004): 661–86.

14. Stephen C. Shulman, "Ukrainian Nation-Building under Kuchma," *Problems of Post-Communism* 52, no. 5 (September/October 2005): 32–47.

15. His daughter Elena Franchuk, married to the powerful oligarch Viktor Pinchuk, is now a celebrated London socialite and an anti-AIDS philanthropist.

16. After he discovered and published evidence of corruption in highest places, web journalist Georgy Gongadze was kidnapped and murdered but only his headless body was ever recovered. Kuchma and his aide Volodymyr Lytvyn were implicated, having had been recorded wishing him dead, but the hit was allegedly ordered by interior minister Yuri Kravchenko, while General Alexei Pukach was the hitman. In 2005 Kravchenko was shot in the head twice and died, which the authorities ruled as suicide. Pukach was apprehended in 2009. See "Ukraine Says Late Minister Ordered Gongadze Murder," Committee to Protect Journalists, (September 16, 2010), http://cpj.org/2010/09/ukraine-says-late-minister-ordered-gongadze-murder.php.; Olena Nikolayenko, "Press Freedom during the 1994 and 1999 Presidential Elections in Ukraine: A Reverse Wave?" *Europe-Asia Studies* 56, no. 5 (July 2004): 661–86; Marta Dyczok, "Was Kuchma's Censorship Effective? Mass Media in Ukraine before 2004," *Europe-Asia Studies* 58, no. 2 (March 2006): 215–38; Adrian Karatnycky, "Meltdown in Ukraine," *Foreign Affairs* 80, no. 3 (May–June 2001): 73–86; Nadia Diuk and Myroslava Gongadze, "Post-Election Blues in Ukraine," *Journal of Democracy* 13, no. 4 (October 2002): 157–66; Taras Kuzio, "Transition in Post-Communist States: Triple or Quadruple?" *Politics* 21, no. 3 (September 2001): 168–77.

17. See Verena Fritz, *State-Building: A Comparative Study of Ukraine, Lithuania, Belarus, and Russia* (Budapest: Central European University Press, 2007), Chapter 8, "The Second Transition in Ukraine," 175–210; Anders Åslund and Michael McFaul, eds., *Revolution in Orange: The Origins of Ukraine's Democratic Breakthrough* (Washington, DC: Carnegie Endowment for International Peace, 2006); Andrew Wilson, *Ukraine's Orange Revolution* (New Haven, CT: Yale University Press, 2005); Taras Kuzio, "From Kuchma to Yushchenko: Ukraine's 2004 Presidential Elections and the Orange Revolution," *Problems of Post-Communism* 52, no. 2 (2005): 29–44; Paul D'Anieri, "The Last Hurrah: The 2004 Ukrainian Presidential Elections and the Limits of Machine Politics," *Communist and Post-Communist Studies* 38, no. 2 (2005): 231–49; Ararat L. Osipian and Alexandr L. Osipian, "Why Donbass Votes for Yanukovych: Confronting the Ukrainian Orange Revolution," *Demokratizatsiya: The Journal of Post-Soviet Democratization* 14, no. 4 (Fall 2006): 495–517; Lyudmyla Pavlyuk, "Extreme Rhetoric in the 2004 Presidential Campaign: Images of Geopolitical and Regional Division," *Canadian Slavonic Papers* 47, no. 3/4 (September–December 2005): 293–316; Marta Dyczok, "Breaking through the Information Blockade: Election and Revolution in Ukraine 2004," *Canadian Slavonic Papers/Revue canadienne des slavistes* 47, no. 3 (2005): 241–64; Ralph S. Clem and Peter R. Craumer, "Orange, Blue and White, and Blonde: The Electoral Geography of Ukraine's 2006 and 2007 Rada Elections," *Eurasian Geography and Economics* 49, no. 2 (2008): 127–51; Ralph S. Clem and Peter R. Craumer, "Shades of Orange: The Electoral Geography of Ukraine's 2004 Presidential Elections," *Eurasian Geography and Economics* 46, no. 5 (2005): 364–85; Valerii Polkovsky, "The Language of the Presidential Election Campaign in Ukraine," *Canadian Slavonic Papers/Revue canadienne des slavistes* 47, no. 3 (2005):

317–32; Maksym Strikha and Evgeniia Kononenko, "The Ukrainian Elections of 2004: Epilogue and Prologue," *Ukrainian Quarterly* 61, no. 12 (2005): 16–28; Olena Yatsunska, "Image Myths in the 2004 Ukrainian Presidential Election Campaign," *Canadian Slavonic Papers/Revue canadienne des slavistes* 47, no. 3 (2005): 333–60; Olena Yatsunska, "Mythmaking and Its Discontents in the 2004 Ukrainian Presidential Campaign," *Demokratizatsiya: The Journal of Post-Soviet Democratization* 14, no. 4 (Fall 2006): 519–33; Paul D'Anieri, "What Has Changed in Ukrainian Politics? Assessing the Implications of the Orange Revolution," *Problems of Post-Communism* 52 no. 5 (September–October 2005): 82–91; Viktor Stepanenko, "How Ukrainians View Their Orange Revolution: Public Opinion and the National Peculiarities of Citizenry Political Activities," *Demokratizatsiya* 13, no. 4 (Fall 2005): 595–616; Alexei Trochev, "Meddling with Justice: Competitive Politics, Impunity, and Distrusted Courts in Post-Orange Ukraine," *Demokratizatsiya: The Journal of Post-Soviet Democratization* 18, no. 2 (Spring 2010): 122–47; Kerstin Zimmer, "The Comparative Failure of Machine Politics, Administrative Resources and Fraud," *Canadian Slavonic Papers* 47, no. 3/4 (September–December 2005): 361–84; Misha Myagkov, Peter C. Ordeshook, and Dimitry Shakin, "The Disappearance of Fraud: The Forensics of Ukraine's 2006 Parliamentary Elections," *Post-Soviet Affairs* 23, no. 3 (2007): 218–39.

18.   There has been some disinformation about Yushchenka's alleged corruption and oligarchic ties in the early 1990s. For an example of such an attack, cut-and-pasted on an American website, but unavailable at its alleged original places of posting (respectively, a Russian news site, which published the original Russian-language article at http://informacia.ru/facts/ushenko-facts.htm, and a British Helsinki Human Rights Group, which published its English translation at http://www.bhhrg.org/LatestNews.asp?ArticleID=53) see the response to the headline "Yushchenko WINS Ukrainian Elections," by frontdeboeuf, post no. 20, "Yushchenko is the demon-rats' man in Eurosthan [sic]," (December 27, 2004), http://freerepublic.com/focus/f-news/1309142/posts.

19.   According to an unattributed source, the US State Department refused to help Yushchenko because Washington did not wish to antagonize Moscow. It was feared that the blood and toxicology tests would show that the dioxin originated in a Russian lab. However, in a typical display of intergovernmental rivalry, the Pentagon did help by surreptitiously dispatching its top toxicologist, who is also affiliated with the University of Virginia, to Vienna, where a medical team intervened fortuitously, saving Yushchenko. At any rate, the alleged main perpetrator, Vladimir (Volodymyr) Satsyuk, has Russian citizenship and the Kremlin has refused to extradite him. For various versions see "President Claims the Kremlin Is Shielding His Would-Be Killers," *The Times* (September 13, 2009), http://www.timesonline.co.uk/tol/news/world/europe/article6832223.ece; "Yushchenko to Russia: Hand Over Witnesses," *Kyiv Post* (September 28, 2009), http://www.kyivpost.com/news/nation/detail/49610/.

20.   Taras Kuzio, "The Orange Revolution at the Crossroads," *Demokratizatsiya: The Journal of Post-Soviet Democratization* 14, no. 4 (Fall 2006): 477–95; Nicklaus Laverty, "The Problem of Lasting Change: Civil Society and the Colored Revolutions in Georgia and Ukraine," *Demokratizatsiya: The Journal of Post-Soviet Democratization* 16, no. 2 (Spring 2008): 143–62.

21.   See David R. Marples, *Heroes and Villains: Creating National History in Contemporary Ukraine* (New York and Budapest: CEU Press, 2007); Bohdan Harasymiw, "Memories of the Second World War in Recent Ukrainian Election

Campaigns," *Journal of Ukrainian Studies* 32, no. 1 (2007): 97–108; David R. Marples, "Anti-Soviet Partisans and Ukrainian Memory," *East European Politics and Societies* 24, no. 1 (Winter 2010): 26–44. See also Taras Kuzio, "Ukraine: Coming to Terms with the Soviet Legacy," *The Journal of Communist Studies and Transition Politics* 14, no. 4 (December 1998): 1–27.

22. See Clifford J. Levy, "'Hero of Ukraine' Splits Nation, Inside and Out," *The New York Times* (March 1, 2010), http://www.nytimes.com/2010/03/02/world/europe/02history.html?_r=1&ref=viktorayushchenko.

23. Januki (Yanuki) is outside of Vitebsk (Witebsk), one of the easternmost provinces of the Commonwealth of Poland-Lithuania, but it also belonged within the borders of the interwar Poland. The graves in the village's Catholic cemetery have tombstones with Polish inscriptions. The few remaining denizens identify themselves as "locals," rather than Poles. Yanukovych's Catholic grandfather migrated to eastern Ukraine either right before or during World War I. His son married a Russian Orthodox woman, and, thus, his grandson, Ukraine's President Yanukovych, identifies himself as "Orthodox." But the chief of state freely admits his Polish roots: one of his grandmothers was born in Warsaw, her stepmother was from Wilno, and the rest are Poles of the former Grand Duchy of Lithuania, including his grandfather who was born in Dokrzyce near Januki. See Andrzej Pisalnik, "Polskie strony Janukowycza," (Yanukovych's Polish Neighborhood) *Rzeczpospolita* (February 22, 2010), http://www.rp.pl/artykul/437991.html; Marcin Wojciechowski, "Janukowycz zmienia konstytucję Ukrainy, przedłuża sobie kadencję i podkreśla polskie korzenie," *Gazeta Wyborcza* (February 1, 2011) http://wyborcza.pl/1,75248,9037863,Janukowycz_zmienia_konstytucje_Ukrainy__przedluza.html.

24. See Marek Jan Chodakiewicz, "Co z Ukrainą," ("What about Ukraine?") *Tygodnik Solidarność* (October 22, 2010); Alexander J. Motyl, "Deleting the Holodomor: Ukraine Unmakes Itself," *World Affairs: A Journal of Ideas and Debate* (September–October 2010), http://www.worldaffairsjournal.org/articles/2010-SeptOct/full-Motyl-SO-2010.html; Taras Kuzio, "Viktor Yanukovych's First 100 Days: Back to the Past, But What's the Rush?" *Demokratizatsiya: The Journal of Post-Soviet Democratization* 18, no. 3 (Summer 2010): 208–18; Taras Kuzio, "Yanukovych Provides a Krysha for Organized Crime," *Eurasia Daily Monito* 9, no. 34 (February 17, 2012), posted at http://www.jamestown.org/single/?no_cache=1&tx_ttnews%5Btt_news%5D=39024&tx_ttnews%5BbackPid%5D=7&cHash=692be4a3bb7db2b91eae3373c738437e; James Marson, "Trials and Tribulations in Ukraine," *Business New Europe* (June 27, 2011), http://www.bne.eu/story2754/Trials_and_tribulations_in_Ukraine; Alex Brideau, "Did Ukraine Just End the Orange Revolution?" *Foreign Policy* (October 5, 2010), http://eurasia.foreignpolicy.com/posts/2010/10/05/did_ukraine_just_end_the_orange_revolution; "Tymoshenko found guilty," *Business New Europe* (October 11, 2011); "Kyiv – the New Minsk," *BNE: Business New Europe Monthly* (December 2011): 17–18, http://issuu.com/businessneweurope/docs/bne_December_2011_poverty_of_nation?mode=window&viewMode=singlePage. One of the most acerbic and vigilant Yanukovych watcher in the United States is Alexander J. Motyl who blogs ("Ukraine's Orange Blues") at http://www.worldaffairsjournal.org/new/blogs/bios/motyl/bio-motyl.html.

25. Lowell Barrington, "The Geographic Component of Mass Attitudes in Ukraine," *Post-Soviet Geography and Economics* 38, no. 10 (December 1997): 601–14.

26. For electoral results between 1994 and 2007 see Wolfram Nordsieck, "Parties and elections in Europe: Ukraine," http://www.parties-and-elections.

de/ukraine2.html and http://www.parties-and-elections.de/ukraine.html.
See also Sarah Birch, *Elections and Democratization in Ukraine* (New York:
St. Martin's Press, 2000); Evhen I. Golovakha and Nataliya V. Panina, "The
Development of a Democratic Political Identity in Contemporary Ukrainian
Political Culture," in *Nationalism, Ethnicity, and Identity: Cross National and
Comparative Perspectives*, ed. Russell F. Farnen (New Brunswick, NJ: Transac-
tion Publishers, 1994), 403–25; and James L. Gibson, "The Resilience of Mass
Support for Democratic Institutions and Processes in the Nascent Russian
and Ukrainian Democracies," in *Political Culture and Civil Society in Russia
and the New States of Eurasia*, ed. Vladmir Tismăneanu (Armonk, NY: M.E.
Sharpe, 1995), 53–111. For detailed treatment of each of Ukraine's elections
see Sarah Birch, "Electoral Systems, Campaign Strategies, and Vote Choice in
the Ukrainian Parliamentary and Presidential Elections," *Political Studies* 46,
no. 1 (March 1998): 96–114; Taras Kuzio, "The 1994 Parliamentary Elections
in Ukraine," *The Journal of Communist Studies and Transition Politics* 11, no.
4 (December 1995): 335–61; Marko Bojcun, "The Ukrainian Parliamentary
Elections in March–April 1994," *Europe-Asia Studies* 47, no. 2 (1995): 229–49;
Robert S. Kravchuk and Victor Chudowsky, "Ukraine's 1994 Elections as an
Economic Event," *Communist and Post-Communist Studies* 38, no. 2 (2005):
131–65; Peter R. Craumer and James I. Clem, "Ukraine's Emerging Electoral
Geography: A Regional Analysis of the 1998 Parliamentary Elections," *Post-
Soviet Geography and Economics* 40, no. 1 (1999): 1–26; Bohdan Harasymiw,
"Elections in Post-Communist Ukraine, 1994–2004: An Overview," *Canadian
Slavonic Papers: Revue canadienne des slavistes* 47, no. 3 (2005): 191–240;
Sarah Birch and Andrew Wilson, "Voting Stability, Political Gridlock: Ukraine's
1998 Parliamentary Elections," *Europe-Asia Studies* 51, no. 6 (1999): 1039–68;
Melvin J. Hinich, Valeri Khmelko, and Peter C. Ordeshook, "Ukraine's 1998
Parliamentary Elections: A Spatial Analysis," *Post-Soviet Affairs* 15, no. 2 (1999):
149–85; Melvin J. Hinich, Valeri Khmelko, and Peter C. Ordeshook, "Ukraine's
1999 Presidential Election: A Spatial Analysis," *Post-Soviet Affairs* 18, no. 3
(2002): 250–69; Thomas F. Klobucar, Arthur H. Miller, and Gwyn Erb, "The
1999 Ukrainian Presidential Election: Personalities, Ideology, Partisanship,
and the Economy," *Slavic Review* 61, no. 2 (2002): 315–44; Mikhail Myagkov
and Peter C. Ordeshook, "The Trail of Votes in Ukraine's 1998, 1999, and 2002
Elections," *Post-Soviet Affairs* 21, no. 1 (2005): 56–71; Oleksandr Sushko, "The
2002 Parliamentary Elections as an Indicator of the Sociopolitical Development
of Ukraine," *Demokratizatsiya* 10, no. 4 (Fall 2002): 568–76; Misha Myagkov,
Peter C. Ordeshook, and Dimitry Shakin, "The Disappearance of Fraud: The
Forensics of Ukraine's 2006 Parliamentary Elections," *Post-Soviet Affairs* 23, no.
3 (2007): 218–39; Melvin Hinich, Valerii Khmelko, and Peter C. Ordeshook,
"A Coalition Lost, Then Found: A Spatial Analysis of Ukraine's 2006 and 2007
Parliamentary Election," *Post-Soviet Affairs* 24, no. 1 (2008): 63–96; Timothy
J. Colton, "An Aligning Election and the Ukrainian Political Community," *East
European Politics and Societies* 25, no. 1 (Winter 2011): 4–28.

27. See Jerzy Targalski, "Ukraina: Panorama Polityczna, 2008/2009," TMs, Warsaw,
no date [2010], 1–22 (a copy in my collection); Paul D'Anieri, *Understanding
Ukrainian Politics: Power, Politics, and Institutional Design* (Armonk, NY: M.E.
Sharpe, 2007); Sarah Whitmore, *State-Building in Ukraine: The Ukrainian Par-
liament, 1990–2003* (London: Routledge Curzon, 2004); Charles R. Wise and
Trevor R. Brown, "Laying the Foundation for Institutionalization of Democratic
Parliaments in the Newly Independent States: The Case of Ukraine," *Journal of*

Legislative Studies 2, no .3 (Autumn 1996): 216–44; Artur Bilous and Andrew Wilson, "Political Parties in Ukraine," *Europe-Asia Studies* 45, no. 4 (1993): 693–703; Victor Chudowsky, "The Ukrainian Party System," in *State and Nation Building in East Central Europe: Contemporary Perspectives*, ed. John S. Micgiel (New York: Institute on East Central Europe, Columbia University, 1996), 305–21; Mykola Tomenko, "The Political System and Political Parties," in *The Political Analysis of Postcommunism: Understanding Postcommunist Ukraine*, ed. Volodymyr Polokhalo (College Station, TX: Texas A&M University Press, 1997), 131–42; Erik S. Herron, "Causes and Consequences of Fluid Faction Membership in Ukraine," *Europe-Asia Studies* 54, no. 4 (June 2002): 625–39; Vicki L. Hesli, William M. Reisinger, and Arthur H. Miller, "Political Party Developments in Divided Societies: The Case of Ukraine," *Electoral Studies* 17, no. 2 (June 1998): 235–56; Taras Kuzio, "The Multi-Party System in Ukraine on the Eve of Elections: Identity Problems, Conflicts and Solutions," *Government and Opposition* 29 (Winter 1994): 109–27.

28. Ilya Prizel, "Populism as a Political Force in Postcommunist Russia and Ukraine," *East European Politics and Society* 15, no. 1 (Spring 2001): 54–63.

29. See Andrew Wilson, "The Ukrainian Left: In Transition to Social Democracy or Still in Thrall to the USSR?" *Europe-Asia Studies* 49, no. 7 (November 1997): 1293–316; Andrew Wilson, "The Long March of the Ukrainian Left: Backwards towards Communism, Sideways to Social-Democracy or Forwards to Socialism?" *The Masaryk Journal* 3, no. 1 (January 2000): 122–40; Andrew Wilson, "Reinventing the Ukrainian Left: Assessing Adaptability and Change, 1991–2000," *The Slavonic and East European Review* 80, no. 1 (January 2002): 21–59.

30. See Zenovia A. Sochor, "From Liberalization to Post-Communism: The Role of the Communist Party in Ukraine," *Journal of Ukrainian Studies* 21, no. 1–2 (Summer–Winter 1996): 147–63; Joan Barth Urban, "The Communist Parties of Russia and Ukraine on the Eve of the 1999 Elections: Similarities, Contrasts, and Interactions," *Demokratizatsiya* 7, no. 1 (Winter 1999): 111–34; Barbara Ann Chotiner, "Organizational Strength Divorced from Power: Comparing the Communist Parties of the Russian Federation and Ukraine," in *The Communist Successor Parties of Central and Eastern Europe*, ed. András Bozóki and John T. Ishiyama (Armonk, NY: M.E. Sharpe, 2002), 397–419; Olexiy Haran, "Can Ukrainian Communists and Socialists Evolve to Social Democracy?" *Demokratizatsiya* 9, no. 4 (Fall 2001): 570–87; Sarah Oates, William L. Miller, and Ase Grodeland, "Towards a Soviet Past or a Socialist Future? Understanding Why Voters Choose Communist Parties in Ukraine, Russia, Bulgaria, Slovakia and the Czech Republic," in *Party Development and Democratic Change in Post-Communist Europe*, ed. Paul G. Lewis (London: Frank Cass, 2001), 16–31.

31. See Taras Kuzio, "Ukrainian Nationalism," *Journal of Area Studies* no. 4 (1994): 79–95; Paul Kubicek, "Dynamics of Contemporary Ukrainian Nationalism: Empire–Breaking to State Building," *Canadian Review of Studies in Nationalism* 23, no. 1–2 (1996): 39–50; Paul Kubicek, "What Happened to the Nationalists in Ukraine?" *Nationalism and Ethnic Politics* 5, no.1 (Spring 1999): 29–45; V'iacheslav Shved, "The Conceptual Approaches of Ukrainian Political Parties to Ethno-Political Problems in Independent Ukraine," *Journal of Ukrainian Studies* 19, no. 2 (Winter 1994): 69–83.

32. Nicklaus Laverty, "The Problem of Lasting Change: Civil Society and the Colored Revolutions in Georgia and Ukraine," *Demokratizatsiya: The Journal of Post-Soviet Democratization* 16, no. 2 (Spring 2008): 143–62. But see also Viktoriya

Topalova, "In Search of Heroes: Cultural Politics and Political Mobilization of Youths in Contemporary Russia and Ukraine," *Demokratizatsiya: The Journal of Post-Soviet Democratization* 14, no. 1 (Winter 2006): 23–41.

33. See Oksana Khomchuk, "The Far Right in Russia and Ukraine," *Harriman Review* 8, no. 2 (July 1995): 40–44; Taras Kuzio, "Radical Nationalist Parties and Movements in Contemporary Ukraine before and after Independence: The Right and Its Politics, 1989–1994," *Nationalities Papers* 25, no. 2 (June 1997): 211–42; Taras Kuzio, "Radical Right Parties and Civic Groups in Belarus and the Ukraine," in *The Revival of Right-Wing Extremism in the Nineties*, ed. Peter H. Merkl and Leonard Weinberg (London: Frank Cass, 1997), 203–30; Roman Solchanyk, "The Radical Right in Ukraine," in *The Radical Right in Central and Eastern Europe since 1989*, ed. Sabrina P. Ramet (University Park, PA: The Pennsylvania State University Press, 1999), 279–95; Per Anders Rudling, "Organized Anti-Semitism in Contemporary Ukraine: Structure, Influence, and Ideology," *Canadian Slavonic Papers/Revue canadienne des slavistes* XLVIII, no. 1–2 (March–June 2006): 81–119.

34. Among other things, Lytvyn was implicated in the Gongadze affair.

35. Sarah Birch, "Nomenklatura Democratization: Electoral Clientelism in Post-Soviet Ukraine," *Democratization* 4, no.4 (Winter 1997): 40–62.

36. See Yevhen Holovakha, "The Social Pathology of the Postcommunist Society," in *The Political Analysis of Postcommunism: Understanding Postcommunist Ukraine*, ed. Volodymyr Polokhalo (College Station, TX: Texas A&M University Press, 1997), 227–40; Kerstin Zimmer, "The Comparative Failure of Machine Politics, Administrative Resources and Fraud," *Canadian Slavonic Papers* 47, no. 3/4 (September–December 2005): 361–84; Jessica Allina-Pisanno, "Social Contracts and Authoritarian Projects in Post-Soviet Space: The Use of Administrative Resource," *Communist and Post-Communist Studies* 43, no. 4 (December 2010): 373–82; Alexei Trochev, "Meddling with Justice: Competitive Politics, Impunity, and Distrusted Courts in Post-Orange Ukraine," *Demokratizatsiya: The Journal of Post-Soviet Democratization* 18, no. 2 (Spring 2010): 122–47; "AIDS in Ukraine: Still No Cure for Corruption," *Economist* (December 1, 2011), http://www.economist.com/blogs/easternapproaches/2011/12/aids-ukraine; Judy Hague, Rose Aidan, and Marko Bojcun, "Rebuilding Ukraine's Hollow State: Developing a Democratic Public Service in Ukraine," *Public Administration and Development* 15, no. 4 (October 1995): 417–33.

37. See Oleksandr Boukhalov and Serguei Ivannikov, "Ukraine," in *Democratic and Local Governance*, ed. Betty M. Jacob, Krzysztof Ostrowski, and H. Jeune (Honolulu, HI: Matsunaga Institute of Peace, 1993), 225–42; Oleksandr Boukhalov and Serguei Ivannikov, "Ukrainian Local Politics after Independence," *Annals of the American Academy of Political and Social Science* no. 540 (July 1995): 126–36; Adrian Campbell, "Regional and Local Government in Ukraine," in *Local Government in Eastern Europe: Establishing Democracy at the Grassroots*, ed. Andrew Coulson (Aldershot: Elgar, 1995), 115–27; Timo Aarrevaard, "Ukrainian Cities: Weak Soviets and Strong Mayors," *The Journal of Post Communist Studies and Transition Politics* 10, no. 4 (December 1994): 55–70; Theodore H. Friedgut, "Popular Efforts toward Self-Government: Political, Social and Economic Initiatives in Donetsk," in *Trials of Transition: Economic Reform in the Former Communist Bloc*, ed. Michael Keren and Gur Ofer (Boulder, CO: Westview Press, 1992), 39–50; Theodore H. Friedgut, "Pluralism and Politics in an Urban Soviet: Donetsk, 1990–1991," in *Search of Pluralism: Soviet and Post-Soviet Politics*, ed. Carl R. Saivetz and Anthony Jones (Boulder, CO: Westview,

1994), 45–61; Theodore Friedgut, "Perestroika in the Provinces: The Politics of Transition in Donets'k," in *Local Power and Post-Soviet Policies*, ed. Theodore H. Friedgut and Jeffrey W. Hahn (Armonk, NY: M.E. Sharpe, 1994), 162–83; Vitaly Timofeev and Rex A. Wade, "Kharkiv in the Post-Perestroika Days: Some Political Tendencies," *Soviet and Post-Soviet Review* 21, no. 1 (1994): 85–98; Ararat L. Osipian and Alexandr L. Osipian, "Why Donbass Votes for Yanukovych: Confronting the Ukrainian Orange Revolution," *Demokratizatsiya: The Journal of Post-Soviet Democratization* 14, no. 4 (Fall 2006): 495–517; Olena Yatsunska, "Comparative Analysis of the 1994, 1998, and 2002 Election Campaigns for the Nikolayev City Council," *Demokratizatsiya* 11, no. 3 (Summer 2003): 440–48; Olena Yatsunska, "Local Elections in Independent Ukraine: The Case Study of Nikolayev," *Nationalities Papers* 32, no. 3 (2004): 551–63; Kimitaka Matsuzato, "Elites and the Party System of Zakarpattya Oblast': Relations among Levels of Party Systems in Ukraine," *Europe-Asia Studies* 54, no. 8 (December 2002): 1267–99; Roman Szporluk, "The Strange Politics of Lviv: An Essay in Search of an Explanation," in *The Politics of Nationality and the Erosion of the USSR*, ed. Zvi Gitelman (London: Macmillan, 1992), 215–31; Marian Rubchak, "Ethnonationalist Construction of Identity: The Lviv Paradigm," *National Identities* 2, no. 1 (March 2000): 21–34; Martin Aberg, "Putnam's Social Capital Theory Goes East: A Case Study of Western Ukraine and L'viv," *Europe-Asia Studies* 52, no. 2 (March 2000): 295–317.

38. See Arthur H. Miller, Vicki L. Hesli, and William M. Reisinger, "Comparing Citizen and Elite Belief Systems in Post-Soviet Russia and Ukraine," *Public Opinion Quarterly* 59, no. 1 (Spring 1995): 1–40; Victor Stepanenko, "Civil Society in Post-Soviet Ukraine: Civic Ethos in the Framework of Corrupted Sociality?" *East European Politics and Societies* 20, no. 4 (Fall 2006): 571–98; Nikolay Churilov and Tatyana Koshechkina, "Public Attitudes in Ukraine," *Perceptions of Security: Public Opinion and Expert Assessments in Europe's New Democracies*, ed. Richard Smoke (New York: Manchester University Press, 1996), 189–208; Jan Pakulski, "Poland and Ukraine: Elite Transformation and Prospects for Democracy," *Journal of Ukrainian Studies* 20, no. 1–2 (Summer–Winter 1995): 195–208; Hans van Zon, Andre Batako, and Anna Kreslavska, *Social and Economic Change in Eastern Ukraine: The Example of Zaporizhia* (Aldershot: Ashgate, 1998); Nicklaus Laverty, "The Problem of Lasting Change: Civil Society and the Colored Revolutions in Georgia and Ukraine," *Demokratizatsiya: The Journal of Post-Soviet Democratization* 16, no. 2 (Spring 2008): 143–62; Martin Aberg and Mikael Sandberg, *Social Capital and Democratisation: Roots of Trust in Post-Communist Poland and Ukraine* (Burlington, VT: Ashgate, 2003).

39. For a brief introduction see Andrew Wilson, *Belarus: The Last European Dictatorship* (New Haven, CT and London: Yale University Press, 2011), 140–260; Alexander Danilovich, "Understanding Politics in Belarus," ed. Ole Nørgaard and Lars Johannsen, Demstar Research Report, University of Aarhus, Department of Political Science (June 2001): 1–42, http://www.demstar.dk/papers/Belarus.pdf; Central Intelligence Agency, "Belarus," *The World Factbook*, https://www.cia.gov/library/publications/the-world-factbook/geos/bo.html; US State Department's Bureau of European and Eurasian Affairs, "Background Note: Belarus," (October 7, 2010), http://www.state.gov/p/eur/ci/bo/; "Belarus," European Forum For Democracy and Solidarity, Socialist International, http://www.europeanforum.net/country/belarus. For current news from Belarus see the website of Foreign Policy and Security Center at http://forsecurity.org/.

It dubs itself as a Minsk-based NGO staffed by top Belarusian scholars from state universities. It is however hard to imagine that the FPSC can exist in a dictatorship without some form of official consent and funding.

40. See Taras Kuzio, "Belarus: Consolidated Authority," Foreign Policy Association, 20 June 2003, http://www.fpa.org/newsletter_info2497/newsletter_info_sub_list.htm?section=Belarus. For the continuity among the Minsk elite, see, e.g., data on the military top brass of Belarus: Steven J. Main, "The Belarusian Armed Forces: A Military-Political Analysis, 1991–2003," Conflict Studies Research Centre (October 2003): Appendix 1: Leading Personnel in the Belarusian Armed Forces, 80–105, http://www.da.mod.uk/colleges/arag/document-listings/cee/g126. See also Taras Kuzio, "Nationalism and Reform in Belarus and Ukraine," RFE/RL Poland, Belarus, and Ukraine Report, 4, no. 20 (May 21, 2002), http://www.taraskuzio.net/media13_files/3.pdf; Alexander Pershai, "Minor Nation: The Alternative Modes of Belarusian Nationalism," *East European Politics and Societies* 24, no. 3 (Summer 2010): 379–408; Grigory Ioffe, "Culture Wars, Soul-Searching, and Belarusian Identity," *East European Politics and Societies* 21, no. 2 (Spring 2007): 348–82; Grigory Ioffe, "Understanding Belarus: Belarusian Identity," *Europe-Asia Studies* 55, no. 8 (2003): 1241–71; Geraldine Fagan, "Belarus: New concordat gives Orthodox enhanced status," Forum 18 News Service, (June 24 2003), http://www.forum18.org/Archive.php?article_id=89; "Belarus, Orthodox Church sign deal boosting Church's standing," Associated Press, (June 13, 2003), http://www.orthodoxnews.netfirms.com/22/Belarus, %20Orthodox%20Church.htm; Elizabeth Kendal, "Belarus: Rescucitating the Soviet Machine," Assistnews.net, (September 4, 2003), http://www.assistnews.net/Stories/2003/s03090024.htm. Oleksandr Lukashenka famously remarked "I'm an atheist, but an Orthodox [Christian] atheist." See "Białoruska Cerkiew przyznała order Łukaszence," ("The Orthodox Church of Belarus Bestowed a Medal on Lukashenka") *Gazeta Wyborcza* (September 26, 2006), http://wiadomosci.gazeta.pl/Wiadomosci/1,80277,3645202.html.

41. For Lukashenka's tenure see Andrew Wilson, *Belarus: The Last European Dictatorship* (New Haven, CT and London: Yale University Press, 2011), 168–260. On the top cadres of the current regime in Belarus and their connections to the Soviet past see Jerzy Targalski, "Ludzie Aleksandra Łukaszenki," ("Oleksandr Lukashenka's Men") TMs, Warsaw, no date [2009], a copy in my collection. See further Grigory Ioffe, *Understanding Belarus and How Western Foreign Policy Misses the Mark* (Lanham, MD: Rowman & Littlefield Publishers, Inc., 2008); David Riach, "Post-Soviet Belarus," in *New Europe: The Impact of the First Decade*, vol. 2: *Variations on the Pattern*, ed. Teresa Rakowska-Harmstone, Piotr Dutkiewicz, and Agnieszka Orzelska (Warsaw: Institute of Political Studies Polish Academy of Sciences and Collegium Civitas Press, 2006), 2: 101–53; Katja Yafimava, *Post-Soviet Russian-Belarussian Relationships: The Role of Gas Transit Pipelines* (Stuttgart and Hannover: Ibidem-Verlag, 2006); Coit Blacker and Condoleezza Rice, "Belarus and the Flight from Sovereignty," in *Problematic Sovereignty: Contested Rules and Political Possibilities*, ed. Stephen D. Krasner (New York: Columbia University Press, 2001), 224–50; Kathleen Mihalisko, "Political-Economic Assessment: Belarus," in United States Congress, Joint Economic Committee, in *The Former Soviet Union in Transition*, ed. Richard F. Kaufman and John Pearce Hardt (Armonk, NY, and London: M.E. Sharpe, 1993): 1003–18; Vincuk Viacorka, "Away From Europe?" *Uncaptive Minds* 9, no. 1–2 (Winter–Spring 1997); Rett Ludwikowski, *Constitution Making in the Region of Former Soviet Dominance* (Durham, NC: Duke University Press, 1996), 95–102

and Belarus's constitution reproduced at 332–50; Verena Fritz, *State-Building: A Comparative Study Ukraine, Lithuania, Belarus, and Russia* (Budapest: Central European University Press, 2007), Chapter 9, "Averting Institutional Change: The Case of Belarus," 211–42; Rawi Abdelal, *National Purpose in the World Economy: Post-Soviet States in Comparative Perspective* (Ithaca, NY: Cornell University Press, 2001), Chapter 6, "Belarus: Toward Russia and the East," 127–49; Kathleen J. Mihalisko, "Belarus: Retreat to Authoritarianism," in *Democratic Changes and Authoritarian Reactions in Russia, Ukraine, Belarus, and Moldova*, ed. Karen Dawisha and Bruce Parrott (Cambridge: Cambridge University Press, 1997), 223–81. For post-Soviet mythology see Andrew Wilson, *Belarus: The Last European Dictatorship* (New Haven, CT and London: Yale University Press, 2011), 114–17.

42. Grigory Ioffe, "Understanding Belarus: Belarusian Identity," *Europe-Asia Studies* 55, no. 8 (2003): 1241–71; Iryna Maryniak, "Belarus and Ukraine: Nation Building in Babel," *Index on Censorship* 22, no. 2 (March 1993): 20–33.

43. For its website see http://www.sovrep.gov.by/index_eng.php/home.html.

44. According to Lukashenka, both Shushkevich and Pozniak are Poles. See Oleksandr Lukashenka interviewed in "Łukaszenka: Nie dzielcie moich Polaków," ("Do Not Divide My Poles") *Rzeczpospolita* (November 16, 2010), http://www.rp.pl/artykul/559964.html.

45. Lukashenka claims that Kebich (Kiebicz) is of Polish-Jewish origin. See Oleksandr Lukashenka interviewed in "Łukaszenka: Nie dzielcie moich Polaków," ("Do Not Divide My Poles") *Rzeczpospolita* (November 16, 2010), http://www.rp.pl/artykul/559964.html.

46. For electoral results between 1994 and 2004 see Wolfram Nordsieck, "Parties and Elections in Europe: Belarus," http://www.parties-and-elections.de/belarus2.html and http://www.parties-and-elections.de/belarus.html.

47. See Steven M. Eke and Taras Kuzio, "Sultanism in Eastern Europe: The Socio-Political Roots of Authoritarian Populism in Belarus," *Europe-Asia Studies* 52, no. 3 (May, 2000): 523–47; Grigory Ioffe, *Understanding Belarus and How Western Foreign Policy Misses the Mark* (Lanham, MD: Rowman & Littlefield Publishers, Inc., 2008); David Riach, "Post-Soviet Belarus," in *New Europe: The Impact of the First Decade*, vol. 2: *Variations on the Pattern*, ed. Teresa Rakowska-Harmstone, Piotr Dutkiewicz, and Agnieszka Orzelska (Warsaw: Institute of Political Studies Polish Academy of Sciences and Collegium Civitas Press, 2006), 2: 101–53; Katja Yafimava, *Post-Soviet Russian-Belarussian Relationships: The Role of Gas Transit Pipelines* (Stuttgart and Hannover: Ibidem-Verlag, 2006); Coit Blacker and Condoleezza Rice, "Belarus and the Flight from Sovereignty," in *Problematic Sovereignty: Contested Rules and Political Possibilities*, ed. Stephen D. Krasner (New York: Columbia University Press, 2001), 224–50; Kathleen Mihalisko, "Political-Economic Assessment: Belarus," in United States Congress, Joint Economic Committee, *The Former Soviet Union in Transition*, ed. Richard F. Kaufman and John Pearce Hardt (Armonk, NY and London: M.E. Sharpe, 1993): 1003–18; Ronald Koven, "Waiting It Out," *Uncaptive Minds* 6, no. 2 (Summer 1993); Iryna Maryniak, "Belarus and Ukraine: Nation Building in Babel," *Index on Censorship* 22, no. 2 (March 1993): 20–33; Vincuk Viacorka, "Away from Europe?" *Uncaptive Minds* 9, no. 1–2 (Winter–Spring 1997); Verena Fritz, *State-Building: A Comparative Study Ukraine, Lithuania, Belarus, and Russia* (Budapest: Central European University Press, 2007), Chapter 9, "Averting Institutional Change: The Case of Belarus," 211–42; Rawi Abdelal, *National Purpose in the World Economy: Post-Soviet States in Comparative*

Perspective (Ithaca, NY: Cornell University Press, 2001), Chapter 6, "Belarus: Toward Russia and the East," 127–49; Kathleen J. Mihalisko, "Belarus: Retreat to Authoritarianism," in *Democratic Changes and Authoritarian Reactions in Russia, Ukraine, Belarus, and Moldova*, ed. Karen Dawisha and Bruce Parrott (Cambridge: Cambridge University Press, 1997), 223–81.

48. Born in 1954 to a single mother, Ekaterina Tromifovna, who briefly worked at a weaving plant in Orsha, Lukashenka grew up in a kolhoz outside of Mohylev. He studied pedagogy and history in Mohylev, and agriculture in Gorki. Occasionally, the dictator invokes his alleged noble (Polish?) pedigree. The most extensive biography of the dictator so far has been penned by his erstwhile ally. See Александр Иосифович Федута, *Лукашенко: Политическая биография*, (no date [ca. 2004]): 1–365, http://lib.rus.ec/b/296144/read. See also Oleksandr Lukashenka interviewed in "Łukaszenka: Nie dzielcie moich Polaków," ("Do Not Divide My Poles") *Rzeczpospolita* (November 16, 2010), http://www.rp.pl/artykul/559964.html; Zdzisław J. Winnicki, *Szkice kojdanowskie: Kojdanowsko-Polski Region Narodowościowy w BSRR: Uwagi o genezie oraz o przesłankach funkcjonowania: Stan badań problematyki (The Koydani Sketches: Kozdani-Polish Nationality Region in the BSSR: Some Remarks on the Origin and Reasons for Functioning: Researching the Problem)* (Wrocław: Wydawnictwo GAJT, 2005), 7, 43, 69.

49. Андрэй Казакевіч, "Палітычная картаграфія Беларусі ў выніках прэзідэнцкіх выбараў, 1994–2006 гадоў," *ПаліТычная сфера*, no. 7 (2007): 5–18, http://palityka.org/pdf/07/0703.pdf; Jerzy Targalski, "Ludzie Aleksandra Łukaszenki," ("Oleksandr Lukashenka's Men") TMs, no date (2009), a copy in my collection.

50. See David Marples, "Belarus Resists Integration with Russia as Pressure Grows," *Eurasia Daily Monitor* 8, no. 61 (March 29, 2011): http://www.jamestown. org/programs/edm/single/?tx_ttnews%5Btt_news%5D=37712&tx_ttnews %5BbackPid%5D=27&cHash=ec7e4895064ef9b42aefd1ae98f369db; David Marples, "Can Lukashenka Survive?" *Eurasia Daily Monitor* 8, no. 134 (July 13, 2011): http://www.jamestown.org/single/?no_cache=1&tx_ttnews%5Btt_ news%5D=38166&tx_ttnews%5BbackPid%5D=512.

51. Jaroslav Romanchuk [Jarosław Romańczuk], "The Changed Mind Is Changing the Country," in *Freedom Champions: Stories from the Front Lines in the War of Ideas: 30 Case Studies by Intellectual Entrepreneurs Who Champion the Cause of Freedom*, ed. Colleen Dyble and Jean Baugh (Washington, DC: Atlas Economic Research Foundation, 2011), 203–10, quote at 208.

52. See Andrew Wilson, *Belarus: The Last European Dictatorship* (New Haven, CT and London: Yale University Press, 2011), 168–254, 261; David Marples, "Can Lukashenka Survive?" *Eurasia Daily Monitor* 8, no. 134 (July 13, 2011): http://www.jamestown.org/single/?no_cache=1&tx_ttnews%5Btt_ news%5D=38166&tx_ttnews%5BbackPid%5D=512; "Belarus Slides towards the Economic Abyss," *Business New Europe* (August 30, 2011): http://www. bne.eu/storyf2871/Belarus_slides_towards_the_economic_abyss.

53. See Marek Jan Chodakiewicz, "Notatki z post-Sowiecji (część IV)," ("Notes from the Post-Soviet Lands, Part IV") *Najwyższy Czas!*, (October 30–November 6, 2010): XLIII; Rawi Abdelal, *National Purpose in the World Economy: Post-Soviet States in Comparative Perspective* (Ithaca, NY: Cornell University Press, 2001), Chapter 6, "Belarus: Toward Russia and the East," 127–49; Taras Kuzio, "Clawless Tiger, Lurking Dangers," *Transitions-On-Line* (July 17, 2003): http:// www.taraskuzio.net/media8_files/23.pdf; Susanna Eskola, "Signs of Change

in Belarus: Has the Countdown for Lukashenka Begun?" Defense Academy of the United Kingdom, Research & Assessment Branch, Central and Eastern European Series, 9/07 (August 2009): 1–10, http://www.da.mod.uk/colleges/arag/document-listings/cee/09%2807%29%20SE%20mod%20style.pdf; Tom Balmforth, "Belarus on The Brink," RFE/RL, (August 23, 2011), http://www.rferl.org/content/belarus_on_the_brink/24305822.html. See also two essays in Daniel Hamilton and Gerhard Mangott, eds., *The New Eastern Europe: Ukraine, Belarus, Moldova* (Washington, DC: Center for Transatlantic Relations, 2007): Vasily Astrov and Peter Havlik, "Belarus, Ukraine and Moldova: Economic Developments and Integration Prospects," 127–48, and Roland Götz, "Ukraine and Belarus: Their Energy Dependence on Russia and Their Roles as Transit Countries," 149–67, http://transatlantic.sais-jhu.edu/bin/o/y/new_eastern_europe_text.pdf.

54. On April 8, 1999, former chairwoman of Belarus's central bank Tamara Vinnikova was the first to disappear. She was followed by Yuri Zakharenko, who vanished on May 8. Both of them were supporters of former prime minister Mikhail Chigir who wanted to challenge Lukashenka in the upcoming presidential elections. On September 16, 1999, Viktor Gonchar and his publisher Anatoly Krasovski were snatched. In 2001, the BBC reported that a "death squad" operated out of Minsk and, as a result, "up to 30 opposition figures" disappeared. Recently, a prominent security police defector Oleg Alkaev's account, which confirmed Lukashenka's involvement, has been translated into the English. See Oleg Alkaev, *Shooters Team* (Warsaw: Foundation Open Belarus, 2010), and a short synopsis posted at http://www.openbelarus.pl/shooters_gb.html. See also Michael Wines, "Belarus Sees Its Dissidents Disappearing," *The New York Times* (October 4, 1999), http://www.nytimes.com/1999/10/04/world/belarus-sees-its-dissidents-disappearing.html?ref=belarus; Steven Eke, "Belarus Death Squad Reports 'Credible,'" *BBC News* (July 18, 2001), http://news.bbc.co.uk/2/hi/europe/1445607.stm; "Evidence," Khartia'97/Charter'97, (July 18, 2001), http://charter97.org/eng/news/2001/07/18/07; "Yuri Zakharenko," http://www.webmii.es/Result.aspx/Yuri/Zakharenko.

55. On the riots of December 2010 see Jay Nordlinger, "Belarus, Assaulted: The State of Affairs in Europe's Last Dictatorship," *National Review* (February 7, 2011), 24–27; Marek A. Koprowski, "Prowokacja opozycji," (A Provocation by the Opposition) *Najwyższy Czas!*, (January 1–8, 2011): XXXI–XXXII.

56. The opposition has been largely nonviolent. The only exception is a bizarre case of two twenty-five-year-old friends and factory workers of Vitebsk. Vladislav Konovaliou (Konovaliov) and Dmitri Konovalou (Konovalov) are allegedly the culprits behind four terrorist bombings: two in Vitebsk (in 2005) and two in Minsk (2008 and 2011). During the last one 15 people were killed and 300 wounded. The duo was sentenced to death and executed. According to some in the opposition, the dictatorship cooked up the case, perhaps even orchestrated the bombings by the KGB. Others defend the sentenced men out of Christian and humanitarian reasons, including the Catholic Church and Amnesty International. See Nils Naumann, "Minsk Metro Bombers Receive the Death Sentence," *Deutsche Welle* (November 30, 2011): http://www.dw-world.de/dw/article/0,,15569106,00.html. See also Jerome Taylor, "In Europe's Last Dictatorship, All Opposition Is Mercilessly Crushed," *The Independent* (March 8, 2011): http://www.independent.co.uk/news/world/europe/in-europes-last-dictatorship-all-opposition-is-mercilessly-crushed-2235153.html; William Schreiber, "Lukashenko's Least-Favorite Writer: Journalist Andrzej Poczobut

Describes His Life on the Belarusian Dictator's Blacklist," *The Wall Street Journal* (August 30, 2011); David Marples, "Can Lukashenka Survive?" *Eurasia Daily Monitor* 8, no. 134 (13 July 2011): http://www.jamestown.org/single/?no_cache=1&tx_ttnews%5Btt_news%5D=38166&tx_ttnews%5BbackPid%5D=512; James Kirchick, "Belarus, the Land of No Applause," *World Affairs: A Journal of Ideas and Debate* (November 14, 2011): http://www.worldaffairsjournal. org/article/belarus-land-no-applause?utm_source=World+Affairs+Newsle tter&utm_campaign=8746b6887d-Blog_Bachrach_Kirchick_Motyl_11_14_ 2011&utm_medium=email; "How to Dupe the KGB," *Economist* (November 14, 2011): http://www.economist.com/blogs/easternapproaches/2011/11/be-larusian-dissidents.

57.   Grigory Ioffe, *Understanding Belarus and How Western Foreign Policy Misses the Mark* (Lanham, MD: Rowman & Littlefield Publishers, Inc., 2008); David Riach, "Post-Soviet Belarus," in *New Europe: The Impact of the First Decade*, vol. 2: *Variations on the Pattern*, ed. Teresa Rakowska-Harmstone, Piotr Dut-kiewicz, and Agnieszka Orzelska (Warsaw: Institute of Political Studies Polish Academy of Sciences and Collegium Civitas Press, 2006), 2: 101–53; Katja Yafimava, *Post-Soviet Russian-Belarussian Relationships: The Role of Gas Tran-sit Pipelines* (Stuttgart and Hannover: Ibidem-Verlag, 2006); Coit Blacker and Condoleezza Rice, "Belarus and the Flight from Sovereignty," in *Problematic Sovereignty: Contested Rules and Political Possibilities*, ed. Stephen D. Krasner (New York: Columbia University Press, 2001), 224–50; Kathleen Mihalisko, "Political-Economic Assessment: Belarus," in United States Congress, Joint Economic Committee, *The Former Soviet Union in Transition*, ed. Richard F. Kaufman and John Pearce Hardt (Armonk, NY and London: M.E. Sharpe, 1993): 1003–18; Vincuk Viacorka, "Away from Europe?" *Uncaptive Minds* 9, no. 1–2 (Winter–Spring 1997); Verena Fritz, *State-Building: A Comparative Study Ukraine, Lithuania, Belarus, and Russia* (Budapest: Central European University Press, 2007), Chapter 9, "Averting Institutional Change: The Case of Belarus," 211–42; Rawi Abdelal, *National Purpose in the World Economy: Post-Soviet States in Comparative Perspective* (Ithaca, NY: Cornell University Press, 2001), Chapter 6, "Belarus: Toward Russia and the East," 127–49; Kathleen J. Mihalisko, "Belarus: Retreat to Authoritarianism," in *Democratic Changes and Authoritarian Reactions in Russia, Ukraine, Belarus, and Moldova*, ed. Karen Dawisha and Bruce Parrott (Cambridge: Cambridge University Press, 1997), 223–81.

58.   Will Englund, "Letter from Warsaw: Silenced at Home, Belarusan Bands Cross Borders," *The Washington Post* (February 3, 2011).

59.   The LDP is led by Serhiy Haidukevich (Sergei Gaidukevich). For the party web-site see http://www.ldpb.net/. See Taras Kuzio, "Radical Right Parties and Civic Groups in Belarus and the Ukraine," in *The Revival of Right-wing Extremism in the Nineties*, ed. Peter H. Merkl and Leonard Weinberg (London: Frank Cass, 1997), 203–30.

60.   The party is led by Tatyana Holubeva. For the KPB's official website see http:// www.comparty.by/. The PKB was seen as "oppositionist" and "pro-Western" by some pundits, who were apparently confused by the tactical deception and the ongoing political flux of the early 1990s and later. Admittedly, the PKB was more radical rhetorically but differed little ideologically from the KPB. The split was one of tactics: whether or not to adulate the President of Belarus. The PKB's leader Syarhei Kalyakin has claimed that the unification of his group with the KPB was executed by Lukashenka's KGB. The remnant of the KPB

renamed itself the Belarusian Party of the Leftists "Just World" and remains in the opposition. See "Kalyakin: Merger of Communist Parties Is Belarusian Secret Services' Invention," Khartia'97/Charter'97, (June 8, 2006), http://www. charter97.org/eng/news/2006/06/08/kalyakin.

61. That is not to say that every single deputy is a mindless slave as reflected in the elections of a token staunch libertarian in 2008. See Jaroslav Romanchuk [Jarosław Romańczuk], "The Changed Mind Is Changing the Country," in *Freedom Champions: Stories from the Front Lines in the War of Ideas: 30 Case Studies by Intellectual Entrepreneurs Who Champion the Cause of Freedom*, ed. Colleen Dyble and Jean Baugh (Washington, DC: Atlas Economic Research Foundation, 2011), 209. See also Elena A. Korasteleva, "Perspectives on Democratic Party Development in Belarus," *Party Development and Democratic Change in Post-Communist Europe: The First Decade*, ed. Paul G. Lewis (London and Portland, OR: Frank Cass Publishers, 2001), 141–51.

62. For electoral results between 1994 and 2004 see Wolfram Nordsieck, "Parties and Elections in Europe: Belarus," http://www.parties-and-elections.de/belarus2.html and http://www.parties-and-elections.de/belarus.html. For an interesting discussion of voting patterns in Belarus according to ethnicity, culture, and religion see the internet debate, particularly wojtek k., entry of September 24, 2010, in "Wschodniopolska Republika Radziecka," http://www. historycy.org/bez_grafik/index.php/t69261-50.html. See further Helena Głogowska, "Wybory prezydenckie w Białorusi w okresie przemian systemu politycznego," ("Presidential Elections in Belarus during the Transformation of the Political System") *Teoria i praktyka polityki (Materiały i Studia)* no. 1 (1995), http://old.bialorus.pl/index.php?pokaz=wybory_1994&&Rozdzial=wybory_ 2001; Андрэй Казакевіч, "Палітычная картаграфія Беларусі ў выніках прэзідэнцкіх выбараў, 1994—2006 гадоў," *Палітычная сфера* 7 (2007): 5–18, http://palityka.org/pdf/07/0703.pdf.

63. On the elections and riots of December 10, 2010, see Jay Nordlinger, "Belarus, Assaulted: The State of Affairs in Europe's Last Dictatorship," *National Review* (February 7, 2011): 24–27; "Lukashenko's Gulag," *The New York Times* (January 10, 2010): http://www.nytimes.com/2011/01/11/opinion/11tue3. html?_r=1&ref=belarus; Christos Pourgourides, "The Situation in Belarus in the Aftermath of the Presidential Election," Parliamentary Assembly, Committee on Legal Affairs and Human Rights, Doc. 12503, (January 26, 2011), http://assembly.coe.int/Documents/WorkingDocs/Doc11/EDOC12503.pdf; Marek A. Koprowski, "Prowokacja opozycji," ("A Provocation by the Opposition") *Najwyższy Czas!* (January 1–8, 2011): XXXI–XXXII.

64. For the party website see http://narodny.org/; and, in English, http://pages. prodigy.net/dr_fission/bpf/.

65. For the party website see http://www.ucpb.org/.

66. For the party website see http://belgreens.org/.

67. Taras Kuzio, "Radical Right Parties and Civic Groups in Belarus and the Ukraine," *The Revival of Right-Wing Extremism in the Nineties*, ed. Peter H. Merkl and Leonard Weinberg (London: Frank Cass, 1997), 203–30.

68. See Taras Kuzio, "Clawless Tiger, Lurking Dangers," *Transitions-On-Line* (July 17, 2003): http://www.taraskuzio.net/media8_files/23.pdf; Susanna Eskola, "Signs of Change in Belarus: Has the Countdown for Lukashenka Begun?" Defense Academy of the United Kingdom, Research & Assessment Branch, Central and Eastern European Series, 9/07 (August 2009): 1–10, http://www.da.mod. uk/colleges/arag/document-listings/cee/09%2807%29%20SE%20mod%style.

pdf; David Marples, "Can Lukashenka Survive?" *Eurasia Daily Monitor* 8, no. 134 (July 13, 2011): http://www.jamestown.org/single/?no_cache=1&tx_ttnews%5Btt_news%5D=38166&tx_ttnews%5BbackPid%5D=512; Tom Balmforth, "Belarus on The Brink," *RFE/RL* (August 23, 2011), http://www.rferl.org/content/belarus_on_the_brink/24305822.html.

69. For a brief introduction to Moldova see Lars Johannsen, Hanne Jensen, and Jørgen Møller, "State of the State in Moldova," Demstar Research Report no. 24, University of Aarhus, Department of Political Science (November 2004): 1–49, http://www.demstar.dk/papers/SotSMoldova.pdf; Central Intelligence Agency, "Moldova," *The World Factbook*, https://www.cia.gov/library/publications/the-world-factbook/geos/md.html; US State Department's Bureau of European and Eurasian Affairs, "Background Note: Moldova," (October 7, 2010): http://www.state.gov/r/pa/ei/bgn/5357.htm; "Moldova," European Forum For Democracy and Solidarity, Socialist International, http://www.europeanforum.net/country/moldova. For the official site of the President of the Republic of Moldova see http://www.president.md/index.php?lang=eng. See also William E. Crowther, *Moldova: A Country Study*, ed. Helen Fedor (Washington: GPO for the Library of Congress, 1995), http://countrystudies.us/moldova/; "Moldova," in *Eastern Europe, Russia, and Central Asia 2003*, ed. Imogen Bell, 3rd edn. (London: Europa Publications, 2002), 262–87; Yuri Josanu, "Moldova," in *Handbook of Political Change in Eastern Europe*, ed. Sten Bergland, Frank Aarebrot, and Joakim Ekman, 2nd edn. (London: Edward Elgar Publishers, 2003), 549–92; and Steven D. Roper, "Moldova since 1989," in *Central and Southeast European Politics since 1989*, ed. Sabrina Ramet (Cambridge and New York: Cambridge University Press, 2010), 473–91.

70. See Lucan A. Way, "The Weak States and Pluralism: The Case of Moldova," *East European Politics and Societies* 17, no. 3 (Summer 2003): 454–82. See further Thomas Hegarty, *Moldova* (New York: Routledge, 2003); Charles King, *The Moldovans: Romania, Russia, and the Politics of Culture* (Stanford, CA: The Hoover Institution Press, 2000); Donald Leroy Dyer, *The Romanian Dialect of Moldova: A Study in Language and Politics* (Lewiston, NY: Edwin Mellen Press, 1999); Donald Leroy Dyer, ed., *Studies in Moldovan: The History, Culture, Language and Contemporary Politics of the People of Moldova* (New York: Columbia University Press, 1996); Stefan Ihrig: *Wer sind die Moldawier? Rumänismus versus Moldowanismus in Historiographie und Schulbüchern der Republik Moldova, 1991–2006* (Stuttgart and Hannover: Ibidem-Verlag, 2008); Matthew H. Ciscel, *The Language of the Moldovans: Romania, Russia, and Identity in an Ex-Soviet Republic* (Lanham, MD: Lexington Books, 2007); Andrei Brezianu and Vlad Spânu, *Historical Dictionary of Moldova* (Lanham, MD, Toronto, and Plymouth: Scarecrow Press, 2007); Michael Bruchis, *The Republic of Moldova: From the Collapse of the Soviet Empire to the Restoration of the Russian Empire* (New York and Boulder, CO: Columbia University Press and East European Monographs, 1997); Marcel Mitrasca, *Moldova: A Romanian Province under Russian Rule: Diplomatic History from the Archives of the Great Powers* (New York: Algora Publishing, 2002); Nicholas Dima, *Bessarabia and Bukovina: The Soviet-Romanian Territorial Dispute* (New York and Boulder, CO: Columbia University Press and East European Monographs, 1983); Nicholas Dima, *From Moldavia to Moldova: The Soviet-Romanian Territorial Dispute* (New York and Boulder, CO: Columbia University Press and East European Monographs, 1991); Nicholas Dima, *Moldova and the Transdnestr Republic* (New York and Boulder, CO: Columbia University Press and East European Monographs, 2001);

Wim P. Van Meurs, *The Bessarabian Question in Communist Historiography* (New York and Boulder, CO: Columbia University Press and East European Monographs, 1994); Herman Pirchner, Jr., *Reviving Greater Russia? The Future of Russia's Borders with Belarus, Georgia, Kazakhstan, Moldova and Ukraine* (Washington, DC: The University Press of America and American Foreign Policy Council, 2005); Andrei Brezianu and Vlad Spanu, *The A to Z of Moldova*, vol. 232 of *A to Z Guides* (Lanham, MD: Scarecrow Press, 2010); Wim van Meurs, "Moldova," in *New Europe: The Impact of the First Decade*, vol. 2: *Variations on the Pattern*, ed. Teresa Rakowska-Harmstone, Piotr Dutkiewicz, and Agnieszka Orzelska (Warsaw: Institute of Political Studies Polish Academy of Sciences and Collegium Civitas Press, 2006), 329–70. And for a partly fictionalized artist's view of Moldova's last two decades see Constantin Cheianu, *Sex & Perestroika* (Chisinau: Editura Cartier Rotonda, 2009).

71.   See Steven D. Roper, "Regionalism in Moldova: The Case of Transnistria and Gagauzia," in *Ethnicity and Territory in the Former Soviet Union: Regions in Conflict*, ed. James Hughes and Gwendolyn Sasse (London and Portland, OR: Frank Cass, 2002), 101–22; Jeff Chinn and Steven D. Roper, "Territorial Autonomy in Gagauzia," *Nationalities Papers* 26, no. 1(March 1998): 87–101; Paul Goble, "Could Gagauzia Replace Transdniestria as Moscow's Lever of Choice in Moldova?" *Window on Eurasia* (June 5, 2008), http://windowoneurasia. blogspot.com/2008/06/window-on-eurasia-could-gagauzia.html.

72.   See Charles King, "Moldovan Identity and the Politics of Pan-Romanianism," *Slavic Review* 53, no. 2 (Summer 1994): 345–60; Bogdan Ivănel, "Moldova and Romania: Between Unification and Alienation," MSc Thesis, University of Oxford, Trinity College, 2010, http://oxford.academia.edu/BogdanIvanel/Papers/474657/Moldova_and_Romania_-_Between_Unification_and_Alienation; Andrei Panici, "Romanian Nationalism in the Republic of Moldova," *The Global Review of Ethnopolitics* 2, no. 2, (January 2003): 37–51; Alla Skvortsova, "The Cultural and Social Makeup of Moldova: A Bipolar or Dispersed Society," *National Integration and Violent Conflict in Post-Soviet Societies: The Cases of Estonia and Moldova*, ed. Pål Kolstø (Lanham, MD: Rowman & Littlefield, 2002), 159–96; and Igor Munteanu, "Social Multipolarity in Moldova," Defense Academy of the United Kingdom, Conflict Studies Research Centre, Central and East European Series Publication, G80 (November 1999): 1–38, http://www. da.mod.uk/colleges/arag/document-listings/cee/G80-im.pdf, which is a version of Igor Munteanu, "Social Multipolarity and Violence," *National Integration and Violent Conflict in Post-Soviet Societies: The Cases of Estonia and Moldova*, ed. Pål Kolstø (Lanham, MD: Rowman & Littlefield, 2002), 197–232.

73.   The head of *Vorozhdenye* (Renaissance) party, Shevchuk replaced Smirnov in indirect elections in December 2011. He secured 75 percent of the vote. The incumbent was virtually forced out at the request of the Kremlin which was apparently annoyed at the impossibility of foreign perceptions management of Transnistria as a wholesome state due to Smirnov's dictatorial length of tenure. Shevchuk was allegedly not the most favorite candidate of Moscow. However, Russia has no reason to worry. According to some accounts, secret service boss Vladimir Antufeev, a veteran of the KGB, remains the power behind the throne in Transnistria. His tenure has been longer than Smirnov's. Last but not least, given president-elect's post-Communist youth background, connections, and functions, including the speakership of the Transnistrian Supreme Soviet (ostensibly, though, in the opposition "Renewal" party until 2010), Shevchuk will probably be a candidate of continuity. See Marek Jan

Chodakiewicz, "Mołdawska gra," [Moldavian game] *Tygodnik Solidarność,* May 4, 2012; Mykola Siruk, "Yevgeny Shevchuk, New President of Transnistria," *Den'/The Day,* The Weekly Digest no. 77, December 29, 2011, posted at http://www.day.kiev.ua/221560; "Yevgeny Shevchuk wins transnistria [sic] elections," Itar-TASS, December 26, 2011, posted at http://www.itar-tass.com/en/c142/306422.html. On Smirnov see a flattering biography by Anna Volkova, *Lider* [Leader] (Tiraspol': Ol'via Press, 2001), http://www.olvia.idknet.com/soderjanie.htm. See also Vladimir Socor, "Last Moldovan schools under Threat in Trans-dniester," *Eurasia Daily Monitor* 1, no. 55 (July 19, 2004): http://www.jamestown.org/single/?no_cache=1&tx_ttnews%5Btt_news%5D=30120; Rebecca Chamberlain-Creangă and Lyndon K. Allin, "Acquiring Assets, Debts and Citizens: Russia and the Micro-Foundations of Transnistria's Stalemated Conflict," *Demokratizatsiya: The Journal of Post-Soviet Democratization* 18, no. 4 (Fall 2010): 329–56; William H. Hill, "Reflections on Negotiation and Mediation: The Frozen Conflicts and European Security," *Demokratizatsiya: The Journal of Post-Soviet Democratization* 18, no. 3 (Summer 2010): 219–27; Steven D. Roper, "From Frozen Conflict to Frozen Agreement: The Unrecognized State of Transnistria," in *The Quest for Sovereignty: Unrecognised States in the International System,* ed. Tozun Bahcheli, Barry Bartmann, and Henry Srebrnik (London: Frank Cass and Taylor and Francis, 2004), 102–17; Steven D. Roper, "Regionalism in Moldova: The Case of Transnistria and Gagauzia," in *Ethnicity and Territory in the Former Soviet Union: Regions in Conflict,* ed. James Hughes and Gwendolyn Sasse (London and Portland, OR: Frank Cass, 2002), 101–22; Claus Neukirch, "Russia and the OSCE: The Influence of the Interested Third and Disinterested Fourth Parties on the Conflicts in Estonia and Moldova," *National Integration and Violent Conflict in Post-Soviet Societies: The Cases of Estonia and Moldova,* ed. Pål Kolstø (Lanham, MD: Rowman & Littlefield, 2002), 233–48; Graeme P. Herd, "Moldova & The Dniestr Region: Contested Past, Frozen Present, Speculative Futures?" Defence Academy of the United Kingdom, Conflict Studies Research Centre, Central & Eastern European Series, 05/07 (February 2005): 1–17, http://www.da.mod.uk/colleges/arag/document-listings/cee/05%2807%29-GPH.pdf; Igor Munteanu, "Social Multipolarity in Moldova," Defense Academy of the United Kingdom, Central and East European Series Publication, G80 (November 1999): 1–38, http://www.da.mod.uk/colleges/arag/document-listings/cee/g80-im.pdf; William E. Crowther, *The Politics of Ethnic Confrontation in Moldova* (Washington, DC: The National Council for Soviet and East European Research, 1993); Pål Kolstø, Andrei Edemsky, and Natalya Kalashnikova, "The Dniester Conflict: Between Irredentism and Separatism," *Europe-Asia Studies* 45, no. 6 (1993): 973–1000; Phillip Petersen, "Moldova: Improving the Prospects for Peace," *Jane's Intelligence Review* 6, no. 9 (September 1994): 396–400; Charles King, "Moldova and the New Bessarabian Question," *World Today* [London] no. 49 (July 1993): 135–39; Ioan Chiper, "Bessarabia and Northern Bukovina," in *Contested Territory: Border Disputes at the Edge of the Former Soviet Empire,* ed. Tuomas Forsberg (Aldershot: Edward Elgar, 1995), 107–27.

74. Jennifer R. Cash, "Origins, Memory, and Identity: 'Villages' and the Politics of Nationalism in the Republic of Moldova," *East European Politics and Societies* 21, no. 4 (Fall 2007): 588–610. See also Cristina Petrescu, "Contrasting/Conflicting Identities: Bessarabians, Romanians, Moldovans," in *Nation-Building and Contested Identities: Romanian & Hungarian Case Studies,* ed. Balázs Trencsényi, Dragoş Petrescu, Cristina Petrescu, Constantin Iordachi and Zoltán

Kántor (Budapest and Iaşy: Regio Books and Editura Polirom, 2001), 153–78, http://vmek.uz.ua/06000/06046/06046.pdf; and Grigore Ureche, Miron Costin, and Ion Neculce, eds., *Letopisetul Tarii Moldovei* (*Chronicle of the Moldovan Nation*) (Chisinau: Editura Hyperion, 1990).

75. Trevor Waters, "The 'Moldovan Syndrome' & the Re-Russification of Moldova: Forward into the Past!" Defense Academy of the United Kingdom, Conflict Studies Research Centre, Central and East European Series Publication, G105 (February 2002): 1–9, http://www.da.mod.uk/colleges/arag/document-listings/cee/G105.

76. See Marek Jan Chodakiewicz, "Mołdawskość" ("Moldavian Identity") *Tygodnik Solidarność* (July 30, 2010); William E. Crowther, *The Politics of Ethnic Confrontation in Moldova* (Washington, DC: The National Council for Soviet and East European Research, 1993); Donald Leroy Dyer, *The Romanian Dialect of Moldova: A Study in Language and Politics* (Lewiston, NY: Edwin Mellen Press, 1999); Stefan Ihrig, *Wer sind die Moldawier? Rumänismus versus Moldowanismus in Historiographie und Schulbüchern der Republik Moldova, 1991–2006* (Stuttgart and Hannover: Ibidem-Verlag, 2008); Matthew H. Ciscel, *The Language of the Moldovans: Romania, Russia, and Identity in an Ex-Soviet Republic* (Lanham, MD: Lexington Books, 2007).

77. No author, "The Republic of Moldova Armed Forces and Military Doctrine Introduction and Background: Military-Political Developments," Defence Academy of the United Kingdom, Conflict Studies Research Centre, Central & Eastern European Series, (no date [1997?, posted April 2007]): 1–18, http://www.da.mod.uk/colleges/arag/document-listings/cee and http://www.da.mod.uk/colleges/arag/document-listings/cee/THE%20REPUBLIC%20OF%20MOLDOVA.pdf. And see Steven D. Roper, "The Impact of Moldovan Parliamentary Committees on the Process of Institutionalization," in *Committees in the New Democratic Parliaments of Central Europe*, ed. David M. Olson and William E. Crowther (Columbus, OH: The Ohio State University Press, 2003), 154–69; Yuri Josanu, "Political Institutionalization in Post Soviet Republic of Moldova," *Pontes Review of South East European Studies* no. 1 (2004): 141–63; William E. Crowther, "Moldovan Legislative Elites in Transition," in *Central European Parliaments: First Decade of Democratic Experience and Future Perspectives*, ed. Zdenka Mansfeldova, David Olson, and Petra Rakusanova (Prague: Institute of Sociology, Academy of Sciences of the Czech Republic, 2004), 156–71; William E. Crowther, "Development of the Moldovan Parliament One Decade after Independence: Slow Going," in *Post-Communist and Post-Soviet Parliaments: The Initial Decade*, ed. Philip Norton and David M. Olson (London, Frank Cass: 2007).

78. See Kelvin Gosnell, *Belarus, Ukraine and Moldova* (Brookfield, CT: Millbrook Press, 1992); Helen Fedor, ed., *Belarus and Moldova: Country Studies* (Washington, DC: GPO for Federal Research Division, Library of Congress, 1996); Oliver Schmidtke and Serhy Yekelchyk, *Europe's Last Frontier? Belarus, Moldova, and Ukraine between Russia and the European Union* (New York: Palgrave Macmillan, 2008). Compare with William E. Crowther, *Electoral Politics and Transition in Romania* (Washington, DC; The National Council for Soviet and East European Research, 1993).

79. See "Narodnyye deputati Moldavskoy SSR" ("People's Deputies of the Moldavian SSR"), *Sovetskaya Moldaviya* [Chisinau] (March 17, 1990): 4; "Biografile Membrilor Guvernului Republicii Moldova," ("Biographies of the Members of the Government of Moldova") *Moldova Suverana* [Chisinau] (August 20,

1992): 1–2; United States, Central Intelligence Agency, *Top Officials in Moldova* (Washington, DC: Government Printing Office, 1992).

80. William E. Crowther, "Romania and Moldavian Political Dynamics," in *Romania after Tyranny*, ed. Daniel Nelson (Boulder, CO: Westview Press, 1992), 239–59; Vladimir Socor, "Moldavia Builds a New State," *RFE/RL Research Report* 1 (January 3, 1992): 42–45; William E. Crowther, "Moldova," in *Belarus and Moldova Country Studies*, ed. Helen Fedor (Washington, DC: Library of Congress, Federal Research Division, 1995), 95–179.

81. Steven D. Roper, "From Semi-Presidentialism to Parliamentarism: Regime Change and Presidential Power in Moldova," *Europe-Asia Studies* 60, no. 1 (January 2008):113–26.

82. For the official biography see "Б И О Г Р А Ф И Я господина Мирчи СНЕГУРА, Президента Республики Молдова (1990–1996 гг.)," http://www.presedinte.md/crono.php?lang=rus&page=602. And its English translation http://www.president.md/crono.php?lang=eng&page=602.

83. Jeff Chinn and Steven D. Roper, "Ethnic Mobilization and Reactive Nationalism: The Case of Moldova," *Nationalities Papers* 23, no. 2 (June 1995): 291–325; William Crowther, "Ethnic Politics and the Post-Communist Transition in Moldova," *Nationalities Papers* 26 no. 1 (March 1998): 147–64.

84. For a sample of the President's demagogy see Mircea Snegur, "Poporul Trebuie Întrebat si Ascultat" ("The People Must Ask and Be Heard"), *Moldova Suverana* [Chisinau] (December 26, 1992), 1–2. See also Liviu Man, "Moldavia, Past and Present: Why the Communists Won Elections," *Uncaptive Minds* 7, no.1 (25) (Winter–Spring 1993–1994); William E. Crowther, *The Politics of Ethnic Confrontation in Moldova* (Washington, DC: The National Council for Soviet and East European Research, 1993); William E. Crowther, *Moldova: A Country Study*, ed. Helen Fedor (Washington: GPO for the Library of Congress, 1995), http://countrystudies.us/moldova/.

85. See Bogdan Ivănel, "Moldova and Romania: Between Unification and Alienation," MSc Thesis, University of Oxford, Trinity College, 2010, http://oxford.academia.edu/BogdanIvanel/Papers/474657/Moldova_and_Romania_-_Between_Unification_and_Alienation; William E. Crowther, *The Politics of Ethnic Confrontation in Moldova* (Washington, DC: The National Council for Soviet and East European Research, 1993); Jeff Chinn and Steven D. Roper, "Ethnic Mobilization and Reactive Nationalism: The Case of Moldova," *Nationalities Papers* 23, no. 2 (June 1995): 291–325; Liviu Man, "Moldavia, Past and Present: Why the Communists Won Elections," *Uncaptive Minds* 7, no.1 (25) (Winter–Spring 1993–1994). Compare with: Ronald D. Bachman, ed., *Romania: A Country Study* (Washington, DC: Government Printing Office, 1991); Daniel Nelson, ed., *Romania after Tyranny* (Boulder, CO: Westview Press, 1992); and William E. Crowther, *Electoral Politics and Transition in Romania* (Washington, DC; The National Council for Soviet and East European Research, 1993).

86. See Kester Eddy, "Moldova Still Labours under Its Past," *Business New Europe* (July 26, 2011), http://www.bne.eu/story2801/Moldova_still_labours_under_its_past; Matthew Gorton and John White, "The Politics of Agrarian Collapse: Decollectivisation in Moldova," *East European Politics and Societies* 17, no. 2 (Spring 2003): 305–32; Steven D. Roper, "The Politics of Economic Reform in Moldova," *Balkanistica* 12, no. 1 (June 1999): 95–118. See also Moldova, Departamentul de Stat pentru statistica al Republicii Moldova, *Anuar statistic: Economia Nationala a Republicii Moldova, 1990 (Narodnoye khozyaystvo respubliki Moldova)*, ed. N. Pasternacov and V. Frunza (Chisinau: Universitas,

1991); Moldova, Departamentul de Stat pentru statistica al Republicii Moldova, *Economia Nationala a Republicii Moldova* (Chisinau: Universitas, 1992); International Monetary Fund, *Moldova* (Economic Review Series) (Washington, DC: International Monetary Fund, 1992); International Monetary Fund, *Moldova* (IMF Economic Reviews) (Washington, DC: International Monetary Fund, 1993); World Bank, *Moldova: Moving to a Market Economy* (World Bank Country Study) (Washington, DC: World Bank, 1994).

87.   See Irina Culic, "Eluding Exit and Entry Controls: Romanian and Moldovan Immigrants in the European Union," *East European Politics and Societies* 21, no. 1 (Winter 2008): 145–66; Kester Eddy, "Moldova Still Labours under Its Past," *Business New Europe* (July 26, 2011): http://www.bne.eu/story2801/ Moldova_still_labours_under_its_past; Paul Goble, "Gastarbeiters in Russia Sending a Third Less Money Home This Year than Last," *Window on Eurasia* (September 10, 2009): http://windowoneurasia.blogspot.com/2009/09/window-on-eurasia-gastarbeiters-in.html; Paul Goble, "Gastarbeiter Transfer Payments from Russia to Homelands Decline by Half since Last Fall," *Window on Eurasia* (May 25, 2009): http://windowoneurasia.blogspot.com/2009/05/window-on-eurasia-gastarbeiter-transfer.html; Paul Goble, "Economic Crisis in Russia Cuts Transfer Payments to Many Post-Soviet States," *Window on Eurasia* (October 14, 2008): http://windowoneurasia.blogspot.com/2008/10/window-on-eurasia-economic-crisis-in.html.

88.   Gabriel Badescu, Paul Sum, and Eric M. Uslaner, "Civil Society Development and Democratic Values in Romania and Moldova," *East European Politics and Societies* 18, no. 2 (Spring 2004): 316–40.

89.   Dan Ionescu, "Back to Romanian?" *Transition* 1, no. 15 (25 August 1995): 54–57; William E. Crowther, "Development of the Moldovan Parliament One Decade after Independence: Slow Going," in *Post-Communist and Post-Soviet Parliaments: The Initial Decade*, ed. Philip Norton and David M. Olson (London: Frank Cass, 2007).

90.   William Crowther, "The Politics of Democratization in Postcommunist Moldova," in *Democratic Changes and Authoritarian Reactions in Russia, Ukraine, Belarus, and Moldova*, ed. Karen Dawisha and Bruce Parrott (Cambridge: Cambridge University Press, 1997), 282–329; William Crowther and Steven D. Roper, "A Comparative Analysis of Institutional Development in the Romanian and Moldovan Legislatures," in *The New Parliaments of Central and Eastern Europe*, ed. David M. Olson and Philip Norton (London: Routledge, 1996), 133–60.

91.   For the official biography see "BIOGRAFIA Domnului Petru LUCINSCHI, ex-Preşedinte al Republicii Moldova," http://www.president.md/crono. php?lang=eng&page=603.

92.   For his views at the time see P.K. Lucinschi, "Aspectete Politice al Restructurare si Activitatea Partidului Comunist Moldovenesti sub Conditiile Noi," ("Political Aspects of Restructuring and the Activity of the CPM under the New Conditions"), *Moldova Socialista* [Chisinau] (March 3, 1990): 1–3; P.K. Lucinschi, "Ob itogakh XXVIII s'yezda KPSS," ("On the Results of the XXVIII CPSU Congress: Report of P.K. Lucinschi, First Secretary of the CC, CPM [Speech to the Central Committee of the CPM]"), *Sovetskaya Moldova* [Chisinau] (August 6, 1990): 2–3.

93.   "Petru Lucinschi, Presedintele Parlamentului Republicii Moldovei," ("Petru Lucinschi, President of the Parliament of Moldova"), *Moldova Suverana* [Chisinau] (February 6 1993): 1.

94. Vladimir Socor, "Quo vadis, Moldova?" *Prism* 4, no. 9 (May 1, 1998), http://www. jamestown.org/single/?no_cache=1&tx_ttnews%5Btt_news%5D=7442.
95. Vladimir Socor, "'Double Vector,' Double Game: Moldova's Centrist Opposition and Moscow," *Eurasia Daily Monitor* 2, no. 43 (March 2, 2005): http://www. jamestown.org/single/?no_cache=1&tx_ttnews%5Btt_news%5D=27632.
96. The Moldovan criminal underground consists of several major gangs, some of them ethnically Russian. Their main transborder pursuit is human trafficking, women for prostitution, in particular. But smuggling weapons and ammunition is also common. There have also been persistent and grim allegations of illegal sales of human organs for transplantation, which included donor intimidation. A kidney sale reportedly fetches the donor $3,000.00 in Moldova. Some have alleged government involvement in the lurid transactions. As far as illegal domestic activities, they concern extortion, racketeering, and money laundering where the nexus between the government and the mafia is palpable. See The Organized Crime and Corruption Reporting Project (OCCRP), "The Proxy Platform," http://www.reportingproject.net/proxy/ and http://www. reportingproject.net/proxy/the-proxy-platform, in particular "Opening the Door: Proxy Platform Revealed," http://www.reportingproject.net/proxy/opening-the-door-proxy-platform-revealed; "The Phantom Accounts," http://www. reportingproject.net/proxy/the-phantom-accounts; "The Money Carousel," http://www.reportingproject.net/proxy/the-money-carousel; "Slum Millionaire: The Moldovan Proxy," http://www.reportingproject.net/proxy/slum-millionaire-the-moldovan-proxy; and "Money from Moldova," http://www. reportingproject.net/proxy/money-from-moldova. See also "Moldova Launches MMM [My Mozhem Mnogo, "We can do a lot"] Pyramid Probe," RIA Novosti, April 4,2012, http://en.rian.ru/world/20120404/172599096.html; Kester Eddy, "Moldova Still Labours under Its Past," *Business New Europe* (July 26, 2011): http://www.bne.eu/story2801/Moldova_still_labours_under_its_past; "Ferenc Banfi: Moldova's approach to combating organized crime needs to change," *All Moldova* (August 14, 2009): http://www.allmoldova.com/en/int/interview/frent-banfi-140809.html; Sam Vaknin, "Organ Trafficking in Eastern Europe," (July 3, 2005): http://www.globalpolitician.com/2383-organ; Alison Weir, "Israeli Organ Harvesting: From Moldova to Palestine," *Washington Report on Middle East Affairs* (November 2009) (which is full of incendiary allegations about alleged Israeli "organ tourism"), http://www.wrmea.com/component/content/article/6410-israeli-organ-harvesting-from-moldova-to-palestine. html; Lada L. Roslycky, "Organized Transnational Crime in the Black Sea Region: A Geopolitical Dilemma?" no date (2006), http://www.harvard-bssp. org/static/files/327/Organized_Crime_in_Black_Sea.pdf; Breffni O'Rourke, "Europe: Council Of Europe Report Says Organized Crime Poses Threat to Democracy," *Radio Free Europe/Radio Liberty* (January 26, 2005): http://www. rferl.org/content/article/1057094.html.
97. For an unauthorized look at Voronin (referred to as "the Moldavian Mao") see Д.Ю. Соин, ed., *Голый Воронин: Сборник статей* (Tiraspol: n.p., 2005), and a synopsis of "ГОЛЫЙ ВОРОНИН: СКЕЛЕТ В ШКАФУ: ЕГО СОМНИТЕЛЬНОЕ ПРОИСХОЖДЕНИЕ," http://zhurnal.lib.ru/s/soin_d_j/goliy.shtml. A word of caution: The Russian-language book came out in Transnistria and the source is allegedly Moldova's conservative paper *Timpul*, both hardly impartial parties.
98. Klemens Büscher, "Moldova after the Parliamentary Elections: A Second Chance for Reform," *SEER-Southeast Europe Review for Labour and Social Affairs*

no. 3 (1998): 69–79; R.J. Hill, "Profile - Moldova Votes Backwards: The 2001 Parliamentary Election," *Journal of Communist Studies and Transition Politics* 17, no. 4 (2001): 130–39; William E. Crowther, "Development of the Moldovan Parliament One Decade After Independence: Slow Going," in *Post-Communist and Post-Soviet Parliaments: The Initial Decade*, ed. Philip Norton and David M. Olson (London: Frank Cass, 2007).

99.   Vladimir Socor, "Moldova's presidential institution increasingly dysfunctional," *Eurasia Daily Monitor* 4, no. 149 (August 1, 2007): http://www.jamestown.org/single/?no_cache=1&tx_ttnews%5Btt_news%5D=32913.

100. See Paul D. Quinlan, "Back to the Future: An Overview of Moldova under Voronin," *Demokratizatsiya: The Journal of Post-Soviet Democratization* 12, no. 4 (Fall 2004): 485–504; Trevor Waters, "The 'Moldovan Syndrome' & the Re-Russification of Moldova: Forward into the Past!" Defense Academy of the United Kingdom, Conflict Studies Research Centre, Central and East European Series Publication, G105 (February 2002): 1–9, http://www.da.mod.uk/colleges/arag/document-listings/cee/G105; Vladimir Socor, "Moldova's Political Sea Change," *Eurasia Daily Monitor* 2, no. 70 (April 11, 2005): http://www.jamestown.org/single/?no_cache=1&tx_ttnews%5Btt_news%5D=30241.

101. Born in 1963, Tarlev is an ethnic Bulgarian from Bessarabia. He worked as a driver on a state farm, and later studied engineering in Chişinău, graduating in 1990. He worked in a number of technocratic and managerial posts, primarily for SA Bucuria, which he headed from 1995. Between 1997 and 2000, Tarlev also served on the Economic Council of the head of the government. In 2001, he was selected as prime minister by Voronin, and, in 2005, elected to the parliament on the Communist list. In 2008, after his unexpected ouster, Tarlev first joined the Russophile and oligarchic Centrist Union of Moldova (CUM) and served briefly as its president (http://www.ucm.md/). Then, he organized its alliance with the post-Communist Social Democratic Party (SDP), and unsuccessfully ran on a joint ticket for parliament. Subsequently, Tarlev quarreled bitterly with his CUM associates. Meanwhile, the former head of government exposed some corruption in Voronin's entourage, including the shady privatization deals of the National and Codru hotels as well as the Mezon enterprise. Tarlev even claimed that the riots of April 7, 2009, which saw the destruction of some of the government financial records, were a cover-up of massive embezzlement by the oligarchs tied to the Communist president. The erstwhile PM briefly maintained his own website: www.tarlev.md. See "Moldova's PM Vasile Tarlev Resigns," Formae Mentis: Technical Assistance NGO, March 19, 2008, http://formaementis.wordpress.com/2008/03/19/moldovas-pm-vasile-tarlev-resigns/; "Report: 7 April riots in Moldova provoked by the communists," Moldova.org, July 22, 2009, http://social.moldova.org/news/report-7-april-riots-in-moldova-provoked-by-the-communists-202886-eng.html; "Ex-PM says president's entourage buy up state assets cheaply," Moldova.org, July 24, 2009, http://social.moldova.org/news/expm-says-presidents-entourage-buy-up-state-assets-cheaply-202922-eng.html; "CUM demands compensation of moral damage from ex-premier Vasile Tarlev," Totul News, August 12, 2009, http://totul.md/en/newsitem/1410.html; "Vasile Tarlev withdraws from UCM," Moldova Azi, November 19, 2009, http://www.azi.md/en/story/7056.

102. In January 2002, Christian democrats and others organized street demonstrations against the compulsory Russian-language instructions in Moldova's grade schools. The government delegalized the parties taking part in the protest. See Vladimir Solonari, "Narrative, Identity, State: History Teaching in Moldova,"

East European Politics and Societies 16, no. 2 (Spring 2002): 314–46; Steven D. Roper, "The Politicization of Education: Identity Formation in Moldova and Transnistria," *Communist and Post-Communist Studies* 38, no. 4 (December 2005):501–14; "People's Christian Democratic Party," http://www.parties.e-democracy.md/en/parties/ppcd/.

103. Iurie Roşca, "Moldova's Orange Evolution," *Demokratizatsiya: The Journal of Post-Soviet Democratization* 13, no. 4 (Fall 2005): 537–43; Steven D. Roper, "From Semi-Presidentialism to Parliamentarism: Regime Change and Presidential Power in Moldova," *Europe-Asia Studies* 60, no. 1 (January 2008):113–26; Menno Fenger, "The Diffusion of Revolutions: Comparing Recent Regime Turnovers in Five Post-Communist Countries," *Demokratizatsiya: The Journal of Post-Soviet Democratization* 15, no. 1 (Winter 2007): 5–28; Taras Kuzio, "Democratic Breakthroughs and Revolutions in Five Postcommunist Countries: Comparative Perspectives on the Fourth Wave," *Demokratizatsiya: The Journal of Post-Soviet Democratization* 16, no. 1 (Winter 2008): 97–109.

104. For the history of Voronin's zig zagging vis-à-vis the Kremlin see Vladimir Socor, "Moldova's Drift Toward Russia," *Eurasia Daily Monitor* 1, no. 20 (May 27, 2004): http://www.jamestown.org/single/?no_cache=1&tx_ttnews%5Btt_news%5D=26584; Vladimir Socor "Moldovan President Wants Out of Russia's Orbit," *Eurasia Daily Monitor* 1, no. 87 (September 16, 2004): http://www.jamestown.org/single/?no_cache=1&tx_ttnews%5Btt_news%5D=26871; Vladimir Socor, "Moldova's President Kremlin Visit Does Not Unfreeze Relations," *Eurasia Daily Monitor* 3, no. 155 (August 10, 2006): http://www.jamestown.org/single/?no_cache=1&tx_ttnews%5Btt_news%5D=31959; Vladimir Socor, "Voronin's Six Point Plan to Putin: A Calculated Risk," *Eurasia Daily Monitor* 4, no. 183 (October 4, 2006): http://www.jamestown.org/single/?no_cache=1&tx_ttnews%5Btt_news%5D=32097; Vladimir Socor, "Moldova's President Cornered by Putin," *Eurasia Daily Monitor* 4, no. 107 (June 1, 2007): http://www.jamestown.org/single/?no_cache=1&tx_ttnews%5Btt_news%5D=32778.

105. See Ellen Barry, "Protests in Moldova Explode, With Help of Twitter," *The New York Times* (April 7, 2009): http://www.nytimes.com/2009/04/08/world/europe/08moldova.html?_r=1; "Police Retake Moldova Parliament," *BBC News* (April 8, 2009): http://news.bbc.co.uk/2/hi/europe/7988893.stm; "Moldova's 'Twitter Revolution," *Radio Free Europe/Radio Liberty* (April 8, 2009): http://www.rferl.org/content/Moldovas_Twitter_Revolution/1605005.html; "Fearing Uprising Russia Backs Moldova's Communists," *Spiegel Online* (April 10, 2009): http://www.spiegel.de/international/europe/0,1518,618563,00.html; Stela Popa, *100 de zile* (Bucharest: Tritonic, 2010); Vladimir Socor, "Violent Riots Devastate Moldovan Presidential and Parliament Buildings," *Eurasia Daily Monitor* 6, no. 68 (April 9, 2009): http://www.jamestown.org/single/?no_cache=1&tx_ttnews%5Btt_news%5D=34832; Vladimir Socor, "Moldova Tense after Post-election Violence in Chisinau," *Eurasia Daily Monitor* 6, no. 68 (April 9, 2009): http://www.jamestown.org/single/?no_cache=1&tx_ttnews%5Btt_news%5D=34833; Vladimir Socor, "Moldovan Authorities Caught Unprepared by Violent Riots," *Eurasia Daily Monitor* 6, no. 73 (April 16, 2009): http://www.jamestown.org/single/?no_cache=1&tx_ttnews%5Btt_news%5D=34863; Vladimir Socor, "Moldova's Body Politic in Gridlock after Elections and Riots," *Eurasia Daily Monitor* 6, no. 73 (April 16, 2009): http://www.jamestown.org/single/?no_cache=1&tx_ttnews%5Btt_news%5D=34864; Marek Jan Chodakiewicz, "Rumuno Post-Sowieci," (Rumanian Post-Soviets) *Tygodnik Solidarność* (May 15, 2009).

106. See Vladimir Socor, "Moldova's Political Crisis Deepens," *Eurasia Daily Monitor* 6, no. 79 (April 24, 2009): http://www.jamestown.org/single/?no_cache=1&tx_ttnews%5Btt_news%5D=34900; "Presidential Vote in Moldova Fails: New Elections on the Way," (June 3, 2009): http://www.europeanforum. net/news/617/presidential_vote_in_moldova_fails_new_elections_on_the_way.

107. Born in 1953 in a peasant family, Mihai Ghimpu graduated law school in 1978. Afterward, he served as a legal advisor and a judge, which most certainly entailed joining the Communist party. As a "reform" Communist he became involved with the National Front (FPM) at the end of the 1980s and supported Moldova's independence under the national Bolshevik leadership. He entered the Supreme Soviet on a National Front ticket, but soon broke with the pan-Romanians and cofounded the post-Communist/liberal Congress of the Intelligentsia, which put him in the parliament in 1994. Then, in 1997, Ghimpu switched to the Party of Reform (established in 1993), which changed its name to the Liberal Party of Moldova (in 2005) but failed to enter the legislature until 2009. Having until then had concentrated on municipal politics, Ghimpu was re-elected to the parliament both in April and July 2009. He became Speaker of the House in August 2009, and the Republic's President in September. After his tenure ended, Ghimpu assumed chairmanship of the Liberal Party. See Paul Goble, "Moldovan Leader Marks Day of Soviet Occupation Despite Opposition from Moscow and Governing Coalition in Chisinau," *Window on Eurasia* (June 28, 2010): http://windowoneurasia.blogspot.com/2010/06/window-on-eurasia-moldovan-leader-marks.html.

108. Born in 1969 in a tiny rural settlement of Lăpușna, the blink-of-an-eye acting president Vladimir (Vlad) Filat first studied agriculture in Moldova but then moved to Romania, where he graduated from the law faculty of the University of Iași in 1992. A moderate leader of a pan-Romanian association of Moldovan students in Romania, he focused on promoting economic exchange between both countries. Active in the private business sector (including, allegedly, in cigarette smuggling), in 1995 Filat joined the Democratic Party of Moldova (DPM), which, ostensibly, champions social democracy but, in reality, is perceived as a vehicle of the post-Communist oligarchic business interests. In 1999, he was tapped to head the Moldovan government's privatization bureaucracy under the kleptocrats of Lucinschi. Elected to the legislature on a DPM ticket in 2005, he switched parties two years later, joining the Liberal Democratic Party of Moldova (LDPM, and its website: http://www.pldm.md/) as its president. He won the parliamentary polls of April and July 2009 and fostered an anti-Communist coalition dubbed the Alliance for European Integration. Except for two days when he was acting president, Filat has served as Prime Minister (2009–present) under the *pro tempore* regime. For his blog see "Vlad Filat: Start Moldova!," http://www.filat.md/blog/. See also "Vladimir Filat: Start Implicare, Stop Nepăsare," http://www.filat2007.md/; and Vladimir Socor, "Moldova's Post-Communist Government Takes Office Amidst Crisis," *Eurasia Daily Monitor* 6, no. 181 (October 2, 2009): http://www.jamestown. org/single/?no_cache=1&tx_ttnews%5Btt_news%5D=35571.

109. Marian Lupu was born in Moldova's second largest city, Bălți, in 1966, but grew up in a family of Communist intellectuals and true believers in Chișinău. His mother was a university French language instructor and his father, Ilie Ion Lupu, was a mathematics professor and a staunch Soviet. At fourteen, Marian Lupu joined the Communist Youth (Komsomol) and, at twenty-four the

Communist party, which was delegalized three years later. Meanwhile, Lupu junior studied Marxist-Leninist economics in Chişinău and Moscow, where he earned his doctorate in 1991. Afterward, he fluctuated between unreformed Communists and kleptocratic post-Communists as a technocratic expert with the Ministry of Economy. His post allowed him to enjoy stints at the International Monetary Fund in Washington, DC, in 1994, and at the World Trade Organization in Geneva in 1996. From 1997 he worked as the head of the Ministry's foreign trade department. Brought on board by Voronin, Lupu joined Vasile Tarlev's cabinet as deputy minister of economy in 2001. Two years later he took over the ministerial portfolio (2003–2005). He entered the parliament on the Communist ticket in 2005 and became Speaker of the House (2005–2009), distinguishing himself as a moderate. In June 2009 he defected from the PCRM after Voronin passed Lupo to succeed him as president in favor of Zinaida Greceanîi (prime minister from March 2008 to September 2009). Lupo then joined the Democratic Party of Moldova. He succeeded in his electoral quest in July 2009, afterward cofounding the ruling coalition, the Alliance for European Integration. From December 2010 to March 2012 he served as president pro tempore. See Graham Stack, "Moldova's Turncoat President?" *Business New Europe* (August 19, 2009): http://www.bne.edu/story1731; and also http://grahamstack.wordpress.com/2009/08/15/moldovas-turncoat-president/ (which is a website of East of Europe: The BRUK states: Business and politics in Belarus, Russia, Ukraine and Kazakhstan (BRUK)); Vladimir Socor, "A New Face of Moldovan Politics," *Eurasia Daily Monitor* 4, no. 149 (August 1, 2007): http://www.jamestown.org/single/?no_cache=1&tx_ttnews%5Btt_news%5D=32914; "Moldova's Centrist Party Courts Communist Defector," *Radio Free Europe/Radio Liberty*, (June 11, 2009): http://www.rferl.org/content/Moldovan_Centrist_Party_Courts_Communist_Defector/1752206.html; Graham Stack, "Moldova's Turncoat President?" *Business New Europe* (August 19, 2009): http://www.bne.eu/story1731.

110. Timofti's candidacy was promoted by the three-party Alliance for European Integration (AEI). His election was secured by the defection of three Communist deputies to the post-Communist camp, namely the (Russophilic) Party of Socialists. Although in any functioning parliamentary democracy such horse trading would be quite normal, in Moldova the allegations of bribery surfaced immediately as did the accusations of Moscow's interference. Be that as it may, however, it is obviously too early to judge the newest president. A peasant child born in Citulesci in 1948, the only bright spots in his Soviet past are a grandfather who died in the Gulag and a mother who taught him about religion. As the president-elect put it himself, "we must believe in something and I believe in God." Otherwise, Timofti's roots are firmly in the Communist legal nomenklatura. He graduated from law school of the University of Chişinău in 1972 and served in the Red Army until 1976. Only four years after entering the legal profession, he was tapped for the Supreme Court of the MSSR. From 1990, he operated in the murky obscurity of the post-Communist judiciary where strong links to the criminal underworld are rumored. He held appointments first at the Appellate Court in Chişinău, then (2005) the Higher Judicial Chamber, and, lastly (2011), the Supreme Council of Magistrates, which he chaired. As other Moldovan post-Communists, the president supports his nation's accession to the EU and pursues "liberal" policies. His situation is complicated by the fact that Moldova's largest party, the Communists, do not recognize the legality of the sitting parliament. The legislature had only been

elected with a one year mandate to pick a president, which it failed to do in the allotted time (it took more than twice as long: 917 days); hence, the Communists deny the validity of Timofti's selection as chief of state. See Marek Jan Chodakiewicz, "Mołdawska gra," [Moldavian game] *Tygodnik Solidarność*, 4 May 2012; "Nicolae Timofti finally elected Moldova President," BBC, March 16, 2012, posted at http://www.bbc.co.uk/news/world-europe-17398641; Vladimir Socor, "Moldova: A Democracy Promoter's Dream and Nightmare," *Eurasia Daily Monitor* 9, no. 54 (March 16, 2012), posted at http://www.jamestown.org/single/?no_cache=1&tx_ttnews%5Btt_news%5D=39145&tx_ttnews%5BbackPid%5D=7&cHash=0572486b2c8ad8e23b5fa9d2bde61c99; Vladimir Socor, "Moldova Finally Elects A Head of State," *Eurasia Daily Monitor* 9, no. 55 (March 19, 2012), posted at http://www.jamestown.org/programs/edm/single/?tx_ttnews%5Btt_news%5D=39153&tx_ttnews%5BbackPid%5D=27&cHash=6bc7339e1a55c9937f69c5037f2fa7ff; Robert Coalson, Valentina Ursu, and Mircea Ticudean, "Profile: Who is Moldova's President Elect?" Radio Free Europe/Radio Liberty, March 16, 2012, posted at http://www.rferl.org/content/who_is_moldovas_new_president/24518350.html; "Moldova finally gets a president," *Economist*, March 17, 2012, posted at http://www.economist.com/blogs/easternapproaches/2012/03/moldovas-politics?fsrc=nlw%7Cnew e%7C3-19-2012%7Cnew_on_the_economist. For a more hopeful outlook see Matthew Rojansky and Lyndon Allin, "Moldova's Revolution in Slow Motion," *World Politics Review* (February 3, 2011): http://www.worldpoliticsreview.com/articles/7768/moldovas-revolution-in-slow-motion and http://www.carnegieendowment.org/publications/index.cfm?fa=view&id=42521&prog=zru.

111. For the election results in 1994, 1998, and 2001 see Annex A in Trevor Waters, "The 'Moldovan Syndrome' & the Re-Russification of Moldova: Forward into the Past!" Defense Academy of the United Kingdom, Conflict Studies Research Centre, Central and East European Series Publication, G105 (February 2002): 6–7, http://www.da.mod.uk/colleges/arag/document-listings/cee/G105. For electoral results between 1994 and 2009 see Wolfram Nordsieck, "Parties and Elections in Europe: Moldova," http://www.parties-and-elections.de/moldova2.html and http://www.parties-and-elections.de/moldova.html. See also United States, Commission on Security and Cooperation in Europe, *Report on the Moldovan Parliamentary Elections, February 27, 1994: Chisinau, Northern Moldova, Transdniestria, Varnitsa*. (Washington, DC: Government Printing Office, April 1994); Liviu Man, "Moldavia, Past and Present: Why the Communists Won Elections," *Uncaptive Minds* 7, no.1 (25) (Winter–Spring 1993–1994); William Crowther, "The Politics of Democratization in Postcommunist Moldova," in *Democratic Changes and Authoritarian Reactions in Russia, Ukraine, Belarus, and Moldova*, ed. Karen Dawisha and Bruce Parrott (Cambridge: Cambridge University Press, 1997), 282–329; Vladimir Socor, "Quo vadis, Moldova?" *Prism* 4, no. 9 (May 1, 1998): http://www.jamestown.org/single/?no_cache=1&tx_ttnews%5Btt_news%5D=7442; Vladimir Socor, "Moldova's Political Crisis Deepens," *Eurasia Daily Monitor* 6, no. 79 (April 24, 2009): http://www.jamestown.org/single/?no_cache=1&tx_ttnews%5Btt_news%5D=34900; Vladimir Socor, "'Double Vector,' Double Game: Moldova's Centrist Opposition and Moscow," *Eurasia Daily Monitor* 2, no. 43 (March 2, 2005): http://www.jamestown.org/single/?no_cache=1&tx_ttnews%5Btt_news%5D=27632; Vladimir Socor, "Moldova's Politics Remain Centered on the Communist Party," *Eurasia Daily Monitor* 6, no. 148 (August 3, 2009): http://www.jamestown.org/single/?no_cache=1&tx_ttnews%5Btt_news%5D=35353; Vladimir Socor,

"Moldova's Stunted Post-Soviet Transition Resumes after Elections," *Eurasia Daily Monitor* 6, no. 148 (August 3, 2009): http://www.jamestown.org/single/?no_cache=1&tx_ttnews%5Btt_news%5D=35352; Klemens Büscher, "Moldova after the Parliamentary Elections: A Second Chance for Reform," *SEER-Southeast Europe Review for Labour and Social Affairs*, no. 3 (1998): 69–79; R.J. Hill, "Profile - Moldova Votes Backwards: The 2001 Parliamentary Election," *Journal of Communist Studies and Transition Politics* 17, no. 4 (2001): 130–39; Menno Fenger, "The Diffusion of Revolutions: Comparing Recent Regime Turnovers in Five Post-Communist Countries," *Demokratizatsiya: The Journal of Post-Soviet Democratization* 15, no. 1 (Winter 2007): 5–28.

112. Irina Arishvili-Hanturia, Iurie Rošca, and Philip Dimitrov, "Georgia, Moldova and Bulgaria: Dismantling Communist Structures Is Hardly Extremism," *Demokratizatsiya: The Journal of Post-Soviet Democratization* 12, no. 2 (Spring 2004): 311–20.

113. See Imogen Bell et al., eds., *Eastern Europe, Russia and Central Asia 2003*, 3rd edn. (London: Europa Publications, 2002), 281 (which is a short laundry list of Moldova's political parties at the threshold of the twenty-first century); Wolfram Nordsieck, "Parties and Elections in Europe: Moldova," http://www.parties-and-elections.de/moldova2.html and http://www.parties-and-elections.de/moldova.html; "Parliamentary Elections in the Republic of Moldova," http://www.e-democracy.md/en/elections/parliamentary/.

114. In 1999, the Christian democrats voted with the Communists to dismiss the cabinet of Ion Struza and to replace him with the government of Dumitru Braghis, both post-Communists. In 2005, the Christian democrats cast the decisive votes to elect the unreformed Communist Voronin for president. See Vladimir Socor, "Moldova's Political Sea Change," *Eurasia Daily Monitor* 2, no. 70 (April 11, 2005): http://www.jamestown.org/single/?no_cache=1&tx_ttnews%5Btt_news%5D=30241.

115. Most of the current political parties of Moldova are briefly described at http://www.e-democracy.md; and Jerzy Targalski, "Mołdowa: Partie Polityczne," ("Moldova: Political Parties") TMs, no date (2010), 1–15 (a copy in my collection). See also William E. Crowther, "Political Parties," in *Moldova: A Country Study*, ed. Helen Fedor (Washington: GPO for the Library of Congress, 1995), http://countrystudies.us/moldova/33.htm; "Moldova," in *Eastern Europe, Russia, and Central Asia 2003*, ed. Imogen Bell, 3rd edn. (London: Europa Publications, 2002), 280–81; William E. Crowther, "Development of the Moldovan Parliament One Decade after Independence: Slow Going," in *Post-Communist and Post-Soviet Parliaments: The Initial Decade*, ed. Philip Norton and David M. Olson (London, Frank Cass: 2007); Vladimir Socor, "Moldova's Political Landscape on the Eve of General Elections: Part One," *Eurasia Daily Monitor* 6, no. 53 (March 19, 2009), http://www.jamestown.org/single/?no_cache=1&tx_ttnews%5Btt_news%5D=34732; Vladimir Socor, "Moldova's Political Landscape on the Eve of General Elections: Part Two," *Eurasia Daily Monitor* 6, no. 53 (March 19, 2009), http://www.jamestown.org/single/?no_cache=1&tx_ttnews%5Btt_news%5D=34733; Vladimir Socor, "Moldova's Political Landscape on the Eve of General Elections: Part Three," *Eurasia Daily Monitor* 6, no. 54 (March 20, 2009), http://www.jamestown.org/single/?no_cache=1&tx_ttnews%5Btt_news%5D=34737; Vladimir Socor, "Moldova Embarks on Election Campaign in Tension-Filled Atmosphere," *Eurasia Dialy Monitor* 6, no. 119 (June 22, 2009), http://www.jamestown.org/single/?no_cache=1&tx_ttnews%5Btt_news%5D=35156; Vladimir Socor,

"Moldova's Stunted Post-Soviet Transition Resumes after Elections," *Eurasia Daily Monitor* 6, no. 148 (August 3, 2009), http://www.jamestown.org/single/?no_cache=1&tx_ttnews%5Btt_news%5D=35352.

116. On the enduring legacy of the now-defunct Interfront and its former cadres continued service to the Kremlin see, e.g., Victor Soccor, "US Embassy in Moldova Annoits a False 'Freedom Champion' for Bush," *Eurasia Daily Monitor* 2, no. 40 (February 27, 2005), http://www.jamestown.org/single/?no_cache=1&tx_ttnews%5Btt_news%5D=27605.

117. For the party website see http://www.pcrm.md. For the party profile in English see "Party of Communists of Moldova," http://www.parties.e-democracy.md/en/parties/pcrm/. In 2003, the PCRM absorbed the Party of Civic Dignity of Moldova, which had been founded four years before. See "Party of Civic Dignity of Moldova," http://www.parties.e-democracy.md/en/parties/pdcm/. See also Vladimir Socor, "Limited Communist Victory Deepens Deadlock," *Eurasia Daily Monitor* 6, no. 147 (July 31, 2009), http://www.jamestown.org/single/?no_cache=1&tx_ttnews%5Btt_news%5D=35348; Vladimir Socor, "Moldova's Politics Remain Centered on the Communist Party," *Eurasia Daily Monitor* 6, no. 148 (August 3, 2009), http://www.jamestown.org/single/?no_cache=1&tx_ttnews%5Btt_news%5D=35353.

118. Established in 1992, the Russophilic Socialist Party of Moldova enjoyed the support of the unreformed Communists from the outset. It also prospered under the "agrarians" and, in particular, through the cronyism of Lucinschi and, later, former prime minister Dumitru Braghis. In 1994 it entered the parliament in coalition with the Russian minority Yedinstvo. In 1996 the party split into the supporters and opponents of Lucinschi. The latter renamed themselves as the Socialist Action Party (SAP). The former became the Party of Socialists of the Republic of Moldova "Patria-Rodina" (PSRM) in 1997. Neither managed to enter the parliament in 1998. In 2001, the remnant of the SPM within the "Braghis Alliance" electoral platform returned to the legislature. For the party profile in English see "Socialist Party of Moldova," http://www.parties.e-democracy.md/en/parties/psm/. For the multi-ethnic PSRM see its profile in English "Party of Socialists of the Republic of Moldova 'Patria-Rodina," http://www.parties.e-democracy.md/en/parties/psrm/.

119. In 2004 DAPM changed its name to the Agrarian Party of Moldova (APM). For the party profile in English see http://www.parties.e-democracy.md/en/parties/pdam/.

120. The SDPM changed its name to the Social Democratic Party (SDP) in 2000 and five years later it merged with the Party of Social Democracy (PSD) under Dumitru Braghis, who assumed control of the united organization for a while. For the party website see www.psdm.md. For the party profile in English see "Social-Democratic Party of Moldova," http://www.parties.e-democracy.md/en/parties/psdm/. For Braghis's outfit see "Social Democracy Party of Moldova," http://www.parties.e-democracy.md/en/parties/pdsm/.

121. The "post-Christian democrat" Liberal Party experienced a very long period of birth pangs. First, in 2000, the Pan-Romanian National Liberal Party (NLP, banned in 1947, reestablished in 1993, and again refounded in 2006) and the Socio-Political Movement "Order and Justice" (SPMOJ, created in 1998) united to form the Social Liberal Union Force of Moldova (SLUFM). The SLUFM joined the Reform Party in 2001. To capitalize on its "agrarian" component, the RP endeavored to attract peasantist and other related organizations. Accordingly, in 2002, the National Peasant Christian Democratic Party (NPCP, assembled

in 1993) joined with the Party of Rebirth and Reconciliation (PRR, started in 1995) to unify with the Reform Party. It remained an extraparliamentary entity until it created an electoral coalition called Our Moldova Alliance in 2003 and, within it, rebranded itself as the Liberal Party in 2005. See "Liberal Party," http://www.parties.e-democracy.md/en/parties/pl/; http://www.parties. e-democracy.md/en/parties/pr/; and (in Romanian) http://www.pl.md/.

122. Aside from the "agrarian" Liberal Party, the OMA is a fusion of the Alliance of the Independents of Moldova (AIM), the Social Democratic Alliance of Moldova (SDAM), and People's Democratic Party (PDP). For the OMA website see http://www.amn.md. For the coalition profile in English see "'Moldova Noastra' (Our Moldova) Alliance," http://www.parties.e-democracy.md/en/parties/ pamn/. Founded in 1997, the PDP was a socialist and liberal extraparliamentary outfit. See "Democratic Peoples' Party of Moldova," http://www.parties. e-democracy.md/en/parties/pdpm/. As for the SDAM, it originates from the Socio-Political Civic Alliance for Reforms (CAR), which was established in 1997. It changed its name to the Party of Social Democracy "Furnica" (Ant) in 1998. Three years later it rebranded itself again as the SDAM under former post-Communist "agrarian" prime minister Dumitru Braghis (DAPM). In 2002, the SDAM absorbed Vladimir Babii's Socio-Political Movement "Plai Natal" (Motherland). See "Social Democratic Alliance of Moldova," http://www.parties.e-democracy.md/en/parties/asdm/. Assembled in 2001, the AIM consists of some of the former post-Communist "agrarian" rural apparat and mayors of provincial municipalities, including some of the minority Gagauz. See "Independents' Alliance of the Republic of Moldova," http://www.parties.e-democracy. md/en/parties/airm/.

123. As of 2009, the center-left DPM is led by the formerly unreformed Communist defector Marian Lupu. Most of its electorate switched from the Communists. For the party website see http://www.pdm.md. For the party profile in English see "Democratic Party of Moldova," http://www.parties.e-democracy.md/en/ parties/pdm/. In 2010 a substantial part of the Social Democratic Party (SDP) split to join the DPM. See "Moldova: Large Portion of Small Left-Wing Party Migrates to Democrats," Moldova.org, (February 5, 2010), http://politicom. moldova.org/news/moldova-large-portion-of-small-leftwing-party-migrates-to-democrats-205886-eng.html. In 2008, the DPM absorbed the Social Liberal Party (SLP). Espousing socialism and liberalism, the latter was set up in 2001, through the merger of the Christian Democratic League of Women (founded in 1990) and of the National Youth League of Moldova (established in 1991), as an anti-Communist watch dog. In 2002, it united with the Party of Democratic Forces. See "Social-Liberal Party," http://www.parties.e-democracy.md/en/parties/psl/.

124. The CDNP is often referred to in English as the Christian Democratic Popular Party or the Christian Democratic People's Party. It is led by Iurie Roşca, whose pragmatic pro-Communist tactics have led to mass defections from the party. For the party website see http://www.ppcd.md. For the party profile in English see "People's Christian Democratic Party," http://www.parties.e-democracy. md/en/parties/ppcd/.

125. Established in 2007, the Liberal Democratic Party of Moldova is led by Vlad Filat. It touts itself as "center-right" and its ideology as "conservatism." Filat, of course, was in turn a moderate Pan-Romanian, a social democrat, and a liberal (see above). For the party website see http://www.pldm.md/. See also "Partidul Liberal Democrat din Moldova," http://www.e-democracy.md/parties/pldm/.

126. Of course, there has been a number of radical nationalist organizations putting in but a fleeting appearance on Moldova's political scene, e.g., the loud but ephemeral ultra-Pan Romanian National Christian Party (NCP), which invoked its pre-war inspiration of the same name, only to disappear shortly after the elections of 1994.

127. Moldova's NPL is, in essence, a branch of Romania's NPL. Suppressed by the Communists in Romania in 1947, it was refunded after 1989. It appeared in Moldova in 1993; then it went dormant for a while (with its shell co-opted as a fig leaf by the Reform Party between 2001 and 2005); and it resurfaced again autonomously in 2006. It advocates classical liberalism, liberal nationalism, Christian democracy, a reunion with Romania, and a membership in the European Union. For the party website see http://www.pnl.md. For the party profile in English see "National Liberal Party," http://www.parties.e-democracy.md/en/parties/pnl/.

128. Established in 2001, the NRP stems from a number of organizations of war veterans and victims of Communism. First, in 1990, the Association of the Victims of Communist Repression appeared and a year later the Association of Former Political Detainees and Romanian Army Participants of World War II. In 1992, they united to form the Association of the Victims of the Communist Regime and War Veterans of the Romanian Army, which changed its name to the NRP. It is an extraparliamentary entity. For the party profile in English see "National Romanian Party," http://www.parties.e-democracy.md/en/parties/pnr/.

129. The Green party was founded in 1992. For the party profile in English see "Environmental Party of Moldova 'Green Alliance'," http://www.parties.e-democracy.md/en/parties/peavm/.

130. See Vladimir Socor, "Limited Communist Victory Deepens Deadlock," *Eurasia Daily Monitor* 6, no. 147 (July 31, 2009), http://www.jamestown.org/single/?no_cache=1&tx_ttnews%5Btt_news%5D=35348; Vladimir Socor, "Moldova's Politics Remain Centered on the Communist Party," *Eurasia Daily Monitor* 6, no. 148 (August 3, 2009), http://www.jamestown.org/single/?no_cache=1&tx_ttnews%5Btt_news%5D=35353.

131. See Vladimir Socor, "Moldova on the Threshold of Post-Post-Communism," *Eurasia Daily Monitor* 6, no. 165 (September 10, 2009), http://www.jamestown.org/single/?no_cache=1&tx_ttnews%5Btt_news%5D=35473. And see also Vladimir Socor, "Moldova's Stunted Post-Soviet Transition Resumes after Elections," *Eurasia Daily Monitor* 6, no. 148 (August 3, 2009), http://www.jamestown.org/single/?no_cache=1&tx_ttnews%5Btt_news%5D=35352; Vladimir Socor, "Moldova's Post-Communist Government Takes Office Amidst Crisis," *Eurasia Daily Monitor* 6, no. 181 (October 2, 2009), http://www.jamestown.org/single/?no_cache=1&tx_ttnews%5Btt_news%5D=35571.

132. The persistence of post-Communism in Moldova impacts its national security and imperils future ties with the West. For example, former Communist secret policemen should be considered security risk because of their participation in totalitarian crimes and their continued ties to Moscow. However, the current supervisor of free Moldova's secret services, Colonel Gheorghe Mihai, has served uninterrupted in a variety of security posts: first, commencing in 1979, in the MSSR's KGB, and, then, automatically, in Moldova's National Security Ministry, beginning in 1991. He did not even have to change his office, or his underlings. In 2007, Mihai was shifted to the reserves. In 2009, he was however nominated as Director of the "new" Intelligence and Security Service (SIS), replacing Artur Reshetnikov, an ethnic Russian with an even more distinguished career as a

Chekist. Incidentally, the latter continues to be active in politics. A year or so after loosing his post, when a PCRM candidate for parliament, Reshetnikov claimed that he had been kidnapped, injected with psychotropic drugs, beaten severely, and forced to sign a false confession by "unknown perpetrators" who sought dirt on ex-president Voronin. Physicians determined that the injuries were very superficial. See "Georghe Mihai – New Chief of Moldovan Intelligence Agency," Moldova.org, (September 28, 2009), http://politicom.moldova.org/news/gheorghe-mihai-new-chief-of-moldovan-intelligence-agency-203741-eng.html; Vladimir Socor, "Moldova's Post-Communist Government Takes Office Amidst Crisis," *Eurasia Daily Monitor* 6, no. 181 (October 2, 2009), http://www.jamestown.org/single/?no_cache=1&tx_ttnews%5Btt_news%5D=35571; "Artur Reshetnikov from Hospital: They Put a Gun to My Temple and Sought Information Discrediting Vladimir Voronin," All Moldova, (November 23, 2010), http://www.allmoldova.com/en/moldova-news/1249048929.html; "PCRM Accuses Power of Indifference towards Case of Artur Reshetnikov," Moldova Azi, (November 23, 2010), http://moldova.azi.md/en/story/14946; "Artur Reshetnikov Refuses To Be Examined by Specialized Doctor," Moldova Azi, (November 25, 2010), http://moldova.azi.md/en/story/14988.

133. Vasile Botnaru, Paul Hodorogea, Alla Ceapai, "The Post-Soviet Generation Looks to Future in Europe's Poorest Country," *Radio Free Europe/Radio Liberty* (August 18, 2011), http://www.rferl.org/content/post_soviet_generation_looks_to_future_in_moldova_europes_poorest_country/24300987.html.

134. Vladimir Socor, "Moldova on the Threshold of Post-Post-Communism," *Eurasia Daily Monitor* 6, no. 165 (September 10, 2009), http://www.jamestown.org/single/?no_cache=1&tx_ttnews%5Btt_news%5D=35473.

135. Kristen Ghodsee, *Lost in Transition: Ethnographies of Everyday Life after Communism* (Durham, NC: Duke University Press, 2011) has concluded likewise in her case study of Bulgaria, despite her feminist politics and jargon. Her postmodernist remedies to the malady of post-Communism naturally differ from ours.

19

Lifting the "Velvet Curtain": Geopolitics and Foreign Policy in the Intermarium*

After the First World War, the Versailles treaty was imposed on the Germans, whose hands were thus tied. As a result, Germany rebelled and it began acting unilaterally. At the moment, we have a similar situation with Russia. Just because the West won the Cold War did not mean that Russia had to be humiliated like Germany in the wake of the First World War . . . The Russians want only one thing now: revenge. And sooner or later it will happen.[1]

—Aleksandr Dugin

As the ideological division of Europe has disappeared, the cultural division of Europe between Western Christianity, on the one hand, and Orthodox Christianity and Islam, on the other, has reemerged. The most significant dividing line in Europe . . . may well be the eastern boundary of Western Christianity in the year 1500. This line runs along what are now the boundaries between Finland and Russia and between the Baltic states and Russia, cuts through Belarus and Ukraine separating the more Catholic western Ukraine from Orthodox eastern Ukraine, swings westward separating Transylvania from the rest of Romania, and then goes through Yugoslavia almost exactly along the line now separating Croatia and Slovenia from the rest of Yugoslavia. In the Balkans this line, of course, coincides with the historic boundary between the Hapsburg and Ottoman empires. The peoples to the north and west of this line are Protestant or Catholic; they shared the common experiences of European history—feudalism, the Renaissance, the Reformation, the Enlightenment, the French Revolution, the Industrial Revolution; they are generally economically better off than the peoples to the east; and they may now look forward to increasing involvement in a common European economy and to the consolidation of democratic political systems. The peoples to the east and south of this line are Orthodox or Muslim; they historically belonged to the Ottoman or Tsarist empires and were only lightly touched by the shaping events in the rest of Europe; they are generally less advanced economically; they seem much less likely to develop stable democratic political systems. The Velvet Curtain of culture has replaced the Iron Curtain of ideology as the most significant dividing line in Europe. As the events in Yugoslavia show, it is not only a line of difference; it is also at times a line of bloody conflict.[2]

—Samuel Huntington

Wherever the standard of freedom and independence has been or shall be unfurled, there will her [America's] heart, her benediction and her prayers be. But she goes not abroad, in search of monsters to destroy. She is the well-wisher to the freedom and independence of all. She is the champion and vindicator only of her own[3]

—John Quincy Adams, Independence Day, 1821

Throughout numerous crises, a reasonable settlement often seemed well within Russia's reach, much better in fact what ultimately emerged. Yet Russia always preferred the risk of defeat to compromise. . . . Russia on the march rarely exhibited a sense of limits. Thwarted, it nursed its grievances and bided its time for revenge.[4]

—Henry Kissinger

Since the end of the Cold War Western collective security arrangements have been rudderless for the lack of strategic American leadership. Russia has reasserted itself regionally. Germany's *Ostpolitik* serves as a rough blueprint for the European Union's approach to the post-Soviet space. Its denizens, meanwhile, frantically search for security. Thus, geopolitics of the Intermarium is back with a vengeance. It resembles the interwar balance of power system. The difference is one of degree, hypocrisy, and deception. Because political correctness dictates the need to pay lip service to the idea that in the West the nation state has been superseded by supranational structures, the national actors play the geopolitical game in a much less brazen manner than they did before World War II. Multilateralism tends to be the rule. But it also tends to express the will of the most powerful actors, who are apt at coalition building to achieve their goals. Unilateralism is a strict exception, limited usually to the American hegemon and its most powerful competition. Force naturally remains the ultima ratio. Yet, military power has so far been deployed chiefly for swaggering, except in the Balkans and Georgia, where internal and external actors resorted to violence to assert themselves. But most of the time the players rely on non-violent weapons of political warfare: intelligence gathering, perceptions management, propaganda warfare, and economic warfare (e.g., Russia's energy weapon). The objectives remain the same as always: influence and expansion. The geopolitical game has thus become much more sophisticated.

Geopolitics impacts the Intermarium's component parts from within (relations between and among the post-Soviet successor states) and without (relations with the outside world, near and far). The playing field thus extends beyond the narrow confines of the lands between the Baltic and Black Seas. It encompasses, firstly, the geographic area east of the Adriatic Sea; secondly, the European continent; thirdly, the Eurasian land mass; and, fourthly, the global dimension.[5]

Further, global, regional, national, and local geopolitics permeate and inform one another as well as shape the Intermarium's foreign policy. Various powers and entities interact horizontally and vertically in a number of overlapping combinations involving the post-Soviet sphere. Globally, the Intermarium is reduced to a pawn on the chessboard of giants, the United States, Russia, Germany, and China, to borrow Zbigniew Brzezinski's compelling imagery.[6] But it is also the stage of operation of global supranational organizations, like the United Nations (UN), and nongovernmental entities, including charities and organized crime. Regionally, the Intermarium is an area of competition between various federative and pseudofederative associations, including the European Union (EU) and the Commonwealth of Independent States (CIS), as well as smaller entities like the Visegrad Group (V-4) and Organization for Democracy and Economic Development (GUAM).

On the national level, the Intermarium is a scene of *tête-à-tête* interaction between nation states. This concerns its component parts, its immediate neighbors, and any other nation state that has elected to involve itself directly with any of the post-Soviet successor republics, for example, the transactions between Belarus and Ukraine, or Poland and Estonia, or France and Lithuania. At the local level, we chiefly focus on the transborder relationship between neighboring states and their abutting localities, say, between Yampil and Cosăuți areas, in Ukraine and Moldova, respectively.

Geopolitics is back in the Intermarium for the simple reason that the Soviet monolith splintered into a dozen or so independent actors, including former USSR and its erstwhile central-eastern European dependencies. Each of them has exercised a variety of geopolitical options to square best with its national interest. Those geopolitical combinations concern their immediate neighbors, intermediate entities, and distant powers, the United States, in particular. A balance of power system of sorts has emerged. This is the system comprising the angry and the scared. Russia is angry and wants to reassert itself. That scares everyone else, in particular the nations of the post-Soviet zone east of Germany in general, and in the Intermarium, in particular. At the same time, each actor is eager to make a deal with Moscow, separately if necessary, both to safeguard his independence and take advantage of the Russian markets and resources. The Kremlin, meanwhile, would like to translate the fear and needs of others into strategic dominance. Russia hopes to have found a sympathetic ear in Germany, luring it with a prospect of a condominium over the Intermarium buttressed with sweet economic and resource deals. All of that influences and limits everyone's geopolitical thinking. And thus, geopolitics impacts and informs the region's foreign policy.

Can we talk about coordinated foreign policy of the Intermarium as a bloc? Indeed, no. There is, however, a common thread running through the foreign policies in the borderlands for the simple reason that each of the newly liberated nation states would like to remain independent. Thus, they have a similar objective: to maintain their sovereignty. That includes even Belarus. Preserving independence entails establishing security arrangements, which are often couched in economic engagement terms.[7]

Admittedly, a shared goal of keeping free does not necessarily translate into regional solidarity and cooperation. Further, even when formal and informal collaboration and concord between them obtain, each of the nation states in the Intermarium seeks individual guarantees from outside powers, whether Russia, Germany, the EU, or the United States, even at the expense of abandoning various collective security arrangements concluded previously between the former captive nations.

This equally applies not only to the post-USSR successor states but to the rest of Europe's erstwhile Communist countries. There are several reasons for this jarring lack or solidarity. First and foremost, simply, the successor states in the post-Soviet sphere realize their own impotence and, hence, desperately seek protection among the mighty. Second, history dictates that threats to freedom in and around the Intermarium tend to come from two sources: Russia and Germany. Hence, the erstwhile victims are left with limited options. They can appease either Moscow or Berlin, and rarely both; or they can look for an exotic protector, France and Britain in the interwar period, and the EU and the United States currently. However, because of the fresh memories of the Soviet occupation, Germany is now also seen as a desirable defender, in particular, because it dominates the EU, practices democracy, and dazzles with its economic prowess, even though its consistently cozy relationship with Russia makes the former Soviet satellites quite jittery.

Third, there is lack of solidarity in the post-Soviet zone because, in addition to an early modern heritage of harmony, in particular in the Polish-Lithuanian Commonwealth, there is also the legacy of bitter and nasty, if sometimes petty, neighborly feuds. In general, in and around the Intermarium only the Balts tend to get along and stereotype one another in a rather positive way. This phenomenon finds its closest analogy in Hungarian–Polish amity, which, however, unlike with the Balts, functions more on a symbolic and cultural, rather than political and economic, levels. Cultural compatibilities affect other countries as well. The re-emerging Orthodox consciousness and much vaunted Slav solidarity between Ukraine and Belarus seem still of secondary importance in comparison with the post-Soviet reflexes ingrained in customs and culture of these successor states. But such post-Communist affinities are inimical both to the re-emerging national identity and the nation state project.[8] Further, they are also a terribly corrosive influence on the project of the Intermarium. The post-Soviet cultural features render them compatible only with other entities tainted by them, particularly Russia.

Cast narrowly, as the lands between the Baltic and the Black Seas, the Intermarium functions chiefly (or, one could say, merely) as cordon sanitaire *vis-à-vis* the Kremlin. Wedged between Russia and the West, the Intermarium yet fails to impress geopoliticians as a viable bloc capable of standing on its own. It is simply too weak and divided. The nation states comprising the Intermarium fail even to consider a *modicum* of unity for the entire region, much less achieve it. That is mainly because they recoil from the memories of totalitarian unity forced upon them by the Soviet Union. In their mind, regional centralization means loss of independence. Particularist nationalisms likewise militate against regional unification. But neighborly integration where cultural affinities apply may be something else altogether. Consequently, Moldova is inclined toward Romania. The Baltics prefer Scandinavia first and the EU next. Ukraine straddles the fence between Russia and the West, and Belarus leans rather far to the Russian side.

However, from the point of view of the Intermarium's long-term political, economic, social, and cultural viability, it is perhaps more efficacious to conceptualize it as a component part of the post-Communist successor sphere in Europe than as a mere borderland between the West and the East. In other words, on the theoretical level, we could approach the Intermarium's Estonia, Latvia, Lithuania, Belarus, Ukraine, and Moldova, as a geopolitical entity harmonized best with its erstwhile fellow captive nations: Poland, Hungary, Romania, Bulgaria, Macedonia, Albania, Bosnia, Kosovo, Serbia, Montenegro, Croatia, Slavonia, Slovakia, and the Czech Republic.

Not so long ago, when wishing for the liberation of the captive peoples, one never consigned the slaves of the western rim of the USSR to a lesser category of humans than the prisoners of the satellite nations of the Soviet bloc. The liberation of one was predicated on the liberation of all. Why not apply the same rule to collective security of the post-Communist sphere now? Why not conceptualize the Intermarium broadly, including all the post-Communist lands surrounded by the Black, Baltic, and even Adriatic seas? In practice, at the moment, no entity like this exists of course. What does exist, instead, appears provisional, sometimes chaotic, geopolitics in a state of flux. That is shaping a new future, once again, of central and eastern Europe, including the Intermarium.

A Global Game

As mentioned, the geopolitical game plays itself out on several levels: global, regional, national, and local (transborder). At the global level, it is the joust of the giants. In other words, geopolitics at the global level results in foreign policy that reflects primarily the dynamics between the mighty. In this context the concerns of the Intermarium, collectively, and its component parts, individually, are merely a reflection of, and a function of, the strategic games of the global powers among themselves. Thus, at the global level, any talk of partnership with the newly liberated nations is just diplomatic etiquette and contrived coquettishness on the part of the United States, Russia, China, and the EU, in particular Germany. Naturally enough, each of the mighty considers its relationship with the Intermarium through the prism of the interaction with its great power peers and competitors. Global concerns thus condition regional responses even of the American hegemon.

The United States lacks a coherent geopolitical vision and foreign policy in regards to the post-Soviet sphere, including in Europe. America has been temporarily shaken in its hyperpower status by the economic crisis, moral malaise, and a bout of isolationism brought about by foreign wars, Iraq and Afghanistan, in particular. In relation to the post-Communist sphere, including the Intermarium, Washington has descended from the lofty heights of liberation of the 1980s through crisis management and integration of the 1990s to antiterror coalition building of the 2000s and rudderless drifting of the early 2010s.

The most important accomplishment of the United States was its enormous contribution to create the conditions which eventually led to the demise of the USSR. In the early 1990s, as the Soviet Union was imploding, however, the American record became less stellar. Washington's policy oscillated between fearful improvisation to preserve the status quo and avoid global anarchy, at one extreme; and at the other, a shrewd continuation of the anti-Communist offensive intended to destroy the USSR under the guise of fearful improvisation to preserve the status quo and avoid global anarchy. Afterward the mission was accomplished; the United States turned inward, only to re-engage in the world, in particular, in the post-Soviet sphere from the mid-1990s on.[9] This resulted not only in the American intervention in the Balkans, but also NATO expansion into the post-Communist zone. This was arguably the single-most important act as far as preserving freedom in the Intermarium was concerned.[10]

The initial establishment of the Polish, Hungarian, and Czech NATO alliance belt in 1999 eliminated the security vacuum east of Berlin and paved the way for the accession of other post-Communist nations. In 2004, Slovakia, Romania, and Bulgarian joined the military alliance simultaneously with Estonia, Latvia, and Lithuania. Laudably, in the second stage of expansion, NATO did not differentiate between former Soviet satellites and former

Soviet republics. And neither did the EU, which, in 2004, accepted the Baltics, Poland, Slovakia, Slovenia, Hungary, and the Czech Republic (as well as, outside of the post-Soviet space, of course, Malta and Cyprus).

In the Intermarium, the Baltic states were the chief beneficiaries, symbolically accessing NATO and the EU at the same time. Some among the Ukrainian and other post-Soviet elite still hope to acquire the Western protection yet. US assistance has been greatly appreciated. At one point, Ukraine was receiving more American funds than even the top-ranking Egypt, mostly in conjunction with Kyiv's surrender of its nuclear weapons. But most government to government aid tends to strengthen the target state's bureaucrats and politicians, in this instance post-Communist kleptocrats. Their attitude toward the nation's welfare is parasitical to say the least. Many lack the daring and foresight for a geopolitical paradigm shift away from Moscow. Many among the ruling elite are thus not necessary reliable partners for Washington and its allies.[11]

It remains unclear how serious the West's commitment is to defend freedom of the post-Soviet sphere, including the member states in the Intermarium. First, until 2010 NATO had no detailed practical contingency plans to protect the Baltics militarily.[12] Second, the Cold War formula of NATO is widely considered to have lost its utility and an ideological reason to defend others. Third, no viable solution to the alliance's identity crisis has been proposed as the allies have argued either in favor of a continued Transatlantic force or a new pan-European army. In consequence, fourth, NATO is often perceived as rudderless. America has failed to provide appropriate leadership. Its "War on Terror" is very unpopular among the old EU members, while "New Europe" supports the United States mostly hoping for reciprocity in future times of peril. It appears then that for the post-Soviet sphere NATO membership has primarily a symbolic value at the moment. It is an expression of kind wishes, and not a firm commitment. A lack of the sense of security in the post-Soviet zone has mostly to do with the moral malaise currently gripping the United States as well as a host of other issues.[13]

Washington's Intermarium approach is subordinated, chiefly, to its Russia policy. However, the United States differentiates between various component parts of the former Soviet empire, treating the sovereign aspirations of the Baltics as more legitimate than those of Ukraine, Belarus, and Moldova. Everywhere, the White House at the minimum pays lip service to democracy and human rights. Sometimes it follows through with its idealistic priorities even at the pain of antagonizing the Kremlin. At other times, it gives primacy to *Realpolitik* and turns a blind eye to its own freedom-loving rhetorics. All in all, America lacks what John Lenczowski has so aptly described as "full spectrum diplomacy and grand strategy."[14] Despite that, the United States remains a beacon of hope for many of the locals, both governments and the peoples. Without Washington's leadership, it is doubtful the Intermarium and the rest will be able to persevere as a viable entity.

Perhaps America's lackluster performance can be explained by the realization that it is against Russia's wishes and interests to see an intermediate area, particularly one enjoying freedom and prosperity, outside of the tutelage of Moscow. The Kremlin's aim is clear: to reimpose its control over the Intermarium in the short run and over the rest of the post-Communist sphere in a long run.[15] To this end, Russia is the most important economic investor in the region as well as the largest supplier of its energy. Moscow has so far preferred economic control over an outright military occupation. The former translates into overt and covert political influence, sometimes exercised nefariously through the active measures and propaganda techniques of its intelligence agencies, the FSB and the GRU. The success of the Russian imperial reintegration project is quite feasible not only because of the passivity of the United States, but also because of the tacit acquiescence of Europe's greatest power, the newly resurgent Germany. Berlin tends to support Moscow reflexively, for example, in the case of the perennial irritant of Transnistria.[16] The ostensible rationale for such unabashed Russophilia is tactical: to secure a steady flow of energy supplies to Europe, a concern deeply shared by the rest of the western part of the continent. Therefore, Germany enjoys, more often than not, the support of France and Italy in its dealings with the Kremlin. Brussels tends also to defer to Berlin in its relations with Moscow.[17]

It appears that, to a degree, the EU's foreign policy toward Russia is largely an extension of Germany's own *Ostpolitik*.[18] And the latter, in turn, is strategically structured to appease Russia and secure its acquiescence to Berlin's spectacular reemergence as a major power. And the appeasement appears to be at the expense of the lands west of Moscow. Therefore, for the nations of the post-Soviet sphere, including the Intermarium, the attitude of the German Federal Republic (and, by extension, the EU) toward the Kremlin appears eerily to resemble the familiar dynamics of the *Ostpolitik* from its eighteenth-century origins through its nineteenth-century triumphs and the twentieth-century disaster, appeasement, and, finally, success resulting in the German reunification.[19] We may very well be witnessing the customary phase of Russo-German amity necessary for Berlin, on the one hand, to strengthen itself for the mastery of western and central Europe, and, for Moscow, on the other, to dominate eastern Europe and enjoy access to the West's economy and technology. Thus, a potentially dangerous partnership is operational once again.

China's presence in the area poses a different challenge altogether. Not since the Mongol invasion has a far eastern power wielded so much influence in the Intermarium. China may be perceived as an awkward interloper in its geopolitical game in post-Communist Europe. But Beijing certainly is not a novice in the area, as evidenced by its sustained influence in Tirana in the 1960s as well as its curt interference in the USSR's business during the upheavals in Poland and Hungary in 1956. Currently, in the early twenty-first century, China sees the post-Soviet sphere as a doorway both into the EU and Russia. Moscow bristles at this apparent attempt at encirclement, even though Beijing's endeavor is chiefly economic. Having penetrated deep into Central Asia, the Chinese now have invested in Belarus and, to a much lesser extent, Ukraine. They have moved gingerly into the Baltics. Their initial business venture into Poland has been unsuccessful so far, but they have pressed on. They have also established a promising foothold in Hungary and Slovakia. The Chinese still lag far behind the western Europeans, Russians, and even Americans as far as connections, activities, and strategies in the Intermarium are concerned. But the Kremlin has duly taken note of the potentially dangerous interloper from the Middle Kingdom.[20]

Since they also operate at the global level, it is worth considering the geopolitical and foreign policy objectives of the UN and major NGOs. Naturally, whether anyone wants to admit it or not, the transnational organizations take advantage of the protection afforded by the world ordered by the great powers. Even if their agents appear in chaotic, lawless, and war zones, the UN and the NGOs as institutions remain still anchored in the global environment of stability and peace. What is their business in the Intermarium? The realist view would be that the UN is in charge of pious pronouncements about human rights, tolerance, peace, democracy, and stability. They are often couched in anti-American terms reflecting the numerical dominance of Washington's great power competitors and Third World detractors. Yet, in practice, particularly in times of crisis, as reflected by the debacle in the Balkans, for example, the UN's performance oscillates between disastrous and embarrassing. The influence of the UN, and other similar international organizations, is overall quite negligible outside of the secular moral sphere driven by the media. It matters mostly so far as the global powers want to support and fund the UN's endeavors in the area. Even with the US and EU muscle behind them, the impact of the UN and related entities is much greater among democratic and small nations than authoritarian and powerful ones. The concerns expressed by, say, the Organization for Security and Cooperation in Europe (OSCE) will receive a more attentive hearing in Westernized Lithuania, than in post-Communist Belarus. Ukraine and Moldova fall in between, but all look to the OSCE, and other such organizations, for protection against Russia and for solutions to regional problems. Without American muscle, however, the UN, OSCE, and other such entities are helpless.[21]

At the grassroots, the major NGOs seem to be more effective than the UN. The work of such outfits as Caritas Internationalis and Transparency International is much needed, appreciated, and admired in the post-Soviet zone. The NGOs are usually Western-based or at least Western-funded (although Saudi-based Islamic charities have also made an appearance in the Intermarium, the Baltics, for example).[22] At the philosophical level, the charitable non-state agents are intended to foster a successor state's civil society which, in turn, we are promised, results in democracy. Their activities verge from grassroots infrastructural projects, including English-language education, water purification, re-forestation, and microloans, through admirable anticorruption programs to arrogant social engineering performances, often implemented under the guise of human or animal rights. Thus, with some NGOs "gay liberation" trumps restoring national consciousness and "environmental imperative" overshadows economic development. There are also various social and economic endeavors combining all facets of charity work with missionary undertakings. Some of it is traditionally religious, other trendy postmodernist. The former replants faith amidst the ruins of post-Communist nihilism. The latter imposes moral relativism under the post-modernist label of "geopolitics of tolerance." Thus, the agenda of some of the major NGOs may be quite salubrious and laudable or culturally imperialistic and nefarious. It depends how one interprets the goals of the project of "exporting liberal pluralism." In economically depressed areas of post-Communism well-funded NGOs can make an enormous impact, either as unscrupulous social engineers or wholesome agents of reconstruction. They can also be a tool of Western influence in the region, or, more precisely, of Western lobbying groups, as well as cultural preferences and ideological orientations such NGOs are either compatible or connected with.[23]

Like NGOs, organized crime operates globally, regionally, nationally, and locally. Unlike NGOs, its roots are usually local in the Intermarium. The local mafia can be family, clan, neighborhood, ethnicity, or even sports club based. Even if an analogous outfit from another region appears, it usually either forms an alliance with, or integrates itself with, or subcontracts a local criminal group for its services. The activities span the range of gun and drug running, black market operations, racketeering, prostitution, and human trafficking. Usually local criminal gangs simply find victims, recruit perpetrators, or organize the logistics of smuggling in their area. Sometimes more successful thugs branch out nationally and regionally, challenging, or amalgamating with, similar outfits throughout the Intermarium and beyond. The most ambitious and dynamic operate internationally, including in the United States. Some of the gangs affiliate for mercenary or, less frequently, ideological reasons with the terrorist underworld, which had enjoyed connections with the Communist secret services; and it has continued to act in the post-Soviet zone after 1989. The terrorists tend to treat the region as a transit, shopping, and, to a lesser extent, safe house venue. This primarily concerns the Balkans, but also impacts Moldova and the Baltics. Whether lone wolves or affiliated ideological extremists of the Al-Qaeda or the Real IRA, they rely on the criminal underground to a varied extent.[24]

The mafias did rather well under the Soviet system. But they positively thrive in post-Communism and globalism, because of increased levels of corruption, porous borders, and liberal law enforcement. Of course, at the global level, ironically, the gangs and the NGOs take advantage of the system put in place chiefly by the United States and its allies after the implosion of the Soviet Union. Thus, globalization has facilitated both charity and pathology, not to mention a new race for power among the former contenders of the Cold War.

A Regional Game

Some of the mighty state actors at the global dimension, because of their continental geopolitical location, operate also at the regional, national, and local levels in the Intermarium. This concerns primarily Russia and the EU. The former is undoubtedly the most important player of all at all levels. Russia's supremacy can be gauged by all indicators, including cultural, political, military, and, especially, economic. Russian investments, both state and private, formal and informal, are impressive by any standards. They are most extensive in Ukraine, followed by the Baltics and Moldova, and the Russian business interests continue to make important inroads in Belarus.

Further, the Kremlin offers the Intermarium a pseudofederative structure, the CIS.[25] This is a loose association of twelve post-Soviet republics with nebulous political, security, and economic arrangements. Russia, Belarus, Ukraine, and Moldova have nominally belonged to the association since its foundation in December 1991. Others joined later. Only the Baltics have kept away from the start. Nonetheless, the CIS has served as a tool of asserting Moscow's influence and, potentially, it can function as integrative framework for the restoration of the Russian dominion in the Intermarium and elsewhere. Its military alliance counterpart is the Collective Security Treaty Organization (CSTO). Its explicit task is to oppose NATO. CSTO enrolls mostly Central Asian countries under Russia's leadership. The only Intermarium nation to belong is Belarus.[26] Minsk is also formally fused with Moscow. However, aside of an official name, the Union State of Belarus and Russia, it is more of a virtual state entity than a functioning one. Despite the efforts of the Kremlin, there has been polite interest about joining the Union State only from seven other post-Soviet countries, mostly minor, and from Serbia. Nonetheless, the persistence and variety of offers emanating from the Kremlin is indication enough that imperial reintegration remains foremost on Russia's mind.[27]

Toward the same end, Moscow has successfully wooed Minsk and Astana to create a Eurasian customs union. The Kremlin next hopes to ensnare Ukraine in this gigantic Eurasian enterprise that intends to replicate the USSR economically. Kyiv has vacillated for now. According to Russian prime minister Vladimir Putin, "This is truly an event of great interstate and geopolitical significance... For the first time since the collapse of the Soviet Union, the first real step has been made towards restoring natural economic and trade ties in the post-Soviet space."[28] The Kremlin's dream is to create a

Lisbon–Vladivostok economic sphere, and Moscow needs the consent of Berlin for that. So far, it has been forthcoming rather gladly. But this does not translate into the EU's unequivocal support for the project, and more broadly for Russia.

Although its *Ostpolitik* is dominated by Germany, the EU's role in the Intermarium is multifarious and not always congruent with the agenda of Berlin and Moscow. Its influence is both direct and indirect, the latter, in particular, in the sphere of the economy.[29] As far as the post-Soviet zone, Brussels operates both within and without its boundaries. On the one hand, it integrates new member states in a variety of ways, including the Baltics (e.g., by subsidizing culture).[30] On the other hand, the EU reaches out to the rest of the Intermarium through a multitude of venues. It engages all actors, including the most unwilling one, Belarus.[31] Some of the undertakings of Brussels, the push for democracy and human rights, in particular, tend to undermine the *Realpolitik* of the *Ostpolitik* by challenging both Russian influence and post-Communist pathologies in the region. Further, despite the Eurocratic pretensions of its bureaucracy, Brussels lacks a rigid enforcement mechanism to discipline its wayward members who fail to appreciate Berlin's Russophilia (and, hence, disregard the Moscow-centric spirit prevailing at the EU's capital). There are enough contradictions, inconsistencies, and competing visions in the European system for those not smitten by Moscow, in particular, in the post-Soviet sphere, primarily new EU members, to exercise some autonomy in their foreign policy regarding the Intermarium and, by extension, Russia and Germany. The membership of the non-Russophiles in the EU does not have to be an impediment to an alternative foreign policy to that championed by Berlin.[32]

Because of the anti-*Ostpolitik* dissidents, the EU, on the one hand, has extended to the Soviet successor states programs like the "Northern Dimension" or "Eastern Partnership," a tempting promise of cooperation and, tacitly, integration into the European economic and security structures. On the other hand, the EU allows its member nations to play group and individual roles in setting the pace and parameters of multilateral and bilateral cooperation with the post-Communist non-member states in Europe. Both efforts are often complementary. Despite Germany's lead in *Ostpolitik*, other voices are also heard. And, sometimes, action follows.

The eldest entity devoted to the post-Soviet space and its western neighbors is Central European Initiative (CEI). Established in 1989, it now consists of eighteen states.[33] CEI was conceived as a forum of regional cooperation between Hungary, Austria, Italy, and Yugoslavia. It was soon joined by Czechoslovakia (1990) and Poland (1991) and it continued to expand afterward, including the Balkan nations and the Intermarium's Belarus and Ukraine (1995) as well as Moldova (1996). At the regional level, CEI focuses on facilitating economic and social compatibility between the EU and the nations aspiring to membership.

Another such collective effort is the Visegrad Group (V-4), comprising of Poland, Hungary, Slovakia, and the Czech Republic.[34] Initially founded in 1991 to expedite the access of those nations to the EU, the V-4 is intimately involved with the Intermarium. It fosters cultural and economic engagement with the post-Soviet western zone. It further promotes cooperation and security within the region as well as lobbies in Brussels on its behalf. To an extent, it can count on the support of the rest of the "New Europe," including Romania, Bulgaria, and the Baltics. Romania's historic interest in Moldova is particularly palpable, if not always reciprocated.[35] But unlike Warsaw, Bucharest and Sofia are sometimes reluctant to involve themselves in collective initiatives such as GUAM and Eastern Partnership that tend to anger Moscow and Berlin. Instead, Bulgaria and Romania prefer to join other regional associations that are perceived as much more innocuous by the Kremlin.[36]

The Poles, in particular, have been active in the affairs of the successor states of the former USSR. They consider it indispensable to their quest for national security. One of the most important priorities within this framework is Poland's energy security. Dependent on Russia for the bulk of its supplies, Warsaw is forced to accommodate Moscow's whims in the short run but endeavors to find viable alternatives, including in the post-Soviet space, in a long run.[37] The Poles also views stability and prosperity as intrinsically tied to liberty. Therefore, arguably, no one more than Poland has been supportive of democratic reforms and critical of dictatorial abuses, in particular, in Belarus. In 2008, with Sweden's backing, the Poles officially introduced the initiative of engagement with the Intermarium and Caucasus, which led to the establishment of Eastern Partnership a year later.[38] The program reaches out to Ukraine, Moldova, and Belarus (as well as Georgia, Azerbaijan, and Armenia). It has been enthusiastically pushed by Warsaw. Berlin's reaction has been tepid at best. Moscow is positively annoyed. Undeterred, the Poles have attempted to involve the Americans in the project with little luck so far.[39] Although it ostensibly avoids the vexing topic of EU expansion, Eastern Partnership facilitates close cooperation with the Soviet successor states as far as free trade and travel are concerned. It complements a similar initiative, Northern Dimension. Launched in 1997 by the Scandinavians, it tackled similar issues around the Baltic Sea, eventually paving the way to the accession of Estonia, Latvia, and Lithuania to the EU.[40]

Both within the framework of the EU and on their own, the Poles have been dynamically expanding into the former Soviet Union. Poland's relations with the nations of the Intermarium tend to be cordial. There are two exceptions: Belarus and Lithuania. The Polish anger burns bright against the dictatorship in Minsk. The Poles object mainly to the suppression of the Belarusian democratic opposition and Polish minority activists. As for Vilnius, the row is about shoddy treatment accorded since independence to the Polish minority in Lithuania, which Warsaw has commenced to complain about only just recently.[41] Otherwise, the Polish foray into the Intermarium has been quite positive, supportive, and constructive. Even as far as Lithuania and Belarus, Poland has attempted to cooperate with both of them.

Much to Moscow's irritation, the Poles tend to be a part of most regional initiatives and structures. They are particularly active in Lithuania and Ukraine (e.g., purchasing an oil refinery from Vilnius and supporting the Orange Revolution).[42] They are engaged with Belarus (e.g., by backing the democratic opposition).[43] Last but not least, they are also involved in the Caucasus (in conjunction chiefly with the Odessa–Brody pipeline and the Russo-Georgian War of 2008). However, the Poles are vulnerable to the Russian energy carrot-and-stick policies. Sometimes, even they abandon regional solidarity in favor of a better gas and oil deal with the Kremlin. This obtains, in particular, when the post-Communists or left-liberals rule in Warsaw.[44] Further, as far as its activities in the post-Soviet sphere, Poland cannot compete easily with western European economic powerhouses who, after initial reluctance, have now engaged themselves energetically in the area: Germany, France, Italy, Spain, Holland, Sweden, Denmark, Finland, and Great Britain.

Since the early 1990s Germany has become gradually omnipresent in the Intermarium, at first via Poland.[45] Berlin's initial focus was on the USSR's area of Kaliningrad. The swath of land around a formerly East Prussian city of Königsberg (Królewiec) contains an outsized contingent of Russian troops with probably the largest concentration of nuclear weapons anywhere in the world. Wedged between Poland and Lithuania, Kaliningrad constitutes a potentially explosive Russian enclave with serious internal problems and strategic challenges for the West. During the implosion of the Soviet Union, Germany allegedly expressed its interest in reclaiming it. That would have been tantamount to restoring East Prussia. If only for that reason, the enclave should have been awarded to Lithuania. That would have neutralized both Russian and German threats in the area.[46]

After the initial honeymoon period between Berlin and Warsaw, the Germans have pointedly marginalized the Poles in their eastward operations. They even limit their Polish investments largely to the western areas of Poland that used to be the Reich until 1945. The joint German–Polish diplomatic attempt to sway Minsk to moderation in 2010 was a notable exception. Otherwise, Berlin can get visibly annoyed with what it views as Warsaw's busybody meddling in the Intermarium, if not its outright Russophobia. As far as the Soviet successor states, Germany's political and economic activities are spread rather proportionally, albeit apparently favoring Ukraine. But Berlin nearly always defers to Moscow in its regional activities. Germany usually enjoys the support of France and Italy in its Russophile course.

Other EU nations are less averse to stepping on the Kremlin's toes. The Scandinavian countries are thus heavily involved in Estonia, Latvia, and Lithuania. There they directly compete with Russia on the economic field. This is a part of a larger effort of the Scandinavians to integrate the nations of the Baltic Sea coast, including Poland. The latter is also the key to Italian endeavors in the region. Although loudly Russophile, Italy radiates its economic influence from its Polish base eastward, chiefly targeting Ukraine. Meanwhile, France, because of cultural affinities, operates primarily out of Romania, focusing first on Moldova but also casting its net in Ukraine. British and Spanish presence in the Intermarium is more ginger, although both have interests in the Baltics and have branched out quietly southward.

Naturally enough, because they are a part of the EU, the Baltic states have been the most prominent targets of Western economic expansion as well as aid of Brussels and its member states. Yet, because of its size and potential, Ukraine remains the most coveted prize for everyone involved. So far, however, despite an impressive level of Western presence, Russia is the most engaged party in the region: economically and politically. Popular culture is the only field Moscow is positively overshadowed on by the West. Here Hollywood and Madison Avenue still rule supreme. Or at least they appear so. This is particularly the case among the youth. How serious a challenge does the apparent domination by Western popular culture constitute to the Russian designs for control of the Intermarium? It seems that it is quite a negligible factor. The apparent triumph of consumerism, rock 'n' roll, and their derivatives among the young in the Russian Federation has failed to prevent the Kremlin from asserting control over the Russian society. If anything, Western pop culture is simply a vacuous veneer that either weakens the indigenous civilization or fails to alter it significantly and even mobilizes its adherents to extremism (as evidenced by the recent developments in the Muslim world). Blue jeans do not make a democrat. Nor does hip hop. And, incidentally, Russia has already begun to appropriate Western pop culture by plagiarizing it and purveying it in the post-Soviet space, the Intermarium included. Russian rap may be a joke in Harlem, but it is not in Odessa. Neither are pirated American movies dubbed in Russian and sold at a fraction of their original cost. Again, Moscow increasingly wins as the gateway to and interpreter of the West among the Russophones.

Of the non-EU states, except for Russia, involved in the Intermarium at the regional and national level, Turkey is arguably the most significant.[47] As NATO member, its influence is important for the West. Despite its internal identity crisis, Turkey remains intimately interested in the immediate post-Soviet sphere abutting it, including the Intermarium. First, Ankara sees itself as a leader of the Turkic people of the former USSR. Second, it has expressed interest in the fate of former Ottoman possessions in the Caucasus, the Crimea, and the Balkans. Third, it has championed post-Soviet governments which are both secular and Muslim-based. Fourth, it has sought to organize, facilitate, and lead economic and political cooperation among the nations of the Black Sea. Fifth, Turkey is involved in providing an alternative venue for the flow of Central Asian gas and oil to Europe, including the so-called Nabucco pipeline project, thus directly challenging Moscow's monopoly on supplying Europe.[48]

In congruence with such considerations, the Turks have supported the Crimean Tartars in their plight against the Ukrainians and Russians as well as the Gagauz *contra* the Moldovans (and the Pomaks versus Bulgarians). Turkey has further backed Azerbaijan over Armenia; it has supported Georgia as an energy-transit nation (e.g., Baku–Tbilisi–Ceyhan pipeline), but it has opposed Kyiv's reversal of the Odessa–Brody pipeline which would sideline Ankara.[49] Obviously, energy policy is of paramount importance to Turkey. However, Ankara also pays attention to such issues as the plight of the Turkish and Muslim minority in Moldova, Ukraine (Crimea), and Bulgaria; Middle Eastern drug smuggling through Romania; human trafficking through the Balkans into the EU; and terrorist activities in the region.[50]

To keep an eye on the developments in the post-Soviet zone, Turkey maintains observer status with the Organization for Democracy and Economic Development (GUAM).[51] It comprises of the southern Intermarium's Ukraine and Moldova as well as the Caucasus' Georgia and Azerbaijan. Denounced by Moscow as an arm of American influence, the organization is a rare example of constructive cooperation among the successor states. It concerns economic, political, and even military spheres. Its efficiency and efficacy reflect, naturally, domestic political developments. For example, following the Orange Revolution, Ukraine tended to disregard Moscow more readily in its relations with the other partners in GUAM for a few years. Outside of that structure, Ukraine and Moldova are reduced to dealing with regional issues through either bilateral means or the Kremlin-dominated CIS.

A National Game

Bilateral and trilateral relations between the countries of the Intermarium focus primarily on three important areas: mopping up the Soviet legacy, dealing with Russia, and handling the West, the EU and the United States, in particular. The main bones of contention between any Soviet successor state concern effecting border delineation, expediting transborder trade, harmonizing infrastructural projects, and facilitating economic cooperation. Most of the problems can be traced back to the recent Communist past, but some stem from the reconceptualization of the successor countries as independent nation states. In the Intermarium, the support for and opposition against economic and political reforms often run along the ethnic lines. The economic assumptions of the Soviet times failed to translate successfully into economic realities of freedom. Assets turned into liabilities, gargantuan steel industries and single ware enterprises, in particular.[52] At times the infrastructural projects of one country tended to ignore their lack of compatibility with the options offered by the neighboring nations, including, say, roads to nowhere in the border areas. Solutions to such problems are often difficult when there is no good will and understanding. Belarus, of course, is the least cooperative toward most of its neighbors. For example, it took the parliament in Minsk twelve years to consider ratifying a border delineation agreement signed with Kyiv back in 1997. Ukraine and Moldova continue to work out minor, if irritating, issues.[53] The Baltics have been able to compromise best among themselves because of cultural affinities, pre-existing legal and infrastructural arrangements stemming from interwar-independent statehood, and common membership in the EU.

As far as the Intermarium's relations with Russia, there is a common fear but no united policy vis-à-vis Moscow. The fear has been greatly compounded by the Russian invasion of Georgia in August 2008.[54] The Kremlin's aggression has thus strengthened the conventional assumption that the greater the integration of the area into the EU and other Western economic and security structures, the safer the post-Soviet successor states will be.[55] For example, Estonia's highly injudicious decision in 2011 to enter the eurozone when the EU's currency remained gripped by an acute crisis can chiefly be explained by the desire to preserve Tallinn's independence from Moscow.[56] Like in the interwar period, also now Estonia is hardly viable on its own from a strictly economic point of view. But the Estonians prefer to sit free on the periphery of the West, than become subjugated to "enjoy" the alleged benefits of Russia's enormous market.

At least the Estonians and other Balts no longer have the dubious pleasure of hosting Russian Federation troops on their soil. This sordid legacy of the USSR is just fine with Belarus. Minsk permits rent-free two Russian military base outside of Baranovichi and Vileyka. However, lately president Oleksandr Lukashenka would like to profit from them, preferably through preferential energy deals. Ukraine oscillates between attempting to accommodate the Russian armed forces and to get rid of them. This concerns, in particular, Moscow's Black Sea Fleet and its base at Sevastopol. Ultimately, Ukraine's continued consent to allow Moscow to occupy the base for the next twenty-five years has earned Kyiv a hefty 30 percent discount on energy prices. Moldova simply wants the Russian units out of its Transnistrian territory. But Chişinău lacks any leverage. Hence, Moscow does as it pleases without really having to resort to the energy carrot in the Moldovan case. Instead, it consistently humiliates Chişinău.[57]

For the obvious reason of disparity of strength, the Kremlin dictates the political discourse in the Intermarium. On the positive side, at least from a short-term perspective, the Russian Federation has greatly encouraged transborder trade and traffic in its eastern rim. In fact, there are virtually no border controls between Russia, on the one hand, and Ukraine, Belarus, and Moldova, on the other. Anyone is free to come and go as one pleases. It allows not only for easier economic expansion of Russian businesses westward, but also facilitates migrations of the denizens of the Intermarium in search of work eastward. Some citizens of Ukraine, Belarus, and Moldova feel more comfortable working and living in the post-Soviet sphere, Russia included, than in the West. It appears culturally and linguistically familiar, even if the use of the Russian language declines at home.[58] And Russia welcomes the migrants. Much vaunted pan-Slav solidarity may be a joke to a Pole and may not translate automatically into political cooperation between Minsk, Kyiv, and Moscow. But many Ukrainians and Belarusians at the grassroots, in the east of those nations, in particular, believe that their common Slavic roots do reinforce their common post-Soviet affinities. Thus, open borders in the east of the Intermarium facilitate greatly the policy of its creeping economic, social, and cultural reintegration into Russia, even if elite nationalism of the leadership of the Soviet successor states serves as a tentative counterweight.[59]

In distinction, the EU's short-sighted policy of barring access to the non-members from the Intermarium reinforces only the message of Moscow's attractiveness to many in the post-Communist nations.[60] It also undermines economic, social, and cultural exchanges at the local level as evidenced by the virtual collapse of transborder economies and trade in western Moldova and eastern Romania; western Ukraine and the abutting eastern Slovakia, eastern Hungary, and south-eastern Poland; in the Brest (Brześć) and Białystok regions on the Belarus–Polish border; and the Polish–Russian–Lithuanian zone surrounding Kaliningrad. There are hopeful signs that at least the Poles will prevail upon Brussels to be able to restore some local traffic with the Russian enclave. However, free trade with eastern and southern Intermarium is out of the question at the moment. Smuggling obtains, but it cannot substitute for free exchange of goods. Lack of free trade and movement benefits the Kremlin.

Meanwhile, Moscow has shored up its position regionally in two other important ways. It skillfully wields the stick of its energy policy externally and Russian minorities internally in bilateral negotiations with the successor states. We have mentioned minority issues earlier and shall deal with them more fully later.[61] For now suffice it to say that only in Belarus the Russian minority is considered virtually not to be a problem. Much of the country is so thoroughly Sovietized and Russified that any Muscovite can feel at home there. Minsk views this as strength, protecting it from Western influences and securing Moscow's support and economic assistance. Flaunting its post-Soviet cultural compatibility, Belarus has derived tangible benefits from such arrangements as a customs union with Russia (and Kazakhstan) and the membership in the Union State. The apparent lack of a Russian minority problem does not guarantee gas and oil deliveries to Minsk, though, but it makes the relations with the powerful eastern neighbor more congenial.[62]

Elsewhere the Russian minorities have been considered a destabilizing factor. Some view them as the Kremlin's Trojan horse in the successor states. In Ukraine it is a threat to the very integrity of the state as the eastern part of the realm is very Russian and Russified. Consequently, the Ukrainian polity tends to vote along the east-west cultural–geographic divide.[63] Further, national divisions are exacerbated by Moscow's routine meddling, including by its "political technologists" who are routinely unleashed during the elections in Ukraine and elsewhere in the "near abroad."[64] In Moldova the Russian minority parties have been an important factor on the political scene, capable of breaking or making a governmental coalition. The local Russians facilitate economic transactions, which entrench Russian business influence, including the pathological underworld of the mafia. Sometimes there appears to be an open collusion between Moldova's Russian minority and the Kremlin, as during the elections of 2005.[65]

Likewise in the Baltics the Russian minority parties occupy a prominent perch on the political and social scene. Additionally, they can count on an unreserved support of the EU, the United States, and Western NGOs, which have been quick to amplify real and alleged discrimination of the Russians by the majority Estonians, Latvians, and Lithuanians. As a result, fewer ethnic Russians depart the Baltics for the Russian Federation than is the case among the member nations of the CIS.[66] Amazingly, the West is much less strident toward Minsk and Kyiv and their minority issues, the local Poles, in particular. Of course, the apparent contumaciousness of the West in championing the rights of the minorities magically recedes when it concerns the Russian Federation, in particular, when the EU and others solicit the Kremlin's good will as far as the energy issue.

The energy weapon is a serious tool to whip the Intermarium into obedience. Both Kyiv and Minsk have felt Moscow's gas and oil lash most acutely.[67] But it has also been deployed periodically against others, including both in the former satellites and western Europe. The Kremlin's ire can be triggered off not only by the Ukrainian and Belarusian refusal to pay fair market prices for energy delivered, but also by such apparently trivial issues as the sale of an oil refinery in Lithuania to Poland. Or perhaps it was not trivial at all. Moscow strives to control the entire process of energy marketing: the raw material, the venues of its transport, the means to process it, and the ways of selling it throughout the post-Soviet zone. No one should stand in its way.

Whereas energy and Russian minority issues remain permanent problems in the Intermarium, there are also several local irritants. For example, at the Kremlin's refusal, Estonia's border with Russia remains symptomatically not delineated. The problem of Transnistria is a much more serious issue. The secessionists have prevailed against the central government. For Moldova it means a de facto loss of its national territory. Here the Kremlin has successfully played the role of the champion of the Russian and Russian-speaking minority to achieve an outcome that Moscow desired: a stalemate. For now, Transnistria is a de facto enclave of Russia, something similar to Kaliningrad, wedged between Ukraine and Moldova and armed to the teeth. Even the involvement of the US-led OSCE failed to produce a solution. Chişinău's latest requests for NATO to remove the Russian army from Transnistria predictably fell on deaf ears.[68]

One fears that this particular outcome portends a worrisome future for the Intermarium. The Kremlin perseveres patiently and achieves its objectives one by one, while the successor states lose their independence gradually, and the West watches impotently and objects piously afterward. If this sounds far fetched, we need only to recall that in nearly every single instance of conflict between Russia and Ukraine the West has tended to appease Moscow, including stripping Kyiv of its nuclear arsenal and refusing to expand NATO further east.[69] Ukraine is the ultimate prize that Russia covets in the area. On the other hand, the Ukrainian elites have done little to act in concert either with other Intermarium states or among themselves in critical times, as evidenced by their inability to respond coherently to the Russian invasion of Georgia in August 2008.[70]

A Federation?

Until the Intermarium, nay, the entire post-Soviet sphere in Europe, learns how to work in solidarity together, its perspectives for the future are rather bleak. No successor state can stand up to Moscow successfully on its own. Without close cooperation they will be overcome sooner or later. Therefore it is also obvious that dismantling the EU to restore the Mount Pelerin Society's vision of free trade and open borders without supranational bureaucracy, as enticing as it may sound, would not solve the national and regional security problem of the Intermarium.

What to do? Why not champion "a federal alternative to the European Union," as Jonathan Levy does?[71] How to go about it? One idea would be to establish lateral federative structures that double the EU and the CIS without, however, initially at least, abandoning those supranational entities. Let us call the process a creeping federalization from within and without. In essence, it can parallel the endeavor behind the EU expansion. There would be five batches of nations involved: central and southern Intermarium, the Baltic states, the Visegrad Four, eastern Balkans, and western Balkans. Altogether twenty nation states would participate: Estonia, Latvia, and Lithuania; Belarus, Ukraine, and Moldova; Romania and Bulgaria; Macedonia, Kosovo, Albania, Serbia, Bosnia-Herzegovina, Montenegro, Croatia, and Slovenia; Poland, Hungary, Slovakia, and the Czech Republic. The process would graduate from local to national and regional. It would require a multitude of bilateral, trilateral, and multilateral agreements between the Black, Baltic, and Adriatic seas. The process would commence at the lowest rung with the most minute arrangements, regarding trade, transportation, and such. Mutually beneficial economic exchange would be the key to the project's success. That means as few government regulations as possible.

First, at the local level, there should be transborder engagement between each participant. Open borders for local traffic should be the rule. EU-member nations already have that arrangement between themselves, and so do the CIS participants. Now, the transborder Belarusian citizens should be permitted to enter the Baltics and Poland, while the local Ukrainians should be allowed to cross into Slovakia, Hungary, and Romania at will. And vice versa. This should not be difficult. There are already such solutions favoring the local communities hugging the border between Poland and Ukraine, for instance. Kaliningrad should be brought promptly into the local travel and trade arrangements, too, but no more unless it becomes autonomous or independent from Moscow, which should be encouraged, of course. After a while, the system ought to be extended to apply bilaterally between neighboring post-Soviet sphere nation states to include all citizens, and not just the transborder local denizens.

As the next step, Belarus, Ukraine, and Moldova would have to undertake a bilateral and trilateral integration among themselves.[72] They would have to coordinate their systems at a level compatible with Lithuania, Latvia, and Estonia.[73] At the same time, each nation of the first trio would execute bilateral agreements with each nation of the other batch.[74] Next, the nations of both federations in the Intermarium would commence a mutual integration process, leading the first trio to abandon the CIS gradually.[75] Simultaneously, a similar multistep process would be executed between Ukraine and Moldova, on the one hand, and Romania and Bulgaria, on the other. The Visegrad Four would follow the same pattern, likewise engaging with its immediate neighbors, as well as the Balkan states without, however, leaving the EU.[76] The "New Europe" nation-members of the EU would serve as an anchor in the process. The Visegrad Four would be the pivot. Around it, the eastern Balkan states would integrate with the western ones and pull them into the EU; and then the Baltic states would accomplish the same with central and southern Intermarium, which would next harmonize with the Balkans and the Visegrad Four. Sitting at the heart of the operation, the V-4 would stabilize the entire enterprise.[77]

Admittedly, this is a complex operation.[78] Some may even suspect deception here. But why? If the EU is a project in the making and no one can really predict the outcome of the integration process and the shape the system will take, then one should not worry about the improvisation attendant to constructing a parallel regional federation in the Intermarium and the rest of Central and Eastern Europe. Admittedly, the makers of the lateral federation would have to be flexible as far as the EU law is concerned. However, that would just be emulating other member states, Italy in particular, which is quite adept at selecting which EU regulations to enforce and to what extent. This will be nothing new then for the Eurocracy. Further, according to Renata Juzikiene, Lithuania and Poland have already been dealing with such challenges by obfuscating laws, and asserting the primacy of their own constitutional principles routinely. Fortunately, Brussels is so mired in bureaucracy that at this stage it cannot possibly tackle a myriad cases of transborder crossings from the Intermarium. Moreover, it has so far lacked a sufficient enforcement mechanism to compel the "New Europe" to obey everything the EU center contrives.[79] Also, who says that all ideas about local, national, and regional integration should come from Brussels?

Thus, there is no deception, just imaginative gaming of the system all around. Perhaps it is then most judicious, and efficacious, first to pull the Intermarium along with the rest of central and eastern Europe as well as the rest of the southeastern Europe, into the EU and NATO, and only then to begin to construct a separate de facto bloc of the post-Communist nations within the pre-existing structures. That is what has already occurred in Europe to a certain extent. And that may augur well for the United States, if Washington assumes a leadership role in the process. The nations of "New Europe" tend to be more pro-American. They tend to cooperate with Great Britain for the most part in the trans-Atlanticist project. However, the affinity for the United States, which stems from the legacy of the Cold War and gratitude for liberation, should not be assumed in perpetuity, in particular, in light of an absence of any strategic vision on the part of Washington and consistency of US foreign policy.

To harmonize the Intermarium with its national interest, Washington must master geopolitical realities at the global, regional, national, and local levels. If it decides that it has no business in Europe, it should promptly withdraw, or limit its involvement to Great Britain, for otherwise it just dispenses false hope to the scared and downtrodden. But if its stated goals of supporting freedom and democracy are not just rhetorical gimmicks, the United States ought to prioritize its objectives accordingly. It should pick its friends accordingly. Should it stick with an increasingly socialistic and post-modernist western Europe, which is mired in nihilism and anti-Americanism? Or should it embrace increasingly revanchist Russia? Or, perhaps, should it support the people most compatible with the American ideal, most notably the Poles and their neighbors to the east, as Edwin Dyga has persuasively argued?[80]

If it bets on the post-Soviet sphere, including the Intermarium, America should become intimately aware of the internal developments there. There is a potentially dangerous political and cultural realignment on the way in central and eastern Europe, including the Intermarium. Whereas right-wing and conservative orientations tend to remain rather sympathetic to the United States and its objectives, left-wing and liberal parties tend to be notably less so. The latter, whether in or out of the EU, have embraced fashionable western European anti-Americanism. In some instances it is simply an updated version of old-style Soviet Yankee bashing. These trends will continue to mount, exacerbated by the Intermarium's heavily post-Communist politics and culture. That is the case even in the Baltics. Paradoxically, Estonia, Latvia, and Lithuania's membership in the EU has helped to conserve post-Communist pathologies by refusing to eradicate them through vigorous de-Communization and de-KGBzation. And anti-Americanism remains one of the strongest features of post-Sovietism. Here, indeed, a convergence occurred with western European leftist America-bashing.

Washington should observe further that, outside of the Baltics, Brussels has played a rather ambiguous role in the region. First, its regulations hamper travel and trade, having greatly constrained the freedom of movement for all nonmember nations east of Poland. Second, the EU tends to prefer to deal chiefly with Russia, rather than Ukraine and Belarus, thus strengthening the Kremlin's hand in the region. Third, the EU's social and economic system relies on etatism and its radical counter-culture and political correctness attacks Western tradition, and that the post-Soviets in the Intermarium find quite congenial and compatible with the preferred order of their own.

Last but not least, the United States should take a long look at itself. The most charitable description would be that both previous and current administrations have been wedded to Moscow-centrism and have ignored the region, treating it traditionally as subordinate to the White House's Russian policy. Should Russia become more assertive, Washington will improvise for lack of strategic thinking. This will be likewise the case when the United States needs some kind of assistance when challenged by either Russia or the EU. However, America may no longer take for granted the support of its foreign policy by the nations of the post-Soviet sphere unless Washington helps create a federative entity in the Intermarium and its environs in whose interest it would be to support the United States. In essence, promoting a pro-American bloc in the middle of Europe, either to complement or counterbalance the increasingly anti-American western Europe, would be indispensable to return the US influence to the old continent.[81]

Does this sound like a fantasy? Admittedly, to accomplish this, a great miracle is needed. But it is not impossible. So long as there is no war, a creeping federalization is feasible. It all depends on Russia's reaction, Berlin's attitude, and America's leadership. As for geopolitics, if the United States leads, it can count on the nations of the Intermarium. Otherwise, they stand to lose everything. Moreover, the British will support a combination that restores the mechanism of the old balance of power system. London can immediately recognize the utility of siding with a weaker party so no hegemon would arise on the continent. The Intermarium federation would be the weaker party.

And there is, of course, a historical precedent for the project. The American-led undertaking can draw on a rich legacy of federative theory and practice, starting with the Polish-Lithuanian Commonwealth of the early modern period. In more recent times, liberation and federation have had a long and illustrious pedigree: From the nineteenth-century Romantics and their slogan "For Our and Your Freedom" vowing to smash "Russia—the prison of nations"; through the interwar Promethean movement[82] to free the Soviet Union's captive nations effort; up to the wartime and postwar plans of the Central and Eastern European federation, based upon a Polish-Czechoslovak union.[83] Most of such ideas emanated from the Poles. There are still traces of such thinking in Poland's support of Ukraine's Orange Revolution in 2004 and of Georgia's integrity in the wake of the Russian invasion in 2008. But even Warsaw falls well short of calling for an association of central and eastern Europe; instead, it advocates the integration of the Intermarium and other rim nations as far afield as the Caucasus, Georgia in particular, into the Western economic and military security structures, notably the EU and NATO. Without American leadership, support, and assistance, however, all this is an empty talk, including the pious wringing of the hands over the retreat of freedom and democracy in the post-Soviet sphere in the last decade.[84]

Ultimately, the question is: Should the Intermarium be a periphery of the EU and Russia? Should it be the EU's buffer or Russia's? Or a playground for the mighty? Or should it become a cohesive unit, a piece of a larger puzzle fitting both in the West and the East on its own terms? Should it become a crucial and hitherto missing element of the balance of power in Europe? Should it serve as a pivot of regional stability? Why not a federation then? After all, the Baltic states have agreed to surrender a chunk of their independence to enter one: the EU. And because the people of Estonia, Latvia, and Lithuania have the most developed sense of national consciousness of anyone in the Intermarium, it is plain then that nationalism is not a major obstacle to participate in a federation. What is then?

There are several factors militating against a federation. It is, first, the lack of will, imagination, and audacity on the part of the post-Communist elites and their allies to accomplish such a great project. Hence, they have followed the path of least resistance by submitting to the EU, or aspiring to. Also, there is a realization that at the moment, because they lack reliable allies and nuclear weapons, the locals cannot defend themselves against any outside power, Russia, in particular. A federation of the Intermarium and neighboring former Communist states would be a direct challenge to Moscow and, possibly even, a casus belli. And no one sane wants war.

Next, the Soviet successor states fear that one of the larger local nations, Ukraine or Poland, may become dominant and subjugate the rest. Therefore, Brussels as a federative center is preferable over, say, Kyiv, because it is perceived as remote, nebulous, democratic, prosperous, nonviolent, and postmodernist, hence nonnationalist. This is the curious case of the Western devil one does not know being preferable to the Eastern one which is familiar, a reversal of intuitive choices. For most of the people of the Intermarium, the abstract EU lacks any association with what was the staple of one's experience in the twentieth century and earlier: violence and terror. Only if tied to

Berlin can Brussels appear menacing (except for the Baltics whose historical experience perhaps dictates a preference for Germany over Russia).[85] Last but not least, the elites and the people of the Intermarium have not yet agreed on a universal dimension that would bind them together to execute the federalist project. They have not discovered yet a cause greater than themselves worth dying for. What would a human being defend to the death? One thing for sure: No one is ready to die for the euro. It is conceivable, however, for one to fight for freedom together with other human beings who, although not the same ethnically, perceive the value of freedom in the same way as indispensable to the common weal. No one in the Intermarium is yet ready to conceptualize freedom as a common good, stemming from common roots, universal to all. In other words, the denizens of the post-Soviet zone have not yet come to grips with the idea and reality of ethno-cultural plurality in their midst.[86] They have not learned quite yet how to make it compatible with their newly formed, or re-established, nation states. Are nation states commodious enough for such plurality? Perhaps they are for now. But what's next? To consider this, we shall therefore look at the majorities and the minorities in the Intermarium.

Notes

*   A version of this chapter has been published in Great Britain as Marek Jan Chodakiewicz, "The West's overshadowed borderlands," *Quarterly Review: Culture & Current Affairs* 12, no. 1 (Spring 2012): 9–26.
1.   "Rosjanie chcą jedynie rewanżu: Rozmowa z Aleksandrem Duginem," in Filip Memches, *Słudzy i wrogowie Imperium: Rosyjskie rozmowy o końcu historii (Servants and Enemies of the Empire: Russian Conversations about the End of History)* (Kraków: Dziennik-Arcana, 2009), 229.
2.   Samuel P. Huntington, "The Clash of Civilizations?" *Foreign Affairs* 72, no. 3 (Summer 1993): 22–28.
3.   John Quincy Adams, Address of July 4, 1821, in *John Quincy Adams and American Continental Empire*, ed. Walter LaFeber (Chicago, IL: Times Books, 1965), 45.
4.   Henry Kissinger, *Diplomacy* (New York: Simon & Schuster, 1994), 172–73.
5.   For some geopolitical observations on the Intermarium see Marek Jan Chodakiewicz, "Geopolityka Intermarium," *Tygodnik Solidarność* (July 15, 2011); Marek Jan Chodakiewicz, "Szachownica," ("The Chessboard") *Tygodnik Solidarność* (October 29, 2010); Oliver Schmidtke and Serhy Yekelchyk, *Europe's Last Frontier? Belarus, Moldova, and Ukraine between Russia and the European Union* (New York: Palgrave Macmillan, 2008); Susanne Michele Birgerson, *After the Breakup of a Multi-Ethnic Empire: Russia, Successor States, and Eurasian Security* (Westport, CT: Praeger/Greenwood, 2002); Jerzy Kłoczowski, ed., *East-Central Europe's Position within Europe: Between East and West* (Lublin: Instytut Europy Środkowo-Wschodniej [East-Central European Institute], 2004); "The Western States," *Russia and the Independent States*, ed. Daniel C. Diller (Washington, DC: Congressional Quarterly, 1993), 275–94; Wojciech Materski, "Eastern Poland," in *Contested Territory: Border Disputes at the Edge of the Former Soviet Empire*, ed. Tuomas Forsberg (Aldershot: Elgar, 1995), 143–55; Lynn M. Tesser, "The Geopolitics of Tolerance: Minority Rights under

EU Expansion in East-Central Europe," *East European Politics and Societies* 17, no. 3 (Summer 2003): 483–532; Volodymyr Polokhalo, ed., *The Political Analysis of Postcommunism: Understanding Postcommunist Ukraine* (College Station, TX: Texas A&M University Press, 1997), in particular the following essays: Oleksandr Dergachov, "The New Geopolitical Situation after the Fall of Communism," (243–64), Volodymyr Sidenko, "Geoeconomic Problems Facing the Postcommunist States," (285–300), James Mace, "Geopolitical Implications of Ethnopolitics," (301–20), Yevhen Pashchenko, "The Realities and Logic of Myth in Inter-Slavic Relations," (321–32), and Sherman W. Garnett, "Ukrainian-Russian Relations and Western Policy," (333–48); George Friedman, "Geopolitical Journey with George Friedman," http://www.stratfor.com/theme/special_series_geopolitical_journey_george_friedman, and consisting of eight parts: "Part 1: The Traveler," "Part 2: Borderlands," "Part 3: Rumania," "Part 4: Moldova," "Part 5: Turkey," "Part 6: Ukraine," "Part 7: Poland," "Part 8: Returning Home." (Also accessible at http://www.stratfor.com/node/175486/archive). See further Timothy Snyder, *The Reconstruction of Nations: Poland, Ukraine, Lithuania, Belarus, 1569–1999* (New Haven, CT and London: Yale University Press, 2003), 232–93, which, however, eulogizes the pivotal role of Poland's post-Communist and liberal elites in the Intermarium's re-emergence and reintegration with the West; and the following two essays in Daniel Hamilton and Gerhard Mangott, eds., *The New Eastern Europe: Ukraine, Belarus, Moldova* (Washington, DC: Center for Transatlantic Relations, 2007): Angela Stent, "The Lands in between: The New Eastern Europe in the Twenty-First Century," (1–24) and Gerhard Mangott, "Deconstructing a Region," (261–86), http://transatlantic.sais-jhu.edu/bin/o/y/new_eastern_europe_text.pdf. For the Intermarium as a central-eastern European federation see Tadeusz Marczak interviewed by Jarosław Kozakowski, "Niezrealizowana koncepcja Międzymorza," ("The Unfulfilled Idea of the Intermarium") KlubyPatriotyczne.pl, no date (2010), http://www.klubypatriotyczne.pl/index.php?option=com_content&view=article&id=467:niezrealizowana-koncepcja-midzymorza&catid=22:aktualnoci. On Europe's geostrategic influence see an informative essay by William Anthony Hay, "Geopolitics of Europe," *Orbis* (Spring 2003), http://www.fpri.org/orbis/4702/hay.geopoliticseurope.html. On the geopolitical impact of Eurasia see Alexandros Petersen, *The World Island: Eurasian Politics and the Fate of the West* (Santa Barbara, CA: Praeger, 2011). More broadly, on geopolitics, see Colin S. Gray and Geoffrey Sloan, eds., *Geopolitics: Geography and Strategy* (London and Portland, OR: Frank Cass, 1999); Gearóid Ó Tuathail, Simon Dalby, and Paul Routledge, eds., *The Geopolitics Reader*, 2nd edn. (London and New York: Routledge, 2006), which is, as far as editorializing, a leftist exercise in deconstruction and postmodernism in geopolitics (self-described "critical geopolitics"). Otherwise, the textbook contains some useful primary sources.

6. See Zbigniew Brzezinski, *The Grand Chessboard: American Primacy and Its Geostrategic Imperatives* (New York: BasicBooks, 1997). Considering Transnistria, Abkhazia, Nagorno Karabakh, and South Ossetia, an American scholar has noted that whereas conflict in the post-Soviet sphere is generated and maintained locally, its solution can be imposed only by the global powers. See William H. Hill, "Reflections on Negotiation and Mediation: The Frozen Conflicts and European Security," *Demokratizatsiya: The Journal of Post-Soviet Democratization* 18, no. 3 (Summer 2010): 219–27.

7. For the initial stage see Karen Dawisha and Bruce Parrot, *Russia and the New States of Eurasia: The Politics of Upheaval* (Cambridge: Cambridge University

Press, 1994); Mark Webber, *The International Politics of Russia and the Successor States* (Manchester: Manchester University Press, 1996).

8. See José Casanova, "Ethno-Linguistic and Religious Pluralism and Democratic Construction in Ukraine," in *Post-Soviet Political Order: Conflict and State Building*, ed. Barnett R. Rubin and Jack Snyder (London: Routledge, 1998), 81–103; Ilya Prizel, *National Identity and Foreign Policy: Nationalism and Leadership in Poland, Russia, and Ukraine* (Cambridge: Cambridge University Press, 1998); Rich Fawn, ed., *Ideology and National Identity in Post-Communist Foreign Policies* (London: Frank Cass, 2004); David D. Laitin, *Identity in Formation: The Russian-Speaking Populations in the Near Abroad* (Ithaca, NY: Cornell University Press, 1998); Mordechai Altshuler, "Some Soviet and Post-Soviet National and Linguistic Problems in the Slavic Republics (States): Russia, Ukraine, Belarus" in *Quest for Models of Coexistence: National and Ethnic Dimensions of Changes in the Slavic Eurasian World*, ed. Kōichi Inoue and Tomohiko Uyama (Sapporo: Slavic Research Center, Hokkaido University: 1998), 111–132, also posted at http://src-h.slav.hokudai.ac.jp/sympo/97summer/alt.html; Volodymyr Polokhalo, ed., *The Political Analysis of Postcommunism: Understanding Postcommunist Ukraine* (College Station, TX: Texas A&M University Press, 1997), in particular: James Mace, "Geopolitical Implications of Ethnopolitics," (301–20), and Yevhen Pashchenko, "The Realities and Logic of Myth in Inter-Slavic Relations," (321–32); Ray Taras, "Redefining National Identity after Communism: A Preliminary Comparison of Ukraine and Poland," in *National Identities and Ethnic Minorities in Eastern Europe*, ed. Ray Taras (New York: St. Martin's, 1995), 84–112; Dominique Arel and Valentyn Khmelko, "The Russian Factor and Territorial Polarization in Ukraine," *The Harriman Review* 9, no. 1–2 (March 1996): 81–91; Sarah Birch, "Interpreting the Regional Effect in Ukrainian Politics," *Europe-Asia Studies* 52, no. 6 (September 2000): 1017–41; Ian Bremmer, "The Politics of Ethnicity: Russians in the New Ukraine," *Europe-Asia Studies* 46, no. 2 (1994): 261–83; Roman Laba, "The Russian-Ukrainian Conflict: State Nation and Identity," *European Security* 4, no. 3 (Autumn 1995): 457–87; Paul Kolstoe, "The Eye of the Whirlwind: Belarus and Ukraine," in *Russians in the Former Soviet Republics*, ed. Paul Kolstoe (Bloomington, IN: Indiana University Press, 1995), 170–99.

9. See Peter Schweizer, *Victory: The Reagan Administration's Secret Strategy that Hastened the Collapse of the Soviet Union* (New York: Atlantic Monthly Press, 1994); Don Oberdorfer, *From the Cold War to a New Era: The United States and the Soviet Union, 1983–1991* (Baltimore, MD: The Johns Hopkins University Press, 1998); Raymond L. Garthoff, *The Great Transition: American-Soviet Relations and the End of the Cold War* (Washington, DC: The Brookings Institution, 1994); Zbigniew Brzezinski, *The Choice: Global Domination or Global Leadership* (New York: Basic Books, 2004); Zbigniew Brzezinski, *Second Chance: Three Presidents and the Crisis of American Superpower* (New York: Basic Books, 2008); Marek Jan Chodakiewicz, "Wspomnienie: Ronald Reagan," (A Recollection) in Ronald Reagan, *Moja wizja Ameryki* (My Vision of America) ed. Marek Jan Chodakiewicz and Paweł Toboła Pertkiewicz (Warszawa: Wydawnictwo Arwil, 2004), 9–25; Carole Foryst, "US Intelligence and the Oval Office as the USSR Collapses: Bush Plays Gorbachev as an Asset in Place," TMs, Honors Thesis, The Institute of World Politics, Washington, DC, May 8, 2010. And see Chapter 13.

10. Janusz Bugajski, *America's New Allies: Central-Eastern Europe and the Transatlantic Link* (Washington, DC: CSIS Press/Center for Strategic and International

Studies, 2006); Andrew A. Michta, *The Limits of Alliance: The United States, NATO, and the EU in North and Central Europe* (Lanham, MD: Rowman & Littlefield, 2006).

11. Askold S. Lozynskyj, "Ukraine's Quest for Mature Nation Statehood: What the U.S. Should Do to Further the Quest?" *The Ukrainian Quarterly* 56, no. 4 (Winter 2000): 383–94; F. Stephen Larrabee, "Ukraine and NATO," in *The New Eastern Europe: Ukraine, Belarus, Moldova*, ed. Daniel Hamilton and Gerhard Mangott (Washington, DC: Center for Transatlantic Relations, 2007), 239–57, http://transatlantic.sais-jhu.edu/bin/o/y/new_eastern_europe_text.pdf.

12. Matthieu Chillaud, "La démarche stratégique des États baltes dans l'architecture européenne de sécurité et de defense: Une politique fondée sur une dialectique identitaire et militaire," PhD thesis, Université Montesquieu – Bordeaux IV, March 30, 2007, http://tel.archives-ouvertes.fr/docs/00/28/22/64/PDF/These_Chillaud.pdf.

13. See Janusz Bugajski, *America's New Allies: Central-Eastern Europe and the Transatlantic Link* (Washington, DC: CSIS Press/Center for Strategic and International Studies, 2006); Andrew A. Michta, *The Limits of Alliance: The United States, NATO, and the EU in North and Central Europe* (Lanham, MD: Rowman & Littlefield, 2006); Ivan Dinev Ivanov, *Transforming NATO: New Allies, Missions, and Capabilities* (Lanham, MD: Lexington Books, 2011); David T. Jones, "NATO at Sixty – Time for Reassessment," *Foreign Policy Research Institute*, E-Notes (March 2009), http://www.fpri.org/enotes/200903.jones.nato60.html. See also Marek Jan Chodakiewicz, "NATO po macoszemu," [NATO as your stepmother], *Tygodnik Solidarność*, 27 April 2012; "NATO sobie, a tymczasem . . . ," ("NATO on its own, and meanwhile") *Tygodnik Solidarność*, 1 June 2012.

14. John Lenczowski, *Full Spectrum Diplomacy and Grand Strategy: Reforming the Structure and Culture of U.S. Foreign Policy* (Lanham, MD: Lexington Books, 2011).

15. See Bruce Clarke, *An Empire's New Clothes: The End of Russia's Liberal Dream* (London: Vintage, 1996); Janusz Bugajski, *Cold Peace: Russia's New Imperialism* (Westport, CT: Greenwood Publishing Group, 2004); Marshall I. Goldman, *Petrostate: Putin, Power and the New Russia* (New York: Oxford University Press, 2010); Pavel Baev, *Russian Energy Policy and Military Power: Putin's Quest for Greatness* (London: Routledge, 2008); Jeffrey Mankoff, *Russian Foreign Policy and the Return of Gret Power Politics* (Lanham, MD: Rowman and Littlefield, 2009); Andrei P. Tsygankov and Pavel A. Tsygankov, eds., *New Directions in Russian International Studies* (Stuttgart and Hannover: Ibidem-Verlag, 2005); Marlene Laruelle, ed. *Russian Nationalism and the National Reassertion of Russia* (London: Routledge, 2009); Marlene Laruelle, *In the Name of the Nation: Nationalism and Politics in Contemporary Russia* (New York: Palgrave Macmillian, 2009); Marlène Laruelle, *Russian Eurasianism: An Ideology of Empire* (Washington, DC: Woodrow Wilson Center Press, 2008); Andreas Umland, ed., *The Nature of Russian "Neo-Eurasianism": Approaches to Aleksandr Dugin's Post-Soviet Movement of Radical Anti-Americanism* (Armonk, NY: M.E. Sharpe 2009). A scholar has argued astutely that Russia's economic, demographic, and political decline will impact adversely its imperial ambitions. However, historically, Moscow has dealt with such exigencies precisely by pursuing its imperial goals, i.e., expanding. See Casimir Dadak, "A New 'Cold War'?", *The Independent Review* 15, no. 1 (Summer 2010): 89–107.

16. Vladimir Socor, "German Diplomacy Tilts toward Russia on Transnistria Negotiations," *Eurasia Daily Monitor* 8, no. 108 (June 6, 2011): http://www.jamestown.org/single/?no_cache=1&tx_ttnews%5Btt_news%5D=38017; Vladimir Socor, "German Initiatives Favor Russia on Transnistria Talks," *Eurasia Daily Monitor* 8, no. 110 (June 8, 2011): http://www.jamestown.org/programs/edm/single/?tx_ttnews%5Btt_news%5D=38024&cHash=45d4871a77719406c37bf9aced6ef813.

17. On Russia's energy weapon see Marek Jan Chodakiewicz, "Petrorusodolary," ("Petroruskiedollars") *Najwyższy Czas!*, 2 June 2012, XXXIV–XXXV. See further Bruce Clarke, *An Empire's New*. For a thoughtful analysis of Berlin's current foreign policy evolution see Peter Zeihan and Marko Papic, "Germany's Choice: Part 2," *Stratfor* (July 26, 2011): http://app.response.stratfor.com/e/es.aspx?s=1483&e=328223&elq=ee77c05153484fa78262474495ef6c7d. See also Marko Papic and Peter Zeihan, "Germany's Choice," *Stratfor* (February 8, 2010): http://www.stratfor.com/weekly/20100208_germanys_choice; Peter Zeihan, "Germany: Mitteleuropa Redux," *Stratfor* (March 16, 2010): http://www.stratfor.com/weekly/20100315_germany_mitteleuropa_redux.

18. Federiga Bindi, ed., *The Foreign Policy of the European Union: Assessing Europe's Role in the World* (Washington, DC: The Brookings Institution Press, 2010); T. R. Reid, *The United States of Europe: The New Superpower and the End of American Supremacy* (New York: the Penguin Group, 2004); Rockwell A. Schnabel with Francis X. Rocca, *The Next Superpower? The Rise of Europe and Its Challenges to the United States* (Lanham, MD: Rowman & Littlefield Publishers, Inc, 2007).

19. See Hajo Holborn, *A History of Modern Germany: 1648–1840* (Princeton, NJ: Princeton University Press, 1982); Hajo Holborn, *A History of Modern Germany: 1840–1945* (Princeton, NJ: Princeton University Press, 1982); G. Barraclough, *The Origins of Modern Germany* (New York and London: W. W. Norton & Company, Inc., 1984); Gordon A. Craig, *Germany: 1866–1945* (New York and Oxford: Oxford University Press, 1980); Mary Fulbrook, *The Divided Nation: A History of Germany 1918–1990* (New York and Oxford: Oxford University Press, 1992); Walter Laqueur, *Russia and Germany: A Century of Conflict* (New Brunswick and London: Transaction Publishers, 1990); Timothy Garton Ash, *In Europe's Name: Germany and the Divided Continent* (New York: Random House, 1993); and Bogdan Musiał, "Od Breżniewa do Putina: Polityka Niemiec Zachodnich a upadek reżimów komunistycznych w krajach Europy Środkowej i Wschodniej oraz rozpad Związku Sowieckiego," ("From Brezhnev to Putin: West Germany's Policy and the Fall of Communist Regimes in Central and Eastern Europe and the Disintegration of the Soviet Union") in *Racja stanu: Janowi Olszewskiemu w 80. rocznice urodzin (Raison d'etat: A Festschrift to Jan Olszewski for his 80th birthday)* (Poznań: Zysk i ska, 2011), 187–203.

20. See Marek Jan Chodakiewicz, "Chiny i Białoruś," ("China and Belarus") *Tygodnik Solidarność* (January 1, 2012); and, for an official website, http://http://belaruschina.by.

21. Natalie Mychajlyszyn, "The OSCE and Regional Conflicts in the Former Soviet Union," in *Ethnicity and Territory in the Former Soviet Union: Regions in Conflict*, ed. James Hughes and Gwendolyn Sasse (London and Portland, OR: Frank Cass, 2002), 194–219.

22. Harry Norris, *Islam in the Baltics: Europe's Early Muslim Community* (London and New York: Tauris Academic Studies, an imprint of I.B. Tauris Publishers, 2009).

23.   See Will Kymlicka and Magda Opalski, eds., *Can Liberal Pluralism Be Exported? Western Political Theory and Ethnic Relations in Eastern Europe* (Oxford: Oxford University Press, 2001); Rachel A. Epstein, *In Pursuit of Liberalism: International Institutions in Postcommunist Europe* (Baltimore, MD: Johns Hopkins University Press, 2008); Alex Pravda and Jan Zielonka, eds., *International Influences on Democratic Transition in Central and Eastern Europe* (Oxford: Oxford University Press, 2001); Bernd Rechel, ed., *Minority Rights in Central and Eastern Europe* (London: Routledge, 2009); Scott D. Orr, "Identity and Civil Society in Latvia, Poland, and Ukraine: Women's NGOs," *East European Politics and Societies* 22, no. 4 (Fall 2008): 856–79; Lidia Varbanova, "The European Union Enlargement Process: Culture in between National Policies and European Priorities," *The Journal of Arts Management, Law, and Society* 37, no. 1 (Spring 2007): 48–64. See also Stephen Deets, "Reconsidering East European Minority Policy: Liberal Theory and European Norms," *East European Politics and Societies* 16, no. 1 (Spring 2001): 30–55; Lynn M. Tesser, "The Geopolitics of Tolerance: Minority Rights under EU Expansion in East-Central Europe," *East European Politics and Societies* 17, no. 3 (Summer 2003): 483–532; Peter Vermeersch, *The Romani Movement: Minority Politics and Ethnic Mobilization in Contemporary Central Europe* (New York: Berghahn Books, 2006); "AIDS in Ukraine: Still No Cure for Corruption," *Economist* (December 1, 2011): http://www.economist.com/blogs/easternapproaches/2011/12/aids-ukraine. Compare with a case study of an NGO in Hungary see Mimi Larsson, "Civil Society in a New Democracy – A Look at Local Realities," Demstar Research Report No. 7 (May 2002): 1–26, http://www.demstar.dk/papers/CivilSociety. pdf. On salubrious influences of the NGOs and international cooperation (as well as freedom and democracy) to address the issue of environmental pollution see Marek Jan Chodakiewicz, "An Environmental Battleground: Eco-Politics in Poland," in *Managing the Environment: An East European Perspective*, ed. O.P. Dwivedi and Joseph G. Jabrra (Willowdale, ON: de Sitter, 1995).

24.   A few observations on the mafia in Marek Jan Chodakiewicz, "Wolność i patologia a Rosja (część 1)," ("Freedom and pathology and Russia [part 1]") *Najwyższy Czas!*, 16 June 2012, XXXIV–XXXV; Marek Jan Chodakiewicz, "Wolność i patologia a Rosja (część 2)," ("Freedom and pathology and Russia [part 2]") *Najwyższy Czas!*, 23 June 2012, XXXIV–XXXV; Marek Jan Chodakiewicz, "Czekiści, mafia i państwo" ("The Chekists, Mafia, and the State") *Tygodnik Solidarność* (August 6, 2010); Marek Jan Chodakiewicz, "Notatki z post-Sowiecji (część I)," ("Notes from the Post-Soviet Lands, Part I") *Najwyższy Czas!* (October 9, 2010): XXXV; and Marek Jan Chodakiewicz, "Notatki z post-Sowiecji (część II)," (Notes from the Post-Soviet Lands, Part II) *Najwyższy Czas!* (October 16, 2010): XXXV. On some legal and logistical problems prosecuting the mafia in the post-Soviet sphere see George Ginsburgs, *The Soviet Union and International Cooperation in Legal Matters* (Norwell, MA, and Dordrecht, the Netherlands: Martinus Nijhoff Publishers and Kulwer Academic Publishers, 1994), 281–323, which is Chapter VI: "Russia and the Successor States." See also David Satter, *Age of Delirium: The Decline and Fall of the Soviet Union* (New Haven, CT and London: Yale University Press, 2001); David Satter, *Darkness at Dawn: The Rise of the Russian Criminal State* (New Haven, CT and London: Yale University Press, 2003); Arkady Vaksberg, *The Soviet Mafia* (New York: St. Martin's Press, 1991); Federico Varese, *The Russian Mafia: Private Protection in a New Market Economy* (New York: Oxford University, 2001, 2nd edn. 2005); Stephen Handelman, *Comrade Criminal: Russia's New Mafiya* (New Haven,

CT: Yale University Press, 1995); Paul Klebnikov, *Godfather of the Kremlin: Boris Berezovsky and the Looting of Russia* (New York: Harcourt, Inc., 2000).

25. See Zbigniew Brzezinski and Paige Sullivan, eds., *Russia and the Commonwealth of Independent States: Documents, Data, and Analysis* (Armonk, NY: M.E. Sharpe, 1997); Dov Lynch, *Russian Peacekeeping Strategies in the CIS: The Cases of Moldova, Georgia, and Tajikistan* (London: Royal Institute of International Affairs and Macmillan, 2000); Paul Beaver, ed., *Jane's Sentinel: The Unfair Advantage: Commonwealth of Independent States: Regional Security Assessment* (Coulsdon: Jane's Information Group, 1994); Bertil Nygren, *The Rebuilding of Greater Russia: Putin's Foreign Policy towards the CIS Countries* (London and New York: Routledge, 2008); Herman Pirchner, Jr., *Reviving Greater Russia? The Future of Russia's Borders with Belarus, Georgia, Kazakhstan, Moldova and Ukraine* (Washington, DC: The University Press of America and American Foreign Policy Council, 2005). Occasionally, a junior member has attempted to assert itself against Russia. See Michael Dobbs, "Three Former Soviet Republics Decline to Sign CIS Charter," *Washington Post* (January 23, 1993): A15; Vladimir Socor "Moldovan President Wants Out of Russia's Orbit," *Eurasia Daily Monitor* 1, no. 87 (September 16, 2004): http://www.jamestown. org/single/?no_cache=1&tx_ttnews%5Btt_news%5D=26871.

26. Established in May 1992, CSTO includes Russia, Armenia, Belarus, Kazakhstan, Kyrgyzstan, Tajikistan, and Uzbekistan (which joined only in 2006). Tellingly, the charter was signed in Chişinău in October 1992 but Moldova refused to participate. CSTO is envisioned as a partner of the Shanghai Cooperation Organization (SCO), a far eastern economic and political collaboration platform, but it also complements a large chunk of the CIS. CSTO has continuously involved and includes now, among others, peacekeeping, counternarcotic, counterterrorist, and cyberwarfare capabilities. Russia naturally controls the entity. For the official website see http://www.odkb.gov.ru/start/index_aengl.htm, and "Charter of the Collective Security Treaty Organization," http://untreaty.un.org/ unts/144078_158780/5/9/13289.pdf. See also "Former Soviet republics hope to contain NATO," RT.com, (August 12, 2011), http://rt.com/politics/security-table-csto-summit/; Major (P) John A. Mowchan, "The Militarization of the Collective Security Treaty Organization," Center for Strategic Leadership, US Army War College, Issue Paper, vol. 6–09 (July 2009): 1–6, http://www.csl.army. mil/usacsl/publications/IP_6_09_Militarization_of_the_CSTO.pdf; Richard Weitz, "Is the Collective Security Treaty Organization the Real Anti-NATO?" *World Politics Review* (January 23, 2008), http://www.worldpoliticsreview. com/articles/1531/is-the-collective-security-treaty-organization-the-real-anti-nato.

27. The Union State was formally established in April 1996. Since then Serbia and seven separate post-Soviet entities and states (Transnistria, South Ossetia, Abkhazia, Kirgyzstan, Kazakstan, Moldova, and Ukraine) have expressed interest in joining at one time or another but the results have been rather disappointing for Moscow. For the Union's official websites see http://www.soyuzinfo.ru/; and http://www.soyuz.by/en/.

28. Putin quoted in Neil Buckley, "Putin Sets Sights on Eurasian Economic Union," *Financial Times* (August 16, 2011), http://www.ft.com/intl/cms/s/0/a7db2310-b769-11e0-b95d-00144feabdc0.html#axzz1VL1UnMTl. The customs union was launched in 2010.

29. Admittedly, the EU expansion has encouraged the private sector, including banks, to move in to formerly high risk areas (including Serbia, Bosnia,

Montenegro, Albania, Bulgaria, and Georgia). The results have been mixed, albeit sometimes encouraging, at least until the recent global crisis. See Ingrid Matthäus-Maier and J.D. von Pischke, eds., *EU Accession – Financial Sector Opportunities and Challenges for Southeast Europe* (Berlin, Heidelberg, and New York: Springer and KFW Entwicklungsbank, 2005); Ingrid Matthäus-Maier and J.D. von Pischke, eds., *The Development of the Financial Sector in Southeast Europe: Innovative Approaches in Volatile Environments* (Berlin, Heidelberg, and New York: Springer and KFW Entwicklungsbank, 2004); and, more generally, Ingrid Matthäus-Maier and J.D. von Pischke, eds., *New Partnerships for Innovation in Microfinance* (Berlin, Heidelberg, and New York: Springer and KFW Entwicklungsbank, 2008). About the role of the private sector in stabilizing former Yugoslavia through microfinances see Dominik Ziller, "The European Fund for Southeast Europe: An Innovative Instrument for Political and Economic Stabilization," in *Microfinance Investment Funds: Leveraging Private Capital for Economic Growth and Poverty Reduction*, ed. Ingrid Matthäus-Maier and J.D. von Pischke (Berlin, Heidelberg, and New York: Springer and KFW Entwicklungsbank, 2006), 193–212.

30.   Alas, all too often the EU's cultural subsidies amount to importing anti-Western counter-culture to the Intermarium. For an inquiry into the EU subsidies for culture to the new member states, including Estonia, Latvia, and Lithuania see Lidia Varbanova, "The European Union Enlargement Process: Culture in between National Policies and European Priorities," *The Journal of Arts Management, Law, and Society* 37, no. 1 (Spring 2007): 48–64.

31.   Russia ostensibly supports the engagement of Belarus with the EU. See "Lavrov: Russia – is for European Belarus," Khartia'97/Charter'97, (November 23, 2010), http://www.charter97.org/en/news/2010/11/23/34028/. See also Ann Lewis, ed., *EU and Moldova: On a Fault-Line of Europe (Europe's Eastern Borders)* (London: The Federal Trust for Education and Research, 2004); Luis Moreno, "The Genesis of the European Union's Relations with Ukraine and Belarus," *Demokratizatsiya: The Journal of Post-Soviet Democratization* 14, no. 4 (Fall 2006): 535–44; and also the following essays in Daniel Hamilton and Gerhard Mangott, eds., *The New Eastern Europe:Ukraine, Belarus, Moldova* (Washington, DC: Center for Transatlantic Relations, 2007): Rainer Lindner, "Neighborhood in Flux: EU-Belarus-Russia: Prospects for the European Union's Belarus Policy," (55–76), Elena Kovalova, "Ukraine's Role in Changing Europe," (171–94), and Michael Emerson, "Ukraine and the European Union," (215–38), http://transatlantic.sais-jhu.edu/bin/o/y/new_eastern_europe_text.pdf. For the genesis of the EU's involvement in the Baltics see Ainius Lasas, "Guilt, Sympathy, and Cooperation: EU-Baltic Relations in Early 1990s," *East European Politics and Societies* 22, no. 2 (Spring 2008): 347–72. One of the reasons for the EU's guilt was that the United States and some other Western states never formally recognized the occupation of the Baltics by the Soviets. Hence, they considered their governments-in-exile as legal until the re-establishment of freedom in the successor states in the 1990s. See John Hiden, Vahur Made, and David J. Smith, *The Baltic Question During the Cold War* (New York and London: Routledge, 2008); James McHugh and James S. Pacy, *Diplomats without a Country: Baltic Diplomacy, International Law, and the Cold War* (Westport, CT: Greenwood Publishing Group, 2001); Stefan Talmon, *Recognition of Governments in International Law: With Particular Reference to Governments in Exile* (Oxford, NY: Clarendon Press, 1998).

32. Michael Artis, Anindya Banerjee, and Massimiliano Marcellino, eds., *The Central and Eastern European Countries and the European Union* (Cambridge, UK and New York: Cambridge University Press, 2006); Joan DeBardeleben, *The Boundaries of EU Enlargement: Finding a Place for Neighbours* (Basingstoke, Hampshire and New York: Palgrave Macmillan, 2008).
33. For the official website see http://www.ceinet.org/.
34. At first it was dubbed the Visegrad Triangle (V-3), as Czechoslovakia was a single entity. One of its most valuable achievements was the Central European Free Trade Agreement (CEFTA) of 1992. Otherwise, the group lacked internal cohesion and solidarity. This stemmed from different interpretation of national interest by each nation. The Czechs, in particular, felt they would be more successful in their bid for EU membership if they went it alone as, unencumbered by economically depressed and underdeveloped Slovakia, the Czech Republic seemed to be economically a much more appealing candidate for Brussels than the remaining countries. Also, Prague succeeded in de-Communization and de-KGBzation of its political elite to a much greater extent than its neighbors. Ultimately, the Czech Republic was admitted together not only with its fellow V-4 members, but also the Baltics on May 1, 2004. One of the V-4's most effective means of engagement in the Intermarium has been the International Visegrad Fund (established belatedly in 2000), which sponsors educational and cultural activities, among others. Further, the V-4 nations plan to commence joint military maneuvers as part of the NATO Response Force in 2013 and to set up a V-4 "battle group" under Polish leadership in 2016. There is talk of inviting Ukraine to join but Turkey has been left out so far, an injudicious omission. For the official sites see http://www.visegradgroup.eu/main.php; and http://visegradfund.org/. See also Adrian A. Basora, "The Value of the Visegrad Four," Foreign Policy Research Institute, E-Notes, 7 March 2011, http://www.fpri.org/enotes/201103.basora.centraleurope.html; George Freedman, "Visegrad: A New European Military Force," *Stratfor* (May 17, 2011), http://www.stratfor.com/weekly/20110516-visegrad-new-european-military-force.
35. See Andrei Panici, "Romanian Nationalism in the Republic of Moldova," *The Global Review of Ethnopolitics* 2, no. 2 (January 2003): 37–51; V. G. Baleanu, "In the Shadow of Russia: Romania's Relations with Moldova and Ukraine," Defense Academy of the United Kingdom, Conflict Studies Research Centre, Central and East European Series Publication, G85 (August 2000): 1–28, http://www.da.mod.uk/colleges/arag/document-listings/cee/G85; Vladimir Socor, "Moldova Refuses Mass Conferral of Romanian Citizenship," *Eurasia Daily Monitor* 4, no. 48 (March 9, 2007): http://www.jamestown.org/single/?no_cache=1&tx_ttnews%5Btt_news%5D=32576. See also Tom Gallagher, *Romania and the European Union: How the Weak Vanquished the Strong* (Manchester: Manchester University Press, 2009).
36. Along with Russia, Turkey, Ukraine, Moldova, and six other nations, Bulgaria and Rumania participate in the Organization of the Black Sea Economic Cooperation. Belarus, Poland, the United States, and ten other states maintain an observer status. For the official website see http://www.bsec-organization.org/Pages/homepage.aspx. Further, in 2006 Bucharest launched the Black Sea Forum for Partnership and Dialogue. In addition to Romania, Ukraine, Moldova, Azerbaijan, Armenia, and Georgia belong to the BSFPD. Turkey and Bulgaria are observers. See http://www.blackseaforum.org/.
37. On energy policy see Joanna A. Gorska, *Dealing with a Juggernaut: Analyzing Poland's Policy towards Russia, 1989–2009* (Lanham, MD: Rowman & Littlefield

Pub Inc, 2010), 101–142; Piotr Naimski, "Ministerstwo Energetyki," ("Ministry of Energy") in *Racja stanu: Janowi Olszewskiemu w 80. rocznice urodzin (Raison d'etat: A Festschrift to Jan Olszewski for his 80th birthday)* (Poznań: Zysk i ska, 2011), 205–217. For the early stages of Poland's involvement with the Intermarium see Glenn E. Curtis, ed., *Poland: A Country Study* (Washington: GPO for the Library of Congress, 1992), http://countrystudies.us/poland/90. htm.

38. For Eastern Partnership's official websites see http://eeas.europa.eu/eastern/index_en.htm; http://eastbook.eu/en/; http://www.easternpartnership.org/; and http://eastbook.eu/. See also Paul Goble, "EU Proposes 'Eastern Partnership' to Six Former Soviet Republics," Window on Eurasia, (December 8, 2008), http://windowoneurasia.blogspot.com/2008/12/window-on-eurasia-eu-proposes-eastern.html; "The Eastern Partnership – An Ambitious New Chapter in the EU's Relations with Its Eastern Neighbours," *Europa*, (December 3, 2008), http://europa.eu/rapid/pressReleasesAction.do?reference=IP/08/1858; "Eastern Relations: EU Partnership Launched with Six East European Countries," (May 8, 2009), http://ec.europa.eu/news/external_relations/090508_en.htm; and Beata Wojna and Mateusz Gniazdowski, eds., "Eastern Partnership: The Opening Report," The Polish Institute of International Affairs (April 2009), http://www.pism.pl/zalaczniki/Report_EP_2009_eng.pdf.

39. See Katarzyna Pisarska, "America and the Eastern Partnership Initiative: From Friend to Meaningful Contributor," *Central Europe Digest,* Issue Brief No. 120 (August 1, 2011): 1–12, http://www.cepa.org/ced/view.aspx?record_id=314 (The Center of European Policy Analysis).

40. Northern Dimension's membership includes Finland, Sweden, Denmark, Germany, Poland, Estonia, Lithuania, and Latvia. It engages Iceland and Norway as well as Russia and, lately, Belarus. Northern Dimension concerns itself further with the Arctic, including its environmental problems. See http://eeas.europa. eu/north_dim/index_en.htm. For Moscow's bilateral oil game with Oslo as far as the Arctic see Marek Jan Chodakiewicz, "NATO sobie, a tymczasem . . . ," ("NATO on its own, and meanwhile") *Tygodnik Solidarność*, 1 June 2012.

41. Both Vilnius and Minsk bristle at what they consider as interference in their domestic affairs. Warsaw is much more involved with Belarus, including supporting its oppositionists and funding anti-Lukashenka media. See TVP, Telewizja Polska, "'TV Belsat': Independent Satellite Television Channel for Belarus, Project description (February 2007): 1–16 (a copy in my collection); "Notatka informacyjna nt. Radia Racja," no date (2008) (a copy in my collection); and www.racyja.com. For some official Polish voices see Bogdan Borusewicz interviewed by Piotr Kościński, "Polonia jest nam potrzebna," ("We Need the Polonia") *Rzeczpospolita* (March 31, 2009); Maciej Płażyński interviewed by Piotr Kościański, "Rozmowa o Polonii," ("A Conversation about the Polonia") *Rzeczpospolita* (March 31, 2009); Marek Borowski interviewed by Piotr Kościański, "Polonia i Polacy za granicą," ("Polonia and the Poles Abroad") *Rzeczpospolita* (March 31, 2009); Andżelika Borys, "Sytuacja Związku Polaków na Białorusi," ("The Situation of the Union of Poles in Belarus") *Rzeczpospolita* (March 31, 2009); "Trzeba załatwić sprawy polskiej mniejszości," ("The Problems of Polish Minority Should Be Taken Care Of") *Rzeczpospolita* (May 8, 2009); Jerzy Haszczyński, "Polacy nie chcą pustych obietnic Litwinów," ("The Poles Do Not Want the Empty Promises of the Lithuanians") *Rzeczpospolita* (May 10, 2009); Dr. Artur Górski, "Traktat polsko-litewski: Martwe zapisy," ("Polish-Lithuanian Treaty: Dead Letters") *Nasz Dziennik* (May 9–10, 2009).

42. For a Russian commentary on Lithuania's national security issues, including its energy policy and Poland's involvement, see "Литва - Польша: уже пахнет Косово: Литва за неделю," ("Lithuania-Poland: It Smells Like Kosovo") *Regnum* (November 5, 2010), http://regnum.ru/news/polit/1343487.html. See also Minton F. Goldman, "Polish-Russian Relations and the 2004 Ukrainian Presidential Elections," *East European Quarterly* 40, no. 4 (Winter 2006): 409–28; Minton F. Goldman, "Polish Policy toward Ukraine: The Impact on Polish-Russian Relations in 2008–2009," *The Polish Review* LIV, no. 4 (2009): 451–76.

43. For a scathing critique of Poland's policy toward Belarus see Lech Z. Niekrasz, ed., *Wojna z "reżimem Łukaszenki"* (*The War against the Lukashenka Regime*) (Warszawa: Wydawnictwo Prasy Lokalnej and Biblioteczka *Myśli Polskiej*, 2010), which is a Polish National Democratic/National Bolshevik compilation freely mixing rants, facts, and punditry.

44. In 2010 Russia offered Poland a multiyear, heavily discounted contract for gas and oil delivery. The EU strenuously objected and intervened to kill the deal. See Judy Dempsey, "Europe Seeks to Block Polish Gas Contract," *The New York Times* (October 10, 2010), http://www.nytimes.com/2010/10/11/business/energy-environment/11gazprom.html. For a brilliantly incisive analysis of Poland's foreign policy in the region see Walter Jajko, "Poland: Strategically Active or Passive?" remarks delivered at the Annual Thanksgiving Dinner of the Washington Division of the Polish American Congress, Washington, DC, (November 13, 2011), also published in the *Sarmatian Review* XXXII, no. 1 (January 2012): 1630–34, and available at http://www.iwp.edu/docLib/20120125_jajko.pdf.

45. The German focus on the Poles pre-dates 1989, of course, but the official engagement was formalized in 1991, when Berlin, assisted by Paris, embraced Warsaw as a junior partner of the so-called Weimar Triangle. For some, it is a tool of German influence over Poland. For others, it was a generous gesture resulting in economic assistance and sponsorship, which eventually, led to Warsaw's accession to the EU. Perhaps most importantly, Berlin intended to assuage Polish fears, while Germany was reuniting, the Soviets were withdrawing, and Poland needed its western border officially recognized. Poland's western boundaries were officially recognized by Berlin but the treaty failed to solve the vexing problem of compensation for property lost by Germans in the territories that became Polish following World War II. See Phillip A. Buhler, *The Oder-Neisse Line: A Reappraisal Under International Law* (Boulder, CO and New York: East European Monographs and Columbia University Press, 1990); W. W. Kulski, *Germany and Poland: From War to Peaceful Relations* (Syracuse, NY: Syracuse University Press, 1976); Robert L. Nelson. *Germans, Poland, and Colonial Expansion to the East: 1850 through the Present* (New York: Palgrave Macmillan, 2009).

46. Had Lithuania received Kaliningrad, it would have sharpened its anti-Moscow stance, distanced it from Berlin, and tied it closer to Warsaw. See Marek Jan Chodakiewicz, "Królewiecka Solidarność," ("The Kaliningrad Solidarity") *Tygodnik Solidarność* (February 26, 2010); Marek Jan Chodakiewicz, "Królewieckie S-400," ("Kaliningradian S-400") *Tygodnik Solidarność*, April 20, 2012; Matthieu Chillaud and Frank Tetart, "The Demilitarization of Kaliningrad: A 'Sisyphean Task?'" *Baltic Security & Defense Review* 9 (2007): 171–86; Ingmar Oldberg, "The Changing Military Importance of the Kaliningrad Region," *Journal of Slavic Military Studies* 22, no. 3 (2009): 352–66; Yury Zverev, "Kaliningrad: Problems and Paths of Development," *Problems of Post-Communism* 54, no. 2 (2007): 9–25; W. Alejandro Sanchez Nieto, "Assessing Kaliningrad's Geostrategic Role:

The Russian Periphery and A Baltic Concern," *Journal of Baltic Studies* 42, no. 4 (December 2011): 465–89, http://dx.doi.org/10.1080/01629778.2011.621737.

47.　Ankara is at a crossroads. It ostensibly yearns to be integrated into the European Union, but that would undermine both its secular, Kemalist constitution and its religious, Islamic society. The former is steadily on the wane, the latter is newly resurgent as reflected by the electoral triumphs of Turkey's Islamist government in the last two decades. Paradoxically, the Kemalist constitution ushered in modernity in Turkey but it is tied to military supremacy over civilians. The potentially obscurantist Islamist government has asserted civilian control over the armed forces under the guise of "joining Europe." A rosy scenario is an Islamist parliamentary democracy within or without the EU. The result may very well be neither the EU nor modernization but either a semi-theocracy or a military *coup d'etat*, bringing Ankara closer to Islamabad, rather than Brussels. See Marek Jan Chodakiewicz, "Tureckie spiski," ("Turkish plots") *Tygodnik Solidarność* (January 29, 2010). Parenthetically, it is important to note that, whenever the Turks appear intractable, Russia plays its Middle Eastern cards, cooperating closely with Iran and Syria. Further, Moscow always stresses its "special relationship" with Athens. Greece is, indeed, a special case. Its cultural affinity with Russia, grounded in common religion, should not be underestimated. Greece has further served as an intermediary between Russia and the EU. Although Russia's involvement in Greece's economy and society are rather well known, in particular in tourism, banking, and energy, including the Burgas-Alexandrupolis pipeline, the Greek participation in the post-Soviet space is much less appreciated. And that includes contacts with the Intermarium's Orthodox everywhere, but in eastern Ukraine in particular, as well as with the post-Soviet Greek diaspora in Odessa. See Marek Jan Chodakiewicz, "Grecki mały brat," ("The Greek little brother") *Tygodnik Solidarność*, 18 May 2012; Marek Jan Chodakiewicz, "Cypryjska furtka Rosji," ("The Cypriot gate of Russia") *Tygodnik Solidarność*, 25 May 2012; Marek Jan Chodakiewicz, "Śródziemnomorska energia," ("Mediterrean Energy") *Tygodnik Solidarność*, 8 June 2012; "An Orthodox Friendship: Russian Tourists are Pouring into Greece, Investors May Follow," *Economist*, April 7, 2012, http://www.economist.com/node/21552240.

48.　See "Europe's Gas Pipelines: The Abominable Gas Man: How Technological Change and New Pipelines Improve Energy Security," *The Economist* (October 14, 2010): http://www.economist.com/node/17260657.

49.　The idea was to use the Odessa terminal to accept gas and oil from the Caspian Sea, Azerbaijan in particular, and send it through Poland to the EU. Hitherto, Odessa pumped Russian gas and oil onto tankers to be sold to the West. See Alexander Serafimovich, "Ukraine Reverses Odessa Brody Pipeline Flow," *Oil and Gas Eurasia*, no. 9 (September 2008): http://www.oilandgaseurasia.com/articles/p/82/article/703/. See also Fyodor I. Kushnirsky, "Free Economic Zones in Ukraine: The Case of Odessa," *Ukrainian Economic Review* 2, no. 3 (1996): 117–24.

50.　Ankara undoubtedly pays attention to anti-Turkic sentiment. For instance, it was not appreciated that at a meeting with Gagauz minority voters, former president Vladimir Voronin lashed out: "You are not a nation. You are an idiot!" Ironically, the verbal altercation erupted because the politician was taken to task for having broken his promise to establish Russian as the official language of Moldova. Voronin defended "Moldovan" as the language of the land. See "'Вы не народ! Вы - идиот!' - экс-президент Молдовы пообщался с избирателями," ("You Are Not a Nation! You Are an Idiot!' – Ex-President of Moldova Quarreled with Voters") Comments.ua, (November 22, 2010), http://world.comments.ua/2010/11/22/211140/vi-narod-vi-idiot-.html. See also Harun Gungor, *Gagauzlar* (*The Gagauz*) (Istanbul: Otuken Nesriyat, 2004).

51. Founded in 1996, GUAM is a cooperation platform for the post-Soviet countries of the Black Sea rim. It stands for Georgia, Ukraine, Azerbaijan, and Moldova. In 1999 Uzbekistan joined GUAM (GUUAM), only to drop out in 2005. The association's charter was formalized in 2001. Turkey and Latvia participate as observers. GUAM also maintains relations with the United States, Japan, and Poland. See http://www.guuam.org/. See also Paul Goble, "GUAM Will Add New Members if Moscow Forces Moldova Out," Window on Eurasia, (March 12, 2008), http://windowoneurasia.blogspot.com/2008/03/window-on-eurasia-guam-will-add-new.html; and Paul Goble, "GUAM Crosses the Former Soviet Border," Window on *Eurasia* (February 25, 2008), http://windowoneurasia. blogspot.com/2008/02/window-on-eurasia-guam-crosses-former.html.

52. On economic matters see Rawi Abdelal, *National Purpose in the World Economy: Post-Soviet States in Comparative Perspective* (Ithaca, NY: Cornell University Press, 2001), vii–ix, and Chapter 2, "A Nationalist Perspective of International Political Economy," 24–44, Chapter 3, "Economic Relations among Post-Soviet States," 45–83, Chapter 7, "Political Economy after Empire," 150–201; Volodymyr Sidenko, "Geoeconomic Problems Facing the Postcommunist States," in *The Political Analysis of Postcommunism: Understanding Postcommunist Ukraine*, ed. Volodymyr Polokhalo (College Station, TX: Texas A&M University Press, 1997), 258–300; International Monetary Fund, *Common Issues and Interrepublic Relations in the Former USSR* (Economic Review Series) (Washington, DC: International Monetary Fund, 1992); Fyodor I. Kushnirsky, "Free Economic Zones in Ukraine: The Case of Odessa." *Ukrainian Economic Review* 2, no. 3 (1996): 117–124. On boundary claims with overlapping ethnicities see Stephen Rapawy, *Ukraine and the Border Issue* (Washington, DC: Center for International Research, US Bureau of the Census, 1993); Istvan Madi, "Carpatho-Ukraine," in *Contested Territory: Border Disputes at the Edge of the Former Soviet Empire*, ed. Tumoas Forsberg (Aldershot: Elgar, 1995), 128–42; Judy Batt, "Transcarpathia: Peripheral Region at the 'Centre of Europe,'" *Regional and Federal Studies* 12, no. 2 (Summer 2002): 155–77; Raymond A. Smith, "Indigenous and Diaspora Elites and the Return of Carpatho-Ruthenian Nationalism, 1989–1992," *Harvard Ukrainian Studies* 21, no. 1–2 (June 1997): 141–60; Hugo Lane, "Rusyns and Ukrainians Yesterday, Today, and Tomorrow: The Limitations of National History," *Nationalities Papers* 29, no. 4 (December 2001): 689–96; Susyn Yvonne Mihalasky, "Ethno-National Orientation among Lemkos in Poland," in *National Identities and Ethnic Minorities in Eastern Europe*, ed. Ray Taras (New York: St. Martin's, 1995), 208–224. Russians and, to a lesser extent, Russian speakers tend to oppose reforms resulting in Westernization (NATO and EU admission, privatization) more frequently as the majority population in Ukraine. See, e.g., Stephen C. Shulman, "National Identity and Public Support for Political and Economic Reform in Ukraine," *Slavic Review* 64, no. 1 (Spring 2005): 59–87. For a discussion of the analogous situation in the Baltics see below.

53. See "Belarus to ratify border agreement with Ukraine," *Interfax-Ukraina* (November 5, 2009), http://www.interfax.com.ua/eng/main/23910/; Vasily Astrov and Peter Havlik, "Belarus, Ukraine and Moldova: Economic Developments and Integration Prospects," in *The New Eastern Europe: Ukraine, Belarus,*

Moldova, ed. Daniel Hamilton and Gerhard Mangott (Washington, DC: Center for Transatlantic Relations, 2007), 127–148, http://transatlantic.sais-jhu. edu/bin/o/y/new_eastern_europe_text.pdf; Vitaly Kulik, "Impediments on the path of Ukrainian-Moldovan cooperation under Eastern Partnership: Kiev's stance," EAP Community, (October 27, 2010), http://www.easternpartnership. org/publication/politics/2010-10-27/impediments-path-ukrainian-moldovan-cooperation-under-eastern-partne.

54. For some thoughtful observations see Harvey Sicherman, "A Clarifying Act of Violence: Russia, Georgia, and The West," Foreign Policy Research Institute, E-Notes (August 2008), http://www.fpri.org/enotes/200808.sicherman. clarifyingactrussiageorgia.html. Sicherman wrote: "Russia's attack on Georgia, although superficially an outburst of ill temper over a minor issue, reflects the increasingly muscular foreign policy of the Putin era. Put plainly, the Russian Prime Minister and his circle do not regard the post-Cold War settlement in Europe as legitimate. They mean to contain and then roll back Western influence, preferably through diplomatic and economic pressure and, failing that, if possible, by the threat or use of military force. Putin's demand for greater respect of Russian interests has become the Cold War by other means—and sometimes by the same means. The United States and its European allies are now forewarned. Will they be forearmed?" See also "Russia's New Military Doctrine Approved," RT.com, (February 5, 2010), http://rt.com/usa/news/russia-military-doctrine-approved/; Steven J. Blank, ed., *Russian Military Politics and Russia's 2010 Defense Doctrine* (Carlisle, PA: Strategic Studies Institute, Army War College, March 2011), 1–196, http://www.strategicstudiesinstitute. army.mil/pubs/display.cfm?pubid=1050.

55. See Tim Sandole, "Post-Soviet Identity and Foreign Policy Formation in Ukraine, Estonia, and Latvia," *SIPA News* (Columbia University School of International and Public Affairs), (January 2012): 20–21; Sten Berglund, Kjetil Duvold, and Joakim Ekman, "The Baltic States and the European Challenge: Independence versus Security," in *Political Culture: Values And Identities In The Baltic Sea Region*, ed. Sten Berglund, Bernd Henningsen, and Mai-Brith Schartau (Berlin: Berliner Wissenschafts-Verlag, 2006), 139–182; Piret Ehin, "Determinants of Public Support for EU Membership: Data from the Baltic Countries," *European Journal of Political Research* 40, no. 1 (August 2001): 31–56; Ainius Lasas, "Guilt, Sympathy, and Cooperation: EU-Baltic Relations in Early 1990s," *East European Politics and Societies* 22, no. 2 (Spring 2008): 347–72. See further Aleksander Lust, "Familiarity Breeds Contempt: Strategies of Economic Reform and Popular Attitudes toward the European Union in Lithuania and Estonia," *East European Politics and Societies* 23, no. 3 (Summer 2009): 339–71; Andrejs Plakans, "Latvia: Normality and Disappointment," *East European Politics and Societies* 23, no. 4 (Fall 2009): 518–26; and the following three essays in Ryszard Żelichowski, ed., *Pierwsza pięciolatka: Małe państwa Europy środkowo-wschodniej w Unii Europejskiej (First Five Years: Small States of Central-Eastern Europe in the European Union)* (Warszawa: Instytut Studiów Politycznych Polskiej Akademii Nauk, 2010): Mindaugas Degutis, "Lithuania – Five Years in [sic—the] European Union," (61–69), Tomasz Otocki, "W cieniu kryzysu. Doświadczenia łotewskie 2004–2009," ("In the Shadow of a Crisis: The Latvian Experience") (70–85), Aleksander Gubrynowicz, "Estonia – pięć lat w Unii Europejskiej," ("Estonia: Five Years in the European Union") (119–34).

56. Estonia fled the (Soviet) Rouble at the first opportunity in 1992. It then pegged its Kroon to the German mark and, in 2002, to the euro. See Tovio U. Raun,

"Estonia after 1991: Identity and Integration," *East European Politics and Societies* 23, no. 4 (Fall 2009): 526–535; Neil Dennis, "Euro Falls as Estonia Joins the Eurozone," *Financial Times* (January 3, 2011), http://www.ft.com/intl/cms/s/0/0e1b1ca0-1730-11e0-badd-00144feabdc0.html#axzz1UTBoUzTJ; "Estonia becomes 17th member of euro zone," *BBC News* (December 31, 2010): http://www.bbc.co.uk/news/world-europe-12098513; Jack Ewing, "As Euro Struggles, Estonia Readies for Entry in Currency," *The New York Times* (December 30, 2010): http://www.nytimes.com/2010/12/31/business/global/31euro.html. On Estonia's economic miracle prior to joining the EU, see John Gillingham, *European Integration, 1950-2003: Superstate or New Market Economy?* (New York: Cambridge University Press, 2003), 422–26.

57. See "Russian Military Bases in Belarus Should Be Paid For, Lukashenko," Telegraf.by, (April 26, 2010), http://telegraf.by/2010/04/russian_bases_in_belarus_should_be_paid_for_lukashenko; Nikolai Troitsky, "The Unequal Sides of the Slavic Triangle," *RIA Novosti* (April 24, 2010), http://en.rian.ru/analysis/20100427/158776387.html; "Молдова просить НАТО видворити з Придністров'я війська РФ," ("Moldova Asks NATO to Eject Russian Federation Army from Transnistria") TSN.UA, (November 12, 2010), http://tsn.ua/svit/moldova-prosit-nato-vidvoriti-z-pridnistrov-ya-viyska-rf.html; "Регионалы объяснили, в каком случае Янукович расторгнет договор о флоте," ("Regionaires Explain under What Conditions Yanukovich Signs the Fleet Agreement"), Unian.net, (April 25, 2010), http://www.unian.net/rus/news/news-374111.html. See also Zdzislaw Lachowski [Zdzisław Lachowski], "Foreign Military Bases in Eurasia," Stockholm International Peace Research Institute, SIRPI Policy Paper no. 18 (June 2007), 1–78 (Table 5.1 at 46, Moldova at 59–60, Ukraine at 60–62, and Belarus at 62), http://books.sipri.org/files/PP/SIPRIPP18.pdf.

58. On open borders see "Страны Таможенного союза открывают внутренние границы," ("The Parties to the Customs Union Open Their Borders") *Bagnet* (November 22, 2010), http://www.bagnet.org/news/summaries/one_day_of_planet/2010-11-22/84467; and see below. On the decline of the use of Russian throughout the post-Soviet sphere see Paul Goble, "Post-Soviet States Increasingly Diverge in Use of Russian, Study Shows," *Window on Eurasia* (May 2, 2008): http://windowoneurasia.blogspot.com/2008/05/window-on-eurasia-post-soviet-states.html. On the status of local languages see Michał Łesiów, "An Important New Role of National Languages in the Former Soviet Republics which Became Independent States in 1991," in *The Future of East-Central Europe*, ed. Andrzej Dumała and Ziemowit Jacek Pietraś (Lublin: Maria Curie-Skłodowska University Press, 1996), 605–09; Dominique Arel, "Language Politics in Independent Ukraine: Towards One or Two State Languages?" *Nationalities Papers* 23, no. 3 (September 1995): 597–622; Anna Fournier, "Mapping Identities: Russian Resistance to Linguistic Ukrainisation in Central and Eastern Ukraine," *Europe-Asia Studies* 54, no. 3 (May 2002): 415–33; Jan G. Janmaat, "Language Politics in Education and the Response of the Russians in Ukraine," *Nationalities Papers* 27, no. 3 (September 1999): 475–501; Dominique Arel, "Interpreting 'Nationality' and 'Language' in the 2001 Ukrainian Census," *Post-Soviet Affairs* 18, no. 3 (July–September 2002): 213–49.

59. See Yevhen Pashchenko, "The Realities and Logic of Myth in Inter-Slavic Relations," in *The Political Analysis of Postcommunism: Understanding Postcommunist Ukraine*, ed. Volodymyr Polokhalo (College Station, TX: Texas A&M University Press, 1997), 321–32; Mordechai Altshuler, "Some Soviet and Post-Soviet National and Linguistic Problems in the Slavic Republics (States):

Russia, Ukraine, Belarus" in *Quest for Models of Coexistence: National and Ethnic Dimensions of Changes in the Slavic Eurasian World*, ed. Kōichi Inoue and Tomohiko Uyama (Sapporo: Slavic Research Center, Hokkaido University: 1998), 111–32, also http://src-h.slav.hokudai.ac.jp/sympo/97summer/alt.html; Ilya Prizel, *National Identity and Foreign Policy: Nationalism and Leadership in Poland, Russia, and Ukraine* (Cambridge: Cambridge University Press, 1998); David D. Laitin, *Identity in Formation: The Russian-Speaking Populations in the Near Abroad* (Ithaca, NY: Cornell University Press, 1998); Paul Kolstoe, "The Eye of the Whirlwind: Belarus and Ukraine," in *Russians in the Former Soviet Republics*, ed. Paul Kolstoe (Bloomington, IN: Indiana University Press, 1995), 170–99; Ian Bremmer, "The Politics of Ethnicity: Russians in the New Ukraine," *Europe-Asia Studies* 46, no. 2 (1994): 261–83; Roman Laba, "The Russian-Ukrainian Conflict: State Nation and Identity," *European Security* 4, no. 3 (Autumn 1995): 457–87; Klemens Buscher, *Transnationale Beziehungen Der Russen in Moldova Und Der Ukraine: Ethnische Diaspora Zwischen Residenz- Und Referenzstaat* (Frankfurt am Main: Peter Lang, 2004).

60.   The case in point is the annual hassle by Lithuanian Poles to visit the graves of their ancestors in Belarus. The Belarusian Poles face the same predicament. The distance involved is about 15 miles, but they have to wait at the border for hours, in particular during the Feast of All Souls. The border, in essence, split the Wilno land in two. There have been attempts to remedy the problem, most notably through the introduction of short term multiple entry visas. See Robert Mickiewicz, "Rozdzieleni granicą," ("Divided by the Border") *Rzeczpospolita* (March 31, 2009); "Европа начала процесс отмены виз для украинцев," ("Europe Has Commenced the Process of Changing Visas for the Ukrainians") Epoch Times.com, (November 22, 2010), http://www.epochtimes.com.ua/ru/ukraine/ ukraine/evropa-nachala-process-otmen-vyz-dlja-ukrayncev-95239.html. For some sage advice for the UE (while the author pretends that the Russian factor does not exist) see Alexander J. Motyl, "Orange Blues: What Should Europe Do about Ukraine?" *World Affairs: A Journal of Ideas and Debate* (December 2, 2011), http://www.worldaffairsjournal.org/blog/alexander-j-motyl/what-should-europe-do-about-ukraine.

61.   Marek Jan Chodakiewicz, "Minority Rights and Imperial Reintegration," http://www.iwp.edu/news/newsID.477/news_detail.asp; and *Nasza Gazeta: The Gazette of the Polish Cultural Foundation* [Clark, NJ] 1, no. 3 (October 2008): 4.

62.   Admittedly, Lukashenka is a shrewd and ruthless, if an opportunistic player. An inveterate politician, he initially attempted to use his power hive in Belarus to catapult himself into Russia's politics under the banner of restoring the Soviet Union or, at least, effecting a political and economic union between Minsk and Moscow. Later, the Belarusian leader pretended to balance between Moscow and Brussels (and even Washington), while at the same time flirting shamelessly with Beijing. In 2011 he openly regained his pro-Kremlin bearings once again, but still not enough to allow Belarus to be absorbed by Russia. See Steven J. Main, "The Bison and the Bear: Belarusian – Russian Relations 2003–2006," Defense Academy of the United Kingdom, Conflict Studies Research Centre, Central and East European Series, 06/06 (February 2006): 1–16, http://www.da.mod. uk/colleges/arag/document-listings/cee/06%2806%29sjm.pdf; Susanna Eskola, "Signs of Change in Belarus: Has the Countdown for Lukashenka Begun?" Defense Academy of the United Kingdom, Research & Assessment Branch, Central and Eastern European Series, 9/07 (August 2009): 1–10, http://www.da.mod.

uk/colleges/arag/document-listings/cee/09%2807%29%20SE%20mod%20style.
pdf; David Marples, "Belarus Resists Integration with Russia as Pressure Grows,"
Eurasia Daily Monitor 8, no. 61 (March 29, 2011): http://www.jamestown.
org/programs/edm/single/?tx_ttnews%5Btt_news%5D=37712&tx_ttnews
%5BbackPid%5D=27&cHash=ec7e4895064ef9b42aefd1ae98f369db; David
Marples, "Can Lukashenka Survive?" *Eurasia Daily Monitor* 8, no. 134 (July
13, 2011): http://www.jamestown.org/single/?no_cache=1&tx_ttnews%5Btt_
news%5D=38166&tx_ttnews%5BbackPid%5D=512; "Лукашенко не считает
Медведева президентом России: Белоруссия за неделю," ("Lukashenka
Does Not Consider Medvedev To Be Russia's President") *Regnum* (November 16, 2010): http://regnum.ru/news/1346653.html#667627832; "Страны
Таможенного союза открывают внутренние границы," ("The Parties to the
Customs Union Open Their Borders") *Bagnet* (November 22, 2010): http://www.
bagnet.org/news/summaries/one_day_of_planet/2010-11-22/84467.

63.   See Sven Holdar, "Torn between East and West: The Regional Factor in Ukrainian Politics," *Post-Soviet Geography* 36, no. 2 (February 1995): 112–32; Roman
Solchanyk, "The Politics of State Building: Centre-Periphery Relations in Post-
Soviet Ukraine," *Europe-Asia Studies* 46, no. 1 (1994): 47–68; Dominique Arel
and Valentyn Khmelko, "The Russian Factor and Territorial Polarization in
Ukraine," *The Harriman Review* 9, no. 1–2 (March 1996): 81–91; George Liber,
"Imagining Ukraine: Regional Differences and the Emergence of an Integrated
State Identity," *Nations and Nationalism* 4, no. 2 (April 1998): 187–206; Sarah
Birch, "Interpreting the Regional Effect in Ukrainian Politics," *Europe-Asia
Studies* 52, no. 6 (September 2000): 1017–41; Gwendolyn Sasse, "The 'New'
Ukraine: A State of Regions," in *Ethnicity and Territory in the Former Soviet
Union: Regions in Conflict*, ed. James Hughes and Gwendolyn Sasse (London
and Portland, OR: Frank Cass, 2002), 69–100.

64.   See Tim Sandole, "Post-Soviet Identity and Foreign Policy Formation in Ukraine,
Estonia, and Latvia," *SIPA News* (Columbia University School of International
and Public Affairs), (January 2012): 20–21; Zenovia A. Sochor, "Political Culture and Foreign Policy: Elections in Ukraine 1994," in *Political Culture and
Civil Society in Russia and the New States of Eurasia*, ed. Vladmir Tismăneanu
(Armonk, NY: M.E. Sharpe, 1995), 208–224; Taras Kuzio, "Russian Policy toward Ukraine during Elections," *Demokratizatsiya: The Journal of Post-Soviet
Democratization* 13, no. 4 (Fall 2005): 491–517; Anna Makhorkina, "Ukrainian
Political Parties and Foreign Policy in Election Campaigns: Parliamentary
Elections of 1998 and 2002," *Communist and Post-Communist Studies* 38, no.
2 (2005): 251–67; Ilya Khineyko, "The View from Russia: Russian Press Coverage of the 2004 Presidential Elections in Ukraine," *Canadian Slavonic Papers*
47, no. 3/4 (September/December 2005): 265–291; Alexander Etkind and
Andrei Shcherbak, "The Double Monopoly and Its Technologists: The Russian
Preemptive Counterrevolution," *Demokratizatsiya: The Journal of Post-Soviet
Democratization* 16, no. 3 (Summer 2008): 229–239.

65.   See Klemens Buscher, *Transnationale Beziehungen Der Russen in Moldova
Und Der Ukraine: Ethnische Diaspora Zwischen Residenz-Und Referenzstaat*
(Frankfurt am Main: Peter Lang, 2004); Ioan Chiper, "Bessarabia and Northern
Bukovina," in *Contested Territory: Border Disputes at the Edge of the Former
Soviet Empire*, ed. Tuomas Forsberg (Aldershot: Edward Elgar, 1995), 107–27;
Igor Munteanu, "Social Multipolarity in Moldova," Defense Academy of the
United Kingdom, Conflict Studies Research Centre, Central and East European Series Publication, G80 (November 1999): 1–38, http://www.da.mod.

uk/colleges/arag/document-listings/cee/G80-im.pdf; Trevor Waters, "Security Concerns in Post-Soviet Moldova: Still no Light at the End of the Tunnel," Defense Academy of the United Kingdom, Conflict Studies Research Centre, Central and East European Series Publication, G94 (April 2001): 1–14, http://www.da.mod.uk/colleges/arag/document-listings/cee/G94; Trevor Waters, "The 'Moldovan Syndrome' & the Re-Russification of Moldova: Forward into the Past!" Defense Academy of the United Kingdom, Conflict Studies Research Centre, Central and East European Series Publication, G105 (February 2002): 1–9, http://www.da.mod.uk/colleges/arag/document-listings/cee/G105; Vladimir Socor, "Moldova: The Kremlin's Next Target after Ukraine?" *Eurasia Daily Monitor* 1, no. 135 (November 28, 2004): http://www.jamestown.org/single/?no_cache=1&tx_ttnews%5Btt_news%5D=27207; International Crisis Group, "Moldova's Uncertain Future," in *The New Eastern Europe: Ukraine, Belarus, Moldova*, ed. Daniel Hamilton and Gerhard Mangott (Washington, DC: Center for Transatlantic Relations, 2007), 77–124, http://transatlantic.sais-jhu.edu/bin/o/y/new_eastern_europe_text.pdf.

66. See Heather A. Conley and Theodore P. Gebel (with further contributions by Lucy Moore and Mihaela David), *Russian Soft Power in the 21st Century: An Examination of Russian Compatriot Policy in Estonia* (Washington, DC: Center for Strategic and International Studies, A Report of the CSIS Europe Program, August 2011), 1–58, http://csis.org/files/publication/110826_Conley_RussianSoftPower_Web.pdf; Timofey Agarin, *A Cat's Lick: Democratisation and Minority Communities in the post-Soviet Baltic* (New York and Amsterdam: Rodopi, 2010); Andreas Selliaas, "Different Faces of Different Phases: Estonia, Latvia and the EU Minority Rights Standards," in *Political Culture: Values and Identities in the Baltic Sea Region*, ed. Sten Berglund, Bernd Henningsen, and Mai-Brith Schartau (Berlin: Berliner Wissenschafts-Verlag, 2006), 135–58; David J. Galbreath, "Still 'Treading Air'? Looking at the Post-Enlargement Challenges to Democracy in the Baltic States," *Demokratizatsiya: The Journal of Post-Soviet Democratization* 16, no. 1 (Winter 2008): 87–96; David J. Galbreath and Ainius Lasas, *Continuity and Change in the Baltic Sea Region: Comparing Foreign Policies* (New York and Amsterdam: Rodopi, 2008); and the following three essays in Ryszard Żelichowski, ed., *Pierwsza pięciolatka: Małe państwa Europy środkowo-wschodniej w Unii Europejskiej (First Five Years: Small States of Central-Eastern Europe in the European Union)* (Warszawa: Instytut Studiów Politycznych Polskiej Akademii Nauk, 2010): Mindaugas Degutis, "Lithuania – Five Years in [sic—the] European Union," (61–69), Tomasz Otocki, "W cieniu kryzysu. Doświadczenia łotewskie 2004–2009," ("In the Shadow of a Crisis: The Latvian Experience") (70–85), Aleksander Gubrynowicz, "Estonia – pięć lat w Unii Europejskiej," ("Estonia: Five Years in the European Union") (119–134). See also Paul Goble, "Russian Flight from CIS Countries Greater than from Baltic States," *Window on Eurasia* (June 5, 2007), http://windowoneurasia.blogspot.com/2007/06/window-on-eurasia-russian-flight-from.html. For the role of the Russian minority in opposing the EU and NATO expansion see Michael Ardovino, "Imagined Communities in an Integrating Baltic Region," *Demokratizatsiya: The Journal of Post-Soviet Democratization* 17, no. 1 (Winter 2009): 5–18; Piret Ehin, "Determinants of Public Support for EU Membership: Data from the Baltic Countries," *European Journal of Political Research* 40, no. 1 (August 2001): 31–56. See also Rich Fawn, ed., *Ideology and National Identity in Post-Communist Foreign Policies* (London: Frank Cass, 2004); David D. Laitin, *Identity in Formation: The Russian-Speaking*

Populations in the Near Abroad (Ithaca, NY: Cornell University Press, 1998); Leon Gudkov, "The Disintegration of the USSR and Russians in the Republics," in *Soviet Transition: From Gorbachev to Yeltsin,* ed. Stephen White, Rita di Leo, and Ottorino Cappelli (London and Portland, OR: Frank Cass, 1993), 75–88.

67. See Katja Yafimava, *Post-Soviet Russian-Belarussian Relationships: The Role of Gas Transit Pipelines* (Stuttgart and Hannover: Ibidem-Verlag, 2006); Roland Götz, "Ukraine and Belarus: Their Energy Dependence on Russia and their Roles as Transit Countries," in *The New Eastern Europe: Ukraine, Belarus, Moldova,* ed. Daniel Hamilton and Gerhard Mangott (Washington, DC: Center for Transatlantic Relations, 2007), 149–67, http://transatlantic.sais-jhu.edu/bin/o/y/new_eastern_europe_text.pdf; "Беларусь рызыкуе атрымаць ад Расеі яшчэ і пошліны на газ," ("Belarus Risks Receiving from Russia Fuel and Gas") Khartia'97/Charter'97, (October 15, 2010), http://www.charter97.org/be/news/2010/10/15/32977.

68. For a comparative perspective on Transnistria and related phenomena see Nina Caspersen, *Unrecognized States: The Struggle for Sovereignty in the Modern International System* (Cambridge: Polity Press, 2011); and Nina Caspersen and Gareth Stansfield, eds., *Unrecognized States in the International System* (New York: Routledge, 2011). See further "Молдова просить НАТО видворити з Придністров'я війська РФ," ("Moldova Asks NATO to Eject Russian Federation Army from Transnistria") TSN.UA, (November 12, 2010), http://tsn.ua/svit/moldova-prosit-nato-vidvoriti-z-pridnistrov-ya-viyska-rf.html; Steven D. Roper, "From Frozen Conflict to Frozen Agreement: The Unrecognized State of Transnistria," in *The Quest for Sovereignty: Unrecognised States in the International System,* ed. Tozun Bahcheli, Barry Bartmann, and Henry Srebrnik (London: Frank Cass and Taylor and Francis, 2004), 102–17; Pål Kolstø, Andrei Edemsky, and Natalya Kalashnikova, "The Dniester Conflict: Between Irredentism and Separatism," *Europe-Asia Studies* 45, no. 6 (1993): 973–1000; Stuart J. Kaufman and Stephen R. Bowers, "Transnational Dimensions of the Transnistrian Conflict," *Nationalities Papers* 26, no. 1 (1998): 129–146; Rebecca Chamberlain-Creangă and Lyndon K. Allin, "Acquiring Assets, Debts and Citizens: Russia and the Micro-Foundations of Transnistria's Stalemated Conflict," *Demokratizatsiya: The Journal of Post-Soviet Democratization* 18, no. 4 (Fall 2010): 329–356; Steven D. Roper, "Regionalism in Moldova: The Case of Transnistria and Gagauzia," in *Ethnicity and Territory in the Former Soviet Union: Regions in Conflict,* ed. James Hughes and Gwendolyn Sasse (London and Portland, OR: Frank Cass, 2002), 101–22; Claus Neukirch, "Russia and the OSCE: The Influence of the Interested Third and Disinterested Fourth Parties on the Conflicts in Estonia and Moldova," *National Integration and Violent Conflict in Post-Soviet Societies: The Cases of Estonia and Moldova,* ed. Pål Kolstø (Lanham, MD: Rowman & Littlefield, 2002), 233–48; Graeme P. Herd, "Moldova & The Dniestr Region: Contested Past, Frozen Present, Speculative Futures?" Defence Academy of the United Kingdom, Conflict Studies Research Centre, Central & Eastern European Series, 05/07 (February 2005): 1–17, http://www.da.mod.uk/colleges/arag/document-listings/cee/05%2807%29-GPH.pdf; International Crisis Group, "Moldova's Uncertain Future," in *The New Eastern Europe: Ukraine, Belarus, Moldova,* ed. Daniel Hamilton and Gerhard Mangot (Washington, DC: Center for Transatlantic Relations, 2007), 77–124, http://transatlantic.sais-jhu.edu/bin/o/y/new_eastern_europe_text.pdf; Paul Goble, "Is Moscow Preparing a Grand Compromise on Moldova?", *Window on Eurasia*

(March 28, 2008), http://windowoneurasia.blogspot.com/2008/03/window-on-eurasia-is-moscow-preparing.html. For detailed reports on the developments regarding Transnistria see Vladimir Socor, "Commentary: How to Turn Moldovans into a Minority in Their Own Land," *Eurasia Daily Monitor* 1, no. 63 (July 29, 2004): http://www.jamestown.org/single/?no_cache=1&tx_ttnews%5Btt_news%5D=26687; Vladimir Socor, "Unedifying Debut to 5+2 Negotiations on Moldova," *Eurasia Daily Monitor* 2, no. 203 (November 1, 2005): http://www.jamestown.org/single/?no_cache=1&tx_ttnews%5Btt_news%5D=31047; Vladimir Socor, "Moldovan Experts Blast Russia-OSCE Military Plan," *Eurasia Daily Monitor* 2, no. 226 (December 6, 2005): http://www.jamestown.org/single/?no_cache=1&tx_ttnews%5Btt_news%5D=31174; Vladimir Socor, "OSCE-Russia Plan for Moldova Criticized in Vienna," *Eurasia Daily Monitor* 2, no. 232 (December 14, 2005): http://www.jamestown.org/single/?no_cache=1&tx_ttnews%5Btt_news%5D=31215; Vladimir Socor, "Russian-Ukrainian Delegation in Moldova/Transnistria Short-Circuits the Negotiating Process," *Eurasia Daily Monitor* 3, no. 31 (February 14, 2006): http://www.jamestown.org/single/?no_cache=1&tx_ttnews%5Btt_news%5D=31385; Vladimir Socor, "New Broom at U.S.-Led OSCE Mission in Moldova," *Eurasia Daily Monitor* 3, no. 168 (September 13, 2006): http://www.jamestown.org/single/?no_cache=1&tx_ttnews%5Btt_news%5D=32032; Vladimir Socor, "Voronin Negotiates with the Kremlin on Transnistria," *Eurasia Daily Monitor* 4, no. 146 (July 27, 2007): http://www.jamestown.org/single/?no_cache=1&tx_ttnews%5Btt_news%5D=32901; Vladimir Socor, "Transnistria Settlement and Political Power in Moldova," *Eurasia Daily Monitor* 4, no. 147 (July 30, 2007): http://www.jamestown.org/single/?no_cache=1&tx_ttnews%5Btt_news%5D=32905; Vladmir Socor, "Another Precondition Set for Political Negotiations for Transnistria," *Eurasia Daily Monitor* 5, no. 73 (April 17, 2008): http://www.jamestown.org/single/?no_cache=1&tx_ttnews%5Btt_news%5D=33556; Vladimir Socor, "Voronin-Medvedev Accord Demolishes Moldova's Negotiating Position on Transnistria," *Eurasia Daily Monitor* 6, no. 54 (March 20, 2009): http://www.jamestown.org/single/?no_cache=1&tx_ttnews%5Btt_news%5D=34736; Vladimir Socor, "Russia Moving from Conflict-Solving to Conquest-Guaranteeing in Transnistria," *Eurasia Daily Monitor* 6, no. 57 (March 25, 2009): http://www.jamestown.org/single/?no_cache=1&tx_ttnews%5Btt_news%5D=34751; Vladimir Socor, "Moldova's President Surrenders Long-Held Positions in Joint Declaration with Medvedev," *Eurasia Daily Monitor* 6, no. 58 (March 26, 2009): http://www.jamestown.org/single/?no_cache=1&tx_ttnews%5Btt_news%5D=34761; Vladimir Socor, "Moldova's Post-Communist Government Adopts Previous Policy on Transnistria," *Eurasia Daily Monitor* 6, no. 184 (October 7, 2009): http://www.jamestown.org/single/?no_cache=1&tx_ttnews%5Btt_news%5D=35594.

69.　　See David R. Marples, "'After the Putsch': Prospects for Independent Ukraine," *Nationalities Papers* 21, no. 2 (Fall 1993): 35–46; F. Stephen Larrabee, "Ukraine: Europe's Next Crisis?" *Arms Control Today* (July–August 1994): 14–19; Orysia Lutsevych, "The Case for Ukraine to Maintain Its Nukes," in *The Future of East-Central Europe*, ed. Andrzej Dumała and Ziemowit Jacek Pietraś (Lublin: Maria Curie-Skłodowska University Press, 1996), 260–65; Sherman W. Garnett, "Ukrainian-Russian Relations and Western Policy," in *The Political Analysis of Postcommunism: Understanding Postcommunist Ukraine*, ed. Volodymyr Polokhalo (College Station, TX: Texas A&M University Press, 1997), 333–48; John A. Armstrong, "Ukraine Evolving Foreign Policy in a New State," *World Affairs: A Journal of Ideas and Debate*, 167, no. 1 (Summer 2004): 31–39; and the following two essays in Daniel Hamilton and Gerhard Mangott, eds., *The New Eastern Europe:Ukraine, Belarus, Moldova* (Washington, DC: Center for Transatlantic Relations, 2007): Elena Kovalova, "Ukraine's Role in Changing Europe," (171–94) and Dmitri Trenin, "Russia and Ukraine," (195–214), http://transatlantic.sais-jhu.edu/bin/o/y/new_eastern_europe_text.pdf. See also Natalie Mychajlyszyn, "The OSCE and Regional Conflicts in the Former Soviet Union," in *Ethnicity and Territory in the Former Soviet Union: Regions in Conflict*, ed. James Hughes and Gwendolyn Sasse (London and Portland, OR: Frank Cass, 2002), 194–219.

70.   Taras Kuzio, "Strident, Ambiguous and Duplicitous: Ukraine and the 2008 Russia-Georgia War," *Demokratizatsiya: The Journal of Post-Soviet Democratization* 17, no. 4 (Fall 2009): 350–72. Moldova also failed to act decisively at the time of the conflict, but ex-President Vladimir Voronin, once out of power, has tried hard to compensate through rude anti-Russian posturing. He met with Georgia's President Mikheil to annoy Moscow. See "Екс-президент Молдови Воронін відмовився зустрічатися з Саакашвілі," ("Former Moldovan President Voronin Intends to Meet Saakashvili") TSN.UA, (November 22, 2010), http://tsn.ua/svit/eks-prezident-moldovi-voronin-vidmovivsya-zustrichatisya-z-saakashvili.html.

71.   Jonathan Levy, *The* Intermarium*: Wilson, Madison, & East Central European Federalism* (Boca Raton, FL: Dissertation.com, 2006) is blissfully unaware of the heritage of the Polish-Lithuanian Commonwealth. Instead, he grounds his argument in the Founding Fathers of the United States, James Madison in particular, and Wilsonian idealism.

72.   See William E. Crowther, "Moldova: The Domestic Scene," in *The EU and Moldova: On a Fault-line of Europe*, ed. Ann Lewis (London: The Federal Trust for Education and Research, 2004), 27–48; Vasily Astrov and Peter Havlik, "Belarus, Ukraine and Moldova: Economic Developments and Integration Prospects," in *The New Eastern Europe: Ukraine, Belarus, Moldova*, ed. Daniel Hamilton and Gerhard Mangott (Washington, DC: Center for Transatlantic Relations, 2007), 127–148, http://transatlantic.sais-jhu.edu/bin/o/y/new_eastern_europe_text.pdf.

73.   For bilateral integration among the Baltic states see "Estonia and Latvia," Estonia Ministry of Foreign Affairs, (August 5, 2011), http://www.vm.ee/?q=en/node/91; "Estonia and Lithuania," Estonian Ministry of Foreign Affairs, (March 18, 2011), http://www.vm.ee/?q=en/node/85. And for tri-lateral unification ideas see Linas Jegelevicius, "A (Con)Federation of Three Baltic States?", *New Eastern Europe: A Quarterly Journal Dedicated to Central and Eastern European Affairs*, January 31, 2012, http://www.neweasterneurope.eu/node/171. The federation's tongue-in-cheek name would be Latlitestia. See also David J. Galbreath and Ainius Lasas, *Continuity and Change in the Baltic Sea Region: Comparing Foreign Policies* (New York and Amsterdam: Rodopi, 2008).

74.   There is cooperation between Belarusians and the Balts. See Nadezhda Khalimanovich, "Obshchaia kharakteristika dvustronnikh otnoshenii Belarusi so stranami Baltii" (1990–2002 gg.), *Belorusskii Zhurnal Mezhdunarodnogo Prava i Mezhdunarodnykh Otnoshenii*, no. 2 (2003), http://www.evolutio.info/index. php?option=com_content&task=view&id=628&Itemid=54. For a proposal for a Poland-Belarus union and even "the United States of Intermarium," see "Belarus Referendum and the Intermarium," April 12, 2012, posted at http://www.iwp. edu/news_publications/detail/belarus-referendum-and-the-intermarium; K. Волох, "Соединенные Штаты Межморья, или геостратегическое значение польско-белорусского союза," April 24, 2012, posted at http://www.iwp.

edu/news_publications/detail/belarus-referendum-and-the-intermarium, and in English as K. Woloh, "The United States of Intermarium, or Geostrategic Importance of the Polish-Belarusian Union," April 24, 2012, posted at http://www.bramaby.com/analiz/1-latest-news/200--usi-en-. At least a few Ukrainians support a close relationship with the Poles. See Stepan Trohimchuk, "Polish-Ukrainian Integration as a Foundation of Peace and Security in East-Central Europe," *The Future of East-Central Europe*, ed. by Andrzej Dumała and Ziemowit Jacek Pietraś (Lublin: Maria Curie-Skłodowska University Press, 1996), 311–13.

75. To this end, they should copy many of the pre-existing arrangements imposed by the EU. Some of them should only be assumed *pro forma*. The trick is to avoid taking seriously the bureaucratic insanity purveyed by Brussels for it will cripple the parallel federation from the outset by paralyzing its free market economy; undermining national cohesiveness; and reinforcing its post-Communist pathologies. The point is to federate the Intermarium and the rest of Central and Eastern Europe without subjugating them to either Brussels or Berlin and without imbibing the EU's knee-jerk anti-Americanism. See Pierre Manent, *Democracy Without Nations? The Fate of Self-Government in Europe* (Wilmington, DE: ISI Books, 2007); John McCormick, *The European Union: Politics and Policies* (Boulder, CO: Westview Press, 2008); John Gillingham, *European Integration, 1950–2003: Superstate or New Market Economy* (Cambridge and New York: Cambridge University Press, 2003); John Van Oudenaren, *Uniting Europe: An Introduction to the European Union*, 2nd edn. (Lanham, MD: Rowman and Littlefield Publishers, Inc, 2005); Beate Sissenich, *Building States without Society: European Union Enlargement and the Transfer of EU Social Policy to Poland and Hungary* (Lanham, MD: Lexington Books, 2007); T. R. Reid, *The United States of Europe: The New Superpower and the End of American Supremacy* (New York: The Penguin Group, 2004); Rockwell A. Schnabel with Francis X. Rocca, *The Next Superpower? The Rise of Europe and its Challenges to the United States* (Lanham, MD: Rowman & Littlefield Publishers, Inc, 2007); Roy H. Ginsberg, *Demystifying the European Union: The Enduring Logic of Regional Integration* (Lanham, MD: Rowman and Littlefield Publishers, 2007); Neill Nugent, *The Government and Politics of the European Union* (Durham: Duke University Press, 2006); Federiga Bindi, ed., *The Foreign Policy of the European Union: Assessing Europe's Role in the World* (Washington, DC: The Brookings Institution Press, 2010); Antonin Rusek, et al., eds., *The Economic Performance of the European Union: Issues, Trends and Policies* (Houndmills: Palgrave Macmillan, 2009); Shinichi Ichimura, Tsuneaki Sato, and William James, *Transition from Socialist to Market Economies: Comparison of European and Asian Experiences* (Basingstoke and New York: Palgrave Macmillan, 2009).

76. Admittedly, the Balkans may be the toughest part of the project. Yet, even there the process is already under way. See Sharon Fisher, *Political Change in Post-Communist Slovakia and Croatia: From Nationalist to Europeanist* (New York: Palgrave Macmillan, 2006); Sabrina P. Ramet and Danica Fink-Hafner, eds., *Democratic Transition in Slovenia: Value Transformation, Education, and Media* (College Station, TX: Texas A&M University Press, 2006). However, see Clarissa De Waal, *Albania Today: A Portrait of Post-Communist Turbulence* (London: I. B. Tauris, 2005); William E. Crowther, "The European Union and Romania: The Politics of Constrained Transition," in *The European Union and Democratization*, ed. Paul J. Kubicek (London: Routledge, 2003), 87–110.

77. This would be in congruence with past Polish federalist plans in Central and Eastern Europe. See Tadeusz Marczak interviewed by Jarosław Kozakowski, "Niezrealizowana koncepcja Międzymorza," ("The Unfulfilled Idea of the Intermarium") KlubyPatriotyczne.pl, no date (2010), http://www.klubypatriotyczne. pl/index.php?option=com_content&view=article&id=467:niezrealizowanakoncepcja-midzymorza&catid=22:aktualnoci.

78. There is no blueprint for the integration of the Intermarium and other successor states but see Alan W. Ertl, *Toward and Understanding of Europe: A Political Economic Précis of Continental Integration* (Boca Raton, FL: Universal Publishers, 2008).

79. In theory, EU law overrides national law. See "Infringements of EU Law," http://ec.europa.eu/eu_law/infringements/infringements_en.htm; and "Europe and the Law: The Supremacy of EU Law," http://labspace.open.ac.uk/mod/resource/view.php?id=376467. In practice, compare: DG INTERNAL POLICIES OF THE UNION, Policy Department: Economic and Scientific Policy, "Status of Implementation of EU Environmental Laws in Italy," (IP/A/ENVI/IC/2006-183), November 2006, 1–64, http://www.europarl.eu/comparl/envi/pdf/externalexpertise/implementation_of_eu_environmental_laws_in_italy.pdf; and Renata Juzikiene, "The Supremacy of the EU Law as a Challenge to National Constitution," paper prepared for the International seminar "The European Integration Process as a Challenge to National Constitutional Law," Cologne, Germany, October 18–21, 2006, 1–9, http://www.ostrecht.uni-koeln.de/fileadmin/dateien/internationale_kooperationen/Europaeische_Seminare/WS06_07/juzikiene.pdf.

80. Edwin Dyga, "Eastern promise – Why the West Needs *Mitteleuropa,*" *Quarterly Review* (Summer 2011): 10–34.

81. Two thoughtful observers have put it as follows: "The Russians are feeling opportunistic. They have always been distrustful of the European Union, since it, like NATO, is an organization formed in part to keep them out. In recent years the union has farmed out its foreign policy to whatever state was most affected by the issue in question, and in many cases these states has been former Soviet satellites in Central Europe, all of which have an ax to grind. With Germany rising to leadership, the Russians have just one decision-maker to deal with. Between Germany's need for natural gas and Russia's ample export capacity, a German–Russian partnership is blooming. It is not that the Russians are unconcerned about the possibilities of strong German power—the memories of the Great Patriotic War burn far too hot and bright for that—but now there is a belt of 12 countries between the two powers. The Russo-German bilateral relationship will not be perfect, but there is another chapter of history to be written before the Germans and Russians need to worry seriously about each other. Those 12 countries are trapped between rising German and consolidating Russian power. For all practical purposes, Belarus, Ukraine and Moldova have already been reintegrated into the Russian sphere. Estonia, Latvia, Lithuania, Poland, the Czech Republic, Slovakia, Hungary, Romania and Bulgaria are finding themselves under ever-stronger German influence but are fighting to retain their independence. As much as the nine distrust the Russians and Germans, however, they have no alternative at present. The obvious solution for these "Intermarium" states—as well as for the French—is sponsorship by the United States. But the Americans are distracted and contemplating a new period of isolationism, forcing the nine to consider other, less palatable, options. These include everything from a local Intermarium alliance that would

be questionable at best to picking either the Russians or Germans and suing for terms. France's nightmare scenario is on the horizon, but for these nine states—which labored under the Soviet lash only 22 years ago—it is front and center." See Peter Zeihan and Marko Papic, "Germany's Choice: Part 2," *Stratfor* (July 26, 2011), http://app.response.stratfor.com/e/es.aspx?s=1483&e=328223 &elq=ee77c05153484fa78262474495ef6c7d.

82. Officially established in Paris in 1926 by the émigré governments in exile (Ukrainian, Georgian, Azeri, Armenian, Turkmeni, Don and Cuban Cossack, and others), the Promethean movement received support of the government of Poland, which became a main hub of its activities: intellectual and political (including anti-Soviet intelligence gathering). One of the principal leaders was Ukrainian Professor Roman Smal-Stocki (Stocky) who headed the Instytut Wschodni (Eastern Institute) in Warsaw. See M. K. Dziewanowski, *Joseph Piłsudski: A European Federalist, 1918–1922* (Stanford, CA: Hoover Institution Press, 1969); Timothy Snyder, *Sketches from a Secret War: A Polish Artist's Mission to Liberate Soviet Ukraine* (New Haven, CT: Yale University Press, 2005); Włodzimierz Bączkowski, *O wschodnich problemach Polski: Wybór pism* (About Eastern Problems of Poland: A Selection) (Kraków: Ośrodek Myśli Politycznej, Księgarnia Akademicka, 2000); Marek Kornat, *Polska szkoła sowietologiczna, 1930–1939* (Polish Sovietological School) (Kraków: Arcana, 2003); Ireneusz Piotr Maj, *Działalność Instytutu Wschodniego w Warszawie, 1926–1939 (Activities of the Eastern Institute in Warsaw)* (Warszawa: Instytut Studiów Politycznych PAN, Oficyna Wydawnicza Rytm, and Fundacja "Historia i Kultura", 2007); Sergiusz Mikulicz, *Prometeizm w polityce II Rzeczypospolitej (Prometheism in the Policy of the Second Republic)* (Warszawa: Książka i Wiedza, 1971). For a neo-Promethean movement and ideas see http://prometheanreview.com/.

83. For the Intermarium conceptualized as a federation by Polish interwar conservatives of Wilno see Jacek Gzella, *Między Sowietami a Niemcami: Koncepcje polskiej polityki zagranicznej konserwatystów wileńskich zgrupowanych wokół "Słowa" 1922–1939 (Between Soviets and Germans: Polish Foreign Policy Ideas of the Wilno Conservatives of the "Word" Newspaper)* (Toruń: Wydawnictwo Naukowe Uniwersytetu Mikołaja Kopernika, 2011); and by Polish émigré intellectuals see Sławomir Łukaszewicz, *Trzecia Europa: Polska myśl federalistyczna w Stanach Zjednoczonych, 1940–1971 (Third Europe: Polish Federalist thought in the United States, 1940–1971]* (Warszawa and Lublin: Instytut Pamięci Narodowej-Komisja Ścigania Zbrodni przeciwko Narodowi Polskiemu, 2010). See further A. T. Lane and Marian Wolanski, *Poland and European Integration: The Ideas and Movements of Polish Exiles in the West, 1939–91* (Houndmills: Palgrave Macmillan, 2009).

84. For a brilliantly incisive analysis of Poland's foreign policy in the region see Walter Jajko, "Poland: Strategically Active or Passive?" remarks delivered at the Annual Thanksgiving Dinner of the Washington Division of the Polish American Congress, Washington, DC, November 13, 2011, also published in the *Sarmatian Review* XXXII, no. 1 (January 2012): 1630–634, and available at http://www.iwp.edu/docLib/20120125_jajko.pdf. See further Joerg Forbrig and Pavol Demes, "Reclaiming Democracy in Central and Eastern Europe," Foreign Policy Research Institute, E-Notes (April 2007), http://www.fpri.org/ enotes/200704.forbrigdemes.democracycentraleasterneurope.html; Adrian A. Basora, "The Continued Retreat of Democracy in Postcommunist Europe and Eurasia?," Foreign Policy Research Institute, E-Notes (November 2007), http://www.fpri.org/enotes/200711.basora.retreatdemocracypostcommunist.

html; "Countering Democratic Regression in Europe and Eurasia: Findings from an October 16, 2009 conference at the Johns Hopkins University School of Advanced International Studies," Foreign Policy Research Institute, E-Notes (November 2009), http://www.fpri.org/enotes/200911.basoraorenstein. counteringdemocraticregression.html. Meanwhile, in lieu of strategic vision, the White House considers its priority both globally and regionally in the Intermarium to support and promote radical life styles and their ideology. See Scott Wilson, "Obama Orders U.S. Diplomats to Increase Efforts to Fight LGBT Discrimination Abroad," *The Washington Post* (December 6, 2011): http://www. washingtonpost.com/blogs/44/post/obama-orders-us-diplomats-to-increase-efforts-to-fight-lgbt-discrimination-abroad/2011/12/06/gIQA93mdZO_blog. html?wpisrc=nl_politics.

85.   John Hiden and Martyn Housden, *Neighbors or Enemies: Germans, the Baltic, and Beyond* (New York and Amsterdam: Rodopi, 2008).
86.   James Mace, "Geopolitical Implications of Ethnopolitics," in *The Political Analysis of Postcommunism: Understanding Postcommunist Ukraine*, ed. Volodymyr Polokhalo (College Station, TX: Texas A&M University Press, 1997), 301–20.

20

The Majorities and the Minorities

—How is your relationship with other faiths, because the Orthodox and the Muslims live here?

—I have emulated older priests. I remember their relationships; they served as my paradigm. I invited an Orthodox clergyman for Easter. He came and he wished me well. Lately, with a group of clerics from Grodno, I have visited the mullah Suleiman of Iwie. He welcomed us cordially; he explained things beautifully; and the relations between us are very good. People here are very nice and they wish each other well.[1]

—A Soviet-born Polish Roman Catholic priest
in Belarus to a Polish journalist, summer 2003

Vilnius? Minsk? L'viv? Those aren't real cities . . . Vilnius — without us, Vilnius would be nothing. Vilnius is a Russian city, Russian. It was built with Russian architects. Nothing Lithuanian about it . . . What? You write about Lithuania? Ukraine? Those are not real places, those are places we invented. Russians built Lithuania, Russians built Ukraine.[2]

—A Russian smuggler to an American journalist, a day after
Lithuania reestablished her independence, March 11, 1990

We have been forgotten by the Poles in Poland, because the Poles in Poland are not real Poles at all. . . . They don't value their home-land because they don't have to fight for it. . . . We are the real Poles, we here in the kresy [the Borderlands], we are the only ones left who believe in Polishness and who believe in tradition. . . . Them—Koroniarze![3]

—A Polish minority activist in Lithuania, 1991

Since the last wave of liberation after 1989, the Intermarium's majorities and the minorities, locally, nationally, and regionally, have entered a new stage of coexistence.[4] Each successor state has a majority population and minority groups. The dominant nationalities in their respective countries are Ukrainian, Belarusian, Romanian, Lithuanian, Estonian, and Latvian. But members of the majorities are often found also as minorities in neighboring countries. In addition to ethnicity, the citizens are also differentiated by the length of their residence in the Intermarium. Thus, minority groups are divided into indigenous people and postwar arrivals. The latter are often considered "interlopers" both by the indigenous minorities and by the majority population. The postwar transplants are usually Russian-speakers, but they are not necessarily ethnic Russians. They represent the hodge-podge of all Soviet nationality groups. Many are mixed, for instance, Russian and Korean. Further, both the indigenous and the interlopers in the Intermarium can be of the same ethnic background, for instance, an eastern Ukrainian from Donbass transplanted to Lviv. Their mentality is usually vastly different. A Polish Tatar whose family has lived in the Wilno-land for the past 600 years baffles his fellow Tatar from the Soviet Tatarstan who was resettled in Vilnius by the Kremlin in the 1960s. Same applies to Polish-speaking Poles from Riga and Russian-speaking Poles from Odessa. An "indigenous" Armenian of Chernivtsi (Czerniowce/Tschernovits) in Ukraine's Bukovina touts his Polonized heritage (dating from the old Commonwealth) to the great chagrin of both a Russified Soviet Armenian transplanted from Moscow in the 1970s and a recent Armenian emigrant from the original homeland. In the Intermarium, Russian remains the *lingua franca*, including for such eminently non-Russian people like the Jewish minority, who lost command of their native Yiddish. In many places varieties of local patois are spoken, including the *surazhok* in Kyiv, a Russo-Ukrainian hybrid. Some of those people truly do not know who they are. Whereas confusion obtains among some, the post-Soviets in particular, others rely on nationalism to define them.

Peasant (or "folkish") nations, once again, as in the interwar period, have to deal with historic and nonhistoric minorities in their midst. The outcome so far has been gingerly encouraging. Democracy and freedom not only thawed out the old grudges, which the parties involved can openly vent about now, but also fostered cooperation and understanding. Generally, even though there have been a few snags, liberty has been good for both the majorities and the minorities. In most cases, members of the ethnic minorities acquired full citizen rights in the countries of their residence. In Latvia and Estonia, citizenship can be claimed by any post-Soviet resident willing to learn the native languages.[5]

Of course, there are a number of outstanding issues. Property restitution is one. Common history is another. There is bitter division in Poland, for example, whether one should even remember the Intermarium's Polish past.[6]

There are also competing visions of its history in the successor states.[7] Fortunately, the healing process has started.[8] And nothing, from the perspective of the West, in general, and the United States, in particular, is more important than the attitude of the majorities toward the Intermarium's Jewish people. Once again, the Poles have led the way here. They have been applauded specifically for tackling the thorny issue of the behavior of some of their citizens toward Jews during World War II. There are hopeful signs that the Balts, Ukrainians, Russians, and, perhaps, even the Belarusians will eventually move up the same path.[9]

The restoration of the Jewish experience to the national histories of Estonia, Latvia, Lithuania, and Ukraine seems to be underway. There is some nationalist resistance, in particular, where native collaboration in the Holocaust was strong. Nonetheless, the restoration of memory proceeds apace because of cultural shifts, international pressure, wide academic interest, and genuine concern among at least some of the intelligentsia and the young. Local initiatives to preserve Jewish monuments and folklore are also not uncommon, especially in Poland. The progress on Jewish issues is smoother than that on the projects concerning other minorities because of the absence of sizable unassimilated Jewish communities between Estonia and Moldova. Hence, at the national level the undertaking remains often an abstract intellectual enterprise with few immediate practical implications. Those include generating goodwill in the West, instituting a new narrative on Jewish issues, reconceptualizing school curricula, and grappling with the controversial issue of property restitution. All in all Jews are back in the public square usually as a historical phenomenon, if not exactly as a vibrant and numerous community they once were.

Other local minorities are very much present in the Intermarium. Yet, they have largely failed to elicit Western interest or support, though, with a striking exception of the Russians, whose numbers have dwindled dramatically since the liberation.[10] Although they were once more numerous, ubiquitous, and prominent in the Intermarium than the Russians, the Poles have failed to attract much outside attention. Yet, they still matter. The local attitude toward the Polish minority is important because it reflects the understanding by the majorities of their own histories and their current attitudes vis-à-vis the West.[11] Simply put, the Poles used to represent and symbolize the West in the Intermarium. Their treatment can often be a gauge of the majority's attitude to Western heritage and its adherence to Western standards. Further, because, unlike Jews, other minorities are very much alive and visible in the Borderlands, their history is of concern to the majority populations. Often a minority interpretation of the past is seen as a threat to the majority. At times, however, it may be a venue to general reconciliation. Most politicians have duly taken note of that, including in a positive way.

On the negative side, some political actors, domestic and foreign, exacerbate the relationship between the majorities and the majorities. Internally, they use the minority issue either to mobilize the majority against the other ethno-cultural groups through populism and integral nationalism or to curry favor with Western protectors of the minorities. External actors play the minority card to exert their influence in the Intermarium. Russia, in particular, meddles in local politics to exercise its power in the region. The Kremlin's recent "Compatriot Project" serves this end, fostering cultural separatism based on Russian nationalism, Soviet nostalgia, and Orthodox religion. Meanwhile, the European Union, the United States, and the Western NGOs implement their globalist agenda both by promoting genuine liberty and human rights, on the one hand, and by socially engineering the region in congruence with their postmodernist ideology of "liberal pluralism," which means support for multiculturalism, radical lifestyles, and extreme environmentalism, on the other hand.[12]

The Baltic lands are the most congruent with the West as far as minority policies are concerned. Ukraine and Moldova hover between the Western model and the Belarusian one, which is often roundly criticized by the international observers. Each successor state of the Intermarium has inherited plenty of challenges from the past. The local majority responses to the minorities and their external champions tend to vary from place to place except, generally, in two of the Baltic states, where they are rather uniform.

Estonia and Latvia

Estonia and Latvia face a similar predicament, so we shall consider them together. Their political discourse is liberal nationalist, inclusive, and civic. Thus, it is open to anyone who is ready to jettison one's totalitarian baggage. It embraces interwar history and anti-Communist resistance, the postwar "forest brothers" (*meža brāļi* in Latvian and *metsavennad* in Estonian) in particular. Therefore, the Latvians and Estonians have had a great deal of trouble including their large, Russian-speaking minorities in the historical narrative of their countries. The Russians and, sometimes, other non-Balts are cast as invaders or at least foreigners. The local Poles are usually excluded from this cliché.

On the other hand, the Russian speakers make it hard to integrate them in the national stories. Often ethnically Russian (although, really, a hybrid of all Soviet nationalities), many of them defy assimilation. They refuse to learn Estonian or Latvian. They are firmly ensconced in Soviet mythology, complete with the delusion that Stalin had "liberated" the Baltic states. Many of them bemoan the demise of the Soviet Union and look to Moscow for protection. They are the ultimate postcolonial former elite offended at the natives for regaining their independence. And these post-Soviets vehemently reject the Balts' celebration of their anti-Soviet resistance. Instead, they continue to embrace the Kremlin myth of the "anti-fascist struggle," which, of course, includes the crushing of Estonia and Latvia's independence in 1940 and 1944.

Admittedly, the Balts lack sensitivity on occasion as the poor timing of the dismantling of the Soviet war memorial in Estonia's capital demonstrated in April 2007. This should not obscure the fact that the Baltic people have overall shown great moderation toward their erstwhile oppressors following nearly half a century of totalitarian rule. Yet, both the West's human rights establishment and the European Union politically correct bureaucracy have problems understanding the Baltic experience from the point of view of the victims from the majority group who simply wish to feel at home at last. And one cannot really be comfortable staring at a Lenin couchant or NKVD man rampant, both frozen in marble in the city central square. That is not obvious to many in the West, who are quick to dismiss the past as irrelevant. The very same individuals in Paris, London, and other places who bend over backwards to show solidarity with the Third World peoples removing the symbols, institutions, and personnel of western European colonialism are completely incapable of relating to the victims of Soviet imperialism trying to accomplish the same. Moscow-centrism and political correctness facilitate Western sympathy for the minority Russians. The Westerners are also seemingly oblivious to the nefarious influences of the Kremlin, the oligarchs, and the post-Soviet mafia among the Russian minority in the Baltics, including their meddling in the local politics, which sometimes undermines the democratic process. And the Balts tend to comply with Western gripes for the most part because both Latvia and Estonia are member states of the EU. Despite that, the numbers of Russians in the Baltics have dwindled, as the majority moves back to Russia, sulking. In distinction, Estonia and Latvia's Jewish communities stay put and are rather satisfied.[13]

Are the challenges with the minorities similar everywhere in the Baltics? No. The Latvians and Estonians would like their former colonial overlords who are now a sizable minority to recognize and respect the sovereignty of their hosts by following the majority rules, including learning the languages. In contrast, the Lithuanians would like to assimilate the local minorities, the Poles in particular, who are indigenous to their lands. This makes the predicament of Lithuania much different than Estonia and Latvia.

Lithuania

In Lithuania, the folkish leaders of the dominant ethnic majority sometimes behave as if they wanted to replicate the interwar integral model as far as nationalities policies are concerned. But the minorities demand their rights; they invoke the laws of the land and the European Union. The larger a minority, the more problematic its relationship with the Lithuanians seems to be. The tiny communities of the Karaites (Karaim) and the Tatars outside of Trakai (Troki) are the most understated. They have reached out to other Karaite and Tatar communities, principally in the post-Soviet zone, to restitch themselves. In addition, the Tatars have secured some international support from Turkey and Tatarstan. At home, both the Karaim and the Tatars merely expect local and religious rights, which they generally can enjoy.[14]

The Jewish community, which mostly congregates in Vilnius, also has several concerns, including property restitution and the Lithuanian vision of twentieth-century history. The Jewish citizens are divided between a secular and a religious wing. Each regards the other with a tad of suspicion. Further, acrimony obtains within the religious orientation itself as evidenced in a bitter struggle over a synagogue in Vilnius, culminating in its temporary closing twice in 2004. Lithuania's Jews agree, however, on the importance of preserving the memory of the Jewish victims of the Nazis, commemorating the Holocaust. The Jewish community members are also very apprehensive about Lithuanian nationalism and defensive about the allegations about the Jewish–Soviet collaboration during and after World War II. The Jews of Vilnius enjoy strong support of other Jewish communities, in particular in Israel and the United States, which often translates into diplomatic pressure on the Lithuanian government.[15]

The Russians also invoke minority rights. They usually vote for post-Communist, leftist, and populist parties, in particular well-funded outfits set up by oligarchs of Russian origin. They also expect and receive assistance from Moscow. As far as Lithuania's Poles, Warsaw has largely ignored them until quite recently. They tactically cooperate with the Russian minority. They also tend to vote for leftist parties, although their political vehicle of choice is always an ethnic Polish organization, most recently The Electoral Action of the Poles in Lithuania (*Akcja Wyborcza Polaków na Litwie*). Although Vilnius is quite apprehensive about its Russian minority because of the Kremlin, it focuses its ire mostly on the local Poles. This attitude stems from history, both ancient and recent.

Starting from the contemporary times, Lithuania's last bid for independence was almost entirely a Lithuanian affair. It was a great nationalist surge that unified ethnic Lithuanians against the Soviets between 1988 and 1992. Initially, the Russian, Belarusian, and Polish minorities opposed Lithuanian statehood for the most part, fearful of the resurgence of Lithuanian nationalism. Ultimately, however, a clear majority of Poles voted in favor of Lithuania's sovereignty. But that outcome obtained only after a lengthy and bitter struggle within and without the local Polish community. Their own ethnic activism took on an organizational form already in 1988, predating Sąjūdis. At first, the Poles wanted an outright autonomy. In September 1990, some of their grassroots representatives proclaimed the Polish National Territorial Country (*Polski Kraj Narodowo Terytorialny*) in the southern part of the Lithuanian Soviet Socialist Republic.[16] With tacit blessings from Moscow, they almost succeeded in replicating either Transnistria or Nagorno Karabakh.

In 1989, as also now, the Poles constituted the largest minority group, residing mostly in compact communities around the capital city of Vilnius/

Wilno. Much of the local Polish leadership and the bulk of the active Polish population initially sided with the Soviets, which may be surprising given that membership in the Communist party was considerably lower among Poles than other groups, particularly Lithuanians. This not only reflected a stunning success of the Kremlin's *divide et impera* policy (which had uniquely in the Lithuanian SSR supported some linguistic and cultural rights for Poles), but was also a classic example of a minority population seeking protection of an outside power against the majority perceived as menacing. Further, there was a historical resentment among the local Poles toward the Lithuanians. The former felt (and still do) that they were at home and the Lithuanians were merely interlopers in the Vilnius/Wilno land. That feeling tallied with the interbellum status quo and ignored all developments since.[17]

On the other hand, the Lithuanians have felt similarly about the Poles.[18] In congruence with the prewar integral nationalist ideology, they patronizingly consider the local Polish population as "lost Lithuanians" who only needed to be re-Lithuanized to revert to their former identity that had been "stolen" by the Poles sometime in the sixteenth century and after. Somewhat incongruously, they also regard the contemporary Wilno Poles to be uncouth and uneducated peasants well beneath "true" Lithuanians.[19] Further, the latter believed (and still do) that Poland appropriated their historical capital Vilnius/Wilno from them in 1918, in spite of the fact that a 1916 German census confirmed that less than 2 percent of the population identified itself as Lithuanian, with the Poles constituting about 54 percent, and the Jews circa 41 percent. (The preponderance of Poles in the countryside was considerably higher.) Therefore, the Lithuanians consider their acceptance of Vilnius/Wilno from the Soviets and its subsequent occupation in both 1920 and 1939 as fully justified. The Poles think of it as inexcusable aggression. They eulogize the struggle of their underground Home Army against the Nazis, Soviets, and Lithuanians, whereas no Lithuanian patriot can view the AK other than a nefarious agent of Polish imperialism.

In the 1990s such attitudes led to the Lithuanian majority democratically curbing the rights of the Polish minority in the areas of property restitution, bilingual services, and equal access to education in one's native tongue. The official Lithuanian stance vis-à-vis the local Poles has fluctuated since 1990. Generally, when the post-Communists are in power, they apply less stringent measures toward the minorities. With the right ascendant the opposite is true. For example, in 2009, the Lithuanian government ordered bilingual municipal signs taken down in Polish minority-dominated townships. The Polish spelling of Polish surnames is forbidden; the Poles are forced to accept documents and deeds with their names misspelled in Lithuanian. This has bred resentment among the Poles, especially since it is common knowledge that the Lithuanians in Poland enjoy this right without any restrictions. It is also congruent with the practices throughout the EU of which both

Poland and Lithuania are members. Consequently, the Polish leadership in the Wilno area is split. Some have elected to cooperate with the Lithuanian government, the left in particular. Others have alternated between sulking in passive opposition and conducting a campaign of civil disobedience that intensified seriously in 2011.[20]

Such historically fueled conflicts frequently spill over the western border. However, former Wilno-land Poles, AK veterans in particular, in contemporary Poland and abroad have failed to influence the Polish government to take any anti-Lithuanian measures. In fact, no Polish politician or community activist has advocated retaliating against the tiny Lithuanian minority in Poland. Instead, Poland's Lithuanians have been democratically granted equal rights. They can spell their names anyway they please. Their settlements have bilingual signs; and their schools face no limitations. There is no compulsory Polonization. Further, Poland had consistently supported Lithuania in its endeavors to join NATO and the EU. Warsaw has also kept rather quiet about the unfair treatment of the Polish minority by Vilnius at least until recently. Last but not least, Polish intellectuals in contemporary Poland have been extremely indulgent and forgiving toward the ethnic Lithuanians, while scathingly dismissive and patronizing toward the Lithuanian Poles. This stems from liberal Warsaw's admiration toward the Lithuanian "Other," on the one hand, and its scorn of the Wilno-land Poles as bumpkins and unreconstructed Catholic nationalists who can derail Poland's pro-successor state eastern policy, on the other.[21]

For those reasons in the past twenty years the Lithuanians and their government seem to have relaxed, at least partly, their latent fear of "Polish imperialism" emanating from Warsaw. They have not yet fully come to grips with the recent past, though. For example, the standard Soviet view that the Home Army was a criminal organization, collaborating with the Nazis and ethnically cleansing Lithuanians in the Wilno/Vilnius region still enjoys a wide currency, including among some prominent Vilnius intellectuals.[22] Nonetheless, at least some Lithuanians try to incorporate the Polish experience into their history. For instance, the parliaments of both nations have taken to celebrating jointly the anniversary of the Constitution of May 3, 1791. Further, on May 9, 2005, Home Army veterans were invited by the Government of Lithuania for the first time ever to an official function marking the end of World War II. The Lithuanian Forest Brothers (*miškų broliai/vietinė rinktinė*) of the anti-Soviet insurrection and Red Army servicemen were also welcomed. This was an important first step in the process of national reconciliation.[23] Moreover, on June 11, 2005, at a ceremony marking the 1944 pacification of two villages—one Polish (Glinciszki/Glitiškės), the other Lithuanian (Dubingiai/Dubinki), ex-servicemen of a German-sponsored Lithuanian military formation and Home Army veterans publicly reconciled. The Lithuanians have even lately dropped their former disdain for their Polonized aristocracy. In

September 2009, two powerful Radziwiłł princes of the sixteenth century were reinterred in an official state ceremony. The family was invited from Poland and elsewhere. Contemporary Lithuania seems to have finally, if fleetingly, embraced the old Grand Duchy in a nonintegral nationalist way.[24]

The Republic of Lithuania is a member of the EU; it is also a democracy. The obligation of the nation to act according to the liberal standards as far as its nationalities is obvious. But Vilnius straddles the fence as far as minority rights are concerned. Its leaders would like to run a large chunk of the former Grand Duchy of Lithuania like the folkish nationalists did the interwar Samogitian Kaunas-based integrist state. This just will not do.

Ukraine

Ukraine also has its share of nationality problems. They concern not only the Poles, but other minority ethnicities as well.[25] The attitude toward the Poles (both at home and abroad), however, is a litmus test of Ukraine's readiness for national and regional cooperation with the West. Thus, the Ukrainian treatment of its Polish minority translates often into Ukraine's official attitude toward Poland.

There have been some positive developments. Most significantly, the Uniate Catholic (i.e., Byzantine-rite Roman Catholics) and (Latin-rite) Roman Catholic Churches work strenuously for making mutual amends for the sins of the Ukrainians and Poles against each other.[26] On the secular plane, the Ukrainian government countenances cultural and social cooperation. For instance, it permits Polish art historians and artisans to restore Polish historical buildings, usually sacral structures. It also allows the Poles to exhume and reinter their dead from wartime mass burial pits. They can repair neglected and abandoned Polish graveyards. After more than a decade of bickering, the town administration of Lviv/Lwów finally agreed to open officially a Polish military cemetery which had been partly bulldozed by the Soviets and restored by the Poles in the last few years. This important event of mutual reconciliation, which was nearly derailed by a resolution of the Ukrainian Parliament passed just a few days prior, took place on June 24, 2005, in the presence of the presidents of Poland and Ukraine, with churchmen of all faiths joining in.[27] However, the Polish–Ukrainian rift is much deeper than the Polish–Lithuanian one and it will take much longer to heal.

The official policy of Warsaw toward Kyiv has been almost as gentle as that in regards to Vilnius. The Polish authorities have largely failed to pressure their Ukrainian counterparts to improve the lot of the Polish minority. Poland granted extensive rights to her Ukrainians without any reciprocity.[28] The attitude of the Poles toward their Ukrainian neighbor has been selflessly generous and extremely supportive. As far as the other side, good will has so far either appeared only tentatively from time to time or failed to materialize at all. Warsaw routinely apologizes to Kyiv for various historical Polish transgressions; it invariably takes the Ukrainian side in most international disputes; and it consistently backs Ukraine's drive for freedom and democracy. On the other hand, Poland hardly ever asks for anything back (except, as noted above, the permission to bury the dead and to fund and execute the restoration of Polish objects of art and architecture in Ukraine).

The Polish government has limited itself mostly to securing symbolic gestures, including most notably Ukraine's support to commemorate the Polish victims of Soviet terror. At the same time, Warsaw has eschewed encouraging Kyiv to deal with the bitter legacy of the ethnic cleansing campaign against the Poles by the Ukrainian nationalists during World War II. Already in August 1990 Poland's Senate passed a resolution condemning the internal deportation of Ukrainians in the so-called "Akcja Wisła" (Vistula Operation) of 1946. Yet, the Polish authorities made no effort to commemorate the fiftieth anniversary of the ethnic cleansing of Poles in Volhynia in 1993 and they largely downplayed the sixty-fifth anniversary in 2008. Further, the Polish government has assisted Ukraine's bid for a closer association with the EU and NATO. Warsaw has kept silent on property restitution issues for Ukraine's Polish community, while returning some private and ecclesiastical properties to its Ukrainian citizens. And Poland is rather mum about the complaints of anti-Polish discrimination in ecclesiastical matters in Ukraine.[29] Last but not least, the Poles, both officials and the public at large, supported overwhelmingly and wholeheartedly the "Orange Revolution" and its aftermath.[30]

Poland's backing for the Orange movement constituted a significant breakthrough in Polish–Ukrainian relations, which was warmly acknowledged in Ukraine. For example, on December 9, 2004, a few score of Ukrainian intellectuals in Kiev sent "An Open Letter to the Poles."

> Dear Friends, we have constantly felt your fraternal sympathy with which you support us in our struggle for the truth in this historic moment, when we as a nation have risen against the lawlessness of the regime which attempted to falsify the presidential elections and when in the name of democracy and human rights we have launched a struggle against the post-Soviet system of the government. . . When you struggled for freedom under the banner of 'Solidarity,' we were praying for you with our hearts and together with you we were singing 'Poland has not perished yet.' It succeeded and the Polish nation prevailed. Today you in the entire country of Poland have been singing 'Ukraine has not perished yet' and you wish us luck. Therefore, on behalf of the Ukrainian nation, we would like to thank each of you cordially. Our struggle for the truth and democracy continues, but God is with us and therefore we are certain of victory.[31]

The long-term effects of such commendable sentiments are yet to be translated into concrete intellectual rapprochement in the field of common history. Despite a series of conferences in which Polish and Ukrainian scholars have attempted to iron out their vastly divergent interpretations of the Polish–Ukrainian conflict that came to a head during World War II, serious dissonance persists.[32] There are but a few hopeful signs among the grass roots.[33] For the most part, however, many Ukrainians still harbor deep historical suspicions about the "Polish lords" and "Polish imperialism." They equally denounce the legacy of "feudal oppression" and Poland's abandonment of Symon Petlura's Ukrainian government after the Polish–Bolshevik War (1919–1921). They further resent the treatment of the Ukrainian minority by the prewar Polish State.[34] They view the Home Army as a force inimical to Ukraine's independence. Last but not least, many Ukrainian intellectuals and regular folk also refuse to come to terms with the massive ethnic cleansing campaign in Volhynia and elsewhere.

This issue came to the fore when President Aleksander Kwaśniewski of Poland and President Leonid Kuchma of Ukraine read a Joint Parliamentary and Joint Presidential Resolution "On Reconciliation on the 60th Anniversary of the Tragic Events in Volhynia" at the unveiling of a monument in the Volhynian village of Poryck, now known as Pavlivka, on July 11, 2003, to commemorate the massacre of its Polish inhabitants by the Ukrainian Insurgent Army. The matter resurfaced again in Pawłokoma in 2006, where Polish President Lech Kaczyński and his Ukrainian counterpart Victor Yushchenko met to express sorrow for the killing of the local Ukrainians by the Polish forces. That the meeting at that level took place at all should be viewed as success on the path of reconciliation. But by September 2009, the mutual relations had again deteriorated to the point that both politicians canceled their presence at the unveiling of a new monument to the Ukrainian victims of the Home Army (AK) at Sahryń. The Poles have officially refused to honor the fallen Ukrainians without any reciprocity on the part of the Government of Ukraine as far as acknowledging the Volhynian massacres. Polish deportees and veterans boycotted the ceremony as well.[35]

Further, most Poles are not ready to embrace the Organization of Ukrainian Nationalists (OUN) and the Ukrainian Insurgent Army, Українська Повстанська Армія, Ukrainskaia Povstanska Armia (UPA) as freedom fighters. They recoil at the cult of wartime nationalist leader Stepan Bandera which is widespread in western Ukraine in particular. The most radical in the Polish camp talk about "the hydra of Ukrainian fascism" which "has been lifting its head again."[36] The problem, however, is that, aside from the 14th Waffen-SS *Galizien* division, the UPA and the OUN are virtually the only organizations that the western Ukrainians are prepared to tout as champions of their independence during World War II and its aftermath. Therefore, after 2005, the Ukrainian authorities resolved, over considerable opposition from Ukrainians in the eastern part of the country and especially those who fought in the ranks of the victorious Soviet army, to incorporate the legacy of the

OUN and UPA into the national historical continuum, which includes also such controversial formations as the seventeenth-century Cossacks of Hetman Bohdan Khmelnytsky. This honorable recognition of wartime extremists has greatly titillated and energized their integral nationalist successors in the present. But it sadly set back the cause of Polish–Ukrainian reconciliation.[37]

The Polish–Ukrainian dialogue is only one of a few important planks necessary for Kyiv to come to grips with the past. Most importantly, internal reconciliation is also far off among Ukrainians themselves. The eastern parts of the country are more prone to cling to the Soviet national Bolshevik mythology and are reluctant to embrace the western nationalist lore increasingly promoted by the authorities in Kyiv, at least until 2010. The eastern parts of the country are also more inclined to identify with Russia and its culture. Many citizens, in fact, list their nationality as Russian.[38]

There are also religious divisions, which exacerbate ethnic and interethnic conflicts in Ukraine.[39] The split within Christian confessions is a serious one. Roman Catholicism is still perceived as a "Polish religion." Protestant denominations are ostracized as dangerous foreign sects. Significantly, there is further a great deal of hostility between Ukraine's Orthodox Church which recognizes the Moscow Patriarchate and the Ukrainian Autocephalic Orthodox Church which preaches independence. Next, both Orthodox Churches feud with the Uniate Church.[40] Further, in the Crimea, the Muslims cause the ire of both the Orthodox and Uniates. Or, to put it in another way, the Tatars returning from Stalinist exile experience hostility from the Russians and Ukrainians as they attempt to reclaim their properties or simply squat. The conflict includes, of course, their different perceptions of history as it is learned and relearned by everyone involved.[41]

Last but not least, Jewish–Ukrainian relations have not been vetted nearly as thoroughly as on the Polish side of the border. Ukraine's Jewish community tends to stand at the sidelines. Organized Ukrainian Jewry is rather small. Most people of Jewish descent neither know or nor care about their roots. They were absorbed into the "Soviet nation" and are very reluctant to emerge as Jews. The obvious exception is over 230,000 people of (allegedly) Jewish origin who emigrated from Ukraine to Israel and elsewhere after the implosion of the USSR. But they are now largely missing from the Intermarium, except for a few who return periodically for business, pleasure, or community organizing. Meanwhile, the assimilated and the indifferent vigorously participate in Ukrainian politics.[42] According to Israeli scholar Vladimir Khanin, "the percentage of Jewish deputies in the Supreme Rada (parliament) of Ukraine is five times larger than the percentage of Jews in the general population."[43] However, most conscious Jews in Ukraine tend to eschew politics and, instead, focus on restoring social, religious, and cultural life of the community. They also deal with the usual issues of community property restitution and historical memories as well as occasional expressions of overt anti-Jewish sentiment from fringe groups. Like elsewhere in the east and south of the Intermarium, Ukraine's both official and unofficial sensitivity about Jewish issues lags far behind the United States and the EU, including to an extent the Baltics. This also concerns other minorities and their narratives.

Belarus

If recovering and synthesizing memories is difficult in Ukraine, it is almost hopeless in Belarus. Dubbed "Europe's last dictatorship," the unhappy place remains heavily Sovietized and thoroughly Russified. Its people tend to be confused about their national identity.[44] And the state exacerbates the confusion by promoting a hybrid understanding of what it means to be "Belarusian." The hybrid includes historical Soviet myths and Marxist class references to local peasantry and their urban relations ("the people"), who happen to live in Belarus as the majority, among others, the minorities, who are not exactly like them. In this telling, they are all one happy post-Soviet people. In reality, however, confusion reigns supreme about the nature of the Belarusian identity.[45] Further, we are told, there is really no need for Belarusian language because almost everyone in Belarus speaks Russian as the first language, and relatively few a literary Belarusian.[46] A scholar has even wondered whether, therefore, Belarus is "a state without a nation."[47] The confusion obtains because the reigning strongman, Oleksandr Lukashenka, and his minions undertook a disingenuous synthesis of Soviet Communist and Belarusian nationalist myths. Those mostly concern World War II. Namely, Minsk has embraced the Soviet partisan movement as an expression of Belarusian nationalism in a national Bolshevik form. Accordingly, the Polish underground continues to be regarded as Nazi collaborators and killers of innocent Belarusians.[48]

The official tale is hard to challenge. Free speech is squelched. No organized response to the official myth purveyed by the dictatorship is permitted. Ordinary Belarusian citizens, including the sizable Polish minority,[49] "prefer not to talk because they can offend the authorities." As one of them has put it, "Fear is the disease of the local Poles, often incurable, a bit genetic and stemming from history."[50] So far the community leaders, like organizer Andżelika Borys and journalist Andrzej Poczobut, have borne the brunt of the official anger at alternative narratives and alternative associations, particularly those unsanctioned by the government.[51] Ethnic Belarusians keep silent on the topic of the Home Army as well, even though some of its units were heavily Belarusian and even Orthodox Christian. And they fear to divulge the truth about the atrocities of the Soviet partisans against the Belarusian peasants. No one really talks about the anti-Bolshevik struggle of the local Greens. Thus, anti-Communist Belarusians are considered perhaps even worse than the Poles. As for other ethnicities, there is no "Russian minority problem," we are told, since everyone speaks Russian. A few thousand Tatars are largely ignored.[52] About 70,000 Jews are tolerated to be, in turn, showcased for

Westerners or castigated before the locals. However, the Jews of Belarus are heavily Sovietized and mostly devoid of their Jewish identity and customs with a few exceptions.[53] Neither the Tatars nor the Jews are welcome to share their past, unless it is congruous with government propaganda. Citizens of Belarus are thus permitted to identify only with the official national Bolshevik state mythology.[54]

In a way then, genuine Belarusianness is a minority orientation in Belarus. Accordingly, the only bright spots are rare, grassroots manifestations of Belarusian peasant mythology and, to a lesser extent, Belarusian anti-Communism. The latter concern almost exclusively the unofficial commemorations of the victims of the crimes of the NKVD and Soviet partisans. As a direct challenge to the official state mythology, they have aroused the official ire quite a bit.[55] A few non-Soviet and non-national Bolshevik Belarusian myths do persist as "collective memories" here and there in the countryside. Some of them have to do with the Polish-Lithuanian Commonwealth and its nobility. Many of the surviving tales are positively charming.[56]

As far as ancient history at the official state level, in a seeming contradiction, the dictatorship in Minsk has recently even made overtures to some exiled Polish-Ruthenian aristocrats. For example, the regime invited the Radziwiłł family to inspect one of its principal, newly restored palaces in Nieśwież/Nesvyezh in 2009. This is congruent with the new official policy of upholding the heritage of the Grand Duchy of Lithuania because Belarus claims to be its heir. The post-Communist regime thus endeavors to steal the thunder of the nationalist opposition who has claimed the legacy as its own from the end of the 1980s. By playing "historical politics" with its distant past, Minsk further would like to demonstrate to everyone that it is not identical with Moscow.[57]

Moldova

In Moldova, the post-Soviet minority picture is even more complex. In the east, the secessionist Transnistria, or Pridniestrovian Moldavian Republic, functions as a de facto separate country. Its Russian, Ukrainian, and Turkic Gagauz population is stuck in a Soviet-time warp. Most look up to Russia for guidance. And the Kremlin is not shy about interfering. In Cisnistrian Moldova, meanwhile, the ruling Communists (who have not even bothered to change their name) promote a national Bolshevik version of the past. They insist that "Moldavians" are a separate ethnic nationality. The majority Romanian speakers are confused. Their brief flirt with pan-Romanianism is but a fuzzy memory of the early 1990s. They are also heavily Sovietized and Russified, because for half a century they experienced Moscow's mailed fist, which included forcing them to use the Cyrillic alphabet. Hence, in the official census, most declare themselves to be of "Moldovan nationality" (75.81 percent). But they also list "Romanian" as their mother tongue (76.51 percent).

The Communists insist that the country's majority tongue is "Moldovan," as is the majority ethnic group. Romanians are a minority in this context. Thus, the nation suffers an acute identity crisis.

There are three forces exacerbating the crisis. First, the Kremlin interferes in matters pertaining to the Russophone minorities and uses them to advance Moscow's agenda. The interference intensifies both the obligatory separatism of the minorities and the reflexive nationalism of the majority. Second, to keep themselves in power, the Communist rulers are bent on forging a national identity derived from Moldovian regionalism. Since the Soviet rule is identified not only with terror and misery but also with Russian domination, that necessitates gradual concessions to the legacy of anti-Sovietism and anti-Communism. The policy tends to jar the Russophone minorities and to excite Romanian nationalists. Third, the Romanian nationalists have touted their creed, both liberal and integrists, which forces the post-Communists and Communists to espouse some of its tenants, on the one hand, and the minorities and Moscow to oppose them, on the other. The pan-Romanians have also made vain attempts to unite with Romania either directly or via entering the European Union. The latter option has resonated rather favorably even with some of the minority Russians, Ukrainians, and Gagauz. Other minorities, including Jews and Poles, are too tiny to matter as an electoral force. Yet, because of self-organization and outside assistance from home countries, they are probably farther advanced on the path of healing themselves by restoring their ethno-cultural memories than the "Moldovans" are. Moldova is perhaps in better shape than Belarus, which renders its situation a bit less pathological. That is somewhat of an improvement for its long suffering people.[58]

As far as the majority–minority relations, the Intermarium is not yet at peace with itself. On the one hand, we deal with the odious continuity of the Communist mendacity. On the other hand, as a radical antidote, we are offered integrist nationalisms of the prewar and wartime types. Whoever manages to frame the national discourse, wins and maintains power. Sustained propaganda assaults by post-Communism and integral nationalism leave very little room for the organic, evolutionary process necessary to restore memories and provide for salubrious cultural continuity at the local, national, and regional levels.

Individual recollections, collective stereotypes, false consciousness, and national memories remain almost hopelessly entangled in the lands between Estonia and Moldavia. To disentangle them, freedom needs to be perpetuated. The process of restoring collective memories is a gradual one. First, individuals need to open up and talk. Then, the national groups have to map out the parameters of their ethnocentric versions of history. Next, each nation should endeavor to incorporate other ethnic discourses into its understanding of the past. The majorities need to listen to the minorities and vice versa. Last but not least, a general synthesis ought to be undertaken of the history of all and sundry in the Eastern Borderlands of the West. This will take years. Without this gradual process the locals cannot even begin to conceptualize themselves outside of either the Soviet or ethno-nationalist paradigms. Therefore, without remembrance and forgiveness which foster concord and co-existence the denizens of the Intermarium cannot aspire to regional solidarity and unity. They cannot even perceive themselves as the Intermarium. They cannot relate to their current condition of freedom as a continuity of the times past and as a contradiction of much of the twentieth century. In essence, they cannot yet act in concert for the most part. How to facilitate solidarity among them? How to encourage unity? It is a daunting task.

One way to tackle it is to foster the revival of the spirit of the Commonwealth of the Crown of Poland and the Grand Duchy of Lithuania, including, of course, the Ruthenian principalities. By fostering the spirit we mean the study of its history and institutions, learning its lessons, propagating its universalism, and modernizing its message. This will entail an exercise in utmost gradualism and sensitive diplomacy. Otherwise the denizens of the Intermarium, led by their high-strung folk nationalists, rabid national Bolsheviks, and cynical post-Communists, will savage the project as a deception operation to rehabilitate Polish chauvinism and imperialism. To state the obvious, this cannot be a Polish project. It should be a local and national Intermarium elite project. It also ought to be a Western project. And it only stands a chance of success if it enjoys the support of the United States. The alternative for Washington is to surrender its responsibilities to Moscow and Berlin, the latter lately disguised as Brussels.

Notes

1. Quoted in Teresa Siedlar-Kołyszko, *Byli, są. Czy będą . . .?* (*They Were, They Are. Will They Be . . .?*) (Kraków: Oficyna Wydawnicza "Impuls," 2006), 109 (afterward *Byli, są. Czy będą . . .?*). For a similar attitude see the recollections about a Latvian Catholic priest by Adam Hlebowicz, "Kurlandzki Sarmata z wyboru: Ksiądz Augustyn Mednis (1932–2007)," ("A Courlander Sarmatian Out of Choice: Father Augustyn Mednis") *Biuletyn Instytutu Pamięci Narodowej* no. 1–2 (96–97) (January–February 2009): 125–29.

2. Anne Applebaum, *Between East and West: Across the Borderlands of Europe* (New York: Pantheon Books, 1994), 301–302 (afterward *Between East and West*).

3. *Koroniarze*: the inhabitants of the lands of the Crown of Poland, i.e., central and western Poland, as opposed to the Grand Duchy of Lithuania. See Applebaum, *Between East and West*, 63.

4. On the statistics of the minorities in the Intermarium and its environs see Jan Skarbek, ed., *Białoruś, Czechosłowacja, Litwa, Polska, Ukraina: Mniejszości w świetle spisów statystycznych XIX–XX w.: Liczebność i rozmieszczenie, stosunki narodowościowe, polityka narodowościowa: materiały z międzynarodowej konferencji Samoidentyfikacja narodowa i religijna a sprawa mniejszości narodowych i religijnych w Europie Środkowo-Wschodniej, Lublin 19–21 października*

1993 (*Belarus, Czechoslovakia, Lithuania, Poland, Ukraine: The Minorities According to Statistical Tallies in the 19th and 20th Centuries*) (Lublin : Instytut Europy Środkowo-Wschodniej, 1996); Zygmunt Sułowski and Jan Skarbek, ed., *Mniejszości narodowe i religijne w Europie Środkowowschodniej w świetle statystyk XIX i XX wieku: Materiały z międzynarodowej konferencji "Mniejszości narodowe i religijne w pokomunistycznej Europie Środkowo-Wschodniej" Lublin 20–22 października 1992 roku* (*National and Religious Minorities in Central-Eastern Europe According to the Statistics of the 19th and 20th Century*) (Lublin: IEŚ-W, 1995); Piotr Eberhardt, *Ethnic Groups and Population Changes in Twentieth-Century Central-Eastern Europe: History, Data, Analysis* (Armonk, NY and London: M.E. Sharpe, 2003).

5. The literature on majority nationalisms and the plight of the minorities is vast, in particular the Jewish community during World War II. For insights on the Jewish minority in Hungary, Moldova, Russia, Ukraine, and Poland see Zvi Gitelman, Barry Kosmin, and András Kovács, eds., *New Jewish Identities: Contemporary Europe and Beyond* (Budapest: Central European University Press, 2003). See also Fredrika Björklund, "The East European 'ethnic nation'– Myth or Reality?" *European Journal of Political Research* 45, no. 1 (January 2006): 93–121; Valerii Tishkov, "Inventions and Manifestations of Ethno-Nationalism in and After the Soviet Union," in *Ethnicity and Conflict in a Post-Communist World: The Soviet Union, Eastern Europe and China*, ed. Kumar Rupesinghe et al. (London: Macmillan, 1992), 41–65; Lowell Barrington, "The Domestic and International Consequences of Citizenship in the Soviet Successor States," *Europe-Asia Studies* 47, no.5 (July 1995): 731–53; and Sonia Alonso and Rubén Ruiz-Rufino, "Political Representation and Ethnic Conflict in New Democracies," *European Journal of Political Research* 46, no. 2 (March 2007): 237–67.

6. See Krzysztof Jasiewicz, "Nie drażnijmy sąsiadów!" ("Let Us Not Annoy the Neighbors!") *Rzeczpospolita, Plus-Minus* (January 16–17, 2009); and a rejoinder by Tomasz Kwaśnicki, "Poświęćmy Kresy!" (Let Us Sacrifice the Borderlands!) *Rzeczpospolita, Plus-Minus* (January 23–24, 2009). See also Agnieszka Biedrzycka, Fr. Roman Dzwonkowski, Janusz Kurtyka, and Janusz Smaza interviewed by Barbara Polak, "Kresy pamiętamy," ("We Remember the Borderlands") *Biuletyn Instytutu Pamięci Narodowej* no. 1–2 (96–97) (January–February 2009): 2–26; and Adam Hlebowicz, Tomasz Łabuszewski, and Piotr Niwiński interviewed by Barbara Polak, "Kresy utracone" ("The Lost Borderlands") in *Stół bez kantów i inne rozmowy Biuletynu IPN z lat 2003–2005* (*A Non-Crooked Table and Other Conversations of the Biuletyn IPN, 2003–2005*) (Warszawa: Instytut Pamiąci Narodowej, 2008), 255–75, which was first published in the *Biuletyn Instytutu Pamięci Narodowej* no. 12 (47) (December 2004).

7. Timothy Snyder, "The Polish-Lithuanian Commonwealth since 1989: National Narratives in Relations among Poland, Lithuania, Belarus and Ukraine," *Nationalism and Ethnic Politics* 4, no. 3 (Autumn 1998): 1–32.

8. In the West, the Polish émigré periodical *Kultura* (*Culture*) and its editor-in-chief Jerzy Giedroyc (1906–2000) continued Poland's interwar "Promethean" tradition, which aimed at liberating the captive people of Soviet Russia's empire and itself maintained a similar trend from the nineteenth century. Giedroyc's influence in Communist-occupied Poland was enormous. Thus, already from the 1960s, much of Poland's non-Communist and, in particular, anti-Communist intelligentsia, including Bohdan Skaradziński, Jan Jarco, and Father Leon Kantorski, championed the idea of freedom for the Baltics, Belarus, Ukraine, and other nations under the Soviet yoke. These sentiments increased significantly

during the 1980s. They were wholeheartedly espoused by many in "Solidarity" as reflected in the "Message to the Working People of Eastern Europe." See "Pionierzy pojednania," ("Pioneers of Reconciliation") *Rzeczpospolita* (November 5, 2005); Timothy Garton Ash, *The Polish Revolution: Solidarity* (New Haven, CT and London: Yale University Press, 2002), 221–22.

9.	Polish intellectuals are most open to deal with Jewish history. See in particular the methodological segment in Część VIII, "Jak pisać o trudnej historii," ("How to Write about Difficult History") in Jasiewicz, *Świat Niepożegnany*, 813–942. See also Konstanty Czawaga, "Przed wywiadem z ostatnim Żydem: Skutki społeczne i psychologiczne nieobecności Żydów na dawnych ziemiach południowo-wschodnich Rzeczpospolitej," ("Before Interviewing the Last Jew: The Social and Psychological Results of the Absence of the Jews in the Former South-Eastern Lands of the Commonwealth") in Jasiewicz, *Europa nieprowincjonalna* 1220–25. For the Lithuanian effort see Hektoras Vitkus, "Istorinė atmintis ir holokaustas: problemos samprata," ("Historical Memory and the Holocaust: Perception of the Problem"), *Genocidas ir reistencija* no. 1 (17) (2005): http://www.genocid.lt/Leidyba/17/vitkus.htm; Šarūnas Liekis, "Žydai: 'kaimynai' ar 'vetimieji'? Etninių mažumų problematika," ("Jewish: 'Neighbors' or 'Alien'? Discussion of Ethnic Minorities in Lithuanian Historical Scholarship") *Genocidas ir reistencija* no. 2 (12) (2002): http://www.genocid. lt/Leidyba/12/liekis.htm. At least one Lithuanian scholar anchors this question in a broader perspective of collaboration. See Vytautas Tininis, "'Kolaboravimo' sąvoka Lietuvos istorijos kontekste," ("Lithuanian 'Collaboration' in Its Historical Context") *Genocidas ir reistencija* no. 1 (9) (2001): http://www.genocid. lt/Leidyba/9/vytautas.htm. See also Sigitas Jegelevičius, "Lietuvių savivalda ir vokiečių okupacinė valdžia: tarp kolaboravimo ir rezistencijos" *Genocidas ir reistencija* no. 1 (7) (2000): http://www.genocid.lt/Leidyba/8/arunas8.htm. For an overview of recent developments in the Jewish community of the Intermarium and its neighbors see Antony Polonsky, *The Jews in Poland and Russia*, vol. 3: *1914 to 2008* (Oxford and Portland, OR: The Littman Library of Jewish Civilization, 2012), 3: 763–830; Hans-Christian Petersen and Samuel Salzborn, eds., *Antisemitism in Eastern Europe: History and Present in Comparison* (Frankfurt am Mein: Peter Lang, 2010), and, in particular, Svetlana Bogojavlenska, "Antisemitism in Latvia," 113–34 and Mordechai Zalkin, "Antisemitism in Lithuania," 135–70.

10.	As many as 3 million Russians have left the Intermarium since the early 1990s. The West's interest in the Russian minority outside of Russia stems from both respect for the power of the Kremlin and liberal sensibilities. Thus, Western scholarship on the Russians is plentiful. In distinction, there are hardly any English-language works on the Polish minority in the Intermarium. See Lowell Barrington, "Russian-speakers in Ukraine and Kazakhstan: 'Nationality,' 'Population,' or Neither?" *Post-Soviet Affairs* 17.2 (April–June 2001): 129–58; Chauncy D. Harris, "Ethnic Tensions in Areas of the Russian Diaspora," *Post-Soviet Geography* 34, no. 4 (April 1993): 233–39; Graham Smith et al., *Nation-Building in the Post-Soviet Borderlands: The Politics of National Identities* (Cambridge, UK: Cambridge University Press, 1998); Graham Smith and Andrew Wilson, "Rethinking Russia's Post-Soviet Diaspora: The Potential for Political Mobilisation in Eastern Ukraine and North-East Estonia," *Europe-Asia Studies* 49, no.5 (July 1997): 845–64; Zhanna Zaionchkovskaia, "Interethnic Tensions and Demographic Movement in Russia, Ukraine, and Estonia," in *Ethnic Conflict in the Post-Soviet World*, ed. Leokadia Drobizheva, Rose Gottemoeller, and

Catherine McArdle Kelleher (Armonk, NY: M.E. Sharpe, 1996), 327–36; Rick Fawn, *Ideology and National Identity in Post-communist Foreign Policies* (London: Frank Cass Publishers, 2004); Pal Kolstø, *Political Construction Sites: Nation-building in Russia and the Post-Soviet States* (Boulder, CO: Westview Pess, 2000); Neil Melvin, *Russians beyond Russia: The Politics of National Identity* (London: Royal Institute of International Affairs, 1995); David D. Laitin, *Identity in Formation: The Russian-Speaking Populations in the Near Abroad* (Ithaca, NY: Cornell University Press, 1998); Mordechai Altshuler, "Some Soviet and Post-Soviet National and Linguistic Problems in the Slavic Republics (States): Russia, Ukraine, Belarus," in *Quest for Models of Coexistence: National and Ethnic Dimensions of Changes in the Slavic Eurasian World*, ed. Kōichi Inoue and Tomohiko Uyama (Sapporo: Slavic Research Center, Hokkaido University: 1998), 111–32, also http://src-h.slav.hokudai.ac.jp/sympo/97summer/alt.html; Paul Kolstoe, "The Eye of the Whirlwind: Belarus and Ukraine," in *Russians in the Former Soviet Republics*, ed. Paul Kolstoe (Bloomington, IN: Indiana University Press, 1995), 170–99. And see two preceding chapters as well as see below.

11. Z. Anthony Kruszewski, "Poles in the Newly Independent States of Lithuania, Belarus and Ukraine," in *National Identities and Ethnic Minorities in Eastern Europe*, ed. Ray Taras (New York: St. Martin's, 1995), 131–47; Tamara J. Resler, "Dilemmas of Democratization: Safeguarding Minorities in Russia, Ukraine, and Lithuania," *Europe-Asia Studies* 49, no.1 (1997): 89–106.

12. See Heather A. Conley and Theodore P. Gebel (with further contributions by Lucy Moore and Mihaela David), *Russian Soft Power in the 21st Century: An Examination of Russian Compatriot Policy in Estonia* (Washington, DC: Center for Strategic and International Studies, A Report of the CSIS Europe Program, August 2011), 1–58, http://csis.org/files/publication/110826_Conley_RussianSoftPower_Web.pdf; Will Kymlicka and Magda Opalski, eds., *Can Liberal Pluralism Be Exported? Western Political Theory and Ethnic Relations in Eastern Europe* (Oxford: Oxford University Press, 2001); Alex Pravda and Jan Zielonka, eds., *International Influences on Democratic Transition in Central and Eastern Europe* (Oxford: Oxford University Press, 2001); Bernd Rechel, ed., *Minority Rights in Central and Eastern Europe* (London: Routledge, 2009).

13. Between 1989 and 2009, the number of Russians in Estonia declined from 474,834 (30.32 percent) to 341,700 (25.50 percent). The number of Estonians fell from 963,281 (61.51 percent) to 921,920 (68.80 percent) of the total population. See Jerzy Targalski, ("Estonia – liczba ludności (z podziałem na narodowości) w latach 1989 i 2009," ("Estonia: Population Statistics [According to Nationality] of 1989 and 2009") TMs, Warsaw, no date (2010), three pages with tables (a copy in my collection). For our most recent report on the Baltics see Marek Jan Chodakiewicz, "Notatki z post-Sowiecji (część I)," ("Notes from the Post-Soviet Lands, Part I") *Najwyższy Czas!* (October 9, 2010): XXXV. For minority issues see Heather A. Conley and Theodore P. Gebel (with further contributions by Lucy Moore and Mihaela David), *Russian Soft Power in the 21st Century: An Examination of Russian Compatriot Policy in Estonia* (Washington, DC: Center for Strategic and International Studies, A Report of the CSIS Europe Program, August 2011), 1–58, http://csis.org/files/publication/110826_Conley_RussianSoftPower_Web.pdf.; and Timofey Agarin, *A Cat's Lick: Democratisation and Minority Communities in the post-Soviet Baltic* (New York and Amsterdam: Rodopi, 2010). For some raw data on polling of the Russian minority in the Baltics between 1993 and 2004 see "Russians in Russia and Russians in the Baltic – Trends," Centre for the Study of Public Policy, University of Aberdeen,

http://www.balticvoices.org/russia/trends.php?S776173303132=32238329d6
05a6f7c35ac88272097d11. For a confused multicultural and Moscow-centric
argument see David J. Smith, *Estonia: Independence and European Integra-
tion* (London and New York: Routledge, 2001); David J. Smith, "Narva Region
within the Estonian Republic: From Autonomism to Accommodation?" in
Region, State and Identity in Central and Eastern Europe, ed. Judy Batt and
Kataryna Wolczuk (London: Frank Cass, 2002), 89–110; and David Smith,
"Cultural Autonomy in Estonia: A Relevant Paradigm for the Post-Soviet
Era?" a working paper posted at http://www.one-europe.ac.uk/pdf/wp19.pdf.
For a spirited rejoinder to politically correct charges of bigotry and racism, as
well as other accusations against the majority Latvians, by a Finish journalist
see Jukka Rislakki, *The Case for Latvia: Disinformation Campaigns Against a
Small Nation: Fourteen Hard Questions and Straight Answers about a Baltic
Country* (Amsterdam and New York: Rodopi, 2008). For a more scholarly look
see Vello Pettai and Klara Hallik, "Understanding Processes of Ethnic Control:
Segmentation, Dependency and Cooptation in Post-Communist Estonia,"
Nations and Nationalism 8, no. 4 (October 2002): 505–30; Andreas Selliaas,
"Different Faces of Different Phases: Estonia, Latvia and the EU Minority Rights
Standards," in *Political Culture: Values And Identities in the Baltic Sea Region*,
ed. Sten Berglund, Bernd Henningsen, and Mai-Brith Schartau (Berlin: Berliner
Wissenschafts-Verlag, 2006), 135–58; Alexei Grigorievs, "The Controversy over
Citizenship in Latvia," *Uncaptive Minds* 4, no. 4 (18) (Winter 1991–1992). See
also "A Bashkir in Estonia: A Conversation with Urszula Doroszewska," *Uncap-
tive Minds* 6, no. 3 (24) (Fall 1993). For a useful overview on Estonia and Latvia
see Michał Buchta, "Karczmy zajezdne mocarstw? Kraje bałtyckie a problem
mniejszości rosyjskiej," ("The Travel Inns of Empires? The Baltic States and the
Russian Minority Problem") in *Źródła nienawiści: Konflikty etniczne w krajach
postkomunistycznych* (*Sources of Hatred: Ethnic Conflict in Post-Communist
Countries*) ed. Kamil Janicki (Kraków and Warszawa: Instytut Wydawniczy
Erica and Histmag.org, 2009), 333–64. For a nostalgic, short travelogue of Latvia
see Tadeusz Żubiński, "Tędy i owędy wokół Wenty," ("Here and There around
Wenty") *Glaukopis* no. 15–16 (2009): 381–85. The Latvians (and the local Poles,
of course) have acted very hospitably toward visiting Polish aristocrats, the
Platers in particular, who held a family reunion near their old estate of Krasław
by the river Dźwina in 2002. Consideration for historic "Polish" families is the
rule everywhere in the Intermarium. Sometimes it is even state policy. See
Roman Aftanazy interviewed by Janusz Miliszkiewicz, "Nikt już nie mówi o
krwiopijcach," ("No one Talks About Bloodsuckers Anymore") *Rzeczpospolita*,
Plus-Minus, January 4, 2003; and see below. See also Walter C. Clemens, Jr.,
Baltic Independence and Russian Empire (New York: St. Martin's Press, 1991);
Anatol Lieven, *The Baltic Revolution: Estonia, Latvia, Lithuania, and the Path
to Independence* (New Haven, CT: Yale University Press, 1993); Rein Taagepera,
Estonia: Return to Independence (Boulder, CO: Westview Press, 1993); Toivu
U. Raun, *Estonia and The Estonians* (Stanford, CA: The Hoover Institution
Press, 2001); Ernest Gellner, "Ethnicity and Faith in Eastern Europe," in *Eastern
Europe..., Central Europe..., Europe*, ed. Stephen R. Graubard (Boulder, CO,
San Francisco, Oxford: Westview Press, 1991), 275–78; Lars Johannsen, "The
Baltic States: A Miracle?" in *New Europe: The Impact of the First Decade*, vol. 2:
Variations on the Pattern, ed. Teresa Rakowska-Harmstone, Piotr Dutkiewicz,
and Agnieszka Orzelska (Warsaw: Institute of Political Studies Polish Academy
of Sciences and Collegium Civitas Press, 2006), 49–100.

14. There are about 250 Karaites left in Lithuania. See Liliana Czerniawska, "Troki – Wysepka Karaimów," ("Troki – An Island of the Karaim") *Magazyn Wileński* (March 4, 2002): http://www.magwil.lt/archiwum/2002/mmw3/marc4.htm; Ewa Wołkanowska, "Karaimi – emigranci, którzy strzegli księcia," *Wilnoteka* (December 14, 2010): http://www.wilnoteka.lt/pl/artykul/karaimi-emigranciktorzy-strzegli-ksiecia; Tapani Harviainen, "Signs of New Life in Karaim Communities," The third Nordic conference on Middle Eastern Studies: Ethnic encounter and culture change, Joensuu, Finland, June 19–22, 1995, http://www.smi.uib.no/paj/Harviainen.html. Lithuania's Tatar community can be estimated at around 5,000 members (including ca. 2,000 postwar arrivals from Soviet Tatarstan). At first, the Tatars, who relaunched their community organization, the Lithuanian Tatar Cultural Society (Stowarzyszenie Kulturalne Tatarów Litewskich), in 1988, cooperated with the Poles and Russians. From 1995, in Soleczniki outside of Wilno, the hub of the Poles, they published their newspaper *Lietuvos Totoriai* (Lithuanian Tatars) in three languages: Polish, Russian, and Lithuanian. In 1998, the editors under Galim Sitdykow moved to Kaunas, where the Tatar community reclaimed a mosque (later it would regain three more: in Rejże, Sorok Tatary, and Niemież), and published their newssheet exclusively in Lithuanian until 2006. The pro-Lithuanian course failed. The funding dried out. And there were tensions within the community in Kaunas. Afterward, Sitdykow and his paper moved back to Soleczniki and restarted its trilingual edition. Meanwhile, the Union of the Communities of the Tatars of Lithuania (*Związek Wspólnot Tatarów Litwy*) under Adas Jakubaskas continues to work with the government in Vilnius. Nonetheless, they keep in touch with their fellow ethnics and coreligionists in Poland. See Antoni Radczenko "Tatarzy litewscy," ("Lithuanian Tatars") *Kurier Wileński: Dziennik polski na Litwie*, July 9, 2010, http://kurierwilenski.lt/2010/07/09/litewscy-tatarzy/; "Litwa: Tatarzy wznieśli pomnik Grunwaldu," ("Lithuania: The Tatars Erected a Monument to Grunwald") PAP, June 28, 2010, http://przewodnik.onet.pl/wiadomosci/litwa-tatarzy-wzniesli-pomnik-grunwaldu,1,3312702,artykul.html; Emir Szabanowicz, "Tatarzy na Litwie i w Polsce: Tatarzy litewscy," ("The Tatars in Lithuania and Poland: Lithuanian Tatars") *Nasza Gazeta* no. 8 (497) (2000): http://archiwum2000.tripod.com/497/tatar.html; Michał Łyszczarz, "Skąd przybyli do Europy? I jak żyją dzisiaj, również w Polsce," *Histmag.org*, April 10, 2006, http://histmag.org/?id=384; "Lithuanian Tatars," http://alka.mch.mii.lt/visuomene/totoriai/trumpa.en.htm.

15. For the secular Jewish community website see http://www.lzb.lt/lt/; for one of the religious orientations, the Chabad Lubavicher, see http://www.fjc.ru/communities/default.asp?AID=84425.

16. The issue of Polish autonomy germinated at the grassroots in Wilnoland and then it was briefly toyed with by the Soviet leadership at the Moscow center, including Gorbachev. The drama played itself out mostly within Polish organizations in Lithuania. However, it is unclear how much of it reflected the preferences of the grassroots, and how much stemmed from outside inspiration of the Kremlin, working through the local Polish Soviet Communist leadership. First, the initiative unexpectedly surfaced in Moscow. In 1989 two newly elected Soviet Communist deputies of Polish origin, Jan Ciechanowicz and Anicet Brodawski, proposed on the forum of the Supreme Soviet of the USSR to create an Eastern Polish Soviet Socialist Republic (EPSSR). The project fluctuated in scope. One of the most persistent ideas was to unite Polish-speaking areas of BSSR and LSSR. At minimum, however, the postulated EPSSR

would consist of Wilnoland. At maximum, this entity would encompass all territories of interwar Poland occupied by the Red Army following September 17, 1939. That would entail truncating the Lithuanian SSR, Byelorussian SSR, and Ukrainian SSR. It is doubtful that the two deputies would even float such a potentially explosive proposal without some kind of official backing at the Kremlin. This was allegedly put forth in conjunction with Gorbachev's threats that Lithuania could only be granted independence in its interwar shape, i.e., without Klaipeda and Wilnoland. Although it seems far fetched today, the idea of EPSSR was advanced concomitantly with, and closely followed the blueprint for, Transnistria and Nagorno Karabakh, both bids to maintain the Kremlin's influence in the region; neutralize majority nationalisms in the area; and prevent the bid for independence of Moldova and Azerbaijan. At any rate, the idea of autonomy enjoyed quite a bit of support among Lithuania's Polish community. It was the most important issue in the power struggles within the leadership of their ethnic organizations. In 1988, the Cultural Society of the Poles in Lithuania (*Stowarzyszenie Kulturalne Polaków na Litwie*) was launched. In 1990, it changed its name to the Union of Poles in Lithuania (*Związek Polaków na Litwie—ZPL*). Most of the top leaders were Soviet Communists of Polish ethnicity. Nonetheless, some of them supported Lithuania's independence and gradually came to dominate the ZPL. Their idea was that autonomy was possible only in a free Lithuania. Their hopes seemed to have been fulfilled in January 1990 with the resolution of the Supreme Soviet of the LSSR which promised autonomy to the Poles within the so-called Polish National Territorial Country (*Polski Kraj Narodowo Terytorialny*). Accordingly, a Polish Coordinating Council (*Rada Koordynacyjna*) was set up in the Soleczniki and Wilno raions to implement the resolution. However, in March 1990 Lithuania proclaimed its independence and the ZLP activists and their supporters were henceforth ignored by the new state. Meanwhile, their Polish Soviet Communist opponents had argued all along that autonomy required Moscow's ultimate blessing and not feckless Lithuanian promises. The pro-Moscow fraction was popular particularly in the countryside of Wilno/Vilnius. In response to Lithuania's reneging on the issue of autonomy, the Communist and Polish activist (and Supreme Soviet of the USSR deputy) Jan Ciechanowicz launched the Party for the Rights of Man (*Partia Praw Człowieka*) to compete with the ZPL in May 1990. It took up the cause of the Polish autonomy in Lithuania and advocated for the right of return by the Polish Gulag survivors and their descendants from central and eastern parts of the USSR. Initially, Ciechanowicz and his comrades, most notably, Czesław Wysocki and Anicet Brodawski, envisioned the Polish National Territorial Country as limited to the Wilnoland's areas with a clear Polish majority. Later, the concept changed. The dynamics of the development of this idea are unclear and the sources of inspiration remain murky. For instance, one of the leading lights behind the autonomy initiative was the second secretary of the Central Committee of the Communist Party of Lithuania Władysław Szwed (Vladislav Shved). After the failure of the initiative and specter of legal prosecution for treason by free Lithuania the ostensibly Polish patriotic Szwed fled to Moscow, where he is one of the leading deniers of Soviet responsibility for the Katyn forest murders – see his *Tayna Katyni* (Moscow: Algorithm, 2007), which was written in collaboration with Sergei Strigin. See Marek Jan Chodakiewicz, "Polscy Sowieci i sowieccy Polacy," ("Polish Soviets and Soviet Poles") *Najwyższy Czas!* (November 26, 2011): XXXVI–XXXVII; Aleksander Graf Pruszyński, "Litwa – Białorus i polska dyplomacja," ("Lithuania

and Polish Diplomacy") *Expatpol* (July 28, 2005): http://expatpol.com/index.
php?stsid=25839&kid=39; "Autonomia Wileńska," ("The Wilno Autonomy")
Kresy.pl (January 20, 2009): http://www.kresy.pl/publicystyka,analizy?zobacz/
autonomia-wilenska; Marek A. Koprowski, "Niespełnione nadzieje," ("Unfulfilled Hopes") *Rzeczpospolita*, a supplement: *Bezkresy* no. 2, (May 6, 2009);
Egidijus Meilūnas, "Kto chciał polskiej autonomii?" ("Who Wanted Polish
Autonomy?") *Rzeczpospolita*, a supplement: *Bezkresy*, no. 3, (June 5, 2009);
Robert Majka, "'Republika Wschodniej Polski' w byłej ZSRR," *Solidarność
Walcząca Katowice* (January 7, 2010): http://swkatowice.mojeforum.net/temat-
vt8465.html; "Autonomia Wileńszczyzny," Naukowy.pl, http://www.naukowy.
pl/encyklopedia/Autonomia_Wile%C5%84szczyzny. See further an internet
debate on "Wschodniopolska Republika Radziecka," http://www.historycy.
org/bez_grafik/index.php/t69261-50.html. On Szwed see Aleksiej Pamiatnych
[Alexei Pamiatnikh], "Rosyjskie publikacje ostatnich miesięcy na temat Katynia:
Film Andrzeja Wajdy i jego rola w problematyce katyńskiej w Rosji," ("Russian
Latest Publications on Katyn: Andrzej Wajda's Movie and Its Role in the Katyn
Debate in Russia") a conference paper (delivered in Polish), Warsaw, Poland,
April 8, 2008, http://ru-katyn.livejournal.com/18245.html.

17. The local Poles differentiate between the local Lithuanians and the Lithuanians
who were settled in the Wilno-land after the war. The latter are referred to
as "Samogitians" (*Żmudzini*), stressing their origin in the Kaunas area. For a
thoughtful study of national consciousness among the Poles of Lithuania see
Dorota Jaworska-Matys, "Kształty polskości," ("The Shapes of Polishness") *Biuletyn Instytutu Pamięci Narodowej* no. 1–2 (96–97) (January–February 2009):
149–155. For Lithuania's Polish minority views see wilnoteka.lt; kurierwilenski.
lt; znadwilli.lt; and www.awpl.lt. See also John Radziłowski, "An Overview of the
History of Poles in Modern Lithuania," *Nihil Novi: The Bulletin of the Kościuszko
Chair in Polish Studies, Miller Center of Public Affairs, University of Virginia*
no. 2 (Fall 2002): 29–30; Aleksander Srebrakowski, *Polacy w Litewskiej SRR
1944–1989* (*Poles in the Lithuanian SSR, 1944–1989*) (Toruń: Wydawnictwo
Adam Marszałek, 2000); Aleksander Srebrakowski, "Polacy litewscy wobec
Komunistycznej Partii Litwy i komunizmu," ("Lithuanian Poles vis-à-vis the
Communist Party of Lithuania and Communism") *Wrocławskie Studia z Historii
Najnowszej* 6 (1999): 251–70. For an example of a Wilno Pole's anti-Lithuanian
attitude in the early 1990s see Waldemar Franciszek Wilczewski, "Dziennik
Kazimierza Sakowicza," *Biuletyn Instytutu Pamięci Narodowej* no. 1–2 (96–97)
(January–February 2009): 86–94.

18. See Henryk Ilgiewicz, "Litewska kontestacja pojęcia 'Kresy Wschodnie,"
("The Lithuanian Objection to the Use of the Term 'Eastern Borderlands'")
in Jasiewicz, *Europa nieprowincjonalna*, 124–31; Applebaum, *Between East
and West*, 57–70; Marek Jan Chodakiewicz, "Notatki z post-Sowiecji (część
I)," ("Notes from the Post-Soviet Lands, Part I") *Najwyższy Czas!* (October 9,
2010): XXXV.

19. Audrius Bačiulis interviewed by Maja Narbutt, "Walka z uprzedzeniami jeszcze
potrwa," ("The Struggle against Prejudice Will Last Some More"), *Rzeczpospolita*
(May 5, 2009). The worst that can be said about the condition of the Lithuanian
minority in Poland is that some unknown perpetrators vandalized Lithuanian
language signs in the countryside outside of Suwałki in the summer of 2011.
See Robert Mickiewicz and Tomasz Nieśpiał, "Kto zniszczył litewskie napisy,"
("Who Destroyed Lithuanian Signs") *Rzeczpospolita* (August 23, 2011). Some
other unknown perpetrators on the Lithuanian side retaliated and desecrated

the graves of Polish soldiers of World War I and its aftermath. See "Atak wandali na groby polskich legionistów w Święcianach," *Kurier Wileński* (October 27, 2011): http://kurierwilenski.lt/2011/10/27/atak-wandali-na-groby-polskich-legionistow-w-swiecianach/.

20. Occasionally, the simmering resentment surfaces as when, on December 13, 2005, about 2,000 ethnic Poles demonstrated in Wilno to demand Polish language education and property restitution, which has proceeded restrictively in Polish-speaking areas. The demonstrators levied the charges of "de-Polonization" at the Lithuanian authorities. Later, the local Poles objected when the Lithuanian Post Office issued envelopes, which depicted Hitler, Stalin, and Piłsudski as equal occupiers of Lithuania. The most massive protest action was launched to object to Lithuania's educational measures. See Waldemar Moszkowski, "Polacy przeciw depolonizacji Wileńszczyzny," ("Poles against the De-Polonization of the Wilno Land") *Nasz Dziennik* (December 14, 2005); "Antypolska hysteria na Litwie," ("Anti-Polish Hysteria in Lithuania") *Nowa Myśl Polska* (May 4–11, 2003); Anna Wiejak, "Po ziemię jak po grudzie," ("Tough to Get the Land Back") *Nasz Dziennik* (November 20, 2007); Witold Janczys, "Państwowy urząd przyznał, że mniejszości narodowe na Litwie są dyskryminowane," ("A Government Office Has Admitted that National Minorities Are Discriminated against in Lithuania") *Kurier Wileński* (February 7, 2008); "Atypolski skandal w Wilnie," ("Anti-Polish Scandal in Wilno"), *Nasz Dziennik* (September 26, 2008); Katarzyna Zuchowicz, "Jak Polacy są dyskryminowani," ("How the Poles Are Discriminated") *Rzeczpospolita* (May 5, 2009); Robert Mickiewicz, "Szkoła strażnicą polskości," ("School – The Fortress of Polishness") *Rzeczpospolita* (May 5, 2009); Waldemar Tomaszewski interviewed by Maja Narbut, "Nie chcę mówić o dyskryminacji," ("I Do Not Want to Talk about Discrimination") *Rzeczpospolita* (May 5, 2009); Maciej Płażyński, "Polityka depolonizacji Wileńszczyzny," ("A Policy of De-Polonizing of the Wilno Land") *Rzeczpospolita* (May 5, 2009); Maja Narbutt, "Honor i pieniądze Polaka na Litwie," ("Honor and Money of a Pole in Lithuania") *Rzeczpospolita* (May 5, 2009); Maja Narbutt, "Polakowi zawsze wiatr w oczy," ("The Pole Always Gets It Tough") *Rzeczpospolita* (May 5, 2009); Piotr Kościński, "Chcemy pomagać Polakom na Wschodzie," ("We Want to Help Poles in the East") *Rzeczpospolita* (May 5, 2009); Dr. Artur Górski, "Traktat polsko-litewski: Martwe zapisy," ("Polish-Lithuanian Treaty: Dead Letters") *Nasz Dziennik* (May 9–10, 2009); Marta Ziarnik, "Litwa ignoruje Polaków," ("Lithuania Ignores the Poles") *Nasz Dziennik* (May 11, 2009); Mariusz Bober, "Waszej ziemi już nie ma," ("Your Land Is No More") *Nasz Dziennik* (August 19, 2009); "Polskie tablice będą usunięte," ("Polish Signs Will Be Removed") *Nasz Dziennik* (September 18, 2009); Michał Olszewski, "Litwo, ojczyzno moja?" ("Lithuania, My Fatherland?") *Tygodnik Powszechny* (September 7, 2010), http://tygodnik.onet.pl/1.52329.html; Maja Narbutt, "Po braterstwie nie został ślad," ("No Trace of Fraternity"), *Rzeczpospolita* (October 26, 2010), http://www.rp.pl/artykul/554530.html; Rytas Staselis, "Bariery w naszych głowach" ("The Barriers in Our Heads") *Rzeczpospolita* (November 2, 2010): http://www.rp.pl/artykul/557886.html; Maja Narbut, "Polacy dostaja szkole," ("The Poles Are Taught a Lesson") *Rzeczpospolita, Plus-Minus* (September 10–11, 2011): http://www.rp.pl/artykul/61991,714739-Polskie-szkoly-na-Litwie-nie-przetrwaja-bez-wsparcia-.html; Michał Wilczyński, "Zakazane tablice w *Švogieriu Šalis*," ("Forbidden Boards in the Law of Bothers-in-Law [i.e., Nepotism]") *Glaukopis* no. 23–24 (2011–2012): 318–21. For the on-going conflict over how to spell Polish names see the Associated Press's dispatch

by Liudas Dapkus, "Poles in Lithuania Want Their 'w' Back," *The Washington Post* (January 12, 2011): http://www.washingtonpost.com/wp-dyn/content/article/2011/01/12/AR2011011202418_2.html.

21. See Andrzej Ajnenkiel, "Wpływ historii na stosunki z sąsiadami: Kilka uwag o relacjach polsko-litewskich," ("The Influence of History on the Relations with Neighbors: A Few Remarks about Polish-Lithuanian Relations") in Jasiewicz, *Europa nieprowincjonalna* 1187–92; and Timothy Snyder, *The Reconstruction of Nations: Poland, Ukraine, Lithuania, Belarus, 1569–1999* (New Haven, CT, and London: Yale University Press, 2003), 239–41, 249–55, who praises effusively Poland's foreign policy vis-à-vis Lithuania, which was predicated on ignoring the plight of the local Poles, after 1989. However, for a Lithuanian pundit's scathing critique of Warsaw's most recent moves toward Vilnius and the Lithuanian Poles, singling out Foreign Minister Radek Sikorski as the chief culprit, see Eldoras Butrimas, "Litwa tez czeka na wybory w Polsce," ("Lithuania also Awaits the Elections in Poland") *Rzeczpospolita* (October 7, 2011), http://www.rp.pl/artykul/9157,728802-Stosunki-polsko-litewskie-i-wybory-parlamentarne-2011.html.

22. On March 13, 2005, Lithuania's Channel 3 TV aired a documentary expressing such views. Among prominent intellectuals endorsing them were Dalia Kuodytė, the director of Lithuania's Center for Research on Genocide and Resistance, who supports the rehabilitation of General Povilas Plechavičius, and historians: Arvydas Anušauskas, Antanas Tyla, and Kazimieras Garšva, who coauthored the controversial work *Armija Krajova Lietuvoje* (*The Home Army in Lithuania*) (Vilnius: "Vilnijos" draugija, Lietuvos Politinių tremtinių ir kalinių sąjunga, 1999), which is a curious combination of Soviet Communist and Lithuanian nationalist myths about the Polish underground. See "Uknuli prowokację," ("They Plotted a Provocation") *Tygodnik Wileńszczyzny* (March 17–23, 2005): http://www.tygodnik.lt. On the other hand, on December 3, 1999, there was a joint Polish-Lithuanian conference on "The Resistance Movement, 1939–1945," held in Vilnius/Wilno and cosponsored by Lietuvos gyventojų genocido ir rezistencijos tyrimo centras (Lithuania's Center for Research on Genocide and Resistance), Vilniaus universiteto Istorijos fakultetas (the Faculty of History at the University of Vilnius), Stowarzyszenie Naukowców Polaków Litwy (the Association of Polish Scholars of Lithuania), and Światowy Związek Żołnierzy Armii Krajowej Okręg Wileński (the Wilno District of the World Union of Soldiers of the Home Army). Over a score of Lithuanian, Polish, and Polish-Lithuanian scholars participated, freely exchanging their opinions, although failing to reach a consensus. See http://www.genocid.lt/GRTD/Konferencijos/eng/seminar.htm. However, it is much easier to find common ground in the field of anti-Communist resistance in Poland and Lithuania. See, e.g., the joint Polish-Lithuanian conference on "Societal Resistance and Security Apparatus during the Occupation and Communist Regimes in Lithuania and Poland from 1944 to 1956," (November 6–7, 2003): http://www.genocid.lt/GRTD/Konferencijos/eng/intern4.htm. And on the question of patriotic commemorations among the Polish expellees from the Wilno area (mostly AK veterans) living now in post-Communist Poland see Helena Pasierbska, "Wileńskie rocznice," ("Wilno Anniversaries") *Nasz Dziennik* (September 18, 2009).

23. The function was not a complete success. According to a journalist, "some Lithuanian veterans refused to participate claiming that they did not want to sit in the same room with Soviets." See Robert Mickiewicz, "Próba pojednania," ("An Attempt at Reconciliation") *Rzeczpospolita* (May 9, 2005).

24. On June 20, 1944, the Lithuanian police killed thirty-nine Polish hostages in Glinciszki and, in revenge, the Home Army shot twenty-seven Lithuanians in Dubinki. Significantly, it was not the Lithuanian ex-policemen who asked the Poles for forgiveness but the veterans of the *Lietuvos Vietinė Rinktinė*, or the so-called "Local Formations" of General Povilas Plechavičius. This outfit was founded in March 1944 and dissolved in May 1944 after it proved itself to be inept in fighting the AK and its leaders refused to fight for the Germans outside the territory of the Lithuanian Republic. The soldiers of the *Lietuvos Vietinė Rinktinė* did not participate in the massacre of Glinciszki. See Robert Mickiewicz, "Wreszcie zgoda" (Finally Reconciliation) and "Wreszcie prawda," (Finally the Truth) *Rzeczpospolita* (June 13, 2005). See also Robert Daniłowicz, "Wojna domowa," (A Civil War) *Rzeczpospolita* (October 13, 2007) (which is a journalistic description of contemporary Dubinki and its history, including the execution in 1944); Marcin Szymaniak, "Litwa żegna Radziwiłłów," (Lithuania Bids Farewell to the Radziwiłłs) *Rzeczpospolita* (September 7, 2009); Maja Narbutt, "Powrót do Wielkiego Księstwa," (The Return to the Grand Duchy) *Rzeczpospolita*, Plus-Minus, (September 18–19, 2009). The Lithuanians have also acted very hospitably toward the Count Przeździecki family, inviting its members to the official opening of a museum in their former palace in Rakiszki. See Roman Aftanazy interviewed by Janusz Miliszkiewicz, "Nikt już nie mówi o krwiopijcach," [No one Talks About Bloodsuckers Anymore] *Rzeczpospolita*, Plus-Minus, January 4, 2003.

25. According to a recent study published by Professor Vil Bakirov, Dr. Alexandr Kizilov, and Dr. Kseniya Kizilova of the East-Ukrainian Foundation for Social Research, Kharkiv, among Ukraine's non-Russian minorities, there are Belarusians (0.6 percent), Tatars (0.5 percent), Moldovans (0.6 percent), Bulgarians (0.4 percent), Hungarians (0.3 percent), Romanians (0.3 percent), Poles (0.2 percent), Jews (0.2 percent), Armenians (0.2 percent), and others (1.7 percent). The study invokes the census of 2001 and shows, based upon several hundred interviews, the attitudes of Ukraine's Poles and Hungarians toward their Slavic neighbors. The Poles are more inclined to view their Ukrainian, Russian, and Belarusian fellow citizens in a positive light. See "Poles and Hungarians in contemporary Ukraine: identities, representations, social capital," ENRI-East, no date (after 2001), http://www.enri-east.net/wp-content/uploads/Kizilova_SK_presentation.pdf. See also Orest Deychakiwsky, "National Minorities in Ukraine," *The Ukrainian Quarterly* 50, no. 4 (Winter 1994): 371–89; John Jaworsky, "Nationality Policy in Ukraine and the Potential for Inter-ethnic Conflict," in *Managing Diversity in Plural Societies: Minorities, Migration and Nation-Building in Post-Communist Europe*, ed. Magda Opalski (Ottawa, ON: Forum Eastern Europe, 1998), 104–27; Natalya Panina, "Interethnic Relations and Ethnic Tolerance in Ukraine: An In-Depth Analytical Report," in *Post-Soviet Puzzles: Mapping the Political Economy of the Former Soviet Union* (4 vols.), ed. Klaus Segbers and Stephan De Spiegeleire, vol. 4: *The Emancipation of Society as a Reaction to Systematic Change: Survival, Adaptation to New Rules and Ethnopolitical Conflicts* (Baden-Baden: Nomos, 1995), 4: 101–21; Andrew Wilson, "The Ukrainians: Engaging the 'Eastern Diaspora,'" in *Nations Abroad: Diaspora Politics and International Relations in the Former Soviet Union*, ed. Charles King and Neil J. Melvin (Boulder, CO: Westview Press, 1998), 103–31.

26. The process of reconciliation has been slow in coming to fruition since the first statement of reconciliation offered by Poland's Primate, Józef Cardinal Glemp, on October 8 and 17, 1987, in Rome, on the eve of the 1,000th anniversary of

the baptism of Kievan Rus', was not reciprocated fully by Ukraine's Myroslav Ivan Cardinal Lubachivsky. The Polish hierarch invoked the Christian commandment to "forgive and seek reconciliation," based upon the formula of the German–Polish ecclesiastical rapprochement of the 1960s ("We forgive and beg for forgiveness"), while his Ukrainian counterpart talked about "extending a fraternal hand to the Poles as a sign of reconciliation and love," but not forgiveness. See Józef Mirski, "Historyczne spotkanie," ("A Historical Meeting") *Kultura* (Paris), no. 3 (486) (March 1988): 113–17; "Pojednać w modlitwie," ("A Reconciliation in Prayer") *Rzeczpospolita* (June 6, 2005); "Przeprośmy Boga za nienawiść," ("Let Us Apologize to the Lord for Hatred") *Rzeczpospolita* (June 20, 2005). See also Letter of Bishops of Poland and Ukraine on Reconciliation, Warsaw-Lviv, (June 19–26, 2005), http://www.zenit.org/english/visualizza.phtml?sid=75653.

27. The so-called Lvovian "Eagle-Cubs" (Orlęta lwowskie) necropolis was built in the interwar period to honor the Poles, Americans, and French who had fallen in the Polish–Ukrainian war of 1918–1919 and the Polish–Bolshevik war of 1919–1921 which restored the city and Eastern Galicia to Poland. The Ukrainian authorities have been very uneasy about allowing any mention of the Polishness of Lviv/Lwów. In particular, the city council and administration, both dominated by hard nationalists, tend to be quite hostile. Ultimately, a compromise inscription was agreed to by officials of both the Polish and Ukrainian governments but the city council threatened to veto it and refused to acknowledge the fallen American and French volunteers who fought on the Polish side. They backed down only after concerted interventions from President Viktor Yushchenko who enjoys considerable popular support among Western Ukrainians because of his overtures to the nationalists. The opening of the cemetery was further put in doubt when, surprisingly, the Ukrainian Parliament passed a last minute resolution, supported by Prime Minister Yulia Tymoshenko's party, calling on the city council to annul its decision. Reason prevailed and this compromising resolution was soon overturned. To reciprocate President Aleksander Kwaśniewski undertook to erect a cross in Pawłokoma, a Ukrainian village that was attacked and obliterated by Polish partisans in March 1945, after several of its Polish inhabitants had been kidnapped and murdered by Ukrainian underground. See Roman Szporluk, "The Strange Politics of Lviv: An Essay in Search of an Explanation," in *The Politics of Nationality and the Erosion of the USSR*, ed. Zvi Gitelman (London: Macmillan, 1992), 215–31; Marian Rubchak, "Ethnonationalist Construction of Identity: The Lviv Paradigm," *National Identities* 2, no. 1 (March 2000): 21–34; Maja Narbutt, "Niepewny los Cmentarza Orląt," ("The Uncertain Fate of the Eagle-Cub Cemetery") *Rzeczpospolita* (June 10, 2005); Piotr Kościński, "Deputowani przeciw Orlętom," ("Deputies against the Eagle Cubs") *Rzeczpospolita* (June 23, 2005); Łukasz Adamski and Anna Gorczyca, "Martwi przeciw Orlętom," ("The Dead against the Eagle Cubs") *Gazeta Wyborcza* (June 24, 2005); Piotr Kościński, "Spór o groby," ("A Quarrel over the Graves") *Rzeczpospolita* (June 24, 2005); Andrzej Kaczyński, "Trudny bój o pamięć," ("A Difficult Battle for Memory") *Rzeczpospolita* (June 24, 2005); Piotr Kościński, "Koniec sporu o bohaterów," ("The End of the Quarrel over Heroes") *Rzeczpospolita* (June 24, 2005); "Symbol Pojednania," ("A Symbol of Reconciliation") *Rzeczpospolita* (June 25, 2005). Soon after, following ten years of procrastination, the Ukrainian authorities permitted the erection of a cross in Huta Pieniacka, where, in February 1944, the Ukrainian SS, elements of the Ukrainian underground (UPA), and some local Ukrainians massacred the Pol-

ish Catholic inhabitants. See Piotr Kościński, "Krzyż zamiast wioski," ("A Cross Instead of the Village") Sławomir Popowski, "Rozbrajanie historii," ("Dis-Arming History") and Professor Myrosław Popowycz interviewed by Tatiana Serwetnyk, "Dla Ukraińców to też byli zbrodniarze," ("They Were Criminals also As Far As the Ukrainians Are Concerned") *Rzeczpospolita* (October 22, 2005).

28. The same applies to Poland's other minorities, including Jews, Germans, Lithuanians, Belarusians, and others. See Katarzyna Krzywicka, "National Minorities: The Polish Position," in *The Future of East-Central Europe*, ed. Andrzej Dumała and Ziemowit Jacek Pietraś (Lublin: Maria Curie-Skłodowska University Press, 1996), 344–50; Cezary Żołędowski, *Białorusini i Litwini w Polsce, Polacy na Białorusi i Litwie* (*Belarusians and Lithuanians in Poland, Poles in Belarus and Lithuania*) (Warszawa: ASPRA-JR, 2003). See also Bozenna Kisielowska-Lipman, "Poland's Eastern Borderlands: Political Transition and the 'Ethnic Question," in *Region, State and Identity in Central and Eastern Europe*, ed. Judy Batt and Kataryna Wolczuk (London: Frank Cass, 2002), 133–54. And for a nostalgic attempt to accommodate various traditions in Lwów see Włodzimierz Paźniewski, "Tylko we Lwowie," ("Only in Lwów") *Rzeczpospolita*, Plus-Minus (September 13–14, 2008).

29. The Lemko and Boyko Ruthenian minorities were able to reclaim much of their properties stolen by the Communists. Poland's Ukrainians, who were compensated with post-German property after being resettled in the western and northern territories, have tried law suits and administrative action with much less success. Some Uniate Church properties have been returned, but by no means all, since many church buildings were destroyed. By comparison, hardly any Polish property restitution has taken place in Ukraine. The return of a small number of Latin-rite Catholic churches has often run into obstacles, as most of the buildings were taken over by the Uniate Church or, sometimes, the Orthodox Church. Catholic Church properties had been built by local Polish communities, often before 1917, were expropriated by the Bolsheviks, and now have been retained by the Ukrainian state or privatized. Further, the Ukrainian Poles complain that the Polish language masses are on the decrease, being replaced with services in Ukrainian. The same applies to Belarus, but it seems to be a Vatican policy to propitiate the majority nationality to make the faith more popular and debunk its image from being identical with Polishness. The policy undoubtedly pleases both the Ukrainian ecclesiasts and nationalists. See Eugeniusz Tuzow-Lubański and Anna Wiejak, "Zagrabione kościoły nie wrócą do właściciela," ("Expropriated Churches Will Not Return to the Owner") *Nasz Dziennik* (August 7, 2008); Susyn Yvonne Mihalasky, "Ethno-National Orientation among Lemkos in Poland," in *National Identities and Ethnic Minorities in Eastern Europe*, ed. Ray Taras (New York: St. Martin's, 1995), 208–24; ks. prof. Roman Dzwonkowski SAC, "Dramat Polaków w Kościele katolickim na Białorusi i Ukrainie," ("The Polish Drama in the Catholic Church in Belarus and Ukraine") *Nasz Dziennik* (September 22–23, 2007); Robert Daniłowicz, "Lenin na bocznym torze," ("Lenin on a Side Rail Link") *Rzeczpospolita* (March 31, 2009); Cezary Gmyz, "Język polski znika z kościoła," ("Polish Language Disappears from the Church") *Rzeczpospolita* (May 11, 2009).

30. See Minton F. Goldman, "Polish-Russian Relations and the 2004 Ukrainian Presidential Elections," *East European Quarterly* XL, no. 4 (Winter 2006): 417–25; Minton F. Goldman, "Polish Policy toward Ukraine: The Impact on Polish-Russian Relations in 2008–2009," *The Polish Review* LIV, no. 4 (2009): 451–76. And see also Andrew Wilson, "Ukraine's 'Orange Revolution' of 2004:

The Paradoxes of Negotiation," in *Civil Resistance and Power Politics: The Experience of Non-violent Action from Gandhi to the Present*, ed. Adam Roberts and Timothy Garton Ash (Oxford: Oxford University Press, 2009): 335–53.

31.   See "Podziękowania z Ukrainy: List otwarty do Polaków," ("Thanks from Ukraine: An Open Letter to the Poles") *Rzeczpospolita* (December 27, 2005).

32.   The eleven conferences held from 1997 to 2005 resulted in the publication of ten volumes of conference papers and discussion materials under the title *Polska-Ukraina: Trudne pytania* (Warszawa: Karta, 1998–2006); however, in many areas Polish and Ukrainian historians failed to agree to conclusions that the participants on both sides could sign. Initially, the conferences were co-sponsored by the World Association of Soldiers of the Home Army (Światowy Związek Żołnierzy Armii Krajowej) and the Association of Ukrainians in Poland (Związek Ukraińców w Polsce), but the latter strongly pro-nationalist organization backed out of the project before the conferences held in 2001. The conferences have also been criticized by the Polish side (including its organizer Jan Niewiński) and nonnationalist Ukrainians (notably Wiktor Poliszczuk) for, among other things, their selection of participants and avoiding certain topics. See also Bogumił Grott, ed., *Polacy i Ukraińcy dawniej i dziś (Poles and Ukrainians in the Past and Now)* (Kraków: Wydawnictwo Uniwersytetu Jagiellońskiego, 2002). For a follow up see "Polacy – Ukraińcy: Trudna przeszłość," (Poles-Ukrainians: A Difficult Past) *Biuletyn Instytutu Pamięci Narodowej* no. 7–8 (2010), an issue entirely devoted to Polish–Ukrainian relations. For some issues of Ukrainian and Polish historiography see Krzysztof Łada, "Creative Forgetting: Polish and Ukrainian Historiographies on the Campaigne [sic] Against the Poles in Volhynia During World War II," *Glaukopis* 2/3 (2004–2005): 343–78; Per Anders Rudling, "Theory and Practice: Historical Representation of the Wartime Accounts of the Activities of the OUN-UPA (Organization of Ukrainian Nationalists – Ukrainian Insurgent Army)," *East European Jewish Affairs* 36, no. 2 (December 2006): 163–89; Piotr Kosiewski and Grzegorz Motyka, eds., *Historycy polscy i ukraińscy wobec problemów XX wieku (Polish and Ukrainian Historians Confronting Problems of the Twentieth Century)* (Kraków: Universitas, 2000).

33.   See passing remarks about cordial and inviting atmosphere toward the Poles among at least some parishioners at a town in Podolia in Andrzej W. Kaczorowski, "Czerwonogród – Perła Podola," *Biuletyn Instytutu Pamięci Narodowej* no. 1–2 (96–97) (January–February 2009): 156–61.

34.   See Tomasz Stryjek, "Kresy z perspektywy Ukrainy: Ziemie zachodnie Ukrainy w *derżawnyćkiej* (państwowej) historiografii ukraińskiej okresu międzywojennego," ("The Borderlands from the Ukrainian Perspective: Western Ukraine in State Ukrainian Historiography of the Interwar Period") in Jasiewicz, *Europa nieprowincjonalna* 132–44; Marek Jan Chodakiewicz, "Notatki z post-Sowiecji (część II)," ("Notes from the Post-Soviet Lands, Part II") *Najwyższy Czas!* (October 16, 2010): XXXV.

35.   As noted by Bilinsky, Yulia Tymoshenko opposed the 2003 declaration that barely passed the Ukrainian Parliament, but was resoundingly endorsed by Poland's *Sejm*. Pro-nationalist Ukrainian commentators have reinterpreted the events as a mutual massacre provoked by the Poles, who were but a small minority in Volhynia, and denied the responsibility of the Ukrainian Insurgent Army. See Yaroslav Bilinsky, "60th anniversary of the Polish-Ukrainian Tragedy of Volyn," *The Ukrainian Quarterly: A Journal of Ukrainian & International Affairs* LIX, no. 3–4 (Fall–Winter 2003): 236–54. On an earlier 1997 declaration

of reconciliation by the Polish and Ukrainian presidents see Piotrowski, *Poland's Holocaust*, 256–58. See also Tomasz Nieśpiał, "W Sahryniu nie będzie pojednania," ("No Reconciliation in Sahryń") *Rzeczpospolita* (September 7, 2009); Marcin Austyn, "Okoliczności wskazały na odmowę," ("The Circumstances Dictated a Refusal") *Nasz Dziennik* (September 8, 2009).

36. Józef Matusz, "Protest Ukrainy," ("The Objection of Ukraine") *Rzeczpospolita* (June 6, 2005). This was the sentiment expressed at a historical conference on "Genocide and Deportations of the Polish Population in the Eastern Borderlands of the Polish Republic, 1939–1947," held in Przemyśl on June 5, 2005. The Ukrainian Embassy in Warsaw, the Union of Ukrainians in Poland, and the head of the Uniate Catholic Church in Poland protested in unison, criticizing the organizers and participants for allegedly inciting anti-Ukrainian sentiment. See also Mariusz Kamieniecki, "Prawda o zbrodni wciąż żywa," ("The Truth about the Crime Is Still Alive") *Nasz Dziennik* (June 6, 2005); Czesław Partacz interviewed by Mariusz Kamieniecki, "Polityka nie może rządzić historią," ("Politics Cannot Rule History") *Nasz Dziennik* (June 6, 2005); and Piotr Kościński and Tatiana Serwetnyk, "Dwie legendy Stepana Bandery," ("Two Legends of Stepan Bandera") *Rzeczpospolita*, Plus-Minus (August 22–23, 2009); Andrzej Chojnowski interviewed by Piotr Zychowicz, "Kult Bandery będzie dzielił Polaków i Ukraińców," ("The cult of Bandera Will Divide Poles and Ukrainians") *Rzeczpospolita* (August 19, 2009). See further Catherine Wanner, *Burden of Dreams: History and Identity in Post-Soviet Ukraine* (University Park, PA: Pennsylvania State University Press, 1998); Bohdan Harasymiw, "Memories of the Second World War in Recent Ukrainian Election Campaigns," *Journal of Ukrainian Studies* 32, no. 1 (2007): 97–108; David R. Marples, "Anti-Soviet Partisans and Ukrainian Memory," *East European Politics and Societies* 24, no. 1 (Winter 2010): 26–44.

37. For a scathing critique of the Ukrainian government's official approval of, and accommodation with, the integral nationalist organizations see Wiktor Poliszczuk, "'Pomarańczowa rewolucja' i cień Bandery," ("'Orange Revolution' and the Shadow of Bandera") *Dziś: Przegląd Społeczny* (June 2005): http://www.dzis.com.pl/main.php3?strona=wiecej17. For an earlier (1996) petition of ninety-five leftist Ukrainian parliamentarians condemning the activities of the Organization of Ukrainian Nationalists and Ukrainian Insurgent Army see Piotrowski, *Poland's Holocaust*, 255–56. As yet the issue of granting combat status to members of the Ukrainian Insurgent Army has not been resolved. However, the OUN has plenty of present day political admirers. Arguably, the OUN itself is not the most extremist of Ukraine's radical nationalist groups. See Taras Kuzio, "Radical Nationalist Parties and Movements in Contemporary Ukraine before and after Independence: The Right and Its Politics, 1989–1994," *Nationalities Papers* 25, no. 2 (June 1997): 211–42; Taras Kuzio, "Radical Right Parties and Civic Groups in Belarus and the Ukraine," in *The Revival of Right-Wing Extremism in the Nineties*, ed. Peter H. Merkl and Leonard Weinberg (London: Frank Cass, 1997), 203–30; Roman Solchanyk, "The Radical Right in Ukraine," in *The Radical Right in Central and Eastern Europe since 1989*, ed. Sabrina P. Ramet (University Park, PA: The Pennsylvania State University Press, 1999), 279–95; Per Anders Rudling, "Organized Anti-Semitism in Contemporary Ukraine: Structure, Influence, and Ideology," *Canadian Slavonic Papers/Revue canadienne des slavistes* XLVIII, no. 1–2 (March–June 2006): 81–119.

38. See Evgenii Golovakha, Natalia Panina, and Nikolai Churilov, "Russians in Ukraine," in *The New Russian Diaspora: Russian Minorities in the Former*

Soviet Republics, ed. Vladimir Shlapentokh, Munir Sendich, and Emil Payin (Armonk, NY: M.E. Sharpe, 1994), 59–71; Neil Melvin, "Russians, Regionalism and Ethnicity in Ukraine," in Neil Melvin, *Russians beyond Russia: The Politics of National Identity* (London: Royal Institute for International Affairs, 1995), 78–99; Paul Kolstoe, "The Eye of the Whirlwind: Belarus and Ukraine," in *Russians in the Former Soviet Republics*, ed. Paul Kolstoe (Bloomington, IN: Indiana University Press, 1995), 170–99; Mordechai Altshuler, "Some Soviet and Post-Soviet National and Linguistic Problems in the Slavic Republics (States): Russia, Ukraine, Belarus" in *Quest for Models of Coexistence: National and Ethnic Dimensions of Changes in the Slavic Eurasian World*, ed. Kōichi Inoue and Tomohiko Uyama (Sapporo: Slavic Research Center, Hokkaido University: 1998), 111–132, also http://src-h.slav.hokudai.ac.jp/sympo/97summer/alt.html; Klemens Buscher, *Transnationale Beziehungen Der Russen in Moldova Und Der Ukraine: Ethnische Diaspora Zwischen Residenz-Und Referenzstaat* (Frankfurt am Main: Peter Lang, 2004). And see the preceding chapter.

39.   See two essays in Vladmir Tismăneanu, ed., *Political Culture and Civil Society in Russia and the New States of Eurasia* (Armonk, NY: M.E. Sharpe, 1995): Dominique Arel, "Ukraine: The Temptation of the Nationalizing State" (157–88), and Orest Subtelny, "Russocentrism, Regionalism, and the Political Culture of Ukraine" (189–207). See also Serhiy Naboka, "Nationalities Issues in Ukraine," *Uncaptive Minds* 5 no.1 (19) (Spring 1992): 75–80; Iryna Maryniak, "Belarus and Ukraine: Nation Building in Babel," *Index on Censorship* 22, no. 2 (March 1993): 20–33; Robert Monyak and Valentin Sazhin, "Contemporary Relations among Nationalities in Ukraine," *Nationalities Papers* 21, no. 2 (Fall 1993): 160–62; V'iacheslav Shved, "The Conceptual Approaches of Ukrainian Political Parties to Ethno-Political Problems in Independent Ukraine," *Journal of Ukrainian Studies* 19, no. 2 (Winter 1994): 69–83; Catherine Wanner, *Burden of Dreams: History and Identity in Post-Soviet Ukraine* (University Park, PA: Pennsylvania State University Press, 1998); M. K. Flynn, "Reconstructing Ukraine: Memory and Imagining the Nation-State," *Ethnic and Racial Studies* 23, no. 1 (January 2000): 143–47; David R. Marples, *Heroes and Villains: Creating National History in Contemporary Ukraine* (New York and Budapest: CEU Press, 2007); and Tadeusz Andrzej Olszański, "Ukraine," in *New Europe: The Impact of the First Decade*, vol. 2: *Variations on the Pattern*, ed. Teresa Rakowska-Harmstone, Piotr Dutkiewicz, and Agnieszka Orzelska (Warsaw: Institute of Political Studies Polish Academy of Sciences and Collegium Civitas Press, 2006), 487–523.

40.   About real and perceived divisions in Ukraine see an incisive, but controversial, analysis by Grzegorz Górny, "Dwie Ukrainy," ("Two Ukraines") *Rzeczpospolita* (December 3, 2004). The author discounts the existence of Russian nationalism among 11 million Russian-speakers in eastern Ukraine. He also doubts the validity of the Orthodox-Uniate-Catholic split. Instead, he sees the conflict in Ukraine as pitting the Moscow Orthodox Patriarchate against all Ukrainian Christians, including the Ukrainian Autocephalic Orthodox Church. For another view of the Ukrainian-Russian and Uniate-Orthodox conflict see Sophia Senyk, "The Ukrainian Catholic Church Today: Universal Values versus Nationalist Doctrines," *Religion, State & Society* 30, no. 4 (2002): 320–32.

41.   On the Crimea and its Tatars and other considerations see Taras Kuzio, *Ukraine-Crimea-Russia: Triangle of Conflict* (Stuttgart and Hannover: Ibidem-Verlag, 2007); Edward Allworth, ed., *Tatars of the Crimea: Their Struggle for Survival: Original Studies from North America, Unofficial and Official Documents from Czarist and Soviet Sources* (Durham, NC and London: Duke University Press,

1988); Alan Fisher, *The Crimean Tatars* (Stanford, CA: Hoover Institution Press, 1987); Azade-Ayşe Rorlich, *The Volga Tatars: A Profile in National Resilience* (Stanford, CA: Hoover Institution Press, 1986); and Lily Hyde, *Dream Land: One Girl's Struggle to Find Her True Home* (London, England: Walker Books Ltd., 2008), which is a literary expression of the Tatar predicament in the Crimea. A brief history of the history of the conflict see Dariusz Wierzchoś, "Krym: Od Scytów do Rosjan," ("The Crimea: From the Scythians to the Russians") in *Źródła nienawiści: Konflikty etniczne w krajach postkomunistycznych* (*Sources of Hatred: Ethnic Conflict in Post-Communist Countries*) ed. Kamil Janicki (Kraków and Warszawa: Instytut Wydawniczy Erica and Histmag.org, 2009), 365–408.

42. There are no reliable statistics on the Jewish community in Ukraine. According to an Israeli estimate of 1999, there may from 400,000 to 685,000 persons of Jewish origin there, a decrease of between about 300,000 and 500,000 since 1989, mostly because of emigration. The estimates of the number of Jews leaving Ukraine in the wake of the Soviet collapse vary from 30 percent to 70 percent of the total from their peak in the 1980s. A bit over 100,000 people self-identified as Jews during the census in 2001. Jews congregate in large towns, primarily Odessa, Kharkiv, Kyiv, Dnipropetrovsk, and Lviv. They operate around 250 communal institutions, including a few Zionist outfits. In early twenty-first century over 120 Jewish newspapers appeared in Ukraine. See Vladimir Levin, "Ukraine," in *The Cambridge Dictionary of Judaism and Jewish Culture*, ed. Judith R. Baskin (Cambridge and New York: Cambridge University Press, 2011), 619–620; Betsy Gidwitz, "Jewish Life in Ukraine at the Dawn of the 21st Century: Part One," *Jerusalem Letter* no. 451 (8 Nisan 5761/1 April 2001), http://www.jcpa.org/jl/jl451.htm; Betsy Gidwitz, "Jewish Life in Ukraine at the Dawn of the 21st Century: Part Two," *Jerusalem Letter* no. 452 (22 Nisan 5761/15 April 2001), http://www.jcpa.org/jl/jl452.htm; Vladimir Khanin, "Judaism and Organized Jewish Movements in the USSR/CIS after World War II: The Ukrainian Case," *Jewish Political Studies Review* 11, no.1–2 (Spring 1999), http://www.jcpa.org/cjc/cjc-khanin-s99.htm. The participation of the local people in the Holocaust is the main unresolved issue of memory. A national debate on the topic is yet to take place in Ukraine. Some contextualizing may help. For example, according to Henry Abramson, historical Ukrainian–Jewish conflict stems from social and economic issues, rather than racism. However, there are a number of extremist organizations that rely on anti-Semitism to mobilize supporters. See Per Anders Rudling, "Organized Anti-Semitism in Contemporary Ukraine: Structure, Influence, and Ideology," *Canadian Slavonic Papers/Revue canadienne des slavistes* XLVIII, no. 1–2 (March–June 2006): 81–119; Henry Abramson, "The Scattering of Amalek: A Model for Understanding the Ukrainian-Jewish Conflict," *East European Jewish Affairs* 24, no. 1 (1994): 39–47; "Ukraine 2009," The Steven Roth Institute for the Study of Antisemitism and Racism, Tel Aviv University, no date [2010], http://www.tau.ac.il/Anti-Semitism/asw2009/ukraine.html; Irena Cantorovich, "Antisemitism in 2010 Ukrainian Presidential Campaign," Stephen Roth Institute for the Study of Contemporary Antisemitism and Racism, Tel Aviv University, Topical Brief no. 5 (2010): 1–6, http://www.tau.ac.il/Anti-Semitism/articles/topicalbrief5.pdf; Ingmar Oldberg, "Both Victim and Perpetrator: Ukraine's Problematic Relationship with the Holocaust," Balticworlds.com, (August 1, 2011), http://balticworlds.com/ukraine%E2%80%99s-problematic-relation-ship-to-the-holocaust/.

43. See Vladimir Khanin, "Judaism and Organized Jewish Movements in the USSR/ CIS after World War II: The Ukrainian Case," *Jewish Political Studies Review* 11, no.1–2 (Spring 1999), http://www.jcpa.org/cjc/cjc-khanin-s99.htm.

44. The statistics are confusing. According to the Soviet census of 1959, 81 percent of the inhabitants declared themselves as Belarusians; 16 percent as Poles; 1 percent as Ukrainians; and 1 percent as Russians. In 1989, there were 10,151,806 people in Belarus, including Belarusians (77.9 percent), Russians (13.2 percent), Poles (4.1 percent), Ukrainians (2.9 percent), and Jews (1.1 percent), while Tatars, Gypsies, Lithuanians, and others accounted for the remaining 0.8 percent. In 1999 and 2009, the proportions were 81.2 percent and 83.7 percent for Belarusians, 11.4 percent and 11.3 percent for Russians, 3.9 percent and 3.1 percent for Poles, 2.4 percent and 1.7 percent for Ukrainians, and 0.3 percent and 0.1 percent for Jews. Between 1999 and 2009 the population also declined from 10,045,000 to 9,504,000. It appears that the Belarusians declined the least of all groups. See Jerzy Targalski, "Białoruś: Statystyka," ("Belarus: Statistics") TMs, Warsaw, no date (2011), two pages of tables (a copy in my collection).

45. Even the integral nationalists of Belarus have had problems imagining themselves and, even more so, packaging themselves attractively enough to entice followers. Some Belarusian activists have complained that the name of their nation is too close to the "Russians," making them appear as "lesser Russians." Incidently, similar sentiments concerned once the "Little Ruthenians" who renamed themselves Ukrainians partly to escape their inferior status vis-à-vis Muscovy's Great Ruthenians (Russians). At any rate, some Belarusian nationalists have taken to calling themselves the "Litvins" (Lithuanians), a moniker harkening back to the Grand Duchy of Lithuania. The Litvins is a Polonism, undoubtedly used to avoid the old Muscovite term the "Litovtsi," which denotes anyone from the Grand Duchy, including Lithuanians, Poles, and White Ruthenians. To confuse things more, "Litovtsi" is also a Belarusian term for modern Lithuanian ethno-nationalists (who sometimes are referred to likewise as Letuvisy). So far the influence of the Litvins is limited to music and art, both confined largely to the internet and, thus, still failing to reach the cyber-deprived Belarusian masses. One of the top leaders of the Litvins is Viktor Nagniebeda, who champions the concept of the "Great Litva," meaning Belarus. See http://litvania.org; vkl. name; bramaby.com; http://www.youtube.com/watch?v=jGEM5qtZxaw; and http://www.youtube.com/watch?v=jSwmW3OxquY. See also Alexander Pershai, "Minor Nation: The Alternative Modes of Belarusian Nationalism," *East European Politics and Societies* 24, no. 3 (Summer 2010): 379–408; Grigory Ioffe, "Culture Wars, Soul-Searching, and Belarusian Identity," *East European Politics and Societies* 21, no. 2 (Spring 2007): 348–82; Grigory Ioffe, "Understanding Belarus: Belarusian Identity ," *Europe-Asia Studies* 55, no. 8 (2003): 1241–71; Iryna Maryniak, "Belarus and Ukraine: Nation Building in Babel," *Index on Censorship* 22, no. 2 (March 1993): 20–33.

46. The problem with such argument is that most Belarusians (60.8 percent) declare "Belarusian" as their native tongue; 36.9 percent indicate Russian as their mother language; 0.04 percent—Ukrainian; and 0.01 percent—Polish. However, declaring Belarusian as one's "native" language and actually using it may be another story. See Национального статистического комитета Республики Беларуси, 2009, http://belstat.gov.by/homep/ru/perepic/2009/itogi1.php. See further Paul Kolstoe, "The Eye of the Whirlwind: Belarus and Ukraine," in Paul Kolstoe, *Russians in the Former Soviet Republics* (Bloomington, IN: Indiana University Press, 1995), 170–99; Mordechai Altshuler, "Some Soviet and

Post-Soviet National and Linguistic Problems in the Slavic Republics (States): Russia, Ukraine, Belarus" in *Quest for Models of Coexistence: National and Ethnic Dimensions of Changes in the Slavic Eurasian World*, ed. Kōichi Inoue and Tomohiko Uyama (Sapporo: Slavic Research Center, Hokkaido University: 1998), 111–32, also http://src-h.slav.hokudai.ac.jp/sympo/97summer/alt.html.

47. See Roman Sidorski, "Białoruś: Państwo bez narodu?" ("Belarus: A State without a Nation?") in *Źródła nienawiści: Konflikty etniczne w krajach postkomunistycznych* (*Sources of Hatred: Ethnic Conflict in Post-Communist Countries*) ed. Kamil Janicki (Kraków and Warszawa: Instytut Wydawniczy Erica and Histmag.org, 2009), 409–57. Even a very sympathetic observer has called the Belarusan identity "still malleable." See Andrew Wilson, *Belarus: The Last European Dictatorship* (New Haven, CT and London: Yale University Press, 2011), 121–39 (quote at 139).

48. For the partisan myth see Andrew Wilson, *Belarus: The Last European Dictatorship* (New Haven, CT and London: Yale University Press, 2011), 114–17. Tellingly, the intellectual current in Belarus follows the official Russian patterns. Gleb Pavlovskii, the leading advisor of President Vladimir Putin, deploys Natalia Yeliseeva as his top specialist in Polish history. According to her neo-Stalinist take, the Home Army was "a German-fascist *agentura*," and "Polish fascist formations." While pondering the problems of "terrorism," other "specialists" compare the war in Chechnya to the situation in Poland after the Soviet takeover in 1944. See Bartłomiej Sienkiewicz, "Rosjanie przetwarzają historię," ("The Russians Recycle Their History") *Rzeczpospolita* (February 24, 2005).

49. See *Problemy natsional'nogo soznaniia pol'skogo naseleniia na Biel'arusi: Materialy ezhdunarodnoi nauchnoi konferentsii, Grodno, 16–18 noiabria 2001 goda* (*The Problems of the National Question of the Polish Population of Belarus*) (Grodno: Związek Polaków na Białorusi, 2003); Zdzisław Julian Winnicki, "'Polski pas' na Białorusi," ("'The Polish Belt' in Belarus") *Rzeczpospolita* (March 31, 2009). For some interesting remarks on Polish voting patterns in Belarus see the internet debate, particularly wojtek k., entry of September 24, 2010, in "Wschodniopolska Republika Radziecka," http://www.historycy.org/bez_grafik/index.php/t69261-50.html.

50. Quoted in Maja Narbutt, "Żyjcie ciszej," ("Live More Quietly") *Rzeczpospolita*, Plus-Minus (May 21–22, 2005).

51. See William Schreiber, "Lukashenko's Least-Favorite Writer: Journalist Andrzej Poczobut describes his life on the Belarusian dictator's blacklist," *The Wall Street Journal* (August 30, 2011); Andrzej Kaczyński, "Nasilają się represje przeciw Polakom," ("The Repressions against the Poles Intensify") *Rzeczpospolita* (June 9, 2005); "KGB przeciw Polakom," ("KGB against the Poles") *Gazeta Wyborcza* (May 31, 2005); Andrzej Pisalnik, "Szkoła polskiej kultury," ("School of Polish Culture") *Rzeczpospolita* (March 31, 2009); and Andżelika Borys and Józef Porzecki interviewed by Barbara Polak, "Pod Białym Orłem na Białorusi," ("Under the White Eagle in Belarus") *Biuletyn Instytutu Pamięci Narodowej* no. 1–2 (96–97) (January–February 2009): 135–42. For dissenting voices, denying any persecution of the Poles and Polish culture in Belarus, see Lech Z. Niekrasz, ed., *Wojna z "reżimem Łukaszenki"* (*The War against the Lukashenka Regime*) (Warszawa: Wydawnictwo Prasy Lokalnej and Biblioteczka Myśli Polskiej, 2010). See also Oleksandr Lukashenka interviewed in "Łukaszenka: Nie dzielcie moich Polaków," ("Do Not Divide My Poles") *Rzeczpospolita* (November 16, 2010), http://www.rp.pl/artykul/559964.html. Lukashenka denies that anything like

"a Polish minority" exists in Belarus. He stresses that "there are ethnic Poles, citizens of Belarus. We do not recognize a concept of 'a national minority'. They are our Poles whom we fully respect." For the Polish ethnic organization of Belarus recognized by Lukashenka see http://www.polacy.by/; and unrec by him see http://www.zpb.org.pl/. A Russian scholar, Vladislav Gulevich, has charged that the Polish minority is in essence the West's Fifth Column. See "Эксперт: Белорусским полякам отвели роль «передового тарана западной демократии»" ("Expert: Belarusian Poles have been Assigned the Role of a Forward Battering Ram of Western Democracy"), NewsBalt.ru, March 9, 2012, posted at http://newsbalt.ru/detail/?ID=3683.

52. There are probably 6,000 Tatars in contemporary Belarus. They congregate mostly around Iwie, which boasts the only working mosque in the entire country. For a touching vignette see Ryszard Sławczyński "Z wizytą u Tatarów na Białorusi," (Visiting the Tatars of Belarus) Tatarzy.pl, (September 24, 2008), http://www.tatarzy.pl/historia/tatarzy_bialorus.html; and pictures of Iwie are posted at http://www.skyscrapercity.com/showthread.php?t=472239&page=21; Siedlar-Kołyszko, *Byli, są. Czy będą ... ?*, 97–102. For ecumenical contacts focused on the Muslim community, see Harry Norris, *Islam in the Baltics: Europe's Early Muslim Community* (London and New York: Tauris Academic Studies, an imprint of I.B. Tauris Publishers, 2009), 75–139.

53. There are no reliable statistics on the Jewish population of Belarus, also because it is hard to determine who qualifies as Jewish. The Soviet Jewish community stood at about 120,000 in 1989. Most of them left for Israel. The remaining Jews of Belarus tend to live in Minsk (20,000 people), Grodno, Iwieńce, Bobruisk, and other towns. There is a cultural and religious revival, but the local Jewish population continues to dwindle through emigration. Lukashenka is anti-Israel. But he is not overtly anti-Semitic; he is also not one to restrain himself. He complained once on the radio that "this is a Jewish city, and the Jews are not concerned for the place they live in. They have turned Bobruisk into a pigsty. . . . I call on all Jews who have money to come back to Bobruisk." His government has feebly assisted in cultural restoration projects, including of synagogues, but that should be seen chiefly as propaganda stunts for Western consumption. The state also runs a Jewish university and a few schools in Minsk. On the Jewish community, including the religious, see "Belarus," http://www. worldjewishcongress.org/en/communities/show?id=83; "Belarus," http://www. europeanjewishfund.org/index.php?/communities/belarus/; "Jewish Belarus," http://www.haruth.com/JewBelarus.html; "Jewish Belarus," http://www.jew-ishbelarus.org/; Jessica Naiman, "Being Jewish in Belarus," Chabad.org, (May 2011), http://www.chabad.org/library/article_cdo/aid/1510157/jewish/Be-ing-Jewish-in-Belarus.htm; Judith Matloff, "The Last Shtetl Jews of Belarus: Elderly and Ill, They Struggle against Loneliness," *Forward* (October 15, 2010): http://www.forward.com/articles/131838/; Ronny Sofer, "Belarus President Attacks Jews," Ynetnews.com, (October 18, 2007), http://www.ynetnews.com/articles/0,7340,L-3461548,00.html; "Jews of Belarus Move to Save Their Past: Major Initiative with Government Will Preserve Historic Jewish Sites: Union of Religious Jewish Congregations Undertakes Bold Initiative," http://kehilalinks. jewishgen.org/slonim/jews_of_belarus_move_to_save_the.htm.

54. Even Belarusian historiography published in Poland tends to be rather hermetic and reluctant to take other views under the consideration. It blends curiously nationalist, pro-Communist, and even sometimes pro-German strains. The representatives of this school strive to advocate a theory of the continuity

of the Belarusian "statehood" and "nationality" from early medieval times. Consequently, at least one scholar celebrates the Soviet invasion of Poland on September 17, 1939, as "unification," while another advances irredentist claims to the territory of the present-day Polish State based on the Wilsonian idea of national self-determination. See Анатоль Трафімчык, "Аб'яднанне Беларусі 17 верасня 1939 г.," ("The Unification of Belarus, September 17, 1939") *Białoruskie Zeszyty Historyczne* no. 21 (2004): 199–206, http://kamunikat.fontel.net/pdf/bzh/21/15.pdf. For other contentious assertions see also Васіль Кушнер, "Асвятленне гісторыі Заходняй Беларусі 1921–1941 гадоў у сучаснай беларускай гістарыяграфіі," ("The Problem of the History of Western Belarus, 1921–1941, and Contemporary Belarusian Historiography") *Białoruskie Zeszyty Historyczne* no. 13 (2000), http://kamunikat.fontel.net/www/czasopisy/bzh/13/13art_kusznier.htm; Уладзімір Калаткоў, "Грамадска-палітычнае жыццё ў Заходняй Беларусі ў 1939–1941 гадах паводле сучаснай беларускай гістарыяграфіі," ("Community and Political Life in Western Belarus, 1939–1941, and Contemporary Belarusian Historiography") *Białoruskie Zeszyty Historyczne* no. 13 (2000), http://kamunikat.fontel.net/www/czasopisy/bzh/13/13kom_kalatkou.htm; Людміла Малыхіна, "Праблемы гістарыяграфіі Літоўска-Беларускай ССР," ("The Problems of Historiography of the Lithuanian-Belorussian SSR") *Białoruskie Zeszyty Historyczne* no. 20 (2003), http://kamunikat.fontel.net/www/czasopisy/bzh/20/06.htm; Уладзімір Снапкоўскі, "Беларуская дыпламатыя ў XX ст.—асэнсаванне знешнепалітычнага вопыту БНР, БССР і Рэспублікі Беларусь," ("Belarusian Diplomacy in the 20th Century") *Białoruskie Zeszyty Historyczne* no. 16 (2001), http://kamunikat.fontel.net/www/czasopisy/bzh/16/16art_snapkouski.htm.

55. In April 2008, a commemorative mass was prayed and a cross erected in Druzha outside of Minsk to mark the 65th anniversary of a massacre of Belarusian villagers by Soviet partisans on April 14, 1943. Although described as an attack on the Belarusian collaborationist police of the Nazis, the victims were mostly civilian. Twenty five people died, chiefly women and children, and thirty-four farmsteads were torched. The post-Communist authorities proclaimed the mass "an illegal gathering," threatened the participants and surviving witnesses, launched a media propaganda campaign against the organizers (who were branded as "libelous liars" and "foreign agents"), and destroyed the cross. In May 2008, a Belarusian journalist, Viktar Khursik, was sentenced to fifteen days in jail ostensibly for having erected the cross, although in reality for having self-published his research, printing 150 copies of a book on the massacre. Further, Viatseslav Sichuk, a leader of "The Belarusian Voluntary Society to Protect the Monuments of History of Culture," was also given two weeks in jail in the same case. In August 2010, a court in Minsk heard a libel case lodged by a Communist against a local newspaper which had dared to report on Soviet guerrilla atrocities against the Belarusian peasants. See Marek Jan Chodakiewicz, "Notatki z post-Sowiecji (część III)," ("Notes from the Post-Soviet Lands, Part III") *Najwyższy Czas!* (October 23, 2010): XXXV; "Wiaczesław Siczuk przeprowadził za kratami 15 dób," ("Viatslav Sluchik led 15 days Behind Bars," which is a very poor translation into Polish that should be: "Viatseslav Sichuk Sentenced to 15 Days Behind Bars") (April 24, 2008), http://www.belarus-live.eu/pl/artykul.php5?idA=1101@idM=6; Andrzej Poczobut, "Białorusin skazany za ustawienie krzyża," ("A Belarusian Sentenced for Putting Up a Cross") *Gazeta Wyborcza*, (May 17, 2008); Viktar U. Khursik [Chursik], *Krou i popel Drazna: Historiya*

partyzanckaha zlatsynstva (*The Blood and Ashes of Drazhno: The History of a Partisan Evil-Doing*) (Minsk: By the author, 2006).

56.   According to a Western anthropologist, who visited the Soviet Union in the 1960s, the Belarusian peasants still displayed considerable sentiment toward the Polish times, including the nobility: "'The *pan*,' I heard, 'was a real gentleman.' . . . But what is interesting that the story was told me by the offspring of the peasantry, not with resentment, but with a kind of sentimental admiration. He was a real pan." See Ernest Gellner, "Ethnicity and Faith in Eastern Europe," in *Eastern Europe . . ., Central Europe . . ., Europe*, ed. Stephen R. Graubard (Boulder, San Francisco, and Oxford: Westview Press, 1991), 267–68. This local fondness for the non-Communist past has continued into the post-Soviet times. For example, in 1996, during his first visit in over half a century to his ancestral Spusza, Prince Eustachy Sapieha was welcomed warmly by all he met and everyone there either recognized him or heard about him and his family. Some locals recalled important events from the prewar times, including the splendid wedding of his sister. In particular, however, the Prince was regaled separately by several unconnected persons with a tale of his English governess's daily peregrinations, "riding on a white horse," to bring flowers to the local church. The admiring locals turned this "fact" into a symbol of Christian piety. In reality, the governess, Florence Levey, delivered the flowers weekly on a small horse-drawn cart. See Sapieha, *Tak było* 373–88.

57.   On the visit by the Radziwiłłs see Andrzej Pisalnik, "Znów w Nieświeżu," *Rzeczpospolita*, ("Again in Nieśwież") (June 20, 2009); Maciej Radziwiłł interviewed by Katarzyna Jaruzelska-Kastory, "Jestem obywatelem Wielkiego Księstwa," ("I Am a Citizen of the Grand Duchy"), *Rzeczpospolita*, Plus-Minus (June 20–21, 2009); Maja Narbutt, "Powrót do Wielkiego Księstwa," ("The Return to the Grand Duchy") *Rzeczpospolita*, Plus-Minus (September 18–19, 2009). See also Gregory Ioffe, *Understanding Belarus and How Western Foreign Policy Misses the Mark* (Lanham, MD: Rowman & Littlefield Publishers, Inc, 2008); David Riach, "Post-Soviet Belarus," in *New Europe: The Impact of the First Decade*, vol. 2: *Variations on the Pattern*, ed. Teresa Rakowska-Harmstone, Piotr Dutkiewicz, and Agnieszka Orzelska (Warsaw: Institute of Political Studies Polish Academy of Sciences and Collegium Civitas Press, 2006), 101–53; Katja Yafimava, *Post-Soviet Russian-Belarussian Relationships: The Role of Gas Transit Pipelines* (Stuttgart and Hannover: Ibidem-Verlag, 2006); and Coit Blacker and Condoleezza Rice, "Belarus and the Flight from Sovereignty," in *Problematic Sovereignty: Contested Rules and Political Possibilities*, ed. Stephen D. Krasner (New York: Columbia University Press, 2001), 224–50.

58.   See Marek Jan Chodakiewicz, "Rumuno post-Sowieci," ("Rumanian Post-Soviets") *Tygodnik Solidarność* (May 15, 2009); Marek Jan Chodakiewicz, "Mołdawskość" ("Moldavian Identity") *Tygodnik Solidarność* (July 30, 2010); Charles King, *The Moldovans: Romania, Russia, and the Politics of Culture* (Stanford, CA: The Hoover Institution Press, 2000); Stefan Ihrig, *Wer sind die Moldawier? Rumänismus versus Moldowanismus in Historiographie und Schulbüchern der Republik Moldova, 1991–2006* (Stuttgart and Hannover: Ibidem-Verlag, 2008); Matthew H. Ciscel, *The Language of the Moldovans: Romania, Russia, and Identity in an Ex-Soviet Republic* (Lanham, MD: Lexington Books, 2007); Andrei Brezianu and Vlad Spânu, *Historical Dictionary of Moldova* (Lanham, MD, Toronto, and Plymouth: Scarecrow Press, 2007); Michael Bruchis, *The Republic of Moldova: From the Collapse of the Soviet Empire to the Restoration of the Russian Empire* (New York and Boulder, CO:

Columbia University Press and East European Monographs, 1997); Nicholas Dima, *Moldova and the Transdnestr Republic* (New York and Boulder, CO: Columbia University Press and East European Monographs, 2001); Wim P. Van Meurs, *The Bessarabian Question in Communist Historiography* (New York and Boulder, CO: Columbia University Press and East European Monographs, 1994); Herman Pirchner, Jr., *Reviving Greater Russia? The Future of Russia's Borders with Belarus, Georgia, Kazakhstan, Moldova and Ukraine* (Washington, DC: The University Press of America and American Foreign Policy Council, 2005); Wim van Meurs, "Moldova," in *New Europe: The Impact of the First Decade*, vol. 2: *Variations on the Pattern*, ed. Teresa Rakowska-Harmstone, Piotr Dutkiewicz, and Agnieszka Orzelska (Warsaw: Institute of Political Studies Polish Academy of Sciences and Collegium Civitas Press, 2006), 329–70; Klemens Buscher, *Transnationale Beziehungen Der Russen in Moldova Und Der Ukraine: Ethnische Diaspora Zwischen Residenz-Und Referenzstaat* (Frankfurt am Main: Peter Lang, 2004). On the German minority see Albert Kern, *Homeland Book of the Bessarabian Germans* (Fargo, ND: Germans from Russia Heritage Collection, North Dakota State University Libraries, 1998); and on the Jews: Yosef Govrin, *In the Shadow of Destruction: Recollections of Transnistria and the Illegal Immigration to Eretz Israel* (Portland, OR: Valentine Mitchell, 2007); Miriam Weiner, *Jewish Roots in Ukraine and Moldova: Pages from the Past and Archival Inventories* (The Jewish Genealogy Series) (Secaucus, NJ: Miriam Weiner Routes to Roots Foundation, 1999); David Noevich Goberman, Robert Pinsky, and Gershon Hundert, *Carved Memories: Heritage in Stone from the Russian Jewish Pale* (New York: Rizzoli, 2000).

Part IV

Chain of Memory

We die with the dying;
See, they depart, and we go with them.
We are born with the dead;
See, they return, and bring us with them.[1]

—T. S. Eliot

21

An Overview

A casual, even repeated traveler passing through the Intermarium, as well as a seasoned, expert visitor, will be struck how much has changed in the past twenty years there. Western influences are evident everywhere, most notably the economy and popular culture. But discontinuities from the Communist past, many of them salubrious and welcome, are matched by as many, and perhaps more, continuities of the Soviet way. Further, the resurrection of various traditions of the pre-Bolshevik history has greatly reinvigorated, in some cases at least, the political, social, cultural, and economic scene of the Intermarium. The restoration of tradition has aided the journey of self-rediscovery and self-assertion of the majorities, but also can be a cause for concern for the minorities. And vice versa, the majorities can find uncomfortable, if not outright menacing, the newly found freedom of the minorities to self-identify as such with all that entails, including building, or, rather, rebuilding, community institutions; maintaining contact with the home country; and networking with other minority groups.

All this brings pain, anxiety, joy, and exhilaration all at once. Any change unsettles, including change for the better. This pertains to alterations to the people's consciousness by bringing back the past. To restore collective memories is a confusing and a necessary process which progresses in sprouts and elicits contradictory reactions and feelings, where pride and denial mingle freely. And modernity intrudes constantly. It demands of the locals to jettison some of the newly restored bits once again. It encourages them to remember more acutely other segments. It introduces a new, unknown dimension to their post-Soviet routine. It challenges and negates the Communist ways, but it often lacks patience for the old, traditional arrangements that have painfully reemerged from under the debris of totalitarianism and endeavored to reassert themselves, sometimes awkwardly oblivious to the passage of time and the requirements of change. In other ways, a selection process is under way where the old, the Soviet, and the new compete, collide, and self-correct. What can emerge will be a hybrid of the three, hopefully anchored in Western tradition grounded in local peculiarities as already had once been the case during the Polish-Lithuanian Commonwealth. Restoring memories is a project in the making.

To appreciate the intricacies of the process, we shall first describe the landscape and impressions of the Intermarium. Next, we shall deal with false consciousness among its inhabitants. Then, we shall focus on individual recollections and national stereotypes. And, finally, to illustrate the above we shall shock the reader with a case study of a massacre where the standard victim–victimizer roles are reversed.

Note

1. T. S. Eliot, "Little Gidding," in *Four Quartets*, http://www.tristan.icom43.net/quartets/ (accessed October 11, 2011).

22

Landscapes and Impressions

In this decayed hole among the mountains
In the faint moonlight, the grass is singing
Over the tumbled graves, about the chapel
There is the empty chapel, only the wind's home.
It has no windows, and the door swings,
Dry bones can harm no one.[1]

—T. S. Eliot

Constant contemplation of Lenin monuments or plaques reading 'Lenin Street' or honoring some other former Soviet official is very harmful to the human psyche. Any monuments and sites associated with the dignitaries of the communist regime should be eliminated. Streets should be given instead such names that are liked by the majority of the population of the area in question. I'm not saying that these should be the names of, say, Ukrainian independence fighters, which are popular in western Ukraine. People themselves should decide on the name and the respective council should approve the choice. Streets may be named not only after some political figures or ideas, but also to highlight the area's nature or history, or they may be given completely neutral names, such as Long Street, Wide Street or Sunny Street. People resist renaming streets today out of sheer inertia, as they have become accustomed to some current name and do not want to change it.[2]

—Ihor Yukhnovsky, a Ukrainian historian

At this point of our journey through the Intermarium we would like to offer some journalistic impressions deriving from the cumulative experience of our trips to the region.[3] They concern the post-Soviet zone's both diversity and uniformity, an economic development theory, social mores of its inhabitants, and the cultural geography of symbols.

Regional, state, ethnic, cultural, economic, social, and political diversity remains the most salient feature of the post-Soviet sphere. In the Intermarium, similarities and differences are unevenly distributed throughout the region.

Not only does each successor state have a different flavor, but there also variations within each of them. Regional differences reflect the history of the region. But so do its uniform features.

The most important common ingredient is the legacy of the USSR. Post-Sovietism and post-Communism continue to inform the nature of the successor states. The length of the Soviet occupation determines the extent and depth of its social engineering experiments, including the scale of terror, as well as their atomizing durability into the present. Thus, the farther east the more crippling the legacy of Communism grinds on. However, a variety of mitigating features, existing in each of the regions, has assisted the locals with dealing with Communism and its aftermath. By the mitigating features we mean pre-Soviet institutions and attitudes. These cushioning phenomena are also grounded in history. Geographically, their strongest manifestations can be conceptualized as existing within two partly overlapping spheres. First, it is the westernmost area enclosed by the former borders of the interwar Poland and the Baltics. Next, it is the region reaching the eastern boundaries of the historic Polish-Lithuanian Commonwealth. In the latter location the mitigating features operate to a much lesser extent and with greatly diminished strength than in the former. Beyond the easternmost reaches of the old Commonwealth's borderlands, the cushioning phenomena are few and far between. Much of culture and civic life there is steeped in Muscovite and Soviet ways.

The Soviet inheritance notwithstanding, one of the most potent forces in the Intermarium has been the legacy of interwar independence. Here the Baltic states are obviously at an advantage. A brief spell of freedom made them strong spiritually. This is compounded by the fact that their occupation by the Soviet Union lasted "only" about forty-five years. It can favorably be contrasted with the Belarusian and Ukrainian historical experience of statelessness, including in the interwar period. Further, both Belarus and Ukraine's eastern territories endured about seventy-five years of the Communist occupation. Only western parts of Belarus and Ukraine were lucky enough to escape with "just" forty-five years under Bolshevism.

Poland's interwar rule in western Belarus and Ukraine was relatively free. It facilitated the creation and maintenance of independent Belarusian and Ukrainian civic life (notwithstanding the Polish bouts of repression, chiefly against the extremist elements, but also, shamelessly, against the Orthodox religion). This interwar legacy allowed the inhabitants of those regions to weather the superseding Soviet regime with more resilience. Still more, the Ukrainians (except the Volhynians) were at a distinct advantage over the Belarusians in this respect because, prior to 1914, they had experienced a rather benign form of government by the liberal Habsburgs, who encouraged most forms of Ukrainian national life. On the other hand, the Belarusians were under the autocratic Romanovs and, therefore, their civil society remained embryonic until 1918. They made only modest strides in national development during the interwar period, all too often in a suicidal alliance with the Bolsheviks, and, hence, found themselves under the Soviet tyranny less equipped to resist than either the Balts or western Ukrainians.

For those reasons, the interwar *cordon sanitaire*, which followed the borders of Poland, Lithuania, Latvia, and Estonia, continues to constitute an important dividing line within the Intermarium. This may be the case now even to a greater extent that in the Soviet times. Partly because of it, in the Intermarium's west, the material culture, political attitudes, local flavor, and the choice of symbols differ, sometimes markedly, from the east. Admittedly, there is a fair degree of mixing with "eastern" features jutting westwards, and "western" attitudes penetrating eastwards.

There is also an intermediate sphere between the east and the west of the Intermarium where "eastern" and "western" attitudes both mesh and clash most visibly. It roughly encompasses the lands all the way east to the furthermost span of the Polish-Lithuanian Commonwealth. Naturally, the intermediate sphere lacks uniformity and invites fascinating exceptions which impact the nature of each region. For example, at the end of the eighteenth century the old Commonwealth's Volhynia was taken over by Moscow's tsars but was recaptured by Poland in 1918. Thus, the Romanov (Volhynian) Ukrainians were more Russified than the Habsburg ones (making the former more akin in their experience to Belarusians), but, unlike eastern Ukrainians and Belarusians, the Volhynian Ukrainians were lucky enough to live under the Polish rule in the interwar period (mostly under a long lasting and very liberal provincial governor). Hence, their direct experience with the Soviets was limited to forty-five years "only."[4]

The intermediate sphere is a virtual alchemist's vial of disparate, mostly conflicting, phenomena. They endeavor to coexist uneasily while encroaching upon each other's prerogatives sometimes by the force of inertia, but at other times by the dynamics of the continued transformation of the region. Those features include primarily the ideologies of post-Communism and nationalism (of various intensity), religion (of a number of confessions), and commercialization and globalization (of different forms of corruption, crudity, and superficiality, on the one hand, and of various degrees of initiative, ingenuity and diligence, on the other).

Naturally, those phenomena do exist as well in the Intermarium's east but to a much lesser extent (save for post-Communism) and in a much more uniform shape (reflecting the enduring virulence of the Bolshevik experience). Although the east is also diverse, it is a diversity of a Soviet imperial kind. It is largely devoid of the ingredients easily recognizable as belonging to Western Civilization which percolate ebulliently to various degree elsewhere in the Intermarium. The exception in the east is of course commercialization and globalization, which were appropriately post-Sovietized via corruption and sloth to function at all in their new environment.

We have purposefully chosen to refer to the commercialization and globalization (instead of free-market capitalism) at the national level because in most of the Intermarium, save for the Baltics, in Estonia chiefly, free markets are stifled by post-Communism. Everywhere a mixed economy of sorts exists with the state heavily regulating the market. Socialism permeates and over-whelms local economies, while permitting, at times, a various degree of individual market initiatives. Property rights are nowhere secure (save, to a certain extent, for the Baltics, in particular Estonia, which has even executed extensive property restitution). Ugly crony capitalism dominates in Ukraine and Moldova. Belarus eyes covetously the Chinese model of the neo-NEP circa 1990.

Yet, the benefits of (even partial) economic freedom in the Intermarium are indubitably manifold. It impacts, slowly, but surely, everything including the local culture. The natives endeavor to emulate the economic success of the West on a variety of levels. This can be best appreciated by observing what we have dubbed "the hotel paradigm" and "the gas station model." The former registers on macroscale. The latter is mostly visible on microscale.

The hotel paradigm refers to the multifarious implications of the endeavor to improve the business and tourism infrastructure. Usually, this endeavor has adhered to the following pattern. First, a Western company, usually a chain, almost always with the local state partners, built a recreational/hous-ing facility in a major city, most likely the capital. Western managers were brought in to run it and to train a local work force. A few of the lucky locals would even be dispatched to the West for training. The Westerners insisted on stringent business requirements for their native workers and contrac-tors. The management stressed the importance of service to deliver quality goods. That excluded the socialist work "ethic," and rewarded diligence and professionalism instead. Further, the employees were expected to maintain appropriate sartorial standards, hygiene, demeanor, and manners. All this was simply shocking in the early post-Soviet context. It also proved extremely appealing.

The hotel would become an instant hit not only with foreign visitors (who, admittedly, had very few choices), but also, perhaps primarily, with the locals. All aspired to visit, if only a few could afford it. The local elite, usually the post-Communists, Mafiosi, and so-called businessmen, often overlapping categories, made the hotel the focus of their lives. Most of them wanted to emulate the glitz, the lifestyle, and the glamour of "the West" as refracted via the hotel. This, in fact, was "the West" in miniature brought home to them to scrutinize. Whether or not, say, the Hyatt Regency in Kyiv or the Crown Plaza in Minsk, truly reflected the reality of the West mattered not. What mattered was the perception that it did. Most importantly, from the point of view of the mentality of the Soviets and, soon, post-Soviets, the natives acquired a local, tangible point of reference against which to scrutinize their own sordid existence. Their reaction was seemingly confusing: to admire, covet, emulate, and, ultimately, resent.

Meanwhile, as the system was unraveling, the local oligarchs either took over old Soviet hotels and rigged them to resemble the Western operation or built themselves new ones based upon this exciting and novel Western paradigm. Pretty soon, to compete successfully and to set themselves off from the Communist past, the oligarchs forced their own employees to emulate the hotel workers of the Western chains down to the most minute detail of the sartorial appearances, or at least so they thought. The hotel was an ideal to emulate, an alternative universe to be built at home. From there the Western standards began to trickle down to the rest of the population. Even if that occurred in a distorted form, it still was a vast improvement over the shoddiness, grimness, and inefficiency of the dreary Soviet norm.

However, the hotel paradigm was of limited utility on microscale because it could not be experienced by the masses. Ritzy establishments were off-limits to mere mortals, who could only gape from the outside. Instead, therefore, it was the gas station that exerted the greatest influence at the grassroots level because of its ubiquity and accessibility. In a way, the gas station was a mini hotel. Yet, it was much more versatile. First, it was clean, including its bathrooms inside and lawns outside. Second, it was usually open twenty-four hours a day. Third, it commonly had a well-supplied mini-mart. Fourth, its personnel was pleasant, competent, and tidy. All this was a shocking convenience in a universe where the Soviet store clerks named their own hours or failed to open at all for the lack of wares as well as exercised with a gusto their proverbial rudeness in deigning to grace the cowed petitioners with scraps of the leftover products that the retail personnel had failed either to sell at the black market or to supply to family and friends. The Soviet norm was thus lethally challenged by the Western way of the gas station.

With car ownership steadily increasing in the post-Soviet sphere, almost everyone had to visit a gas station. And everyone had a good look at its operations over and over again. At the lowest level, the people not only began to aspire to what they saw at the gas station (including hygienic standards), but they also came to expect other local businesses to conform to the model, including, for example, the dreadful Soviet-style grocery stores. And the increasingly emancipated customers came to expect less rudeness from the once-lordly clerks. Imagine that!

Thus, even within the crippling context of post-Communism, the free-market hotel paradigm and gas station model proved hugely successful in fostering the Western way in the Intermarium. Naturally, one should remember that the successful implementation of both was greatly facilitated by other manifestations of freedom. Clearly, the transitional ride has been rather bumpy. It inches at the top, because of the constraints of socialism and the rest of the post-Soviet legacy; it accelerates at times at the grassroots, where individuals can surprise themselves and others with an astonishing degree of emancipation from Communism and post-Communism. Naturally, the story is not one of uninterrupted progress. At times, grassroots economic initiatives in Hradna (Grodno) are interrupted by an *ukase* from Minsk regulating internet cafes; a dour-faced local bureaucrat objecting to the new proprietor's desire to restore a historic building in Ivano Frankyvsk (Stanisławów); or neighborhood mafia strong arming an owner of a successful pizza parlor in Chişinău to make him sell the business at a pittance.[5] That happens all too frequently. Then the locals try again. That kind of initiative in itself is a vast improvement over the Soviet-style inertia.

What is a threat to free markets usually constitutes a danger to democracy, too. It is the individual freedom within that allows one to remain gingerly hopeful for the Intermarium. Some grassroots entrepreneurs are discouraged; some emigrate. But others return from abroad and chip away at the posttotalitarian structure. Still others who have never left join them in the endeavor. Most people appear docile, but the Soviet experience has ironically taught them the utility of black marketeering, and of ignoring the state and the mafia thugs, often connected to the secret police. That means that most contribute to the restoration of free markets, if only a little. The sum total of self-empowered individual wills may yet translate into a cathartical emancipation of the collective mentality of the former Soviet slaves.

Mentality, of course, is the most resilient to change. The most salient feature of the posttotalitarian mentality is mistrust of one's fellows. For economic, social, and political success of the region there must be mutual trust. But there is precious little of it. After all, the people who populate the area were mostly born in the USSR, subjected to and affected by its propaganda, institutions, mores, and terror or at least its memory. Experience dictates caution and even fear. Consequently, the very ingredients indispensable for a healthy body politics, for a salubrious civil society, are in short supply.

Take the reflexes that once upon a time in the West were considered "Christian," and nowadays, although less frequent, are still considered decent. The common secular name for them is "altruism." For instance, in the post-Soviet sphere the acts of spontaneous kindness for strangers, Westerners in particular, do occur, but are by no stretch of anyone's imagination the rule. If anything, one should expect their opposite. Some of the nihilistic reactions of the denizens of the Intermarium are purely Soviet: suspicion, intolerance, rudeness, faithlessness, slovenliness, callousness, close-mindedness, lack of manners, disregard for diligence, disrespect for the law, respect for power, a resort to violence, mocking of the notion of honor, inability to express oneself directly, support for black and grey economy, and a penchant for intrigue and conspiracy theories.

That is not to say that other cultures are happily devoid of such attitudes. On the contrary, they abound elsewhere, too. The Japanese, for instance, delight in conspiracies real and imagined.[6] Garbage strewn on the streets of any Third World country is the norm. However, as far as the Intermarium, we simply would like to observe that those negative phenomena manifest themselves dialectically, and predictably, in the Soviet way. It was the Communists who fostered and encouraged them as a negation of the "bourgeois norms." For the same reasons, the east Germans are yet to rediscover their once much-vaunted "Protestant work ethic." And the Poles need to learn to respect the law. As David Satter astutely shows, the nefarious persistence of post-Communist pathologies stems from the nihilistic lack of faith. The near annihilation of religion impacts adversely both the elite and the people on the political, social, cultural, and economic levels in the Intermarium.[7]

Paradoxically, some of the outside influences, appearing under the labels of "Westernization" and "globalization," both sharply challenge the post-Soviet ways and incongruously reinforce them. We are referring here to the basic freedoms, including the freedom of speech, movement, and vote, as guaranteed by a parliamentary democracy, and economic freedom, as promised by free-market capitalism. The opportunities are there and some have taken advantage of them with various results.

In particular, the young of the Intermarium have been free to travel and compare their status quo with that of their peers elsewhere, most often in western Europe. On the one hand, some have taken advantage of the new opportunities to better themselves and their stations, in particular those who emigrated. The returnees enjoy a much smaller degree of success than they would in the West. But most have improved their lot economically. They learned new skills, including trade. They invested their earnings into improving their standard of living at home. Their mentalities are now infused with inventiveness acquired abroad.

However, the losers among the repatriates and among those who stayed put covet impotently what they failed to acquire. For most of them the largess of the West is still inaccessible. But it is irksome because of its visual ubiquity at home, principally on TV. For most of the post-Soviet losers, hardly anything has changed. Among the idle and frustrated young, their unfulfilled desires are the main source of nostalgia for the Soviet times. They make a common cause with other economically downtrodden: chiefly collective farmers and pensioners. Their grievances are echoed by the post-Soviet minorities, the Russians in particular. Chafing at the assertive nationalism of the newly liberated majorities, the minorities harken back to the alleged era of Soviet egalitarianism. The Russians additionally resent the loss of their prestige as the former colonial overlords. This is most pronounced in the Baltics, where the Russian dissatisfaction with the restoration of freedom of Estonia, Latvia, and Lithuania is only secondarily tied to economic grievances. Everywhere, the dissatisfied tend to express themselves in anticapitalist ways.

Yet, the importance of a flowering free-market economy for the salubrious development of the Intermarium is undeniable as is its impact on the mentality of the locals. Western consumerism currently entering the region in a variety of forms and through a variety of venues has changed from a trickle into a torrent; for some it is a flood of unfulfilled promises and unmet expectations. In a long run, however, it can probably reshape the post-Soviet mentality in a hospitable manner to foster freedom on every level. But the young lack patience to appreciate anything promised to them in a distant future. They want change for the better and they want it now. Rampant unemployment does not help.

As a result, in many cases, the young naturally enough marry their post-Soviet nihilism, inherited from their elders, with the postmodernist malaise found in Western liberalism. The result is to reinforce the existing pathologies, not only at the lower depths of the crime world but also, say, in post-Soviet academia, where the original political correctness of Marxism-Leninism has been increasingly refitted with the straight jacket of the smelly pet peeves of the Western universities in their gender, queer, and other guises. This is an awful tragedy because at its most sublime the success of the Intermarium is predicated on the return of faith, empiricism, and logocentrism.[8]

All in all, intellectually and intuitively, the post-Soviets endeavor to make sense of their old-new world. They often thrash around for a solid point of reference. And nothing embeds itself more permanently in the subconscious and nothing allows us to relate to the world more comfortably than the permanent features that surround us. Monuments, buildings, and various other structures are the most enduring man-made features of our landscape. They are our most basic symbols. They can have a soothing influence on one's psyche. We surrender to their power because we routinely take them for granted. And only a few initiated among us can relate consciously to, including either embracing or taking offense at, the symbols that surround our space since before our birth or even that of our grandparents. If certain new structures blend effortlessly into the familiar background, we accept them too, the more so readily the greater utility they have.

In this context, in the Intermarium, whereas nowadays hotels and gas stations unify the area in an agreeable manner as harbingers of positive change, the cultural monuments divide it. In fact, the local monuments are perhaps the most graphic illustrations of the jarring contradictions within the post-Soviet zone. They are also the most handy tools to depict the confusion and chaos as well as political and cultural trends in the area. They function as often conflicting symbols of the past and the present. They are the pivots around which the locals try to maintain or reconstruct their identity. Yet, apparently, despite their contradictory nature the cultural monuments do not bother the natives enough to cause them to destroy them. At the least it can be said that not everywhere did the monuments mobilize the population spontaneously to eliminate symbols of the past.

In the east, in particular in western Russia, but also eastern Ukraine, the Soviet and Communist monuments remain swaggeringly ubiquitous. They blend in with few surviving structures denoting the glory of pre-revolutionary mother Russia. However, both have been recently augmented with the newly resurrected symbols of Orthodox Christianity. Smolensk is a good case in point here: a Lenin street, a Kutuzov monument, and the Uspensky Sobor, all, more or less, within walking distance. Thus, a Putinesque continuity zygotically joined the Bolshevik demigod with a Tsarist general and an Orthodox church. The text on a newly remounted plaque on the Uspensky Sobor provides the cement for this artificial construct: "To commemorate the 300th anniversary of the defense of Smolensk from the Poles, 1609–1611."[9] Never mind that Smolensk, within and without the Commonwealth, had defended itself from the Muscovites for years. Never mind that "the Poles" were really Ruthenians, Lithuanians, Poles, and others who defended Western Civilization from the Muscovite tyranny. There is not a peep about that either in Smolensk or, for that matter, virtually anywhere in the Intermarium. The permissible symbols are reduced to "defeating the Polish lords" in the name of "Mother Russia" here or some folk ethnonationalism elsewhere in the region. The grotesquely ridiculous life-sized puppets of the "Polish nobles" *sans* their family rings at the castle of Kamieniec Podolski come to mind in Ukraine. The southern town of Odessa is an exception here: there are some ugly Bolshevik plaques and Soviet monuments, but also some charming Russian and other cultural symbols of the port city's less sanguinary past of the nineteenth century.

Ukraine's east is virtually a post-industrial wasteland. In Donbass in particular the cities are ravaged with urban blight, the depressing projects in particular, but decorated with some Western-style commercial advertising. The countryside is monotonous and pockmarked with erstwhile state and collective farms in various states of decrepitude. From time to time, gaudy kleptocratic residences can be spotted, but access to the area may be restricted both in the town and country. Some enjoy a prime location. Oligarch Rinat "Botanik" Akhmetov's sprawling 250-acre estate at Donetsk's public Botanical Garden is a case in point, awarded to him by the fawning town council, and repossessed by the state in the wake of the Orange Revolution.

From Kremenchug to Poltava, from Kharkiv/Kharkov to Lukhans'k, from Dnipropetrovsk/Dnepropetrovsk to Kerch, there are only a few pearls of architecture, mostly sacral. New and renovated Orthodox churches appear here and there, for example Spasko Preobrazhensky Cathedrals in Dnepropetrovsk and Donetsk. Arguably, the most impressive churches are in Kharkiv. Dating from the seventeenth century, the Pokrovsky Sobor's construction commenced under the Hetmanate as a fortress but later expanded to include a cloister and several places of worship. The Moscow Patriarchate maintains the Blagoveshchensky Sobor, whose construction was launched the late nineteenth century. The Uspensky Sobor dates from the same era, but it has not been returned to the faithful. Instead, it continues to serve as a concert hall.

Everywhere Soviet monuments command the public square. Most popular are to the victorious Red Army. But Lenin also continues to seduce from his pedestal in many places. Stalin has made a comeback of sorts. In May 2010 the Communists of Zaporozhye unabashedly unveiled a statue to "Uncle Joe." It was mercifully blown up, presumably by anti-Communists, on January 1, 2011, obliterating the dictator's image completely and also damaging the local Bolshevik party headquarters.

There has been at least one successful effort to commemorate a capitalist. The recent monument of Welshman John James Hughes in Donetsk in recognition to his contribution to his founding of the city is long overdue. Some also remember the forbidden dead. Kharkiv's modest "wall of memory" adorned with St. Andrew's Cross for the Ukrainian victims of the Great Purge (1937–1938) at Piatykhatky is a shockingly exceptional anti-Communist memento as is the memorial stone to blind Ukrainian bagpipers shot by the NKVD at that time. Stone images of earlier heroes, including the Romantic bard Taras Shevchenko and Ruthenian prince Yaroslav the Wise, are rather rare. In lower Dnieper, on an islet on the Kakhovka Reservoir, the government reconstructed a Cossack base a few years ago. The legendary *Sich* is alas completely overshadowed by the monstrous Soviet-era dam and electricity generating enterprise located next to it. This amply reflects the story of eastern Ukraine: a few very feeble signs of recovering or even constructing national memories in a swamp of post-Soviet survivals.

In central Ukraine, however, the imposing Communist structures share the landscape with a few demure Ukrainian nationalist symbols, mostly from premodern and early modern times, and Western (Catholic) and Orthodox architectural monuments. In Khmelnitsk (Płoskirów), the imposing statue of Hetman Bohdan Khmelnytsky, a seventeenth-century anti-Commonwealth rebel, caters both to the adherents of the Communist class struggle narrative and the ethno-nationalist haters of "the Polish lords." Kyiv sports much of that as well but also a new feature invoking the nation's unity through anti-Communism. Namely, Ukraine's capital has recently acquired a monument to the victims of the Terror-Famine (*Holodomor*). This is a welcome addition to the still ubiquitous Soviet-era images, which are less than admired by some Ukrainians, as evidenced by the around-the-clock volunteer Communist guard at the gigantic status of Lenin, which has been as yet an unsuccessful target of the ultranationalist bombers. There are also Kyivian architectural wonders of ecclesiastic nature, albeit currently mired in an Orthodox Christian *monachomachia*, the war of the monks, between the adherents of the

Moscow Patriarchate and its opponents in Ukraine. It includes at least one hastily built and highly visible grave, in essence a public monument, to spite the Muscovite enemy who has quite recently refused to bury an autocephalic Ukrainian Orthodox ecclesiast inside a Moscow-controlled monastery at the center of Kyiv. In Kamenets Podolsk the odious Lenin statue was toppled, but the "tank-liberator" of the Red Army retained. It is complemented by a highly abstract sculpture to the victims of the Soviet war in Afghanistan, and surrounded by a variety of beautifully renovated churches of every possible denomination: Russian Orthodox, Greek Catholic, Roman Catholic, Armenian Orthodox, and others. A Madonna sits above the Roman Catholic cathedral, perched triumphant on the top of a former minaret, a legacy of a brief Ottoman occupation. The Madonna is a legacy of the old Commonwealth, a votive gift erected after the reconquest of the fortress from the Turks.

Zhitomir is another good example of heterodoxy. There two Catholic churches neighbor two Orthodox places of worship. At least one of the latter, the Preodbrazhensky Sobor, recognizes the Moscow Patriarchate. Inside the Sobor, there is a handmade wall-mounted pictorial tribute to the Red Army of "liberation," in particular a parishioner's grandfather and grandmother. On its grounds, in the shadow of a rather large monument to the millennium of Ruthenia's Christianity built under Gorbachev, there sits a symbolic grave to two obscure Ukrainian nationalist (OUN) heroes who perished there in 1941. Whether they were killed by the Soviets or the Nazis is left unsaid. Outside of the Sobor fence, in the square, a monument-tank (or, more precisely, a self-propelled gun) of the "Soviet liberation" menacingly towers over everything else unchallenged. On the opposite side of the Preodbrazhensky Sobor, at a square down the street, Lenin waves to the passer-by gaily from his monument.[10]

It is also a worker paradisiacal *déjà vu* in Hradna in Belarus, where Lenin looms goodnaturedly, blessing the merrymakers and strollers promenading in a park across Dzherzhinsky Street.[11] A little bit up the street, as we pass the plaque to commemorate a felicitously brief sojourn of the Cheka founder in the town in 1920 and a monument to a Soviet military leader of World War II fame, we reach the Soviet Square (*Sovetskaia Ploshchad'*, aka the Batory Mall of interwar Poland). The authorities have hoisted a huge banner over it: "I love you, Belarus," it screams in white letters over red background. Right across the street, there is a Catholic cathedral. Its frontón carries the eternal message of hope: "Sursum Corda." On the other side of the square, at the feet of the old Bernardine Catholic church, a Soviet tank-liberator is frozen on a slight incline, an enduring and ubiquitous monument to the Communist occupation.

In Belarus, the authorities have appropriated the Soviet symbols and endowed them with a parallel meaning as monuments to Belarusian (post-Soviet) nationalism. In the successor state's east and center, they share the public space with the Orthodox Christian structures. Lenin and St. Nicholas the

Miracle Worker can be found in Minsk, Brest, Orsha, and really everywhere else. However, Western Christian symbols have also made their reappearance here and there, in particular many proudly renovated Catholic churches and chapels in west Belarus. A precious few restored Protestant places of worship are limited mostly to the Baltics.[12]

In the north-west and west of the Intermarium (save for Belarus), the Soviet and Communist monuments are on the wane. They persevere either by the force of inertia or by the anger of the Russian minority population (and their few native Communist supporters), who defend them staunchly from destruction. Nonetheless, in the Baltics, some of the Soviet monuments have been overthrown, while others are forced to coexist with the local national-ist ones. More precisely, the native nationalist structures seem to dominate along the coast and the west of the Baltic states, including the capital cities. The Crosses to commemorate the anti-Communist forest brothers have been erected in a number of localities in the countryside, including along major highways and side roads in Lithuania, Latvia, and Estonia. This is now state-mandated, even though it originated as a grassroots initiative. Deeper inland, the numbers of the Crosses diminish, yielding to the usurpation of space by an offensive slew of Soviet-era monuments, in both Estonia and Latvia. This concerns mostly the eastern rim of both Baltic successor states.[13]

An early 1950s monumental stone tablet to mark the founding of a local *kolkhoz* some way south of Tartu is disturbing in its casual celebration of a human tragedy wrought about by the official violence. The ghoulish solitary "Bolshevik" on the Dvina bank in Daugavpils (Dynaburg) is arguably the most nauseating example of such art. It is only overshadowed in its sheer unaes-thetic horror by the socialist realist mausoleum to the Red Army "Liberators" or "Unknown Soldiers" in Riga, a sculpture the local Latvian wags refer to as the "Monument to the Unknown Rapists." The Estonians removed theirs. The situation is similar in Lithuania, although the Soviet remnants seem fewer and the native ones more numerous. A curious variation occurs in the eastern and southeastern part of the country, where Polish nationalist monuments, includ-ing some restored and renovated as well as a few new ones, in the cemeteries in particular, are notable, increasing in size and ubiquity toward the border with Belarus and Poland, but also present in certain locations of the capital city, Vilnius. The necropolis at Rossa in Vilnius is as splendid a testimony to the area's Polish past as is the Łyczakowski burial ground in Lviv.[14]

Speaking of Ukraine, last but not least, the Soviet and Communist monu-ments have been almost completely purged from its western part, where they were replaced with a multitude of nationalist structures. Ivano Frankyvsk, for instance, celebrates the nationalist leader Stefan Bandera, who was as-sassinated by the Soviets following World War II. We can admire Bandera crouchant, Bandera rampant, Bandera pensive, and a Soviet-style mausoleum to Bandera's followers: all quite bombastic, quite gauche, quite socialist realist. Modest OUN and UPA mounds (*kurhani*) to the fallen anti-Communist fighters dotting the countryside in the Carpathians seem much more appropriately decent.[15] Instead of inviting coexistence with other traditions, this outpouring of integral nationalist symbolism intimidates other Ukrainian traditions into obscurity. Where is a worthy monument to the great Metropolitan Andriy Sheptitsky (Count Andrzej Szeptycki, 1865–1944), for example? A modest bust of the ecclesiastic aristocrat in Truskavets is perhaps a good beginning but fails to give justice to his accomplishments. Perhaps the plans to have a statue to Sheptitsky erected in Lviv will bear positive fruit in more ways than one, in particular by diversifying the Ukrainian nationalist discourse and its symbols. Integral nationalist imagination and attitude also hardly leave any place for Polish mementos except in churches and cemeteries. There are even fewer Jewish artifacts visible in the public space. Nonetheless, there remain synagogues and other Jewish community properties, spread throughout the Intermarium. But they are usually under state ownership. Only a few of them have been returned to the rightful owners.[16]

Notes

1. T. S. Eliot, *The Waste Land*, 1922, http://www.bartleby.com/201/1.html.
2. Valerii Kostiukevych, "Olevsk frees itself from the Soviet legacy," *Den'/The Day*, no. 77, December 29, 2011, posted at http://www.day.kiev.ua/221557/.
3. In particular, our observations concern the trip of the summer of 2010. A full report in Marek Jan Chodakiewicz, "Notatki z post-Sowiecji (część I)," ("Notes from the Post-Soviet Lands, Part I") *Najwyższy Czas!* (October 9, 2010): XXXV; "Notatki z post-Sowiecji (część II)," ("Notes from the Post-Soviet Lands, Part II") *Najwyższy Czas!* (October 16, 2010): XXXV; "Notatki z post-Sowiecji (część III)," ("Notes from the Post-Soviet Lands, part III") *Najwyższy Czas!* (October 23, 2010): XXXV; "Notatki z post-Sowiecji (część IV)," ("Notes from the Post-Soviet Lands, Part IV") *Najwyższy Czas!* ("October 30–November 6, 2010): XLIII. Compare with George Friedman's travelogue-cum-geopolitical incongruous musings, which can be infuriatingly uninformed about the particulars, on the one hand, and verging on brilliant about the generalities, on the other: George Friedman, "Geopolitical Journey with George Friedman," http://www.stratfor.com/theme/special_series_geopolitical_journey_george_friedman, and consisting of eight parts: "Part 1: The Traveler," "Part 2: Borderlands," "Part 3: Rumania," "Part 4: Moldova," "Part 5: Turkey," "Part 6: Ukraine," "Part 7: Poland," "Part 8: Returning Home." (Also accessible at http://www.stratfor.com/node/175486/ archive). For interwar Volhynia's liberal governor see, Timothy Snyder, *Sketches from a Secret War: A Polish Artist's Mission to Liberate Soviet Ukraine* (New Haven, CT.: Yale University Press, 2005).
4. For some pertinent observations about Ukraine alone see Alexander J. Motyl, "Ukraine's Orange Blues: The Underdevelopment of the Donbas," *World Affairs: A Journal of Ideas and Debate* (October 7, 2011): http://www.worldaffairsjournal.org/new/blogs/motyl/The_Underdevelopment_of_the_Donbas?utm_sou rce=World+Affairs+Newsletter&utm_campaign=9038d2bade-Blog_Chang_ Kara_Murza_Motyl_10_7_2011&utm_medium=email.

5. Breffni O'Rourke, "Europe: Council of Europe Report Says Organized Crime Poses Threat to Democracy," *Radio Free Europe/Radio Liberty* (January 26, 2005): http://www.rferl.org/content/article/1057094.html.

6. Michael Shapiro, "The Elders of Zion in Tokyo," *The New York Times Book Review* (February 5, 1995): 12; Tom Tugend, "Magazine Folds Following Article Denying Holocaust," *Jewish Chronicle* (February 3, 1995): 60.

7. On Soviet and post-Soviet social mores see David Satter, *Age of Delirium: The Decline and Fall of the Soviet Union* (New Haven, CT and London: Yale University Press, 2001); David Satter, *Darkness at Dawn: The Rise of the Russian Criminal State* (New Haven, CT and London: Yale University Press, 2003); David Satter, *It Was a Long Time Ago, and It Never Happened Anyway: Russia and the Communist Past* (New Haven, CT and London: Yale University Press, 2012). His observations pertain to the whole of the post-Soviet sphere, and not only Russia. See also Adele Marie Barker, ed., *Consuming Russia: Popular Culture, Sex, and Society since Gorbachev* (Durham, NC and London: Duke University Press, 1999). For the post-Soviet pathology in its criminal practice see Arkady Vaksberg, *The Soviet Mafia* (New York: St. Martin's Press, 1991); Federico Varese, *The Russian Mafia: Private Protection in a New Market Economy* (New York: Oxford University, 2001, 2nd edn. 2005); Stephen Handelman, *Comrade Criminal: Russia's New Mafiya* (New Haven, CT: Yale University Press, 1995); Paul Klebnikov, *Godfather of the Kremlin: Boris Berezovsky and the Looting of Russia* (New York: Harcourt, Inc., 2000); Misha Glenny, *McMafia: A Journey through the Global Criminal Underworld* (New York: Alfred A. Knopf, 2008).

8. See "Ni ma jak Lviv?" ("There Ain't Nothing like Lviv?") *Glaukopis* no. 5/6 (2006): 490–97, which is a review of John Czaplicka, ed., *Lviv: A City in the Crosscurrents of Culture* (Cambridge, MA: Distributed by Harvard University Press for the Harvard Ukrainian Research Institute, 2005), where some of the authors pay respect to fashionable multiculturalism, failing to anchor the Lvovian shibboleths in the context of Western universalism.

9. Marek Jan Chodakiewicz, "Notatki z post-Sowiecji (część III)," ("Notes from the Post-Soviet Lands, Part III") *Najwyższy Czas!* (October 23, 2010): XXXV.

10. Marek Jan Chodakiewicz, "Notatki z post-Sowiecji (część II)," ("Notes from the Post-Soviet Lands, Part II") *Najwyższy Czas!* (October 16, 2010): XXXV. A few small towns in central Ukraine have nonetheless begun to de-Communize their streets and other public spaces, for instance Olevsk outside of Zhitomir. See Valerii Kostiukevych, "Olevsk frees itself from the Soviet legacy," *Den'/The Day*, no. 77, December 29, 2011, posted at http://www.day.kiev.ua/221557/.

11. In 2005, the Minsk government rebuilt the manor house in Dzierżynowo, former estate of the Polish patriotic Dzierżyński (Dzherzhinsky) family outside of Iwieniec (near Grodno), and established a museum to "bloody Felix". The secret services of the CSI countries resolved to honor their founder thus. Annually, the graduating class of the Belarus KGB academy holds its swearing in ceremony at the manor. Incidently, the Nazis burned the manor and killed the Dzierżyński family for their participation in the Polish Home Army during World War II. For a journalistic account see Andrzej Pisalnik, "Feliks – symbol szlachty i . . . terroru," ("Feliks – the symbol of the nobility and . . . terror") *Rzeczpospolita* (March 31, 2009).

12. Lenin is ubiquitous in Belarus. His images were dismantled in very few places. For a story of a drawn-out battle between Soviet and Catholic and Polish symbols and monuments in Łyntupy in Belarus, where the local faithful with their priest, Count Jan Tyszkiewicz aka Father Jan Szutkiewicz, first opposed the erection

of the Lenin monument by putting up a cross, and then sabotaged the Soviet deity, only to kidnap it one night and sink in the marches during the implosion of the USSR (as well as removed a red star and replaced it with a cross to commemorate 150 local Poles shot by the Nazis) see Robert Daniłowicz, "Lenin na bocznym torze," ("Lenin on a Side Rail Link") *Rzeczpospolita* (March 31, 2009). See also Marek Jan Chodakiewicz, "Notatki z post-Sowiecji (część III)," ("Notes from the Post-Soviet Lands, Part III") *Najwyższy Czas!* (October 23, 2010): XXXV; and Marek Jan Chodakiewicz, "Notatki z post-Sowiecji (część IV)," ("Notes from the Post-Soviet Lands, Part IV") *Najwyższy Czas!* (October 30–November 6, 2010): XLIII. For a scathing indictment of the ubiquity of Communist symbols and monuments in Poland and Belarus see the editorial introduction in *Glaukopis* no. 21–22 (2011): 2–3.

13.   For example, a monument to Soviet partisans mars the central square of Lucyn/ Lutsin, Latvia's oldest town, Ludza (Lucyn). A huge plaque outside of the city informs the visitor that the town was founded by a Ruthenian ("Russian") Prince Rurik Rostislavovich in 1177. In fact, the evidence is quite flimsy, because the Ruthenian *latopis* mentions Lutshin, an unidentified locality, between Novgorod and Smolensk, quite a way off from contemporary Latvia. One of the streets celebrates the Tsarist General Yakov Kulniv. There is also a museum for the General. Meanwhile, the medieval fortress of the Teutonic Knights dominating the landscape of the city is in ruins. And so is the Catholic cemetery, while the local Catholic church is demurely hidden away. Of the Poles, only some 300 remain. Probably none of them knows much about the past, including the fact that the world famous writer Ferdynand Ossendowski was born in Lucyn. Last but not least, there is virtually no trace of the Jewish community, which used to dominate this town of the Polish-Lithuanian Commonwealth. The majority of the population is Russian. See Robert Daniłowicz, "Tartak pełen znakomitości," ("A Saw Mill Full of Significant Ones") *Rzeczpospolita* Plus-Minus, (February 23, 2008).

14.   Marek Jan Chodakiewicz, "Notatki z post-Sowiecji (część I)," ("Notes from the Post-Soviet Lands, Part I") *Najwyższy Czas!* (October 9, 2010): XXXV.

15.   Marek Jan Chodakiewicz, "Notatki z post-Sowiecji (część II)," ("Notes from the Post-Soviet Lands, Part II") *Najwyższy Czas!* (October 16, 2010): XXXV.

16.   Omer Bartov, *Erased: Vanishing Traces of Jewish Galicia in Present-Day Ukraine* (Princeton and Oxford: Princeton University Press, 2007).

23

False Consciousness

People bond with ancient families not only by blood, but also through the stories about the past. They are sustained and nourished not only by the heritage, but also the living and flowing stream of stories which are handed down.[1]

—Stanisław Vincenz

If the Party could thrust its hand into the past and say of this or that event, it never happened—that, surely, was more terrifying than mere torture and death.[2]

—George Orwell, 1984

A radical discontinuity exists between the historical fact and the collective perception of the history of World War II and its aftermath (1939–1947), as well as, really, anything else ancient and not, in the newly independent states on the western fringes of the former Soviet Union. Namely, the Communist system succeeded in instilling false consciousness into its subjects.

This situation results from the very nature of the totalitarian Soviet occupation of the Baltic States, Belarus, and Ukraine. Totalitarianism aims to control every sphere of human life. To control the present, it is necessary to reshape the past. The Communist objective was to destroy collective memories, indispensable for the maintenance of conscious local nationalisms, and replace them with false memories, to maintain monolithic Soviet nationalism among the captive peoples. In other words, a pluralistic chain of memory was interrupted and the incorrigible barbed wire of Soviet "memories" linked all the hapless Soviet subjects together. The occupiers halted and annihilated the natural, organic process of free information exchange indispensable for the formation and persistence of collective memories.[3] Only through freedom, including the medium of vigorous historical research conducted in congruence with empirical, logocentric, and deductive methodology enshrined in the

476

tradition of a liberal learning process, can atomized individual recollections fuse into collective memories and overcome false consciousness.[4]

On the collective level, false consciousness characterizes almost everyone who lived under the Soviets, in particular anyone not old enough to have experienced the catastrophic period himself. First, totalitarianism cauterized individual memories by killing, imprisoning, or exiling the leaders and terrorizing the rest of the occupied people into silence through police repression and censorship. Second, the Soviet occupiers barred individual experiences to be freely discussed and exchanged, and, thus, the Communists prevented them from becoming interwoven in a natural tapestry of national remembering. Third, the Soviet propaganda—schools, mass media, and individual and group indoctrination sessions—concocted a uniform, politically correct, mendacious, and Orwellian image of the putative "past" and imposed it upon the captive population with grim zeal. Ewa M. Thompson perceptively notes that the Kremlin extirpated violently the indigenous memories and poured a nearly lethal dose of "Soviet nationalism" into the wound.[5]

Thus, instead of a rainbow of individual recollections aligned in a variety of ways reflecting multifaceted and multifarious experiences of heterodox peoples, the captive nations had their wealth of memories substituted with a Procrustean contraption of artificial Communist myths devised by Moscow. Native memories were raped and exterminated. False consciousness was implanted, a sine qua non for the success of the totalitarian enterprise. Collective amnesia was greatly expedited by mass accommodation and individual collaboration. Compliance with the regime was enforced initially through terror, then through its legacy enhanced with material incentives and the desperately sad sense of permanence of the Soviet occupation regime.[6]

In 1946, an exceptionally perceptive Western intellectual, T. S. Eliot, reflecting on Stalin's crimes in the Intermarium, noted that

> We are, in fact, in a period of conflict between cultures—a conflict which finds the older cultures in a position of disadvantage: from lack of confidence in themselves, from divisions both internal and between each other, from the inheritance of old abuses from the past aggravated by abuses due to the hasty introduction of novelties. The Liberal still thinks in terms of political differences which can be settled by negotiation, and of religious differences which have ceased to matter; he assumes further that the cultural conflict is one which can, like political conflict, be adjusted by compromise, or, like religious conflict, be resolved by tolerance. But the culture conflict is the religious conflict on its deepest level: it is one whole pattern of life against another . . . [This] is a document for the study of the methods of destroying a culture, one pattern of life, and imposing another pattern. We do not yet know to what extent such a transformation can be effected; we do not know to what extent a people can be altered

by the power of planned ignorance. The mutilation of a people by the destruction of its upper and middle classes is serious enough: but that is an injury which a people can inflict upon itself. Whether a culture can survive systematic destruction from without, depends less upon its forces of active revolt, than upon the stubbornness of the unconscious masses, the tenacity with which they cling to habits and customs, their instinctive resistance to change. . . . Respect for the culture, the pattern of life, of other people—which is not the same thing as indifference to other people's crimes against humanity—is respect for history: and by history we set no great store.[7]

Fifty years later it appeared to some that the foreign occupier had won in the Intermarium. All was obliterated. Nothing was left. In 1996, an aristocratic Polish émigré, who returned to his ancestral land (now in Belarus) for a visit, reflected on what he saw with the utmost pessimism:

A man visits this post-war new creation, equalized the Soviet way. Yet, this is a country where we have had our roots planted deep down for the past 500 years. After all, we consider ourselves 100% Poles and for several hundred years every generation of us fought for this country. There is no room here to explain the phenomenon of Ruthenia [Ruś]. According to all my documents, I can claim that I am a Belarusian. I was born there, I was baptized there, my mother fed me there, I was reared there, and that was my love. Nowadays no one outside of the circle of the secret-keepers can understand what the Grand Duchy of Lithuania was once upon a time and the labyrinth of its history. It was falsified over the centuries by Russia and Prussia, capitalizing on the antagonisms among the local inhabitants. The Commies pounded a mendacious image of history into the Polish heads. Today the phenomenon of the country [the Grand Duchy of Lithuania] is hard to grasp for the post-war generations, not to mention the Western Europeans . . . I bent down, the sole remaining witness that there once had been civilization here and that there had been SOMETHING here. They destroyed it, burned it, and robbed it blind. No archeologist will ever find anything here. They even dug up every single little stone from the foundation [capitalized in the original].[8]

Nonetheless, if one is not an octogenarian Polish-Ruthenian-Lithuanian aristocrat, the situation does not appear as gloomy.[9] An outside observer has been able reflexively to sense, even contrary to his own antinationalist and antitraditionalist prejudices, a stilted strain of the variety stemming from the past. According to one such leftist Western scholar, writing in 1989,

Western Byelorussia had been under Polish rule and domination between the two world wars. Staying with Byelorussian peasants, on a visit from Moscow, one had no feeling that the time was remembered with resentment. On the contrary, the Poles had left behind precisely the kind of romantic image with which they are associated and with which they like to be associated. . . .

Society in those days was markedly plural. For one thing, the pan [noble lord] provided small holdings, or khutors, for veterans of the Polish Legion who had fought . . . for Polish independence during the First World War. But in any case, there had locally been both Orthodox and Catholic communities. The Catholics considered themselves a kind of gentry even when, economically, they were no better off than the Orthodox. In local speech, a different term is used for "church" according to whether it is Orthodox or Catholic: *tserkov* or *kostel*. An Orthodox priest is remembered who tried to campaign for the conversion of the Catholic peasantry. In the village, there had been a number of inns run by Jews where one could rest horses and drink. Now there are none: here as in Russia, there is that curious lack of public or communal space, driving people to accentuate the privacy and home-based nature of social relations. There is of course the *kolkhoz* club, but these places tend to be used in a formal and stilted way and to contribute little to informal socializing . . .

In the local town, the quarter around the market had been inhabited mainly by Jews. The synagogue building still stands. Relations between Byelorussians and Jews seem to have been markedly less bad than those between Ukrainians and Jews. . . .

The Jews and the Poles have gone. The Poles fled or were deported. The Jews perished during the German occupation. Byelorussian nationalism, as nationalisms within the Soviet Union go, is relatively muted. Byelorussian parents are not averse to sending their children to Russian schools, which gives their children better access to advancement . . . In the village, the older inhabitants remember having to have their schooling, such as it was, in Polish; but they remember it without any bitterness. On the contrary, they were eager to try out their Polish on me. The village retained an attractive insularity: if a man did not speak Byelorussian, why then naturally he must speak Polish . . . In the nearby town, the historic local Polish church, an early specimen of Polish baroque, is well preserved despite the absence of a congregation, and the inscriptions in Polish and Latin commemorating erstwhile local dignitaries and their achievements, and thus testifying to an order which is no longer, are piously preserved. The seat of the greatest local nobles, the Radziwils [sic Radziwiłł], a great polonized Lithuanian lineage lately intermarried with the Kennedys, is now preserved as a monument and a convalescence home.[10]

The Western scholar quoted above inexplicably marveled at the "sentimental admiration" of the locals toward the past. However, unlike many Western liberal intellectuals, at least some of the captive elite realized that the ties to a pluralistic past were a sine qua non for their successful trip to a free future. They appreciated the importance of culture, history, and custom. Therefore, in the wake of the collapse and disintegration of the Soviet Union, the newly independent states and their citizens began an arduous process of self-definition.

The restoration of collective memories is a function indispensable for the reconstruction of one's self-identity. It concerns the individual, the local community, and the nation. The process has taken place on two planes: official and unofficial. The former is largely a state-run, comprehensive scholarly effort by the universities, archives, and other cultural institutions. The unofficial endeavor is simply a continuation, albeit on a much broader scale, of one of the most important aspects of the dissident work: collecting and preserving individual memories.

The oral history undertaking has evolved from clandestine story-telling by a few survivors who were bold enough to talk to a precious few who were bold enough to listen. Thus, after the Soviet takeover, a tiny, elite band of usually unconnected individuals preserved select, forbidden memories in a manner akin to that of an early tribal society. Unlike the elders in a tribal society, however, the memory keepers in the captive nations of the Soviet Union lacked the freedom to pass their knowledge to the collective. So they passed it on to their own individual apprentices, usually family members. Memory preservation was a strictly individual endeavor in the first three decades of the Communist occupation after 1944.[11]

By the 1980s an important readjustment took place, however. At that time a number of unofficial groups began forming in defense of the environment and historical monuments ravaged by the Soviet system. Some activists joined the pre-existing, state-approved (but hitherto largely moribund) entities; others operated outside the state-sanctioned limits. At least a few of the latter realized the importance of learning about their nation's history. They began actively searching out the witnesses of their national past, earning their trust, and soliciting their recollections. Family connections expedited the process. Thus, individual memory keepers entrusted their secrets to the next generation: the dissidents. Unlike the original purveyors, the dissidents endeavored to disseminate their knowledge to the broadest possible audiences. This was done mostly in oral form or in *samizdat*, an underground publication. The audiences remained relatively small and self-selected as the dissidents hardly ever reached anyone outside their elite circles. Also, the audiences tended to be uni-ethnic, even (or, perhaps, in particular) when more than one captive nation occupied the same space. Nonetheless, because of the dissident endeavor, the memories were no longer confined to isolated senior citizens on the verge of death or a few of their trusted family members or friends, who kept publicly and privately silent for the most part.

According to a participant in the oral history project,

Estonia's first major opposition movement—the Estonian Heritage Society—took the lead in gathering this information. Realizing that most written historical accounts had been destroyed, the Heritage Society sought out the people who had experienced the postwar era in order to record their recollections of events. Under the society's sponsorship, I recorded the first stories in the summer of 1985. In 1986, I worked with a large group of young people collecting personal accounts in southern Estonia. We rode from village to town on bicycles and wrote down old people's narratives. By the summer of 1987, a large number of similar youth groups were working in Estonia. Naturally, the KGB took a great deal of interest in our operations. We were harassed and our work was disrupted.

By the end of 1987, an opposition [underground] magazine published my first in-depth survey of the terror that the Soviet occupation had wrought upon Estonia. The KGB initiated criminal proceedings against me. I was accused of "slandering the Soviet regime". . . .

After that, our work could continue. To date [1992], the archives of the Estonian heritage Society have collected more than 30,000 pages of recollections, original documents, photographs, etc. The past, left for dead by the aggressors, lives again. The Heritage Society archives, preserving a nation's history as told by its own people, are awe-inspiring.[12]

In Belarus, another individual recalls his journey as follows:

I was born in a Polish family in Nowogródek [in Soviet-occupied Belarus in the 1960s]. I heard for the first time about the Home Army from my father when I was 13 or 14. My father, who was a Home Army soldier in the Iwie-Juraciszki area, had decided that I was ready to learn the secret. That is how I understood this initiation. At that time one talked about the Home Army only among the closest relatives, often lowering one's voice. My interest in the past of the Nowogródek area, the history of the AK in particular, gradually converted itself into a passion which led me to earn a university degree in history.

The recollections of the elderly and a few AK soldiers who managed to survive the war and Stalinist camps were the basic source of knowledge about the Polish underground and guerrillas in my home of the Nowogródek Land. Soviet books informed one that the AK consisted of bandits and nationalists. One was not allowed into the archives. The change came only after the disintegration of the USSR. Access to the archives was liberalized. Historical monographs about the Home Army began flowing from Poland.

Good luck had it that [after the transformation of Communism] Professor Tomasz Strzembosz, a human being of great heart and knowledge, was among the first Polish historians who arrived in Minsk to look for source materials to study the history of the Polish underground in the Eastern Borderlands. Thanks to his help I was able to secure a graduate fellowship from the Polish Ministry of National Education. This enabled me to spend several years in the archives and to attend the seminars of Professor Tomasz Strzembosz, who was also my dissertation advisor. My Ph.D. thesis considered the relations between the Soviet partisan movement and the AK in the Nowogródek region during the German occupation.[13]

The dissident quest for memory served a variety of functions. First, and most important, it had a moral dimension: It enabled the dissidents to juxtapose the resurrected Truth with the Soviet Lie. Second, the quest provided an exhilarating experience of struggle in which the re-emergent national elite was forged. Third, the search for memory supplied ammunition to recreate the framework of national self-identification, a step indispensable to re-awaken and rally the Sovietized multitude of nationalities.

In 1988 and after, the quest for memory bore positive fruit.[14] As the imperial center began to relax and, later, disintegrate, the non-Soviet nationalities finally rebelled, gaining their freedom by 1992. Estonia, Latvia, Lithuania, Ukraine, Belarus, and Moldova became independent and separate states precisely because their leaders were able to conceptualize their people not only without the Soviet Union but also outside of Russia. Arguably, the process of separation based upon the idea of national self-identification as dictated by historical memories was most advanced in the Baltic States. In Moldova it was evident throughout the land with decreasing intensity eastward; in Ukraine, it was largely limited to its western part; and in Belarus the process registered only modestly throughout.

Therefore, it would be disingenuous to argue that the quest for memory and the resulting upsurge of hitherto dormant nationalism were the only factors accounting for the liberation of the captive nations. They *were* nonetheless very important reasons that expedited the dissolution of the Soviet Union.[15] Further, one can argue that memory translates into freedom not only during the initial stage of the struggle for national liberation but also after the victory is achieved. Simply put, nations possessing the highest degree of indigenous memory and, thus, national self-identification, aspire to freedom to a greater degree than those who have not yet succeeded in liberating themselves fully from the Soviet stereotypes. Once the self-aware have achieved or recouped freedom they are more prepared to conserve it than the successor state entities either devoid of the indigenous self-identification or ridden with conflicting and contradictory national narratives. Hence, now, Estonia, Latvia, and Lithuania are, overall, almost model liberal democracies.[16]

That is not to say that even in the Baltics the citizens have attained full self-awareness. It is not the case. In fact, one of the greatest challenges facing the post-Soviet successor states is that of self-definition. A part of the process involves restoring hitherto hidden history. Naturally, among many of the restorationists, on the one hand, there is an overwhelming tendency to reject everything Soviet. On the other hand, there is a temptation to explicate the past through a constrained lens of ethnocentric genre. However, because in most successor states pluralism and democracy prevail to a greater or lesser degree, there is no monopoly on telling the past.

There is also no agreement yet on how to conceptualize history of the Intermarium. The search for memory inevitably resurrects nationalism in a form that may be quite incongruous with the multiethnic and regional diversity of the newly independent states. The dilemmas of their peoples and elites are perhaps best explicated by a Ukrainian linguist. According to him,

I do not know what people mean when they say Ukraine. There are many Ukraines. There is Kiev, central Ukraine . . . There is eastern Ukraine, the heart of the Kievan Rus from which we were descended—oh, they speak the most lovely, the most pure Ukrainian in Kiev. There is eastern Ukraine—Donetsk, Kharkov, Dnipropetrovsk—which has been sadly Russian for so many years . . . that the language is even lost, they speak a bastardized Russian there, a kind of slang. Then there is the Black Sea coast—Crimea, Odessa . . . They also speak Russian, but by history, by right, the Crimean Tartaria belongs to Ukraine. . . . Then there is the northern Bukovyna—and the beautiful town of Czernowitz . . .—and southern Bessarabia—land of the Gagauz, the Turks. Those regions were taken from Romania at the end of the last war, and there they speak Ukrainian and Moldovan and a kind of mix of the two. . . . And western Ukraine (here I mean L'viv . . .), which was once Polish—why, you could probably get away with speaking Polish there, no one would notice you were speaking a different language. . . . And, of course, Ruthenia—Transcarpathia—owned so long by Hungary and then Czechoslovakia. . . . Listen to the language there—it is not my Ukrainian, it is not Kiev Ukrainian, just listen to it! It is Transcarpathian Ruthenian!

All of this variety . . . but they tried to knock it out of us. We are all Soviet people now, *Homo sovieticus*. They concreted us together . . . and told us to speak Russian. Ideology for this Marxist movement, it had to be completely simple, and absolutely primitive and absolutely contrary to everything that had gone in the past. Bang, they eliminate everything and tell us we are all the same, they tell Ukrainians that a Soviet Ukrainian is a Soviet Ukrainian and there is no more story. They teach us Russian, they tell us to forget these silly dialects. They teach us to be Ukrainian in a Soviet way.

So now we have democratization, and democratization goes with new nationalism, it is inevitable. We have new Ukrainian nationalism.

We are a society that is to such an extent destroyed that we needed the simplest ways to pull people into the process and the simplest way is national revival . . . I am afraid that this nationalism will be unifying in a bad way. Our people will not recognize the value of their differences. . . . they will want Ukrainians to be the same. And then some will oppose this, some will feel Ukrainization, this is a bad thing. But the Ukrainians, they know only one model, the Soviet model, and that model said that strength lay in unity. But strength is in the differences. Variety, that is the beauty of Ukraine . . . that is its treasure.[17]

But where are the roots of the variety? Where did the Intermarium's plurality come from? Surely, neither from Muscovy nor from the Soviet Union nor from postmodernism. It originated among the Ruthenians and the Balts, flowered in the Polish-Lithuanian Commonwealth, and its greatly reduced image persevered in interwar Poland. Afterward, this variety was destroyed almost completely by the totalitarians. There are traces of it, here and there. However, they cannot be reassembled from the above by either integral nationalists, kleptocratic or post-Communists, or the politically correct commissars of multiculturalism.[18] The roots of the variety need to resprout, individually, one by one. One individual soul at the time needs to re-emerge self-conscious, before it, once again, can fit into the pluralistic framework. And that is one of the greatest projects under way in the Intermarium.

Let an inspiring story of a libertarian born in 1966 in the Soviet Socialist Republic of Belarussia serve as our example of the individual self-liberation:

I was born in the USSR in a small town. . . . The town used to be a Polish settlement. . . . When I was a child I used to hear the words I could hardly understand, 'When we lived free before Soviet occupation'. Much later when I was sent to the Soviet army for two years as a conscript I heard from officers, 'Oh, you are a Pole, a potential enemy of our state. You and your compatriots should go to Siberia'. . . .

I was leader of a school [Communist] pioneer organization . . . I thought that you were born with certain things like the sun, the seasons, 'granny Lenin' and leader Leonid Brezhnev. . . .

The only kinds of ideas available at that time were communist ideas. But I was brought up in a Catholic family, which is why there was a kind of hybrid ideology, with some ideas borrowed both from communism and Catholicism. That is why even in childhood I was somehow confronted with a choice, either official propaganda or family values. At the same time people around me did not talk much about politics and the past. Much later I discovered that my grandfathers were sent to Siberia and did not survive. Only later I discovered that people were afraid to talk because the truth could bring you to prison or to a psychiatric clinic. . . .

There was little information available about the outside world. The Iron Curtain was so tight that it effectively blocked any 'unauthorized' news. My friends and I were typical victims of the Soviet brainwashing machine. We thought that we were lucky to be born in the freest country in the world.

As a teenager I began to listen to so-called 'enemy voices' over the radio ('Radio Liberty,' 'Voice of America'). . . . I started asking questions and I asked them basically wherever it was possible. . . . Those were the times of dramatic historic change. The Soviet Union collapsed. I took part in my first demonstration against the August 1991 coup. . . . Being an anticommunist . . . I was a strong supporter of capitalism. . . . In the 1990s I became general director of a foreign company. . . . Those were the times of chaotic liberalism in independent Belarus. [Eventually] You were given the choice of working for the state or for the mafia. I hated these two options . . . The decision to stop doing business and to take up an intellectual career came easily. By that time I had learnt one name that was the key to my intellectual career—Ayn Rand. . . .

I arranged 'People-to-People' tours during which Americans visited Belarus. . . . They talked about rather controversial things such as the morality of capitalism, the benevolence of entrepreneurship and self-esteem. They later sent me *Atlas Shrugged*. . . . I decided to make Rand ideas and the ideology of capitalism known in Belarus and in all of the Russian-speaking world. I ordered more and more books. Mises, Hayek, Rothbard, Friedman, Menger, Bastiat—I discovered a gold mine of ideas![19]

Intellectual self-liberation was possible because freedom finally dawned in the Intermarium. Today the person whose story we quoted at length above, Jarosław Romańczuk (Jaroslav/Yaroslav Romanchuk), heads a libertarian think tank in Minsk. He is one of the top leaders of the libertarian-conservative United Civic Party (UCP). In 2008, despite official restrictions, Romańczuk managed to get himself elected to the "legislature" on a libertarian ticket. In and out of the "parliament" he was a persistent campaigner for a flat personal income tax, which Belarus enacted in 2009. In 2010, the Randian enthusiast unsuccessfully ran for president of Belarus as the official UCP candidate. Afterward, he flatly turned down Lukashenka's offer of prime ministership.[20] We can call this the liberation of one. What about the others? Obviously, the exceptional "objectivist" cannot be the norm. And the norm at the level of an average denizen of the Intermarium usually reflects some form of a nationalist narrative.

A preliminary inquiry suggests that the restored discourse of the erstwhile captive nations is colored by separate national considerations. It also deemphasizes the tales of other people involved in the same space. Once again, the degree of flexibility in reconstructing of a national history, its willingness to accommodate and face honestly other national discourses, depends on the degree of freedom and democracy enjoyed by a given people. Once again, the Baltics are much more open than Ukraine and Moldova, and, in particular, Belarus.

Yet, freedom does not automatically create a collective memory. Freedom merely creates conditions which facilitate the re-emergence of individual recollections. That should eventually lead to restoring the collective memory. But first national stereotypes should be distilled reflecting long-suppressed individual recollections. Frozen in time and brutally stifled, over fifty years ago, in the age of nationalism rampant, individual recollections currently have often re-acquired their original, anachronistic, integral nationalist flavor. Under the circumstances most eyewitnesses could hardly be expected to produce any other outcome. A series of singularly ethnic views of the past have resulted.[21] And those, naturally, color the present and influence the future.

Notes

1. "Ludzie nie tylko krwią wiążą się z dawnymi rodami, lecz i wieściami o dawności. Nie tylko dziedzictwem trzymają i karmią, lecz także żywą strugą wieści przekazanych." Stanisław Vincenz, *Na wysokiej połoninie: Prawda starowieku: Obrazy, dumy i gawędy z wierchowiny huculskiej* (Sejny: Pogranicze, 2002), 64. This is a reprint of a 1938 edition.

2. Emphasis in the original. See George Orwell, *1984* (New York: New American Library, HBJ Books, 1981), 32.

3. On the synergy between individual and collective remembering in the posttotalitarian setting see Marek Jan Chodakiewicz, "Poland's *Fragebogen*: Collective Stereotypes, Individual Recollections," in *Poland's Transformation: A Work in Progress*, ed. Marek Jan Chodakiewicz, John Radzilowski, and Dariusz Tolczyk (Charlottesville, VA: Leopolis Press, 2003), 223–67.

4. On methodology see Marek Jan Chodakiewicz, "Wędrówki historyka: Kilka słów o metodologii," ("Peregrinations of a Historian: A Few Words on Methodology") *Aparat represji w Polsce Ludowej, 1944–1989: Studia i materiały, (The Apparatus of Repression in People's Poland, 1944–1989: Studies and Documents)* vol. 1 (2004): 13–25.

5. Ewa M. Thompson also posits a continuity between the Tsarist and Soviet measures against the captive nations. See Ewa M. Thompson, *Imperial Knowledge: Russian Literature and Colonialism* (Westport, CT: Greenwood Press, 2000). Mikhail Dolbilov, "The Stereotype of the Pole in Imperial Policy: The 'Depolonization' of the Northwestern Region in the 1860s," *Russian Studies in History* 44, no. 2 (Fall 2005): 44–88, argues, inter alia, that "the Pole was perceived as an antagonist of the popular masses and as an alien element in the social organism, on the people's soil." However, "the Pole was an enemy of the [Russian] nation but was not an enemy that was national in its essence" (63). The Pole was not only the "lord" and a "fanatical Catholic" but also a "pan-European . . . revolutionary." Thus, during the Partitions, the Russian Imperial propaganda sometimes denied the existence of the Polish nationhood and set the Poles apart as the ultimate cosmopolitan, "European" Other. For a discussion of the ideological propaganda measures applied during the enslavement of Lithuania see Juozapas Romualdas Bagušauskas, "Komunistų partijos ideologinė apologe-

tika slopinant tautos pasipriešinimą (1944–1953 m.)," ("Ideological Apologetics of the Communist Party in Suppressing National Resistance [1944–1953]"), *Genocidas ir reistencija* no. 2 (16) (2004): http://www.genocid.lt/Leidyba/16/bagusaus.htm. For a critical look at Soviet propaganda intended mostly for the Western consumption see, e.g., Herbert Romerstein, "Divide and Conquer: The KGB Disinformation Campaign against Ukrainians and Jews," *The Ukrainian Quarterly* (Fall 2004): http://www.iwp.edu/news/newsID.139/news_detail.asp.

6. On religious and national collaboration see Otto Luchterhandt, "Die Kollaborationsproblematik im Verhältnis von Religionsgemeinschaften und kommunistischen Einparteistaat (ausgehend vom Fall 'Sowjetunion')," in *"Kollaboration" in Nordosteuropa: Erscheinungsformen und Deutungen im 20. Jahrhundert*, ed. Joachim Tauber (Wiesbaden: Harrassowitz Verlag, 2006), 443–52. For the case of accommodation of a single Polish Catholic priest before, during, and after his Gulag experience in the USSR see Father Stanisław Ryżko, *"Trzeba zostać"* (Lublin: Norbertinum, 1999); Father Stanisław Ryżko, *Z Panem Bogiem w łagrach* (Lublin: Norbertinum, 2004); Father Stanisław Ryżko, *Kronika kościoła rzymsko-katolickiego w Łahiszynie: Listy i notatki z lat 1956–1984* (Warszawa: Księża Orioniści, 1995). For the experience of the Soviet Polish ethnic group and others connected to the Poles in the USSR see Yuras Krmanau, "Vet of famed WWII unit honored on 103rd birthday," Associated Press, (December 17, 2008), which is a report on Aleksander Szekal, a Gulag survivor and Monte Cassino veteran, who returned from England to Belarus in 1999, but had been unable to visit his wife there until 1976; Jakub Konan interviewed by Andrzej Poczobut, "Białorusin spod Monte Cassino," ("Belarusian from Monte Cassino") *Gazeta Wyborcza* (May 13, 2008); Dominik Smyrga, "Spod Monte Cassino do gułagu," ("From Monte Cassino to the Gulag"), *Rzeczpospolita* (May 20, 2009); Przemysław P. Romaniuk, ed., *Spod Monte Cassino na Sybir: Deportacje byłych żołnierzy Polskich Sił Zbrojnych na Zachodzie z Białorusi, Litwy i Ukrainy w 1951 roku* (*From Monte Cassino to Siberia: Deportations of Former Polish Soldiers of the Polish Armed Forces in the West from Belarus, Lithuania, and Ukraine in 1951*) (Warszawa: Centralne Archiwum Ministerstwa Spraw Wewnetrznych i Administracji, 1998); Jerzy Grabowski, "Powojenne losy żołnierz Polskich Sił Zbrojnych na Zachodzie po powrocie na Białoruś," ("Post-War Fate of the Soldiers of the Polish Armed Forces in the West Following Their Return to Belarus") *Pamięć i Sprawiedliwość* no. 1 (11) (2007): 227–44; Bożena Kącka and Stanisław Stępka, eds., *Repatriacja ludności polskiej z ZSRR 1955–1959: Wybór dokumentów* (*The Repatriation of the Polish Population from the USSR 1955–1959: A Selection of Documents) (Warszawa: SGGW, 1994*); Małgorzata Ruchniewicz, *Repatriacja ludności polskiej z ZSRR w latach 1955–1959* (The Repatriation of the Polish Population from the USSR, 1955–1959) (Warszawa: Volumen, 2000); Anatol F. Vialiki, *Belarus'—Pol'shcha u XX stahoddzi: Neviadomaia repatryiatsyia,1955–1959 hh.: Manahrafyia* (*Belarus-Poland in the 20th Century: The Unknown Repatriation, 1955–1959: A Monograph*) (Minsk: BDPU, 2007); Krzysztof Renik, *Podpolnicy - rozmowy z ludźmi Kościoła na Litwie, Łotwie, Białorusi i Ukrainie 1990–1991* (*The Undergrounders: Conversations with the Lay People of the Church in Lithuania, Latvia, Belarus, and Ukraine, 1990–1991*) (Warszawa: Oficyna Wydawnictwa *Przeglądu Powszechnego*, 1991); Father Roman Dzwonkowski, *Polacy na dawnych Kresach Wschodnich: Z problematyki narodowościowej i religijnej* (*Poles in the Former Eastern Borderlands: Nationality and Religion Problems*)

(Lublin: Oddział Lubelski Wspólnoty Polskiej, 1994); Father Dzwonkowski Roman et al., *Za wschodnią granicą 1917–1993 (Beyond the Eastern Border, 1917–1993)* (Warszawa: Wspólnota Polska and Apostolicum, 1993); Aleksander Srebrakowski, *Polacy w Litewskiej SRR 1944–1989 (Poles in the Lithuanian SSR, 1944–1989)* (Toruń: Wydawnictwo Adam Marszałek, 2000); Antoni Kuczyński, ed., *Kościół katolicki na Syberii: Historia - Współczesność - Przyszłość (The Catholic Church in Siberia: History-Modernity-Future)* (Wrocław: Silesia, 2002); Father Edward Walewander, ed., *Polacy i Niemcy w Rosji (Poles and Germans in Russia)* (Lublin: Wspólnota Polska-Lublin, 1993); Father Edward Walewander, ed., *Polacy w Estonii mówią o sobie (Poles in Estonia Talk about Themselves)* (Lublin: Oddział Lubelski Stowarzyszenia Wspólnota Polska, 1997); Father Edward Walewander, ed., *Polacy w Mołdowie mówią o sobie (Poles in Moldova Talk about Themselves)* (Lublin: Oddział Lubelski Stowarzyszenia Wspólnota Polska, 1995); Father Edward Walewander, ed., *Polacy w Rosji mówią o sobie (Poles in Russia Talk about Themselves)*, 3 vols., (Lublin: Wydawnictwo KUL, 1994–1995).

7.   T. S. Eliot, "Preface," in [Zoe Zeidler], *The Dark Side of the Moon* (New York: Charles Scribner's Sons, 1947), vii–xi.

8.   Eustachy Sapieha, *Tak było: Niedemokratyczne wspominienia Eustachego Sapiehy (That's How It Was: Undemocratic Memoirs of Eustachy Sapieha)* (Warszawa: Wydawnictwo Safari Poland, 1999), 373, 382 (afterward *Tak było*). Prince Eustachy Sapieha (1916–2004) was a Polish-Ruthenian-Lithuanian aristocrat and a combat veteran, living in Nairobi, Kenya, since the end of World War II. See Piotr Zychowicz, "Cisza wśród szeregów: Wspomnienie o księciu Eustachym Sapiesze (1916–2004)," ("Silence in the Ranks: A Recollection about Prince Eustachy Sapieha [1916–2004]") *Rzeczpospolita*, (May 27, 2004).

9.   Grzegorz Górny, "Zobaczyć Kresy," ("To See the Borderlands") *Rzeczpospolita* Plus-Minus, (August 23–24, 2008).

10. Ernest Gellner, "Ethnicity and Faith in Eastern Europe," in *Eastern Europe . . ., Central Europe . . ., Europe*, ed. Stephen R. Graubard (Boulder, CO, San Francisco, Oxford: Westview Press, 1991), 267–69. Although it reflects accurately the attitude of the country folk in this particular part of the Intermarium, this short quote displays the woeful inadequacy of historical research and the sad lack of context. Gellner does not seem to know that in the wake of the Polish–Bolshevik war only a few Polish landed nobles rewarded a small number of petty gentry and peasantry with land grants. However, what the locals remembered during the Soviet times was the comprehensive program by the interwar Polish government to allot land plots to the anti-Communist veterans. Further, Gellner probably refers to the Radziwiłł estate in Nieśwież, although there had been many others throughout the Grand Duchy and the Crown. Next, during the Soviet times, there was no "absence of the congregation." Simply, the Communists forbade the locals to attend Church, and fiercely persecuted the faithful. Geller's original observations on Soviet-occupied Belarus most likely date from the 1960s when he was a doctoral student focusing on the countryside. His recollections from the USSR are particularly notable for what he failed to see and understand. A known critic of Western Civilization and its tradition, he is an enemy of the variety to the extent that he opposes national cultures. Like his Marxist colleague Eric Hobsbawm and others of their ilk, Gellner anticipates the demise of nations as did Marx, Engels, and Lenin, among other "classics." See Ernest Gellner, *Nations and Nationalism* (Ithaca, NY: Cornell University Press, 1983); Ernest Gellner, *Nationalism* (New York: University of New York

Press, 1997); Benedict Anderson, *Imagined Communities: Reflections on the Origin and Spread of Nationalism* (London: Verso, 1991); Eric Hobsbawm, *Nations and Nationalism since 1780: Programme, Myth, Reality* (Cambridge: Cambridge University Press, 1990); Eric Hobsbawm and Terence Ranger, eds., *The Invention of Tradition* (Cambridge: Cambridge University Press, 1983). Hobsbawm is an unreformed Stalinist, a member of the Communist party until its end. See also Anthony D. Smith, *The Ethnic Origins of Nations* (Cambridge: Basil Blackwell Ltd., 1986) (Smith contradicts Gellner and others); Walker Connor, *Ethnonationalism: The Quest for Understanding* (Princeton, NJ: Princeton University Press, 1994); John Breuilly, *Nationalism and the State* (Chicago, IL: University of Chicago Press, 1982); Rogers Brubaker, *Nationalism Reframed: Nationhood and the National Question in the New Europe* (Cambridge: Cambridge University Press, 1996); Yael Tamir, *Liberal Nationalism* (Princeton, NJ: Princeton University Press, 1993); James Mayall, *Nationalism and International Society* (Cambridge: Cambridge University Press, 1990). Hugh Seton-Watson, *Nationalism and Communism: Essays, 1946–1963* (New York: Frederick A. Praeger, 1964) remains as perhaps the most perceptive student of nations and nationalism, particularly valuable because of its astute observations on Communism, and, thus, applicable in the Intermarium. See further Hugh Seton-Watson, *Nations and States* (Boulder, CO: Westview Press, 1977).

11.   It was even the case in the least terrorized of all Soviet colonial satellites, Poland. After she was told at home about her father, who fought against the Nazis and Soviets in the Home Army outside of Wilno, an uncle, who had been deported to the Gulag but later struggled in the ranks of the Free Polish Armed Forces in the West, and another uncle, who was shot by the NKVD in the Katyn forest, Maria Kaczyńska recalls that as a little girl "I knew I was unable to talk about everything at school. I was always cautious but this split personality in historical matters pained me quite a bit." Until her tragic death on April 10, 2010, she was the First Lady of Poland. See Marzanna Stychlerz-Kłucińska, "Szatynka z temperamentem," *Tygodnik Solidarność* (December 23–30, 2005): http://www.tygodniksolidarnosc.com/2005/51/22_sza.html. The dissidents in the 1970s spoke up on behalf of the Poles of the Intermarium publicly only once, signing an open letter to the Communist regime to that effect. More significantly, there was semi-clandestine research and popularizing effort by at least two intrepid souls, Witold Szolginia (who immortalized Lwów) and Roman Aftanazy (who saved for posterity the memories of the noble palaces and manor houses in the Intermarium). Decades after the war, both of them were permitted to publish some of their research, which was heavily censored by the Communists. See the following essays in *Biuletyn Instytutu Pamięci Narodowej* no. 1–2 (96–97) (January–February 2009): Norbert Wójtowicz, "W obronie pozostałych na Wschodzie," ("In Defense of Those Left in the East") (107–10); Andrzej Kaczorowski, "Arcylwowianim – Witold Szolginia (1923–1996)," [Arch-Lvovian] (117–24); and Tadeusz Kukiz, "Roman Aftanazy," (130–34). Most, however, kept things very private if they wished to talk about the Intermarium and their youth there. See two private accounts about trips to Wilno in *Glaukopis*, no. 15–16 (2009): Longin Łokuciewski, "Druga podróż do Wilna," ("Second Trip to Wilno") (22–33); and Michał Kondratowicz, "Reminiscencje," ("Remembering") (343–370). In fact, the Communist secret police terrorized the survivors to prevent the publishing of any accounts of their free life, including underground exploits from World War II. See Piotr Niwiński, *Działania komunistycznego aparatu represji wobec środowisk kombatantów wileńskiej AK, 1945–1980* (*The*

Activities of the Communist Apparatus of Repression against the Milieu of the Veterans of the Wilno Home Army) (Warszawa: Instytut Studiów Politycznych PAN and Oficyna Wydawnicza Rytm, n.d. [2008]).

12. Mart Laar, *War in the Woods: Estonia's Struggle for Survival, 1944–1956* (Washington, DC: The Compass Press, 1992), xxiii–xxiv (afterward *War in the Woods*). The author later became Estonia's prime minister.

13. Zygmunt Boradyn, *Niemen—rzeka niezgody: Polsko-sowiecka wojna partyzancka na Nowogródczyźnie, 1943–1944* (*Niemen—the river of discord: Polish-Soviet Partisan War in the Nowogródek Region, 1943–1944*) (Warszawa: Oficyna Wydawnicza Rytm, 1999), 9 (afterward *Niemen—Rzeka niezgody*).

14. At least one Western scholar, focusing chiefly on Lithuania, recognizes the importance of continuity in the grassroots struggle for freedom from the 1940s to the 1990s. Unfortunately, his work is of limited utility. Petersen is rather unreliable on issues outside of Lithuania. His comparativist ventures barely transcend the theoretical musings of a sociologist; he is unaware of much of the scholarship on Central and Eastern Europe, where he largely failed to conduct any archival research. See Roger Dale Petersen, *Resistance and Rebellion: Lessons from Eastern Europe* (Cambridge: Cambridge University Press, 2001).

15. For the factors leading to the dissolution of the Soviet Union see Chapters 13 and 14 above.

16. One should not, however, underestimate the problems of assimilating of the remnant of the post-Soviet, postcolonialist, Russian-speaking groups in the Baltics.

17. Quoted in Anne Applebaum, *Between East and West: Across the Borderlands of Europe* (New York: Pantheon Books, 1994), 195–96 (afterward *Between East and West*).

18. Broader on the topic of the involvement of international organizations in the post-Soviet sphere see Will Kymlicka and Magda Opalski, eds., *Can Liberal Pluralism Be Exported? Western Political Theory and Ethnic Relations in Eastern Europe* (Oxford: Oxford University Press, 2001); Rachel A. Epstein, *In Pursuit of Liberalism: International Institutions in Postcommunist Europe* (Baltimore, MD: Johns Hopkins University Press, 2008); Alex Pravda and Jan Zielonka, eds., *International Influences on Democratic Transition in Central and Eastern Europe* (Oxford: Oxford University Press, 2001); Bernd Rechel, ed., *Minority Rights in Central and Eastern Europe* (London: Routledge, 2009).

19. Jaroslav Romanchuk [Jarosław Romańczuk], "The Changed Mind Is Changing the Country," in *Freedom Champions: Stories from the Front Lines in the War of Ideas: 30 Case Studies by Intellectual Entrepreneurs Who Champion the Cause of Freedom*, ed. Colleen Dyble and Jean Baugh (Washington, DC: Atlas Economic Research Foundation, 2011), 203–05. The author was born in Sopotskin/Sopoćkinie near Hrodna/Grodno.

20. Romańczuk carefully avoids to appear anti-Lukashenka. He cooperates with the regime believing that change can come from within (*vide* his success with flat tax). The libertarian not only condemned the postelectoral violence in Minsk in December 2010, but also blamed it on the rabble rousers among the opposition rather than on the government. However, he flatly turned down Lukashenka's offer of prime ministership in the wake of the riots. See "Belarus opposition nominate 2011 presidential election candidate," (May 31, 2010), http://en.beta.rian.ru/world/20100531/159229800.html; "Ex-candidate Yaroslav Romanchuk condemns December 19 protests in Belarus," (January 1, 2011), http://www.topix.com/forum/world/belarus/TUFP4OUC7COGT6RIB; Marek

A. Koprowski, "Prowokacja opozycji," ("A Provocation by the Opposition") *Najwyższy Czas!* (January 1–8, 2011): XXXI–XXXII.

21.   This concerns not only the post-Soviet East but also the West, Israel and the United States in particular. About 600 memorial books (*Yizkor Bikher*) have been published chronicling the experience of Jewish communities before, during, and after World War II. Their collective authors, often not the eye-witnesses, frequently fail to consider any other views but those of their own ethno-religious group. For an extensive bibliography see Jack Kugelmass and Jonathan Boyarin, eds., *From a Ruined Garden: The Memorial Books of Polish Jewry*, 2nd exp. edn. (Washington, DC: United States Holocaust Memorial Museum and Indiana University Press, 1998), 273–339.

24

A Sample of Individual Recollections

A fair sample of such views appears in Anne Applebaum's entertaining and astute travelogue through the Intermarium. They were collected during her peregrinations between 1990 and 1993.[1] They range from hilarious through curious to downright noxious. On the one hand, they reflect the region's false consciousness, Soviet indoctrination, base ignorance, ethnic prejudice, general confusion, gloomy pessimism, and acute insecurity. On the other hand, they also glitter with national pride, cultural accomplishment, deep faith, tenacious custom, and unbridled optimism. The opinions of the newly liberated people also underscore the uneven level of national consciousness, including even its utter lack in some cases.

In Vilnius/Wilno, a Lithuanian politician revealed his fears that the local Poles were in cahoots with the KGB, while their brethren to the West wanted to seize the capital of Lithuania. "They want to invade us again."[2] A Lithuanian academic was firmly convinced that "there are no true Poles in the Vilnius region. Never were."[3] Meanwhile, a local Polish minority journalist complained acrimoniously that "the Lithuanians? They lie," because they refused to allow Polish schools. Consequently, "children are forgetting their language. . . . When they forget their language, they lose their history, and then they know nothing." According to the journalist, it was the Poles who brought civilization into Lithuania: "who built Wilno? . . . Who were the great citizens of Wilno, the statesmen and the writers? . . . Poles, not Lithuanians, but Poles. Back when the Poles were building palaces, the Lithuanians were peasants on farms, speaking a forgotten language that nobody else could understand!"[4] The man also readily admitted his preference for the defeated Russians over the ascendant Lithuanian nationalists.

In Hermaniszki, two elderly Polish women complained in all seriousness about the loss of Poland. The culprits were the Communists and others. "They stole it all from us, they did. This is Poland, madam, not Belarus, and our president is [Marshal Józef] Piłsudski. This is not godless Russia, we are not godless Russians, madam, we are Catholics, we have always tried to do the right thing."[5]

Meanwhile, in Brest (formerly Brześć), Vasily Ptashitz sang the peans of Polesian nationalism. "He believed that the Polesians had the right to have their own state." According to Ptashitz, "the inhabitants of Brest are Polesians . . . but they just don't know it yet." The Polesians were allegedly heirs to the Baltic Yatvingians, themselves supposedly of Celtic and Germanic origin. Ptashitz's confederate in Pinsk (Pińsk) argued that

> If you want to know about Polesian, I can tell you the exact composition of our language. It is 40 percent Ukrainian, 5 percent Belarusian, 5 percent Polish, and 50 percent Polesian. I can tell you that Polesian culture is 30 percent Ukrainian, 3 percent Belarusian, 2 percent Polish, and 65 percent uniquely Polesian. And I can tell you that the propagation of Polesian language and culture is a healthy phenomenon: the Bolsheviks made everybody speak Russian, and look what happened. Now the Ukrainians and Belarusians will make everybody speak Ukrainian and Belarusian. The result will be worse.[6]

In Paberžė, after admitting that he had taken his monastic vows "for Lithuania," a Lithuanian monk hinted that he was sorry that it was the Poles who brought Western Christianity to Lithuania for "they cannot accept that we are farther advanced than they in spiritual matters. They cannot accept that our intuition, our feeling for the poor and downtrodden, is far more important than their learning and tradition."[7] Also in the same locality, a priest admitted to having been born into a noble Polish family. However, already before World War II he elected to become a Lithuanian: "We were all Lithuanians, Polonized Lithuanians." Hence, the Polish nobleman Stanisław Dobrowolski became Father Stanislovas Dobrovolskis and remained true to his newly minted Lithuanian identity during the Soviet occupation and after. In the Gulag, he suffered for Lithuania and the Church.[8]

In Radun (Raduń), the ancient Meyer Chaimovich stubbornly insisted that "people were happy when the Soviet soldiers arrived here . . . They said the Soviet Union would be better than Poland. And they were right. It is better. . . . In Polish times there were no televisions, only radios."[9] Chaimovich, who was a Communist and a former anti-German guerrilla, also refused to acknowledge that the principal victims of the Nazis in his *shtetl* should be identified as Jews. "They were peaceful Soviet citizens . . . That's what they were."[10] At the same time, the man remembered vividly the Jewish inhabitants of Radun and, indeed, failed to shed his Jewish identity altogether.

In Novahrudak (Nowogródek), a ninety-something-year-old descendant of Polish gentry, gross, obese, dirty, lonely, and destitute, spewed bitter venom against "the Jews": "Things were better in Polish times. . . . Except that there were too many Jews . . . Hitler got rid of them for us. . . . Hitler killed them all off. He did terrible things, Hitler, he killed those nuns in the parish church, but he did us a service when he got rid of all the Jews."[11] The woman was a staunch Polish nationalist. However, her granddaughter was confused about her own identity. Svetlana confessed that she learned Polish poetry, Adam Mickiewicz's forbidden verse, in particular, from her paternal grandmother. However, when prompted whether she was Polish, Svetlana responded: "No . . . I am Soviet. I mean—I am Russian." After a while, nonetheless, she confided in her interlocutor that

> The Poles here, they hate the others, they hate the Belarusians, they hate us Russians. But the Poles in Poland are not like them. They are more open, they are friendly, they are not closed and hard like our people here. They know about [sic the] West, they know about God. So now I go to the Catholic Church. I am the only Russian there. I used to be proud to be Soviet, but there is no more Soviet Union. Now I want—to be with them. I want to be one of them. I want to be a Pole. I want to be Polish.[12]

Svetlana in Novahrudak was luckier than Yelena in Kamieniec Podolski/ Kamenets Podolsk. The latter was completely lost. She despised her surroundings; she refused to associate with anyone. "Yelena was Ukrainian, but her surname was Polish and her family had spoken Russian for four generations. Her mother once lived in a town house in the center of Kiev, but the family lost everything in the Revolution. Yelena had grown up in the Crimea . . . Now, Yelena belonged nowhere."[13]

In Bieniakonie, when quizzed "about the nationality of the local people," Pole Michał Wołosiewicz dismissed his neighbors with scorn: "these people here aren't Polish or Russian or Belarusian or Lithuanian or anything, they are Bieniakonian. They speak Bieniakonian, their own dialect; it doesn't have proper grammar at all . . . Some used to be Polish—I remember from back then—but now their interests changed and they have switched their tongue and pen."[14]

In Brest, where "Poles, or people pretending to be Poles, were everywhere"[15] to take advantage of the black market, a Polish Catholic priest explained to a visiting American that

> All I can say is that whatever they told you in Minsk, no one around here knows if he is Belarusian, Polish, Russian, *tutejszy*—it means local—or what. They just have no real identity at all . . . or they choose an identity for personal gain . . . Slowly, some people are coming to me because I give them a language with poetry and grammar, and I give them a faith with real values. . . . But slowly. Very, very, very slowly.[16]

Thus, at the outset of freedom, the confusion about one's identity was often widespread. Many of the newly liberated Ukrainians, Lithuanians, Belarusians,

Poles, and others were frequently at a loss about how to conceptualize themselves in their new surroundings. Most were unmoored; some of them relied on the force of inertia to carry them wherever the economic, cultural, or political wind blows. Others observed the public scene cautiously. Still others actively searched for the answers. Culture and religion tended to attract one to a particular ethnicity.[17]

This is because culture and religion inevitably trigger specific memories. They support and perpetuate certain customs and modes of conduct. Material issues seem of secondary importance. To end confusion and to find oneself, the newly liberated people have strived to re-establish their identity by searching for memories. The search is selective and ethno-centric. It is as if, once liberated, the national elites lacked the imagination to extend the search for memories from their fellow coethnics to their neighbors. Instead, each national story is reassembled in separation and, often, in contradiction to others.

Notes

1. These included a particularly long trip which lasted several months in 1991, when the bulk of the information was collected. See Anne Applebaum to Marek Jan Chodakiewicz, November 17, 2005.
2. Applebaum, *Between East and West*, 59.
3. Ibid., 67.
4. Ibid., 61–62.
5. Ibid., 105.
6. Ibid., 181–82.
7. Ibid., 77–78.
8. Ibid., 72.
9. Ibid., 96–97.
10. Ibid., 99.
11. The nuns were executed for sheltering Jews, which the woman did not mention to the American journalist. Later, upon learning that her interlocutor was Jewish, the woman prayed: "Lord . . . forgive me for what I have said to this girl." See Applebaum, *Between East and West*, 137–39.
12. Ibid., 131–32.
13. Ibid., 264.
14. Ibid., 110.
15. Ibid., 184.
16. Ibid., 187.
17. This is quite evident in another fascinating travelogue which concentrates mostly on the Polish Catholic minority in the Intermarium. Nonetheless, the travelogue confirms most of Applebaum's astute observations, in particular about the post-Soviet ethno-cultural confusion and malaise. The author has been traveling in the Intermarium for about fifteen years and has produced several books on her experience. See Teresa Siedlar-Kołyszko, *Byli, są. Czy będą . . .? (They Were, They Are. Will They Be . . .?)* (Kraków: Oficyna Wydawnicza "Impuls," 2006) (afterward *Byli, są. Czy będą . . .?*); Teresa Siedler-Kołyszko, *Od Smoleńska po Dzikie Pola (From Smolensk to Wilde Plains)* (London: PFK, 1998); Teresa Siedler-Kołyszko, *Między Dźwiną a Czeremoszem - reportaże z ziem I i II*

Rzeczypospolitej (*Between Dzvina and Cheremosh: Reporting from the Lands of the 1st an 2nd Commonwealth*) (London: Polska Fundacja Kulturalna, 1998). See also Krzysztof Renik, *Podpolnicy - rozmowy z ludźmi Kościoła na Litwie, Łotwie, Białorusi i Ukrainie 1990–1991* (*The People of the Underground: Conversation with Church Persons in Lithuania, Latvia, Belarus, and Ukraine, 1990–1991*) (Warszawa: Oficyna Wydawnictwa Przeglądu Powszechnego, 1991); Father Roman Dzwonkowski, *Polacy na dawnych Kresach Wschodnich: Z problematyki narodowościowej i religijnej* (*Poles in the Former Eastern Borderlands: Nationality and Religious Problems*) (Lublin: Oddział Lubelski Wspólnoty Polskiej, 1994); Father Dzwonkowski Roman et al., *Za wschodnią granicą 1917–1993* (*Beyond the Eastern Border*) (Warszawa: Wspólnota Polska and Apostolicum, 1993); Father Edward Walewander, ed., *Polacy w Estonii mówią o sobie* (*Poles in Estonia Talk about Themselves*) (Lublin: Oddział Lubelski Stowarzyszenia Wspólnota Polska, 1997); Father Edward Walewander, ed., *Polacy w Mołdawie mówią o sobie* (*Poles in Moldavia Talk about Themselves*) (Lublin: Oddział Lubelski Stowarzyszenia Wspólnota Polska, 1995); Father Edward Walewander, ed., *Polacy w Rosji mówią o sobie* (*Poles in Russia Talk about Themselves*), 3 vols., (Lublin: Wydawnictwo KUL, 1994–1995).

25

National Stereotypes

This logical outcome of totalitarian repression creates a number of problems, including how the individual perceives the past. First, most peoples from Estonia to Moldova (and, indeed, both east and west of that swath of land) feel that they are victims. Second, each national group has indeed a legitimate claim to the status of a victim. Third, each group believes it is the victim. Fourth, consequently, each group tends to overlook, belittle, or even deny the claims to victimhood of other groups. To stereotype, members of the majority group (e.g., the Poles in Wilno-land) tend to feel that they suffered the most not only at the hands of the Nazis and Communists but also at the hands of the minorities, who were, allegedly, at best uniformly indifferent and at worst hostile to the plight of the majority. Conversely, the representatives of the minority groups feel that they were persecuted not only by the foreign invaders but also by the local majority as well as other minorities.

Predictably many, if not most, individuals identifying with a national group seem incapable of particularizing outside of their own ethnicity. Namely, say, a Polish Christian eyewitness is usually perfectly capable of recalling which individual Poles cooperated with the Nazis and which resisted them but never would the eyewitness argue that the entire Polish national group was collaborating with either the Third Reich or the Soviet Union. Rather, the standard eyewitness conclusion is that "the entire nation" resisted. The same Polish witness can usually list a couple of Soviet collaborators who happened to be Jewish or a few Nazi auxiliaries who happened to be Ukrainian and, next, without batting an eye, volunteer that all Jews were "Communists" or all Ukrainians "fascists."[1]

The same inability to discern various attitudes among individuals outside of one's ethnic group afflicts everyone else. It seems that neither the Poles, nor the Estonians, nor the Latvians, nor the Lithuanians, nor the Jews, nor the Ukrainians, nor the Belarusians, nor the Moldovans, nor anyone else are able to synthesize fairly their individual recollections. Perhaps we should expect neither individual victims nor their descendants to be able to do so. However, we should expect the scholars to accomplish that.

Admittedly, it has not been an easy task to handle. Wartime propaganda of both the Axis and the Allies was cast largely in a nationalistic way. Even

Communist propaganda of "Soviet nationalism" stressed the Russian nationalist narrative, which only sometimes admitted the validity of other "fraternal" narratives. Subsequent punditry and historiography likewise continued the trend. Further, the witnesses have tended to narrate their stories in ethno-centric terms. Hence, the historians have generally had a tough time conceptualizing the war and its aftermath in any other form.[2] Moreover, both the witnesses and at least some of the scholars have tended to favor a particular ethnicity, whichever they are culturally conditioned to, starting with their own, and narrate the story from its point of view. Native historians usually like to champion their own nationality, while foreign academics tend to treat some ethnic groups in a kinder manner than others. All that reflects a variety of factors, including ethnic biases and/or cultural prejudices.

In the Intermarium, privately, ethnocentrism was the rule at least until 1992 and, officially, it persists to a certain extent until today. As one scholar put it about two competing ethnocentric interpretations of history, "Polish and Ukrainian historiographies on the campaign of ethnic cleansing against the Poles in Volhynia differ enough to have been created in a mind of a schizophrenic."[3] However, the ethnocentric approach is inadequate in the multicultural setting that the Borderlands of Europe were and, to a large extent, continue to be. This much is obvious. Therefore, at least some historians have been able to consider the problem in a more comprehensive manner. Those scholars understand that investigating the past requires familiarizing themselves not only with the recollections of individual witnesses but also with the ethnic histories, including ethnocentric myths. The task at hand is to combine the singular experience of individuals and the separate experiences of each ethnicity to arrive at a fair synthesis of the collective experience of all ethnic groups.

This is an indispensable process to restore the past and facilitate the reemergence of collective memory. It is also a painful and shocking process as demonstrated by the case of the massacre in Koniuchy/Kaniūkai/Koniukhi near Ejszyszki/Eišiškės/Eishyshok in the Wilno/Vilnius/Vilna region. The case of Koniuchy is controversial because it challenges Stalinist propaganda, ethnic stereotypes about victimhood and victimization, and Western scholarship, which overwhelmingly tends to view the Intermarium through the singular prism of the Holocaust.

Notes

1.   This observation is based not only on our interviews of hundreds of Polish Christian survivors, but also on examination of tens of thousands of pages of oral depositions, contemporary underground reports, and other documents, including assessments of charitable organizations, at the Hoover Institution Archives, Stanford, California; Archiwum Akt Nowych in Warsaw, Poland; Archiwum Państwowe in Białystok; Archiwum Państwowe in Łomża; Archiwum Państwowe in Lublin; Archiwum Państwowe in Kraśnik; Archiwum

Muzeum Regionalnego in Kraśnik; Archiwum Diecezjalne in Lublin; Archiwum Diecezjalne in Łomża; Archiwum Instytutu Historii Polskiej Akademii Nauk in Warsaw; Archiwum Związku Żołnierzy Narodowych Sił Zbrojnych in Lublin; Archiwum Brygady Świętokrzyskiej NSZ in Chicago (later at Orchard Lake, MI, and currently at the Jagiellonian University in Cracow); The Polish Museum of America Archives, Chicago, IL; the Institute of National Remembrance Archives in Warsaw; The State Archive of the Russian Federation in Moscow; and The Russian State Archive of Socio-Political History in Moscow. However, there were naturally exceptions that transcended the ethnic paradigm in the archives mentioned above. Further, Christian depositions collected at the Archives of the Jewish Historical Institute in Warsaw and at the United States Holocaust Memorial Museum in Washington, DC, usually display an ethno-religiously universal approach. For a sample of Polish Christian attitudes see, e.g., a collection of depositions from the Borderlands in *Wschodnie losy Polaków* (*Eastern Fates of the Poles*), 6 vols. (Łomża: Oficyna Wydawnicza Stopka, 1991–1996). For a fairly typical Polish Christian memoir from a single town in the Borderlands see Tadeusz Wróbel, *Borysław nie śmieje się: Opowieść o rodzinnym mieście* (*Boryslav Is Not Laughing: A Story about My Native Town*) (Warszawa: Wydawnictwo LTW, 2003).

2.   Predictably enough, there have been attempts by moral relativists to view the calamity from extremist feminist or ecological perspectives. The former compares, for example, the alleged crimes of the "Jewish patriarchate" ("sexism" and "exploitation") against Jewish women and children to Nazi terror, including "Nazi sexism." The ecological perspective endeavors "to decenter" the narrative from its human aspect and, instead, focuses on the environmental impact of dumping human ashes into rivers and otherwise polluting nature. Both perspectives are tantamount to Holocaust revisionism but they are not usually billed as such. See the views of Joan Ringelheim and R. Ruth Linden as quoted in Gabriel Schoenfeld, "The 'Cutting Edge' of Holocaust Studies," *The Wall Street Journal* (May 21, 1998): A16.

3.   See Krzysztof Łada, "Creative Forgetting: Polish and Ukrainian Historiographies on the Campaigne [sic] against the Poles in Volhynia during World War II," *Glaukopis: Pismo społeczno-historyczne* 2/3 (2004–2005): 343.

26

Koniuchy: A Case Study[*]

Koniuchy was a remote village in the vicinity of the Rudniki Forest (*Puszcza Rudnicka*). The area was inhabited by Polish and some Lithuanian Catholics. A few of the former had tenuous links to the Polish underground. During the Nazi occupation, these peasants were forced to surrender the mandatory food quota to the Germans which seriously threatened their survival. Further, following the breakdown of law and order in the countryside, the villages in this area experienced frequent raids by common bandits and Soviet partisans, who had their bases in the Rudniki Forest. Banditry was a widespread plague in the countryside at that time. However, the Soviets lacked support among the local population and, hence, resorted to expropriations to supply themselves.

Brutalized, exasperated, and on the brink of starvation, the inhabitants of Koniuchy created a village self-defense unit. Its members armed themselves with a few discarded Soviet weapons of dubious quality. The village watchmen patrolled the village perimeter nightly but failed to build any fortifications. However, to prevent Nazi reprisals, the Polish self-defense men sought and secured official blessing for their enterprise from a Lithuanian auxiliary police unit garrisoned by the Germans in Rakliszki, a locality a few miles away. Thus, with indirect German permission, the villagers successfully fended off several partisan raids on their village.

The Soviets considered these as hostile acts by "White Poles" and "fascist collaborators." On January 29, 1944, to punish the defenders and to set an example for other villagers, the Soviet partisans completely destroyed the village and killed indiscriminately around forty inhabitants of both sexes and all ages. There was virtually no armed resistance; some lucky villagers saved themselves through flight. After the return of the Red Army in July 1944, the Soviet secret police conducted an investigation and arrested a number of local Polish survivors implicated in the self-defense affair. They were shipped off to the Gulag.

The events regarding the massacre in Koniuchy can now be restored to collective memory after a careful study based upon a variety of sources, including contemporary German, Soviet, Lithuanian, and Polish reports as well as witness testimonies. Until 1989, only Jewish accounts were available in the West. After the fall of Communism, other eyewitnesses fearfully began to identify themselves and speak about the massacre in Koniuchy. Also, independent scholars penetrated the hitherto sealed Soviet archives.

The operation was carried out on orders of the First Secretary of the Lithuanian Communist Party Antanas Sniečkus, who was also the commander in chief of the Lithuanian Communist Partisan Movement. The action was overseen by Henokh Ziman aka Genrikas Zimanas aka Genrikh Ziman, the Yiddish-speaking top Soviet guerrilla commander and party secretary of "Southern Area" in the Vilnius/Wilno region. According to Ziman,

> The joint forces of the Vilnius [Wilno] partisan units "Death to the Occupants," Margiris and General Headquarters Special Intelligence Group [Soviet Military Intelligence–GRU] destroyed Kaniūkai [Koniuchy], the village with the fiercest self-defense in the Eishy-shok [Ejszyszki] area. Kaniūkai had not only objected to the Soviet partisans entering the village but used to organize ambushes on the roads, was attacking villages friendly to the partisans and forced villages that were neutral to the partisans to arm themselves. The [village] self-defense suffered heavy casualties. We did not have casualties on our side.[1]

The report of the Lithuanian auxiliary police serving with the Nazis confirms Ziman's account:

> 1944.01.29 at 6 a.m., around 150 bandits (Jews and Russians) armed with 1 heavy machine gun, 3 light machine guns, machine pistols, rifles and grenades, attacked Koniuchy village. The village was burnt down, people were killed and cattle were slaughtered (35 were killed in action and 15 wounded.) Bandits had arrived from Daučiunai [Dawciuny] and WLK Salky [Wielkie Sałki] directions. They spent one hour there. Then they retreated in the same directions.[2]

Further, in a dispatch of February 5, 1944, the *Wehrmacht* also confirmed that a massacre took place in Koniuchy, which was torched, and that the perpetrators, Russians and Jews, killed thirty-six persons and wounded fourteen.[3] Neither the Soviet, nor the German, nor the Lithuanian, nor the Polish military dispatches mention anything about any German casualties or any German presence in Koniuchy.

The perpetrators of the massacre included Jewish guerrillas, fugitives from the Kaunas and Wilno/Vilnius ghettos, who were subsequently the first to describe the attack in their memoirs, in particular in the West. According to their accounts, Koniuchy was a veritable Nazi fortress with a strong German garrison. Allegedly, the villagers were all Nazi collaborators and bandits who received arms from the Germans and distributed them to other inhabitants in the area, agitating against Jews and Soviets, and even murdering them. In other words, many Jewish witnesses simply repeated Soviet propaganda clichés about Koniuchy, adding anti-Semitism as an important factor in the tragedy.

The first mention of Koniuchy appears as a log entry in a contemporary journal of a Jewish partisan detachment fighting on the Soviet side. "In the operation to destroy the armed village of Koniuchy, 30 fighters took part, of the units of 'Avenger' and 'To Victory.'"[4] The *Black Book of Russian Jewry*, based on Jewish testimonies compiled by Ilya Ehrenburg and Vasily Grossman in 1944, reported that the Jewish partisan units "Avenger" and "To Victory" carried out a "series of military operations" in the vicinity of Rudniki forest, and "helped destroy a German garrison in the heavily fortified town of Konyukhi [sic]."[5]

The first-ever published extensive Jewish account about Koniuchy reads like a Soviet propaganda lecture, which is unsurprising considering that it came out in Moscow in 1948 with the blessing of the official censor:

> Having got reinforcements from Kovno [Kaunas] ghetto group "Death to Invaders" received an opportunity to participate in large opera- tions alongside other groups from Rudnizky [Rudniki] forest.
>
> In village Koniukhi [Koniuchy], some 30 kilometres from the partisan base a German garrison took up position. Fascists followed partisans, set up ambushes on the roads. Several partisan groups, among them the "Death to Invaders," were ordered to liquidate this bandit cell.
>
> At first the Germans were ordered to stop their actions and hand in weapons. When they refused to do so people's avengers decided to act according to the law: "If the enemy does not give in, the enemy should be eliminated."
>
> Having left their base in the evening and gone through marshes and forests the partisans reached suburbs of the village by morn- ing time. Red rocket was a signal for the start of the attack. Twenty partisans from the group "Death to Invaders," headed by unit leader Mikhail Trushin, went entered [sic] the village. Germans occupied several houses and started drum-fire from their submachine- and machine-guns. Every house had to be stormed. Incendiary bullets, hand grenades, flares were used to exterminate the Germans. Kovno partisans Dovid Teper, Jankl Ratner, Peisach Volbe, Leiser Zodikov and others charged the enemy in the face of bullets. Strong Leib Zaiats stormed one of the buildings after using all his bullets, wrestled a rifle from a German and proceeded hitting the enemy with a butt so that the butt broke.[6]

Subsequent Jewish accounts appeared in the West and were somewhat more restrained. However, for the most part, the framework set up by Stalin's propaganda masters remained intact. Some brief accounts, however, failed to mention any German presence in Koniuchy. In his depositions of 1960 and 1961, Zalman Wyłożny of the "Death to Fascists" unit notes briefly that "among other things, I participated in an important operation to liquidate the village of Koniuchy, whose inhabitants collaborated with the Germans. The peasants of this village caused a lot of evil to the local [Soviet] partisans. In revenge, the entire village of 80 farmsteads was burned to the ground and its inhabitants were murdered."[7] According to Israel Weiss of the "Victory" detachment, "we succeeded in wresting considerable quantities of arms and ammunition from villages who collaborated with the Germans and were supplied with arms by them. Punitive measures were undertaken against collaborators; and one village [Koniuchy] which was notorious for its hostility to the Jews was burned down completely."[8]

Ruzhka Korchak of the "Avenger" unit published in Israel the following Russian-language account of the massacre. Here, for the first time, allegations of the villagers having murdered partisans are advanced, though no victims are named and no Soviet document corroborates this serious charge:

At the [Soviet partisan] brigade headquarters they considered what means to employ for revenge. It was obvious that if no decisive measure was undertaken, most villages could refuse to obey [the Communists]. If there was no reaction to the instances of the killing of partisans, all their activities could be endangered and the prestige of the [Soviet] brigade would be undermined. The Lithuanian [sic] village of Koniuchy was known for its actions against the partisans. Its inhabitants collaborated actively with the Germans and the Lithuanians of Plechavičius. They distributed weapons they received among the peasants and organized them [for self-defense]. The village itself was large and well fortified; the partisans eschewed coming up to the village. The inhabitants of Koniuchy organized ambushes; they captured two guerrillas from the [Soviet] Lithuanian outfits and tortured them to death.

The staff of the brigade decided to carry out a great punitive expedition against the village. . . . All partisan forest units contributed fighters for the operation; altogether circa 150 persons participated, including about 40 Jewish fighters. A Soviet officer from the Šilas unit was appointed commander. The Jewish fighters were led by Iakov Prener.

Some partisans surrounded the village and entered it. . . . Hand to hand combat commenced. Many Lithuanians succeeded in fleeing the village. They began running toward the German garrison. They were ambushed. They were slaughtered; only a few saved themselves.

Seeing that the attempt to take Koniuchy by surprise failed, the commanding officer sent couriers to the partisans manning the ambush site and ordered them to assist the fighters in the village. . . . The partisans burned down one farmstead after another. Many peasants, women, and children fell from their bullets. Only very few saved themselves. The village was erased from the face of the earth.

The following day the superior Gestapo authorities from Vilnius arrived on the spot along with soldiers. The ruins and the bodies of the fallen were photographed and then the pictures were published as proof of the bestiality of the "red bandits," who ruthlessly destroyed the peaceful population.

Both the operation and German propaganda shook everyone around. The staff of the brigade undertook damage control. Leaflets were disseminated in the villages telling the truth about Koniuchy. The leaflets also contained a warning that everyone collaborating with the enemy would meet the same end. However, those who assisted the partisans would be rewarded. One can suspect that the village inhabitants were influenced not so much by admonitions, agitation, and leaflets, but by fear of revenge by the partisans. The story of Koniuchy tamed other villages of the region for a long time.

The punitive operation, and the way it was carried out, caused a great consternation and sharp criticism of many fighters in the Jewish camp. ... this cruel operation [against Koniuchy] ... during which men, women, and children were killed indiscriminately, caused such a reaction. Many of the participating Jewish fighters returned to the base shocked and depressed.[9]

Jewish partisan Chaim Lazar of the "Avenger" detachment believes that Koniuchy was targeted as "a nest of bands and the center of intrigues against the [Soviet] partisans. Its residents, known for their villainy [sic], were organizing the people in the area, distributing arms among them which they received from the Germans, and leading every attack on the partisans."[10] According to him,

The Brigade Headquarters decided to raze Koniuchy to the ground to set an example to others.

One evening a hundred and twenty of the best partisans from all the camps, armed with the best weapons they had, set out in the direction of the village. There were about 50 Jews among them, headed by Yaakov (Jacob) Prenner. At midnight they came to the vicinity of the village and assumed their proper positions. The order was not to leave any one alive. Even livestock was to be killed and all property was to be destroyed ...

The signal was given just before dawn. Within minutes the village was surrounded on three sides. On the fourth side was the river and the only bridge over it was in the hands of the partisans. With torches prepared in advance, the partisans burned down the houses, stables, and granaries, while opening heavy fire on the houses. ... Half-naked peasants jumped out of windows and sought escape. But everywhere fatal bullets awaited them. Many jumped into the river and swam towards the other side, but they too, met the same end. The mission was completed within a short while. Sixty households, numbering about 300 people, were destroyed, with no survivors. . . . The next day, the Gestapo heads came from Vilna [Wilno] with large army forces. The Germans photographed the ruins and the charred corpses and publicized the photos accompanied by biting articles on the cruelty of the partisans.[11]

Another erstwhile Jewish guerrilla remembers that

Our base commander gave the order that all able-bodied men should be prepared in an hour to leave for an operation. . . .
When we were closing in on our destination, I saw that partisans were coming from all directions, from various detachments. . . .
Our detachment got the order to destroy everything that was moving and burn the village down to its roots.
At the exact hour and minute all partisans from all four corners of the village started pouring rifle and machine-gun fire, with incendiary bullets, into the village. This caused the straw roofs of the houses to catch fire.
The villagers and the small German garrison answered back with heavy fire, but after two hours the village with the fortified shelter was completely destroyed.
Our only casualties were two men who were lightly wounded.
When, later we had to go through Koniuchi [sic] we did not encounter any sniper shots, because it was like crossing through a cemetery.[12]

The most detailed and graphic account of a participant in the assault on Koniuchy was penned by Paul (Pol) Bagriansky. Although he failed to mention any German garrison in the village, Bagriansky confabulated about the activities, and the arms and ammunition in the possession, of the villagers. His claim that the Partisan Headquarters in Moscow reprimanded and punished the people who initiated and led the assault on the village is also a fabrication. Bagriansky wrote as follows:

Before we started, the commanding officer told us briefly in Russian what our mission was about. Many villages in the radius of about 20 kilometers from Koniuchi [sic] decided to bring their cows and hogs during the night to the village of Koniuchi. Koniuchi was well armed by the Nazis and soldiers from Armia Krajowa. Partisans who went for food to the surrounding villages would find them empty. Very often the Germans would come there overnight to protect the village of Koniuchi. Therefore, the commanding officer told us, we are going to teach Koniuchi a lesson. . . .

I understood that our purpose is to destroy the entire village including all the villagers. I asked why such harsh inhuman treatment? The answer was that this is what the high command had decided to do. We cannot permit such heav[il]y armed villages to disrupt our partisan activities. This lesson will teach the other villages to think twice before they try again with Nazi's [sic] help to arm and to oppose us. . . .

Some units had the task of setting the huts on fire while the others had to close the escape routes. Exactly at midnight the village was set on fire and in a few minutes the stored ammunition started to explode. . . . When I reached my unit I saw one of our people holding the head of a middle aged woman against a big stone and hitting her head with another stone. Each blow was accompanied by sentences like: this is for my murdered mother, this is for my killed father, this is for my dead brother, etc. . . .

When I reached the unit to tell them their new assignment, I saw an awful, gruesome picture. . . . In a small clearing in the forest six bodies of women of various ages and two bodies of men were lying around in a half circle. . . . One man at a time was shooting in between the legs of the dead bodies. When the bullet would strike the nerve the body would react as if were alive. . . . All men of the unit were participating in this cruel play, laughing, in a wild frenzy. I was first petrified by this performance, and then started to be sickly interested.

On my way back to the command post I saw several bodies of the peasants who had been shot on their way to escape. . . .

The village Koniuchi was now a memory full of ashes and of dead bodies. The lesson had been taught. The commanding officer assembled all units, thanked them for their well accomplished job. . . The people were tired but their faces looked satisfied and happy with the accomplished assignment. . . .

As we learned the next day, the other units got a heros' [sic] welcome for destroying Koniuchi and they drank and ate and sang all night. They enjoyed the killings, the destruction and most of all the drinking.[13]

Writing in the late 1990s, both Joseph Harmatz of the "To Victory" unit and Alex Faitelson of the "Death to Occupiers" detachment likewise confirm the ruthlessness of the massacre. They also provide vivid details of frequent Soviet partisan "supply," or provision-gathering expeditions. However, Faitelson, Harmatz, and other partisans refuse to see the link between Soviet partisan robberies and violence, on the one hand, and legitimate self-defense by the peasants, on the other. They view the massacre in Koniuchy through the prism of collaboration with the Nazis and justified revenge.[14]

Rachel Margolis, a member of the "To Victory" detachment, published her memoirs in 2006, but in many ways they were a throwback to much earlier accounts.

In the village of Kaniuki [sic] there was a Fascist garrison that covered the partisans' route to the larger region and was very dangerous for us. The brigade command decided to engage the garrison in battle and to send all its detachments there. Fania [Jocheles, later Brantsovsky] went on this mission with the group from the "Avenger" detachment. Our people also went.

They returned after a few days, bringing the wounded. The battle was very protracted. The partisans had surrounded the garrison, but the Fascists were exceptionally well armed and repelled all attacks. They broke the flanks of the Jewish detachments, and the partisans withdrew precipitously. Then [Elhanan] Magid jumped on a rock and yelled: "We are Jews. We will show them what we are capable of. Forward, comrades!"

This sobered the boys up; they ran back and were victorious. . . . Everyone was elated: they returned from the victory, in spite of the numerical preponderance of the enemy. The garrison in Kaniuki did not exist anymore.[15]

No eyewitness testimonies about the massacre of Koniuchy were published either in the Soviet Union (aside from Gelpern's book in Yiddish) or in "people's" Poland. According to a sixty-year-old teacher, Antoni Wierżyński, a Pole who was born in Soviet-occupied Lithuania and lives near the village today, "For a long time I myself did not know anything about what really happened in Koniuchy." He was indoctrinated to admire the Soviet Union, including the Soviet partisans. Perversely, when Wierżyński was a schoolboy, the Communist authorities took him and his schoolmates to pay tribute to the perpetrators of the massacre at the Soviet partisan museum in the Rudniki Forest. Later, as a teacher, Wierżyński ferried his own pupils to the same museum and likewise indoctrinated them, albeit unwittingly for he believed in the Communist lie. As a result, "the Polish youth learned about the tragedy in Koniuchy only last year [2004] when a monument was erected there through the efforts of the Union of Poles in Lithuania."[16]

As far as the free Poles in the West were concerned, the first public, if very brief, acknowledgment of the massacre appeared in an émigré periodical only in 1973. A Polish underground Home Army commissioned officer, who was a second-hand witness, testified that the Soviets pacified the village, destroying it completely and killing thirty-four persons.[17]

Only after 1989 did non-Jewish witness begin to speak out more openly. Interviewed in 2005, a Soviet partisan stated he "is proud" of his role in the massacre. Anatolii M. Kotskin, who lives near Koniuchy, fought in the "For the Fatherland" unit. He readily admits that he killed "not a few enemies," including women, but in the chaos of battle "he was not paying attention." According to Kotskin,

> There were well over one hundred of us . . . There were also comrades from the Jewish outfits. We surrounded the village. We were told that the Germans were garrisoned there. The order was to kill everyone and this time around to take neither animals nor food. Burn everything.[18]
> However, Polish Christian victims of the massacre are still traumatized.[19]

According to Edward Tubin,

> the first time they [the Soviets] came, it was to us alone. They told us to harness our horse . . . They took the keys to the storehouse and stable, they chased everyone into a corner, one of them watched us with an automatic weapon. They took everything. Then they came at the end and said that 'there'll be no mercy: If you report us, we'll come and burn you down.' . . . The next time more of them came. They came in the early evening and went to take, to rob in the entire village. They came to us and also ordered us to harness our horse. . . . When they were leaving, two of them burst into our home. There was nothing in the house. I was sleeping on the bed with my brother Leon. We were covered with a village coverlet of our own making. They burst in, saw that there was nothing, and tore the coverlet off us. My father said to them, "Comrades, the children won't have anything to cover themselves with." So one of them said using a really dirty word, "shit on your children." And they left.[20]

Anna Suckiel recalls that

> There were no Germans here with us. There was an outpost of the Lithuanian police close by in Rakliszki . . . The watch was organized by Władek Woronis called Wadas. The boys went on patrols every night, several of them from each side of the village. They were protecting their own wives, children, cows. They had enough weapons, because they were left over from the wars—in 1939 and, later, in 1941, when the Germans chased the Soviets.
> After yet another robbery the boys grabbed their arms and took a short cut in pursuit of the thieves. They intercepted them and shot at them with sawed-off guns on the bridge in Gierwiszki. The partisans were scramming so fast that they almost lost their hats. They even abandoned a wagon with the loot. From then on the boys of Koniuchy guarded the village regularly.[21]

On January 29, 1944, the Soviets returned in full force:

The partisans murdered everyone without any distinction regarding sex and age. Stanisława Jankowska was paralyzed and was unable to escape from her blazing home. She was burned alive. Right here on the spot where the cross has been erected with a list of names of my fallen neighbors the partisans finished Urszula Parwicka off with stones. I survived miraculously. That night haunts me every day of my entire life.[22]

Another survivor remembers that

automatic weapons started to go off and we see fire, it's burning. The thatched roofs were made of straw. People started to run away, they rushed into the forest, into those bushes. . . .

My mother and I ran to a hollow to hide, and I see them [Soviet partisans] running from the cemetery—there may have been twelve of them—they're shooting. Maybe if I were older I would have followed my mother, but I left her, ran across the village, to our neighbor . . . My [eleven-year-old] brother Leon was there. And Leon and I ran to the river. I saw incendiary bombs dropping. . . . We ran up to the river. We look and see a large alder that had grown on the other side of the river. A hole had been hollowed out. And we look and see a neighbor sitting there who had run and hidden with his family near that river. And we went there.

We sat there and heard shots on the other side. The Pilżys family lived there. We saw how they came for them, they entered their house. They shot them. That's to say they shot the two daughters, the father and the mother. They left the house and set it on fire. They set fire to everything. Then we see how quite near us, well maybe about 50 meters away, Woronis, an elderly man, was running and fell into the water with his sheepskin coat. Two men with automatic weapons ran right behind him. They ran to the river and sprayed a series from the automatic weapons into the river . . . They thought they'd killed him and so they turned back. Thank God they did not look to the left, where we sat under that little hill. . . .

We thought that [Woronis] had perished . . . We look and look, he crawled out of the water on the other side . . . They had wounded his hand very seriously . . . The partisans killed his wife, his daughter and his son. . . .

My mother had run to that hollow and fell in. They probably knew . . . They approached. My sister was sitting nearby with her young daughter. They sprayed her with shots from the automatic weapon. . . . My sister may have been around thirty. She had a young girl, four years old, in her hands. They shot at the girl in her hand and killed her. My sister sat there, and another man saw her and said that she's still alive

509

and raised his rifle. Another fellow said to leave the woman alone . . . But he shot at my sister. She was sitting, and he fired at her head diagonally right in the cheek and through the jaw. The bullet ripped through her teeth and jaw. My sister fell. So that the bullet entered through her jaw and ripped out part of her breast.

And my brother who was nearby in the bushes ran. That's how they encountered him and sprayed him on the head with the automatic weapon. His head was shattered in half . . .

Stanisław Bandalewicz was burned in his house with two sons. I myself saw him lying on the veranda with his burned bones . . . His children had hidden under the stove and were burned, they had suffocated. . . .

There was no difference, they killed whomever they caught. Even one woman who ran toward the cemetery to the forest, they didn't shoot her but killed her with a rock, a rock to the head. When they killed my mother, they sprayed about eight bullets in her chest.[23]

According to another witness, Józef Bondalewicz,

We were awoken from our sleep by the shooting and the glow of fire in our windows. It was as light as day and crawling with partisans, who fired at everyone who tried to get out of their homes. The noise from the fire and crash of buildings falling apart were reminiscent of a thunderstorm. From various sides one could hear the desperate moans of people being burned alive in their homes and the groaning of animals locked in their sheds.

When I ran out of my house I saw a mother with an infant in her hands running out of the neighboring Wójtkiewicz house. Two women whom I recognized by their voices to be Jewish, since there were no [other] women in Soviet units, mowed her down with a series of bullets from their automatic weapons. One of them darted toward the dying woman, tore her child away, and threw it into a burning cottage. The terror and uncanny heat forced everyone who made it out of the buildings to take flight without delay. Out of breath I managed to reach friendly brushwood from where I made my way to the village of Kuże.[24]

Antoni Gikiewicz testified that "they surrounded the entire village and started murdering everyone, one after another." Stanisława Woronis recalled that "whomever the Soviets found in the bushes or in a hole in the ground, they killed." According to Stanisław Wojtkiewicz, "they didn't even spare pregnant women."[25] Anna Suckiel wonders "why did they murder so many women and children? . . . What did little Molis do to them? She was not even two years old. Or the Bandalewicz boys—one was eight and the other nine."[26] Uncharacteristically, Stanisława Woronis and her three-year-old daughter were spared by a Soviet guerrilla, who showed her a safe escape route: "He was a partisan; I pray for him until this day. One can find a human being even among bandits."[27]

The massacre at Koniuchy was a nonevent in Soviet or Polish Communist historiography between 1944 and 1989. Polish historians discovered it only afterward. The leading specialist in the field of resistance in the northeastern provinces of Poland, Kazimierz Krajewski, confirmed that there were no fortifications in the village and the self-defense was armed "with a few rusty rifles." In fact, "the only 'fault' of the inhabitants of Koniuchy was the fact that they had had enough of the daily—or, rather, nightly—robberies and assaults, and they wanted to organize a self-defense. The Bolsheviks from Rudniki forest decided to level the village to the ground to terrorize into submission the inhabitants of other settlements."[28] Other Polish-language scholars and investigators concur.[29] In March 2001, the Commission for the Investigation of Crimes against the Polish Nation of Poland's Institute of National Memory launched a still ongoing formal investigation.

Meanwhile, the massacre has hardly registered in the Western scholarship. Mark Paul, an independent scholar in Canada, is the single notable exception. Paul has written the most exhaustive study of Koniuchy in any language so far. His findings fully confirm and expand on the version championed by Krajewski and others.[30]

A few Israeli historians and two Western authors wrote on the topic. Among the "operations" carried out by the "Avenger" detachment, historian Dov Levin, who was a member of the "Death to the Occupiers" unit, lists "reprisals and punishment" which resulted in the killing of "a number of peasants who collaborated with the enemy."[31] Historian Yitzhak Arad, who also fought with the Soviet partisans in this area, speaks of "punitive raids against hostile villages."[32] Like Levin, he blames the Home Army for instigating the conflict and murdering Soviets and Jews.[33] Nechama Tec, an American sociologist who alludes to the massacre in a recent study, curiously classified it as an example of "anti-German military missions."[34] She is aware neither of any original sources other than Jewish witness accounts nor of any recent scholarship on the topic. Neither is American writer Rich Cohen. According to his recently published journalistic account, Koniuchy was a

> pro-Nazi town on the edge of the forest. There was an enemy garrison nearby, and the Germans used Konyuchi [sic] as a staging point for sweeps and raids. They built towers around the town and organized a local militia; the militia had recently captured two partisans and tortured them to death . . . Konyuchi was a village of dusty streets and squat, unpainted houses. . . . The partisans—Russians, Lithuanians and Jews—attacked Konyuchi from the fields, the sun at their backs. There was gunfire from the guard towers. Partisans returned the fire. The peasants ducked into houses. Partisans threw grenades onto roofs and the houses exploded into flame. Other houses were

torched. Peasants ran from their front doors and raced down the streets. The partisans chased them, shooting men, women, children. Many peasants ran in the direction of the German garrison, which took them through a cemetery on the edge of town. The partisan commander, anticipating this move, had stationed several men behind the gravestones. When these partisans opened fire, the peasants turned back, only to be met by the soldiers coming up from behind. Caught in a cross fire, hundreds of peasants were killed.[35]

The accounts of "second generation survivors" (i.e., children of Jews who lived through the Holocaust) go even further in embellishing the historical record. Michael Bart, the son of Leizer Bart, who was a policemen in the Wilno ghetto before joining the partisans in Rudniki forest, eagerly justifies his father's participation in the massacre.

Abba Kovner began meeting with other Jewish, Russian, and Lithuanian partisan leaders to plan a response against the Polish villagers who had attacked them. One particular town, Koniuchi [sic], was notorious for its enthusiastic support of the Nazis against the partisans. The Germans had helped the residents fortify their village by building defense trenches and lookout towers, and organizing the men of the town into an antipartisan militia, armed with German rifles and even machine guns.

One day in April [sic] a scout returned from Koniuchi. Because he looked "Aryan" and spoke unaccented Polish, he had been able to enter the village posing as a member of a pro-Nazi militia from another village. In the village he had seen the corpses of two Jewish partisans, who had been killed and afterward placed on public display.

When Kovner heard this, he reported the event to the Russian partisan commander, with whom the leaders had already been discussing retaliation against hostile villages. The commander ordered an unprecedented call-up of all available fighters from the various Jewish and non-Jewish brigades in Rudnicki [sic] for an attack on Koniuchi.

Leizer [Bart] and the other Avengers would be part of a small army of well-armed and trained partisan fighters. They would surround the town from all sides and destroy it. No building was to be left standing. All residents who resisted in any way were to be killed. . . .

By dawn the strike force had surrounded the three land-locked sides of the village and taken control of the river on the forth side. Several partisans had torched houses, stables, and granaries on the outskirts of the village, while the others began riddling the town with gunfire and incendiary bullets.

The people of Koniuchi returned fire from their houses and defensive positions. The straw roofs burst into flames, and within minutes the German ammunition hidden inside homes began to explode. Soon the whole town was ablaze. Half-clothed villagers, roused from their sleep, jumped out of windows and escaped across the river. Anyone in the town who surrendered was told to leave, but those who fought back or ignored calls for surrender were killed. Within two hours the mission was complete. The town had been leveled, three dozen people were dead, and another dozen had been injured.

Leizer and the other Avengers came back safely from Koniuchi. All any of them had to say was that it was done and that Koniuchi would not be a problem anymore. Once other nearby villages saw the price to be paid, they would most likely not be problems either. Kovner had once said that, unlike the Nazis, the Jewish partisans didn't kill because they wanted people to die. Making an example of Koniuchi had been necessary for their survival, and the validity of their cause made the choice between their survival and that of the people of Koniuchi a defensible one. After the war, when recounting their exploits, Koniuchi was rarely spoken of. [36]

This is indeed sad. Despite clear evidence that there was no German garrison in the village and the perpetrators sustained no casualties, Stalinist propaganda survives unwittingly in the West. Further, Cohen and Tec seem to be throwbacks to pre-1989 times when history was written from an ethno-nationalist point of view and other perspectives were ignored either consciously or subconsciously. They are aided and abetted by postmodernist "scholarship" of juggling selective facts and amplifying them to fit one's prejudice of identity politics. Such shoddy academic practices then are often translated into popular culture and spread in a multitude of ways through novels, cartoons, TV shows, documentaries, and movies. They are singularly unhelpful in our mission to liberate the past from the totalitarian nightmare.[37] Now, with the archives open to all, there are no more excuses not to research thoroughly, checking and cross-checking facts and juxtaposing various accounts to reconstruct the past, however controversial it may be. For the sake of restoring collective memory, we must move beyond a narrowly defined ethnic history and consider the past in all its complexity.

Theory and Reality

The case study of Koniuchy amply demonstrates how much more old-fashioned empirical research is needed before we can allow ourselves the luxury of theorizing. Theorizing tends to substitute for research in contemporary academia. And that just would not do. Because we have enjoyed such a long spell of academic freedom, Western history has been researched plenty and overtheorized even more. This is not the case in the newly liberated former Soviet colonies. Here we deal with the handicap of underresearching and overtheorizing on the part of many nontraditional Western historians.

Even the postmodernists should support research. After all, we can only deconstruct that which exists. Deconstructing theory may be exciting for some in *l'art pour l'art* sort of a way. But deconstructing an incomplete and inadequate picture of the past is flawed deconstruction. Would it not be more exciting to deconstruct a complete picture? Let the traditional scholars do their work before pouncing on them. Eschew erecting sand castles of "theory" before delving into the archives. Stop pretending that sexy effusions are a fit substitute for research. That is something a postmodern intellectual should care about, never mind the old-fashioned logic and truth that is the domain of the traditional scholar.

Perhaps all these admonitions are in vain. In mainstream French, German, and, to a lesser extent, American academia, words ceased to mean what Aristotelian logic dictates. The notion of logocentrism, an idea of a well-ordered logical universe based on pre-Enlightenment reason, has been jettisoned. Extreme nominalist heresy tends to be the rule in the humanities and social sciences. These branches of knowledge have been gripped by a powerful malady of postmodernism.[38]

Perhaps then the best remedy is to ignore the mainstream until the disease burns itself out and the logocentric normalcy returns triumphant. However, because the infinite capacity of the left for mischief is undeniable, we should also prepare ourselves for the *Reconquista*. There are already hopeful signs that it is possible. In the United States probably the bulk of the important work in social sciences and humanities takes place in think tanks, and not universities, which are increasingly irrelevant. On the individual level, the traditionalist scholar does his bit by simply carrying on the traditional, empirical, and logocentric way. In this particular instance of the Intermarium, we need many more case studies before we can be tempted to produce a definitive synthesis of its past. For now, however, we can suggest another preliminary outline, as we did earlier in this work.

The brief outline of history during World War II and its aftermath presented above is based upon the fruit of almost two decades of unfettered scholarship in the east. It could only be undertaken because of the implosion of Communism and, ultimately, the dissolution of the Soviet Union. Further, the outline is a synthesis of research by Estonian, Latvian, Lithuanian, Ukrainian, Belarusian, Russian, Moldovan, Jewish, Polish, and Western scholars, most of whom, it seems, write from an ethno-centric perspective. That is only natural. At first, one tends to focus on the affairs of one's own. One must master the most immediate requirements and delve into the most burning issues which deal with self-identity. Soon, however, the time comes to cast one's eye about at the research and opinion of others. Comparative studies should only be conducted after local studies have been completed, including case histories. What if we know the minute details of the experience of, say, a Jewish survival group in the Rudniki forest, when we are completely unaware of the context it operated in, including the story of its Christian neighbors? However, by judiciously combining the particular ethnic experiences those ethno-centrist scholars describe we can restore a collective history of all the peoples of the Intermarium.[39] This is probably the best first step to reconciling divergent accounts of World War II and its aftermath in the lands between Estonia and Moldova. Without healing the past, there will be no harmony and cooperation in each of the newly independent states of the Borderlands and between each of them.[40]

Notes

*   This section is based upon Marek Jan Chodakiewicz, *Żydzi i Polacy, 1918–1955: Współistnienie, Zagłada, Komunizm (Jews and Poles, 1918–1955: Coexistence, Extermination, Communism)* (Warszawa: Fronda, 2000); Marek Jan Chodakiewicz, ed., *Ejszyszki: Kulisy zajść w Ejszyszkach: Epilog stosunków polsko-żydowskich na Kresach, 1944–45: Wspomnienia-dokumenty-publicystyka (Ejszyszki: The Background to the Events in Ejszyszki: An Epilogue to Polish-Jewish Relations in the Eastern Borderlands: Recollections, Documents, Essays)* (Warszawa: Fronda, 2002 [2003]); Rimantas Zizas, "Pacyfikacja wsi Koniuchy (Kaniūkai), *Biuletyn Historii Pogranicza* (Polskie Towarzystwo Historyczne, Oddział w Białymstoku), no. 4 (2003): 33–57; Ryszard Tyndorf, "Zwyczajna pacyfikacja: Źródła żydowskie o zagładzie wsi Koniuchy," ("An Ordinary Pacification: Jewish Sources about the Extermination of Koniuchy") *Glaukopis* 2/3 (2004–2005): 376–84; Piotr Gontarczyk, "Tragedia Koniuchów," ("The Tragedy of Koniuchy"), *Gazeta Polska* (March 3, 2006): 25–29; Piotr Gontarczyk, "Nikt nie wymknął się z okrążenia," ("No one Fled the Encirclement") *Rzeczpospolita* (July 26, 2008); Mark Paul, *A Tangled Web: Polish-Jewish Relations in Wartime Northeastern Poland and the Aftermath*, Part Three (Toronto: PEFINA, 2008), http://www.kpk-toronto.org/2008-fundusz_obrony.html. See also a forthcoming monograph by Piotr Gontarczyk, *Zwyczajna pacyfikacja: Koniuchy, luty 1944 (An Ordinary Pacification: Koniuchy, February 1944)*.

1.   LVOA fond 1, in. 1, file 410, page 173, quoted in Mark Paul, *A Tangled Web*, Part Three.

2.   Report No. 53 of January 31, 1944, from the commander of the Lithuanian Police post in Bołcieniki to Vladas Zibas, the commander of the 253rd Lithuanian Police Battalion, LCSA F.R–666, In. 1, file 7, page 29, in Mark Paul, *A Tangled Web*, Part Three. See also Arūnas Bubnys, "253-iasis lietuvių policijos batalionas (1943–1944)," ("253rd Lithuanian Police Battalion [1943–1944]") *Genocidas ir rezistencija* no. 2 (4) (1998), http://www.tdd.lt/genocid/Leidyba/4/arunas3.htm; and Rimantas Zizas, "Žudynių Kaniūkuose pėdsakais," *Genocidas ir rezistencija* no. 1 (11) (2002), http://www.genocid.lt/Leidyba/11/genocida.htm.

3.   Archiwum Akt Nowych, Materiały aleksandryjskie (Alexandria Collection), T-454, Reichministerium für die besetzten Ostgebiete, Reel 19. This collection was donated to Poland by the United States.

4.   "Operations Diary of a Jewish Partisan Unit in Rudniki Forest, 1943–1944," in *Documents of the Holocaust: Selected Sources on the Destruction of the Jews of Germany and Austria, Poland, and the Soviet Union*, ed. Yitzhak Arad, Yisrael Gutman, and Abraham Margaliot (Jerusalem: Yad Vashem, 1981), 463–71.

5.   Ilya Ehrenburg and Vasily Grossman, *The Complete Black Book of Russian Jewry* (New Brunswick, NJ and London: Transaction Publishers, 2002), 289.

6. Dmitri Gelpernus, *Kovno Ghetto Diary* (Moscow: State Publishing House "Der Ermes," 1948), as translated at http://www.jewish.gen.org/yizkor/kaunas/. For the Yiddish original see Meir Yelin and Dmitri Gelpern, *Partizaner fun Kaunaser geto* (Partisans from the Kaunas Ghetto) (Moscow: "Der Ermes," 1948).

7. See the deposition of Zalman Wyłożny, December 24, 1960, January 11 and 15, 1961, Yad Vashem Archives, 0.3 2272 (formerly 1503/80-1) reproduced in Tyndorf, "Zwyczajna pacyfikacja," 380.

8. Israel Weiss in *Pinkas Hrubieshov: Memorial to a Jewish Community in Poland*, ed. Baruch Kaplinsky (Tel Aviv: Hrubieshov Associations in Israel and U.S.A., 1962), xiii.

9. Ruzhka Korchak, *Plamia pod peplom* (Tel Aviv: Biblioteka-Alija, 1977), 319–21.

10. See Chaim Lazar, *Destruction and Resistance* (New York: Shengold Publishers in Cooperation with The Museum of Combatants and Partisans in Israel, 1985), 174–75.

11. Ibid.

12. Isaac Kowalski, *A Secret Press in Nazi Europe: The Story of a Jewish United Partisan Organization* (New York: Central Guide Publishers, 1969), 333–34.

13. Paul Bagriansky, "Koniuchi," *Pirsumim* (Tel Aviv: Publications of the Museum of the Combatants and Partisans), no. 65–66 (December 1988): 120–24.

14. Joseph Harmatz, *From the Wings* (Sussex, Anglia: The Book Guild, 1998), 96, 84–85; Alex Faitelson, *Heroism & Bravery in Lithuania, 1941–1945* (Jerusalem: Gefen Publishing House, 1996), 307, 332–33.

15. Rakhil Margolis, *Nemnogo sveta vo mrake: Vospominaniia* (Vilnius: Gosudarstvennyi Evreiskii muzei imeni Vilniusskogo Gaona, 2006), 408–9.

16. Antoni Wierżyński quoted in Jerzy Danilewicz, "Zbrodnia bez kary," ("Crime without Punishment") *Newsweek* [Warsaw] (May 15, 2005): 38.

17. See Z. S. Siemaszko, "Rozmowy z kapitanem Szabunią," ("Conversations with Captain Szabunia") *Zeszyty Historyczne* no. 25 (1973): 146.

18. Anatolii M. Kotskin quoted in Jerzy Danilewicz, "Zbrodnia bez kary," *Newsweek* [Warsaw] (May 15, 2005), 38.

19. See Czesław Malewski, "Masakra w Koniuchach," ("The Massacre in Koniuchy") *Nasza Gazeta* (Vilnius), (March 8, 2001); Liliana Narkowicz, "'Siła w cierpieniu (z zeznań naocznego świadka)," ("Strength in Suffering [from the Testimony of an Eyewitness]") *Nasza Gazeta* (Wilno), March 29–April 4, 2001; Edward Tubin interviewed by Andrzej Kumor, "Nie przepuścili nikomu . . .: Z naocznym świadkiem pacyfikacji wsi Koniuchy rozmawia Andrzej Kumor," ("They Spared No One: Andrzej Kumor Interviews an Eyewitness of the Pacification of the Village of Koniuchy") *Gazeta* (Toronto) (May 4–6, 2001).

20. Edward Tubin interviewed by Andrzej Kumor, "Nie przepuścili nikomu . . .:: Z naocznym świadkiem pacyfikacji wsi Koniuchy rozmawia Andrzej Kumor," ("They Did Not Let Anyone go . . .:: Andrzej Kumor Talks to an Eyewitness of the Pacification of Koniuchy") *Gazeta* (Toronto) (May 4–6, 2001).

21. Anna Suckiel quoted in Jerzy Danilewicz, "Zbrodnia bez kary," *Newsweek* [Warsaw] (May 15, 2005): 37.

22. Anna Suckiel quoted in Andrzej Kaczyński, "Nikomu nie darować życia: Zagłada Koniuchów, 29 stycznia 1944," ("Spare No one's Life: The Annihilation of Koniuchy") *Rzeczpospolita: Dodatek specjalny: Cmentarze-Przeszłość-Pamięć* (October 30, 2004). However, elsewhere, Anna Suckiel gave a different name of the victim: "They finished off the wounded Mrs. Woronis with a rock." See

Czesław Malewski, "Masakra w Koniuchach," *Nasza Gazeta* (Vilnius) (March 8, 2001).

23. Edward Tubin interviewed by Andrzej Kumor, "Nie przepuścili nikomu . . .:: Z naocznym świadkiem pacyfikacji wsi Koniuchy rozmawia Andrzej Kumor," *Gazeta* (Toronto) (May 4–6, 2001).

24. Czesław Malewski, "Masakra w Koniuchach," *Nasza Gazeta* (Vilnius), (March 8, 2001).

25. Ibid.

26. Anna Suckiel quoted in Jerzy Danilewicz, "Zbrodnia bez kary," *Newsweek* [Warsaw] (May 15, 2005): 37.

27. Stanisława Woronis quoted in Jerzy Danilewicz, "Zbrodnia bez kary," *Newsweek* [Warsaw] (May 15, 2005): 37.

28. Kazimierz Krajewski, *Na Ziemi Nowogródzkiej: "NÓW" – Nowogródzki Okręg Armii Krajowej* ("NOW – the Nowogródek District of the Home Army") (Warszawa: Instytut Wydawniczy PAX, 1997), 511–12.

29. See Chodakiewicz, *Żydzi i Polacy*, 330; Chodakiewicz, *Ejszyszki*, 1: 52–54; Czesław Malewski, "Masakra w Koniuchach," *Nasza Gazeta* (Vilnius) (March 8, 2001); Czesław Malewski, "Masakra w Koniuchach (II)," *Nasza Gazeta* (Vilnius) (March 29, 2001); Jerzy Danilewicz, "Zbrodnia bez kary," *Newsweek* [Warsaw] (May 15, 2005): 36–38; Anna Gałkiewicz, "Informacja o śledztwach prowadzonych w OKŚZpNP w Łodzi w sprawach o zbrodnie popełnione przez funkcjonariuszy sowieckiego aparatu terroru," *Biuletyn Instytutu Pamięci Narodowej* no. 7 (August 2001): 22; Oddziałowa Komisja w Łodzi, "Informacja o stanie śledztwa w sprawie zabójstwa przez partyzantów sowieckich, w styczniu 1944 roku, mieszkańców wsi Koniuchy gm. Bieniakonie pow. Lida woj. nowogródzkie," (March 1, 2002); Oddziałowa Komisja w Łodzi, "Śledztwo w sprawie zabójstwa przez partyzantów sowieckich, w styczniu 1944 roku, mieszkańców wsi Koniuchy gm. Bieniakonie pow. Lida woj. Nowogródzkie," (September 5, 2002); Anna Gałkiewicz, "Omówienie dotychczasowych ustaleń w śledztwach w sprawach o zbrodnie w Nalibokach i Koniuchach," (May 15, 2003); Robert Janicki, "Investigation in the Case of the Murder by Soviet Partisans of Koniuchy Inhabitants: Investigation S 13/01/Zk, August 5, 2003"; "Informacja o działalności Instytutu Pamięci Narodowej–Komisja Ścigania Zbrodni przeciwko Narodowi Polskiemu w okresie 1 lipca 2003 r.–30 czerwca 2004 r.," Warsaw, January 2005 (Łódź sygnatura akt S 13/01/Zk); "Information on the Investigation in the Case of Crime Committed in Koniuchy," (September 13, 2005); Oddziałowa Komisja w Łodzi, "Śledztwo w sprawie zabójstwa przez partyzantów sowieckich, w styczniu 1944 roku, mieszkańców wsi Koniuchy gm. Bieniakonie pow. Lida woj. nowogródzkie," (May 16, 2006); Oddziałowa Komisja w Łodzi, "Śledztwo w sprawie zabójstwa przez partyzantów sowieckich, w styczniu 1944 roku, mieszkańców wsi Koniuchy gm. Bieniakonie pow. Lida woj. nowogródzkie," (October 12, 2007).

30. Mark Paul, *A Tangled Web: Polish-Jewish Relations in Wartime Northeastern Poland and the Aftermath*, http://www.kpk-toronto.org/2008-fundusz_obrony. html. See also the collection of documents in the dossier "The Massacre in Koniuchy," http://www.kpk-toronto.org/viewpoints/KONIUCHY_MASSA-CRE_rev.pdf.

31. Dov Levin, *Fighting Back: Lithuanian Jewry's Armed Resistance to the Nazis, 1941–1945* (New York and London: Holmes & Meier, 1985), 182.

32. Yitzhak Arad, *Ghetto in Flames: The Struggle and Destruction of the Jews in Vilna in the Holocaust* (Jerusalem: Yad Vashem Martyrs' and Heroes' Remembrance

Authority, and Anti-Defamation League of B'nai Brith in New York, 1980), 460.

33. Ibid., 459.

34. See Nechama Tec, "Reflections on Resistance and Gender," in *Remembering for the Future: The Holocaust in an Age of Genocide*, ed. John K. Roth and Elisabeth Maxwell (Houndmills and New York: Palgrave, 2001), 1: 559.

35. Rich Cohen, *The Avengers* (New York: Alfred A. Knopf, 2000), 144–45. The tid-bit about torturing two Soviet partisans to death can be traced to Ruzhka Korchak's account but is not substantiated by any other sources.

36. Michael Bart and Laurel Corona, *Until Our Last Breath: A Holocaust Story of Love and Partisan Resistance* (New York: St. Martin's Press, 2008), 228–30.

37. Such ignorance, of course, informs politics. The United Kingdom's Labor leader Gordon Brown himself opined in favor of one of the participants of the Koniuchy massacre without really researching anything much about the event. See Gordon Brown, "Women of Courage: Rachel Margolis," *The Independent* (March 9, 2011): http://www.independent.co.uk/news/people/profiles/women-of-courage-rachel-margolis-2236081.html?origin=internalSearch.

38. The best explication of the affliction is Ewa Thompson "Postmodernizm, pamięć, logocentryzm," ("Postmodernism, Memory, Logocentrism") in *(Nie)obecność: Pominięcia i przemilczenia w narracjach XX wieku (Absence/Presence: Omissions and Silencing in the 20th Century Narrations)*, ed. Hanna Gosk and Bożena Karwowska (Warsaw: ELIPSA, 2008), 54–75. For an overview of some of the major problems in Western universities see Hilton Kramer and Roger Kimball, eds., *The Future of the European Past* (Chicago, IL: Ivan R. Dee, 1997); Keith Windschuttle, *The Killing of History: How Literary Critics and Social Theorists Are Murdering Our Past* (San Francisco: Encounter Books, 2000); David Gelernter, "Back to Basics, Please," *The Wall Street Journal* (October 14, 2005); Robert Conquest, "History, Humanity, and Truth," the 1993 Jefferson Lecture in the Humanities (Stanford, CA: Hoover Institution on War, Revolution and Peace, 1993).

39. There have already been a few attempts, mostly Polish-led, to address this issue. Aside from several collective works with the participation of international scholars and edited by Krzysztof Jasiewicz, the most notable effort has been a collection of essays by multi–ethnic authors (Lithuanians, Belarusians, Poles, and Ukrainians) in Roman Wapiński, ed., *Czas XX wieku – nie tylko w polskiej perspektywie (The Time of the 20th Century: Not Only from the Polish Perspective)* (Ostaszewo Gdańskie: Wydawnictwo "Stepan Design," 2000); and Roman Wapiński, ed., *Polska na styku narodów i kultur: W kręgu przeobrażeń narodowościowych i cywilizacyjnych w XIX i XX wieku, (Poland on the Edge of Nations and Cultures: On the National and Civilizational Transformations of the 19th and 20th Century)* 3 parts (Gdańsk: Wydawnictwo "Stepan Design," 2001–2002).

40. The healing process was initiated by Poland's unequivocal public support for their eastern neighbor's freedom. See Mirosław Boruta, *Wolni z wolnymi, równi z równymi: Polska i Polacy o niepodległość wschodnich sąsiadów Rzeczypospolitej (Free with Free, Equal with Equal: Poland and the Poles about the Independence of the Eastern Neighbors of the Commonwealth)* (Kraków: Wydawnictwo Arcana, 2002); Tomasz Stryjek, "Historiografia a konflikt o Kresy Wschodnie w latach 1939–1953: Radzieckie, rosyjskie, ukraińskie i polskie prezentacje dziejów ziemi wschodnich dawnej Rzeczypospolitej jako część wojny ideologicznej w okresie lat trzydziestych-pięćdziesiątych XX wieku," ("Historiography and the

Conflict about the Eastern Borderlands, 1939–1953: Soviet, Russian, Ukrainian, and Polish Points of View on the History of the Eastern Lands of the Old Commonwealth as a Part of the Ideological War between the 1930s and 1950s") in Jasiewicz, *Tygiel Narodów*, 429–564. For the Poles, there is also a self-healing process of reclaiming the cultural heritage of the Intermarium to share it with others. See Grzegorz Rąkowski interviewed by Andrzej W. Kaczorowski, "Sto podróży," ("One Hundred Trips") *Biuletyn Instytutu Pamięci Narodowej* no. 1–2 (96–97) (January–February 2009): 162–67.

Conclusion

Hoc tempore obsequium amicos, veritas odium parit.[1]

—Terence

I wrote the truth, at least the way I comprehended it, that I love both my countrymen and all other people; that as a human and Christian I condemn all hatred both private and national; that, while loving people, I condemn only those flaws of theirs that, having made them deaf to all the lessons of the past, plant pernicious seeds into their future. Evil principles are more dangerous than evil deeds, and I have dared to proclaim a war on the former ones only.[2]

—Henryk Rzewuski

The duty of every thinking man is to ponder the causes of phenomena, and to extract the truth through separating the seed from the chaff, and not mixing everything into one mindless pot.[3]

—Józef Mackiewicz

Since the Mongol invasions of the thirteenth century, the Intermarium has been a staunch defender of Western civilization. Understood as a morally ordered universe of freedom, Western Civilization is only one of several cultures present in the Intermarium. It can appear paradoxical then that this heterodox cultural space should be such a formidable champion of the West. Yet, it is precisely in the interest of the multifarious to defend Western freedom. Western civilization—at its best—uniquely can provide the context in which other cultures can fulfill themselves and be fulfilled in the most decent manner. Only within the Western cultural framework can they coexist, converge, and, yes, sometimes clash—albeit without annihilating one another totally. Only Western civilization displays true flexibility in its

520

tolerance toward the "Other." To put it differently, no other cultural climate is as ambient to the cohabitation of a variety of cultures because no other civilization is predicated on freedom. Non-Western civilizations tend to reject the essence of the West and Western heresies like Nazism and Communism attempted to negate it. Therefore, for freedom to obtain in the Intermarium, its nations should aim at restoring the spirit of the golden age of the Commonwealth of Poland-Lithuania. To do so, they first have to remember who they are and where they came from. It is necessary for the people of the Intermarium to heal themselves from the horrible wounds inflicted on them by the totalitarians.

Estonia, Latvia, Lithuania, and, to a lesser extent, Ukraine and Moldova, but hardly Belarus, are on their way to achieve closure for their nightmarish twentieth-century experiences. It is often a painful process requiring a collective soul-searching, where well-founded pride stemming from the antitotalitarian resistance encounters dark ghosts of the past, including the collaboration with the very totalitarians and the participation in ethnic massacres. The process exposes those still-fragile civil societies to cruel blows and a barrage of accusations often directed from abroad as well as from the domestic minorities. The pain is necessary, though, for the rebirth of the formerly captive nations and their collective memories.[4]

Perhaps the most important aspect of the process is the need for objective, detached, rigorous, and skilled scholars to manage and guide it. A new generation of historians is already at work. They must beware of fads, however, and never sacrifice their scholarly integrity on the altar of political expediency, even if it currently dons a liberal democratic form. There is great hope that given time, provided there be no foreign invasion, the reconstructors of collective memories and guardians of the past will be successful.

According to an astute observer of the region,

> Perhaps the most urgent need before the people who have recently undergone a change of regime, no matter how incomplete, . . . is the need to carve out an identity. A sense of purpose and self-definition is almost as basic as nourishment. This is one of the main reasons for the need to properly understand—not simply, and simplistically, condemn—post-Communist nationalism. If it can be attained, an honest self-definition may well provide a healthy sense of self-worth and renewed confidence. Equipped with an instrument of continuity to their past and their rich—if sometimes checkered—traditions, there is hope that the nations of Eastern and Central Europe will be able to breathe, survive, and create once more. . . .
>
> Over the past four decades, each nation of East-Central Europe has had to systematically rewrite its entire chronology from a Marxist-Leninist point of view. Regardless of the relative value of each nation, the valor of its people or its cowardice, the richness of its culture or

its mediocrity, erasing the nation's history altogether might have been easier to survive than the distortion. Books must now be rewritten, rediscovered, resuscitated. . . .

Having had to lie—not only about one's own past, but even about the present, about the matter before one's own eyes—for fear of the secret police, for fear of destruction and retaliation not only against oneself but one's own children and parents, has created a deep sense of insecurity. No matter how clear it is that such fear is perfectly justified, the sense that one should have sacrificed everything in the interest of truth is impossible to erase completely. . . .

This Faustian legacy weighs heavily on the people of East-Central Europe. . . . 'Living in truth' . . . cannot help those who, sometimes quite deliberately, usually half-consciously, and sometimes even unconsciously, went along with the Big Lies of their corrupt Marxist regimes. They cannot forgive themselves. . . .

Marxist-Leninist "newspeak" was designed specifically to affect people's perceptions of reality to make easier the distortions that had been required by socialist reconstruction. New words were invented, old ones redefined. Slogans permeated ordinary speech, and some words became outlawed outright. People's relationships with each other were redrawn in the attempt to create "the new socialist man." In the process, one became alienated from one's most immediate instrument of communication with one's innermost reality: language. Never before had such an experiment been undertaken. For the imposition of a foreign dialect or an alien tongue does not affect one's original language. This was rather a mutilation, a sacrilege—and was perceived as such.[5]

Thus, the problems of restoring history to its rightful place are legion. In addition to those enumerated above, there are a few others. First, the old guard of Communist historians resists any changes. Second, some of the middle-generation former Communist regime and collaborating scholars have reinvented themselves and now re-serve the old Communist propaganda in a liberal garb, a form usually quite palatable for their Western colleagues, many of them leftists. Third, they have been grooming eager postmodernist young clones as their successors. This unholy alliance of the post-Communist leftists, East and West, has combined to retard the organic process of reconstructing the collective memories. Instead, they have attempted to impose a straight jacket of political correctness, afflicting liberal Western academia, upon the newly liberated Eastern Borderlands of the West. Postmodernist history conveniently disregards the facts. What matters is their selective interpretation and shrill propagation by the nefarious union of academic postmodernists and Hollywood pop-culture, eerily reminiscent of the Bolshevik propaganda apparatus.

This will just not do. We vehemently reject "the neo-Stalinist discourse," as John Radziłowski has aptly dubbed it.[6] We brazenly affirm the primacy of Western logocentrism. The old-fashioned empirical method serves our mission best. Thus, the undertaking to restore hidden history should not be confused with historical revisionism. Instead, it should be looked upon as an archeological endeavor. Since what we "know" about the twentieth-century history of the newly independent nations is mostly a concoction of Soviet propaganda and woefully inadequate Western attempts to understand the area,[7] we can endeavor to obtain the true picture only through an arduous process of applying the traditional, empirical rules of historical scholarship. Namely, we need to return to the archives to excavate, as it were, hitherto inaccessible documents. Next, we should combine archival knowledge with oral history accounts collected from the memory keepers. Oral history projects ought to be encouraged and survivor memoirs published not only for history's sake but also to rebuild local communities by fostering the links between the dead and the living, the old and the young. Then, we should juxtapose the resulting product with Soviet propaganda and Western scholarship, including original sources generated in the East and West (published documents, memoirs, and unpublished individual depositions).

Scholars everywhere need to embark on a much-needed corrective quest. Three areas should be addressed especially: Communist lies, ethnocentric myths, and Western distortions. Communist lies are the most poisonous legacy of totalitarianism. Ethnocentric myths are, on the one hand, understandable exercises in self-defense to preserve historic memories under totalitarianism and, on the other, woefully inadequate products of selective understanding of the past through the limited, and limiting, prism of an incomplete experience of a single national group.

Western distortions are a logical outcome of the lack of academic freedom under Communist totalitarianism that barred the way to the archives, the witnesses, and any comprehensive, independent inquiry into the past of the captive nations. Western distortions can also be blamed on the cultural prejudices of the West. Those expressed themselves in the tendency to ignore, patronize, or disregard the concerns of the losers of World War II: Poland, Estonia, Latvia, Lithuania, Belarus, Ukraine, and Moldova, among others.[8] Hence, lacking sophistication, including geographic, ethnographic, and linguistic skills, few Western scholars undertook any solid study of the East. Further, Western distortions result from the unintended consequences of the overwhelming tendency to study the Intermarium during World War II and its aftermath through the prism of the Holocaust. Last but not least, there is a widespread Western tendency to view nationalism as the generic boogeyman.

If Central and Eastern Europeans are to remember anything, including the Holocaust, they should remember everything. That entails restoring collective memories in all their beauty and ugliness, and everything in between; and restoring them also means dealing with nationalism without hostile hysteria. Western intellectuals ought to heed the sagely advice of one of their own, who uniquely understood Central and Eastern Europe. According to the celebrated author Rebecca West,

> Here was the nationalism which the intellectuals of my age agreed to consider a vice and the origin of the world's misfortunes. I cannot imagine why. Every human being is of sublime value, because of his experience, which must be in some measure unique, gives him a unique view of reality, and the sum of such views should go far to giving us the complete picture of reality, which the human race must attain if it is ever to comprehend its destiny. Therefore every human being must be encouraged to cultivate his consciousness to the fullest degree. It follows that every nation, being an association of human beings who have been drawn together by common experience, has also its unique view of reality, which must contribute to our deliverance, and should therefore be allowed a like encouragement to its consciousness. Let people, then, hold to their own language, their own customs, their own beliefs, even if this inconveniences the tourist. There is not the smallest reason for confounding nationalism, which is the desire of a people to be itself, with imperialism, which is the desire of a people to prevent other peoples from being themselves. Intense nationalist spirit is often, indeed, an effort by a people to rebuild its character when an imperialist power has worked hard to destroy it. . . . It surprised me that many Englishmen and Americans, who professed to be benevolently concerned about the future of man, were not in the least exalted by this prospect. The left wing, especially, was sharply critical of the new states [of Central and Eastern Europe] and all that they did. This was inconsistent in those who believed, often to a point far beyond the practical, that the individual must be free to determine his own destiny, and it was partly due to a theory, so absurd that not even its direct opposite has any chance of being true, that nationalism is always anti-democratic and aggressive, and that internationalism is always liberal and pacific. Yet nationalism is simply the determination of a people to cultivate its own soul, to follow the customs bequeathed to it by its ancestors, to develop its traditions according to its own instincts. It is the national equivalent of the individual's determination not to be a slave. The fulfillment of both those determinations is essentially a part of the left programme. But the liberation of an individual or a people may lead to all sorts of different consequences, according to their different natures.[9]

Precisely because there can be different consequences with different people and different settings, it is important to encourage individual freedom to foster collective memories rather than rely on the state to restore them according to immediate political needs and ideological fads. Remembering empowers the individual and restores his community from the nightmare of totalitarianism. Remembering also emboldens the scholar to produce competitive sets of interpretations, all indispensable for freedom to flourish.

Thus, as for the final product, collective memory must contain the story of all who are not with us whether they are politically, socially, culturally, and politically convenient or not. That entails a comprehensive picture of history. Such depiction of the past must embrace the majorities, minorities, interlopers, and invaders considered from a multitude of angles, including the most controversial and unsavory ones.

Individually, one victim is equal to another victim. Death is death, and suffering is suffering, whether we consider an Estonian, a Jew, or anyone else. Nonetheless, it should be possible to establish a hierarchy of victims from a historical perspective. Above, we have described the horrific carnage in the Intermarium in the first half of the twentieth century. A minimum of over thirteen million and a maximum of more than nineteen million human beings perished between 1914 and 1953 (see Appendix 1). Nazis and Communists were chief perpetrators. Lenin and Stalin killed more people than Hitler, albeit over a longer period of time (thirty-five years compared to four years). This was democide *par excellence*, defined superbly by R. J. Rummel as "death by government," political mass murder perpetrated to maintain oneself in power, often in service of a totalitarian ideology. In some instances, the killing fields of the Intermarium also bore the unmistakable marks of genocide, however.[10]

The slaughter had its dynamics, timing, and inner logic. Soviet mass murder spiked in the late teens and early twenties; it peaked in the early thirties with Terror-Famine, only to swallow fewer humans when it rematerialized in the late thirties and early forties, as well as, once again, to a much lesser extent, in the mid-forties. The Nazis butchery came in successive waves between 1941 and 1944, the most ferocious at the initial stage, leveling off and then picking up again in the middle, and somewhat abating at the end. Murder consistently tended to impact everyone, if not always to the same degree. For example, although in the interwar USSR at large Jews were exceptionally underrepresented among the casualties of the Red terror, earlier, during World War I, Bolshevik revolution, and Civil War, the Jewish community proportionally suffered at least as much as other nationalities in the Intermarium. However, at certain periods specific ethno-cultural groups were singled out for unspeakable bouts of bloodlust precisely because of their national origin. The Jews slaughtered in the Holocaust by the Nazis are the best known example (1941–1944). But, *toute proportion gardée*, there were also the Soviet Poles during the "Polish operation" of the NKVD (1937–1938). In each instance, the perpetrators *specifically* defined their victims by their ethno-cultural roots.

At other times there was no such clear cut designation. The Ukrainians constituted the largest category of the dead in Stalin's Terror-Famine, both in absolute numbers in Soviet Ukraine and percentagewise among all the nationalities of the USSR, though the murderers identified them as class enemies ("kulaks") to be exterminated and not as a national community per se. But the lack of a clear cut official designation by national criteria of the victims of forced collectivization in Ukraine should not stunt us. Killing peasants in Ukraine where the majority of farmers were Ukrainian means de facto murdering Ukrainians. The Soviet leadership was perfectly aware of this "happy coincidence." Further, since before and after the anti-kulak operation the Kremlin took bloody measures against the Ukrainian intelligentsia, both national Bolshevik and not, it is perfectly legitimate to view this general democide of the peasantry in the USSR also as a specific genocide of the Ukrainians. Under the Soviet terror ethnic and class categories often overlapped, in particular as far as minority peoples were concerned. In the Nazi savagery some of the non-Jewish victims experienced a combination of class-cum-race struggle as well. For instance, the Germans designated specifically the "Polish leadership stratum" for extermination both as "Slavic subhumans" (an ethnic/racial designation) and as representatives of the elite (the educated and upper class).

Precise statistics of death may never be known. So far we have estimated the following. Between 1914 and 1953, people of Ruthenian origin constituted the single largest category of victims in the Intermarium. In sheer numbers, the Ukrainians have the dubious distinction to have lost the most individuals of any group between the Black and Baltic seas. The Belarusians account for the largest losses relative to the size of that majority population in its domicile, in particular during World War II. Both the absolute and proportional losses of the Balts were relatively moderate, even though still staggering by Western European standards. The Christian Romanians and local non-Jewish minorities of the Moldavian lands incurred the smallest losses of anyone. This was mostly because, first, they were briefly liberated by Romania (1941-1944), whose forces treated the locals, their Romanian fellow compatriots, even much more gently than the Germans handled the Balts. Second, the relatively low level of casualties in the Moldavian lands stems from the fact that the Red terror before (1940-41) and after (1944-53) was comparable to the repression in the Baltics.

As for the minorities in the Intermarium, the Polish elite suffered horribly; it was virtually eliminated between 1917 and 1946. The non-elite Poles sustained losses proportional to the overall death statistics of the area or even locality they resided in. For instance, the Polish minority in Latvia suffered much less than its Polish counterparts in the White Ruthenian (Belarusian) lands. There were of course local variations; for instance, the Poles of Volhynia experienced far greater proportional and, possibly, numerical losses than the

Ukrainian population of that particular province. There was virtually no safe haven for Jews, of course. Under the jurisdiction of the Third Reich, their domicile made little difference in their ultimate fate: death to every Jewish child, woman, and man. They were even exterminated in the lands reconquered by Romania from the Soviets.

World War II was a watershed of far greater importance than anything else in the twentieth century Intermarium. It represented a nearly complete and seemingly final extermination of its society as it had been organically shaped and stratified for several hundred years by the Polish-Lithuanian Commonwealth. This cataclysm impacted everyone. It decimated the majority populations and it eliminated the traditional elites and the minorities. Chronologically, under the Soviet occupation between 1939 and 1941, it was the majority group in each state incorporated into the USSR that suffered most. This applies to the national elite, in particular. In absolute numbers, and the range and intensity of terror, the Christian Poles were the most victimized group followed by the Balts and others. The Poles were also the most common target of ordinary terror under the Nazi occupation. However, because the Jewish experience under Nazi rule was so extraordinarily horrific, the Jews were overall the most victimized group. Simply put, no one else but the Jews was slated for immediate and wholesale extermination. Denying this is a nationalist lie. And national history cannot rest on a lie; a nationalist lie is a lie all the same, even if it is intended to replace the lie of Communism.[11]

Thus, we need to reintegrate the Jewish past into the history of the Intermarium without denying the singularity of the Holocaust. But to do so, we need to restore the history of the Borderlands and to contextualize the great Jewish tragedy within the catastrophic experience of the Estonians, Latvians, Lithuanians, Ukrainians, Belarusians, Romanians (Moldovans), Poles, and others. Local history should be fostered, in particular, for it is the key to overcoming the terrible legacy of totalitarian atomization. The pursuit of the local past restores human links through oral history projects and case studies at the lowest rung of the newly free societies. And the universalistic message of the Polish-Lithuanian Commonwealth should be reconsidered as well since it is the principal historical phenomenon philosophically and spiritually binding the newly independent post-Soviet nations to the West. This must be accomplished not only for the sake of intellectual integrity, but also national security and regional stability.

Security and Stability

For now the post-Soviet sphere remains an area severely neglected at the strategic level by the US government. This neglect consistently cripples America's foreign policy endeavors on both regional and global dimensions. The chief problem is the lack of a proper perspective and, indeed, basic facts about the politics of Russia and its neighbors. This stems from flawed scholarship, particularly, most recently, "post-Sovietology"—the study of the post-Soviet sphere, which continues in the footsteps of Sovietology, the scholarship on Russia and the USSR undertaken during the Cold War.

Both Sovietology and post-Sovietology tend to be primarily focused on "theory." In other words, all too often they view their objects of interest through the lenses of theoretical constructs fashionable in the West. (A well-known Sovietological example was the application of "interest group" theory of modern political science to the Soviet system—an exercise that produced a severely distorted understanding of how that system actually worked). However, no political science or international relations theory envisioned the demise of the Soviet Union. Similarly, no amount of theorizing has been able to tackle the post-Soviet situation successfully. This is despite the enormous amount of resources made available to the postmodernist "theorizers" who, more often than not, scorn the empirical approach both to contemporary and historical problems.

Post-Sovietology has inherited many of the prejudices of its forerunner, Sovietology. It has conditioned US policymakers and academics to express four main attitudes. First, there is a tendency to concentrate on the Moscow center to the detriment of the periphery, which consists of the former Soviet republics and satellites, now constituted as a collection of sovereign nation states. Second, there is a reluctance to look at the period before the post-Soviet times (pre-Soviet developments, in particular) to comprehend the rich history and complex regional entanglements of the successor nation states. Third, there is a reflex to demonize the nationalisms of small nations. Fourth, there is a propensity to misunderstand, ignore, or downplay the political phenomenon of "post-Communism" in the post-Soviet sphere (just as previously there was a tendency to ignore nationalism in the early stages of the Cold War and underestimate the institutionalized tenacity of Soviet ideology in its latter stages). Post-Communism is a complex phenomenon consisting partly of: totalitarian-style institutional arrangements and personnel; socialist, statist ideology; and tactical mechanisms of Marxist-Leninist dialectics retained by the post-Communist elites to triumph in both foreign and domestic power struggles. Thus, post-Communism is mostly about continuities in behavior in the post-Soviet sphere.

As a result, American policy makers have largely failed to grasp the post-Soviet space on its own terms. Instead, the United States tends to address it via the unidimensional prism of our own latest trendy concerns, including globalism, multiculturalism, and sexual politics (including feminism and gay rights). All this is exacerbated by the penchant of an influential part of America's intellectual elite to conceptualize external reality, including US foreign policy, through academic trends such as postmodernism, deconstructionism, and other antirationalist currents. Thus, Cold War mirror-imaging, which adversely affected US foreign policy toward the Soviet Union, has now metastasized to afflict the post–Cold War era analysis of the Russian Federation and other successor states. The remedy to this situation necessitates relegating trendy intellectual propositions to the side and tackling the post-Soviet problem on its own terms. Policymakers and academics must be supplied with knowledge tainted neither by postmodernism and other antirational and antiempirical "methodologies" nor by the Moscow-centric *Weltanschauung* pandemic in both Sovietology and post-Sovietology. Such knowledge must derive from empirical studies of each of the significant national elements of the vast mosaic of the post-Soviet sphere.

Unfortunately, case studies of the non-Russian nations are still scarce. The few that exist often fail to appreciate their regional setting, sometimes tending to treat them even as anomalies. For example, a few years ago Yale University Press published a book *The Ukrainians: Unexpected Nation*. But Ukraine's statehood reaches back, from one perspective, a thousand years to Kievan *Rus'* or, from another perspective, five hundred to the Polish-Lithuanian-Ruthenian Commonwealth. And modern Ukrainian nationalism has been around for well over one hundred years. So what is the "unexpected nation?" It is only that which modern analysts fail to understand because of pervasive lack of knowledge of history and local nationalisms—an ignorance that would give novel discontinuities primacy and prominence over obscured continuities. Thus, *Rus'* and its history lamentably remain hidden or Russified and, therefore, Moscow-centric, and the Soviet Union sadly continues to serve as our universal frame of reference, despite its obvious interloper status in the area, not to mention its rumored demise, downsizing, and rebranding as the Russian Federation.

As a result, the United States is at a loss not only how to craft a successful global strategy vis-à-vis the Russian Federation in response to its attempted re-emergence as a global superpower but also how to react to "unexpected" local contingencies (the Russo-Georgian War of August 2008, the Russian cyberinvasion of Estonia in November 2008, the Russo-Ukrainian gas clash of December 2008,; the Russo-American joust over the air base in Kyrgyzstan of February 2009, the anti-Communist and anti-Russian youth riots in Moldova of April 2009, and the tragic Polish presidential plane crash[12] at Smolensk, Russia, of April 2010, to name a few). A successful response entails elucidating a regional policy toward the resurgent power of Moscow. It means understanding both Russia's neighbors and the Kremlin's reintegrationist ambitions. The latter are often expressed in terms of the old-fashioned spheres of influence. However, historically, for Moscow, the interference in the affairs of its neighbors has just been a prelude to full domination. This history remains mostly unknown.

The prospect of the post-Soviet nation states succumbing to Russia would be a dramatic reversal of the West's victory in the Cold War. It would also be a colossal waste of the enormous energy and resources the United States has poured into the post-Soviet sphere in the last twenty years. Last but not least, it would demonstrate plainly to the world's public opinion that the United States does not take its commitments to freedom and democracy seriously.

To restate, during the Cold War, America's foreign policy was simple. We only had to deal with a single adversary: the Soviet Union. Only the USSR constituted a grave threat to the United States. Only the Kremlin could have destroyed us with a push of a button. Other nations, Soviet allies or ideological comrades, including China, throughout the world were of much lesser importance to our national security concerns. Some of them, most notably the Warsaw Pact nations and the "Soviet nationalities," were directly subordinated to Moscow and had no autonomous foreign policy. Others, in particular Third World leftist tyrannies of the nonaligned movement, usually mimicked the Kremlin in their anti-Americanism, while using such hostile posturing to procure US and Western aid for themselves.

Having concentrated on the USSR, we neglected its enslaved minority peoples and its captive satellite nations. This stemmed from several sources. It partly reflected our tendency to treat the Communist behemoth as a monolith in congruence with the totalitarian paradigm. It also underscored the lazy preference of many American foreign policy experts to concentrate on the Soviet center and to ignore the peripheries. Simply, it was more convenient to deal with the single Moscow fount of power than to seek out and address the many confusing alternatives in the imperial provinces and satellites. Most of all, however, America's undifferentiated thinking about the USSR originated in the Moscow-centric view of the Soviet universe promoted by the Communist propaganda, which drew its inspiration from the pre-1917 Russian tradition. According to this tradition, there is nothing but Russia and the Russians in the Russian/Soviet/post-Soviet sphere.

The systemic neglect of the non-Moscow-centric Soviet areas and peoples was remedied somewhat by the robust US foreign policy of the 1980s. However, that policy was quickly discontinued and the post-Soviet space fell into oblivion. Once again, the Moscow-centric approach serves many an American policymaker as a guide post to post-Communist Russia. Once again, it is to our detriment that we ignore the alternatives. The woeful inadequacy of the Moscow-centric paradigm haunts us periodically.

The strategic necessity of a study of the Intermarium, in general, and its most combustive ideological forces, nationalism and (post-)Communism, is becoming more apparent over time. Russian National Security Doctrine has portended the reabsorption of these areas into the Russian political space since 1992. How would it impact the American interests? First, a Russian takeover would indubitably crush local democracies, political systems compatible with ours, which we helped to re-establish after the collapse of Communism. Second, it would eliminate the most pro-American part of Europe from the international scene, that part which has been more supportive of US foreign policies than many of our other traditional European allies have been. Third, it would close the emerging markets of Central and Eastern Europe to the United States. Fourth, it would deny our European allies access to alternative suppliers of energy resources and make them even more dependent on Moscow. Fifth, it would seriously undermine American credibility among our allies in Western Europe and throughout the world. Sixth, by the same token, US inactivity before a Muscovite aggression would embolden rogue regimes and their emulators everywhere. Seventh, it would be a strategic disaster for the balance of power in Europe exposing the EU to the tender mercies of the Kremlin and tempting it to switch alliances.

Although Russia has vowed to subjugate the Intermarium, or, "the near abroad," as the Kremlin calls it, the prevention of such a contingency is essential for the protection of American natural interests for several reasons. The most important relates to the region's value in enabling the United States to continue in its pre-eminent position in Europe. The debate over NATO expansion highlighted the strategic necessity of our maintaining this pre-eminence on the Old Continent. So long as the newly independent nations of Central and Eastern Europe could enjoy the same benefits of peace and security afforded by NATO's protective umbrella, they had a greater incentive to build democracy and bury old irredentist ambitions and historic grudges thus contributing not only to peace but to prosperity of the continent. Maintaining this peace and prosperity has proven and, if managed properly by American diplomacy, will continue to prove to be an enormously cost-effective investment in our own security and continental interests. But this diplomacy necessarily entails the delicate task of preventing Russia's military and political expansion westward, while encouraging its economic and cultural engagement with us. It also involves the proper management of the geo-strategic attributes of the Intermarium—its strategic resources, particularly energy, and its transit routes. This, in turn, necessitates attention to European energy independence and preventing Russia from its persistent policy of energy embargo as a way of pressuring both Eastern and Western Europe.

The continued presence of the United States in Europe guarantees that the European Union remains on the trans-Atlanist political course and Brussels refrains from asserting itself against Washington. Otherwise, the EU, under Berlin's newly assertive leadership, might seek a realignment of its alliance system with Moscow, and given China's emerging power, possibly even with Beijing. A Brussels/Berlin–Moscow–Beijing axis would be a geostrategic calamity for the United States. To offset such a possibility, Washington should not only maintain its traditional ties with London, but also with the newly independent European nations of the post-Soviet sphere. It is in the best interest of America to foster the success of democratic and free political systems there because, at the least, it is more convenient to deal with nations that share similar values as we do, rather than with dictatorships or "sovereign democracies," as some at the Kremlin like to refer to the Russian Federation and its allies. Last but not least, recognition of the affinities of the nations of the Intermarium with the United States has strategic implications for third areas. For example, it is those countries of "New Europe" who have been more supportive of US policies in the Middle East than the countries of "Old Europe." The United States must not forget that it is better to have allies on some of these policy issues than no allies at all.

To summarize, after the Partitions of the Polish-Lithuanian Commonwealth, two world wars, Soviet colonization, political realism, and a huge dose of home-grown and Soviet-imported leftism, only recently has the Intermarium begun to emerge in America's consciousness. On a negative plane, it serves as a backdrop to the Holocaust; on a positive one, it evokes Poland's "Solidarity" and other nonviolent national liberation movements as well as late Pope John Paul II and the "New Europe," populated by reliable allies of the United States.

For US foreign policy and academia the Intermarium constitutes a serious challenge but also presents potential benefits. History is alive in the east. Sorting out the past is the key to the future.

Notes

1. Nowadays flattery wins friends, the truth begets hatred.
2. "Pisałem prawdę, przynajmniej tak, jak ją pojmowałem, że miłuję i moich ziomków, i wszystkich ludzi; że jako człowiek i chrześcijanin potępiam wszystkie nienawiści, tak prywatne, jako i narodowe, że miłując ludzi, nienawidzę tylko te ich wady które, robiąc ich głuchymi na wszelkie nauki przeszłości, na ich przyszłość zgubne rzucają nasiona. Złe zasady są niebezpieczniejsze od złych uczynków, i tylko tym pierwszym odważyłem się wypowiedzieć wojnę." See Henryk Rzewuski, *Listopad* [November] (Kraków: Universitas, 2000), 63–64. This is a reprint of the 1936 edition; the original was first published in three volumes in 1845–1846 in St. Petersburg.
3. "Otóż obowiązkiem każdego myślącego człowieka jest zastanawianie się nad przyczynami zjawisk, wydobywanie prawdy przez oddzielanie ziarna od plew, a nie mieszanie wszystkiego w jeden bezmyślny korzec." See Józef Mackiewicz, "Na zgliszczach Polski," ("On the Smoldering Ruins of Poland") in *Gazeta Codzienna* (March 23–25, 1940) [Wilno], reprinted in *Nudis Verbis* (London: Kontra, 2003), 273.
4. For restoring memory about the Borderlands see Adam Wierciński, *Przywracanie pamięci* (Opole: Wydawnictwo Uniwersytetu Opolskiego, 1997). See also an interesting literary endeavor regarding the Crimean Tatars: Lily Hyde, *Dream Land: One Girl's Struggle to Find Her True Home* (London: Walker Books, 2008).
5. Juliana Geran Pilon, *The Bloody Flag: Post-Communist Nationalism in Eastern Europe: Spotlight on Rumania* (New Brunswick, NJ and London: Transaction Publishers, 1992), 1, 32–33, 35.
6. John Radziłowski, "The Neo-Stalinist Discourse in Polish Historical Studies in the United States," *Golden Harvest or Hearts of Gold? Studies on the Fate of Warteime Poles and Jews*, ed. by Marek Jan Chodakiewicz, Wojciech Jerzy Muszyński, and Paweł Styrna (Washington, DC: Leopolis Press, 2012), 239–53.

7.   Western efforts were woefully inadequate, first, because the Communists either outright barred Western scholars from the archives or showed them only small parts of their documentary collections. Further, many Western academics who dealt with populations under the Soviet yoke were Communists, other leftists, or liberals at least somewhat sympathetic to the ruling regime. Peter Stachura makes this point best in regards to Poland. See Peter Stachura, *Poland, 1918–1945: An Interpretive and Documentary History of the Second Republic* (London and New York: Routledge, 2004). And see my review of his work in *The Polish Review* XLIX, no. 4 (2004): 1155–59. Last but not least, recently, more than a few Western scholars have been too enamored of "theory" (deconstruction, historicism, etc.) to apply themselves to solid research. As a result, they produce a skewed picture of history of the captive nations. This brought them praise among the like-minded in Western academia but failed to assist in any way in restoring history as it was. See, e.g., Brian Porter, *When Nationalism Began to Hate: Imagining Modern Politics in Nineteenth-Century Poland* (New York: Oxford University Press, 2000); its review by John Radziłowski in *Kosmas: Czechoslovak and Central European Review* 15, no. 1 (Fall 2001): 97–99; and my review of Porter's work in "Nacjonalizm wyobrażony," ("Nationalism Imagined") *Arcana* no. 6 (60) (2004): 167–86. See also a somewhat novice attempt to come to grips with the western part of the former Soviet empire in Timothy Snyder, *The Reconstruction of Nations: Poland, Ukraine, Lithuania, Belarus, 1569–1999* (New Haven, CT and London: Yale University Press, 2003). For a much deeper understanding of the area see Oscar Halecki, *Borderlands of Western Civilization: A History of East Central Europe* (New York: The Ronald Press Company, 1952); Piotr Wandycz, *A History of East Central Europe from the Middle Ages to the Present*, 2nd edn. (London and New York: Routledge, 2001); and the travelogue of Anne Applebaum, *Between East and West: Across the Borderlands of Europe* (New York: Pantheon Books, 1994).

8.   This sorry state of affairs is amply documented in John J. Kulczycki, "Eastern Europe in Western Civilization Textbooks: The Example of Poland," *The History Teacher* 38, no. 2 (February 2005): 153–77.

9.   Rebecca West, *Black Lamb and Grey Falcon: A Journey through Yugoslavia* (New York and London: Penguin Books, 1994), 842–43, 1100–1101.

10. See R. J. Rummel, *Death by Government* (New Brunswick, NJ: Transaction Publishers, 1997); Raphael (Rafal) Lemkin, "Genocide—A Modern Crime," *Free World* (April 1945): 39–43; Raphael (Rafal) Lemkin, "Genocide as a Crime Under International Law," *American Journal of International Law* 41, no. 1 (January 1947): 145–51; G. A. Finch, "The Genocide Convention," *American Journal of International Law* 43, no. 4 (October 1949): 732–38; William A. Schabas, *Genocide in International Law: The Crime of Crimes* (New York, NY: Cambridge University Press, 2009). See further Jacques Semelin, *Purify and Destroy: The Political Uses of Massacre and Genocide* (New York: Columbia University Press, 2007); Ben Kiernan, *Blood and Soil: A World History of Genocide and Extermination from Sparta to Darfur* (New Haven, CT and London: Yale University Press, 2007).

11. See Alain Besançon, *A Century of Horrors: Communism, Nazism, and the Uniqueness of the Shoah* (Wilmington, DE: ISI Books, 2007); and Omer Bartov, *Erased: Vanishing Traces of Jewish Galicia in Present-Day Ukraine* (Princeton, NJ and Oxford: Princeton University Press, 2007).

12. The Smolensk plane crash of April 10, 2010—resulting in the tragic death of the Polish Presidential couple, Lech and Maria Kaczyński, and their entire entourage

consisting of Poland's political and military elite, a grand total of ninety-six victims—had an important and detrimental impact on the geopolitics of the Intermarium. Poland's liberal government feared antagonizing Moscow to the point of failing to perform the most elementary due diligence in the wake of the crash. Hence, the black boxes and the wreck of the Polish Tupolev remain in Russia two years after the crash. The Russian stonewalling and the Polish government's pusillanimity have even prompted some to suggest that President Kaczyński, a leader hated at the Kremlin, was actually assassinated. Whatever the exact cause of the air disaster, it certainly shattered Kaczyński's policy of rallying the nations of the Intermarium around Warsaw. Following the crash, this grand strategy was reversed in favor of appeasing Moscow. Meanwhile, the United States did virtually nothing either to investigate the suspicious death of leaders of one of its staunchest NATO allies or to counter Russia's political warfare in the wake of the disaster. See *The Smolensk White Book*, forthcoming from IWP/Leopolis Press.

Appendix I

The Death Toll in the Intermarium during the Twentieth Century (in millions)

Number of deaths as result of:	Belarus	Estonia	Latvia	Lithuania	Moldova	Poland**	Ukraine
World War I: 1914–1918	n/a	n/a	.009	n/a	n/a	.5	.496
Communist revolution, civil war in former Russian Empire, Polish–Bolshevik War: 1917/18–1921	n/a	.0023	n/a	n/a	n/a	.04	1.5
Soviet genocide of Poles/NKVD "Polish Operation": 1937–1938	n/a		n/a		n/a	n/a	.111*** / .250
Terror-Famine/*Holodomor*: 1932–1933	n/a		n/a		n/a	n/a	3 / 6
Other Soviet policies: 1917–1939	2(?)		n/a		n/a	n/a	n/a
Soviet terror in occupied territories: 1939–1941	n/a		.005		.008	.058 / .1	n/a
World War II and German occupation: 1939–1944/45	.4		.015		.150 / .161	4.2 / 7****	1
Communist policies: 1944/45–1953	.03		.035		.216	.03	.085
Totals:	2.03		.0663		.374 / .385	4.8 / 7.67	6.2 / 9.33
Grand total:	Minimum:				13.47		
	Maximum:				19.48****		

Note: In many cases mentioned above, the data is incomplete or simply unavailable due to restrictions in accessing archives and other factors. Once more information surfaces, the death statistics will most likely increase (e.g., collectivization and Great Terror in Soviet Belarus).

† In split cells, the number above represents the minimum figure while the figure below is a maximum one.

†† We are referring to the citizens of the Polish state within its interwar frontiers before 1945. Figures after 1945 refer to Poland's postwar boundaries.

††† The "Polish Operation" of the NKVD took place not only in the Ukrainian SSR but also in Belarusian SSR and the Soviet Russian interior. About two-thirds of the victims were killed in areas adjacent to the Soviet–Polish frontier in the Ukrainian and Belarusian SSRs.

†††† Includes approximately 2.9–3.2 million Polish Jews murdered by the Nazis.

††††† It is important to juxtapose these figures with the death toll in the USSR, which, according to Robert Conquest, claimed approximately 30 million lives. In turn, the meticulous R. J. Rummel argues that as many as 62 million people may have been exterminated by the Bolshevik regime. Divorcing these numbers from the death statistics in the Intermarium is, of course, quite challenging due to overlapping numbers, as in the case of the Terror-Famine in the Soviet Ukraine

Appendix II

Maps

Map 1.
Early Slavic Settlement, c. Eighth Century AD

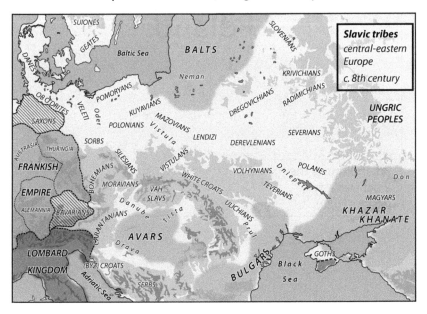

Map 2.
Early Medieval Poland, c. 1020

Old Prussia

Lithu-
ania

Veleti
Union

Kievan
Rus'

Misnia

Poland

Bohemia

Poland under the
Piast Dynasty
(about 1020)

Hungary

Map 3.
The Intermarium under the Jagiellonian Dynasty, c. 1500

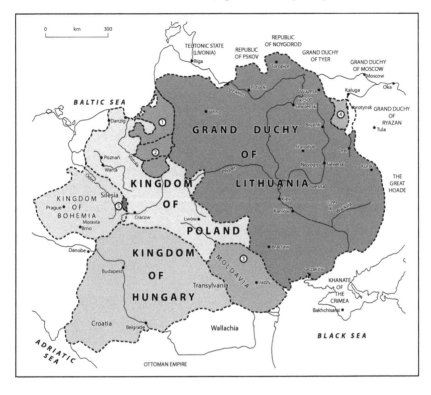

Map 4.
The Polish-Lithuanian Commonwealth, Seventeenth Century

Map 5.
The Partitions of the Commonwealth, Late Eighteenth Century

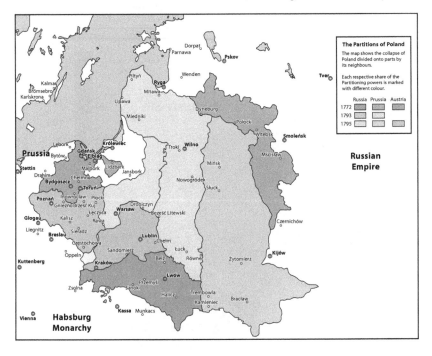

Map 6.
The Jewish Pale of Settlement in the Romanov Empire Nineteenth Century
(percentage of Jewish population)

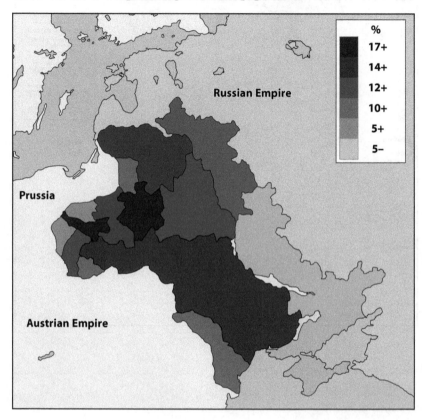

Map 7.
Central and Eastern Europe c. 1910

- – – – International boundaries
- ——— Boundaries of semi-independent kingdoms, duchies, principalities, and free cities
- – – – – Provincial boundaries
- ·············· Boundaries of counties, districts, and departments

- ⊕ State capitals
- ⦿ Capitals of kingdoms, duchies, and principalities
- ○ Provincial capitals
- ○ Departmental centers
- KOSOVA Names of provinces other than capitals

Scale 1:8 890 000

0 ——— 150 miles
0 ——— 150 kilometers

Map 8.
The Intermarium between the World Wars (c. 1921)

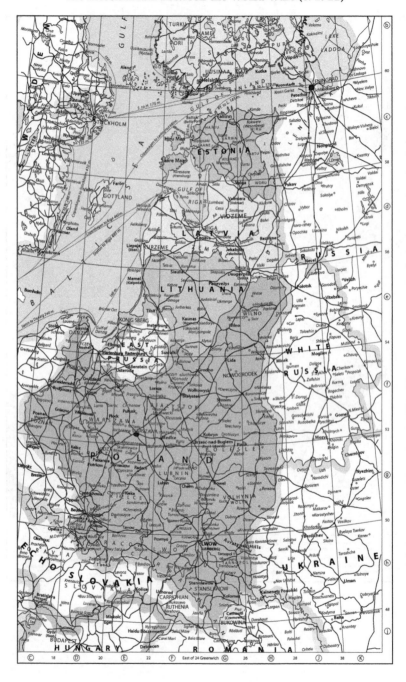

Map 9.
Central and Eastern Europe in the Wake of World War II

Map 10.
The Postcommunist Intermarium after the Soviet Collapse

Bibliography

Primary Sources

Public Archives and Depositories:

Archiwum Akt Nowych (AAN, Archive of New Records), Warsaw, Poland.

Archiwum Instytutu Historii Polskiej Akademii Nauk (Archive of the Institute of History of the Polish Academy of Sciences), Warsaw, Poland.

Archiwum Państwowe (State Archive), Białystok, Poland.

Archiwum Państwowe (State Archive), Lublin, Poland.

Archiwum Zakładu Historii Ruchu Ludowego (AZHRL, the Archive of the Institute for the History of the Peasant Movement), Warsaw, Poland.

Archiwum Żydowskiego Instytutu Historycznego (AŻIH, Archives of the Jewish Historical Institute), Warsaw, Poland.

Genocido aukų muziejus (Museum of Genocide Victims), Vilnius, Lithuania.

Gosudarstvennyi Arkhiv Rossiiskoi Federatsii (GARF, the State Archive of the Russian Federation), Moscow, Russia.

Hoover Institution Archives (HIA), Stanford, California.

Instytut Pamięci Narodowej (IPN, Institute of National Remembrance), Warsaw, Poland.

Latvijas Okupācijas muzejs (Museum of the Occupation of Latvia 1940–1991), Riga, Latvia.

Lietuvos Visuomenes Organizaciju Archyvas (LVOA, Lithuanian Archives of Public Organizations), Vilnius, Lithuania.

Okupatsioonide Muuseum (Museum of Occupations), Tallin, Estonia.

Rossiiskaya Gosudarstvennaya Biblioteka (Russian State Library), Moscow, Russia.

Rossiiski Gosudarstvennyi Arkhiv Sotsialno-Politicheskoi Istorii (Russian State Archive of Social-Political History), Moscow, Russia.

Rossiiski Gosudarstvennyi Voennyi Arkhiv (Russian State Military Archive), Moscow, Russia.

United States Holocaust Memorial Museum, Washington, DC, USA.

Yad Vashem Archives, Jerusalem, Israel.

Published Documentary Collections:

Akcja "Wisła," 1947 (Warsaw and Kiev: Instytut Pamięci Narodowej KŚZpNP, Archiwum MSWiA RP, Państwowe Archiwum Służby Bezpieczeństwa Ukrainy, 2006).

Allworth, Edward, ed., *Tatars of the Crimea: Their Struggle for Survival: Original Studies from North America, Unofficial and Official Documents from Czarist and Soviet Sources* (Durham and London: Duke University Press, 1988).

Aptekar, P. A., Chizhov, L. B., and Eliseeva, N. E., eds., *Krest'anskoe vosstanie na Tambovshchine (1921–22 gg.): Komplekt dokumentov iz fondov TsGASA (Peasant Rising in the Tambov Area: A Collection of Documents)* (Moscow: TsGASA, 1991).

Aptekar, P. A., Chizhov, L. B., and Eliseeva, N. E., eds., *Povstancheskie dvizheniia na Ukraine 1921 g.: Komplekt dokumentov iz fondov TsGASA (Insurgent Activities in the Ukraine: A Collection of Documents)* (Moscow: TsGASA, 1991).

Arad, Yitzhak, Gutman, Yisrael, and Margaliot, Abraham, eds., *Documents of the Holocaust: Selected Sources on the Destruction of the Jews of Germany and Austria, Poland, and the Soviet Union* (Jerusalem: Yad Vashem, 1981).

Bordiugow, Giennadij A. et al., eds., *Polska–ZSRR: Struktury podległości: Dokumenty WKP(b), 1944–1949 (Poland–USSR: The Structures of Dependence: Documents of the VKP(b), 1944–1949)* (Warsaw: ISP PAN and Stowarzyszenie Współpracy Polska-Wschód, 1995).

Chernoglazova, R. A., ed., *Tragediia evreev belorussii v gody nemetskoi okkupatsii (1941–1945): Sbornik materialov i dokumentov (The Tragedy of the Jews of Belarussia during the German Occupation)* (Minsk: Ia. B. Dremach, 1995).

Chodakiewicz, Marek Jan, and Muszyński, Wojciech Jerzy, *Żeby Polska była polska: Antologia publicystyki konspiracyjnej podziemia narodowego, 1939–1950 (Let Poland be Polish: An Anthology of the Nationalist Press during the Nazi and Soviet Occupations)* (Warsaw: Instytut Pamięci Narodowej, 2010).

Chodakiewicz, Marek Jan, Gontarczyk, Piotr, and Żebrowski, Leszek, eds., *Tajne Oblicze: Dokumenty GL-AL i PPR, 1942–1945,* 3 vols. (*Secret Face: Documents of the Communist Underground*) (Warsaw: Burchard Edition, 1997–1999).

Deportatsii z zakhodni zemli Ukrainy kintsia 30-kh – pochatku 50-kh r.r.: Dokumenty, materiali, spokhadi, (Deportations from Western Ukraine from the End of the 1930s until the Beginning of the 1950s: Documents, Materials, Essays) 3 vols. (Lviv: Natsional'na Akademia Nauk Ukrainy im. I. Krypiakevycha, 2003).

Dudek, Antoni, ed., *Zmierzch dyktatury: Polska lat 1986–1989 w świetle dokumentów,* vol 1: *(lipiec 1986–maj 1989) (The Twilight of the Dictatorship: Poland during 1986–1989 According to Documents (July 1986–May 1989))* (Warszawa: Instytut Pamięci Narodowej, KŚZpNP, 2009).

Gnatowski, Michał, *Niepokorna Białostocczyzna: Opór społeczny i polskie podziemie niepodległościowe w regionie białostockim w latach 1939–1941 w radzieckich źródłach* (*The Unbending Bialystok Region: Civil Resistance and the Polish Independentist Underground in the Bialystok Area, 1939–1941, According to Soviet Documents*) (Białystok: Instytut Historii Uniwersytetu w Bialymstoku, 2001).

Holodomor: The Great Famine in Ukraine, 1932–1933 (Warsaw-Kiev: The Institute of National Remembrance-Commission of the Prosecution of Crimes against the Polish Nation, Ministry of Interior and Administration, Republic of Poland, The Security Services of Ukraine Branch State Archives, Institute of Political and Ethno-National Studies at the National Academy of Sciences of Ukraine, 2009).

Isaievych, Iaroslav, ed., *Volyn i Kholmshchyna 1938–1947 rr.: Polsko-ukrainske protystoiannia ta ioho vidlunnia. Doslidzhennia, dokumenty, spohady* (*Volhynia and the Chełm Area, 1938–1945: Polish-Ukrainian Relations*) (Lviv: Natsionalna akademiia nauk Ukrainy, Instytut ukrainoznavstva im. I. Krypiakevycha, 2003).

Kącka, Bożena, and Stępka, Stanisław, eds., *Repatriacja ludności polskiej z ZSRR 1955–1959: Wybór dokumentów* (*The Repatriation of the Polish Population from the USSR 1955–1959: A Selection of Documents*) (Warsaw: SGGW, 1994).

Kostiushko, I.I., ed., *Pol'sko-sovetskaia voina, 1919–1920: Ranee ne opublikovannye dokumenty i materialy* (*Polish-Soviet War, 1919–1920: Formerly Unpublished Documents and Material*), 2 vols. (Moscow: Institut slavianovedeniia i balkanistiki RAN, 1994).

Miliakova, Lidia B., ed., *Kniga pogromov: Pogromy na Ukraine, v Belorussii i evropeiskoi chaste Rossii v period Grazhdanskoi voiny 1918–1922 gg. Sbornik dokumentov* (*The Book of Pogroms: Pogroms in Ukraine, Belarus, and European Russia during the Civil War Period of 1918–1922: A Collection of Documents*) (Moscow: ROSSP-EN, 2007).

Mozgunova, G. N., Korsak, A. V., and Levitin, M. N., eds., *Sud'by natsional'nykh men'shinstv na Smolenshchine, 1918–1938 gg. Dokumenty i materialy Arkhivnogo upravleniia Administratsii Smolenskoi oblasti* (*The Fate of National Minorities in the Smolensk Region, 1918–1938: Documents and Materials from the Archival Authority of the Administration of the Smolensk Region*) (Smolensk: Gosudarstvennyi arkhiv Smolenskoi oblasti, 1994).

Mykhailychenko, H. M., Shatalina, I. P., and Kul'chyt'skyi, S. V., eds., *Kolektyvizatsiia i holod na Ukraini, 1929–1933. Zbirnyk dokumentiv i materialiv* (*Collectivization and Hunger in the Ukraine: A Collection of Documents and Materials*) (Kiev: Naukova dumka, 1993).

Noskova, A. F., et al., eds., *NKVD i polskoe podpole, 1944–1945 (Po "Osobym papkam" I. V. Stalina)* (*NKVD and the Polish Underground, 1944–1945 (Stalin's Personal File)*) (Moskva: Institut slavianovedeniia i balkanistiki RAN, 1994).

Petrusheva, L. I., Teplova, E. F., and Trukan, G. A., eds., *Rossiia antibol'shevistskaia: Iz belogvardeiskikh i emigrantskikh arkhivov* (*Anti-Bolshevik*

Russia: From White Guard and Emigré Archives) (Moscow: Institut Rossiiskoi istorii RAN, 1995).

Polacy i Ukraińcy między dwoma systemami totalitarnymi, 1942–1945 (Poles and Ukrainians between Two Totalitarian Systems, 1942–1945) (Warsaw and Kiev: Wydawnictwo Rytm, Instytut Pamięci Narodowej KŚZpNP, Archiwum MSWiA RP, Państwowe Archiwum Służby Bezpieczeństwa Ukrainy, 2005).

Polskie podziemie 1939–1941: Lwów, Kołomyja, Stryj, Złoczów (Polish Underground, 1939–1941: Lwów, Kołomyja, Stryj, Złoczów) (Warsaw and Kiev: Wydawnictwo Rytm, IPN KśZpNP, Archiwum MSWiA RP, Państwowe Archiwum Służby Bezpieczeństwa Ukrainy, 1998).

Polskie podziemie na terenach Zachodniej Ukrainy i Zachodniej Białorusi w latach 1939–1941, (Polish Underground in Western Ukraine and Western Belarus between 1939 and 1941) 2 vols. (Warsaw and Moscow: Wydawnictwo Rytm, Ministerstwo Spraw Wewnętrznych i Administracji Rzeczpospolitej Polskiej and Służba Bezpieczeństwa Federacji Rosyjskiej, 2001).

Powstanie Warszawskie 1944 w dokumentach z archiwów służb specjalnych (Warszawa and Moscow: Instytut Pamięci Narodowej, Komisja Ścigania Zbrodni przeciwko Narodowi Polskiemu, Ministerstwo Spraw Wewnętrznych i Administracji Rzeczpospolitej Polskiej and Służba Bezpieczeństwa Federacji Rosyjskiej, 2007).

Pyrih, R. Ia., et al., ed., *Holod 1932–1933 rokiv na Ukraini. Ochyma istorykiv, movuiu dokumentiv (Hunger of 1932–1933 in the Ukraine: According to Historians and Documents)* (Kiev: Vydavnytstvo politichnoi literatury Ukrainy, 1990).

Segel, Harold B., ed., *Political Thought in Renaissance Poland: An Anthology in English* (New York: PIASA Books, 2003).

Romano, Andrea, Tarkhova, N. S., and Bettanin, Fabio, eds., *Krasnaia Armiia i kollektivizatsiia derevni v SSSR, 1928–1933 gg. Sbornik dokumentov iz fondov Rossiiskogo gosudarstvennogo voennogo arkhiva (Red Army and Collectivization of Agriculture in the USSR, 1928–1933: A Collection of Documents from the Russian State War Archive)* (Napoli: Istituto universitario orientale, 1996).

Verstiuk V. F., et al., eds., *Ukrainska Tsentralna Rada: Dokumenty i materialy (Ukrainian Central Council: Documents and Materials)*, 2 vols. (Kiev: Naukova dumka, 1996–1997).

Vladimirtsev, N. I., and Kokurin, A. I., eds., *Sbornik dokumentov: NKVD-MVD SSR v bor'be s banditizmom i vooruzhennym natsionalisticheskim podpol'em na Zapadnoi Ukraine, v Zapadnoi Belorussii i Pribaltike (1939–1956) (A Collection of Documents: NKVD-MVD of the USSR against Banditry and Armed Nationalist Underground in Western Ukraine, Western Belarus, and the Baltics)* (Moscow: Ob'iedinennaia redaktsia MVD Rossii, 2008).

Diaries, Memoirs, Recollections, Travelogues:

Applebaum, Anne, *Between East and West: Across the Borderlands of Europe* (New York: Pantheon Books, 1994).

Chodakiewicz, Marek Jan, "Notatki z post-Sowiecji ," (Notes from the Post-Soviet Lands), parts I–IV, *Najwyższy Czas!* (October/November 2010).

Friedman, George, "Geopolitical Journey with George Friedman," http://www.stratfor.com/theme/special_series_geopolitical_journey_george_friedman.

Korchak, Ruzhka, *Plamia pod peplom* (Tel Aviv: Biblioteka-Alija, 1977).

Kramer, Mark, *Travels with a Hungry Bear: A Journey to the Russian Heartland* (New York: Houghton Mifflin, 1996).

Kuberska, Maria, *To było życie . . . Wspomnienia z Kazachstanu 1936–1996* (*This Was Life: A Memoir from Kazakhstan, 1936–1996*) (Warszawa: Pax, 2006).

Łoziński, Mieczysław, *Polonia nieznana* (*The Unknown Polonia*) (Kłodawa and Konin: Drukarnia Braci Wielińskich, 2005).

Meysztowicz, X. Walerian, *Poszło z dymem: Gawędy o czasach i ludziach* (*Up in Smoke: The Tales of Times and People*) (London: Polska Fundacja Kulturalna, 1973).

Puttkamer Żółtowska, Janina, *Inne czasy, inni ludzie* (*Different Times, Different People*) (London: Polska Fundacja Kulturalna, 1998).

Renik, Krzysztof, *Podpolnicy - rozmowy z ludźmi Kościoła na Litwie, Łotwie, Białorusi i Ukrainie 1990–1991* (*The People of the Underground: Conversation with Church Persons in Lithuania, Latvia, Belarus, and Ukraine, 1990–1991*) (Warszawa: Oficyna Wydawnictwa Przeglądu Powszechnego, 1991).

Ryżko, Father Stanisław, *"Trzeba zostać"* (*We Must Remain*) (Lublin: Norbertinum, 1999).

Ryżko, Father Stanisław, *Kronika kościoła rzymsko-katolickiego w Łahiszynie: Listy i notatki z lat 1956–1984* (*A Chronicle of the Roman Catholic Church in Łahiszyn: Letters and Notes from 1956–1984*) (Warszawa: Księża Orioniści, 1995).

Ryżko, Father Stanisław, *Z Panem Bogiem w łagrach* (*With the Lord God in the Camps*) (Lublin: Norbertinum, 2004).

Sapieha, Eustachy, *Tak było: Niedemokratyczne wspominienia Eustachego Sapiehy* (*That's How It Was: Undemocratic Memoirs of Eustachy Sapieha*) (Warszawa: Wydawnictwo Safari Poland, 1999).

Siedlar-Kołyszko, Teresa, *Byli, są. Czy będą . . .?* (*They Were, They Are. Will They Be . . .?*) (Kraków: Oficyna Wydawnicza "Impuls," 2006).

Świderski, Józef, *Śmierć na czarnoziemie* (*Death on Black Soil*) (Łódź: By the author, 2000).

West, Rebecca, *Black Lamb and Grey Falcon: A Journey through Yugoslavia* (New York and London: Penguin Books, 1994).

Wschodnie losy Polaków (*Eastern Fates of the Poles*), 6 vols. (Łomża: Oficyna Wydawnicza Stopka, 1991–1996).

Government Publications, Atlases, Reports, and Demographic Studies:

"Government Portal: Web Portal of the Ukrainian Government," http://www.kmu.gov.ua/control/.

Bater, James H., *The Soviet Scene: A Geographical Perspective* (New York: Edward Arnold, 1989).

Bruchis, Michael, *The USSR: Language and Realities: Nations, Leaders, and Scholars* (New York: Columbia University Press, 1988).

Drengsgaard, Linda, and Hansen, Ole Hersted, "State of the State in Estonia," Demstar Research Report no. 12, Department of Political Science, University of Aarhus (March 2003): 1–56, http://www.demstar.dk/papers/EstoniaSOTS.pdf.

Drengsgaard, Linda, Hansen, Ole Hersted, and Brøgger, Line, "State of the State in Lithuania," Demstar Research Report no. 19, University of Aarhus, Department of Political Science (July 2004): 1–41, http://www.demstar.dk/papers/SotSLithuania[1].pdf.

Eberhardt, Piotr, *Przemiany ludnościowe na Ukrainie XX wieku (Demographic Transformation in Ukraine in the 20th Century)* (Warszawa: Biblioteka "Obozu," 1994).

Eberhardt, Piotr, *Przemiany narodowościowe na Białorusi (Demographic Transformation in Belarus)* (Warszawa: Editions Spotkania, [1994]).

Eberhardt, Piotr, *Przemiany narodowościowe na Litwie (Demographic Transformation in Lithuania)* (Warszawa: Przegląd Wschodni, 1997).

Frucht, Richard, *Eastern Europe: An Introduction to the People, Lands, and Culture* (Santa Barbara, CA: ABC-CLIO, 2005).

International Monetary Fund, *Moldova* (IMF Economic Reviews) (Washington, DC: International Monetary Fund, 1993).

Kozlov, Viktor, *The Peoples of the Soviet Union* (The Second World Series), trans. Pauline M. Tiffen (Bloomington, IN: Indiana University Press, 1988).

Magocsi, Paul Robert, *Historical Atlas of Central Europe* (Seattle, WA: University of Washington Press, 2002).

Maryański, Andrzej, *Przemiany ludnościowe w ZSRR (Demographic Transformations in the USSR)* (Warsaw and Kraków: Centrum Badań Wschodnich Uniwersytetu Warszawskiego i Wyższa Szkoła Pedagogiczna w Krakowie, 1995).

Newton, Melanie, and Tolz, Vera, eds. *The USSR in 1991: A Record of Events* (Boulder, CO: Westview Press, 1993).

Newton, Melanie, and Tolz, Vera, eds., *The USSR in 1989: A Record of Events* (Boulder, CO: Westview Press, 1990).

Newton, Melanie, and Tolz, Vera, eds., *The USSR in 1990: A Record of Events* (Boulder, CO: Westview Press, 1992).

Nørgaard, Ole, Hansen, Ole Hersted, Ostrovska, Ilze, and Møller, Louise Pape, "State of the State in Latvia," Demstar, Research Report no. 1, University of Aarhus, Department of Political Science (May 2000): 1–51, http://www.demstar.dk/papers/LatviaStateOf.pdf.

Olson, James Stuart, Pappas, Lee Brigance, and Pappas, Nicholas C. J., *Ethnohistorical Dictionary of the Russian and Soviet Empires* (Westport, CT: Greenwood Press, 1994).

Poland: A Country Study (Washington, DC: GPO for the Library of Congress, 1992), http://countrystudies.us/poland/90.htm.

Ramet, Sabrina, ed., *Central and Southeast European Politics since 1989* (Cambridge and New York: Cambridge University Press, 2010).
Sulimierski, Filip, Chlebowski, Bronisław, and Walewski, Władysław, *Słownik geograficzny Królestwa Polskiego i innych krajów słowiańskich* (*Geographic Dictionary of the Polish Kingdom and Other Slavic Countries*), 15 vols. (Warszawa: Wydawnictwa Artystyczne i Filmowe, 1975–1977).
The First Book of Demographics for the Republics of the Former Soviet Union, 1951–1990 (Shady Side, MD: New World Demographics, 1992).
The Historical Atlas of Poland (Warszawa and Wrocław: Państwowe Przedsiębiorstwo Wydawnictw Kartograficznych, 1986).
US State Department's Bureau of European and Eurasian Affairs.
Wixman, Ronald, *The Peoples of the USSR: An Ethnographic Handbook* (Armonk, NY: M.E. Sharpe, 1984).
Wnuk, Rafał et al., eds., *Atlas polskiego podziemia niepodległościowego: The Atlas of the Independence Underground in Poland, 1944–1956* (Warsaw and Lublin: Instytut Pamięci Narodowej, 2007).
World Bank, *Statistical Handbook: States of the Former USSR* (Studies of Economies in Transformation, No. 3) (Washington, DC: The World Bank, 1992).
World Factbook (CIA).
Zickel, Raymond E., ed., *Soviet Union: A Country Study* (Washington, DC: GPO, 1991).

Press:

Boston Globe
Economist
Financial Times
Gazeta Wyborcza
Guardian
Los Angeles Times
Moldova Socialista
Nasz Dziennik
New York Times
Newsweek
Pravda
Rzeczpospolita
Times
Tygodnik Solidarność
Wall Street Journal
Washington Post
Washington Times

Secondary Sources

Scholarly Monographs:

Applebaum, Anne, *Gulag: A History* (New York and London: Doubleday, 2003).

Artis, Michael, Banerjee, Anindya, and Marcellino, Massimiliano, eds., *The Central and Eastern European Countries and the European Union* (Cambridge, UK and New York: Cambridge University Press, 2006).

Berman, Ilan and Waller, J. Michael, eds., *Dismantling Tyranny: Transitioning beyond Totalitarian Regimes* (Lanham, MD: Rowman & Littlefield Publishers, 2006).

Biskup, Marian and Labuda, Gerard, *Dzieje Zakonu Krzyżackiego w Prusach: Gospodarka – Społeczeństwo – Państwo – Ideologia* (*A History of the Teutonic Order in Prussia: Economy, Society, State, Ideology*) (Gdańsk: Wydawnictwo Morskie, 1988).

Bozo, Frederic, ed. [et al.], *Europe and the End of the Cold War: A Reappraisal* (London and New York: Routledge, 2008).

Budnitskii, Oleg Vital'evich, *Rossiiskie evrei mezhdu krasnymi i belymi, 1917–1920* (*Russian Jews between Reds and Whites, 1917–1920*) (Moscow: ROSSP-EN, 2005).

Bugajski, Janusz, *America's New Allies: Central-Eastern Europe and the Transatlantic Link* (Washington, DC: CSIS Press/Center for Strategic and International Studies, 2006).

Bugajski, Janusz, *Cold Peace: Russia's New Imperialism* (Westport, CT: Greenwood Publishing Group, 2004).

Cenckiewicz, Sławomir, *Długie ramię Moskwy: Wywiad wojskowy Polski Ludowej, 1943–1991* (*Moscow's Long Arm: Military Intelligence of People's Poland*) (Poznań: Zysk i Ska, 2011).

Cenckiewicz, Sławomir, *Śladami bezpieki i partii: Studia-źródła-publicystyka* (*Tracking the Secret Police and the Party: Studies, Sources, Journalism*) (Łomianki: LTW, 2009).

Chertoprud, Sergei, *НКВД - НКГБ в годы Великой Отечественной войны: Неизвестные страницы* (*NKVD-NKGB during the Great Fatherland War: The Unknown Chapters*) (Moscow: Iaza/Eskimo, 2005).

Chirot, Daniel, ed., *The Origins of Backwardness in Eastern Europe: Economics and Politics from the Middle Ages until the Early Twentieth Century* (Berkeley, Los Angeles and London: University of California Press, 1989).

Chmielowiec, Piotr, ed., *Okupacja sowiecka ziem polskich (1939–1941)* (*The Soviet Occupation of Polish Lands*) (Rzeszów and Warsaw: Instytut Pamięci Narodowej—Komisja Ścigania Zbrodni przeciwko Narodowi Polskiemu, 2005).

Chodakiewicz, Marek Jan, *After the Holocaust: Polish-Jewish Conflict in the Wake of World War II* (Boulder, CO: East European Monographs, 2003).

Chodakiewicz, Marek Jan, *Between Nazis and Soviets: Occupation Politics in Poland, 1939–1947* (Lanham, MD: Lexington Books, 2004).

Chodakiewicz, Marek Jan, ed., *Ejszyszki: Kulisy zajść w Ejszyszkach: Epilog stosunków polsko-żydowskich na Kresach, 1944–45: Wspomnienia-dokumenty-publicystyka* (*Ejszyszki: The Background to the Events in Ejszyszki: An Epilogue to Polish-Jewish Relations in the Eastern Borderlands: Recollections, Documents, Essays*) (Warsaw: Fronda, 2002 [2003]).

Chodakiewicz, Marek Jan, *Narodowe Siły Zbrojne: "Ząb" przeciw dwu wrogom* (*National Armed Forces: "Ząb" Against Two Enemies*) (Warsaw: Fronda, 1999).

Chodakiewicz, Marek Jan, Radziłowski, John, and Tolczyk, Dariusz, eds., *Poland's Transformation: A Work in Progress* (Charlottesville, VA: Leopolis Press, 2003).

Chodakiewicz, Marek Jan, *The Massacre in Jedwabne, July 10, 1941: Before, during, after* (New York and Boulder, CO: Columbia University Press and East European Monographs, 2005).

Chodakiewicz, Marek Jan, *Żydzi i Polacy, 1918–1955: Współistnienie, Zagłada, Komunizm* (*Jews and Poles, 1918–1955: Coexistence, Extermination, Communism*) (Warsaw: Fronda, 2000).

Cienciała, Anna M., Lebedeva, Natalia S., and Materski, Wojciech, eds., *Katyn: A Crime Without Punishment* (New Haven, CT and London: Yale University Press, 2008).

Conquest, Robert, *The Great Terror: A Reassessment* (New York and Oxford: Oxford University Press, 1990).

Conquest, Robert, *The Harvest of Sorrow: Soviet Collectivization and the Terror-Famine* (New York and Oxford: Oxford University Press, 1986).

Courtois, Stéphane et al., *The Black Book of Communism: Crimes, Terror, Repression* (Cambridge, MA, and London: Harvard University Press, 1999).

Crozier, Brian, *The Rise and Fall of the Soviet Empire* (Roseville, CA: Forum and Prima Publishing, 2000).

Davies, Norman, *God's Playground: A History of Poland*, 2 vols. (New York: Oxford University Press, 1982).

Davies, Norman, *No Simple Victory: World War II in Europe, 1939–1945* (New York: Viking, 2006).

Davies, Norman. *White Eagle, Red Star: The Polish-Soviet War, 1919–20* (London: Orbis Books Ltd., 1983).

Davies, Norman, *Rising'44: The Battle for Warsaw* (New York: Viking, 2004).

DeBardeleben, Joan, *The Boundaries of EU Enlargement: Finding a Place For Neighbours* (Basingstoke, and New York: Palgrave Macmillan, 2008).

Djilas, Milovan, *The New Class: An Analysis of the Communist System* (New York: Frederick A. Praeger, Publisher, 1957).

Dobroszycki, Lucjan, and Gurock, Jeffrey S., eds., *The Holocaust in the Soviet Union: Studies and Sources on the Destruction of the Jews in the Nazi Occupied Territories of the USSR, 1941–1945* (Armonk, NY and London: M.E. Sharpe, 1990).

Dvornik, Francis, *The Slavs in European History and Civilization* (New Brunswick, NJ: Rutgers University Press, 1962).

Edwards, Lee, ed., *The Collapse of Communism* (Stanford, CA: Stanford University, 2000).

Fountain II, Alvin Marcus, *Roman Dmowski: Party, Tactics, Ideology, 1895–1907* (Boulder and New York: East European Monographs and Columbia University Press, 1980).

Gitelman, Zvi, ed., *The Politics of Nationality and the Erosion of the USSR* (London: Macmillan, 1992).

Głębocki, Henryk, *Kresy Imperium: Szkice i materiały do polityki Rosji wobec jej peryferii (XVIII-XXI wiek) (The Borderlands of the Empire: Essays and Materials on Russia's Policy toward Its Peripheries between the 18th and 21st Centuries)* (Kraków: Arcana, 2006).

Glenny, Misha, *McMafia: A Journey through the Global Criminal Underworld* (New York: Alfred A. Knopf, 2008).

Gottfried, Paul Edward, *The Strange Death of Marxism: The European Left in the New Millennium* (Columbia and London: University of Missouri Press, 2005).

Hilberg, Raul, *The Destruction of the European Jews*, 2nd revised edition (New York and London: Holmes & Meier, 1985).

Holborn, Hajo, *A History of Modern Germany: 1648–1945*, 3 vols. (Princeton, NJ: Princeton University Press, 1982).

Hosking, Geoffrey, *Rulers and Victims: The Russians in the Soviet Union* (Cambridge, MA, and London: The Belknap Press of Harvard University Press, 2006).

Jasienica, Paweł, *Jagiellonian Poland* (Miami, FL: The American Institute of Polish Culture, 1978).

Jasienica, Paweł, *Piast Poland* (Miami, FL and New York: The American Institute of Polish Culture and Hippocrene Books, 1985).

Jasiewicz, Krzysztof, ed., *Europa nieprowincjonalna: Przemiany na ziemiach wschodnich dawnej Rzeczpospolitej (Białoruś, Litwa, Ukraina, wschodnie pogranicze III Rzeczpospolitej Polskiej) w latach 1772–1999 (Non-provincial Europe: Transformations in the Eastern Lands of the Old Commonwealth (Belarus, Lithuania, Ukraine, and the Eastern Borderlands of the III Polish Commonwealth), 1772–1999)* (Warszawa and London: Instytut Studiów Politycznych Polskiej Akademii Nauk, Oficyna Wydawnicza Rytm, Polonia Aid Foundation Trust, 1999).

Jelavich, Barbara, *History of the Balkans: Eighteenth and Nineteenth Centuries* (New York: Cambridge University Press, 1983).

Joachim Tauber, ed., *"Kollaboration" in Nordosteuropa: Erscheinungsformen und Deutungen im 20. Jahrhundert* (Wiesbaden: Harrassowitz Verlag, 2006).

Kamiński, Andrzej Sulima, *Republic vs. Autocracy: Poland-Lithuania and Russia, 1686–1697* (Cambridge, MA: Distributed by Harvard University Press for the Harvard Ukrainian Research Institute, 1993).

Kann, Robert A., *A History of the Habsburg Empire, 1526–1918* (Berkeley, Los Angeles, and London: University of California Press, 1980).

Karolevitz, Robert F. and Fenn, Ross S., *Flight of Eagles: The Story of the American Kosciuszko Squadron in the Polish-Russian War, 1919–1920* (Sioux Falls, SD: Brevet Press, Inc., 1974).

King, Charles, *The Moldovans: Romania, Russia, and the Politics of Culture* (Stanford, CA: The Hoover Institution Press, 2000).

Kotkin, Stephen, *Armageddon Averted: The Soviet Collapse, 1970–2000* (Oxford and New York: Oxford University Press, 2001).

Krasnodębski, Zdzisław, Garsztecki, Stefan, and Ritter, Rüdiger eds., *Last der Geschichte? Kollektive Identität und Geschichte in Ostmitteleuropa: Belarus, Polen, Litauen, Ukraine* (Hamburg: Verlag Dr. Kovač, 2008).

Kulik, Anatoly and Pshizova, Susanna, eds., *Political Parties in Post-Soviet Space: Russia, Belarus, Ukraine, Moldova, and the Baltics* (Westport, CT and London: Praeger Publishers, 2005).

Kuromiya, Hiroaki, *Freedom and Terror in the Donbas: A Ukrainian-Russian Borderland, 1870s–1990s* (Cambridge, UK: Cambridge University Press, 1998).

Kuzio, Taras and D'Anieri, Paul, *Dilemmas of State-Led Nation Building in Ukraine* (Westport, CT: Praeger, 2002).

Laruelle, Marle?ne, *Russian Eurasianism: An Ideology of Empire* (Washington, DC: Woodrow Wilson Center Press, 2008).

Lenczowski, John, *Full Spectrum Diplomacy and Grand Strategy: Reforming the Structure and Culture of U.S. Foreign Policy* (Lanham, MD: Lexington Books, 2011).

Lenczowski, John, *The Sources of Soviet Perestroika* (Ashland, OH: Ashbrook Center, Ashland University, 1990).

Lieven, Anatol, *The Baltic Revolution: Estonia, Latvia, Lithuania and the Path to Independence* (New Haven, CT: Yale University Press, 1993).

Lieven, Dominic, *Empire: The Russian Empire and Its Rivals* (New Haven, CT and London: Yale University Press, 2001).

Magocsi, Paul Robert, *A History of Ukraine* (Seattle, WA: University of Washington Press, 1996).

Magocsi, Paul Robert, *The Roots of Ukrainian Nationalism: Galicia as Ukraine's Piedmont* (Toronto, ON: University of Toronto Press, 2002).

Malia, Martin, *The Soviet Tragedy: A History of Socialism in Russia, 1917–1991* (New York: The Free Press, 1994).

Martin, Terry, *The Affirmative Action Empire: Nations and Nationalism in the Soviet Union, 1923–1939* (Ithaca and London: Cornell University Press, 2001).

Materski, Wojciech, and Szarota, Tomasz, eds., *Polska 1939–1945: Straty osobowe i ofiary represji pod dwiema okupacjami* (*Poland 1939–1945: Individual Losses and Victims of Repression under Both Occupations*) (Warszawa: Instytut Pamięci Narodowej, 2009).

Mawdsley, Evan, *The Russian Civil War* (Edinburgh: Birlinn Ltd., 2000).

Michta, Andrew A., *The Limits of Alliance: The United States, NATO, and the EU in North and Central Europe* (Lanham, MD: Rowman & Littlefield, 2006).

Musial, Bogdan, *Kampfplatz Deutschland: Stalins Kriegspläne gegen den Westen* (Berlin: Propyläen, 2008).

Norris, Harry, *Islam in the Baltics: Europe's Early Muslim Community* (London and New York: Tauris Academic Studies, an imprint of I.B. Tauris Publishers, 2009).

Nowak, Andrzej, *Od Imperium do Imperium: Spojrzenie na historię Europy Wschodniej* (*From Empire to Empire: A Look at the History of Eastern Europe*) (Kraków and Warszawa: Arcana and Instytut Historii PAN, 2004).

Nygren, Bertil, *The Rebuilding of Greater Russia: Putin's Foreign Policy towards the CIS Countries* (London and New York: Routledge, 2008).

Persak, Krzysztof, and Kamiński, Łukasz, eds., *Czekiści: Organy bezpieczeństwa w europejskich krajach bloku sowieckiego, 1944–1989* (*The Chekists: Security Organs in the European Countries of the Soviet Bloc, 1944–1989*) (Warszawa: Instytut Pamięci Narodowej, 2010).

Pilon, Juliana Geran, *The Bloody Flag: Post-Communist Nationalism in Eastern Europe: Spotlight on Rumania* (New Brunswick, NJ and London: Transaction Publishers, 1992).

Piotrowski, Tadeusz, *Poland's Holocaust: Ethnic Strife, Collaboration with Occupying Forces and Genocide in the Second Republic, 1918–1947* (Jefferson, NC: McFarland & Company, 1998).

Pipes, Richard, *The Russian Revolution* (New York: Vintage Books, 1990).

Plakans, Andrejs, *A Concise History of the Baltic States* (Cambridge and New York: Cambridge University Press, 2011).

Politkovskaya, Anna, *Putin's Russia: Life in a Failing Democracy* (New York: Henry Holt and Company, 2007).

Prizel, Ilya, *National Identity and Foreign Policy: Nationalism and Leadership in Poland, Russia, and Ukraine* (Cambridge: Cambridge University Press, 1998).

Prusin, Alexander V., *The Lands between: Conflict in the East European Borderlands, 1870–1992* (New York and Oxford: Oxford University Press, 2010).

Racja stanu: Janowi Olszewskiemu w 80. rocznice urodzin (*Raison d'etat: A Festschrift to Jan Olszewski for His 80th Birthday*) (Poznań: Zysk i ska, 2011).

Riasanovsky, Nicholas, *Nicholas I and Official Nationality in Russia, 1825–1855* (Berkeley, Los Angles, and London: University of California Press, 1959).

Rothschild, Joseph, *Return to Diversity: A Political History of East Central Europe since World War II* (New York: Oxford University Press, 2000).

Rybakov, Boris, *Киевская Русь и русские княжества XII-XIII вв.* (*Kievan Rus' and Russian Principalities in XII–XIII Centuries*) (Moscow: Nauka, 1993).

Satter, David, *Darkness at Dawn: The Rise of the Russian Criminal State* (New Haven, CT and London: Yale University Press, 2003).

Schmidtke, Oliver and Yekelchyk, Serhy, *Europe's Last Frontier? Belarus, Moldova, and Ukraine between Russia and the European Union* (New York: Palgrave Macmillan, 2008).

Schweizer, Peter, *Victory: The Reagan Administration's Secret Strategy that Hastened the Collapse of the Soviet Union* (New York: Atlantic Monthly Press, 1994).

Seton-Watson, Hugh, *The Russian Empire, 1801–1917* (Oxford: the Clarendon Press, 1990).

Siemaszko, Władysław, and Siemaszko, Ewa, *Ludobójstwo dokonane przez nacjonalistów ukraińskich na ludności polskiej Wołynia 1939–1945,*

(*Genocide Perpetrated by the Ukrainian Nationalists Against the Polish Population of Volhynia, 1939–1945*) 2 vols. (Warsaw: von borowiecky, 2000).

Slezkine, Yuri, *The Jewish Century* (Princeton, NJ and Oxford: Princeton University Press, 2004).

Snyder, Timothy, *Bloodlands: Europe between Hitler and Stalin* (New York: Basic Books, 2010).

Snyder, Timothy, *The Reconstruction of Nations: Poland, Ukraine, Lithuania, Belarus, 1569–1999* (New Haven, CT and London: Yale University Press, 2003).

Stachura, Peter, *Poland, 1918–1945: An Interpretive and Documentary History of the Second Republic* (London and New York: Routledge, 2004).

Staliūnas, Darius, *Making Russians: Meaning and Practice of Russification in Lithuania and Belarus After 1863* (Amsterdam and New York: Rodopi, 2007).

Sukiennicki, Wiktor, *East Central Europe during World War I: From Foreign Domination to National Independence*, 2 vols. (Boulder, CO: East European Monographs, 1984).

Suziedelis, Saulius, *The Sword and the Cross: A History of the Church in Lithuania* (Huntington, IN: Our Sunday Visitor Publishing, 1988).

Tazbir, Janusz, *A State without Stakes: Polish Religious Toleration in the Sixteenth Century* (New York and Warsaw: The Kościuszko Foundation, Twayne Publishers, and Państwowy Instytut Wydawniczy, 1973).

Thompson, Ewa M., *Imperial Knowledge: Russian Literature and Colonialism* (Westport, CT and London: Greenwood Press, 2000).

Umland, Andreas, ed., *The Nature of Russian "Neo-Eurasianism": Approaches to Aleksandr Dugin's Post-Soviet Movement of Radical Anti-Americanism* (Armonk, NY: M.E. Sharpe 2009).

Vaksberg, Arkady, *The Soviet Mafia* (New York: St. Martin's Press, 1991).

Vermeersch, Peter, *The Romani Movement: Minority Politics and Ethnic Mobilization in Contemporary Central Europe* (New York: Berghahn Books, 2006).

Vialiki, A. F. [Anatol Fiodaravich], *Na razdarozhzhy: Belarusy i paliaki ŭ chas peresialennia, 1944–1946 hh.* (Minsk: BDPU, 2005).

Waller, J. Michael, *Secret Empire: The KGB in Russia Today* (Boulder, CO: Westview and Harper Collins, 1994).

Wandycz, Piotr S., *The Lands of Partitioned Poland, 1795–1918* (Seattle, WA and London: University of Washington Press, 1984).

Wellisz, Stanisław, *The Economies of the Soviet Bloc: A Study of Decision Making and Resource Allocation* (New York and Toronto: McGraw-Hill Book Company, 1966).

Wheeler-Bennett, John W., *Brest Litovsk: The Forgotten Peace, March 1918* (New York: W.W. Norton and Company, 1971).

Wynot, Edward D., *Cauldron of Conflict: Eastern Europe, 1918–1945* (Wheeling, IL: Harlan Davidson, 1999).

Periodicals:

Arcana
Białoruskie Zeszyty Historyczne (*Belarussian Historical Notebooks*)
Biuletyn Instytutu Pamięci Narodowej (*The Bulletin of the Institute of National Remembrance*)
Canadian Slavonic Papers
Communist and Post-Communist Studies
Demokratizatsiya: The Journal of Post-Soviet Democratization
East European Jewish Affairs
East European Politics and Societies
East European Quarterly
Europe-Asia Studies
Genocidas ir rezistencija (*Genocide and Resistance*)
Glaukopis
Holocaust and Genocide Studies
Journal of Cold War History
Journal of Social, Political, and Economic Studies
Journal of Soviet Nationalities
Kritika: Explorations in Russian and Eurasian History
Nationalism and Ethnic Politics
Nationalities Papers
Pontes Review of South East European Studies
Problems of Post-Communism
Russian Review
Sarmatian Review
Slavic Review
Southeastern Political Review
Soviet Analyst: An Intelligence Commentary
Uncaptive Minds
World Affairs

Index

Lightning Source UK Ltd.
Milton Keynes UK
UKHW02f2050180218
318084UK00016B/527/P